Print

HDEV delivers all the key terms and all the content for the **Human Development** course through a visually engaging and easy-to-review print experience.

Digital

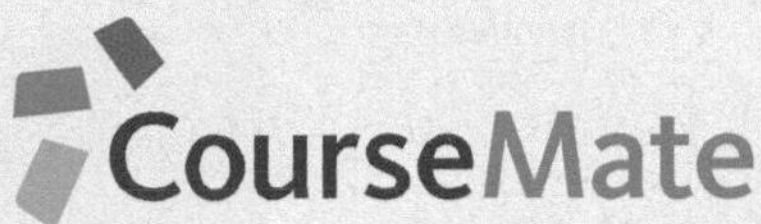

CourseMate enables you to stay organized and study efficiently by providing a single location for all your course materials and study aids.

1. Open the Access Card included with this text.
2. Follow the steps on the card.
3. Study.

Student Resources

- Chapter in Review Cards
- Build a Summary Activities
- Observing Development Videos
- Flashcards
- Pre-Tests and Post-Tests
- Practice Quizzes
- Weblinks

Students: **nelson.com/student**

Instructor Resources

- All Student Resources
- Engagement Tracker
- LMS Integration
- Test Bank
- PowerPoint Slides
- Image Library
- Instructor Prep Cards

Instructors: **nelson.com/instructor**

NELSON

HDEV, Third Canadian Edition

by Spencer A. Rathus, Shauna Longmuir, Laura Ellen Berk, and Rebecca Rogerson

Publisher, Digital and Print Content:
Lenore Taylor-Atkins

Marketing Manager:
Ann Byford

Content Manager:
Lisa Berland

Photo and Permissions Researcher:
Karen Hunter

Production Project Manager:
Jennifer Hare

Production Service:
MPS Limited

Copy Editor:
Elspeth McFadden

Proofreader:
MPS Limited

Indexer:
MPS Limited

Design Director:
Ken Phipps

Higher Education Design PM:
Pamela Johnston

Interior Design Revisions:
Ken Cadinouche

Cover Design:
Ken Cadinouche

Cover Image:
OJO Images/Getty Images

Compositor:
MPS Limited

Printed and bound in Canada
3 4 5 21 20 19 18

For more information contact Nelson Education Ltd., 1120 Birchmount Road, Toronto, Ontario, M1K 5G4. Or you can visit our Internet site at nelson.com

Library and Archives Canada Cataloguing in Publication Data

Rathus, Spencer A., author
HDEV / Spencer A. Rathus, Shauna Longmuir, Laura Ellen Berk, Rebecca Rogerson. — Third Canadian edition.

Includes bibliographical references.
ISBN 978-0-17-665745-1 (softcover)

1. Developmental psychology—Textbooks. 2. Child development—Textbooks. 3. Aging—Psychological aspects—Textbooks. 4. Textbooks. I. Longmuir, Shauna, author II. Berk, Laura Ellen, 1972-, author III. Rogerson, Rebecca, 1974-, author IV. Title. V. Title: Human development.

BF713.R377 2017 155
C2017-900423-9

ISBN-13: 978-0-17-665745-1
ISBN-10: 0-17-665745-2

HDEV Brief Contents

leungchopan/Shutterstock.com

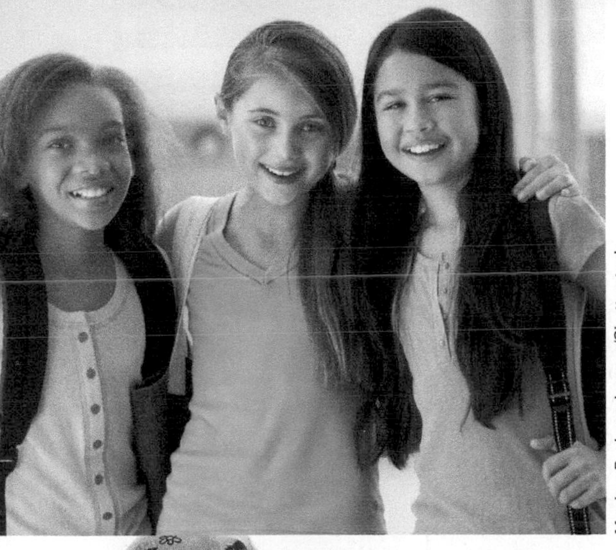
Monkey Business Images/Shutterstock

© Jim West/PhotoEdit

HDEV Contents

PART ONE Introduction

1 HISTORY, THEORIES, AND METHODS 1

(t) Brand X Pictures/Jupiterimages; (b) jh Fotografie/Shutterstock.com

2 HEREDITY AND PRENATAL DEVELOPMENT 20

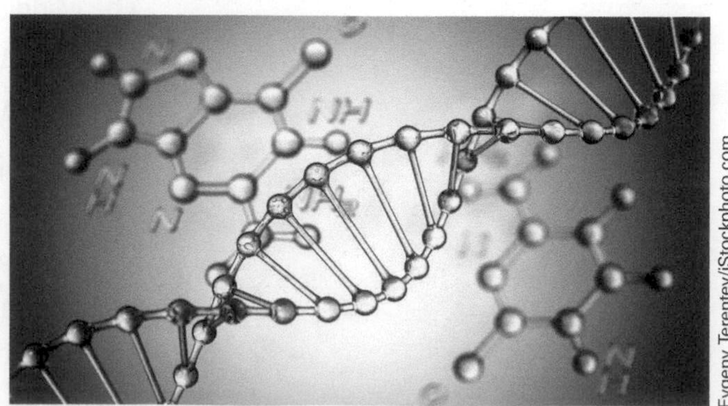

Evgeny Terentev/iStockphoto.com

PART TWO Birth and Infancy

3 BIRTH AND THE NEWBORN BABY: IN THE NEW WORLD 45

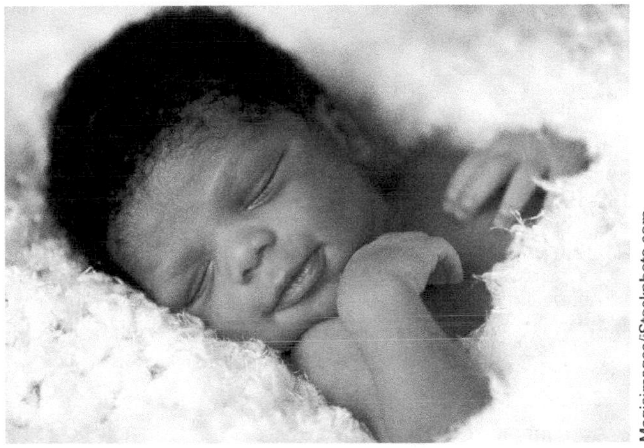

Magiaimages/iStockphoto.com

4 INFANCY: PHYSICAL DEVELOPMENT 65

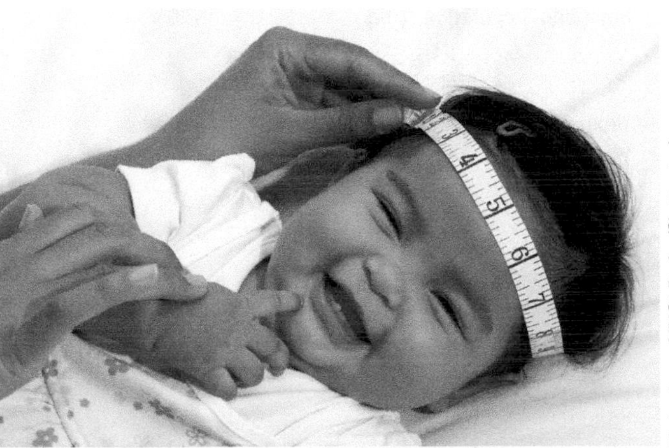

Marlon Lopez MMG1 Design/Shutterstock.com

5 INFANCY: COGNITIVE DEVELOPMENT 82

Kevin Reid/Getty Images

6 INFANCY: SOCIAL AND EMOTIONAL DEVELOPMENT 100

Stephanie Rausser/Getty Images

PART THREE Early and Middle Childhood

7 EARLY CHILDHOOD: PHYSICAL AND COGNITIVE DEVELOPMENT 119

Rebekah Littlejohn Photography www.littlejohnphotography.com

8 EARLY CHILDHOOD: SOCIAL AND EMOTIONAL DEVELOPMENT 139

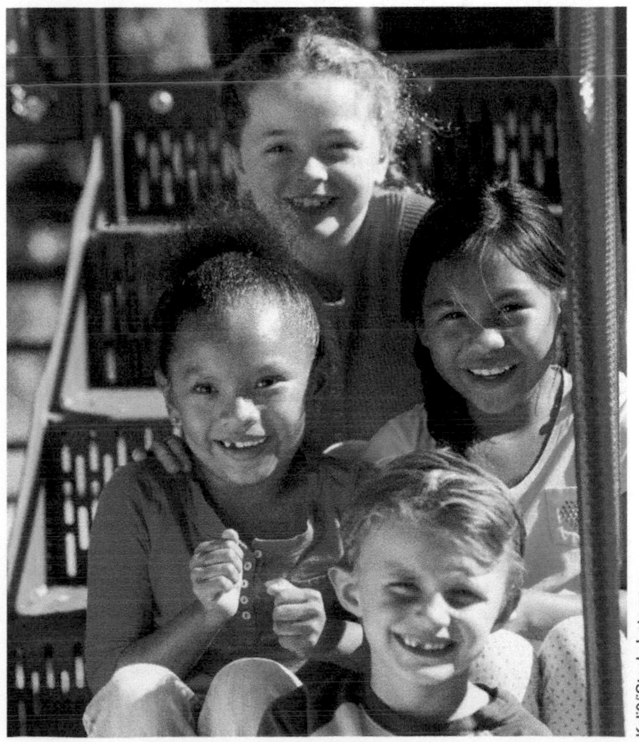

Kali9/iStockphoto.com

Hemis/Alamy Stock Photo

Sean Locke Photography/Shutterstock.com

PART FOUR Adolescence and Early Adulthood

11 ADOLESCENCE: PHYSICAL AND COGNITIVE DEVELOPMENT 194

© Design Pics/Kristy-Anne Glubish

12 ADOLESCENCE: SOCIAL AND EMOTIONAL DEVELOPMENT 210

David Pereiras/Shutterstock.com

13 EARLY ADULTHOOD: PHYSICAL AND COGNITIVE DEVELOPMENT 225

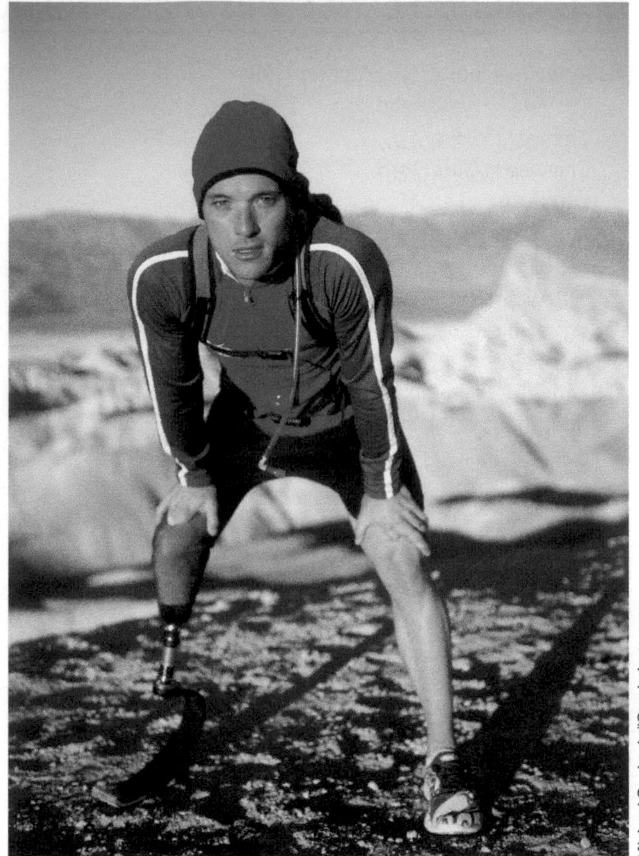

Michael Svoboda/iStockphoto.com

14 EARLY ADULTHOOD: SOCIAL AND EMOTIONAL DEVELOPMENT 240

oliveromg/Shutterstock.com

PART FIVE Middle and Late Adulthood

15 MIDDLE ADULTHOOD: PHYSICAL AND COGNITIVE DEVELOPMENT 257

Andresr Imaging/iStockphoto.com

16 MIDDLE ADULTHOOD: SOCIAL AND EMOTIONAL DEVELOPMENT 272

Jupiterimages/Getty Images

17 LATE ADULTHOOD: PHYSICAL AND COGNITIVE DEVELOPMENT 284

Tomas Rodriguez/Getty Images

18 LATE ADULTHOOD: SOCIAL AND EMOTIONAL DEVELOPMENT 301

© Brand X Pictures/Jupiterimages

19 LIFE'S FINAL CHAPTER 316

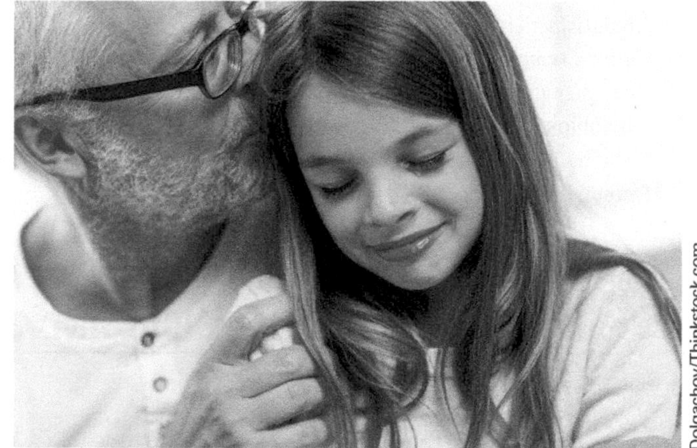

Dolgachov/Thinkstock.com

What's New in the Third Canadian Edition

Christopher Futcher/iStockphoto.com

Overall

- Greater ethnic diversification and inclusion of cultures and people with disabilities, reflective of the current Canadian population
- Updated statistics, figures, tables, and photos that highlight the most recent research and developments in the field of human development
- Updated material on social media
- More detailed information about bullying, including bullies, bystanders, cyberbullying, and outcome research
- Updated and expanded coverage of issues concerning LGBTQ and gender role socialization
- Expanded information about various issues concerning Indigenous peoples in Canada
- Increased exploration of mental health and issues of stress
- A more complete look at family structure

Chapter 1

- Coverage of the evolution of development studies for better understanding of the field
- Expanded discussion of gender

© Blend Images/Jupiterimages

Chapter 2

- A new section on assisted reproductive technology (ART), including reasons for its use
- A new section on the Motherisk program

Chapter 3

- More complete and updated coverage of midwifery in Canada
- Updated research on newborns' sense of smell, the importance of touch for newborns, postpartum depression, and infant mortality

Chapter 4

- New and updated information on infant nutrition issues, including breastfeeding and bottle-feeding
- A new section on malnutrition
- Added information on immunization and the anti-vaccination movement

© Brand X Pictures/Jupiterimages

Chapter 5

- Supplemented coverage of Piaget's stages with added examples and a new illustration that includes accompanying milestones for each stage
- More information about Canadian resources for speech and language delays

Chapter 6

- The adult working model added to the discussion of attachment theory, as well as more information about the stability of attachment style and reactive detachment disorder
- Updated discussion of autism spectrum disorder that aligns with the recent changes in DSM5
- An updated and expanded discussion of sex and gender

What's New in the Third Canadian Edition

Chapter 7

- New Canadian research added to theory of mind section
- Information about nutrition in preschool years and being overweight later in life added
- A new discussion of issues around the requirement for children in kindergarten to be toilet trained

Chapter 8

- Expanded and updated section on the impact of divorce on early childhood
- Reworked section on gender development, including a new discussion of gender-neutral parenting

Chapter 9

- Expanded and updated information on childhood obesity and new emphasis on healthy eating
- Emotional intelligence added as a theory of intelligence
- More information on bilingualism

Chapter 10

- New discussions of step-parents and blended families, single parents, and grandparents as caregivers
- Discussions of bullying added: cyberbullying, bystanders and their impact on bullying, and bullying intervention

Chapter 11

- Updated research on the environmental factors of early menarche
- Discussion of LGBTQ youth and their unique challenges and issues during puberty
- New discussion of the role of social media in body image and eating disorders among youth, including boys

Chapter 12

- Up-to-date information on cyberbullying with current Canadian examples
- New section on STIs in adolescence
- Expanded discussion of the unique issues of LGBTQ youth
- More information on teen suicide, including how to help teens

Ton Koene/age fotostock/First Light

Wavebreakmedia/Shutterstock.com

Rubberball/Mike Kemp/Getty Images

What's New in the Third Canadian Edition

Andresr/Shutterstock.com

Svetlana Braun/iStockphoto.com

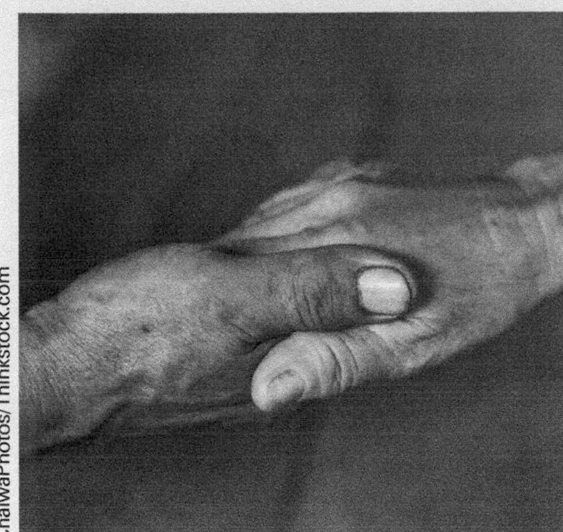
ChaiwaPhotos/Thinkstock.com

Chapter 13

- Updated sexual orientation section, including recent news and events
- Updated information about sexual consent
- Updated information on legislation concerning medical cannabis use

Chapter 14

- Updated information on post-partum depression, stress, and work overload
- New information on failure to launch in young adults
- More discussion of issues surrounding culture, LGBTQ, and people with disabilities

Chapter 15

- Updated information about the causes of death in middle adulthood
- Added Indigenous peoples' issues to discussion of health matters
- New section on mental health and issues of stress

Chapter 16

- Indigenous perspectives of middle adulthood included
- Updated research on the sandwich generation
- Men included in the discussion of empty nest syndrome

Chapter 17

- Added information on poverty among seniors in Canada
- Updated research on substance abuse in seniors
- Updated information on theories of aging
- Up-to-date information about dementia in Canada

Chapter 18

- New information on social media usage among seniors
- Added positive examples and research on seniors and aging well
- Indigenous perspectives on late adulthood and the treatment of seniors included
- Updated section on mental health, including a depression fact sheet

Chapter 19

- Greater cultural diversity added to the discussion of dying, death, and funerals
- Updated ethics and legislation related to death and dying and physician-assisted dying
- Tips provided on how to support a child or teen when someone has died
- A critique and alternatives for the stages of grief and pathologizing of grief included

PART ONE

CHAPTER 1

Julia Margaret Cameron ca. 1864.

History, Theories, and Methods

LEARNING OUTCOMES

LO1 Explain the history of the study of human development

LO2 Compare and contrast theories of human development

LO3 Enumerate key controversies in human development

LO4 Describe ways in which researchers study human development

> "You are unique, and things will happen to you, and because of you, that have never happened before."

This book has a story to tell. It is an important story—it is your story. It is about the remarkable journey you have already taken through childhood. It is about the unfolding of your adult life. Learning about the history of the study of human development and key theories in child development help us to understand our origin and where we might be headed.

LO1 The History of the Study of Human Development

Scientific inquiry into human development has existed for little more than a century. However, in ancient times and in the Middle Ages, children often were viewed as innately evil, and discipline was harsh. Children were nurtured until they were 7 years old, which was considered the "age of reason." After that age, they were expected to work alongside adults in the home and in the field.

DID YOU KNOW?

During the Middle Ages, children were often treated as miniature adults.

Though more was expected of them, they weren't given additional privileges.

The Study of Child Development

The transition to modern thinking about children is marked by the writings of philosophers such as John Locke and Jean-Jacques Rousseau. Englishman John Locke (1632–1704) believed that the child came into the world as a *tabula rasa*—a "blank tablet" or clean slate—that was written on by experience. Locke did not believe that inborn predispositions toward good or evil played an important role in the conduct of the child. Instead, he focused on the role of the environment or of experience. Locke believed that social approval and disapproval are powerful shapers of behaviour. On the other hand, Jean-Jacques Rousseau (1712–1778), a Swiss–French philosopher, argued that children are inherently good and that, if allowed to express their natural impulses, they will develop into generous and moral individuals.

During the Industrial Revolution, family life came to be defined in terms of the nuclear unit of mother, father, and children rather than the extended family. Children became more visible, fostering awareness of childhood as a special time of life. Still, children often laboured in factories from dawn to dusk through the early years of the 20th century.

In the 20th century, laws were passed to protect children from strenuous labour, to require that they attend school until a certain age, and to prevent them from getting married or being sexually exploited. Whereas children were once considered the property of parents to do with as they wished, laws now protect children from abuse by

Locke viewed children as a blank slate, or *tabula rasa*. What life experiences have been, and will be, written on your blank slate?

marekuliasz/iStockphoto.com

Lewis Hein, ca. 1908, public domain.

parents and other adults. Today, youth criminal justice courts ensure that children who break the law receive appropriate treatment according to their age and stage of development in the criminal justice system. For well over a century, childhood has been understood to be a distinct psychological stage of development; children are in need of protection and consideration of their specific and unique needs.

Pioneers in the Study of Child Development

By the start of the 20th century, child development had emerged as a distinct scientific field of study. In the United States of America, G. Stanley Hall (1844–1924) is credited with having founded child development as an academic discipline. Furthermore, French psychologist Alfred Binet (1857–1911) worked with Theodore Simon to develop the first standardized intelligence test near the beginning of the 20th century. Binet's purpose was to identify elementary school children who were at risk of falling behind their peers in academic achievement (see Chapter 9 for further discussion).

The Study of Human Development

Traditionally, the focus of human development has been on childhood and adolescence because of the dramatic physical and cognitive changes that occur during those years. Many theorists today focus on the emerging adulthood, a relatively new period of development that occurs just after adolescence before an individual is ready to enter the adult world. The marked decline of late adulthood is also of great significance given that people's life expectancy has increased in Canada over the years.

Developmental psychology is the biological, psychological, and socio-cultural study of development across the lifespan (see Table 1.1). Developmental psychology examines the progressive challenges and changes that an individual encounters from cradle to grave, which are prompted by maturation and the learning process.

developmental psychology the biological, psychological, and socio-cultural study of human change across the lifespan

behaviourism Watson's view that science must study observable behaviour only and investigate relationships between stimuli and responses

LO2 Theories of Human Development

Give me a dozen healthy infants, well-formed, and my own specified world to bring them up in, and I'll guarantee to train them to become any type of specialist I might suggest—doctor, lawyer, merchant, chief, and, yes, even beggar and thief, regardless of their talents, penchants, tendencies, abilities, vocations, and the race of their ancestors.

—Watson, 1924, p. 82

John B. Watson, the founder of North American **behaviourism**, viewed development in terms of learning theory. He generally agreed with Locke that children's ideas, preferences, and skills are shaped by experience. The study of children has been subject to a long-standing nature–nurture debate. In Watson's theoretical approach to understanding children, he came down on the side of nurture—the importance

TABLE 1.1

The Biopsychosocial Framework of Development

The study of human growth and development is built on the disciplines of biology, psychology, and sociology. This focus explains the formatting of your textbook. Each stage of development is addressed in a chapter focusing on biological and cognitive studies, followed by a chapter examining the psychological and sociological issues that shape lifespan development. These issues are then examined within the context of life-cycle forces.

Biological Force	How do genetics, health, and cognition shape our experiences?
Psychological Force	How do our perceptions and interpretations shape our inner world?
Sociological Force	How do the communities and cultures that we come in contact with influence our life experiences?
Life-Cycle Force	How is the same life event experienced by people in different stages of the lifespan?

maturation
the unfolding of genetically determined traits, structures, and functions

psychosexual development
the process by which libidinal energy is expressed through different erogenous zones during different stages of development

stage theory
a theory of development characterized by distinct periods of life

defence mechanism
a method to reduce anxiety when the id and superego are too demanding

of the physical and social environments—as evidenced by parental training and approval.

Arnold Gesell expressed the opposing idea that biological maturation was the main principle of development: "All things considered, the inevitability and surety of maturation are the most impressive characteristics of early development. It is the hereditary ballast which conserves and stabilizes growth of each individual infant" (Gesell, 1928, p. 378). Whereas Gesell focused mainly on physical aspects of growth and development, Watson discussed the behaviour patterns that children develop. This interplay between nature and nurture has long been debated by developmental researchers. (See section "Nature and Nurture" on page 15 of this chapter for more details).

Theories such as those just mentioned—learning theory and maturational theory—help developmentalists to explain, predict, and influence the events they study. Let us consider popular theories that are studied by developmental researchers today. They fall within broad perspectives on development including the Psychoanalytic Perspective, the Learning Perspective, the Cognitive Perspective, the Biological Perspective, and the Ecological Perspective.

The Psychoanalytic Perspective

Many theories fall within the psychoanalytic perspective. Each of these theories owes its origin to Sigmund Freud, and each views children—and adults—as caught in an internal conflict. Early in development, the conflict is between the child and the world outside. The expressions of basic drives, such as sex and aggression, are in conflict with parental expectations, social rules, moral codes, even laws. But the external limits—parental demands and social rules—are brought inside or internalized. Once internalization occurs, the conflict takes place between opposing inner forces. The child's observable behaviour, thoughts, and feelings reflect the outcomes of these hidden battles.

Let us consider Freud's theory of psychosexual development and Erik Erikson's theory of psychosocial development. Each is a stage theory that sees children as developing through distinct periods of life. Both Freud and Erikson propose that children's early experiences during their formative years affect both their emotional and social development throughout their lives.

Sigmund Freud's Theories of Development: Structural and Psychosexual

Sigmund Freud's (1856–1939) Structural Theory focused on three parts of one's personality: *id, ego,* and *superego*. First, the id is present at birth; it is unconscious. It represents biological drives and demands instant gratification, as suggested by a baby's wailing when hungry. The ego, or the conscious sense of self, begins to develop when children learn to obtain gratification consciously, without screaming or crying. The ego curbs the appetites of the id and makes plans that are in keeping with social conventions so that a person can find gratification but avoid social disapproval. It does this through the use of defence mechanisms, which are designed to keep an individual from feeling anxiety by keeping certain knowledge away from conscious experience. Finally, the superego develops throughout infancy and early childhood. It brings inward the wishes and morals of the child's caregivers and other members of the community.

According to Freud, psychosexual development has five stages: oral, anal, phallic, latency, and genital (see Figure 1.1). If a child receives too little or too much gratification during a stage, the child can become fixated at that stage. For example, during the first year of life, which Freud termed the *oral stage,*

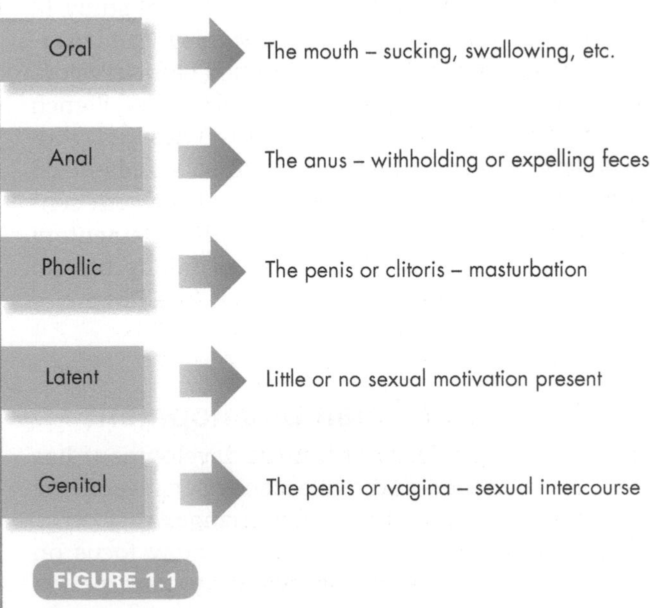

FIGURE 1.1

Freud's Stages of Psychosexual Development

A body part is the source of gratification at every stage of psychosexual development.

Source: Saul McLeod. (2008). Psychosexual Stages. *Simply Psychology*. Retrieved from http://www.simplypsychology.org/psychosexual.html

Artzone/Thinkstock.com

The pull between "right" and "wrong" can be said to be the inner battle of the superego and the id, leaving the ego to make decisions.

"oral" activities such as sucking and biting bring pleasure and gratification. A child who is weaned too early or breastfed too long may become fixated on oral activities such as nail-biting or smoking, or may even show a "biting wit" as they become older.

In the second, or *anal*, stage, gratification is obtained through control and elimination of feces. Excessively strict or permissive toilet training can lead to the development of anal-retentive traits, such as perfectionism and neatness, or anal-expulsive traits, such as sloppiness and carelessness.

In the third stage, the *phallic stage,* parent–child conflict may develop over masturbation, which many parents treat with punishment and threats. According to Freud's psychoanalytical perspective, it is normal for children in the phallic stage to develop strong sexual attachments to the parent of the opposite sex and to begin to view the parent of the same sex as a rival. He termed this rivalry the **Oedipal Complex** for boys and the **Electra Complex** for girls. At the end of this stage of development, children learn that they cannot possess their opposite sex parent but rather learn to identify with the parent of the same sex.

Freud believed that by the age of 5 or 6 years, children enter a *latency stage,* during which sexual feelings remain unconscious; children turn to schoolwork, and they typically prefer playmates of their own sex.

The final stage of psychosexual development, the *genital stage,* begins with the biological changes that usher in adolescence. Adolescents generally desire sexual gratification through intercourse with a partner. Freud believed that oral or anal stimulation, masturbation, and male–male or female–female sexual activity are immature forms of sexual conduct that reflect fixations at early stages of development.

Oedipal Complex the rivalry between a boy and his father for his mother's love

Electra Complex the rivalry between a girl and her mother for her father's love

Evaluation: Freud's views about the anal stage have influenced childcare workers to recommend that toilet training not be started too early or handled punitively. His emphasis on the emotional needs of children has influenced educators to be more sensitive to the possible emotional reasons behind a child's misbehaviour. Freud's work has also been criticized. For example, Freud developed his theory on the basis of contacts with adult patients (mostly women) (Schultz & Schultz, 2008), not by observing children directly. Freud may also have inadvertently guided patients into expressing ideas that confirmed his views. Although Freud's theory forms the basis of many psychological theories, many suggest that his ideas need to be placed within a more modern context that recognizes the role of relationships and the desire to achieve. Furthermore, it is impossible to study the unconscious and so his theories can never be proven either correct or incorrect.

Why Study Freud Today?

The question remains as to why we study Freud in the first place if his theories have never been proven accurate. He was one of the most influential thinkers of the 20th century; his ideas live on today in

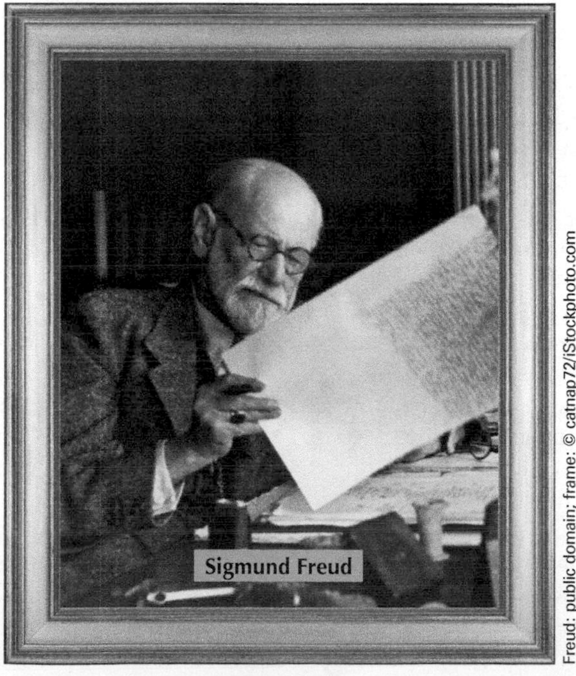

Sigmund Freud

Freud: public domain; frame: © catnap72/iStockphoto.com

psychosocial development Erikson's theory, which emphasizes the importance of social relationships and conscious choice throughout eight stages of development

life crisis an internal conflict that attends each stage of psychosocial development

such well-known terms as Freudian slips, unconscious motives, defence mechanisms, and catharsis. Freud's theories helped to explain social and emotional development and childhood origins of such issues in adulthood as dependence, obsessive neatness, and internal conflict. Although controversial, his ideas paved the way for others to explore topics and ideas that were never studied before contributing to our understanding of early childhood development today.

Erik Erikson's Theory of Psychosocial Development

Erik Erikson (1902–1994) modified and advanced Freud's work by extending his stages of development to include the adult years. Erikson's theory, like Freud's, focuses on the development of emotional life and psychological traits, but differs in its focus on social relationships rather than unconscious motivations, such as sexuality or aggressive instincts. Erikson emphasized the desire to achieve and to help others. Therefore, Erikson speaks of **psychosocial development** rather than of psychosexual development. Furthermore, Erikson places greater emphasis on the ego, or the sense of self. Erikson (1963) extended Freud's five stages to eight to include the concerns of adulthood. Rather than label his stages after parts of the body, Erikson labelled them after the **life crisis** that people might encounter during that stage (see Table 1.2). These life stages form the structure of lifespan development (and the structure of your textbook). Together we will explore these life challenges in the context of the changing world around us.

Erikson proposed that social relationships and physical maturation give each stage its character. For example, the parent–child relationship and the infant's dependence and helplessness are responsible for the nature of the earliest stages of development. Early experiences affect future developments.

TABLE 1.2

Erik Erikson's Psychosocial Stages of Lifespan Development

Psychosocial Stage	Personality Crisis (Challenge)	Important Life Event	Outcome
Infancy (birth to 18 months)	Trust vs. Mistrust	Feeding	Trust is developed when caregivers are reliable and affectionate. Mistrust is developed when care is unpredictable and/or lacking in affection.
Early Childhood (19 months to 3 years)	Autonomy vs. Shame and Doubt	Toilet Training	Children develop a sense of personal control, skill, and independence. Success leads to feelings of self-rule and independence, whereas failure results in feelings of shame and self-doubt.
Preschool (4 to 5 years)	Initiative vs. Guilt	Exploration	Children need to take control over their own environment, leading to a sense of purpose. If children exert too much power, they will encounter disapproval, which will result in guilt. Failure to control their environment will lead to a sense of inadequacy.
School Age (6 to 11 years)	Industry vs. Inferiority	School	Children learn to cope with new social and academic demands. Success leads to a sense of ability and accomplishment. In contrast, failure leads to a sense of nagging inferiority.
Adolescence (12 to 18 years)	Identity vs. Role Confusion	Social Relationships	Teens develop a sense of their personal identity. Success leads to their being able to clearly define themselves and to stay true to who they believe they are. Failure leads to unclear standards and a weak sense of self.
Young Adulthood (19 to 39 years)	Intimacy vs. Isolation	Relationships	Young adults need to form intimate and loving relationships. Success leads to patterns of strong relationship building. Failure to enter into loving relationships results in loneliness and isolation.
Middle Adulthood (40 to 64 years)	Generativity vs. Stagnation	Work and Parenthood	Adults thrive when they create and nurture things that will outlast them. Raising children or creating a positive change leads to feelings of usefulness and accomplishment. Failure results in shallow involvement and a realization that they will leave nothing lasting behind.
Later Life (65 to death)	Ego Integrity vs. Despair	Reflection on Life (Life Review)	Older adults need to actively look back on life and feel a sense that their life mattered. Success at this stage leads to feelings of wisdom and of contribution. Death is the logical next step and is received with grace. Failure to navigate this stage results in regret, bitterness, and despair. Death is feared.

Time & Life Pictures/Getty Images

Erik Erikson was married to his Canadian wife, Joan, for 64 years.

Erikson's views, like Freud's, have influenced child rearing, early childhood education, and child therapy. For example, Erikson's views about an adolescent identity crisis have entered the popular culture and have affected the way many parents and teachers deal with teenagers. Some schools help students master the crisis by means of life-adjustment courses and study units on self-understanding in social studies and literature classes.

Evaluation: Erikson's views are appealing because they emphasize the importance of human consciousness and choice, and they portray us as social beings, whereas Freud portrayed us as creatures who are selfish and need to be compelled to comply with social rules. Empirical findings support the Eriksonian view that positive outcomes of early life crises help put us on the path to positive development (Hoegh & Bourgeois, 2002).

The Learning Perspective: Behavioural and Social Cognitive Theories

Behaviourism

John B. Watson argued that a scientific approach to development must focus on observable behaviour only and not on activities, such as thoughts, fantasies, and other mental images that cannot be made into data.

Classical conditioning is a simple form of learning in which an originally neutral stimulus is paired with an unconditioned stimulus enough times that the neutral stimulus brings on the same response as that unconditioned stimulus. For example, Pavlov's famous study reveals that dogs salivate when food is presented. No learning has occurred because it is an automatic response or reflex. However, if a neutral stimulus such as a bell is sounded every time food is placed in front of a dog, after enough pairings of bell and food, the sound of the bell alone will bring on salivation for that dog because the dog has been conditioned to make that response. Another word for conditioning is learning.

identity crisis according to Erikson, a period of inner conflict during which individuals examine their values and make decisions about their life roles

classical conditioning a simple form of learning in which one stimulus comes to bring forth the response usually brought forth by a second stimulus as a result of being paired repeatedly with the second stimulus

operant conditioning a simple form of learning in which an organism learns to engage in behaviour that is reinforced

reinforcement the process of providing stimuli following responses in an effort to increase the frequency of the responses

Another example to illustrate this occurs when opening a can of dog food. Opening of the can does not initially elicit a response from a dog. But once the dog learns to associate the opening of a can with being fed, then anytime the dog hears the opening of a can, it will run toward that familiar sound from anywhere in the house. The can might contain dog food or beans, but either way, the dog will associate the sound of it being opened with the act of being fed.

Operant conditioning is another type of learning; it takes place when individuals learn to either continue or stop a behaviour due to its consequences. B.F. Skinner introduced the key concept of reinforcement. Reinforcers are stimuli that are

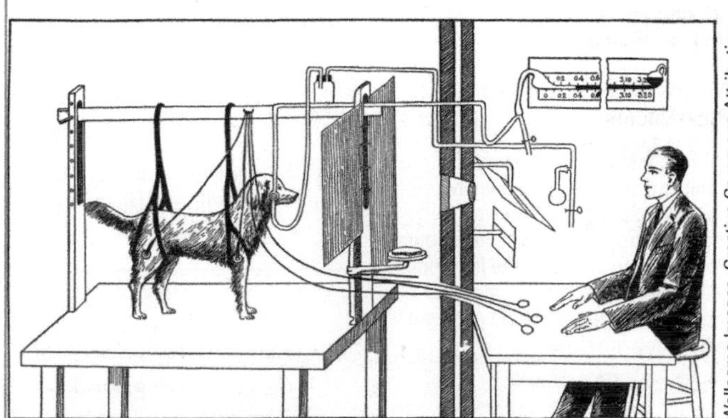

Wellcome Images, Creative Commons Attribution 4.0 International, https://commons.wikimedia.org/wiki/File:Pavlov_experiments_with_dog_Wellcome_M0014738.jpg

The sound of a can opening will bring a dog running whether it is a can of dog food or a can of chicken noodle soup.

positive reinforcer
a reinforcer that, when applied, increases the frequency of a response

negative reinforcer
a reinforcer that, when removed, increases the frequency of a response

punishments
aversive events that suppress or decrease the frequency of the behaviour they follow

intended to increase the frequency of the behaviour they follow. Most children learn to adjust their behaviour to conform to social codes and rules so they can earn reinforcers, such as the attention and approval of their parents and teachers. Other children, ironically, learn to misbehave because misbehaviour also draws attention. Any stimulus that increases the frequency of the responses preceding it serves as a reinforcer.

Skinner distinguished between positive and negative reinforcers. Positive reinforcers increase the frequency of behaviours when they are applied. Food and approval are common positive reinforcers. Negative reinforcers increase the frequency of behaviours when they are removed. Fear is a negative reinforcer because its removal increases the frequency of the behaviours preceding it. Figure 1.2 compares positive and negative reinforcers.

Skinner: Nina Leen/The LIFE Picture Collection/Getty Images; frame: © catnap72/iStockphoto.com

A punishment is the application of something aversive or the removal of something pleasant; a punishment suppresses or decreases the frequency of a behaviour they follow. (Figure 1.3 compares negative

FIGURE 1.2

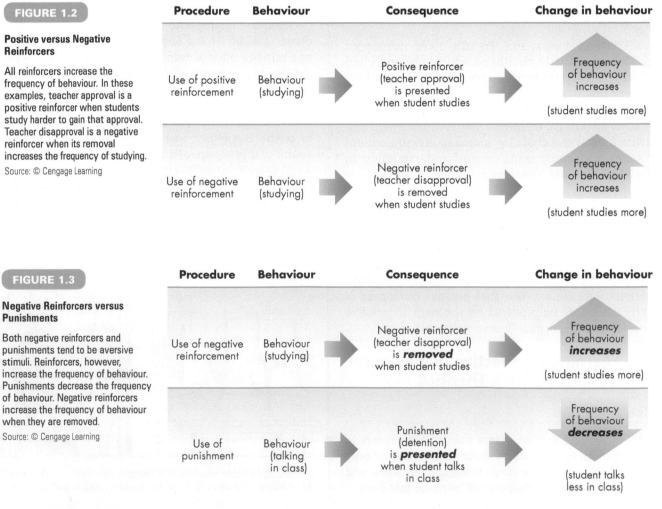

Positive versus Negative Reinforcers

All reinforcers increase the frequency of behaviour. In these examples, teacher approval is a positive reinforcer when students study harder to gain that approval. Teacher disapproval is a negative reinforcer when its removal increases the frequency of studying.

Source: © Cengage Learning

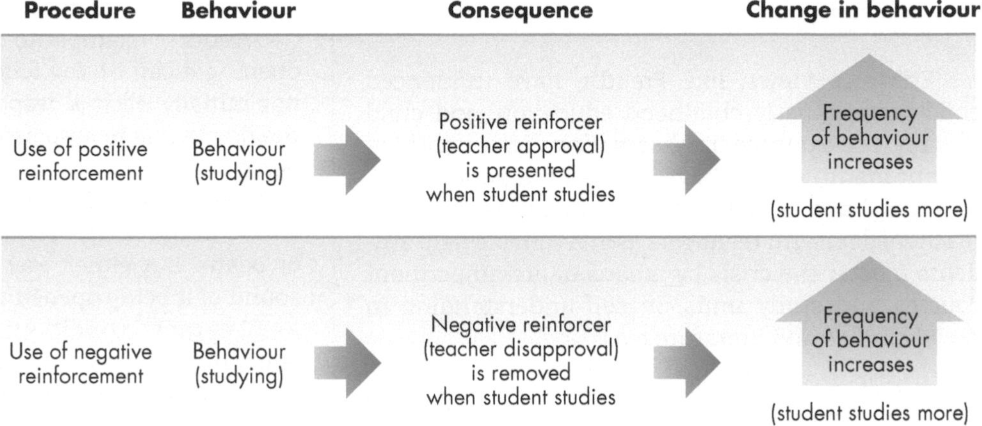

Procedure
Behaviour
Consequence
Change in behaviour
Use of positive reinforcement
Behaviour (studying)
Positive reinforcer (teacher approval) is presented when student studies
Frequency of behaviour increases
(student studies more)
Use of negative reinforcement
Behaviour (studying)
Negative reinforcer (teacher disapproval) is removed when student studies
Frequency of behaviour increases
(student studies more)

FIGURE 1.3

Negative Reinforcers versus Punishments

Both negative reinforcers and punishments tend to be aversive stimuli. Reinforcers, however, increase the frequency of behaviour. Punishments decrease the frequency of behaviour. Negative reinforcers increase the frequency of behaviour when they are removed.

Source: © Cengage Learning

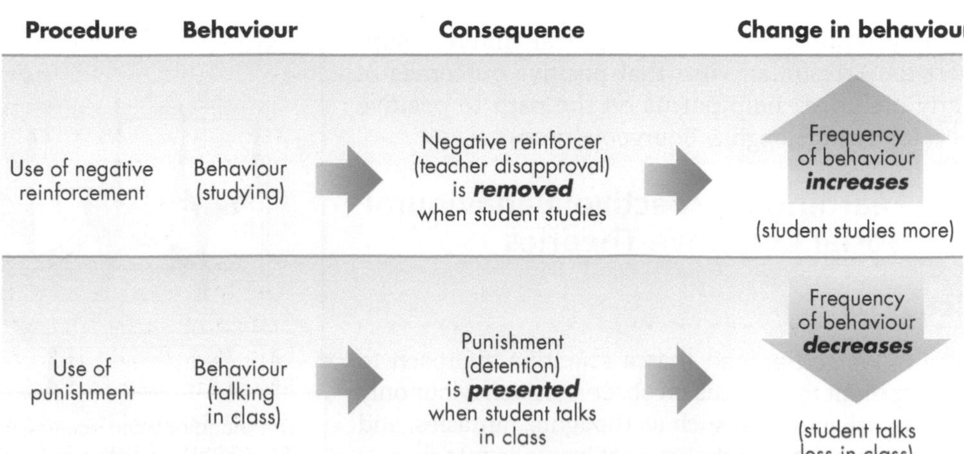

reinforcers with punishments.) Many learning theorists agree that punishment should be used sparingly in child rearing and that punishment is most appropriate when mild and prompt, such as the case with time outs. (A time out is when children who behave disruptively are placed in a restrictive environment for a specified time period, such as 10 minutes.)

Punishment on its own does not suggest an alternative, preferred behaviour and can lead to anger and resentment. Inappropriate behaviour will not stop unless punishment is consistent.

Extinction results when operant behaviour is no longer reinforced. After a number of trials when the stimuli are not reinforced, the operant behaviour is no longer shown. Children's temper tantrums and crying at bedtime can often be extinguished by parents' remaining out of the bedroom after the children have been put to bed.

Research suggests that when teachers praise and attend to appropriate behaviour and ignore misbehaviour, studying and classroom behaviour improve while disruptive and aggressive behaviours decrease (McIlvane & Dube, 2003; Takahashi & Sugiyama, 2003). By ignoring misbehaviour or by using time outs—removing the child from the environment that is causing the misbehaviour in the first place—caregivers can avoid reinforcing children's misbehaviour.

Social Cognitive Theory

Finally, we also learn by observation. Canadian-born Albert Bandura (1986, 2006a, 2006b) is well known for his theory of observational learning also called modelling. We also learn by observing other people, and by reading or viewing individuals in the media. People may need practice to refine their skills, but they can acquire the basic know-how through observation and modelling. For example, we may learn to hit by watching characters on television hit each other. In other words, learning does not always require conditioning.

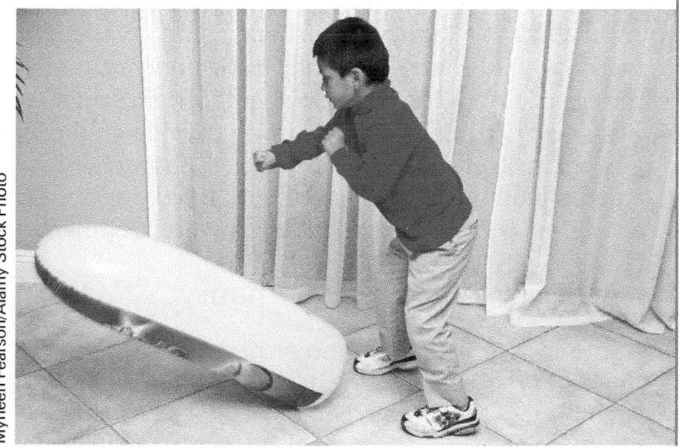

Myrleen Pearson/Alamy Stock Photo

Observational learning occurs when children notice how parents cook, clean, or interact with one another. It takes place when adults watch supervisors interact in the workplace or make important decisions. In social cognitive theory, the people after whom we pattern our own behaviour are termed *models*.

extinction the cessation of a response that is the result of the absence of reinforcement

social cognitive theory a cognitively oriented learning theory that emphasizes observational learning

cognitive-developmental theory the stage theory that suggests that children's abilities to mentally represent the world and solve problems are a result of the interaction of experience and the maturation of neurological structures

Evaluation of Learning Theories

Learning theories allow us to explain, predict, and influence many aspects of behaviour. Parenting magazines and websites are filled with tips for parents who want to learn how to control, observe, and make positive changes using the basics of learning theory. Many of the teaching approaches used in children's educational television are also based on these learning principles.

The Cognitive Perspective

Cognitive theorists focus on people's mental processes. They investigate how children perceive and mentally represent the world and how they develop thinking, logic, and problem-solving ability. One cognitive perspective is cognitive-developmental theory, advanced by Swiss biologist Jean Piaget (1896–1980) and further developed by many theorists. The theories of Lev Semenovich Vygotsky, for example, are discussed later in this chapter. Another cognitive perspective is information-processing theory.

Cognitive-Developmental Theory

During adolescence, Jean Piaget studied philosophy, logic, and mathematics; he took his Ph.D. in biology. In 1920, he obtained a job at the Binet Institute in Paris, where research on intelligence tests was being conducted. Through his studies, Piaget realized that when children answered questions incorrectly, their wrong answers still often reflected consistent—although illogical—mental processes. Piaget regarded children as natural physicists who actively intend to learn about and take intellectual charge of their worlds. In the Piagetian view, children who squish their food and laugh enthusiastically are often acting as budding scientists. They are studying both the texture and

schema
an action pattern or mental structure involved in the acquisition and organization of knowledge

adaptation
the interaction between the organism and the environment, consisting of assimilation and accommodation

assimilation
the incorporation of new events or knowledge into existing schemas

accommodation
the modification of existing schemas to permit the incorporation of new events or knowledge

equilibration
the creation of an equilibrium, or balance, between assimilation and accommodation

the consistency of their food, as well as their parents' response.

Piaget used concepts such as *schemas, adaptation, assimilation, accommodation,* and *equilibration* to describe and explain cognitive development. Piaget defines the **schema** as a pattern of action or mental structure involved when acquiring or organizing knowledge. For example, newborn babies might be said to have a sucking schema (others call it a *reflex*) because they respond to objects put in their mouths as "things I can suck" versus "things I can't suck."

Adaptation refers to the interaction between the organism and the environment. According to Piaget, all organisms adapt to their environment. Adaptation consists of assimilation and accommodation, which occur throughout life (Figure 1.4 illustrates the adaptation process). Cognitive **assimilation** refers to the process by which we respond to new objects or events according to existing schemas or ways of organizing knowledge. A 2-year-old who refers to horses as "doggies" is assimilating horses into the dog schema. But sometimes a novel object or event cannot be made to fit into an existing schema. In that case, the schema may be changed or a new schema may be created to incorporate the new event. This process is called **accommodation**. Consider the sucking reflex. Infants accommodate by rejecting objects that are too large, that taste bad, or that are of the wrong texture or temperature.

> "It is with children that we have the best chance of studying the development of logical knowledge, mathematical knowledge, physical knowledge, and so forth."
>
> —Piaget

Piaget theorized that when children can assimilate new events to existing schemas, they are in a state of cognitive harmony, or equilibrium. When they encounter something that does not fit, their state of equilibrium is disturbed and they may try to accommodate. The process of restoring equilibrium is termed **equilibration**. Piaget believed that the attempt to restore equilibrium lies at the heart of a child's natural curiosity.

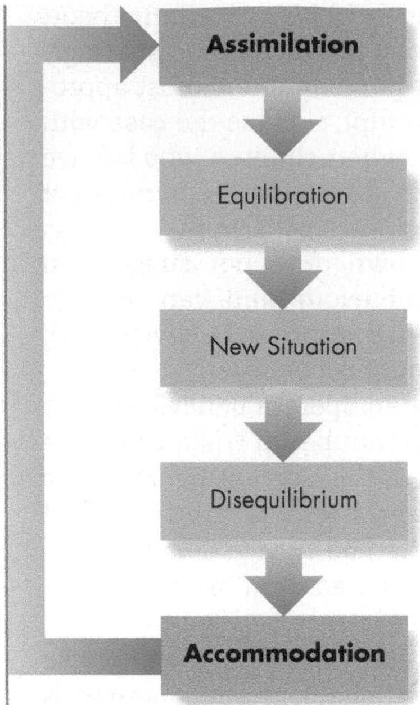

Assimilation → Equilibration → New Situation → Disequilibrium → Accommodation → (back to Assimilation)

FIGURE 1.4

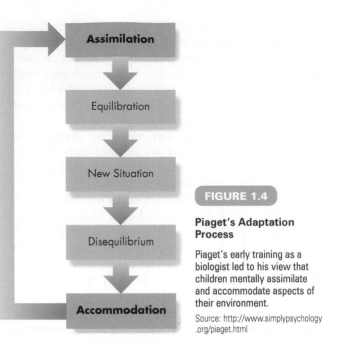

Piaget's Adaptation Process

Piaget's early training as a biologist led to his view that children mentally assimilate and accommodate aspects of their environment.

Source: http://www.simplypsychology.org/piaget.html

Piaget's Stages of Cognitive Development

Piaget (1963) hypothesized that children's cognitive processes develop in an orderly sequence, or series, consisting of four stages: sensorimotor, preoperational, concrete operational, and formal operational. These stages are discussed in greater detail in subsequent chapters.

Because Piaget's theory focuses on cognitive development, its applications are primarily in educational settings and provide the foundation for curriculum decisions made throughout the public school system in Canada. Teachers following Piaget's views actively engage children in solving problems. They gear instruction to children's developmental level and offer activities that challenge children to advance to the next level.

Evaluation: Many researchers, using a variety of methods, find that Piaget may have underestimated the ages when children are capable of certain activities. Also, many cognitive skills seem to develop gradually and not in distinct stages. Nevertheless, Piaget has provided a strong theoretical foundation for researchers concerned with sequences in cognitive development.

Information-Processing Theory

Another face of the cognitive perspective is information processing (Flavell et al., 2002; Siegler & Alabali, 2005). Many psychologists speak of people's

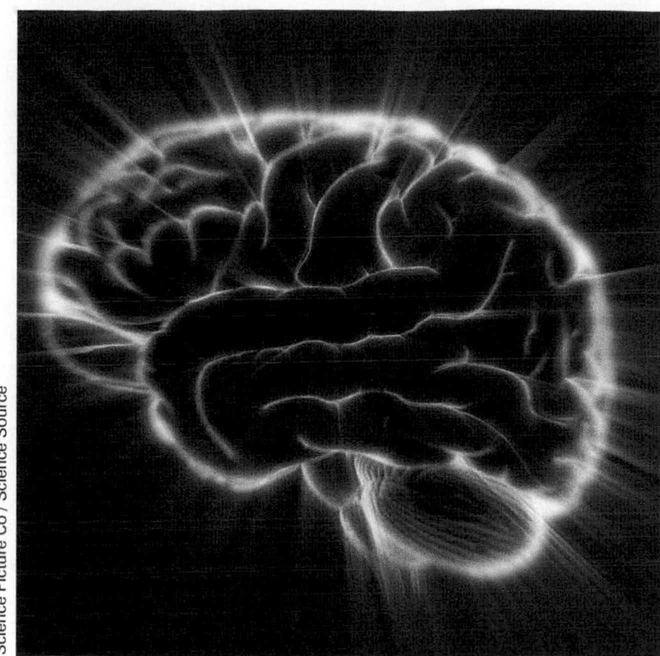

Science Picture Co / Science Source

The human brain is very similar to a computer.

working, or short-term, memory and a more permanent long-term memory (storage). If information has been placed in long-term memory, it must be retrieved before we can work on it. Retrieving information from our own long-term memories requires certain cues; otherwise, the information may be lost.

Thus, many cognitive psychologists focus on people's information processing—the processes people use to encode (input) information, store it (in long-term memory), retrieve it (place it in short-term memory), and manipulate it to solve problems. Our strategies for solving problems are sometimes referred to as our "mental programs" or "software." In this computer metaphor, our brains are the "hardware" that runs our mental programs. Our brains—containing billions of brain cells called *neurons*—become our most "personal" computers. When psychologists who study information processing contemplate cognitive development, they are likely to talk in terms of the size of the person's short-term memory.

Birds raised in isolation from other birds will build nests during the mating season even if they have never seen a nest or have never seen another bird building a nest.

The Biological Perspective

The biological perspective directly relates to physical development: to gains in height and weight; to development of the brain; and to developments related to hormones, reproduction, and heredity. Here we consider one biologically oriented theory of development, ethology.

ethology the study of behaviour specific to a species from the evolutionary perspective

fixed action pattern (FAP) a stereotyped pattern of behaviour that is evoked by a "releasing stimulus"; an instinct

Ethology: "Doing What Comes Naturally"

Ethology was heavily influenced by the 19th-century work of Charles Darwin and by the work of 20th-century ethologists Konrad Lorenz and Niko Tinbergen (Washburn, 2007). Ethology is concerned with instinctive, or inborn, behaviour patterns.

The nervous systems of most, and perhaps all, animals are "prewired" to respond to some situations in specific ways. For example, birds raised in isolation from other birds will build nests during the mating season even if they have never seen a nest or have never seen another bird building a nest. Nest-building could not have been learned. Birds raised in isolation also sing the songs typical of their species. These behaviours are "built in," or instinctive. They are also referred to as inborn fixed action patterns (FAPs).

Evaluation: Research into the ethological perspective suggests that instinct may play a role in human behaviour. Research seeks to answer two questions: Do human behaviour and human development involve instincts? If so, how powerful are human instincts?

Ronnie Howard/Shutterstock.com

Nesting is an instinctive behaviour, not a learned behaviour.

ecology
the branch of biology that studies the relationships between living organisms and their environment

ecological systems theory
the view that explains child development in terms of the reciprocal influences between children and their environmental settings

microsystem
the immediate settings with which the child interacts, such as the home, the school, and peers

mesosystem
the interlocking settings that influence the child, such as the interaction of the school and the larger community

The Ecological Perspective

Ecology is the branch of biology that studies the relationships between living organisms and their environment. The ecological systems theory of development addresses aspects of psychological, social, and emotional development as well as aspects of biological development. Development is explained in terms of the interaction between people and the settings in which they live (Bronfenbrenner & Morris, 2006).

According to Urie Bronfenbrenner (1917–2005), for example, we need to focus on the two-way interactions between the child and the parents, not just maturational forces (nature) or child-rearing practices (nurture). Bronfenbrenner (Bronfenbrenner & Morris, 2006) suggested that we can view the setting or contexts of human development as consisting of multiple systems, each embedded within the next larger context. From narrowest to widest, these systems are the microsystem, the mesosystem, the exosystem, the macrosystem, and the chronosystem (see Figure 1.5).

The microsystem involves the interactions of the child with other people in the immediate setting, such as the home, the school, or the peer group. Initially, the microsystem is small, involving care-giving interactions with the parents or others, usually at home. As children get older, they do more, with more people, in more places.

The mesosystem involves the interactions of the various settings within the microsystem. For instance, the home and the school interact during parent–teacher conferences. The school and the larger community interact when children

FIGURE 1.5

The Contexts of Human Development

An understanding of the interactions of systems is valuable for people employed in social work, community justice services, and child and youth services.

Source: © Cengage Learning

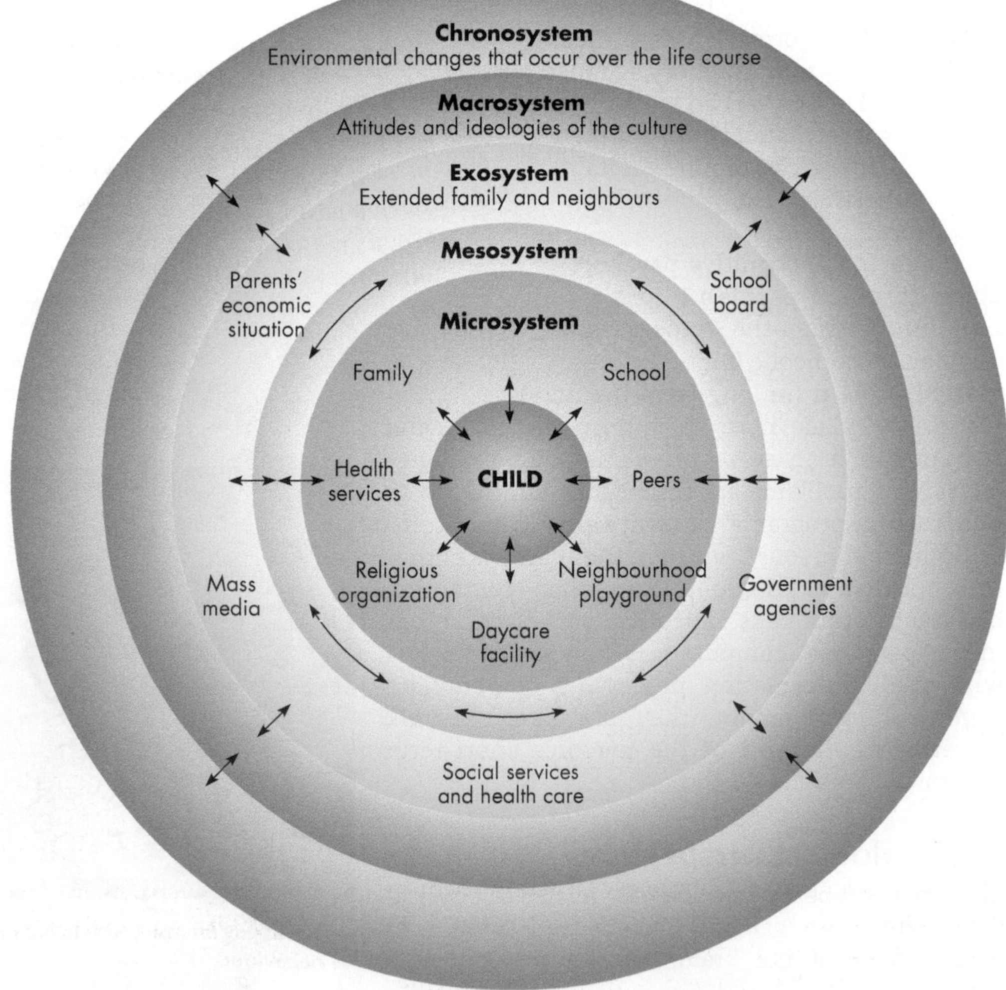

go on field trips. The ecological systems approach addresses the joint effect of two or more settings on the child.

The **exosystem** refers to the institutions in which the child does not directly participate but which exert an indirect influence on the child. For example, the school board is part of the child's exosystem because board members design programs for the child's education, determine the textbooks to be used, and so forth. In similar fashion, parents' workplaces and their economic situations determine the hours when they are available to the child, and so on (Kaminski & Stormshak, 2007).

The **macrosystem** refers to the interaction of children with the beliefs, values, expectations, and lifestyles of their socio-economic and cultural settings. Cross-cultural studies examine children's interactions with their macrosystem. In Canada, three different macrosystems are the dual-earner family; the low-income, single-parent household; and the family with father as sole breadwinner. Each has its lifestyle, set of values, and expectations (Bronfenbrenner & Morris, 2006; Silbereisen, 2006).

The **chronosystem** considers the changes that occur over time. For example, the effects of divorce peak about a year after the event, and then children begin to recover. The ecological approach broadens the strategies for intervention in issues such as prevention of teenage pregnancy, child abuse, youth in conflict with the law, and substance abuse (Kaminski & Stormshak, 2007).

The Socio-Cultural Perspective

The socio-cultural perspective teaches that people are social beings who are affected by the cultures in which they live. Russian psychologist Lev Semenovich Vygotsky (1896–1934), who was concerned with the biological transmission of traits from one generation to the next, did not view learning in terms of conditioning. Rather, he focused on how the child's social interaction with adults, mostly in the home, organizes a child's learning experiences in such a way that the child can obtain cognitive skills—such as computation or reading skills—which the child uses to acquire information. One key concept in Vygotsky's theory is the **zone of proximal development (ZPD)**, which refers to a range of tasks that a child can carry out with the help of someone who is more skilled, as in an apprenticeship (Ash, 2004; Umek, Podlesek, & Fekonja, 2005; Vygotsky, 1962).

Another key concept in Vygotsky's theory is **scaffolding**. A *scaffold* is a temporary skeletal structure that enables workers to fabricate a building or another permanent structure. According to Vygotsky, teachers and parents provide children with problem-solving methods that serve as cognitive scaffolding while the child gains the ability to function independently. A *scaffold* is a temporary skeletal structure that enables workers to fabricate a building or another permanent structure.

Gender and the Feminist Perspective

Gender is an aspect of human diversity that is no longer defined by physiological traits. Gender is now characterized more by social constructs, identity, and expression, and it varies within communities and societies. Gender is not fixed or definitive. Sex, on the other hand, refers to biological traits, which include physiological and anatomical characteristics such as sex organs and hormonal schemas.

Expectations of females and males are often polarized by cultural rules. That is, gender differences may be exaggerated, as is the case

exosystem
community institutions and settings that indirectly influence the child, such as the school board and the parents' workplaces

macrosystem
the basic institutions and ideologies that influence the child

chronosystem
the environmental changes that occur over time and have an effect on the child

zone of proximal development (ZPD)
Vygotsky's term for the range of tasks a child can carry out with the help of someone who is more skilled

scaffolding
Vygotsky's term for temporary cognitive structures or methods of solving problems that help children as they learn to function independently

gender
characterized by social constructs and identity, not fixed or definitive. It isn't as simple as physiology or anatomy

According to Vygotsky's theory, teachers and parents provide children with problem-solving methods that serve as cognitive scaffolding.

Gloria E. Anzaldúa, a cultural feminist and queer theorist, suggested that we move away from gender binaries, and that identification of ourselves through labelled sexes inhibits our capacity. "I change myself, I change the world."

with "boys" and "girls" toys, clothes, and games. Gender has played an important role, for example, when historically, females have been discouraged from careers in the sciences, politics, technology, policing, sports, and business. However, women today have made inroads into academic and vocational spheres that were traditionally male preserves—such as medicine, law, engineering, and the military. It is worth noting that, until relatively recently, women were not considered qualified for education. And even today, in many parts of the world, women are still prevented from obtaining an education.

Judith Butler, a prolific feminist and queer theorist, questioned the "naturalness" of gender, suggesting that gender is a kind of performance that is learned. Heterosexuality, which is deemed "normal" and "acceptable," is part of societal behaviours that are learned, or forced upon individuals and society. Butler questions how individuals constitute themselves, and how convention and "norms" may really determine who we are.

The Socio-Cultural Perspective and Human Diversity

The socio-cultural perspective asserts that we cannot understand individuals without awareness of the richness of their diversity (Fouad & Arredondo, 2007). For example, people differ in their ethnicity, gender, and socio-economic status.

People's ethnic groups involve their cultural heritage, their race, their language, and their common history. Figure 1.6, from the website of Citizenship

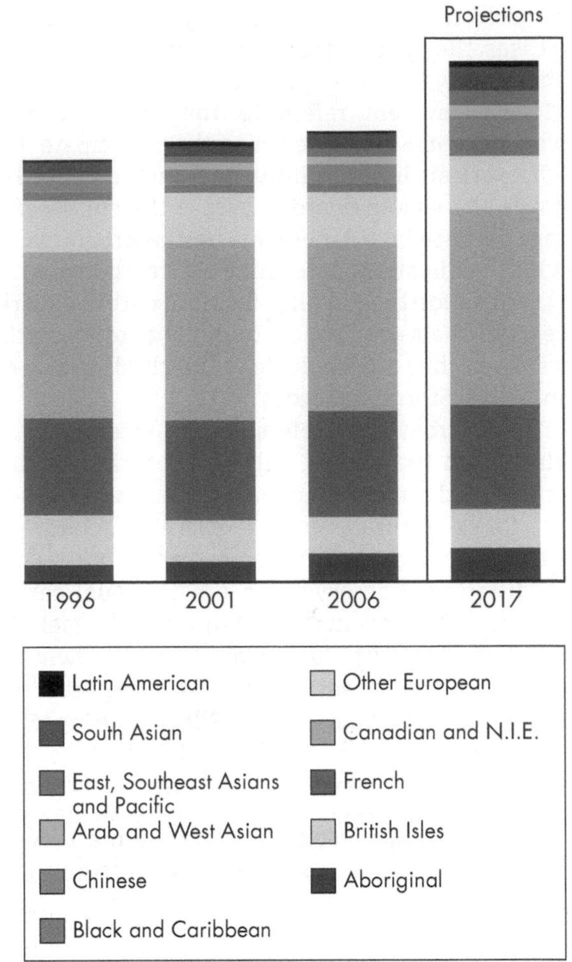

FIGURE 1.6

Diversity in Canada 1996–2006, and 2017 Projections

Source: Content courtesy of the Department of Canadian Heritage © All rights reserved. *Annual Report on the Operation of the Canadian Multiculturalism Act 2007-2008*. Reproduced with the permission of the Minister of Canadian Heritage, 2016.

and Immigration Canada, highlights more than 200 multicultural groupings that populate our country. Canadian society is built on the acceptance and promotion of diversity within the Canadian population, which must not be taken for granted but should be fostered and developed.

EMERGING CANADA

Canadians are better educated than they were a decade ago and have some of the highest graduation rates in the free world. More Canadian women graduate from high school and postsecondary institutions than men, but women continue to earn far less in the workplace (Morrow, 2010).

LO3 Debates in Human Development

The discussion of theories of development reveals that developmentalists can see things in very different ways. Let us consider how they react to three of the most important debates in the field.

Nature and Nurture

Researchers are continually trying to sort out the extent to which human behaviour is the result of nature (heredity) and of nurture (environmental influences). What aspects of human behaviour originate in our genes and are biologically programmed to unfold as time goes on, as long as we receive minimal nutrition and social experience? What aspects of human behaviour can be traced mostly to such environmental influences as nutrition and learning?

Most researchers agree that both nature and nurture play important roles in nearly every area of development. Consider the significant health threat that cardiovascular disease presents to Canadians. A person may be genetically predisposed to this disease (nature), but lifestyle choices (nurture) will also strongly affect this person's health outcome. Modern theorists rarely view nature and nurture as mutually exclusive.

Continuity and Discontinuity

Some developmentalists view human development as a continuous process, in which the effects of learning increase gradually, with no sudden major qualitative changes. In contrast, other theorists believe that numerous rapid qualitative changes usher in new stages of development. Maturational theorists point out that the environment, even when enriched, provides us with little benefit until we are ready, or mature enough, to develop in a certain way. For example, newborn babies will not imitate their parents' speech, even when parents speak clearly and deliberately, because developmentally, babies are not yet ready to speak. Stage theorists such as Sigmund Freud and Jean Piaget saw development as discontinuous. They saw biological changes as providing the potential for psychological changes.

nature
the processes within an organism that guide it to develop according to its genetic code

nurture
environmental factors that influence development

empirical
based on observation and experimentation

> **EMERGING CANADA**
>
> In Canada, tens of thousands of people die every year from heart disease or stroke. Over the past 40 years, the rate has significantly declined as a result of education and changes in lifestyle. The rate has declined 25% over the past 10 years, 50% over the past 20 years, and 70% between 1956 and today (Heart and Stroke Foundation, 2013).

Active and Passive Roles

Historical views of children as willful and unruly suggest that people have generally viewed children as being active, even if mischievous (at best) or evil (at worst). John Locke introduced a view of children as passive beings (blank tablets); he believed that experience "wrote" features of personality and moral virtue on children.

At one extreme, educators who view children as passive may assume that instructors must motivate children to learn. Such educators are likely to provide a rigorous traditional curriculum with a powerful system of rewards and punishments to promote absorption of the subject matter. At the other extreme, educators who view children as active may assume that children have a natural love of learning. Such educators are likely to argue for open education and encourage children to explore and pursue their unique likes and talents, focusing on a love of learning for learning's sake.

These debates are theoretical. Scientists value theory for its ability to tie together observations and suggest new areas of investigation, but they also follow an empirical approach. That is, to find evidence for or against various theoretical positions, they engage in research methods, such as those described in the next section.

Tomas 111/Shutterstock.com

Sari O'Neal/Shutterstock.com

Those viewing development as discontinuous recognize distinct changes comparable to the caterpillar and the butterfly.

Blend Images / Alamy Stock Photo

Girls usually spurt in growth before boys do, which these graduating grade eights are very much aware of.

LO4 How Do We Study Human Development?

Gathering Information

Researchers use various methods to gather information. For example, they ask teachers or parents to report on the behaviour of children, use interviews or questionnaires with adults, or study statistics compiled by the government or the United Nations. They also directly observe children in the laboratory, the playground, or the classroom. Let us discuss two ways of gathering information: the naturalistic-observation method and the case-study method.

Naturalistic Observation

Naturalistic-observation studies are conducted in "the field," that is, in the natural, or real-life, settings in which the activities being studied occur. For example, in field studies, investigators observe the natural behaviour of children in settings such as homes, playgrounds, and classrooms. Because researchers do not want their presence to interfere with children's normal behaviour, they may try to blend in and sit quietly in the back of a classroom or observe the class through a one-way mirror.

case study
a carefully written account of the behaviour of an individual

standardized test
a test that compares an individual's score with the scores of a group of similar individuals

The Case Study

The case study is a carefully written account of the behaviour of an individual. Parents who keep diaries of their children's activities are writing informal case studies. Case studies themselves often use different kinds of information. In addition to direct observation, case studies may include questionnaires, standardized tests, and interviews. Information gleaned from public records may also be included. Scientists who use the case-study method try to record all relevant factors in a person's behaviour, and they are cautious in drawing conclusions about the source of any behaviour.

Surveys

Researchers also collect information by posing well-designed questions to gather statistics on a wide variety of topics. For example, Statistics Canada collects data to ensure that the government can make appropriate planning decisions while collecting the most recent and accurate information on Canadian trends. The long-form census is gathered every 5 years and is mandatory for every citizen to complete.

The Canadian Psychological Association also routinely conducts surveys. This initiative aids in the collecting of information concerning the characteristics of the clients they assess and treat. The survey results are used to address the data gap that exists in the area of mental health needs in Canada.

Remember that survey results are subject to interpretation. The individual analyzing the results is responsible to give the collected information significant meaning. Throughout this textbook, you will read Emerging Canada features that describe the information being collected on emerging Canadian trends. Your challenge is to apply this information in a meaningful way, by going beyond the statistics presented.

Correlation: Putting Things Together

Researchers use the correlational method to determine whether one behaviour or trait being studied relates to, or correlates with, another. Consider intelligence and achievement. These variables are assigned numbers such as intelligence test scores

Jeffrey Greenberg / Science Source

The researcher is able to observe children in this two-way mirror without disrupting their play. The children are unaware they are being observed.

EMERGING CANADA

Mental illness indirectly affects all Canadians at some time through personal experience, or through the experience of a family member, friend, or colleague. Consider that 20% of Canadians will personally experience a mental illness in their lifetime, and suicide accounts for 24% of all deaths among 15- to 24-year-olds and 16% of all deaths among 25- to 44-year-olds. In other words, 1 in 5 Canadians will experience mental illness, and suicide is one of the leading causes of death for young Canadians (Canadian Mental Health Association, 2013c). What questions arise from this finding? Why is there a stigma connected with mental health when it is clearly a significant Canadian issue?

and grade point averages. The numbers or scores are then mathematically related and expressed as a correlation coefficient—a number that varies between +1.00 and −1.00.

In general, the higher people score on intelligence tests, the more likely they are to have better academic performance (and income). The scores attained on intelligence tests are positively correlated (about +0.60 to +0.70) with overall academic achievement (and income). A negative correlation exists between adolescents' grades and delinquent acts. That is, the higher an adolescent's grades, the less likely he or she is to engage in criminal behaviour. Figure 1.7 illustrates positive and negative correlations.

Limitations of Correlational Information

Correlational information can reveal relationships between variables but does not show cause and effect. Assuming that exposure to violent media makes people more aggressive may seem logical, but it may also be that more aggressive people choose violent media. This research bias is termed a *selection factor.*

To investigate cause and effect, researchers turn to the experimental method.

The Experiment: Trying Things Out

The experiment is the preferred method for investigating questions of cause and effect. In the experiment, one group of subjects receives a treatment and another group does not. The subjects are then observed to determine whether the treatment changes their behaviour. Experiments are usually undertaken to test a hypothesis. For example, a researcher might hypothesize that TV violence will cause aggressive behaviour in children.

Independent and Dependent Variables

In an experiment to determine whether TV violence causes aggressive behaviour, subjects in the experimental group would be shown a TV program containing violence, and then its effects on behaviour would be measured. TV violence would be considered an independent variable, a variable whose presence is manipulated by the experimenters so that its effects can be determined. The measured result—in this case, the child's behaviour—is called a dependent variable. Its presence or level presumably depends on the independent variable.

correlation coefficient
a number ranging from +1.00 to −1.00 that expresses the direction (positive or negative) and strength of the relationship between two variables

positive correlation
a relationship between two variables in which one variable increases as the other increases

negative correlation
a relationship between two variables in which one variable increases as the other decreases

experiment
a method of scientific investigation that seeks to discover cause-and-effect relationships by introducing independent variables and observing their effects on dependent variables

hypothesis
a proposition to be tested

independent variable
a condition in a scientific study that is manipulated so that its effects can be observed

dependent variable
a measure of an assumed effect of an independent variable

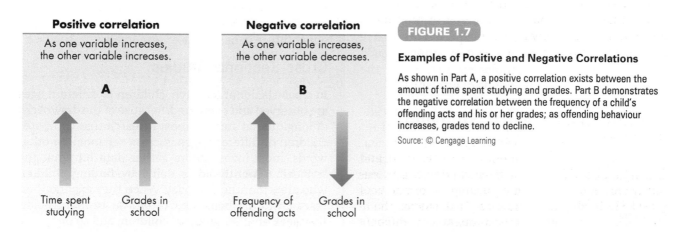

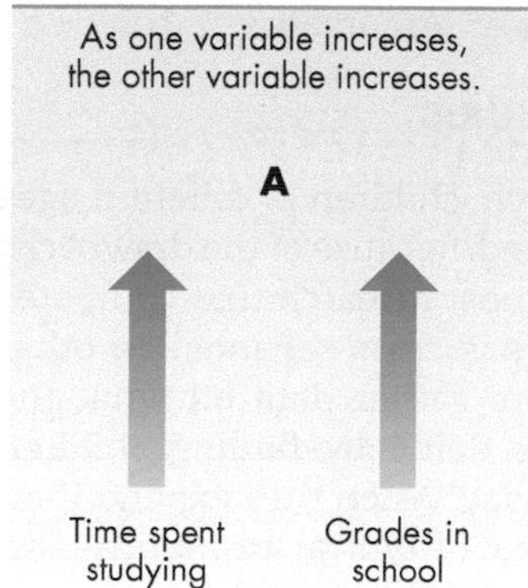

Negative correlation

As one variable increases, the other variable decreases.

B

Frequency of offending acts

Grades in school

FIGURE 1.7

Examples of Positive and Negative Correlations

As shown in Part A, a positive correlation exists between the amount of time spent studying and grades. Part B demonstrates the negative correlation between the frequency of a child's offending acts and his or her grades; as offending behaviour increases, grades tend to decline.

Source: © Cengage Learning

experimental group
a group of subjects who receive a treatment in an experiment

control group
a group of subjects in an experiment who do not receive the treatment but for whom all other conditions are comparable with those of the experimental group

longitudinal research
the study of developmental processes by taking repeated measures of the same group of participants at various stages of development

cross-sectional research
the study of developmental processes by taking measures of participants of different age groups at the same time

Experimental and Control Groups

Experiments use experimental and control groups. Subjects in the experimental group receive the treatment, whereas subjects in the control group do not. All other conditions are held constant for both groups. Thus, we can have confidence that experimental outcomes reflect the treatments and not chance factors.

Random Assignment

Subjects should be assigned to experimental or control groups on a chance or random basis. We could not conclude much from an experiment on the effects of TV violence if the children were allowed to choose whether they would be in a group that watched TV violence or in a group that did not. In such an experiment, a selection factor, not the treatment itself might be responsible for the results of the experiment.

Ethical and practical considerations also prevent researchers from doing experiments on the effects of many life circumstances, such as divorce or different patterns of child rearing. It is also impossible to randomly assign parents to rearing their children in an authoritarian or permissive manner. In some areas of investigation, we must settle for correlational or empirical evidence.

When experiments cannot ethically be performed on humans, researchers sometimes carry them out with animals and try to generalize the findings to humans. No researcher would separate human infants from their parents to study the effects of isolation on development, yet experimenters have deprived monkeys of early social experience. Such research has helped psychologists investigate the formation of parent–child bonds of attachment.

Longitudinal Research: Studying Development over Time

The processes of development occur over time, and researchers have devised different strategies for comparing children of one age with children or adults of other ages. In longitudinal research, the same people are observed repeatedly over time, and researchers record their changes in development, such as gains in height or changes in mental abilities.

> **DID YOU KNOW?**
>
> **Research with monkeys has helped psychologists understand the formation of attachment in humans.**
>
> Scientists cannot ethically research the formation of attachments on humans, so they conduct tests on animals that are genetically similar to people and then extrapolate their findings.

Longitudinal Studies

The National Longitudinal Survey of Children and Youth (NLSCY) began in Canada in 1994. The NLSCY collects information on the factors that influence children's social, emotional, and behavioural development and studies the impact of these factors on children's development over time. Also gathered are data concerning Canadian children's social environment (family, friends, schools, and communities) (Statistics Canada, 2008c).

> **DID YOU KNOW?**
>
> **To learn how a person develops over a lifetime, researchers have tracked some individuals for more than 50 years.**
>
> Lewis Terman's Genetic Studies of Genius, which began in the 1920s and will continue until the last member of the sample dies, has tracked the professional achievements of male subjects with high IQs.

These studies allow long-term vision; however, they are also costly and require an extensive time commitment.

Longitudinal studies have drawbacks. For example, researchers find it difficult to enlist volunteers to participate in a study that will last a lifetime. Many subjects fall out of touch as the years pass; others die. The researchers must be patient or arrange to enlist future generations of researchers.

Cross-Sectional Studies

In cross-sectional research, children of different ages are observed and compared. Because of the drawbacks of longitudinal studies, most research that compares children of different ages is cross-sectional. In other words, most investigators gather data on what the "typical" 6-month-old is doing by finding children who are 6 months old today. When they expand their research to the behaviour of typical 12-month-olds, they seek another group of children, and so on.

Zurijeta/Shutterstock.com

Cross-sectional research involves observations and measurement of developmental processes of different aged participants at the same time.

A major challenge to cross-sectional research is the cohort effect. A cohort is a group of people born at about the same time. As a result, they experience cultural and other events unique to their age group. In other words, children and adults of different ages are not likely to have shared similar cultural backgrounds. For example, people who are 80 years old today grew up without TV. Today's children grow up taking iPods and the Internet for granted.

cohort effect similarities in behaviour among a group of peers as a result of being of approximately the same age

Children of past generations also grew up with different expectations about gender roles and appropriate social behaviour.

In longitudinal studies, we know that we have the same individuals as they have developed over 5, 25, even 50 years or more. In cross-sectional research, we can only hope that the individuals being studied will be comparable.

Nina Leen/The LIFE Picture Collection/Getty Images

Harlow's research in 1958 sought to understand bonds of attachment between mothers and newborns. When "tactile comfort" (McLeod, 2009) wasn't given to rhesus monkeys, they engaged in self-mutilating and aggressive behaviours. Interestingly, the monkeys spent more time with the cloth mother than the wire one, as it provided a "safe base."

Ethical Considerations

The Canadian Psychological Association (2000) has designed a 32-page Code of Ethics for psychologists conducting research in Canada. Although this document often makes the completion of research more difficult, it ultimately safeguards the welfare of Canadians.

Some of the governing principles of the document include the following:

1. Respect for the Individual, including standards such as informed consent, confidentiality, and protection for vulnerable persons (including children, seniors, and those with intellectual disabilities);
2. Responsible Care, such as risk/benefit analysis and minimizing harm;
3. Integrity in Relationships, including honesty, lack of bias, and complete disclosure; and
4. Responsibility to Society, including the pursuit of beneficial research for the development of society.

This strict and detailed code of ethics reflects the responsibility and integrity that must govern all psychological research conducted in Canada. The code promotes the dignity of the individual, fosters human welfare, and maintains scientific integrity.

STUDY TOOLS CourseMate **CHAPTER 1**

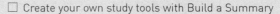

Located at **nelson.com/student**

- ☐ Prepare for tests with a variety of exercises and activities
- ☐ Review Key Terms Flashcards (online or print)
- ☐ Create your own study tools with Build a Summary
- ☐ Watch Observing Development videos to expand your knowledge

CHAPTER 2

Heredity and Prenatal Development

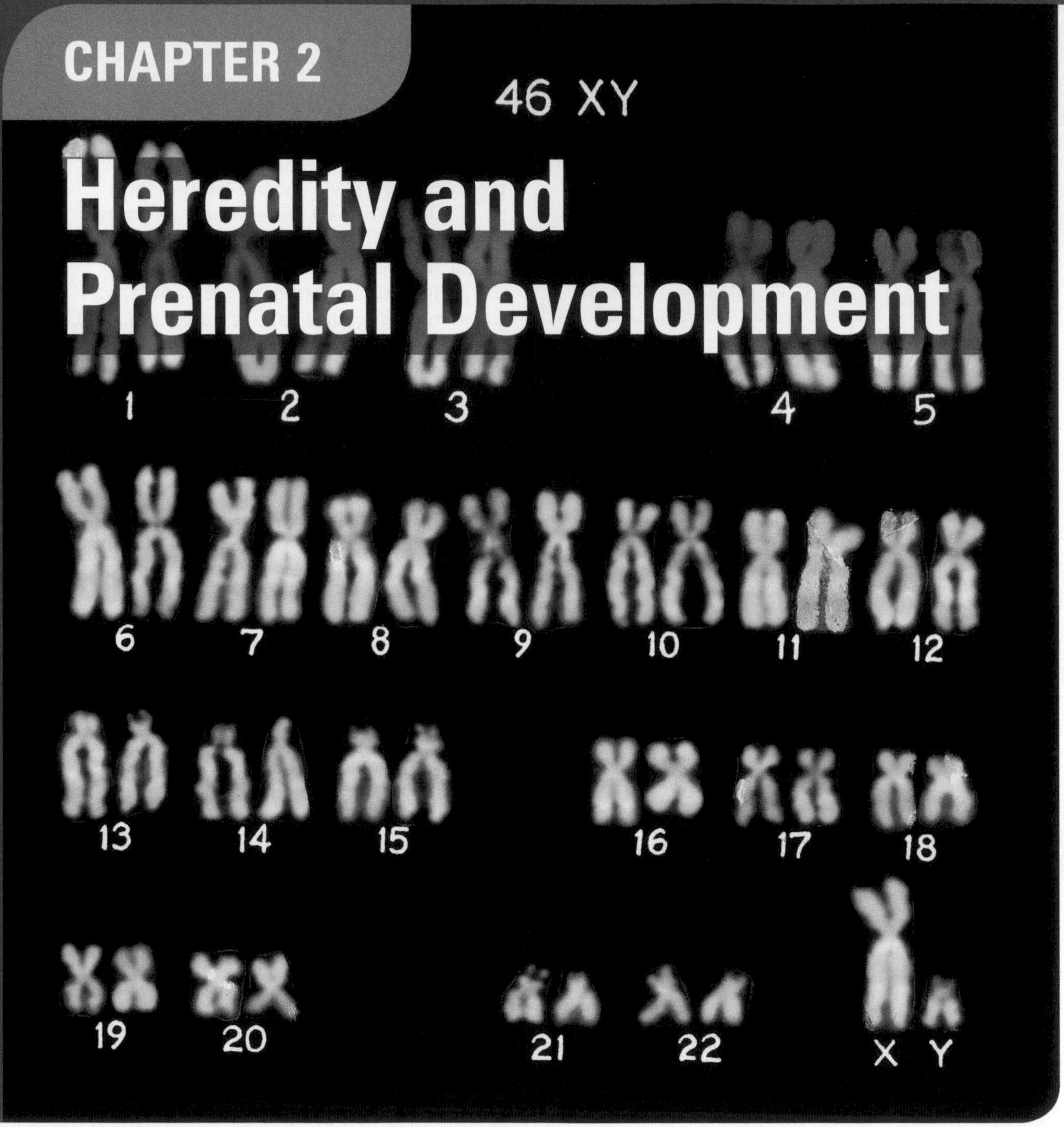

46 XY

1 2 3 4 5

6 7 8 9 10 11 12

13 14 15 16 17 18

19 20 21 22 X Y

BIOPHOTO ASSOCIATES/Getty Images

LEARNING OUTCOMES

LO1 Describe the influences of heredity on development

LO2 Describe the influences of the environment on development

LO3 Explain what happens in the process of conception

LO4 Recount the major events of prenatal development

> "The structures we inherit make our behaviour possible and place limits on it."

LO1 The Influence of Heredity on Development

Heredity makes all things humanly possible. Heredity is the transmission of genetic material from one generation to another. The structures we inherit make our behaviour possible and place limits on it. The field of biology that studies heredity is called genetics.

Genetic influences are fundamental in the transmission of physical traits, such as height, hair texture, and eye colour. Genetics also appears to play a role in psychological traits such as intelligence, activity level, sociability, shyness, anxiety, empathy, effectiveness as a parent, happiness, and even interest in arts and crafts (Johnson & Krueger, 2006; Knafo & Plomin, 2006a, 2006b; Leonardo & Hen, 2006). Genetic factors are also involved in psychological problems such as schizophrenia; depression; and dependence on nicotine, alcohol, and other substances (Farmer, Elkin, & McGuffin, 2007; Hill et al., 2007; Metzger et al., 2007).

Chromosomes and Genes

Traits are transmitted by chromosomes and genes. Chromosomes are rod-shaped structures found in cells. Typical human cells contain 46 chromosomes organized into 23 pairs. Each chromosome contains thousands of segments called genes. Genes are the biochemical materials that regulate the development of traits. Some traits, such as blood type, appear to be transmitted by a single pair of genes, one derived from each parent. Other traits are polygenic; that is, they are determined by many (poly) pairs of genes.

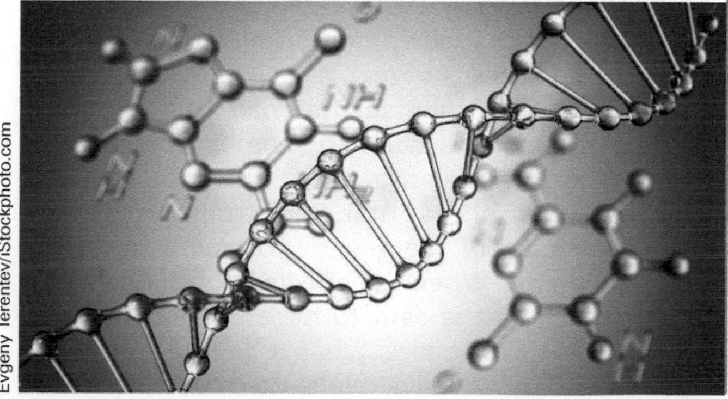
Evgeny Terentev/iStockphoto.com

Our heredity is governed by 20,000 to 25,000 genes (International Human Genome Sequencing Consortium, 2006). Genes are segments of strands of deoxyribonucleic acid (DNA). DNA takes the form of a double spiral, or double helix, similar to a twisting ladder.

Mitosis and Meiosis

We begin life as a single cell, or zygote, that divides repeatedly. There are two types of cell division: *mitosis* and *meiosis*. In mitosis, strands of DNA break apart, or "unzip" (see Figure 2.1). The double helix then duplicates. The DNA forms two camps on either side of the cell, and then the cell divides. Each incomplete rung combines with the appropriate "partner" to form a new complete ladder. The two resulting identical copies of the DNA strand will separate when the cell divides so that each becomes a member of a newly formed cell. As a result, the genetic code is identical in new cells unless mutations occur through radiation or other environmental influences. Mutations also occur by chance, but not often.

heredity transmission of genetic material from one generation to another

genetics the branch of biology that studies heredity

chromosomes rod-shaped structures that are composed of genes and are found within the nuclei of cells

genes the basic units of heredity. Genes are composed of deoxyribonucleic acid (DNA)

polygenic resulting from many (poly) genes

deoxyribonucleic acid (DNA) genetic material that takes the form of a double helix and is composed of phosphates, sugars, and bases

mitosis the form of cell division in which each chromosome splits lengthwise to double in number. Half of each chromosome combines with chemicals to retake its original form and then moves to the new cell.

mutation a sudden, or accidental, variation in a heritable characteristic that affects the composition of genes

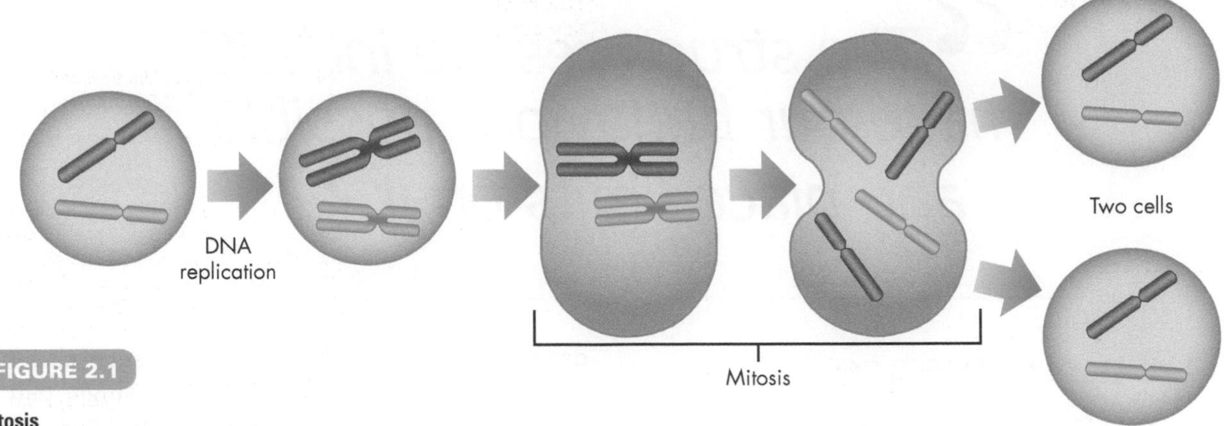

FIGURE 2.1

Mitosis

Sperm and ova (egg cells) are produced through **meiosis**, or *reduction division*. In meiosis, the 46 chromosomes within the cell nucleus first line up into 23 pairs. The DNA ladders then unzip, leaving unpaired halves of chromosomes. When the cell divides, one member of each pair goes to each newly formed cell. Each new cell nucleus contains only 23 chromosomes, not 46.

Source: Adapted from the *Science Primer*, a work of the National Center for Biotechnology Information, part of the National Institutes of Health, US Federal Government.

meiosis
the form of cell division in which each pair of chromosomes splits so that one member of each pair moves to the new cell. As a result, each new cell has 23 chromosomes.

autosome
a pair of chromosomes (with the exception of sex chromosomes)

sex chromosome
a chromosome in the shape of a Y (male) or X (female) that determines the sex of the child

monozygotic (MZ) twins
twins that derive from a single zygote that has split into two; identical twins. Each MZ twin carries the same genetic code.

dizygotic (DZ) twins
twins that derive from two separate zygotes; fraternal twins with different genetic codes

allele
a member of a pair of genes

homozygous
having two identical alleles

heterozygous
having two different alleles

ovulation
the releasing of an ovum from an ovary

When a sperm cell fertilizes an ovum (egg cell), we receive 23 chromosomes from our father's sperm cell and 23 from our mother's ovum, and the combined chromosomes form 23 pairs. Twenty-two of the pairs are autosomes—pairs that look alike and possess genetic information concerning the same set of traits. The 23rd pair, the sex chromosomes, looks different from the autosome pairs and determines our sex. We all receive an X sex chromosome (so called because of its X shape) from our mother. Our father supplies either a Y or an X sex chromosome. If we receive an X sex chromosome from our father, we develop into a female, and if we receive a Y chromosome (named after its Y shape), we develop into a male.

DID YOU KNOW?

Your father determined whether you are female or male.

Males supply either an X or a Y chromosome, which determines the sex of the baby. Imagine how shocked King Henry VIII would be if he were a student in this class. Many women were isolated in medieval times for "their" inability to produce a male heir.

Identical and Fraternal Twins

Now and then, a zygote divides into two cells that separate so that each develops into an individual with the same genetic makeup. These individuals are identical twins, or monozygotic (MZ) twins. In very rare cases, the eggs do not completely separate on the 13th day after conception, and the result is conjoined twins, as was the case for Tatiana and Krista, born in British Columbia in March 2007. If a woman produces two ova in the same month, and each is fertilized by different sperm cells, they develop into fraternal twins, or dizygotic (DZ) twins (see Figure 2.2). DZ twins run in families. If a woman is a twin, if her mother was a twin, or if she has previously borne twins, the likelihood that she will bear twins increases (Office of National Statistics, 2006).

Dominant and Recessive Traits

Traits are determined by pairs of genes. Each member of a pair of genes is termed an allele. When both of the alleles for a trait, such as hair colour, are the same, the person is said to be homozygous for that trait. When the alleles for a trait differ, the person is heterozygous for that trait. Some traits result from an "averaging" of the genetic instructions carried by the parents. When the effects of both alleles are shown, the trait is said to have incomplete dominance, or codominance. When a dominant allele is paired with a recessive allele, the trait determined

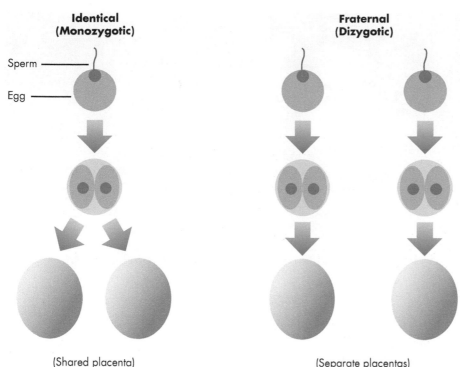

Identical
(Monozygotic)

Sperm

Egg

(Shared placenta)

Fraternal
(Dizygotic)

(Separate placentas)

FIGURE 2.2

Difference between Identical and Fraternal Twins Cell Division

As women reach the end of their child-bearing years, ovulation becomes less regular, resulting in months when more than one ovum is released. Thus, the chances of twins increase with parental age (National Guideline Clearinghouse, 2007). Adding to this likelihood is the social reality in Canada that women are postponing parenting later than their mothers and grandmothers. Of the mothers who gave birth in 2005, 48.9% were 30 years of age or older, more than double the percentage in 1974 (Human Resources and Skills Development Canada, 2010a). Fertility drugs also enhance the chances of multiple births by causing more than one ovum to ripen and be released during a woman's cycle (National Guideline Clearinghouse, 2007). Finally, multiple births (more than one baby born from a single pregnancy) have increased with the greater number of in vitro fertilization procedures that have been performed in Canada.

Source: https://commons.wikimedia.org/wiki/File:Identical-fraternal-sperm-egg.svg

by the dominant allele appears in the offspring. For example, the offspring from the crossing of brown eyes with blue eyes have brown eyes, suggesting that brown eyes are a dominant trait and blue eyes are a recessive trait.

If one parent carried genes for only brown eyes and if the other parent carried genes for only blue eyes, the children would invariably have brown eyes. But brown-eyed parents can also carry recessive genes for blue eyes, as shown in Figure 2.3. If the recessive gene from one parent combines with the recessive gene from the other parent, the recessive trait will be shown. As suggested by Figure 2.3, approximately 25% of the children of brown-eyed parents who carry recessive blue eye colour will have blue eyes. Table 2.1 shows some dominant and recessive traits in humans.

People who bear one dominant gene and one recessive gene for a trait are said to be carriers of the recessive gene. In the cases of recessive genes that cause illness, carriers of those genes are fortunate to have dominant genes that cancel the effects of the recessive genes but they may still pass on the illness to their children. This is the case for cystic fibrosis and sickle-cell anemia.

Chromosomal or genetic abnormalities can cause health problems. Some chromosomal disorders reflect abnormalities in the 22 pairs of autosomes (e.g., Down syndrome); others reflect abnormalities in the sex chromosomes (e.g., XYY syndrome). Some genetic abnormalities, such as cystic fibrosis, are caused by a single pair of genes; others are caused by combinations of genes. Diabetes mellitus, epilepsy, and peptic ulcers are multifactorial problems; they reflect both a genetic predisposition and environmental contributors.

Chromosomal Abnormalities

People normally have 46 chromosomes. Children with more or fewer chromosomes usually experience

dominant trait
a trait that is expressed

recessive trait
a trait that is not expressed when the gene or genes involved have been paired with **dominant genes**

carrier
a person who carries and transmits characteristics but does not exhibit them

multifactorial problems
problems that stem from the interaction of heredity and environmental factors

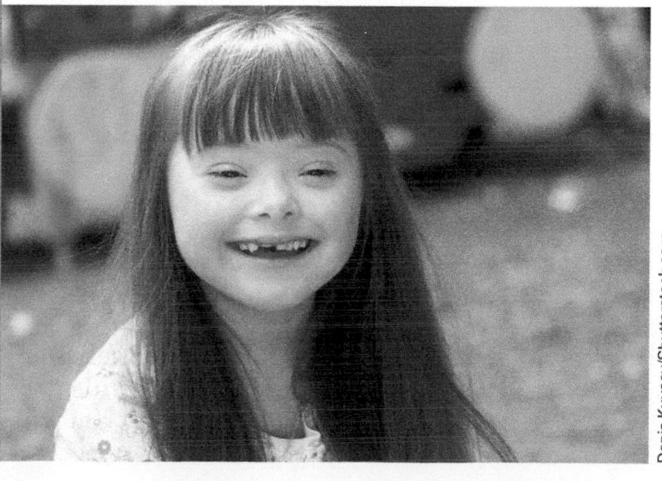

Denis Kuvaev/Shutterstock.com

Down syndrome
a chromosomal abnormality characterized by intellectual challenges and caused by an extra chromosome in the 21st pair

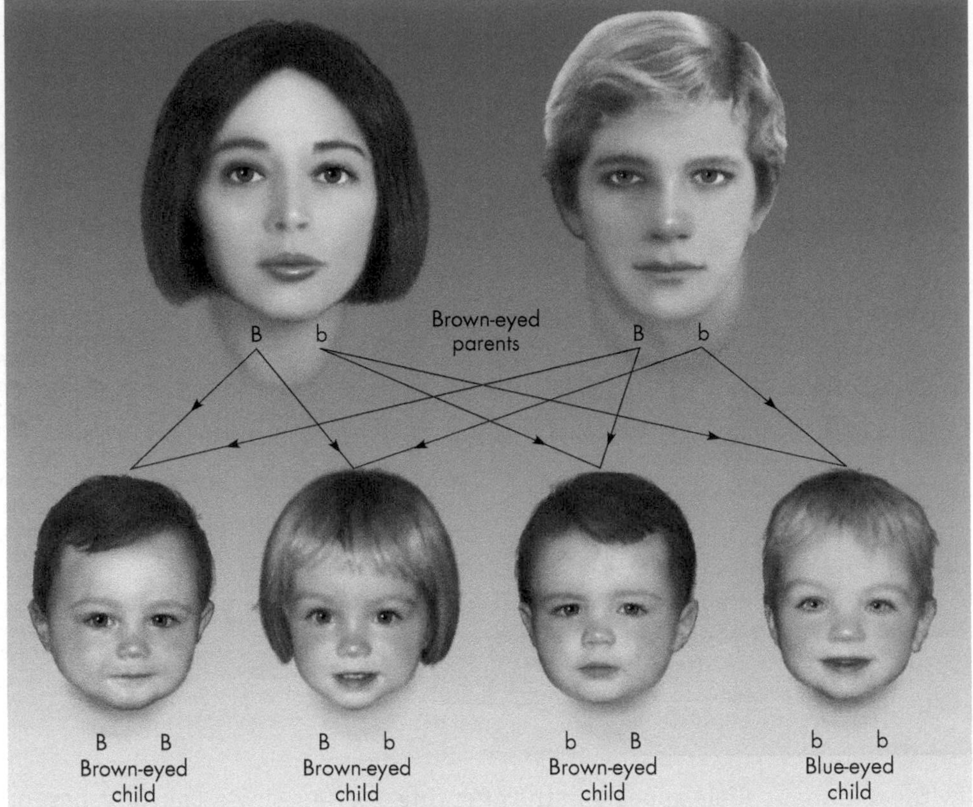

FIGURE 2.3

Transmission of Dominant and Recessive Traits

These two brown-eyed parents each carry a gene for blue eyes. Their children have an equal opportunity of receiving genes for brown eyes and blue eyes.

Source: © Cengage Learning

TABLE 2.1

Examples of Dominant and Recessive Traits in Humans

Dominant Trait	Recessive Trait
Dark hair	Blond hair
Dark hair	Red hair
Curly hair	Straight hair
Normal colour vision	Red-green colour blindness
Normal vision	Myopia (nearsightedness)
Farsightedness	Normal vision
Normal pigmentation	Deficiency of pigmentation in skin, hair, and retina (albinism)
Normal sensitivity to touch	Extremely fragile skin
Normal hearing	Some forms of deafness
Dimples	Lack of dimpling
Type A blood	Type O blood
Type B blood	Type O blood

Source: © Cengage Learning

health problems or behavioural abnormalities. The risk of chromosomal abnormalities rises with the age of the parents (American Fertility Association, 2007).

Down Syndrome

Down syndrome is usually caused by an extra chromosome on the 21st pair, resulting in 47 chromosomes. It occurs in approximately 1 in 781 live births in Canada (Canadian Down Syndrome Society, 2016). The probability of having a child with Down syndrome increases with the age of the parents. People with Down syndrome have characteristic features that include a rounded face; a protruding tongue; a broad, flat nose; and a sloping fold of skin over the inner corners of the eyes. They show varying deficits in cognitive development (Rondal & Ling, 2006) and motor development (Virji-Babul et al., 2006) and usually die from pneumonia and cardiovascular problems by middle age, although modern medicine has extended their life expectancy to approximately 60 years (Pitetti, Baynard, & Agiovlasitis, 2013).

EMERGING CANADA

The Canadian Down Syndrome Society (CDSS) is proud to celebrate World Down Syndrome Day, March 21. This day of recognition celebrates the lives of people with Down syndrome all around the world. The goal of this day is to promote inclusion of individuals with Down syndrome so that they may participate fully and equally with others in society.

Sex-Linked Chromosomal Abnormalities

Numerous disorders stem from an abnormal number of sex chromosomes and are therefore called sex-linked chromosomal abnormalities. Most individuals with an abnormal number of sex chromosomes are infertile. Beyond that common finding, these individuals experience many differences, some of them associated with "maleness" or "femaleness" (Wodrich, 2006).

Genetic Abnormalities

Numerous disorders have been attributed to genes, such as phenylketonuria, Huntington disease, sickle-cell anemia, Tay-Sachs disease, and cystic fibrosis.

Phenylketonuria

The enzyme disorder phenylketonuria (PKU) is transmitted by a recessive gene. The Canadian PKU and Allied Disorders organization estimates that 1 in 15,000 newborns in Canada have PKU (Pailone, 2013). Children with PKU cannot metabolize an amino acid called phenylalanine, which builds up in their bodies and impairs the functioning of the central nervous system, resulting in intellectual challenges, psychological disorders, and physical problems. PKU has no cure, but in Canada, newborns are screened for PKU at birth. Those testing positive can be placed on diets low in phenylalanine within 3 to 6 weeks of birth and will develop normally (Brazier & Rowlands, 2006).

Huntington Disease

Huntington disease (HD) is a fatal, progressive degenerative disorder and a dominant trait. According to the Huntington Society of Canada (n.d.), one in every 10,000 Canadians has HD and the prevalence of the disorder has increased over the last 50 years in North America. Physical symptoms include uncontrollable muscle movements (Jacobs, Levy, & Marder, 2006). Psychological symptoms include loss of intellectual functioning and personality change (Robins Wahlin, Lundin, & Dear, 2007). Although there is a juvenile type of the disorder, most individuals are not diagnosed until middle adulthood; consequently, many individuals with the defect have borne children only to discover years later that they and possibly half their offspring will inevitably develop the disorder. Medicines can help deal with some symptoms; however, the disease is terminal.

Genetic Abnormalities

Phenylketonuria
Huntington Disease
Sickle-Cell Anemia
Tay-Sachs Disease
Cystic Fibrosis
Hemophilia
Muscular Dystrophy

sex-linked chromosomal abnormalities abnormalities that are transmitted from generation to generation and are carried on the sex chromosome

phenylketonuria (PKU) a genetic abnormality in which phenylalanine builds up and causes intellectual challenges

Huntington disease (HD) a fatal genetic neurological disorder whose onset takes place in middle age. It is a dominant trait, which is rare for a fatal genetic disorder

sickle-cell anemia a genetic disorder that decreases the blood's capacity to carry oxygen

Tay-Sachs disease a fatal genetic neurological disorder that causes degeneration and premature death

Sickle-Cell Anemia

Sickle-cell anemia is caused by a recessive gene. Sickle-cell anemia is most common among black North Americans. In Canada, many refer to sickle-cell anemia as the "neglected disease" because Health Canada does not keep precise statistics on the prevalence of the disease (CBC News, 2003). It is estimated that between 3,000 to 7,000 patients live with the disease in Canada and approximately 5% of the world population are carriers of the gene (Canadian Haemoglobinopathy Association, 2014). In sickle-cell anemia, red blood cells take on the shape of a sickle and clump together, obstructing small blood vessels and decreasing the oxygen supply. The reduced oxygen supply can impair cognitive skills and academic performance (Hogan et al., 2005; Ogunfowora et al., 2005). Episodes of acute pain are also common, as are complications such as blindness and failure of the heart, kidney, and liver, which can be fatal.

Tay-Sachs Disease

Tay-Sachs disease is also caused by a recessive gene, which leads to an absence of an enzyme that is required for neurological functioning. This absence causes the cells to become damaged leading to degeneration of the central nervous system, ultimately resulting in death. The disorder is commonly found among children in Jewish families of Eastern European background and French Canadians, where 1 person in 27 carries the recessive gene (National Tay-Sachs and

cystic fibrosis
a fatal genetic disorder in which mucus obstructs the lungs and pancreas

hemophilia
a genetic disorder in which blood does not clot properly

sex-linked genetic abnormalities
abnormalities resulting from genes that are found on the X sex chromosome. They are more likely to be shown by male offspring (who do not have an opposing gene from a second X chromosome) than by female offspring.

Allied Diseases Association, 2016). Such genetic concerns have led doctors to recommend Tay-Sachs testing for Canadians who either have a family history of the disease or live in a population with a high incidence of the disease (WebMD, 2010). Children with the disorder progressively lose control over their muscles, experience sensory losses, develop intellectual challenges, become paralyzed, and usually die by about the age of 5 years.

Cystic Fibrosis

Cystic fibrosis, also caused by a recessive gene, is the most common fatal hereditary disease among Canadian children and young adults, according to the Canadian Cystic Fibrosis Foundation (2014). Approximately 1 in every 3,500 children in Canada is born with this disease. Children with the disease suffer from excessive production of thick mucus that clogs the pancreas and lungs. Mucus and protein build up in the digestive tract, resulting in extreme difficulty digesting food and absorbing adequate nutrients. Most victims die of respiratory infections in their 20s although many individuals are living well into their 30s and 40s due to advances in medicine and treatment. One such treatment is lung transplantation. This can enable individuals with end-stage lung disease to regain their health. Canada, however, has a limited number of organ donors. The Canadian Cystic Fibrosis Foundation supports organ donor awareness and encourages Canadians to discuss organ donation with their loved ones.

Sex-Linked Genetic Abnormalities

Some genetic defects, such as **hemophilia** and colour blindness, are carried only on the X sex chromosome. For this reason, they are referred to as **sex-linked genetic abnormalities**. These defects also involve recessive genes. Females, who have two X sex chromosomes, are less likely than males to show sex-linked disorders because the genes that cause the disorder need to be present on both of a female's sex chromosomes for the disorder to be expressed. Sex-linked diseases are more likely to afflict sons of female carriers because males have only one X sex chromosome, which they inherit from their mothers. Females have two X chromosomes, which means that in order for the female to have a disorder that affects only the X chromosome, she would have to inherit the condition from both of her parents. (See Figure 2.4.)

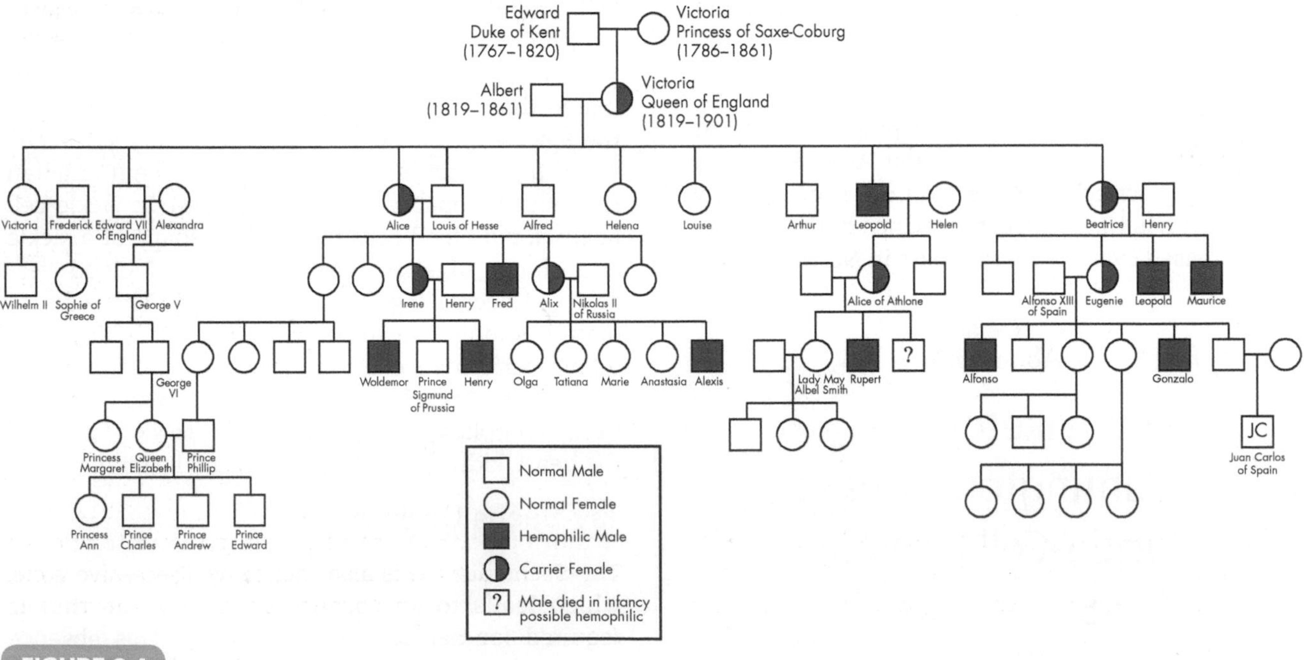

FIGURE 2.4

How Parents Pass Sex-Linked Gene to Offspring

Queen Victoria was a carrier of hemophilia and transmitted the sex-linked blood disorder to many of her children, who in turn carried it into many of the ruling houses of Europe. For this reason, hemophilia has been dubbed the "royal disease."

Source: "Hemophilia: The Royal Disease" by Yelena Aronova-Tiuntseva and Clyde Freeman Herreid. ©National Center for Case Study Teaching in Science (NCCSTS), University at Buffalo, State University of New York.

One form of muscular dystrophy, Duchenne muscular dystrophy, is sex-linked. Muscular dystrophy is characterized by a weakening of the muscles, which can lead to a wasting away of the muscles, an inability to walk, and sometimes death. Other sex-linked abnormalities include diabetes, colour blindness, and some types of night blindness.

Colour blindness is a sex-linked condition that makes it difficult for affected individuals to differentiate various colours. Red–green colour blindness is the most common type. For most people with the condition, colour blindness doesn't interfere with daily life. Of Caucasians, 8% of males and 1% of females have either red or green colour blindness. The condition is rare among people of Asian, First Nations, and African decent (Colour Blindness Awareness, n.d.).

Genetic Counselling and Prenatal Testing

Genetic counsellors can detect the genetic abnormalities that are responsible for many diseases. They compile information about a couple's genetic heritage to explore whether their children might develop genetic abnormalities. Couples who face a high risk of passing genetic defects to their children sometimes choose to adopt or to not have children rather than conceive on their own. In addition, prenatal testing can indicate whether the embryo or fetus carries genetic abnormalities.

> **DID YOU KNOW?**
>
> **In many provinces in Canada, it is legal to terminate a pregnancy up to 24 weeks after gestation.**
>
> Abortion is legal when the child has a genetic condition such as a neural tube defect, Down syndrome, or Tay-Sachs disease. A pregnancy can also be terminated if the mother's life is at risk.

Amniocentesis

Amniocentesis is usually performed on the mother at 14 to 16 weeks after conception, although many physicians now perform the procedure earlier ("early amniocentesis"). During this procedure, the health professional uses a syringe (needle) to withdraw fluid from the amniotic sac (see Figure 2.5). The fluid contains cells that have been sloughed off by the fetus. The cells are separated from the amniotic fluid, grown in a culture, and then examined microscopically for genetic and chromosomal abnormalities.

Amniocentesis has become routine among Canadian women who become pregnant past the age of 35 because the chances of Down syndrome and other chromosomal abnormalities increase dramatically as women approach or pass the age of 40. In Canada, the risk of fetal loss because of an amniocentesis procedure is 0.5% of all pregnancies (Wilson, Langlois, & Johnson, 2007). Amniocentesis is not conducted simply to learn the sex of the child, which can be determined earlier through an ultrasound.

Chorionic Villus Sampling

Chorionic villus sampling (CVS) is similar to amniocentesis but is carried out earlier, between the 9th and 12th weeks of pregnancy. A small syringe is inserted through the vagina or abdomen into the placenta and removes some threadlike projections (chorionic villi) that are then tested. Results are available within days. CVS has not been used as frequently as amniocentesis because CVS carries a slightly greater risk of spontaneous abortion. Studies suggest that both amniocentesis and CVS increase the risk of miscarriage (Alfirevic, Sundberg, & Brigham, 2003; Philip et al., 2004).

Ultrasound

Health professionals also use sound waves that are too high in frequency to be heard by the human ear—ultrasound—to obtain information about the fetus. Ultrasound waves are reflected by the fetus, and a computer uses the information to generate a picture of the fetus. The picture is termed an ultrasound (see Figure 2.6).

Ultrasound is used to guide the syringe in amniocentesis and CVS by determining the position of the fetus. It is also used to establish the growth of the fetus, including its age and the baby's sex, and to detect multiple pregnancies and structural abnormalities.

muscular dystrophy
a chronic disease characterized by a progressive wasting away of the muscles

colour blindness
a sex-linked condition that makes it difficult to differentiate various colours

prenatal
before birth

amniocentesis
a procedure for drawing and examining fetal cells sloughed off into amniotic fluid to determine the presence of various disorders

chorionic villus sampling (CVS)
a method for the prenatal detection of genetic abnormalities that samples the membrane enveloping the amniotic sac and fetus

placenta
the organ that provides oxygen and vital nutrients to the fetus and removes waste products from the blood

ultrasound
sound waves too high in pitch to be sensed by the human ear

alpha-fetoprotein (AFP) assay a blood test that assesses the mother's blood level of alpha-fetoprotein, a substance that is linked to fetal neural tube defects

reaction range the interaction between nature (genetic potential) and nurture (the set of circumstances that we encounter in life)

genotype the genetic form or constitution of a person as determined by heredity

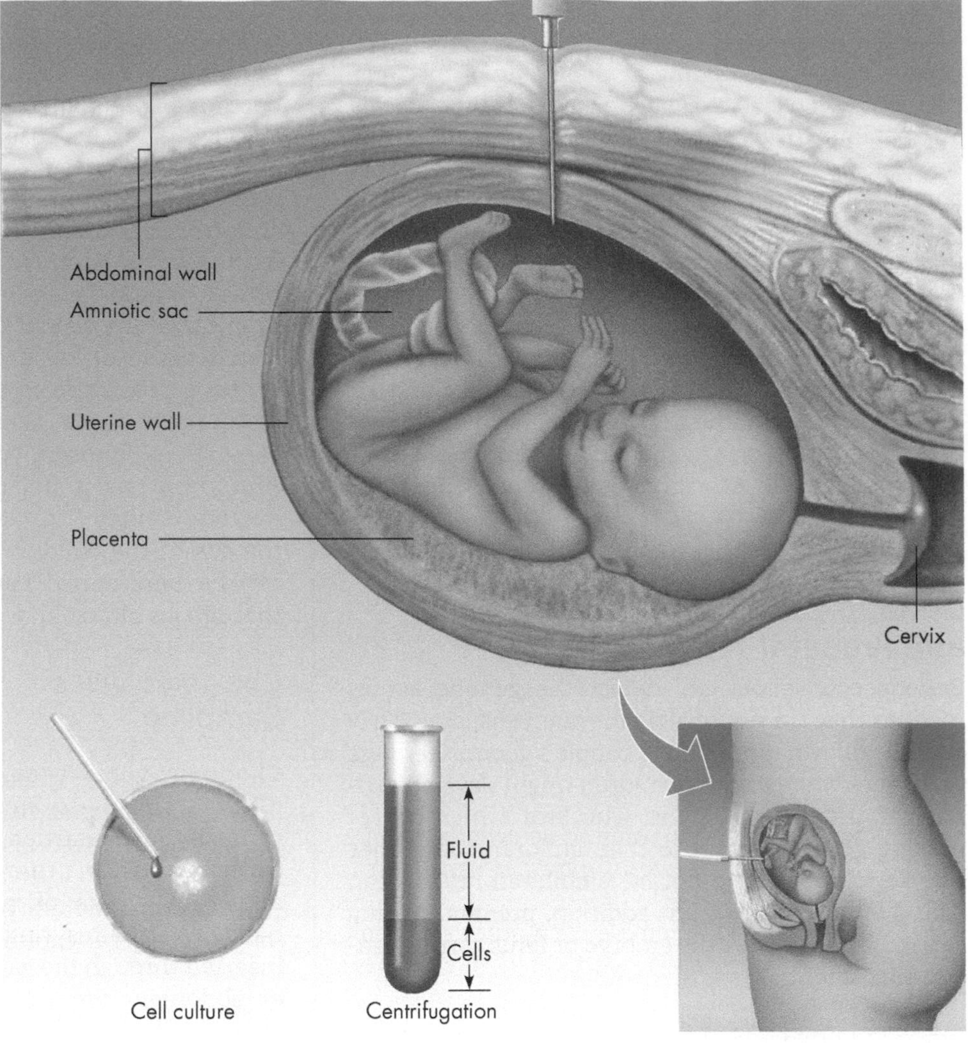

FIGURE 2.5

Amniocentesis

Amniocentesis allows prenatal identification of certain genetic and chromosomal disorders by examining genetic material sloughed off by the fetus into amniotic fluid.

Source: © Cengage Learning

Blood Tests

Parental blood tests can reveal the presence of genetic disorders such as sickle-cell anemia, Tay-Sachs disease, and cystic fibrosis. The alpha-fetoprotein (AFP) assay is used to detect neural tube defects such as spina bifida and certain chromosomal abnormalities. Neural tube defects cause an elevation in the AFP level in the mother's blood. Elevated AFP levels also are associated with increased risk of fetal death. Because the mother's blood is tested, the fetus is not at risk.

FIGURE 2.6

3-D Ultrasound Image

In the ultrasound technique, sound waves are bounced off the fetus to provide an image that enables medical professionals to detect various abnormalities. 3-D ultrasounds now give a much more complete view of the fetus. Parents often refer to 3-D ultrasounds as simply an ultrasound.

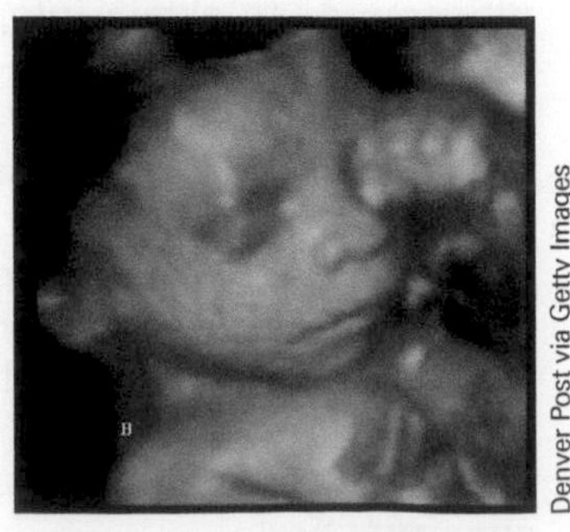

Denver Post via Getty Images

LO2 Heredity and the Environment

The development of our traits is influenced by inheritance and by nutrition, learning, exercise, and—unfortunately—accident and illness. Reaction range refers to the interaction between nature (genetic potential) and nurture (the set of circumstances that we encounter in life). A potential Shakespeare who is reared in poverty and never taught to read or write will not create a *Hamlet*. Our traits and behaviours represent the interaction of heredity and environment. The sets of traits that we inherit from our parents are referred to as our genotypes. The actual sets of traits that we exhibit are called our phenotypes. Our phenotypes reflect both genetic and environmental influences.

Researchers have developed numerous strategies to help sort out the effects of heredity and the environment on development.

Kinship Studies

Researchers study the distribution of a trait or behaviour among relatives who differ in their degree of genetic closeness. The more closely people are related, the more genes they have in common. For example, parents and children have a 50% overlap in their genetic endowments, as do siblings. Aunts and uncles have a 25% overlap with nieces and nephews, as do grandparents with grandchildren. First cousins share 12.5% of their genetic endowment. If genes are implicated in a trait, people who are more closely related are more likely to share it.

Twin Studies: Looking in the Genetic Mirror

Monozygotic (MZ) twins share 100% of their genes, whereas dizygotic (DZ) twins have a 50% overlap, similar to other siblings. When MZ twins show greater similarity on some trait or behaviour than DZ twins do, a genetic basis for the trait or behaviour is indicated.

But do MZ twins resemble each other so closely in part because they are often treated so similarly? One way to answer this question is to compare MZ twins who were reared apart. Except for the uterine environment, similarities between MZ twins reared apart would appear to be a result of heredity. In the Minnesota Study of Twins Reared Apart (Bouchard et al., 1990; DiLalla et al., 1999; Lykken, 2006b), researchers have been measuring the physiological and psychological characteristics of 56 sets of MZ adult twins who were separated in infancy and reared in different homes. The MZ twins reared apart are about as similar as MZ twins reared together on measures of intelligence, personality, temperament, occupational and leisure-time interests, and social attitudes. These traits would thus appear to have a genetic underpinning.

DID YOU KNOW?

Twins who were separated at birth and raised in different homes give researchers a wonderful opportunity for research.

Twin studies allow researchers to examine which characteristics are genetic and which characteristics are due to living in the same environment. Research from The Minnesota Twin Study of Adult Development has indicated that twins reared apart from each other are just as similar on aspects of personality, interests, and attitudes as twins raised in the same home. (Bouchard et al., 1990; DiLalla et al., 1999; Lykken, 2006b). This suggests that it is genetics that plays a strong role in our development of these characteristics.

phenotype
the actual form or constitution of a person as determined by heredity and environmental factors

conception
the union of a sperm cell and an ovum that occurs when the chromosomes of each of these cells combine to form 23 new pairs

DID YOU KNOW?

In Canada, more than 6,000 twins are born every year.

Approximately 3% of live births in Canada are multiple births—two or more children born at the same time (Statistics Canada, 2011b).

Adoption Studies

Adoption studies in which children were separated from their natural parents at an early age and reared by adoptive parents provide special opportunities for looking at the effects of nature and nurture. When children reared by adoptive parents exhibit a trait more similar to their natural parents, a powerful argument is made for a genetic role in the appearance of that trait.

LO3 Conception: Against All Odds

Conception is the union of an ovum and a sperm cell; it occurs when one of several hundred thousand ova produced by the woman unites with one of hundreds of millions of sperm produced by the man in the average ejaculate.

Ova

At birth, women already have all the ova they will ever have: some 400,000. The ova, however, are immature in form. The ovaries also produce the female hormones estrogen and progesterone. At puberty, in response to hormonal command, some ova begin to mature. Each month, an egg (occasionally more than one) is released from its ovarian follicle about midway through the menstrual cycle and enters a nearby fallopian tube. An egg might take 3 to 4 days to be propelled by small, hairlike structures called cilia and, perhaps, by contractions in the wall of the tube (perhaps resulting in cramping), along the several centimetres (a few inches) of the fallopian

endometrium
the inner lining of the uterus

spontaneous abortion
unplanned miscarriage of the developing organism

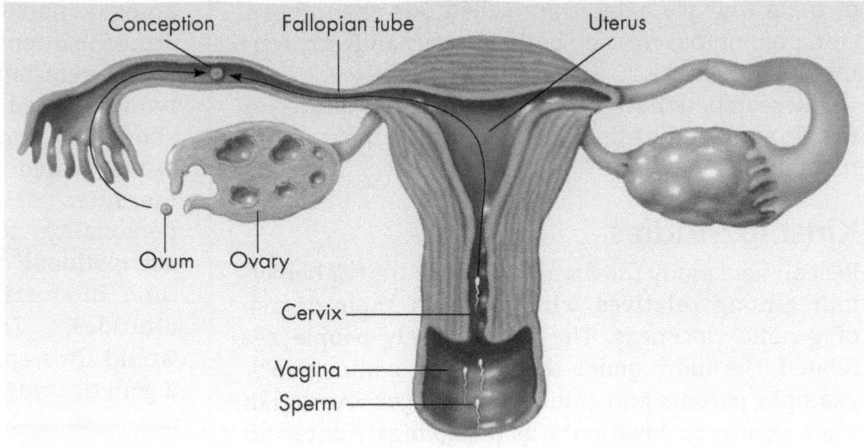

FIGURE 2.7

Female Reproductive Organs

Source: © Cengage Learning

tube to the uterus. Unlike sperm, eggs do not propel themselves.

If the egg is not fertilized, it is discharged through the uterus and the vagina in the menstrual flow along with the endometrium that had formed to support an embryo. During a woman's reproductive years, about 400 ova (that is, 1 in 1,000) will ripen and be released.

Ova are much larger than sperm but also are a single cell. Human ova are barely visible to the eye, but their bulk is still thousands of times larger than that of sperm cells.

Sperm Cells

Sperm cells begin with 46 chromosomes, but after meiosis, each sperm has 23 chromosomes, half with X sex chromosomes and half with Y. Each sperm cell is about 1/200 cm (1/500 in.) long, making it one of the smallest cells in the body. Sperm with Y sex chromosomes appear to swim faster than sperm with X sex chromosomes. This difference contributes to the conception of 120 to 150 boys for every 100 girls. However, compared with female fetuses, male fetuses have a higher rate of spontaneous abortion, often during the first month of pregnancy and likely before the mother is aware of being pregnant. At birth, boys outnumber girls by a ratio of only 106 to 100. Boys also have a higher incidence of infant mortality, which further equalizes the numbers of girls and boys.

DID YOU KNOW?

Approximately 120 to 150 boys are conceived for every 100 girls.

Sperm with Y chromosomes swim faster, resulting in the conception of more boys than girls.

The 150 million or so sperm in the ejaculate may seem to be a wasteful investment because only one sperm can fertilize an ovum, but only 1 in 1,000 sperm will ever approach an ovum. Millions of sperm deposited in the vagina flow out of the woman's body because of gravity. Gravity and normal vaginal acidity kill millions of the sperm before they can begin their journey. The surviving sperm then need to swim against the current of fluid coming from the cervix (see Figure 2.7).

Sperm that survive these initial obstacles may reach the fallopian tubes 60 to 90 minutes after ejaculation. About half the sperm enter the tube without the egg. Perhaps 2,000 enter the correct tube. Fewer still manage to swim the final 5 cm (2 in.) against the currents generated by the cilia that line the tube. Sperm travel towards the egg as though they are being "egged on" by the change in calcium ions that occurs when an ovum is released (Angier, 2007). Fianlly, one sperm cell of approximately 50 million per ejaculation may be successful in penetrating the egg (Kennard, 2012).

Of all the sperm swarming around the egg, only one enters (see Figure 2.8). Ova are surrounded by a gelatinous layer that must be penetrated for fertilization to occur. Many of the sperm that have completed their journey to the ovum secrete an enzyme that briefly thins the layer, but it enables only one sperm to penetrate. Once a sperm cell has entered, the layer thickens, locking out other sperm.

DID YOU KNOW?

Sperm do not travel about at random inside the woman's reproductive tract.

The direction that sperm travel is guided by a change in calcium ions that occurs when an ovum is released.

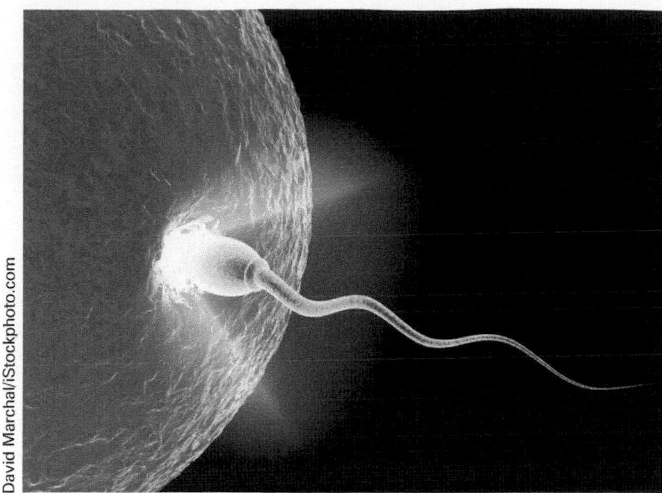

David Marchal/iStockphoto.com

FIGURE 2.8

Egg and Sperm at Time of Conception

This image shows the egg and sperm at the moment of conception. Fertilization normally occurs in a fallopian tube. Thousands of sperm may wind up in the vicinity of an ovum, but only one fertilizes it.

Infertility

Approximately one in six Canadian couples will have difficulties conceiving a child. Beverly Hanck, the executive director of the Infertility Awareness Association of Canada, recommends that couples begin planning their families in their 20s because a woman's reproduction begins to decline in her mid- to late 20s (Health Journal, 2010). The social reality in Canada is that women are beginning their families at older ages than past generations. In 2011, slightly more than half of all Canadian births (52%) were to women ages 30 and older, a significant increase from 24% in 1981 (Pew Research Center, 2013). The fertility rate for women ages 40 to 44 years has also increased, doubling from 1988 to 2008 (Statistics Canada, 2011). Taken together, Canadian women are waiting longer to begin families, and this decision could collide with human biology.

Female Infertility

The most common problem in women is irregular ovulation or lack of ovulation. This problem can have many causes, including irregularities among the hormones that govern ovulation, stress, and malnutrition. So-called fertility drugs (e.g., *clomiphene* and *pergonal*) are made up of hormones that cause women to ovulate. These drugs may cause multiple births by stimulating more than one ovum to ripen during a month (Legro et al., 2007).

Infections may scar the fallopian tubes and other organs, impeding the passage of sperm or ova. Such infections include pelvic inflammatory disease (PID). PID can result from bacterial or viral infections, including the STIs gonorrhea and chlamydia. Health Canada is particularly concerned that women aged 15 to 19 have chlamydia infections at a rate nine times the national average, which could significantly affect these women when, later in life, they wish to start families (Bissell & McKay, 2005). Antibiotics are usually helpful in treating bacterial infections, but infertility may be irreversible.

pelvic inflammatory disease (PID) an infection of the abdominal region that may have various causes and may impair fertility

endometriosis inflammation of endometrial tissue sloughed off into the abdominal cavity rather than out of the body during menstruation; the condition is characterized by abdominal pain and sometimes infertility

motility the movement of sperm

Endometriosis can obstruct the fallopian tubes, where conception normally takes place. Endometriosis has become fairly common among women who delay childbearing. Each month, tissue develops to line the uterus in case the woman conceives. This tissue—the endometrium—is then sloughed off during menstruation. For women who have endometriosis, some of this tissue backs up into the abdomen through the fallopian tubes. It then collects in the abdomen, where it can cause abdominal pain and reduce the chances of conception. Physicians may treat endometriosis with hormones that temporarily prevent menstruation or with surgery.

Male Infertility

Infertility was once viewed as a problem of the woman, but it turns out that the problem lies with the man in about 40% of cases. A low sperm count—or lack of sperm—is the most common infertility problem in men. Men's fertility problems have a variety of causes: genetic factors, environmental poisons, diabetes, sexually transmitted infections (STIs), overheating of the testes (which is sometimes experienced by athletes, such as long-distance runners), pressure (as from using narrow bicycle seats), aging, and certain prescription and illicit drugs (Hatcher et al., 2007). Sometimes the sperm count is adequate, but the sperm may have been deformed or deprived of their motility by other factors, such as prostate or hormonal problems. Motility can also be impaired by the scar tissue from infections, such as STIs.

SolStock/iStockphoto.com

EMERGING CANADA

Some provinces—Ontario, for example—provide funding for IVF procedures for eligible women. One cycle of IVF is covered today by the Ontario government. A woman's eggs will be retrieved after only one cycle. Thus, if none of the eggs implant, in most cases the government won't pay for her to have the procedure done a second time. Eligibility for government funding includes being under the age of 43 years and determination that IVF is an appropriate course of treatment. The program is available to anyone regardless of sex, gender, sexual orientation, or family status (Ministry of Health and Long-Term Care, 2015). Prior to this new funding, Ontarians were spending thousands of dollars to have this procedure performed.

artificial insemination injection of sperm into the uterus to fertilize an ovum

in vitro fertilization (IVF) fertilization of an ovum in a laboratory dish

donor IVF the transfer of a donor's ovum, fertilized in a laboratory dish, to the uterus of another woman

assisted reproductive technology (ART) the term for any medical assistance provided that enables conception to take place

Other Ways of Becoming Parents

Assisted Reproductive Technology (ART)

Assisted reproductive technology (ART) is the technical term for any medical assistance that is provided to an individual who would like to conceive a child; it includes drug treatment, artificial insemination, in vitro fertilization, and surrogacy. There are many people for whom ART is necessary, including same-gender couples, single parents wanting to start a family, and couples who are having infertility issues after one year of trying to conceive on their own. Accordingly, the number of ART cycles has increased by 30% in Canada in 2011 as compared to 2010 (Gunby, n.d.).

DID YOU KNOW?

Surrogacy contracts are illegal in Canada.

In 2004, the Assisted Human Reproductive Act was passed in the Senate. It makes commercial surrogacy contracts as well as the sale of sperm, eggs, and embryos illegal in Canada. This Act also prevents producing embryos for the purpose of research, and cloning (Government of Canada, 2016).

Artificial Insemination

Men with low sperm counts can collect multiple ejaculations, which are then quick-frozen. The sperm can then be injected into the woman's uterus at the time of ovulation. This method is one procedure of artificial insemination. Sperm from a man with low sperm motility can also be injected into his partner's uterus so that the sperm can begin their journey closer to the fallopian tubes. When a man has no sperm or an extremely low sperm count, his partner can be artificially inseminated with the sperm of a donor who may or may not resemble the man in physical traits. Artificial insemination is also used by some women who want a baby but do not have a partner.

In Vitro Fertilization

So called "test-tube babies" are not actually grown in a test tube but are conceived through in vitro fertilization (IVF), a method of conception in which ripened ova are removed surgically from the mother and placed in a laboratory dish. The father's sperm are combined with the egg in the dish or sometimes the sperm is injected into the egg directly. After several days, a group of cells called a *blastocyst* is formed; the blastocyst is then implanted in the mother's uterus.

IVF may be used when the fallopian tubes are blocked because the ova need not travel through them. A variation known as donor IVF can be used when the intended mother does not produce ova. An ovum from another woman is fertilized and injected into the uterus of the mother-to-be.

Because only a minority of attempts lead to births, several attempts may be needed to achieve a pregnancy. Several embryos may be injected into the uterus at once, heightening the odds and increasing the chance of multiples. IVF remains costly, which excludes many Canadians from exploring this option, although several provinces are now covering the procedure but for one cycle

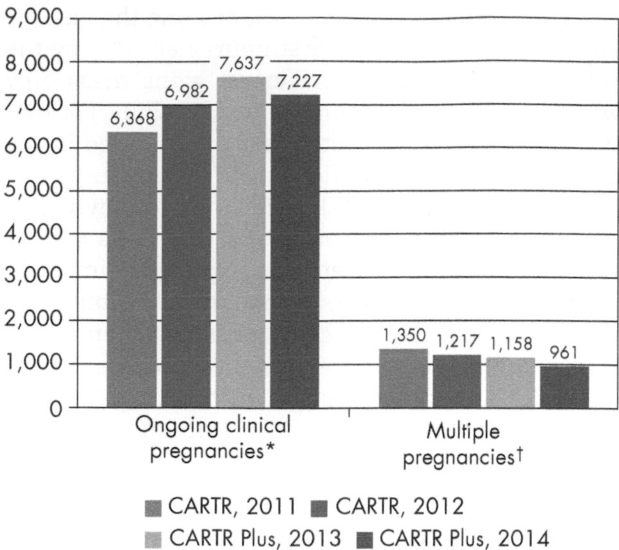

** Ongoing clinical pregnancy: clinical pregnancy with ≥1 fetal heart beat on ultrasound*
† Multiple pregnancy: ongoing clinical pregnancy with >1 fetal heart beat on ultrasound

FIGURE 2.9

Number of Total Pregnancies and Multiple Pregnancies as a Result of All Types of Assisted Reproductive Technology (ART) Treatments from 2011 to 2014

Source: Canadian Assisted Reproductive Technologies Registry (CARTR) Plus. (2015, October). Preliminary treatment cycle data for 2014. Better Outcomes Registry & Network Ontario. Ottawa, ON.

only. Multiple eggs are retrieved after one cycle, resulting in several embryos that are frozen and implanted at later dates. For funded IVF treatment, only one embryo may be planted at a time to prevent multiples. (See Figure 2.9.)

IVF is a routine procedure, but it has a significant failure rate especially for women over the age of 40 years. In 2011, only 23.9% of IVF cycles resulted in a birth of a child (Gunby, n.d.)

Selecting the Sex of Your Child

Today, a reliable method is available for selecting the sex of a child prior to implantation: preimplantation genetic diagnosis (PGD). PGD was developed to detect genetic disorders, but it also reveals the sex of the embryo. In PGD, ova are fertilized in vitro. After a few days of cell division, a cell is extracted from each developing organism, and its sex chromosomal structure is examined microscopically to learn of its sex. Embryos of the desired sex are implanted in the woman's uterus, where one or more can grow to term. However, successful implantation cannot be guaranteed. In 2004, sex selection was made illegal in Canada according to the Assisted Human Reproductive Act, though it is available in other countries. This issue raises interesting ethical concerns, such as those noted at the end of this chapter.

Nathan Gleave/iStockphoto.com

Adoption

Adoption is another option for people to become parents. Despite occasional conflicts that pit adoptive parents against biological parents who change their minds about giving up their children, most adoptions result in the formation of new loving families. Many Canadians find it easier, or more desirable, to adopt infants from other countries or with special needs although with new laws in place, it has become increasingly difficult to adopt internationally compared to in the past.

LO4 Prenatal Development

Prenatal development is divided into three periods: the germinal stage (approximately the first 2 weeks), the embryonic stage (the third through the eighth weeks), and the fetal stage (the third month until birth).

The Germinal (Zygotic) Stage

Within 36 hours after conception, the zygote divides into two cells. It then divides repeatedly as it undergoes its 3- to 4-day journey to the uterus.

germinal (zygotic) stage
the period of development between conception and the implantation of the embryo

blastocyst
a cluster of cells that are formed around a cavity of fluid; some of the cells will become the fetus and some of the cells will become the placenta that nourishes the fetus

embryonic disk
the platelike inner part of the blastocyst that differentiates into the ectoderm, mesoderm, and endoderm of the embryo

embryonic stage
the stage of prenatal development that lasts from implantation through the eighth week of pregnancy; it is characterized by the development of the major organ systems

cephalocaudal
from head to tail

proximodistal
from the inner part (or axis) of the body outward

Within another 36 hours, it has become approximately 32 cells. The mass of dividing cells wanders about the uterus for another 3 to 4 days before it begins to implant in the uterine wall. Implantation takes another week or so. The period from conception to implantation is called the **germinal (zygotic) stage** (see Figure 2.10). Newly fertilized egg cells survive for more than a week without any nourishment from the mother. As a result, they make no gains in mass.

A few days into the germinal stage, the dividing cell mass takes the form of a fluid-filled ball of cells called a **blastocyst**. In the blastocyst, cells begin to separate into groups that will eventually become different structures. The inner part of the blastocyst has two distinct layers that form a thickened mass of cells called the **embryonic disk**.

The cluster of cells that will become the embryo and then the fetus is at first nourished only by the yolk of the egg cell. A blastocyst gains mass only when it receives nourishment from outside. For that to happen, the blastocyst must be implanted in the uterine wall. Implantation may be accompanied by bleeding (often mistaken for a period), which is usually normal; but bleeding can also be a sign of miscarriage. Most women who experience implantation bleeding, however, do not miscarry, but have normal pregnancies. Miscarriage usually stems from abnormalities in the developmental process. Nearly one third of pregnancies end in miscarriage, most occurring in the first 3 months (National Library of Medicine, 2007).

The Embryonic Stage

The **embryonic stage** begins with implantation and covers the first 2 months, during which the major organ systems differentiate. Development follows **cephalocaudal** (Latin for "head to tail") and **proximodistal** (Latin for "near to far") trends. Growth of the head takes precedence over growth of the lower parts of the body. You can also think of the body as containing a central axis that coincides with the spinal cord. The growth of the organ systems near the spine occurs earlier than growth of the extremities. Relatively early maturation of the brain and organs that lie near the spine allows them to play key roles in further development. (See Figure 2.11.)

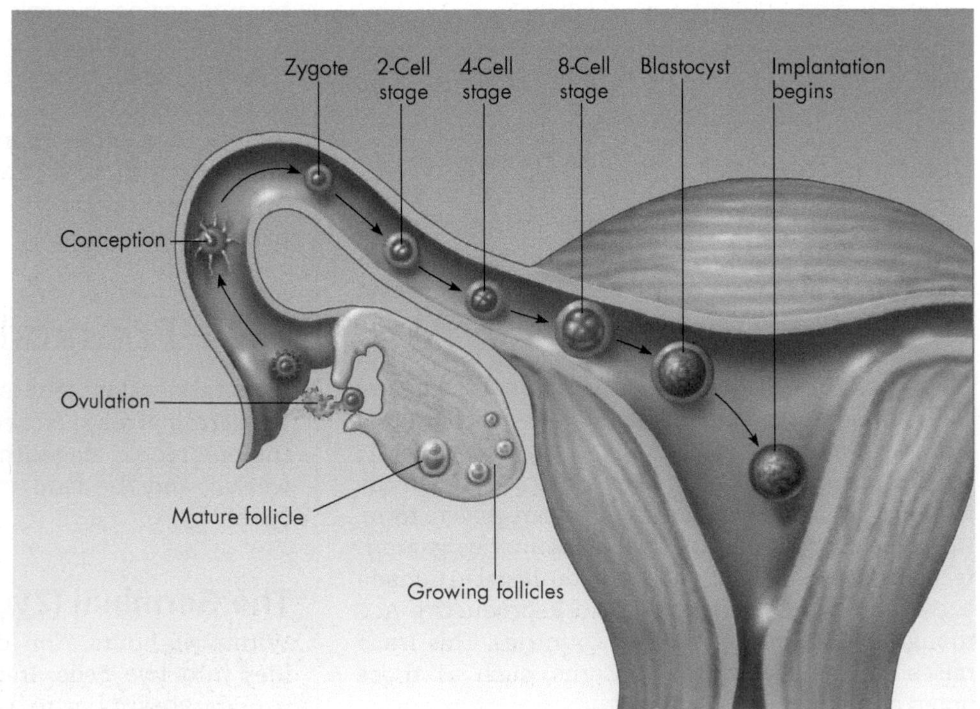

FIGURE 2.10

The Ovarian Cycle, Conception, and the Early Days of the Germinal Stage

Division of the zygote creates the hollow sphere of cells termed the blastocyst, which becomes implanted in the uterine wall.

Source: © Cengage Learning

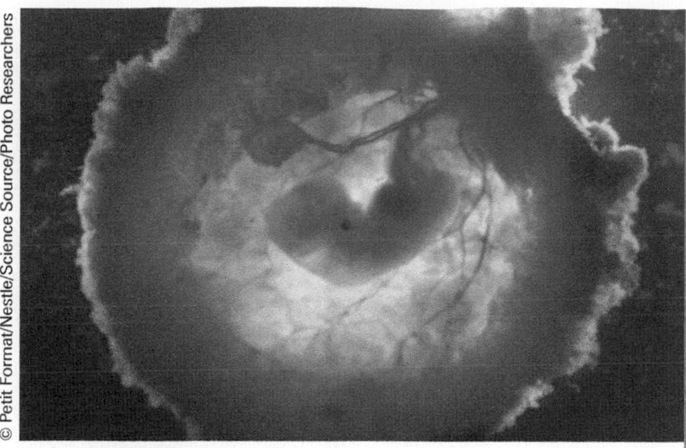

© Petit Format/Nestle/Science Source/Photo Researchers

FIGURE 2.11

A Human Embryo at 7 Weeks

In this embryo at 7 weeks, the head is oversized in relation to the rest of the body.

During the embryonic stage, the outer layer of cells of the embryonic disk, or ectoderm, develops into the nervous system, sensory organs, nails, hair, teeth, and outer layer of skin. At approximately 21 days, two ridges appear in the embryo and fold to compose the neural tube, from which the nervous system will develop. The inner layer, or endoderm, forms the digestive and respiratory systems, the liver, and the pancreas. A bit later, the mesoderm, a middle layer of cells, becomes differentiated. The mesoderm develops into the excretory, reproductive, and circulatory systems, the muscles, the skeleton, and the inner layer of the skin.

During the third week after conception, the head and blood vessels begin to form. Your heart started beating when you were only 0.6 cm (1/4 in.) long and weighed just a few grams (a fraction of an ounce). The major organ systems develop during the first 2 months. Arm buds and leg buds begin to appear toward the end of the first month. Eyes, ears, nose, and mouth begin to take shape. By this time, the nervous system, including the brain, has also begun to develop. During the second month, the cells in the nervous system begin to "fire"; that is, they send messages among themselves. By the end of the second month, the embryo begins to look human. The head has the lovely, round shape of your own, and the facial features have become quite distinct. All this detail is inscribed on an embryo that is only about 2.5 cm (1 in.) long and weighs about 10 g (1/3 oz.). The embryo's kidneys filter acid from the blood, and its liver produces red blood cells.

DID YOU KNOW?

The head develops more rapidly than the rest of the body during the embryonic stage.

By 8 weeks after conception, the head constitutes half the entire length of the embryo. The brain develops more rapidly than the spinal cord. Arm buds form before leg buds. Most newborn babies have a strong, well-defined sucking reflex, although their legs are spindly and their limbs move back and forth only in diffuse excitement or agitation. Infants can hold up their heads before they gain control over their arms, their torsos, and, finally, their legs. They can sit up before they can crawl and walk.

The lower parts of the body, because they get off to a later start, must do more growing to reach adult size. The head doubles in length between birth and maturity, but the torso, arms, and legs increase in length by three, four, and five times, respectively.

ectoderm
the outermost cell layer of the newly formed embryo from which the skin and nervous system develop

neural tube
a hollowed-out area in the blastocyst from which the nervous system develops

endoderm
the inner layer of the embryo from which the lungs and digestive system develop

mesoderm
the central layer of the embryo from which the bones and muscles develop

androgens
male sex hormones

Sexual Differentiation

By 5 to 6 weeks, the embryo is only 0.6 to 1.2 cm (1/4 to 1/2 in.) long. At this stage of development, both the internal and the external genitals resemble primitive female structures. By about the seventh week, the genetic code (XY or XX) begins to assert itself, causing sex organs to differentiate. Genetic activity on the Y sex chromosome causes the testes to begin to develop. If the Y chromosome is *absent*, the ovaries begin to be distinguished. By about 4 months after conception, males and females show distinct external genital structures. Once the testes have developed in the embryo, they begin to produce male sex hormones, or androgens, the most important of which is testosterone. Female embryos and fetuses produce small amounts of androgens, but they are usually not enough to cause

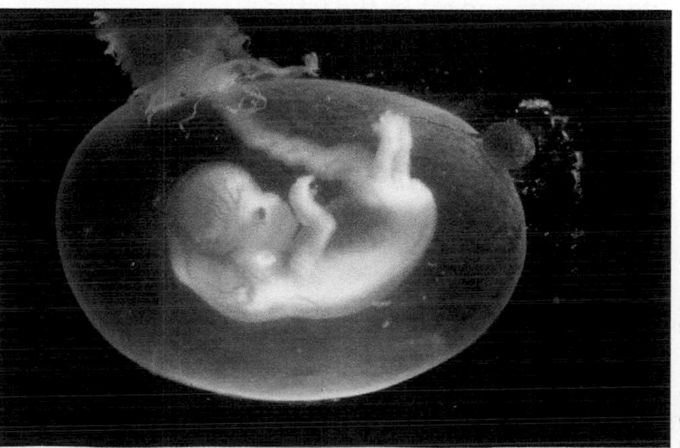

Dr G. Moscoso/Science Source

amniotic sac
the sac containing the fetus

amniotic fluid
fluid within the amniotic sac, which suspends and protects the fetus

fetal stage
the stage of development that lasts from the beginning of the ninth week of pregnancy through birth; it is characterized by gains in size and weight and by maturation of the organ systems

sexual differentiation along male lines.

The Amniotic Sac

The embryo and fetus develop within a protective amniotic sac in the uterus. This sac is surrounded by a clear membrane and contains amniotic fluid. The fluid serves as a kind of natural airbag, allowing the embryo and fetus to move around without injury. It also helps maintain an even temperature.

The placenta is a mass of tissue that permits the embryo (and later, the fetus) to exchange nutrients and wastes with the mother. The placenta is unique in origin. It grows from material supplied by both the mother and the embryo. The fetus is connected to the placenta by the umbilical cord. The mother is connected to the placenta by blood vessels in the uterine wall.

The Placenta: A Filtration System

Mother and embryo have separate circulatory systems. The pancake-shaped placenta contains a membrane that acts as a filter, permitting oxygen and nutrients to reach the embryo from the mother and permitting carbon dioxide and waste products to pass to the mother from the embryo. The mother then eliminates the waste through her lungs and kidneys. Some harmful substances can also sneak through the placenta, including various "germs," such as the ones that cause syphilis and German measles. On the other hand, human immunodeficiency virus (HIV), the virus that causes acquired immunodeficiency syndrome (AIDS), is more likely to be transmitted through childbirth. Some drugs—aspirin, narcotics, alcohol, tranquilizers, and others—cross the placenta and affect the fetus.

The placenta also secretes hormones that preserve the pregnancy, prepare the breasts for nursing, and stimulate the uterine contractions that prompt childbirth. After the birth of the baby, the placenta passes from the birth canal, which is why it is also called the afterbirth.

DID YOU KNOW?

A fetus will suck its thumb, sometimes for hours on end.

The fetus already demonstrates a right- or left-handed preference in utero.

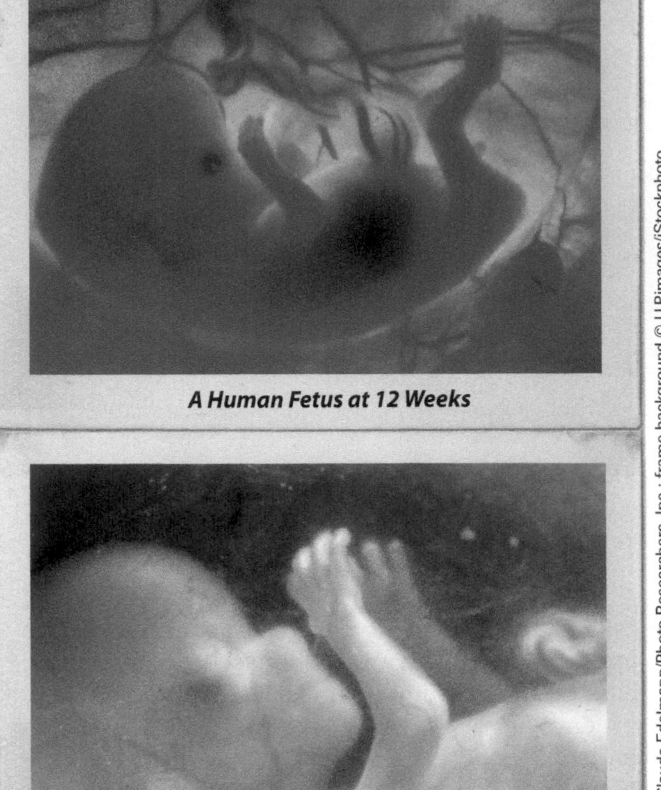

A Human Fetus at 12 Weeks

A Human Fetus at 4½ Months

The Fetal Stage

The fetal stage lasts from the beginning of the third month until birth. The fetus begins to turn and respond to external stimulation at about the ninth or tenth week. By the end of the first trimester, the major organ systems have been formed. The fingers and toes are fully formed. The eyes and the sex of the fetus can be clearly seen.

The second trimester is characterized by further maturation of fetal organ systems and dramatic gains in size. The brain continues to mature, contributing to the fetus's ability to regulate its own basic body functions. The fetus advances from a weight of 28 g (1 oz.) to 0.9 kg (2 lb.) and grows four to five times in length, from about 7.5 cm (3 in.) to 35.5 cm (14 in.). By the end of the second trimester, the fetus opens and shuts its eyes, sucks its thumb, alternates between wakefulness and sleep, and perceives light and sounds.

During the third trimester, the organ systems mature further. The fetus gains about 2.5 kg (5.5 lb.) and doubles in length. During the seventh month, the fetus normally turns upside down in the uterus so that delivery will be headfirst. By the end of the seventh month, the fetus will have almost doubled in weight, gaining another 0.8 kg (1 lb. 12 oz.), and will have increased another 5 cm (2 in.) in length. If born now, chances of survival are nearly 90%. If born at the end of the eighth month, the odds are overwhelmingly in favour of survival. By the time they are born, boys average about 3.4 kg (7.5 lb.) and girls about 3.2 kg (7 lb.).

Fetal Perception

By the 13th week of pregnancy, the fetus responds to sound waves. One of the first experiments of its kind, Sontag and Richards (1938) rang a bell near the mother's abdomen, and the fetus responded with movements similar to those of the startle reflex shown after birth. During the third trimester, fetuses respond to sounds of different frequencies through a variety of movements and changes in heart rate, suggesting that they can discriminate pitch (Lecanuet et al., 2000).

An experiment by Anthony DeCasper and William Fifer (1980) is even more intriguing. In this study, women read the Dr. Seuss book *The Cat in the Hat* out loud twice daily during the final month and a half of pregnancy. After birth, each baby was given a special pacifier. Sucking on the pacifier in one way would activate recordings of the baby's mother reading *The Cat in the Hat*, and sucking on them in another way would activate the mother reading from a book that was written in very different rhythms. The newborns "chose" to hear *The Cat in the Hat*. Fetal learning may be one basis for the development of attachment to the mother (Krueger et al., 2004; Lecanuet et al., 2000).

We once believed that the womb was a dark and uneventful place, but because of ultrasound technology, scientists have discovered a virtual sensory playground housing the developing baby. The fetus responds to its parents' voices and other sounds in the room. It also reacts to light and dark shadows as the mother moves from place to place and even tumbles as the mother shifts positions. Experts believe that these experiences cause physiological changes in the fetus's sensory system, which are help the baby to grow (WebMD, 2013).

Fetal Movements

The mother usually feels the first fetal movements in the middle of the fourth month (Adolph & Berger, 2005). By 29 to 30 weeks, the fetus moves its limbs so vigorously that the mother may complain of being kicked. The fetus also turns somersaults, which are clearly felt by the mother. The umbilical cord will not break or become dangerously wrapped around the fetus, no matter how many acrobatic feats the fetus performs. As the fetus grows, it becomes cramped in the uterus and movement is constricted, so that the fetus becomes markedly less active during the ninth month of pregnancy.

stillbirth
the birth of a dead fetus

Environmental Influences on Prenatal Development

The developing fetus is subject to many environmental hazards. Scientific advances have made us keenly aware of the types of things that can go wrong and what we can do to prevent these problems.

Nutrition

A common misconception is that fetuses "take what they need" from their mothers. In actuality, maternal malnutrition has been linked to low birth weight, prematurity, retardation of brain development, cognitive deficiencies, behavioural problems, and even cardiovascular disease (Giussani, 2006; Guerrini, Thomson, & Gurling, 2007; Morton, 2006). The effects of fetal malnutrition can sometimes be overcome by a supportive, care-giving environment. Experiments with children who suffered from fetal malnutrition show that enriched daycare programs enhance intellectual and social skills by 5 years of age (Ramey et al., 1999). Supplementing the diets of pregnant women who might otherwise be deficient in their intake of calories and protein also shows modest positive effects on the motor development of infants (Morton, 2006).

On the other hand, maternal obesity is linked with a higher risk of stillbirth (Fernandez-Twinn & Ozanne, 2006) and neural tube defects. Over the course of pregnancy, women who do not restrict their diet normally will gain 11.3–15.8 kg (25–35 lb.). Overweight women may gain less, and slender women may gain more. Regular weight gains of about 0.2 kg (1/2 lb.) per week during the first half of pregnancy and 0.5 kg (1 lb.) per

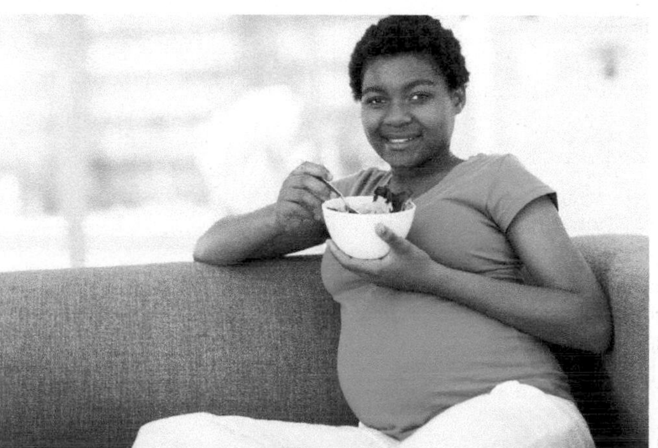

Michael Jung/Shutterstock.com

Maternal malnutrition has been linked to low birth weight, prematurity, retardation of brain development, cognitive deficiencies, behavioural problems, and even cardiovascular disease.

teratogens
environmental influences or agents that can damage the embryo or fetus

toxemia
a life-threatening disease that can afflict pregnant women; characterized by high blood pressure

Rh incompatibility
a condition in which antibodies produced by the mother are transmitted to the child, possibly causing brain damage or death

critical periods
periods during which an embryo is particularly vulnerable to a certain teratogen

week thereafter are desirable (Christian et al., 2003; Hynes et al., 2002).

Teratogens and Health Problems of the Mother

Teratogens are environmental agents that can harm the embryo or fetus. They include illegal substances such as heroin and cocaine, and addictive substances such as marijuana, alcohol, and cigarettes. Prescription drugs, food-borne bacteria, environmental agents such as pesticides, and illnesses such as Rubella are also considered to be teratogens as many of these substances or illnesses pass through the placenta and damage the fetus. The amount of substance as well as the time during development when the substance is ingested impact the degree of severity of malformation that occurs. For example, during the first 2 weeks of development, teratogens usually kill the embryo (Chung, n.s.). Additionally, health problems such as toxemia or Rh incompatibility are health problems that impact both mother and child during pregnancy.

Critical and Sensitive Periods of Vulnerability

Exposure to particular teratogens is most harmful during critical periods that correspond to the times when organs are developing. For example, the heart develops rapidly in the third to sixth weeks after conception. As you can see in Figure 2.12, the heart is most vulnerable to certain teratogens at this time. The eyes, which develop later, are most vulnerable in the fourth through eighth weeks. Because the major organ systems differentiate during the embryonic stage, the

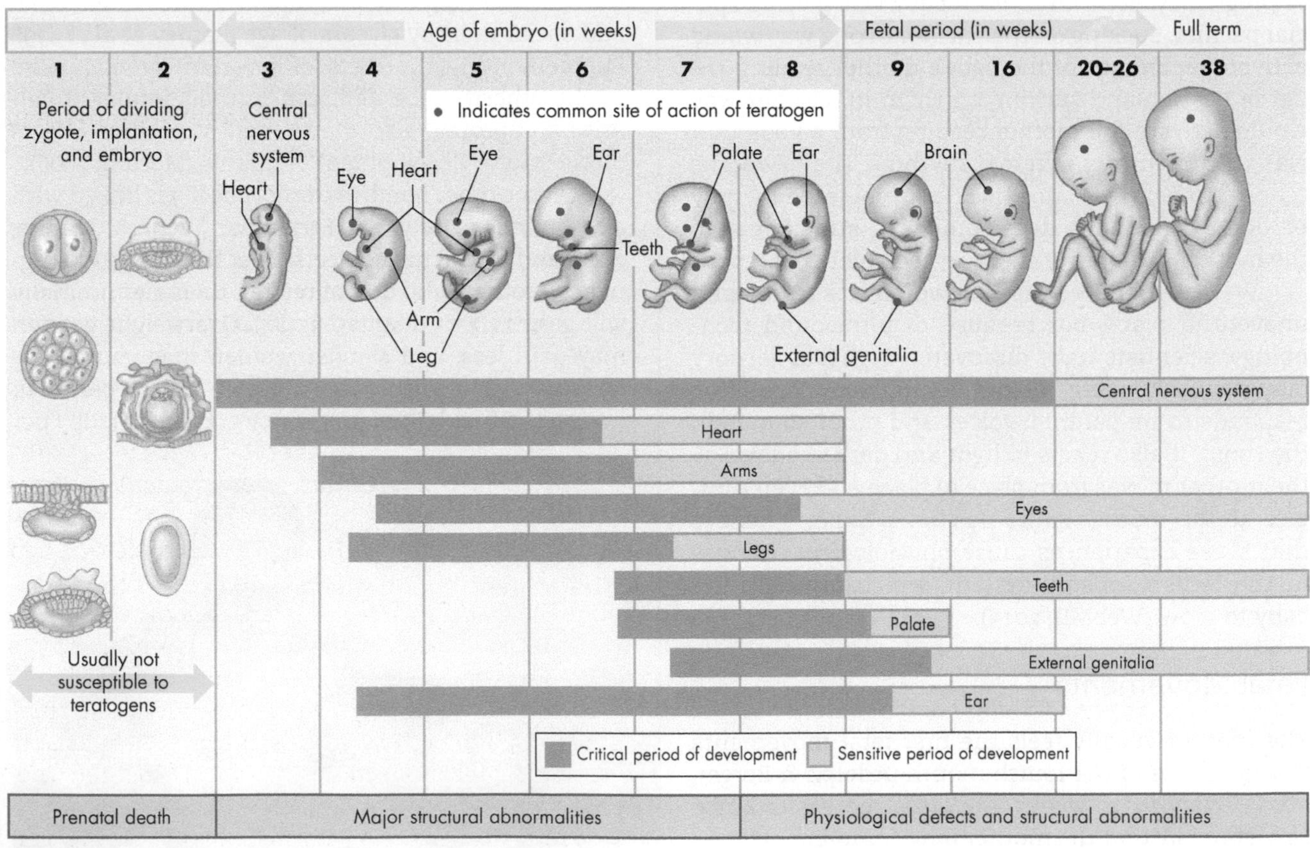

FIGURE 2.12

Critical and Sensitive Periods in Prenatal Development

Specific teratogens are most harmful during critical periods of prenatal development, indicated by the darker sections of the bars. During sensitive periods of development, indicated by the lighter sections of the bars, teratogens are less likely to be harmful, but the embryo and fetus are still at risk.

Source: © Cengage Learning

embryo is generally more vulnerable to teratogens than the fetus. During sensitive periods, the fetus and embryo have less risk, but development can still be disrupted if teratogens are encountered; and a sensitive period for development of one part of the fetus may be a critical period for another part. Many teratogens are, therefore, harmful throughout the entire course of prenatal development. For example, thalidomide was marketed in the 1960s as a treatment for insomnia and nausea. It was later found that thalidomide taken pregnancy almost invariably caused birth defects such as missing or stunted limbs as a fetus's extremities undergo rapid development during the second month of pregnancy when this drug was administered. (See Figure 2.12.)

Illegal or Addictive Substances Taken by the Parents

Even commonly used medications, such as aspirin, can be harmful to the fetus. If a woman is pregnant or thinks she may be pregnant, she should consult her obstetrician before taking any drugs, not just prescription medications. A physician usually can recommend a safe and effective substitute for a drug that could potentially harm a developing fetus.

Heroin and Methadone

Maternal addiction to heroin or methadone is linked to low birth weight, prematurity, and toxemia. Narcotics such as heroin and methadone readily cross the placental membrane. Expectant mothers who are regular narcotics users may cause addictions in their fetuses (Lejeune et al., 2006). Addicted newborns may be given the narcotic or a substitute shortly after birth so that they will not suffer serious withdrawal symptoms. The drug is then withdrawn gradually. Addicted newborns may show such symptoms as tremors, abnormal sucking, vomiting, increased respiratory difficulties, and a high-pitched cry (Nelson, 2013).

Marijuana (Cannabis)

Smoking marijuana during pregnancy poses numerous risks for the fetus, including slower growth (Hurd et al., 2005) and low birth weight (Visscher et al., 2003). The babies of women who regularly used marijuana show increased tremors and startling, suggesting immature development of the nervous system (Huestis et al., 2002).

Research into the cognitive effects of maternal prenatal use of marijuana shows mixed results. Some studies suggest that there may be no impairment (Fried & Smith, 2001). Others suggest that cognitive skills, including learning and memory, may be impaired (Huizink & Mulder, 2006). One study assessed the behaviour of 10-year-olds who had been exposed prenatally to maternal use of marijuana (Goldschmidt, Day, & Richardson, 2000) and suggested that prenatal use of marijuana was significantly related to increased hyperactivity, impulsivity, problems in paying attention, and increased delinquency and aggressive behaviour.

thalidomide
a treatment for insomnia and nausea given in the 1960s that caused birth defects

fetal alcohol spectrum disorder (FASD)
a cluster of symptoms shown by children of women who drank heavily during pregnancy, including characteristic facial features and intellectual challenges. A spectrum disorder indicates a range of linked conditions.

Cocaine

Pregnant women who abuse cocaine increase the risk of stillbirth, low birth weight, and birth defects. Infants are often excitable and irritable, or lethargic; sleep is disturbed (Schuetze, Lawton, & Eiden, 2006). Some delays in cognitive development have been suggested, even at 12 months of age (Singer et al., 2005).

Children who are exposed to cocaine prenatally also show problems at later ages. One study compared 189 children at 4 years of age who had been exposed to cocaine in utero with 185 4-year-olds who had no exposure (Lewis et al., 2004). The children exposed to cocaine had much lower receptive and expressive language abilities.

Alcohol

Because alcohol passes through the placenta, when a pregnant woman drinks alcohol, she poses risks for the embryo and fetus. Heavy drinking is associated with deficiencies and deformities in growth and can be lethal. Some children of heavy drinkers develop fetal alcohol spectrum disorder (FASD) (Connor et al., 2006; see Figure 2.13). Babies with FASD are often smaller than normal, as are their brains. They have distinct facial features: widely spaced eyes, an underdeveloped upper jaw and a flattened nose. Their psychological characteristics appear to reflect dysfunction of the brain (Guerrini et al., 2007).

The facial deformities of FASD diminish as the child moves into adolescence, and most children catch up in height and weight; but their intellectual, academic, and behavioural deficits of FASD persist to varying degrees (Guerrini et al., 2007). Children with FASD commonly have maladaptive behaviours such as poor judgment, distractibility, and difficulty perceiving social cues (Schonfeld, Mattson, & Riley, 2005). Although some health professionals have in the past allowed pregnant women a glass of wine with dinner, research now suggests that even moderate drinkers place their offspring at increased risk (Newburn-Cook et al., 2002). The First Nations and Inuit Health

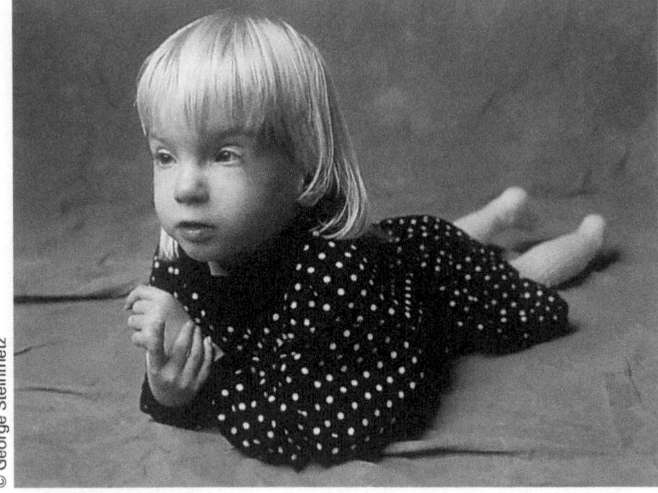

© George Steinmetz

FIGURE 2.13

Fetal Alcohol Spectrum Disorder (FASD)

Many children of mothers who drank alcohol during pregnancy exhibit fetal alcohol spectrum disorder (FASD). This spectrum disorder is characterized by a range of developmental lags and facial features such as an underdeveloped upper jaw, a flattened nose, and widely spaced eyes.

Committee proactively promotes to all Canadian women that since a safe amount of alcohol to consume is unknown, it's best to have none (Assembly of First Nations, 2008). FASD is an abnormality that is completely preventable.

Cigarettes

Cigarette smoke contains many ingredients, including the stimulant nicotine, the gas carbon monoxide, and hydrocarbons ("tars"), which are carcinogens. Nicotine and the carbon monoxide pass through the placenta and reach the fetus. Nicotine stimulates the fetus, but its long-term effects are uncertain. Carbon monoxide decreases the amount of oxygen available to the fetus. Oxygen deprivation is connected with impaired motor development, academic delays, learning disabilities, intellectual challenges, and hyperactivity (Secker-Walker & Vacek, 2003). Second-hand smoke and even third-hand smoke (smoke residue found after smoking has occurred) are also topics of interest in prenatal research.

The First Nations and Inuit Health Committee promotes the idea that since a safe amount of alcohol to consume is unknown, it is best to have none when pregnant.

Yuri Arcurs/iStockphoto.com

EMERGING CANADA

Drug use during pregnancy is risky, and the accompanying stigma makes it difficult for women who use drugs to receive help and support. The reality is that some women still use drugs. The most commonly used drugs are these:

Nicotine – 20%	Marijuana – 3%
Alcohol – 19%	Cocaine – 1%

The risk of taking drugs significantly increases when the mother is using both nicotine and alcohol (Kang, 2004).

Pregnant women who smoke are likely to deliver smaller babies than non-smokers (Bernstein et al., 2005). Their babies are also more likely to be stillborn or to die soon after birth (Cnattingius, 2004). Babies of fathers who smoke have higher rates of birth defects, infant mortality, lower birth weights, and cardiovascular problems (Goel et al., 2004).

Prescribed Medications and Food-Borne Issues

Drugs that are prescribed by doctors may also cause damage to the fetus. For example, it is recommended that pregnant women consume limited quantities of fish such as tuna during pregnancy for fear that the mercury content may be consumed at toxic levels affecting the unborn child. Also, certain cheeses made from unpasteurized milk contain bacteria such as listeria and can be dangerous. Eating food such as meat, fish, and eggs that have not been properly cooked could also contain salmonella, listeria, or other harmful bacteria. Through the Motherisk Program, the Hospital for Sick Children in Toronto conducts research and provides information about drugs and other products that may be damaging to the fetus or that might pass through breast milk causing harm to an infant. Motherisk counsellors offer support and guidance for pregnant and nursing women as well as for health-care professionals regarding the risk of consuming drugs, alcohol, and other substances. They also provide information about exposure to radiation, chemicals, and other environmental hazards. In addition,

Emin Kuliyev/Shutterstock.com

The Motherisk program conducts research and provides guidance to the public and to health professionals on exposure to drugs, chemicals, disease, radiation, and environmental agents that affect the fetus or that may impact the safety of breast milk.

Motherisk counsellors provide support for women experiencing nausea and vomiting during pregnancy.

Accutane (Isotretinoin)

Accutane (isotretinoin) is a prescription treatment for severe acne. It is an extremely powerful human teratogen that results in a 20 to 35% risk of physical damage to a fetus exposed to accutane during pregnancy. These defects include craniofacial, cardiovascular, and neurological damage.

In an article released by the *Canadian Medical Association Journal*, Choi and colleagues (2013) explore the finding that 7–59% of Canadian women prescribed Accutane did not use a contraceptive or, if they did, they used the contraceptive ineffectively. Pregnancy tests were not administered to 36% of these women before taking the drug for the first time. Intervention is needed to provide improved education for patients and healthcare providers. Proper control of drug distribution is required. Furthermore, time must be taken with women to explain the high risks associated with this prescription medicine, particularly teenagers who are more likely to be prescribed this medication (Choi, Koren, & Nulman, 2013).

accutane (isotretinoin) a frequently prescribed acne medication that can cause significant physical and neurological birth defects

progestin a hormone used to maintain pregnancy that can cause masculinization of the fetus

DES diethylstilbestrol, an estrogen that has been linked to cancer in the reproductive organs of children whose mothers used the hormone when pregnant

Hormones

Women at risk for miscarriages have been prescribed hormones to help maintain their pregnancies. Progestin is chemically similar to male sex hormones and can masculinize the external sex organs of female embryos. DES (short for diethylstilbestrol), a powerful estrogen, often prescribed during the 1940s and 1950s to help prevent miscarriage, has been shown to have caused cervical and testicular cancer in some offspring. Among daughters of DES users, about 1 in 1,000 will develop cancer in the reproductive tract (Centers for Disease Control and Prevention, 2005).

Vitamins

Although pregnant women are often prescribed multivitamins to maintain their own health and to promote the development of their fetuses, high doses of vitamins A and D have been associated with central nervous system damage, small head size, and heart defects (National Institutes of Health, 2002). Special maternal vitamins reduce the risk of neural tube defects in unborn babies and can promote postpartum health for the mother.

Caffeine

Many pregnant women consume caffeine in the form of coffee, tea, soft drinks, chocolate, and non-prescription drugs. Research findings on

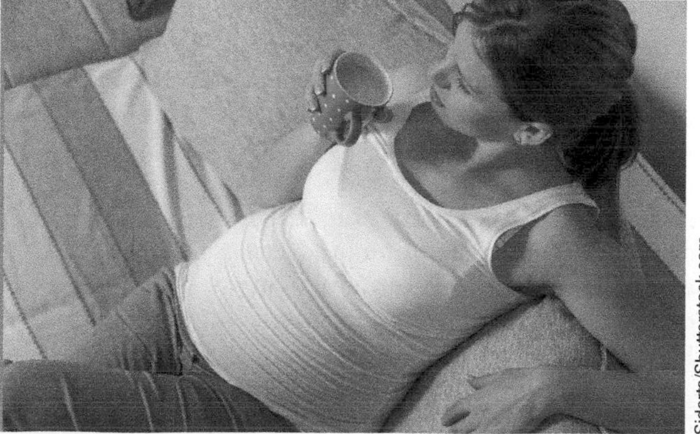

Sidarta/Shutterstock.com

pathogenic anything that causes disease

syphilis a sexually transmitted infection that, in advanced stages, can attack major organ systems

congenital present at birth; resulting from the prenatal environment

HIV/AIDS HIV stands for the human immunodeficiency virus, which cripples the body's immune system. AIDS stands for acquired immunodeficiency syndrome, a condition in which the immune system is weakened such that it is vulnerable to diseases it would otherwise be able to fight off.

rubella a viral infection that can cause retardation and heart disease in the embryo. Also called German measles

toxemia a life-threatening disease that can afflict pregnant women; characterized by high blood pressure

premature born before the full term of gestation. Also referred to as preterm

caffeine's effects on the developing fetus have been inconsistent (Signorello & McLaughlin, 2004). Some studies report no adverse findings, but other studies do (Weng, Odouli, & Li, 2008).

Teratogens of a Pathogenic Nature

Pathogenic means anything that causes disease. Included in this section are maternal conditions that impact the safety of both mother and child such as toxemia and Rh incompatibility

Sexually Transmitted Infections

The syphilis bacterium can cause miscarriage, stillbirth, or congenital syphilis. Routine blood tests early in pregnancy can diagnose syphilis. The syphilis bacterium is vulnerable to antibiotics. The fetus will probably not contract syphilis if an infected mother is treated with antibiotics before the fourth month of pregnancy (Centers for Disease Control and Prevention, 2006). If the mother is not treated, the baby may be infected in utero and develop congenital syphilis. About 12% of babies infected die.

HIV/AIDS (human immunodeficiency virus/acquired immunodeficiency syndrome) disables the body's immune system and leaves victims prey to a variety of fatal illnesses, including respiratory disorders and cancer. The prognosis for a person with HIV/AIDS is not favourable unless a treatment of antiviral drugs is followed. Even then, the drugs do not work for everyone, and the eventual outcome remains in doubt (Rathus, Nevid, & Fichner-Rathus, 2008).

HIV can be transmitted by sexual relations, blood transfusions, sharing hypodermic needles, childbirth, and breast feeding. About one-fourth of babies born to HIV-infected mothers become infected themselves (Coovadia, 2004). During childbirth, blood vessels in the mother and baby rupture, enabling an exchange of blood and the transmission of HIV. HIV is also found in breast milk. If interventions are not implemented, the risk of mother to child transmission of HIV during breastfeeding is 5–20% (World Health Organization, 2004).

About one fourth of babies born to mothers infected with HIV become infected themselves.

Rubella

Rubella (German measles) is a viral infection. Women who are infected with rubella during the first 20 weeks of pregnancy stand at least a 20% chance of bearing children with birth defects such as deafness, intellectual challenges, heart disease, or eye problems, including blindness (Food and Drug Administration, 2004; Reef, Zimmerman-Swain, & Coronado, 2004).

Many adult women had rubella as children and are therefore immune. Women who are not immune should be vaccinated before they become pregnant if the pregnancy is planned. A mother can be inoculated during pregnancy, if necessary. Inoculation has led to a dramatic decline in the number of North American children born with defects caused by rubella, from approximately 2,000 cases in 1964–1965 to 21 cases in 2001 (Food and Drug Administration, 2004; Reef et al., 2004).

Toxemia

Toxemia, a life-threatening disease characterized by high blood pressure, may afflict women late in the second trimester or early in the third trimester. Women with toxemia often have premature or undersized babies. Toxemia is also a cause of pregnancy-related maternal deaths (Rumbold et al., 2006). Toxemia appears to be linked to malnutrition, but the causes are unclear. Women who do not receive prenatal care are much more likely to die from toxemia than those who receive prenatal care (Scott, 2006). Universal healthcare in Canada is a protection for both mother and the developing baby, provided the services are accessed.

Rh Incompatibility

In Rh incompatibility, antibodies produced by the mother are transmitted to a fetus or newborn infant and cause brain damage or death. Rh is a blood protein found in the red blood cells of some individuals. Rh incompatibility occurs when a woman who does not have this factor—and is thus Rh negative—is carrying an Rh-positive fetus, which can happen when the father is Rh positive. The negative–positive combination occurs in approximately 10% of Canadian couples and becomes a problem in some resulting pregnancies. Rh incompatibility does not affect a first child because women will not have formed Rh antibodies. The chances of an exchange of blood are greatest during childbirth. If an exchange occurs, the mother produces Rh-positive antibodies to the baby's Rh-positive blood. These antibodies can enter the fetal bloodstream during subsequent deliveries, causing anemia, mental deficiency, or death.

If an Rh-negative mother is injected with Rh immunoglobulin within 72 hours after delivery of an Rh-positive baby, she will not develop the antibodies. This series of injections is provided to affected Canadian mothers after the delivery of their first child and during subsequent pregnancies.

Environmental Hazards

Mothers know when they are ingesting drugs, but they may unknowingly take in other harmful substances from the environment. These substances are environmental hazards to which we are all exposed, and we refer to them collectively as pollution.

Prenatal exposure to heavy metals such as lead, mercury, and zinc threatens to delay mental development at 1 and 2 years of age (Heindel & Lawler, 2006). Polychlorinated biphenyls (PCBs), used in many industrial products, accumulate in fish that feed in polluted waters. Among Canada's First Nations, a growing body of research and concerns are focused on the health effects posed to children and unborn fetuses as a result of exposures to toxic chemicals and other environmental hazards. Recent research has linked environmental contaminants to adverse child health outcomes, including learning and developmental disabilities, birth defects, low birth weight, some cancers, and asthma (Assembly of First Nations, 2008).

Experiments with mice show that fetal exposure to radiation in high doses can damage the eyes, central nervous system, and skeleton (e.g., Hossain, Chetana, & Devi, 2005). Pregnant women are advised to avoid unnecessary exposure to X-rays. (Ultrasound, which is not an X-ray, has not been shown to harm the fetus.) Even a house cat can pose a life-threatening risk to a fetus if the mother is exposed (through litter boxes or gardening) to cat feces infected with the tiny parasite that causes toxoplasmosis. Exposure to this parasite can result in severe birth defects or even death for the fetus (Kidshealth, 2010).

Parents' Ages

What about the parents' ages? During a parental "age window," the health of the baby is better ensured. For example, sperm production slows in old age but remains throughout men's lifespan, though older fathers are more likely to produce abnormal sperm. The mother's age also matters. From a biological vantage point, the 20s may be the ideal age for women to bear children in terms of reducing the risk of genetic abnormalities. The offspring of teenage mothers have a higher incidence of infant mortality and are more likely to have a low birth weight (Phipps, Blume, & DeMonner, 2002; Save the Children, 2004). Girls who become pregnant in their early teens may place a burden on their bodies, which may not have adequately matured to facilitate pregnancy and childbirth (Berg et al., 2003).

Women's fertility declines gradually until the mid-30s, after which it declines more rapidly. Women who wait until their 30s or 40s to have children also

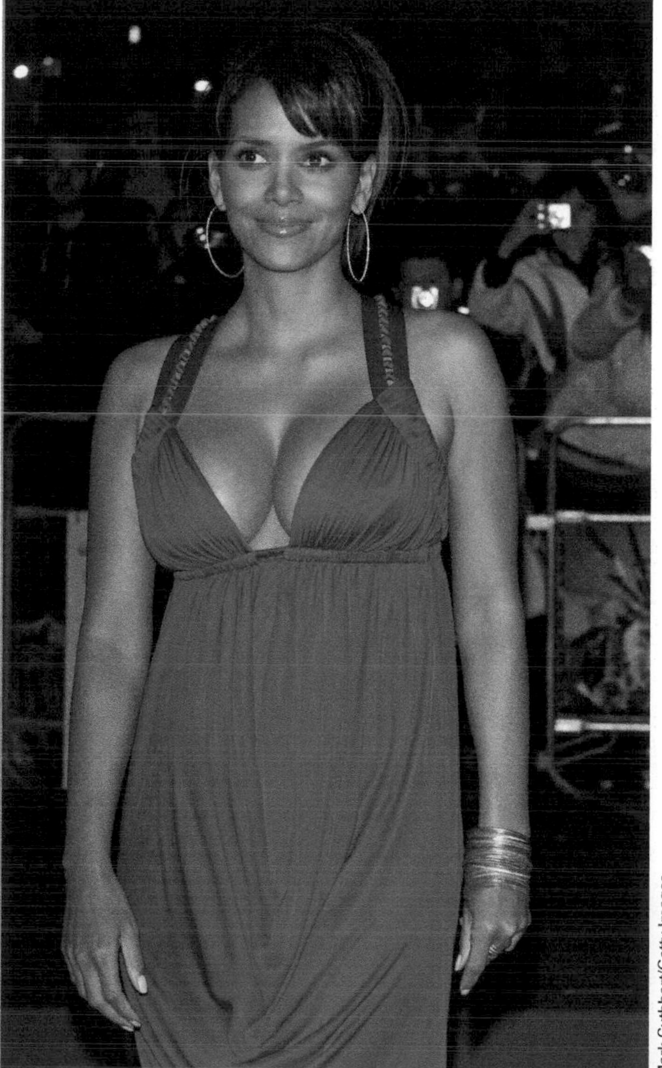
Mark Cuthbert/Getty Images

Medical Discovery versus Bioethics

In 1996, the cloning of Dolly the Sheep (or the Dolly Lamba, as she is often called) prompted Canada and the world to examine how far they were willing to stretch the boundaries of medical discovery and ethics. The Canadian government enacted legislation in March of 2004 banning human and stem cell cloning, rent-a-womb contracts, the sale of human eggs and sperm, and the creation of people with animal DNA. This legislation was designed to keep children safe and to ensure research into new reproductive technology is ethically sound (CBC News, 2009a). Canada has limited research to the use of embryos that have been created for reproductive purposes but are now no longer required. Permission to use the embryos must be obtained from the parents for whom the embryos were created. In the case of experimental stem cell research, should Canadian parents be able to create an embryo so that they can harvest the stem cells later? What are your thoughts?

AP Photo/Paul Clements/CP Images

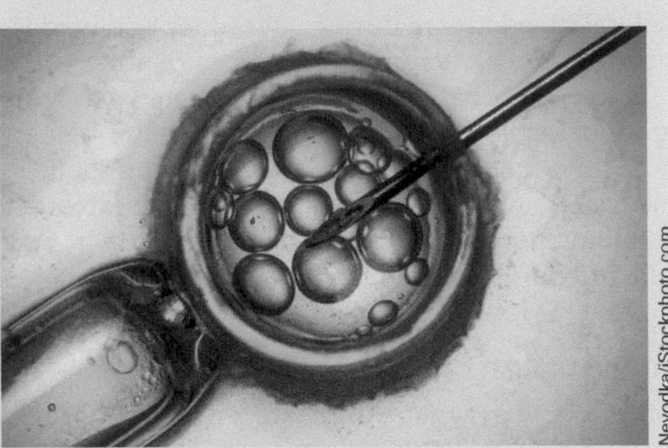

Nevodka/iStockphoto.com

increase the likelihood of having stillborn or preterm babies (Berg et al., 2003). With adequate prenatal care, however, the risk of bearing a premature or unhealthy baby still is relatively small, even for older first-time mothers (Berg et al., 2003).

Whatever the age of the mother, the events of childbirth provide some of the most memorable moments in the lives of parents. In Chapter 3, we continue our exploration with the process of birth and the characteristics of the newborn child.

EMERGING CANADA

In 2009, the average age of mothers at the birth of their children was 29.4 years. This age has been increasing over the past three decades. Half of all mothers who gave birth in 2009 were age 30 or older. Births to teenage mothers have been decreasing constantly from 30 births per 1,000 in 1974 to 12 in 2009 (Human Resources and Skills Development Canada, 2013a).

STUDY TOOLS

CHAPTER 2

Located at **nelson.com/student**

- ☐ Prepare for tests with a variety of exercises and activities.
- ☐ Review Key Terms Flashcards (online or print)
- ☐ Create your own study tools with Build a Summary
- ☐ Watch Observing Development videos to expand your knowledge

PART TWO

CHAPTER 3

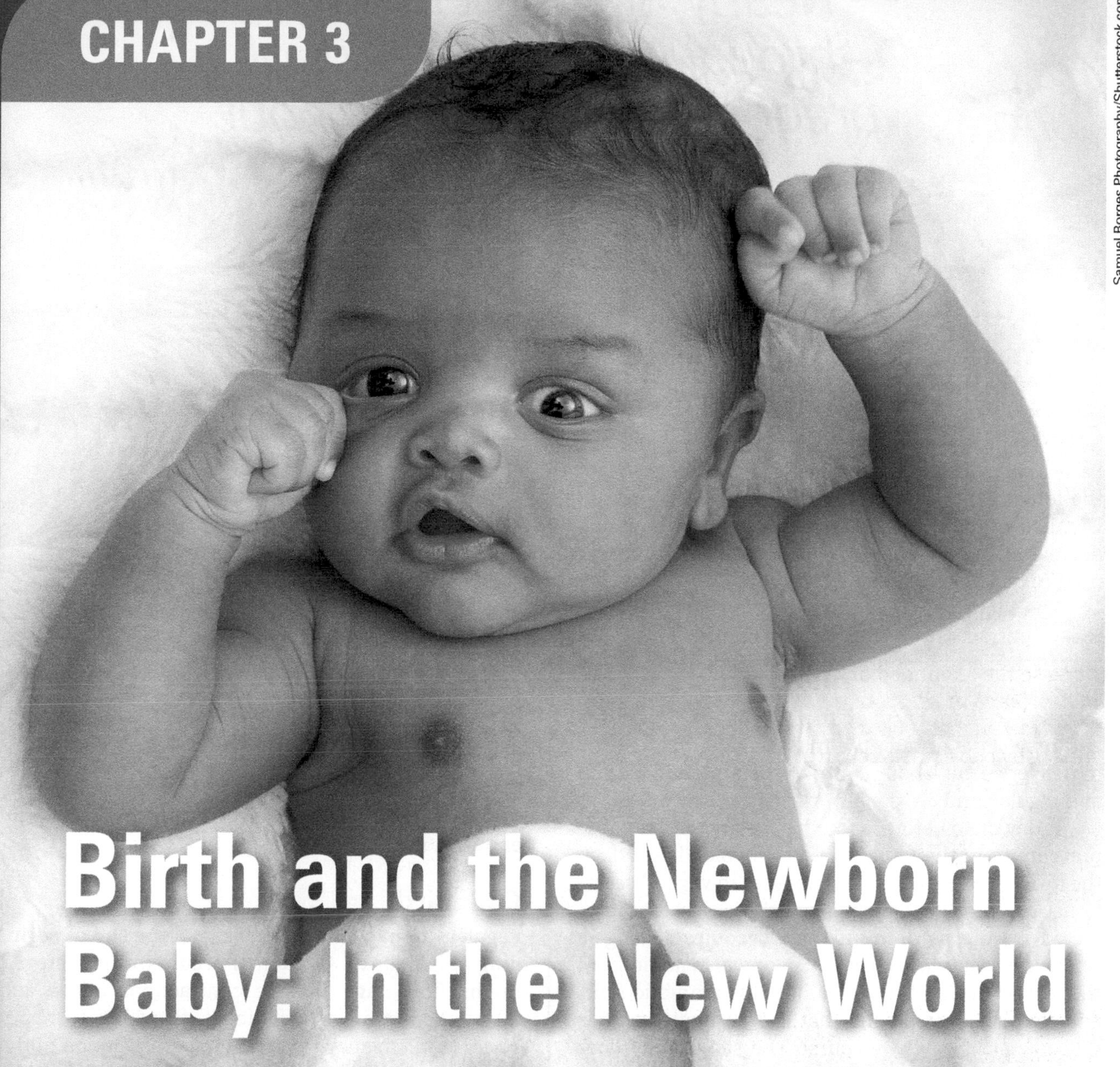

Samuel Borges Photography/Shutterstock.com

Birth and the Newborn Baby: In the New World

LEARNING OUTCOMES

LO1 Identify the stages of childbirth

LO2 Describe the different methods of childbirth

LO3 Discuss potential problems with childbirth

LO4 Describe the key events of the postpartum period

LO5 Describe the characteristics of the newborn

> “Nearly all mothers struggle through the last weeks of pregnancy and worry about the mechanics of delivery.”

LO1 The Stages of Childbirth

Countdown...

Early in the last month of pregnancy, the head of the fetus settles in the mother's pelvis. This process is called dropping or lightening. Because lightening decreases pressure on the diaphragm, the mother may, in fact, feel lighter.

The first uterine contractions are called Braxton-Hicks contractions, or false labour contractions. They are relatively painless and may be experienced as early as the sixth month of pregnancy. These contractions increase in frequency as the pregnancy progresses and may serve to tone the muscles that will be used in delivery. True labour contractions are more painful and regular, and are usually intensified by walking.

A day or so before labour begins, increased pelvic pressure from the fetus may rupture blood vessels in the birth canal so that blood appears in vaginal secretions. Mucus that had plugged the cervix and protected the uterus from infection becomes dislodged. About 1 woman in 10 has a rush of warm liquid from the vagina at this time. This liquid is amniotic fluid, and its discharge means that the amniotic sac has burst. The sac usually does not burst until the end of the first stage of childbirth, as described later. Other signs that labour is beginning include indigestion, diarrhea, an ache in the small of the back, and cramps.

Braxton-Hicks contractions the first, usually painless, contractions of childbirth

prostaglandins hormones that stimulate uterine contractions

oxytocin a hormone that stimulates labour contractions

efface to become thin

dilate to widen

The fetus may actually signal the mother when it is ready to be born by secreting hormones that stimulate the placenta and uterus to secrete prostaglandins (Snegovskikh, Park, & Norwitz, 2006). Prostaglandins cause

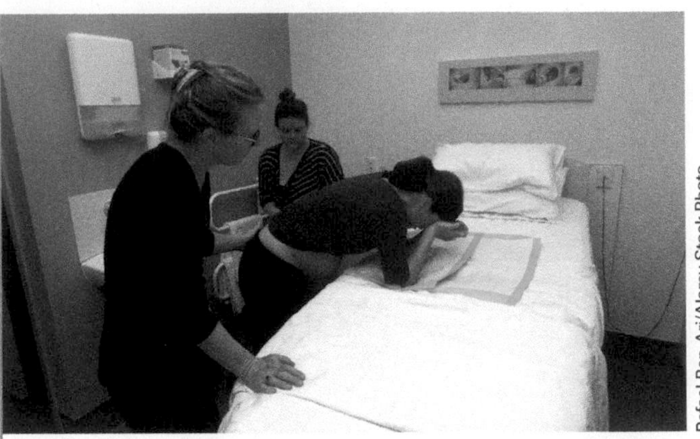

Rafael Ben-Ari/Alamy Stock Photo

the cramping women may feel before or during menstruation, and they also excite the muscles of the uterus to engage in labour contractions. As labour progresses, the pituitary gland releases the hormone oxytocin, which stimulates contractions powerful enough to expel the baby.

Childbirth

Regular uterine contractions signal the actual beginning of childbirth. Childbirth occurs in three stages. In the first stage, uterine contractions efface and dilate the cervix, which needs to widen to about 10 cm (4 in.) to allow the baby to pass. Dilation of the cervix causes most of the pain of childbirth.

The first stage of childbirth is the longest. For first-time mothers, this stage may last from a few hours to more than a day. Subsequent pregnancies take less time. The first contractions are not usually painful. They are spaced 10 to 20 minutes apart and may last from 20 to 40 seconds each. As the process continues, the contractions become more powerful, frequent, and regular. Women are usually advised to go to the hospital or birthing centre when the contractions are 4 to 5 minutes apart. Until the end of the first stage of labour, the mother is usually in a labour room.

During the first stage of childbirth, fetal monitoring may be used. One kind of monitor is an electronic device strapped around the woman's abdomen that measures both the fetal heart rate and the mother's contractions. When the cervix is nearly fully dilated, the head of the fetus begins to move into the vagina. This process is called **transition**. During transition, which lasts 30 minutes or less, contractions are frequent and strong.

The second stage of childbirth begins when the baby appears at the opening of the vagina (now called the birth canal; see Figure 3.1). The second stage is briefer than the first, possibly lasting minutes or a few hours and ending with the birth of the baby. For this stage, the woman may be taken to a delivery room.

The contractions of the second stage stretch the skin surrounding the birth canal farther and propel the baby forward. The baby's head is said to have crowned when it begins to emerge from the birth canal. Once crowning has occurred, the baby normally emerges completely within minutes.

The physician, nurse, or midwife may perform an episiotomy once crowning takes place. The purpose of the episiotomy is to prevent random tearing when the area between the birth canal and the anus becomes severely stretched. The incision may cause itching and discomfort as it heals. In 1992, half of all women who had vaginal deliveries in Canada had an episiotomy. This rate fell to 14.1% in 2012 (Chalmers et al., 2012). According to research conducted at the Ottawa Hospital Research Institute, an episiotomy provides no advantage other than speeding up the delivery.

transition
movement of the head of the fetus into the birth canal

To clear any obstructions from the passageway for breathing, mucus is suctioned from the baby's mouth when the head emerges from the birth canal. When the baby is breathing adequately on his or her own, the umbilical cord is clamped and severed (Figure 3.2). Mother and infant are now separate beings. The stump of the umbilical cord will dry and fall off on its own in about 7 to 10 days.

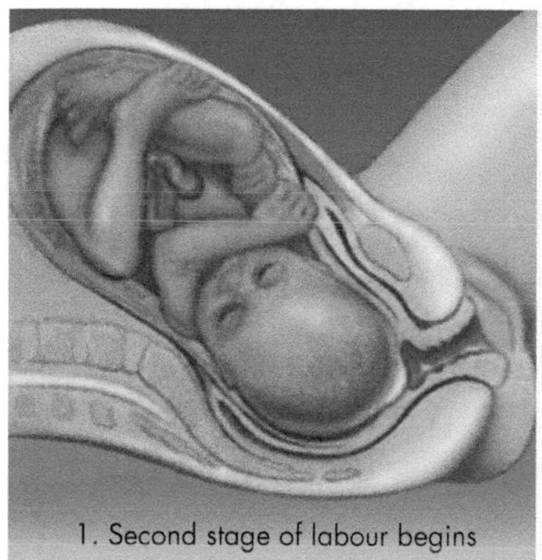
1. Second stage of labour begins

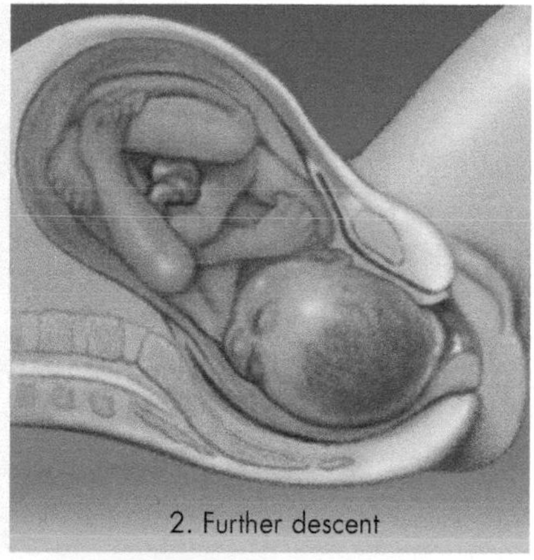
2. Further descent

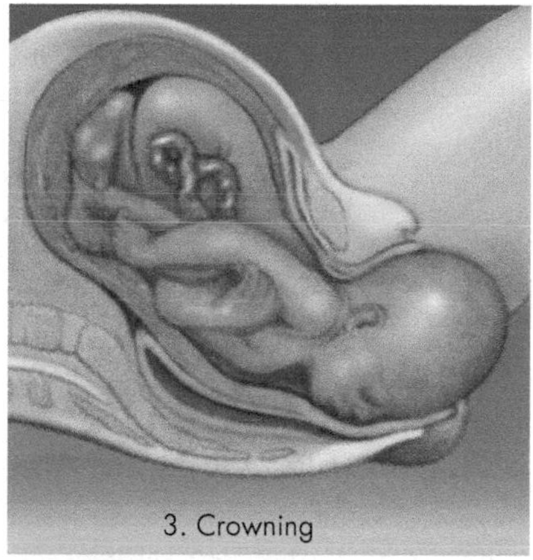
3. Crowning

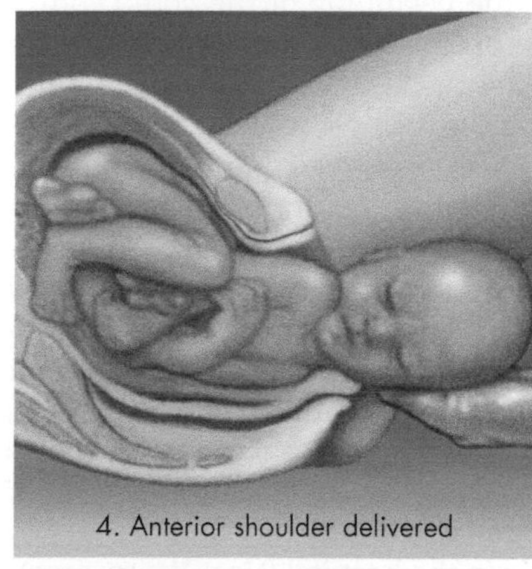
4. Anterior shoulder delivered

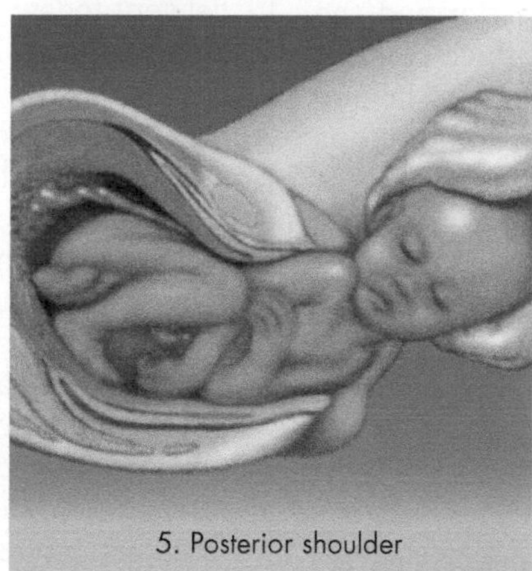
5. Posterior shoulder

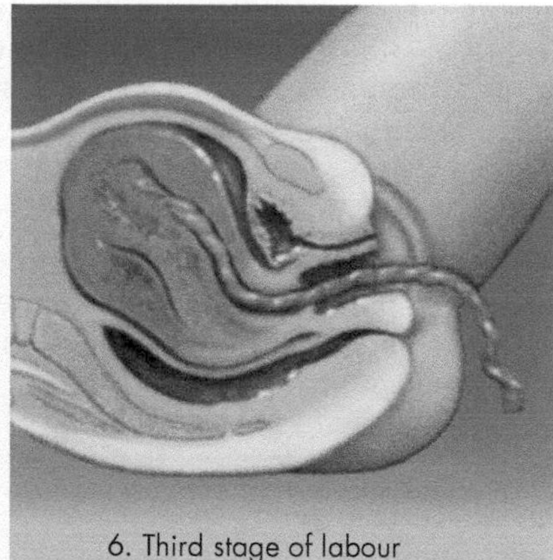
6. Third stage of labour

FIGURE 3.1

Stages of Childbirth

In the first stage, uterine contractions efface and dilate the cervix. The second stage begins with movement of the baby into the birth canal and ends with birth of the baby. During the third stage, the placenta separates from the uterine wall and is expelled through the birth canal.

Source: © Cengage Learning

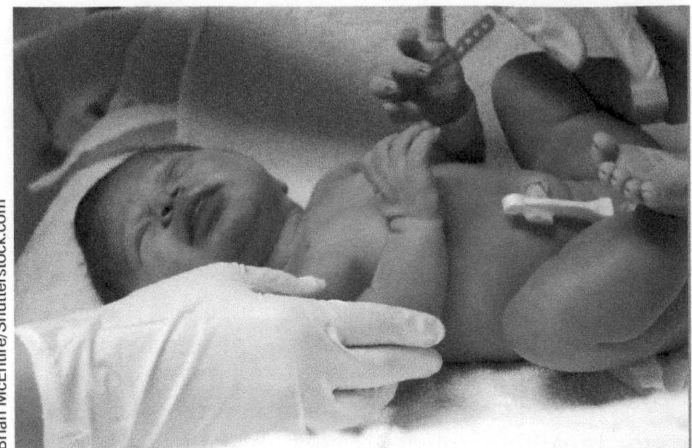

Brian McEntire/Shutterstock.com

FIGURE 3.2

A Clamped and Severed Umbilical Cord

The stump of the umbilical cord dries and falls off in about 10 days.

midwife
an individual who cares for women during pregnancy, labour and delivery, and after the child is born

The baby is now often whisked away by a nurse, who will perform various procedures, including footprinting the baby, supplying an ID bracelet, administering antibiotic ointment or drops of silver nitrate into the baby's eyes to prevent bacterial infections, and injecting the baby with vitamin K to help its blood clot properly if it bleeds (newborn babies do not manufacture vitamin K). In Canada, one drop of blood is taken from newborns to screen for more than 50 obscure disorders and anomalies (such as PKU) that may be treatable if detected early (CBC News, 2007b).

While these procedures are being performed, the mother is in the third stage of labour, which can last from minutes to hours. During this stage of labour, the placenta separates from the uterine wall and is expelled through the birth canal. Some bleeding is normal. The obstetrician then sews the episiotomy, if one has been performed, and determines whether the entire placenta has been expelled; if a part of the placenta is not expelled, hemorrhaging (excessive bleeding) could occur.

DID YOU KNOW?

Slapping babies on the bottom to stimulate breathing is an outdated Hollywood image.

Though this image is often seen in old movies, it does not happen in today's hospitals. To allow for independent breathing, mucus is suctioned from the baby's nose and mouth when the head emerges from the birth canal.

LO2 Methods of Childbirth

Childbirth was once a more intimate procedure that usually took place in the woman's home and involved the mother, perhaps a **midwife**, and family members. This pattern is followed in many less developed nations today. About 10% of babies born in Canada are delivered by midwife (numbers vary by province). Using a midwife is a growing trend in Canada, particularly within the Aboriginal population. Modern medicine has undeniably saved countless lives of both newborn babies and their mothers, but childbearing has also become more impersonal. Some argue that modern methods take control from women over their own bodies. The major methods of delivery involve greater degrees of intervention. They include a natural, vaginal delivery (no medical intervention given), medically assisted vaginal birth, and Caesarean section (removal of child through mother's abdomen). Each of these methods will be discussed in turn.

EMERGING CANADA

As of 2012, Otis Kryzanauskas was Canada's only registered, practising male midwife. His mother practises midwifery and he was inspired to join the profession after being involved in the delivery of his brother (Bradshaw, 2012).

From Midwifery to Care by Physician: A Historical Perspective

How did a change take place from predominant use of midwifery at the turn of the 20th century to a small but growing group of women choosing this method of delivery today? At the beginning of the 20th century, hospitals were like poor houses. Physicians cared for middle and upper class individuals in their own homes (Noel-Weiss, 2007). Thus, using a midwife was acceptable; however, this also resulted in more infant mortality and more maternal deaths during childbirth than childbirth by physician. With the advent of new technology, medicines, and surgeries, the opinion of many changed and hospitals were no longer taboo. As physicians asserted authority over healthcare, nurses sought to separate from midwifery legitimizing the profession. Consequently, the midwifery came to be perceived as being old-fashioned, and the childbirth preference of Canadian women transformed to care and delivery by physician and nurse in the hospital (Noel-Weiss, 2007).

Midwives

Today, about 10% of childbirths are performed by a midwife, as midwife-assisted births have grown in popularity over the past two decades (McCracken,

2015). Midwife literally means "with mother." In Canada, midwives are regulated healthcare professionals who receive specialized training in the birth and care of infants and their mothers, using natural childbirth methods including relaxation and breathing techniques. They may also provide induction, anaesthesia, and the use of antibiotics to treat infection when required. Women who deliver with a midwife must be low risk for complications that require medical intervention. Midwives may deliver infants in the woman's home or in the hospital. What makes this type of healthcare special is the amount of individualized planning that is involved in the birthing process and the continuity of care provided to mother and infant both before and after delivery. In 2010, Ontario became the first province to regulate and legislate midwives. Women using midwives report being more satisfied with their prenatal care and maternity experiences than women using any other healthcare professional. Women using midwives also receive fewer medical interventions than any other patients (O'Brien et al., 2011).

Prepared Childbirth

In the Lamaze method, women engage in breathing and relaxation exercises that reduce fear and pain and distract them from discomfort. The mother-to-be attends Lamaze classes with a "coach"—most often, her partner—who will aid her in the delivery room by massaging her, timing the contractions, offering social support, and coaching her in patterns of breathing and relaxation. Women using the Lamaze method often report less pain and ask for less medication (Yeo, 2010), but these experiences could have more to do with psychological preparation than a reduction in actual pain. Prepared childbirth is a form of natural childbirth.

DID YOU KNOW?

Midwives perform 10% of all births today.

In Canada, women can choose to use a midwife instead of a physician for prenatal care and delivery of their child. Provinces vary in the number of registered midwives available, and there are more midwives available in urban than in rural areas. When a woman learns that she is pregnant, she would discuss her preference to use a midwife rather than a physician with her general practitioner (family doctor). Her GP would refer her to the midwives in her area, or she could call a clinic directly and set up her first appointment. If she is unaware of the clinics in her area, she could also telephone the association of midwives related to her province for a referral. One of the benefits of using a midwife is the option to give birth in the mother's own home if the pregnancy is deemed low risk. For example, about half of all births by midwives were delivered at home in Alberta (Alberta Association of Midwives, 2015).

natural childbirth
childbirth without medical intervention, including anaesthesia, being given to the mother during labour and delivery

Lamaze method
a childbirth method in which women are educated about childbirth, breathe in patterns that reduce pain during birth, and have a coach present

anaesthetics
agents that lessen pain

general anaesthesia
an agent that eliminates pain by putting a person to sleep

local anaesthetic
an agent that reduces pain in an area of the body

Hospital Delivery with Medical Intervention

In Canada, the majority of childbirths (98.5) are performed in a hospital (Picard, 2013). Approximately 20% of all hospital deliveries are performed by Caesarean section and 10% of vaginal births involve medical interventions such as forceps and suction extraction (Picard, 2013). A study by Chalmers and associates (2012) assessed the birthing experience of women who delivered in hospitals and found that many medical interventions are used to deliver babies, including inducing labour (30.9%), use of an epidural (53.7%), and the use of an episiotomy (14.1%).

Anaesthesia

Two types of anaesthetics are used to lessen the pain associated with childbirth. General anaesthesia achieves its anaesthetic effect by putting the woman to sleep by means of an injected barbiturate or through tranquilizers, oral barbiturates, and narcotics. General anaesthesia reduces the responsiveness of the baby shortly after birth when parents are eager to interact with their new arrival, but there is little evidence that the anaesthetic has any long-term negative effects (Caton et al., 2002).

More commonly used than general anaesthetics are regional or local anaesthetics, which reduce anxiety and the perception of pain without putting the mother to sleep. The mother's external genitals are numbed by local injection. With an epidural block and the spinal block, anaesthesia is injected into the spinal canal or spinal cord, temporarily numbing the body below the waist. Local anaesthesia has minor depressive effects on newborns shortly after birth, but the effects have not been shown to linger (Caton et al., 2002; Eltzschig, Lieberman, & Camann, 2003).

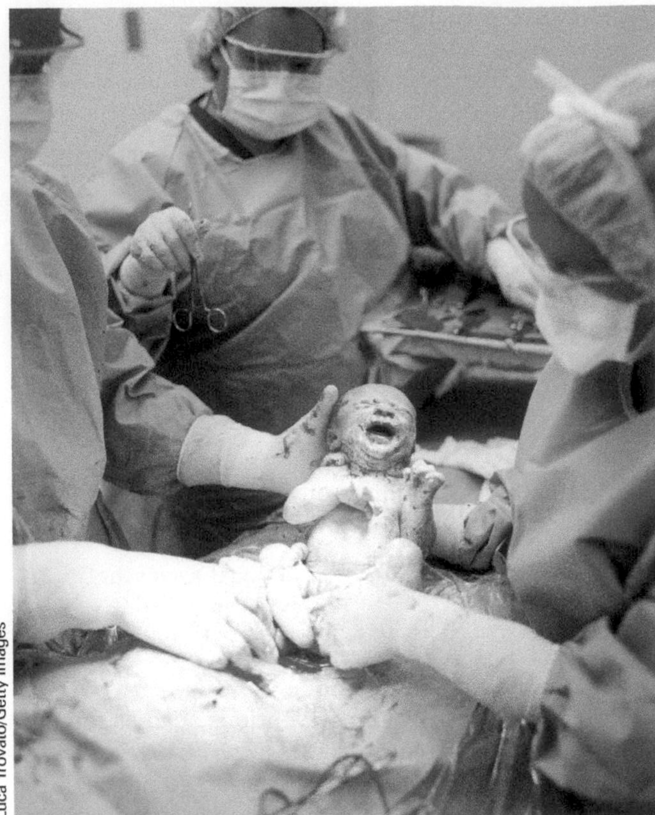
Luca Trovato/Getty Images

Caesarean section (C-section)
delivery of a baby by abdominal surgery

anoxia
absence of oxygen

hypoxia
less oxygen than required

Caesarean Section

In a Caesarean section (C-section), the physician delivers the baby by abdominal surgery. The physician cuts through the mother's abdomen and uterus to physically remove the baby. The incisions are then sewn.

Physicians prefer C-sections to vaginal delivery when they believe that normal delivery may threaten the mother or child or may be more difficult than desired. Reasons to perform C-sections include risks to the infant—issues with the umbilical cord, baby in breech position, and size of infant—as well as maternal issues—heart disease, high blood pressure, placenta previa (blocked cervix), and other conditions. Today, nearly one of every five births in Canada is by C-section (Pittman, 2010).

In 2012, 8.1% of Canadian women requested a Caesarean section before delivery. Fear of vaginal delivery and concern for the safety of the baby are offered as reasons for this new trend. Some mothers view a C-section as providing convenience (Gallagher et al., 2012). C-sections are also performed when the physician wants to prevent the circulatory systems of the mother and baby from mixing, as might occur when (normal) bleeding occurs during vaginal delivery. C-sections in such cases help prevent transmission of the viruses that cause genital herpes and AIDS.

DID YOU KNOW?

In Canada, nearly one of every five births is by Caesarean section.

According to the World Health Organization, although it can save lives, Caesarean section is often performed without medical need, putting women and their babies at risk of short- and long-term health problems. (Murphy, 2015)

LO3 Birth Problems

Although most deliveries are unremarkable from a medical standpoint, some problems can and do occur.

EMERGING CANADA

Stem cells are cells that are blank slates, holding the potential to be developed into virtually any cell in the human body (see Medical Discovery versus Bioethics on page 44). A newborn's umbilical cord is rich with stem cells that can be preserved and potentially used to save the life of the baby or a member of the baby's family. A new Canadian trend is to pay a private stem cell bank to store these valuable cells, which could be the subject of a new medical discovery (CBC Digital Archives, 2013). Canadian researchers are at the forefront of stem cell research—and ethical controversy.

Oxygen Deprivation

Researchers use two terms to discuss oxygen deprivation: anoxia and hypoxia. Anoxia derives from roots meaning "without oxygen." Hypoxia derives from

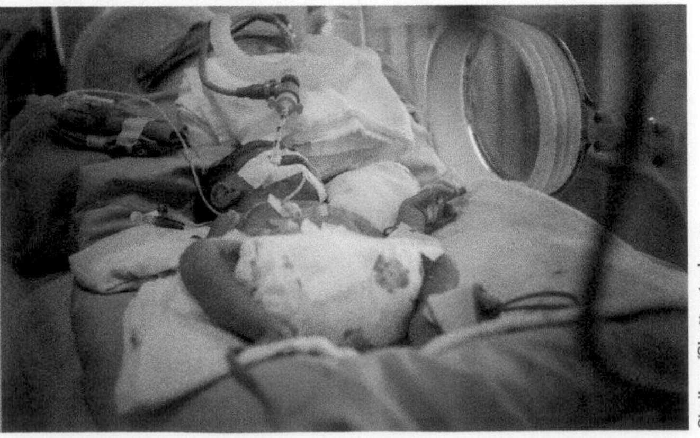
Chaikom/Shutterstock.com

massage, and human touch in general—helps improve weight gain in newborns, especially premature babies still developing.

Low-Birth-Weight Infants

A baby is considered to have a low birth weight when it weighs less than about 2.5 kg (5.5 lb.). When a baby is low in birth weight, despite being born at full term, it is referred to as being small for dates. Mothers who smoke, abuse drugs, or are malnourished place their babies at risk of being small for dates. Small-for-dates babies tend to remain shorter and lighter than their age-mates and show slight delays in learning and problems in attention when compared with their age-mates (O'Keeffe et al., 2003). Pregnant women who experience abuse are also at elevated risk of having a low-birth-weight baby (Canadian Institute of Child Health, 2010).

Risks Associated with Low Birth Weight

Newborns are often referred to as neonates, *neo* meaning "new" and *nate* meaning "born." Newborns weighing between 1.475 kg (3.25 lb.) and 2.5 kg (5.5 lb.) are seven times more likely to die than infants of normal birth weight, whereas those weighing less than 1.5 kg (3.3 lb.) are nearly 100 times as likely to die (Nadeau et al., 2003). In general, the lower a child's birth weight, the more poorly he or she fares on measures of neurological development and cognitive functioning throughout the school years (Dorling et al., 2006; Nadeau et al., 2003; Wocadlo & Rieger, 2006).

Low birth weight is a key determinant of infant survival, health, and development. Low-birth-weight infants are at a greater risk of developing chronic health problems and of dying during the first year of life. In 2010, 6.2% of infants in Canada were born at low birth weight with the rate of low birth weight being 5.7% for infant boys and 6.7% for infant girls. Mothers aged 35–49 seem to be at a slightly higher risk for developing a low-birth-weight baby (7.6%) (Human Resources and Skills Development Canada, 2013c).

small for dates
description of newborns who are small for their age

LO4 The Postpartum Period

The postpartum period refers to the weeks following delivery; it has no specific limit. The family's long wait is over. Concerns about pregnancy and labour have subsided; fingers and toes have been counted, and despite some local discomfort, the mother finds her "load" to be lightened—literally.

Maternal Depression

One feature of the postpartum period for many mothers is depression. According to the Canadian Paediatric Society (Province of British Columbia, 2010), about 80% of new mothers can expect to

postpartum period
the period immediately following childbirth

Maternal and Infant Mortality around the World

Modern medicine has made vast strides in decreasing the rates of maternal and infant mortality, but the advances are not equally spread throughout the world. Save the Children, a nonprofit relief and development organization, tracks the likelihood that a woman will die in childbirth and that an infant will die during its first year. The likelihood of maternal and infant mortality relates to such factors as the percentage of births that are attended by trained people, the literacy rate of adult women (one measure of women's level of education), and the participation of women in national government (one measure of the extent to which a society empowers women). In Afghanistan, one woman in six will die as a result of pregnancy, and 165 children of 1,000 will die during their first year. In Afghan society, the literacy rate for women is only 21%, only 12% of women receive any professional assistance during childbirth, and women have virtually no role in government.

In Canada, the infant mortality rate in 2007 was 5.1 per 1,000 babies born (Statistics Canada, 2010b). Factors contributing to this number are our system of universal healthcare, our high literacy rate (99%), and strong female leadership within the country. However, compared to other industrialized countries, Canada ranks second highest rate of first-day infant mortality (The Canadian Press, 2013). The rate is 2.4 per 1,000 births. This may be due in part to the number of infants that are conceived using assisted reproductive technology resulting in multiple births. Infants born prematurely or of low birth weight are at greater risk of mortality. Another factor is that the number of infant deaths among the aboriginal community is four times higher than the national average (Canadian Press, 2013).

UNICEF Report: Leaving No Child Behind

In the past 20 years, the world has reduced the infant mortality rate by 30%. If we can achieve this change in some of the poorest nations in the world, why are infant mortality rates for some Aboriginal communities much higher than they are for other Canadian children (see Table 3.1)? In 2009, UNICEF asked why Aboriginal children are generally not as healthy as other Canadian children (UNICEF Canada, 2009).

TABLE 3.1

United Nations Statistics on the Health of Canadian Children

1 in 9 On average, the number of Canadian children living in poverty	1 in 4 The number of children in First Nations communities living in poverty
5 Infant deaths per 1,000 infants born in Canada	16 Infant deaths per 1,000 infants born in Nunavut (where 85% of the population is Inuit)
3 out of 177 Canada's ranking in the Human Development Index (HDI), a United Nations standard that measures a country's achievements in three basic aspects of human development: health, knowledge, and decent standard of living	68 out of 177 The HDI ranking of Canada's First Nations communities
85 The percentage of all children in Canada who accessed a doctor in 2000–01	63 The percentage of First Nations children on selected reserves who accessed a doctor in 2000–01
21 The percentage of non-Aboriginal children in census metropolitan areas living in low-income families	45 The percentage of Inuit children in census metropolitan areas living in low-income families
2 to 3× The multiple by which First Nations, Inuit, and Métis children are worse off than other Canadian children. They are less likely to see a doctor. As teens, they are more likely to become parents, and they are more likely to commit suicide.	

Source: Adapted from UNICEF, *The State of the World's Children 2009: Aboriginal Children's Health: Leaving No Child Behind*, Canadian supplement.

Christopher Futcher/iStockphoto.com

In the past, Canadians attributed their health to biological and medical causes. Then we began to factor in the effects of lifestyle choices. Now we know that our health is much more complicated. Health depends on a web of economic, social, political, and environmental factors. Some of the factors affecting the health of Aboriginal children include the following: poverty, a lack of education, substandard housing, poor nutrition, lack of access to health care and social services, in addition to a legacy of family, community, and cultural breakdown left by residential school policies.

Prenatal care and infant mortality rates are the starting point of a child's health. We have the knowledge, technology, and information to make changes. The UNICEF document states the priority of leaving no child behind. We are, however, leaving some Canadian children behind, a situation that must change.

Source: Adapted from UNICEF, *The State of the World's Children 2009: Aboriginal Children's Health: Leaving No Child Behind*, Canadian supplement.

experience periods of tearfulness, sadness, and irritability called the "baby blues."

Problems related to maternal depression range from the "baby blues" to more serious disturbances in mood including postpartum depression, and much less often, postpartum psychosis. Baby blues are so common that they are statistically normal (Gavin et al., 2005). Researchers believe that the blues are often due to hormonal changes that follow delivery (Kohl, 2004). They last about 10 days and are generally not severe enough to impair the mother's functioning.

Perhaps as many as 13% of Canadian mothers will encounter the more serious mood disorder

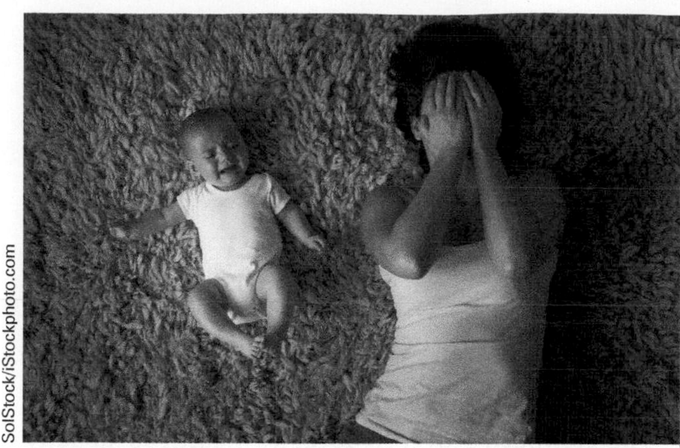
SolStock/iStockphoto.com

referred to as postpartum depression (PPD), which begins about a month after delivery and may linger for weeks or months. PPD is characterized by feelings of sadness every day almost all day long; feelings of hopelessness, helplessness, and worthlessness; difficulty concentrating; mood swings; and major changes in appetite (usually loss of appetite) and sleep patterns (frequently insomnia). Some women show obsessive concern for the well-being of their babies in addition to feeling overwhelmed.

Many researchers suggest that PPD is caused by a sudden drop in estrogen (Kohl, 2004). The focus is on physiological factors because of the major changes in body chemistry during and after pregnancy and because women around the world seem to experience similar disturbances in mood, even when their life experiences and support systems are radically different from those found here in Canada (Cohen et al., 2006). Other causes of postpartum depression include fatigue, a lack of social support, transitioning to motherhood, pain following childbirth, stress on the marriage or partnership, and feelings of isolation.

postpartum depression (PPD) serious maternal depression following delivery; characterized by sadness, apathy, and feelings of worthlessness

bonding formation of parent–infant attachment

In extreme cases, mothers may experience a break from reality (psychotic episode) that may lead to delusional thoughts about harming their infant. This is called postpartum psychosis. The infant is often at risk of injury or death. This illness was brought to the forefront of Canadian news when 37-year-old Suzanne Killinger-Johnson leapt in front of a moving subway with her sleeping child. Killinger-Johnson had a psychotherapy practice. Her mother was a psychotherapist who had written books on stress, depression, and anxiety, and her father was a medical doctor. The tragic irony was that even those trained in the field can fall victim to the despair of depression that, when left untreated, can lead to violent outcomes (CBC News, 2000).

Women who experience PPD usually benefit from social support, counselling, and psychoeducation. A woman's physician, public health nurse, or midwife could refer a depressed mother for care in the community or find her other resources as part of the Healthy Baby Healthy Children initiative. Some women are prescribed psychotropic medication such as antidepressants or they may be prescribed other medication to increase estrogen levels. Unfortunately, some medications may pass through breast milk and the long-term exposure on baby's neurological functioning are unknown leaving many women with the difficult decision of whether or not to terminate their breastfeeding practices earlier than expected.

DID YOU KNOW?

Fathers can experience postpartum depression too; it's called paternal postpartum depression or PPPD.

Roughly 10% of men experience depressive affect starting the first trimester of their partner's pregnancy to 6 months after the birth of the child (Rosen, 2012). This may be due to adjusting to parenthood, stress in the marriage, anxiety, and feeling out of control. It may even be due to fluctuating hormones as testosterone drops after the birth of a child and estrogen increases possibly to help father bond with the infant (Rosen, 2012). The symptoms of depression are often different in men than in women, complicating awareness of this disorder. Men often experience agitation, anger, and irritability rather than sadness. They may feel worthless, lose interest in sex and other activities they previously enjoyed, and exhibit signs of anxiety (Rosen, 2012). The risk of PPPD is twice as likely if the father's partner also experiences postpartum depression.

DID YOU KNOW?

It is normal to feel depressed following childbirth.

A disturbance in mood after childbirth is so common, it is called the "blues." Approximately 80% of women experience the blues after childbirth, regardless of whether the pregnancy was planned, and even in the case of adoption. Fortunately, the symptoms usually lessen or end 14 days after the birth of the infant.

Bonding

Bonding—that is, the formation of bonds of attachment between parents and their children—is essential to the survival and well-being of children.

Parent–child bonding has been shown to be a complex process involving desire to have the child;

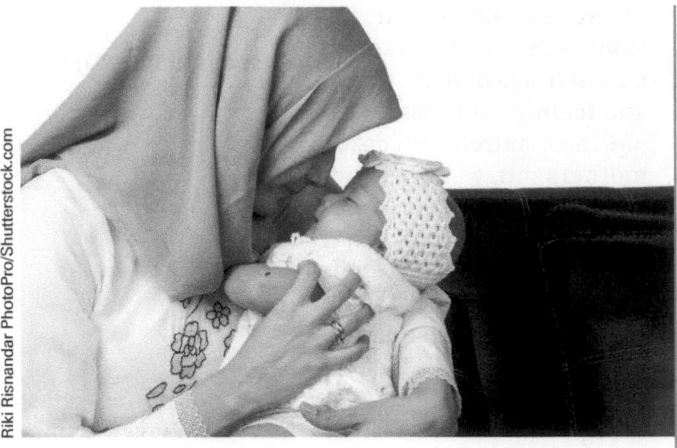

Riki Risnandar PhotoPro/Shutterstock.com

Apgar scale a measure of a newborn's health that assesses appearance, pulse, grimace, activity level, and respiratory effort

Brazelton Neonatal Behavioural Assessment Scale a measure of a newborn's motor behaviour, response to stress, adaptive behaviour, and control over physiological state

parent–child familiarity with one another's sounds, odours, and tastes; and caring. On the other hand, serious maternal depression can delay bonding with newborns (Klier, 2006), and a history of parental rejection can interfere with women's bonding with their own children (Leerkes & Crockenberg, 2006).

Parents do not, however, require early contact with their newborn children for adequate bonding to occur. Many parents, for instance, adopt children at advanced ages and bond closely with them.

DID YOU KNOW?

Parents do not require early contact with their newborn child for adequate bonding to occur.

For instance, many parents adopt children at advanced ages and bond closely with them.

EMERGING CANADA

In December 2000, Canada made family a social priority by making important changes to maternity and parental leave. As part of the new benefits package, after a baby is born or adopted, either the mother or father can take 35 weeks of parental leave, or the parents can share the leave to better accommodate the needs of their family and the new family member. For eligible parents, the benefits equal 55% of the average weekly insurable wage (up to 80% for low-income families), up to a maximum of $537 per week in 2016 (Service Canada, 2013).

LO5 Characteristics of Newborns

Many newborns come into the world seeing things a bit fuzzy, but even though they are utterly dependent on others, they are probably more aware of their surroundings than you can imagine. Newborns also make rapid adaptations to the world around them.

Assessing the Health of Newborns

The newborn's overall level of health is usually evaluated at birth according to the Apgar scale (Table 3.2). Apgar scores are based on five signs of health: appearance, pulse, grimace, activity level, and respiratory effort. For each sign, the newborn is assigned a score of 0, 1, or 2. The total Apgar score can therefore vary from 0 to 10. A score of 7 or more usually indicates that the baby is not in danger. Parents should not be concerned if a baby does not receive a perfect score as its breathing may not be functioning perfectly but quickly rebounds. A score of less than 4 suggests that the baby is in critical condition and requires medical attention. By one minute after birth, most normal babies attain scores of 8 to 10 (Clayton & Crosby, 2006).

Used when a newborn is not doing well, the Brazelton Neonatal Behavioural Assessment Scale measures newborns' reflexes and other behaviour patterns. This test screens for behavioural and neurological problems by assessing four areas of behaviour: motor behaviour, response to stress, adaptive behaviour, and control over physiological state.

TABLE 3.2

The Apgar Scale

Points	0	1	2
Appearance: Colour	Blue, pale	Body pink, extremities blue	Entirely pink
Pulse: Heart Rate	Absent (not detectable)	Slow—below 100 beats/minute	Rapid—100–140 beats/minute
Grimace: Reflex Irritability	No response	Grimace	Crying, coughing, sneezing
Activity level: Muscle tone	Completely flaccid, limp	Weak, inactive	Flexed arms and legs; resists extension
Respiratory effort: Breathing	Absent (infant is not breathing)	Shallow, irregular, slow	Regular breathing; lusty crying

Reflexes

Reflexes are unlearned, automatic responses that occur without thinking and are elicited by certain types of stimulation. Of these reflexes, most are exhibited by newborns shortly after birth, disappear within a few months, and—if the behaviours still serve a purpose—are replaced by corresponding voluntary actions.

Pediatricians learn about a newborn's neural functioning by testing the newborn's reflexes. The absence or weakness of a reflex may indicate immaturity (as in prematurity), slowed responsiveness (which can result from anaesthetics used during childbirth), brain injury, or retardation.

The rooting and sucking reflexes are basic to survival. In the **rooting reflex**, the baby turns its head and mouth toward a stimulus that strokes its cheek, chin, or corner of the mouth. The rooting reflex facilitates finding the mother's nipple in preparation for sucking. Babies will suck almost any object that touches their lips. The sucking reflex grows stronger during the first days after birth and can be lost if not stimulated, which can lead to difficulty feeding and may result in malnourishment. As the months go on, reflexive sucking becomes replaced by voluntary sucking.

In the startle reflex, or **Moro reflex**, the back arches and the legs and arms are flung out and then brought back toward the chest, with the arms in a hugging motion. The Moro reflex occurs when a baby's position is suddenly changed or when support for the head and neck is suddenly lost. It can also be elicited by loud noises or sudden movements. The Moro reflex ensures that if the infant falls, he or she will land bottom-first, reducing injury. This reflex is usually lost within 6 to 7 months after birth. Absence of the Moro reflex can indicate immaturity or brain damage.

During the first few weeks following birth, babies show an increasing tendency to reflexively grasp fingers or other objects pressed against the palms of their hands. In this **grasping reflex**, or palmar reflex, they use four fingers only (the thumbs are not included). Absence of the grasping reflex may indicate depressed activity of the nervous system, which can stem from use of anaesthetics during childbirth. The grasping reflex is usually lost within 3 to 4 months of age, and babies generally show voluntary grasping within 5 to 6 months.

Within 1 or 2 days after birth, babies show a reflex that mimics walking. When held under the arms and tilted forward so that the feet press against a solid surface, a baby will show a **stepping reflex** in which the feet advance one after the other. A full-term baby "walks" heel to toe, whereas a preterm infant is more likely to remain on tiptoe. The stepping reflex usually disappears by about 3 to 4 months of age.

In the **Babinski reflex**, the newborn fans or spreads its toes in response to stroking of the underside of the foot from heel to toes. The Babinski reflex normally disappears toward the end of the first year, to be replaced by the toes curling downward.

The **tonic-neck reflex** is observed when the baby is lying on its back and turns its head to one side.

reflexes
unlearned responses to a stimulus

rooting reflex
the response of turning the mouth and head toward the stroking of the cheek or the corner of the mouth

Moro reflex
the response of arching the back, flinging out the arms and legs, and drawing them back to the chest in response to a sudden change in position

grasping reflex
the response of grasping objects that touch the palms.

stepping reflex
the response of taking steps when held under the arms and leaned forward so the feet press the ground

Babinski reflex
the response of fanning the toes when the soles of the feet are stroked

tonic-neck reflex
the response of turning the head to one side, extending the arm and leg on that side, and flexing the limbs on the opposite side

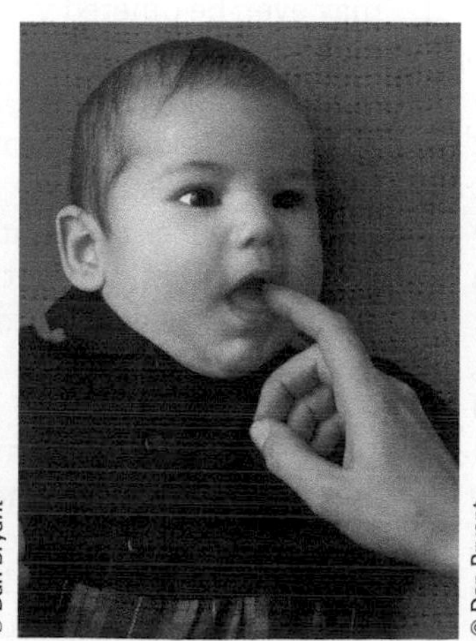

© Dan Bryant © Dan Bryant © Dan Bryant

The Rooting Reflex

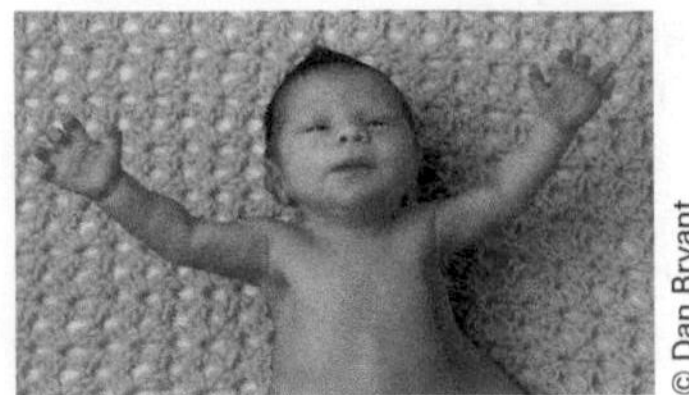
© Dan Bryant

The Moro Reflex

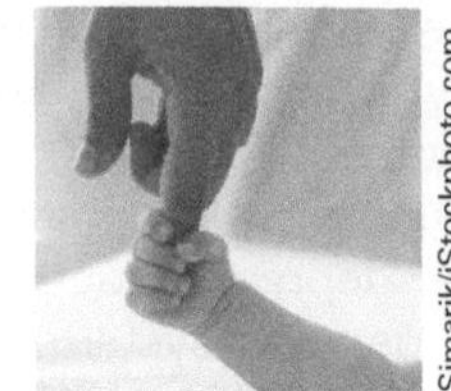
Simarik/iStockphoto.com

The Grasping Reflex

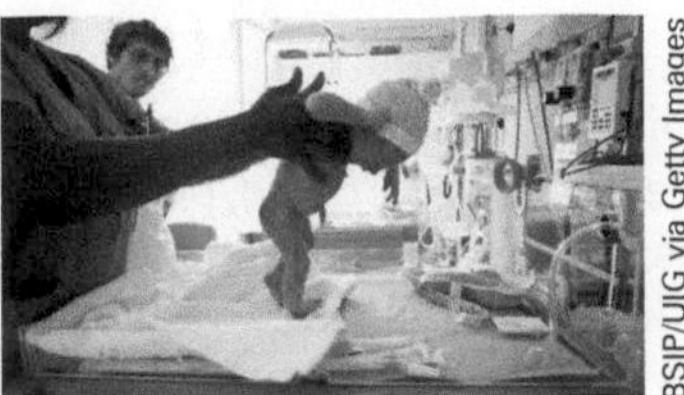
BSIP/UIG via Getty Images

The Stepping Reflex

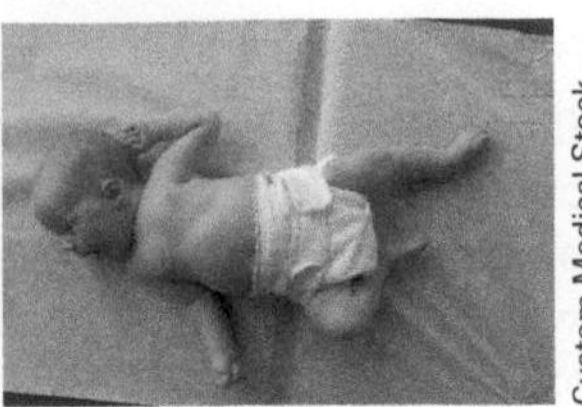
Custom Medical Stock Photo/Alamy Stock Photo

The Tonic-Neck Reflex

visual accommodation
automatic adjustments of the lenses of the eyes to focus on objects

convergence
inward movement of the eyes to focus on an object that is drawing nearer

amplitude
loudness (of sound waves)

pitch
highness or lowness (of a sound), as determined by the frequency of sound waves

The arm and leg on that side extend, while the limbs on the opposite side flex. This reflex is believed to aid the baby in the rolling process later on when greater mobility is apparent.

Sensory Capabilities

In 1890, William James, a founder of modern psychology, wrote that the newborn must sense the world "as one great blooming, buzzing confusion." We now study the sensory capabilities of newborns, and we see that James, for all his eloquence, exaggerated their disorganization.

Vision

Newborns can see, but they are nearsighted. They can best see objects that are about 18 to 23 cm (7 to 9 in.) from their eyes (Kellman & Arterberry, 2006), which is roughly the distance of a caregiver's face when a baby is being held. Newborns also do not have the peripheral vision of older children (Candy, Crowell, & Banks, 1998). They can visually detect movement, and many infants can visually follow, or track, movement the first day after birth. In fact, they appear to prefer (i.e., they spend more time looking at) moving objects to stationary objects (Kellman & Arterberry, 2006).

© Design Pics/Leah Warkentin

Visual accommodation refers to the self-adjustments made by the eye's lenses to bring objects into focus. Newborns show little or no visual accommodation; rather, they see as through a fixed-focus camera. Objects placed about 18 to 23 cm (7 to 9 in.) away are in clearest focus for most newborns, but visual accommodation improves dramatically during their first 2 months (Kellman & Arterberry, 2006).

Newborns do not have the muscle control to converge their eyes on an object that is close to them. For this reason, parents should not be concerned if their babies appear cross-eyed. **Convergence** with nearby objects does not occur until 7 or 8 weeks of age (Kellman & Arterberry, 2006).

The degree to which newborns perceive colour remains an open question. By 4 months, however, infants can see most, if not all, colours of the visible spectrum (Franklin, Pilling, & Davies, 2005). To stimulate infants, distinct black and white patterns should be used (Boston Children's Hospital, 2011).

Even at birth, babies do not simply passively respond to visual stimuli. Babies placed in absolute darkness will open their eyes wide and search around (Kellman & Arterberry, 2006).

Hearing

Fetuses respond to sound for months before they are born, and expecting parents might discover that a baby may kick or jump in response to loud noises and may even be quieted with soft, soothing music (Boston Children's Hospital, 2011). Although myelination of the auditory pathways is not complete before birth, a fetus's middle and inner ear normally reach their mature shape and size before birth. A newborn typically hears well unless its middle ears are clogged with amniotic fluid (Priner et al., 2003). Usually, a newborn will turn its head toward unusual sounds, such as the shaking of a rattle.

Newborns have the capacity to respond to sounds of different **amplitude** and **pitch**. They are more likely to respond to high-pitched sounds than to low-pitched sounds—especially voices (Trehub & Hannon, 2006). By contrast, softly speaking or singing to infants, in a relatively low-pitched voice, can have a soothing effect (Volkova, Trehub, & Schellenberg, 2006). The sense of

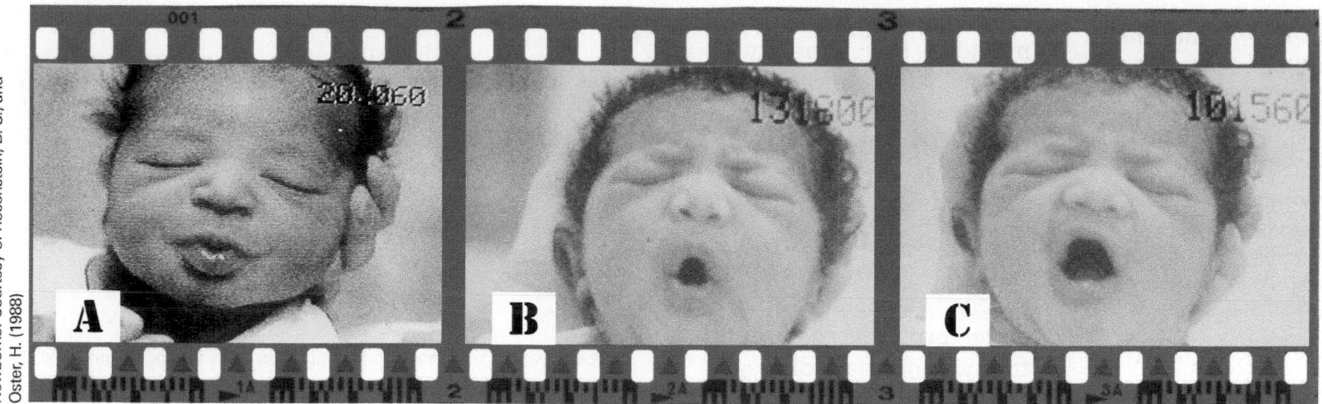

Newborns: Courtesy of Rosenstein, D. S., and Oster, H. (1988)

Filmstrip: © Nicholas Belton/iStockphoto.com

FIGURE 3.4

Facial Expressions Elicited by Sweet, Sour, and Bitter Solutions

Newborns are sensitive to different tastes, as shown by their facial expressions when tasting (a) sweet, (b) sour, and (c) bitter solutions.

hearing may play a role in the formation of affectional bonds between newborns and mothers that goes well beyond the soothing potential of the mothers' voices.

Smell

Newborns can discriminate distinct odours, such as those of onions and licorice. They show more rapid breathing patterns and increased bodily movement in response to powerful odours. They also turn away from unpleasant odours, such as ammonia and vinegar, as early as the first day after birth (Werner & Bernstein, 2001). The nasal preferences of newborns are similar to those of older children and adults (Werner & Bernstein, 2001).

Within the first few days of life, infants show a preference for the smell of their own mother, especially her breast milk (Boston Children's Hospital, 2011). Like hearing, the sense of smell may provide a vehicle for mother–infant recognition and attachment. Newborns may be sensitive to the smell of milk because, when held by the mother, they tend to turn toward her nipple before they have had a chance to see or touch it. In one classic experiment, Macfarlane (1975, 1977) placed nursing pads above and to the sides of newborns' heads. One pad had absorbed milk from the mother, while the other was clean. Newborns less than 1 week old spent more time turning to look at their mothers' pads than at the new pads. Smell may contribute to the early development of recognition and attachment.

Taste

Taste buds begin to form early in fetal development. Thus, newborns are sensitive to different tastes; their preferences, as suggested by their facial expressions in response to various fluids, are like those of adults (Werner & Bernstein, 2001). When distilled water is placed on the tongue, newborns swallow without showing any facial expression suggestive of a positive or negative response. Sweet solutions, however, are met with smiles, licking, and eager sucking, as in Figure 3.4a (Rosenstein & Oster, 1988). Newborns discriminate among solutions with salty, sour, and bitter tastes, as suggested by reactions in the lower part of the face (Rosenstein & Oster, 1988). Sour fluids (Figure 3.4b) elicit pursing of the lips, nose wrinkling, and eye blinking. Bitter solutions (Figure 3.4c) stimulate spitting, gagging, and sticking out the tongue.

Sweet solutions have a calming effect on newborns (Blass & Camp, 2003). Babies also show a strong preference for breast milk (Boston Children's Hospital, 2011).

Touch

Touch is the most advanced of all senses at birth. Physical contact between mother and baby is thus very important for healthy development as

© Blend Images/Jupiterimages

rapid-eye-movement (REM) sleep a sleep period when dreams are likely, as suggested by rapid eye movements

non-rapid-eye-movement (non-REM) sleep a sleep period when dreams are unlikely

skin-against-skin contact provides the infant with feelings of comfort and security that may be major factors in the formation of bonds of attachment between infants and their caregivers. Consequently, infants who are not touched, such as those in large orphanages around the world, may die as a result of a lack of touch because they become so depressed, they stop eating. For example, the infant mortality rate in some orphanages has been reported to be as high as between 30 and 40% (Szalavitz, 2010). Not only is skin-to-skin contact important for the bonding process, physical parental touch is important for brain development too. A gentle stroke has been found to help the infant create a coherent sense of self as this allows them to gain an understanding of their bodies or body ownership (Bergland, 2013).

Throughout the last months of pregnancy, a baby is snugly cocooned in the uterus with arms and legs tucked inward. At birth, babies are suddenly thrust into a bright, cold world where their arms and legs can move about freely. The newborn might feel insecure, so cuddling the baby closely can make her or him feel more protected. Swaddling (wrapping snugly in a blanket) is an effective technique for soothing an infant. Baby massage has also become an increasingly popular method of promoting a relationship between baby and caregiver.

Sleeping and Waking

As adults, we spend about one-third of our time sleeping. Newborns, on the other hand, spend two thirds of their time, or about 16 hours per day, in sleep. However, newborns do not sleep their 16 hours consecutively, as every parent who is wakened in the middle of the night is aware. The extra sleep of infants is likely necessary for the brain's development, as the brain isn't fully developed at birth.

Several different states of sleep and wakefulness have been identified in newborns and infants, as shown in Table 3.3 (Cornwell & Feigenbaum, 2006; Salzarulo & Ficca, 2002; Wulff & Siegmund, 2001). Although individual babies differ in the amount of time they spend in each of these states, sleep clearly predominates over wakefulness in the early days and weeks of life.

Different infants require different amounts of sleep and follow different patterns of sleep, but virtually all infants distribute their sleeping throughout the day and night through a series of naps. The typical infant has about six cycles of waking and sleeping in a 24-hour period. The longest nap typically approaches 4½ hours, and the newborn is usually awake for a little more than 1 hour during each cycle.

After a month or so, the infant has fewer but longer sleep periods and will usually take longer naps during the night. By the ages of about 6 months to 1 year, many infants begin to sleep through the night. Some infants start sleeping through the night even earlier (Salzarulo & Ficca, 2002). Some infants begin to sleep through the night for a week or so only to revert to their wakeful ways again for a period of time.

TABLE 3.3

States of Sleep and Wakefulness in Infancy

State	Comments
Quiet sleep (non-REM)	Regular breathing, eyes closed, no movement
Active sleep (REM)	Irregular breathing, eyes closed, rapid eye movement, muscle twitches
Drowsiness	Regular or irregular breathing, eyes open or closed, little movement
Alert inactivity	Regular breathing, eyes open, looking around, little body movement
Alert activity	Irregular breathing, eyes open, active body movement
Crying	Irregular breathing, eyes open or closed, thrashing of arms and legs, crying

Source: © Cengage Learning

REM and Non-REM Sleep

Sleep can be divided into rapid-eye-movement (REM) sleep and non-rapid-eye-movement (non-REM) sleep (see Figure 3.5). REM sleep is characterized by rapid eye movements that can be observed beneath closed lids. About 80% of adults who are roused during REM sleep report that they have been dreaming. Is the same true of newborns?

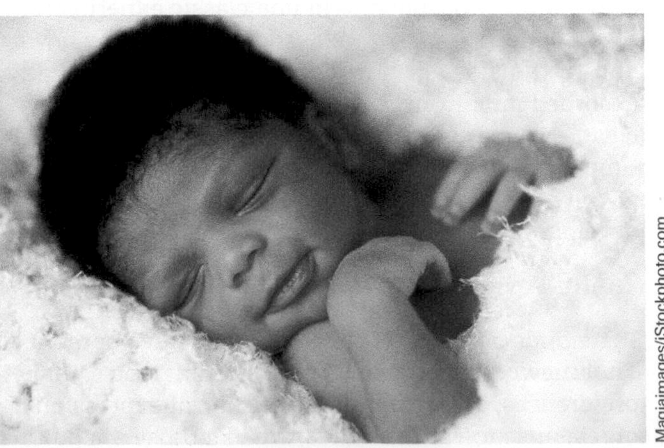

Magiaimages/iStockphoto.com

sudden infant death syndrome (SIDS) the death, while sleeping, of apparently healthy babies who stop breathing

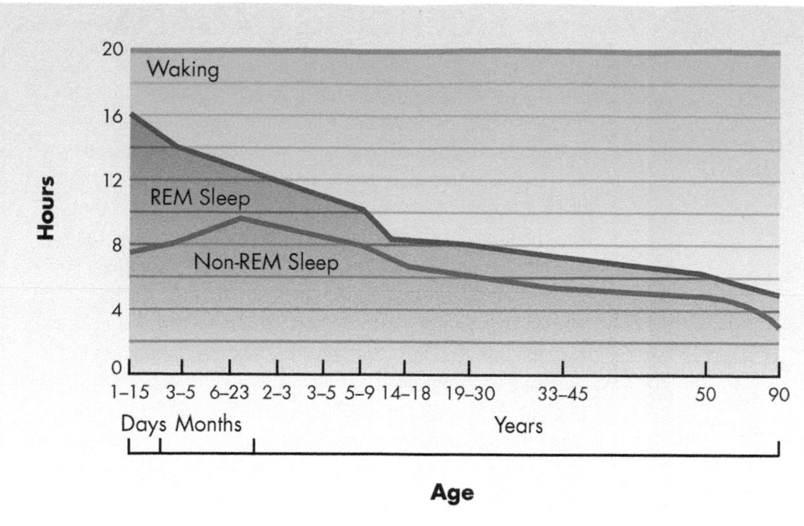

FIGURE 3.5

REM Sleep and Non-REM Sleep

The percentage of time spent in REM sleep declines as people age.

Source: Roffwarg, Muzio, & Dement, 1966.

Note from Figure 3.5 that newborns spend about half their time sleeping in REM sleep. As they develop, the percentage of sleeping time spent in REM sleep declines. By 6 months or so, REM sleep accounts for only about 30% of the baby's sleep. By 2 to 3 years, REM sleep drops off to 20–25% (Salzarulo & Ficca, 2002). As we develop, we experience a dramatic falling-off in the total number of hours spent in sleep (Salzarulo & Ficca, 2002).

What is the function of REM sleep in newborns? Research with humans and animals, including kittens and rat pups, suggests that the brain requires a certain amount of stimulation for the creation of proteins that are involved in the development of neurons and synapses (Dang-Vu et al., 2006). Perhaps newborns create this stimulation by means of REM sleep, which most closely parallels the waking state in terms of brain waves. Preterm babies spend an even greater proportion of their time in REM sleep, perhaps because they need relatively more stimulation of the brain.

Sudden Infant Death Syndrome (SIDS)

For some unknown reason, infants may die in their sleep, a fear shared by all parents. When an infant under the age of 1 year dies suddenly and without explanation, this is called **sudden infant death syndrome (SIDS)**. More children die from SIDS than from cancer, heart disease, pneumonia, child abuse, AIDS, cystic fibrosis, and muscular dystrophy combined (Lipsitt, 2003). SIDS—also known as crib death—occurs when a baby goes to sleep, apparently in perfect health, and is later found dead. There is typically no sign that the baby struggled or was in pain. The awareness campaign "Back to Sleep" was initiated in 1994, encouraging parents to have their babies sleep on their backs; however, despite a 50% decrease in incidence, each week in Canada, three babies succumb to SIDS (Canadian Foundation for the Study of Infant Deaths, 2005).

The incidence of SIDS has been declining, but each year many infants in Canada still die of SIDS. It

SIDS is more common among the following (Hunt & Hauck, 2006; Paterson et al., 2006):

- Babies aged 2–4 months
- Babies who are put to sleep on their stomachs or their sides
- Premature and low-birth-weight infants
- Male babies
- Babies whose mothers smoked during or after pregnancy or whose mothers used narcotics during pregnancy

Note that these characteristics are risk factors for, not causes of, SIDS.

© Radius Images/Jupiterimages

is the most common cause of death during the first year, and most of these deaths occur between 2 and 5 months of age (Paterson et al., 2006; Public Health Agency of Canada, 2012). New parents frequently live in dread of SIDS and check a sleeping baby regularly to observe its breathing. Babies occasionally suspend their breathing for a moment, which heightens caregiver anxiety.

What should *you* do about SIDS? Place your baby to sleep on his or her back. Keep current with research data on SIDS by checking with your pediatrician and by exploring websites such as the Public Health Agency of Canada (2014) and Baby's Breath Canada.

Crying

The first form of communication that all parents are quite familiar with is crying. There are different reasons why babies cry—from hunger or pain, to sleepiness and discomfort. However, studies suggest that the main reason babies cry seems to be pain (Gormally et al., 2001; Zeifman, 2004). Whether crying is healthy remains an open question, but some crying among babies seems to be universal.

More Canadian children die from sudden infant death syndrome (SIDS) than die from cancer, heart disease, pneumonia, child abuse, AIDS, cystic fibrosis, and muscular dystrophy combined.

EMERGING CANADA

The health of First Nations children was the focus of a discussion paper published by the Assembly of First Nations in Canada. The aim of this paper was to provide a basic overview of the issues and concerns that affect the health of First Nations children. A major point of concern is that First Nations infant mortality rate is 1.5 times higher than the mainstream Canadian population. Several studies also show that SIDS rates range from 3 to 10 times higher among First Nations than across Canada (Assembly of First Nations, 2008). The Assembly of Manitoba Chiefs created an education campaign to help protect First Nations families in a culturally relevant way. Education is a key strategy in protecting all parents and families against the risk factors associated with Sudden Infant Death Syndrome (Assembly of First Nations, 2008).

Andrew Stewart/First Light

Before parenthood, many people wonder whether they will be able to recognize the meaning of their babies' cries, but it usually does not take them long. Parents typically learn to distinguish cries that signify hunger, anger, and pain. The pitch of an infant's cries appears to provide information (Zeifman, 2004). Adults perceive high-pitched crying to be more urgent, distressing, and sick-sounding than low-pitched crying (Zeifman, 2004). A sudden, loud, insistent cry associated with flexing and kicking of the legs may indicate colic—that is, pain resulting from gas or other sources of distress in the digestive tract. Crying from colic can be severe and persistent; it may last for hours (Barr et al., 2005). Much to the relief of parents, colic tends to disappear by the third to sixth month, as a baby's digestive system matures.

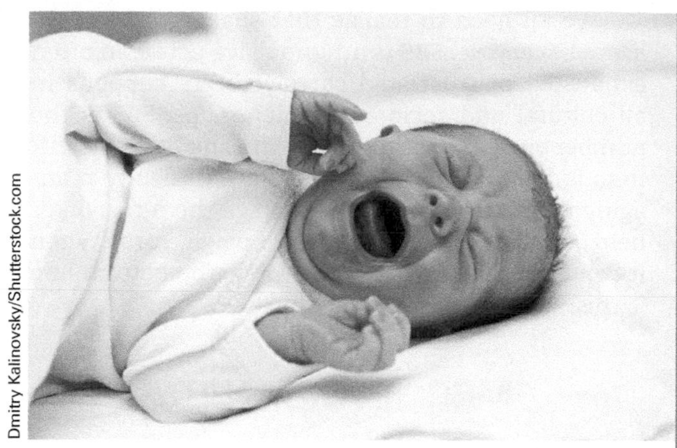

Dmitry Kalinovsky/Shutterstock.com

Certain high-pitched cries, when prolonged, may signify health problems. The cries of chronically distressed infants differ from those of non-distressed infants in both rhythm and pitch. Patterns of crying may be indicative of chromosomal abnormalities, infections, fetal malnutrition, and exposure to narcotics (Zeifman, 2004).

Infant crying increases after birth, peaking at around 5 to 6 weeks; it goes away by about 3 months. This early period of crying can be a source of great concern for parents. During early infancy, the pattern of crying has some significant differences. For example, depending on the child, the age at which crying peaks can range from 3 to 12 weeks. The amount of crying also varies, ranging from a daily total crying duration of less than 20 minutes in mild cases, to more than 3 hours in severe cases. Many infants continue to have symptoms after 3 months (Shinohara & Kodama, 2012). At first, crying communicates pain and hunger, which are easy for a caregiver to take care of. Because persistent crying can strain the mother–infant relationship, it is important to provide support for new caregivers (Reijneveld et al., 2004).

In extreme cases of crying, parents can become very frustrated. Extended crying can be confusing and concerning and is often labelled as colic. Because crying sounds like an illness, it can seem abnormal, but crying is a very normal developmental phase. Dr. Ronald Barr, a developmental pediatrician who studies infant crying, came up with the phrase "the period of purple crying." Purple does not refer to the colour a baby turns. It is an acronym that stands for P(peak of) U(unexpected) R(resists) P(pain-like) L(long) E(evening). PURPLE crying begins at about 2 weeks of age and continues until about 3 to 4 months of age. The baby seems to resist soothing and nothing helps. Parents often say their baby looks like he or she is in pain yet the baby is healthy and happy at other times during the day. This crying is a very normal part of development and, although frustrating, is only temporary—this period will come to an end. The best thing a caregiver can do is stay calm, which may sound simple but is very difficult when you are tired, frazzled, and worried about your baby (Barr, n.d.).

Shaken baby syndrome is the result of an impulsive act of an often exhausted or frustrated caregiver. SBS cases happen in all cultural and socio-economic groups.

pacifier
a device such as an artificial nipple or teething ring that soothes babies when sucked

shaken baby syndrome (SBS)
the violent shaking of an infant, often to stop the infant from crying

Soothing

To comfort a crying baby, soothing methods must be developed. One of the best methods to soothe a crying infant is allowing them to suck. Sucking seems to be a built-in tranquilizer. Sucking on a pacifier decreases crying and agitated movement in hungry newborns (Field, 1999). The soothing function of sucking need not be learned through experience because it is an automatic reflex, done even in utero. Babies are equipped at birth to suck in order to self-soothe.

Other methods that parents use to soothe infants are picking them up, patting them, caressing and rocking them, swaddling them, and speaking to them in a low voice. Parents then usually try to find the specific cause of the distress by offering a bottle or pacifier or checking the diaper. Parents learn by trial and error the types of embraces and movements that are likely to soothe infants.

Infants learn quickly that crying is followed by being picked up or other interventions. Whether it is possible to spoil a crying baby remains a hotly debated question.

Shaken Baby Syndrome (SBS)

Unfortunately, there are times when infants' crying can have a devastating end. Shaken baby syndrome (SBS) and abusive head trauma (AHT) are terms used to describe the injuries sustained by an infant or young child who is roughly shaken often to stop her or him from crying. Damage can occur in as little as five seconds (Higuera, 2016). Since an infant has a soft brain and weak neck muscles, when an infant is shaken vigorously, the brain hits his or her skull causing bleeding, bruising, and swelling (Higuera, 2016). Another consequence of forcibly shaking an infant is that the brain

Monkey Business Images/Shutterstock.com

cells do not receive enough oxygen, causing further damage. The result is permanent brain damage. Other injuries include broken bones and damage to the eyes, neck, and spine. Babies who are victims of SBS are most often shaken between the ages of 6 and 8 weeks when crying is the most intensive (Higuera, 2016).

We all need to realize that shaking a baby *can happen to anyone*. SBS is an impulsive act of an often exhausted or frustrated caregiver. SBS happens in all cultural and socio-economic groups. SBS is the number one type of child abuse in Canada. If you witness individuals who seem to have difficulty managing their baby's crying, encourage them to ask for help (Alberta SBS Prevention Campaign, 2010). When it comes to shaken baby syndrome, the bottom line is this: Take a Break—Don't Shake.

EMERGING CANADA

In a Canadian study of 364 victims of SBS and AHT who were admitted to hospital (King et al., 2003), 81% of the children survived but suffered neurological deficit, visual impairment, and ongoing care issues; the other 19% died. The authors concluded that any estimate of the number of SBS cases was likely just the "tip of the iceberg," as the incidence of SBS and AHT is likely significantly underestimated due to misdiagnoses and underreporting.

STUDY TOOLS

CHAPTER 3

Located at **nelson.com/student**

- ☐ Prepare for tests with a variety of exercises and activities
- ☐ Review Key Terms Flashcards (online or print)
- ☐ Create your own study tools with Build a Summary
- ☐ Watch Observing Development videos to expand your knowledge

Sergey Dolgikh/Shutterstock.com

CHAPTER 4

Infancy: Physical Development

LEARNING OUTCOMES

LO1 Describe the physical development of the infant

LO2 Explain the development of the brain and the nervous system in infancy

LO3 Describe the development of gross motor milestones during infancy

LO4 Outline patterns of sensory and perceptual development in infancy

> "Three key sequences of physical development are cephalocaudal development, proximodistal development, and differentiation."

What a fascinating creature the newborn is: tiny, delicate, apparently oblivious to its surroundings, yet perfectly formed and fully capable of letting its caregivers know when it is hungry, thirsty, or uncomfortable. And what a fascinating creature is this same child 2 years later: running, playing, talking, hugging, and kissing.

It is hard to believe that only 2 short years —the years of infancy—bring about so many changes. It seems that nearly every day brings a new accomplishment. But as we will see, not all infants share equally in the explosion of positive developments. Therefore, we will also enumerate some developmental problems and what can be done about them.

LO1 Physical Growth and Development

During the first 2 years, children make enormous strides in physical growth and development. In this section, we explore sequences of physical development, changes in height and weight, and nutrition. As we will see, development is "head first."

Sequences of Physical Development

Three key sequences of physical development are cephalocaudal development, proximodistal development, and differentiation (see Chapter 2 to review these terms).

Cephalocaudal Development

Development proceeds from the upper part of the head to the lower parts of the body (tip to toe). When we consider the central role of the brain, which is contained within the skull, the cephalocaudal sequence appears quite logical. The brain regulates essential functions, such as heartbeat. Through the secretion of hormones, the brain also regulates the growth and development of the body and influences basic drives, such as hunger and thirst.

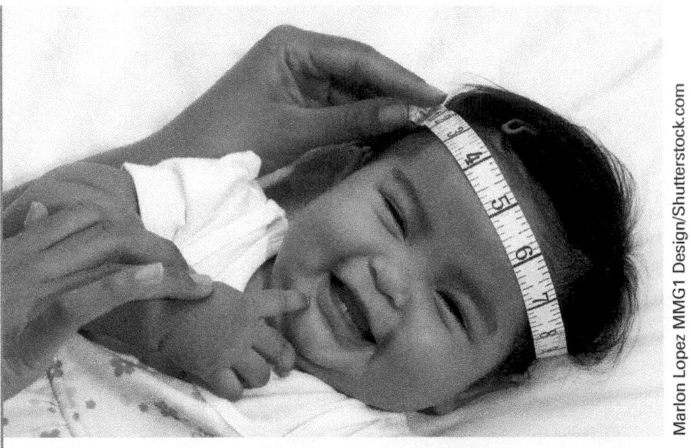

Marlon Lopez MMG1 Design/Shutterstock.com

DID YOU KNOW?

The head of the newborn child doubles in length by adulthood, but the legs increase in length by about five times.

The torso increases by about three times and the arms by four.

Proximodistal Development

Growth and development also proceed from the trunk outward (from the centre out), from the body's central axis toward the periphery. The proximodistal principle, too, makes sense. The brain and spinal cord follow a central axis down through the body, and it is essential that the nerves be in place before the infant can gain control over the arms and legs. Consider also that the life functions of the newborn baby—heartbeat, respiration, digestion, and elimination of wastes—are all carried out by organ systems close to the central axis. These functions must be in operation or ready to operate when the child is born.

In terms of motor development, infants gain control over their trunks and their shoulders before they can control their arms, hands, and fingers. Similarly, infants gain control over their hips and upper legs before they can direct their lower legs, feet, and toes.

Differentiation

As children mature, their physical reactions become less global and more specific. The tendency of behaviour to become more specific and distinct is called **differentiation**. If a newborn's finger is pricked or burned, he or she may withdraw the finger but also thrash about, cry, and show general signs of distress. Toddlers may also cry, show distress, and withdraw the finger, but they are less likely to thrash about wildly. Thus, the response to pain has become more specific. An older child or adult is also likely to withdraw the finger, but less likely to wail (sometimes) and show general distress.

Growth Patterns in Height and Weight

The most dramatic gains in height and weight occur during prenatal development. Within a span of 9 months, children develop from a zygote about 0.015 cm (1/175th of an inch) long to a newborn about 50 cm (20 in.) in length. Weight increases by billions.

During the first year after birth, gains in height and weight are also dramatic, although not by the standards of prenatal gains. Infants usually double their birth weight in about 5 months and triple it by the first birthday (Murray, 2013). Height increases by about 50% in the first year, so that a child whose length at birth was 50 cm (20 in.) is likely to be about 75 cm (30 in.) tall at 12 months.

> **DID YOU KNOW?**
>
> **Infants, on average, triple their birth weight within a year.**
>
> Infants usually double their birth weight in about 5 months and triple it by the first birthday if development is proceeding according to the norm.

Growth in infancy has long been viewed as a slow and steady process, but more recent research indicates that infants grow in spurts. In a new study, 23 sets of parents of newborns kept daily sleep records. Infant sleep time was compared with infant growth in length. Growth spurts tended to follow increased sleeping and nap time and occurred within two days of the increased sleep. Exactly how sleep and growth are interrelated is not fully understood but measureable growth followed sleep (Mann, 2011). The growth rates of taller-than-average infants, as a group, tend to slow down; however, the growth rates of shorter-than-average infants, as a group, tend to speed up. Tall infants, as a group, achieve a taller adult height than the adult height achieved by short infants, but in most cases not by as much as seemed likely during infancy.

differentiation the processes by which behaviours and physical structures become specialized

Changes in Body Proportions

Development proceeds in a cephalocaudal manner. A few weeks after conception, an embryo is almost all head. At the beginning of the fetal stage, the head is about half the length of the unborn child. In the newborn, it is about one-fourth the length of the body. The head gradually diminishes in proportion to the rest of the body, even though it doubles in size by adulthood.

Typically, an adult's arms are nearly three times the length of the head. The legs are about four times as long. Among newborns, the arms and legs are about equal in length. Each is only about one and a half times the length of the head. By the first birthday, the neck has begun to lengthen, as have the arms and legs. The arms grow more rapidly than the legs at first; by the second birthday, the arms are actually longer than the legs, but soon the legs catch up with and surpass the arms in length.

Failure to Thrive

Haley is 4 months old. Her mother, as she puts it, is breastfeeding Haley "all the time" because she is not gaining weight. Not gaining weight for a while is normal, but Haley is also irritable and feeds fitfully, sometimes refusing the breast entirely.

failure to thrive (FTT) a disorder of infancy and early childhood characterized by variable eating and inadequate gains in weight

canalization the tendency of growth rates to return to normal after undergoing environmentally induced change

Her pediatrician is evaluating her for a syndrome called failure to thrive (FTT).

FTT is a serious disorder that impairs growth in infancy and early childhood (Simonelli, Monti, & Magalotti, 2005). Yet FTT is sometimes an unclear diagnosis. Historically, researchers have spoken of biologically based (or "organic") FTT versus nonbiologically based ("nonorganic") FTT. The idea is that in organic FTT, an underlying health problem accounts for FTT. Nonorganic FTT (NOFTT) apparently has psychological roots, social roots, or both. In either case, the infant does not make normal gains in weight and size (Simonelli et al., 2005).

Regardless of the cause or causes, feeding problems are central. As in Haley's case, infants are more likely to be described as variable eaters and less often as hungry (Wright & Birks, 2000). FTT is linked not only to slow physical growth but also to cognitive, behavioural, and emotional problems (Simonelli et al., 2005). The long-term consequences of FTT on cognitive development and future academic performance remain unclear (Cole & Lanham, 2011).

Catch-Up Growth

A child's growth can be slowed from its genetically predetermined course by many environmental factors, including illness and malnutrition. If the problem is alleviated, the child's rate of growth frequently accelerates to approximate its normal course (van IJzendoorn & Juffer, 2006). The tendency to return to one's genetically determined pattern of growth is referred to as canalization. Once Haley's parents receive counselling and once Haley's FTT is overcome, Haley will put on weight rapidly and catch up to the norms for her age.

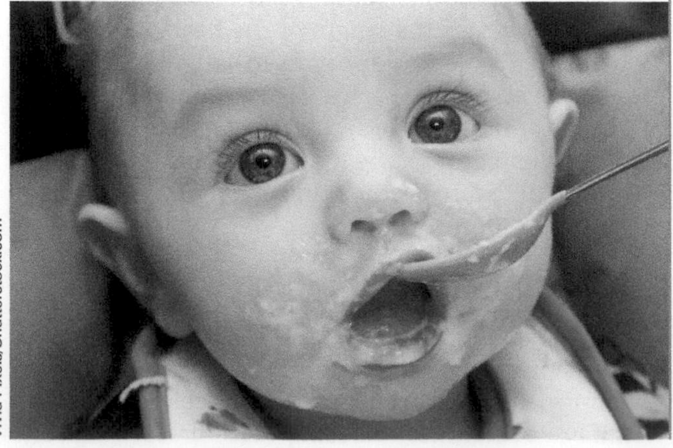

Vivid Pixels/Shutterstock.com

Nutrition: Fuelling Development

The nutritional status of most children in Canada is good compared with that of children in developing countries (Arija et al., 2006). However, infants and young children from low-income families are more likely than other children to display signs of poor nutrition, such as anemia and FTT (National Center for Children in Poverty, 2004).

From birth, infants should be fed either breast milk or an iron-fortified infant formula. The Canadian Paediatric Society recommends exclusive breastfeeding for the first six months of life for healthy term infants. However, the rate of breastfeeding infants until 6 months of age in Canada varies from province to province anywhere from 22.8% in Quebec to 35.9% in Nova Scotia (Statistics Canada, 2014).

Breast milk is the optimal food for infants, and breastfeeding may continue for up to 2 years and beyond, as recommended by the World Health Organization (WHO) (2016a), for mothers who are socially comfortable with this practice. The introduction of solid foods is not recommended until about 4 to 6 months of age. Infants typically begin a solid-food diet by eating iron-enriched cereal, followed by strained fruits, vegetables, meats, poultry, and fish. Introducing whole cow's milk is normally delayed until the infant is 9 to 12 months old. Finger foods such as teething biscuits are introduced in the latter part of the first year. Parents who are looking for information about how to keep their infants healthy and safe may turn to Health Canada's resource guide for new parents.at http://www.hc-sc.gc.ca/hl-vs/babies-bebes/index-eng.php.

Here are some useful guidelines for infant nutrition (National Institutes of Health, 2007):

- Build up to a variety of foods. Introduce new foods one at a time. Because the infant may be allergic to a new food, introducing foods one at a time helps identify any possible allergens.
- Pay attention to the infant's appetite to avoid overfeeding or underfeeding.
- Generally avoid items that have added sugar and salt.
- Encourage eating of high-iron foods; infants need more iron, pound for pound, than adults do.

Canadians live in a very diet-conscious society, but low-fat, high-fibre diets and sugar substitutes are not healthy for infants.

Breastfeeding versus Bottle-Feeding

Breast milk is considered by most health professionals to be the "medical gold standard," although the practice of breastfeeding is not as common in the developing world as it is in Canada (Cai, Wardlaw, & Brown, 2012). Despite this, an 8% global increase in

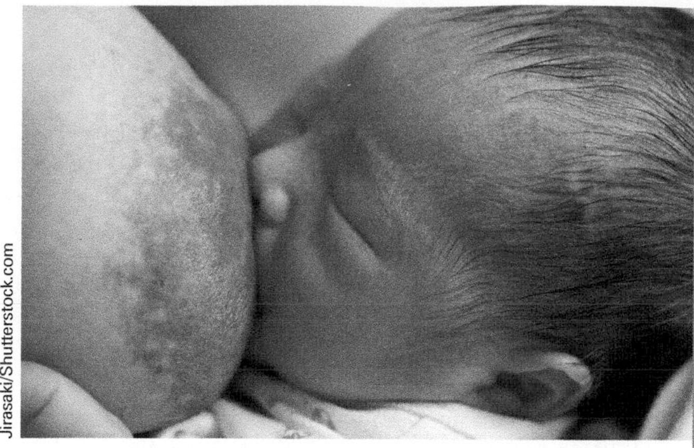
Jirasaki/Shutterstock.com

exclusive breastfeeding to 6 months is estimated to have reduced infant mortality by 1,000,000, decreased fertility by 600,000, and saved countries billions of dollars in unneeded breast milk substitutes (UNICEF, 2010). To promote breastfeeding, the Breastfeeding Committee of Canada has made several recommendations regarding formula and other supplements. Advertisements of infant formula should not be directly shown to the public, no free samples of formula should be given to mothers, no words or phrases that idealize breast milk substitutes should be mentioned on packaging, and that all substitutes include on their packaging both the benefits of breastfeeding and the hazards of artificial feeding substitutes (Breastfeeding Committee for Canada, 2011). Unfortunately, many of these recommendations have not been enforced.

Over the past few decades, breastfeeding has gained popularity, largely because of increased knowledge of its health benefits (Sloan et al., 2006). Today, most Canadian mothers—more than 88.4%—initiate breastfeeding in the hospital, but this practice drops considerably by 6 months to approximately 30% (Statistics Canada, 2015b). Many factors affect the mother's decision to breastfeed, including age, education, and even geographic location. Older women and more highly educated women are more likely to breastfeed.

Many mothers choose to bottle-feed because they need to return to work, and breastfeeding poses complicated logistics. Caregivers give their children bottles during the day. Some mothers pump their milk and bottle it for use when they are away. Some parents bottle-feed because it permits both parents to share in feeding. Breastfeeding is a bonding experience for the mother and the child especially since oxytocin, a bonding hormone, is released in the milk; however, it can also lead to a stressful relationship requiring support if any breastfeeding problems occur. The top five reasons why the mothers surveyed chose not to breastfeed were medical reasons (20.5%), a belief that the bottle was easier (19.8%), a belief that breastfeeding was unappealing (19%), birthing complications (9.8%), and the belief that formula was just as good (6.6%) (Health Canada, 2012).

The reason breast milk is considered to be the gold standard of infant nutrition is that it has numerous advantages, according to Health Canada (2007a):

- Breastfeeding is associated with better neural and behavioural organization in the infant.
- Breast milk contains the mother's antibodies and reduces the infant's incidence of infection.
- Breast milk enhances cognitive development.
- Breastfed infants are less likely to develop allergic responses and diarrhea.
- Breastfed infants are less likely to die of Sudden Infant Death Syndrome (SIDS).
- Breastfeeding also has health benefits for the mother:
- Breastfeeding reduces the risk of early breast cancer and ovarian cancer.
- Breastfeeding builds the strength of bones, which can reduce the likelihood of the hip fractures that may result from osteoporosis following menopause.
- Breastfeeding helps shrink the uterus after delivery and hastens post-birth weight loss.

Breastfeeding has some downsides. For example, breast milk is one of the bodily fluids that transmit HIV. As many as one-third of the world's infants who have HIV/AIDS were infected in this manner (UNAIDS, 2006). Also transmitted through breast milk are alcohol, many drugs, and environmental hazards such as polychlorinated biphenyls (PCBs). Moreover, for breast milk to contain the necessary nutrients, the mother must be adequately nourished herself. The mother also encounters the physical demands of producing and expelling milk, a tendency for soreness in the breasts, and the emotional demands of being continually available to meet the infant's feeding needs.

Bottle-feeding has its downsides too. In addition to the lack of benefits found in breast milk, bottle-feeding is expensive, preparations are time-consuming, and formula is not readily available in the same way as breast milk. Furthermore, infants fed formulas made with tap water are at risk of lead poisoning, because water pipes sometimes contain lead. Lead causes neurological damage and may result in lowered cognitive functioning and other delays.

Malnutrition

Malnutrition in infancy impairs development. Malnourished children are more likely to sustain a developmental delay, weight loss, and/or serious illness as a result of a lack of protein, calories, and other nutrients

micronutrients
nutrients required in small doses, such as vitamins and minerals, that are required for physical growth

macronutrients
nutrients required in large quantities, such as protein, carbohydrates, and fat, that are responsible for physical growth

vaccines
a small amount of dead or weakened germs that, when taken in by the infant's body, allows the immune system to protect itself against the disease by creating antibodies

neurons
cells in the nervous system that transmit messages

(Orphan Nutrition, 2016). Malnourished children have compromised immune systems. Furthermore, malnour-ished children often experience gastrointestinal issues that further stunt their growth. Malnourishment affects brain development resulting in Attention Deficit Hyperactivity Disorder, learning disabilities, social skill limitations, and reduced problem-solving and language skills (Orphan Nutrition, 2016).

Growth retardation caused by malnourishment is prevalent in developing countries. Several micronutrients, nutrients required in small doses, such as vitamins and minerals, are required for growth; however, it is unclear which ones are most important to prevent retardation among infants in developing countries. Insufficient macronutrients, nutrients required in large quantities, such as protein, carbohydrates, and fat, are also responsible for growth retardation among infants in developing countries.

Growth retardation can occur when there is a lack of food, poor sanitation, or gastrointestinal illness and other illnesses. Other causes of infant malnutrition include inadequate prenatal and postnatal care of the mother, poor prenatal diet, premature birth or low birth weight, improperly prepared formula, and lack of exposure to sunlight (Orphan Nutrition, 2016). In Canada, people in the Aboriginal community are more vulnerable to malnutrition as they experience significantly greater food insecurity (27.1%) as compared to the non-Aboriginal population (11.5%) (Hassmann, 2014).

Minor Illnesses

Minor illnesses include respiratory infections, such as colds, and stomach upsets, such as nausea, vomiting, and diarrhea. These conditions are normal in that most children experience them. Minor illnesses typically last a few days or less and are not life threatening. Although diarrheal illness in Canada is usually mild, it is a leading killer of children in developing countries (UNICEF, 2006).

People are born with about 100 billion neurons, most of which are in the brain.

DID YOU KNOW?

Some diseases are normal.

Minor illnesses are generally normal, insofar as most children get them and may actually be healthier in adulthood as a result of the immunities they acquire.

Canadian children will have lots of colds, some as many as 8 to 10 each year before they are 2 years old (Canadian Paediatric Society, 2010). Childhood illnesses can lead to the creation of antibodies that may prevent children from coming down with the same illnesses in adulthood, when illnesses can do more harm.

Vaccinations

Vaccines contain a small amount of dead or weakened germs. As a result of receiving a small amount of vaccine, the infant's immune system learns how to protect itself against the disease by creating antibodies. In Canada, infants are routinely introduced to vaccinations that prevent numerous diseases, such as measles, polio, and whooping cough. Each of these diseases can be fatal if contracted. The safety of vaccines is of utmost importance to all Canadians. It takes approximately 10 years of research and development before a vaccine will be approved for use by Health Canada (Government of Canada, 2014). Some parents have chosen not to vaccinate their children due to the concern that vaccinations can lead to autism. Research conducted on the relationship between vaccination use and autism has been conducted worldwide. To date, no evidence linking vaccination and autism has been found (Immunization Action Coalition, n.d.).

LO2 Development of the Brain and Nervous System

The nervous system is a system of nerves involved in heartbeat, visual–motor coordination, thought, language, and so on.

Development of Neurons

The basic units of the nervous system are cells called neurons. Neurons receive and transmit messages from one part of the body to another. The messages account for such phenomena as reflexes, the perception of an itch from a mosquito bite, the visual–motor coordination of a skier, the composition of a concerto, and the solution of a math problem.

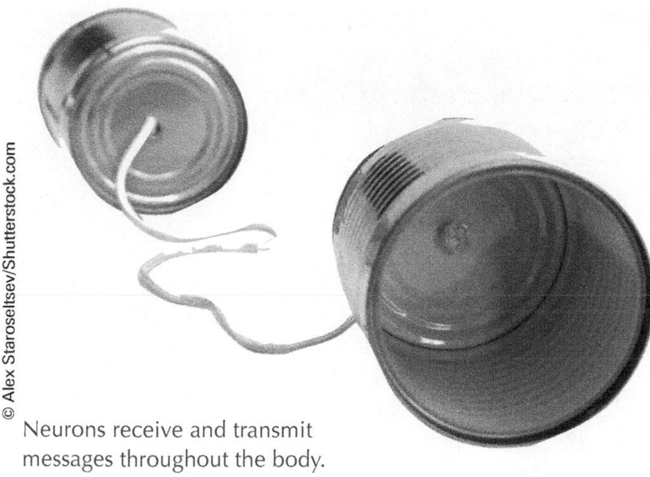
© Alex Staroseltsev/Shutterstock.com

Neurons receive and transmit messages throughout the body.

Neurons vary according to their functions and locations in the body. Some neurons in the brain are only a fraction of a centimetre in length, whereas neurons in the leg can grow to more than a couple of metres (several feet) long. Each neuron possesses a cell body, dendrites, and an axon (see Figure 4.1). Dendrites are short fibres that extend from the cell body and receive incoming messages from up to 1,000 adjoining transmitting neurons. The axon extends trunk- like from the cell body and accounts for much of the difference in length in neurons. An axon can be up to a couple of metres (several feet) in length if it is carrying messages from the toes upward. Messages are released from axon terminals in the form of chemicals called neurotransmitters. These messages are received by the dendrites of adjoining neurons, muscles, or glands. As the child matures, axons lengthen, and dendrites and axon terminals proliferate.

dendrites rootlike parts of neurons that receive impulses from other neurons

axon a long, thin part of a neuron that transmits impulses to other neurons through branching structures called axon terminals

neurotransmitters chemicals that transmit neural impulses across a synapse from one neuron to another

myelin sheath a fatty, whitish substance that encases and insulates axons

Myelin

Many neurons are tightly wrapped with white, fatty myelin sheaths that give them the appearance of a

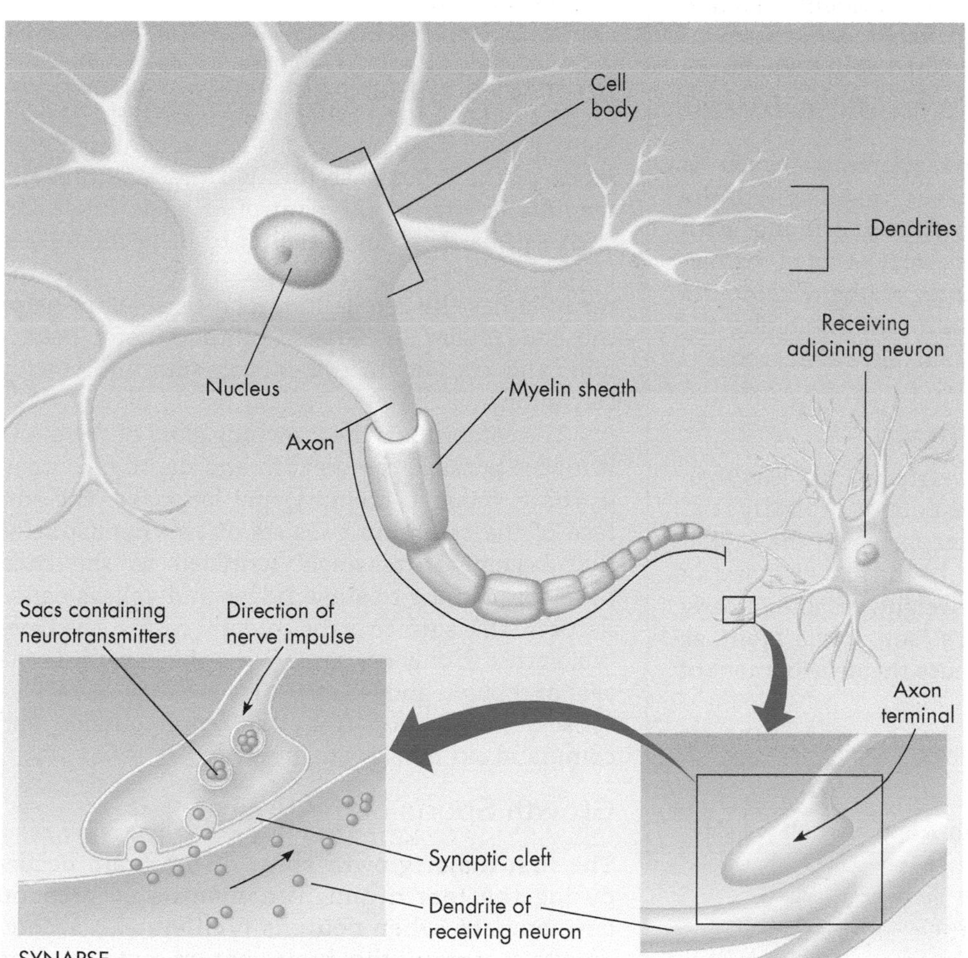

FIGURE 4.1

Anatomy of a Neuron

Source: © Cengage Learning

myelination
the coating of axons with myelin

multiple sclerosis
a disorder in which hard fibrous tissue replaces myelin, impeding neural transmission

medulla
an area of the hindbrain involved in heartbeat and respiration

cerebellum
the part of the hindbrain involved in coordination and balance

cerebrum
the part of the brain responsible for learning, thought, memory, language, and muscle control

string of white sausages. The high fat content of the myelin sheath insulates the neuron from electrically charged atoms in the fluids that encase the nervous system. In this way, leakage of the electric current being carried along the axon is minimized, and messages are conducted more efficiently.

The term myelination refers to the process by which axons are coated with myelin. Myelination is not complete at birth; it is part of the maturation process that leads to the ability to crawl and walk during the first year after birth. Myelination of the brain's prefrontal matter continues into the second decade of life and relates to advances in working memory and language ability (Aslin & Schlaggar, 2006; Pujol et al., 2006). Breakdown of myelin is believed to be associated with Alzheimer's disease, a source of cognitive decline that typically begins later in life.

In the disease multiple sclerosis, myelin is replaced by hard, fibrous tissue that disrupts the timing of neural transmission, interfering with muscle control (Stankoff et al., 2006). One of the disorders we discussed in Chapter 2, phenylketonuria (PKU), causes mental retardation by inhibiting the formation of myelin in the brain (Sirrs et al., 2007).

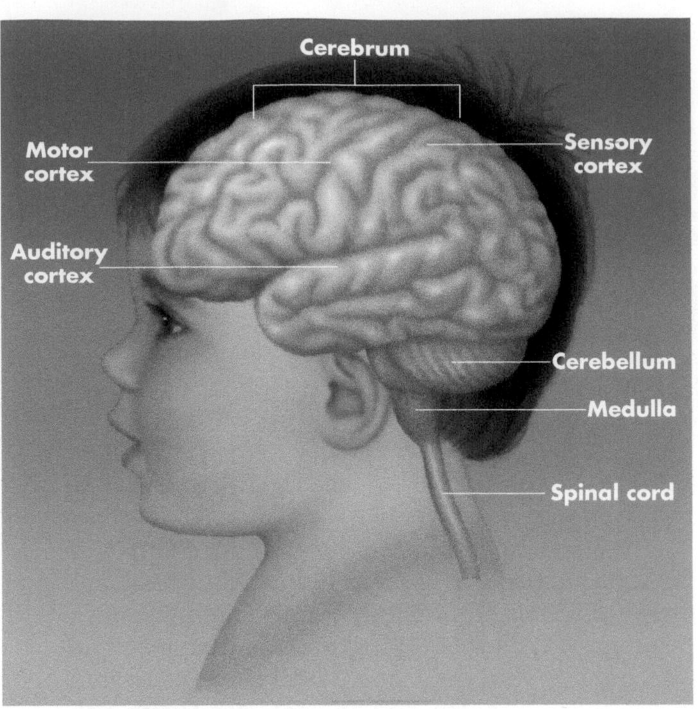

FIGURE 4.2

Structures of the Brain

Source: © Cengage Learning

Development of the Brain

The brain of the newborn weighs a little less than half a kilogram (less than one pound), or nearly one-fourth its adult weight. In keeping with the principles of cephalocaudal growth, by the first birthday, an infant's brain has tripled in weight, reaching nearly 70% of its adult weight. Let's look at the brain, as shown in Figure 4.2, and discuss the development of the structures within.

> **DID YOU KNOW?**
>
> **A child's brain reaches more than half its adult weight by the age of 1 year.**
>
> By the first birthday, a child's brain has usually tripled in weight at birth, reaching roughly 70% of its adult weight.

Structures of the Brain

Many nerves that connect the spinal cord to higher levels of the brain pass through the medulla. The medulla is vital in the control of basic functions, such as heartbeat and respiration. The medulla is part of an area called the brain stem. Above the medulla lies the cerebellum. The cerebellum helps the child maintain balance, control motor behaviour, and coordinate eye movements with bodily sensations.

The cerebrum is the crowning glory of the brain. It makes possible the breadth and depth of human learning, thought, memory, and language. The surface of the cerebrum consists of two hemispheres that become increasingly wrinkled as the child develops, coming to show ridges and valleys called fissures. This surface is the cerebral cortex. The cerebral cortex is only 0.3 cm (1/8 in.) thick, yet it is the seat of thought and reason. It is here that we receive sensory information from the world outside and command our muscles to move.

Growth Spurts of the Brain

The first major growth spurt of the brain occurs during the fourth and fifth months of prenatal development, when neurons proliferate. A second growth spurt in the brain occurs between the

25th week of prenatal development and the end of the second year after birth. Whereas the first growth spurt of the brain is due to the formation of neurons, the second growth spurt is due primarily to the proliferation of dendrites and axon terminals.

DID YOU KNOW?

The cerebral cortex—the outer layer of the brain that is vital to human thought and reasoning—is only 0.3 cm (1/8 in.) thick.

Despite its thinness, the cerebral cortex houses our individual thoughts and reasoning.

Brain Development in Infancy

What infants are able to do is linked to their myelination. At birth, the parts of the brain involved in heartbeat and respiration, sleeping and arousal, and reflex activity are fairly well myelinated and functional. Myelination of motor pathways allows newborns to show stereotyped reflexes, but otherwise their physical activity tends to be random and unorganized. Myelin develops rapidly along the major motor pathways from the cerebral cortex during the last month of pregnancy and continues after birth. The development of intentional physical activity coincides with myelination as the movements of the newborn come under increasing control. Myelination of the nerves to muscles is largely developed by the age of 2, although myelination continues to some degree into adolescence (Wozniak & Lim, 2006).

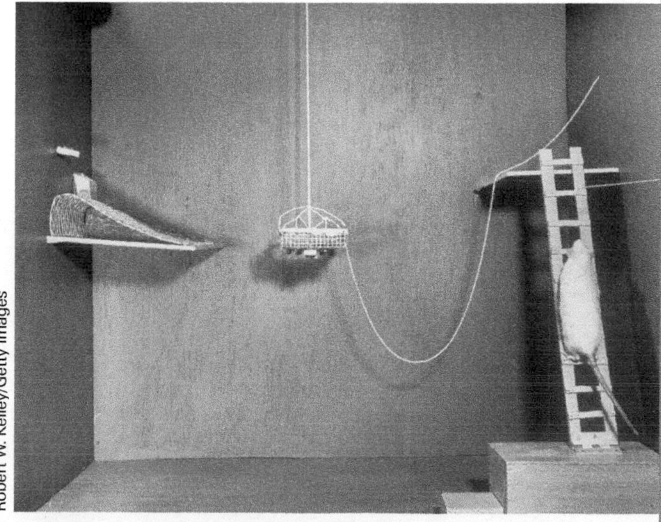

Robert W. Kelley/Getty Images

Research with rats demonstrates how a rich environment sparks brain growth.

Although newborns respond to touch and can see and hear quite well, the areas of the cortex that are involved in vision, hearing, and the skin senses are not fully myelinated at birth. As myelination progresses and the interconnections between the various areas of the cortex thicken, children become increasingly capable of complex and integrated sensorimotor activities (Wozniak & Lim, 2006).

Myelination of the neurons involved in the sense of hearing begins at about the sixth month of pregnancy. Myelination of these pathways is developing rapidly at term and continues until about age 4. The neurons involved in vision begin to myelinate only shortly before full term, but then they complete the process of myelination rapidly. Within 5 to 6 months after birth, vision has become the dominant sense.

Nature and Nurture in Brain Development

Development of the areas of the brain that control sensation and movement begins as a result of maturation, but sensory stimulation and physical activity during early infancy also spur the development of these areas (Güntürkün, 2006; Posner & Rothbart, 2007).

The brain is also affected by experience. Infants actually have more connections among neurons than adults do. Connections that are activated by experience survive; the others do not (Tsuneishi & Casaer, 2000; Weinberg, 2004) and are pruned over time.

The great adaptability of the brain appears to be a double-edged sword. Adaptability allows us to develop different patterns of neural connections to meet the demands of different environments, but lack of stimulation—especially during critical early periods of development—can impair adaptability. Many parts of the brain have specialized functions,

EMERGING CANADA

Most parents want their baby to be happy and healthy, and they want their baby to make the most of its potential. But in our highly competitive world, some parents take things too far, by focusing on achievement of the skill rather than true learning. "Super Baby Syndrome" refers to a parental attitude that intends for a child to achieve more skills earlier than other children; it often results in an infant or toddler being pushed to do more than is ordinarily expected of such a young child. We have all shared a playground, or an activity, with parents that take things too far in the hope that their child will be the best.

plasticity the ability of the brain to compensate for injuries in particular areas by developing new neural pathways

palmar grasp grasping objects between the fingers and the palm

pincer grasp grasping objects between the fingers and the thumb

locomotion movement from one place to another

allowing our behaviour to be more complex. But this specialization also means that injuries to certain parts of the brain can result in loss of these functions. However, the brain also shows plasticity, or the ability to compensate for injuries to particular areas by forming new neural pathways. Plasticity is greatest at about 1 to 2 years of age and then gradually declines (Kolb & Gibb, 2007; Nelson, de Haan, & Thomas, 2006).

LO3 Motor Development

Motor development involves the activity of muscles, leading to changes in posture, movement, and coordination of movement with the infant's developing sensory apparatus. Motor development provides some of the most fascinating changes in infants because so much happens so fast.

Like physical development, motor development follows cephalocaudal and proximodistal patterns and differentiation. Infants gain control of their head and upper torso before gaining effective use of their arms. This trend illustrates cephalocaudal development. Also infants can control their trunk and shoulders before using hands and fingers, demonstrating the proximodistal trend.

Lifting and Holding the Torso and Head

Newborns can move their head slightly to the side. Because of this ability, they avoid suffocation. Thus, if they lie face down and their nose or mouth is obstructed by bedding, they are likely to find air to breathe. At about 1 month, infants can raise their head. By about 2 months, they can also lift their chest while lying on their stomach.

When holding newborns, caregivers must support the head. By 3 to 6 months of age, infants can generally manage to hold their own head quite well; supporting the head is no longer necessary. Unfortunately, even though infants can normally support their head, they cannot do so when being lifted or being moved about in a jerky manner; if they are handled carelessly, they can thus develop neck injuries and, in extreme cases, shaken baby syndrome (SBS) (see section "Shaken Baby Syndrome (SBS)" in Chapter 3, page 63).

Control of the Hands: Getting a Grip

The development of hand skills is an example of proximodistal development. Infants will track slowly moving objects with their eyes shortly after birth, but they will not reach for the objects. Voluntary reaching and grasping require visual–motor coordination. By about 3 months, infants will make clumsy swipes at objects. Between 4 to 6 months, infants become more successful at grasping objects (Piek, 2006; Santos, Gabbard, & Goncalves, 2000). However, they may not know how to let go and may hold an object indefinitely, until their attention is diverted and the hand opens accidentally. Four to 6 months is a good age for giving children rattles, large plastic spoons, mobiles, and other brightly coloured toys that can be grasped but are harmless if they end up in the mouth.

Grasping is reflexive at first. Voluntary holding replaces reflexive grasping by 3 to 4 months. Infants first use a palmar grasp, holding objects clumsily between their fingers and their palm. By 4 to 6 months, they can transfer objects back and forth between hands. The opposable thumb comes into play at about 9 to 12 months, enabling infants to pick up tiny objects in a pincer grasp. By about 11 months, infants can hold objects in each hand and inspect them in turn.

Another aspect of visual–motor coordination is stacking blocks. On average, children can stack two blocks at 15 months, three blocks at 18 months, and five blocks at 24 months (Wentworth, Benson, & Haith, 2000).

Locomotion

Locomotion is movement from one place to another. Children gain the capacity to move their bodies through a sequence of activities that includes rolling over, sitting up, crawling, creeping, walking, and running (see Figure 4.3). The ages when infants first engage in these activities can vary. Although the sequence mostly

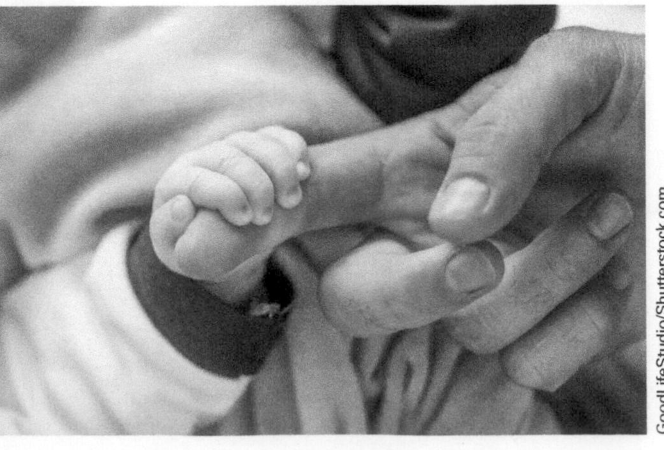

GoodLifeStudio/Shutterstock.com

FIGURE 4.3

Motor Development in Infancy

Motor development proceeds in an orderly sequence, but the timing of marker events may have considerable variation.

Source: © Cengage Learning

remains the same, some children will skip a step. For example, some infants move on their bottoms to get around without ever having crawled.

Most infants can roll over, from back to stomach and from stomach to back, by about the age of 6 months. By about 7 months, infants usually begin to sit up by themselves. At 8 to 9 months, babies begin to crawl; they move themselves along, often on their hands and knees, although there is a lot of variation and some infants never perform this motor skill. Some infants will crawl backwards at the beginning before learning to move forward.

toddler
child who walks with short, uncertain steps

Standing overlaps with crawling. Most 8- or 9-month-olds can remain in a standing position by holding on to something. At this age, they may also be able to walk a bit with support. About 2 months later, they can pull themselves to a standing position by holding on to the sides of their cribs or other objects and can stand briefly without holding on. By 12 to 15 months or so, they walk by themselves, earning them the name **toddler**.

Toddlers soon run about, supporting their relatively heavy heads and torsos by spreading their legs in a bowlegged fashion. Because they are top-heavy and inexperienced, they fall frequently. Many toddlers are able to navigate slopes (Adolph & Berger, 2005). They walk down shallow slopes but prudently choose to slide or crawl down steep slopes. Walking gives children new freedom. It allows them to get about rapidly and to grasp objects that were formerly out of reach.

Parents often worry when their children aren't walking by 18 months. According to one Canadian researcher, failure to walk on its own is rarely cause for concern. It is important to observe the other skills infants have acquired, such as their social skills, fine motor skills, and speech. "If they can crawl or scoot around on their bottom—in other words, if they have the capacity to travel—then leave them alone, and watch and wait" (Seto, 2012).

As children mature, their muscle strength, bone density, and balance and coordination

leungchopan/Shutterstock.com

Pincer Grasp

Crawling

Walking

Polaroid frame: © U.P.images/iStockphoto.com

improve (Metcalfe et al., 2005). By the age of 2 years, they can climb steps one at a time, placing both feet on each step. They can run well, walk backward, kick a large ball, and jump several inches.

Both maturation (nature) and experience (nurture) are involved in motor development. Certain voluntary motor activities are not possible until the brain has matured in terms of myelination and the differentiation of the motor areas of the cortex. Although the newborn shows stepping and swimming reflexes, these behaviours are controlled by more primitive parts of the brain. The behaviours disappear when cortical development inhibits some functions of the lower parts of the brain; and, when they reappear, they differ in quality.

Can training accelerate the appearance of motor skills? In a classic study with identical twins, Arnold Gesell (1929) gave one twin extensive training in hand coordination, block building, and stair climbing from early infancy. The other twin was allowed to develop on his own. At first, the trained twin had better skills, but as time passed, the untrained twin became just as skilled. Thus, the development of motor skills can be accelerated by training (Adolph & Berger, 2005; Zelazo, 1998), but the long-lasting effect seems slight.

Nature provides the limits—the "reaction range"—for the expression of inherited traits. Nurture determines whether the child will develop skills that reach the upper limits of the range. Even such a fundamental skill as locomotion is determined by a complex interplay of maturational and environmental factors (Adolph & Berger, 2005). There may be little purpose in trying to train children to enhance their motor skills before they are ready. Once they are ready, however, teaching and practice do make a difference. People do not become Olympic athletes without "good genes," but they also usually do not become Olympic athletes without solid training.

Unfortunately, social conditions can lead to circumstances that are tragic from a developmental perspective. For example, in the 1990s, the world became aware of horrible conditions in Romania where severely malnourished children were being held in orphanages. They had profound growth delays and had received only limited social interaction and stimulation. Canadians rescued these children, providing safe homes for them, but many developmental questions remained unanswered. In a study, 36 of these severely deprived children were measured for long-term developmental effects at 11 months, 4.5 years, and 10.5 years. Could growth rebound under such severe conditions?

Observations indicated severe negative impact at periods one and two of the study. By period three, dramatic growth catch-up had taken place. Further, the children were as healthy as Canadian-born children. Despite their severe early deprivation, the adopted Romanian children seemed to be able to make remarkable gains in the areas of physical growth and health. Continued study of these children will expand our knowledge of the importance of early life experiences on physical growth, physical health, and the body's ability to recover from extreme negative circumstances (Le Mare & Audet, 2006).

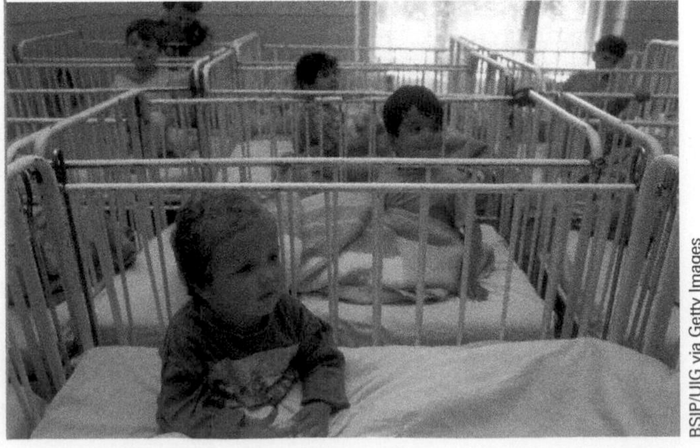

BSIP/UIG via Getty Images

LO4 Sensory and Perceptual Development

Many things that are obvious to us are not so obvious to infants. You may know that a coffee cup is the same whether you see it from above or from the side, but make no such assumptions about the infant's knowledge. You may know that an infant's mother is the same size whether she is standing next to the infant or approaching from two blocks away, but do not assume that the infant agrees with you.

Development of Vision

Development of vision involves development of visual acuity or sharpness, development of peripheral vision (seeing things at the sides while looking ahead), visual preferences, depth perception, and perceptual constancies—such as knowing that an object remains the same object even though it may look different when seen from a different angle.

Development of Visual Acuity and Peripheral Vision

Newborns are extremely nearsighted, with vision beginning at about 20/600. The most dramatic gains in visual acuity are made between birth and 6 months of age, with acuity reaching about 20/50 (Haith, 1990; Skoczenski, 2002). By 3 to 5 years, visual acuity generally approximates adult levels (20/20 in the best cases).

Newborns also have poor peripheral vision (Cavallini et al., 2002; Skoczenski, 2002). Adults can perceive objects that are nearly 90 degrees off to the side (i.e., directly to the left or right), although objects at these extremes are unclear. Newborns cannot perceive visual stimuli that are off to the side by an angle of more than 30 degrees, but their peripheral vision expands to an angle of about 45 degrees by the age of 7 weeks. By 6 months, their peripheral vision is about equal to that of an adult.

Let us now consider the development of visual perception. We will see that infants frequently prefer the strange to the familiar but will avoid going off the deep end—sometimes.

By the age of 8 to 12 weeks, most infants show a distinct preference for curved lines over straight ones.

Visual Preferences

Newborns look at stripes longer than at blobs. This finding has been used in much of the research on visual acuity. Classic research found that by the age of 8 to 12 weeks, most infants also show a distinct preference for curved lines over straight ones (Fantz, Fagan, & Miranda, 1975).

Robert Fantz (1961) also wondered whether something intrinsically interesting about the human face drew the attention of infants. To investigate this question, he showed 2-month-old infants the six disks in Figure 4.4. One disk contained human features, another newsprint, and still another, a bull's-eye. The remaining three disks were featureless but coloured: one red, one white, and one yellow. In this study, the infants fixated significantly longer on the human face.

Some studies suggest that the infants in Fantz's (1961) study may have preferred the human face because it had a complex, intriguing pattern of dots (eyes) within an outline,

Constance Bannister Corp/Archive Photos/Getty Images

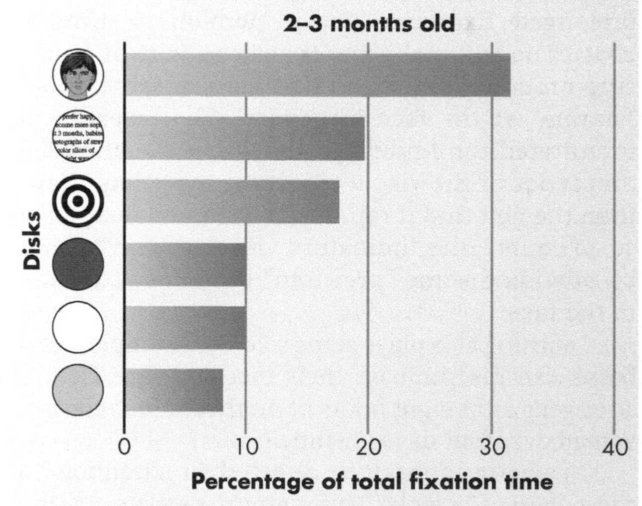

FIGURE 4.4

Preferences for Visual Stimuli in 2-Month-Olds

Infants seem to prefer complex visual stimuli over simpler stimuli. By the age of 2 months, they tend to show a preference for the human face.

Source: © Cengage Learning

Pedalist/Shutterstock.com

Infants prefer human faces over other stimuli.

not because it was a face. But de Haan and Groen (2006) assert that "reading" faces (interpreting facial expressions) is important to infants because they do not understand verbal information as communicated through language.

Researchers therefore continue to ask whether humans come into the world "prewired" to prefer human stimuli over other stimuli that are just as complex, and—if so—what it is about human stimuli that draws attention. Some researchers—unlike de Haan and Groen—argue that neonates do not "prefer" faces because they are faces per se but because of the structure of their immature visual systems (Simion et al., 2001). A supportive study of 34 neonates found that infants' longer fixations on facelike stimuli resulted from a larger number of brief fixations (looks) rather than from a few prolonged fixations (Cassia, Simion, & Umilta, 2001). The infants' gaze, then, was sort of bouncing around from feature to feature rather than "staring" at the face in general. The researchers interpreted the finding to show that the stimulus properties of the visual object are more important than the fact that it represents a human face. Even so, of course, the "immature visual system" would be providing some "prewired" basis for attending to the face.

Learning also plays some role. For example, newborns can discriminate their mother's face from a stranger's after eight hours of mother–infant contact spread over four days (Bushnell, 2001).

Newborns appear to direct their attention to the edges of objects. This pattern persists for the first several weeks (Bronson, 1991). When they are given the opportunity to look at human faces, 1-month-old infants tend to pay most attention to the "edges," that is, the chin, an ear, or the hairline. The eye movements of 2-month-old infants move in from the edge. Infants focus particularly on the eyes, although they also inspect other features such as the mouth and nose (Nelson & Ludemann, 1989).

Some researchers (e.g., Haith, 1979) explain infants' tendencies to scan from the edges of objects inward by noting that for the first several weeks, infants seem to be concerned with *where* things are. Their attention is captured by movement and sharp contrasts in brightness and shape, such as those found where the edges of objects stand out against their backgrounds. But by about 2 months, infants tend to focus on the *what* of things, scanning systematically within the boundaries of objects (Bronson, 1990, 1997). As infants grow older, their preferences can be shaped by the objects that others find interesting. This effect shows the infant's integration of the biological process of seeing with the social aspect of interacting with those nearby. This effect also lays the groundwork for social referencing, which will be discussed in greater detail in Chapter 6 (Flom & Johnson, 2011).

Development of Depth Perception

Infants generally respond to cues for depth by the time they are able to crawl (8 to 9 months of age or so), and most have the good sense to avoid "going off the deep end," that is, crawling off ledges and tabletops into open space (Campos et al., 1978).

In a classic study on depth perception, Gibson and Walk (1960) placed infants of various ages on a fabric-covered runway that ran across the centre of a clever device called a *visual cliff* (see Figure 4.5). The visual cliff is a sheet of Plexiglas that covers a cloth with a checkerboard pattern. On one side, the cloth is placed immediately beneath the Plexiglas; on the other, the cloth drops about 1.2 m (4 ft.). In the Gibson and Walk study, 8 out of 10 infants who had begun to crawl refused to venture onto the seemingly unsupported surface, even when their mothers beckoned encouragingly from the other side.

Psychologists can assess infants' emotional responses to the visual cliff long before infants can crawl. For example, Campos and his colleagues (1970) found that 1-month-old infants showed no change in heart rate when placed face down on the "cliff." They apparently did not perceive the depth of the cliff. At 2 months, infants showed decreases in heart rate when so placed, which psychologists interpret as a sign of interest. But the heart rates of 9-month-olds accelerated on the cliff, which is interpreted as a fear response. The study appears to suggest that infants benefit from some experience crawling about (and, perhaps, accumulating some bumps) before they develop fear of heights, which was the experience of the 9-month-olds but not the 2-month-olds. Other studies support the

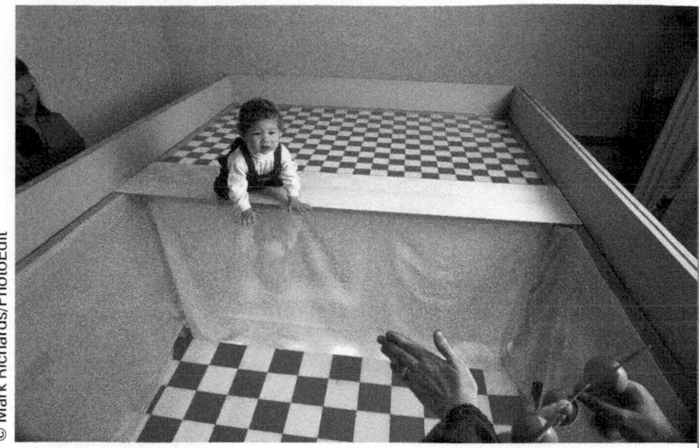

© Mark Richards/PhotoEdit

FIGURE 4.5

The Visual Cliff

This young explorer has the good sense not to crawl out onto an apparently unsupported surface, even when mother beckons from the other side.

view that infants usually do not develop fear of heights until they can move around (Sorce et al., 2000; Witherington et al., 2005).

In 2010, a follow-up study was conducted (Lin, Reilly, & Mercer, 2010) to determine whether depth perception at crawling age differed among infants who were born preterm and those born at term. The studies determined that both groups of infants were able to perceive the depth change. What differed, however, was that the babies born at term showed more motor strategies and avoidance techniques when they encountered the visual cliff.

Development of Hearing

Neonates can crudely orient their heads in the direction of a sound (Saffran, Werker, & Werner, 2006). By 18 months of age, the accuracy of sound-localizing ability approaches that of adults. Sensitivity to sounds increases in the first few months of life (Saffran et al., 2006). As infants mature, the range of the pitch of the sounds they sense gradually expands to include the adult's range of 20 to 20,000 cycles per second. The ability to detect differences in the pitch and loudness of sounds improves considerably throughout the preschool years. Auditory acuity also improves gradually over the first several years (Saffran et al., 2006). Sometimes, infants' hearing can be so acute that many parents complain their napping infants will awaken at the slightest sound; this is especially true when parents have been overprotective in attempting to keep their rooms as quiet as possible. Infants who are normally exposed to a backdrop of moderate noise levels become habituated to them and are not likely to awaken unless they hear a sudden, sharp noise.

By the age of 1 month, infants perceive differences between speech sounds that are highly similar. In a classic study relying on the **habituation** method, infants of this age could activate a recording of "bah" by sucking on a nipple (Eimas et al., 1971). As time went on, habituation occurred, as shown by decreased sucking to hear the "bah" sound. Then the researchers switched from "bah" to "pah." If the sounds had seemed the same to the infants, their lethargic sucking patterns would have continued; but they immediately sucked harder, suggesting that they had perceived the difference. Other researchers have found that within another month or two, infants reliably discriminate three-syllable words such as *marana* and *malana* (Kuhl et al., 2006).

habituation becoming used to a stimulus and therefore paying less attention to it

Infants can discriminate the sounds of their parent's voices by 3 1/2 months of age. In classic research, infants of this age were oriented toward their parents as they reclined in infant seats. The experimenters (Spelke & Owsley, 1979) played recordings of their mother's or father's voices while the parents themselves remained inactive. The infants reliably looked at the parent whose voice was being played.

Young infants are capable of perceiving most of the speech sounds present in the world's languages. But after exposure to one's native language, infants gradually lose the capacity to discriminate those sounds that are not found in the native language (Werker et al., 2007), as shown in Figure 4.6.

Infants also learn at an early age to ignore small, meaningless variations in the sounds of their native language—for instance, those caused by accents or head colds—as early as 6 months of age (Kuhl et al., 2006). Kuhl and her colleagues (1997) presented American and Swedish infants with pairs of sounds in either their own language or the other language. The infants were trained to look over their shoulder when they heard a difference in the sounds and to ignore sound pairs that seemed to be the same. The infants routinely ignored variations in sounds that were part of their language, because they apparently perceived them as the same sound. But the infants noticed slight variations in the sounds of the other language. Another study demonstrated the same ability in infants as young as 2 months (Marean, Werner, & Kuhl, 1992).

Development of Coordination of the Senses

Young infants can recognize that objects experienced by one sense (e.g., vision) are the same as those experienced through another sense (e.g., touch).

FIGURE 4.6

Declining Ability to Discriminate the Sounds of Foreign Languages

Infants show a decline in the ability to discriminate sounds not found in their native language. Before 6 months of age, infants from English-speaking families could discriminate sounds found in Hindi (red bars) and Salish, a Native American language (blue bars). By 10 to 12 months of age, they could no longer do so.

Source: Werker, 1989.

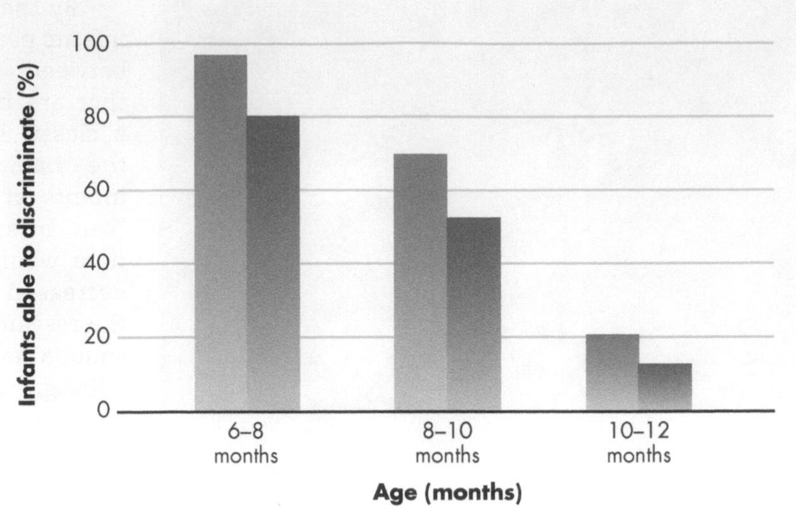

This ability has been demonstrated in infants as young as 1 month of age (Bushnell, 1993). One experiment demonstrating such understanding in 5-month-olds showed that infants of this age tend to look longer at novel rather than familiar sources of stimulation. Féron and her colleagues (2006) first allowed 5-month-old infants to handle groups of either two or three objects, presented one by one to their right hand. The infants were then shown visual displays of either two or three objects. The infants looked longer at the group of objects that differed from the one they had handled, showing a transfer of information from the sense of touch to the sense of vision.

Vanessa Davies/Getty Images

The Active–Passive Controversy in Perceptual Development

Newborns have more sophisticated sensory capabilities than you would expect. Still, their ways of perceiving the world are largely mechanical, or passive. Newborns seem to be generally at the mercy of external stimuli. When a bright light strikes, they attend to it. If the light moves slowly across the plane of their vision, they track it.

As time passes, broad changes occur in the perceptual processes of children, and the child's role in perception appears to become decidedly more active. Developmental psychologist Eleanor Gibson (1969, 1991) noted several of these changes:

1. Intentional action (scanning and exploration) replaces "capture" (automatic responses to stimulation).
2. Systematic search replaces unsystematic search.
3. Attention becomes selective regardless of environmental confusion.
4. Irrelevant information (such as the noise of cars in the street or the playing of a radio in another room) becomes ignored when the child is focused on playing.

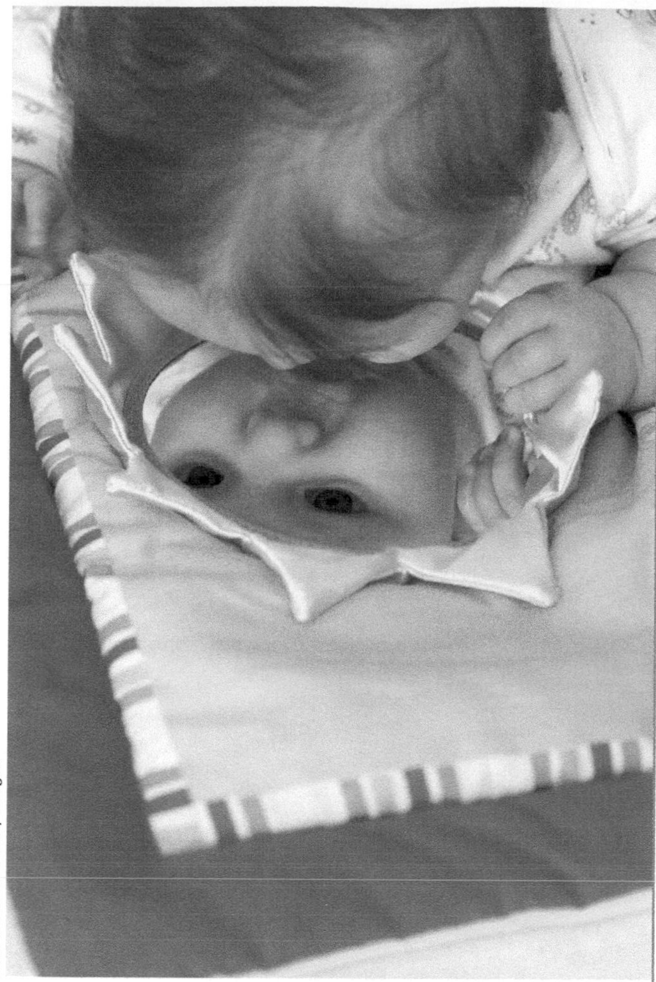

Ruth Jenkinson/Getty Images

In short, children develop from passive, mechanical reactors to the world about them into active, purposeful seekers and organizers of sensory information.

Nature and Nurture in Perceptual Development

The nature–nurture issue is found in perceptual development, as in other areas of development.

Evidence for the Role of Nature

Compelling evidence supports the idea that inborn sensory capacities play a crucial role in perceptual development. Newborns arrive in the world with many perceptual skills. They can see nearby objects quite well, and their hearing is usually fine. They are born with tendencies to track moving objects, to systematically scan the horizon, and to prefer certain kinds of stimuli. Preferences for different kinds of visual stimuli appear to unfold on schedule as the first months wear on. Sensory changes, as with motor changes, appear to be linked to maturation of the nervous system.

Evidence for the Role of Nurture

Evidence is also compelling that experience plays a crucial role in perceptual development. Children and lower animals have critical periods in their perceptual development. Failure to receive adequate sensory stimulation during these periods can result in permanent sensory deficits (Greenough, Black, & Wallace, 2002). For example, if health problems require that a child's eye be patched for an extensive period of time during the first year, the child's visual acuity in that eye may be impaired.

Today most developmentalists agree that nature and nurture interact to shape perceptual development. In the next chapter, we see how nature and nurture influence the development of thought and language in infants.

STUDY TOOLS

CHAPTER 4

Located at **nelson.com/student**

- ☐ Prepare for tests with a variety of exercises and activities.
- ☐ Review Key Terms Flashcards (online or print)
- ☐ Create your own study tools with Build a Summary
- ☐ Watch Observing Development videos to expand your knowledge

CHAPTER 5

Anatoliy Samara/Thinkstock.com

Infancy: Cognitive Development

LEARNING OUTCOMES

LO1 Examine Jean Piaget's studies of cognitive development

LO2 Discuss the information-processing approach

LO3 Identify individual differences in intelligence among infants

LO4 Examine language development in children

> "Cognitive development focuses on the development of children's ways of perceiving and mentally representing the world."

Alana plays in the bathtub slapping the water making sounds and bubbles. She does the same movements over and over . . . just as she did the day before. She pours water from one cup to the other and back again.

Is this a description of a scientist at work? In a way, it is. Swiss psychologist Jean Piaget (1963 [1936]) felt that children frequently act like scientists, performing what he called "experiments in order to see."

LO1 Cognitive Development: Jean Piaget

Cognitive development focuses on the development of children's ways of perceiving and mentally representing the world. Piaget labelled children's concepts of the world schemas. A schema is a mental structure that categorizes knowledge so that information that is similar is grouped together. He hypothesized that children use assimilation to absorb new information into existing schemas. When assimilation does not allow the child to make sense of novel events, children try to modify existing schemas to fit the newly acquired information through accommodation.

schema
a mental structure that categories information based on similarity

assimilation
new information is added to an existing schema

accommodation
new information must be modified to fit an existing schema as new information is acquired

Piaget (1963 [1936]) hypothesized that cognitive processes develop in an orderly sequence of stages. Some children may advance more quickly than others, but the sequence remains constant (Flavell, Miller, & Miller et al., 2002; Siegler & Alibali, 2005). Piaget identified four stages of cognitive development: sensorimotor, preoperational, concrete operational, and formal operational. In this chapter, we discuss the sensorimotor stage (see Table 5.1).

The Sensorimotor Stage

Piaget's sensorimotor stage refers to the first 2 years of cognitive development, a time during which infants progress from responding to events with reflexes, or

TABLE 5.1

Jean Piaget's Stages of Cognitive Development

Stage	Approximate Age	Comments
Sensorimotor	Birth–2 years	At first, the child lacks language and does not use symbols or mental representations of objects. In time, reflexive responding ends, and intentional behaviour begins. The child develops the object concept and acquires the basics of language.
Preoperational	2–7 years	The child begins to represent the world mentally, but thought is egocentric. The child does not focus on two aspects of a situation at once and therefore lacks conservation. The child shows animism, artificialism , and objective responsibility for wrongdoing. (See Chapter 7 for more information about animism and artificialism.)
Concrete operational	7–12 years	Logical mental actions—called operations—begin. The child develops conservation concepts, can adopt the viewpoints of others, can classify objects in series, and shows comprehension of basic relational concepts (such as one object being larger or heavier than another).
Formal operational	12 years and older	Mature, adult thought emerges. Thinking is characterized by deductive logic, consideration of various possibilities (mental trial and error), abstract thought, and the formation and testing of hypotheses.

Source: From Rathus. Childhood and Adolescence: Voyages in Development, 5E. © 2014 South-Western, a part of Cengage Learning, Inc. Reproduced by permission. www.cengage.com/permissions (italicize Childhood and Adolescence: Voyages in Development)

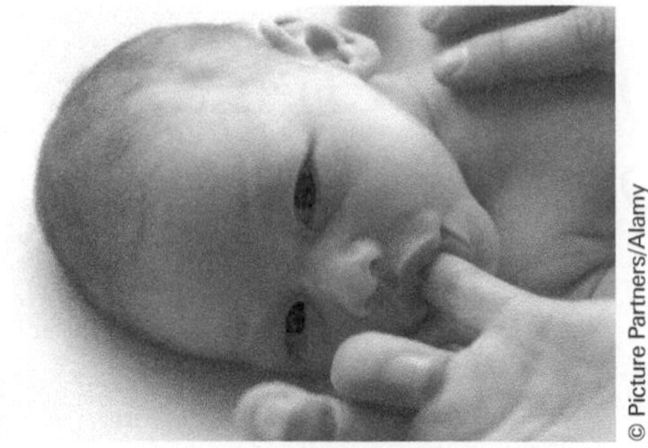
© Picture Partners/Alamy

At birth, neonates assimilate objects into reflexive responses.

© Picture Partners/Alamy

Infants repeat actions that involve their bodies (primary circular reactions).

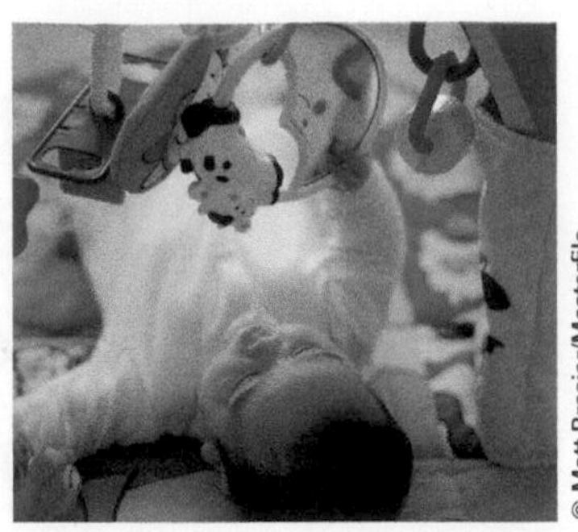
© Matt Brasier/Masterfile

Patterns of activity are repeated because of their effect on the environment (secondary circular reactions).

primary circular reactions the repetition of actions that first occurred by chance and that focus on the infant's own body.

secondary circular reactions the repetition of actions that produce an effect on the environment

ready-made schemas, to goal-oriented behaviour. Piaget divided the sensorimotor stage into six sub-stages. In each sub-stage, earlier forms of behaviour are repeated, varied, and coordinated.

Simple Reflexes

The first sub-stage covers the first month after birth. It is dominated by the assimilation of sources of stimulation into inborn reflexes such as grasping or visual tracking. At birth, reflexes seem like automatic responses but even within the first few hours, neonates begin to modify reflexes as a result of experience. For example, infants will adapt their patterns of sucking to the shape of the nipple and the rate of flow of fluid. During the first month or so, however, infants apparently make no connection between stimulation perceived through different sensory modalities. They make no effort to grasp objects that they visually track. Another example of a simple reflex is that infants will startle in response to a loud noise such as loud clapping hands.

Primary Circular Reactions

The second sub-stage, primary circular reactions, lasts from about 1 to 4 months of age and is characterized by the beginnings of the ability to coordinate various sensorimotor schemas. Infants tend to repeat stimulating actions that first occurred by chance. For example, an infant may lift its arm repeatedly to bring it into view. **Primary circular reactions** focus on the infant's own body rather than on the external environment.

In terms of assimilation and accommodation, the child is attempting to assimilate the motor schema (moving the hand) into the sensory schema (looking at it). But the schemas do not automatically fit. Several days of apparent trial and error pass, during which the infant seems to be trying to make accommodations so that they will fit. By the third month, infants may examine objects repeatedly and intensely. It seems that the infant is no longer simply looking and seeing but is now "looking in order to see." Another example is that an infant will learn to suck its thumb at first by accident. With repetition, it brings its thumb to its mouth repeating the movement until it becomes proficient.

Piaget considers the desire to prolong stimulation to be as "basic" as the drives of hunger or thirst.

Secondary Circular Reactions

The third sub-stage lasts from about 4 to 8 months and is characterized by **secondary circular reactions**, in which patterns of activity are repeated because of their effect on the environment; the focus of attention shifts from their bodies to external objects and environmental events. Infants may now learn to pull strings in order to make a plastic face appear or to shake an object in order to hear it rattle. Babies at this

Creativa Images/Shutterstock.com

Dave Long/iStockphoto.com

stage are first interested in the game peek-a-boo as the caregiver's face appears behind their hands.

Coordination of Secondary Schemas

In the fourth sub-stage, infants ages 8 to 12 months no longer act simply to prolong interesting occurrences. Now they can coordinate schemas to attain specific goals. Infants begin to show intentional, goal-directed behaviour in which they differentiate between the means of achieving a goal and the goal or end itself. For example, they may lift a piece of cloth to reach a toy that they had seen a parent place there earlier. In this example, the schema of picking up the cloth (the means) is coordinated with the schema of reaching for the toy (the goal or end). This example indicates that the infant has mentally represented the toy placed under the cloth. Other examples are reaching for a bib at feeding time or hiding from Mom at bedtime.

During the fourth sub-stage, infants also gain the capacity to imitate gestures and sounds that they had previously ignored. The imitation of a facial gesture implies that an infant has mentally represented his or her own face and, through feedback from facial muscles, can tell what parts of the face he or she is moving.

DID YOU KNOW?

For 2-month-old infants, "out of sight" is "out of mind."

Infants delight at playing peek-a-boo because once you disappear from view they don't realize you still exist!

tertiary circular reactions the purposeful adaptation of established schemas to new situations

Tertiary Circular Reactions

In the fifth sub-stage, which lasts from about 12 to 18 months of age, Piaget looked on the behaviour of infants as characteristic of budding scientists. Infants now engage in **tertiary circular reactions**, or purposeful adaptations of established schemas to specific situations. Behaviour takes on a new experimental quality, and infants may vary their actions dozens of times in a deliberate trial-and-error fashion to learn how things work. Examples include putting shapes into a shape sorter toy or putting puzzle pieces together.

Invention of New Means through Mental Combinations

The sixth sub-stage lasts from about 18 to 24 months of age. It serves as a transition between sensorimotor development and the development of symbolic thought. External exploration is replaced by mental exploration. At about 18 months, children may also use imitation to symbolize or stand for a plan of action.

Piaget noticed that at the age of 18 months, his own children studied various problematic situations

© Laura Dwight/PhotoEdit Inc. All rights reserved.

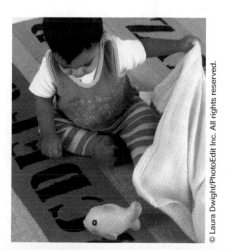

Infants coordinate their behaviour to attain specific goals (coordinating secondary schemas).

© David Mendelsohn/Masterfile

Infants use trial and error to learn how things work (tertiary circular reactions).

object permanence recognition that objects continue to exist when they are not in view

for a few moments rather than engage in trial and error learning. For example, each child grasped a stick that was outside of its playpen, turned it upright, and brought it into the playpen with little overt effort. They apparently mentally represented the stick and the bars of the playpen and then perceived that the stick would not fit through as it was. They then needed to rotate the mental image of the stick until they perceived a position that would allow the stick to pass between the bars and were able to do so. Other examples during this stage include playing the role of mother or father, playing other dress-up games and using their imagination.

Development of Object Permanence

Object permanence is an important aspect of sensorimotor development. Object permanence is the recognition that an object or person continues to exist even when out of sight. For example, your textbook continues to exist when you leave it in the library after studying for a test, and an infant's mother continues to exist even when she leaves the child at daycare. Object permanence requires that the child be able to form a mental representation of that object. The development of object permanence is tied into the development of infants' working memory and reasoning ability (Aguiar & Baillargeon, 2002; Saiki & Miyatsuji, 2007).

Newborns show no tendency to respond to objects that are not within their immediate sensory grasp. By the age of 2 months, infants may show some surprise if an object (such as a toy duck) is placed behind a screen and then taken away so that when the screen is lifted, it is absent. However, they make no effort to search for the missing object (see Figure 5.1). Moreover, if something special were missing in their crib like their favourite stuffed animal, they wouldn't notice or look for it. Through the first 6 months or so, when the screen is placed between the object and the infant, the infant behaves as though the object is no longer there.

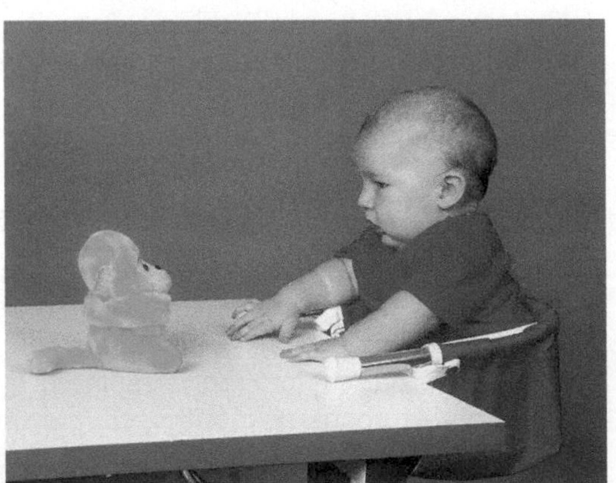

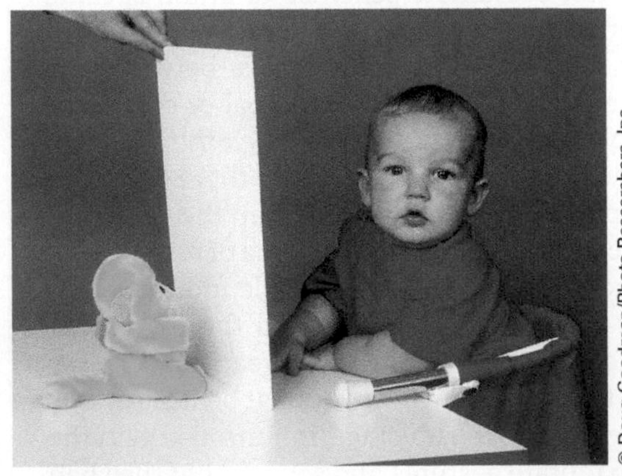

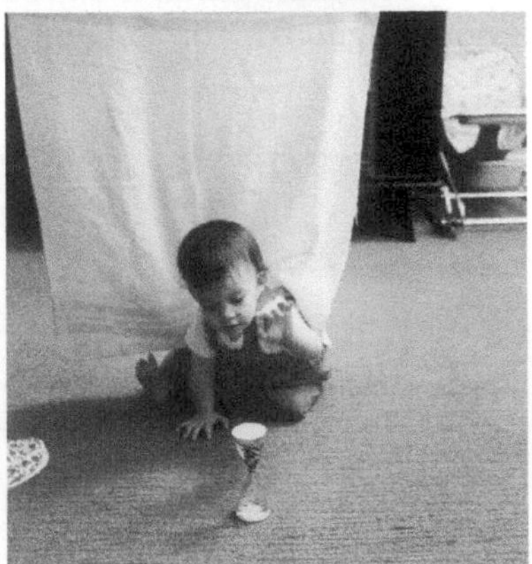

FIGURE 5.1

Object Permanence

To the infant who is in the early part of the sensorimotor stage, out of sight is truly out of mind. After a sheet of paper is placed between the infant and the toy monkey (top two photos), the infant loses all interest in the toy. Using similar evidence, Piaget concluded that the infant does not have a mental representation of the toy. The bottom series of photos shows a child in a later part of the sensorimotor stage. This child does mentally represent objects, indicated by his pushing through a towel to reach an object that has been obstructed.

Apparently, they do not yet reliably mentally represent objects they see. For 2-month-old infants, "out of sight" is truly "out of mind."

By about the sixth month, some interesting advances occur in the development of the object concept (Piaget's sub-stage 3). For example, an infant at this age will tend to look for an object that has been dropped, behaviour that suggests some form of object permanence. We have reason to believe that a 6-month-old perceives a mental representation (image) of an object, such as a favourite toy, in response to sensory impressions of part of the object. This perception is shown by the infant's reaching for an object that is partly hidden.

By 8 to 12 months of age (Piaget's sub-stage 4), infants will seek to retrieve objects that have been completely hidden. At this point, infants might start to cry if they go to sleep without their favourite blanket or stuffed toy. But in observing his own children, Piaget (1963 [1936]) noted an interesting error known as the A-not-B error. Piaget repeatedly hid a toy behind a screen (A), and each time, his infant removed the screen and retrieved the toy. Then, as the infant watched, Piaget hid the toy behind another screen (B) in a different place. Still, the infant tried to recover the toy by pushing aside the first screen (A). It was as though the child had learned that a certain motor activity would reinstate the missing toy. The child's concept of the object did not, at this age, extend to recognition that objects usually remain in the place where they have been most recently mentally represented.

Under certain conditions, 9- to 10-month-old infants do not show the A-not-B error (Bremner & Bryant, 2001; Marcovitch & Zelazo, 2006). If infants are allowed to search for the object immediately after seeing it hidden, the error often does not occur. But if they are forced to wait 5 or more seconds before looking, they are likely to commit the A-not-B error (Wellman, Cross, & Bartsch, 1986).

Deferred Imitation

Deferred imitation is imitation of an action that may have occurred hours, days, or even weeks earlier. Piaget believed that children demonstrate deferred imitation at the age of 18 months, when they are able to mentally represent behaviour patterns or events. For example, children will watch their parents cook and then pull out the pots and pans from the drawer and pretend to cook, starting at this age. Children may see a child at daycare throw a tantrum and be rewarded with the attention of the caregivers, and later engage in the same behaviour at home. Piaget explained that children are unable to engage in deferred imitation until 18 to 24 months because to do so requires the ability to make internal representation of that behaviour or event. In other words, when children do not have the chance to imitate behaviour they have just witnessed, they form a memory representation of that behaviour; later, they may engage in the same behaviour when in a similar situation (Jones & Herbert, 2006).

deferred imitation imitation of a behaviour that was seen earlier

Evaluation of Piaget's Theory

Piaget's theory remains a comprehensive model of infant cognition. Many of his observations of his own infants have been confirmed by others. The pattern and sequence of events he described have been observed among infants in North America, Europe, Africa, and Asia (Werner, 1988). Still, research has raised questions about the validity of many of Piaget's claims (Siegler & Alibali, 2005).

First, most researchers now agree that cognitive development is not as tied to discrete stages as Piaget suggested (Krojgaard, 2005; Siegler & Alibali, 2005). Although later developments seem to build on earlier ones, the process appears to be more gradual than discontinuous.

Second, Piaget emphasized the role of maturation, almost to the point of excluding adult and peer influences on cognitive development. However, these interpersonal influences have been shown to play important roles in cognitive development (Kuhn, 2007; Maratsos, 2007).

Third, Piaget appears to have underestimated infants' competence (Siegler & Alibali, 2005). For example, infants display object permanence earlier than he believed (Wang, Baillargeon, & Paterson, 2005). Moreover, Piaget's argument that deferred imitation appeared around the age of 18 months has been contradicted by other research (Barr, Rovee-Collier, & Campanella, 2005; Campanella & Rovee-Collier, 2005) that has indicated infants as young as 6 months of age could imitate an action after a time delay. For example, a child can observe an adult push a button to produce a beep and after a time delay, they can reproduce the same action. One day later, when the infants were given a chance to play with the same objects, many of them imitated the actions they had witnessed.

Thanks in part to computer technology, investigators have found new ways to measure object permanence. Instead of assessing object permanence as the infant's response to objects in their reach, researchers may measure an infant's visual response to objects that are hidden; this is based on the assumption that infants will look at things longer if they have never been seen before. The results of various studies indicate that infants as young as 3.5 months are aware that objects exist even when hiding behind a screen, can retain the height of the object as it should appear behind the screen, and were surprised in a situation when objects should have appeared but were blocked (Baillargeon & Devos, 1991; Rosander & Hofsten, 2004). Thus, infants as young as 3.5 months demonstrate some object permanence although it may be limited to the specific experimental situation. By 1 year of age however, infants have a greater understanding of object permanence in many different situations than they did when they were younger.

LO2 Information Processing

The information-processing approach to cognitive development focuses on how children manipulate or process information that is coming in from the environment or is already stored in the mind. Infants' tools for processing information include their memory and imitation.

Infants' Memory

Many of the cognitive capabilities of infants—recognizing the faces of familiar people, developing object permanence, and, in fact, learning in any form—depend on one critical aspect of cognitive development: their memory (Daman-Wasserman et al., 2006; Hayne & Fagen, 2003). Even newborns demonstrate their memory for stimuli for which they have previously been exposed. For example, as mentioned in Chapter 2, neonates adjust their rate of sucking to hear a recording of their mother reading a story she had read aloud during the last weeks of pregnancy, (DeCasper & Fifer, 1980; DeCasper & Spence, 1991). Much of our current understanding of infant perceptions and cognitive abilities comes from the study of the visual habituation–dishabituation model. Habituation takes place when the infant encodes information and begins to predict outcomes. Dishabituation takes place when memory performance becomes apparent. In other words, infants disengage from the source of interest and shift their attention to something new (Kavšek, 2012).

Memory improves dramatically between 2 and 6 months of age and then again by 12 months (Pelphrey et al., 2004; Rose, Feldman, & Jankowski, 2001). The improvement may indicate that older infants are more capable than younger ones at encoding information so that it may be stored, retrieving information already stored, or both (Hayne & Fagen, 2003).

Imitation: Infant See, Infant Do?

Imitation is the basis for much of human learning. To assist infants remembering imitated acts, a practice period enhances success of deferred imitation. But in one study, 12-month-old infants were prevented from practising the behaviour they imitated. However, they were able to demonstrate it 4 weeks later, suggesting that they had mentally represented the act (Klein & Meltzoff, 1999).

DID YOU KNOW?

A 1-hour-old infant may imitate an adult who sticks out his or her tongue.

True, but that imitation may be reflexive rather than an action of choice.

But infants can imitate certain actions at a much earlier age. Neonates only 0.7 to 71 hours old have been found to imitate adults who open their mouths or stick out their tongues (Meltzoff & Prinz, 2002; Rizzolatti et al., 2002; see Figure 5.2).

Before you become too impressed with this early imitative ability of neonates, you should know that some studies have not found imitation in early infancy (Abravanel & DeYong, 1991). One key factor may be the infants' age. Most of the studies that find imitation were done with very young infants—up to

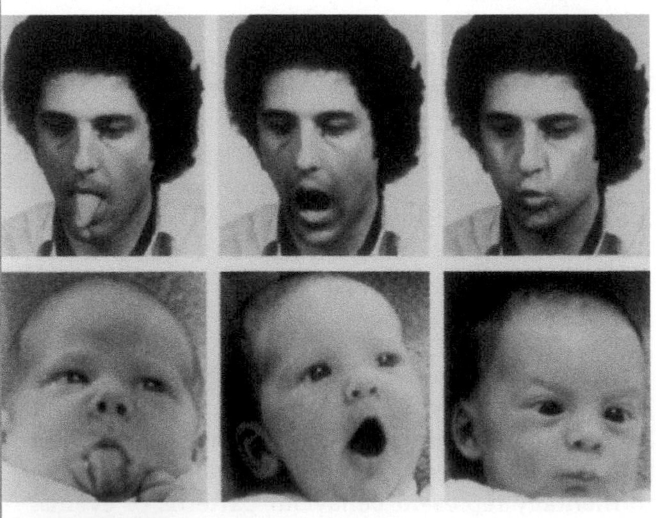

FIGURE 5.2

Imitation in Infancy

These 2- to 3-week-old infants are imitating the facial gestures of an adult experimenter. How are we to interpret these findings? Can we say that the infants "knew" what the experimenter was doing and "chose" to imitate the behaviour, or is there another explanation?

Source: A. N. Meltzoff and M. K. Moore. (1977). Imitation of facial and manual gestures by human neonates. *Science, 198*, 75–78.

R. Eko Bintoro/iStockphoto.com

Photo by Stephen Ausmus/Courtesy of the USDA

The Bayley scales measure an infant's mental and motor development.

2 weeks old—whereas the studies that do not find imitation tended to use older infants. Therefore, the imitation of neonates is likely to be reflexive. Thus, imitation might disappear when reflexes are "dropping out" and then re-emerge when it has a firmer cognitive footing.

Why might newborns possess some sort of imitation reflex? Answers lie in the realm of speculation. One possibility is that such a built-in response would contribute to the formation of caregiver–infant bonding and the survival of the newborn (Meltzoff & Prinz, 2002). Some theorists speculate that the imitation reflex is made possible by *mirror neurons* that are found in human brains. Such neurons are maintained by evolutionary forces because they enhance the probability of survival as a result of caregiving (Oztop, Kawato, & Arbib, 2006; Rizzolatti et al., 2002).

LO3 Individual Differences in Intelligence among Infants

Cognitive development does not proceed in the same way or at the same pace for all infants (Newman et al., 2006; Rose, Feldman, & Jankowski, 2001, 2005). Efforts to understand the development of infant differences in cognitive development have relied on so-called scales of infant development or infant intelligence.

Measuring cognition, or intelligence, in infants is quite different from measuring it in adults. Infants cannot, of course, be assessed by asking them to explain the meanings of words, the similarity between concepts, or the rationales for social rules. Very different kinds of items are used in the Bayley Scales of Infant Development (BSID), first constructed in 1933 by psychologist Nancy Bayley, and now in its third edition (BSID III). This is one of the most commonly used tests of cognitive functioning in high risk and premature infants (Hack et al., 2005).

The Bayley Scale for Infant and Toddler Development, 3rd edition (Bayley-III), currently consists of 178 mental-scale items and 111 motor-scale items. The mental scale assesses verbal communication, perceptual skills, learning and memory, and problem-solving skills. The motor scale assesses gross motor skills, such as standing, walking, and climbing, and fine motor skills, as shown by the ability to manipulate the hands and fingers. Also used is a behaviour rating scale that is based on an examiner's observation of the child during the test. The behaviour rating scale assesses attention span, goal directedness, persistence, and aspects of social and emotional development.

This test is often used with preterm infants to determine their neurological functioning and for screening of a developmental delay. It remains unclear how well results obtained on the Bayley-III completed in infancy predict intellectual functioning at later ages. For example, only 18% of infants who had low scores on the Bayley-II Mental Development Index (MDI) had low scores at 5 years of age (Colombo & Carlson, 2012; Hack et al., 2005).

DID YOU KNOW?

Psychologists can begin to measure intelligence in infancy.

This is true, but they use different test items from those used with older children and adults. We can't ask infants to explain themselves, so we need to observe their behaviours and draw conclusions instead.

EMERGING CANADA

Baby Einstein and other popular baby DVDs are designed and marketed to promote infant learning. Dr. Hoecker (2011), of the Mayo Clinic, argues that these videos might grab the child's attention but they aren't likely to promote development. A 2007 study of children aged 8 to 16 months concluded that infants exposed to baby DVDs scored lower on language development than children with no screen time. Another study in 2009 of 2-month-olds to 4-year-olds indicated that turning on the television actually reduces interaction time between caregivers and children. Reading does boost language ability for babies and toddlers. If you enjoy baby DVDs, then it might be a productive way to spend time with a child but be cautious about their value and use.

Sebcz/Dreamstime.com

Testing Infants: Why and with What?

As you can imagine, testing an infant is no easy matter. The test items must be administered on a one-to-one basis by a psychometrist, someone specially trained to administer test questions; and it can be difficult to judge whether the infant is showing the targeted response. Why, then, do we test infants?

One reason is to screen infants for atypical development. A psychometrist may be able to detect early signs of sensory or neurological problems, as suggested by development of visual–motor coordination. In addition to the Bayley scales, several other tests have been developed to screen infants for such difficulties, including the Brazelton Neonatal Behavioural Assessment Scale (see Chapter 3) and the Denver Developmental Screening Test.

Instability of Intelligence Scores Attained in Infancy

Researchers have also tried to use infant scales to predict development, but this effort has been unsuccessful. One study found that scores obtained during the first year of life correlated moderately at best with scores obtained a year later (Harris et al., 2005). Certain items on the Bayley scales do appear, however, to predict related intellectual skills later in childhood. For example, Bayley items measuring infant motor skills predict subsequent fine motor and visual–spatial skills at 6 to 8 years of age (Siegel, 1992). Bayley language items also predict language skills at the same age (Siegel, 1992).

One study found that the Bayley scales and socio-economic status were able to predict cognitive development among low-birth-weight children from 18 months to 4 years of age (Dezoete, MacArthur, & Tuck, 2003). But overall scores on the Bayley and other infant scales apparently do not reliably predict school grades or IQ scores among schoolchildren (Colombo, 1993). Perhaps the sensorimotor test items used during infancy are not strongly related to the verbal and symbolic items used to assess intelligence at later ages.

The overall conclusion seems to be that the Bayley scales can identify gross lags in development and relative strengths and weaknesses. However, they are only moderate predictors of intelligence scores even one year later, and are still poorer predictors of scores taken beyond longer stretches of time.

Dung Vo Trung/Eurelios/Look at Sciences/Science Photo Library

Infant intelligence scores are unstable; that is, a score in infancy cannot be considered to have accurate predictive power for intelligence scores obtained in childhood.

Use of Visual Recognition Memory

In a continuing effort to find aspects of intelligence and cognition that might remain consistent from infancy through later childhood, researchers have recently focused on visual recognition memory (Courage, Howe, & Squires, 2004). **Visual recognition memory** is the ability to discriminate previously seen objects from novel objects. This procedure is based on habituation.

Let us consider longitudinal studies of this type. Susan Rose and her colleagues (Rose, Feldman, & Wallace, 1992) showed 7-month-old infants pictures of two identical faces. After 20 seconds, the pictures were replaced with one picture of a new face and a second picture of a familiar face. The amount of time the infants spent looking at each face in the second set of pictures was recorded. Some infants spent more time looking at the new face than at the familiar face, suggesting that they had better memory for visual stimulation. The children were given standard IQ tests every 12 months from ages 1 through 6 years. It was found that the children with greater visual recognition memory later attained higher IQ scores. Rose and her colleagues (2001) also showed that, as children grow older, their visual recognition memory remains stable. This is one of many aspects that determine our intelligence.

Moreover, it appears that the speed at which a baby habituates to an object it has seen numerous times is related to intelligence, as visual recognition is an important determinant of intelligence. Babies will look longer at novel as opposed to familiar stimuli. Thus, Joseph Fagan developed a test of visual information processing called the Fagan Test of Infant Intelligence (Fagan, 2005; Fagan & Detterman, 1992). This test is especially useful for infants with special needs who may have difficulty performing the items found on the Bayley scales. Research has found a modest correlation between infant visual recognition memory and intelligence in childhood (Rose, Feldman & Jankowski, 2004) as well as a relationship between information processing ability in infancy (6 to 12 months) and academic achievement in adulthood (age 21 years) Fagan, Holland, and Wheeler (2007). Taken together, measures of intelligence in infancy may be useful as screening devices (the Bayley Scales of Infant Development) and hold promising avenues for predicting intelligence in later years (Fagan Test of Infant Intelligence).

LO4 Language Development

In physical development, the most dramatic developments come early—fast and furious—long before the child is born. Language does not come quite as early, and its development may not seem quite so fast and furious. Nevertheless, during the years of infancy, most children develop from creatures without language to little people who understand nearly all the things that are said to them and who relentlessly sputter words and simple sentences for everyone to hear.

visual recognition memory the kind of memory shown in an infant's ability to discriminate previously seen objects from novel objects

prelinguistic vocalizations made by the infant before the use of language

cooing prelinguistic vowel-like sounds that reflect feelings of positive excitement

babbling the child's first vocalizations that have the sounds of speech

Early Vocalizations

Children develop language according to an invariant sequence of steps, or stages, as outlined in Table 5.2. Infants typically begin with **prelinguistic** vocalizations. True words are symbols of objects and events. Prelinguistic vocalizations, such as cooing and babbling, do not represent objects or events, so infant crying is not a primitive form of language.

Newborns, as parents are well aware, have an unlearned but highly effective form of verbal expression: crying and more crying. Crying is about the only sound that infants make during the first month. During the second month, infants begin **cooing**. Infants use their tongues when they coo. For this reason, coos are more articulated than cries. Coos are often vowel-like and may resemble extended "oohs" and "ahs." Cooing appears to be linked to feelings of pleasure or positive excitement. Infants tend not to coo when they are hungry, tired, or in pain.

Cries and coos are innate but can be modified by experience (Volterra et al., 2004). When parents respond positively to cooing, such as by talking to their infants, smiling at them, and imitating them, cooing increases. Early parent–child "conversations," in which parents respond to coos and then pause as the infant coos, may foster infant awareness of taking turns as a way of verbally relating to other people.

By about 8 months of age, cooing decreases markedly. Somewhere between 6 and 9 months, children begin to babble. **Babbling** is the first vocalizing that sounds like human speech. When babbling, infants frequently combine consonants and vowels, as in *ba*, *ga*, and, sometimes, the much valued *dada*

DID YOU KNOW?

Infant crying is not a primitive form of language.

Cries do not represent objects or events, so they are not considered language.

TABLE 5.2

Milestones in Language Development in Infancy

Approximate Age	Vocalization and Language
Birth	Cries
12 weeks	Cries less Smiles when talked to and nodded at Engages in squealing and gurgling sounds (cooing) Sustains cooing for 15–20 seconds
16 weeks	Responds to human sounds more definitely Turns head, searching for the speaker Chuckles occasionally
20 weeks	Cooing becomes interspersed with consonant-like sounds Vocalizations differ from the sounds of mature language
6 months	Cooing changes to single-syllable babbling Neither vowels nor consonants have fixed pattern of recurrence Common utterances sound like *ma*, *mu*, *da*, or *di*
8 months	Continuous repetition (reduplication) enters into babbling Patterns of intonation become distinct Utterances can signal emphasis and emotion
10 months	Vocalizations mixed with sound play, such as gurgling and bubble blowing Effort made to imitate sounds made by others, with mixed success
12 months	Identical sound sequences replicated more often Words (e.g., *mama* or *dada*) emerge Many words and requests understood (e.g., "Show me your eyes")
18 months	Repertoire of 3–50 words Explosive vocabulary growth Babbling consists of several syllables with intricate intonation Little effort to communicate information Little joining of words into spontaneous two-word utterances Understanding of nearly everything spoken
24 months	Vocabulary more than 50 words, naming everything in the environment Spontaneous creation of two-word sentences Clear efforts to communicate

Note: Ages are approximations. Slower development does not necessarily indicate language problems.

Source: © Cengage Learning; Table items adapted from Lenneberg (1967), pp. 128–130.

(Stoel-Gammon, 2002). At first, *dada* is purely coincidental (sorry, you dads), despite the family's jubilation over hearing it.

In verbal interactions between infants and adults, the adults frequently repeat the syllables produced by their infants. They are likely to say *dadada* or *bababa* instead of simply *da* or *ba*. Such redundancy apparently helps infants discriminate these sounds from others and further encourages them to imitate their parents (Elkind, 2007; Tamis-LeMonda et al., 2006).

echolalia the automatic repetition of sounds or words

intonation the use of pitches of varying levels to help communicate meaning

receptive vocabulary the number of words a person understands

expressive vocabulary the number of words a person can use in the production of language

> Most infants develop from creatures without language to little people who understand nearly all the things that are said to them.

After infants have been babbling for a few months, parents often believe that their children are having conversations with themselves. At 10 to 12 months, infants tend to repeat syllables, showing what linguists refer to as echolalia. Parents overhear them going on and on, repeating consonant–vowel combinations (*ah-bah-bah-bah-bah*), pausing, and then switching to other combinations. Because of the repetition of sounds or words, echolalia is often called "parroting." Echolalia is part of normal development; for example, infants and children may repeat parts of songs, conversations and other sounds. Infants outgrow this phase by the age of 30 months (Stokes, n.d.). Infants and children who are diagnosed with autism spectrum disorder or Tourette syndrome, however, often display echolalia well past this age range (Stokes, n.d.).

Toward the end of the first year, infants use patterns of rising and falling intonation that resemble the sounds of adult speech. It may sound as though the infant is trying to speak the parents' language. For example, if our pitch rises at the end of a sentence, we assume someone is asking a question. If our pitch falls, we believe the person is making a statement. Infants are able to make use of intonation as early as 6 to 12 months of age.

Development of Vocabulary

Vocabulary development refers to the child's learning of the meanings of words. In general, children's receptive vocabulary development outpaces their expressive vocabulary development (Lickliter, 2001; Ouellette, 2006). In other words, at any given time, they can understand more words than they can use. One study, for example, found that 12-month-olds could speak an average of 13 words but could comprehend the meaning of 84 (Tamis-LeMonda et al., 2006). Infants usually understand much

DID YOU KNOW?

Albert Einstein did not talk until the age of 3.

A child's first word typically is spoken between the ages of 11 and 13 months, but anywhere between 8 and 18 months is considered normal. But slower development does not necessarily indicate language problems.

of what others are saying well before they themselves utter any words. Their ability to segment speech sounds into meaningful units—or words—before 12 months is a good predictor of their vocabulary at 24 months (Newman et al., 2006).

Kevin Reid/Getty Images

Infants have a rapidly expanding vocabulary that helps them identify objects in their environment.

The Child's First Words

Ah, that long-awaited first word! What a milestone! Sad to say, many parents miss it. They are not quite sure when their infants utter their first word, often because the first word is not pronounced clearly or because pronunciation varies from usage to usage.

A child's first word typically is spoken between the ages of 11 and 13 months, but a range of 8 to 18 months is considered normal (Hoff, 2006; Tamis-LeMonda et al., 2006). First words tend to be brief, consisting of one or two syllables. Each syllable is likely to consist of a consonant followed by a vowel. Vocabulary acquisition is slow at first. It may take children 3 or 4 months to achieve a vocabulary of 10 to 30 words after the first word is spoken (de Villiers & de Villiers, 1999).

By about 18 months of age, children may be producing up to 50 words. Many of them are quite familiar, such as *no, cookie, mama, hi,* and *eat*. Others, such as *all gone* and *bye-bye,* may not be found in the dictionary, but they function as words. That is, they are used consistently to symbolize the same meaning.

More than half (65%) of children's first words make up "general nominals" and "specific nominals" (Hoff, 2006; Nelson, 1973). General nominals are similar to nouns in that they include the names of classes of objects (*car, ball*), animals (*doggy, cat*), and people (*boy, girl*), but they also include both personal and relative pronouns (*she, that*). Specific nominals are proper nouns, such as *Daddy* and *Rover*. Words expressing movement are frequently found in early speech.

At about 18 to 22 months of age, children have a rapid burst in vocabulary (Tamis-LeMonda et al., 2006). The child's vocabulary may increase from 50 to more than 300 words in only a few months. This vocabulary spurt could also be called a naming explosion because almost 75% of the words added during this time are nouns. The rapid pace of vocabulary growth continues through the preschool years, with children acquiring an average of nine new words per day (Hoff, 2006).

referential language style use of language primarily as a means of labelling objects

expressive language style use of language primarily as a means of engaging in social interaction

overextension use of words in situations in which their meanings become extended

Referential and Expressive Styles in Language Development

Some children prefer a referential approach in their language development, whereas others take a more expressive approach (Hoff, 2006; Nelson, 1981). Children who show a **referential language style** use language primarily to label objects in their environment. Children who use an **expressive language style** use language primarily to engage in social interactions (Tamis-LeMonda et al., 2006).

Overextension

Young children try to talk about more objects than they have words for. To accomplish their linguistic feats, children often extend the meaning of one word to refer to things and actions for which they do not have words (McDonough, 2002). This process is called **overextension**. Eve Clark (1973, 1975) studied diaries of infants' language development and found that overextensions are generally based on perceived similarities in function or form between the original object or action and the new one. She provides the example of the word *mooi*, which one child originally used to designate the moon. The child then overextended *mooi* to designate

holophrase
a single word that is used to express complex meanings

telegraphic speech
type of speech in which only the essential words are used

syntax
the language rules for placing words in an order to form sentences

all round objects, including the letter o and cookies and cakes. Overextensions gradually pull back to their proper references as the child's vocabulary and ability to classify objects develop (McDonough, 2002). Another common example is a child using the word *dog* to refer to other animals they see, including pets or small animals at the zoo.

Holophrases

Holophrases are single words that are used to express complex meanings. For example, *Mama* may be used by the child to signify meanings as varied as "There goes Mama," "Come here, Mama," and "You are Mama." Most children readily teach their parents what they intend by augmenting their holophrases with gestures, intonations, and reinforcers. That is, they act delighted when parents do as requested and howl when they do not (Tamis-LeMonda et al., 2006). Infants are between the ages of 9 to 18 months when holophrases begin.

Development of Sentences

The infant's first sentences are typically one-word utterances, but they express complete ideas and therefore can be thought of as sentences. Roger Brown (1973), a psychologist who studied children's linguistic development, referred to brief expressions that have the meanings of sentences as **telegraphic speech**. This term originated from old telegrams that were sent; their cost was determined by the number of words used. Thus, the principles of syntax were removed from all the unnecessary words. For example, the telegram "Home Tuesday" might have stood for "I expect to be home on Tuesday." Similarly, only the essential words are used in children's telegraphic speech—in particular, nouns, verbs, and some modifiers.

Two-Word Sentences

When the child's vocabulary consists of 50 to 100 words (usually between 18 and 24 months of age), telegraphic two-word sentences begin to appear (Tamis-LeMonda et al., 2006). In the sentence "That ball," the words *is* and *a* are implied.

Two-word sentences, although brief and telegraphic, show understanding of **syntax** (Slobin, 2001). The child will say "Sit chair," not "Chair sit," to tell a parent to sit in a chair. The child will say "My shoe," not "Shoe my," to show possession. "Mommy go" means Mommy is leaving, whereas "Go Mommy" expresses the wish for Mommy to go away. See Figure 5.3 for samples of the average number of morphemes used in toddler communication.

Speech and Language Delays

Although infants will start talking at different rates, there are indicators when speech and language development is atypical and requires further investigation. Close attention should be given to the following signs:

- Doesn't smile or interact with others (birth–3 months)
- Doesn't babble (4–7 months)
- Makes few sounds (7–12 months)
- Does not use gestures (e.g., waving, pointing) (7–12 months)
- Doesn't understand what others say (7 months–2 years)
- Says only a few words (12–18 months)
- Doesn't put words together to make sentences (1.5–2 years)
- Says fewer than 50 words (2 years) (American Speech Language Hearing Association, n.d.)

If a child has a speech or language delay, there are several resources that are available for support in Canada, such as the College of Audiologists and Speech–Language Pathologists of Ontario or other provinces (http://www.caslpo.com) and Speech–Language and Audiology Canada (http://www.sac-oac.ca/public/home).

Theories of Language Development

Billions of children have learned the languages spoken by their parents and have passed them down, with minor changes, from generation to generation. But

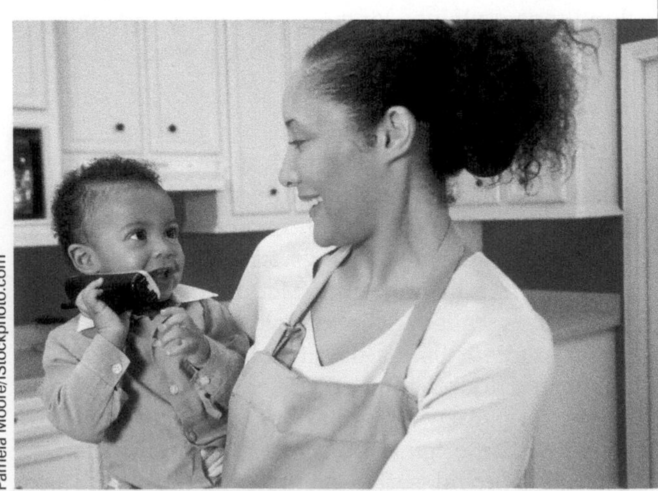

Pamela Moore/iStockphoto.com

Language development in young children is enhanced when caregivers engage the infant "in conversation."

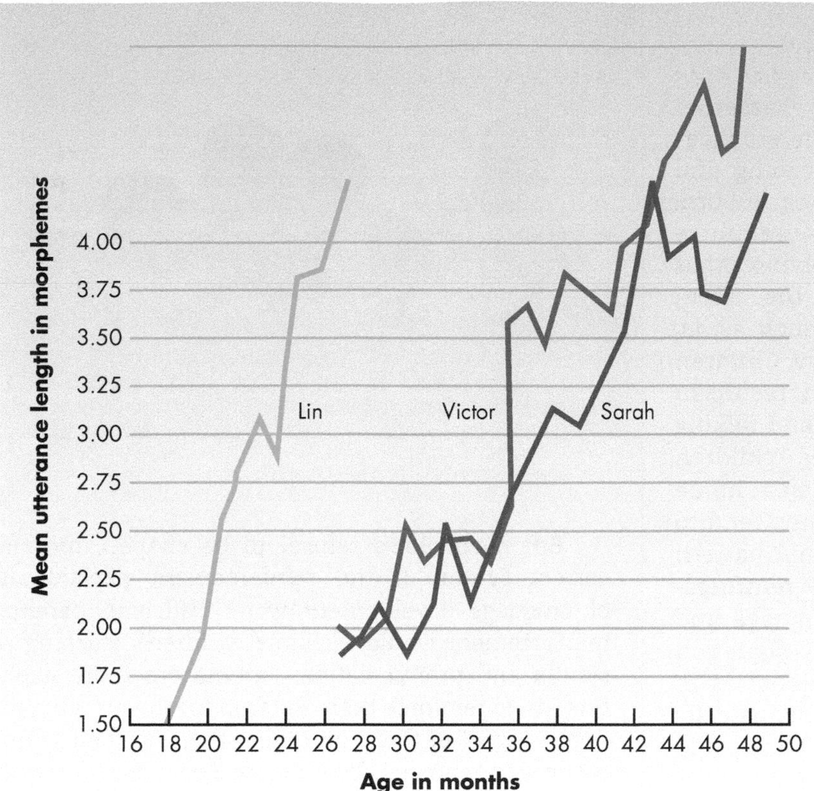

FIGURE 5.3

Mean Length of Utterance for Three Children

The mean length of utterance (MLU) increases rapidly once speech begins.

Source: © Cengage Learning

how do they do so? In discussing this question—and so many others—we refer to the possible roles of nature and nurture. Learning theorists have come down on the side of nurture, and those who point to a basic role for nature are said to hold a nativist view.

Views that Emphasize Nurture

Learning plays an obvious role in language development. Children who are reared in English-speaking homes learn English, not Japanese or Russian. Learning theorists usually explain language development in terms of imitation and reinforcement.

The Role of Imitation

From a social cognitive perspective, parents serve as **models**. Children learn language, at least in part, by observation and imitation. Many vocabulary words, especially nouns and verbs, are learned by imitation. But imitative learning does not explain why children spontaneously utter phrases and sentences that they have never heard (Tamis-LeMonda et al., 2006). Parents, for example, are unlikely to model utterances such as "Bye bye sock" and "All gone Daddy" but children say them. And children sometimes steadfastly avoid imitating certain language forms suggested by adults, even when the adults are insistent. Note the following exchange between 2-year-old Ben and a very frustrated adult (Kuczaj, 1982, p. 48):

Ben: I like these candy. I like they.

Adult: You like them?

Ben: Yes, I like they.

Adult: Say them.

Ben: Them.

Adult: Say "I like them."

Ben: I like them.

Adult: Good.

Ben: I'm good. These candy good too.

Adult: Are they good?

Ben: Yes. I like they. You like they?

Ben is not resisting the adult because of obstinacy. He does repeat "I like them" when asked to do so. But when given the opportunity afterward to construct the object *them*, he reverts to using the subjective form *they*. Ben is likely at this period in his development to use his (erroneous) understanding of syntax spontaneously to actively produce his own language, rather than just imitate a model.

models
in learning theory, those whose behaviours are imitated by others

extinction decrease in the frequency of a response due to the absence of reinforcement

shaping gradual building of complex behaviour by reinforcing successive approximations to the target behaviour

The Role of Reinforcement

B. F. Skinner (1957) asserted that prelinguistic vocalizations such as cooing and babbling may be inborn. But parents reinforce children's babbling that approximates the form of real words, such as *da*, which, in English, resembles *dog* or *daddy*. Children do, in fact, increase their babbling when it results in adults smiling at them, stroking them, and talking to them. As the first year progresses, children babble the sounds of the language spoken at home with increasing frequency; foreign sounds tend to drop out. The behaviourist explains this pattern of changing frequencies in terms of reinforcement of the sounds of the adults' language and extinction of foreign sounds. Another explanation is that children actively attend to the sounds in their linguistic environments and are intrinsically motivated to utter them. For example, when a child babbles and it sounds like a common word, caregivers become ecstatic and say that word repeatedly so as to reinforce the child's behaviour. As a result, the child repeats the word.

From Skinner's perspective, children acquire their early vocabularies through shaping. That is, parents require that children's utterances to be progressively closer to actual words before they are reinforced. In support of Skinner's position, research has shown that reinforcement accelerates the growth of vocabulary in children (August et al., 2005; Kroeger & Nelson, 2006).

Jay Directo/AFP/Getty Images

To enhance language growth, let the child guide the interaction. Toddler: "My doll!" Caregiver: "Yes, your doll is pretty."

Nancy Brown/Getty Images

But recall Ben's refusal to be shaped into the correct syntax. If the reinforcement explanation of language development were sufficient, parents' reinforcement would facilitate children's learning of syntax and pronunciation. Parents are more likely, though, to reinforce their children for the accuracy, or "truth value," of their utterances than for their grammatical correctness according to Roger Brown (1973). The child who points down and states, "The grass is purple," is not likely to be reinforced, despite correct syntax. But the enthusiastic child who shows her empty plate and blurts out, "I eated it all up," is likely to be reinforced, despite the grammatical incorrectness of "eated."

Learning theory cannot account for the invariant sequences of language development and for children's spurts in acquisition. The types of questions used, passive versus active sentences, and so on, always emerge in the same order.

On the other hand, aspects of the child's language environment do influence the development of language. Studies show that language growth in young children is enhanced when adults use "Motherese" (see the box entitled "Motherese" on page 97) when speaking to their child, read to their child regularly, are attuned to their child's language development, talk to their child often, ask questions to encourage further dialogue, and are engaged. For example, adults relate their speech to the child's utterance by saying, "Yes, your doll is pretty," in response to the child's statement, "My doll" (Tamis-LeMonda et al., 2006).

DID YOU KNOW?

You can advance children's development of pronunciation by correcting their errors.

Maybe, but their vocabulary will not develop as rapidly if you focus on pronunciation.

Motherese

Adults influence the language development of infants through the use of baby talk, or "Motherese," known more technically as child-directed speech, or infant-directed speech. But Motherese is a misnamed term because grandparents, fathers, siblings, and older children also use Motherese when talking to infants (Kidd & Bavin, 2007; Snedeker, Geren, Shafto, 2007). In fact, one study found that women often talk to their pets in Motherese (Prato-Previde, Fallani, & Valsecchi, 2006). Motherese occurs in languages as varied as Arabic, English, Comanche, Italian, French, German, Xhosa (an African language), Japanese, and Mandarin Chinese (Nonaka, 2004; Trainor & Desjardins, 2002).

Jonas Unruh/iStockphoto.com

Many individuals worry that speaking in Motherese will prevent their child from learning adult speech due to the lack of modelling. They also worry that their grammar will be restricted due to the use of Motherese (Eisenbeiss, 2015). However, it has been found that the short, simple sentences and high pitches used are more likely to produce a response from the child and enhance vocabulary development than complex sentences and lower-pitched speech. Children who hear their utterances repeated and recast seem to learn from the adults who are speaking to them (Tamis-LeMonda et al., 2001; Trevarthen, 2003). In sum, Motherese may help foster children's language development.

Motherese has several characteristics:

1. Motherese is spoken slowly, at a higher pitch, and with pauses inserted between ideas.
2. Sentences are brief.
3. Sentences use simple grammar.
4. Keywords come at the ends of sentences and are spoken in a higher and louder voice.
5. The diminutive morpheme *y* is frequently added to nouns: *Dad* becomes *Daddy*, and *horse* becomes *horsey*.
6. Adults repeat sentences several times using minor variations, as in "Show me your nose." "Where is your nose?"
7. Motherese includes reduplication. *Yummy* becomes *yummy-yummy*. *Daddy* may alternate with *Da-da*.
8. Vocabulary is concrete, referring, when possible, to objects in the immediate environment. Stuffed lions may be referred to as "kitties."
9. Objects may be overdescribed by being given compound labels. Rabbits may become "bunny rabbits," and cats may become "kitty cats."
10. Parents speak for the children, as in, "We want to take our nap now, don't we?"

© C Squared Studios/Photodisc/Getty

sensitive period the period from about 18 months to puberty when the brain is especially capable of learning language

Views that Emphasize Nature

The nativist view of language development holds that inborn factors cause children to attend to and acquire language in certain ways. From this perspective, children bring an inborn tendency in the form of neurological "prewiring" to language learning. According to Steven Pinker and Ray Jackendoff (2005), the structures that enable humans to perceive and produce language evolved in bits and pieces. Those individuals who possessed these "bits" and "pieces" were more likely to reach maturity and transmit their genes from generation to generation because communication ability may have increased their chances of survival.

> **DID YOU KNOW?**
>
> **Children are "prewired" to listen to language in such a way that they come to understand rules of grammar.**
>
> Brain development suggests a biological component to language acquisition.

Canada is increasingly becoming a multilingual society so, more than ever before, Canadian children are exposed to two or more languages. In the 2011 Canadian census, more than 200 different languages were reported as a home language, or mother tongue (Statistics Canada, 2013d). In this same census, 17.5% of Canadians reported speaking two languages at home, up from 14.2% in 2006 (Statistics Canada, 2013d). A recent study conducted by Diane Poulin-Dubois from Concordia University in Montreal concluded that the cognitive benefits to toddlers who are bilingual come much earlier than indicated by previous studies. Bilingual toddlers outperform their unilingual peers in doing tasks while being distracted. The bilingual advantage provides an enhancement in attention control (Science Daily, 2011).

The Sensitive Period

The brain is most capable and efficient at learning language during the **sensitive period**, which begins around 18 to 24 months and lasts until puberty (Clancy & Finlay, 2001; Uylings, 2006). Evidence for a sensitive period is found in some people's recovery from brain injuries. Injuries to the hemisphere that controls language (usually the left hemisphere) can

The Genie Project

The best way to determine whether people are capable of acquiring language once they have passed puberty would be to run an experiment in which one or more children were reared in such severe isolation that they were not exposed to language until puberty. Of course, for ethical reasons, such an experiment could not be conducted. However, human circumstance sometimes presents such an opportunity, such as the disturbing case history of Genie (Fromkin et al., 2004; LaPointe, 2005).

The PBS *Nova* documentary "Secret of the Wild Child" (Garmon, 1997) explores Genie's tragic life. Genie's father locked her in a small room at the age of 20 months and kept her confined until she was 13 years old. Her social contacts during this period were limited to her mother, who entered the room only to feed Genie, and her father, who beat her. When Genie was rescued, she weighed only about 27 kg (60 lb.), did not speak, had not been toilet trained, and could barely stand. Numerous physicians, psychologists, psychiatrists, and linguistic professors observed her linguistic ability and played a role in teaching her language and socialization, in what was termed the *Genie Project*. Her language development followed the normal sequence of much younger children in several ways.

Five years after her liberation, however, Genie's language remained largely telegraphic. She still showed significant problems with syntax, such as failing to reverse subjects and verbs to phrase questions. Unfortunately, when she left the hospital and was no longer cared for by the numerous people who tried to help her, she lost most of the language she had developed.

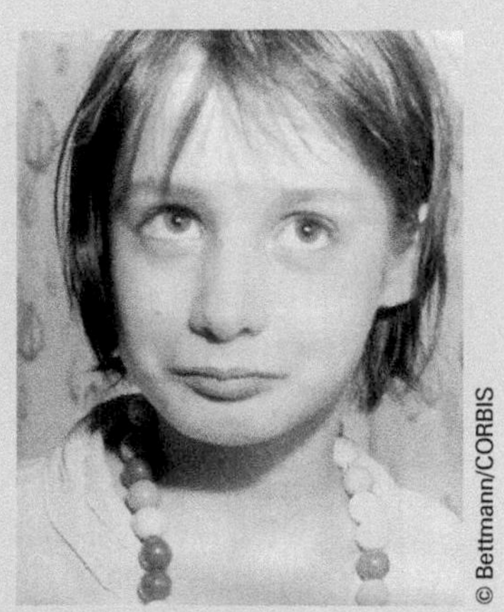
© Bettmann/CORBIS

Genie's language development provides support for the sensitive-period hypothesis, although her language problems might also be partly attributed to her years of malnutrition and abuse. Her efforts to acquire English after puberty were laborious, and the results were not favourable, when compared with the language development of many 2- and 3-year-olds. She never acquired the linguistic or social skills of an adult, perhaps as a result of what is called synaptic pruning: the synapses that could have facilitated this learning may have simply disappeared through the lack of use.

In sum, the development of language in infancy represents the interaction of environmental and biological factors. Children are born with a built-in readiness for the task of language acquisition. However, it would seem that children must also have the opportunity to hear spoken language and to interact verbally with others to be able to speak it fluently. In the next chapter, we see how interaction with others affects social development.

impair or destroy the ability to speak (Werker & Tees, 2005). But before puberty, children who have left-hemisphere injuries frequently recover a good deal of their speaking ability due to brain plasticity. In young children, left-hemisphere damage may encourage the development of language functions in the right hemisphere. But adaptation ability wanes in adolescence, when brain tissue has reached adult levels of differentiation (Snow, 2006).

Early Deprivation and the Brain

Research indicates that early deprivation has significant impact on the brain. Children who suffer from severe neglect and deprivation will have cognitive impairments that will last well into adulthood (Makinodan et al., 2012). Evidence suggests that social deprivation prevents the growth of cells that make up white matter in the brain; white matter is responsible for producing myelin, which acts as insulation allowing the transmission of long-distance messages to be sent in the brain (Science Daily, 2012). This explains why children who are raised in orphanages or who are extremely maltreated experience lasting cognitive deficits throughout their lives (see the box entitled "The Genie Project" on page 98).

STUDY TOOLS

CHAPTER 5

Located at **nelson.com/student**

- ☐ Prepare for tests with a variety of exercises and activities
- ☐ Review Key Terms Flashcards (online or print)
- ☐ Create your own study tools with Build a Summary
- ☐ Watch Observing Development videos to expand your knowledge

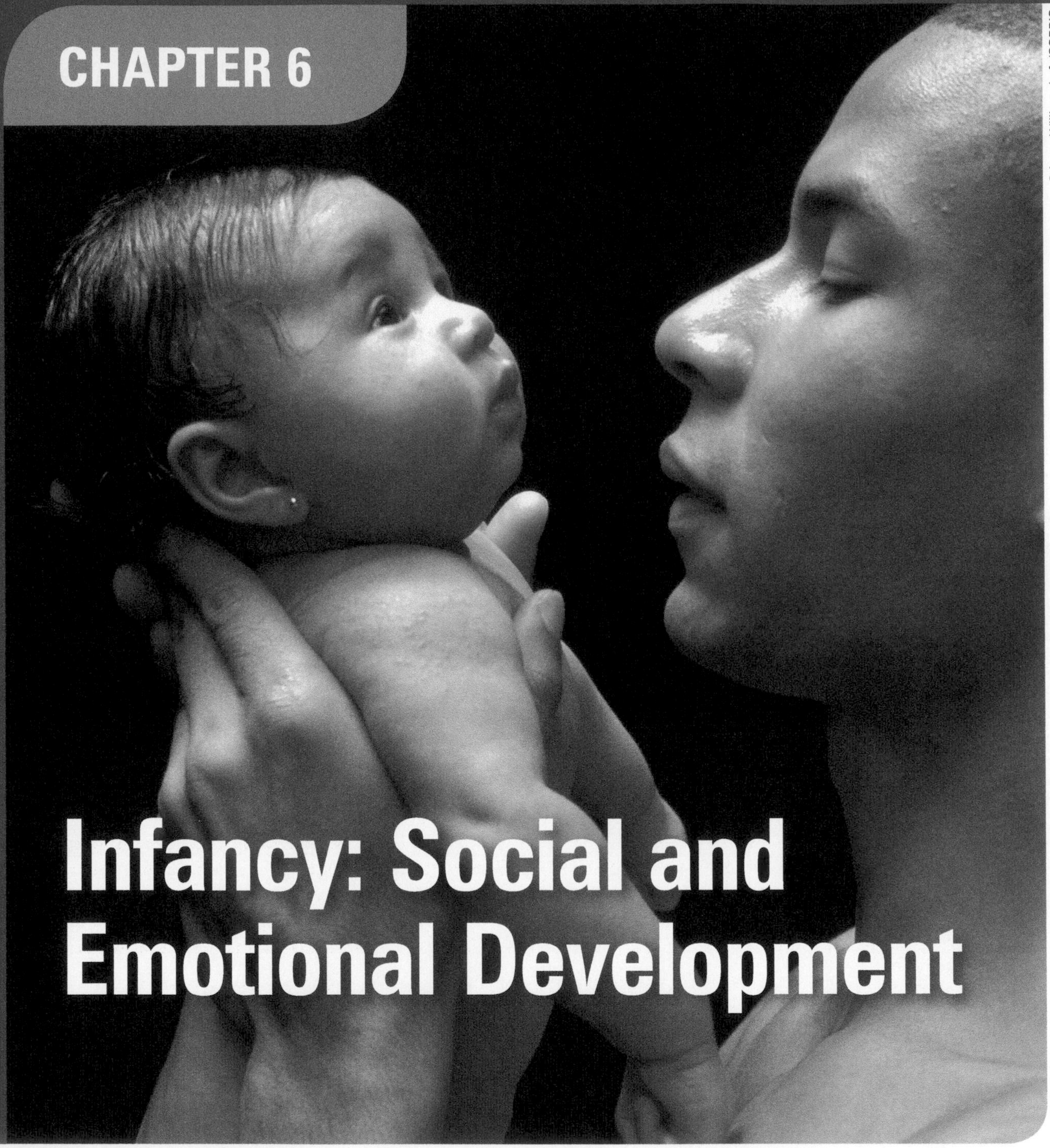

© Larry Williams/zefa/CORBIS

CHAPTER 6

Infancy: Social and Emotional Development

LEARNING OUTCOMES

- **LO1** Describe the development of attachment in infancy and theoretical views of how it evolves
- **LO2** Discuss the effects of social deprivation, abuse and neglect, and autism spectrum disorders on attachment
- **LO3** Discuss the effects of childcare on development
- **LO4** Describe the emotional development of the infant
- **LO5** Describe the personality development of the infant, focusing on the self-concept, temperament, and sex differences

> **"Babies are born with behaviours—crying, smiling, clinging—that stimulate caregiving from adults."**

As discussed in Chapter 1, Erikson's theory of psychosocial development focuses on age-based stages of development. Each stage has a specific developmental "crisis," or challenge. When the challenge is handled successfully, it leads to a sense of mastery that sets the groundwork for the next developmental challenge. When a stage is not successfully navigated, it may lead to a sense of inadequacy. During each developmental period, the potential for personal growth is high—but so is the potential for failure. We explore Erikson's first stage of psychosocial development: trust versus mistrust.

LO1 Attachment: Bonds That Endure

Attachment is what most people refer to as affection or love. Canadian-born Mary Ainsworth (1989) defines attachment as an enduring emotional bond between one animal or person and another. John Bowlby adds that attachment is essential to the survival of the infant (Bowlby, 1988). He notes that babies are born with behaviours—crying, smiling, clinging—that encourage caregiving from adults. Infants seek out attachment figures when they are scared, tired, or in pain, or when the caregiver appears inaccessible (Bowlby, 1980).

attachment
an affectional bond characterized by seeking closeness with another when distressed, especially after separation

separation anxiety
fear of separation from an attachment figure

Infants try to maintain contact with caregivers to whom they are attached. They engage in eye contact, pull and tug at them, and ask to be picked up. When they cannot maintain contact, they show separation anxiety—thrash about, fuss, cry, screech, or whine.

Several theories have been developed to explain attachment behaviour in humans and animals. Psychoanalytic theory explains that attachment is the result of oral gratification; learning theories, on the other hand, explain attachment as the consequence of being provided with care and thus being reinforced. Cognitive theory explains that attachments occur when the child has developed object permanence. The most prominent perspective today stems from ethological theory, which explains attachment as a biological need that is formed to guarantee survival.

Erikson Today

Time & Life Pictures/Getty Images

Stage 1: Basic Trust versus Mistrust (birth to 18 months)

The initial task of the ego is the development of trust. Infants are not able to care for themselves and are therefore completely dependent on primary caregivers for all of their needs. The development of trust is an ongoing challenge that will have to be reconciled throughout the lifespan, but it has particular importance during the first stage of development. Children must develop a sense that their primary caregivers will be both reliable and predictable. This occurs when the caregiver responds adequately and consistently to meet the infants' needs. The quality of care received during this period will set the stage for all other social interactions that follow. If a caregiver is unreliable or inconsistent, a sense of mistrust is established, which may become the template for future relationships.

Consider THIS

Can you spoil your baby?

Please see page 105 for a discussion on this topic.

Caregiver as a Source of Contact Comfort

Harry and Margaret Harlow conducted classic experiments to demonstrate that feeding is not critical to the attachment process, as Freud had suggested (Harlow & Harlow, 1966). In one infamous study, rhesus monkey infants were placed in cages with two surrogate mothers (see Figure 6.1). One "mother" was made from wire mesh, from which a baby bottle was extended. The other surrogate mother was made of soft, cuddly

Nina Leen/The LIFE Picture Collection/Getty Images

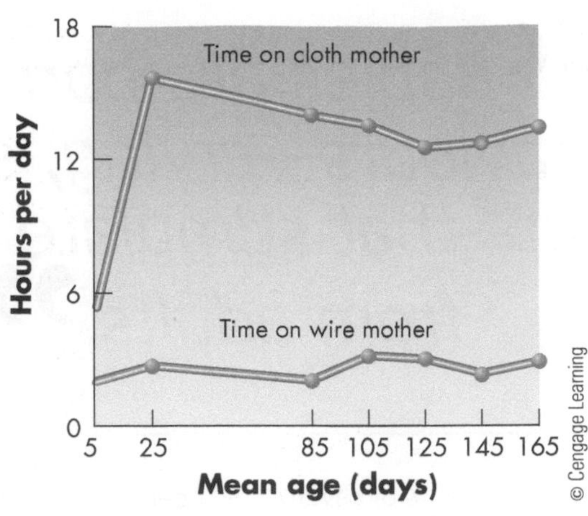

© Cengage Learning

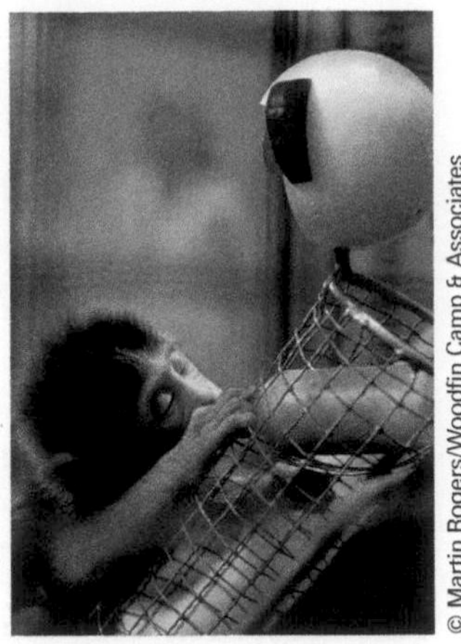
© Martin Rogers/Woodfin Camp & Associates

FIGURE 6.1

Contact Comfort

Although this rhesus monkey infant is fed by the "wire-mesh mother," it spends most of its time clinging to a soft, cuddly "terry-cloth mother."

contact comfort the pleasure derived from physical contact with another

ethologists scientists who study the behaviour patterns characteristic of various species

social smile a smile that occurs in response to a human voice or face

critical period a period during which imprinting can occur

imprinting the process by which waterfowl become attached to the first moving object they follow

pre-attachment phase lasts from birth to 6 weeks; characterized by random attachment

terry cloth. Infant monkeys spent most of their time clinging to the cloth mother, even though she did not offer food. When frightened, the monkeys were also observed running to and clutching the surrogate cloth mother until the fear passed. It was concluded that monkeys—and perhaps humans—have a need for contact comfort that is as basic as the need for food.

Ethological View of Attachment

Ethologists note that for many animals, attachment is an inborn, or instinctive, response to a specific stimulus. Some researchers theorize that a baby's cry stimulates caregiving in women. By 2 to 3 months of age, the human face begins to elicit a social smile in infants, helping to ensure survival by eliciting affection (Ainsworth & Bowlby, 1991; Bowlby, 1988). In circular fashion, the mother's social response to her infant's face can reliably produce infant smiling by 8 months of age (Jones & Hong, 2005). The pattern contributes to a mutual attachment.

In many nonhumans, attachment occurs during a critical period of life. Waterfowl become attached during this period to the first moving object they encounter. Because the image of the moving object

Inna G/Shutterstock.com

seems to become "imprinted" on the young animal, the process is termed imprinting. Another example of imprinting is when baby chicks are observed to follow their mother wherever she goes.

Ethologist Konrad Lorenz (1962, 1981) became well known when pictures of his "family" of goslings (baby geese) were made public. Lorenz acquired his "following" by being present when the goslings hatched and allowing them to follow him. The critical period for geese and ducks begins when they first engage in locomotion and ends when they develop fear of strangers. The goslings followed Lorenz persistently, ran to him when frightened, honked with distress at his departure, and tried to overcome barriers placed between them. If you substitute crying for honking, it sounds quite human.

Bowlby

Bowlby (1980) adopted the idea of a critical period from the ethological perspective and applied the concept to human infants. A critical period is a time when infants must attach to their caregivers. This occurs because infants are programmed to behave in a way that draws their caregiver's attention, such as crying, smiling, or vocalization. In turn, this behaviour increases the chance infants will receive love and protection from adults. Caregiving in humans is largely learned and not inborn. Thus, the critical period for attachment in humans extends to months or years (Ainsworth & Bowlby, 1991; Verissimo & Salvaterra, 2006).

Stages of Attachment

Bowlby (1980) identified the following four phases of attachment:

1. The initial pre-attachment phase lasts from birth to about 6 weeks and is characterized by random attachment.
2. The attachment-in-the-making phase occurs at about 6 weeks to 6 months and is characterized by preference for familiar figures.
3. The clear-cut-attachment phase occurs at about 6 or 7 months until 18 to 24 months and is characterized by intensified dependence on the primary caregiver, usually the mother.
4. Formation of reciprocal relationships occurs from 18 months until 2 years and beyond and is characterized by awareness of factors that predict the parent's return.

Internal Working Model

Based on these four phases of attachment, Bowlby (1980) said that infants develop an internal working model of attachments that includes beliefs and expectations as to whether they are worthy of love and whether others are available and able to protect or soothe them when necessary. The internal working model also includes a general belief about the self and others. Internal working models are complementary in that if a child views that caregivers are rejecting and untrustworthy, the child feels unloveable and worthless. However if the child's finds others to be consistent and caring, the infant's internal working model is that of being loveable and competent (Bretherton, Ridgeway and Cassidy, 1990). The fact that this is a *working* model indicates that the child's expectations are subject to change in the future; attachments may become more or less secure moving into adulthood.

PeopleImages/iStockphoto.com

attachment-in-the-making phase occurs from 6 weeks to 6 months; characterized by preference for familiar figures

clear-cut attachment phase occurs from 6 to 7 months and lasts until 18 to 24 months; characterized by dependence on the primary caregiver, usually the mother

formation of reciprocal relationships occurs from 18 months until 2 years and beyond; characterized by awareness of factors that predict the parent's return

internal working model a set of expectations and beliefs about the self, others, and the relationship between self and others

secure attachment a type of attachment characterized by mild distress when a caregiver leaves and being readily soothed by reunion

Patterns of Attachment

Another way to view attachments is to examine the patterns of attachment identified by Ainsworth and her colleagues (1978). The results of her work indicate that infants show either a secure attachment style or three different types of insecure attachment styles. Most North American children are securely attached (Belsky, 2006a; McCartney et al., 2004).

Ainsworth developed the strange-situation method as a way of measuring the development of attachment (see Figure 6.2). In this method, an infant is exposed to a series of separations

EMERGING CANADA

Mary (Salter) Ainsworth (1913–1999) was born in Ohio and moved to Canada when she was 5 years old. She attended the University of Toronto, where she earned her Ph.D. She was offered a teaching position at Queen's University in 1939; however, two weeks later, her offer of employment was withdrawn, as the Senate refused to appoint a woman. This refusal is not surprising, given the time period. After four years in the army, Ainsworth returned to the University of Toronto, where she met her future husband. After marriage, Ainsworth and her husband moved to England. There, she was offered a position with John Bowlby, studying the effects of early separation from mothers and personality development. She used this learning to support her naturalistic observation of attachment between caregivers and children. Ainsworth proudly considered herself a feminist, though some claimed her groundbreaking work on attachment and early caregiving was used to argue that mothers should stay at home with their children in the early years. Ainsworth commented, saying that attachment in early childhood is vital; however, if she had been blessed with the children that she had wanted, she believed she could have balanced the responsibilities of motherhood with the demands of a career (Held, 2010).

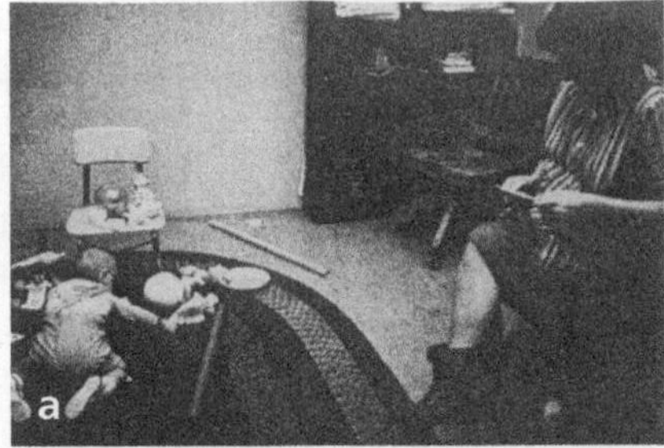
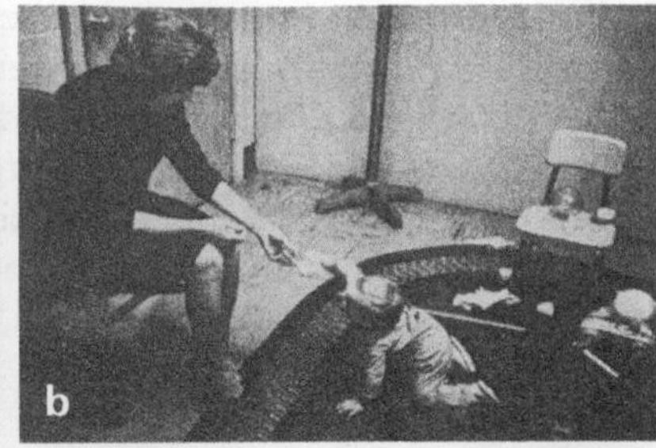

FIGURE 6.2

The Strange Situation

These historic photos show a 12-month-old child in the Strange Situation. In (a), the child plays with toys, glancing occasionally at the mother. In (b), the stranger approaches with a toy. While the child is distracted, the mother leaves the room. In (c), the mother returns after a brief absence. The child crawls to her quickly and clings to her when picked up. In (d), the child cries when the mother again leaves the room.

avoidant attachment a type of insecure attachment characterized by apparent indifference to leave-takings by and reunions with an attachment figure

anxious–ambivalent attachment a type of insecure attachment characterized by severe distress at the caregiver's departure and ambivalent behaviour at reunions

disorganized–disoriented attachment a type of insecure attachment characterized by dazed and contradictory behaviours toward an attachment figure

reactive attachment disorder characterized as disturbed or inappropriate social interactions across a number of social situations, developed before age 5 years

prototype hypothesis the belief that the initial relationship between child and caregiver serves as the foundation of all other relationships, including romantic ones

and reunions either with a caregiver (usually the mother) or with a stranger who is working with the researchers. In the test, secure infants mildly protest their mother's departure, seek interaction upon reunion, and are readily comforted by her.

Insecurity, or "insecure attachment," can be divided into two types: avoidant attachment and anxious–ambivalent attachment. Infants who show avoidant attachment are the least distressed by their mothers' departure. They play without fuss when alone and ignore their mothers upon reunion. Anxious–ambivalent babies are the most emotional. They show severe signs of distress when their mothers leave and, upon reunion, show ambivalence by alternately clinging to their mothers and pushing them away. This may be seen as a "protest" reaction in order to resume contact with the primary caregiver.

Additional categories of insecure attachment have been proposed, including disorganized–disoriented attachment, exhibited by babies who seem dazed, confused, or disoriented. They may show contradictory behaviours, such as moving toward the mother while looking away from her. This type of attachment is often developed as a result of abuse or neglect or when a healthy attachment is suddenly disrupted (Stinehart, Scott, & Barfield, 2012).

Not surprisingly, secure infants and toddlers are happier, more sociable, and more cooperative with caregivers. At ages 5 and 6, they get along better with peers and are better adjusted in school than insecure children (Belsky, 2006; McCartney et al., 2004; Spieker et al., 2003). Insecure attachment at 1 year of age predicts psychological disorders by age 17 (Sroufe, 1998; Steele, 2005a).

Attachment and Quality of Care

Attachment is related to the quality of infant care (Belsky, 2006; Coleman, 2003). Compared with parents of insecure infants, the parents of secure infants tend to be more affectionate, cooperative, and predictable. These parents also respond more sensitively to their infants' smiles and cries (Harel & Scher, 2003).

Security is also related to the infant's temperament (Belsky, 2006; Kerns et al., 2007). The mothers of so-called "difficult" children tend to be less responsive to them and report feeling more distant from them (Morrell & Steele, 2003; Stams et al., 2002). On the other hand, infants that are insecurely attached tend to be less likely to explore their environment and to develop friendships. As adults, they tend to have relationships that don't last as long and issues that affect their mental health such as depression, anxiety, and low self-esteem (McAdams, Rijsdijk, Neiderhiser, Narusyte, Shaw, Natsuaki et al., 2015). Moreover, children with a disorganized attachment style are more likely to display aggressive behaviour in childhood (Lyons-Ruth, Easterbrooks, & Davidson, 1997).

Involvement of Fathers

How involved is the average father with his children? The brief answer, in developed nations, is more so than in the past (Grossmann et al., 2002). But mothers typically engage in more interactions with their infants. Most fathers are more likely to play with their children than to feed or clean them. Fathers, more often than mothers, engage in rough-and-tumble play, whereas mothers are more likely to play games involving toys, patty-cake, and peek-a-boo (Laflamme, Pomerleau, & Malcuit, 2002).

How strongly, then, do infants become attached to their fathers? The more affectionate the interaction between father and infant, the stronger the attachment (R. A. Thompson, Easter rooks, & Padilla-Water, 2003).

Adoption and Attachment

A question that often emerges when studying attachment is whether adopted infants develop the same secure attachments as non-adoptive children. Children adopted at various ages can become securely attached to adoptive parents (Verissimo & Salvaterra, 2006). Furthermore, one study found that infants who were adopted before the age of 6 months and who were not institutionalized at birth develop the same secure attachment style as non-adoptive children. However, infants born in orphanages with little care provided do not have the opportunity to bond with a caregiver due to the lack of consistent caregiving (Strickert, 2004). This may lead to a reactive attachment disorder.

Stability of Attachment and the Prototype Hypothesis

Evidence that attachment patterns are moderately stable over the first 19 years of life has been found (Fraley, 2002). Stability of attachment styles is related to the prototype hypothesis, the idea that the initial relationship between the infant and caregiver serves as a foundation for all other relationships. Patterns of attachment tend to persist when caregiving

Consider THIS

Can you spoil your baby?

All new parents fear that they will make a mistake that will scar their child for a lifetime. Complicating the matter is that we were all raised in different families and may have grown up with varying expectations. Our early family experiences often become our parenting templates. Babies do not have language, and they use crying to communicate that they are hungry, are soggy, or simply want attention and affection.

According to Erikson, at this first stage of ego development, newborns are establishing whether their parents are reliable and predictable. But parents may be aware of looks of disapproval from expert parent observers and whispers of "You're spoiling them. They are going to rule your household." It's no wonder many new parents worry that their decisions may have long-reaching developmental effects. According to attachment theory and research, early child–parent relationships lay the foundation for children's later social, emotional, and academic functioning (Appleyard & Berlin, 2007).

Current research suggests that babies are unable to understand cause and effect until at least 8 or 10 months of age (Faris & McCarroll, 2010) and thus cannot be spoiled. In *The Attachment Parenting Book* (2001), Sears and Sears redefined a modern relationship between mother and baby; they recommended breastfeeding—into toddlerhood if desired—as well as immediately responding to a baby's cries, co-sleeping, and baby-carrying ideas.

Parents need to do their own research and also be aware of cultural beliefs that influence how quickly they respond to the demands and needs of their babies. Ultimately, parents must decide what approach to parenting works best for them.

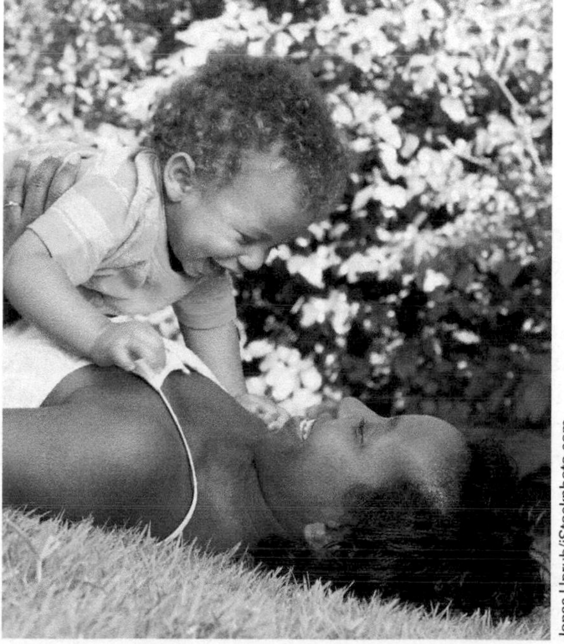

Jonas Unruh/iStockphoto.com

physical abuse any type of deliberate force that leads to non-accidental injury to any part of the body

sexual abuse the molestation or exploitation of a child

conditions remain constant (Ammaniti, Speranza, & Fedele, 2005; Karavasilis, Doyle, & Markiewicz, 2003). But children can also become less securely attached to caregivers when home life deteriorates (Belsky, 2006).

Early attachment patterns tend to endure into middle childhood, adolescence, and even adulthood (Ammaniti et al., 2005; Karavasilis et al., 2003), but they may also change from insecure to secure. For example, when caregivers improve their skills or when infants develop strong bonds with adults outside of their immediate family, insecure children are less likely to develop adjustment issues (NICHD Early Child Care Research Network, 2006). What seems to be important is that an individual's ability to work through early attachment injuries due to negative experiences with caregivers may lead to positive relationships with others in adulthood (McCarthy & Maughan, 2010).

But most infants have more than one adult caregiver and are likely to form multiple attachments: to the father, childcare providers, grandparents, and other caregivers, as well as to the mother.

LO2 When Attachment Does Not Develop

What happens when children are reared with little or no contact with caregivers, when they are abused, or when they have disorders that prevent them from attaching to their caregivers?

Social Deprivation

Studies of children reared in institutions where they receive little social stimulation from caregivers are limited because they are correlational. In other words, family factors that led to the children's placement in those institutions may also have contributed to their developmental problems. Tragic real-life examples, such as the Romanian orphans studied earlier, are thankfully few and far between. Ethical considerations prevent us from conducting experiments in which children are randomly assigned to social deprivation. Such experiments have been undertaken with rhesus monkeys, and the results are consistent with correlational studies of children.

Experiments with Monkeys

As discussed earlier, Harlow and his colleagues conducted a study of rhesus monkeys that were reared apart from their natural mothers and "raised by" wire-mesh and terry-cloth surrogate mothers. In later studies, rhesus monkeys were reared without even this questionable "social" support—without seeing any other animal, monkey, or human (Harlow, Harlow, & Suomi, 1971).

Harlow and his colleagues (1971) found that rhesus infants reared in this most solitary confinement later avoided other monkeys. They cowered in the presence of others and made little attempt to fend off attacks by other monkeys. Rather, they sat in the corner, clutching themselves and rocking back and forth. The isolated females who later bore children ignored or abused them.

Can the damage from social deprivation be overcome? When monkeys deprived for six months or more are placed with younger, 3- to 4-month-old females for a couple of hours a day, the younger monkeys attempt to interact with their deprived elders. After a few weeks, many of the deprived monkeys begin to play with the youngsters, and many eventually expand their social contacts to older monkeys (Suomi, Harlow, & McKinney,1972). Similarly, socially withdrawn 4- and 5-year-old children make gains in their social and emotional development when provided with younger playmates (Furman, Rahe, & Hartup, 1979). Although we need to be cautious when drawing connections between animal studies and the human population, similarities are indisputable.

Child Maltreatment

Child maltreatment includes physical, sexual, or emotional maltreatment, as well as neglect/failure to provide. **Physical abuse** includes any type of deliberate force that leads to non-accidental injury to any part of the body, including hitting, burning, and shaking. Often physical abuse is confused with physical discipline. **Sexual abuse** includes molestation or sexual

Anthony Asael/Art in All of Us/Getty Images

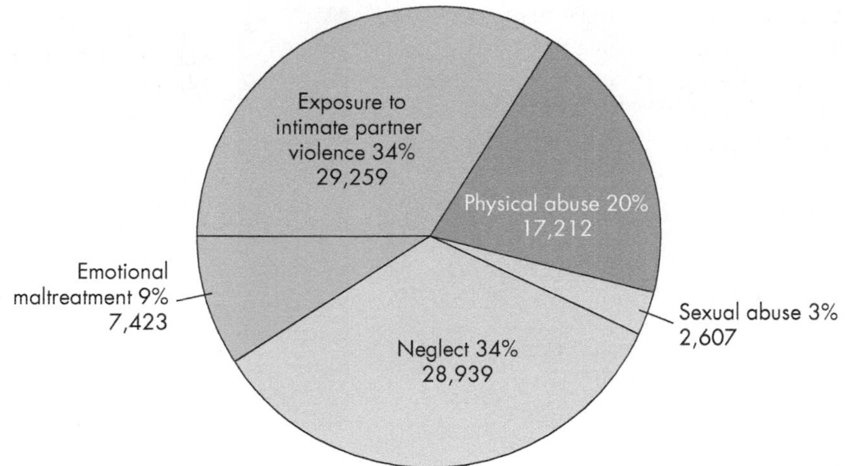

FIGURE 6.3

Primary Categories of Substantiated Child Maltreatment in Canada in 2008*

*Total estimated number of substantiated investigations is 85,440, based on a sample of 6,163 substantiated investigations.

exploitation of a child. Emotional abuse includes verbal abuse or inadequate attention, and neglect includes failing to supervise a child, which may result in the child's injury. Another category that is often not considered as abuse but requires reporting to Children's Aid is exposure to domestic violence. This includes witnessing physical abuse to a family member.

The Canadian Incidence Study (CIS) of Reported Child Abuse and Neglect is a national attempt to profile levels of child abuse in Canada. The 2008 report is the third attempt at such Canadian data collection (Public Health Agency of Canada, 2010a). However, because of the secrecy that often surrounds cases of child abuse, gathering reliable data is very difficult, if not impossible (Statistics Canada, 2013f). Figure 6.3 represents the primary categories of substantiated child maltreatment in Canada in 2008.

As can be seen in Figure 6.3, the most common categories of substantiated child maltreatment cases in Canada are neglect (34%) and exposure to intimate partner violence (34%), followed by physical abuse (20%), emotional maltreatment (9%), and sexual abuse (3%).

Figure 6.4 reports the number of child maltreatment investigations in Canada. Figure 6.5 depicts the type of child maltreatment investigations and level of substantiation of these investigations, in Canada in 2008. Together these charts give us a more complete picture of the issues associated with child abuse in Canada. Changes in rates from 1998 to 2008 may be due to changes in public awareness, changes in legislation and definitions, and/or actual changes in the rates of maltreatment.

Consequences of Child Abuse

Consequences of child abuse and neglect vary widely, depending on the circumstances of the abuse and the resilience of the child. Several studies have shown a physical consequence of abuse reflected in the relationship between abuse and poor health. The immediate emotional effects of abuse and neglect—isolation, fear, and an inability to trust—can translate into lifelong depression, relationship difficulties, and low self-esteem. Not all survivors of abuse experience these behaviour consequences; however, those who experienced abuse are more likely to encounter delinquency, risky sexual behaviour, and substance abuse. They are also more likely to display abusive behaviour themselves.

emotional abuse verbal abuse or inadequate attention

neglect failing to supervise a child, which may result in the child receiving injury

Society pays the toll of maintaining costly welfare systems to support individuals who experience

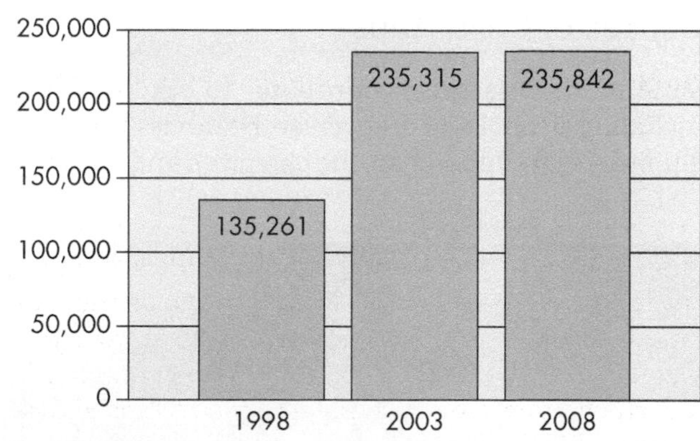

FIGURE 6.4

Number of Child Maltreatment Investigations in Canada in 1998, 2003, and 2008*

*Based on a sample of 7,633 investigations in 1998; 14,200 in 2003; and 15,980 in 2008.

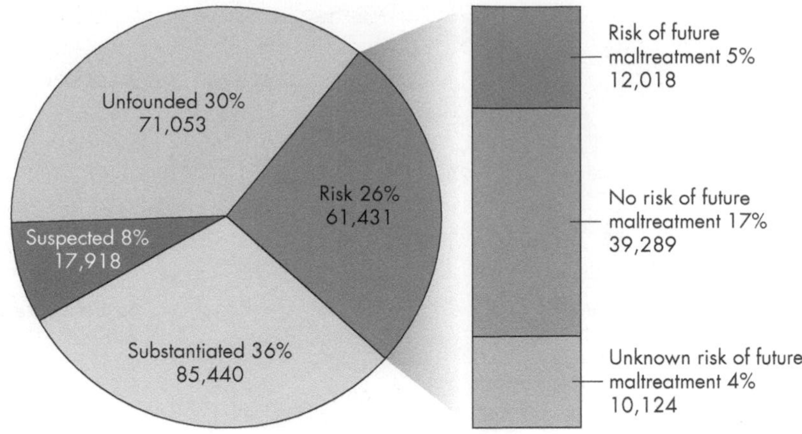

FIGURE 6.5

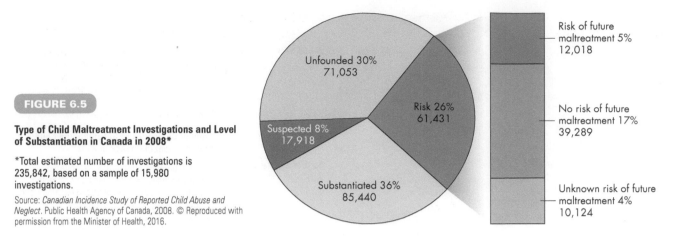

Type of Child Maltreatment Investigations and Level of Substantiation in Canada in 2008*

*Total estimated number of investigations is 235,842, based on a sample of 15,980 investigations.

Source: *Canadian Incidence Study of Reported Child Abuse and Neglect*. Public Health Agency of Canada, 2008. © Reproduced with permission from the Minister of Health, 2016.

these indirect consequences of abuse and neglect. Early intervention and proactive support reduce the impact of abuse; but the widespread effects of abuse are felt by the child, the family, and society as a whole (Child Welfare Information Gateway, 2013). For example, it has been found that children who were physically abused have poor academic performance, cognitive delays, and difficulties relating to their teachers and other adults; also, they have fewer friends and are are more aggressive than securely attached children (Kurtz, 1993; Stevenson, 1999).

DID YOU KNOW?

Thirty-two percent of Canadian adults have reported experiencing abuse at some point in their lives.

Causes of Child Abuse

Various risk factors contribute to child abuse, including alcohol and drug abuse, health issues, inadequate social supports for the caregiver, and a history

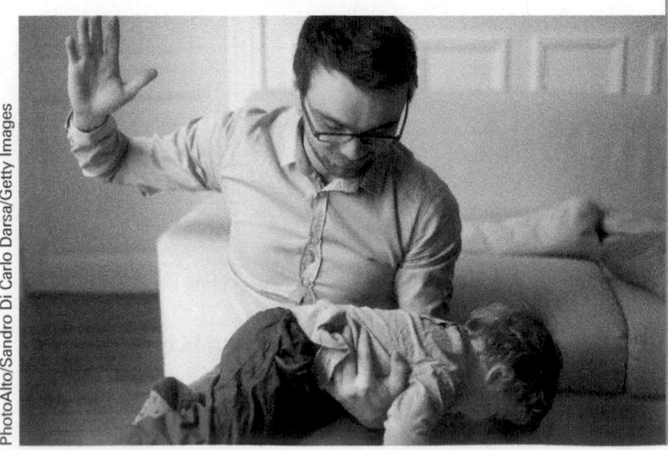

PhotoAlto/Sandro Di Carlo Darsa/Getty Images

Consider THIS

Should spanking still be legal in Canada?

The Liberal government plans to cancel a law that allows parents to spank their children as a form of discipline. According to Section 43 of the Criminal Code of Canada,

> Every schoolteacher, parent or person standing in the place of a parent is justified in using force by way of correction toward a pupil or child, as the case may be, who is under his care, if the force does not exceed what is reasonable under the circumstances. (Criminal Code, RSC 1985, c C-46 s 745)

On January 30, 2004, the Supreme Court of Canada decided that Section 43 does not violate the Canadian Charter of Rights and Freedoms (Barnett, 2008). According to the Supreme Court decision, parents may use physical punishment with these provisos: the children are between the ages of 2 to 12 years; the punishment is not degrading, humiliating, or harmful; the punishment is delivered when one is collected and not angered; and the punishment is used to correct or teach the child.

According to Schafer (2007), a well-known psychotherapist in Canada, parents hit because they have not figured out another method to discipline their children and they believe it is best thing to do. Parents need to learn alternatives to hitting and attend parent education classes to understand why the child is misbehaving in the first place. If they get to the root of the problem, they will not have to rely on a short-term solution like hitting as a way to correct the problem. The problem with the law is determining when "force does not exceed what is reasonable"; moreover, hitting of any kind is likely to be humiliating and degrading. Furthermore, "[i]t is not a radical thing to say that in a society where we don't hit people, we also don't hit children," said Mary Birdsell, executive director of Justice for Children and Youth, a nonprofit legal aid clinic in Toronto (Smith, 2015).

of domestic violence (Public Health Agency, 2010a). Many abusive parents were abused as children and have a low tolerance for what is considered normal infant or child behaviour. They misinterpret their children's behaviour as negative, and rely on coercion and physical punishment to control their behaviour (Emery, 1989). Another significant risk factor for abuse is stress due to social isolation, poverty, and conflict in the home. Children who have a developmental delay are at greatest risk. One Canadian study found that such children are 4.4 times more likely than the average child to be abused (Brown & Schormans, 2003).

DID YOU KNOW?

Abused children are at a greater risk for delinquency, risky sexual behaviour, and substance abuse in later life.

Numerous techniques have been developed to help prevent child abuse. One approach focuses on strengthening parenting skills among the general population, while providing information about abuse and providing support for families. Another approach focuses on groups at high risk for abuse, such as people living in poverty and single teenage mothers. In some programs, home visitors help new parents develop their care-giving and home-management skills (Duggan et al., 2004).

Autism Spectrum Disorders

Research indicates that 1 in 68 children will be diagnosed with autism spectrum disorder (ASD) in their lifetime (Bhat, Acharya, Adeli, Bairy et al., 2014). The diagnosis of autism as a spectrum disorder was substantially revised in 2013 with the introduction of the *Diagnostic and Statistical Manual*, 5th Edition (DSM 5). Prior to 2013, disorders such as Asperger disorder (which included many of the features of autism disorder without the language delay), Rett's disorder or childhood disintegrative disorder were diagnosed as separate conditions. This is no longer the case, as these disorders were removed from the current DSM 5 and replaced with autism spectrum disorder. This means that ASD is now diagnosed on a continuum ranging in severity. These changes were made partially to allow for greater funding to meet the needs of all children who were diagnosed with an ASD.

autism spectrum disorders (ASDs) developmental disorders characterized by impairment in social communication and social interaction across various contexts, and by repetitive, stereotyped behaviour

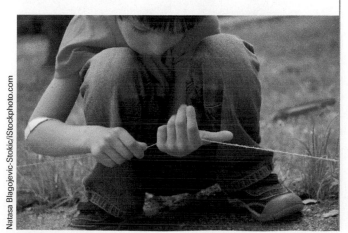

ASD is characterized by impairment in social communication and social interaction across contexts, as well as restricted, repetitive patterns of behaviour, activities, or interests. It also must be present in early childhood although presentation of many symptoms may not be evident until social demands of childhood increase (see Table 6.1). Some children with autism show limited interest in social interaction and may avoid eye contact. The disorder may accompany intellectual impairment or language impairment; it may be associated with a known medical condition or environmental factor; it may be associated with another neurological disorder and even catatonia.

ASD is four to five times more common among boys than girls (Autism Society of Canada, 2009). In Canada, the prevalence of ASD for children between the ages of 2 and 14 has increased, depending on the study, between 9.7% and 14.6% (Ouellette-Kuntz, et al., 2013). What are the possible reasons to explain this increase? Possible explanations for the increased rate of ASD include these: ASD has in fact become more common, there is greater awareness of

Natasa Blagojevic-Stokic/iStockphoto.com

TABLE 6.1

Early Signs of Autism Spectrum Disorder

Signs of autism spectrum disorder that may be evident to parents/caregivers first:

- No big smiles or other warm, joyful expressions by six months or thereafter
- No back-and-forth sharing of sounds, smiles, or other facial expressions by nine months
- No babbling by 12 months
- No back-and-forth gestures such as pointing, showing, reaching, or waving by 12 months
- No words by 16 months
- No meaningful, two-word phrases (not including imitating or repeating) by 24 months
- Any loss of speech, babbling, or social skills at any age

Source: Adapted from Autism Speaks Canada, 2016.

mutism
refusal to speak

echolalia
automatic repetition of sounds or words

the disorder among parents and professionals, and/or there are better diagnostic tools and a broader diagnosis (Coo, Ouellette-Kuntz, Lloyd, Kasmara et al., 2008).

Other features of autism include communication problems, difficulty adapting to change, and ritualistic or stereotypical behaviour (Georgiades et al., 2007). Some individuals with autism demonstrate self-harming behaviours, such as slapping their faces or biting their hands. Parents of children with autism often say they were "good babies," which usually means they made few demands. But as children with autism develop, they tend to shun traditional forms of affectionate contacts such as hugging, cuddling, and kissing.

Speech development is often delayed, with little babbling and few communicative gestures during the first year. Children with autism may show mutism, echolalia, and pronoun reversal, referring to themselves as "you" or "he." By middle childhood, approximately half of all children with autism use language, but their speech is often unusual.

The Autism Society of Canada warns that we need to distinguish between clinical descriptions and our knowledge of people who live with ASDs. Many terms are seen as labels that have limiting effects, often "medicalizing" people to the point that, despite their unique skills, abilities, and values, they become forgotten by communities or eclipsed by their "disorder." When referring to children with autism, take care to use person-first language. That is, use "child with autism" in place of the dated reference to "the autistic child," where the word *autism* defines the child.

EMERGING CANADA

Because child welfare is a provincial and territorial responsibility, each province and territory and each Aboriginal child welfare organization has a different mandate regarding the duty to report. Our laws require that anyone who has reasonable grounds to suspect child abuse must report that situation. Reasonable grounds refer to any suspicions of abuse that an average person would identify, given that person's training, background, and experience, when exercising normal and honest judgment. This duty to report is ongoing, which means that even if a previous report has been made, additional reasonable grounds must also be reported. The reporting person must communicate directly with the appropriate provincial or territorial protection agency and cannot rely on anyone else to report on his or her behalf. The reporter has no responsibility to collect any information, a task that is best left to the authorities. Reporting may be done anonymously. Parents who experience difficulty in controlling their aggressive impulses toward their children are also encouraged to call for support (Ontario Association of Children's Aid Societies, 2010).

Causes of Autism

Research evidence shows no correlation between the development of autism and deficiencies in child rearing (Mackic-Magyar & McCracken, 2004). Various lines of evidence suggest biological factors play a key role in autism. For example, very low birth weight and advanced maternal age may heighten the risk of autism (Maimburg & Vaeth, 2006). A role for genetic mechanisms is suggested by kinship studies (Constantino et al., 2006; Gutknecht, 2001). The concordance (agreement) rates for autism are about 60% among pairs of identical (MZ) twins, who fully share the same genes, compared with about 10% for pairs of fraternal (DZ) twins, whose genetic codes overlap by half (Plomin et al., 1994).

Biological factors focus on neurological involvement. Many children with autism have abnormal brain wave patterns or seizures (Canitano, 2007; Roulet-Perez & Deonna, 2006). Other researchers have found that the brains of children with autism have abnormal sensitivities to neurotransmitters

Burger/Phanie/Getty Images

Autism is a spectrum disorder. Many individuals with autism are able to thrive in a supportive environment.

such as serotonin, dopamine, acetylcholine, and norepinephrine (Bauman et al., 2006). Researchers also note unusual activity in the motor region of the cerebral cortex (Mueller et al., 2001) and less activity in some other areas of the brain (Lam, Aman, & Arnold, 2006; Penn, 2006).

Individuals with autism should be valued for their differences and not viewed as persons who should be changed.

Treatment for Autism

Treatment for autism is mainly based on principles of learning, although investigation of biological approaches is also under way (Strock, 2004).

Because children with autism show behavioural deficits, behaviour modification is used to help them develop new behaviours. Although children with autism often experience difficulty relating to people, many can be taught to accept people or animals as reinforcers, rather than objects, by pairing praise with food treats (Drasgow et al., 2001). Praise can then be used to encourage speech and social play.

The most effective treatment programs focus on individualized instruction (Rapin, 1997). In a classic study conducted by Lovaas and colleagues (1989), children with autism received more than 40 hours of one-to-one behaviour modification a week for at least two years. Significant intellectual and educational gains were reported for 9 of the 19 children (47%) in the program. Less intensive educational programs have yielded some positive results with toddlers who have autism (Stahmer, Ingersoll, & Koegel, 2004).

Researchers are studying biological approaches for the treatment of autism. For example, drugs that enhance serotonin activity (selective serotonin reuptake inhibitors, or SSRIs) can help prevent self-injury, aggressive outbursts, depression, anxiety, and repetitive behaviour (Kwok, 2003). Drugs that are usually used to treat schizophrenia—so-called "major tranquilizers"—are helpful with stereotyped behaviour, hyperactivity, and self-injury, but not with cognitive and language problems (Kwok, 2003; McClellan & Werry, 2003).

Autistic behaviour generally continues into adulthood to one degree or another, but many individuals with autism go on to be productive, happy, and successful individuals.

Recent research on autism has introduced animal intervention as a treatment technique for working with children with autism spectrum disorder. Marguerite E. O'Haire and colleagues compared the social interactions of 5- to 13-year-old children with ASD after they had played with two guinea pigs as opposed to toys. They found that in the presence of animals, the children presented more social behaviours, such as talking, face gazing, and making physical contact. They were also more open to social advances from peers in the presence of animals than when they were playing with toys. The presence of the animals increased the frequency of smiling and laughing and reduced negative social behaviours such as frowning, whining, and crying (Science Daily, 2013).

DID YOU KNOW?

Many children with autism spectrum disorder grow up to be independent, productive, and successful professionals. We must resist the stereotypes and consider the individual.

Temple Grandin, for example, is a spokesperson for autism and expert in animal behaviour who is known all over the world.

LO3 Childcare

Have you seen the bumper sticker that suggests we should choose our children's childcare wisely because our children will one day choose our retirement home? Most parents, including mothers with infants, are in the workforce (Carey, 2007a). About 54% of Canadian children aged 6 months to 5 years receive some type of non-parental childcare (Bushnik, 2006).

Many parents wonder whether childcare will affect their children's attachment to them. The issue is not whether their children should attend childcare, but the quality of their children's childcare and the number of hours in care, as well as the age of the child in care (Johnson, 2008). Childcare centres should do more than provide routine care; they should be warm and nurturing environments. Whenever possible, the child's diaper should be changed by the same person. Meals should be eaten together, and the care provider should be emotionally available for activities with the children. Attachment with a care provider does not replace the love of a parent. The parent and the caregiver should work together. The child's development benefits from having numerous opportunities to form a secure attachment. Despite parents' concerns, research finds that, for the most part, infants who attend full-time childcare are as securely attached as infants raised at home, provided they have a strong parent–child bond before receiving childcare (Timmerman, 2006).

Some studies report that infants with childcare experience are more peer-oriented and play at higher developmental levels than do home-reared infants. Children in high-quality childcare are more likely to share their toys. They also tend to be more independent, self-confident, outgoing, affectionate, and more helpful and cooperative with peers and adults (Lamb & Ahnert, 2006; Pierce & Vandell, 2006). Participation in childcare is also linked to better academic performance in elementary school (Belsky, 2006b).

A study funded by the National Institute on Child Health and Human Development (NICHD) agrees that high-quality childcare can result in scores on tests of cognitive skills that rival or exceed those of the children reared in the home by their mothers (Belsky et al., 2007). The quality of the childcare was defined in the study in terms of the richness of the learning environment (availability of toys, books, and other materials), the ratio of caregivers to children (high-quality meant grater ratio of caregivers to children), the amount of individual attention received by the child, and the extent to which caregivers talked to the children and asked them questions.

DID YOU KNOW?

About 54% of Canadian children aged 6 months to 5 years attend some type of non-parental childcare.

However, researchers have also found that children placed in childcare may be less cooperative and more aggressive toward peers and adults than children who are reared in the home. (Clarke-Stewart, 1992). Teacher ratings found that children who had attended childcare were significantly more likely than children cared for in the home to interrupt in class and to tease or bully other children (Belsky et al., 2007). The degree of disturbance generally remained "within normal limits." *The quality of the childcare centre made no difference.* Children from high-quality childcare centres were also more likely to be disruptive than children cared for in the home. Moreover, the behavioural difference persisted through Grade 6.

Jupiterimages/Thinkstock.com

EMERGING CANADA

Canada is experiencing a repeat baby boom, referred to as an echo boom (an echo of the earlier baby boom that followed World War II). The population of children 4 years of age and younger increased 11.0% between 2005 and 2011 to the highest birth rate since the baby boom of 1956–61 (Statistics Canada, 2012b). In 2002–2003, 54% of Canadian children aged 6 months to 5 years attended some type of non-parental childcare, up 42% in the previous eight years (CBC News, 2009b). In addition, government statistics show that half of all Canadian mothers who gave birth were older than age 30. Women are waiting longer to start their families, as they establish themselves in their careers (Human Resources and Skills Development Canada, 2013a), and they are choosing to return to work soon after they have their children. All of these factors combine to establish the need to be proactive in demanding the provision of high-quality daycare.

LO4 Emotional Development

An emotion is a state of feeling that has physiological, situational, and cognitive components. Physiologically, when emotions are strong, our hearts may beat more rapidly and our muscles may tense. Situationally, we may feel anger when frustrated, or pleasure or relief when being held by a loved one. Cognitively, anger may be triggered by the idea that someone is purposefully withholding something we need.

It is unclear how many emotions babies have, and they cannot tell us what they are feeling. We can only observe how they behave, including changes in their facial expressions (Oster, 2005). Facial expressions appear to be universal in that they are recognized in different cultures around the world, so they are considered a reliable index of emotion.

Researchers have long debated whether newborns are born with specific emotions (Soussignan & Schaal, 2005). They have asked whether the newborn baby's crying is nothing more than a reflex in response to discomfort. It seems clear enough that as infants develop through the first year, their cognitive appraisal of events, including their interaction with their caregivers, becomes a key part of their emotional life and their emotional expression (Camras et al., 2007; Soussignan & Schaal, 2005).

Infants' initial emotional expressions appear to comprise two basic states of emotional arousal: a positive attraction to pleasant stimulation, such as the caregiver's voice or being held, and withdrawal from aversive stimulation, such as a sudden loud noise. By the age of 2 to 3 months, social smiling has replaced reflexive smiling. Social smiling is usually highly endearing to caregivers. At 3 to 5 months, infants laugh at active stimuli, such as repetitively touching their bellies or playing "Peek-a-boo!"

> Infants' initial emotional expressions appear to comprise two basic states of emotional arousal: a positive attraction to pleasant stimulation and withdrawal from aversive stimulation.

In sum, researchers agree that infants show only a few emotions during the first few months. They agree that emotional development is linked to cognitive development and social experience. They do not necessarily agree, however, on exactly when specific emotions are first shown or whether discrete emotions are present at birth (Camras et al., 2007).

Fear of Strangers

We live in an increasingly transient world where many adult children find themselves living across the country, or at least in a different province, from their parents. It is a proud moment to introduce your child to your parents for the first time. The new grandparents expectantly shower their grandchild with joy and affection, only to be met by screams that rival any carefully scripted horror movie. What have they done wrong? They simply existed within sight of their grandchild, who is going through the cognitive stage of stranger anxiety.

Fear of strangers—also called *stranger anxiety*—is normal. Most infants develop it. Stranger anxiety appears at about 6 to 9 months of age. By 4 or 5 months of age, infants may compare the face of a stranger with their mother's face, looking back and forth. Older infants show distress by crying, whimpering, gazing fearfully, and crawling away. Fear of strangers often peaks at 9 to 12 months, just in time for that first picture with Santa Claus, and declines in the second year.

Children who have a fear of strangers show less anxiety when their mothers are present (Thompson & Limber, 1990). Children are also less fearful when

DID YOU KNOW?

Fear of strangers is normal among infants.

Most infants develop some form of stranger anxiety around 6 to 9 months of age. This behaviour is not an indicator of an insecure attachment.

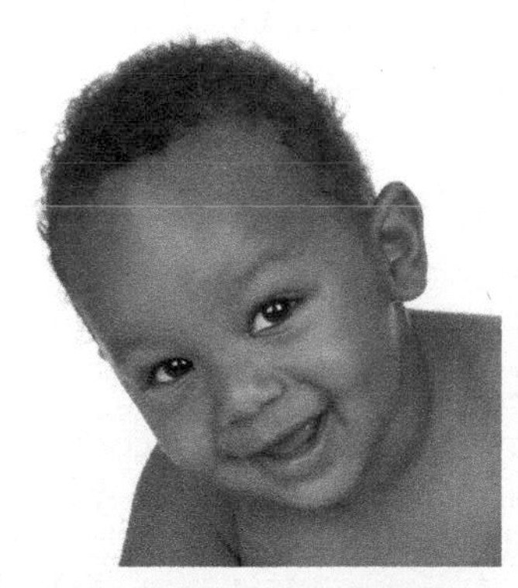

Top row (left to right): Gelphi/Shutterstock.com; Leung Chopan/Shutterstock.com; NChoochat/Shutterstock.com; Bottom row (left to right): Tommaso Lizzul/Shutterstock.com; Szefei/Shutterstock.com; Photomak/Shutterstock.com

social referencing
using another person's reaction to a situation to form one's own response

emotional regulation
techniques for controlling one's emotional states

they are in familiar surroundings, such as their homes, rather than in new and unfamiliar environments (Sroufe, Waters, & Matas, 1974).

Social Referencing

Social referencing is the seeking out of another person's perception of a situation to help us form our own view of it (Hertenstein & Campos, 2004). Leslie Carver and Brenda Vaccaro (2007) suggest that social referencing requires three components: (1) looking at another, usually older individual in a novel, ambiguous situation; (2) associating that individual's emotional response with the unfamiliar situation; and (3) regulating one's own emotional response in accord with the response of the older individual.

Infants also display social referencing, as early as 6 months of age. They use caregivers' facial expressions or tone of voice as clues on how to respond (Hertenstein & Campos, 2004). In one study, 8-month-old infants were friendlier to a stranger when their mothers exhibited a friendly facial expression in the stranger's presence than when she looked worried (Boccia & Campos, 1989). Parents quickly learn that smiling when their child has a gentle fall will help to diffuse the situation. A parent may need to suppress a personal fear of spiders and play with one to keep a child free from that same fear.

Emotional Regulation

Emotional regulation refers to the ways in which young children control their own emotions. Even infants display certain behaviours to control unpleasant emotional states. For example, an infant may look away from a disturbing event or suck her or his thumb as a way to control emotional discomfort (Rothbart & Sheese, 2007). Caregivers help infants learn to regulate their emotions. A two-way communication system develops, in which the infant signals the caregiver that help is needed and the caregiver responds. Claire Kopp (1989, p. 347) provides an example of such a system:

> A 13-month-old, playing with a large plastic bottle, attempted to unscrew the cover, but could not. Fretting for a short time, she initiated eye contact with her mother and held out the jar. As her mother took it to unscrew the cover, the infant ceased fretting.

Research evidence suggests that the children of secure mothers are not only likely to be securely attached themselves but also are likely to regulate their own emotions in a positive manner (Grolnick, McMenamy, & Kurowski, 2006; Thompson & Meyer, 2007). A German longitudinal study (Zimmermann et al., 2001) related emotional regulation in adolescence with patterns of attachment during infancy, as assessed using the strange-situation method. Forty-one adolescents, aged 16 and 17, were placed in complex problem-solving situations with friends. Those adolescents who were secure as infants were more capable of regulating their emotions to interact cooperatively with their friends.

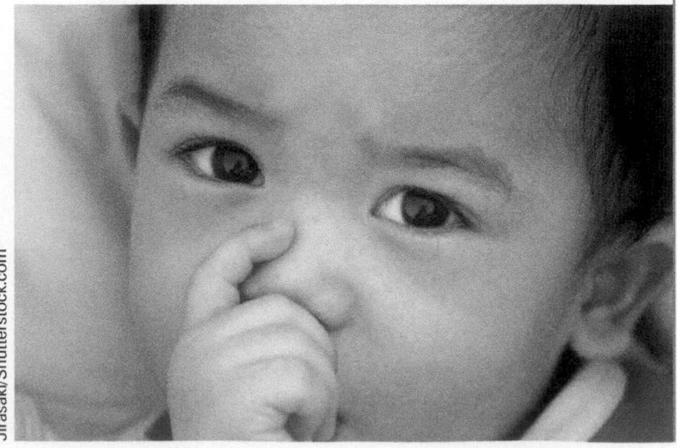

Jirasaki/Shutterstock.com

LO5 Personality Development

In this section, we look at the emergence of the self-concept. We then turn to a discussion of temperament. Finally, we consider sex differences in behaviour.

The Self-Concept

At birth, we may find the world to be a confusing blur of sights, sounds, and inner sensations—yet the "we" may be missing, at least for a while. When we first see our hands, we do not yet realize that the hands belong to us and that we are separate and distinct from the world outside.

The self-concept appears to emerge gradually during infancy. At some point, infants understand that the hands they are moving in and out of sight are their own hands. At some point, they understand that their own bodies extend only so far and then external objects and the bodies of others begin.

Development of the Self-Concept

Psychologists have devised ingenious methods to assess the development of the self-concept among infants. One of these methods uses the mirror technique, which involves a mirror and a dot of lipstick. Before the experiment begins, the researcher observes the infant for baseline data on how frequently the infant touches his or her nose. The mother then applies a red lipstick dot on the infant's nose and places the infant in front of a mirror. While looking in the mirror, infants do not touch their own nose until about the age of 18 months (Campbell et al., 2000; Keller et al., 2005). Nose touching suggests that children recognize themselves and that they perceive the red dot to be an abnormality.

Most 2-year-olds can point to pictures of themselves, and they begin to use "I" or their own name spontaneously (Smiley & Johnson, 2006). In other words, they have developed a sense of "self."

Self-awareness affects the infant's social and emotional development (Foley, 2006). Knowledge of the self permits the infant and child to develop notions of sharing and cooperation. In one study, 2-year-olds with a better-developed sense of self were more likely to cooperate with other children (Brownell & Carriger, 1990).

Self-awareness also facilitates the development of self-conscious emotions such as embarrassment, envy, empathy, pride, guilt, and shame (Foley, 2006). In one study, Deborah Stipek and her colleagues (1992) found that children older than 21 months often seek their mother's attention and approval when they have successfully completed a task, whereas younger toddlers do not.

Psychoanalytic Views of the Self-Concept

Margaret Mahler, a psychoanalyst, has proposed that development of self-concept comes about through a process of **separation–individuation**, which lasts from about 5 months until 3 years of age (Mahler, Pine, & Bergman,1975). Separation involves the child's growing perception that her or his mother is a separate person. Individuation refers to the child's increasing sense of independence and autonomy.

One of the ways toddlers demonstrate growing autonomy, much to the dismay of caregivers, is by refusing to comply with caregivers' requests. "No!" becomes a universal reply to many parental interactions. Studies of toddlers and preschoolers between the ages of 1.5 and 5 years have found that as children grow older, they adopt more skillful ways of expressing resistance to caregivers' requests (Smith et al., 2004; Stifter & Wiggins, 2004). For example, young toddlers are more likely to ignore a caregiver's request or defy it. Older toddlers and preschoolers are more likely to make excuses or negotiate.

Temperament: Easy, Difficult, or Slow to Warm Up?

separation–individuation the process of becoming separate from and independent of the mother

temperament individual difference in style of reaction, which is present early in life

Each child has a characteristic **temperament**, a stable way of reacting and adapting to the world, which is present early in life (Wachs, 2006). Many researchers believe that temperament involves a strong genetic component (Goldsmith et al., 2003; Wachs, 2006). The child's temperament includes many aspects of behaviour, including activity level, smiling and laughter, regularity in eating and sleep habits, approach or withdrawal, adaptability to new situations, intensity of responsiveness, general cheerfulness or unpleasantness, distractibility or persistence, and soothability (Gartstein, Slobodskaya, & Kinsht, 2003; Thomas & Chess, 1989).

Types of Temperament

Thomas and Chess (1989) found that from the first days of life, many of the children in their study (65%) could be classified into one of three types of temperament: "easy" (40% of their sample), "difficult" (10%), and "slow to warm up" (15%). Some of the differences among these three types of children are shown in Table 6.2. The easy child is generally cheerful, has regular sleep and feeding schedules, approaches new situations (such as a new food or a new school) enthusiastically, and adapts easily to change. Some children, though, are more inconsistent and show a mixture of temperament traits. The difficult child, for example, has irregular sleep and feeding schedules, is slow to accept new people and situations, takes a long time to adjust to new routines, and responds to frustrations with tantrums and crying. The slow-to-warm-up child falls between the other two.

Creativa Images/Shutterstock.com

TABLE 6.2

Types of Temperament

Temperament Category	Easy	Difficult	Slow to Warm Up
Regularity of biological functioning	Regular	Irregular	Somewhat irregular
Response to new stimuli	Positive approach	Negative withdrawal	Negative withdrawal
Adaptability to new situations	Adapts readily	Adapts slowly or not at all	Adapts slowly
Intensity of reaction	Mild or moderate	Intense	Mild
Quality of mood	Positive	Negative	Initially negative; gradually more positive

Sources: Chess & Thomas, 1991; Thomas & Chess, 1989.

goodness of fit agreement between the parents' expectations of a child and the child's temperament

sex a way of classifying individuals usually as male or female, due to a combination of biological and physiological features

intersex individuals who are born with variations to their chromosomes or genitals such that their sex doesn't match binary notions of male or female

gender cultural view of what it means to be masculine or feminine according to one's sex

Stability of Temperament

Although not all children are born with the same temperament, as Thomas and Chess found, at least moderate consistency is shown in the development of temperament from infancy onward (Wachs, 2006). The infant who is highly active and cries in novel situations often becomes a fearful toddler. Difficult children are, in general, at greater risk for developing psychological disorders and adjustment problems later in life (Pauli-Pott, Mertesacker, & Beckmann, 2003; Rothbart, Ellis, & Posner, 2004). A longitudinal study tracked the progress of infants with a difficult temperament from 1.5 through 12 years of age (Guerin, Gottfried, & Thomas,1997). A difficult temperament correlated both with parental reports of behavioural problems from ages 3 to 12 and with teachers' reports of problems with attention span and aggression.

© Radius Images/Jupiterimages

DID YOU KNOW?

Children are born with varying temperaments that are believed to have a significant genetic component.

Though not all children are born with the same temperament, at least moderate consistency is shown in the development of temperament from infancy onward.

Goodness of Fit: The Role of the Environment

The environment also affects the development of temperament. An initial biological predisposition to a certain temperament may be strengthened or weakened by the parents' reaction to the child. Parents may react to a difficult child by imposing rigid care-giving schedules, which in turn can cause the child to become even more difficult (Schoppe-Sullivan et al., 2007). This example illustrates a poor fit between the child's behaviour style and the parents' response.

On the other hand, parents may modify a child's initial temperament in a more positive direction to achieve a goodness of fit between child and parent. Realization that their youngster's behaviour does not mean that the child is weak or deliberately disobedient, or that they are bad parents, helps parents modify their attitudes and behaviour toward the child, whose behaviour may then improve (Bird, Reese, & Tripp, 2006; Schoppe-Sullivan et al., 2007).

Sex Differences

Sex is a way of classifying individuals (usually male and female or boy and girl) due to a combination of biological and physiological features. Some individuals are born intersex, with variations to their chromosomes or genitals that do not match the binary notion of male and female (The Critical Media Project, 2016). Gender refers to a cultural view of what it means to act masculine or feminine according to one's sex. It is socially constructed, which means that gender means different things to individuals in various parts of the world and across history. At an early age, infants are socialized to act and conform to their gender role. This, in turn, shapes how infants view themselves.

Behaviour of Infant Girls and Boys

Physical differences in infancy have been found regarding motor development, as girls tend to advance more rapidly than boys. Girls tend to sit, crawl, and walk earlier than boys (Matlin, 2008). Although a few studies have found that infant boys are more active and irritable than girls, others have not (Matlin, 2008). Girls and boys are similar in their social behaviours. They are equally likely to smile at people's faces, for example, and they do not differ in their dependency on adults (Maccoby & Jacklin, 1974).

Socialization of boys and girls stems from old beliefs that differences between the sexes exists particularly regarding aptitude in math and verbal skills, communication, nurturance, aggression, leadership, and self-esteem. These gender stereotypes are damaging because they limit opportunities for boys and girls to act authentically. Girls may wish to be firefighters and boys may wish to grow up to be dancers, however they are told that they must conform. Actual differences between males and females are minimal when it comes to cognitive abilities and reasoning (Rivers & Barnett, 2011). Neuroscience supports the notion that there is little difference in the brains of boys and girls. "Neuroscientists have yet to identify distinct 'male' and 'female' neural circuits underlying any sexually differentiated behavior, in spite of widespread belief in such circuits" (Eliot, 2011, p.897).

It has been found that girls and boys differ early in their preference for certain toys and play activities. By 12 to 18 months of age, girls tend to play with dolls, doll furniture, dishes, and toy animals; boys more commonly play with transportation toys (trucks, cars, airplanes, and the like), tools, and sports equipment as early as 9 to 18 month of age (Campbell et al., 2000; Serbin et al., 2001). Given that there is little evidence for actual differences in the brain, one must question whether this is due to actual preferences or the way boys and girls have been socialized and nurtured. By 24 months, both girls and boys appear to be aware of which behaviours are considered appropriate or inappropriate for their sex, according to their culture's gender stereotypes (Hill & Flom, 2007). It is believed that this is the result of learning which toys to play with through modelling and reinforcement.

Socialization of Gender Stereotypes

Adults interact differently with girls and boys. Researchers have presented adults with an unfamiliar infant who is dressed in boy's clothes and has a boy's name or an infant who is dressed in girl's clothing and has a girl's name. (In reality, it is the same baby who simply is given different names and clothing.) When adults believe they are playing with a girl, they are more likely to offer "her" a doll; when they think the child is a boy, they are more likely to offer a football or a hammer. "Boys" also are encouraged to engage in more physical activity than "girls" (Worell & Goodheart, 2006).

Parents, especially fathers, are more likely to encourage rough-and-tumble play in sons than daughters (Eccles et al., 2000; Fagot, Rodgers, & Leinbach, 2000). On the other hand, parents talk more to infant daughters than to infant sons. They smile more at daughters and are more emotionally expressive toward them (Powlishta et al., 2001).

Infant girls are likely to be decked out in a pink or yellow dress and embellished with ruffles and lace, whereas infant boys wear blue or red (Eccles et al., 2000; Powlishta et al., 2001). Parents tend to provide baby girls and boys with different bedroom decorations and toys, sometimes even before they are born. Examination of the contents of rooms of children from 5 months to 6 years of age found that boys' rooms were often decorated with animal themes and with blue bedding and curtains. Girls' rooms featured flowers, lace, ruffles, and pastels. Girls owned more dolls; boys had more vehicles, military toys, and sports equipment.

Parents react favourably when their infant daughters play with "girls' toys" and their sons play with "boys' toys." In spite of best efforts not to stereotype their children, adults, especially fathers, show more negative reactions when girls play with boys'

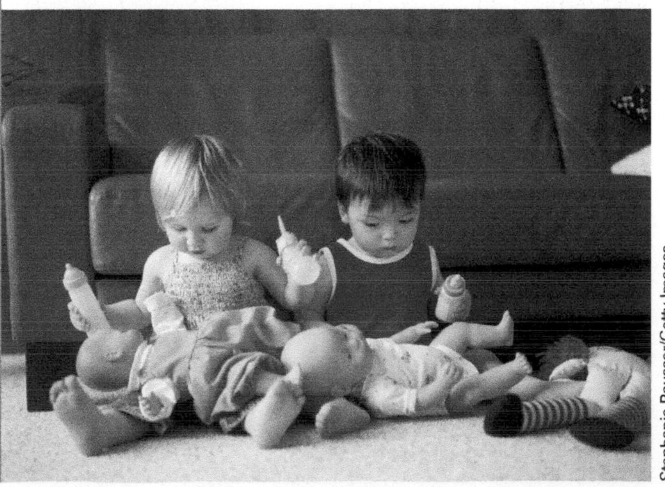
Stephanie Rausser/Getty Images

toys and boys play with girls' toys (Martin, Ruble, & Szkrybalo, 2002; Worell & Goodheart, 2006). Parents thus try to shape their children's behaviour during infancy and lay the foundation for development in early childhood, without even realizing it.

Parents tend to provide baby girls and boys with different bedroom decorations and toys, sometimes before they are even born.

Infant–Father Interaction as a Predictor of Later Infant Behaviour

Recently, research has increasingly focused on the earliest years of life. Relatively few studies have focused on father–infant interactions despite the importance of this relationship on child behavioural development. A recent study conducted by Ramchandani et al. (2013) studied whether father–infant interactions at age 3 months independently predicted child behavioural problems at 1 year of age. Fathers and their children were observed in their own homes in two different play scenarios. Fathers were asked to play with their child in each setting without toys or other object for three minutes. When fathers were disengaged and remote (lost in their thoughts or simply "going through the motions"), their negative interaction reliably predicted early behavioural problems. Interestingly, boys seemed more sensitive to this pattern of association. This study reinforces the importance of the father–infant relationship and promotes an opportunity for preventative intervention (Ramchandani et al., 2013).

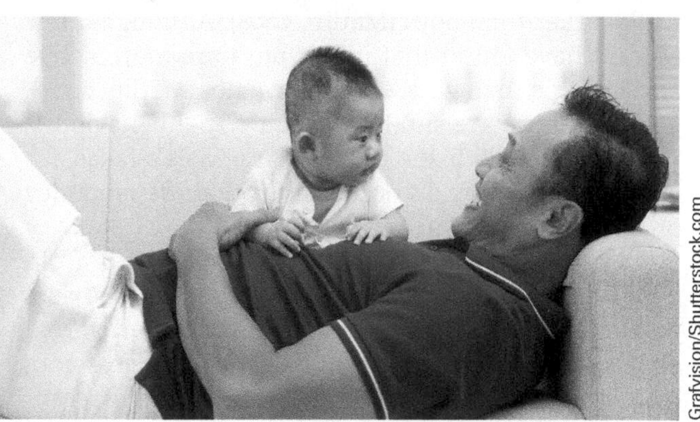
Grafvision/Shutterstock.com

STUDY TOOLS CourseMate **CHAPTER 6**

Located at **nelson.com/student**

- ☐ Prepare for tests with a variety of exercises and activities
- ☐ Review Key Terms Flashcards (online or print)
- ☐ Create your own study tools with Build a Summary
- ☐ Watch Observing Development videos to expand your knowledge

PART THREE

CHAPTER 7

Early Childhood: Physical and Cognitive Development

Rebekah Littlejohn Photography www.littlejohnphotography.com

LEARNING OUTCOMES

LO1 Outline trends in physical development in early childhood

LO2 Describe motor development in early childhood

LO3 Describe nutritional needs in early childhood

LO4 Describe trends in health and illness in early childhood

LO5 Explain sleep patterns in early childhood

LO6 Discuss elimination disorders

LO7 Describe Piaget's preoperational stage

LO8 Discuss influences on cognitive development in early childhood

LO9 Explain how theory of mind affects cognitive development

LO10 Outline memory development in early childhood

LO11 Outline language development in early childhood

> "During the preschool years, physical and motor development proceeds, literally, by leaps and bounds."

The ages from 2 to 6 years are referred to as early childhood, or the preschool years, even though many Canadian children begin junior kindergarten as early as 3 years 8 months of age. During early childhood, physical growth is slower as compared to growth in infancy. Children become taller and leaner, and, by the end of early childhood, they look more like adults than infants. As their motor skills develop, children become stronger, faster, and better coordinated.

Language improves enormously, and children begin to carry on conversations with others. As cognitive skills develop, a new world of make-believe, or "pretend" play, emerges. Most preschoolers are curious and eager to learn. Increased physical and cognitive capabilities enable children to emerge from total dependence on others to exploring the broader world outside the family.

LO1 Growth Patterns

During the preschool years, significant fluctuations in physical and motor development occur. First we will examine the physical growth that occurs and then we will discuss changes in motor development during this age group.

Height and Weight

After the dramatic gains in height in a child's first two years, the growth rate slows during the preschool years (Kuczmarski et al., 2002). Girls and boys tend to gain about 5 to 8 cm (2 to 3 in.) in height per year, and weight gains remain fairly even at about 2 to 3 kg (4 to 6 lb.) per year. Children become increasingly slender as they gain in height and shed some "baby fat." Boys as a group become slightly taller and heavier than girls. Noticeable variations in growth occur from child to child.

Development of the Brain

The brain develops more quickly than any other organ in early childhood and needs to be supported by proper nutrition. At 2 years of age, the brain already has attained 75% of its adult weight. By the age of 5 years, the brain has reached 90% of its adult weight, even though the body weight of the 5-year-old is barely one-third of what it will be as an adult (Tanner, 1989).

The increase in brain size is due in part to the continuing myelination of nerve fibres. Completion of myelination of the neural pathways that link the cerebellum to the cerebral cortex facilitates development of fine motor skills, balance, and coordination (Nelson & Luciana, 2001; Paus et al., 1999).

Brain Development and Visual Skills

Brain development also improves the processing of visual information (Yamada et al., 2000), which facilitates learning to read. The parts of the brain that enable the child to sustain attention and screen out distractions (reticular formation) become increasingly myelinated between the ages of about 4 and 7 years (Nelson & Luciana, 2001), enabling most children to focus on schoolwork. The speed of processing visual information improves throughout childhood, reaching adult levels at the onset of adolescence (Chou et al., 2006; Paus et al., 1999).

Right Brain, Left Brain?

We often hear people described as being "right-brained" or "left-brained." The notion is that the hemispheres of the brain are involved in different kinds of intellectual and emotional activities. Research does suggest that in right-handed individuals, the left hemisphere is relatively more involved in intellectual undertakings that require logical analysis, problem-solving language, and computation (Grindrod & Baum, 2005; O'Shea & Corballis, 2005). In contrast, the right hemisphere is usually superior in visual–spatial functions (such as piecing puzzles together), aesthetic and emotional responses, and understanding metaphors.

But it is not true that some children are left-brained and others are right-brained. The functions of the left and right hemispheres overlap, and the hemispheres respond simultaneously when we focus on one thing or another. They are aided in "cooperation" by the myelination of the **corpus callosum**, a thick bundle of nerve fibres that connects the hemispheres (Kinsbourne, 2003). This process is largely complete by the age of 8 years, enabling the integration of logical and emotional functioning.

Plasticity of the Brain

Many parts of the brain have specialized functions, allowing our behaviour to be more complex. But this specialization also means that injuries to certain parts of the brain can result in loss of these functions. However, the brain shows **plasticity**, or the ability to compensate for injuries to particular areas. Plasticity is greatest at about 1 to 2 years of age and then gradually declines (Kolb & Gibb, 2007; Nelson, de Haan, & Thomas, 2006). When we, as adults, experience damage to the areas of the brain that control language, we may lose the ability to speak or understand language. However, when the same damage occurs in a preschooler, other areas of the brain may assume these functions. As a result, preschoolers with brain damage may regain the ability to speak or comprehend language (Nelson et al., 2006). Neurological factors that enable plasticity include the growth of new dendrites ("sprouting") and the redundancy of neural connections (Nelson et al., 2006; Szaflarski et al., 2006).

Tom Merton/Getty Images

corpus callosum the thick bundle of nerve fibres that connects the left and right hemispheres of the brain

plasticity the tendency of new parts of the brain to take up the functions of injured parts

gross motor skills skills employing the large muscles used in locomotion

LO2 Motor Development

The preschool years witness an explosion of motor skills, as children's nervous systems mature and their movements become more precise and coordinated.

Gross Motor Skills

Gross motor skills involve the large muscles used in locomotion (see Table 7.1). At about the age of 3 years, children can balance on one foot. By age 3 or 4 years, they can walk up stairs as adults do, by placing one foot on each step. By age 4 or 5 years, they can skip and pedal a tricycle (McDevitt

TABLE 7.1

Development of Gross Motor Skills in Early Childhood

2 Years (24–35 Months)	3 Years (36–47 Months)	4 Years (48–59 Months)	5 Years (60–71 Months)
• Runs well straight ahead • Walks up stairs, two feet to a step • Kicks a large ball • Jumps a distance of 10 to 35 cm (4 to 14 in.) • Throws a small ball without falling • Pushes and pulls large toys • Hops on one foot, for two or more hops • Tries to stand on one foot • Climbs on furniture to look out of window	• Goes around obstacles while running • Walks up stairs, one foot to a step • Kicks a large ball easily • Jumps from the bottom step • Catches a bounced ball, using torso and arms to form a basket • Goes around obstacles while pushing and pulling toys • Hops on one foot, for up to three hops • Stands on one foot • Climbs on playground equipment	• Turns sharp corners while running • Walks down stairs, one foot to a step • Jumps from a height of 30 cm (12 in.) • Throws a ball overhand • Turns sharp corners while pushing and pulling toys • Hops on one foot, for four to six hops • Stands on one foot for 3 to 8 seconds • Climbs ladders • Skips on one foot • Rides a tricycle well	• Runs lightly on toes • Jumps a distance of 1 m (3 ft.) • Catches a small ball, using hands only • Hops on one foot for 2 to 3 m (2 to 3 yd.) • Stands on one foot for 8 to 10 seconds • Climbs actively and skillfully • Skips on alternate feet • Rides a bicycle with training wheels

Note: The ages are averages; there are individual variations.

Source: © Cengage Learning

fine motor skills skills employing the small muscles used in manipulation, such as those in the fingers

& Ormrod, 2002). Older preschoolers are better able to coordinate two tasks at the same time, such as singing and running. In general, preschoolers appear to acquire motor skills by teaching themselves and observing other children. At this age, imitating other children is influential in advancing physical development.

Throughout early childhood, girls and boys are similar in motor skills. Girls are generally better at balance and precision. Boys show some advantage in throwing and kicking (McDevitt & Ormrod, 2002).

Throughout early and middle childhood, individual differences are more significant than differences due to sex. Some children are genetically predisposed to developing better coordination or more strength. For example, some girls are excellent skaters and love to play hockey whereas many boys become interested in the coordination of dance routines. Motivation and practice play an important role in the development of motor skills.

Physical Activity

Preschoolers spend an average of more than 25 hours a week in large-muscle activity (Campbell, Eaton, & McKeen, 2002). Younger preschoolers are more likely than older preschoolers to engage in physically oriented play, such as grasping, banging, and mouthing objects (D. W. Campbell et al., 2002).

Motor activity level begins to decline after 2 or 3 years of age. Children become less restless and are able to sit still longer. Between the ages of 2 and 4 years, children show an increase in sustained, focused attention.

Rough-and-Tumble Play

Rough-and-tumble play consists of running, chasing, fleeing, wrestling, hitting with an open hand, laughing, and making faces. Rough-and-tumble play is not the same as aggressive behaviour, which involves hitting with a fist, pushing, taking, grabbing, and angry looks. Rough-and-tumble play helps develop physical and social skills (Fry, 2005; Smith, 2005).

Grafvision/Shutterstock.com

Rough-and-tumble play, which is not the same as aggressive behaviour, helps develop physical and social skills.

Active Parents Have Active Children

A recent study suggests that active parents raise active children. Regular parental activity seems to protect children from the risk of obesity (Khamsi, 2007).

Several reasons may explain this relationship. First, active parents may serve as role models for activity. Second, sharing of activities by family members may have an influence. Active parents may be more likely to encourage their child's participation in physical activity. In other words, children seem to learn physical activity habits through example.

Fine Motor Skills

Fine motor skills develop gradually and later as compared to gross motor skills. Fine motor skills involve the small muscles used in manipulation

EMERGING CANADA

Increasingly, Canadians are becoming more and more involved in their children's lives. Children spend less time alone than ever before, and when they are alone, they are often monitored closely, sometimes without their knowledge. Inuit culture provides a very different experience. Children, and even infants, are more likely to be encouraged to make their own choices and to explore and build independence. Learning is encouraged through individual effort and at a pace that is set by the child and his or her interest level. This approach provides the groundwork for encouraging Inuit values of self-reliance, resourcefulness, and patience. Inuit children enjoy a much greater degree of freedom than other Canadian children, and their limitations are guided only by the potential for harm to self or others (Pauktuutit Inuit Women of Canada, 2006). This cultural practice raises the question of whether Western culture underestimates the abilities of the young children. Does the approach used in Western culture result in underdevelopment in children?

Ton Koene/age fotostock/First Light

TABLE 7.2

Development of Fine Motor Skills in Early Childhood

2 Years (24–35 Months)	3 Years (36–47 Months)	4 Years (48–59 Months)	5 Years (60–71 Months)
• Builds tower of 6 cubes • Copies vertical and horizontal lines • Imitates folding of paper • Prints on easel with a brush • Places simple shapes in correct holes	• Builds tower of 9 cubes • Copies circle and cross • Copies letters • Holds crayons with fingers, not fist • Strings 4 beads using a large needle	• Builds tower of 10 or more cubes • Copies square • Prints simple words • Imitates folding paper three times • Uses correct hand grip to hold a pencil • Strings 10 beads	• Builds 3 steps from 6 blocks, using a model • Copies triangle and star • Prints first name and numbers • Imitates folding a piece of square paper into a triangle • Traces around a diamond drawn on paper • Laces shoes

Note: The ages are averages; there are individual variations.

Source: © Cengage Learning

and coordination. Control over the wrists and fingers enables children to hold a pencil properly, dress themselves, and stack blocks (see Table 7.2). Preschoolers can labour endlessly trying to tie their shoelaces and get their jackets zipped, as their fine motor skills develop.

Children's Drawings

The development of drawing is linked to the development of motor and cognitive skills. Children first begin to scribble during the second year of life. Initially, they seem to make marks for the sheer joy of it (Eisner, 1990). Rhoda Kellogg (1959, 1970) found a meaningful pattern in the scribbles. She identified 20 basic scribbles that she considered the building blocks of art (see Figure 7.1).

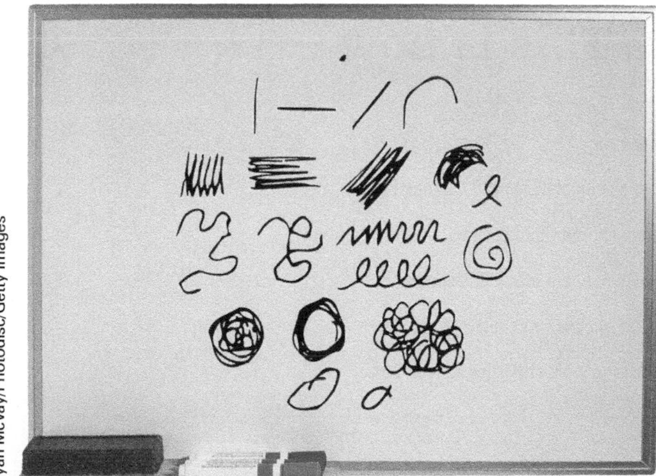

Ryan McVay/Photodisc/Getty Images

FIGURE 7.1

The 20 Basic Scribbles

By the age of 2, children can scribble. Rhoda Kellogg has identified these 20 basic scribbles as the building blocks of young children's drawings.

Source: © Cengage Learning

Two-year-olds scribble in various locations on the page (e.g., in the middle of the page or near one of the borders). By age 3 years, children are starting to draw basic shapes: circles, squares, triangles, crosses, Xs, and odd shapes. As soon as they can draw shapes, children begin to combine them in the design stage. Between ages 4 and 5 years, children reach the pictorial stage, when their designs begin to resemble recognizable objects.

A more recent study by Yang and Noel (2006) confirmed earlier findings by Kellogg that 4- and 5-year-olds prefer single line drawings with centred placement patterns. This preference is possibly because their hand–eye coordination is still developing, so centred drawings dominate over pictures on other areas of the paper. The concept of symmetry is evolving, which may explain why a child often considers a drawing in the centre of the page to be complete. Another finding of this study is that drawings help to encourage emerging literacy. Children seem to prefer the letters in their own name as compared to other random letters and readily add their names to their drawings. Yang and Noel (2006) concluded that children should be encouraged to freely explore scribbles and placement patterns in their drawings; adding names to their pictures is a great way to practise name writing.

Handedness

Handedness emerges during infancy. By the age of 2 to 3 months, a rattle placed in an infant's hand is held longer with the dominant hand (Fitzgerald et al., 1991). By 4 months of age, most infants show a clear-cut right-hand preference when exploring objects (Streri, 2002). Preference for grasping with one hand over the other increases markedly between 7 and 11 months (Hinojosa, Sheu, & Michel, 2003); however, handedness becomes more strongly established during early childhood

(McManus et al., 1988). Most people are right-handed, although 12% of the population is left-handed (Mastin, 2012).

A study conducted by Rat-Fischer and colleagues (2012) had 16- to 22-month-olds reach for a toy rake. Most of the younger infants used their hand of preference, while most older infants used the hand that would provide the easiest retrieval. Older children were better able to anticipate the most successful strategy and could use either hand.

The origins of handedness apparently have a genetic component (Geschwind, 2000; McManus, 2003). If both of your parents are right-handed, your chances of being right-handed are about 92%. If both of your parents are left-handed, your chances of being left-handed are about 50% (Annett, 1999; Clode, 2006). An environmental component also comes into play if children are discouraged from using their left hand.

Left-Handedness

Being a "lefty" was once seen as a deficiency, but today, the 12% of the population that identify themselves as left-handed are usually quite proud of their uniqueness. Being left-handed may matter because it appears to be related to language problems, such as dyslexia and stuttering, and with health problems, such as high blood pressure and epilepsy (Andreou et al., 2002; Bryden, Bruyn, & Fletcher, 2005). Left-handedness is also related to psychological disorders, including schizophrenia and depression (Annett & Moran, 2006; Dollfus et al., 2005).

Even so, being left-handed has its advantages. A disproportionately high percentage of math whizzes are left-handed, as found on the math portion of the SAT among 12- and 13-year-olds (O'Boyle & Benbow, 1990). Twenty percent of the highest-scoring group was left-handed, while only 12% of the general population is left-handed.

Left-handedness (and ambidexterity, the use of both hands with similar or equal dexterity) also has been associated with success in athletic activities such as handball, fencing, boxing, basketball, and baseball (Coren, 1992; Dane & Erzurumluoglu, 2003). Higher frequencies of left-handedness are found among musicians, architects, and artists (Natsopoulos, Kiosseoglou, & Zeromeritou, 1992).

DID YOU KNOW?

A disproportionately high percentage of math whizzes are left-handed.

Twenty percent of the highest-scoring group on the math SATs was left-handed, while only 12% of the general population is left-handed.

LO3 Nutrition

Today's generation of children has been referred to as "Generation XL," which is a comment on the most overweight generation of children our country has known. Statistics Canada reports that 31% of Canadian children between the ages of 5 and 17 are either overweight or obese (Roberts et al., 2012).

When it comes to our food, we have bought into the notion that bigger is better. Today's children are

That was then ... This is now

20 Years Ago	Today
Two pieces of pizza: 500 calories	Two pieces of pizza: 850 calories
Cheeseburger: 333 calories	Cheeseburger: 590 calories
Movie popcorn tub: 270 calories	Movie popcorn tub: 630 calories
Can of coke (351 ml): 145 calories	Bottle of coke (500 ml): 242 calories
Kids who walk or bike to school: 58%	Kids who walk or bike to school: 28%

Sources: Boyle, T. (2013, May 21). Canadian children don't walk to school, study says. *Toronto Star*, retrieved from http://www.thestar.com/life/health_wellness/2013/05/21/canadian_children_dont_walk_to_school_study_says.html; Gottesman, N. (2012). Generation XL. *Parenting School Years, 26*(7), p. 76; Monte, L. (2013). Portion size, then and now. Retrieved from http://www.divinecaroline.com/self/wellness/portion-size-then-vs-now

The following are some tips given by Nancy Gottesman (2012):

- Use smaller dishware (Cornell University scientists have proven we eat and drink less when using smaller dishes).
- Use the palm of your hand to gauge portions. Consider that many portions purchased in restaurants are usually 2 to 3 times the daily recommended serving size.
- When grabbing snacks, one serving size is what you can grab in one hand, not what comes in a prepackaged serving size.

part of the supersizing phenomenon. For example, many cookies today are 700% bigger than they were in the 1970s (Gottesman, 2012). Look at the following comparisons of common food servings compared with the 1970s.

Health Canada recommends that a healthy diet for children should focus on the number of food guide servings, not on calorie intake (Health Canada, 2007b) (see Figure 7.2). During the second and third years, a child's appetite typically varies, but because the child is growing more slowly than in infancy, he or she needs fewer calories. Children who eat little at one meal may compensate by eating more at another (Cooke, Breedlove, & Jordan, 2003).

Many children eat too much sugar and salt, which can be harmful to their health. Preferences for these foods containing sugar and salt increase with repeated exposure. Parents serve as role models in the development of food preferences (Hannon et al., 2003). The preschool age is an important time for parents to intervene, as preschool-aged children who are overweight are five times more likely than other children to be overweight at age 12 years (Nader, O'Brien, Houts, Belsky, Crosnoe, et al., 2006). Another study examined factors that contribute to the risk of being overweight among children 5 years of age; results included not eating breakfast, drinking more than two glasses of a sugary drink, playing outside less than one hour, and watching more than two hours of television a day (Veldhuis et al., 2012). Educating parents about the risk factors associated with obesity in young children and its long-term effects is an important first step towards prevention.

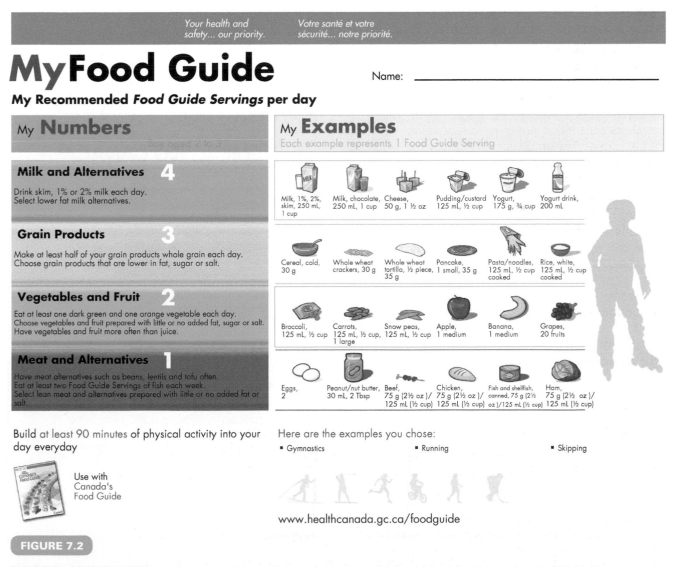

Your health and safety... our priority. *Votre santé et votre sécurité... notre priorité.*

MyFood Guide

Name: ______________________

My Recommended *Food Guide Servings* per day

My **Numbers** Boy aged 2 to 3	My **Examples** Each example represents 1 Food Guide Serving					
Milk and Alternatives 4 Drink skim, 1% or 2% milk each day. Select lower fat milk alternatives.	Milk, 1%, 2%, skim, 250 mL, 1 cup	Milk, chocolate, 250 mL, 1 cup	Cheese, 50 g, 1 ½ oz	Pudding/custard 125 mL, ½ cup	Yogurt, 175 g, ¾ cup	Yogurt drink, 200 mL
Grain Products 3 Make at least half of your grain products whole grain each day. Choose grain products that are lower in fat, sugar or salt.	Cereal, cold, 30 g	Whole wheat crackers, 30 g	Whole wheat tortilla, ½ piece, 35 g	Pancake, 1 small, 35 g	Pasta/noodles, 125 mL, ½ cup cooked	Rice, white, 125 mL, ½ cup cooked
Vegetables and Fruit 2 Eat at least one dark green and one orange vegetable each day. Choose vegetables and fruit prepared with little or no added fat, sugar or salt. Have vegetables and fruit more often than juice.	Broccoli, 125 mL, ½ cup	Carrots, 125 mL, ½ cup, 1 large	Snow peas, 125 mL, ½ cup	Apple, 1 medium	Banana, 1 medium	Grapes, 20 fruits
Meat and Alternatives 1 Have meat alternatives such as beans, lentils and tofu often. Eat at least two Food Guide Servings of fish each week. Select lean meat and alternatives prepared with little or no added fat or salt.	Eggs, 2	Peanut/nut butter, 30 mL, 2 Tbsp	Beef, 75 g (2½ oz)/ 125 mL (½ cup)	Chicken, 75 g (2½ oz)/ 125 mL (½ cup)	Fish and shellfish, canned, 75 g (2½ oz)/125 mL (½ cup)	Ham, 75 g (2½ oz)/ 125 mL (½ cup)

Build at least 90 minutes of physical activity into your day everyday

Here are the examples you chose:

- Gymnastics
- Running
- Skipping

Use with Canada's Food Guide

www.healthcanada.gc.ca/foodguide

FIGURE 7.2

Canada's Food Guide for a Toddler

Source: *My Food Guide*. Healthy Canadians, 2016. Adapted and reproduced with permission from the Minister of Health, 2016.

EMERGING CANADA

Currently, 14% of Canadian children in the early childhood age group are overweight, and 6% are obese. Without strong intervention, these numbers will increase as these children age. Experts believe that tackling the Canadian obesity epidemic will require tackling the early childhood age group. Cardiologists are now focusing on early childhood to prevent weight-related diabetes, heart disease, and stroke.

The Hospital for Sick Children and Toronto Public Health has launched Canada's first obesity program targeting 3- to 5-year-olds. The focus of the program is less on obesity and more on the healthy, active living of young children and their families. This cutting-edge program focuses on physical games, meal planning, and family activities to create healthy habits that can last a lifetime (Alphonso, 2012).

LO4 Health and Illness

Major Illnesses

Advances in immunization and the development of antibiotics and other medications have dramatically reduced the incidence and effects of serious childhood diseases in Canada. Because most preschoolers and schoolchildren have been inoculated against major childhood illnesses such as rubella (German measles), measles, tetanus, mumps, whooping cough, diphtheria, and polio, these diseases no longer pose the threat they once did.

Although many major childhood diseases have been largely eliminated in Canada and other industrialized nations, they remain fearsome killers of children in developing countries. Around the world, 8 to 9 million children die each year from only six diseases: pneumonia, diarrhea, measles, tetanus, whooping cough, and tuberculosis (UNICEF, 2006). Half of these deaths are preventable by simple intervention like vaccinations. Air pollution from the combustion of fossil fuels used for heating and cooking causes many respiratory infections, which are responsible for nearly one death in five among children under the age of 5 years (UNICEF, 2006). Diarrhea kills nearly 2 million children under the age of 5 years each year. Diarrheal diseases are mostly related to unsafe drinking water, inadequate sanitation, and poor hygiene (UNICEF, 2006). Children are at greater risk of dying if they live in rural areas, are from poor households, and/and or are born to mothers who are uneducated (World Health Organization, 2016b). In Canada, the number one cause of death of preschool aged children (1 to 4 years) due to natural causes is cancer at a rate 3.3% (Statistics Canada, 2015a).

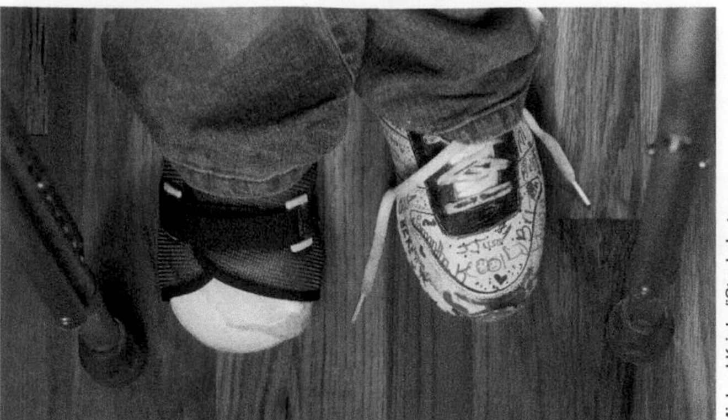
Michael Krinke/iStockphoto.com

Accidents

Accidents cause more deaths in early childhood than the next six most frequent causes combined (National Center for Injury Prevention and Control, 2007a). The single most common cause of death in early childhood is motor vehicle accidents. Boys are more likely than girls to incur accidental injuries at all ages and in all socio-economic groups. Children living in poverty are five times as likely as other children to die from fires and more than twice as likely to die in motor vehicle accidents (National Center for Injury Prevention and Control, 2007a).

EMERGING CANADA

The Canadian Lung Association educates Canadians about the health risks associated with second-hand smoke. Children are especially vulnerable because they have less developed immune systems than adults and they have a faster breathing rate, which means their bodies absorb more smoke. Children also have less control about whether their environment will be smoke-free or not. The nonprofit group Physicians for a Smoke-Free Canada estimates that in Canada, second-hand smoke is responsible for the following:

- 13% of ear infections
- 13% of asthma cases
- 16% of physician visits for cough
- 20% of lung infections in children younger than age 5
- 15 deaths per year due to deaths from fires
- 80–270 deaths per year from Sudden Infant Death Syndrome

Data collected by Health Canada in 2007 reported that 7% of children younger than age 12 are exposed to second-hand smoke at home (Canadian Lung Association, 2012).

LO5 Sleep

According to the National Sleep Foundation, toddlers need 12 to 14 hours of sleep in a 24-hour period. Getting the right amount of sleep may be difficult in a world that has become increasingly demanding and

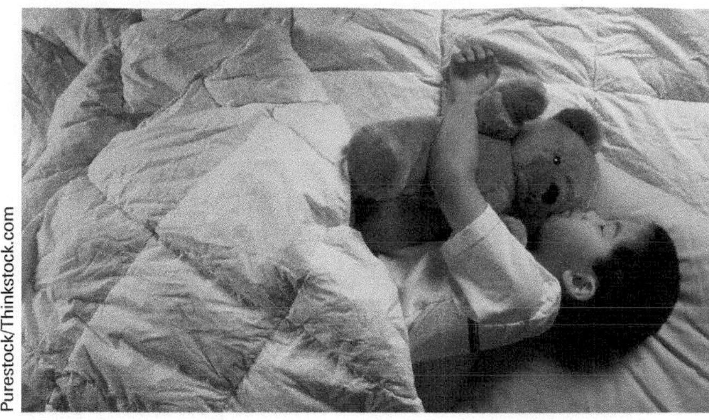
Purestock/Thinkstock.com

fast paced. Often the toddler's sleep schedules must be juggled to fit their busy family's routine. Changes in an infant's sleep schedule usually occur at around 18 months of age; children between the ages of 18 months and 4 years take regular naps, usually in the afternoon. If naps are too close to bedtime, sleep issues may surface. Toddlers will sleep better when they have a daily sleep schedule and a consistent bedtime routine. Security objects such as blankets or stuffed animals should be encouraged (National Sleep Foundation, 2011) to help soothe children in bed. If children do not receive sufficient sleep, they may experience changes in their behaviour such as hyperactivity, aggression, crying, or misbehaviour (Peters, 2013). Getting a child to sleep, especially during the day, may be very difficult for parents or caregivers. Children may protest sleep due to a sense of wanting to assert their independence and exercise control over what is happening to them. They may protest sleep also because they are overtired, making it difficult to fall asleep; or they may be experiencing some kind of stress like moving, a new sibling, or even changing rooms at daycare (Johnson, 2008).

Sleep Disorders

In this section, we focus on three sleep disorders that are significant for this age group: sleep terrors, nightmares, and sleepwalking.

Nightmares and Sleep Terrors

Nightmares are dreams of disturbing and vivid content. They take place during lighter, rapid-eye-movement (REM) sleep, when about 80% of normal dreams occur. **Sleep terrors** are extreme nightmares that take place during non-REM or deep sleep. When children awaken as a result of a sleep terror, they are often experiencing feelings of hyperarousal, agitation, sweating, high blood pressure, and enlarged pupils (National Sleep Foundation, 2016) due to the intense fear they are experiencing; this may even result in screaming.

Comstock Images/Jupiterimages

nightmares
dreams of disturbing and vivid content

sleep terrors
frightening dreamlike experiences that occur during the deepest stage of non-REM sleep, shortly after the child has gone to sleep

somnambulism
sleepwalking

Sleep terrors usually begin in childhood or early adolescence and are outgrown by late adolescence. They are sometimes associated with stress, often the result of moving to a new neighbourhood, beginning school, adjusting to parental divorce, or being in a war zone. Children with sleep terrors may wake suddenly with a surge in heart and respiration rates, talk incoherently, and thrash about. Children may then fall back into more restful sleep. The incidence of sleep terrors wanes as children age.

Children who have frequent nightmares or sleep terrors may come to fear going to sleep. They may show distress at bedtime, refuse to get into their pajamas, and insist that the lights be kept on. As a result, they can develop insomnia. Children with frequent nightmares or sleep terrors need caregivers' understanding and affection. They also benefit from a regular routine in which they are expected to get to sleep at the same time each night (Christophersen & Mortweet, 2003).

Sleepwalking

Sleepwalking, or **somnambulism**, is more common among children than adults. As with sleep terrors, sleepwalking tends to occur during deep sleep (Stores & Wiggs, 2001). Onset is usually between the ages of 4 and 8 years.

When children sleepwalk, they may rearrange toys, go to the bathroom, or walk to the refrigerator to get a glass of milk. Then they return to their room and go back to bed. Many myths surround sleepwalking, such as the suggestion that sleepwalkers' eyes are closed, that they will avoid harm, and that they will become violently agitated if awakened during an episode. All these notions are false. In fact, sleepwalking can be very dangerous as children can get hurt tripping on objects, falling down stairs, and even opening their doors and leaving home.

enuresis
failure to control the bladder (urination) once the normal age for control has been reached

bed-wetting
failure to control the bladder during the night

encopresis
failure to control the bowels once the normal age for bowel control has been reached; also called soiling

Thus, sleepwalkers should be brought back to their rooms to return to sleep, and locks should be installed on doors and other safety measures should be taken if this is a common pattern experienced by a child.

Sleepwalking in children is assumed to reflect immaturity of the nervous system. As with sleep terrors, the incidence of sleepwalking drops as children grow older. If a child has persistent sleep terrors or sleepwalking, it may be helpful to talk with a health professional. Information on sleep related disorders can be found on the Canadian Sleep Society website at https://css-scs.ca/resources/brochures#.

LO6 Elimination Disorders

During toilet training, a child's maturation plays a crucial role. During the first year, only an exceptional child can be toilet trained. Most Canadian children are toilet trained between the ages of 2 and 3 years (Bracht, 2007). Expectations around toilet training are culturally influenced, and in our busy Western culture, the initiation of toilet training is sometimes postponed. In a study conducted by Horn and colleagues (2006), both race and socio-economic status seemed to play a role in the age when toilet training was initiated. In this study, Caucasian parents initiated toilet training at 25.4 months, African American parents started at 18.2 months, and other racial groups began at 19.4 months. In addition, higher-income groups also initiated attempts later. The researchers suggest that the reasons for the different ages might include the cost of diapers and a need for day-trained children who will attend daycare.

Although children may be toilet trained during the day, they may continue to have nighttime "accidents" for another year or so. Children who do not become toilet trained within reasonable time frames may be diagnosed with enuresis, encopresis, or both.

DID YOU KNOW?

For most Canadian children, toilet training takes place between the ages of 2 and 3.

It is important to allow the child to set the pace for toilet training. The average age can vary significantly, and nighttime accidents can be expected to occur for an additional year after daytime training has been achieved.

Enuresis

Enuresis is failure to control the bladder (urination) once the "normal" age for achieving bladder control has been reached.

A nighttime "accident" is termed bed-wetting. Nighttime control is more difficult to achieve than daytime control. At night, children must first wake up when their bladders are full. Children would not be considered enuretic unless they wet themselves more than twice a week after age 5 years (Canadian Paediatric Society, 2005). At 5 years of age, 10–15% of Canadian children wet the bed. By 8 years, only 6–8% wet the bed (Canadian Paediatric Society, 2007). Bed-wetting is about twice as common among boys as among girls and tends to occur during the deepest stage of sleep, the stage when sleep terrors and sleepwalking may also occur. The cause of eneuresis is not usually associated with emotional and behavioural issues but with physical maturity of the bladder (Canadian Paediatric Society, 2005).

Just as children outgrow sleep terrors and sleepwalking, they tend to outgrow bed-wetting (Mellon & Houts, 2006). Scientists have discovered a gene for bed-wetting. If one parent wet the bed as a child, the child has a 25% risk of bed-wetting. If both parents wet the bed as children, this likelihood increases to about 65% (Canadian Paediatric Society, 2007).

Encopresis

Soiling, or encopresis, is lack of control over the bowels. Soiling, like enuresis, is more common among boys. About 1–2% of children between the ages of 7 and 8 years have continuing problems

EMERGING CANADA

In Canada, kindergarten children must be toilet trained to attend schools. Teachers do not help children in the washroom as they are worried about being accused of inappropriate behaviour. Consequently, some children sit in their wet or soiled clothes for long periods of time before their parents or caregivers can come and change them. One pediatrician said that he has seen diaper rashes in 4-year-old children because of this policy. Not only does this impact the child physically, but psychologically too as he or she would smell like urine and feces all day (Flanders, 2013). Also some schools with special needs children do not have adequate resources to help children in the washroom. Consequently, children on the autism spectrum who aren't toilet trained may go to the washroom accompanied by a classroom buddy rather than an adult. However, if the same child was attending daycare, he or she would be changed or assisted in the washroom as they do not have the same policies in place.

controlling their bowels (Mellon, 2006; von Gontard, 2007). Soiling, in contrast to enuresis, is more likely to occur during the day. Thus, encopresis can be embarrassing to the child, especially when it occurs at school.

Encopresis stems from both physical causes, such as chronic constipation, and psychological factors (Mellon, 2006; von Gontard, 2007). Soiling may follow harsh punishment of toileting accidents, especially in children who are already anxious or experiencing stress. Punishment may cause the child to tense up on the toilet, whereas moving one's bowels requires relaxation. Soiling, punishment, and anxiety can become a vicious cycle.

LO7 Jean Piaget's Preoperational Stage

According to Piaget, the preoperational stage of cognitive development lasts from ages 2 to 7 years. At this stage, young children's logic is at best "under construction." Preoperational literally means "before operations"; the child is not yet able to put various ideas and concepts together.

Symbolic Thought

Preoperational thought is characterized by the use of symbols to represent objects and relationships among them. According to Piaget, preschoolers' drawings are symbols of objects, people, and events in children's lives. Symbolism is part of pretend play.

Symbolic or Pretend Play

Children's symbolic play—the "let's pretend" type of play—may seem immature to busy adults meeting the realistic demands of the business world, but this type of play requires cognitive sophistication (Feldman & Masalha, 2007; Keen et al., 2007).

Christopher Futcher/iStockphoto.com

Piaget (1962 [1946]) wrote that pretend play usually begins in the second year, when the child begins to symbolize objects. The ability to engage in pretend play is based on children's mental representations of their experiences or things they have heard about.

preoperational stage Piaget's second stage of development, characterized by inflexible and irreversible mental manipulation of symbols

symbolic play play in which children make believe that objects and toys are other than what they are. Also called pretend play

egocentrism putting oneself at the centre of things such that one is unable to perceive the world from another person's point of view

Children first engage in pretend play at about 12 or 13 months. They make believe that they are performing familiar activities, such as sleeping or feeding themselves. By 15 to 20 months, they can shift their focus from themselves to others. A child may pretend to feed his or her doll. By 30 months, a child can make believe that the other object takes an active role. The child may pretend that the doll is feeding itself (Paavola et al., 2006).

Quality of pretend play has been found to influence future academic performance, creativity, and social skills among preschoolers (Russ, 2006; Stagnitti, Unsworth, & Rodger, 2000).

One example of pretend play is engaging with imaginary friends. As many as 65% of preschoolers have imaginary friends; they are most common among first-born and only children (Gleason et al., 2003). Having an imaginary playmate does not mean that the child has problems with real relationships (Gleason, 2004; Hoff, 2005). In fact, children with imaginary friends are usually less aggressive, more cooperative, and more creative than children without them (Gleason, 2002). Moreover, another study found that children who have imaginary friends have more real friends, show greater ability to concentrate, and are more advanced in language development (Taylor, 1999).

DID YOU KNOW?

Children pursuing a relationship with an imaginary friend show many developmental advantages.

Children who have imaginary friends are usually less aggressive, cooperate more, and show greater language development and concentration than children who do not.

Egocentrism: It's All about Me

According to Piaget, during the preoperational stage of development, children are one-dimensional thinkers. A consequence of this is egocentrism. Egocentrism,

precausal
a type of thought in which natural cause-and-effect relationships are attributed to will and other preoperational concepts

transductive reasoning
faulty reasoning that links one specific isolated event to another specific isolated event

in Piaget's use of the term, means that preoperational children do not understand that other people may have different perspectives on the world. When children want to hide from you, they will cover their eyes, thinking that if they can't see anything, neither can you.

Piaget used the "three-mountains test" (see Figure 7.3) to learn whether egocentrism prevents young children from sharing the viewpoints of others. In this demonstration, the child sits at a table before a model of three mountains. One has a house on it, one has a cross at the summit, and one final mountain is covered in snow. Piaget then placed a doll at the other end of the table. The children were permitted to move around the table to observe the mountains from the doll's perspective. They were then asked, "What does the doll see?" Since children this age will have difficulty describing the answer, they may select from various photographs that depict different viewpoints including their own and that of the doll. The 5- and 6-year-olds usually selected photos that correspond to what they themselves saw, their own perspective (Laurendeau & Pinard, 1970).

C Squared Studios/Getty Images

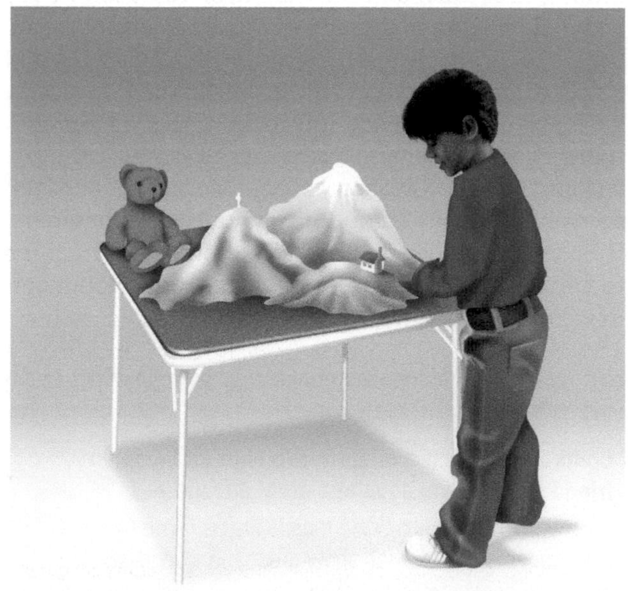

FIGURE 7.3

The Three-Mountains Test

Piaget used the three-mountains test to learn whether children at certain ages are egocentric or can take the viewpoints of others.

DID YOU KNOW?

Two-year-olds tend to assume that their parents are aware of everything that is happening to them, even when their parents are not present.

This attitude is a product of early childhood one-dimensional thinking and egocentrism.

Causality: Why? Because

Preoperational children's responses to questions such as "Why does the sun shine?" is also related to egocentrism. At the age of 2 years or so, they may answer that they do not know, or they may change the subject. Three-year-olds may report themselves as doing things because they want to do them or "Because Mommy wants me to." In egocentric fashion, this explanation of behaviour is extended to inanimate objects. The sun may be thought of as shining because it wants to shine or someone wants it to shine.

Piaget labels this structuring of cause and effect precausal. Unless preoperational children know the natural causes of an event, their reasons are likely to have an egocentric flavour and not be based on science. Consider the question, "Why does it get dark outside?" The preoperational child usually does not have knowledge of Earth's rotation and is likely to answer something like "So I can go to sleep."

In transductive reasoning, children reason by going from one specific isolated event to another. For example, a 3-year-old may argue that she should go to

DID YOU KNOW?

"Because Mommy wants me to" may be a perfectly good explanation for a 3-year-old.

This line of reasoning is also a reflection of early childhood egocentrism.

Jitloac/Shutterstock

sleep because it is dark outside. That is, separate events, darkness and going to sleep, are thought to have cause-and-effect relationships.

Preoperational children also show animism and artificialism in their attributions of causality. In animistic thinking, they attribute life and intentions to inanimate objects. For example, they may cry if you throw their dolls across the room thinking the dolls might be hurt. Artificialism assumes that environmental features such as rain and thunder have been designed and made by people.

Focus on One Dimension at a Time

To gain further insight into preoperational thinking, consider two problems. First, imagine that you pour water from a low, wide glass into a tall, thin glass, as in Figure 7.4(b). Does the tall, thin glass contain more than, less than, or the same amount of water as in the low, wide glass? We won't keep you in suspense. If you said the same amount, you were correct.

Next, if you flatten a ball of clay into a pancake, do you wind up with more, less, or the same amount of clay? If you said the same amount, you are correct once more.

To arrive at the correct answers to these questions, you must understand the law of conservation. The law of conservation holds that properties of substances, such as volume, mass, and number, remain the same—or are conserved—even if you change their shape or arrangement.

Preoperational children tend to focus on only one aspect of a problem at a time, a characteristic of thought that Piaget called centration. Conservation requires the ability to focus on two aspects of a situation at once, such as height and width. A preoperational child focuses, or centres, on only one dimension at a time. To test this, Piaget showed the children the different sized glasses, tall and thin or short and wide. To start, the child is shown two equal size glasses of water and agrees they contain the same amount of water. Then, as he watches, water is poured from one glass (short and wide) into the other glass (tall, and thin) Asked which glass has more water, he points to the tall glass. Why? When he looks at the glasses, he is swayed by the fact that the thinner glass is taller.

animism the attribution of life and intentionality to inanimate objects

artificialism the belief that environmental features were made by people

conservation in cognitive psychology, the principle that properties of substances such as weight and mass remain the same (are conserved) when superficial characteristics such as their shapes or arrangement are changed

The preoperational child's failure to show conservation also comes about because of irreversibility. In the case of the water, the child does not realize that pouring water from the wide glass to the tall glass can be reversed, restoring things to their original condition.

Another conservation experiment conducted with preoperational children involves conservation of number. Make two rows with four balls in each. As the 3-year-old child watches, move the balls in the second row to about 5 cm (2 in.) apart, as in Figure 7.5. Ask the child which row has more balls. When children see the balls in Figure 7.5, they say that the row of balls that is spread further apart contains more balls because it is more spread out and thus larger.

Class Inclusion

Class inclusion, as we are using it here, refers to the inclusion of new objects or categories in broader mental classes or categories. Class inclusion requires children to focus on two aspects of a situation at once. In one of Piaget's class-inclusion tasks, the child

a

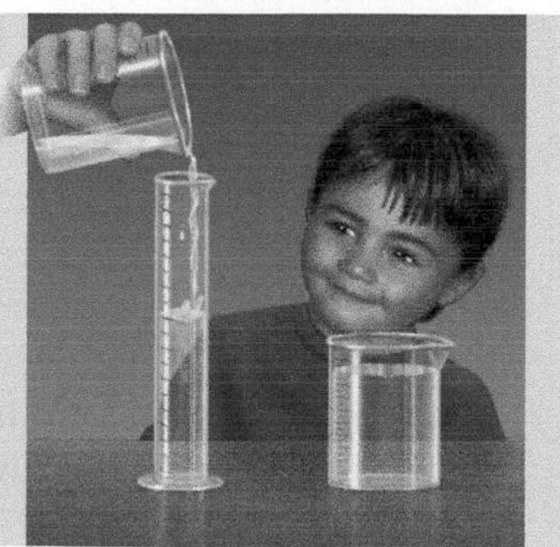
b

c

FIGURE 7.4

Conservation

(a) The boy in this illustration agreed that the amount of water in two identical containers is equal. (b) He then watched as water from one container was poured into a tall, thin container. (c) When asked whether the amounts of water in the two containers are now the same, he says no.

Source: © Cengage Learning

Child is shown two rows of loonies.
Experimenter moves loonies in one row.
Nikola Bilic/Shutterstock.com

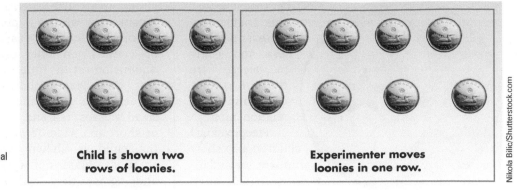

FIGURE 7.5

Conservation of Number

In this demonstration, a preoperational child will think that there are more loonies in the longer row.

scaffolding Vygotsky's term for the situation in which a child carries out tasks with the help of someone who is more skilled, to advance their skills

zone of proximal development (ZPD) the gap between what children are capable of doing now and what they could do with help from others

is shown several pictures from two subclasses of a larger class—for example, four cats and six dogs. She is asked whether there are more dogs or more animals. What do you think she will say? Preoperational children typically answer that there are more dogs than animals (Piaget, 1963 [1936]).

Why do preoperational children make this error? According to Piaget, they cannot think about the two subclasses and the larger class at the same time. Therefore, they cannot easily compare them. Children view dogs as dogs, or as animals, but find it difficult to see them as both dogs and animals at once (Branco & Lourenço, 2004).

LO8 Factors in Cognitive Development

Scaffolding and the Zone of Proximal Development

Different from Piaget, Vygotsky asserted that cognitive development is advanced by social interaction and parental responsiveness. One component of this interaction is scaffolding. Cognitive scaffolding refers to temporary support provided by a parent or teacher to help children learn. The guidance provided by adults decreases as children become capable of carrying out the task on their own (Lengua, Honorado, & Bush, 2007; Sylva et al., 2007). For example, every time parents sit down and review the sounds letters make with their preschool children, scaffolding is occurring. Eventually, with the help of parents, the child will make words from those sounds, as the scaffolding will help them advance. Without scaffolding, it is likely the same child will learn to read, however not as early.

In other words, the key forms of children's cognitive activities develop through interaction with older, more experienced individuals who teach and guide them. Consider working on a jigsaw puzzle with children. They will model your strategies of locating the corners and the edges first. With practice, they will be able to build the puzzle on their own.

A related concept is Vygotsky's zone of proximal development (ZPD). The zone refers to the gap between what children are capable of doing now and what they could do with help from others. For example, at the end of preschool, children may be able to read several 3-letter words on their own. With help from a teacher or parent, they can grow this list significantly, learn other word family groupings, and expand to 4-letter words or more challenging material. Adults or older children can best guide children through this zone by gearing their assistance to children's capabilities (Lantolf & Thorne, 2007; Wennergren & Rönnerman, 2006). In other words, you wouldn't give a preschool child a novel taught in Grade 3 as this would be too difficult and well outside the zone in which they would be able to comprehend. Thus, it is best to help children with material just outside their "zone" as they would learn this material without a struggle.

Effects of Early Childhood Education

Research suggests that preschool education offers children an early start on academic and social achievement in school. Children who have been reared in poverty perform significant lower on standardized intelligence tests than children of higher socio-economic status; they are also at greater risk for school failure as they grow older (Stipek & Hakuta, 2007; Whitehouse, 2006). As a result, preschool programs were begun in the 1960s to enhance children's cognitive development and readiness for elementary school. Canada has one of the earliest educational starts in the world, with children able to enter the school system as early as 3 years 8 months. Children in these programs typically are exposed to letters and words, numbers, books, exercises in drawing, pegs and pegboards, puzzles, and toy animals and dolls—materials and activities that middle-class children usually take for granted.

In First Nation communities, the Aboriginal Head Start on Reserve program encourages the development of locally controlled projects that strive to instill in children a sense of pride and a desire to learn. These programs also aim to enhance parenting skills that contribute to the healthy development of children, to improve family relationships, to foster emotional and social development, and to increase confidence (Health Canada, 2009). Studies of Head Start and other intervention programs show that environmental enrichment can enhance the cognitive development of economically disadvantaged children (Stipek & Hakuta, 2007; P. Wilson, 2004).

EMERGING CANADA

The ability to access quality daycare is becoming a national concern in Canada. Since the late 1990s, demand for daycare spaces has been rapidly rising in both urban and rural centres. In 2005, the Organisation for Economic Co-operation and Development (OECD) released a report that described Canada's childcare system as a chronically underfunded patchwork of programs with no overarching goals. The report ranked Canada last among developed countries in terms of access and public investment in child care. The report also found a shortage of available regulated childcare spaces—enough for fewer than 20% of children aged 6 years and younger whose parents work outside the home. In the United Kingdom, 60% of children find regulated child care; in Belgium, 63%; in France, 69%; and in Denmark, 78%. According to the Child Care Advocacy Association of Canada, the 2009 federal budget allocated no new money to daycare centres; thus, no improvement could be made. In addition, daycare costs are increasing. Statistics Canada reported in 2008 that the consumer price index rose by 2.3% but the average cost of day care across the country was up by 6.1% (CBC News, 2009b).

Television

The National Longitudinal Survey of Children and Youth (NLSCY) reported from data collected in 2004–05 that 27% of children aged 2 to 3 years, and 22% of children aged 4 to 6 years, are watching more than 2 hours of TV per day (Active Healthy Kids Canada, 2010). The good news is that some programs, such as *Sesame Street,* have positive effects on preschoolers' cognitive development (Calvert & Kotler, 2003). The goal of *Sesame Street* is to promote the intellectual growth of preschoolers, particularly those of lower socioeconomic status. Large-scale evaluations of the effects of *Sesame Street* have concluded that regular viewing increases children's learning of numbers and letters, and improves cognitive skills such as sorting and classification (Fisch, 2004). Caregivers are reminded

John Lamparski/WireImage/Getty Images

to limit the number of hours that children spend watching television. TV watching should be a conscious decision that is periodically reviewed. Caregivers should be wary of the trap of television—that it easily becomes a mindless distraction for children.

theory of mind the understanding that people are mental beings who have their own mental states, including thoughts, wishes, and feelings that differ from our own

EMERGING CANADA

The Canadian Paediatric Society recommends that children have no more than 2 hours of screen time daily (from television, DVDs, computers, social media, and video games), but research shows that just 15% of children meet this guideline while the rest exceed it. Studies show that the more time kids spend in front of a screen, the less likely they are to be physically active, which leads to weight issues. Research has also shown excessive screen time to be a risk factor for anxiety, depression, and a low sense of belonging. Caregivers need to set limits in early childhood to avoid the pattern of too much screen time that seems to be developing for older children. Canadians aged 10 to 16 years spend an average of 6 hours watching TV, playing video games, and/or using the computer (Fernandes, 2011).

LO9 Theory of Mind

People are mental beings and as such have their own mental states that impact their thoughts, wishes, and feelings—that is, a **theory of mind**. This is true whether we are thinking of our own thoughts, wishes, and feelings or inferring those of others whose thoughts, wishes, and feelings will differ from our own (Astington & Edward, 2010). Furthermore, theory of mind is also related to knowing the distinction between actual and imagined events and between how things may appear and how they are in reality.

appearance–reality distinction
the difference between real events on the one hand and mental events, fantasies, and misleading appearances on the other hand

Although there is some evidence that theory of mind has an earlier beginning, around the age of 4 years, theory of mind seems to advance. For example, Canadian researcher Janet Wilde Astington has a theory of mind lab at the Ontario Institute for Studies in Education. In one early study, Astington asked children what they believe would be inside a familiar box of chocolates (Gopnik & Astington, 1988). Naturally, they said chocolates, only to find pencils inside. The children were then asked what they thought other children would believe was inside the box. Three-year-olds said they thought others would think pencils were hiding inside, because of what they now believed. Older children (4- and 5-year olds), on the other hand, said that others would also be tricked into believing there were chocolates inside; by that age they had an understanding that people would have their own answers consistent with their own beliefs (Gopnik & Astington, 1988). The results of this study indicate that preschoolers have the ability to accurately predict and explain human action and emotion in terms of mental states (Wellman et al., 2006).

Finally, having a theory of mind influences social relationships because children who have a well-developed theory of mind tend to be better communicators and are able to resolve conflicts with their friends; they are also rated as more socially competent by their teachers and are more popular with their peers, and their pretend play is more advanced (Astington, & Edward, 2010).

Jeff Greenberg/PhotoEdit

As children get older, they realize that appearances can be different from reality.

Origins of Knowledge

Another aspect of theory of mind is how we acquire knowledge. By age 3 years, most children begin to realize that people gain knowledge about something by looking at it (Pratt & Bryant, 1990). By age 4 years, children understand that particular senses provide information about only certain qualities of an object; for example, they understand that we come to know an object's colour through our eyes, but we learn about its weight by feeling it (O'Neill & Chong, 2001). In a study by Daniela O'Neill and Alison Gopnik (1991), 3-, 4-, and 5-year-olds learned about the contents of a toy tunnel in three different ways: they saw the contents, were told about them, or felt them. The children were then asked to state what was in the tunnel and how they knew. Although 4- and 5-year-olds had no trouble identifying the sources of their knowledge, the 3-year-olds had difficulty. For example, after feeling but not seeing a ball in the tunnel, some 3-year-olds told the experimenter that they could tell it was a blue ball. The children did not realize they could not learn the ball's colour by feeling it.

Young children can remember a great deal, but compared with older children, they depend more on cues from adults to help them retrieve their memories.

The Appearance–Reality Distinction

Children must acquire an understanding of the difference between real events and imagined events, fantasies, and misleading appearances (Bialystok & Senman, 2004; Flavell, Miller, & Miller, 2002). This understanding is known as the appearance–reality distinction.

Piaget's view was that children do not differentiate reality from appearances or mental events until the age of 7 or 8 years. In a study by Marjorie Taylor and Barbara Hort (1990), children age 3 to 5 years were shown objects that had misleading appearances, such as an eraser that looked like a cookie. The children initially reported that the eraser looked like a cookie. However, once they learned that it was actually an eraser, they tended to report that it looked like an eraser. Apparently, these children could not mentally represent the eraser as both being an eraser and looking like a cookie.

LO10 Development of Memory

Memory significantly influences intelligence. However, children, like adults, often remember what they want to remember (Ghetti & Alexander, 2004; Sales, Fivush, & Peterson, 2003). By the age of 4 years, children can remember events that occurred at least 18 months earlier (Fivush & Hammond, 1990). Furthermore, young children seem to form scripts, which are abstract, generalized accounts of these repeated events. For example, in describing what happens during a birthday party, a child might say, "You play games, open presents, and eat cake" (Fivush, 2002) because that is what happens at most birthday parties. This script isn't based on a specific memory but rather generalizations of a common event. However, an unusual experience, such as a hurricane, may be remembered for its specific detail for years to come (Fivush et al., 2004).

Even though children as young as 1 and 2 years can remember events, these memories seldom last into adulthood. Memory of specific events—known as autobiographical memory—is facilitated by children talking about the events with others (Nelson & Fivush, 2004).

Factors Influencing Memory

Factors that affect memory include what the child is asked to remember, the interest level of the child, the availability of retrieval cues or reminders, and the memory measure being used. First, children find it easier to remember events that follow a fixed and logical order than events that are random. Children's interests also have impact on their memory. Research consistently shows that most preschool boys are more interested in playing with toys such as cars and weapons, whereas most preschool girls are more interested in playing with dolls, dishes, and teddy bears. Later, the children typically show better recognition and recall for the toys that interest them the most (Martin & Ruble, 2004).

Young children can remember a great deal, but compared with older children, they depend more on cues from adults to help them retrieve their memories. By elaborating on the child's experiences and by asking questions that encourage the child to contribute information to the narrative, adults can generally help children remember an episode (Nelson & Fivush, 2004).

scripts
abstract, generalized accounts of familiar repeated events

autobiographical memory
the memory of specific episodes or events

rehearsal
a strategy that uses repetition to remember information

Memory Strategies: Remembering to Remember

Adults and older children use strategies to help them remember things. One strategy is mental repetition, or rehearsal. If you are trying to remember a new friend's phone number, for example, you might repeat it several times. Another strategy for remembering is to organize things into categories. Most preschoolers do not engage in rehearsal until about 5 years of age (Labrell & Ubersfeld, 2004). They also rarely group objects into related categories to help them remember. By about age 5 years, though, many children have learned to verbalize information silently to themselves by counting mentally, for example, rather than aloud.

LO11 Language Development

Children's language skills mushroom during the preschool years. By the fourth year, children are asking adults and each other questions, taking turns talking, and engaging in lengthy conversations.

Development of Vocabulary

The development of vocabulary proceeds at an extraordinary pace. Preschoolers learn an average of nine new words per day (Tamis-LeMonda et al., 2006). But how can that be possible when each new word has so many potential meanings? Consider the following example. A toddler observes a small, black dog running through the park. His older sister points to the animal and says, "Doggy." The word *doggy* could mean this particular dog, or all dogs, or all animals. It could refer to one part of the dog (e.g., its tail), or to its behaviour (running, barking), or to its characteristics (small, black) (Waxman & Lidz, 2006). Does the child consider all these possibilities before determining what *doggy* actually means?

Myrleen Pearson/Alamy Stock Photo

fast mapping a process of quickly determining a word's meaning, which facilitates children's vocabulary development

overregularization the application of regular grammatical rules for forming inflections to irregular verbs and nouns

Word learning, in fact, does not occur gradually but is better characterized as a **fast-mapping** process in which the child quickly attaches a new word to its appropriate concept (Homer & Nelson, 2005; Waxman & Lidz, 2006). Children apparently have early cognitive biases or constraints that lead them to prefer certain meanings over others (Waxman & Lidz, 2006).

Development of Grammar

A "grammar explosion" occurs during children's third year (Tamis-LeMonda et al., 2006). Children's sentence structure expands to include the words missing in telegraphic speech. Children usually add to their vocabulary an impressive array of articles (*a, an, the*), conjunctions (*and, but, or*), possessive adjectives (*your, her*), pronouns (*she, him, one*), and prepositions (*in, on, over, around, under, through*). Between the ages of 3 and 4 years, children usually show knowledge of rules for combining phrases and clauses into complex sentences, as in "You goed and Mommy goed, too."

Overregularization

The apparent basis of one of the more intriguing language developments—overregularization—is that children acquire grammatical rules as they learn language. At young ages, they tend to apply these rules rather strictly, even in cases that call for exceptions (Jacobson & Schwartz, 2005; Stemberger, 2004). Consider the formation of the past tense and plurals in English. We add *d* or *ed* to regular verbs and s to regular nouns. Thus, *walk* becomes *walked* and *dog* becomes *dogs*. But then there are irregular verbs and irregular nouns. For example, *sit* becomes *sat* and *go* becomes *went*. *Sheep* remains *sheep* (plural) and *child* becomes *children*.

As children become aware of the syntactic rules for forming the past tense and plurals in English, they often misapply them to irregular words. As a result, they tend to make charming errors (Stemberger, 2004). Some 3- to 5-year-olds are more likely to say "Mommy sitted down" than "Mommy sat down" or talk about the "sheeps" on the farm and about all the "childs" they ran into at the playground.

Some parents recognize that their children used to form the past tense of irregular verbs correctly but then begin to make errors. Some of these parents become concerned that their children are "slipping" in their language development and attempt to correct them. However, **overregularization** reflects accurate knowledge of grammar, not faulty language development. In another year or two, *mouses* will be boringly transformed into *mice*, and Mommy will no longer have *sitted* down. Parents might as well enjoy overregularization while they can.

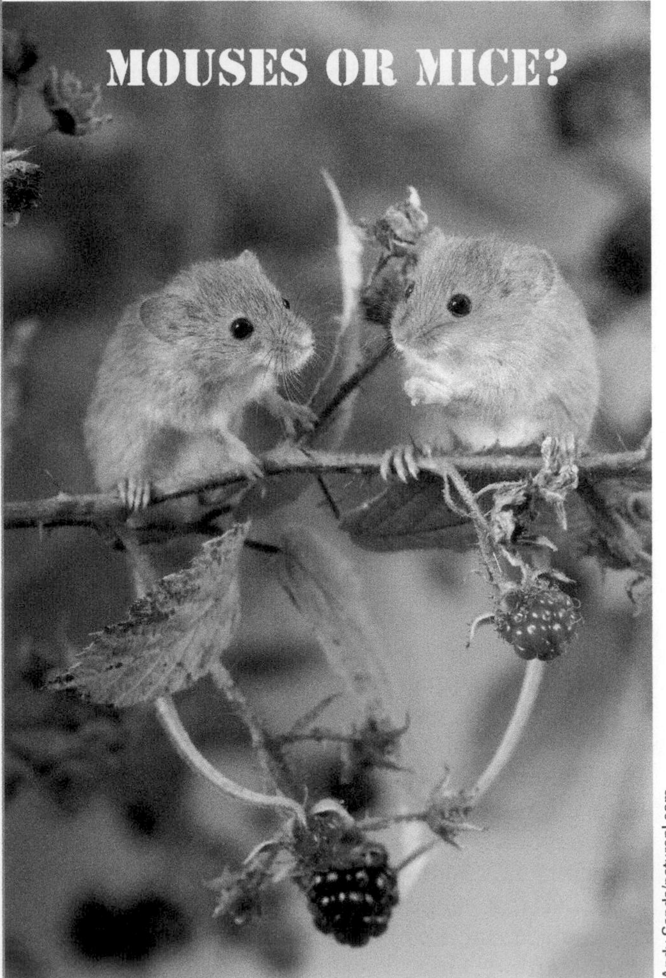

Andy Sands/naturepl.com

Asking Questions

Children's first questions are telegraphic and characterized by a rising pitch at the end, which, in English, signifies a question. Depending on the context, "More milky?" can be translated into "May I have more milk?" or "Would you like more milk?" or "Is there more milk?" Usually toward the latter part of the third year, the *wh* questions start. Consistent with the child's general cognitive development, certain *wh* questions (*what, who,* and *where*) appear earlier than others (*why, when, which,* and *how*) (Tamis- LeMonda et al., 2006). *Why* is usually too philosophical for a 2-year-old, and *how* is too involved. Two-year-olds are also likely to be oriented to the present, so *when* is of little concern. By the fourth year, most children are spontaneously producing *why, when,* and *how* questions. These *wh* words are initially tacked on to the beginnings of sentences. "Where Mommy go?" can stand for "Where is Mommy going?" or "Where did Mommy go?" or "Where will Mommy go?" The meaning must be derived from context. Later on, the child will add the auxiliary verbs *is, did,* and *will* to indicate whether the question concerns the present, past, or future.

Pragmatics

Pragmatics refers to the practical aspects of communication. Children show pragmatism when they adjust their speech to fit the social situation (Nelson, 2006). For example, children show greater formality in their choice of words and syntax when their make-believe games include role-playing high-status figures, such as teachers or physicians. They say "please" more often when making requests of high-status people. Another example of this is they use Motherese when talking to someone younger whether real or imagined.

Due to their egocentricity, when 2-year-olds tell another child, "Gimme my book," without specifying which book, they assume that the other child knows which book they want. Once children can perceive the world through the eyes of others, they advance in their abilities to make themselves understood. Children can then recognize that the others need a description of the book or of its location to carry out the request.

Language and Cognition

Language and cognitive development are interwoven (Homer & Nelson, 2005; Waxman & Lidz, 2006). For example, the child gradually gains the capacity to discriminate between animals on the basis of distinct features, such as size, patterns of movement,

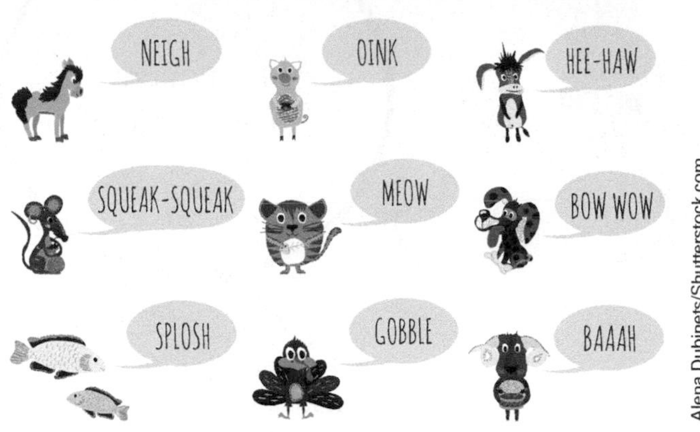

Alena Dubinets/Shutterstock.com

and the sounds they make. At the same time, the child is acquiring words that represent broader categories, such as *mammal* and *animal*.

pragmatics
the practical aspects of communication, such as adaptation of language to fit the social situation

But which comes first? Does the child first develop concepts and then acquire the language to describe them, or does the child's increasing language ability lead to the development of new concepts? To answer these questions, we turn to again to Piaget.

The Relationship between Cognitive and Language Development

Piaget (1976) believed that cognitive development precedes language development. He argued that children must understand concepts before they use words to describe them. From Piaget's perspective, children learn words to describe classes or categories that they have already created (Nelson, 2005). Children can learn the word *kitty* because they have perceived the characteristics that distinguish cats from other things; in other words, they have a schema for cat.

Some studies support the notion that cognitive concepts may precede language. For example, the vocabulary explosion that occurs at about 18 months of age is related to the child's ability to group a set of objects into two categories, such as "dolls" and "cars" (Gopnik & Meltzoff, 1992). On the other hand, other research suggests that young children need to experience an action themselves or by observation to learn the meaning of a verb (Pulverman et al., 2006).

Although many theorists argue that cognitive development precedes language development, others reverse the causal relationship and claim that children create cognitive classes to understand things that are labelled by words (Clark, 1983). When children hear the word *dog*, they try to understand

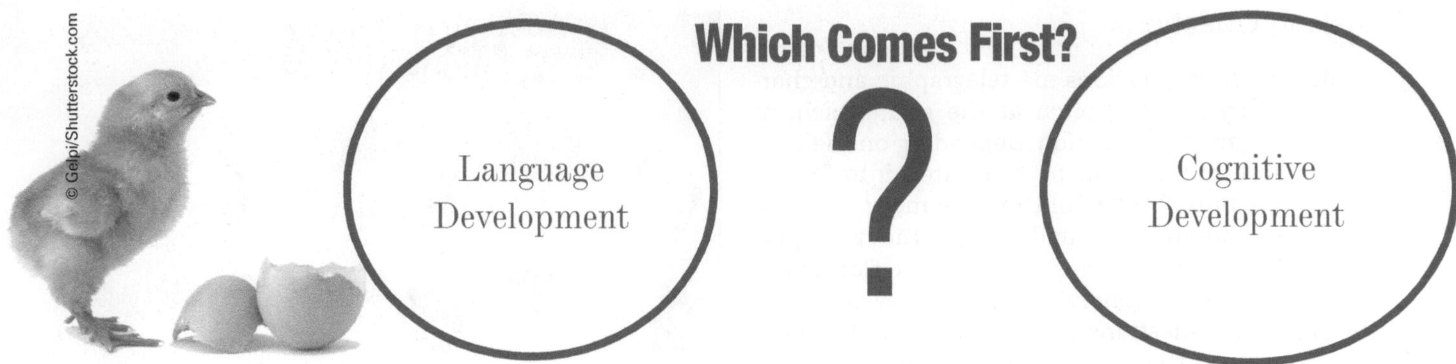

inner speech Vygotsky's concept of the ultimate binding of language and thought. Inner speech originates in vocalizations that may regulate the child's behaviour and become internalized by age 6 or 7.

it by searching for characteristics that separate dogs from other things.

Today, most developmental researchers find something of value in each of these cognitive views (Waxman & Lidz, 2006). In the early stages of language development, concepts often precede words, and many of the infant's words describe classes that have already developed. But later, language influences thought.

The Interactionist View: Outer Speech and Inner Speech

Vygotsky believed that during most of the first year, vocalizations and thought are separate. But during the second year, thought and speech are combined. Children discover that objects have labels. Their learning of the labels becomes more self-directed. Children ask what new words mean. Learning new words fosters the creation of new categories, and new categories become filled with labels for new things.

Vygotsky's concept of **inner speech** is a key feature of his position. At first, children's thoughts are spoken aloud. You can hear the 3-year-old instructing herself as she plays with toys. At this age, her vocalizations serve to regulate her behaviour, but they gradually become internalized. What was spoken aloud at ages 4 and 5 years becomes an internal dialogue by age 6 or 7 years. Inner speech is the ultimate binding of language and thought. It facilitates learning and is involved in the development of planning and self-regulation.

STUDY TOOLS

CourseMate CHAPTER 7

Located at **nelson.com/student**

- ☐ Prepare for tests with a variety of exercises and activities
- ☐ Review Key Terms Flashcards (online or print)
- ☐ Create your own study tools with Build a Summary
- ☐ Watch Observing Development videos to expand your knowledge

CHAPTER 8

Early Childhood: Social and Emotional Development

Kali9/iStockphoto.com

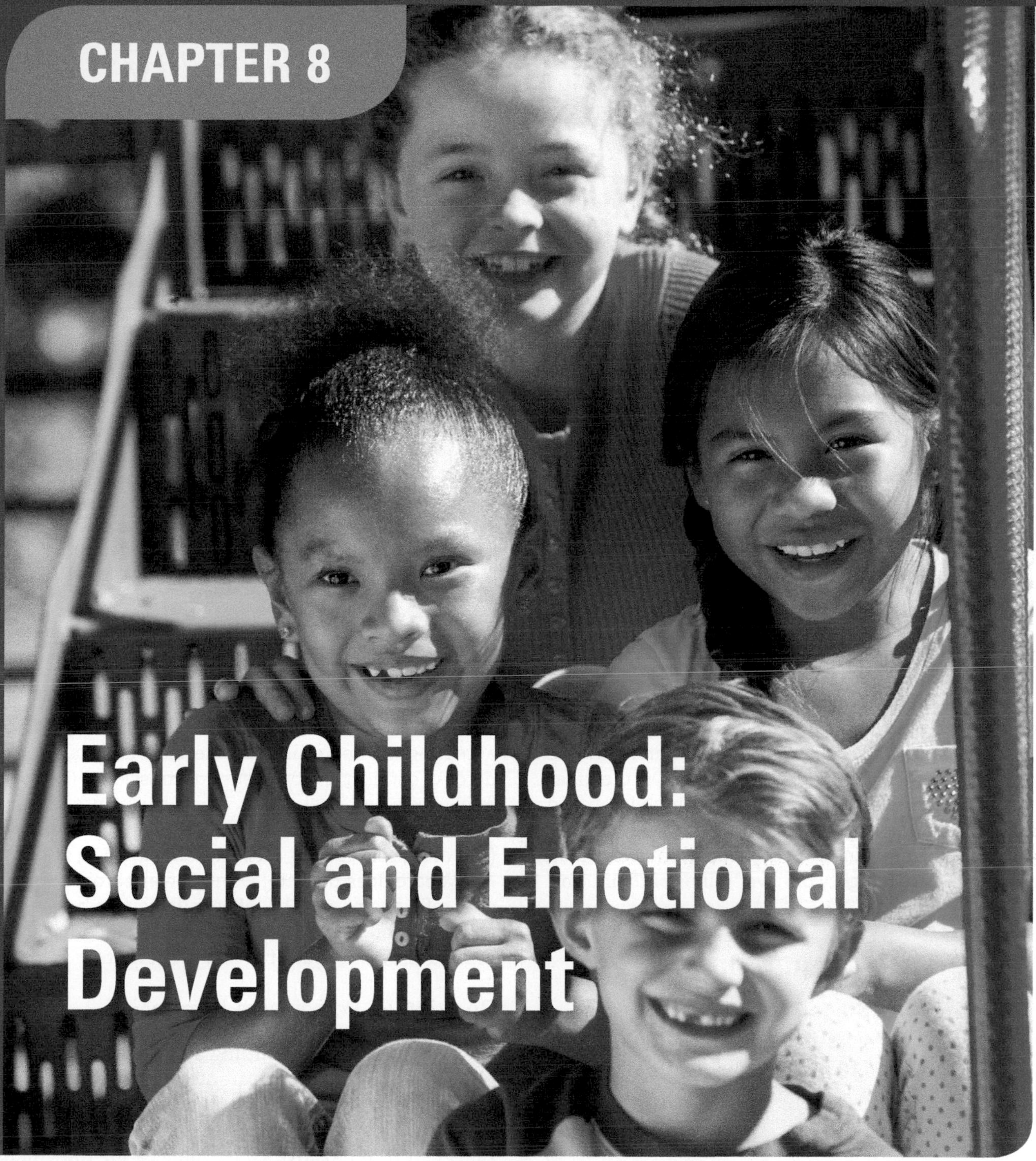

LEARNING OUTCOMES

LO1 Describe the dimensions of child rearing and parenting styles

LO2 Explain how siblings, birth order, peers, and other factors affect social development during early childhood

LO3 Discuss personality and emotional development during early childhood, focusing on the self, Erikson's views, and fears

LO4 Discuss the development of gender roles and sex differences

> "Most parents want preschoolers to develop a sense of responsibility and develop into well-adjusted individuals."

LO1 Child Rearing

Parents have different approaches to rearing their children. In this chapter, we will be looking at various child-rearing approaches. One way to classify parental patterns of child rearing is to determine where parents fall on two broad dimensions: warmth–coldness and restrictiveness–permissiveness (Baumrind, 1989, 2005).

Dimensions of Child Rearing

Warm–Cold Dimension

Warm parents are affectionate toward their children. They are caring and supportive, hugging, kissing, and smiling at them frequently. They communicate their enjoyment of being with their children. Moreover, warm parents are less likely than cold parents to use physical discipline (Bender et al., 2007). On the other hand, cold parents may not enjoy their children and may have few feelings of affection towards them. They are likely to complain about their children's behaviour, saying they are naughty or have "minds of their own."

Time & Life Pictures/Getty Images

Erikson Today

Stage 2: Autonomy versus Shame and Doubt (18 months to 3 years)

The next step along the road of personality development involves the challenge of autonomy vs. shame and doubt. As children become older and are able to explore their own environment, they need to develop a sense of autonomy or control. Between the ages of 18 months and 3 years, children have the opportunity to build self-esteem as they learn new skills and the difference between right and wrong. Well-cared-for children will explore their environment with pride rather than shame. This stage focuses on the ability (or inability) to master certain skills, as children become the controllers of their universe by mastering such social and cultural rules as toilet training and sleep schedules.

Time & Life Pictures/Getty Images

Erikson Today

Stage 3: Initiative versus Guilt (4 to 5 years)

The third piece of the puzzle focuses on the life stage when children begin to copy the important people in their lives by taking initiative in creating play situations. They make up stories and play out character roles in their pretend universe. They experiment with their ideas of who people are, both within the context of their family and in the world around them.

Clearly, it is better to be warm than cold toward children. The children of parents who are warm and accepting are more likely to develop internal standards of conduct, a moral sense or conscience (Bender et al., 2007; Lau et al., 2006). Parental warmth also is related to the child's social and emotional well-being (Lau et al., 2006; Leung, McBride-Chang, & Lai, 2004).

Where does parental warmth come from? Some of it reflects parental beliefs about how to best rear children, and some reflects parents' tendencies to imitate the behaviour of their own parents.

Restrictive–Permissive Dimension

Restrictiveness means putting standards or rules in place. It is not true that parents who are strict and demand mature behaviour end up raising rebellious children. Consistent control and firm enforcement of rules can have positive consequences for the child, particularly when combined with strong support and affection (Grusec, 2006). On the other hand, if "restrictiveness" means physical punishment, interference, or intrusiveness, it can give rise to disobedience, rebelliousness, and lower levels of cognitive development (Paulussen-Hoogeboom et al., 2007; Rudy & Grusec, 2006).

Permissiveness means not having or enforcing a standard of behaviour. Permissive parents do not present as authority figures or role models. Since there are few if any rules in place, children with permissive parents learn to regulate themselves; they make up their own rules and live by them.

Consider THIS

Can you be your child's friend?

See page 143 for a discussion of this topic.

Parenting Styles: How Parents Transmit Values and Standards

Diana Baumrind (1989, 1991b) focused on the relationship between parenting styles and the development of competent behaviour in young children. She used the dimensions of warmth–coldness and restrictiveness–permissiveness to develop a grid of four parenting styles based on whether parents are high or low in each dimension (see Table 8.1).

The parents of the most capable children are rated high in both dimensions, called **authoritative** parenting. They are highly restrictive and make strong demands for maturity. However, they also reason with their children and show strong support and feelings of love; they know what they want their children to do but also respect their children and are warm towards them.

Compared with other children, the children of authoritative parents tend to show self-reliance and independence, high self-esteem, high levels of activity and exploratory behaviour, and social competence. They are highly motivated to achieve and do well in school (Baumrind, 1989, 1991b; Grusec, 2006).

"Because I say so" could be the motto of parents whom Baumrind labels **authoritarian**. Students often confuse the endings of this parenting style and the previous one as they sound similar, but their impact on child rearing could not be more different. Authoritarians value obedience for its own sake. They have strict guidelines for right and wrong and demand that their children accept those guidelines without question. Like authoritative parents, they are controlling, but unlike authoritative parents, their enforcement methods rely on force. Moreover, authoritarian parents do not communicate well with their children or respect their children's viewpoints. Most researchers find them to be generally cold and rejecting (Grusec, 2002).

authoritative
a child-rearing style in which parents are restrictive and demanding yet communicative and warm

authoritarian
a child-rearing style in which parents demand submission and obedience

permissive–indulgent
a child-rearing style in which parents are warm and not restrictive

rejecting–neglecting
a child-rearing style in which parents are neither restrictive and controlling nor supportive and responsive

Baumrind found the sons of authoritarian parents to be relatively hostile and defiant and the daughters to be low in independence and dominance (Baumrind, 1989). Other researchers have found that the children of authoritarian parents are less competent socially and academically than children of authoritative parents. Children of authoritarian parents tend to be anxious, irritable, and restrained in their social interactions (Grusec, 2002). As adolescents, they may be conforming and obedient but have low self-reliance and self-esteem.

Baumrind found two types of parents who are permissive as opposed to restrictive. One is permissive–indulgent and the other rejecting–neglecting. **Permissive–indulgent** parents are low in their attempts to control their children and in their demands for mature behaviour. They are easy-going and unconventional. This type of parenting style is also accompanied by high nurturance (warmth and support). Because they supervise their children less closely than restrictive parents, permissive parents allow their children to do what is "natural," such as make noise, treat toys carelessly, and experiment with their bodies. They may also allow their children to show some aggression, intervening only when its continuation presents a danger. The children of permissive–indulgent parents are less competent in school and show more misconduct and substance abuse than children of more restrictive, controlling parents. But children from permissive–indulgent homesare fairly high in social competence and self-confidence.

Rejecting–neglecting parents are also low in their demands for mature behaviour and in their attempts to control their children. Unlike indulgent parents, however, they are low in support and responsiveness. The children of neglectful parents are the least competent, least responsible, and least mature of all children. The children of neglectful parents, like those of permissive–indulgent parents, are less competent in school and

TABLE 8.1

Baumrind's Patterns of Parenting

Parental Style	Restrictiveness and Control	Warmth and Responsiveness
Authoritative	↑	↑
Authoritarian	↑	↓
Permissive–Indulgent	↓	↑
Rejecting–Neglecting	↓	↓

inductive
parenting technique based on an attempt to foster understanding of the principles behind parental demands; characteristic of disciplinary methods, such as reasoning

show more misconduct and substance abuse than children of more restrictive, controlling parents. But children from neglectful homes are low in social competence and self-confidence (Baumrind, 1991a).

How Parents Enforce Restrictions

Inductive methods of child rearing aim to teach knowledge that will enable children to generate desirable behaviour on their own. The main inductive technique is "reasoning," or explaining why one kind of behaviour is good and another is not. Reasoning with a 1- or 2-year-old will be basic. "Don't do that—it hurts!" qualifies as reasoning with toddlers. "It hurts!" is an explanation, though brief. The inductive approach helps the child understand moral behaviour and fosters prosocial behaviours such as helping and sharing (Paulussen-Hoogeboom et al., 2007).

Power-assertive methods include physical punishment and denial of privileges. Parents often justify physical punishment with sayings such as "Spare the rod, spoil the child." Parents may insist that power assertion is necessary because their children are noncompliant. However, use of power assertion is related to both parental authoritarianism and children's behaviour (Roopnarine et al., 2006; Rudy & Grusec, 2006). Parental power assertion is associated with children's lower acceptance by peers, poorer grades, and more antisocial behaviour. The more parents use power-assertive techniques, the less children appear to develop internal standards of conduct. Parental punishment and rejection are often linked to children's aggression and delinquency.

Consistent control and firm enforcement of rules can have positive consequences for the child, particularly when combined with strong support and affection.

Didesign021/Shutterstock.com

Parents prefer power assertion to induction when they believe that children understand the rules they have violated and are capable of acting appropriately. Stress also contributes to the parents' use of power.

Some parents control children by threatening the withdrawal of love. They isolate or ignore misbehaving children. Because most children need parental approval and contact, loss of love can be more threatening than physical punishment. Although withdrawal of love may foster compliance, it may also instill guilt and anxiety (Grusec, 2002).

Preschoolers more readily comply when asked to do something than when asked to *stop* doing something (Kochanska, Coy, & Murray, 2001). One way to manage children who are doing something wrong or bad is to direct them towards a different activity. This is called redirecting.

Some recommended techniques that parents can use to help control and guide their children's behaviour without simply asserting their power are listed in Table 8.2.

Effects of the Situation and the Child on Parenting Styles

Parenting styles are not merely a one-way street, from parent to child. Parenting styles also depend partly on the situation and partly on the characteristics of the child (Grusec, 2006). For example, parents are most likely to use power-assertive techniques when dealing with their child's aggressive behaviour (Casas et al., 2006; Lipman et al., 2006).

Hartup has discussed the bidirectional relationship between parents and their children's behaviour. Individuals are changed by relationships just as changes in relationships are precipitated by changes in the individual (Hartup, 1986). In other words, relationships influence individual's behaviour just as individuals impact relationships, making it difficult to know when a problematic reaction began (Hartup, 1986). Is it that the child's temperament leads to inappropriate behaviour and this leads the parent to treat the child harshly in return, or does the parent's treatment of the child lead him or her to act negatively?

One study found that authoritative parenting styles mediate the relation between negative emotionality (an aspect of temperament) and problematic behaviours (Paulussen-Hoogeboom et al., 2008). When parents learn to respond to their child's negative reactions without reacting harshly themselves, the parent–child

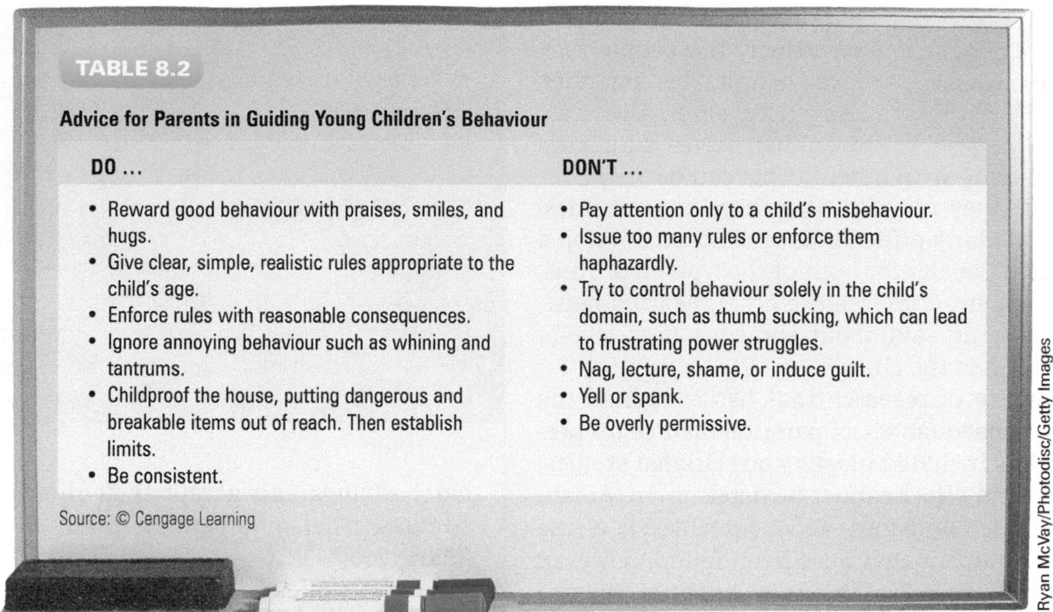

TABLE 8.2

Advice for Parents in Guiding Young Children's Behaviour

DO ...	DON'T ...
• Reward good behaviour with praises, smiles, and hugs. • Give clear, simple, realistic rules appropriate to the child's age. • Enforce rules with reasonable consequences. • Ignore annoying behaviour such as whining and tantrums. • Childproof the house, putting dangerous and breakable items out of reach. Then establish limits. • Be consistent.	• Pay attention only to a child's misbehaviour. • Issue too many rules or enforce them haphazardly. • Try to control behaviour solely in the child's domain, such as thumb sucking, which can lead to frustrating power struggles. • Nag, lecture, shame, or induce guilt. • Yell or spank. • Be overly permissive.

Source: © Cengage Learning

Ryan McVay/Photodisc/Getty Images

relationship becomes more rewarding, reducing the child's problematic behaviours in the present and in the future (Paulussen-Hoogeboom et al., 2008).

Consider THIS

Can you be your child's friend?

Many well-meaning parents want to be their child's friend. They want to have a close relationship with their child, sharing experiences that would be better shared with others their own age. By making the child their confidante, parents are saying that the child is a joint decision maker who is equipped to make appropriate decisions (Lehman, 2016).

Certainly, asking for children's preferences may be helpful, but children also need to hear the word "no" as this helps them to set limits. If parents are their children's friends, they may have a hard time setting boundaries, and this may have long-term consequences when other authority figures put demands on them. Said differently, "a parent should be the one person a child feels he can talk to about anything, while at the same time being the person who sets the rules, boundaries and expectations for behaviors" (Kidsafe Foundation, 2016).

The Effects of Divorce on Early Childhood

It is estimated that the 35% of children in Canada are impacted by divorce (Ambert, 2009). Twenty-two percent of Canadian children who live in one-parent families headed by females live in poverty. Also, the number of couples who tell their children they will be separating and how life will be different is only 5% (Ambert, 2009); the children are given no preparation for the transition that is taking place in their family, and they are given no say in their living arrangement.

Preschool-aged children are completely dependent on their parents for survival. When parents are divorcing, children's sense of security and safety is threatened. Preschool children worry about abandonment and separation. Furthermore, children may be shuffled in and out of their parents' homes weekly disrupting their routines, or they may not have access to one parent altogether. All of the changes related to their new family structure will significantly impact a young child's sense of stability.

Parents are reminded that young children experience divorce much differently from adults. Young children have a limited ability to understand the complex emotions they are experiencing; they are unable to regulate their emotions often leading to greater distress (Amato & Keith, 1991). According to one Canadian researcher, children between the ages of 4 to 10 years are most negatively affected by divorce because they are unable to process their loss and change in family structure (Ambert, 2009).

Often preschool-aged children view themselves as the cause of their parents' separation, and they believe or hope that their parents will ultimately get back together. Because early childhood is a time when children build their sense of self by watching and interacting with their parents, those children who witness their parents arguing often experience it as though they were personally involved. It is hard

regression
a return to behaviour characteristic of earlier stages of development

for preschoolers to understand why the people they love cannot be together, especially since the children themselves are always told to get along with others. This can be very confusing. Also, they may feel they have to take sides. This is particularly difficult since children develop a deep sense of loyalty for both of their parents. Thus, when one parent criticizes the other, hearing negative things being said about someone they love is very upsetting to the child.

The review of research that has examined the long-term consequences of parental divorce on preschoolers has included mostly correlational studies; thus cause and effect cannot be determined (Amato & Keith, 1991; Landsford, 2009; Leon, 2003). Some general conclusions that have been found, however, include a relationship between parental divorce when a child is under the age of 5 years and the likelihood of an anxious–ambivalent attachment style and less attachment to parents (Leon, 2003). Parental separation at a younger age seems to be related to behaviour issues (aggression, hyperactivity, fighting), academic and social difficulties, and emotional distress including anxiety, depression, and low self-esteem (Ambert, 2009; Amato & Keith, 1991; Landsford, 2009; Leon, 2003). However, it has also been found that many children emerge after the first 2 years of divorce without long-term negative consequences (Landsford, 2009; Leon, 2003).

LO2 Social Behaviours

During early childhood, children make tremendous advances in social skills and behaviour. Their play increasingly involves other children. They learn how to share, cooperate, and comfort others. But young children, like adults, can be aggressive as well as loving and helpful.

Influence of Siblings

Siblings serve many functions in the social development of a preschool child, including giving physical care, providing emotional support and nurturance, offering advice, serving as role models, providing social interaction that helps develop social skills, making demands, and imposing restrictions (McHale, Kim, & Whiteman, 2006; Parke & Buriel, 2006).

In early childhood, siblings' interactions have positive aspects (cooperation, teaching, nurturance) and negative aspects (conflict, control, competition) (Parke & Buriel, 2006). Older siblings tend to be more caring but also more dominating than younger siblings. Younger siblings are more likely to imitate older siblings and accept their direction. In many cultures, older girls care for their younger siblings (Clark, 2005).

Szefei/Shutterstock.com

Parents often urge their children to stop fighting among themselves, and at times, these conflicts look deadly. But sibling conflict can enhance children's social competence, their development of self-identity (who they are and what they stand for), and their ability to rear their own children (Ross et al., 2006). More conflicts occur between siblings when the parents play favourites (Scharf, Shulman, & Avigad-Spitz, 2005). Conflict between siblings is also greater when the relationship between the parents or between the parents and children are troubled (Kim et al., 2006).

Adjusting to the Birth of a Sibling

The birth of a sister or brother leads to changes in family relationships, and these changes are often a source of stress for preschoolers (Volling, 2003). When a new baby comes into the home, the mother pays relatively more attention to that child and spends less time with the older child. As a result, the older child may feel displaced and resentful.

Children show a mixture of negative and positive reactions to the birth of a sibling. Negative responses include regression to baby-like behaviours, such as increases in clinging, crying, and toilet accidents. Anger and naughtiness may also increase. But the same children may also show more independence and maturity, insisting on feeding or dressing themselves and helping to care for the baby (Volling, 2003). Parents can help a young child cope with the arrival of a baby by explaining in advance what is to come (Kavcic & Zupancic, 2005).

Birth Order

Differences in personality and achievement have been linked to birth order. First-born children, as a group, are more highly motivated to achieve than later-born children (Latham & Budworth, 2007). First-born and only children perform better academically and are more cooperative (Healy & Ellis, 2007). They are more adult-oriented and less aggressive than later-born children (Beck, Burnet, & Vosper, 2006; Zajonc, 2001). They obtain higher standardized test scores, including IQ and SAT scores (Kristensen & Bjerkedal, 2007; Sulloway, 2007). On the negative side, first-born and only children show greater anxiety and are less self-reliant than later-born children.

Later-born children may learn to act aggressively to compete for the attention of their parents and older siblings (Carey, 2007b). Their self-concepts tend to be lower than those of first-born or only children, but the social skills later-born children acquire from dealing with their family position seem to translate into greater popularity with peers (Carey, 2007b). They also tend to be more rebellious and liberal than first-born children (Beck et al., 2006; Zweigenhaft & Von Ammon, 2000).

By and large, parents are more relaxed and flexible with later-born children. Many parents see that the first-born child is turning out well and perhaps they assume that later-born children will also turn out well.

> **DID YOU KNOW?**
>
> **First-born children are more highly motivated to achieve than later-born children.**
>
> As a group, this is true, but individual variances always occur.

Blend Images/Shutterstock.com

First-born children tend to be more cooperative, and later-born children tend to be more social.

Peer Relationships

Peer interactions foster social skills—sharing, helping, taking turns, and dealing with conflict. Groups teach children how to lead and how to follow. Physical and cognitive skills develop through peer interactions. Peers also provide emotional support (Dishion & Stormshak, 2007; Grusec, 2006).

By about 2 years of age, children imitate one another's play and engage in social games such as follow-the-leader (Fontaine, 2005; Kavanaugh, 2006). Also, 2-year-old children show preferences for particular playmates—an early sign of friendship (Sherwin-White, 2006). Friendship is characterized by shared positive experiences and feelings of attachment (Grusec, 2002). Even early friendships can be fairly stable (Rubin, Bukowski, & Parker, 2006).

When preschoolers are asked what they like about their friends, they typically mention the toys and activities they share (Gleason & Hohmann, 2006). Primary-school children usually report that their friends are the children with whom they do things and have fun (Gleason & Hohmann, 2006). They also live in close proximity to their friends such as on their street and in their neighbourhood. Thus the repeated exposure makes them more favourable. Another important determinant of friendship among preschool aged children is similarity (Cook & Cook, 2010). Children spend a lot of time together sharing toys, activities, and playing games. The importance to friendship of friends' traits and notions of trust, communication, and intimacy do not emerge until late childhood and adolescence.

dramatic play play in which children enact social roles

The Importance of Play

Play is more than fun; it is also meaningful, voluntary, and internally motivated (Elkind, 2007). Play helps children develop motor skills and coordination. It contributes to social development, as children learn to share their play materials, take turns, and, through **dramatic play**, try on new roles (Elkind, 2007). Play also supports the development of such cognitive qualities as curiosity, exploration, symbolic thinking, and problem solving. Play may even help children learn to control impulses (Elkind, 2007).

Play and Cognitive Development

Play contributes to and expresses milestones in cognitive development. Jean Piaget (1962 [1946]) identified kinds of play, each characterized by increasing cognitive complexity:

- *Functional play.* Beginning in the sensorimotor stage, the first kind of play involves repetitive motor activity, such as rolling a ball or running and laughing.
- *Symbolic play.* Also called pretend play, imaginative play, or dramatic play, symbolic play emerges toward the end of the sensorimotor stage and increases during early childhood. In symbolic play, children create settings, characters, and scripts (Kavanaugh, 2006).
- *Constructive play.* Children use objects or materials to draw or make something, such as a tower of blocks.
- *Formal games.* Games with rules include board games, which are sometimes enhanced or invented by children, and games involving motor skills, such as marbles and hopscotch, ball games involving sides or teams, and video games. Such games may involve social interaction as well as physical activity and rules. People play such games for a lifetime.

EMERGING CANADA

The "hot toy list" published by The Canadian Toy Association for 2016 includes droids and robots such as BB-8 from *Star Wars*, Finding Dory: Let's Speak Whale, and Paw Patrol Air Patrollers. Other popular toys include HEXBUG AquaBot, which is an electromagnetic toy that can be used in water, and KIDIzoom Smartwatch, which allows children to take photos and videos and to play games. What influences are at play when it comes to the toys we choose for our children?

Simple is better for most children. When toys become equipped with flashing lights and moving parts, there is less for the child to do so they quickly lose interest (Abel, 2016). The top toys of all time include blocks, building toys, dolls, play dough, and other arts and crafts as well as dress-up clothes (Abel, 2016). All of these toys require imagination and promote interaction with other children.

How do smart phones, tablets, and other gaming equipment that is geared for preschoolers impact their play? Children between the ages of 0 to 6 years spend approximately two hours daily on screen time (Malik, 2007). There is evidence that screen time from such sources as tablets, television, and computers can become addictive. Furthermore, many experts believe that screen time reduces a child's much needed time to daydream, process their experiences with parents, and receive reassurance. When children are given electronic equipment for a ride in the car, the ability to engage in discussions with parents, leading to the opportunity for support, is limited. Screen time limits time for social interactions that take place one-on-one and there is also evidence that it reduces a child's ability to recognize emotions (Summers, 2014).

Another well-documented finding is that by age 2 years, many children begin to prefer playmates of the same sex. Girls tend to develop this preference earlier than boys (Fagot, 1990; Hay, Payne, & Chadwick, 2004). This tendency strengthens during middle childhood.

Prosocial Behaviour

Prosocial behaviour, also known as altruism, refers to behaviour that is intended to benefit another without expectation of reward. Prosocial behaviour includes sharing, cooperating, and helping and comforting others in distress (Strayer & Roberts, 2004). This behaviour is exhibited by children in their preschool and early school years (Knafo & Plomin, 2006a, 2006b) and is linked to the development of empathy and perspective taking.

Empathy

Empathy refers to sensitivity to the feelings of others; it is demonstrated by such activities as sharing and cooperating. An early example of empathy is that infants frequently begin to cry when they hear other children crying, although this agitated response may be largely reflexive (Strayer & Roberts, 2004). Empathy promotes prosocial behaviour and decreases aggressive behaviour, and these links are evident by the second year (Hastings et al., 2000). During the second year, many children approach other children and adults who are in distress and try to help them. They may hug a crying child or tell the child not to cry. On the other hand, toddlers who are rated as emotionally unresponsive to the feelings of others are more likely to behave aggressively throughout their school years (Olson et al., 2000).

Girls show more empathy than boys (Strayer & Roberts, 2004). It is unclear whether this sex difference reflects genetic factors or the socialization of girls to be attuned to the emotions of others.

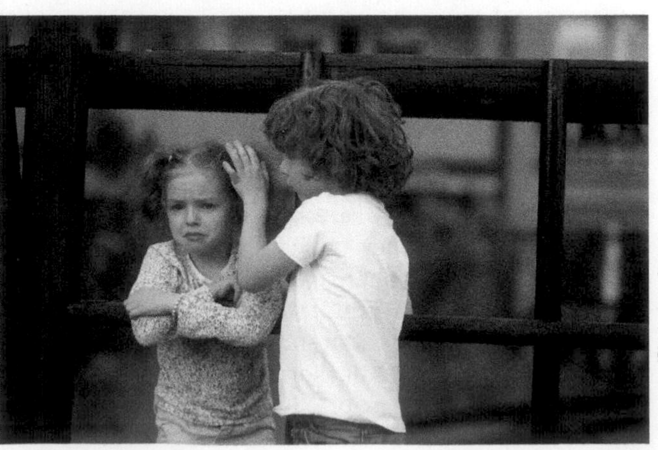

unguryanu/Shutterstock.com

Perspective Taking

According to Piaget, preoperational children tend to be egocentric. They tend not to be able to see things from the vantage points of others. Various cognitive abilities, such as being able to take another person's perspective, are related to knowing when someone is in need or distress. Perspective-taking skills improve with age, as do other prosocial skills. Among children of the same age, those with better-developed perspective-taking ability also show more prosocial behaviour and less aggressive behaviour (Hastings et al., 2000).

Influences on Prosocial Behaviour

Altruistic behaviour is often defined as prosocial behaviour that occurs in the absence or without the expectations of rewards; but altruism is, in reality, influenced by rewards and punishments. Nursery-school children who are cooperative, friendly, and generous have peers who respond more positively to them as compared to children whose behaviour is self-centred (Hartup, 1983). Children who are rewarded for acting prosocially are likely to continue these behaviours (Knafo & Plomin, 2006a, 2006b).

Parents foster prosocial behaviour when they use inductive techniques such as explaining how behaviour affects others ("You made Josh cry. It's not nice to hit."). Parents of prosocial children are more likely to expect mature behaviour from their children. They are less likely to use power-assertive techniques of discipline (Strayer & Roberts, 2004).

Development of Aggression

Aggression refers to behaviour intended to hurt or injure another person. Children, like adults, can be aggressive.

Aggressive behaviour, similar to other social behaviour, seems to follow developmental patterns. The aggression of preschoolers is frequently instrumental or possession oriented (Persson, 2005). For example, younger preschoolers tend to use aggression to obtain the toys or to get what they want, such as a favoured seat at the table or in the car. Anger and aggression in preschoolers usually causes other preschoolers to reject them (Henry et al., 2000; Walter & LaFreniere, 2000).

Older preschoolers are more likely to resolve conflicts over toys by sharing rather than fighting (Caplan et al., 1991). By age 6 or 7 years, aggression becomes hostile and person oriented. Children taunt and criticize one another and call one another names; they also attack one another physically.

Aggressive behaviour appears to be generally consistent over time and predictive of social and emotional problems later on, especially among boys (Nagin & Tremblay, 2001; Tapper & Boulton, 2004). Toddlers who are perceived as difficult and defiant are more likely than others to behave aggressively throughout their school years (Olson et al., 2000).

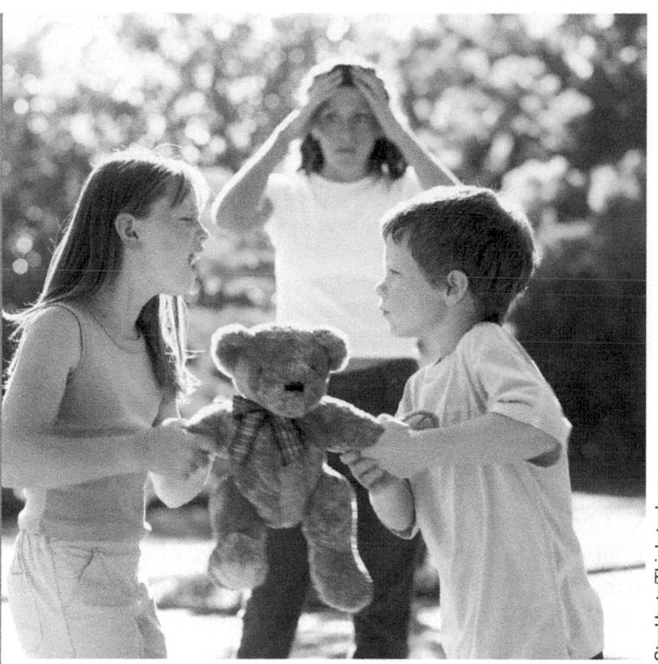
Stockbyte/Thinkstock.com

Theories of Aggression

Evidence suggests that genetic factors may be involved in aggressive behaviour, including criminal and antisocial behaviour (Hicks et al., 2007; Lykken, 2006a; E. O. Wilson, 2004). If genetics is involved in aggression, genes may do their work at least in part through the male sex hormone testosterone. Testosterone is apparently related to feelings of self-confidence, high activity levels, and—the negative side—aggressiveness (Archer, 2006; Cunningham & McGinnis, 2007; Popma et al., 2007).

Social cognitive explanations of aggression focus on environmental factors such as reinforcement and observational learning. Cognitive research with primary-school children has found that children who believe that aggression is an acceptable way to settle matters are more likely to behave aggressively when provoked (Tapper & Boulton, 2004). When children repeatedly push, shove, and hit to grab toys or break into line, other children usually let them have their way (Kempes et al., 2005). Children who are thus rewarded for acting aggressively are likely to continue to use aggressive means, especially if they have no other means to achieve their ends. Aggressive children may also associate with peers who value and encourage aggression (Stauffacher & DeHart, 2006).

Children who are physically punished are more likely to be aggressive themselves than children who

disinhibit stimulate a response that has been suppressed by showing a model engaging in that response

are not physically punished (Patterson, 2005). Physically aggressive parents serve as models for aggression and also stoke their children's anger.

Myrleen Pearson/Alamy Stock Photo

DID YOU KNOW?

Children who are physically punished are more likely to be aggressive than children who are not physically punished.

This fact raises important discipline issues.

Media Influences

Real people are not the only models of aggressive behaviour in children's lives. A classic study by Albert Bandura and his colleagues (1963) suggested that televised models had a powerful influence on children's aggressive behaviour. One group of preschoolers observed a film of an adult model hitting and kicking an inflated Bobo doll, whereas a control group saw an aggression-free film. The experimental and control children were then left alone in a room with the same doll as hidden observers recorded their behaviour. The children who had observed the aggressive model showed significantly more aggressive behaviour toward the doll. Many children imitated the bizarre attack behaviours they had observed in the film, behaviours they would not have thought up themselves.

greenland/Shutterstock.com

Consider the ways in which depictions of violence contribute to actual violence:

- *Observational learning.* Children learn from observation (Holland, 2000). TV violence supplies models of aggressive "skills," which children may acquire.
- *Disinhibition.* Punishment inhibits behaviour. Conversely, media violence may disinhibit aggressive behaviour, especially when characters "get away" with it.
- *Increased arousal.* Media violence and aggressive video games increase viewers' level of arousal. People are more likely to be aggressive under high levels of arousal.
- *Priming of aggressive thoughts and memories.* Media violence "primes," or arouses, aggressive ideas and memories (Bushman, 1998; Meier, Robinson, & Wilkowski, 2006).
- *Habituation.* We become used to repeated stimuli. Children exposed to violence are more likely to assume that violence is acceptable or normal and become desensitized to it (Holland, 2000).

DID YOU KNOW?

Children who watch 2 to 4 hours of TV a day will see 8,000 murders and another 100,000 acts of violence by the time they have finished elementary school.

What are our children watching?

DID YOU KNOW?

Children mechanically imitate the aggressive behaviour they view in the media.

According to social cognitive theory, a direct connection cannot be drawn between exposure to media violence and violence in real life. But what about the indirect effects?

Although exposure to violence in the media increases the probability of violence by viewers, media violence has no simple one-to-one connection to violence in real life. According to social cognitive theory, we also choose whether to imitate the behaviour we observe.

EMERGING CANADA

Albert Bandura was born in the small town of Mundare, Alberta. He attended a two-teacher school, which he believes was an advantage because it encouraged him to be inquisitive. He fell in love with the field of psychology and earned his Ph.D. from the University of British Columbia. His early research focused on human motivation, action, and thought. He then worked with Richard Walters to explore social aggression. Bandura challenged the notion that punishment and rewards were primary factors in behaviour, suggesting that our behaviour was also based on the behaviours of others. This work led him to conduct his famous Bobo doll experiment. He concluded that aggressive behaviour was learned through exposure to aggressive behaviour in others. Bandura developed social cognitive theory from a holistic view of human cognition in relation to social awareness and influence. Albert Bandura has been listed as one of the most influential figures in modern psychology and has been described as "the greatest living psychologist" (GoodTherapy.org, 2013). He recently received an appointment to the Order of Canada for his significant contribution to the field of social psychology.

LO3 Personality and Emotional Development

In early childhood, children's sense of self—who they are and how they feel about themselves—develops and grows more complex. They begin to acquire a sense of their own abilities and their increasing mastery of the environment. As they move out into the world, they also face new experiences that may cause them to feel fearful and anxious.

The Self

The sense of self, or the self-concept, emerges gradually during infancy. Infants and toddlers visually begin to recognize themselves and differentiate themselves from other individuals such as their parents.

categorical self the definitions of the self that refer to external traits

In the preschool years, children continue to develop their sense of self. Almost as soon as they begin to speak, they describe themselves in terms of certain categories, such as age groupings (baby, child, adult) and sex (girl, boy). Self-definitions that refer to concrete external traits have been called the categorical self.

One aspect of the self-concept is self-esteem. Children with high self-esteem are more likely to be securely attached and to have parents who are attentive to their needs (Booth-LaForce et al., 2006; Patterson & Bigler, 2006). Also, they are more likely to exhibit prosocial behaviour (Salmivalli et al., 2005).

By the age of 4 years, children begin to make evaluative judgments about two different aspects of themselves (Harter & Pike, 1984). One is their cognitive and physical competence (e.g., being good at puzzles, counting, swinging, tying shoes), and the second is their social acceptance by peers and parents (e.g., having lots of friends, being read to by Mom). But preschoolers do not yet clearly

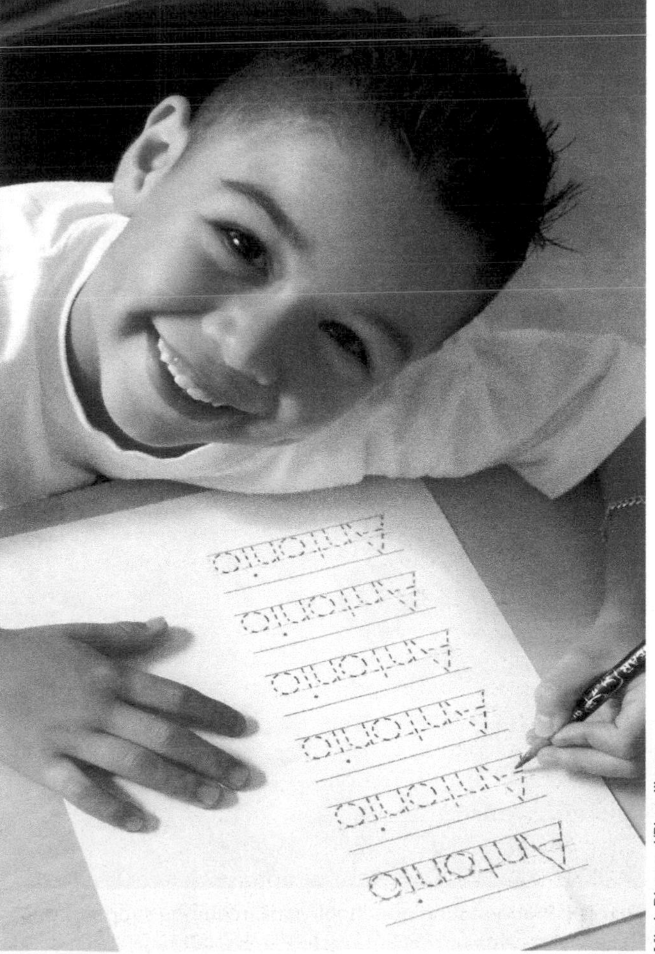

Mitch Diamond/Photolibrary

distinguish between different areas of competence. A child is not likely to report being good academically but poor in physical skills. One is either "good at doing things" or not (Clark & Symons, 2000; Piek, Baynam, & Barrett, 2006).

Fears: The Horrors of Early Childhood

In Erikson's view, fear of violating parental prohibitions can be a powerful force in a young child's life. Children's fears change as they move from infancy into the preschool years. The number of fears seems to peak between 2.5 and 4 years and then tapers off (Miller, Boyer, & Rodoletz, 1990). Fear of social disapproval is just beginning to develop among children of this age group. Preschoolers are most likely to fear animals, imaginary creatures, the dark, and personal danger (Field, 2006; Muris et al, 2003). Young children's fantasies frequently involve stories they are told and images they see in the media. Frightening images of imaginary creatures can remain in the child's mind for a long time. Many preschoolers are reluctant to have the lights turned off at night for fear that such creatures may appear or even assault them. Real objects and situations also cause many preschoolers to fear for their personal safety. These sources of fear include lightning, thunder and other loud noises, high places, sharp objects and being cut, blood, unfamiliar people, strange people, and insects.

DID YOU KNOW?

The types of fears children experience from preschool age to middle childhood differ, but they remain a significant hurdle for children.

Fear of the dark, monsters under the bed, thunder and lightning, and being alone are among the top worries children report.

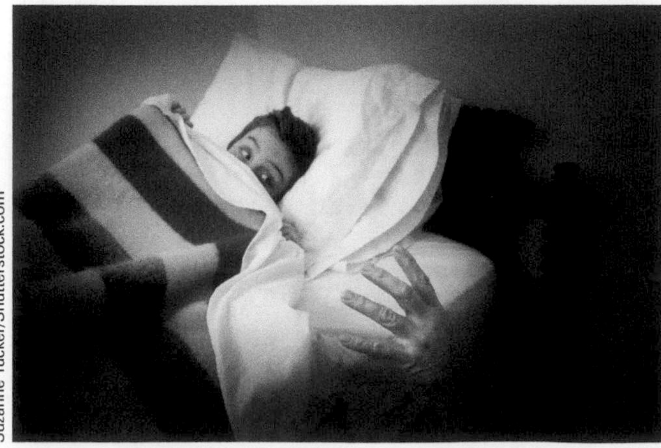

Suzanne Tucker/Shutterstock.com

Fear is common in the preschool years, requiring support from trusted caregivers.

LO4 Development of Gender Roles and Sex Differences

Although the terms *gender* and *sex* are often used interchangeably, they have very different meanings. As defined in Chapter 6, gender refers to sociocultural factors (social role, behaviour, and identity). Gender is considered on a continuum instead of just using the binary terms *male* and *female*. On the other hand, sex refers to the biological features of male or female (genitalia, chromosomes, and hormones) (Mikkola, 2016). Males have XY chromosomes and females to have XX chromosomes. It has long been the norm to identify sex according to two biologically driven categories, male and female. However, some people are born with biological characteristics of both sexes; they are called *intersex* (Pflag, 2016). Intersex features may not be visible at birth but may become more noticeable as a child hits puberty.

Theories of Gender Development

What roles do biology and socialization play in gender development?

Nature: The Roles of Heredity and Sex Hormones

According to evolutionary psychologists, sex differences were fashioned by natural selection in response to problems in adaptation that were repeatedly encountered by humans over thousands of generations (Buss & Duntley, 2006; Geary, 2006). The story of the survival of our ancient ancestors is etched in our genes. Genes that bestow attributes that increase an organism's chances of surviving to produce viable offspring are most likely to be transmitted to future generations. Thus, from an evolutionary perspective, women stayed with the children because their bodies were designed to bear children and feed them. If women were the hunter–gatherers, the chance of survival for all would be limited if something were to happen to them (such as being eaten by a wild animal). Consequently, men's brains and bodies evolved genetically to be the hunter–gatherers as this would ensure survival. Unfortunately, research that has focused on the biological differences between the sexes to account for differences in behaviour has relied mostly on animal studies.

On the other hand, research that has examined the impact of hormones on development provides some support for the notion that hormones play at least a partial role in gender development. Sex hormones and other chemical substances fuel the prenatal differentiation of sex organs. Toward the end of the embryonic stage, androgens—male sex hormones—sculpt the male genital organs. Girls and boys have both sex hormones; however, the amount of each and the impact it has on various body parts differs (McLeod, 2014). Thus, researchers believe that gender identity is the result of prenatal androgen exposure and virilization. Even research (Berenbaum, & Bailey, 2002; Reiner & Gearhart, 2004) examining children who were born with rare genetic conditions that resulted in sex reassignment at birth found mixed results. Many males who are reassigned as females develop male identities; some subjects develop female identities, while others fail to report their sexual identities altogether. Thus biology is only partially responsible for gender development; gender identity is much more than just biology.

Gender Role Socialization

In addition to biology, gender role socialization is important in gender development. **Gender role socialization** is the process of females learning to become women and to acquire feminine traits and behaviour (Mikkola, 2016), and of males learning to become men and to acquire masculine traits and behaviour. Gender role socialization results in stereotypes that are socially constructed and based on social learning.

It is believed that gender-role stereotypes develop in stages. First, children learn to label the sexes. By age 3 years, they display knowledge of gender stereotypes for toys, clothing, work, and activities (Campbell et al., 2004). Children become increasingly traditional in their stereotyping of activities, jobs, and personality traits between the ages of 3 and 9 or 10 years (Miller, Trautner, & Ruble, 2006). For example, the trait of "repairs broken things" is viewed as masculine, and the trait of "cooks and bakes" is seen as feminine.

gender roles socialization learning to acquire clusters of traits and behaviours that are considered stereotypical of females and males

Oleg Kozlov/Shutterstock.com
Glenda/Shutterstock.com

Socially constructed stereotypes of what it is to be a "girl" and what it is to be a "boy" are powerful influences.

Children and adolescents perceive their own gender in a slightly better light. For example, girls perceive other girls as nicer, more hard-working, and less selfish than boys. Boys, on the other hand, think that they are nicer, more hard-working, and less selfish than girls (Matlin, 2008; Miller et al., 2006).

Social Cognitive Theory

Social cognitive theorists (Bandura, 1986) consider the roles of rewards and punishments (reinforcement) in gender typing as well as the shaping of sex-role behaviours by parents or caregivers. Parents purchase specific toys and clothes for their child and encourage their children to participate in certain activities that are considered gender appropriate. Furthermore, when children play with the gender-appropriate toy, they are rewarded with smiles and respect and companionship, as is the case when they display "gender-appropriate" behaviour. Children are punished with frowns and loss of friends when they display "inappropriate" behaviour. Boys are encouraged to be independent, whereas girls are more likely to be restricted. Boys are allowed to roam farther from home at an earlier age and are more likely to be left unsupervised after school (Miller et al., 2006).

This theory explains further that children learn from observing others and decide which behaviours are appropriate for them. Children learn much about what society considers "masculine" or "feminine" by observing and imitating models of the same sex. These models may be their parents, other adults, other children, and even characters in electronic media such as TV and video games. Furthermore, socialization also plays a role. Parents, teachers, other adults—even other children—provide children with information about the gender-typed behaviours expected of them (Sabattini & Leaper, 2004). These stereotypes are socially constructed and based on social learning.

Primary-school children show less stereotyping when their mothers frequently engage in traditionally

gender identity
a person's innate, deeply felt sense of being male or female (sometimes even both or neither)

gender stability
the concept that one's sex is unchanging

gender constancy
the concept that one's sex remains the same despite changes in appearance or behaviour

gender-schema theory
the view that society's gender-based concepts shape our assumptions of gender-typed preferences and behaviour patterns

"masculine" tasks such as washing the car, taking children to ball games, or assembling toys (Powlishta, 2004). Maternal employment is associated with less polarized gender-role concepts for girls and boys (Sabattini & Leaper, 2004; Powlishta, 2004). Taken together, children benefit from being allowed to choose careers or develop interests based on personal preference and not due to what society determines is appropriate for them based on socially constructed concept such as gender.

DID YOU KNOW?

In 2012, Sweden introduced a gender-neutral term to replace him or her called "hen."

There is an attempt to remove gender-specific toys, clothes, and language in schools, daycare settings, and homes (Anwar, 2014). Furthermore, the Swedish are making more gender-neutral toys and leading the way in removing socially constructed gender stereotypes from store shelves. They are removing the words *boys* and *girls* and using the plural *children* in books and in the classrooms. Children are encouraged to wear what they wish and in whatever colour they prefer in an effort not to pigeonhole children into displaying gender stereotypes (Anwar, 2014).

Cognitive-Developmental Theory

According to Lawrence Kohlberg (1966), the acquisition of gender-role identity emerges in three stages: gender identity, gender stability, and gender constancy. The first step in gender-role identity is labelling oneself as a boy or a girl; this stage is called gender identity. By age 2 years, most children can say whether they are a boy or girl. By the age of 3 years, many children can discriminate anatomic sex differences (Campbell et al., 2004; Ruble, Martin, & Berenbaum, 2006). Different from Kohlberg, a current way of viewing gender identity is a person's innate, deeply felt sense of being male or female (sometimes even both or neither) (Gender Diversity, 2016).

At around age 4 or 5 years, most children develop the concept of gender stability, according to Kohlberg. They recognize that people retain their sexes for a lifetime. For example, boys believe they will grow up to be men and girls imagine they will grow up to be women.

By the age of 5 to 7 years, Kohlberg believes that most children develop the more sophisticated concept of gender constancy and recognize that people's sex does not change, even if they change their dress or behaviour. For example, a girl who dresses in a Buzz Lightyear costume for Halloween realizes she is still a girl regardless of her costume. Once children have established concepts of gender stability and constancy, they seek to behave in ways that are consistent with their sex (Martin & Ruble, 2004).

The opposite of this view of gender constancy is the idea of gender fluidity. Gender fluidity is the idea that gender expression can vary greatly. One's interests and behaviours may change even on a daily basis (Gender Diversity, 2016). Gender-fluid individuals are not restricted to stereotypical boundaries and thus they may feel more masculine on some days and more feminine on other days, or neither. Their identity is fluid.

Gender-Schema Theory

Gender-schema theory proposes that children use sex as one way of organizing their perceptions of the world (Bem, 1981). A gender schema is a cluster of concepts about male and female physical traits, behaviours, and personality traits. For example, consider the dimension of strength–weakness. Children learn that strength is linked to the male gender-role stereotype and weakness is linked to the female stereotype. They also learn that some dimensions, such as strength–weakness, are more relevant to one gender than the other—in this case, to males.

From the viewpoint of gender-schema theory, gender identity alone can lead to "gender-appropriate" behaviour (Ruble et al., 2006). As soon as children understand the labels "girl" and "boy," they seek information concerning gender-typed traits and try to live up to them. A boy may fight back when

Jay Lazarin/iStockphoto.com

It is important to expose children to examples that contradict gender-role stereotypes so that they become more open to diversity.

DGLimages/Shutterstock.com

provoked because boys are expected to do so. A girl may be gentle and kind because those traits are expected of girls. Both boys' and girls' self-esteem will depend on how they measure up to the gender schema.

Studies indicate that children organize information according to a gender schema. For example, boys show better memory for "masculine" toys, activities, and occupations, whereas girls show better memory for "feminine" toys, activities, and occupations (Martin & Ruble, 2004). However, gender-schema theory does not address the issue of the biological forces also at play in gender identity

Contrary to Kohlberg's theory, according to gender-schema theory children do not have to understand that gender is constant to begin to form a schema for being male or female. Also, as children age, they become more flexible in their ability to adopt characteristics outside of their perceived gender.

A growing number of parents are choosing to be gender-neutral (see Emerging Canada below). **Gender-neutral parenting (GNP)** is the decision not to assign a specific gender to children based on their biological sex (Lucas-Stannard, 2013). Children should be able to put on a tutu and dance regardless of their gender. GNP is allowing children to have more choices and fewer limitations. There are many myths around GNP, including that it pushes androgyny on children, that it will lead a child to a same-gender sexual orientation, and that it is anti-feminine or anti-masculine. In reality, GNP does not force androgyny on children just as it doesn't force gender stereotypes of any kind on children. It is about allowing children to choose what they prefer based on their preferences and not what is ascribed to them (Lucas-Stannard, 2013). GNP does not influence sexual orientation, and it gives children the confidence to choose their comfort level on the gender spectrum. It has been found that "85% of **gender bending** children/youth are **cisgender** and identify as heterosexual in adulthood." In other words applying nail polish to a boy will not influence his sexual orientation. Finally, GNP isn't just giving children opposite gender toys to play with but rather encouraging children to think critically about gender binaries and gendered hierarchies (Lucas-Stannard, 2013).

gender-neutral parenting (GNP) the decision not to assign a specific gender to children based on their biological sex

gender bending when an individual dresses or acts in a manner opposite of their identified gender or in a gender-neutral way

cisgender when an individual's gender is consistent with their biological sex

EMERGING CANADA

Baby Storm was born in Toronto, Ontario, on New Year's Day in 2011. When Storm was introduced to family and friends by email, the parents announced they would not be telling anyone whether Storm was a boy or a girl. They wanted Storm to be a tribute to freedom and choice, instead of being subject to limitations. Storm's sex (a biological identity) would not be disclosed to the world, which would leave Storm's gender (a sociological construct) also undeclared. The media frenzy was immediate (Poisson, 2011).

Storm's parents say they are fighting conformity to gender stereotypes. They have raised their other two children, Kio, now 7 years, and Jazz, now 10 years, to be as gender-neutral as possible. Storm's brother, Jazz, identifies as a transgendered girl, and began her transitioning three days before her seventh birthday. Kio identifies as non-binary and prefers the pronoun "they." Storm herself now self-identifies as female. The family saw the withholding of Storm's gender as an opportunity to protect this child from even further strict gender expectations and the possibility of gender-based bullying. As a family, they are fighting conformity to gender stereotypes. Jazz's favourite activities are math and sports; Kio prefers Suduku puzzles and reading whereas Storm prefers to play with stuffed animals (Botelho-Urbanski, 2016).

Bernard Weil/Toronto Star via Getty Images

LEARNING OUTCOMES

LO1 Describe trends in physical development in middle childhood

LO2 Describe changes in motor development in middle childhood

LO3 Discuss ADHD and learning disabilities

LO4 Describe Piaget's concrete operational stage

LO5 Discuss Kohlberg's theories of moral development

LO6 Describe developments in information processing in middle childhood

LO7 Describe intellectual development in middle childhood, focusing on theories of intelligence

LO8 Describe language development in middle childhood, including reading and bilingualism

> "Boys are slightly heavier and taller than girls through to the age of 9 or 10. Girls then begin their adolescent growth spurt."

LO1 Growth Patterns

Middle childhood occurs when children reach age 7 to 12 years. This period is marked with changes in both height and weight, motor development, and educational achievement as children are now required to attend school. Middle childhood is also marked by moral and language development.

Following the growth trends of early childhood, boys and girls continue to gain a little more than 5 cm (2 in.) in height per year until the adolescent growth spurt. The average gain in weight between the ages of 6 and 12 years is 2.25 to 3 kg (5 to 7 lb.) a year, but children grow less stocky and more slender (Kuczmarski et al., 2002).

Nutrition and Growth

In middle childhood, the average child's body weight doubles. Children also spend a good deal of energy in physical activity and play. To fuel this growth and activity, schoolchildren eat more than preschoolers. According to Canada's Food Guide, average 6- to 7-year-olds need 1,400 calories per day if they are inactive, and the average 8- to 10-year-old requires 1,600 calories a day (Health Canada, 2014).

Nutrition involves more than calories. Good nutrition requires making healthy choices from Canada's Food Guide, including fruits and vegetables, fish, poultry (without skin), and whole grains and a limited intake of fats, sugar, and starches. Good nutrition at this stage is challenging, however, because most foods in school cafeterias and elsewhere are heavy in sugar, animal fats, and salt (Bauer, Yang, & Austin, 2004). Portions have also grown over the decades, especially at fast-food restaurants (Nielsen & Popkin, 2003).

Sex Similarities and Differences in Physical Growth

Boys are slightly heavier and taller than girls through to the age of 9 or 10 years. Girls then begin their adolescent growth spurt and surpass boys in height and weight until about age 13 or 14 years, when boys grow taller and heavier than girls. The steady gains in height and weight in middle childhood are paralleled by increased muscle strength in both sexes. Beginning at about age 11 years, boys develop relatively more muscle, and girls develop relatively more fat.

growth spurt
a period during which growth advances at a dramatically rapid rate compared with other periods

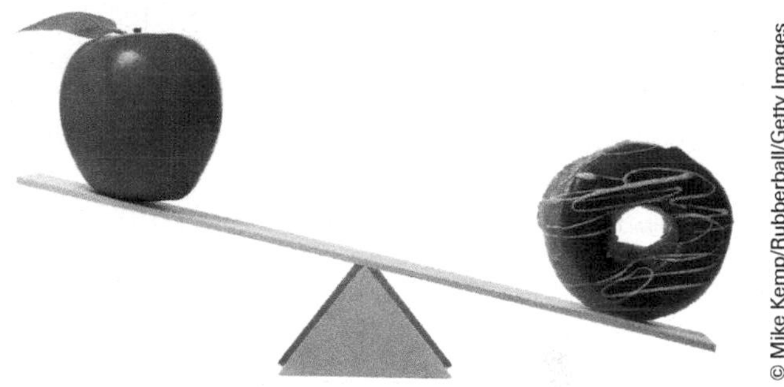
© Mike Kemp/Rubberball/Getty Images

Encouraging healthy food choices is important.

Overweight Children

In 2015, Statistics Canada reported that 33.4% of Canadian children were overweight or obese. Although parents often assume that heavy children will outgrow their "baby fat," most overweight children become overweight adults (Daniels, 2006; Roberts et al., 2012). Furthermore, excessive weight in childhood has been linked to insulin resistance, type 2 diabetes, hypertension, poor emotional health, and diminished social well-being (Roberts et al., 2012). Overweight children are often rejected by peers or become a focus of ridicule (Storch et al., 2007). They are usually poor at sports and less likely to be considered attractive in adolescence (Storch et al., 2007). Figure 9.1 shows how common it has become for Canadians aged 5 to 17 years to be overweight or obese.

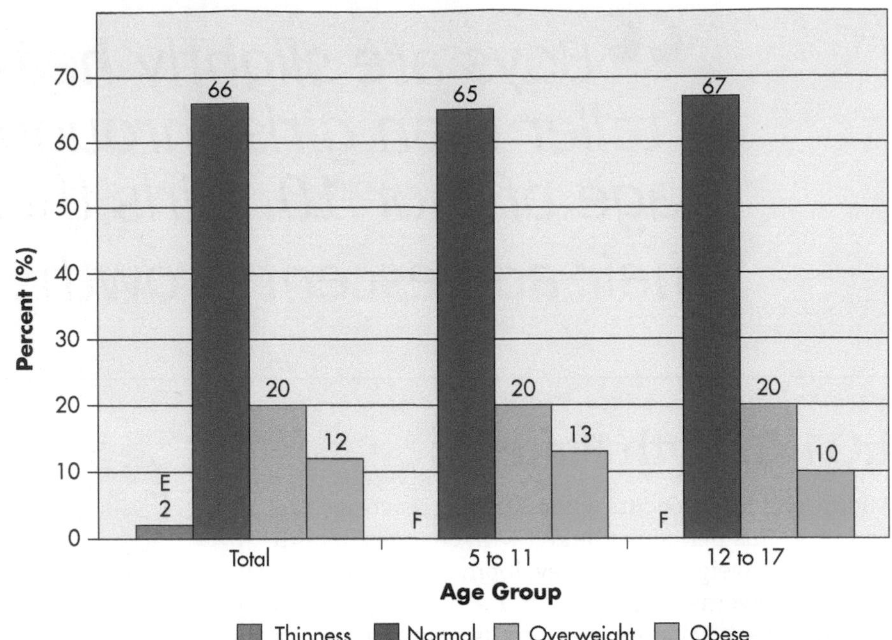

FIGURE 9.1

Body Mass Index of Canadian Children and Youth, 2009 to 2011

Distribution of Household Population Aged 5–17, by Body Mass Index Norms† and age group, Canada, 2009 to 2011

Overweight and obesity is becoming common for Canadians aged 5 to 17.

E Use with caution (data with a coefficient of variation (CV) from 16.6% to 33.3%)

F Too unreliable to be published (data with a coefficient of variation (CV) greater than 33.3%; suppressed due to extreme sampling variability)

†BMI classification based on de Onis, M., et al.

Source: Statistics Canada. Overweight and obesity rates, by age group, household population aged 2 to 17, Canada excluding territories, 1978/79 and 2004. 2004 Canadian Community Health Survey: Nutrition; Canada Health Survey 1978/79. (http://www.statcan.gc.ca/pub/82-620-m/2005001/c-g/child-enfant/4053584-eng.htm)

DID YOU KNOW?

"Baby fat" in early childhood can remain a lifelong struggle.

Statistically, most overweight children become overweight adults.

Sedentary Lifestyle

In addition to less healthy eating, the lack of physical fitness has been an issue among Canadian children over the past several decades. A sedentary lifestyle is on the increase and this is true regardless of age, gender, and ethnicity. Sedentary behaviour can be defined as behaviour that involves little physical movement and low energy use, including sitting and watching television, sitting at the computer, and playing video games (Tremblay, LeBlanc, Janssen, Kho, Hicks, Murumets et al., 2011). Children who watch a lot of TV burn fewer calories and are more likely to become overweight adolescents than children who exercise frequently (Schumacher & Queen, 2007).

Exercise is important because it reduces the risk of heart disease, stroke, diabetes, and certain forms of cancer (Atkinson & Davenne, 2007). However, more than half of Canadians aged 5 to 17 years are not active enough for optimal growth and development (Heart and Stroke Foundation of Canada, 1993).

To reduce the negative effects of a sedentary lifestyle, various guidelines have been suggested. Screen time should be limited to no more than 2 hours a day, children should walk to school regularly, and caregivers should encourage children to spend time outdoors in active play (Tremblay et al., 2011). Sadly, only 8.4% of children aged 6 to 17 years met these guidelines in 2013 (Statistics Canada, 2015c). Instead, studies have found that Canadian children spend 7.5 hours a day entertaining themselves with their cellphones, watching television or movies, playing video games, or surfing the internet (Rowan, 2011). Some children engage in as much as 11 hours of entertainment a day as most parents fail to put restrictions on these activities and 75% of children have these devices in their bedrooms (Rowan, 2011).

Other Causes of Childhood Obesity

Heredity plays a role in being overweight. Some people inherit a tendency to burn up extra calories, whereas others inherit a tendency to turn extra calories into fat (Kolata, 2007). Family, peers, and environmental factors can influence children's eating habits (Moens, Braet, & Soetens, 2007). Overweight parents may serve as examples of poor exercise habits, encourage overeating, and keep unhealthy foods in the home. Dining out frequently can become an unhealthy family habit.

Other causes of childhood obesity include reduced resources for physical education, hectic family schedules that limit family mealtime, and the food industry, which advertises inexpensive, high-calorie foods to children (Canadian Obesity Network, n.d.). Canadian schools have seen a decline in physical education programming over several decades (Physical and Health Education Canada, 2009).

Interestingly, one study found that children who are overweight or obese do not differ significantly from children who are normal weight in the number of minutes they spend in physical activity (Sharma, 2011). Thus, it appears to be the combination of many factors together that is implicated in obesity. What appears to be different for obese children is that their genetics, possibly combined with a sedentary lifestyle, lead to their increased weight gain (Sharma, 2011).

LO2 Motor Development

The school years are marked by increases in the child's speed, strength, agility, and balance—all all considered to be motor activities.

Gross Motor Skills

Throughout middle childhood, children show steady improvement in their ability to perform gross motor skills. Children are hopping, jumping, and climbing by about age 6 years; by age 6 or 7 years, they are usually capable of balancing and pedalling on a bicycle. By the ages of 8 to 10 years, children are showing the balance, coordination, and strength that allow them to engage in gymnastics and team sports.

During these years, children's muscles grow stronger, and their neural pathways that connect the cerebellum to the cortex become more myelinated. Experience refines their sensorimotor abilities, but some differences are inborn. For example, some people are born with better visual acuity, depth perception, or coordination than others.

EMERGING CANADA

In 2005, Statistics Canada conducted a survey to gather information on Canadian youth in sports. Many factors influence children's participation in sports activities, including gender, age, household income, parental education, parental involvement in sports, geography, and immigrant status of parents.

Boys are more likely than girls to participate in sports, but the gender gap is not as large as it once was. Early teens are more likely to be involved in sports than younger children. Children in higher-income households and those with parents with more than a high-school education are much more likely to be sports participants. The five most popular organized sports in Canada are soccer, swimming, hockey, basketball, and baseball.

Parents who are involved in sports (either as players or spectators) are more likely to enroll their children in sports. Children living in smaller towns and cities are more likely participate in sports than children in Canada's three largest cities. Children of recent immigrants are least likely to participate (Clark, 2009).

Wara Jenny/iStockphoto.com

Reaction time is basic to the child's estimate of when to swing a bat or hit a tennis ball. Children's reaction time gradually improves (i.e., it decreases) from early childhood to about age 18 years, but individual differences are common (Karatekin, Marcus, & White, 2007). Reaction time increases again in adulthood.

reaction time the amount of time required to respond to a stimulus

Fine Motor Skills

By the age of 6 to 7 years, children can usually tie their shoelaces and hold pencils as adults do. Their abilities to fasten buttons, zip zippers, brush teeth, wash themselves, coordinate a knife and fork, and use chopsticks all develop during the early school years and improve during middle childhood (Beilei et al., 2002).

LO3 Children with Disabilities

The school setting requires that a child sit still, pay attention, and master certain academic skills. But some children have difficulty with these demands.

attention-deficit hyperactivity disorder (ADHD) a disorder characterized by excessive inattention, impulsiveness, and hyperactivity

hyperactivity excessive restlessness and overactivity; a characteristic of ADHD

stimulants drugs that increase the activity of the nervous system

Attention-Deficit Hyperactivity Disorder (ADHD)

Attention-deficit hyperactivity disorder (ADHD) is a neurological condition that is marked by excessive inattention, impulsivity, and/or hyperactivity. Additionally, children with ADHD often have difficulty regulating their emotions. The unique constellation of symptoms of a child with ADHD often results in social difficulties. Symptoms of ADHD must be evident in two or more settings, such as home and school, and cause difficulties in either or both academic and social settings (American Psychological Association, 2013) before a child is diagnosed with the condition. ADHD is not a learning disability, although many with the disorder have comorbid disorders including learning disabilities, anxiety disorders, and mood disorders.

The degree of hyperactive behaviour varies for every child diagnosed with ADHD. Some children with the inattentive subtype may not exhibit hyperactivity resulting in misdiagnosis or no diagnosis at all. This is especially the case for inattentive girls (Centre for ADHD Awareness, Canada, n.d.). Children who are disruptive in class require attention immediately, whereas children who are inattentive without being disruptive are often labelled as lazy or daydreaming when a real diagnosable issue is the cause.

ADHD is typically evident by age 7 years. The hyperactivity and restlessness impair children's ability to function in school. They cannot sit still and have difficulty getting along with others. ADHD is diagnosed worldwide to be anywhere from 5% to 12% of school-age children; it is three times more common in boys than in girls (Centre for ADHD Awareness, n.d.).

ADHD is sometimes "overdiagnosed" (Weisler & Sussman, 2007). Some children who misbehave in school are diagnosed with ADHD and medicated to encourage more acceptable behaviour (Reddy & De Thomas, 2007).

DID YOU KNOW?

ADHD often expresses itself differently in girls than in boys.

Girls often engage in excessive talking, and exhibit poor self-esteem, worrying, perfectionism, risk-taking, and nosiness—not the typical hyperactivity and lack of focus that is often seen in boys. Furthermore, girls with ADHD may be socially rejected more often by their peers as compared to boys because girls' friendships often require greater sophistication and more maintenance (Connolly, n. d.).

Causes of ADHD

ADHD may have a genetic component, involving the brain chemical dopamine (Thapar et al., 2007; Walitza et al., 2006). Studies in brain imaging have found differences in the brain chemistry of children with ADHD as compared with children without ADHD. Also, children whose family member has been diagnosed with the disorder are five times more likely to be diagnosed with ADHD too (Centre for ADHD Awareness, n.d.). Nigg and his colleagues (2006) note that ADHD is due to a lack of executive control of the brain over motor and more primitive functions.

DID YOU KNOW?

There are different subtypes of ADHD.

One subtype is called hyperactive. A second subtype is inattentive. In the third subtype, called combined, both hyperactive and inattentive symptoms are evident.

Treatment and Outcome

Stimulants such as Concerta and Dexedrin are common medications prescribed to medically treat ADHD. The longer-lasting non-stimulant Strattera is also used for children who have symptoms that last into the night or who also experience anxiety (CADDAC, n.d.). Stimulants promote the activity of the brain chemicals dopamine and noradrenaline, which arouse the "executive centre" of the brain to control more primitive areas of the brain. Stimulants increase children's attention span and improve their academic performance (Posey et al., 2007). Most children with ADHD continue to have problems in attention, conduct, or learning well into adolescence and adulthood despite receiving treatment for the disorder (Nigg et al., 2004).

Non-medical treatment of ADHD is also recommended. This might involve behaviour modification—shaping appropriate behaviour by using rewards to encourage a desired outcome (Sherman, n.d.). Rewards may include praise, privileges, or a token

DID YOU KNOW?

Stimulants are often used to treat children who are already hyperactive.

Stimulants such as Concerta are the most common treatment for ADHD.

system where children are able to trade in their tokens for something desirable like a new toy.

Learning Disabilities

Children with learning disabilities may have difficulties in math, writing, or reading, in spite of scoring in the average range for intelligence on IQ tests. Some have difficulties in articulating the sounds of speech or in understanding spoken language. Others have difficulties in motor coordination. Children are usually diagnosed with a learning disability when they are performing below the level expected for their age and intelligence, and when the child shows no evidence of other physical issues such as vision or hearing problems, retardation, or socio-economic disadvantage (Joshi, 2003; Lyon, Shaywitz, & Shaywitz, 2003). Learning disabilities may persist through life, but early recognition and remediation can help many children learn how to compensate for their disability (Vellutino et al., 2004). Strategies for adapting are key to success for children with learning disabilities.

Origins of Dyslexia

Dyslexia is a reading disorder characterized by letter reversals, mirror reading, slow reading, and reduced comprehension. It is theorized that sensory and neurological problems contribute to these difficulties with reading. Genetic factors appear to account for this disorder; it has been found that between 25% and 65% of children who have one parent with dyslexia are diagnosed with dyslexia themselves (Plomin & Walker, 2003). Furthermore, about 40% of siblings of children with dyslexia are also diagnosed with this disorder.

Genetic factors lead to neurological and circulation problems in the left hemisphere of the brain (Grigorenko, 2007). The circulation problems result in oxygen deficiency. The part of the brain called the angular gyrus "translates" visual information, such as written words, into auditory information (sounds). Problems in the angular gyrus may give rise to reading problems by making it difficult for the reader to associate letters with sounds (Grigorenko, 2007; Shaywitz, Lyon, & Shaywitz, 2006b).

Most researchers also focus on *phonological processing*. That is, children with dyslexia may not discriminate sounds as accurately as other children (Halliday & Bishop, 2006). As a result, *b*'s and *d*'s and *p*'s may be hard to tell apart, creating confusion that impairs reading ability (Shaywitz et al., 2006a). Figure 9.2 shows a writing sample from a child with dyslexia.

© Will and Deni McIntyre/Science Source/Photo Researchers

FIGURE 9.2

Writing Sample from a Child with Dyslexia

Children with dyslexia may perceive letters as upside down (confusing *w* with *m*) or reversed (confusing *b* with *d*). Their misperception leads to rotations or reversals in writing, as shown here.

learning disabilities disorders characterized by inadequate development of specific academic, language, and speech skills

dyslexia a reading disorder characterized by letter reversals, mirror reading, slow reading, and reduced comprehension

classroom inclusion placing children with disabilities in classrooms with children without disabilities

Educating Children Who Have Exceptionalities

In childhood, treatment of dyslexia focuses on remediation (Bakker, 2006). Children are given highly structured exercises to help them become aware of how to blend sounds to form words, such as by identifying word pairs that rhyme and do not rhyme. Later in life, the focus tends to be on accommodation rather than on remediation. For example, postsecondary students who have dyslexia may be allowed extra time for the reading portion of tests.

A philosophy of classroom inclusion has been adopted in Canada where, whenever possible, children with exceptionalities of any kind are placed in regular classrooms that have been adapted to their needs. Most students who have mild learning disabilities spend most of their school day in regular classrooms (Fergusson, 2007).

EMERGING CANADA

Education is a provincial and territorial responsibility; each province and territory will have different procedures for dealing with students with special educational needs. The Canadian Human Rights Code states that equal treatment for all students is required by law, requiring all schools to make accommodations for students identified as having a special educational need. In Ontario, for example, students with learning disabilities are given an Individual Education Plan (IEP) that ensures they have equal access to education. This written plan describes the services required by students who have been thoroughly assessed and identified as having a learning disability by a school psychologist.

The Individual Education Plan (IEP) is a document that specifies a child's learning needs, and the accommodations required to help students achieve learning expectations given their identified strengths and needs. Students with any type of exceptionality may be given an IEP including those who are gifted or who have a physical condition that impacts their learning. Students do not necessarily have to be diagnosed with a condition in order to receive an individualized plan (Ontario Ministry of Education, 2004). The most common exceptionalities that result in an IEP include a diagnosis on the autism spectrum, visual or hearing impairments, brain injuries, learning disabilities, ADHD, speech and language impairment, orthopaedic issues, and emotional disturbance and/or behavioural issues.

Accommodations that may be given to students who have an IEP include access to computer software, access to a calculator for tests, or provision of a quiet room to write tests with an extra amount of time assigned to the task (Ontario Ministry of Education, 2004). The IEP is monitored by educators, parents, and psychologists to ensure that the specific learning needs identified are met.

Universal Design: The Inclusive Classroom

The Learning Disabilities Association of Canada (LDAC) argues that 1 in 10 Canadians may have a learning disability. The new trend toward educational universal design suggests that the best teaching practices implement accommodations for all students regardless of their identifications. Universal design is built on the educational approach that all students benefit from a variety of teaching strategies that have been designed to promote global student success (Kumar, 2010). Many students may not be sufficiently self-aware to identify their own limitations, or their specific learning challenges may have gone unnoticed by teachers. How could a classroom be set up to promote inclusion of all types of exceptionalities?

LO4 Cognitive Development

At about the age of 11 years, children make enormous strides in their cognitive development as their thought processes and language become more logical and complex.

concrete operations the third stage in Piaget's scheme, characterized by flexible, reversible thought concerning tangible objects and events

decentration simultaneous focusing on more than one aspect or dimension of a problem or situation

Piaget: The Concrete Operational Stage

According to Jean Piaget, the typical child enters the stage of concrete operations by age 7 years and this stage lasts until about age 12 years. At the end of this stage, children show the beginnings of adult logic but generally focus on tangible objects rather than abstract ideas, which is why their activities are known as "concrete" operations.

Concrete operational thought is reversible and flexible. Adding the numbers 2 and 3 to get 5 is an operation. Subtracting 2 from 5 to get 3 reverses the operation. Subtracting 3 from 5 to get 2 demonstrates flexibility.

Concrete operational children are less egocentric than preoperational children. They recognize that people see things in different ways because of different situations and values. Concrete operational children also engage in decentration. They can focus on multiple parts of a problem at once. Thus, they can understand that a wide short glass holds as much liquid as a tall skinny glass, as discussed in Chapter 7. The two dimensions are height and width in this case.

Conservation

Concrete operational children show an understanding of the laws of conservation. A 7-year-old child would say that the flattened ball of clay from the example in Chapter 7 still has the same amount of clay as the round one "because you can roll it up again." The concrete operational child knows that objects can have several properties or dimensions. By attending to both the height and the width of the clay, the child recognizes that the loss in height compensates for the gain in width.

Transitivity

If your parents are older than you are, and you are older than your children, are your parents older than your children? The answer, of course, is yes. But how did you arrive at this answer? If you said yes simply on the basis of knowing that your parents are older

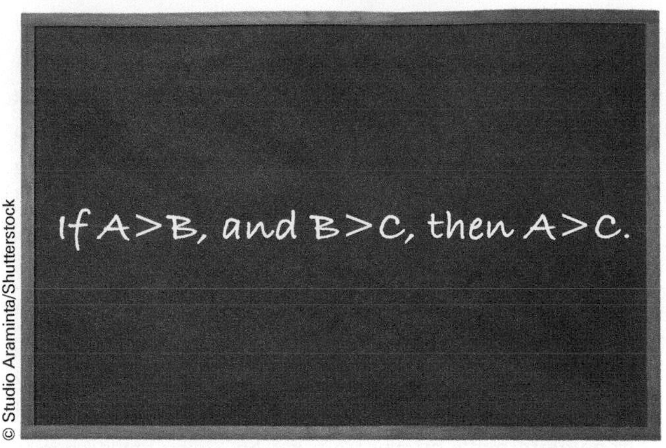

© Studio Araminta/Shutterstock

than your children (e.g., 58 and 56 compared with 5 and 3), your answer did not require concrete operational thought. But one aspect of concrete operational is the principle of **transitivity**: If A exceeds B in some property (say, age or height) and if B exceeds C, then A must also exceed C.

Researchers can assess whether children understand the principle of transitivity by asking them to place objects in a series, or order, according to some property, such as lining up one's family members according to age, height, or weight. Placing objects in a series is termed **seriation**.

Concrete operational children also have the decentration capacity to allow them to seriate in two dimensions at once, unlike preoperational children. Consider a seriation task used by Piaget and Inhelder (1956). In this test, children are given 49 leaves and asked to classify them according to size and brightness (from small to large and from dark to light) (see Figure 9.3). As the grid is completed from left to right, the leaves become lighter. As the grid is filled in from top to bottom, the leaves become larger.

transitivity the principle that if A > B and B > C, then A > C

seriation placing objects in an order or series according to a property or trait

Class Inclusion

Chapter 7 discussed a 4-year-old who was shown pictures of four cats and six dogs. When asked whether there were more dogs or more animals, she said more dogs. This preoperational child apparently could not simultaneously focus on the two subclasses (dogs and cats) and the larger subclass (animals). But concrete operational children are able to do this. Therefore, they are more likely to answer the question about the dogs and the animals correctly (Chapman & McBride, 1992).

Applications of Piaget's Theory to Education

Piaget believed that learning involves active discovery. He also believed that instruction should be geared towards the child's level of development. For example, when teaching concrete operational children about fractions, the teacher should not only describe what fractions are but also allow children to divide concrete objects into parts. Piaget also believed that learning that takes into account the

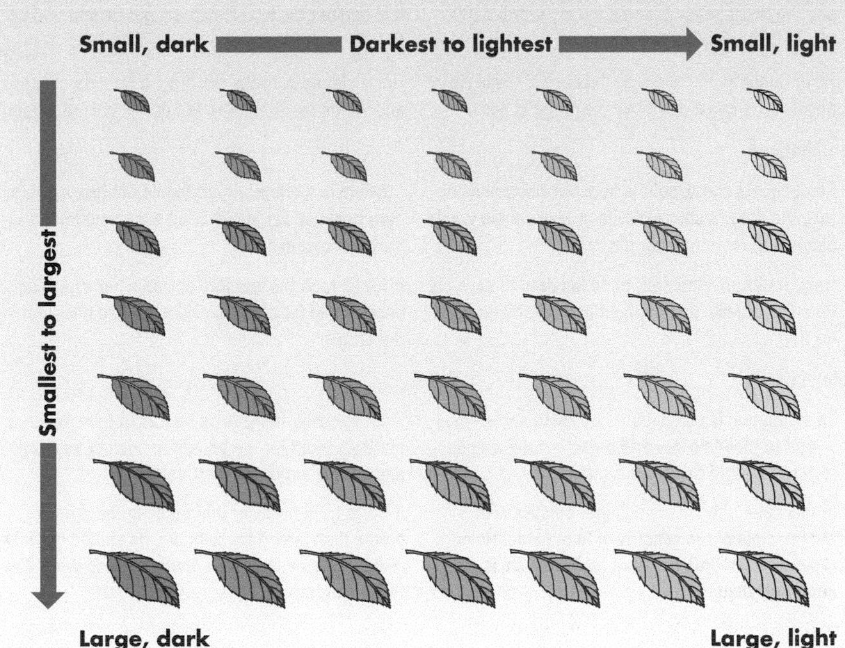

FIGURE 9.3

A Grid for Demonstrating the Development of Seriation

To classify these leaves, children must focus on two dimensions at once: size and lightness. They must also understand the principle of transitivity—that if A > B and B > C, then A > C.

Source: © Cengage Learning

perspectives of others is a key ingredient for developing both cognition and morality.

LO5 Moral Development

On a cognitive level, moral development concerns the basis on which children judge that an act is right or wrong. Lawrence Kohlberg believed that moral reasoning undergoes the same cognitive-developmental pattern around the world. The moral considerations that children display at a given age may be influenced by both the values of their culture and their stage of cognitive development (Lapsley, 2006). As the child's cognitive development advances, so too will her or his moral development.

Kohlberg's Theory of Moral Development

Kohlberg (1981, 1985) advanced the cognitive-developmental theory of moral development by elaborating on the kinds of information children use to make a judgment and on the complexities of their moral reasoning. Before we discuss Kohlberg's views, read the tale that Kohlberg used in his research and answer the questions that follow.

> In Europe, a woman was near death from a special kind of cancer. There was one drug that the doctors thought might save her. It was a form of radium that a druggist in the same town had recently discovered. The drug was expensive to make, but the druggist was charging 10 times what the drug cost him to make. He paid $200 for the radium and charged $2,000 for a small dose of the drug. The sick woman's husband, Heinz, went to everyone he knew to borrow the money, but he could only get together about $1,000 which was half of what it cost. He told the druggist that his wife was dying and asked him to sell it cheaper or let him pay later. But the druggist said: "No, I discovered the drug and I'm going to make money from it." So Heinz got desperate and broke into the man's store to steal the drug for his wife.
>
> —Kohlberg (1969)

Kohlberg emphasized the importance of being able to view the moral world from the perspective of another person (Krebs & Denton, 2005). Look at this situation from Heinz's perspective. What do you think? Should Heinz have tried to steal the drug? Was he right or wrong? As you can see from Table 9.1, the issue is more complicated than a simple yes or no.

TABLE 9.1

Kohlberg's Levels and Stages of Moral Development

Stage of Development	Examples of Moral Reasoning That Support Heinz's Stealing the Drug	Examples of Moral Reasoning That Oppose Heinz's Stealing the Drug
Level I: Preconventional—Typically Begins in Early Childhood[a]		
Stage 1: Judgments guided by obedience and the prospect of punishment (the consequences of the behaviour)	It is not wrong to take the drug. Heinz did try to pay the druggist for it, and it is only worth $200, not $2,000.	Taking things without paying is wrong because it is against the law. Heinz will get caught and go to jail.
Stage 2: Naively egoistic, instrumental orientation (things are right when they satisfy people's needs)	Heinz ought to take the drug because his wife really needs it. He can always pay the druggist back.	Heinz should not take the drug. If he gets caught and winds up in jail, it won't do his wife any good.
Level II: Conventional—Typically Begins in Middle Childhood		
Stage 3: Good-boy/good-girl orientation (moral behaviour helps others and is socially approved)	Stealing is a crime, so it is bad, but Heinz should take the drug to save his wife or else people would blame him for letting her die.	Stealing is a crime. Heinz should not just take the drug because his family will be dishonoured, and they will blame him.
Stage 4: Law-and-order orientation (moral behaviour is doing one's duty and showing respect for authority)	Heinz must take the drug to do his duty to save his wife. Eventually, though, he must pay the druggist for it.	If we all took the law into our own hands, civilization would fall apart, so Heinz should not steal the drug.
Level III: Postconventional—Typically Begins in Adolescence[b]		
Stage 5: Contractual, legalistic orientation (one must weigh pressing human needs against society's need to maintain social order)	This situation is complicated because society has a right to maintain law and order, but Heinz needs to take the drug to save his wife.	I can see why Heinz feels he has to take the drug, but laws exist for the benefit of society as a whole and cannot simply be cast aside.
Stage 6: Universal ethical principles orientation (people must follow universal ethical principles and their own conscience, even if it means breaking the law)	In this case, the law comes into conflict with the principle of the sanctity of human life. Heinz must take the drug because his wife's life is more important than the law.	If Heinz truly believes that stealing the drug is worse than letting his wife die, he should not take it. People need to make sacrifices to do what they think is right.

[a]Tends to be used less often in middle childhood.

[b]May not develop at all.

Willsie/iStockphoto.com

The reason for wrongdoing reflects the individual's level of moral development.

Heinz is caught in a moral dilemma in which legal or social rules (in this case, laws against stealing) are pitted against a strong human need (Heinz's desire to save his wife). According to Kohlberg's theory, children and adults arrive at yes or no answers for different reasons. These reasons can be classified according to the level of moral development they reflect.

Kohlberg theorized three levels of moral development and two stages within each level. He argued that the developmental stages of moral reasoning follow the same sequence in all children. Children progress at different rates; however, not everyone reaches the highest stage. But children must experience Stage 1 before Stage 2, and so on.

The Preconventional Level

At the **preconventional level**, children base their moral judgments on the consequences of their behaviour. Stage 1 is oriented toward obedience and punishment. Good behaviour means being obedient so one can avoid punishment. In Stage 2, good behaviour allows people to satisfy their own needs and, perhaps, the needs of others. In a study of children age 7 through 16, Kohlberg (1963) found that Stage 1 and 2 types of moral judgments were offered most frequently by children 7–10 years of age. Stage 1 and 2 judgments fell off steeply after age 10.

preconventional level
according to Kohlberg, a period during which moral judgments are based largely on expectations of rewards or punishments

conventional level
according to Kohlberg, a period during which moral judgments largely reflect social rules and conventions

postconventional level
according to Kohlberg, a period during which moral judgments are derived from moral principles, and people look to themselves to set moral standards

The Conventional Level

At the **conventional level** of moral reasoning, right and wrong are judged by conformity to conventional (family, religious, societal) standards of right and wrong. According to the Stage 3 "good-boy/good-girl orientation," it is good to meet the needs and expectations of others. Moral behaviour is what is "normal," or what the majority does. In Stage 4, moral judgments are based on rules that maintain the social order. Showing respect for authority and duty is valued highly. Many people do not develop beyond the conventional level. Kohlberg (1963) found that Stage 3 and 4 types of judgments emerge during middle childhood. They are all but absent among 7-year-olds, but are reported by about 20% of 10-year-olds and by a higher percentage of adolescents.

The Postconventional Level

At the **postconventional level**, moral reasoning is based on the person's own moral standards as well as universal, ethical principles that may not fit with one's cultural standards. This level of reasoning is found among adolescents and adults; however, many individuals never reach this stage of development. An example of postconventional moral reasoning was brought to the attention of one of the authors when she met a woman who loves animals. When the woman saw abandoned kittens on the side of the road, she tried for hours to rescue them. Afterwards, she took them home to the dismay of those around her. Critics said she was wrong for taking the kittens because they may be looking for their own mother or because she could have been hurt trying to save them. Afterwards, she found a shelter that adopted the kittens. Her moral standard of caring for animals in the same way she would care for any human being is due to her moral standards of right and wrong.

sensory memory the structure of memory first encountered by sensory input. Information is maintained in sensory memory for only a fraction of a second

short-term memory the structure of memory that can hold a sensory stimulus for up to 30 seconds

Look ahead to Chapter 11 for more information about the postconventional stage of development.

Applying Kohlberg's work to everyday examples is important because children (and adults) are faced with moral dilemmas all the time. Consider cheating in school. When taking a test, some may be tempted to cheat. Their reason to cheat or not to cheat will vary according to their moral development. One child may fear the consequences of getting caught (preconventional reasoning). Others may decide that it is more important to live up to their moral principles than to achieve the highest possible grade (postconventional reasoning). In each case, the child's decision is not to cheat. However, their decisions reflect different levels of reasoning.

Roots of Empathy: Character Education

Roots of Empathy is a school-based curriculum targeting the development of student character in Canada. This character-based educational program is designed to teach empathy as a weapon against bullying. "Roots of Empathy" provides children with an opportunity to see skills modelled, to apply these same skills in real-life situations, and then to reflect on their learning. The program increases the chances that students will develop competencies that will guide their future behaviours and social choices. Research that compared the behaviours of children exposed to the Roots of Empathy program with the behaviour of their peer groups concluded that the Roots of Empathy curriculum led to the following:

- An increase in social and emotional knowledge
- A decrease in aggression
- An increase in prosocial behaviour, including sharing and helping
- Lasting results (Roots of Empathy, 2013)

Debra Pepler, a York University professor and psychologist in Toronto, warns that character should be discussed in the classroom but that it is not the kind of lesson that comes from a workshop. For lasting empathy, children need to learn to think before they act and to have opportunities to practise the lessons they have learned on a regular basis (Hammer, 2012a).

LO6 Information Processing: Learning, Remembering, Problem Solving

Key elements in children's information processing include the following (Pressley & Hilden, 2006):

- Development of selective attention
- Development of memory skills
- Development of the ability to solve problems, such as by finding the correct formula and applying it

Development of Selective Attention

Children's ability to selectively attend while ignoring distractions advances steadily through middle childhood (Rubia et al., 2006). Preoperational children who are engaged in problem solving tend to focus (or centre) their attention on one element of the problem at a time, which is a major reason they lack conservation. On the other hand, concrete operational children can attend to multiple aspects of the problem at once, permitting them to conserve numbers and volume.

Developments in the Storage and Retrieval of Information

Psychologists use the term *memory* to refer to the processes of storing and retrieving information. Many psychologists divide memory functioning into three major processes or structures: sensory memory, short-term or working memory, and long-term memory (see Figure 9.4).

Sensory Memory

When we look at an object and then blink our eyes, the visual impression of the object lasts for a fraction of a second. This is called **sensory memory**. Then the "trace" of the stimulus decays. The concept of sensory memory applies to all of the senses. For example, when we are introduced to a new person, the trace of the sound of the name also decays, but, by focusing on it, we can recall the name.

Short-Term Memory

When children focus on a stimulus in the sensory register, it tends to be retained in **short-term memory** for up to 30 seconds after the trace of the stimulus

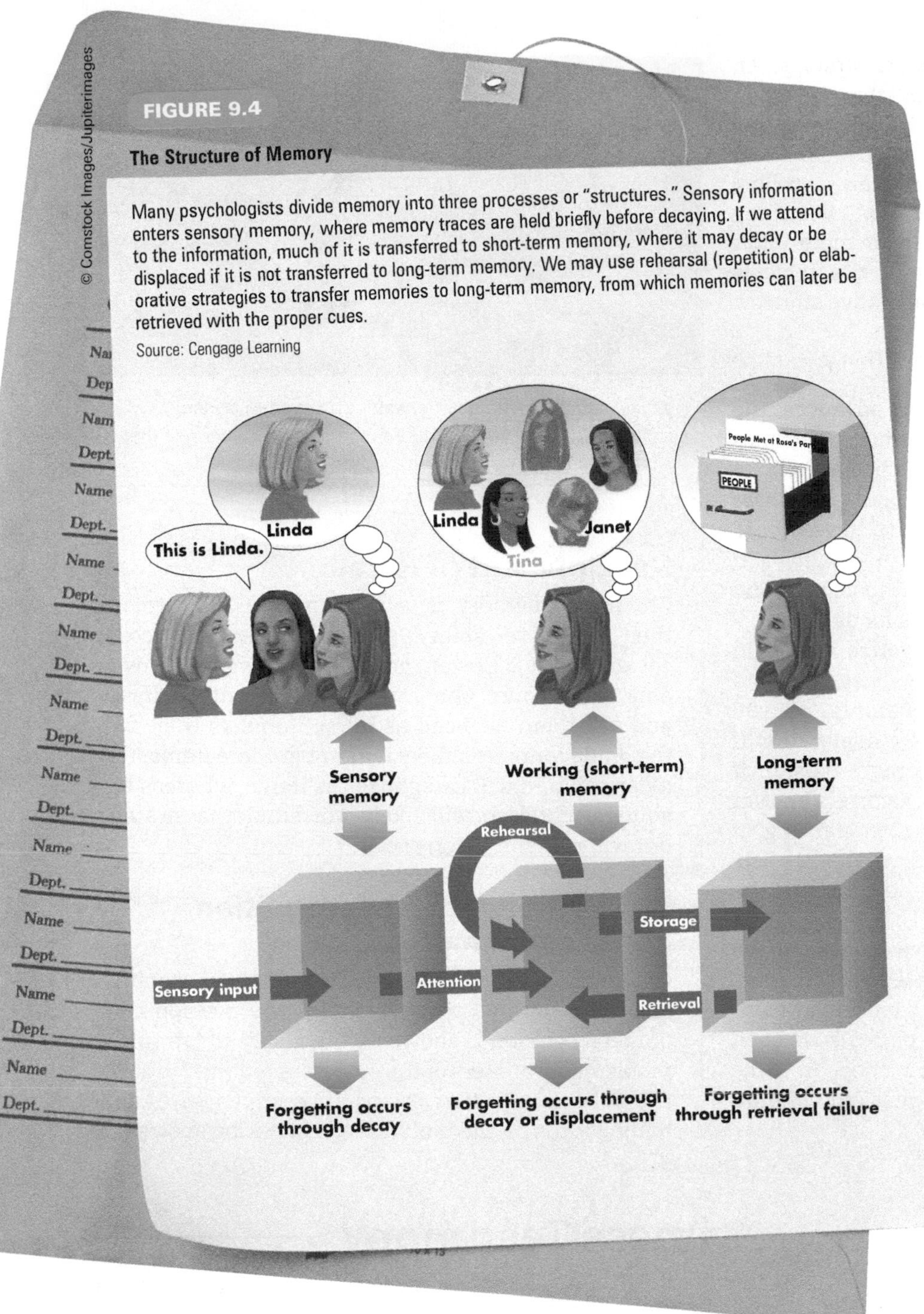

© Comstock Images/Jupiterimages

FIGURE 9.4

The Structure of Memory

Many psychologists divide memory into three processes or "structures." Sensory information enters sensory memory, where memory traces are held briefly before decaying. If we attend to the information, much of it is transferred to short-term memory, where it may decay or be displaced if it is not transferred to long-term memory. We may use rehearsal (repetition) or elaborative strategies to transfer memories to long-term memory, from which memories can later be retrieved with the proper cues.

Source: Cengage Learning

encode to transform sensory input into a form that is more readily processed

rehearsing repetition that aids in recall

long-term memory the memory structure capable of relatively permanent storage of information

decays. The ability to maintain information in short-term memory depends on cognitive strategies and on capacity to continue to perceive a vanished stimulus. Memory function in middle childhood seems largely adult-like in its organization and strategies, and only quantitative improvement is shown through early adolescence (Alloway et al., 2004; Archibald & Gathercole, 2006).

Auditory stimuli can be maintained longer in short-term memory than visual stimuli. For this reason, one strategy for promoting memory is to encode visual stimuli as sounds. The sounds can then be repeated out loud or mentally. In Figure 9.4, mentally repeating or rehearsing the sound of Linda's name helps the other girl remember it.

Long-Term Memory

Think of long-term memory as a vast storehouse of information containing names, dates, and places, as well as personal information such as what Johnny did to you in Grade 2, or what Ashlyn said about you when you were 12 years old. Long-term memories may last days, years, or, for practical purposes, a lifetime.

There is no known limit to the amount of information that can be stored in long-term memory. From time to time, we may seem to have forgotten, or lost, a long-term memory, such as the names of classmates from elementary or high school. But it is more likely that we cannot find the right cues to retrieve the memory. It is "lost" in the same way we misplace an object but know it is still in the house.

Older children are more likely than younger children to use rote rehearsal, or repetition, to try to remember information (Saito & Miyake, 2004; Towse & Cowan, 2005). A more effective method than rote rehearsal is to purposefully relate new material to well-known information, which makes it meaningful. Relating new material to known material is called

elaborative strategy a method for increasing retention of new information by relating it to well-known information

metacognition awareness of and control of one's cognitive abilities

an elaborative strategy. An example of this is when children use new words in sentences to help them remember their spelling and meaning. Searching the Internet for more information about the topic is another elaborative strategy.

Organization in Long-Term Memory

As children's knowledge of concepts advances, the storehouse of their long-term memory becomes organized according to categories. Preschoolers tend to organize their memories by grouping objects that share the same function (Lucariello et al., 2004; Towse, 2003). "Toast" may be grouped with "peanut butter sandwich" because both are edible. In middle childhood, toast and peanut butter are likely to be joined as foods.

When children correctly categorize items in their long-term memory, they are more likely to recall accurate information. For example, do you remember whether whales breathe underwater? If you did not know that whales are mammals, or if you knew nothing about mammals, a correct answer might depend on an instance of rote learning. If children have incorrectly classified whales as fish, they might search their memories and construct the wrong answer.

Knowledge in a particular area increases the capacity to store and retrieve related information. As an example, chess experts are superior to amateurs at remembering where chess pieces have been placed on the board (Gobet & Simon, 2000). In these studies, the experts were 8- to 12-year-old children and the amateurs were adults!

sethakan/iStockphotos.com

Whales do not breathe underwater. This is an important characteristic that allows children to correctly categorize the whale as a mammal in their long-term memory.

Development of Recall

Children's memory is a good overall indicator of their cognitive ability (Gathercole et al., 2004a, 2004b; Towse & Cowan, 2005). If you give grade twos and grade fours one minute to look at 10 items and ask them to recall as many items as they can, the grade fours will likely remember more items. The older children will categorize the items, whereas the younger children will likely not employ a strategy but will rely simply on recall.

Development of Metacognition and Metamemory

Children's knowledge and control of their cognitive abilities is termed metacognition. The development of metacognition is shown by the ability to formulate problems, awareness of the processes required to solve a problem, activation of cognitive strategies, maintaining focus on the problem, and checking answers.

Children's Eyewitness Testimony

The child witness is typically asked questions to prompt information. But such questions may be "leading"; that is, they may suggest an answer. For example, "What happened at school?" is not a leading question, but "Did your teacher touch you?" is. Can children's testimony be distorted by leading questions? By the age of 10 or 11 years, children are no more suggestible than adults; but younger children are more likely to be misled (Bruck, Ceci, & Principe, 2006; Krackow & Lynn, 2003). Research also indicates that repeated questioning may lead children to make up events that never happened to them (Roebers & Schneider, 2002).

What, then, are investigators to do when the only witnesses to criminal events are children? Maggie Bruck and her colleagues (2006) recommend that interviewers avoid leading or suggestive questions to minimize influencing the child's response.

JPR-PROD/Shutterstock.com

When a student in Grade 6 decides which homework assignments to do first, memorizes the provincial and territorial capitals for tomorrow's test, and then tests herself to see which ones she needs to study more, she is displaying metacognition (Flavell et al., 2002; Stright et al., 2001). Metamemory is an aspect of metacognition that refers to children's awareness of the functioning of their memory. Older students are more likely to accurately assess their knowledge.

Older children store and retrieve information more effectively that younger children (Towse & Cowan, 2005). Older children also show more knowledge of strategies that can be used to facilitate memory. Preschoolers will usually use rehearsal if someone suggests they use it, but not until about the age of 6 or 7 do children use it on their own (Flavell et al., 2002). As children develop, they are more likely to use selective rehearsal to remember important information.

LO7 Intellectual Development

At an early age, we gain impressions of how intelligent we are compared with our family members and schoolmates. We associate intelligence with academic success, advancement on the job, and appropriate social behaviour. Despite our sense of familiarity with the concept of intelligence, it is an abstract concept with many definitions and many theories trying to account for its development.

Intelligence is usually perceived as a child's underlying competence or *learning ability*, whereas achievement involves a child's acquired competencies or *performance*. Most psychologists agree that many of the competencies underlying intelligence are seen during middle childhood, when most children are first exposed to formal schooling.

metamemory knowledge of the functions and processes involved in one's storage and retrieval of information

intelligence defined by Wechsler as the "capacity ... to understand the world [and the] resourcefulness to cope with its challenges"

achievement acquired competencies that are attained by one's efforts and are presumed to be made possible by one's abilities

Theories of Intelligence

Let's consider some theoretical approaches to intelligence. Then we will see how researchers and practitioners assess intellectual functioning.

Sternberg's Theory of Intelligence

Psychologist Robert Sternberg (2000) constructed a three-part, or "triarchic," theory of intelligence. The parts are *analytical intelligence*, *creative intelligence*, and *practical intelligence* (see Figure 9.5). Analytical intelligence refers to academic ability. Creative intelligence is defined as the abilities to cope with novel situations and to benefit from experience. Practical intelligence, or "street smarts," enables people to adapt to the demands of their environment, including the social environment.

Gardner's Theory of Multiple Intelligences

Psychologist Howard Gardner (1983, 2006), like Sternberg, believes that intelligence—or intelligences—reflect more than academic ability. Gardner refers to each kind of intelligence in his theory as

Analytical intelligence (academic ability)
Ability to solve problems, compare and contrast, judge, evaluate, and criticize

Creative intelligence (creativity and insight)
Ability to invent, discover, suppose, and theorize

Practical intelligence ("street smarts")
Ability to adapt to the demands of the environment and apply knowledge in practical situations

FIGURE 9.5

Sternberg's Triarchic Theory of Intelligence

Robert Sternberg views intelligence as three-pronged: having analytical, creative, and practical aspects.

Source: © Cengage Learning

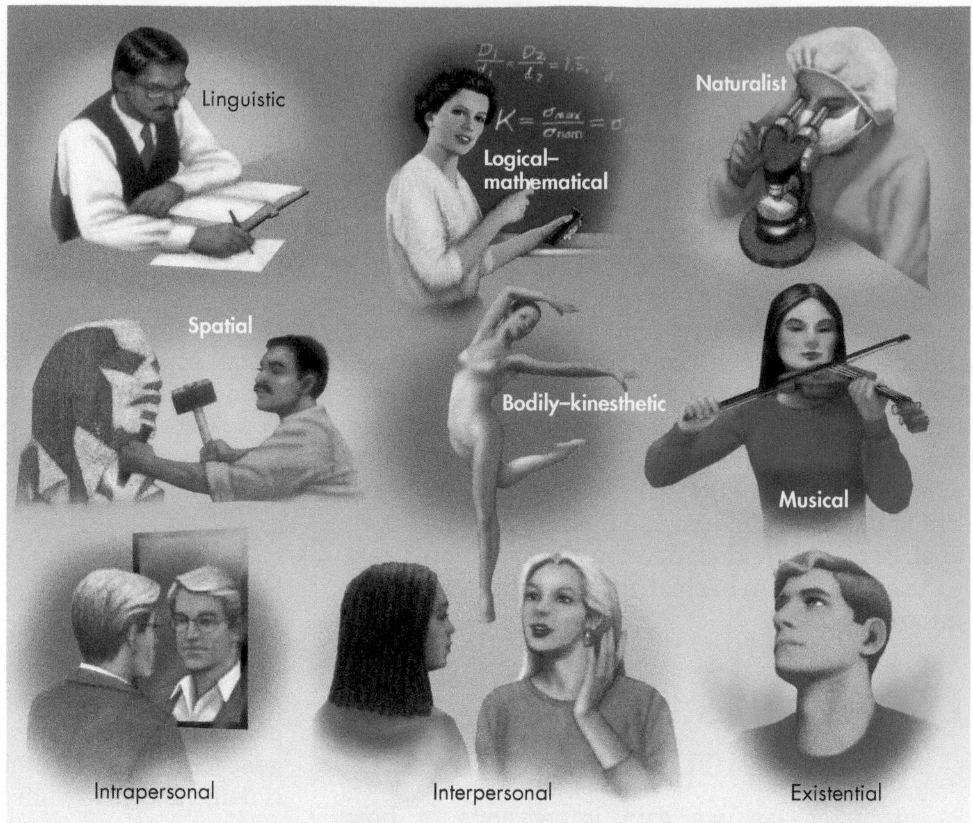

FIGURE 9.6

Gardner's Theory of Multiple Intelligences

Gardner argues that people are capable of many intelligences. Each intelligence has its neurological bases in its own parts of the brain.

Source: © Cengage Learning

intelligence quotient (IQ) a score on an intelligence test

"an intelligence" because each differs in quality (see Figure 9.6).

Three of Gardner's intelligences are verbal ability, logical–mathematical reasoning, and spatial intelligence (visual–spatial skills). Others are bodily-kinesthetic intelligence (as shown by dancers and gymnasts), musical intelligence, interpersonal intelligence (as shown by empathy and ability to relate to others), and personal knowledge (self-insight). Individuals may show great "intelligence" in one area without notable abilities in others. Critics agree that many people have special talents, as in music, but they question whether such talents are "intelligences" (Neisser et al., 1996).

Goleman's Emotional Intelligence

Emotional Intelligence (EI) is a term made popular by Goleman in 1995. It is the ability to understand one's own emotions and those of others, to apply emotional awareness to various tasks such as thinking and problem solving, and to regulate emotions or help others manage their emotions (Mayer, 2009). People who are high in EI could solve emotional problems quickly and effectively. They are able to interpret accurately the nonverbal emotional expression of others (Mayer, 2009). There is some evidence that teaching children social and emotional learning at an early age can improve their academic achievement and that emotional intelligence will be a required skill to work effectively with others in the future (Linder, 2016).

Measurement of Intellectual Development

Although people may disagree about the nature of intelligence, thousands of intelligence tests are administered every day by psychologists and educators to determine various exceptionalities. Licensed school psychologists use standardized tests, one of which determines something called an **intelligence quotient (IQ)**. An IQ is one's total score on a standardized intelligence test. Educators consider IQ scores along with additional information when placing children in special education classes for either cognitively challenged or gifted children.

The Stanford–Binet Intelligence Scale

The SBS originated in the early 1900s, when Alfred Binet and Théodore Simon worked for the French public school system. Binet assumed that intelligence increased with age. Therefore, older children should answer more items correctly. Thus, Binet arranged a series of questions in order of difficulty, from easier to harder. These questions have since undergone revision and refinement.

In 1916, Louis Terman adapted the Binet–Simon scale for use with American children. Because Terman carried out his work at Stanford University, the scale is now named the Stanford–Binet Intelligence Scale. The SB5 (now in its fifth edition) yields an intelligence quotient, or IQ. The SB5 today can be used with children from the age of 2 years up to adulthood. In the past, the IQ was considered to be the relationship between a child's mental age (MA) and his or her actual chronological age (CA). A mental age is the intellectual level at which a child is functioning. For example, an MA of 8 is an above-average score for a 6-year-old but a below average score for a 10-year-old.

Today, IQ scores on the SB5 are derived by comparing children's (and adults) performances with those of other people of the same age. People who answer more items correctly than the average individual in their age group attain IQ scores above 100, and people who answer fewer items correctly attain scores below 100.

DID YOU KNOW?

Two children of different ages can answer exactly the same items on an intelligence test correctly, yet one can be above average in intelligence and the other below average.

IQ tests consider both mental age and chronological age as factors when calculating IQ.

© SSPL/The Image Works

In 1905, in France, Alfred Binet and Théodore Simon introduced the idea of measuring intelligence. This version of the test was produced in 1937 by Lewis Terman and Maude Merrill in the United States and was specifically designed for younger children.

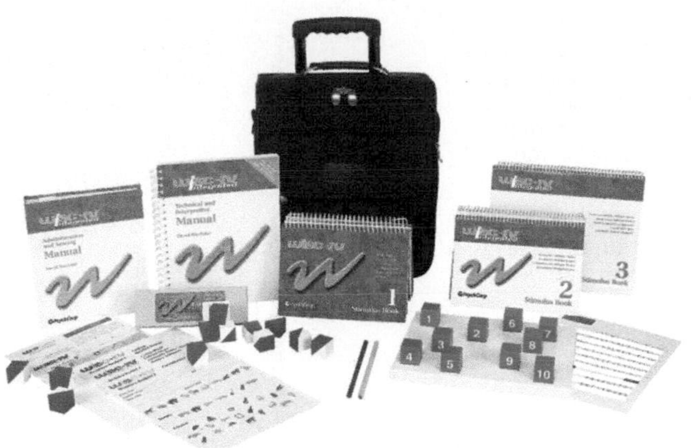

The Wechsler Intelligence Scale for Children is an intelligence test administered to children ages 6 to 16 years.

The Wechsler Intelligence Scale for Children

mental age (MA) the intellectual level at which a child is functioning

chronological age (CA) a person's actual age

The Wechsler Intelligence Scale for Children, now in its fifth edition (WISC-V), is administered to children between the ages of 6 to 16 years. David Wechsler also developed an intelligence test for adults called the Wechsler Adult Intelligence Scale (WAIS-IV), currently in its fourth version. Wechsler also developed a version of the test for children between the ages of 2 to just under 7 years called the Wechsler Preschool and Primary School Intelligence scale, currently in its fourth edition (WPPSI-IV).

The WISC-V group test questions into subtests that measure different intellectual tasks. Subtests compare a person's performance on one type of task (such as defining words) with another (such as using blocks to construct geometric designs). The Wechsler scales thus suggest children's strengths and weaknesses and provide overall measures of intellectual functioning.

Wechsler described some subtests as measuring verbal tasks and others as assessing non-verbal or performance tasks. In general, verbal subtests require knowledge of verbal concepts, whereas performance subtests require familiarity with non-verbal concepts such as spatial–relations.

Figure 9.7 indicates the labels that are assigned to various IQ scores on the WISC-V and the approximate percentages of the population who attain IQ scores at those levels. Most children's IQ

cultural bias
a factor in intelligence tests that provides an advantage for test takers from certain cultural backgrounds

culture-free
descriptive of a test in which cultural biases have been removed

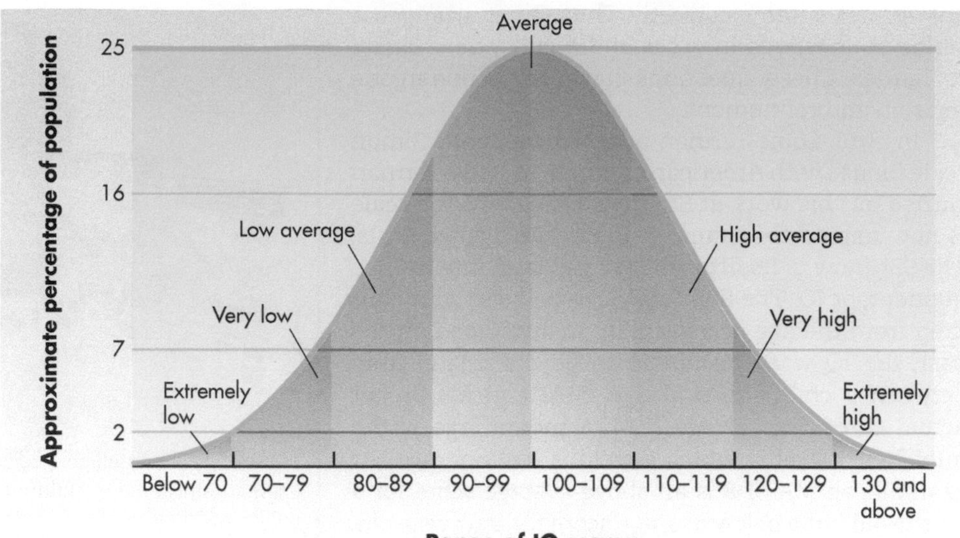

FIGURE 9.7

Variations in IQ Scores

IQ scores generally vary according to a bell-shaped, or "normal," curve.

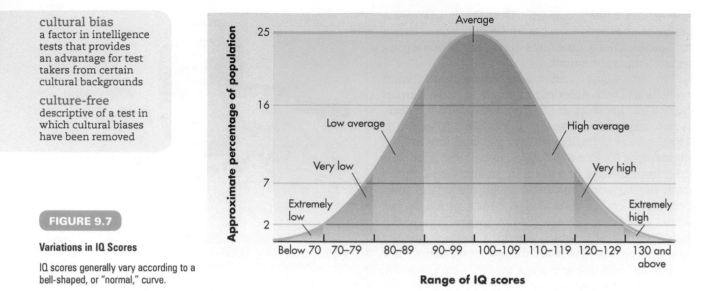

scores on the WISC-V cluster around average. Only about 5% of the population have IQ scores above 130 (Extremely High) or below 70 (Extremely Low).

The Testing Controversy

If scoring well on intelligence tests requires a certain type of cultural experience, the tests are said to have a cultural bias. Most psychologists and educational specialists consider intelligence tests to be culturally biased, at least to some degree, against minority groups and members of lower social classes (Snyderman & Rothman, 1990). For this reason, psychologists have tried to construct culture-free or culture-fair intelligence tests. Such culture-free tests are of particular importance in Canada because of our large multicultural population.

Some tests do not rely on expressive language at all. For example, Raymond Cattell's (1949) Culture-Fair Intelligence Test evaluates reasoning ability through the child's comprehension of the rules that govern a progression of geometric designs, as shown in Figure 9.8.

Culture-free tests have not lived up to their promise. First, middle-class children still outperform lower-class children on these tests (Rushton, Skuy, & Fridjhon, 2003). Middle-class children, for example, are more likely to have basic familiarity with materials such as blocks and pencils and paper. They are also more likely to have played with blocks (a practice relevant to the Cattell test). Second, the purpose of most testing is to predict academic success, but culture-free tests do not predict academic success as accurately as other intelligence tests do (Keogh & Whyte, 2006).

Patterns of Intellectual Development

Intellectual growth seems to occur in at least two major spurts. The first occurs at about the age of 6 years. It coincides with entry into school and also

FIGURE 9.8

Sample Items from Cattell's Culture-Fair Intelligence Test

Culture-fair tests attempt to exclude items that discriminate on the basis of cultural background rather than intelligence.

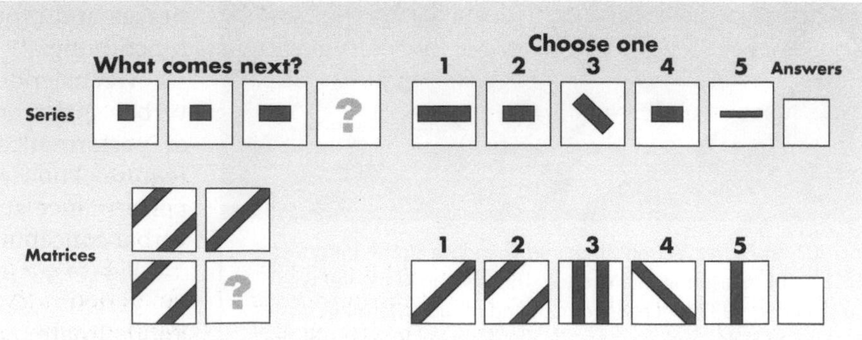

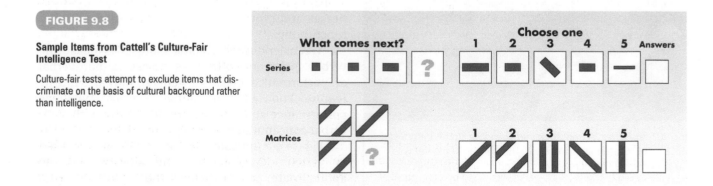

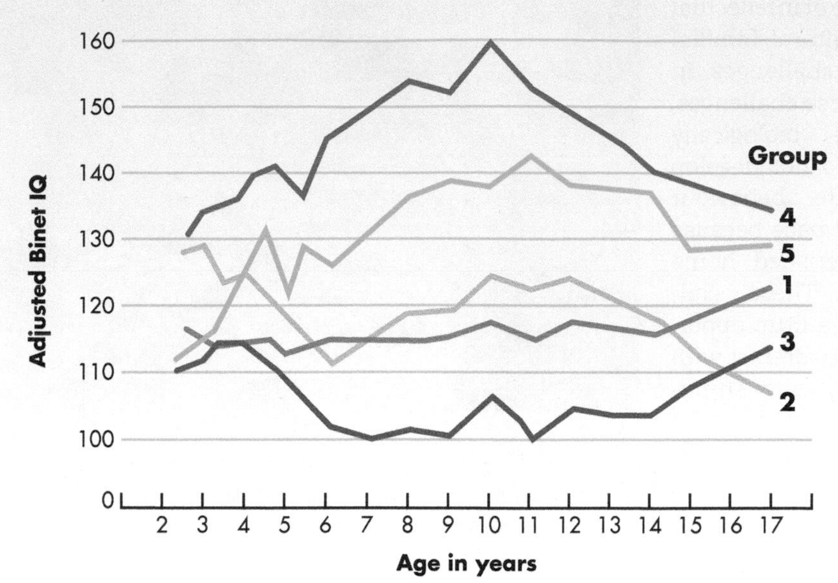

FIGURE 9.9

Five Patterns of Change in IQ Scores for Children in the Fels Longitudinal Study

In the Fels Longitudinal Study, IQ scores remained stable between the ages of 2½ and 17 years for only one of five groups tested.

Source: McCall et al., 1973.

with the shift from preoperational to concrete operational thought. School may help crystallize children's intellectual functioning. The second spurt occurs at about age 10 or 11 years.

Once children reach middle childhood, their gains in intellectual functioning appear to follow more stable patterns, although some spurts still occur (Deary et al., 2004). As a result, by middle childhood, intelligence tests gain greater predictive power. For example, testing at age 11 years shows a moderate to high relationship with scores at age 77 (Deary et al., 2004).

Despite the increased predictive power of intelligence tests during middle childhood, individual differences exist. In the classic Fels Longitudinal Study (see Figure 9.9), two groups of children made reasonably consistent gains in intelligence test scores between the ages of 10 and 17 years, whereas the scores of three groups declined. Another finding was that children who had shown the most intellectual promise at age 10 years went on to show the most precipitous decline, although they still wound up in the highest 2–3% of the population (McCall, Applebaum, & Hogarty, 1973). Many factors influence changes in IQ scores, including changes in the home, socio-economic circumstances, and education (Deary et al., 2004).

Differences in Intellectual Development

The average IQ score for Canadian children is 103.34. About half the children in Canada attain IQ scores in the broad average range from 90 to 110. Nearly 95% attain scores between 70 and 130. Children who attain IQ scores below 70 are generally labelled as "intellectually deficient" or "intellectually challenged." Children who attain scores of 130 or above are usually labelled as "gifted."

Intellectual Challenges

An intellectual challenge refers to limited functioning in both intellectual performance and adaptive skills. This term has been controversial in Canada and is used in limited circumstances. Terminology has evolved from *mental retardation* to *intellectual challenge* to *intellectual delay* to the more currently used term, *intellectual disability*. It is offensive to refer to an individual as "retarded" or as "a retard." These insensitive terms have degrading social implications. But *retardation* is an accepted term from a psychometrical perspective and may be off-putting when students encounter the term for the first time.

Of all children who are intellectually challenged, 80% are at the higher end of the scale. These individuals often receive modifications in their workload and are able to manage the demands of educational institutions and society at large. Many of these children will attend school in regular, inclusive classrooms, not in special-needs classes.

Some causes of intellectual challenge are biological, stemming from chromosomal abnormalities, such as Down syndrome; genetic disorders, such as phenylketonuria (PKU); and brain damage (AAIDD, 2007). Brain damage can have many origins, including childhood accidents, childhood illnesses such as brain cancer, and problems during pregnancy such as maternal alcohol abuse, malnutrition, or diseases.

cultural–familial developmental challenges substandard intellectual performance stemming from lack of opportunity to acquire knowledge and skills

heritability the degree to which the variations in a trait from one person to another can be attributed to genetic factors

Another cause of intellectual challenge is cultural–familial development challenges. In the case of these challenges, children are biologically normal but do not develop age-appropriate behaviour at the normal pace because of an impoverished home environment. These children may have little opportunity either to interact with adults or play with stimulating toys.

Wavebreakmedia/Shutterstock.com

Giftedness

Giftedness involves more than achieving excellence on the tasks provided by standard intelligence tests. In determining who is gifted, most educators include children who have outstanding abilities, such as those who are capable of high performance in a specific academic area—language or mathematics, for example. Children who show creativity, leadership, and distinction in the visual or performing arts, or bodily talents, as in gymnastics and dancing, may receive special training opportunities but they are not designated as gifted in the school setting.

Socio-Economic and Ethnic Differences in IQ

Research has found differences in IQ scores between socio-economic and ethnic groups but most psychologists agree that more research must be completed in the area of intelligence before we have a clear explanation of the effects of nature and nurture (Turkheimer et al., 2003). Lower-class children obtain IQ scores some 10 to 15 points lower than those obtained by middle- and upper-class children. African North American, Latino and Latina North American, and Native North American children all tend to score below the norms for European North Americans (Neisser et al., 1996). Youth of Asian descent frequently outscore youth of European backgrounds on achievement tests in math and science, including the math portion of the SAT (Dandy & Nettelbeck, 2002; Stevenson, Chen, & Lee, 1993).

Asian students and their mothers tend to attribute academic success to hard work (Randel, Stevenson, & Witruck, 2000), whereas North American mothers are more likely to attribute academic success to natural ability (Basic Behavioral Science Task Force, 1996). Thus, Asian students may work harder. Controversial Canadian research conducted by Rushton and Jensen (2005) asserts that denying cognitive differences between different races is not only poor science but also is injurious to unique individuals. Others fear that such research will support systemic discrimination.

Other measures of creativity include suggesting improvements or unusual uses for a familiar toy or object, naming items that belong in the same class, producing words similar in meaning, and writing different endings for a story.

Determinants of Intellectual Development

If heredity is involved in human intelligence, close relatives should have more similar IQ scores than distantly related or unrelated people, even when they are reared separately. Figure 9.10 shows the averaged results of more than 100 studies of IQ and heredity (Bouchard et al., 1990). The IQ scores of identical (monozygotic, or MZ) twins are more alike than the scores for any other pairs, even when the twins have been reared apart. The average correlation for MZ twins reared together is +0.85; for those reared apart, it is +0.67. Correlations between the IQ scores of fraternal (dizygotic, or DZ) twins, siblings, and parents and children are generally comparable, as is their degree of genetic relationship. The correlations tend to vary from about +0.40 to +0.61.

Overall, studies suggest that the heritability of intelligence is between 40% and 60% (Bouchard et al., 1990; Neisser et al., 1996). In other words, about half of the difference between your IQ score and those of others can be explained in terms of genetic factors.

Figure 9.10 also demonstrates that genetic pairs (such as MZ twins) reared together show higher correlations between IQ scores than similar genetic pairs (such as other MZ twins) who were reared apart. This finding holds for MZ twins, siblings, parents, children, and unrelated people. As such, the same group of studies that suggests that heredity plays a role in determining IQ scores also suggests that the environment plays a role.

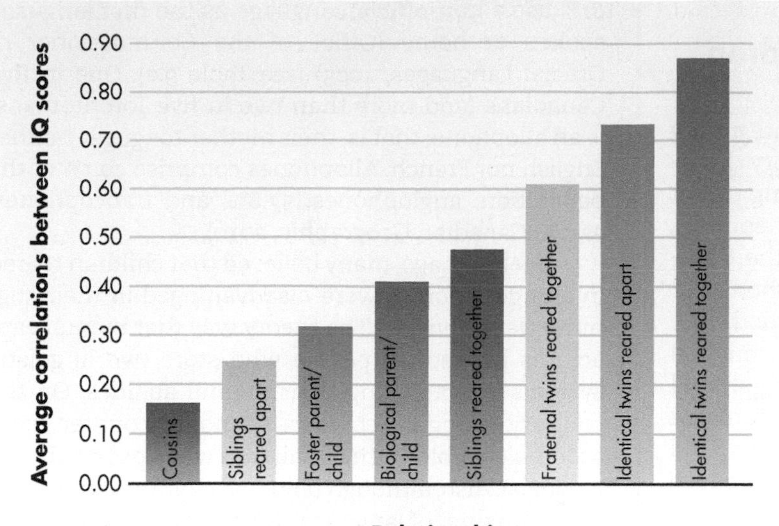

FIGURE 9.10

Findings of Studies of the Relationship between IQ Scores and Heredity

Correlations are stronger for persons who are more closely related and for persons who are reared together or living together, thus supporting both genetic and environmental hypotheses of the origins of intelligence.

Source: Bouchard et al., 1990.

Studies of environmental influences on IQ use several research strategies, including discovering situational factors that affect IQ scores, exploring children's abilities to rebound from early deprivation, and exploring the effects of positive early environments. Children whose parents are responsive and provide appropriate play materials and varied experiences during the early years attain higher IQ and achievement test scores (Bradley, 2006). Graduates of Head Start and other preschool programs also show significant gains in IQ and other test scores (Phillips & Styfco, 2007).

Many psychologists believe that heredity and environment interact to influence intelligence (Lubinski & Benbow, 2000; Winner, 2000). An impoverished environment may prevent some children from living up to their potential. An enriched environment may encourage others to maximize their potential.

LO8 Language Development and Literacy

Children's language ability grows more sophisticated in middle childhood. During this stage, children begin learning to read. Many children are exposed to a variety of linguistic experiences, and these experiences affect their cognitive development.

Vocabulary and Grammar

By the age of 6 years, a child's vocabulary has expanded to nearly 10,000 words. By 7 to 9 years of age, most children realize that words can have different meanings, and they become entertained by riddles and jokes that require semantic sophistication. By the age of 8 or 9, children are able to form "tag questions," such as "You want more ice cream, don't you?" and "You're sick, aren't you?" (Weckerly, Wulfeck, & Reilly, 2004).

Children make subtle advances in articulation and in their capacity to use complex grammar. Moreover, children in middle childhood are able to understand passive sentences such as "The truck was hit by the car" (Aschermann, Gülzow, & Wendt, 2004). During these years, children develop the ability to use connectives, as illustrated by the sentence "I'll eat my spinach, but I don't want to." They also learn to form indirect object–direct object constructions (e.g., "She showed her sister the toy").

Reading Skills and Literacy

Reading involves perceptual, cognitive, and linguistic processes (Smolka & Eviatar, 2006). It relies on the integration of visual and auditory information. Children must accurately perceive the sounds in their language and make basic visual discriminations (Levinthal & Lleras, 2007). Children must perceive the visual differences between letters such as *b* and *d* and *p* and *q*. Children become familiar with their own written languages by books, street signs, names of stores and restaurants, educational television programming, and the writing on packages. Children from homes where books and other sources of stimulation are plentiful learn to read more readily. Reading storybooks with parents in the preschool years helps prepare a child for reading in middle childhood (Raikes et al., 2006).

word-recognition method
a method for learning to read in which children come to recognize words through repeated exposure to them

phonetic method
a method for learning to read in which children decode the sounds of words based on their knowledge of the sounds of letters and letter combinations

sight vocabulary
words that are not decoded but are immediately recognized because of familiarity with their overall shapes

bilingual
using or capable of using two languages with equal or nearly equal facility

Methods of Teaching Children to Read

Children read by integrating visual and auditory information (associating what they see with sounds), whether they use the word-recognition method or the phonetic method. The word-recognition method associates visual stimuli such as seeing the words *cat* and *Robert* with the sound combinations that produce the spoken words. Children usually acquire this capacity is rote learning, or extensive repetition.

In the phonetic method, children learn to associate written letters and letter combinations (such as *ph* or *sh*) with the sounds they indicate. Then they sound out words. The phonetic method provides skills children can use to decode new words, but some children learn more rapidly at early ages through the word-recognition method. The phonetic method can slow down reading of familiar words.

Some English words can be read only by recognition, as with *one* and *two*. Word recognition is useful when it comes to words such as *danger*, *stop*, *poison*, and a child's name because it provides children with a basic sight vocabulary. But decoding skills help children read new words on their own. Most children and adults use both methods in their reading: they read familiar words by word recognition and make some effort to sound out new words.

Bilingualism: Linguistic Perspectives on the World

According to the 2001 Census of Canada, more than 100 mother tongues are spoken in Canada in addition to our indigenous languages and our official languages of English and French. Of all immigrants who arrived in the 1990s, 61% use a non-official language as the first language spoken at home (Office of the Commissioner of Official Languages, 2005) (see Table 9.2). One in five Canadians (and more than two in five Torontonians) is an allophone; that is, their mother tongue is neither English nor French. Allophones comprise 20.1% of the population; anglophones, 57.8%; and francophones, 22.1% (Canadian Geographic, 2010).

A century ago, many believed that children reared in bilingual homes were disadvantaged in their cognitive development. The theory was that mental capacity is limited, so people who store two linguistic systems are crowding their mental abilities. On the contrary, bilingual children do not encounter more academic problems than children who speak only one language. Also, although bilingual children experience some "mixing" of languages (Gonzalez, 2005), they can generally separate the two languages at an early age.

Today, most linguists consider it advantageous for children to be bilingual because knowledge of more than one language contributes to the complexity of the child's cognitive processes (Bialystok & Craik, 2007). For example, bilingual children are more likely to understand that the symbols used in language are arbitrary, whereas monolingual children are more likely to think erroneously that the word *dog* is somehow intertwined with the nature of the beast. Bilingual children therefore tend to have more cognitive flexibility. Furthermore, Canadian research indicates that speaking more than one language at an early age can have a positive impact on the brain as it

TABLE 9.2

Top Ten Languages Spoken at Home in Canada

English
French
Chinese
Italian
German
Punjabi
Spanish
Portuguese
Polish
Arabic
Fancy/Jupiter Images

One in five Canadians (and more than two in five Torontonians) is an allophone; that is, their mother tongue is neither English nor French. Allophones comprise 20.1% of the population; anglophones, 57.8%; and francophones, 22.1%.

Sources: Canadian Geographic. (2010). Who we are: Canada by demographics - Top 10 languages. The Canadian Atlas Online. Retrieved from http://magazine.canadiangeographic.ca/Atlas/themes.aspx?id=whoweare&sub=whoweare_demographics_work&lang=En; Statistics Canada. (2009c). 2006 Consensus: The evolving linguistic portrait, 2006 Census: Sharp increase in population with a mother tongue other than English or French. Retrieved from http://www12.statcan.ca/census-recensement/2006/as-sa/97-555/p2-eng.cfm

Hemis/Alamy Stock Photo

Children who are bilingual have a greater understanding of the symbolic nature of language.

trains executive functioning through language selection (Bialystok, 2015). In other words, when children are bilingual and thus understand more than one language, they are constantly searching for the correct meaning of a word; this strengthens their ability to selectively attend to information.

EMERGING CANADA

Language development is central to how children gain knowledge and learn to participate and grow within their cultures. Children who learn their cultural languages experience all the benefits of other bilingual children, and they remain connected with their culture of origin. Canada's numerous heritage language programs support children in maintaining speaking skills the cultural language of their families. Heritage language programmes range from Italian, to Gaelic, to Mohawk, and typically take place outside of regularly scheduled class time, such as weekends or evenings, or after school.

Low literacy development in Aboriginal languages is a significant issue in Canada. It is largely the result of the policies and practices carried out in residential schools, which instilled a belief among many Aboriginal children, who are now adults, that their language was inferior and their cultural ways were primitive. In addition to providing all the benefits of bilingualism—including, for example, increased cognitive flexibility and improved executive functioning—assisting Aboriginal children in learning their Indigenous language is an excellent way to effectively communicate important thoughts of cultural identity, cultural knowledge, and connectedness with their cultural community (Ball, 2008).

STUDY TOOLS

CHAPTER 9

Located at **nelson.com/student**

- ☐ Prepare for tests with a variety of exercises and activities
- ☐ Review Key Terms Flashcards (online or print)
- ☐ Create your own study tools with Build a Summary
- ☐ Watch Observing Development videos to expand your knowledge

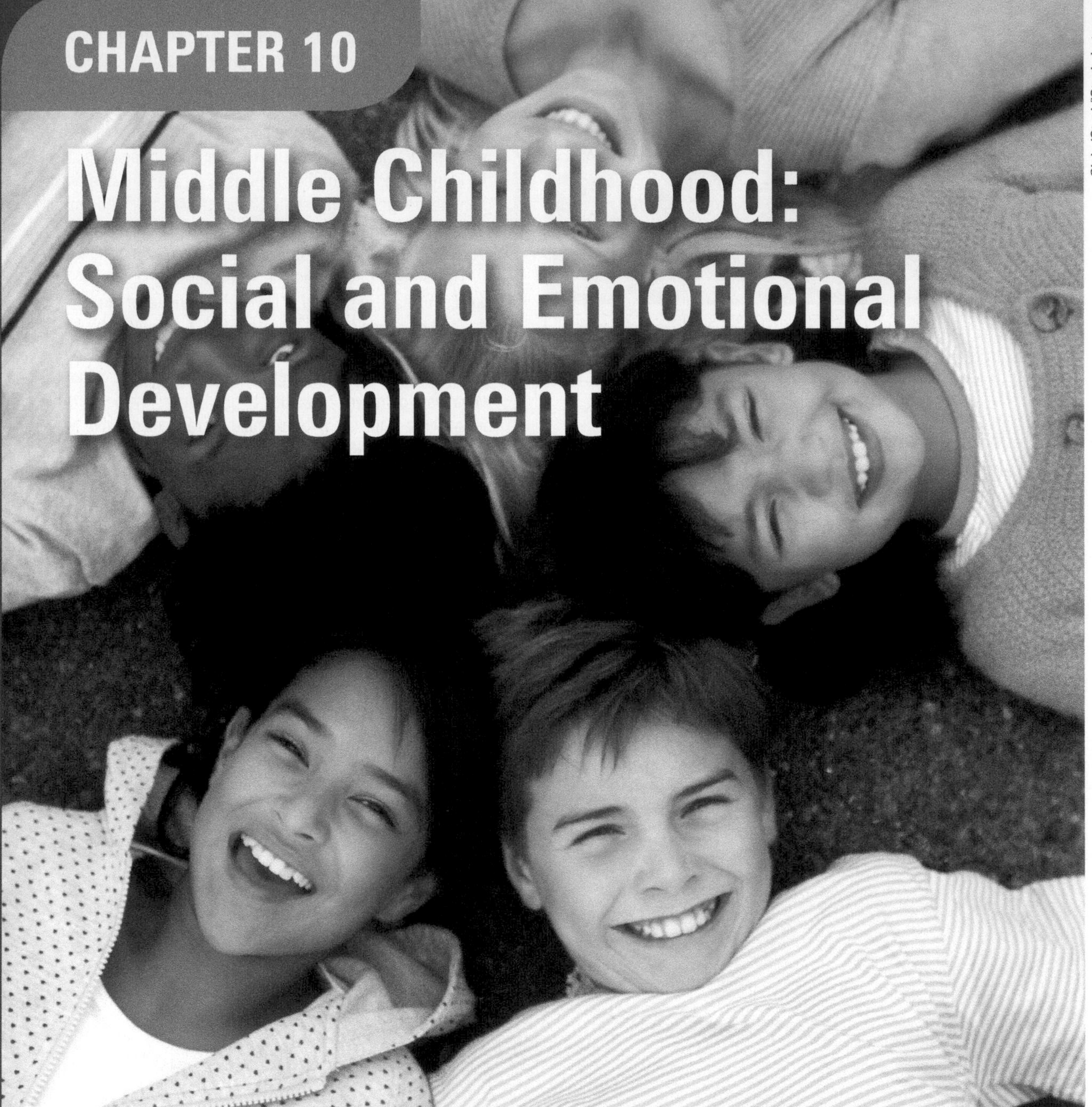

CHAPTER 10

Middle Childhood: Social and Emotional Development

LEARNING OUTCOMES

LO1 Explain theories of social and emotional development in middle childhood

LO2 Discuss the impact of the family on social development in middle childhood

LO3 Outline the influences of peers on social development in middle childhood

LO4 Explain the importance of the school on development in middle childhood

LO5 Discuss social and emotional problems that tend to develop in middle childhood

> "In the years between 6 and 12, peers take on greater importance and friendships deepen."

In the years between 6 and 12, the child's social world expands. Peers take on greater importance and friendships deepen. Entry into school exposes the child to the influence of teachers. Relationships with parents change as children develop greater independence.

LO1 Theories of Social and Emotional Development in Middle Childhood

Social Cognitive Theory

Social cognitive theory, advanced by Albert Bandura, focuses on the importance of rewards and modelling in middle childhood. During these years, children depend less on external rewards and punishments and increasingly regulate their own behaviour. Children are exposed to a wide variety of models, including parents, teachers, other adults, peers, and symbolic models (such as TV characters or the heroine in a story) (Anderson, Gentile, & Buckley, 2007; Oates & Messer, 2007).

Time & Life Pictures/Getty Images

Erikson Today

Stage 4: Industry versus Inferiority (6–11 years)

As children become more capable, they face new developmental challenges. Children's lives become more focused on learning, creating, and accomplishing a variety of new skills and knowledge, which results in a sense of industry. Children begin to look outward to compare themselves with their peers. This constant social comparison can result in unresolved feelings of inadequacy and even inferiority. Ability and self-esteem are at the forefront of this psychosocial challenge to be a productive and important member of the group. Parents are no longer the only authorities in the life of the child, whose world grows in size with the introduction of the classroom, peers, and more unsupervised play experiences.

Bandura also discussed a concept called reciprocal determinism. This is the interplay between the individual's personality, environment, and behaviour. Because all three components interact, a change in one component impacts the other two (Cherry, 2016). For example, a child who is aggressive may grab a toy from another child. The other child who is less confident may give in because he or she does not want to be physically or emotionally hurt by the aggressive child. The aggressive child's behaviour has been reinforced because he or she has the prized toy, and this behaviour will happen again. The children's overall environment is also affected because no one else will dare stand up to the aggressive kid for fear of injury (Cherry, 2016). Taken together, behaviour influences and is influenced by personality and environment all interacting together.

reciprocal determinism
the interplay between one's personality, environment, and behaviour

social cognition
one's understanding of the relationship between oneself and others

Consider THIS

Are the anti-bullying school policies in place across Canada effective at reducing bullying?

Please see page 186 for a discussion on this topic.

Cognitive-Developmental Theory and Social Cognition

According to Piaget, middle childhood coincides with the stage of concrete operations and is partly characterized by a decline in egocentrism and an expansion of the capacity to view the world and oneself from the perspective of others. This cognitive advancement affects the child's social relationships (Mischo, 2004; Zan & Hildebrandt, 2003).

Social cognition refers to perception of the social world, and our concern is the development of children's perspective-taking skills. Robert Selman and his colleagues (Selman, 1980; Selman & Dray, 2006) studied the development of these skills by presenting children with a social dilemma such as the following:

Holly is an 8-year-old girl who likes to climb trees. She is the best tree climber in the neighbourhood. One day while climbing down from a tall tree, she falls off the bottom branch but does not hurt herself. Her father sees her fall. He is upset and asks her to promise not to climb trees any more. Holly promises. Later that day, Holly and her friends meet Sean. Sean's kitten is caught up in a tree and can't get down. Something has to be done right away, or the kitten may fall. Holly is the only one who climbs trees well enough to reach the kitten and get it down, but she remembers her promise to her father (Selman, 1980, p. 36).

The children then were asked questions such as "How will Holly's father feel if he finds out she climbed the tree?" Using the children's responses, Selman (1976) described five levels of perspective-taking skills in childhood (see Table 10.1). Children with better perspective-taking skills tend to have better peer relationships (Selman & Dray, 2006).

Sergey Petrov/Shutterstock.com

Development of the Self-Concept in Middle Childhood

In early childhood, children's self-concepts focus on concrete external traits, such as appearance, activities, and living situations. But as children undergo the cognitive developments of middle childhood, more abstract internal traits, or personality traits, begin to play a role. Social relationships and group memberships take on significance (Harter, 2006; Thompson, 2006).

TABLE 10.1

Levels of Perspective Taking

Level	Approximate Age (Years)	What Happens
0	3–6	Children are egocentric and do not realize that other people have perspectives different from their own. A child of this age will typically say that Holly will save the kitten because she likes kittens and that her father will be happy because he likes kittens, too. The child assumes that everyone feels as she does.
1	5–9[a]	Children understand that people in different situations may have different perspectives. The child still assumes that only one perspective is "right." A child might say that Holly's father would be angry if he did not know why she climbed the tree. But if she told him why, he would understand. The child recognizes that the father's perspective may differ from Holly's because of lack of information. But once he has the information, he will assume the "right" perspective (i.e., Holly's).
2	7–12[a]	The child understands that people may think or feel differently because they have different values or ideas. The child also recognizes that others are capable of understanding the child's own perspective. Therefore, the child is better able to anticipate reactions of others. The typical child of this age might say that Holly knows that her father will understand why she climbed the tree and that he therefore will not punish her.
3	10–15[a]	The child finally realizes that both she and another person can consider each other's point of view at the same time. The child may say something similar to this reasoning: Holly's father will think that Holly shouldn't have climbed the tree. But now that he has heard her side of the story, he will feel that she was doing what she thought was right. Holly realizes that her father will consider how she felt.
4	12 and above[a]	The child realizes that mutual perspective taking does not always lead to agreement. The perspectives of the larger social group also must be considered. A child of this age might say that society expects children to obey their parents and therefore that Holly should realize why her father might punish her.

[a]Ages may overlap.
Source: Selman, 1976.

Self-Esteem

As children enter middle childhood, they evaluate their self-worth in many different areas (Tassi, Schneider, & Richard, 2001). Preschoolers tend to see themselves as either generally "good at doing things" or not. But by 5 to 7 years of age, children are able to judge their performance in seven different areas: physical ability, physical appearance, peer relationships, parent relationships, reading, math, and general school performance. They also report a general self-concept (Harter, 2006).

Children's self-esteem declines throughout middle childhood, reaching an all-time low at age 12 or 13 years. Self-esteem then increases during adolescence (Harter, 2006). What accounts for the decline? Whereas preschoolers are egocentric and thus, their self-concepts may be unrealistic in early childhood, in middle childhood children compare themselves with other children. Consequently, they arrive at a more honest and critical self-appraisal. Gender differences regarding self-esteem among this age group have been found. Girls tend to have more positive self-concepts regarding reading, general academics, and helping others; boys tend to have more positive self-concepts in terms of math, physical ability, and physical appearance (Jacobs et al., 2005; Wang, 2005).

Authoritative parenting apparently contributes to children's self-esteem (Baumrind, 1991a, 1991b; Supple & Small, 2006). Children with a favourable self-image tend to have parents who are restrictive, involved, and loving. Children with low self-esteem are more likely to have authoritarian or rejecting–neglecting parents.

Social acceptance by peers is related to self-perceived competence in academic, social, and athletic domains (Nesdale & Lambert, 2007). Parents and classmates have an equally strong effect on children's self-esteem in middle childhood. Friends and teachers have relatively less influence but also matter (Harter, 2006).

DID YOU KNOW?

Children's self-esteem tends to decline in middle childhood.

Children's self-esteem declines throughout middle childhood, reaching an all-time low at age 12 or 13 years and rising again in adolescence.

LO2 The Family

In middle childhood, the family continues to play a key role in socializing the child, although peers, teachers, and outsiders begin to play a greater role (Harter, 2006).

Parent–Child Relationships

co-regulation a gradual transferring of control from parent to child, beginning in middle childhood

transsexuals individuals who prefer to be of the other sex and who may undergo hormone treatments, cosmetic surgery, or both to achieve the appearance of being of the other sex

Parent–child interactions focus on some new concerns during middle childhood. They include school-related matters, assignment of chores, and peer activities (Collins et al., 2003). Parents do less monitoring of children's activities and provide less direct feedback than they did in the preschool years. Control is gradually transferred from parent to child in a process known as co-regulation (Maccoby, 2002; Wahler, Herring, & Edwards, 2001). Children begin to internalize the standards of their parents.

Children in middle childhood spend less time with their parents than they did in their preschool years, although they typically spend more time with their mother than with their father. Mothers' interactions with school-age children continue to revolve around caregiving; fathers are relatively more involved in recreational activities (Wolfenden & Holt, 2005).

Because of their developing cognitive ability, 10- to 12-year-olds evaluate their parents more harshly than they did in early childhood (Selman & Dray, 2006). But throughout middle childhood, children still rate their parents as their best source of emotional support (Cowan & Cowan, 2005; Katz et al., 2005).

Same-Sex Parents

The number of same-sex married couples tripled between 2006 and 2011 (Milan, 2013). Research on same-sex parenting is divided into two general categories: the general adjustment of children of same-sex parents and whether the children of same-sex parents are more likely than other children to be lesbian or gay. Research by Charlotte Patterson (2006) has generally found that the psychological adjustment of children of same-sex parents is comparable with that of children of heterosexual parents. Similar to their heterosexual counterparts, lesbians and gay men often sustain positive family relationships (Wainright, Russell, & Patterson, 2004). With the legalization of gay marriage in Canada in 2005, social stigmas regarding homosexuality have lessened.

What have researchers learned about the sexual orientation of the children of same-sex parents? Green (1978) observed 37 children and young adults, ages 3 to 20 years, who were being reared—or had been reared—by lesbians or transsexuals. All but one of the children reported or recalled preferences

Juanmomino/Shutterstock.com

PFLAG CANADA

Courtesy of PFLAG Canada

EMERGING CANADA

Fifty years of families in Canada: 1961 to 2011

The traditional family of a mother and a father and three children is no longer the reality in Canadian society. Over the past 50 years, the Canadian family has evolved to the point that there no longer is a "typical" family. Many Canadians live alone, have remarried, are empty nesters, or live with multiple generations in one household. In 1961, the average Canadian family had 3.9 people. In 2011, the average Canadian family had 2.9 people. Anne Milan, a Statistics Canada demographer, observed that the Canadian family is more complex and is definitely more diverse than ever before (Scoffield, 2012).

The following are some of the significant changes to the Canadian family that were observed in the Statistics Canada document titled *Fifty Years of Families in Canada: 1961 to 2011* (Statistics Canada, 2013b):

- Married couples accounted for 91.6% of census families in 1961. By 2011, this number had declined to 76%. This decrease is likely due to the growth of common-law couples.
- The number of married couples rose 19.7%, while the number of common-law couples more than quadrupled, with an increase of 345.2%.
- The percentage of lone-parent families almost doubled, from 8.4% in 1961 to 16.3% in 2011. In 2011, lone-parent families were headed by a parent who was divorced or separated (50.8%), never married (31.5%), or widowed (17.7%).
- Same-sex couples made up only 0.8% of all recorded couples in 2011.
- In 1961, 9.3% of households consisted of one person. In 2011, 27.6% of all Canadian households consisted of one person.

for toys, clothing, and friends (male or female) that were typical for their sex and age. All the 13 older children who reported sexual fantasies or sexual behaviour were heterosexually oriented. It seems that the concerns of those opposed to families with same-sex parents are not supported through research (Foley, 2015).

Divorce and Family Structure

Much of our popular culture information about divorce comes from the United States but Canadians do not divorce at the same rates as our neighbours. The Canadian divorce rate has remained fairly stable, at 37.6 divorces per 100 marriages by the 30th wedding anniversary in 2002 and 38.3 in 2003. However, the divorce rate for remarried individuals is higher (Statistics Canada, 2005). Divorce is most common 14.5 years after marriage (Ambert, 2009). The average age of divorce is 44 years for a man and 41.4 for women (Ambert, 2009).

Many demographic variables have been found to be risk factors for divorce. For example, low income and little education are risk factors as they lead to financial stress in the marriage. Marrying at a young age, parental divorce (one's own parents divorcing), and cohabitation prior to marriage are also risk factors for divorce. In addition, couples with little religious affiliation are at risk, because religious affiliation is related to higher marital happiness (Ambert, 2009).

Divorce may be tough on parents; it can be even tougher on children (Amato, 2000). No longer do children participate with both parents in daily activities such as eating, attending extracurricular activities and social activities, and vacations. Also,

Andresr/Shutterstock.com

the financial strain of parents having to support two homes means fewer resources for the children (Tashiro, Frazier, & Berman, 2006).

Most children live with their mothers after a divorce; only 10% of children live with their fathers exclusively (Ambert, 2009; Amato, 2000). Many fathers remain devoted to their children despite the split, but others tend to spend less time with their children as they move on to other relationships. Ideally, parents will take care in discussing children's emotions about the divorce and providing reassurance that they will always be loved even though the family arrangement will be different.

Step-Parents and Blended Families

In Canada, half of all adults who become step-parents are remarried whereas the remainder are in couples living common-law. The exception is Quebec where 75% of **blended families** are headed by a cohabitating couple (Ambert, 2009). Around 12.6% of Canadian children are living in a stepfamily (Statistics Canada, 2011c). In 2011, in 1% of families headed by couples, the children were either the biological or adopted children of one parent. 4.1% included a biological child of both parents and children from either parent's previous relationship (Statistics Canada, 2011c) as indicated in Table 10.2. A major concern of step-parents is their ability to discipline their stepchildren and to provide them with the same love and affection they feel towards their own children. Step-parents who assume an authoritative parenting style tend to have a positive relationship with their stepchildren, especially when they are supportive of the biological parent's ability to act as an authority (Hetherington, 1989).

blended families families that include the biological children of at least one of the partners in a relationship

Single Parents

According to the 2011 census, 1,527,845 families are living in single parent homes with the majority headed by women (1,200,295) (Statistics Canada, 2011c). Single mothers tend to feel socially isolated and have a reduced income. They tend to communicate less with their children than mothers in two-parent homes. They also feel impatient and less warm towards their children, especially their sons, and they tend to monitor their children's whereabouts less closely than other parents (Hetherington & Stanley-Hagan, 2002).

TABLE 10.2

Distribution (number and percentage) of Couple Families with Children by Stepfamily Status, Canada, 2011

Couple Family with Children[1]	Number	Percentage
All couple families with children	3,684,675	100.0
Intact families[2]	3,220,340	87.4
Stepfamilies	464,335	12.6
Simple stepfamilies	271,930	7.4
Complex stepfamilies	192,410	5.2
Families with child(ren) of both parents and child(ren) of one parent only	149,365	4.1
Families with child(ren) of each parent only and no children of both parents	35,765	1.0
Families with child(ren) of both parents and child(ren) of each parent only	7,275	0.2

[1] Refers to couples with at least one child aged 24 and under.

[2] Couple families with at least one child aged 24 and under for whom it cannot be determined if there are stepchildren present are considered intact families.

Source: Statistics Canada, Census of Population, 2011.

skip-generation families
families whose grandparents parent the grandchildren with little or no help from their adult child

Some recent Canadian research indicates that children from single parent homes fare almost as well as children from two parent homes (Seabrook & Avison, 2015). The single parents in the study tended to have higher education and higher status occupations that they were able to hold for a long period of time. It appears that the level of income in the family is the most important determinant of adjustment for children. Thus, the authors conclude that rather than emphasizing only family structure as an important determinant of children's wellbeing, it is important to provide adequate financial resources and opportunities for education to single parents (Seabrook & Avison, 2015).

In order to reduce isolation and to provide support for each other, it is important that single parents are able to connect with other single parents and to find resources where they can go back to school or take parenting classes. One agency that provides such help is Single Mothers In Progress. Resources can be found on their website at www.singlemothersinprogress.org.

Outcome of Divorce on Middle Childhood

According to research, when compared to their peers whose parents live together, the children of divorce are more likely to experience conduct disorders, drug abuse, and poor grades in school, as well as lowered self-esteem, and disruptions in interpersonal functioning (Ambert, 2009; Amato, 2000; Amato, 2010). Although there is evidence that preschoolers are negatively affected by divorce, there seems to be evidence that long-term consequences for children in middle childhood may be more serious (Wallerstein, 1987). Children whose parents divorced while they were between the ages of 6 to 8 years had painful memories of the divorce 10 years later and felt that they too would not be happy in their romantic relationships in the future (Wallerstein, 1987). The physical health of these children may also decline (Troxel & Matthews, 2004). It should be noted, however, that most children do not develop a serious developmental problem as the result of divorce (Ambert, 2000). In general, the fallout for children is worst during the first year after the breakup. After a couple of years or so, children tend to rebound (Malone et al., 2004).

Some of the difficulties experienced by children after divorce may have to do with factors that were apparent before the separation, such as temperament of the child and/or mental health issues. Thus, it is hard to say whether it is the impact of divorce per se that leads to negative outcomes, as most of the research is correlational in nature. Although the averages are not large, when compared to those whose parents live together, children of divorce are more likely to suffer from mental health issues, such as anxiety and depression, and they have more relationship problems, often due to their behavioural issues (Ambert, 2009).

Should We Remain Married "for the Sake of the Children"?

Many individuals believe—for moral or personal reasons—that marriage and family life must be permanent, no matter what. But—from a purely psychological perspective—what should bickering parents do? The answer seems to relate to how they behave in front of the children. Research shows that severe parental bickering is linked to the same kinds of problems that children experience when their parents separate or divorce (Troxel & Matthews, 2004). When children are exposed to adult or marital conflict, they display a biological "alarm reaction": their bodies react with sharp increases in heart rate, blood pressure, and sweating (El-Sheikh, 2007). Therefore, Hetherington and her colleagues suggest that divorce can be a positive alternative to long-term family conflict (Hetherington, 1989; Wallerstein et al., 2005).

Focused parenting is key to children successfully making this significant social adjustment. Parents who are devoted to their children and are aware of the statistics can protect their children from the harms associated with divorce. Studies have shown that children exhibit fewer adjustment issues after divorce when mothers exhibit a high degree of acceptance and are consistent with their discipline (Wolchik, Wilcox, Tein, & Sandler, 2000).

Grandparents as Primary Caregivers

Skip-generation families is a term used to classify grandparents who parent their grandchildren with little to no help from their adult child. There are some cultural differences. More skip-generation families are of South Asian decent or part of the Aboriginal community. According to the 2011 census, 30,010 children were living with either one or more grandparent (Statistics Canada, 2011c); 1% of all grandparents were living with their grandchildren. In skip-generation homes, grandparents may take on the responsibility of caring for their grandchildren when the child's own parents are unavailable for various reasons, such as emotional difficulties or mental health issues, hospitalization, incarceration, drug or alcohol abuse, or relocating for work (Milan, LaFlamme, & Wong, 2015). Furthermore, sometimes children are removed from their home due to violence or abuse and placed with grandparents (Hoffman, 2009). Although many enjoy the experience, many grandparents may find that they have to put off various plans they had to retire or change how they spend their time in retirement to parent their grandchildren.

When Mom Works

One stereotype is that delinquency results from mothers being in the workforce rather than in the home. Researchers using data on 707 adolescents, age 12 to 14 years, from the National Longitudinal Survey of Youth, examined whether the occupational status of a mother was related to delinquent behaviour (Vander Ven & Cullen, 2004). They found that maternal employment made little difference; rather, delinquency was related to a lack of supervision. When supervision and monitoring of children's behaviour is limited, there is evidence that maternal employment has particularly negative outcomes for boys, including lower school achievement, behavioural issues, and greater parent–child conflict (Crouter et al., 1990). Consistent with this, a longitudinal study that examined maternal employment 6 months after the child was born found small negative effects. However, more important than maternal employment on children were family's income, parental education, and quality of interaction with children (Huerta, Adema, Baxter. Corak, Deding, Gray, et al., 2011).

Maternal employment has benefits. Daughters of employed women are more achievement oriented and set higher career goals for themselves than daughters of non-working women (Hangal & Aminabhavi, 2007). Children of working mothers also tend to be more prosocial, less anxious, and more flexible in their gender-role stereotypes (Nomaguchi, 2006; Wright & Young, 1998). Daughters of working women have higher levels of self-esteem, independence, and achievement, as well as higher career goal aspirations than daughters of non-working mothers (Lucas-Thompson, Goldberg, & Prause, 2010).

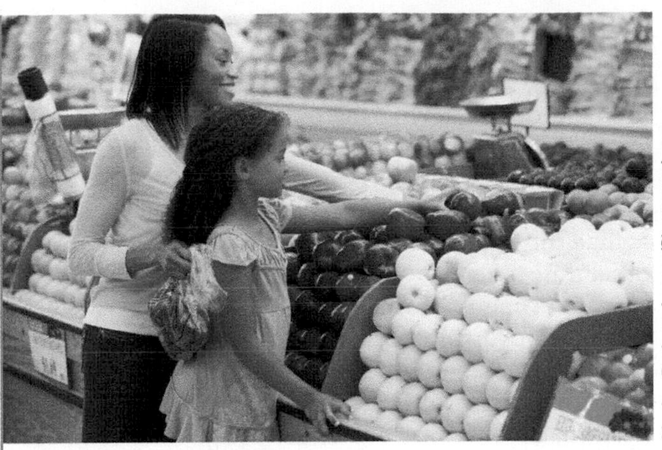
Monkey Business Images/Shutterstock.com

DID YOU KNOW?

The daughters of employed women are more achievement oriented and set higher career goals for themselves than the daughters of non-working women.

This tendency is likely due to the role modelling that takes place between mother and daughter.

LO3 Peer Relationships

Families exert the most powerful influences on children during their first few years. But as children move into middle childhood, peers take on greater importance because, belonging to the same generation, they have similar interests and skills (Molinari & Corsaro, 2000). Peers provide practice in cooperating, relating to leaders, and coping with aggressive impulses, including their own. Peers can also be important confidants (Dunn et al., 2001; Hanlon et al., 2004). Furthermore, children who are at odds with their parents can turn to peers as sounding boards, to compare their feelings and experiences. When children share troubling ideas and experiences with peers, they realize they are normal and not alone (Barry & Wentzel, 2006).

Development of Friendships

In the preschool years and early years of middle childhood, friendships are based on geographic proximity. Friendships are superficial: they are quickly

DID YOU KNOW?

In middle childhood, popular children tend to be attractive and relatively mature for their age.

This is true, though more so for girls in the case of attractiveness.

formed and easily broken. What matters are shared activities and who has a swing set or sandbox to play in (Berndt, 2004; Gleason et al., 2005). Preschool children are more likely to say that friends are nice and share their interests. They increasingly pick friends who are similar in behaviour and personality.

Between the ages of 8 and 11 years, children recognize the importance of friendships that meet each other's needs and what constitutes desirable traits in their friends (Zarbatany, McDougall, & Hymel, 2004). Trustworthiness, mutual understanding, and a willingness to disclose personal information characterize friendships in middle childhood and beyond (Hamm, 2000; Rotenberg et al., 2004). Girls tend to develop closer friendships than boys, in their effort to seek confidantes (Zarbatany et al., 2000).

Robert Selman (1980) described five stages in children's changing concepts of friendship. The stages correspond to the levels of perspective-taking skills discussed earlier. School-age friends are more verbal, attentive, relaxed, and responsive to each other during play than are mere acquaintances (Cleary et al., 2002). Conflicts can occur among friends, but when they do, they tend to be minor disagreements and are typically resolved in positive ways (Wojslawowicz Bowker et al., 2006).

By middle childhood, children will typically report that they have more than one "best" friend (Berndt, Miller, & Park,1989). Nine-year-olds report an average of four best friends (Lewis & Feiring, 1989). Best friends tend to be more like each other than other friends. In middle childhood, boys tend to play in larger groups than girls. Children's friendships are almost exclusively with others of the same sex, continuing the trend of sex segregation (Hartup, 1983).

Peer Acceptance

Acceptance or rejection by peers is important in childhood because problems with peers affect adjustment later on (Wentzel, Barry & Caldwell, 2004). Popular children tend to be attractive, mature for their age, and successful in sports or academics, although attractiveness seems to be more important for girls than boys (Langlois et al., 2000). Children who are accepted show social savvy and know how to join play groups (Bierman, 2003). They are described by their peers as "attractive, athletic, wealthy, nice dressers and not boring" (Kennedy-Moore, 2013). Some children who are popular act in prosocial ways. They are friendly, nurturing, cooperative, helpful, and socially skilled (Xie et al., 2006). They also have high self-esteem. On the other hand, another group of popular children are anti-social. They are the "cool" kids who are socially competent but not kind (Kennedy-Moore, 2013). They act defiantly towards adults and are socially aggressive, gossiping or manipulating others to get ahead. Their peers admire and fear them at the same time.

Research on popularity indicates that by age 11 years, one third of children are in the popular dominant clique (Adler & Adler, 1998). This group engages in mean behaviour to determine who will be accepted or rejected by the clique. Approximately 10% of children fall in a "wannabe" group; these are students who are on the outside of the popular group holding on for dear life, hoping to be included (Adler & Adler, 1998). They get some indications that they are approved by the large, popular group, but they are never completely accepted. About 50% of all children this age have middle social status. They form their own smaller cliques and are loyal to and supportive of each other. They look out for each other and look down at less popular children (Adler & Adler, 1998). Approximately, 10% of students fall into the last category of socially isolated. They are at the bottom of the social hierarchy and are at risk for being targets of bullying (Kennedy-Moore, 2013).

Monkey Business Images/Shutterstock

Peer Rejection

There are two different types of children who are rejected by their peers. The first group is withdrawn–rejected; these children tend to be disliked by their peers because they are perceived to be different in some way. For example, children who are shy, or who are more creative than most others, tend to be rejected. Children who are new immigrants to the country, children who have physical disabilities, and children who engage in unusual behaviour or act different from others are often rejected (Bierman, 2003). Also part of the withdrawn–rejected group are children who are rejected because they miss nonverbal cues; they are unable to read and understand the social meaning of nonverbal behaviour and they have not developed methods for resolving social conflicts

(Nixon, 2010). This issue becomes a vicious cycle in that the rejected children have few opportunities to improve their social skills as they have less opportunity for social interactions. Another reason why children in this group are rejected is their own social anxiety (Bierman, 2003).

Peer rejection tends to be stable and thus once it is established, it is difficult to overcome (Cillessen, 2009). When children who are popular engage in the same behaviour as a withdrawn–rejected child, their behaviour is treated more favourably than it would be if engaged in by the already-rejected child. This occurs because once a child's rejected status is formed, it serves as a bias for the way that child will be viewed and treated by others in the future. Even changing schools does little to help rejected children improve their social status as their reputation often follows them wherever they go. This is called reputational bias (Cillessen, 2009).

The second group of children who are rejected are aggressive–rejected; these children are disruptive and uncooperative. Rejection often occurs for this group because they display more impulsive, immature, or inattentive behaviour, and less prosocial behaviour, like taking turns (Bierman, 2003; Boivin, Vitaro, & Poulin, 2005). Most aggressive children do not learn to conform. Instead, they remain on the fringes of the group and may find aggressive friends who are similar to them (Rose, Swenson, & Carlson, 2004). The difference between aggressive behaviour that leads to rejection and aggression that may be viewed more positively is that aggressive children who are well liked tend to be friendly and have special skills such as athleticism and intelligence. On the other hand, aggressive–rejected children tend to actually hurt others or get their peers into trouble for their behaviour (Hincks-Dellcrest, 2014).

Bullying

Bullying transforms the perception of school from a safe place into a violent place (Batsche & Porter, 2006). An estimated 70–75% of students have reported being bullied at some point in their lifetime (Li, 2007). Public Safety Canada (2010) defines bullying as acts of intentional harm, repeated over time, in a relationship characterized by an imbalance of power. Bullying includes physical actions (e.g., punching, kicking), verbal actions (e.g., threats and insults), and social exclusion (e.g., spreading rumours and ostracizing).

Bullying is not an act of anger but one of contempt for the target. The bully views the victim as worthless and undeserving of respect. The key elements of bullying are intent to harm, repeated behaviour over time, imbalance of power, and the victim's distress (Pepler & Craig, 2000).

peer rejection
when children are rejected by their peers. Divided into two groups: one is withdrawn–rejected; as they are disliked by their peers due to some perceived difference; the other is aggressive–rejected, and these children are rejected due to aggressive, disruptive behaviour.

bullying
an act of intentional harm, repeated over time, in a relationship characterized by an imbalance of power

Canadian researchers Debra Pepler and Wendy Craig have studied bullying, aggression, and violence for over 20 years. Their work has changed the way bullying is viewed in the school; bullying is no longer seen as something "that is a normal part of childhood or that kids will grow out of" (Pepler & Craig, 2000). There are long-term consequences for individuals who bully and for those who have been bullied. The long-term consequences of being bullied include such mental health issues as anxiety and depression, withdrawal, school refusal, somatization (using physical symptoms to cover up psychological distress), and reputation as someone who is victimized (Pepler, & Craig, 2000). Less well known are the long-term effect of bullying: increased rate of conduct disorder (see LO5) and aggressive behaviour, dating violence and sexual harassment, academic problems, and anxiety (Pepler & Craig, 2000).

Students who identify with the lesbian, gay, bisexual, transgender and queer (LGBTQ) community are at even greater risk for bullying. Identifying with the LGBTQ community was reported to be the second most common reason for being bullied (CBC News, 2010a). Fifty-nine per cent of students who identify as belonging to that community reported being bullied as compared to 7% of their non-LBGTQ peers (CBC News, 2010). Individuals from this community also reported being physically harassed, being the target of cyberbullying, feeling unsafe, and not being accepted by their peers as compared to their non-LGBTQ peers (CBC News, 2010). However, bullying was less common in schools that had a gay–straight alliance and anti-bullying policies in place.

DID YOU KNOW?

There are many reasons why bystanders do not intervene to stop bullies despite having the belief that bullying is wrong.

Some of the main reasons why bystanders do not intervene during a bullying episode include not knowing what to do, fear of making the situation worse not better, and being afraid of becoming bullied themselves.

Consider THIS

Are the anti-bullying school policies in place across Canada effective at reducing bullying?

Bullying prevention and finding ways to stop bullying once it has started are complex and difficult to achieve. Most children who witness bullying episodes feel uncomfortable during the event, and most bullying happens in front of others. One way to end victimization is to encourage peers who see bullying taking place to intervene when appropriate (Cappadocia, Pepler, Cummings, & Craig, 2012). These peers are called bystanders and their impact can have a significant impact on the outcome of a bullying episode.

Pepler and Craig (2000) observed children during bullying events—on the playground particularly—and found that 11% of the time, bystanders intervened to end the bullying. However, one third of children who are bystanders reported that they joined in the bullying when it was someone they didn't like (Pepler & Craig, 2000). However, bystanders have a lot of power too; it has been found that they can stop the bullying from happening or they can prolong an episode because the bully has the bystanders' attention (Cappadocia et al., 2012; Craig, Pepler, & Blais, 2007).

There are many reasons why bullying in the playground takes place. First, bullies and bystanders are drawn to the arousal and excitement of aggressive behaviour and over time, they become desensitized to it. Children who bully require greater hurtful and aggressive attacks to bring about the same desired sense of power (Pepler & Craig, 2000). Second, bystanders may increase their social status if they join the bullying taking place, and they may enjoy the sense of group cohesion they experience by being part of something. Third, bullies feel justified in their actions; they have little or no empathy for their victims and attribute the blame to the victim's behaviour. Last, peers who align with the victim may become bullied themselves. Thus, to prevent this, they join in the behaviour (Pepler & Craig, 2000).

Despite what is popularized in the media, many children who are bullied tell the teacher or someone they trust about the bullying behaviour (46% of those bullied have told the teacher about the event). However, there is a discrepancy between the perception of the teachers and the children concerning whether teachers actually intervene when children report bullying behaviour: 25% of children versus 74% of teachers reported that the teacher intervened during the bullying episode. Furthermore, Pepler and Craig (2000) observed teachers in the playground and found that teachers intervened only 14% of the time during classroom episodes and only 4% of the time during playground events.

Finally, there are societal influences that allow for bullying to continue. Popular beliefs around bullying includes "children will grow out of it" and "it is a normal part of childhood". Other myths include that "it is best for children to resolve their own conflicts" and that "conflicts only involve teasing, which isn't really harmful to the child" (Pepler & Craig, 2000). Furthermore, some people believe that the individual who was bullied provoked the attack and that it isn't wise to promote tattling. Parents of bullies accept this form of behaviour and rarely intervene when it has come to their attention that their child engaged in bullying. They do not set limits or monitor their children's behaviour, and they often use power and aggression in their own home to establish desired behaviour (Pepler & Craig, 2000).

bystanders
peers who watch a bullying episode take place but do not take part in the bullying, at least, initially

cyberbullying
using some form of technology to bully and harass another person

Cyberbullying

Cyberbullying means using some form of technology, often social media, or using a cellphone to bully and harass another person. This can include spreading rumours about another individual, making threatening comments, sending or posting unflattering pictures of an individual, or spreading rumours on popular social media websites or in chat rooms, and through text messaging (Kids Help Phone, 2014). Approximately 70% of children who use Kids Help Phone reported being bullied online (Kids Help Phone, 2014).

There are major differences between cyberbullying and face-to-face bullying. First, it is easier to send mean messages to others when they cannot be seen on the receiving end. Second, cyberbullying reaches a larger audience than face-to-face bullying. Cyberbullying has much greater potential to do damage than face-to-face bullying,

Bullying and Pink Shirt Day

A student in Nova Scotia was bullied for wearing a pink shirt to school. To protest the bullying, two students purchased 50 pink T-shirts and handed them out in school the next day. They wanted to support the target and diffuse the power of the bullies. It was the first Pink Shirt Day.

On April 14 each year, many students and schools across Canada now participate in the growing social trend known as Pink Shirt Day. The pink shirts are worn to symbolize intolerance toward bullying. Pink Shirt Day promotes awareness, understanding, and openness about the problem of bullying in a shared commitment to a community solution. Visit www.pinkshirtday.ca for more information or to organize Pink Shirt Day in your school.

KINDNESS
IS ONE SIZE
Fits All

Courtesy of CKNW ORPHANS' FUND/Pink Shirt Day

as everyone, not just one's friend group, witnesses the bullying. Perhaps the most serious difference is that the hurtful comments or images can reappear well after the incident has gone away. Thus, the individual cannot escape from the bullying. This can lead a child to feel anxious, depressed, or even suicidal.

Issues of cyberbullying may have negative consequences for the bully too, in a way that is not realized until much later. For example, when applying for college, university, or employment, issues of cyberbullying may be revealed, costing the individual a position they may have secured otherwise. Even worse, sexting pictures of anyone, particularly those under the age of 18 years, is considered child pornography. This could lead to charges being laid or serious consequences for the child who thought he or she was just pulling a prank on someone.

Bullying Interventions

To end bullying, everyone must be involved, including teachers, parents of the bully and the child being bullied, the principal, school staff, school administrators, and parents in the community. We must create a culture that accepts others who may be different or non-aggressive. In other words, unless adults change their attitude regarding bullying behaviour, the problem of bullying will never be solved. Students on their own will have a difficult time changing the long-standing dynamics that lead to bullying in the first place (Pepler & Craig, 2000).

Other interventions include teaching empathy and perspective-taking skills to children. Children need to recognize what it feels like to be a victim. This could be accomplished using role-play scenarios. Other techniques that have been suggested include encouraging kindness and rewarding such behaviour. Children need to view prosocial behaviour as desirable and not as a sign of weakness (Pepler & Craig, 2000).

LO4 The School

As indicated in the discussion of bullying, the school exerts a powerful influence on many aspects of children's development. Schools, like parents, set limits on behaviour, make demands for mature behaviour, attempt to communicate values, and are oriented toward nurturing positive physical, social, and cognitive development. Schools influence children's IQ scores, achievement motivation, and career aspirations (Aber et al., 2007; Woolfolk, 2008). Schools influence social and moral development (Killen & Smetana, 2006).

EMERGING CANADA

Social awareness issues are being championed by students in initiatives such as Pink Shirt Day. Social media have their risks and dangers, but they have also fuelled a social awareness and social conscience among today's youth. Social media can fuel the rapid communication of messages, as happened when news of the Infinity Project quickly spread among Canadian youth. The Infinity Project was passed through Instagram accounts, Facebook, and Twitter (The Infinity Project, 2013). The message it spread was that kids should speak out and talk to someone they trust, if they are struggling with depression, self-harm, anxiety, or any overwhelming issue. One youth asked, "Have you ever felt alone in life? Like you didn't fit in?" Children acknowledge to one another that these issues hurt and that they live in a world where they are judged by their image. The Infinity Project suggests that students mark an infinity symbol on their wrists to remind each other that they are beautiful and that there is always someone to love you for just who you are.

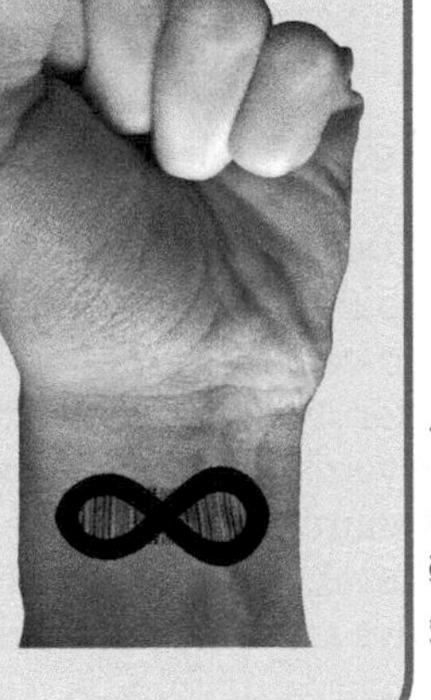
Vlue/Shutterstock.com

Schools are also competitive environments, and children who do too well—and those who do not do well enough—may incur the resentment or ridicule of others. Such treatment from peers has particular significance in this stage of development as children constantly look to their peers for reassurance and as a measure of their own self-worth.

Teachers

Teachers, like parents, set limits, make demands, communicate values, and foster development. They are powerful role models and dispensers of reinforcement. After all, children spend several hours each weekday with teachers.

Teacher Influences on Student Performance

Achievement is enhanced when teachers manage the classroom effectively, allocate most of their available time to academic activities, and expect students to master the curriculum. Students learn more in class when they are actively instructed or supervised by teachers than when they work on their own. The most effective teachers ask questions, give

Pygmalion effect a self-fulfilling prophecy; an expectation that is confirmed because of the behaviour of those who hold the expectation

self-fulfilling prophecy an event that occurs because of the behaviour of those who expect it to occur

sexism discrimination or bias on the basis of a person's sex

personalized feedback, and provide opportunities for drill and practice (Slavin, 2006).

Student achievement is also linked to the emotional climate of the classroom (Slavin, 2006; Woolfolk, 2008). Students do not do as well when teachers rely heavily on criticism, ridicule, threats, or punishment. Achievement is high in classrooms that have a pleasant, friendly—but not overly warm—atmosphere.

Teacher Expectations

There is a saying that "you find what you're looking for." Consider the so-called Pygmalion effect in education. In Greek mythology, the sculptor Pygmalion breathed life into a beautiful statue he had carved. Teachers also try to bring out positive traits they believe dwell within their students. A classic experiment by Robert Rosenthal and Lenore Jacobson (1968) suggested that teachers' expectations can become self-fulfilling prophecies. Rosenthal and Jacobson (1968) first gave students a series of psychological tests. Then they informed teachers that a handful of the students, although average in performance to date, were about to blossom forth intellectually in the current school year.

In education, teachers often find what they are looking for.

In fact, the tests indicated nothing about the "chosen" children. These children had been selected at random. The purpose of the experiment was to determine whether enhancing teacher expectations could affect student performance. It did; the identified children made significant gains in IQ scores.

In subsequent research, however, results have been mixed. Some studies have found support for the Pygmalion effect (Madon et al., 2001; Sarrazin et al., 2005a, 2005b); others have not. But these findings have serious implications for children from ethnic minority and low-income families because of the indication that teachers expect less from children in these groups (Slavin, 2006; Woolfolk, 2008). Teachers who expect less may "find what they are looking for," spending less time encouraging and working with children.

Sexism in the Classroom

Although girls were systematically excluded from formal education for centuries, today we do not expect to encounter sexism among teachers.

In a widely cited study, Myra Sadker and David Sadker (Sadker & Silber, 2007) observed students in Grade 4, 6, and 8 classes from a variety of cultural, urban, suburban, and rural backgrounds. In almost all cases, the findings were depressingly similar. Boys generally dominated classroom communication, regardless of the subject. Despite the stereotype that girls are more likely to talk or even chatter, boys were eight times more likely than girls to call

© Cheryl Casey/Shutterstock.com

What are some of the ways that teachers can help motivate all students to do their best? Anita Woolfolk (2008) suggests the following:

- Make the classroom safe and pleasant and the lessons interesting and inviting.
- Recognize that students' backgrounds can give rise to diverse patterns of needs.
- Help students take appropriate responsibility for their successes and failures.
- Encourage students to perceive the links between their own efforts and their achievements.
- Help students set attainable short-term goals.

out answers without raising their hands. So far, it could be said, we have evidence of a sex difference, but not of sexism. However, teachers were less than impartial in responding to boys and girls when they called out. Teachers, both male and female, were more likely to accept calling out from boys. Girls were more likely to be reminded that they should raise their hands and wait to be called on. Boys, it appears, are expected to be spontaneous, but girls are reprimanded for "unladylike behaviour." Until they saw videotapes of themselves, the teachers were largely unaware they had been treating girls and boys differently.

LO5 Social and Emotional Problems

Many Canadian children experience emotional or behavioural issues. It is estimated that 15% of Canadian children, with the exception of the Aboriginal population, have social–emotional issues that warrant attention from professionals. The most common disorders in middle childhood are mood disorders, anxiety disorders, conduct disorders, and attention-deficit hyperactivity disorder (discussed previously in Chapter 9).

Childhood Depression

An estimated 5–9% of children are seriously depressed in any given year. Depression occurs equally often in girls and boys. Depression in children does not appear the same as it does in adulthood; thus, knowing the symptoms is important for early detection. Children who are depressed appear "unhappy, worried, guilty, angry, fearful, helpless, hopeless, lonely or rejected" (Canadian Mental Health Association, 2013a).

Even children do not recognize depression in themselves often until the age of 7 years or so. When children cannot report their feelings, depression can be inferred from their behaviour, such as their withdrawal from social activity. In some cases, childhood depression is masked by misbehaviour, physical complaints, academic problems, and anxiety.

serotonin
a neurotransmitter that is involved in mood disorders such as depression

Origins of Depression

The origins of depression are complex and varied. Both biological and psychological explanations have been proposed. Some evidence suggests that depression has genetic factors (Kendler et al., 2007). A Norwegian study of 2,794 twins estimated that the heritability of depression in females was 49% and 25% in males (Orstavik et al., 2007). On a neurological level, evidence suggests that depressed children (and adults) "underutilize" the neurotransmitter serotonin (Vitiello, 2006).

Some social cognitive theorists explain depression in terms of relationships between competencies (knowledge and skills) and feelings of self-esteem.

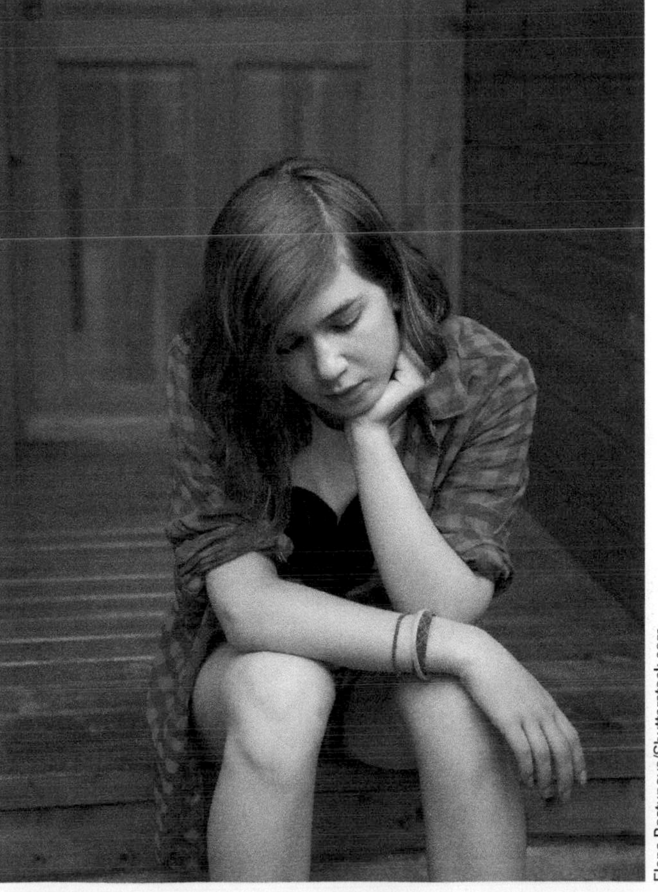

attributional style one's disposition toward interpreting outcomes (successes or failures), as in tending to place blame or responsibility on oneself or on external factors

Children who gain academic, social, and other competencies usually have high self-esteem. Perceived low levels of competence are linked to feelings of helplessness, low self-esteem, and depression.

Longitudinal studies have found that children's feelings of depression can be predicted by their perceived lack of competence in several areas: academics, socializing, physical appearance, and sports (Kistner, 2006). Some competent children might not appropriately credit themselves because of their parents' excessive expectations. Or children may be perfectionists themselves. Perfectionistic children may be depressed because they cannot meet their own high standards.

A tendency to blame oneself (an internal attribution) or others (an external attribution) is called a child's attributional style. Certain attributional styles can contribute to feelings of helplessness and hopelessness and hence to depression (Kagan, MacLeod, & Pote, 2004; Runyon & Kenny, 2002). Some children blame themselves for all the problems in their lives, whether they deserve the blame or not. Research shows that children who are depressed are more likely to attribute the causes of their failures to internal, stable, and global factors, which they are relatively helpless to change (Lewinsohn et al., 2000). Those feelings of helplessness can trigger depression.

Consider the case of two children who do poorly on a math test. John thinks, "I'm a loser! I'm just no good in math! I'll never learn." Jim thinks, "That test was tougher than I thought it would be. I'll have to study harder next time." John perceives the problem as global (he's "a loser") and stable (he'll "never learn"). Jim perceives the problem not as global but as specific (related to the type of math test) and not as stable but as unstable (he can change the results by working harder). In effect, John thinks, "It's me" (an internal attribution). By contrast, Jim thinks, "It's the test" (an external attribution).

DID YOU KNOW?

Some children blame themselves for all the problems in their lives even when they are not responsible for a negative outcome.

Children who are depressed are more likely to attribute the causes of their failures to internal, stable, and global factors that they are relatively helpless to change.

Treatment of Childhood Depression

Parents and teachers can help children alleviate relatively mild feelings of depression by involving them in enjoyable activities, encouraging them to develop skills, praising them when appropriate, and pointing out when they are being too hard on themselves. But if feelings of depression persist, professional treatment is required.

Psychotherapy for depression may include cognitive–behavioural therapy. Children (and adolescents) are encouraged to do enjoyable activities and build their social skills. They are made aware of their tendencies to minimize their accomplishments, exaggerate their problems, and overly blame themselves for any shortcomings (e.g., Ellis & Dryden, 1996). Another method to treat children with depression is to help them learn how to regulate their emotions by becoming aware of them (Robinson, Dolhanty, & Greenberg, 2013). Emotion-focused family therapy is specifically designed to help parents learn how to be emotional coaches for their children. Emotional awareness leads to greater understanding of the reasons behind the depressive affect in the first place, leading to insight and change. For more information about this type of treatment, please go to the following website www.emtionfocusedfamilytherapy.org.

Because depressed children may underutilize serotonin, drugs that increase the action of serotonin in the brain (selective serotonin reuptake inhibitors, or

EMERGING CANADA

If you suspect a child is depressed, make an effort to get help. Depression is treatable with the proper professional intervention. The Canadian Mental Health Association has developed the following questions to help identify children who might need support for dealing with their emotional health:

1. Has there been a change in feelings where the child is showing signs of being unhappy, worried, guilty, angry, fearful, helpless, hopeless, lonely, or rejected?
2. Has there been a change in thinking where the child indicates difficulty concentrating or frequently experiences negative thoughts such as self-dislike or low self-esteem?
3. Have there been changes in behaviour where the child withdraws, cries easily, or is disinterested in activities that he or she would normally enjoy? Are there sudden outbursts of anger or tears over seemingly small incidents?
4. Has the child experienced headaches or general aches and pains? Does the child lack energy, or is the child sleeping too little or too much? Does the child seem to be tired all the time?

Try to openly communicate with the child. Encourage the child to talk about his or her feelings. Caregivers should consider taking the child to the family doctor and making connections with local community supports (Canadian Mental Health Association, 2013a).

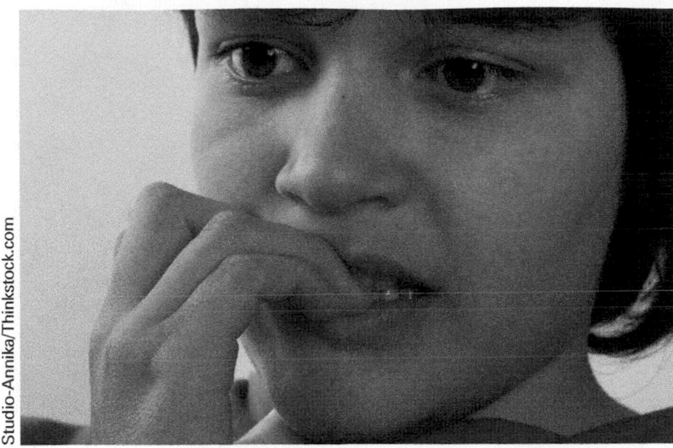

Studio-Annika/Thinkstock.com

SSRIs, such as Luvox, Prozac, and Zoloft) are sometimes used to treat childhood depression. Although SSRIs are often effective, a link may exist between their use and suicidal thinking in children (Harris, 2004).

Childhood Anxiety

Children may show many kinds of anxiety disorders, such as generalized anxiety disorder (GAD), phobias, separation anxiety disorder (SAD), and stage fright (Beidel & Turner, 2007). In 50–60% of cases in children, anxiety is accompanied by depression (Kendler et al., 2007). But many children show anxiety disorders in the absence of depression (Kearney & Bensaheb, 2007).

Separation Anxiety Disorder

It is normal for children sometimes to feel anxious when separated from loved ones or when entering an unfamiliar situation. This is called separation anxiety and it often begins during the first year of a child's life. But the sense of security that is usually provided by bonds of attachment encourages children to explore their environment and become progressively independent.

When anxiety interferes with normal life, the child may have a more serious issue. Approximately 12% of children will suffer from some form of separation anxiety disorder (SAD) before age 18 years. The prevalence of this disorder is 3–5% of children in Canada (Statistics Canada, 2015d). It is characterized by fear of being alone, frequent physical complaints when the child experiences, or even anticipates, separation from an attachment figure, and excessive distress when separated from home or attachment figures. SAD may occur before middle childhood, preventing adjustment to daycare or nursery school; however, it usually becomes a significant problem in middle childhood, when children are expected to adjust to school. SAD has three peaks: between ages 5 and 6 years, 11 and 12 years, and around 14 years (Anxiety BC, 2010), when children usually start new schools. Children who suffer from SAD come from warm, loving homes. SAD is usually brought on by a stressful event such as a death of a member of the family or of the child's pet, change in the home structure, or moving to a new neighbourhood (Statistics Canada, 2015d).

generalized anxiety disorder (GAD) an anxiety disorder in which anxiety appears to be present continuously and is unrelated to the situation

phobias irrational, excessive fears that interfere with one's functioning

separation anxiety disorder (SAD) an extreme form of separation anxiety characterized by anxiety about separating from parents; SAD often takes the form of refusal to go to school

SAD is diagnosed when separation anxiety is persistent and excessive, when it is inappropriate for the child's developmental level, and when it interferes with activities or development tasks, such as attending school. Children with SAD tend to cling to their parents and follow them around the house. They may voice concerns about

Sean Locke Photography/Shutterstock.com

© Photos.com

school phobia
fear of attending school, marked by extreme anxiety at leaving parents

death and dying and may insist that someone stay with them at bedtime. They may complain of nightmares and may have "stomach aches" on school days. They may throw tantrums or plead with their parents not to leave the house.

Separation Anxiety Disorder, School Phobia, and School Refusal

SAD may be expressed as school phobia—fear of school—or refusal to go to school (which can stem from fear or other factors). Children will often exhibit physical symptoms of anxiety in the morning such as stomach-ache, headache, and nausea, and this can be confusing to the caregiver who may believe the child is physically ill. Separation anxiety is not the cause of all instances of school refusal. Some children refuse school because they perceive it as unpleasant, unsatisfying, or hostile—which it may be. Some children are concerned about doing poorly in school or being asked questions in class (in which case, they may have stage fright or social anxiety). High parental expectations may heighten children's anxieties, and difficulties interacting with classmates may also be the root of the issue.

Treatment of School Phobia or School Refusal

Most professionals agree that the first rule in the treatment of school phobia is to have the child return to school as soon as possible. The disorder often improves once the child returns on a regular basis. Knowledge of the reasons for refusal can help parents and educators devise strategies for assisting the child. However, it is probably best not to force the child to return before he or she is ready; forcing the issue may lead to longer school refusal. See the "How Parents Can Help a Child Return to School" box for a list of things that parents can do to get a child back into school.

Antidepressant medication has been used—often in conjunction with cognitive–behavioural methods—with much success, but the medications require close monitoring because some can lead to significant complications, such as suicidal thoughts. In addition, drugs do not teach children how to cope. Children with anxiety will require support to battle the emotional issues they face.

How Parents Can Help a Child Return to School

- Have the child return to school as quickly as possible.
- Secure the cooperation of the child's teacher, principal, or a Board of Education social worker.
- If the child has a specific school-related problem, such as an overly strict teacher, help the child—and teacher—find ways to handle the situation.
- Reward the child for attending school.

DID YOU KNOW?

Children with school phobia should return to school as soon as possible.

Understanding the problem can be helpful, but getting the child back in to school is the most important first step.

Conduct Disorders

Children with conduct disorders persistently break rules or violate the rights of others. They exhibit behaviours such as lying, stealing, fire setting, truancy, cruelty to animals, and fighting (Mental Health Canada, 2013). Conduct disorders typically emerge by 8 years of age and are much more common in boys than girls (Nock et al., 2006). The prevalence of conduct disorder is anywhere from 2–9% of the population and it is more common in boys than in girls because when boys are aggressive, they tend to be physical (American Psychological Association, 2013).

There are two different types of conduct disorders, childhood-onset type (behaviours appear before the age of 10 years) and adolescent-onset type (the behaviours present after the age of 10 years). The behaviour displayed with the childhood-onset type of conduct disorder tends to be more aggressive than other conduct disorders; these children are at greater risk for developing an antisocial personality disorder in adulthood (American Psychological Association, 2013).

Children with conduct disorders are often involved in sexual activity before puberty, and often smoke, drink, and abuse substances. They have a low tolerance for frustration and may have temper flare-ups. They tend to blame other people for their issues. Their academic achievement is usually below grade level, but their intelligence is usually at least average. Many children with conduct disorders also are diagnosed with ADHD (Chronis et al., 2007).

Origins of Conduct Disorders

Conduct disorder may occur when a child has difficulty with self-regulation combined with fear or anger; this leads to dysregulated behaviour. Conduct disorders may have a genetic component (Scourfield et al., 2004). Other contributors include antisocial family members, deviant peers, inconsistent discipline, parental insensitivity to the child's behaviour, physical punishment, and family stress (Black, 2007). Risk factors for conduct disorder that have been noted include low verbal IQ, the experience of parental rejection, sexual abuse, and other maltreatment, and a parent with a history of ADHD and or a conduct disorder himself or herself (Theravive, 2016). Parental overindulgence has also been linked to conduct disorder because this is related to a sense of entitlement, unrealistic expectations, and frustration when their expectations are not met.

conduct disorders disorders marked by persistent breaking of the rules and violations of the rights of others

Treatment of Conduct Disorders

The treatment of conduct disorders is challenging, but cognitive–behavioural techniques involving parent training seem to hold promise (Kazdin, 2000; Sukhodolsky et al., 2005; Theravive, 2016). Children benefit from interventions that fulfill these criteria: the children's behaviour is monitored closely, children face consequences (such as time-outs) for unacceptable behaviour, physical punishment is avoided, and positive social behaviour is rewarded (Cavell, 2001). Community-based supports are available for the child and the family (Mental Health Canada, 2013). To find mental health services for children in Canada, a person may connect with agencies often located in hospitals or search for resources from their provincial government websites to locate appropriate facilities. In Ontario, the website where such services can be located is https://www.ontario.ca/page/mental-health-services-children-and-youth.

It seems unfortunate to depart middle childhood following a discussion of social and emotional problems. Most Canadian children come through middle childhood quite well, in good shape for the challenges and dramas of adolescence.

STUDY TOOLS

CourseMate CHAPTER 10

Located at **nelson.com/student**

- ☐ Prepare for tests with a variety of exercises and activities
- ☐ Review Key Terms Flashcards (online or print)
- ☐ Create your own study tools with Build a Summary
- ☐ Watch Observing Development videos to expand your knowledge

PART FOUR

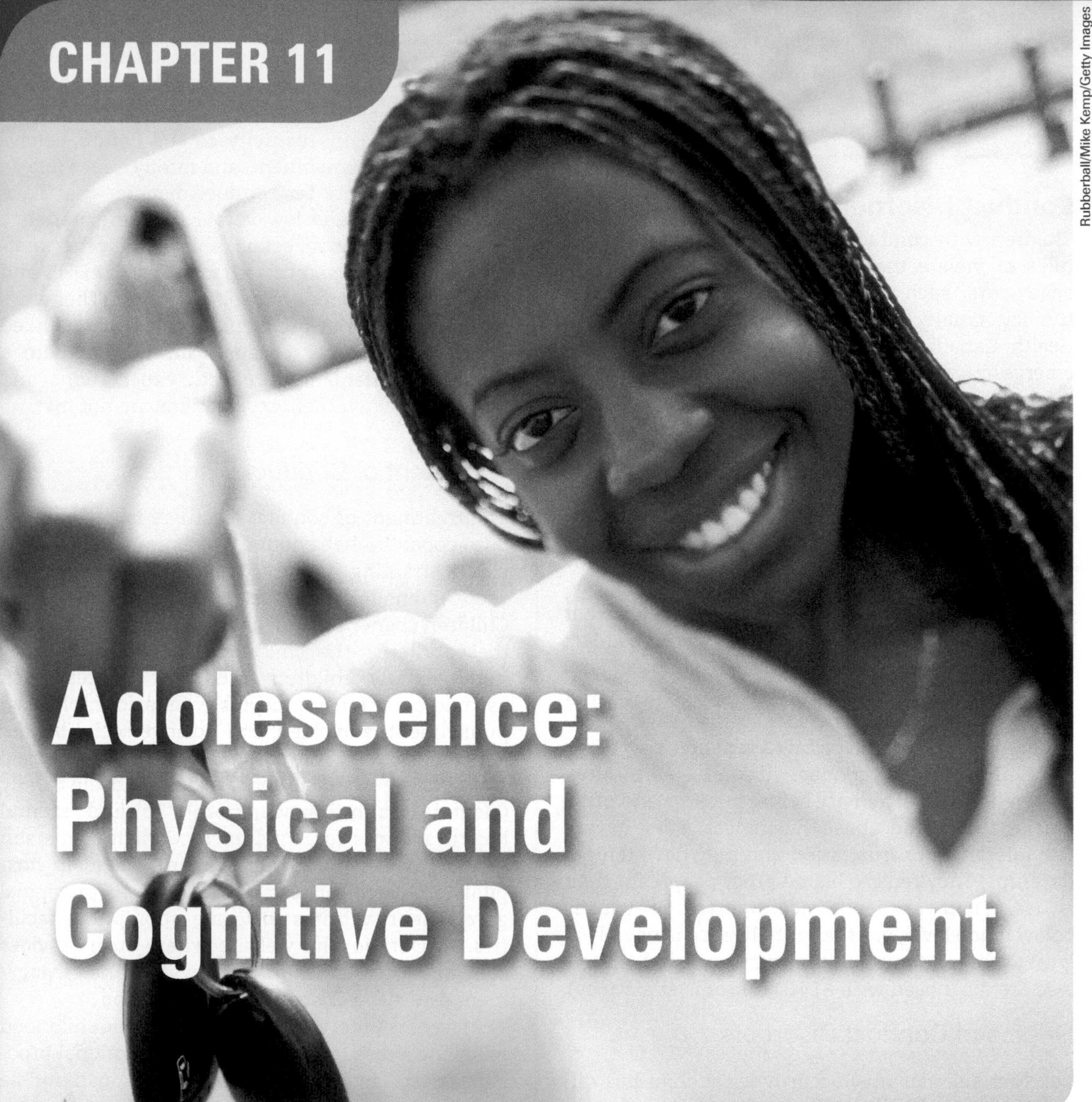

Rubberball/Mike Kemp/Getty Images

LEARNING OUTCOMES

LO1 Describe the key events of puberty and their relationship to social development

LO2 Discuss health in adolescence, focusing on causes of death and eating disorders

LO3 Outline adolescent cognitive development and the key events of Piaget's stage of formal operations

LO4 Discuss sex differences in cognitive abilities

LO5 Discuss Kohlberg's theory of moral development in adolescence

LO6 Explain the roles of the school in adolescence, focusing on dropping out

LO7 Discuss career development and work experience during adolescence

> *"Many teens are taller and stronger than their parents, and they have the responsibilities associated with reproduction. But to their frustration, they face social restrictions in terms of driving, voting, and consuming alcohol."*

Perhaps no other period of life is as exciting—and bewildering—as adolescence. Except for infancy, more changes occur between the ages of 13 and 19 years than at any other time of life. Adolescence is a time of being in between. Adolescents are physically able to become parents yet they cannot attend R-rated films. Given the restrictions placed on adolescents, their growing yearning for independence, and a sex drive heightened by high levels of sex hormones, it is not surprising that adolescents are occasionally in conflict with their parents.

The idea that adolescence is an important and separate developmental stage was proposed by G. Stanley Hall (1904). Hall believed that adolescence is marked by turmoil and used the German term *Sturm und Drang* ("storm and stress") to refer to the conflicts of adolescence. Contemporary theorists no longer see adolescent storm and stress as inevitable (Smetana, 2005). Instead, they see adolescence as a period when biological, cognitive, social, and emotional functioning are reorganized. Nevertheless, adolescents need to adapt to numerous changes.

Krivosheev Vitaly/Shutterstock.com

LO1 Puberty: The Biological Eruption

Puberty is a stage of development characterized by reaching sexual maturity and the ability to reproduce. The onset of adolescence coincides with the advent of puberty. Puberty is controlled by a feedback loop involving the hypothalamus, the pituitary gland, hormones, and the gonads—the ovaries in females and the testes in males. The hypothalamus signals the pituitary gland, which, in turn, releases hormones that control physical growth and the gonads. The gonads respond to pituitary hormones by increasing their production of sex hormones (androgens and estrogens). The sex hormones further stimulate the hypothalamus, perpetuating the feedback loop.

The sex hormones also trigger the development of primary and secondary sex characteristics. The primary sex characteristics are the structures that make reproduction possible. In girls, these are the ovaries, vagina, uterus, and fallopian tubes. In boys, they are the penis, testes, prostate gland, and seminal vesicles. The secondary sex characteristics are physical indicators of

puberty
the biological stage of development characterized by physiological and cognitive changes that are associated with reproduction

feedback loop
a system in which glands regulate each other's functioning through a series of hormonal messages

primary sex characteristics
the structures that make reproduction possible

secondary sex characteristics
physical indicators of sexual maturation—such as changes to the voice and growth of bodily hair—that do not directly involve reproductive structures

asynchronous growth imbalanced growth, such as the growth that occurs during the early part of adolescence and causes many adolescents to appear gawky

sexual maturation that are not directly involved in reproduction. They include breast development, deepening of the voice, and the appearance of facial, pubic, and underarm hair.

The Adolescent Growth Spurt

The stable growth patterns in height and weight that characterize early and middle childhood end abruptly with the adolescent growth spurt. Girls start to spurt in height sooner than boys, at an average age of a little older than 10. Boys start to spurt about 2 years later. Girls and boys reach their peak growth in height about 2 years after the growth spurt begins (see Figure 11.1). The spurt in height for both girls and boys continues for about another 2 years at a gradually declining pace. The Canadian Paediatric Society (2013a) reports the growth spurt for boys and girls can be quite dramatic. They may grow 2 to 8 inches (5 to 20 cm) in one year, but puberty is a long process that will take place over several years.

Adolescents begin to spurt in weight about half a year after they begin to spurt in height. The period of peak growth in weight occurs about a year and a half after the onset of the spurt. As with height, the growth spurt in weight then continues for a little more than 2 years. Because the spurt in weight lags the spurt in height, many adolescents are relatively slender compared with their preadolescent stature. However, adolescents tend to eat enormous quantities of food to fuel their growth spurts. Active 14- and 15-year-old boys may consume 3,000 to 4,000 calories a day without becoming obese.

© James Worrell/Getty Images

Girls' and boys' body shapes begin to differ during adolescence. Girls develop relatively broader hips compared with their shoulders (Canadian Paediatric Society, 2013b), whereas the opposite is true for boys. A girl's body shape is more rounded than a boy's because girls gain almost twice as much fatty tissue as boys. Boys gain twice as much muscle tissue as girls.

Asynchronous Growth

Adolescents may be awkward and gawky due to **asynchronous growth**; different parts of the body grow at different rates. The hands and feet mature before the arms and legs do. As a consequence, adolescent girls and boys may complain of big hands or feet. Legs reach their peak growth before the shoulders and chest. Boys stop growing out of their pants about a year before they stop growing out of their jackets.

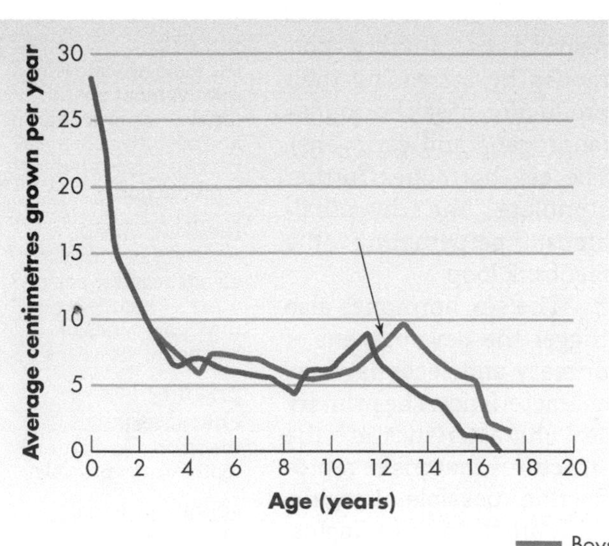

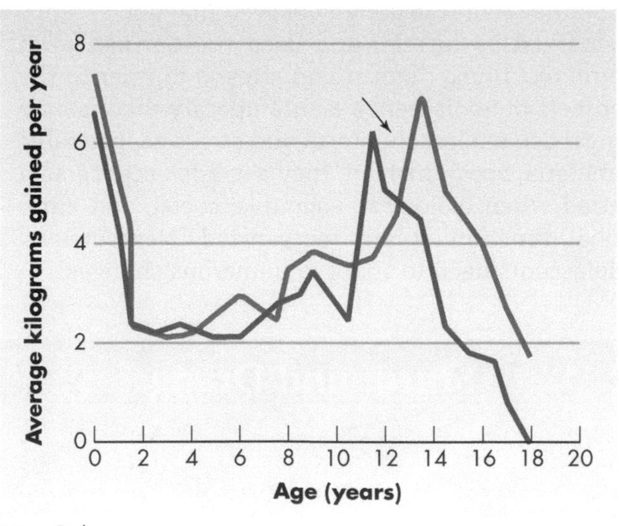

Boys Girls

FIGURE 11.1

Spurts in Growth

The adolescent growth spurt begins at about age 10½ for girls and age 13 for boys.

Source: From Kail/Cavanaugh. (2009). *Human Development*, 2e. © 2009 Nelson Education Ltd. Reproduced by permission. www.cengage.com/permissions

The Secular Trend

During the 20th century, children in the Western world grew dramatically more rapidly and ended up taller than children from earlier times (Sun et al., 2005). This historical trend toward increasing adult height was accompanied by an earlier onset of puberty and is known as the secular trend. This trend, which has been observed worldwide, is likely due to improved healthcare and nutrition.

Research is now revealing that early onset menarche—the earliest stages of menstruation—can be a risk factor in developing breast cancer. In *The Falling Age of Puberty in U.S. Girls*, Steingraber (2007) reveals that the new "normal" of earlier menstruation isn't healthy. Early menstruation shows early responses to the external environment and affects internal functions. Steingraber's ground-breaking research shows that exposure to environmental chemicals disrupts the endocrine systems, which can lead to obesity and insulin issues. It can also lead to shorter times of gestation (the process of pregnancy from conception to birth). Steingraber suggests that children who are exposed continuously to low-level endocrine disruptors in their diets, drinking water, and air supply, as well as various flame retardant materials and even consumer products such as hair products and pesticides, are found to have altered hormone functioning in adolescents (O'Grady, 2008). Traces of polycarbonate plastics, which are used in food container linings, have been detected in the urine of US teenage girls. This early exposure to environmental chemicals may induce early menstruation. More research is needed to examine the full effects of synthetic hormones in adolescence (O'Grady, 2008).

Growth and height are recognized as a measure of the health and wellness of individuals. Adult height is varied among different ethnic groups, with males normally being taller than females within each group. In the 18th and 19th century, European North Americans were the tallest people in the world. Today, the heights of people from many nations (particularly those in Europe) have surpassed the typical heights in the United States. Americans, on average, are taller than Canadians. What human growth and development factors are at play to create such shifts? Table 11.1 shows the average male and female heights reported by selected countries (Disabled World, 2008).

Changes in Boys

At puberty, the pituitary gland stimulates the testes to increase their output of testosterone, leading to further development of the male genitals. The first visible sign of puberty is accelerated growth of the testes, which begins at an average age of about 11½, plus or minus 2 years. Testicular growth further accelerates testosterone production and other pubertal changes. The penis spurts about a year later, and still later, pubic hair begins to spurt.

secular trend
a historical trend toward increasing adult height and earlier puberty

semen
the fluid that contains sperm and substances that nourish and help transport sperm

nocturnal emission
emission of seminal fluid while asleep

gynecomastia
enlargement of breast tissue in males

Underarm and facial hair appears at about age 15. Only half of Canadian boys shave (of necessity) by age 17. At age 14 or 15, the voice deepens because of growth of the "voice box," or larynx, and the lengthening of the vocal cords. The process is gradual, and adolescent boys sometimes encounter an embarrassing cracking of the voice. (See Figure 11.2 for an overview of changes for both boys and girls during puberty.)

Testosterone also triggers the development of acne, which afflicts 75–90% of adolescents (Goldstein, 2004). Severe acne is manifested by pimples and blackheads on the face, chest, and back. Although boys are more prone to acne, we cannot say that girls suffer less from it. A smooth complexion has a higher value for girls.

Males can have erections in early infancy, but erections are infrequent until age 13 or 14. Adolescent males may experience unwanted erections. The organs that produce semen grow rapidly, and boys typically ejaculate seminal fluid by age 13 or 14. About a year later, they begin to have nocturnal emissions, also called wet dreams because of the myth that emissions necessarily accompany erotic dreams. Mature sperm are found in ejaculatory emissions by about the age of 15.

Nearly half of all boys experience enlargement of the breasts, or gynecomastia, which usually declines in a year or two. Gynecomastia stems from the small amount of female sex hormones (estrogen) secreted by the testes.

TABLE 11.1

Average Male and Female Heights in Selected Countries

Country	Average Male Height	Average Female Height
Canada	174 cm (5′ 8.5″)	161.0 cm (5′ 3.4″)
India	165.3 cm (5′ 5″)	165.3 cm (5′ 5″)
Netherlands	184.8 cm (6′ 0.8″)	168.7 cm (5′ 6.4″)
Philippines	163.5 cm (5′ 4.4″)	151.8 cm (4′ 11.8″)
United States	178.2 cm (5′ 10.2″)	164.1 cm (5′ 4.6″)

Source: Used with permission from *Disabled World*.

epiphyseal closure the process by which the cartilage that separates the long end of a bone from the main part of the bone turns to bone

menarche the onset of menstruation

At age 20 or 21, men stop growing taller because testosterone causes epiphyseal closure, which prevents the long bones from making further gains in length. Puberty for males draws to a close.

Changes in Girls

In girls, the pituitary gland signals the ovaries to boost estrogen production at puberty. Estrogen may stimulate the growth of breast tissue ("breast buds") as early as age 8 or 9, but the breasts usually begin to enlarge during the 10th year. The development of fatty tissue and ducts elevates the areas of the breasts surrounding the nipples and causes the nipples to protrude. The breasts typically reach full size in about 4 years, but the *mammary glands* do not mature fully until a woman has a baby. Estrogen also promotes the growth of the fatty and supporting tissue in the hips and buttocks, which, along with the widening of the pelvis, causes the hips to round. Beginning at about the age of 10½ or 11, girls develop pubic and underarm hair. (See Figure 11.2 for an overview of physical changes during puberty.)

Estrogen causes the labia, vagina, and uterus to develop during puberty, and androgens cause the clitoris to develop. The vaginal lining varies in thickness according to the amount of estrogen in the bloodstream. Estrogen typically brakes the female growth spurt some years before testosterone brakes the growth spurt of males.

Menarche

Menarche (first menstruation) commonly occurs between the ages of 11 and 14, plus or minus 2 years

coloroftime/iStockphoto.com

EMERGING CANADA

Canadian society is kinder to boys than it is to girls in terms of issues of physical change. Most parents are proud to see their boys growing stronger and taller and becoming young men. If you are a female helping a male understand his body changes, you may have knowledge but you have no first-hand experience. The following are some concerns young men may have but they may not be prepared to voice:

- Some boys may gain weight before a spurt in height. Reassure that this change is normal and will likely be temporary if he is eating properly and exercising.
- Another source of concern is breast development. Almost half of all boys can expect swelling under the nipples. This growth is also temporary, though boys may be concerned that they are growing breasts or that they have cancer.
- Let the young man know that the penis first grows long and then wide. The process takes several years, and some may be concerned that their penis will never grow.
- Sometimes one testicle grows faster than the other; this difference is normal.
- Erotic dreams accompanied by ejaculation (a wet dream) are also normal but can be alarming if the boy is unprepared.
- Spontaneous erections, though potentially embarrassing, are also normal, as are erections every morning.

Starting a conversation around body changes might be embarrassing at first but establishing that the adolescent can ask you any questions without judgment is important. If you don't know the answers, let them know that together you can find them (Langlois, 2013).

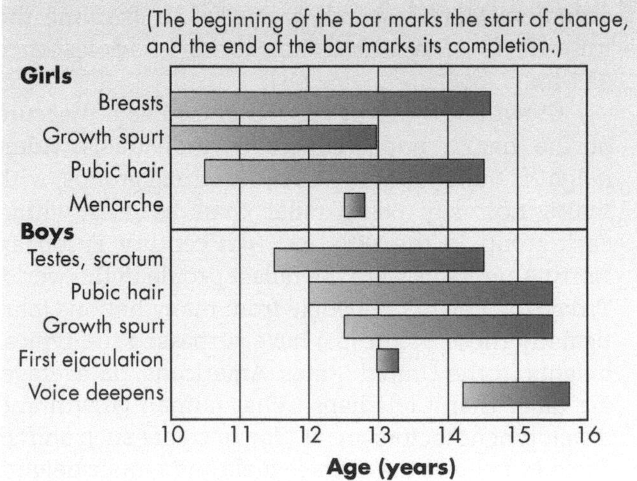

FIGURE 11.2

Average Timing of Pubertal Changes in North American Youth

Because girls' growth spurt occurs earlier, girls are taller and heavier than boys from about age 9 or 10 until about age 13. Once boys begin their spurt, they catch up with girls and eventually become taller and heavier.

Source: From Kail/Cavanaugh. (2009). *Human Development*, 2e. © 2009 Nelson Education Ltd. Reproduced by permission. www.cengage.com/permissions

(Capron, Thérond, & Duyme, 2007; Mendle et al., 2006). The average age of menarche for a Canadian girl is 12½.

What accounts for the earlier age of puberty for girls? One hypothesis is that girls must reach a certain body weight to trigger pubertal changes such as menarche. Body fat could trigger the changes because fat cells secrete a protein that signals the brain to secrete hormones that raise estrogen levels. Menarche comes later to girls who have a lower percentage of body fat, such as athletes and girls with eating disorders (Bosi & de Oliveira, 2006; Frisch, 1997). The average body weight for triggering menarche depends on the girl's height (Frisch, 1994). Today's girls are larger than those of the early 20th century because of improved nutrition and health-care. As a result, menarche now occurs earlier than it did for previous generations.

EMERGING CANADA

Canadian girls can experience changes to their bodies as early as age 8 or 9, when cognitively they are not as prepared to deal with changes to their body as they will be later. Girls changing into young women bring concerns of sexuality, which are prevalent in Canadian society. Speak openly with female adolescents and make sure they know they can ask you any questions they have. The following are some changes that may cause concerns:

- A girl's hips and thighs begin to widen before growth, and she may develop a rounded belly that will be an energy store for puberty. With a healthy diet and active lifestyle, this change will be temporary.
- Budding begins breast growth. These buds may be tender to the touch and may be irritated by clothing and normal play. It is normal for breasts to grow unevenly. One might grow earlier or faster. Reassure that this uneven growth is not a sign of cancer.
- Sweat glands will produce odour, which, if not properly looked after, can lead to ridicule from classmates.
- She will begin to discharge a clear white fluid from her vagina that she will see on her underwear, up to a year before menstruation. This too is normal but should be discussed openly.
- When she sees the clear white fluid, it is a good time for a discussion about her period. If a young girl receives her first period without being prepared, she may think she is hurt or even dying.
- Dysmenorrhea is the medical term for painful menstruation; dysmenorrhea affects every woman at some point in her life. This pain can be particularly difficult when the girl is at school. Symptoms may include severe abdominal cramping, headaches, nausea, and vomiting. Effects can last 2 to 3 days. Serious medical conditions should always be ruled out by visiting a doctor. Sleep and exercise might reduce the effects.
- Skin and hair can become oily and may become a point of frustration in a society that is so driven by appearances.

Working with adolescent girls and establishing a sense of trust allows you to help them to understand and properly care for their bodies. Let them know that if you don't have the answers, you will find them together (Langlois, 2013).

DID YOU KNOW?

Girls are not usually fertile immediately after their first menstrual period.

Girls should not, however, assume they cannot become pregnant at this time because variations in the timing of ovulation are common.

Early versus Late Maturers

Early-maturing boys tend to be both more popular than their late-maturing peers and more likely to be leaders in school (Graber et al., 2004). They are more poised, more relaxed, and good-natured. Their edge in sports and the admiration of their peers heighten their sense of worth. On the negative side, early maturation is associated with greater risks of aggression and delinquency (Lynne et al., 2007) and with abuse of alcohol and other drugs (Costello et al., 2007). Coaches may expect too much of early-maturing boys in sports, and peers may want the early-maturing boys to fight their battles for them. In addition, sexual opportunities may create demands before they know how to respond (Lam et al., 2002).

Late-maturing boys have the advantage of not being rushed into maturity. On the other hand, late-maturing boys often feel dominated by early-maturing boys. They have also been found to be more dependent and more insecure and may be more easily influenced by peer pressure (Ge et al., 2003).

Although boys who mature early usually have higher self-esteem than those who mature late, early-maturing girls may feel awkward because they are among the first of their peers to begin the physical changes of puberty. They become conspicuous with their height and their developing breasts. Early-maturing girls are at greater risk for psychological problems and substance abuse than girls who mature later on (Ge et al., 2003; Lynne et al., 2007). Many girls who mature early obtain lower grades in school and are involved in sexual activity earlier (Lam et al., 2002). For reasons such as these, the parents of early-maturing girls may increase their vigilance and restrictiveness, leading to new child–parent conflicts.

EMERGING CANADA

Precocious puberty (PP) is happening more often in Canada. PP is the onset of puberty before age 7 or 8 in girls, and before age 9 in boys. In general, girls are now developing earlier than ever before, and breast development is the most noticeable marker. Many jump to the conclusion that PP is caused by hormones in food or chemicals in water, but research attributes this change to better nutrition, greater consumption of animal protein, and higher levels of body fat. According to researchers, PP is merely a change in development being experienced across a new generation. PP is confirmed through blood and urine tests that indicate elevated levels of sex hormones and through an X-ray of hands that detects "bone age." Normal early onset of puberty does raise social and emotional concerns but does not appear to have significant lasting physical effects (Curtis, 2012).

LGBTQ adolescents may find puberty particularly difficult. Trying to navigate the stormy waters of puberty with all its physiological and cognitive changes is challenging enough as a teenager, but feeling that you are in the wrong body, have the wrong "parts," or are different from friends or mainstream society can make it even harder. As a result, LGBTQ youth have higher rates of depression, anxiety, and suicide. Parents of LGBTQ youth should help them become aware that they are not alone, and that they are normal, loved, and cared for. Utilizing local LGBTQ agencies and online resources and becoming aware of LGBTQ role models can also help LGBTQ youth navigate puberty and beyond.

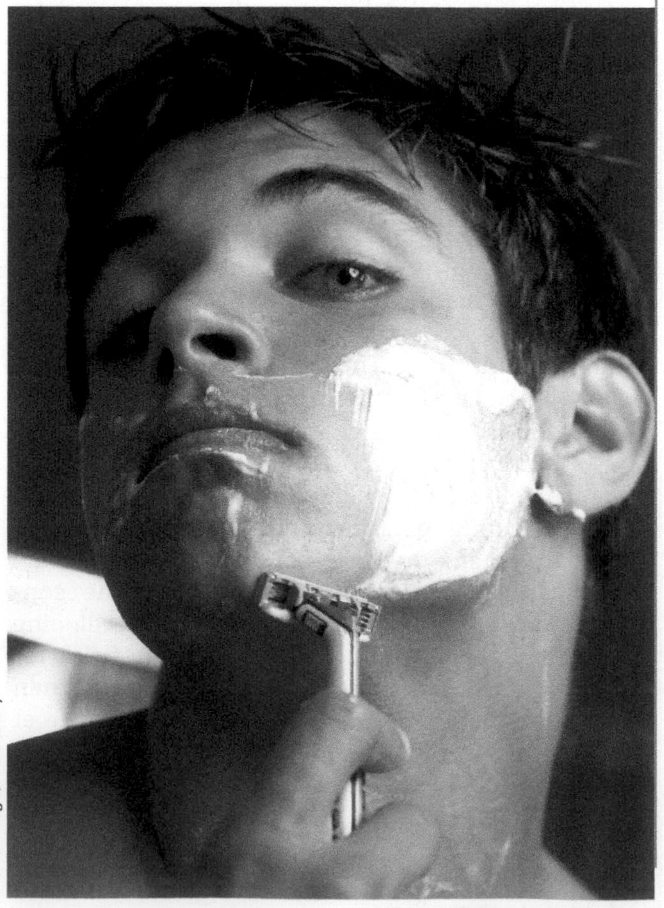

© Susan Vogel/Photolibrary

DID YOU KNOW?

Physical maturity influences boys' and girls' self-esteem differently.

Although boys who mature early often have higher self-esteem, early-maturing girls can encounter negative social experiences.

Body Image

The Public Health Agency of Canada reports that dangerous and unrealistic cultural ideals of slimness (particularly in females) and muscularity (particularly in males) have filtered down to Canadian children and adolescents. Dissatisfaction with body weight and size is, in many situations, reported by young people with a healthy weight (Janssen, 2012). Adolescents tend to be concerned about their physical appearance, particularly in early adolescence, during the rapid physical changes of puberty (Jones & Crawford, 2006). By age 18, girls and boys are more satisfied with their bodies (Eisenberg, Neumark-Sztainer, & Paxton, 2006).

LO2 Health in Adolescence

Death and Injuries

Death rates are, in general, low in adolescence, but they are nearly twice as great for male adolescents as for female adolescents. Unintentional injury is the number one cause of death (73%) with 1 youth dying every 5 hours in Canada (MacDonald, Yanchar, & Hebert, 2007). Motor vehicle accidents cause 60% of these deaths. Since 2008, motor vehicle accidents have steadily decreased for both males and females ages 15–19. In 2012, however, there was an increase in death caused by motor vehicle accidents over the previous year in the 20–24 age group (Statistics Canada 2015e) According to MacDonald, Yanchar, and Hebert (2007), this high rate of teen deaths can be traced to teenagers' increased likelihood of taking chances, their tendency to act impulsively, their overestimation of their skills, and their feeling of invincibility.

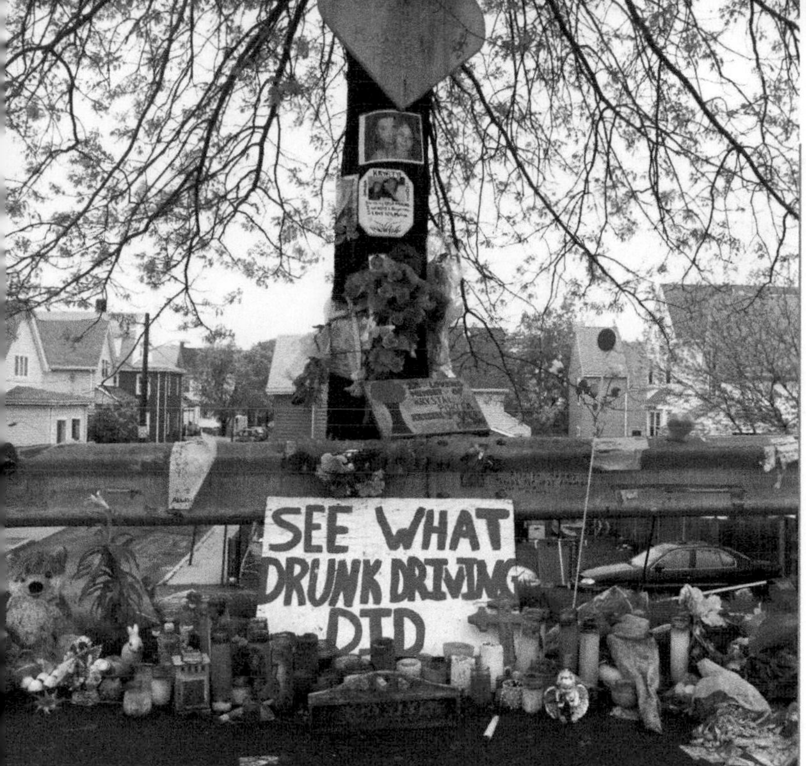

Raymond Forbes/First Light

DID YOU KNOW?

Accidents are the number one cause of death for Canadian adolescents.

Each week, 32 Canadian youths die in motor vehicle accidents (MacDonald et al., 2007).

Nutrition

Physical growth occurs more rapidly in the adolescent years than at any other time after birth, with the exception of the first year of infancy. Health Canada recommends that Canadian teens build a healthy diet based on Canada's Food Guide selections rather than following the dated method of counting calories. Recommendations for female teens include 7 servings of fruits and vegetables, 6 servings of grains, 3 to 4 servings of milk and milk alternatives, and 2 servings of meat and meat alternatives; male teens have slightly higher requirements of 8 servings of fruits and vegetables, 7 servings of grains, 3 to 4 servings of milk and milk alternatives, and 3 servings of meat and meat alternatives (Health Canada, 2007c). The nutritional needs of adolescents vary according to their activity level and stage of pubertal development.

One reason for adolescents' nutritional deficits is their irregular eating patterns. Breakfast is often skipped, especially by dieters (Niemeier et al., 2006). Teenagers may rely on fast food and junk food, which are convenient but high in fat, sugar, and calories. A diet heavy in junk food can lead to being overweight, and being overweight in adolescence can lead to chronic illness and premature death in adulthood (Niemeier et al., 2006).

Teens and Alcohol and Illicit Drugs

Although teens cannot legally use alcohol or illicit drugs, we know that these substances are a significant part of adolescent social life in Canada. The Canadian Medical Association released a 10-year study on alcohol and drug use in Canada. Of the teens surveyed, two thirds had used alcohol, one third had used marijuana, and 1 in 20 had tried LSD, ecstasy, or cocaine.

A closer look at adolescent drug and alcohol use patterns is more revealing. In Alberta, 79% of people over the age of 15 drink. Of Ontario Grade 12 students, 83% reported drinking regularly, and 49% responded that they binge drink. Among Grade 11 students who drink, age 13 was the average age of their first alcoholic drink and 14 was the average age of their first intoxication. The average age of drug use was 15.7 (Teen Challenge Canada, 2013). Teenagers in Canada may not be able to use illicit drugs and alcohol legally; but clearly, alcohol and drug use is an issue that must be discussed openly to protect our youth and to avoid exposure to potential lifelong addictions.

Eating Disorders

The Canadian ideal has slimmed down to the point that most Canadian females of normal weight are dissatisfied with the size and shape of their bodies (Paxton et al., 2005). In the section on cognitive development, we will see that adolescents also tend to think that others are paying a great deal of attention to their appearance. Because of our cultural emphasis on slimness and the psychology of the adolescent, young people are highly vulnerable to eating disorders. These disorders are characterized by gross disturbances in patterns of eating. Overweight and obese young people, particularly girls, are more likely to have mental health problems than young people who have a healthy weight (Janssen, 2012).

With the advent of social media and the "selfie," there is an increased preoccupation with appearance. Teenagers play to an imaginary audience—an egocentric view during adolescence that others are preoccupied with how you look, what you do, and how you sound (we learn more about this in the section "The Imaginary Audience" on page 204). But is this perception all that fantastical? Social media platforms have created a cyber-audience. For generations, youth have been influenced by mainstream media to have better skin, be thinner and paler, and/or have a six-pack; they have come to internalize myths and societal standards of beauty and attraction.

EMERGING CANADA

A disturbing trend dramatically on the rise is teen abuse of prescription drugs.

- 1 in 4 teens has misused or abused a prescription drug at least once, representing a jump of 33% in 5 years.
- Of the teens reporting having used or abused prescription drugs, 20% did so before age 14.
- Of all teens surveyed, 27% mistakenly believe that misusing and abusing prescription drugs to get high is safer than using street drugs.
- Ritalin and Adderal (medications for attention deficit hyperactivity disorder, or ADHD) are among the most commonly abused medications. They are misused as a study aid and an aid to reducing hunger for teens wanting to lose weight.
- Painkillers were taken by 16% of the teens surveyed, and their use seems to be on the decrease.

Knowing that prescription drug abuse is on the rise presents a good opportunity for conversations with teens. Parents must be sure to safely store prescription medications, given the high incidence of abuse. A majority of teens (81%) said they have discussed the use of marijuana with their parents and 80% have discussed alcohol use, but a shockingly low number of teens (16%) say that their parents have discussed the abuse of prescription medication. Talk with teens to discuss the dangers associated with this activity (Nauert, 2013).

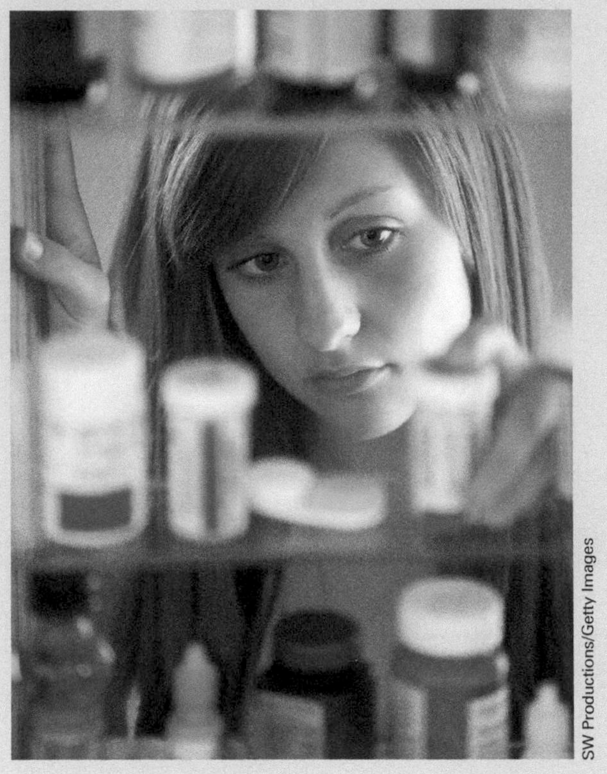

SW Productions/Getty Images

anorexia nervosa an eating disorder characterized by irrational fear of weight gain, distorted body image, and severe weight loss

osteoporosis a condition involving progressive loss of bone tissue

But today's young people are also impacted by social media. They are bombarded with endless images of their friends on Instagram looking "hot"; many teens feel they aren't good enough and may worry about what their online followers and the people they follow think of them.

Anorexia Nervosa

Anorexia nervosa is a life-threatening eating disorder characterized by extreme fear of being heavy, dramatic weight loss, a distorted body image, and resistance to eating enough to maintain a healthful weight. Anorexia nervosa afflicts males as well as females, but most studies put the female-to-male ratio at 10 to 1 or greater (Kjelsås, Bjornstrom, & Götestam, 2004).

Females with anorexia nervosa can drop 25% or more of their weight within a year. Severe weight loss triggers abnormalities in the endocrine system (i.e., with hormones) that prevent ovulation (Nielsen & Palmer, 2003). General health declines. Problems arise in the respiratory system (Forman-Hoffman, Ruffin, & Schultz, 2006) and the cardiovascular system (Katzman, 2005). Females with anorexia are at risk for premature development of osteoporosis (Katzman, 2005). The mortality rate for anorexic females is about 4–5%.

People often develop anorexia nervosa to lose weight after fat gains as a result of changes during puberty (Shroff et al., 2006). However, their dieting and exercise continue well after the weight has been lost, and even after others say they have taken their

© Kristian Dowling/Getty Images

weight loss too far. Denial is a major factor of anorexia nervosa. Distortion of the body image is also a major feature of the disorder.

Bulimia Nervosa

Bulimia nervosa is characterized by recurrent cycles of binge eating and purging. Binge eating often follows on the heels of dieting (Williams, 2004). Various methods of purging are used. Vomiting is common. Other behaviours include strict dieting or fasting, overuse of laxatives, and engaging in demanding exercise regimes. Individuals with eating disorders will not settle for less than their idealized body shape and weight (Kaye et al., 2004). Bulimia, like anorexia, can lead to irregular menstrual cycles in women (Edler, Lipson, & Keel, 2007) and tends to afflict women during adolescence and young adulthood (Nolen-Hoeksema et al., 2007). In males, eating disorders can create muscle weakness, hair loss, heart arrhythmia, and lowered testosterone levels (National Eating Disorders Association, 2016.)

Ted Foxx/Alamy Stock Photo

EMERGING CANADA

According to the Canadian Mental Health Association, eating disorders can be very difficult to detect as Canadian society glamorizes the media-driven "ideal" body. Dieting is also viewed as a very normal activity, which can blur the indications of an eating disorder. When a young person's life is overly focused on weight, calorie consumption, grams of fat consumed, and vigorous exercise, he or she may have an eating issue (Canadian Mental Health Association, 2013b). People who work with youth should be aware of the following statistics:

- In a recent study of Ontario girls between the ages of 12 and 18, 27% reported being engaged in severely problematic food and weight behaviour.
- The annual death rate associated with anorexia is more than 12 times higher than the annual death rate due to all other causes combined for females between 15 and 24 years old.
- In Grades 9 and 10, 4% of boys reported steroid use in a 2002 study, showing that body preoccupation is also an important issue for males.
- Thirty-seven percent of girls in Grade 9 and 40% in Grade 10 perceived themselves as being too fat.
- Even among students of normal weight (based on Body Mass Index, or BMI), 19% believed they were too fat, and 12% reported that they were trying to lose weight.

Source: National Eating Disorder Information Centre, 2012.

LO3 Cognitive Development: Piaget's Stage of Formal Operations

Piaget's Stage of Formal Operations

Concrete operational children are bound by the facts as they are, but the adolescent and the adult can ponder abstract ideas and see the world as it could be.

The stage of **formal operations** is the top level in Jean Piaget's theory. Adolescents in this stage have reached cognitive maturity, even if rough edges remain. Piaget describes the accomplishments of the stage of formal operations in terms of the individual's increased ability to classify objects and ideas, engage in logical thought, and hypothesize, similar to how researchers make hypotheses in their

bulimia nervosa
an eating disorder characterized by cycles of binge eating and vomiting as a means of controlling weight gain

formal operations
the fourth stage in Piaget's cognitive–developmental theory, characterized by the capacity for flexible, reversible operations concerning abstract ideas and concepts, such as symbols, statements, and theories

imaginary audience the belief that others around us are as concerned with our thoughts, appearance, and behaviours as we are; one aspect of adolescent egocentrism

personal fable the belief that our feelings and ideas are special and unique and that we are invulnerable; one aspect of adolescent egocentrism

investigations. Adolescents can follow and formulate arguments from their premises to their conclusions and back again, even if they do not actually believe in them.

Hypothetical Thinking

In formal operational thought, adolescents discover the concept of "what might be." Adolescents can project themselves into situations that transcend their immediate experience and become wrapped up in fantasies. Adolescents can think ahead, systematically trying out various possibilities in their minds.

In terms of career decisions, the wealth of possible directions leads some adolescents to experience both anxiety about whether they will pick the career that is the best fit and a sense of loss because they may be able to choose only one.

Sophisticated Use of Symbols

Formal operational children can grasp the meaning of symbols as seen in high-school math classes. Adolescents intuitively work with *x* variables and with points that have no dimensions, lines that have no width and are infinite in length, and circles that are perfectly round, even though such things are not found in nature. The ability to manipulate these symbols also enables them to work in theoretical physics or to obtain jobs in engineering or architecture.

Formal operational individuals can understand, appreciate, and sometimes produce metaphors—figures of speech in which words or phrases that ordinarily signify one thing are applied to another. *Squeezing* out a living, *hanging by a thread,* or *jumping* to conclusions have new meaning for adolescents who have mastered formal operations.

Adolescent Egocentrism

The Imaginary Audience

Many adolescents fantasize about becoming rock stars or movie stars who are adored by millions. The concept of the **imaginary audience** achieves part of that fantasy. It places the adolescent on stage, but surrounded by critics more than by admirers. Adolescents assume that other people are concerned with their appearance and behaviour, more than they really are (Elkind, 1967, 1985). The self-perception of adolescents as being on stage may account for their intense desire for privacy and their preoccupation with their appearance. Bell and Bromnick (2003) challenged this definition of the imaginary audience. They suggested that adolescents worry about what other people think so much because, at this stage of development, they face real personal and social consequences for their actions. They argued that their concerns, therefore, are based in social reality and are not as imaginary as Elkind suggests.

Sanjagrujic/iStockphoto.com

The Personal Fable

Because of the **personal fable**, many adolescents become action heroes, at least in their own minds. In the personal fable, one believes that one's thoughts and emotions are special and unique (Aalsma, Lapsley, & Flannery, 2006). It also refers to the common adolescent belief that the teen is invulnerable.

The personal fable is connected with such behaviours as showing off and risk taking (Omori & Ingersoll, 2005). Since many adolescents assume that they are invincible, they can smoke without risk. Cancer? "It can't happen to me." They drive recklessly. They engage in spontaneous, unprotected sexual activity, assuming that sexually transmitted infections (STIs) and unwanted pregnancies happen to other people, not to them.

Wunderimages/iStockphoto.com

It is normal for adolescents to think of themselves as action heroes and to act as though they are made of steel.

High-risk behaviours seem to disregard the need to be safe. They are testaments to the belief that "bad things won't happen to me!"

LO4 Sex Differences in Cognitive Abilities

The nature versus nurture discussion is important when analyzing sex differences in cognitive abilities. We can ask, are we pre-wired to think in a particular way because of our gender (nature)? Or, are we socialized to think in specific ways (nurture)? Or is it a combination of both? And, how does nature then relate to people who are intersexual, or fall within the spectrum of LGBTQ?

Although females and males do not differ noticeably in overall intelligence, beginning in childhood, sex differences appear in certain cognitive abilities (Johnson & Bouchard, 2007). Females tend to be superior to males in verbal ability. Males tend to be superior in visual–spatial skills. The picture for mathematics is more complex, with females excelling in some areas and males in others.

Verbal Ability

Verbal abilities include reading, spelling, grammar, oral comprehension, and word fluency. As a group, females surpass males in verbal ability (Halpern, 2003, 2004). These differences show up early. Girls seem to acquire language faster than boys. They make more prelinguistic vocalizations, utter their first word sooner, and develop larger vocabularies. Boys in Canada are more likely than girls to be dyslexic and to read below grade level (Halpern, 2003, 2004).

Visual–Spatial Ability

Visual–spatial ability refers to the ability to visualize objects or shapes and to mentally manipulate and rotate them. This ability is important in such fields as art, architecture, and engineering. Boys begin to outperform girls on many types of visual–spatial tasks starting at age 8 or 9, and the difference persists into adulthood (Johnson & Bouchard, 2007). The sex difference is particularly notable on tasks that require imagining how objects will look if they are rotated in space (see Figure 11.3; Delgado & Prieto, 2004).

One environmental theory is that gender stereotypes influence the spatial experiences of children. Gender-stereotyped "boys' toys," such as blocks, Lego, and Erector sets, provide more practice with spatial skills than gender-stereotyped "girls' toys." Boys are also more likely to engage in sports, which involve moving balls and other objects through space (Halpern, 2004).

a. Spatial visualization

Embedded-figure test. For each of the three pairs of figures, start by studying the line drawing on the left. Now, try to find the same configuration in the black and white figure to the right. The line drawing may need to be shifted to locate it in the black and white figure.

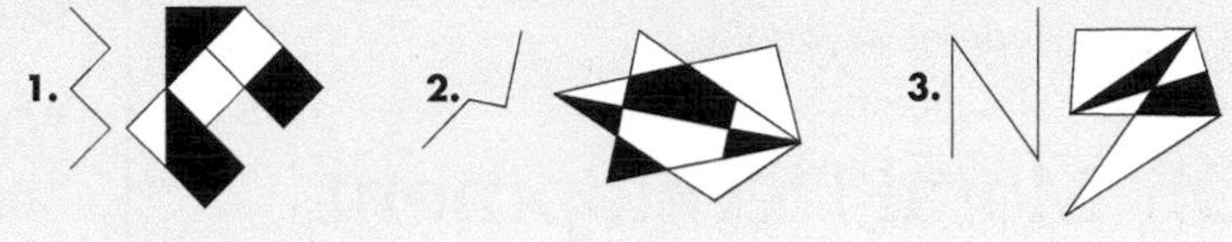

b. Spatial perception

Water-level test. Examine the glass of water on the left. Now imagine that it is slightly tilted, as on the right. Draw in a line to indicate the location of the water level.

c. Mental rotation

Mental-rotation test. If you mentally rotate the figure on the left, which of the five figures on the right would you obtain?

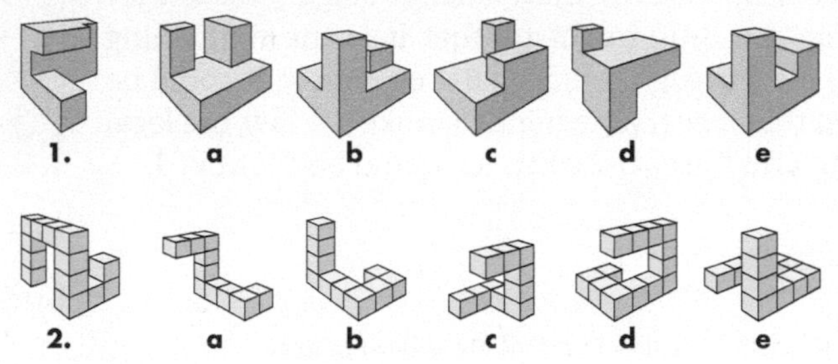

Answers: a. 1: Orient the pattern as if it were a tilted capital M, with the left portion along the top of the white triangle. 2: This pattern fits along the right sides of the two black triangles on the left. 3: Rotate this figure about 100° to the right, so that it forms a Z, with the top line coinciding with the top line of the top white triangle. **b.** The line should be horizontal, not tilted. **c.** 1: c; 2: d.

FIGURE 11.3

Examples of Tests Used to Measure Visual–Spatial Ability

No sex differences are found on the spatial visualization tasks in part (a). Boys tend to perform better than girls on the tasks measuring spatial perception in part (b). The sex difference is greatest on the mental rotation tasks in part (c). What are some possible reasons for these differences? How might nature and nurture play a role?

Source: © Cengage Learning

postconventional level according to Kohlberg, a period during which moral judgments are derived from moral principles and people look to themselves to set moral standards

Mathematical Ability

For half a century or more, we have believed that male adolescents generally outperform females in mathematics, and research has tended to support that belief (Collaer & Hill, 2006; Halpern, 2004). However, a more recent study by Hyde and her colleagues (2008) of some 7 million Grade 2s through Grade 11s found no sex differences for performance in mathematics on standardized tests. The complexity of the test items apparently made no difference. Nevertheless, most North Americans have stereotyped expectations for boys and girls, and these expectations may still dissuade females from entering fields in science and math (Hyde et al., 2008).

LO5 Moral Development

Kohlberg: The Postconventional Level

In the postconventional level, moral reasoning is based on the person's own moral standards. Consider once more the case of Heinz that was introduced in Chapter 9 (see section "Kohlberg's Theory of Moral Development" on page 162 to review the details). Moral judgments are derived from personal values, not from conventional standards or authority figures. In the contractual, legalistic orientation of Kohlberg's Stage 5, it is recognized that laws stem from agreed-on procedures and that many rights have great value and should not be violated (see Table 11.2). But under exceptional circumstances, such as in the case of Heinz, laws cannot bind the individual. A Stage 5 reason for stealing the drug might be that it is the right thing to do, even though it is illegal. Conversely, it could be argued that if everyone in need broke the law, the legal system and the social contract would be destroyed.

Stage 6 thinking relies on supposed universal ethical principles, such as those regarding human life, individual dignity, justice, and reciprocity. Behaviour that is consistent with these principles is considered right. If a law is seen as unjust or contradicts the right of the individual, it is wrong to obey it.

In the case of Heinz, it could be argued from the perspective of Stage 6 that the principle of preserving life takes precedence over laws prohibiting stealing. Therefore, it is morally necessary for Heinz to steal the drug, even if he must go to jail. It could also be asserted, from the principled orientation, that if Heinz finds the social contract or the law to be the highest principle, he must remain within the law, despite the consequences.

By age 16, Stage 5 reasoning was shown by about 20% of adolescents and Stage 6 reasoning was demonstrated by about 5% of adolescents (Commons, Falaz-Fontes, & Morse, 2006; Rest, 1983).

Moral Behaviour and Moral Reasoning

Are individuals whose moral judgments are more mature more likely to engage in moral behaviour? The answer seems to be yes (Emler, Tarry, & St. James, 2007). Adolescents with higher levels of moral reasoning are more likely to exhibit moral behaviour (Maclean, Walker, & Matsuba, 2004). Studies have also found that

KidStock/Blend Images/Getty Images

TABLE 11.2

Kohlberg's Postconventional Level of Moral Development

Stage	Examples of Moral Reasoning That Support Heinz's Stealing the Drug	Examples of Moral Reasoning That Oppose Heinz's Stealing the Drug
Stage 5: *Contractual, legalistic orientation:* One must weigh pressing human needs against society's need to maintain social order.	This issue is complicated because society has a right to maintain law and order, but Heinz needs the drug to save his wife.	I can see why Heinz feels he has to take the drug, but laws exist for the benefit of society as a whole and cannot simply be cast aside.
Stage 6: *Universal ethical principles orientation:* People must follow universal ethical principles and their own conscience, even if it means breaking the law.	In this case, the law comes into conflict with the principle of the sanctity of human life. Heinz must take the drug because his wife's life is more important than the law.	If Heinz truly believes that stealing the drug is worse than letting his wife die, he should not take it. People make sacrifices to do what they believe is right.

Source: © Cengage Learning

group discussion of moral dilemmas elevates delinquents' level of moral reasoning (Smetana, 1990).

Evaluation of Kohlberg's Theory

Evidence supports Kohlberg's view that the moral judgments of children develop in an upward sequence (Boom, Wouters, & Keller, 2007), even though most children do not reach postconventional thought. Postconventional thought, when found, first occurs during adolescence, apparently because formal operational thinking is a prerequisite for it (Patenaude, Niyonsenga, & Fafard, 2003).

LO6 The Adolescent in School

How can we emphasize the importance of the school to the development of the adolescent? Adolescents are highly influenced by the opinions of their peers and their teachers. Their self-esteem rises or falls with the pillars of their skills.

The transition from elementary school to high school is often accompanied by a decline in grades and less participation in school activities. Students may also experience a drop in self-esteem and an increase in stress (Rudolph & Flynn, 2007).

The transition from elementary school appears to be more difficult for girls than boys. Girls are more likely to be undergoing puberty and to earn the attention of boys in higher grades, whereas younger boys are not likely to be of interest to older girls. Girls experience major life changes, and children who experience many life changes at once find it more difficult to adjust (Tobbell, 2003).

Dropping Out

Completing high school is a critical developmental task. The consequences of dropping out can be grim. Dropouts are more likely to be unemployed or have low incomes (Wald & Losen, 2007). They are more likely to resort to criminal behaviour and substance abuse (Donovan & Wells, 2007). (See Figure 11.4 for dropout rates in Canada.)

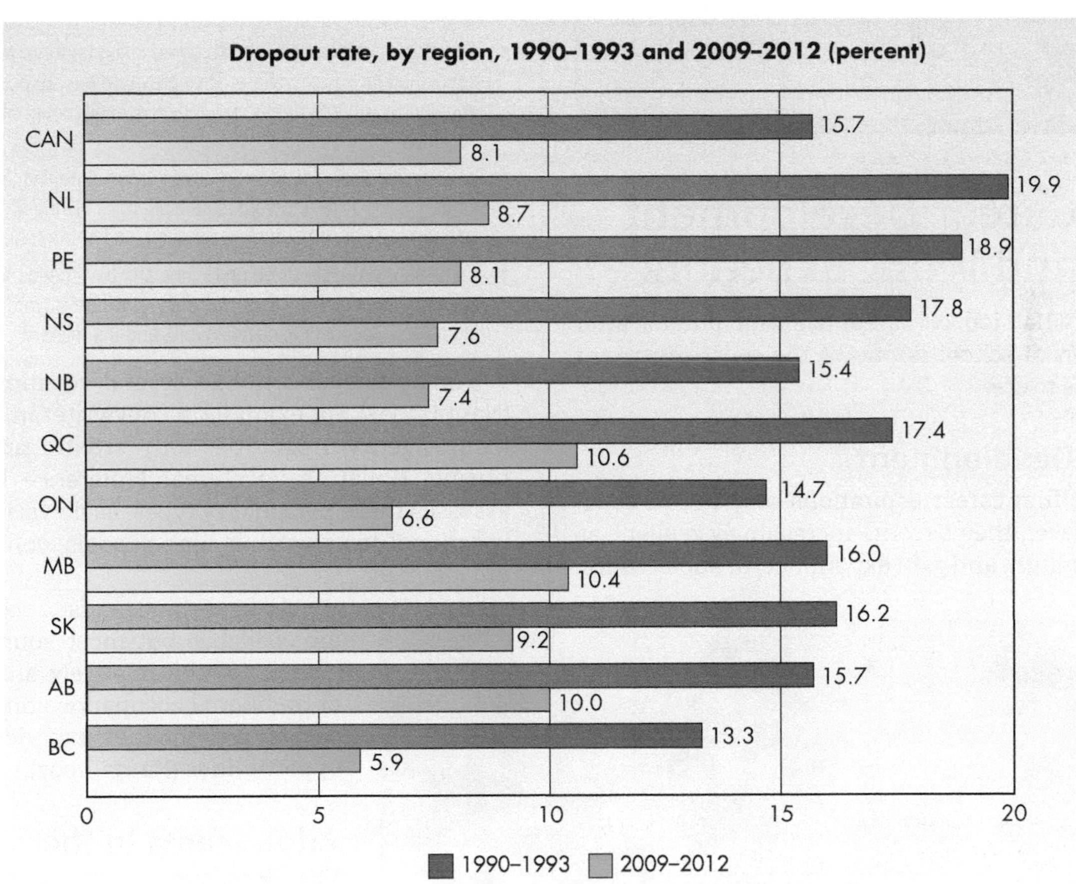

FIGURE 11.4

Canada Dropout Rates by Region (percent)

Source: Data produced by Statistics Canada. (2012). *Labour Force Survey 2012*. Ottawa: Statistics Canada. http://well-being.esdc.gc.ca/misme-iowb/.3ndic.1t.4r@-eng.jsp?iid=32

Two predictors of school dropout are excessive school absence and reading below grade level (Lever et al., 2004). Other risk factors include low grades, low self-esteem, problems with teachers, substance abuse, being old for one's grade level, and being male (South, Haynie, & Bose, 2007). Adolescents who adopt adult roles early, such as marrying or becoming a parent at a young age, are also more likely to drop out (Bohon, Garber, & Horowitz, 2007). Students from low-income households or from large urban areas are at greater risk (National Center for Education Statistics, 2007). Drop-out rates, however, have decreased since 1993 as a result of lower teenage pregnancy rates as well as the growing recognition of the importance of education in order to secure employment.

EMERGING CANADA

Forty thousand Canadian youth drop out of high school each year.

Dropping out of high school is associated with serious labour market issues. For example, in 2009–10, 24% of high-school drop-outs were unable to find a job, and this situation has worsened with the recent economic downturn. Even those who were able to find a job earned significantly less than those with a high-school diploma.

Immigrants have a lower dropout rate, but the dropout rate for Aboriginal youth is higher than the rate for non-Aboriginal youth (Gilmore, 2010).

LO7 Career Development and Work Experience

Deciding what job or career we will pursue after completion of school is one of the most important choices we make.

Career Development

Children's first career aspirations may not be practical; however, they become increasingly realistic as children mature and gain experience. In adolescence, teenagers' ideas about the kind of work they want to do tend to become more firmly established, but a particular occupation may not be chosen until the postsecondary years or later (Rottinghaus, Betz, & Borgen, 2003).

Holland's Career Typology

John Holland's (1997) Vocational Preference Inventory uses Holland's RIASEC method to match six personality types (realistic, investigative, artistic, social, entrepreneurial, and conventional) to various kinds of careers. Within each "type" of career, some are more sophisticated than others and require more education and training.

- Realistic people are concrete in their thinking and are mechanically oriented. They tend to be best adjusted in occupations that involve motor activity, such as attending gas stations, farming, auto repairs, engineering, or construction work.
- Investigative people are abstract in their thinking, creative, and open to experience. They tend to do well in higher-level education, as professors, and in research.
- Artistic people also tend to be creative and open to experience. They are emotional and intuitive. They tend to be content in the visual and performing arts.
- Socially oriented people tend to be outgoing (extroverted) and concerned for social welfare. They gravitate toward occupations in teaching (kindergarten through high school), counselling, and social work.
- Enterprising people tend to be adventurous, outgoing, and dominant. They gravitate toward leadership roles in industry and organizations; they become business owners and entrepreneurs.
- Conventional people thrive on routine and have needs for order, self-control, and social approval. They gravitate toward occupations in banking, accounting, clerical work, and the military.

Many people combine several vocational types (Nauta, 2007). For example, a copywriter in an advertising agency might be both artistic and enterprising. Holland's Vocational Preference Inventory assesses these personality types, as do various other vocational tests used in high schools, colleges, and universities.

© Design Pics/Kristy-Anne Glubish

All in all, thousands of occupations are available, but most young people choose from a relatively small range of traditional occupations on the basis of their personalities, experiences, and opportunities (Nauta, 2007).

Adolescents in the Workforce

Life experiences help shape vocational development. One life experience common among most North American teenagers is holding a job.

Zhang Bo/iStockphoto.com

According to Statistics Canada (2008a), in 2004–05, 31% of high school students between the ages of 15 and 17 held a job. Those not working reported preferring to focus on schoolwork or other activities.

Pros and Cons of Adolescent Employment

The potential benefits of adolescent employment include developing a sense of responsibility, self-reliance, and discipline; learning to appreciate the value of money and education; acquiring positive work habits and values; and enhancing occupational aspirations (Porfeli, 2007). Working a reasonable amount of time per week (less than 10 hours) prompts students to schedule their study time appropriately and lends structure to the week. On the other hand, most working adolescents are in jobs with low pay, high turnover, little authority, and little chance for advancement (Staff, Mortimer, & Uggen, 2004). Some question the benefits of such "McJobs." Students who work lengthy hours—more than 11 to 13 hours per week—report lower grades, higher rates of drug and alcohol use, more illegal behaviour, lower self-esteem, and higher levels of psychological problems than students who do not work or who work only a few hours (Brandstätter & Farthofer, 2003). Students working 30 hours or more per week were the most likely to drop out of high school (Statistics Canada, 2008a). Perhaps the safest course is for parents and educators to limit the number of hours adolescents work, particularly during the school year.

DID YOU KNOW?

The number of hours worked after school can affect school performance.

Working 30 hours per week or more places students at a high risk to drop out of school. Working less than 10 hours can prompt students to manage their time productively.

STUDY TOOLS

CHAPTER 11

Located at **nelson.com/student**

- ☐ Prepare for tests with a variety of exercises and activities
- ☐ Review Key Terms Flashcards (online or print)
- ☐ Create your own study tools with Build a Summary
- ☐ Watch Observing Development videos to expand your knowledge

CHAPTER 12

Adolescence: Social and Emotional Development

Used by permission of Kaitlyn Howden

LEARNING OUTCOMES

LO1 Discuss the formation of identity in adolescence

LO2 Examine relationships with parents and peers during adolescence

LO3 Explain sexuality during adolescence, focusing on sexual identity and teenage pregnancy

LO4 Review the statistics specific to youth in conflict with the law and measures that can reduce youth crime in Canada

LO5 Outline risk factors in adolescent suicide

“Adolescents are preoccupied not only with their present selves but also with what they want to become.”

LO1 Development of Identity: “Who Am I?”

Canadian teens search for an answer to the question “Who am I?” They struggle to balance different selves and contradictory traits and behaviours to determine the “real me.” Adolescents are preoccupied not only with their present selves but also with what they want to become.

Erikson and Identity Development

The primary developmental task is for adolescents to develop ego identity: a sense of who they are and what they stand for. They face choices about their future occupation, political and religious beliefs, and gender roles. Because of formal operational thinking, adolescents can weigh options they have not directly experienced (Roeser et al.,Roeser, Peck, & Nasir, 2006).

One aspect of identity development is what Erikson called a psychological moratorium during which adolescents experiment with different roles, values, beliefs, and relationships (Erikson, 1968). During this time, adolescents often undergo an identity crisis in which they examine their values and make decisions about their life roles. Should they attend college or university? What career should they pursue? Should they become sexually active? With whom? Adolescents in developed nations may feel overwhelmed by their options.

Consider THIS

What issues are associated with social media and identity formation in the teenage years?

Please see page 217 for a discussion on this topic.

Time & Life Pictures/Getty Images

Erikson Today

Stage 5: Identity versus Role Confusion (12–18)

Psychosocial Theory: Up until now, development has been dependent on events that happen to the child. In adolescence, development shifts to focus on what the person does. Adolescents struggle to discover their own identity. While negotiating and struggling in a complex social world, they must find their own sense of self in terms of their morality. Those who do not embrace responsibility will be unsuccessful as they face the challenges of this life stage and, as a result, may experience emotional upheaval and role confusion. Adolescents must construct their own sets of beliefs, ideals, and friends.

Identity Statuses

Building on Erikson’s approach, James Marcia (1991) theorized four identity statuses that represent the four possible combinations of the dimensions of exploration and commitment, which Erikson believed were critical to the development of identity (Schwartz, 2001) (see Table 12.1). *Exploration* involves active questioning and searching among alternatives to establish goals, values, and beliefs. *Commitment* is a stable investment in one’s goals, values, and beliefs.

Identity diffusion is the least advanced status and includes adolescents who neither have commitments nor are trying to form them (Berzonsky, 2005). This stage is characteristic of younger adolescents and of older adolescents who

ego identity
according to Erikson, individuals’ sense of who they are and what they stand for

psychological moratorium
a time-out period when adolescents experiment with different roles, values, beliefs, and relationships

identity crisis
a turning point in development during which people examine their values and make decisions about life roles

identity diffusion
an identity status that characterizes those who are non-committal to specific beliefs and who are not in the process of exploring alternatives

TABLE 12.1

The Four Identity Statuses of James Marcia

Commitment	Exploration
Identity Achievement • Most developed in terms of identity • Has experienced a period of exploration • Has developed commitments • Has a sense of personal well-being, high self-esteem, and self-acceptance • Cognitively flexible • Sets goals and works toward achieving them	*Foreclosure* • Has commitments without considering alternatives • Commitments are based on identification with parents, teachers, or other authority figures • Often authoritarian and inflexible
Moratorium • Actively exploring alternatives • Attempts to make choices with regard to occupation, ideological beliefs, and so on • Often anxious and intense • Ambivalent feelings toward parents and authority figures	*Identity Diffusion* • Least developed in terms of identity • Lacks commitments • Not trying to form commitments • May be carefree and uninvolved or unhappy and lonely • May be angry, alienated, rebellious

foreclosure an identity status that characterizes those who have made commitments without considering alternatives

moratorium an identity status that characterizes those who are actively exploring alternatives in an attempt to form an identity

identity achievement an identity status that characterizes those who have explored alternatives and have developed commitments

drift through life or become alienated and rebellious (Snarey & Bell, 2003).

In the foreclosure status, individuals make commitments without considering alternatives. These commitments are usually established early in life and are often based on identification with parents, teachers, or religious leaders who have made a strong impression (Saroglou & Galand, 2004).

The moratorium status refers to a person who is actively exploring alternatives in an attempt to make choices (Akman, 2007). Such individuals are often anxious, intense, and passionate.

Identity achievement refers to those who have explored alternatives and developed relatively firm commitments. They generally have high self-esteem and self-acceptance (Adams, Berzonsky, & Keating, 2006).

RawPixel.com/Shutterstock.com

Who do I want to become?

Development of Identity Statuses

Before high school, children show little interest in questions of identity. Most are either in identity diffusion or foreclosure statuses. During the high-school and postsecondary years, adolescents increasingly move from the diffusion and foreclosure statuses to the statuses of moratorium and achievement (Snarey & Bell, 2003). The greatest gains in identity formation occur in college and university (Berzonsky & Kuk, 2005). College and university students are exposed to a variety of lifestyles, beliefs, and career choices, which spur their consideration of identity issues. Are you a student who has changed majors once or twice (or more)? If so, you have most likely experienced the moratorium identity status, which is common among postsecondary students. College and university seniors have a stronger sense of identity than first-year students as a result of having resolved their identity crises (Lewis, 2003).

Ethnicity and Development of Identity

The development of self-identity is a key task for all adolescents. This task is more complex for adolescents who are members of ethnic minority groups (Phinney & Ong, 2007). Adolescents who belong to the dominant culture—in this country, European Canadians of Christian heritage—are usually faced with assimilating one set of cultural values into their identities. However, adolescents who belong to ethnic minority groups, such as African Canadians and Islamic Canadians, confront two sets of cultural values: the values of the dominant culture and those of their particular ethnic group (Phinney & Alipuria, 2006). If the cultural values conflict, the adolescent needs to sort out which values are more personally meaningful and incorporate those values into his or her identity. Some adolescents do it cafeteria style, taking a little bit of this and a little bit of that. For example, a young Catholic woman may decide to use artificial means of birth control even though doing so may conflict with the teachings of her religion.

Adolescents from racial and ethnic minority groups often face racism and prejudice, which can take a toll physically and psychologically. Researchers reveal that those who experience prejudice and discrimination are at greater risk for developmental health issues and have higher rates of loneliness, anxiety, depression, sleeplessness, and self-esteem issues (Yip, 2014.)

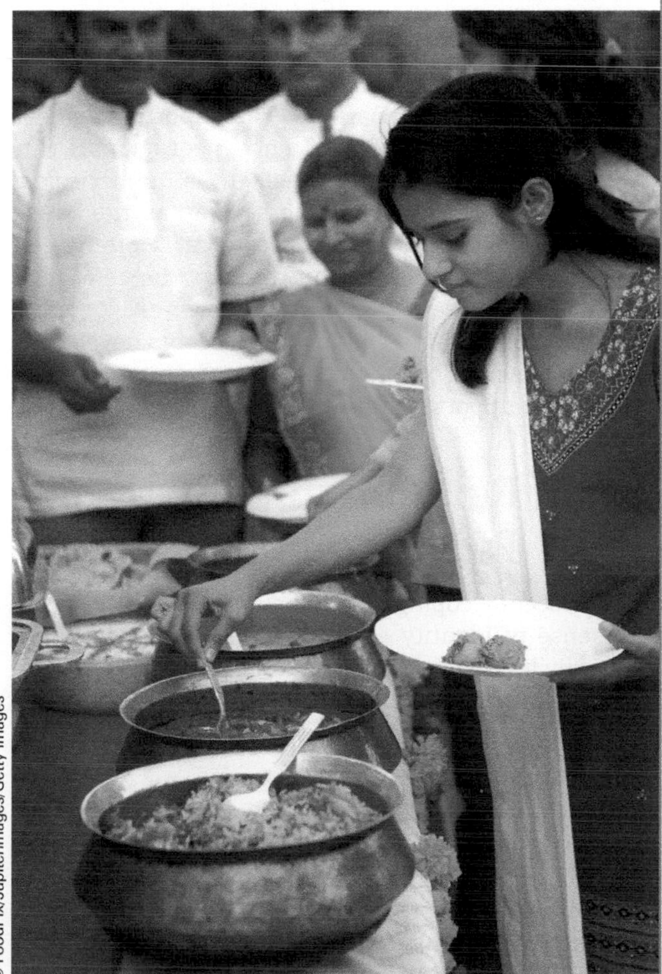
© FoodPix/Jupiterimages/Getty Images

A relative scarcity of successful role models can be a problem, particularly for youth who live in poverty. Identifying too strongly with the dominant culture may also lead to rejection by various racial and ethnic cultures.

Some researchers hypothesize three stages in the development of ethnic identity (Phinney, 2006). The first is unexamined ethnic identity, which is similar to Marcia's ego identity statuses of diffusion or foreclosure. In the second stage, the adolescent embarks on an ethnic identity search. This second stage, similar to Marcia's moratorium, may be based on some incident that makes the adolescent aware of her ethnicity. During this stage, the adolescent may explore her ethnic culture, doing research and participating in cultural events and discussions. In the third stage, individuals have an achieved ethnic identity that involves self-acceptance as a member of one's ethnic group.

ethnic identity
a sense of belonging to an ethnic group

unexamined ethnic identity
the first stage of ethnic identity development; similar to the diffusion or foreclosure identity statuses

ethnic identity search
the second stage of ethnic identity development; similar to the moratorium identity status

achieved ethnic identity
the final stage of ethnic identity development; similar to the identity achievement status

DID YOU KNOW?

The concept of *teenager* was invented.

During the Industrial Revolution when the world was in upheaval due to global conflict, a gap was created between adults and children (Wolf 2014). So began the birth of the teenager, or coming of age. Youth movements have since changed and shaped the world.

Development of the Self-Concept

Before adolescence, children describe themselves primarily in terms of their physical characteristics and their actions. As they approach adolescence, their self-descriptions begin to incorporate psychological characteristics and social relationships (Damon, 1991). Self-concept refers to adolescents' overall evaluation of themselves in terms of self-perceptions of their abilities. In earlier childhood, children tended to develop overly positive self-perceptions because they lacked the maturity to critically evaluate their abilities and integrate information from multiple sources. As adolescents mature, they better understand how others view their skills and abilities, which increases the accuracy of their self-perceptions (Manning, 2007).

EMERGING CANADA

Covenant House reports that there are roughly 35,000 youth per year who do not have a home. Many leave home around age 15. Sixty-four percent are under 25 and most are male, but there are high rates of female youth homelessness too. Half of homeless youth are from economically sound families, but many have been involved in child welfare. A large number of homeless youth are dealing with anger problems, ADHD, and learning disabilities. One in five is LGBTQ. Seventy percent of homeless youth have suffered from abuse. Other causes for homelessness include family breakdown, substance abuse, unemployment, and lack of affordable housing (Covenant House, 2015).

The self-concept becomes more differentiated; adolescents add more categories to their self-description. Also, social roles begin to enter their self-descriptions. Adolescents may describe themselves as anxious or sarcastic with parents but talkative and cheerful with friends. The advanced formal operational skills of the older adolescent allow them to integrate contradictory aspects of the self.

Self-Esteem

Self-esteem tends to decline as a child progresses from middle childhood to about age 12 or 13 (Harter & Whitesell, 2003). Young adolescents' growing cognitive maturity makes them increasingly aware of the disparity between their ideal self and their real self, especially in terms of physical appearance (Durkin, Paxton, & Sorbello, 2007; Seidah & Bouffard, 2007). Boys might fantasize about having the physique of the warriors they see in video games or in the media (Konijn, Bijvank, & Bushman, 2007). The idealized body image in mainstream North American society is currently thin with so many girls are trying to achieve unrealistic body weights.

How would you describe yourself?
✓ anxious
✓ sarcastic
✓ caring
✓ talkative
✓ cheerful
✓ adaptable
✓ quiet

© Radius Images/Jupiterimages

After hitting a low point at about age 13 or 13, self-esteem gradually improves (Harter & Whitesell, 2003). Perhaps adolescents adjust their ideal selves to better reflect reality. Also, as adolescents develop academic, physical, and social skills, they may grow less self-critical (Shirk, Burwell, & Harter, 2003).

For most adolescents, low self-esteem produces temporary discomfort (Harter & Whitesell, 2003). For others, low self-esteem has serious consequences. For example, low self-esteem is often found in teenagers who are depressed or suicidal (Shirk et al., 2003), or are dealing with eating disorders or other mental health issues.

Emotional support from parents and peers is important in maintaining self-esteem. Adolescents who feel highly regarded by family and friends are more likely to feel positive about themselves (Costigan, Cauce, & Etchison, 2007). In early adolescence, support from parents is as important as peer support. But by late adolescence, peer support carries more weight. Low self-esteem is often viewed, particularly in the academic setting, as the cause of all evil, whereas high self-esteem is often seen as the cause of all good. But the importance of high or low self-esteem should not be over-exaggerated; equally important is helping adolescents develop an accurate self-concept within an environment where they are supported (Manning, 2007).

LO2 Relationships with Parents and Peers

Adolescents coping with the task of establishing a sense of identity and direction in their lives are heavily influenced both by parents and peers.

Relationships with Parents

With the advance of adolescence, teens spend less time with their parent(s) and considerably more time with their peers. Each parent continues to play a quality role in their children's lives, but the quantity of time spent together drops. Once again, the importance of parent–child attachment emerges, as children who have secure attachment are associated with less engagement in high-risk behaviours, fewer mental health issues, enhanced social skills, and more effective coping strategies (Moretti & Peled, 2004).

The decrease in time spent with family may reflect the adolescents' striving for independence. A certain degree of distancing from parents may be adaptive, as adolescents form relationships outside the family. However, adolescents continue to maintain love, loyalty, and respect for their parent(s) (Collins & Laursen, 2006). Adolescents who feel close to their parent(s) exhibit more self-reliance and self-esteem, better school performance, and fewer adjustment problems (Costigan et al., 2007).

The relationship between parent(s) and teens is not always rosy, of course. Early adolescence, in particular, is characterized by increased bickering and a decrease in both shared activities and expressions of affection (Smetana, Campione-Barr, & Metzger, 2006). Conflicts typically centre on the everyday details of family life, such as chores, homework, curfews, personal appearance, finances, and dating—often because adolescents believe they should manage matters that were previously controlled by their parents (Costigan et al., 2007). But the parent(s) continue to believe they should retain control in most areas, such as encouraging adolescents to do their homework and clean their rooms. As adolescents get older, they and their parent(s) are more likely to compromise (Smetana et al., 2006). On the other hand, parents and adolescents are usually quite similar in their values and beliefs regarding social, political, religious, and economic issues (Collins & Laursen, 2006). Even though the notion of a generation gap between adolescents and their parents may persist as a stereotype, there is little evidence of such a gap.

As adolescents grow older, parents are more likely to relax controls and less likely to use punishment (Smetana et al., 2006). Although parent–child relationships change, most adolescents feel that they are close to and get along with their parents, even though they may develop a less idealized view of them (Collins & Laursen, 2006).

David Pereiras/Shutterstock.com

DID YOU KNOW?

The idea of adolescents being in a constant state of rebellion against their parents is a stereotype that is no longer true.

Parents and adolescents are usually quite similar in their values and beliefs regarding social, political, religious, and economic issues (Collins & Laursen, 2006).

Parenting Styles

Differences in parenting styles continue to influence the development of adolescents (Costigan et al., 2007). Adolescents from authoritative homes—whose parents are willing to exert control and explain their reasons for doing so—show the most competent behaviour. They are more self-reliant, do better in school, have better mental health, and show the lowest incidence of psychological problems and misconduct, including substance use.

Relationships with Peers

Although adolescents' relationships with parents can remain positive, the role of peers increases as a source of activities, influence, and support. Teens often have friends who represent different interests and groups. These friendships are also dynamic, changing frequently. Teenagers may have base friendships and then move from one group of friends to another. This movement does not signal a lack of loyalty but the teen's migration toward peers who are more similar. This shift sometimes takes time to figure out (de Guzman, 2007).

EMERGING CANADA

In Canada, the reality is that teens spend less time with their parents but their parents continue to be a large influence in their lives. The increase in conflict that is a natural progression toward independence should not be viewed as parental rejection or a signal that parents are less important. Parental relationships tend to be more renegotiated than rejected (de Guzman, 2007). Parents need to reframe conflict as an opportunity to build a relationship with their adolescent child. Staying connected—good communication, mainly in the form of active listening—is key, especially in the face of reduced time spent together. A focus on sensitivity and compassion, as well as being in tune with the teenager, will go a long way in supporting relationships during a time of developmental sensitivity (Moretti & Peled, 2004).

clique
a group of five to ten individuals who may be exclusive of others, and who share activities and confidences

crowd
a large, loosely organized group of people who may or may not spend much time together and who are identified by the activities of the group

Friendships in Adolescence

Friendships in adolescence differ from the friendships of childhood. Adolescents' friendships are more likely to stress acceptance, intimate self-disclosure, and mutual understanding (González, Moreno, & Schneider, 2004). Adolescents' friendships also stress loyalty and trustworthiness (Rotenberg et al., 2004). They may consider a friend as someone who will "stick up for you in a fight" and will "not talk about you behind your back." Adolescents are more likely than younger children to share with their friends and are less likely to compete with them.

RawPixel.com/Shutterstock.com

Friendship networks among girls are smaller and more exclusive than networks among boys (Schraf & Hertz-Lazarowitz, 2003). Girls tend to have one or two close friends, whereas boys tend to congregate in larger, less intimate groups. The activities of girls' and boys' friendship networks also differ. Girls are more likely to engage in unstructured activities, such as talking and listening to music. Boys are more likely to engage in organized group activities, games, and sports.

Social media has added a new dynamic to relationships with peers.

Zeynep Demir/Shutterstock.com

Peer Groups

Most adolescents belong to one or more peer groups: *cliques* and *crowds* (Henzi et al., 2007). A **clique** consists of five to ten individuals who hang around together and share activities and confidences. A **crowd** is a larger group that may or may not spend much time together and is identified by its activities or attitudes. Crowds are usually given labels by other adolescents such as "jocks," "brains," "stoners," or "preps." The most negatively labelled groups ("druggies" and "rejects") show higher levels of substance abuse, illegal behaviour, and stigmatized mental health issues.

Adolescent peer groups function with less adult guidance or control than childhood peer groups (Staff, Mortimer, & Uggen, 2004). Adolescent peer groups may include members of the other sex, which sharply contrasts with the sex segregation of childhood peer groups. Such associations may lead to dating and romantic relationships.

> Adolescent peer groups function with less adult guidance or control than childhood peer groups.

Online Friendships

A new area of research focuses on the online friendships that peers are creating. Buote, Wood, and Pratt (2009) examined the role of attachment style and online friendships. These researchers found that although attachment style alone provides a fairly limited impact on friendship assessment, the context of the online friendship yields different results. Social media are frequently used by most teens, but those with secure attachment styles tend to be more guarded in terms of their self-disclosures. Teens with an insecure attachment style are much more open to disclosures online. In addition, insecurely attached teens were more likely to rate their face-to-face friendships negatively and their online friendships more positively than securely attached teens, who experienced an opposite result. This finding raises important issues regarding the need to "online-proof" our teenagers and to openly discuss social media and the need for safety, limitations, and guidelines.

Dating and Romantic Relationships

Dating serves many functions. First and foremost, people date to have fun. Dating, especially in early adolescence, also serves to enhance prestige with peers. Dating gives adolescents additional experiences in learning to relate to people. Finally, dating prepares adolescents for adult forms of intimacy (Florsheim, 2003).

Dating relationships tend to be casual and short-lived in early adolescence. In late adolescence, relationships tend to become more stable and committed (Connolly, Furman, & Konarski, 2000). Eighteen-year-olds are more likely than 15-year-olds to mention love, trust, and commitment when describing their romantic relationships (Feiring, 1993).

Consider THIS

What issues are associated with social media and identity formation in the teenage years?

Constructing a sense of self is the primary task of today's teenager. But the world is much different for today's teenager than it was even 20 years ago. One of the most significant factors in this new world is the digital age. Teenagers have access to hundreds of their friends and even their "non-friends" with a touch of a button. Facebook has been eclipsed by Twitter, which is rapidly being replaced by Instagram, Snapchat, Vine....

Identity is not preprogrammed; it is a socially constructed attribute. The self-concept is an understanding of who we are, combined with self-awareness and a cognitive knowledge of self (Aronson, Wilson, & Akert, 2010). When forming an identity, young adolescents base their ideas on what they believe the world to actually be. With social media reaching into teenagers' lives, they are basing much of their identity and that of other's on online profiles and "updates."

As many teenagers interact through social media and have fewer face-to-face interactions, social media can also be a place to hide or embellish one's identity. Social media in many senses have improved communication and interconnectivity, but the negative side is that teens and adults may have *so* much autonomy that making cruel or overly judgmental and critical comments becomes the norm. This can unknowingly shape a teen's sense of identity, either inflating their sense of "hotness" or damaging their self-esteem.

Social media has other dangers for adolescents too. Sadly, we now hear many stories of children and teens being targeted by online predators. Amanda Todd was a 15-year-old from British Columbia who took her own life in 2012 after being blackmailed by an online predator. She faced a great deal of cyber- and in-school bulling. She made a video just weeks before she committed suicide sharing her story. In Nova Scotia in 2013, 17-year-old Rehtaeh Parsons committed suicide after pictures showing her in an alleged sexual assault circulated by cellphone throughout her high school. She was shunned and harassed on social media (CBC News, 2013). Often, the solution for cyberbullied teenagers is to leave their school in the hopes of creating a fresh start, but social media can follow them.

What issues are associated with social media and identity formation in the teenage years? Are we doing enough to protect our youth from cyber predators and bullying?

DID YOU KNOW?

Parents should not necessarily fear peer pressure.

Parents and peers are usually complementary rather than competing influences (Reis & Youniss, 2004).

LO3 Sexuality

Because of the flood of sex hormones, adolescents tend to experience a powerful sex drive. In addition, they are bombarded with sexual messages in the media, including scantily clad "twerkers" and hyper-sexualized pop and YouTube stars, print ads for barely there underwear, countless articles on "The 10 things that will drive your boyfriend wild," and endless Instagram pics with duck-face selfies and bum-protruding, "sexy" shots. Teenagers are strongly motivated to follow the crowd, yet they are also influenced by the views of their parents and teachers, who are urging caution. So what is a teen to do?

Sexual activity in adolescence can take many forms. In this section, we consider sexual identity, sexual behaviour, and teenage pregnancy.

Sexual Identity

According to Ritch Savin-Williams and Lisa Diamond (2004; Savin-Williams, 2007), the development of sexual identity in gay males and lesbians involves several steps: attraction to members of the same sex, self-labelling as LGBTQ, sexual contact with members of the same sex, and eventual disclosure of one's sexual orientation to other people. Generally, about a 10-year gap occurs between initial attraction to members of the same sex, which tends to occur at about the age of 8 or 9, and disclosure of one's orientation to other people, often occurring at about age 18. But some gay males and lesbians never disclose their sexual orientation to certain people, such as their parents, or to anyone.

Teens who experience same-sex attractions have begun the first step toward their self-acceptance.

The "Gay Alphabet"

In the past, "gay" was a term used for most non-heterosexual gender orientations. In striving to be inclusive and anti-oppressive, the "gay alphabet" has a variety of acronyms and is continually expanding. These acronyms include, but are not limited to, LGBTQQIP2SA: Lesbian, Gay, Bisexual, Trans, Queer, Questioning, Intersex, Pansexual, 2-spirited, and A-sexual.

In this textbook, we will primarily use LGBTQ, but we acknowledge the other terms and acronyms that strive to be fully representational.

Are We Born Gay?

Epigenetics is the investigation of changes of gene interpretation. Although epigenetics may play a role in sexual orientation, a "gay gene" has not been found and is a controversial issue. Some feel that the concept of a gay gene is empowering as it scientifically validates that "we are born this way"; others feel a search for the "gay gene" is more about pushing political or religious agendas. Scientists suggest that genetic factors (nature) engage with environmental factors (nurture) to impact sexual orientation. We may also ask if it is nature or nurture that makes the majority of people heterosexual.

Many LGBTQ people suggest that it is inconsequential whether it is nature or nurture, or a combination of factors; rather, it is important that people should have a choice in their sexual orientation.

masturbation
sexual self-stimulation

LGBTQ youth may choose to *come out*, which means personally accepting their sexuality, becoming comfortable with who they are, and telling others about their sexual identity. Teens must remember that this decision is solely their own. They should not feel any pressure. Coming out has many benefits and and it has many risks, as identified by the Human Rights Campaign Foundation's *A Resource Guide to Coming Out* (2013). The benefits include the following:

- Living an open and whole life
- Developing closer, more genuine relationships
- Gaining self-esteem by being known and loved for who you really are
- Reducing the stress of hiding
- Connecting with others who have also come out

The risks of coming out include the following:

- Not everyone will be accepting
- People you are close to might have a negative reaction, and their feelings might be permanent
- You may experience harassment, discrimination, or even violence

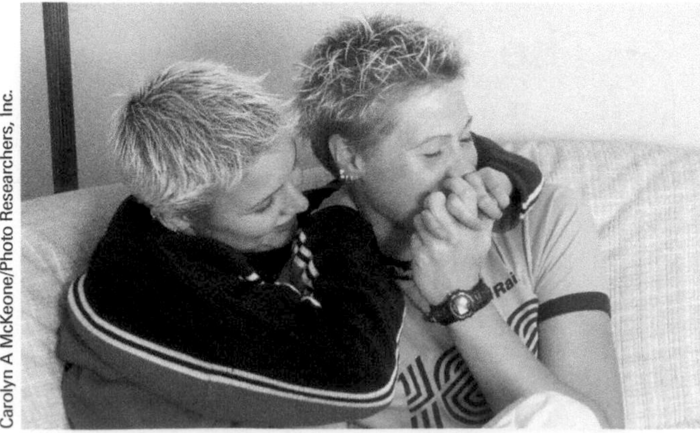
Carolyn A McKeone/Photo Researchers, Inc.

EMERGING CANADA

Egale Canada Human Rights Trust's first national survey on homophobia in Canadian schools (Taylor & Peter, 2011) teaches us that much work is needed in Canada to ensure safe schools for all. Statistics in relation to LGBTQ youth in secondary schools reveal the lack of safety many youth face due to rampant homophobia, transphobia, and biphobia.

- More than 75% of LGBTQ youth reported feeling unsafe at school compared with 20% of straight participants.
- More than 33% of LGBTQ youth have missed a day of school because they felt unsafe compared with 13% of straight participants.
- Fifty percent of LGBTQ participants have come out to only a few friends at school or no one at all.
- Almost 40% of straight participants reported that they made homophobic remarks sometimes or frequently.

The International Day of Silence was founded in 1996 and has become the largest single student-led action toward creating safer schools for all (Toronto District School Board, 2013). Students across Canada participated in the Day of Silence to bring attention to the problem of bullying, letting their classmates know that they are not alone.

LGBTQ youth should think their decisions through carefully and come out on their own terms. If LGBTQ youth place their trust in other students, those students should encourage them to seek out supports and work as an advocate for them.

Masturbation

Masturbation, or sexual self-stimulation, is the most common sexual outlet in adolescence. People masturbate because it feels good, because they are curious, or because it relieves stress. Masturbation has no rules, so long as it is done privately or with a consenting partner. Beliefs that masturbation is harmful and guilt about masturbation lessen the incidence of masturbation (Ortega et al., 2005), although masturbation has not been shown to be physically harmful, despite frequent warnings to discourage this normal activity.

Male–Female Sexual Behaviour

Adolescents today start dating earlier now than in past generations. Teens who date earlier are more likely to engage in sexual activity during high school (Lindberg, Jones, & Santelli, 2007). Teens who initiate sexual activity earlier are also less likely to use contraception and more likely to become pregnant. But early dating does not always lead to early sex, and early sex does not always lead to unwanted pregnancies. Table 12.2 indicates the percentage of Canadian youth, grades 9 and 10, who report having had sexual intercourse.

TABLE 12.2

Percentages of Canadian Adolescents Grade 9 and 10 Who Report Ever Having Had Intercourse, 2002, 2006, 2010

	2002	2006	2010
Male Grade 9	20%	20%	24%
Female Grade 9	18%	19%	19%
Male Grade 10	27%	25%	31%
Female Grade 10	25%	27%	31%

Source: *The health of Canada's young people: a mental health focus.* John G. Freeman, Matthew King, William Pickett, with Wendy Craig, et al., 2011. Adapted and reproduced with permission from the Minister of Health, 2016.

Sexual touching is practically universal among Canadian adolescents. Adolescents use touching to express affection, satisfy their curiosities, heighten their sexual arousal, and reach orgasm while avoiding pregnancy and maintaining virginity. Many adolescents do not consider they have had sex if they stop short of vaginal intercourse (Lindberg et al., 2007). Increasingly heterosexual female teens are having anal sex instead of vaginal sex as they believe it allows them to maintain their virginity, as well as avoid unwanted pregnancies.

Parental Influences

Teenagers who have close relationships with their parents are less likely to initiate sexual activity at an early age (Bynum, 2007). Adolescents who communicate well with their parents also delay the onset of sexual activity (Aspy et al., 2007). If these youngsters do have sexual intercourse, they are more likely to use birth control and have fewer partners.

Peer Influences

A good predictor of sexual activity for adolescents is the sexual activity of their best friends (Dishion & Stormshak, 2007). When teenagers are asked why they do not wait to have sex until they are older, the main reason reported is usually peer influence (O'Donnell et al., 2003). Peers, especially those of the same sex, also serve as a key source of sex education for adolescents. Adolescents report that they are more likely to receive information about sex from friends and media sources—TV shows, films, magazines, and the Internet—than from sex education classes or their parents (Holt, Greene, & Davis, 2003).

Teenage Pregnancy

The age of sexual consent in Canada recently increased from 14 to 16 (with some exceptions). Twelve- and 13-year-olds can consent to sexual activity with peers who are less than two years older than they are. Fourteen- and 15-year-olds can consent to sexual activity with persons who are within 5 years of their age. The age of consent is 18 years if the sexual activity "exploits the young person" (e.g., prostitution, pornography, or a relationship of trust or authority, such as with a teacher or coach) (Department of Justice Canada, 2013).

Many young women have made education and careers their priority and are taking measures to avoid unwanted pregnancies. Why do adolescents get pregnant? Sometimes adolescent girls are given little advice in school or at home about how to deal with sexuality and social pressures. Another reason is failure to use contraception during consensual sex. Some initiate sex at very early ages, when they are least likely to use contraception (Buston, Williamson, & Hart, 2007). Many adolescent girls, especially younger adolescents, do not have access to contraceptive devices. Among those who do, fewer than half use them reliably (Buston et al., 2007). Most girls are impregnated because they and their partners miscalculate the odds of getting pregnant (Buston et al., 2007).

Table 12.3 indicates the numbers of births and abortions among Canadian girls aged 15 to 19.

There are medical, social, and economic consequences of teenage pregnancy, both to the mothers and to the children. If the teenage mother is very young, she can have medical complications and long-term health effects. She is less likely than her peers to graduate from high school or move on to postsecondary education. Therefore, she will likely earn less and be in greater need of public assistance.

In spite of fears that sexuality has dramatically changed among today's youth, this is in fact not the case.

EMERGING CANADA

Project Teen Canada reports an interesting change in teenage female attitudes toward sex. Teens aren't collectively having more sex, but female teens have a drastically different attitude about sex. Rather than passively waiting for a romantic partner to suggest having sex, they are much more likely to have sex on their own terms. According to Reginald Bibby, the lead sociologist on Project Teen, females are "catching up" to their male counterparts. Nearly half of female teens say it's acceptable to have sex after a few times out together, up from 35% in 1984. Male attitudes have not changed during this time. Teen girls also report that "making out" is okay after being out with someone a few times. In 1984, 79% of teen girls felt this was true, compared with 94% of young women today, putting them on par with 96% of young men who say the same (Gulli, 2009).

TABLE 12.3

Birth, Abortion, and Combined Birth/Abortion Rates per 1,000 Canadian Women Aged 15–19: 1996–2009

	1996	1997	1998	1999	2000	2001	2002	2003	2004	2005	2006	2007	2008	2009
Birth	22.1	20.0	19.8	18.6	17.0	16.0	14.9	14.4	13.6	13.3	13.7	14.0	14.3	14.2
Abortion	22.1	21.6	21.6	20.5	20.1	19.4	18.4	17.1	16.3	15.3	14.2			
Total	**44.2**	**41.6**	**41.4**	**39.1**	**37.1**	**35.4**	**33.3**	**31.5**	**29.9**	**28.6**	**27.9**			

Source: Statistics Canada. (n.d.a.). Table 106-9002 – Pregnancy Outcomes. By age group, Canada, provinces and territories, annual, CANSIM (database); Statistics Canada. (n.d.b.). Table 102-4505 – Crude birth rate, age specific and total fertility rates (live births), Canada, provinces and territories, annual, CANSIM (database); Statistics Canada. (n.d.c.). Table 106-9034 – Induced abortions in hospitals and clinics, by age group and area of residence of patient, Canada, provinces and territories, annual, CANSIM database. http://www.sexualityandu.ca/sexual-health/statistics1/statistics-on-canadian-teen-pregnancies

DID YOU KNOW?

Teen sexual activity has not experienced a sharp increase.

Despite social misperceptions, the self-reported incidence of teen sexual activity remains fairly constant.

Few teenage mothers obtain assistance from the babies' fathers. The fathers typically cannot support themselves, much less a family. Teens may also face rejection from peers, although in some towns in Canada, teenage parenthood has become normalized.

In 2009, 22% of all positive HIV tests in Canada were among young adults aged 20 to 29. More females tested positive than males.

Sexually Transmitted Infections (STIs)

The Canadian Federation for Sexual Health (2007) reports that between 1997 and 2004, the reported rates of sexually transmitted infections (STIs) in Canada increased dramatically. Canadians under the age of 30 continue to have the highest reported rates of STIs (in both the homosexual and heterosexual communities). The most commonly occurring STI in young Canadians is chlamydia, a bacterial infection of the vagina or urinary tract that can result in sterility. The next most common STIs are gonorrhea, genital warts, genital herpes, syphilis, and HIV/AIDS (Society of Obstetricians and Gynaecologists of Canada, 2009b). Because of its potential to cause death, HIV/AIDS tends to capture most of the headlines. However, other STIs are more widespread and can also be deadly.

In 2009, 22% of all positive HIV tests in Canada were among young adults aged 20 to 29. More females tested positive than males, leading Canadians to re-examine their perception of HIV as a gay male disease (Public Health Agency of Canada, 2011b).

More than two thirds of chlamydia cases occur among youth (Signal Hill, 2009). Chlamydia is a major cause of pelvic inflammatory disease (PID), which often leads to infertility.

Human papillomavirus (HPV) is transmitted through vaginal, oral, or anal sex, or by skin-to-skin contact. HPV can cause skin warts, genital warts, and pre-cancerous lesions, which can lead to certain types of cancers. An estimated 75% of Canadians will have at least one HPV infection in their lifetime (Society of Obstetricians and Gynaecologists of Canada, 2009b). A controversial vaccine is available that prevents most young women from being infected with HPV and is best administered before they become sexually active (Pichichero, 2006).

HIV/AIDS

HIV/AIDS is the most devastating STI. If left untreated, it is lethal, and the long-term prospects of those who do receive treatment remain unknown.

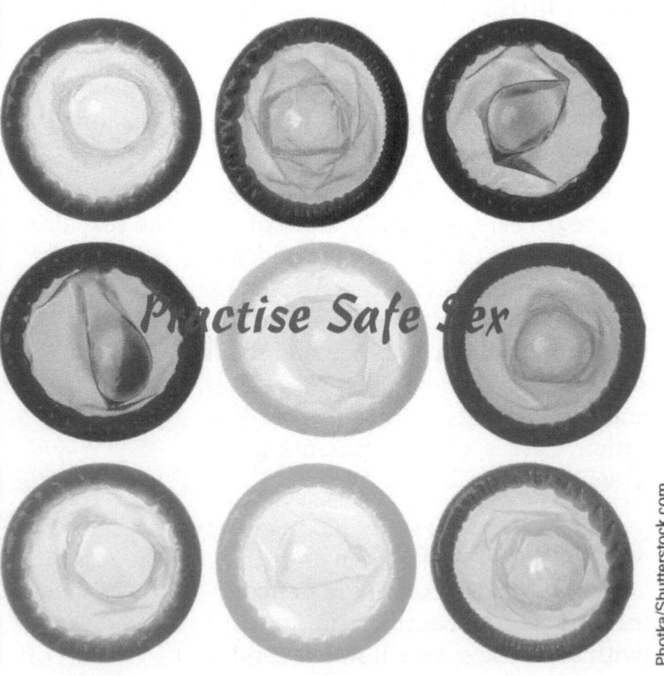

Photka/Shutterstock.com

TABLE 12.4

Overview of Sexually Transmitted Infections (STIs)

STI and Cause	Transmission	Symptoms	Diagnosis	Treatment
Gonorrhea ("clap," "drip"): Gonococcus bacterium (*Neisseria gonorrhoeae*)	Vaginal, oral, or anal sex. To newborns passing through the birth canal of an infected mother.	In men, yellowish, thick discharge, burning urination. Women may be symptom-free or have vaginal discharge, burning urination, or irregular menstruation.	Clinical inspection. Culture of discharge.	Antibiotics
Syphilis: *Treponema pallidum*	Vaginal, oral, or anal sex. Touching an infectious chancre. Congenital.	Hard, painless chancre appears at site of infection within 2–4 weeks. May progress through additional stages if untreated.	Clinical inspection or examination of fluid from a chancre. Blood test.	Antibiotics
Chlamydia and non-gonococcal urethritis: Chlamydia trachomatous bacterium in women	Vaginal, oral, or anal sex. To newborns passing through birth canal of infected mother.	Women and men may be symptom-free or have frequent and painful urination and a discharge.	Analysis of cervical smear in women. Analysis of penile fluid in men.	Antibiotics
Genital herpes: Herpes simplex virus-type 2 (HSV-2)	Vaginal, oral, or anal sex.	Painful, reddish bumps around the genitals, thigh, or buttocks. Bumps become blisters that fill with pus and break, shedding viral particles. Fever, aches, and pains possible.	Clinical inspection of sores. Culture and examination of fluid drawn from sore.	Antiviral drugs may provide relief and help with healing but are not cures.
HIV/AIDS: acronym for human immunodeficiency virus, the cause of acquired immunodeficiency syndrome	Vaginal or anal sex. Infusion of contaminated blood by needle sharing or from mother to baby during childbirth. Breast feeding.	Usually symptom-free for many years. Swollen lymph nodes, fever, weight loss, fatigue, diarrhea. Deadly "opportunistic infections," which are bacteria, viruses, fungi, or protozoa. Examples include types of cancer, tuberculosis, and herpes.	Blood, saliva, or urine tests detect HIV antibodies. Other tests confirm the presence of HIV itself.	HIV/AIDS has no cure. A "cocktail" of highly active antiviral therapy (HAART) prolongs life in many people living with HIV/AIDS.
HPV/Genital warts: human papilloma virus (HPV)	Sexual contact. Contact with infected towels or clothing.	Painless warts resembling cauliflowers on the genitals or anus or in the rectum. Associated with cervical cancer.	Clinical inspection.	A vaccine can prevent infection in most young women. Warts removed by freezing, topical drugs, burning, and surgery.
Pubic lice ("crabs"): *Pthirus pubis* (an insect, not a crab)	Sexual contact. Contact with an infested towel, sheet, or toilet seat.	Intense itching in pubic area and other hairy regions to which lice can attach.	Clinical inspection.	Topical drugs containing pyrethrins or piperonal butoxide.

HIV—the virus that causes AIDS—is spreading rapidly around the world. By the end of the 20th century, it had infected nearly 39 million people (UNAIDS, 2006).

HIV/AIDS is not a disease associated with race, gender, or sexual orientation. It is a human disease that can affect any person who has been sexually active. Young Canadians between the ages of 19 and 30, especially college and university students, are at a particularly high risk for contracting this disease because they tend to be at the height of their sexuality and have opportunities to have several partners during a short period of time. In fact, young people are the fastest growing group to be infected with HIV. Health Canada estimates that 27% of people living with HIV do not know that they have the virus. Awareness is the key to making the choices that will protect you and keep you healthy (HIV Edmonton, 2010). Although knowledge about HIV/AIDS is widespread among youth, only about half modify their sexual practices as a result of it (Santelli et al., 2000). Major risk factors include sex with multiple partners, failure to use condoms, and drug and alcohol abuse (UNAIDS, 2006).

youth in conflict with the law a child or adolescent whose behaviour is characterized by illegal activities

The causes, methods of transmission, symptoms, and (where it exists) treatment of STIs are described in Table 12.4.

LO4 Youth in Conflict with the Law

The term youth in conflict with the law refers to children or adolescents who engage in illegal activities and come into contact with the criminal justice system. At the most extreme end, these youth display behaviours that lead to assault (sexual and physical), robbery, or the selling of drugs. Less serious offences, such as truancy, underage drinking,

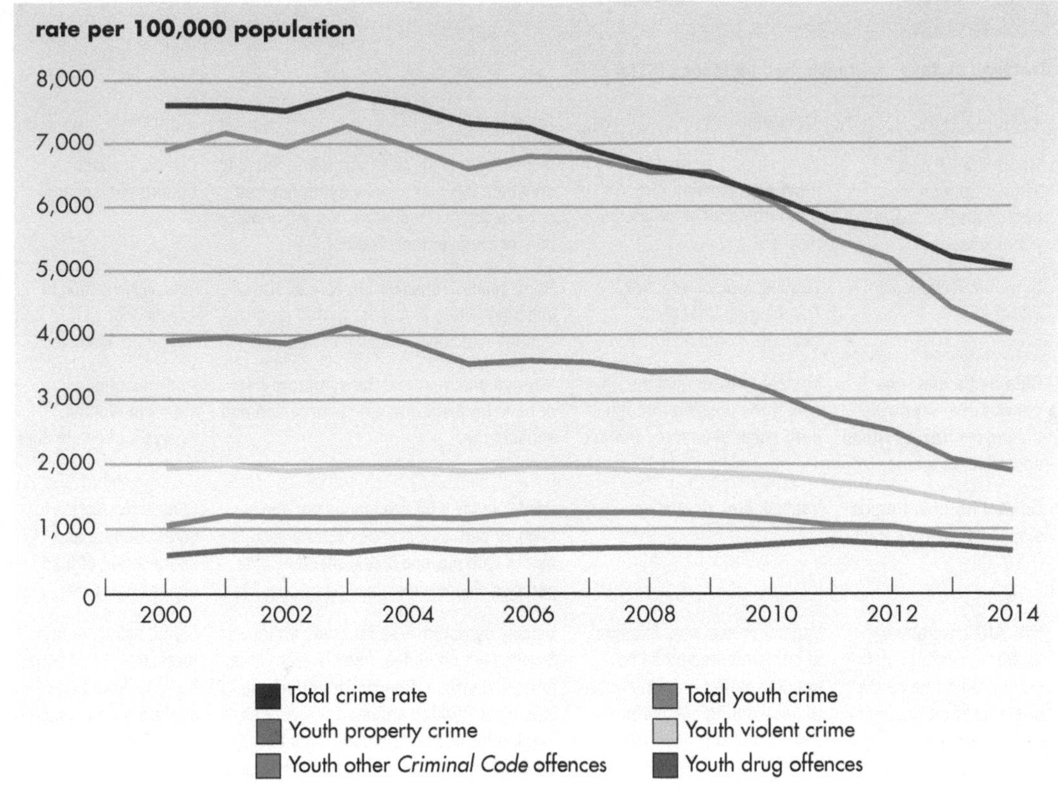

FIGURE 12.1

Youth Crime Trends in Canada, by Offence Type

Source: Statistics Canada. (2016, February 17). *Youth crime in Canada, 2014*. The Daily. http://www.statcan.gc.ca/daily-quotidien/160217/dq160217b-eng.htm

running away from home, shoplifting, and sexual promiscuity, are considered illegal only when performed by minors. Hence, these activities are termed as *status offences*.

Antisocial and criminal behaviours show a dramatic increase in many societies during adolescence and then taper off during adulthood. Whenever possible, the Canadian legal system encourages alternative consequences for adolescents rather than custody punishment. These are called *extrajudicial measures*, and they reduce the long-term effects of being in conflict with the law. Extrajudicial measures can include a police warning, a formal caution, or a referral to an agency that can help the young person make better decisions in the future (Department of Justice Canada, 2009).

In 2012, less than half the youth who were accused of crimes were formally charged with an offence (Perrault, 2013). Those youth who were arrested were mostly dealt with according to the provisions of the Youth Criminal Justice Act (Statistics Canada, 2013e).

Youth Crime in Canada

Few social issues receive as much attention in Canada as youth crime. In 2014 in Canada, young adults between 18 and 24 made up the age group accused often of crimes. Overall, however, youth crime is decreasing (see Figure 12.1).

Factors Associated with Youth Crime in Canada

Relatively few studies have explored the link between ethnicity and youth crime in Canada, but the studies that have been completed indicate that the important link to youth crime is not race or ethnicity but socio-economic deprivation, particularly family poverty, and lack of parental supervision (Bertrand et al., 2013).

Reducing Youth Crime

Contrary to popular Canadian belief, little research evidence supports the effectiveness of punitive sanctions, such as incarceration, in reducing youth crime. Although some offenders need to be incarcerated, many expert criminologists argue that more offenders need to be engaged in community programs that build character, increase self-esteem, and develop life skills. Several studies have demonstrated that youth sport can reduce youth crime. The organized sports programs that are successful at reducing youth crime appear to develop feelings of competence, connectedness, and empowerment (Carmichael, 2008). Developing these feelings

© Jordan Chesbrough/iStockphoto

is one of the primary philosophies of the Youth Criminal Justice Act, which came into force in 2003.

First Nations, Métis, and Inuit youth represent a growing and significant population. Unfortunately, crime is higher in these communities as a result of the effects of residential schooling, generational poverty, and structural oppression. Various successful community-led initiatives engage youth in indigenous cultural and ceremonial practices as a way of solidifying their roles in their communities, and strengthening a sense of identity.

> The important link to youth crime is not race or ethnicity but socio-economic deprivation.

Indigenous Culture and Community Justice

Borrowing from Canadian First Nations, Métis, and Inuit cultures, the Youth Criminal Justice Act relies heavily on the effectiveness of restorative justice. Restorative justice is a philosophy that holds community healing as its cornerstone. It acknowledges and repairs harm that victims experience while also holding young people accountable for their actions in meaningful ways (Centre for Research on Youth at Risk, n.d.). Restorative justice views crime as a violation of one person by another, not simply as a breaking of the law. Community ownership and involvement gives people a voice to address the harm crime brings to victims, offenders, the families and friends of both, and society.

LO5 Suicide in Adolescence

Adolescence is such an exciting time of life. For many, the future is filled with promise and the teen dreams of what lies ahead. One of the tragedies of teenage suicide is the loss of potential years of life. Canadian suicide rates are currently at the highest levels in Canadian history, and the reported number of suicides in Canada is likely lower than the real number, because suicides are often misreported as accidents. This socially sensitive cause of death is underreported. (University of Ottawa, 2013).

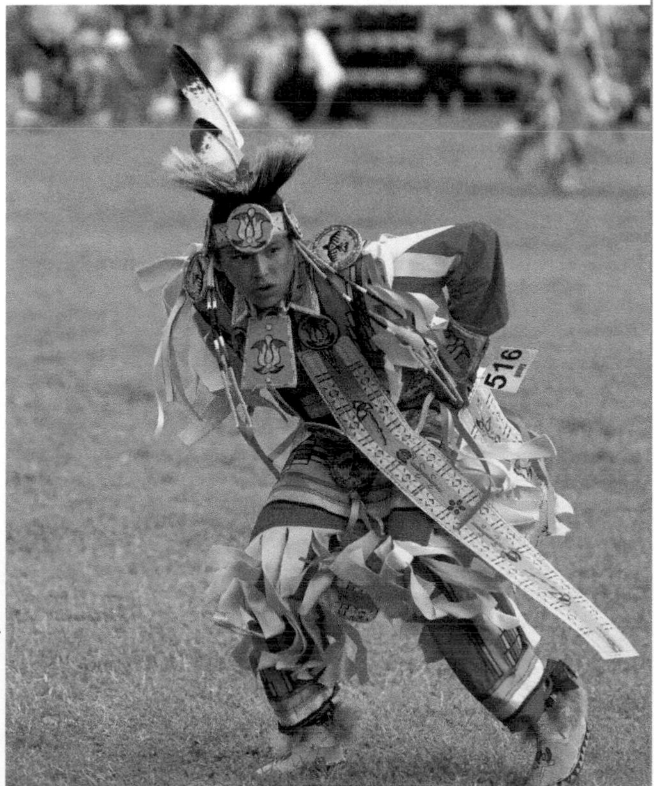

Paul McKinnon/iStockphoto.com

DID YOU KNOW?

Suicide is the second leading cause of death among Canadian adolescents.

Motor vehicle accidents are the number one cause of death among Canadian adolescents; suicide is second.

Risk Factors in Suicide

Most suicides among adolescents and adults are linked to feelings of depression and hopelessness (Cheng & Chan, 2007). Suicide is the second leading cause of death for 10-24 year olds in Canada. Each

EMERGING CANADA

Data from Project Teen 2008 shows that, despite discouraging crime statistics, the majority of indigenous youth see a bright future for themselves. Of all Aboriginal teens living on a reserve, 89% believe that anyone who works hard can rise to the top, 84% expect to get the job they want, and 79% feel they will be more financially comfortable than their parents. The resilience of indigenous youth is encouraging.

Many indigenous youth realize that their upbringing is different from that of other Canadian youth because of their parents' experience being raised in residential schools. The effects of institutional abuse may linger, but the optimism of this new group of teens may have resulted from not directly experiencing the residential schools. Another explanation for their optimism is the impact of social media in connecting indigenous youth across Canada (Mendleson, 2009).

year 294 youths die from suicide, and there are many more attempts. Indigenous teens and LGBTQ teens are at the highest risk of suicide (Canadian Mental Health Association, 2013d).

Adolescent suicide attempts are more common after stressful life events, especially events that entail loss of social support, such as the death of a parent or friend, breaking up with a boyfriend or girlfriend, or a family member's leaving home (Cooper, Appleby, & Amos, 2002). Other contributors to suicidal behaviour include concerns over sexuality, school grades, problems at home, and substance abuse (Conner & Goldston, 2007; Cuellar & Curry, 2007). Suicide is not always precipitated by a stressful event itself, but, instead, it is often triggered by the adolescent's anxiety or fear of being "found out" for something, such as having failed a course or having been arrested.

Female teen suicide is on the rise, whereas male teen suicide is decreasing. Suffocation has overtaken firearms as the most common method of suicide completion.

Traditional patterns of suicide do seem to be changing, with suicide rates among females increasing and among males decreasing.

Suicidal youth will rarely make a direct plea for help (Canadian Mental Health Association, 2013d). The Canadian Mental Health Association (2013d) advises that suicide is most often a process, not a single event. Suicidal youth are in pain. They don't necessarily want to die, but living does not seem like an acceptable alternative. Anytime a parent or other concerned adult observes concerning behaviours, he or she should consider those behaviours as an invitation to enter into open and honest dialogue. The caring adult should establish a basis of trust by talking calmly about suicide, without showing fear or making judgments. The following are warning signs that parents and others should watch for:

- Sudden changes in behaviour (both positive and negative)
- Isolation and withdrawal
- Not caring
- Changes in eating or sleeping patterns
- Depression, moodiness, or hopelessness
- Previous suicide attempt or the recent death by suicide of a friend or family member

10 Things Parents Can Do to Prevent Suicide

Healthychildren.org recommends the following for parents:

1. Not allowing depression or anxiety to get out of control, or overwhelming.
2. Active listening
3. Not ignoring threats of self-harm as being melodramatic
4. Seeking immediate professional support
5. Sharing feelings and concerns
6. Encouraging engagement and not isolation
7. Encouraging teen to be realistic about demands on themselves
8. Encouraging exercise and being active
9. Being patient with treatment results
10. Removing anything that is potentially dangerous such as fire arms

Source: https://www.healthychildren.org/English/health-issues/conditions/emotional-problems/Pages/Ten-Things-Parents-Can-Do-to-Prevent-Suicide.aspx

EMERGING CANADA

On April 16, 2013, another social media trend went viral on Instagram and Tumblr. Canadian teens asked each other electronically to draw a semicolon on their wrists to represent everyone who self-harms, is suicidal, is depressed, has anxiety, is unhappy, has just lost a loved one, or is experiencing emotional pain. The semicolon represents a sentence the author could have ended, but chose not to. The author is the teenager, and the sentence is life (Campos, 2013).

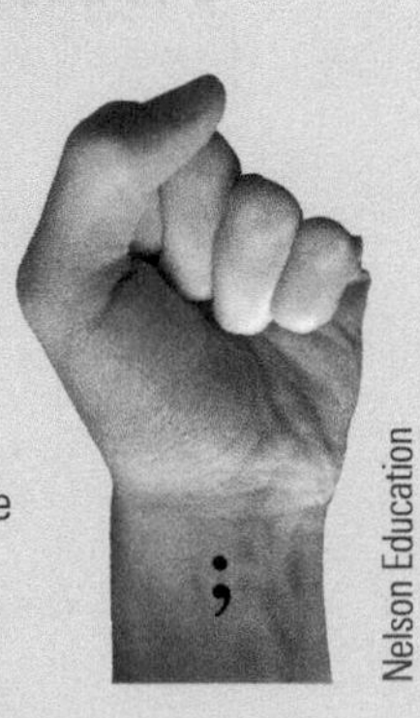
Nelson Education

Michael Jung/Shutterstock.com

CHAPTER 13

Early Adulthood: Physical and Cognitive Development

LEARNING OUTCOMES

LO1 Discuss the (theoretical) stage of emerging adulthood

LO2 Describe trends in physical development in early adulthood

LO3 Examine health in early adulthood, focusing on causes of death, diet, exercise, nutrition, and substance abuse

LO4 Discuss sexuality in early adulthood, focusing on LGBTQ, menstrual problems, sexual coercion, and sexual violence

LO5 Discuss cognitive development in early adulthood, focusing on "postformal" developments and effects of life after high school

LO6 Describe career choice and development during early adulthood

> "Adulthood is usually defined in terms of what people do, not how old they are."

emerging adulthood a theoretical period of development, spanning the ages of 18 to 25, when young people in developed nations engage in extended role exploration

Adulthood is usually defined in terms of what people do, not how old they are. Over the years, developmentalists have considered marriage to be a key standard for adulthood (Carroll et al., 2007). Other criteria include holding a full-time job and living independently. Today, the transition to adulthood is mainly marked by adjustment issues, such as settling on one's values and beliefs, accepting personal responsibility, becoming financially independent, and establishing an equal relationship with one's parents (Gottlieb, Still, & Newby-Clark, 2007).

Adulthood itself has been divided into stages, and the first of these, early adulthood, has been largely seen as the period of life when people focus on establishing their careers or pathways in life, covering ages 18 to about 35 years. The transition to adulthood can be rapid or piecemeal. Many individuals in their late teens and early 20s remain dependent on their parents and are reluctant or unable to make enduring commitments in terms of identity formation or intimate relationships. The question is whether another stage of development bridges adolescence and early adulthood. Many developmental theorists believe in a bridging stage, including Jeffrey Arnett (2007), who terms this stage *emerging adulthood*.

LO1 Emerging Adulthood

Emerging adulthood is theorized to be a distinct period of development found in societies that allow young people an extended opportunity to explore their roles in life. Some parents are affluent enough to continue to support their children through their postsecondary education. Some students will receive assistance from the government by qualifying for student loans. These supports allow young people the luxury of sorting out their identity issues and creating meaningful life plans. But even in Canada, of course, many people cannot afford the luxury of exploring educational opportunities in emerging adulthood.

Overall, Canadian youth and young adults are leading healthy lives and are in a positive transition toward becoming healthy adults. Some young adults, however, will experience significant health issues. Most mental illnesses, which are often an issue throughout life, begin to appear in early adulthood. Eating disorders and intentional self-harm are of particular concern. Accidents are the number one cause of death and injury in young adults; sadly, many of these accidents are preventable. Substance abuse and risky sexual behaviour are also major health issues. On the other hand, several factors have a positive outcome on the life of the young adult. Most young adults report positive relationships with peers and parents. Academic engagement and involvement in extracurricular activities also protect the well-being of young Canadians (Public Health Agency of Canada, 2011b).

LO2 Physical Development

Physical development peaks in early adulthood, when most are at their height of sensory sharpness, strength, reaction time, and cardiovascular fitness. Young adults are at their tallest, and their height remains stable through middle adulthood, declining slightly in late adulthood. A higher percentage of men's body mass is made of muscle, and men are typically stronger than women. Physical strength in both men and women peaks in the 20s and early 30s, then slowly declines (Markham, 2006). Seventy percent of young adults perceive their health as very good or excellent. In spite of this perception, young adults have increasing rates of obesity and the highest rates of sexually transmitted infections (STIs). Asthma, diabetes, cancer, and STIs are the most common illnesses and diseases among Canada's youth and young adults (Public Health Agency of Canada, 2011b).

Sensory sharpness also peaks in the early 20s (Fozard & Gordon-Salant, 2001). Visual acuity remains good until middle adulthood, when a gradual decline leads to farsightedness and, in many people, a need for reading glasses. Hearing tends to decline once people reach their late 20s and early 30s, particularly for tones that are high in pitch.

The changes of aging in the cardiovascular, respiratory, and immune systems begin in early adulthood, but they are gradual. The heart muscle becomes more rigid, decreasing the maximum heart rate and reducing the ability of the heart to pump enough blood to provide oxygen for stressful exercise. But regular exercise increases cardiovascular and respiratory capacity at any age. As people age, their immune system produces fewer white blood cells, and the disease-fighting ability declines in the white blood cells that remain.

Fertility in both sexes declines as early adulthood progresses through the 30s. After age 35, women are usually advised to have their fetuses checked for Down syndrome and other chromosomal abnormalities. Older men may also contribute to chromosomal abnormalities. A major problem in women is a reduced number of ova (egg cells) and a decline in the ovas' quality. But because of advances in reproductive technology, many women give birth to healthy children, including their first children, in their 30s and 40s.

Both sexes may find their hair thinning and greying by the end of early adulthood. Toward the end of early adulthood, and almost certainly in middle adulthood, the skin begins to loosen, grow less elastic, and wrinkle, moreso in women than in men.

LO3 Health and Fitness

As a group, young adults tend to be healthy. Their immune systems are generally functioning well. As Table 13.1 shows, the leading cause of death for young adults in Canada in 2004 was accidents. Deaths among young adults are uncommon, accounting for only 7% of all deaths of Canadians younger than 65 years of age in 2007. Injuries and poisons (both intentional and unintentional) were the most common causes of death (70%), followed by cancers (8%). Nearly three quarters of all deaths (72%) of youth and young adults in 2007 were among adolescent boys and young men. Of these deaths 18% were associated with all-terrain vehicles, motorcycles, and water transport vehicles (Public Health Agency of Canada, 2011b). Interestingly, cancer rates are significantly higher for women than for men. HIV (human immunodeficiency virus) and AIDS (acquired immune deficiency syndrome) have not made the list of causes of death, possibly because these conditions take many years to overwhelm the body's immune system.

TABLE 13.1

Five Leading Causes of Death in Canada for Young Adults by Age Group

Young Men		Young Women	
(ages 15–24)	(ages 25–34)	(ages 15–24)	(ages 25–34)
Accidents 43.7 %	Accidents 31.2 %	Accidents 39.4 %	Cancer 22.0 %
Suicide 23.6 %	Suicide 25.3 %	Suicide 16.4 %	Accidents 21.4 %
Cancer 6 %	Cancer 9.2 %	Cancer 10.2 %	Suicide 13.6 %
Assault 5.8 %	Heart Disease 5.6 %	Heart Disease 4.1 %	Heart Disease 5.6 %
Heart Disease 2.1 %	Assault 4.6 %	Assault 2.9 %	Assault 3.8 %

Source: Statistics Canada. (2008b). Leading causes of death in Canada. Statistics Canada, Catalogue no. 84-215-X. Table 1-3 and Table 1-4. Retrieved from www.statcan.gc.ca/pub/84-215-x/2008000/hl-fs-eng.htm#3

Given that so many young adults are in excellent or good health, it is unfortunate that many are careless about their health or put it on the "back burner." Many are more concerned about their careers, their education, or their social lives; they think of health issues—diet, smoking, sedentary living, excessive drinking—as something they can get to later.

Consider the results of a poll by the Centers for Disease Control and Prevention (CDC) that reported on the health-related behaviour patterns of more than 18,000 young adults aged 18–24 (McCracken, Jiles, & Blanck, 2007). More than three respondents in four (78%) ate fewer than the recommended five fruits and vegetables each day. Forty-three percent reported either no or insufficient physical activity. More than one in four (29%) were smokers, and 30% reported binge drinking—having five drinks in a row on single occasions. About one respondent in four (26%) was overweight (having a body-mass index [BMI] of 25.0–29.9; see Figure 13.1), and another 14% were obese (having a BMI of 30.0 or above).

DID YOU KNOW?

Accidents are the leading cause of death, followed by suicide and then cancer.

Leading causes of death vary between Canadian men and women in this age group. For men, accidents are the leading cause of death; for women, accidents and cancer.

Diet, Weight, and Nutrition

The percentage of Canadians who are overweight or obese has risen dramatically in recent years, mirroring a worldwide phenomenon. According to Statistics Canada (2010d), 18.1% of Canadians 18 and older, according to their BMI, were considered obese

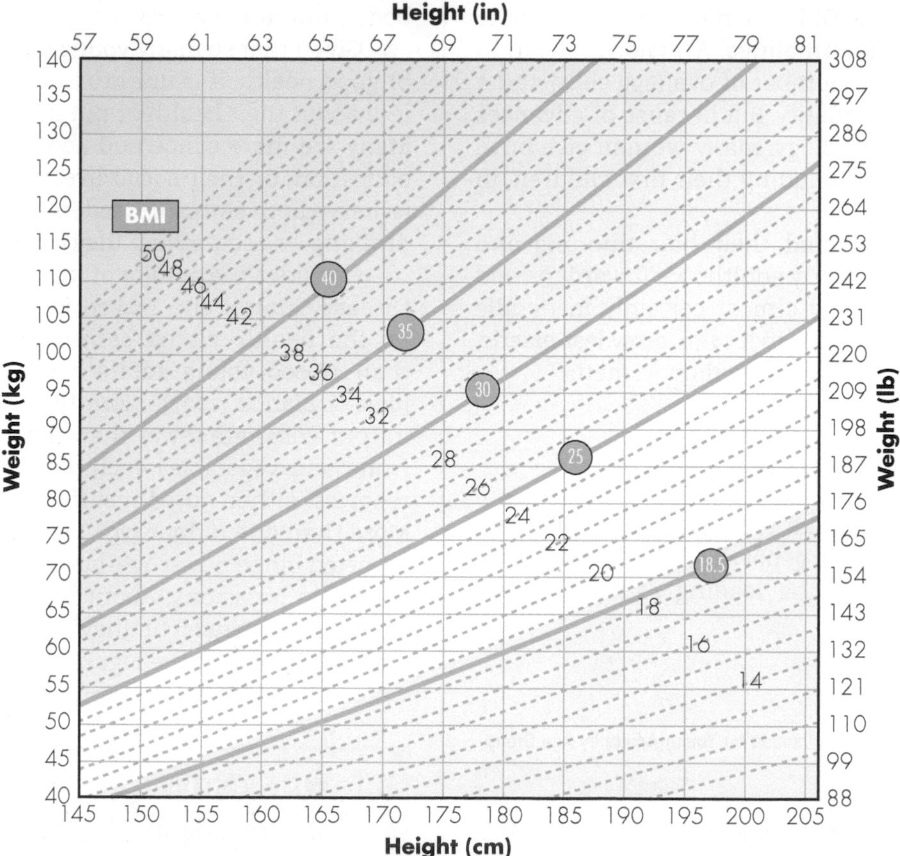

FIGURE 13.1

Body Mass Index

Your BMI is based on your height and weight. Health professionals consider a BMI of 25 to 29 to be overweight, and 30 or above to be obese.

Source: All rights reserved. *Canadian Guidelines for Body Weight Classification in Adults–Quick Reference Tool for Professionals*. Health Canada, 2003. Adapted and reproduced with permission from the Minister of Health, 2016.

in 2010. Obesity rates rose among men between 2003 and 2010 from 16.0% to 19.8%, and among women from14.5% to 16.5%.

Why are so many young adults overweight and obese? Typical North American diets consist of high sodium, fat, and sugars, all of which contribute to obesity. Fast food is convenient and easily accessible, although it isn't as inexpensive as it once was. Young adults may be busy with schooling, work, and relationships; they find it difficult and inconvenient

Michael Svoboda/iStockphoto.com

to take the time to eat correctly, and thus resort to eating fast and frozen foods. Economic factors also play a role in good nutrition. The cost of fresh vegetables in Canada has risen in 2016 by almost 20% and fruit approximately 13% (Canadian Press, 2016). Affordability, especially for lower income early adults, affects healthy eating habits.

adaptive thermogenesis the process by which the body converts food energy (calories) to heat at a lower rate when a person eats less, because of, for example, famine or dieting

Both biological and psychological factors are involved in obesity, including levels of physical activity, access to healthy foods, level of education earned, and income. These influences increase the risk of obesity by shaping individual perceptions, knowledge, and behaviours related to healthy life-styles and healthy weights (Public Health Agency of Canada, 2011).

Being overweight tends to run in families. Studies of monkeys (Kavanagh et al., 2007) and of human twins (Silventoinen et al., 2007) suggest that heredity plays a strong role in being overweight. Efforts by overweight and obese people to maintain a slender profile may be sabotaged by a mechanism that helps to preserve life in times of famine—adaptive thermogenesis. This mechanism causes the body to produce less energy (burn fewer calories) when less food is consumed (Major et al., 2007). This does not mean that overweight people will not lose

The Skinny on Weight Control

The most effective and healthy weight-control programs involve exercising, improving nutritional knowledge, decreasing calorie intake, and changing eating habits by reducing portion sizes and eating less saturated fat and cholesterol. Most health professionals believe that Canadians eat too much animal fat and not enough fruits and vegetables. Dieting plus exercise is more effective for controlling weight than dieting alone. Exercise burns calories and builds muscle tissue, which metabolizes more calories than fatty tissue does.

Cognitive-behavioural methods such as the following also help:

- Establish calorie-intake goals and keep track of whether you are meeting them.
- Eat preplanned low-calorie snacks.
- Take a five-minute break between helpings. Ask yourself, "Am I still hungry?" If not, stop eating.
- Avoid temptations. Plan your meal before entering a restaurant. Shop from a list.
- When you meet your calorie goals, reward yourself (but not with food).
- Mentally rehearse solutions to problems. Plan what you will do when cake is handed out at the office party or when you visit relatives who try to stuff you with food.
- If you binge, don't give up. Resume dieting the next day.

EMERGING CANADA

According to the 2007–2009 Canadian Health Measures Survey, 34% of young men are considered overweight, compared with 21% of young women. Yet 18% of women are considered obese, compared with 13% of men. The following additional factors affect the weight of young Canadians (Public Health Agency of Canada, 2011):

- Young adult immigrants are less likely to be overweight or obese with only 17% being overweight and 5% being obese. (The longer young adults live in Canada, the more likely they are to reflect the Canadian averages.)
- As women's income levels rise, their overweight and obesity rates decrease.
- As men's income levels rise, their overweight and obesity rates increase. Their higher weight might result because they eat out more, or it may be that men who earn less tend to have more physically demanding jobs.
- Young adult males eat out more than any other segment of the Canadian population. Of all young adult males surveyed, 39% reported having eaten at a fast-food restaurant the day before.

substance abuse a persistent pattern of use of a substance characterized by frequent intoxication and impairment of physical, social, or emotional well-being

substance dependence a persistent pattern of use of a substance that is accompanied by physiological addiction

tolerance habituation to a drug such that increasingly higher doses are needed to achieve similar effects

abstinence syndrome a characteristic cluster of symptoms that results from a sudden decrease in the level of usage of a substance

weight by dieting; it means that weight loss will likely take longer than expected. As well, fatty tissue in the body also metabolizes (burns) food more slowly than muscle. For this reason, a person with a high fat-to-muscle ratio metabolizes food more slowly than a person of the same weight who has more muscle.

Psychological factors, such as observational learning, stress, emotional states, and compulsive overeating disorders, also contribute to obesity.

Exercise

Increased levels of sedentary activities (including screen times) have been associated with obesity. Between 2000–2001 and 2009, the percentage of young adults spending 15 or more hours per week on sedentary activities increased from 57% to 75% (Public Health Agency of Canada, 2011a).

Adults 18 and older need 30 minutes of physical activity five or more days a week to be healthy (*Physical Activity Fact Sheet*, 2005). Significant benefits can be reaped from a moderate amount of activity, such as 30 minutes of brisk walking or raking leaves, 15 minutes of running, or 45 minutes of volleyball. You can break 30 to 60 minutes of physical activity into smaller segments of 10 or 15 minutes through the day.

This amount of physical activity can substantially reduce the risk of developing or dying from cardiovascular disease, type 2 diabetes, and certain cancers, such as colon cancer. Exercise also benefits the brain and cognitive performance (Stein et al., 2007). Exercise may even help with psychological disorders such as anxiety and depression (Stein et al., 2007). The "trick" for most young adults is to integrate exercise into their daily routine, perhaps through moderately vigorous activities for 15 minutes two times a day or for 10 minutes three times a day.

Substance Abuse and Dependence

People use drugs not only to cope with medical problems but also to deal with daily tensions, social anxiety, depression and other mental health issues, and even boredom. A recent Canadian survey indicated that tobacco, alcohol, and marijuana are the substances most commonly used by young adults (Public Health Agency of Canada, 2011b). For some, experimentation with these substances may be part of their transition into adulthood. But for others, experimentation can lead to substance abuse. Where does the use of a drug or substance end and substance abuse begin? **Substance abuse** is defined by Canadian researchers and professionals by applying the conditions outlined in the *Diagnostic and Statistical Manual of Mental Disorders* (DSM-IV-TR) (American Psychiatric Association, 1998). Substance abuse is a maladaptive pattern of substance use (within a 12-month period) leading to significant impairment or distress in one or more of the following areas:

- Failure to fulfill obligations at work, at school, or in the home
- Recurrent use of substances in situations that are physically dangerous (e.g., operating a car)
- Recurrent legal problems associated with substance use
- Continued substance use in spite of recurring social problems

It's important to note that many people are functional addicts, or abuse substances while maintaining a seemingly normal life. Substance abuse is, however, progressive; signs and symptoms are likely to worsen over time.

A person who is dependent on a substance loses control over using it. **Substance dependence** means that having it in the body becomes the norm. **Tolerance** develops as the body becomes habituated to the substance; as a result, more of it may be needed to achieve the same effects. Many substances are physically addictive, so when the dosage is lowered, withdrawal symptoms, also known as **abstinence syndrome**, occur. When addicted individuals lower their intake of alcohol, for example, they may experience symptoms such as tremors (shakes), high blood pressure, rapid heart and pulse rate, anxiety, restlessness, and weakness. Three of the most common types of abused substances are depressants, stimulants, and hallucinogens.

Effects of Depressants

Depressants slow the activity of the nervous system. Depressants include alcohol, narcotics derived from the opium poppy (such as heroin, morphine, and codeine), and sedatives (such as barbiturates and methaqualone).

Alcohol lessens inhibitions so that drinkers may do things when drinking that they might otherwise resist (Donohue et al., 2007). Alcohol is also an intoxicant: it distorts perceptions, impairs concentration, hinders coordination, and slurs the speech. Barbiturates are depressants with various legitimate medical uses, such as relief from pain, anxiety, and tension, but people can become rapidly dependent on them.

Effects of Stimulants

Stimulants speed up the heartbeat and other bodily functions. Nicotine, cocaine, and amphetamines are the most common stimulants. Nicotine is the addictive chemical in tobacco. According to researchers, over the past decade in Canada, 21% of all deaths (more than 1 in 5) can be attributed to smoking (Jones, Gulbis, & Baker, 2010). Although Canada's smoking rate of 19.9% in 2011 has decreased from a rate of 25.9% in 2001, smoking remains the leading cause of premature death in Canada (Janz, 2012).

Cocaine accelerates the heart rate, spikes the blood pressure, constricts the arteries of the heart, and thickens the blood, a combination that can cause cardiovascular and respiratory collapse (Mitchell, 2006). Overdoses can cause restlessness, insomnia, tremors, and even death.

Amphetamines can keep users awake for long periods and reduce their appetites. Tolerance for amphetamines develops rapidly. Methamphetamine is very addictive and abuse can cause brain damage, leading to problems in learning and memory (Jonkman, 2006).

Effects of Hallucinogenics

Hallucinogenics give rise to hallucinations, which sometimes can be so strong that they are confused with reality. Marijuana, ecstasy, LSD, and PCP are hallucinogenic drugs. Marijuana, which is typically smoked, helps users relax, elevates mood, increases sensory awareness, and can induce visual hallucinations. Marijuana carries health risks such as impairing perceptual–motor coordination and short-term memory loss (Egerton et al., 2006; Lamers et al., 2006). Marijuana has been illegal due to its hallucinogenic components. Current research demonstrates that it is the TCH levels in cannabis that creates "a high," whereas CBD and other cannabinoids provide pain relief and other medical benefits. Research also shows that cannabinoids are useful in helping a lengthy list of chronic and terminal illnesses. This research led to the legalization of medical marijuana in Canada in 2001. Prime Minister Trudeau in 2015 announced that cannabis for recreational purposes will also be legalized in Canada by 2017.

hallucinogenics drugs that give rise to hallucinations

Is cannabis addictive? Research suggests that regular users of cannabis with TCH levels, may experience withdrawal, which is a sign of addiction (Budney et al., 2007).

Ecstasy, a popular "party" drug, provides the boost of a stimulant and mild hallucinogenic effects. The combination appears to free users from inhibitions and awareness of the consequences of risky behaviour, such as unprotected sex. Ecstasy can also impair working memory, increase anxiety, and lead to depression (Lamers et al., 2006).

LSD is the acronym for lysergic acid diethylamide, another hallucinogenic drug. High doses of hallucinogenics can change the mood, cause paranoid delusions, and impair coordination and judgment. Driving while using hallucinogenic drugs poses grave risks.

EMERGING CANADA

Marijuana use is high among young adults, with 31% of males using cannabis, compared with 17% of females. The next most commonly used illegal drugs among young adults are cocaine (5%), ecstasy (3%), and hallucinogens (2%). Drugs can cause health and social problems among young adults if overused (Public Health Agency of Canada, 2011).

Do You Have a Problem with Alcohol?

How can you tell if you have a drinking problem? Answering the following questions can help you find out (NIAAA, 2005):

Yes	No	Have you ever felt you should cut down on your drinking?
Yes	No	Have people annoyed you by criticizing your drinking?
Yes	No	Have you ever felt bad or guilty about your drinking?
Yes	No	Have you ever had a drink first thing in the morning (as an "eye opener") to steady your nerves or get rid of a hangover?
Yes	No	Has drinking ever caused a social difficulty for you?
Yes	No	Have you ever missed school or work because of drinking?

Just one "yes" answer suggests a possible alcohol problem. Two or more "yeses" make it highly likely that a problem exists. In either case, it is advisable to discuss your answers with your doctor or another health care provider.

Source: Reproduced with permission from the *Journal of the American Medical Association*. 1984. Vol. 252. Issue 14: p. 1905.

Stress and Health

Many factors are commonly used to measure an individual's mental health, including self-assessment, a sense of satisfaction with and control over life, a sense of belonging, and relationships. In 2009, more than 77% of Canadian youth and young adults described their mental health as very good or excellent (Public Health Agency of Canada, 2011). According to a national poll taken by Ipsos Reid (2006), though, nearly half (45%) of Canadians felt they did not have the control over their stress levels that they would like. Stress can have a negative impact on people's psychological and physical health and on their social, academic, and vocational lives (see Figure 13.2).

On the other hand, many Canadians reported positive influences of stress:

- 46% exercise in response to stress
- 48% believe that stress is proof they have important responsibilities
- 31% say that stress improves the quality of their work (BC Partners for Mental Health and Addictions Information, 2004)

EMERGING CANADA

A certain level of anxiety is a normal and healthy reaction to stress. But when the anxiety increases to the point it interferes with everyday functioning, an anxiety disorder may be involved. Panic disorder, phobias, and obsessive-compulsive disorders are all types of anxiety disorders and affect all Canadians. They often begin during young adulthood.

In 2014, 23.0% of Canadians 15 and older reported that most days they felt "quite a bit" or "extremely stressed." For females, the level was 23.7%; for males, 22.3% (Statistics Canada 2014b).

Being a young adult is defined by life transitions. Individuals have new financial responsibilities, they may be away from home for the first time, and they are likely trying on new social roles. Anxiety disorders can disrupt school life, family life, work life, and social life. If anxiety is becoming an issue, a trusted person, counsellor, or doctor should be consulted.

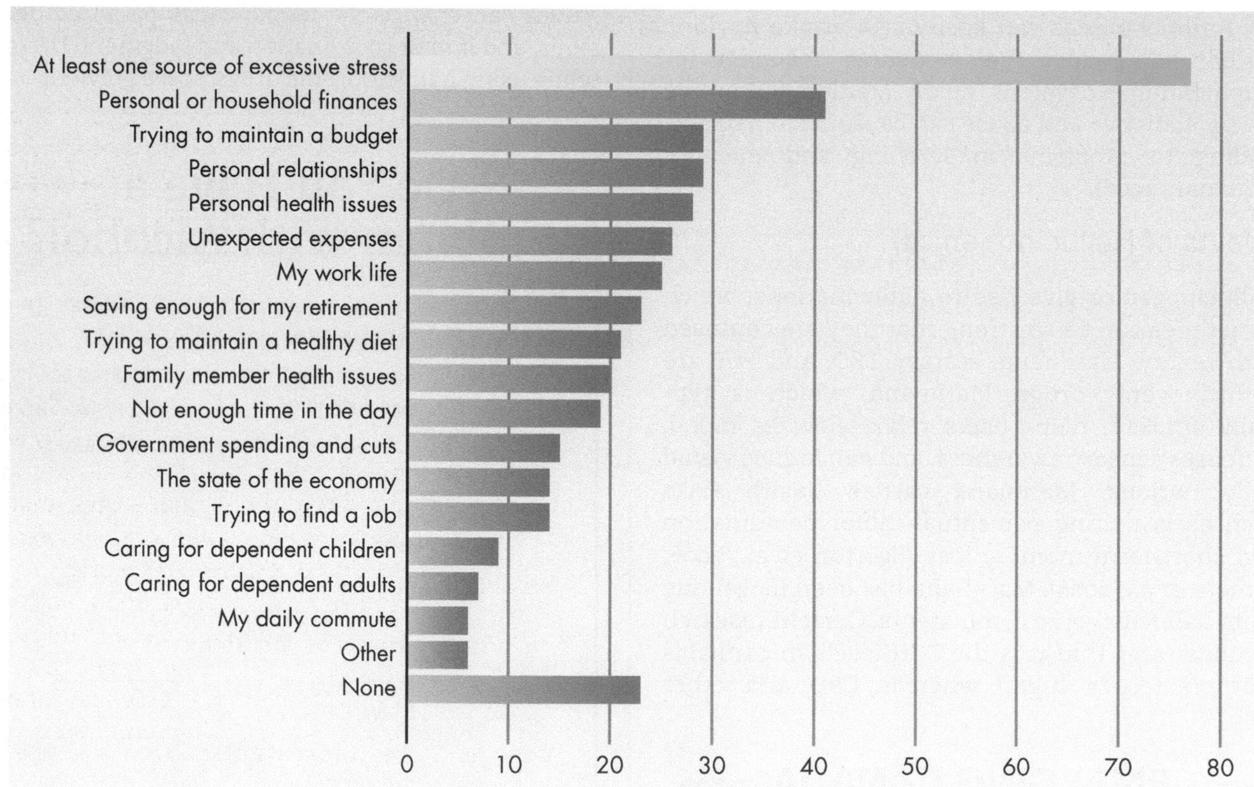

FIGURE 13.2

Sources of Excessive or Uncomfortable Stress

Source: *Sun Life Canadian Health Index 2013*, section 3, page 8; courtesy of Sun Life Assurance Company.

LO4 Sexuality

Sexual activity with a partner usually peaks in a person's 20s. Why does this age group have sex most frequently? The answer is a combination of youth and opportunity. Men and women in this age group are still experiencing the flood of sex hormones that affected them as adolescents. Now, however, they are of an age at which they are likely to be in sexual relationships.

Table 13.2 explores a global study that examined the number of reported sex partners in a lifetime. Clearly, Canadians, as a social group, are comfortable with their sexuality, especially when compared with populations from other countries. Canadians are known for their toques, maple syrup, and hockey, and for being polite and cautious. Apparently, we have been overlooked globally when it comes to our sexuality. Canadians have more sex partners in a lifetime than people in most other countries, and we are also more sexually adventurous, spending more time on foreplay and intercourse, according to a 2007–2008 "Durex Sexual Wellbeing Global Survey" (Lunau, 2009).

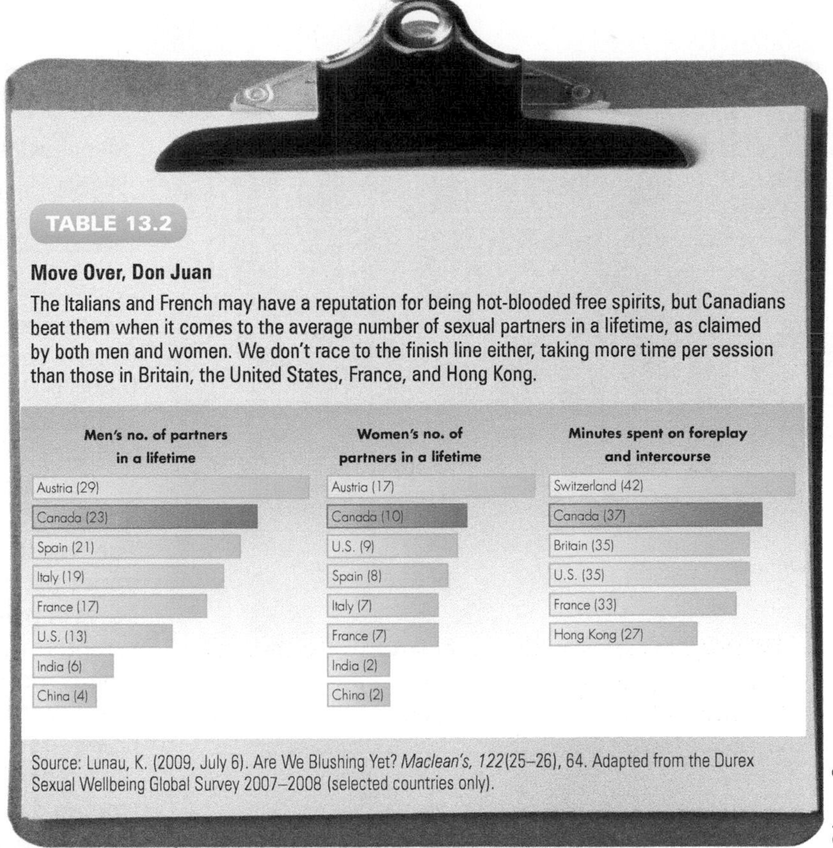

TABLE 13.2

Move Over, Don Juan

The Italians and French may have a reputation for being hot-blooded free spirits, but Canadians beat them when it comes to the average number of sexual partners in a lifetime, as claimed by both men and women. We don't race to the finish line either, taking more time per session than those in Britain, the United States, France, and Hong Kong.

Men's no. of partners in a lifetime	Women's no. of partners in a lifetime	Minutes spent on foreplay and intercourse
Austria (29)	Austria (17)	Switzerland (42)
Canada (23)	Canada (10)	Canada (37)
Spain (21)	U.S. (9)	Britain (35)
Italy (19)	Spain (8)	U.S. (35)
France (17)	Italy (7)	France (33)
U.S. (13)	France (7)	Hong Kong (27)
India (6)	India (2)	
China (4)	China (2)	

Source: Lunau, K. (2009, July 6). Are We Blushing Yet? *Maclean's, 122*(25–26), 64. Adapted from the Durex Sexual Wellbeing Global Survey 2007–2008 (selected countries only).

© Image Source

Sexual Orientation

Pride festivities are celebrated and supported in increasing numbers throughout Canadian towns and cities. The rainbow flag, which symbolizes the inclusion of all, is as diverse as the individuals who populate this community. Canadians have experienced a significant paradigm shift in promoting the diversity of sexuality among our citizens. Our legislation on marriage and adoption reflects social acceptance and inclusion of the Canadian LGBTQ community, but we still have significant social barriers to overcome. According to a Statistics Canada (2009a) survey, the number of LGBTQ who reported having experienced discrimination was three times higher than that of heterosexuals. Rampant homophobia is still a reality throughout the world.

The Orlando nightclub shootings in 2016 provided a shocking reminder of the lack of safety for many LGBTQ people.

On June 12, 2016, a gunman, with his own internalized issues of homophobia and religious fundamentalist beliefs, stormed into a gay nightclub in Orlando, Florida, and killed 49 people and injured 53. This atrocious act is a shocking reminder of the lack of safety for many LGBTQ people.

Red = Life
Orange = Healing
Yellow = Sun
Green = Nature
Royal Blue = Harmony
Violet = Spirit

The colours in the pride flag represent important components of the LGBTQ community. Pride flags are symbols of acceptance and "positive spaces."

nito/Shutterstock.com

DID YOU KNOW

Canadians have more sex partners in a lifetime than people in most other countries.

We are also more sexually adventurous, spending more time on foreplay and intercourse.

Al Diaz/Miami Herald/TNS via Getty Images

49 people were killed in a hate crime in Orlando on June 12, 2016.

DID YOU KNOW

Menstrual discomfort is normal.

Statistically speaking, some form of menstrual discomfort is a normal monthly experience.

Menstrual Problems

dysmenorrhea painful menstruation

prostaglandins hormones that cause muscles in the uterine wall to contract, as during labour

amenorrhea the absence of menstruation

premenstrual syndrome (PMS) the discomforting symptoms that affect many women during the 4- to 6-day interval preceding their periods

premenstrual dysphoric disorder (PMDD) a condition similar to but more severe than PMS

Many women experience at least some discomfort prior to or during menstruation, including dysmenorrhea, menstrual migraines, amenorrhea, premenstrual syndrome (PMS), and premenstrual dysphoric disorder (PMDD) (Sommerfeld, 2000). Dysmenorrhea is the most common menstrual problem, and pelvic cramps are the most common symptom. Cramps are most often brought about by high amounts of hormones called prostaglandins, which cause muscles in the uterine wall to contract, as during labour. In a recent study, 84% of women reported this pain during their periods, and 43% of women experience this pain every month (Grandi et al., 2012). Another symptom of dysmenorrhea is fluid retention in the pelvic region, which may cause bloating.

Amenorrhea is the absence of menstruation and a sign of infertility. Premenstrual syndrome (PMS) describes the combination of biological and psychological symptoms that may affect women during the 4- to 6-day interval that precedes their menses each month. Premenstrual dysphoric disorder (PMDD) is more severe than PMS. Before it can be diagnosed, the woman must have a collection of five or more symptoms, including panic attacks, mood swings, binge eating, low energy, a lack of interest in relationships, and difficulties sleeping and concentrating (A.D.A.M. Medical Encyclopedia, 2012).

Many women experience some degree of PMS. The most common premenstrual symptoms are minor psychological changes, muscular tension, and aches or pains. Only a small minority of women report symptoms severe enough to impair their social, academic, or occupational functioning. Women who suffer with endometriosis—misplaced endometrial lining—tend to have more severe PMS symptoms. This condition affects 10% of women, and half of all women dealing with infertility (American Society for Reproductive Medicine, 2012).

PMS may be caused by the body's responses to changing levels of sex hormones. PMS also appears to be linked to imbalances in neurotransmitters, such as serotonin and gamma-aminobutyric acid (GABA), which are related to the appetite, anxiety, and mood changes (Bäckström et al., 2003). Many treatment options are available for PMS: exercise, dietary control, hormone treatments, and medications that reduce anxiety or increase the activity of serotonin in the nervous system. Women experiencing unusual symptoms of PMS should consult their gynecologist.

Sexual Assault

It is difficult to accurately report statistics on sexual assaults that occur in Canada. According to the Canadian Centre for Justice Statistics, victimization data suggest that fewer than 1 in 10 incidents of sexual assault are reported to police. Further, 94% incidents of sexual touching go unreported, as do 78% of sexual attacks. Although victims may not report these crimes to the police, many do seek support from informal sources, such as friends (72%), family (41%), co-workers (33%), and doctors and nurses (13%). According to a general survey, most (93%) sexual assaults do not result in a physical injury to the victim. The Alberta Association of Sexual Assault Centres reports that 39% of Canadian women have experienced at least one incident of sexual assault since the age of 16 (Brennan & Taylor-Butts, 2008).

In 2015 CBC's popular radio host Jian Ghomeshi was fired after sexual assault allegations erupted. Ghomeshi's case brought forward many allegations from his colleagues and personal relationships spanning decades. In many of the cases, the intimate interactions were said to have turned violent with punching, hitting, slapping, and other forms of assault; Ghomeshi claimed these were consensual sex acts. The case fell on the heels of allegations against Bill Cosby, who was accused by 60 different women of drugging and sexually assaulting them. The first allegation went as far back as 50 years ago.

Both cases left many with a sense of shock and surprise. Cosby, once viewed as an idyllic father figure for the role he played as Heathcliffe on *The Cosby Show*, and Jian Ghomeshi, a seemingly sensitive, intelligent, and "perfect boyfriend" type. The one positive aspect that evolved from both high profile cases was bringing the issue of sexual violence back into the public discourse.

Types of Sexual Assault

Sexual assault includes any form of sexual activity without a person's consent, including kissing, touching, and intercourse. Stalking refers to being followed, receiving threatening or unwanted communications, and being spied on. Stalking acts often occur repeatedly and cause the persons being stalked to fear for their own safety.

Social Attitudes, Myths, and Cultural Factors That Encourage Sexual Assaults

Many people believe the myths about sexual assault: "Women say no when they mean yes," for example, and "The way women dress, they are just asking to have sex" (Maxwell, Robinson, & Post, 2003). Yet another myth is that deep down inside, women want to be overpowered and forced into sex by men. These myths have the effect of justifying sexual assault for both assailants and the public.

Walk a Mile in Her Shoes is an international event in which men, figuratively and literally, walk a mile in women's shoes to raise money and awareness to stop violence against women.

THE CANADIAN PRESS IMAGES/Graham Hughes

These college men are "walking a mile in her shoes" to raise awareness of sexual assault issues.

dating violence
assaults such as verbal threats, pushing, and slapping committed by an individual in an intimate relationship and often leading to injuries that require first aid

> **DID YOU KNOW**
>
> **The majority of sexual assaults are committed by someone the victim knows.**
>
> According to the Ontario Women's Directorate, 69% of women who are sexually assaulted know the person who assaults them. Only 1% of these women will report the assault to the police.

Males are also often reinforced from childhood for aggressive and competitive behaviour, as in sports. Gender typing may lead men to reject in themselves stereotypical "feminine" traits such as tenderness and empathy that might restrain aggression (Yost & Zurbriggen, 2006).

With high rates of sexual violence on college and university campuses, a better understanding of perpetrators' behaviours is important to stop sexual violence. Surveys estimate that 1 in 12 college men commit acts that are legally defined as rape. Of those men, 84% did not consider their actions to be illegal and 8.8% admitted to rape or attempting rape. In another survey, 21–35% of males indicated the possibility of raping if they wouldn't be caught (University of Michigan, n.d.).

Although no two sex offenders are the same, and there isn't a typical abuser profile, offenders do often make up a specific population, with contributing etiological factors (University of Michigan). For example, perpetrators on campus are often white men; most deny the experience of early childhood sexual abuse, and in places where there isn't the likelihood of punishment, sexual violence is higher. Sex offenders often explain away their behaviours, and minimize the violence and the number of people they have victimized (University of Michigan).

Dating Violence

Dating violence is a blanket term that often involves so-called "common assaults," such as verbal threats, pushing, and slapping committed by an individual in

sexual harassment deliberate or repeated unwanted comments, gestures, or physical contact

an intimate relationship and often leading to injuries that require first aid. Statistics Canada reports that this type of violence is on the rise in Canada in different types of relationships, including boyfriends and girlfriends, exes, and various other intimate relationships. The victim can be male or female. In 2010, the number of victims had doubled since 2004. Women in their late 20s and early 30s are at most risk, and statistics for men seem to peak at 35 to 44. The increase seems to have resulted from a complicated set of factors, including a confused notion of acceptable behaviour in a dating situation and the activities considered to be acts of violence. Also contributing to the issue are aggressive dating partners, an increase in harassment on social media, and the acceptance of forceful sex. Open dialogue about healthy and unhealthy relationships and behaviours is an important first step in reversing this unfortunate social trend (Bielski, 2012).

Sexual Harassment

For legal purposes, sexual harassment in the workplace is usually defined as deliberate or repeated unwanted comments, gestures, or physical contact. Sexual harassment makes the workplace or any

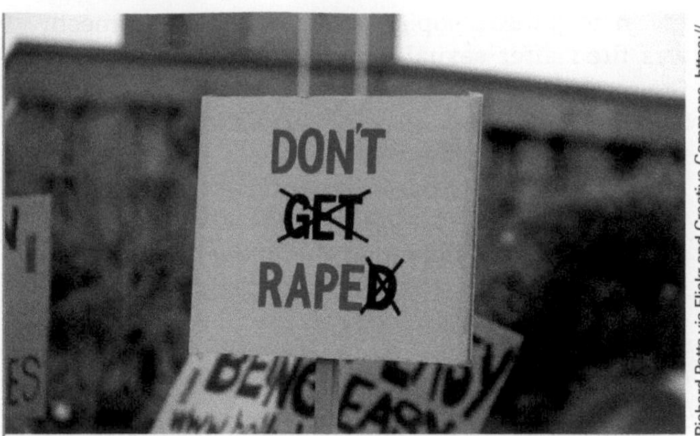

Richard Potts via Flickr and Creative Commons, https://www.flickr.com/photos/cascade_of_rant/5827890190/

other setting a hostile place. Examples range from unwelcome sexual jokes, suggestive comments, verbal abuse, leering at or ogling a person's body, unwelcome physical contact, outright sexual assault, or demands for sex accompanied by threats concerning one's job or student status.

Charges of sexual harassment are often ignored or trivialized by co-workers and employers. The victim may hear, "Why make a big deal out of it? It's not like you were attacked in the street." Yet evidence shows that people who are sexually harassed suffer from the experience. Some become physically ill (Rospenda et al., 2005). Some find harassment on the job so unbearable

What Is Consensual Sex?

RAINN (Rape, Abuse & Incest National Network) is an anti–sexual violence organization that provides clarity about what sexual consent is, how it works, and what it isn't.

What is consent?

Consent is an agreement between participants to engage in sexual activity. There are many ways to give consent, and some of those are discussed below. Consent doesn't have to be verbal, but verbally agreeing to different sexual activities can help both you and your partner respect each other's boundaries.

How does consent work in real life?

When you're engaging in sexual activity, *consent is about communication*. And it should happen every time. Giving consent for one activity, one time, does not mean giving consent for increased or recurring sexual contact. For example, agreeing to kiss someone doesn't give that person permission to remove your clothes. Having sex with someone in the past doesn't give that person permission to have sex with you again in the future. Agreeing to sex, doesn't mean agreeing to all types of sex (i.e. choking, slapping etc.).

You can change your mind at any time.

You can withdraw consent at any point if you feel uncomfortable. It's important to clearly communicate to your partner that you are no longer comfortable with this activity and wish to stop. The best way to ensure both parties are comfortable with any sexual activity is to talk about it, ideally ahead of time.

Positive consent can look like this:

- Communicating when you change the type or degree of sexual activity with phrases like "Is this OK?"
- Explicitly agreeing to certain activities, either by saying "yes" or another affirmative statement, like "I'm open to trying."
- Using physical cues to let the other person know you're comfortable taking things to the next level.

It does NOT look like this:

- Refusing to acknowledge "no"
- Assuming that wearing certain clothes, flirting, or kissing is an invitation for anything more
- Having sexual contact with someone under the legal age of consent, as defined by the government
- Having sexual contact with someone incapacitated because of drugs or alcohol
- Pressuring someone into sexual activity by using fear or intimidation
- Assuming you have permission to engage in a sexual act because you've done it in the past

Source: Courtesy of RAINN (Rape, Abuse & Incest National Network), https://www.rainn.org/articles/what-is-consent

that they resign (Sims, Drasgow, & Fitzgerald, 2005). College students have dropped courses and switched programs to avoid it (Stratton et al., 2005).

One reason that sexual harassment is so stressful is that blame tends to fall on the victim. Some harassers argue that charges of harassment against them were exaggerated. Harassed individuals are demonized if they assert themselves, but remain victimized if they don't (Witkowska & Gådin, 2005).

Sexual harassment has more to do with the abuse of power than sexual desire (Finkelman, 2005). The Canadian justice system recognizes sexual harassment as a form of sex discrimination and holds employers accountable if harassment creates a hostile or abusive work environment.

LO5 Cognitive Development

As with physical development, people are at the height of their cognitive powers during early adulthood. Some aspects of cognitive development, such as memory, show a general decline as people age, yet people typically retain their verbal skills and may even show improvement in vocabulary and general knowledge (Fair, 2007). Performance tends to decline on tasks that require reasoning or problem-solving speed and visual–spatial skills, such as piecing puzzles together.

Consider the difference between crystallized intelligence and fluid intelligence. Crystallized intelligence represents one's lifetime of intellectual attainments and generally increases with age. Fluid intelligence, defined by mental flexibility—the ability to process information rapidly—is more susceptible to the effects of aging (Lachman, 2004).

In terms of brain development, most verbal and quantitative capacities may have developed by late adolescence and early adulthood. However, adolescence carries with it a certain egocentrism that can impair judgment, problem solving, and other areas of cognition. Certain experiences of early adulthood can lead to further cognitive developments, but these experiences are not universal, and many people become set in their cognitive ways long before the arrival of early adulthood.

A New Way of Thinking

Young adults may wonder why their beliefs differ from others' and may seek to justify or revise their thinking and their conclusions. College students' views on what they know and how they get to know what they know become more complex as they are exposed to the complexities of postsecondary thinking (King & Kitchener, 2004; Magolda, 2004). Cognitive development in postsecondary schooling not only rests on exposure to new ideas but also is fostered by being challenged by students from different backgrounds and by instructors whose views differ from those of students (Moshman, 2005).

Students often enter their postsecondary years assuming there are right and wrong answers and that the world can be divided easily into black versus white, good versus bad, and us versus them. This type of thinking is termed dualistic thinking. After a while, in a multicultural society or on a school campus, students may realize that judgments of good or bad are often rooted in a certain belief system, such as a religion or a cultural background, so that such judgments actually represent relativistic thinking rather than absolute judgments (Vukman, 2005).

Numerous studies show that college and university life encourages cognitive development through broadened experiences.

crystallized intelligence one's intellectual attainments, as shown, for example, by vocabulary and accumulated knowledge

fluid intelligence mental flexibility; the ability to process information rapidly

dualistic thinking dividing the cognitive world into opposites, such as good and bad, or us versus them

relativistic thinking recognition that judgments are often not absolute but are made from a certain belief system or cultural background

pragmatic thought decision making characterized by willingness to accept reality and compromise

cognitive–affective complexity a mature form of thinking that permits people to harbour positive and negative feelings at the same time about their career choices and other matters

Labouvie-Vief's Theory of Pragmatic Thought

Gisella Labouvie-Vief's (2006) theory of pragmatic thought notes that adults must typically narrow possibilities into choices, whether these are choices about careers, school, or life partners. The "cognitively healthy" adult is more willing than the egocentric adolescent to compromise and cope within the world as it is, rather than the world as she or he would like it to be. To deal with the real world, adults need to be able to accept living with mixed feelings about their goals. As people mature, Labouvie-Vief found that they tend to develop a cognitive–affective complexity that enables them to harbour both positive and negative feelings about their career choices ("I may never get rich, but when I wake up in the morning, I'll look forward to what I'm doing that day") and their partners ("Okay, he may not be a hunk, but he's stable and he is kind"). Adults function best when they accept reality but choose goals that allow them to experience positive feelings (Labouvie-Vief & González, 2004).

Postformal Thinking

Most developmentalists agree that the cognitive processes of young adults are in many ways more advanced than the cognitive processes of adolescents (Commons, 2004; Gurba, 2005). Young adults maintain most of the benefits of their general secondary educations, and some may have gathered specialized knowledge and skills through opportunities in higher education. Many have also gained knowledge and expertise in the career world.

The thinking of young adults tends to be less egocentric than that of adolescents.

Education

In 2012 the number of students enrolled in postsecondary education increased by 1% over the year before, and the number of those who received a certificate, diploma, or degree increased by 3% from the previous year (Statistics Canada, 2014c).Not everyone who attempts postsecondary education completes it, but clearly college and university education has value for Canadians.

The Diverse Culture of Postsecondary Education

Diversity speaks to the differences we find between groups of people—ethnic and cultural diversity (race, religion, country of origin, language), diversity by socio-economic level, gender, age, and sexual orientation. Many students are exposed to more kinds of people on campus than before they began college or university. They meet people from other backgrounds, places, and walks of life—among them, their instructors.

The following ideas suggest how students can benefit from diversity on their campus to achieve cognitive growth (Association of American Colleges & Universities, 2007):

- Recognize that your way of looking at the world is not universal.
- Embrace opportunities for encountering people who are different.
- Recognize that your initial reaction to cultural difference may be defensive.

LO6 Career Development

The first reason people work is obvious: money. Despite folk wisdom, money does not always buy happiness. Many million-dollar lottery winners who quit their jobs encounter feelings of aimlessness and dissatisfaction afterward (Corliss, 2003). Moreover, within a year of cashing their cheques, lottery winners

THE CANADIAN PRESS/Ian Jackson

"Work is the refuge of people who have nothing better to do."
—Oscar Wilde

generally report happiness (or unhappiness) levels corresponding to their pre-winning levels (Corliss, 2003).

Work offers many rewards: earning a living, fringe benefits, and ensuring future security all inspire people to pursue careers and employment. These external benefits of working are called *extrinsic motives*; however, extrinsic motives alone do not explain why people work.

Many people seek more in life than extrinsic rewards such as a paycheque and financial security. They also want intrinsic rewards, such as engaging in challenging activities, broadening their social contacts, and filling their days with meaningful activity. Work can offer opportunities to engage in stimulating and satisfying activities and to develop one's talents. Employment generates a sense of opportunity and sends the message that the individual is participating in society (Public Health Agency of Canada, 2011).

Intrinsic reasons for working include the following (Duffy & Sedlacek, 2007):

- *The work ethic.* This suggests that we are morally obligated to avoid idleness.
- *Self-identity.* Our occupational identity can become intertwined with our self-identity.
- *Self-fulfillment.* We often express our personal needs and interests through our work.
- *Self-worth.* Recognition and respect for a job well done contribute to self-esteem.
- *Socialization.* The workplace extends our social contacts.
- *Public roles.* Work roles help define our functions in the community.

DID YOU KNOW?

Million-dollar lottery winners often feel aimless and dissatisfied if they quit their jobs after striking it rich.

But wouldn't it be nice to be in a position to conduct this research firsthand!

Stages of Career Development

Employment differs from a career. Careers are chosen paths that can potentially frame a lifetime of satisfaction and growth. Erikson argues that a career is one of the measures of personal lifespan satisfaction. For most of us, career development has numerous stages. Our discussion in this box is informed by psychologist Donald Super's theory of career development, but we have made some changes to reflect contemporary realities.

The first or *fantasy stage* involves the child's unrealistic conception of self-potential and of the world of work, which dominates from early childhood until about age 11. Young children focus on glamour professions, such as acting, medicine, sports, and law enforcement (Auger, Blackhurst, & Wahl, 2005). They show little regard for the fit between these occupations and their abilities. During the second or *tentative choice stage*, from about age 11 through high school, children base their choices on their interests, abilities, and limitations, as well as glamour.

Beyond age 17 or so, in the *realistic choice stage*, choices become narrowed as students weigh job requirements and rewards against their own interests, abilities, and values (Nauta, 2007). They may direct their educational plans to ensure they obtain the knowledge and skills they need to enter their intended occupation. Some follow the paths of role models such as parents or respected members of the community (Auger et al., 2005). Many "fall into" careers not because of particular skills and interests, but because of what is available at the time, family pressures, or the lure of high income or a certain lifestyle. Others may "job hop" through several different career paths before finally finding one that fits well.

During the *maintenance stage*, young adults begin "settling" into their career role, which often happens by their late 30s. Although they may change positions within a company or within a career, as in moving from marketing to management, they often have a sense of their career continuing to develop, a feeling of forward motion. Of course, during this stage, people can also feel "trapped" in dead-end jobs (Savickas, 2005).

Vocational interests tend to be stable over the life course (Rottinghaus et al., 2007). Although people may switch jobs, they generally seek employment that reflects their stable interests.

EMERGING CANADA

For young adults, employment is key to their financial and personal independence. Among young adults, 76% are employed. Of this group, 80% are employed in full-time jobs in contrast to only 30% of 15- to 19-year-olds who hold full-time employment. After postsecondary school is completed, young adults actively seek full-time employment. By the age of 26 to 28, only 15% of young adults are still attending school, and nearly 70% are working full-time. Unemployment was a reality for 7% of young adults in 2008. Those with fewer years of formal education experience statistically higher unemployment rates (Public Health Agency of Canada, 2011).

Developmental Tasks in Beginning a Career

One of the challenges of early adulthood is becoming established in the career world. Different careers hold different challenges, but many challenges are common, such as the following: (Bozionelos & Wang, 2006; Quigley & Tymon, 2006):

- Learning to carry out the job tasks
- Accepting your subordinate status within the organization or profession
- Learning to get along with your co-workers and supervisor
- Showing that you can maintain the job, make improvements, and show progress
- Finding a sponsor or mentor to "show you the ropes"
- Defining the boundaries between the job and other areas of life. Not taking home your troubles on the job
- Evaluating your occupational choice in the light of measurable outcomes of your work
- Learning to cope with daily hassles on the job, frustrations, successes, and failures

STUDY TOOLS

CHAPTER 13

Located at **nelson.com/student**

- ☐ Prepare for tests with a variety of exercises and activities
- ☐ Review Key Terms Flashcards (online or print)
- ☐ Create your own study tools with Build a Summary
- ☐ Watch Observing Development videos to expand your knowledge

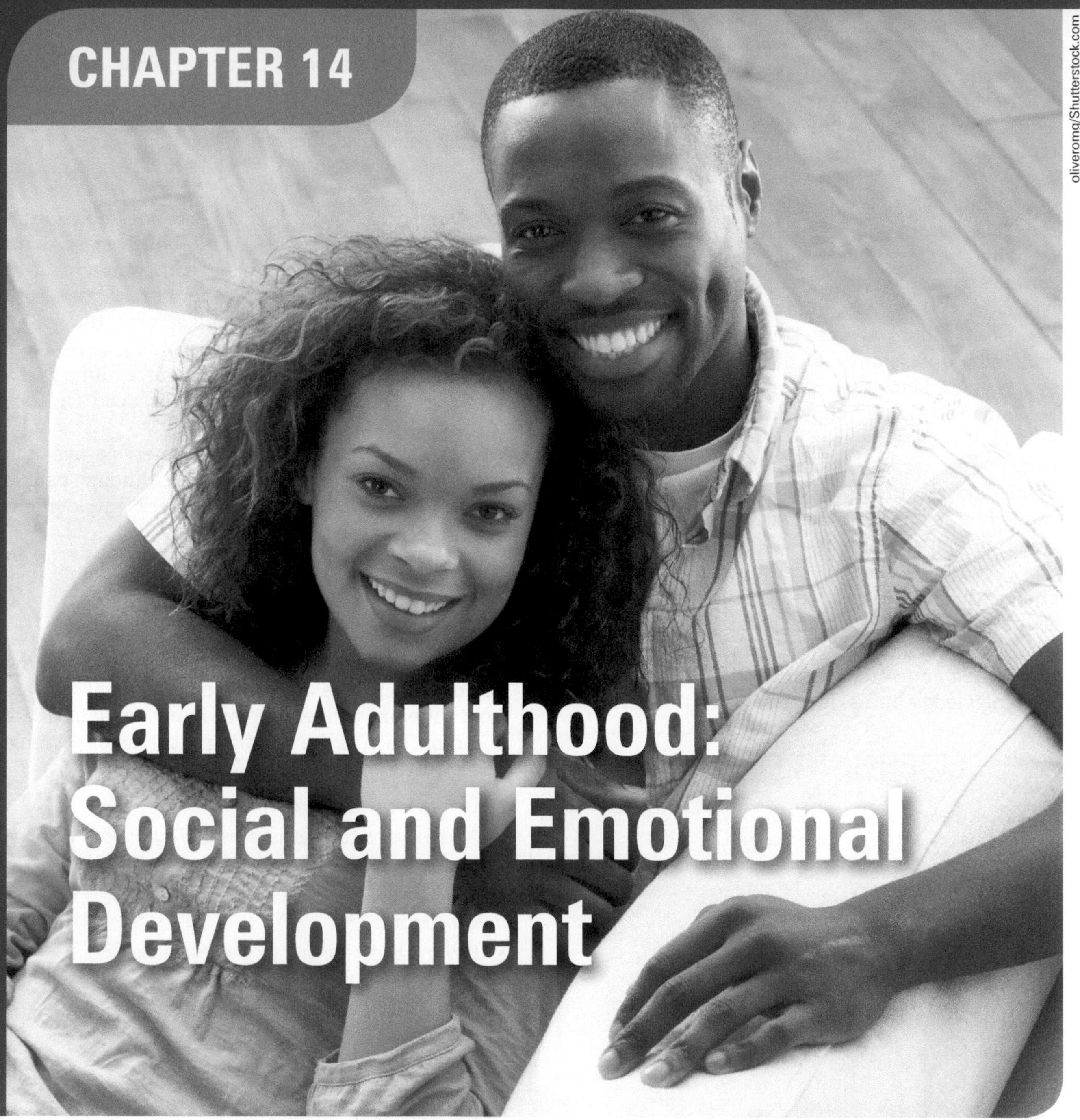

oliveromg/Shutterstock.com

Early Adulthood: Social and Emotional Development

LEARNING OUTCOMES

LO1 Examine the issues involved in early adulthood separation

LO2 Describe the conflict between intimacy and isolation

LO3 Discuss the stage of life for entry into adulthood

LO4 Examine the emotional forces of attraction and love

LO5 Explain why people get lonely and what they do in response

LO6 Discuss the lifestyle of being single

LO7 Describe the practice of living together

LO8 Describe the practice of marriage

LO9 Discuss the state of parenthood

LO10 Discuss divorce and its repercussions

> **"Erik Erikson saw the establishment of intimate relationships as the key "crisis," or challenge, of early adulthood."**

Early adulthood generally covers the two decades from ages 20 to 40, although some theorists suggest this stage begins at age 17 or 18, when the teen goes off to college or university, or enters the workforce. Others believe that since Canadians are living longer, middle age doesn't really start at 40 anymore. The traditional view of development in early adulthood was laid down by developmental psychologist Robert Havighurst (1972) more than 40 years ago. He believed that each stage of development involved accomplishing certain "tasks," and the tasks he describes for early adulthood include the following:

- ✓ 1. Getting started in an occupation
- ✓ 2. Selecting a life partner
- ✓ 3. Learning to live contentedly with one's partner
- ✓ 4. Starting a family and becoming a parent
- ✓ 5. Assuming the responsibilities of managing a home
- ✓ 6. Assuming social responsibilities

Many young adults will laugh at this list of tasks. Others will think that it doesn't sound too bad at all. Does this list remain valid, or does it need to be adjusted for the realities of today's life?

Erikson Today

Time & Life Pictures/Getty Images

Stage 6: Intimacy vs. Isolation (19 to 39)

Psychosocial Theory: If a clear sense of self has been established, the individual will begin to look outward to find companionship and love. The more solidly the earlier foundations of personality development have been constructed, the easier this transition will be. Young adults seek deep intimacy and satisfying relationships. Individuals who are unsuccessful in this challenge will begin to isolate themselves from lasting unions.

For example, many young adults (and older adults) remain single. Some may choose stable and long-term relationships but not the traditional label of marriage to formalize these relationships. Some couples choose not to have children, and others may discover they are infertile. This list is also rather heteronormative—it assumes the belief that heterosexuality and heterosexual relationships between a biological man and woman is what is "natural" or "normal." Havighurst did not list *separation* from one's family of origin, which seems to define today's Canadian reality.

Consider THIS

Are the "boomerang kids" creating a new stage in lifespan development?

Please see page 242 for a discussion on this topic.

LO1 Separation

Young adults leave home at different ages and for different reasons, and some never had a traditional home life to begin with (Minkler & Fuller-Thomson, 2005).

Young adults who enter the job market out of high school, or without completing high school, may live at home for a while to save up some money before venturing out on their own. When they do, they may move in with roommates or into affordable housing. If they are able to, parents may contribute toward their children's next steps.

Other young adults may leave home to go to college or university, or to find work. If the college and university students are attending is local, they may stay at home or move in with roommates. When young adults attend school away from home, a room may be kept for them at home.

If young adults are working within commuting distance of their homes of origin, even after graduating, they may choose to return home to live for

Consider THIS

Are the "boomerang kids" creating a new stage in lifespan development?

The baby boomers have raised their children, and many of these children are leaving home only to return, earning them the title "boomerang kids." The "empty nest" isn't so empty anymore. The 2011 Canadian census report shows that 42.3% of young adults aged 20–29 are living with their parents, compared with 26.9% of adult children in 1981. One of the reasons given by returning adult children is financial difficulties, particularly in light of higher unemployment, student loans to repay, and higher costs of living. Living on their own isn't financially manageable for many young adults. Some young adult children return home because they may need to regroup after a relationship breakup or the loss of a job (Rennie, 2012).

This boomerang group can be divided into two separate age groupings. Young adults in their late 20s don't tend to linger at home very long; they stay just long enough to get back on their feet. The Canadian census reports that only 25.2% of young adults living at home are in the 25–29 age category. More striking is the 59.3% of young adults between the ages of 20 and 24 still living at home with their parents. Their staying at home is likely due partly to the social acceptability of living with parents when you are older (Rennie, 2012).

individuation the young adult's process of becoming an individual by means of integrating his or her own values and beliefs with those of his or her parents and society at large

financial reasons. Entry-level jobs often do not pay well, or the young adult may want to try to save enough for a down payment on an apartment or a house. Some young adult couples move in with a set of parents.

Canadian youth are living at home longer than ever before, delaying financial responsibility and independence. Should we be considering a new stage of development to distinguish adolescents, early adulthood, and the cohort that takes a little bit longer to leave the security of their parents' home?

Failure to launch syndrome is increasingly an issue for twenty-somethings and their parents. It refers to smart, creative, and intelligent young adults who aren't able to "get off the couch," out of the basement; they don't seem able to find a job, have friends, or invest in a relationship. In other words, they're "going nowhere fast" (Wellbeing Institution, 2010). But this situation may not just be about nature versus nurture. If a young adult is exhibiting many of the above listed behaviours as well as feelings of hopelessness, worthlessness, or despair, they may be dealing with other mental health issues like depression or substance abuse.

Separation–Individuation

Whether young adults leave the nest or not, they need to separate from their parents psychologically. Psychologists and educators refer to the relevant processes as separation and individuation—that is, becoming an individual by means of integrating his or her own values and beliefs with those of parents and society.

Most men in our society consider separation and individuation to be key goals of personality development in early adulthood (Blazina et al., 2007). But many psychologists argue that the priorities are different for women, who see the primary importance to be the establishment and maintenance of social relationships (Gilligan, 1990; Jordan et al., 1991). Nevertheless, women need to become their own persons in the sense of separating from their mothers (Brockman, 2003). Males are more likely to show a struggle or a fight for independence (Levpušcek, 2006).

The transition to college, university, or to the workplace can play roles in separation and individuation. Employment and financial independence can reduce feelings of connectedness with parents, whereas college or university can maintain these feelings (Buhl, Wittmann, & Noack, 2003). Feelings of connectedness are related to the amount of financial and emotional support students receive from parents (Tanner, 2006).

LO2 Intimacy versus Isolation

Erikson (1963) saw the establishment of intimate relationships as the key "crisis" of early adulthood (**intimacy versus isolation**). Young adults who have evolved a firm sense of identity during adolescence are now ready to separate from their families of origin and "fuse" their identities with those of other people through a committed relationship and abiding friendships. Erikson warned that we might not be able to commit ourselves to others until we have achieved ego identity, or established stable life roles. Lack of identity is related to the high divorce rate in young marriages. On the other hand, Erikson argued that young adults who do not reach out to develop intimate relationships risk retreating into isolation and loneliness.

Erikson, like Havighurst, has been criticized for suggesting that young adults who choose to remain celibate or single are not developing normally (Hayslip et al., 2006). Today's psychologists argue that intimacy can be achieved in a variety of different relationship situations. Like Havighurst, Erikson appeared to make similar conventional demands of people in middle and late adulthood.

intimacy versus isolation according to Erik Erikson, the central conflict or life crisis of early adulthood, in which a person develops an intimate relationship with a significant other or risks heading down a path toward social isolation

the dream according to Daniel Levinson and his colleagues, the drive to become someone, to leave one's mark on history, which serves as a tentative blueprint for the young adult

LO3 Seasons of Life

On the basis of their in-depth interviews of adult men and women, Yale psychologist Daniel Levinson and his colleagues (Levinson, 1996; Levinson, Darrow, & Klein,1978) formulated a theory of adult development in which people shape their lives according to the goals they consider to be most important. Levinson considers the ages of 17 to 33 to be the entry phase of adulthood for young men—when they leave their parents' home, enter college or university, or the job market, and become emotionally and financially independent. Many young adults also adopt what Levinson calls "**the dream**"—the drive to become someone, to leave their mark on history—which serves as a tentative blueprint for life. Levinson (1996) found that women undergo similar developments, but experience more the social constraints of sexism, both from their families of origin and society in general. Thus women may take longer to leave home

and may feel more pressure to go from one home (their parents') to another (their partner's).

Levinson labelled the ages of 28 to 33 the *age-30 transition*. He found that the late 20s and early 30s are commonly characterized by reassessment: "Where is my life going?" and "Why am I doing this?"

Levinson and his colleagues also found that the later 30s were often characterized by settling down or planting roots. At this time, many people felt a need to make a financial and emotional investment in their home. Their concerns became focused on promotion or tenure, career advancement, mortgages, and, in many or most cases, raising their own families.

Today, Levinson's views seem rather archaic, at least when they are applied to young women (Hayslip et al., 2006). It is now acceptable and widespread for women to lead independent, single lives, for as long as they wish. The great majority of career women and many LGBTQ people in Canadian cities simply would not care what anyone thinks about their marital status or living arrangements. And given the mobility young adults have in Canada today, many will not live in places where people frown upon their lifestyles.

Vince Bucci/Getty Images

Power couples in Hollywood are often identified as "the pretty people."

LO4 Attraction and Love

Young adults separate from their families of origin and (often, not always) join with others. In developed nations, they are free to choose the people with whom they will associate and develop friendships and romantic relationships. The emotional forces that fuel these associations are *attraction* and *love*.

Attraction

Investigators define feelings of attraction as psychological forces that draw people together. Some researchers find that physical appearance is the key factor in consideration of partners for dates, sex, and long-term relationships (Wilson, Tripp, & Boland, 2005). We might like to claim that sensitivity, warmth, and intelligence are more important to us, but we may never learn about other people's personalities if they do not meet our minimal standards for attractiveness (Langlois et al., 2000; Strassberg & Holty, 2003).

Is Beauty in the Eye of the Beholder?

Are our standards of beauty subjective, or do we have broad agreement on what is attractive?

Currently in mainstream Canadian society "thin is in," especially for females (Furnham, Petrides, & Constantinides, 2005; Wilson et al., 2005). Most men in our society are attracted to women with ample bustlines (Hill, Donovan, & Kohama, 2005); and larger "booties" are currently trending.

Nonphysical Traits Affect Perceptions of Physical Beauty

Nonphysical traits also affect our perceptions. For example, the attractiveness of a partner is likely to be enhanced by traits such as familiarity, liking, respect, and sharing of values and goals (Kniffin & Wilson, 2004). People also rate the attractiveness of faces higher when they are smiling than when they are not smiling (O'Doherty et al., 2003).

DID YOU KNOW?

People are considered to be more attractive when they are smiling.

Studies suggest that smiling increases bonding, cooperation, and trust.

Sex Differences in Perceptions of Attractiveness

According to Geoff Kishnick, a University of Washington anthropologist, culture plays a significant role in deciding what makes a mate attractive. Universal features of physical attractiveness are typically thought to have been hard-wired into the brain tens of thousands of years ago. But Kishnick studied foot size to disprove this concept. He argues that the cultural transmission of attractiveness allows humans to adapt to local environments. For example, in the past, many cultures have viewed small feet as being attractive. Rural cultures, however, seem to value larger feet because these women can work better in the fields. Urban women seemed to be highly valued for their small feet, where field work was not a factor (News-Medical.Net, 2013).

Are Preferences Concerning Attractiveness Inborn?

Evolutionary psychology believes that evolutionary forces favour the continuation of sex differences in preferences for mates because certain preferred traits provide reproductive advantages (Buss, 2005). Some physical features are universally appealing to both females and males, such as cleanliness, good complexion, clear eyes, good teeth, good hair, firm muscle tone, and a steady gait (Buss, 2005). Age and health may be relatively more important to a woman's appeal because these characteristics tend to be associated with her reproductive capacity: that is, the "biological clock." Physical characteristics associated with a woman's youthfulness, such as smooth skin, firm muscle tone, and lustrous hair, may thus have become more closely linked to a woman's appeal (Buss, 2005), and may be socio-culturally influenced as well. A man's reproductive value, however, may depend more on how well he can provide for his family than on his age or physical appeal. The value of men as reproducers, therefore, is more intertwined with factors that contribute to a stable environment for child rearing—such as economic status and reliability. Again, behavioural traits and societal influences are also factors. Evolutionary psychologists argue that these sex differences in mate preferences may have been passed down through the generations as part of our genetic heritage (Buss, 2005).

Human behaviour cannot be defined simply genetically, however; it is also important to understand how psychological and socio-cultural mechanisms distinguish behaviour (Buss, Schmitt 2011). Evolutionary psychology has created a great deal of discourse in academic spheres with regards to the nature versus nurture debate. Evolutionary psychology, suggest Buss and Schmitt, can support feminist mandates to address various social concerns (2011). Social and cultural inputs are very important in scientific inquiry into human behaviours, which are enormously flexible due to psychological adaptations (Buss & Schmitt, 2011).

The following short list of rules of attraction has emerged over years of study (Carey, 2006):

1. **Symmetry:** Good symmetry can be a cue that the individual can deliver healthy offspring.
2. **Hips:** Body shape is also important. Anthropologists suggest this cue indicates good potential to deliver offspring.
3. **Facial structure:** Estrogen shapes the female face so that small and sharp features are attractive. Men's faces are shaped by testosterone so a larger face and jaw indicate attractiveness.
4. **Smell:** Pheromones are chemical signals that can communicate reproductive quality.

Anthropologists may argue that, even though the rules of attraction may unconsciously drive our initial mate contact, behaviour also plays a role. But we first need to be attracted to someone before a relationship will be considered.

Are People with Physical Disabilities Seen to Be Equally Attractive to People Without?

Using the *Romantic Attraction Scale*, a study with 41 college students was conducted to assess attitudes toward people with physical disabilities. Students were equally attracted to those with physical disabilities. But explicit attraction was biased toward people without physical disabilities. Social attitudes factor into explicit attraction of people who do not have physical disabilities toward those that do (Rojahn, Komelasky, & Man, 2008).

DID YOU KNOW?

Opposites DO NOT attract.

People who are similar are usually more likely to be attracted to one another.

attraction–similarity hypothesis the view that we tend to develop romantic relationships with people who are similar to ourselves in physical attractiveness and other traits

reciprocity the tendency to respond in kind when we feel admired and complimented

romantic love a form of love fuelled by passion and feelings of intimacy

The Attraction–Similarity Hypothesis: Do "Opposites Attract" or "Do Birds of a Feather Flock Together"?

Do not despair if you are less than magnificent in appearance, along with most of us mere mortals. You may be saved from permanently blending in with the wallpaper by the effects of the attraction–similarity hypothesis. This hypothesis holds that people tend to develop romantic relationships with people who are similar to themselves in attractiveness and other traits (Klohnen & Luo, 2003; Morry & Gaines, 2005). According to Canadian psychologist Philipe Rushton, similar genes influence our choice of both friends and mate selection (Rushton & Bons, 2005). Look around and do some informal research of your own. What do you see?

Attraction can lead to feelings of love.

Researchers have found that people who are involved in committed relationships are not only genetically similar but are also likely to be similar to their partners in their attitudes and cultural attributes (Amodio & Showers, 2005). Our partners tend to be like us in race and ethnicity, age, level of education, and religion.

Reciprocity: If You Like Me, You Must Have Excellent Judgment

Has anyone told you that you are good-looking, brilliant, and emotionally mature to boot? That your taste is excellent? Ah, what amazing judgment! When we feel admired and complimented, we tend to return these feelings and behaviours. This tendency is called reciprocity. Reciprocity is another potent determinant of attraction (Levine, 2000; Sprecher, 1998). Perhaps the power of reciprocity has enabled many couples to become happy with one another and reasonably well adjusted. Reciprocity may take the form of shared responsibilities, mutual respect, and equal generosity.

Love

The experience of romantic love, as opposed to attachment or sexual arousal, occurs within a cultural context in which the concept is idealized (Berscheid, 2003, 2006). Western culture has a long tradition of idealizing the concept of romantic love, as represented, for instance, by romantic fairy tales that have been passed down through the generations. In fact, our exposure to the concept of romantic love may begin with hearing those fairy tales; later perhaps, it continues to blossom through exposure to romantic novels, television and films, and the tales of friends and relatives.

Researchers have found that love is a complex concept, involving many areas of experience (Berscheid, 2003, 2006). Let us consider two psychological perspectives on love, both of which involve emotional arousal.

Love as Appraisal of Arousal

Social psychologists Ellen Berscheid and Elaine Hatfield (Berscheid, 2003, 2006; Hatfield & Rapson, 2002) define romantic love in terms of a state of intense physiological arousal and the cognitive appraisal of that arousal as love. The arousal may be experienced as a pounding heart, sweaty palms, and butterflies in the stomach when a person is in the presence of, or thinking about, his or her love interest. Cognitive appraisal of the arousal means attributing it to some cause, such as fear or love. According to Berscheid and

Prince Charming or just another frog?

Hatfield, then the perception that a person has fallen in love is thus derived from three elements: (1) a state of intense arousal in relation to an appropriate love object (that is, a person, not an event like a rock concert), (2) a cultural setting that idealizes romantic love, and (3) the attribution of the arousal to feelings of love toward another person.

Sternberg's Triangular Theory of Love

Robert Sternberg's (2006a) "triangular theory" of love includes three building blocks, or components, of loving experiences:

1. **Intimacy:** The experience of warmth toward another person that arises from feelings of closeness and connectedness, and the desire to share one's inmost thoughts
2. **Passion:** Intense romantic or sexual desire, accompanied by physiological arousal
3. **Commitment:** Commitment to maintain the relationship through good times and bad

In Sternberg's model, the three components of love can be conceptualized in terms of a triangle in which each vertex represents one of the building blocks (see Figure 14.1). In Sternberg's model, couples are well matched if they possess corresponding levels of passion, intimacy, and commitment (Drigotas, Rusbult, & Verette, 1999; Sternberg, 2006a). According to the model, various combinations of the building blocks of love characterize different types of love relationships. For example, infatuation (passionate love) is typified by sexual desire but not by intimacy and commitment.

intimacy
the experience of warmth toward another person that arises from feelings of closeness and connectedness

passion
intense sexual desire for another person

commitment
the decision to devote oneself to a cause or another person

"Being in love" can refer to states of passion or infatuation, whereas friendship is usually based on shared interests, liking, and respect. Friendship and passionate love do not necessarily overlap. However, nothing prevents people in love from becoming good friends—perhaps even the best of friends, and vice versa. Sternberg's model recognizes that the intimacy we find in true friendships and the passion we find in love are blended in two forms of love—romantic love and consummate love. These love types differ, however, along the dimension of commitment.

Romantic love comprises both passion and intimacy but lacks commitment. Romantic love may burn brightly and then flicker out. Or it may develop into a more complete love, called consummate love,

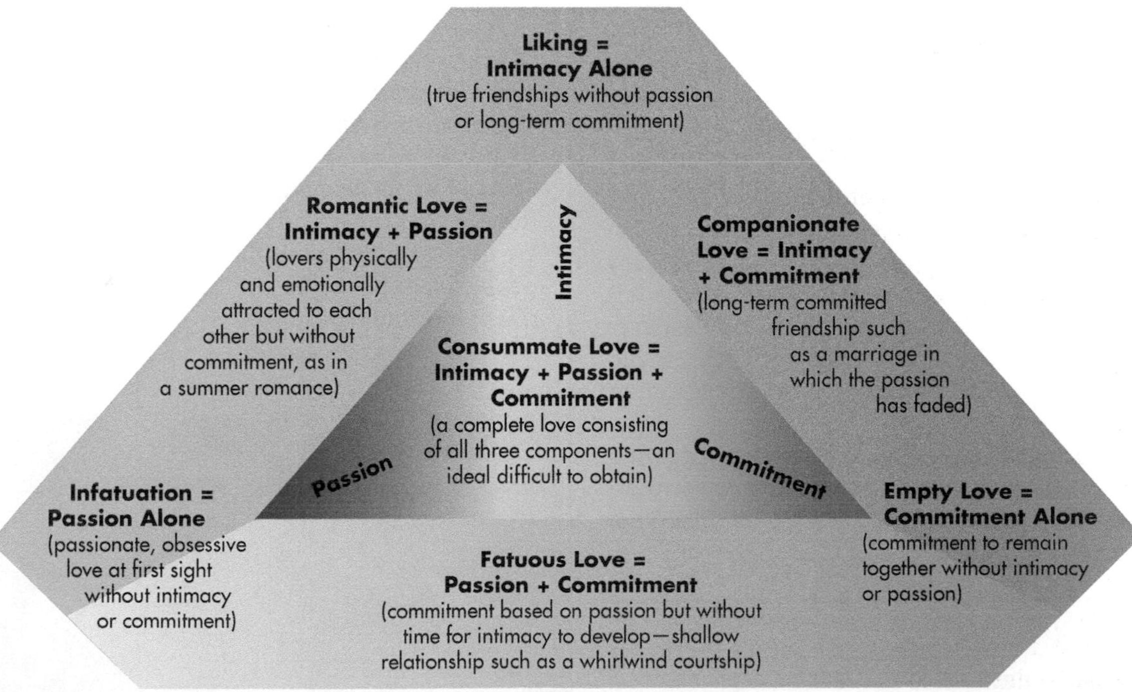

FIGURE 14.1

Sternberg's Triangular Model of Love

Source: Sternberg, Robert J. (1986, April). A triangular theory of love. *Psychological Review, 93*(2), 119–135.

in which all three components flower. Consummate love is an ideal toward which many Westerners strive. Sometimes a love relationship has both passion and commitment but lacks intimacy. Sternberg calls this *fatuous* (foolish) *love*. Fatuous love is associated with whirlwind courtships that burn brightly but briefly as the partners realize they are not well matched. In companionate love, intimacy and commitment are strong, but passion is lacking. Companionate love typifies long-term relationships and marriages in which passion has ebbed but a deep and abiding friendship remains (Hatfield & Rapson, 2002).

DID YOU KNOW?

Couples can remain in love after passion fades.

With companionate love, couples can remain "in love" after passion fades.

Jealousy

O! beware, my lord, of jealousy;

It is the green-ey'd monster . . .

– William Shakespeare, *Othello*

Thus was Othello, the Moor of Venice, warned of jealousy in the Shakespearean play that bears his name. Yet Othello could not control his feelings and wound up killing his beloved (and innocent) wife, Desdemona. Like Othello, some people can become jealous when others show sexual interest in their partners or when their partners show interest in another.

Jealousy can lead to loss of feelings of affection, feelings of insecurity and rejection, anxiety and loss of self-esteem, and feelings of mistrust. Jealousy, therefore, can be one reason that relationships fail. In extreme cases, jealousy can lead to depression or give rise to spouse abuse, suicide, or, as with Othello, murder (Puente & Cohen, 2003; Vandello & Cohen, 2003).

Many young adults—including many college students—play jealousy games. They let their partners know that they are attracted to other people. They flirt openly or manufacture tales to make their partners pay more attention to them, to test the relationship, to inflict pain, or to take revenge for a partner's disloyalty.

DID YOU KNOW?

Jealousy can be destructive to a relationship.

Some milder forms of jealousy may have the positive effect of revealing how much a person cares for her or his partner, but some people use jealousy to control their partner. Beware!

LO5 Loneliness

Many people start relationships because of loneliness. Loneliness tends to peak during adolescence, when peer relationships are beginning to supplant family ties, and individuals are becoming—often—painfully aware of how other adolescents may be more successful at making friends and earning the admiration of others. Loneliness is also often related to feelings of depression. A study of 101 dating couples with a mean age of 21 found that poor relationships contributed to feelings of loneliness and to depression—even though the individuals had partners (Segrin et al., 2003).

Research shows consistently that social support helps people cope with stress, and that stress can lead to health problems (Pressman et al., 2005). Therefore, it is not surprising that loneliness is associated with physical health problems and depression. Social isolation has also been shown to predict cancer, cardiovascular disease, and a higher-than-average mortality rate (Tomaka, Thompson, & Palacios, 2006).

The causes of loneliness are many and complex. Lonely people tend to have several of the following characteristics: lack of social skills, lack of interest in other people, and lack of empathy (Cramer, 2003). The fear of rejection is often connected with self-criticism of their social skills and expectations of failure in relating to others (Vorauer et al., 2003). Lonely people also fail to disclose personal information to potential friends (Solan, Batten, & Parish, 1982), are cynical about human nature (for example, seeing people as only out for themselves), and demand too much too soon.

Nandy Photos/iStockphoto.com

DID YOU KNOW?

Many people remain lonely because they fear being rejected by others.

Being alone is very different from being lonely. Studies show that being lonely is a significant and complex issue for young adults.

LO6 The Single Life

Married people became the minority in Canada for the first time in 2006, according to the census information released by Statistics Canada in its "family portrait"at that time Unmarried persons are defined as those who are divorced, separated, widowed, or have never married. In a study called *A Diamond is Forever and Other Fairy Tales,* thousands of recent divorcees were polled from 2008–2014. The research found that those who dated 3 years or more prior to marriage were 39% less likely to get divorced, and those who dated 1–2 years prior to marriage were 20% less likely to get divorced than people who dated less than 1 year. Ultimately, the shorter the time spent before a proposal, the greater the likelihood of a divorce.

In 2011, single persons represented 27.6% (more than 1 in 4) of all Canadian households. This rate represents an increase of 10.4% from 2006 (Statistics Canada, 2013a) Several factors contribute to the increased proportion of singles. More young adults are postponing marriage to pursue educational and career goals. Many are also deciding to "live together" (cohabit), at least for a while, rather than get married. Also people are getting married later, with the average age at first marriage for men in 2008 being 31.1 years and for women 29.1 years (Human Resources and Skills Development Canada, 2013b).

According to the "family portrait" compiled by Statistics Canada in 2011, 16.3% of families with children were headed by a lone parent. Of those families, about 25% were headed by men, representing a large gender disparity (Statistics Canada, 2013b).

Many young adults see being single as an alternative, open-ended way of life—not a temporary stage that precedes marriage. Single people encounter less social stigma today. They are less likely today than earlier to be perceived as socially inadequate or as failures. As career options for women have expanded, women are not as financially dependent on men as their mothers and grandmothers were; they don't need to be married to afford a decent lifestyle. Other young adults do not choose to be single, but haven't found the right person.

Being single is not without its problems, though. Many single people are lonely. Some singles would like to have a steady, meaningful relationship. Others, usually women, worry about their physical safety. Some young adults who are living alone find it difficult to satisfy their needs for intimacy, companionship, and sex. Despite these concerns, most singles are well adjusted.

There is no distinct "singles scene." Single people differ in their sexual interests and lifestyles. Many achieve emotional and psychological

DID YOU KNOW?

Being single has become a more common Canadian lifestyle over the past few decades.

The evolution of relationships has seen acceptance of a variety of different lifestyle choices.

EMERGING CANADA

Worldwide 100 million people make use of the British Columbia–based company Plenty of Fish for online dating (Canadian Press, 2015). Numerous studies indicate that Canadians are among the world's most active users of social media, so it should not be a surprise that Canadians are also active in online dating. A 2011 survey found that 34% of Canadians ages 18–34 used online dating services (Canadian Press, 2015). But can online dating withstand scientific review? Finkel et al. (2012) have concluded that, from a psychological perspective, online dating has fundamentally altered the romantic meeting process of a compatible match. Online dating offers access to potential partners that people would be unlikely to meet in the traditional dating process. But users should "proceed with caution." Profile browsing can lead to unrealistic "pickiness." Also, people are sometimes not truthful in their profiles; and there is the potential of investing a lot of time before meeting, only to have a disappointing face-to-face encounter.

Andresr/Shutterstock

serial monogamy
a series of exclusive sexual relationships

celibacy
abstention from sexual activity, whether from choice or lack of opportunity

cohabitation
living together with a romantic partner without being married

security through a network of intimate relationships with friends. Many are sexually active and practise serial monogamy (Kulick, 2006). Others have both a primary sexual relationship with one steady partner and occasional flings. A few pursue casual sexual encounters. By contrast, some singles remain celibate, either by choice or lack of opportunity. Some choose celibacy because of health factors or for religious reasons; others choose celibacy to focus on work, or because they are asexual, because they find sex unalluring, or because they fear STIs or pregnancy.

Photographer Mitchel Raphael

Comedian Elvira Kurt kisses friend and musician Carol Pope to raise money. In 2011, 3 in 10 married couples in Canada were same-sex (Statistics Canada, 2015h).

LO7 Living Together

Some social scientists believe that cohabitation has become accepted within the social mainstream. Whether or not this is so, society in general has become more tolerant (Laumann, Mahay, & Youm, 2007). We seldom hear cohabitation referred to as "living in sin" or "shacking up" as we once did. People today are more likely to refer to cohabitation with value-free expressions such as "living together." But some families, influenced by cultural or religious beliefs, frown upon cohabitation.

According to the 2011 census, the number of common-law couples has more than quadrupled in the past 30 years. The number of same-sex married couples nearly tripled between 2006 and 2011 (Statistics Canada, 2013b).

So, when couples cohabit before marriage, are they less likely to divorce? The answer is no. In fact, on average, such couples are more likely to divorce, not only in Canada but also in the United States and Great Britain. Women between the ages of 20 and 30 were 63% likely to separate if they had cohabited first, compared with 33% of women who hadn't cohabited first (Ambert, 2005). We cannot conclude that cohabitation necessarily causes divorce. We must be cautious about drawing causal conclusions from correlational data. Selection factors—the factors that led some couples to cohabit and others not to cohabit—may explain the results. For example, cohabitors tend to be less traditional and less religious than non-cohabitors (Hussain, 2002; Marquis, 2003), and thus tend to be less committed to the values and interests traditionally associated with the institution of marriage. Therefore, the attitudes of cohabitors and not necessarily cohabitation itself are likely to be responsible for their higher rates of divorce.

Young adults cohabit for many reasons. Cohabitation, like marriage, is an alternative to living alone. Romantic partners may have deep feelings for each other but may not be ready to get married. Some couples prefer cohabitation because it provides an abiding relationship without the legal entanglements of marriage (Hussain, 2002; Marquis, 2003). Economic factors also come into play. Young adults may decide to cohabit because of the economic advantages of sharing household expenses. Cohabiting individuals who receive public assistance risk losing support if they get married (Hussain, 2002; Marquis, 2003).

LO8 Marriage

Families, for all of their different descriptions and labels, remain our most common form of Canadian lifestyle. Young adults are likely to get married in a traditional sense of the word. They are mature enough to have completed tertiary schooling or to have established careers.

Why Do People Get Married?

Even in this era of serial monogamy and cohabitation, people continue to marry. Marriage meets many personal and cultural needs. For traditionalists, marriage legitimizes sexual relations. Marriage provides an institution in which children can be supported and socialized. Marriage (theoretically) restricts sexual relations. Unless one or both partners have signed a prenuptial agreement to the contrary, marriage permits the orderly transmission of wealth from one family to another and one generation to another.

Today in mainstream Canadian society, because more people believe that premarital sex is acceptable between two people who feel affectionate toward each other, the desire for sex is less likely to motivate marriage than has been the case in earlier generations. But marriage can provide a sense of security and opportunities to share feelings, experiences, and ideas with someone with whom a special attachment has been formed. Most young adults agree that marriage is important for people who plan to spend the rest of their lives together (Jayson, 2008) and who may be considering having children.

The Future Families Project (Bibby, 2004) was a survey of Canadian values conducted by Reginald Bibby of the University of Lethbridge. Many people want to get married because they believe they will be happier. According to Table 14.1, most married men and women are happier, though their numbers have decreased since the 1970s.

TABLE 14.1

Happy Marriages

Percentage of Married Persons Age 18 and Older Who Said Their Marriages Were "Very Happy," by Period

Period	Men	Women
1973–1976	69.6	68.6
1977–1981	68.3	64.2
1982–1986	62.9	61.7
1987–1991	66.4	59.6
1993–1996	63.2	59.7
1998–2004	64.4	60.4

Source: © Cengage Learning

Types of Marriage

Arranged Marriage

In the Broadway musical *Fiddler on the Roof*, Tevye, the Jewish father of three women of marriageable age in 19th-century Russia, demands that his daughters marry Jewish men to perpetuate their families' religious and cultural traditions. Traditional societies have used—and some continue to use—arranged marriages, in which the families of the bride and groom more or less arrange for the union.

As in *Fiddler*, one of the purposes of arranged marriage is to ensure the bride and groom share similar backgrounds so they will carry on their traditions, secure land or resources, and enhance family and community bonds. Supporters of arranged marriage also argue that it is wiser to follow family wisdom than one's own heart, especially since the attraction many couples feel is often infatuation and not a deep, abiding love. Proponents also claim a lower divorce rate for arranged marriages than for "self-arranged marriages," although this argument doesn't carry too much weight since couples who enter arranged marriages are generally more traditional to begin with.

On marriage

Marriage is a great institution, but I'm not ready for an institution—yet.
Mae West

Marriage is not a word, it is a sentence.
Unknown

When two people are under the influence of the most violent, most insane, most delusive, and most transient of passions, they are required to swear that they will remain in that excited, abnormal, and exhausting condition until death do them part.
George Bernard Shaw

Heteronormative marriage is often idealized in society.

monogamy
the practice of having a sexual relationship with only one person at a time

polyamory
the practice of consenting partners maintaining an "open" sexual relationship

same-sex marriage
marriage between two gay males or between two lesbians

Monogamous Marriage

Traditional marriage relationships are based on monogamy, two partners who are committed to having a sexual relationship with only their partner. In addition to these traditional relationships, a new form of relationship is emerging. U.S. studies have shown a trend of polyamory, whereby consenting partners maintain "open" sexual relationships with other partners. These arrangements are referred to as "relationship orientations" by Canadian helping professionals, in their bid to protect couples from sexual harassment or discrimination (Robinson, 2011).

Same-Sex Marriage

In churches and in politics, there has been a large focus on same-sex marriage—that is, whether LGBTQ couples should be allowed to marry. Although Canada recognizes the equality rights of LGBTQ citizens, such is not the case in many areas of the United States and throughout the world. In 2013, only 14 countries had legalized marriage, nine of them European countries. Canada was one of the others. Figure 14.2 illustrates the growing support in Canada for same-sex marriage.

Committed LGBTQ couples who cannot legally marry may, depending on where they live, choose to enter into civil unions, domestic partnerships, or registered partnerships. Canada is very much a front runner in the domain of LGBTQ rights with a recent and historic amendment to Bill C-279, which now includes transgender people in the prevention of discrimination based on gender identity (OpenParliament, 2015). We need to remember, however, that legal equality must also be supported by social equality, an area where Canada has much work left to do.

Whom Do We Marry: Are Marriages Made in Heaven or in the Neighbourhood?

Although the selection of a mate is theoretically free in our society, factors such as race, social class, and religion often determine the people we seek as

FIGURE 14.2

Growing Support for Same-Sex Marriage

The "millennials" have shown more support than any other generation for same-sex marriage.

Source: Pew Research. (2013). Growing support for gay marriage: Changed minds and changed demographics. Pew Research Centre. http://www.people-press.org/2013/03/20/growing-support-for-gay-marriage-changed-minds-and-changing-demographics/

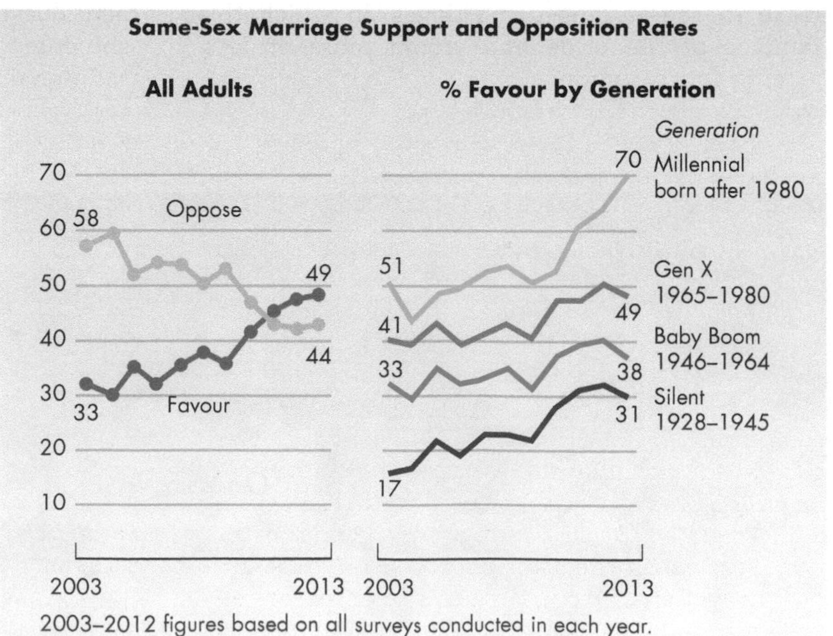

mates (Laumann et al., 2007). Young adults tend to marry others from the same area and social class. Parental approval may not be formally required but is often viewed as desirable. Since neighbourhoods often comprise people from a similar social class, storybook marriages like Cinderella's are fantasy. Young adults tend to marry people who are similar in physical attractiveness, attitudes, background, and interests (Blackwell & Lichter, 2004). Young adults are more often than not similar to their mates in height, weight, personality traits, intelligence, educational level, religion, even in use of alcohol and tobacco (Myers, 2006; Reynolds, Barlow, & Pedersen, 2006). As Canada continues to diversify and embrace a philosophy of diversity, mixed marriages and mixed common-law relationships are increasing. The 2011 National Survey found that 4.6% of all married and common-law couples were in mixed unions, compared to 3.9% in 2006 and.to 2.6% in 1991. Of the 3.9% in 2006, one person in the relationship was a member of a visible minority, and the other not. In 2011, 0.7% of all couples involved two people from different visible ethnic groups (Statistics Canada, 2011c).

The concept of "like marrying like" is termed homogamy. Research shows that marriages between people from similar backgrounds tend to be more stable (Myers, 2006), perhaps because these partners are more likely to share values and attitudes (Willetts, 2006).

Most people also tend to follow *age homogamy*—the selection of a partner who falls in their own age range, with bridegrooms two to five years older than their wives (Buss, 1994; Michael et al., 1994). But age homogamy reflects the tendency to marry in early adulthood. Persons who marry late or who remarry tend not to select partners so close in age.

Marital Satisfaction

The nature of romantic relationships and the satisfaction of the partners strongly affect the well-being of each member of the couple at various stages throughout adulthood (Bertoni et al., 2007). An Italian study of married couples found that the partners' confidence in their ability to influence their relationship for the better contributed to the quality of the marriage (Bertoni et al., 2007). In turn, the quality of the marital relationship appeared to positively affect individuals' physical and psychological health. Another study found that intimacy, which is fuelled by trust, honesty, and the sharing of innermost feelings, is strongly related to marital satisfaction (Patrick et al., 2007). So is the psychological support of one's spouse.

Satisfaction with one's career is positively correlated with marital satisfaction, and both are related to general life satisfaction (Perrone, Webb, & Jackson, 2007). Perhaps general tendencies toward happiness (or depression) manifest themselves in various walks of life, including one's vocational life and romantic relationships. Or perhaps doing very well in one arena can cast a positive glow on other parts of life.

homogamy
marriage between two similar individuals

When one marital partner drinks heavily, or abuses substances, and the other does not, marital satisfaction declines over time (Homish & Leonard, 2007). It doesn't matter who is the user, the man or the woman; in either case, satisfaction declines. Another study followed 172 newlywed couples over 4 years and found that physical aggression preceded sharp declines in marital satisfaction (Lawrence & Bradbury, 2007). Interestingly, the union was more likely to be dissolved when the woman was the aggressor.

LO9 Parenthood

Becoming a parent is a major life event that requires changes in nearly every sphere of life: personal, social, financial, and academic (Redshaw & van den Akker, 2007). In fact, many individuals and couples in contemporary developed nations no longer think of parenthood as a necessary part of marriage or a relationship (Doherty, Carroll, & Waite, 2007).

Just as people are getting married in their later 20s today, they are also delaying parenthood into their later 20s (Arnett, 2007; Popenoe & Whitehead, 2006). And many women do not bear children until they are in their 30s or even their 40s. But bearing children in developed nations is generally seen as ideally occurring in early adulthood, although teenage pregnancy remains a Canadian reality.

Why do people have children? Reliable birth control methods have separated sex acts from reproduction. Except for women living under specific traditions or religious rules, for those dealing with issues of abuse, or where couples have unplanned pregnancies, becoming pregnant is a choice. In developed nations, most couples report that they choose to have children for personal happiness or well-being (Dyer, 2007). In more traditional societies,

DID YOU KNOW?

Research indicates that having a child will not necessarily save a troubled marriage.

In fact, a newborn can often add additional stress to a couple's relationship.

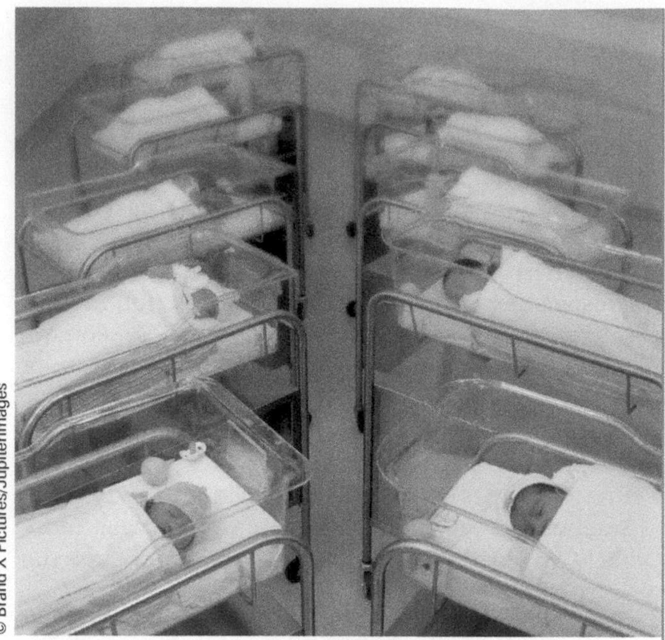
© Brand X Pictures/Jupiterimages

people report having children to strengthen marital bonds, provide social security, assist with labour (as in having more farm hands), provide social status, maintain the family name and lineage, secure property rights and inheritance, and in some places, improve the odds of reincarnation (Dyer, 2007). Of these reasons, having children to care for the parents in their old age ("social security") looms large. In Canada, the Canadian Pension Plan helps support older people, but how many middle-aged people (typically daughters) are running in one direction to rear their children and in another direction to provide emotional and other supports for elderly parents and other relatives?

Having a child is unlikely to save a marriage. Numerous studies show that because of the added stress of caring for a new baby and adjusting to parenthood, relationships often decline significantly throughout the year following delivery (e.g., Lawrence, Nylen, & Cobb, 2007; Simonelli et al., 2007). Researchers in one study, for example, investigated the effects of infants' sleep patterns and crying on marital satisfaction in 107 first-time parent couples during the first year following birth. In general, marital satisfaction decreased as the year wore on, and the baby's crying was apparently the main source of the problem (Meijer & van den Wittenboer, 2007). Parental loss of sleep compounded the difficulties.

Parenthood and Role Overload

Some research has focused on the effects of newborns entering the lives of working-class families, especially when the mother must return to work shortly after the birth (e.g., Perry-Jenkins et al., 2007). Maternity leave for most women in the U.S. is 3 months, for Canadian, Albanian, and Croatian women it is 1 year. Returning to work too soon after becoming a parent can cause parents to be depressed and overwhelmed, and conflicts may emerge. Sometimes conflicts emerge because a father may not be supporting enough with the baby and with household tasks. Often the mother is the primary caregiver (Wall & Arnold, 2007). These mothers encounter role overload, acting both as primary caregiver and, in our demanding economy, one of two primary breadwinners. Role overload is one of the primary reasons that Canada has instituted supportive parental leave programs.

Postpartum depression (PPD) can also contribute to role overload. Returning to work or not, many young parents are overloaded with the balance of career and family life and the expectations of parenting a young child. Additionally, if support isn't in place, parents can struggle to keep up with the day-to-day tasks of parenting.

PPD doesn't only occur immediately after a baby is born. Mothers can experience PPD up to 5 years after having a child. The symptoms include feelings of worthlessness, hopelessness, prolonged sadness, depression, and extreme detachment. PPD affects the mother and child the most, but it also affects the partner and other siblings, if there are any. A more severe type of PPD is postpartum psychosis, which has the same symptoms as PPD but is much more severe, as the mother may want to cause harm to herself or her child. Various interventions and supports are available to women who have PPD and postpartum psychosis, and should be sought out with the first sign of symptoms. (Refer to Chapter 3 for more information about PPD.)

Yet a longitudinal study of 45 couples expecting their first child showed that family life does not need to be overly stressful (McHale & Rotman, 2007). The couples were assessed

© Jamie Grill/Corbis

during pregnancy and from their child's infancy through toddlerhood—at 3, 12, and 30 months after birth. Parents who generally agreed on their beliefs about parenting, and on which parent should do what, experienced a postnatal adjustment that was largely solid and remained stable. In other words, when both members of the couple believed they should share caregiving equally and they lived up to it, their adjustment was good. Parents who also have family or additional supports adjust better to parenting and their various responsibilities.

Parenthood in Dual-Earner Families

The financial realities of contemporary life, and the women's movement, have made the move of women into the workplace the norm in Canadian society. Thus young adults with children, who are married or cohabiting, more often than not make up dual-earner families.

Studies find that the mothers in dual-earner families encounter more stress than the fathers do (Schneewind & Kupsch, 2007; Wall, 2007). Evidence of a powerful sex difference in dual-earner families was also found in analysis of longitudinal survey data on 884 dual-earner couples (Chesley & Moen, 2006). Caring for children was related to declines in well-being for dual-earner women, but, ironically, with increases in well-being for dual-earner men. Dual-earner women with flexible work schedules encountered less stress than women with fixed schedules, apparently because they were more able to manage their role overload.

What happens in the workplace doesn't necessarily stay in the workplace. A study of 113 dual-earner couples found that problems in the workplace contributed to tension in the couples, health problems, and dissatisfaction with the relationship (Matthews, Del Priore, Acitelli, & Barnes-Farrell, 2006).

Because of problems balancing work and family life, when dual-earner families can no longer afford to have a parent out of the home, it is usually the mother and not the father who cuts back on work or drops out of the workforce altogether (Wall, 2007). Because of experience with dual-earner families around them, a sample of 194 adolescents from dual-earner families generally expected that they (if they were female) or their partners (if they were male) would be the ones to cut back or quit work in the future, at least temporarily, if the couple had a child (Weinshenker, 2006). The responses showed little insight into the problems raised by interrupting careers. On the other hand, having a working mother encouraged the adolescents—both females and males—to say they believed in gender egalitarianism.

LO10 Divorce

When Reginald Bibby (2004) surveyed Canadian teenagers, 90% said they expected to marry and stay with the same partner for life. Yet we know that 40% of marriages in Canada will end in divorce (Government of Canada, n.d.). This number increases to 48.4% in Quebec and decreases to 21.6% in Newfoundland and Labrador (Ambert, 2009). Divorce rates sharply increased in 1968 when a new Divorce Act was passed, broadening the grounds for divorce. The increased economic independence of women has also contributed to the divorce rate. More women today have the economic means to leave a troubled marriage. Today, more people consider marriage an alterable condition than in prior generations.

Canadians today also want more from marriage than did their grandparents and they are not as willing to accept less. They expect marriage to be both personally fulfilling and a foundation for family life and rearing children. Dr. John M. Gottam, author of *The Seven Principles for Making Marriage Work*, says that there are key elements that can predict divorce. Gottam suggests that discussions that are sarcastic and critical—which he terms the "harsh start-up"— are predictors of divorce. What he calls "flooding"—negativity run rampant, defensiveness, and contempt—are also indicators. Changes in body language that show physical distress are also concerning, as are partners who are not making an effort to de-escalate tensions. On the other hand, couples who see their struggles in a positive light—as adversity that they have met together—are more likely to have a happy marriage and avoid divorce.

The Cost of Divorce

We have examined divorce from the child's perspective (see Chapters 8 and 10), but now we turn to the impact of divorce on the adult. When a household splits, the resources often cannot maintain the earlier standard of living for each partner. Ambert (2009) warns that divorce brings an increased risk of poverty for mothers and children. Women who have not pursued a career may struggle to compete with younger, more experienced workers when seeking work. Divorced mothers often face the combined stress of the sole responsibility for child rearing and the need to increase their incomes. Divorced fathers may find it difficult to pay alimony and child support while establishing a new lifestyle. On the other hand, Ambert found that 29% of men's disposable incomes increase because they are less likely to receive custody of their children and thus avoid many child-related expenses (Ambert, 2009).

Couple: Dragon Images/Shutterstock.com; money: Ppart/Shutterstock.com

Divorce causes both financial and emotional problems. Divorce can prompt feelings of failure as a spouse and parent, loneliness and uncertainty about the future, and depression. Married people appear to be better able to cope with the stresses and strains of life, perhaps because they can lend each other emotional support. Divorced and separated people have the highest rates of physical and mental illness (Carrère et al., 2000; Lorenz et al., 2006). They also have high rates of suicide (Donald et al., 2006; Lorant et al., 2005). These variables can also be the result of pre-existing conditions and may have contributed to the marital breakdown.

> My wife and I were considering a divorce, but after pricing lawyers we decided to buy a new car instead.
>
> — Henny Youngman

On the other hand, divorce may permit personal growth and renewal and the opportunity to take stock of oneself and establish a new, more rewarding life. But as noted in Chapter 10, children tend to be the biggest losers when parents divorce.

STUDY TOOLS

Located at **nelson.com/student**

- ☐ Prepare for tests with a variety of exercises and activities
- ☐ Review Key Terms Flashcards (online or print)
- ☐ Create your own study tools with Build a Summary
- ☐ Watch Observing Development videos to expand your knowledge

PART FIVE

CHAPTER 15

Middle Adulthood: Physical and Cognitive Development

THE CANADIAN PRESS/Fred Chartrand

LEARNING OUTCOMES

LO1 Describe trends in physical development in middle adulthood

LO2 Discuss the major health concerns of middle adulthood, including cancer and heart disease

LO3 Discuss the functioning of the immune system

LO4 Discuss sexuality in middle adulthood, focusing on menopause and sexual difficulties

LO5 Describe cognitive development in middle adulthood, distinguishing between crystallized and fluid intelligence

LO6 Describe mental health issues in middle adulthood

LO7 Discuss opportunities for exercising creativity and continuing education in middle adulthood

> "Some theorists view middle age as a time of peak performance, whereas others portray it as a time of crisis or decline."

baby boomers postwar babies whose births between 1946 and 1965 spiked the Canadian population by 11%

inter-individual variability the notion that people do not age in the same way or at the same rate

presbyopia loss of elasticity in the lens of the eye, which makes it harder to focus on nearby objects

presbycusis loss of hearing over time

The baby boomers are those people who were born between 1946 and 1965. At that time, Canada saw a population increase of 11% as the result of postwar babies. On average, 3.7 babies were born to each woman, compared with the average of 1.7 more recently (Statistics Canada, 2013c). Most of the baby boomers are now middle-aged adults. Middle adulthood spans the ages of 40 to 65 years.

Some theorists view middle age as a time of peak performance, and others have portrayed it as a time of crisis or decline (Lachman, 2004). Physically speaking, we are at our peak in early adulthood, but in general, those who eat right and exercise will, in many ways, undergo only a gradual and relatively minor physical decline in middle adulthood. As we age, we become more vulnerable to a variety of illnesses, but we also become less prone to irresponsible behaviour that may result in injury or death. On the other hand, some sensory and sexual changes might well become major issues. Cognitively speaking, we are at our peak in many intellectual functions in middle adulthood, but may experience some loss of processing speed and some lapses in memory. Even so, these declines are often made up for in expertise.

LO1 Physical Development

No two people age in the same way or at the same rate. This phenomenon is called inter-individual variability. But whatever individual differences may exist, physiological aging is defined by changes in the body's integumentary system (the body's system of skin, hair, and nails), senses, reaction time, and lung capacity. These changes may well be unavoidable. On the other hand, changes in metabolism, muscle mass, strength, bone density, aerobic capacity, blood-sugar tolerance, and ability to regulate body temperature may be moderated and sometimes reversed through exercise and diet.

Skin and Hair

Hair usually begins to grey in middle adulthood as the production of *melanin*, the pigment responsible for hair colour, decreases. Hair loss also accelerates with aging, especially in men.

Much of the wrinkling of the skin that is associated with aging is caused by exposure to ultraviolet (UV) rays. Beginning gradually in early adulthood, the body produces fewer of the proteins that give the skin its elasticity. The body also produces fewer *keratinocytes*—the cells in the outer layer of the skin that are regularly shed and renewed. Lower levels of keratinocytes leave the skin dryer and more brittle.

Sensory and Auditory Functioning

Normal age-related changes in vision begin to appear by the mid-30s and assert themselves in middle adulthood. Presbyopia (Latin for "old vision") refers to loss of elasticity in the lens that makes it harder to focus on, or accommodate to, nearby objects or fine print. Presbycusis is the loss of hearing over time and is predominant in the aging population. It is estimated that 30–35% of adults between 65 and 75 have hearing loss (Cleveland Clinic, 2016).

Reaction Time

Reaction time—the amount of time it takes to respond to a stimulus—increases with age, mainly because of changes in the nervous system. At age 25 or so, we begin to lose neurons, which are responsible for sensing signals such as sights and sounds and for coordinating our muscular responses.

Lung Capacity

Lung tissue stiffens with age, diminishing the lungs' capacity to expand, such that breathing capacity may decline by half between early and late adulthood. Regular exercise can offset much of this loss, and beginning to exercise regularly in middle adulthood can expand breathing capacity beyond what it was earlier in life.

Lean-Body Mass and Body Fat

Beginning at age 20, we lose nearly 3.2 kg (7 lb.) of lean-body mass with each decade. The rate of loss accelerates after age 45. Fat replaces lean-body mass, including muscles. Consequently, the average person's body mass index (BMI) rises.

Muscle Strength

Loss of muscles reduces strength. However, the change is gradual, and in middle adulthood, exercise can readily compensate, by increasing the size of the remaining muscle cells. Exercise contributes to vigour, health, and a desirable body shape.

Metabolism

Metabolism is the rate at which the body processes or "burns" food to produce energy. The resting metabolic rate—also called the *basal metabolic rate (BMR)*—declines as we age. Fatty tissue burns fewer calories than muscle, and the decline in BMR is largely attributable to the loss of muscle tissue and the corresponding increase in fatty tissue. Since we require fewer calories to maintain our weight as we age, middle-aged people (and older adults) are likely to gain weight more easily.

Bone Density

Bone, which consists largely of calcium, begins to lose density and strength at around the age of 40. As bones lose density, they become more brittle and prone to fracture. Bones in the spine, hip, thigh (femur), and forearm lose the most density as we age. This process can lead to osteoporosis, which we discuss further in Chapter 17.

SportPoint/Shutterstock.com

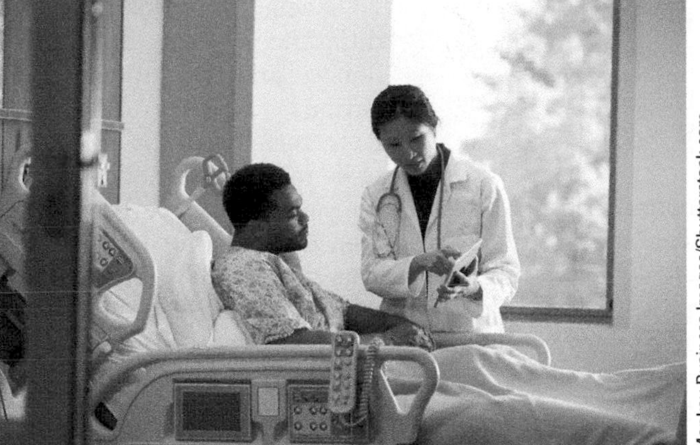
Monkey Business Images/Shutterstock.com

Aerobic Capacity

As we age, the cardiovascular system becomes less efficient. Heart and lung muscles shrink. Aerobic capacity declines as less oxygen is taken into the lungs and the heart pumps less blood. The maximum heart rate declines, but exercise expands aerobic capacity and improves heart health at *any* age.

Blood-Sugar Tolerance

Blood sugar, or glucose, is the basic fuel and energy source for cells. The energy from glucose supports cell activities and maintains body temperature. Glucose circulates in the bloodstream and enters cells with the help of insulin, a hormone secreted by the pancreas.

As we age, the tissues in our body become less capable of taking up glucose from the bloodstream. Body tissues lose their sensitivity to insulin; the pancreas must thus produce more insulin to achieve the same effect. Therefore, blood-sugar levels rise, increasing the risk of adult-onset diabetes.

LO2 Health

The health of people aged 40–65 in developed nations such as Canada is better than ever for most populations. Nearly everyone has been vaccinated for preventable diseases. Many, perhaps the majority, practise preventive healthcare. Once people reach 40, they are advised to have annual physical checkups. Fortunately, more is known today about curing or treating illnesses than ever before.

metastases
new tumours formed by the transference of malignant or cancerous cells to other parts of the body

Racial, ethnic, and sex differences affect the incidence and treatment of various diseases. People from certain groups appear to be more likely to develop certain chronic conditions, such as hypertension and specific types of cancer. Diabetes, for example, is higher among Indigenous and African American populations, in part because of genetic factors and also because of socio-economic factors such as poverty, stress, and access to resources. Canadians are very proud of their healthcare system, but reduced access and lengthy wait times make it apparent that much work is needed to restore healthcare to a level meriting our pride.

As we consider the health of people in middle adulthood, we focus on many things that can go wrong. For many, things go quite well if they get regular medical checkups, pay attention to nutrition and exercise, avoid smoking, drink in moderation if at all, regulate stress, are not living in poverty and—ideally—enjoy supportive relationships.

DID YOU KNOW?

Canadians are proud of their healthcare system.

Reduced access and lengthy wait times make it clear that we need to focus on our healthcare system if we want to protect it.

Leading Causes of Death

In early adulthood, the leading causes of death—accidents and suicide—screamed out their preventability. In middle adulthood, diseases come to the fore (see Figure 15.1). Cancer and heart disease are numbers one and two, and accidents are now in third place. Cancer and heart disease are also preventable to some degree, of course.

Cancer

Although heart disease is the nation's number one cause of death overall, cancer is the leading cause of death in middle adulthood (see Figure 15.1). In many cases, cancer can be controlled or cured, especially when detected early. Cancer Care Ontario (2013) recommends that women have mammograms to screen for breast cancer beginning at age 50, and that both men and women be screened for cancer of the colon also beginning at age 50. Most men should have digital rectal exams (in which the doctor uses a gloved finger to feel the prostate gland) and blood tests for prostate-specific antigen (PSA) beginning at age 40 (Prostate Cancer Canada, 2013).

EMERGING CANADA

Only 56% of Canadians between the ages of 45 to 65 consider themselves to be in very good or excellent health, and 14% say their health is fair or poor (Human Resources and Skills Development, 2013d).

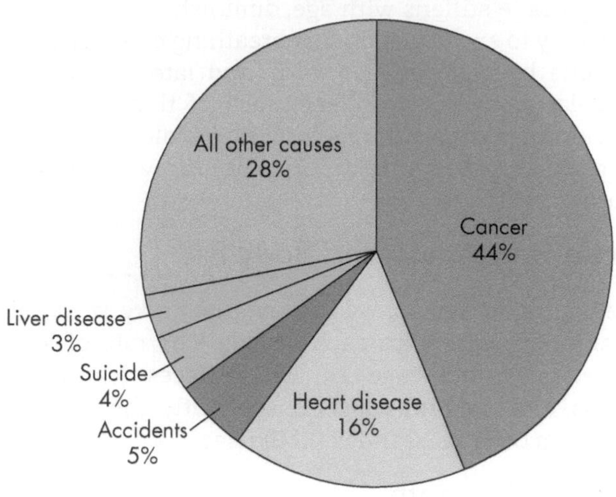

FIGURE 15.1

Leading Causes of Death in Middle Adulthood*

*Not indicated in Figure 15.1 is women's sharply increased incidence of death due to heart disease after menopause.

Source: Statistics Canada. (2011). *The 10 leading causes of death*. http://www.statcan.gc.ca/pub/82-625-x/2014001/article/11896/c-g/c-g01-eng.htm

Cancer is a chronic, non-communicable disease characterized by uncontrolled growth of cells, which form masses of excess tissue called tumours. Tumours can be *benign* (non-cancerous) or *malignant* (cancerous). Benign tumours do not spread and rarely pose a threat to life. Malignant tumours invade and destroy surrounding tissue. Cancerous cells in malignant tumours may also break away from the primary tumour and travel through the bloodstream or lymphatic system to form new tumours, called **metastases**, elsewhere in the body. Metastases damage vital body organs and systems and in many cases lead to death. The incidence of cancer increases dramatically with age (see Figure 15.2).

Cancer begins when a cell's DNA, its genetic material, changes such that the cell divides indefinitely. The change is triggered by mutations in the DNA, which can be caused by internal or external factors. Internal factors include heredity, problems in

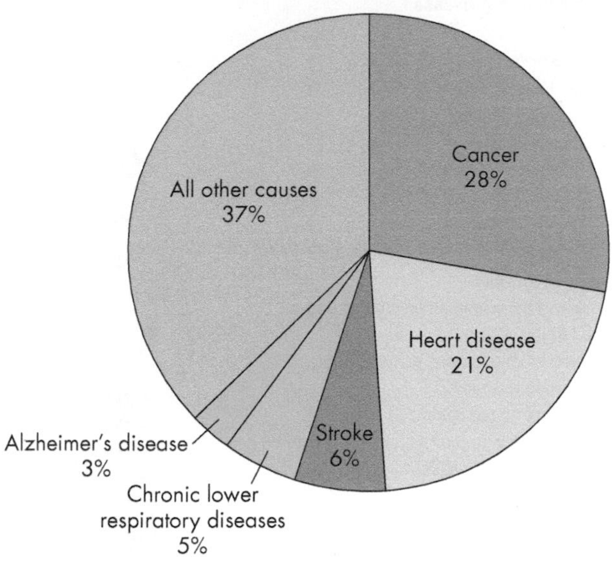

FIGURE 15.2

Leading Causes of Death in Late Adulthood

Source: Statistics Canada, 2015f.

Cancer Incidence and Mortality

Cancer mainly affects Canadians aged 50 and older, but it can occur at any age. Lung, breast, colorectal, and prostate cancer are the most common types of cancer in Canada.

It is estimated that in 2016:

- 102,900 Canadian men will be diagnosed with cancer and 41,700 men will die from cancer.
- 99,500 Canadian women will be diagnosed with cancer and 37,100 women will die from cancer.
- On average, 555 Canadians will be diagnosed with cancer every day.
- On average, 216 Canadians will die from cancer every day.

Lung, breast, colorectal, and prostate cancer are the most common types of cancer in Canada (excluding non-melanoma skin cancer). Based on 2016 estimates:

- These cancers account for half (50%) of all new cancer cases.
- Prostate cancer accounts for about one fifth (21%) of all new cancer cases in men.
- Lung cancer accounts for 14% of all new cases of cancer.
- Breast cancer accounts for about one quarter (26%) of all new cancer cases in women.
- Colorectal cancer accounts for 13% of all new cancer cases.

Source: Canadian Cancer Society's Advisory Committee on Cancer Statistics. Canadian Cancer Statistics 2015. Toronto, ON: Canadian Cancer Society; 2015, www.cancer.ca/Canadian-Cancer-Statistics-2015-EN

the immune system, and hormonal factors. External agents, called carcinogens, include some viruses, chemical compounds in tobacco and elsewhere, and ultraviolet (UV) solar radiation.

Two in five Canadians will eventually develop cancer. Of all Canadians who are diagnosed with cancer, 63% will survive a minimum of five years after being diagnosed, while one in four won't make it (Canadian Cancer Society, 2016).

Although cancer cuts across all racial and ethnic groups, many members of African-American/Canadian, Hispanic, Asian, and Indigenous groups avoid screening by the healthcare system, which they see as impersonal, insensitive, and racist. African Americans have higher than average colorectal cancer incidence and death rates (Cancer Prevention and Control, 2004), and African Canadians have twice the average death rate from prostate cancer. The incidence of cervical cancer in Latina Canadian women is higher than that of other demographic groups. Only 52% of Indigenous women age 40 years and over have had a recent mammogram. Indigenous populations have the poorest survival rate from cancer. Although much of the difference in mortality rates can be attributed to lack of early detection, which would have led to earlier treatment (Health Disparities, 2004), systemic issues of poverty, oppression, and barriers to healthy living and healthcare are also contributing factors.

Despite the many causes of cancer (see Table 15.1) and risk factors that vary among population groups, two out of three cancer deaths are the result of two controllable factors: smoking and diet (Willett, 2005). According to the Canadian Cancer Society, a person has a higher risk of developing cancer if he or she is overweight. Maintaining a healthy body weight helps to reduce cancer risks. A proper diet of fruit, vegetables, high fibre, and low fat and sugar is important. Regular physical exercise has been proven to reduce the risk of cancers, as has avoiding red and processed meats (Canadian Cancer Society, 2016). Cigarette smoking causes 84% of lung cancer deaths in Canada. On average, in 2007, 300 Canadians die each week from lung cancer caused by smoking (Canadian Cancer Society, 2007).

Traditional methods for treating cancer are surgery (surgical removal of cancerous tissue), radiation

DID YOU KNOW?

Eating well, exercising, and not smoking can lower your risk of cancer by 20–30%.

Taking a multivitamin once a day can lower your risk of cancer by 8% (Marchione, 2012).

TABLE 15.1

Factors in Cancer

Biological:

Family history
Physiological conditions:
Obesity

Psychological (personality and behaviour):

Patterns of consumption:
Smoking
Drinking alcohol (especially in women)
Eating animal fats
Unprotected sun exposure (risk of skin cancer)
Prolonged depression
Prolonged stress

Socio-cultural:

Socio-economic status
Access to healthcare
Timing of diagnosis and treatment
Higher death rates are found in nations with higher rates of fat intake

© Goodshoot/Jupiterimages

Source: © Cengage Learning

TABLE 15.2

Factors in Heart Disease

Biological:

Family history
Physiological conditions:
Obesity
High serum cholesterol
Hypertension

Psychological (personality and behaviour):

Type A behaviour
Hostility and holding in feelings of anger
Job strain
Chronic fatigue, stress, anxiety, depression, and emotional strain
Patterns of consumption:
Heavy drinking (but a drink a day may be helpful with heart disease)
Smoking
Overeating
Sudden stressors
Physical inactivity

Socio-cultural:

African Canadians are more prone to hypertension and heart disease than European Canadians
Access to healthcare
Timing of diagnosis and treatment

© Goodshoot/Jupiterimages

Source: © Cengage Learning

arteriosclerosis hardening of the arteries

atherosclerosis the buildup of fatty deposits (plaque) on the lining of arteries

(high-dose X-rays or other sources of high-energy radiation to kill cancerous cells and shrink tumours), chemotherapy (drugs that kill cancer cells or shrink tumours), and hormonal therapy (hormones that stop tumour growth). These methods have their limitations. Anti-cancer drugs and radiation kill both healthy tissue and malignant tissue. They also have side effects, such as nausea, vomiting, loss of appetite, loss of hair, and weakening of the immune system.

Heart Disease

Every seven minutes, a Canadian dies of heart disease or stroke (Heart and Stroke Foundation, 2013). In heart disease, the flow of blood to the heart is insufficient to supply the heart with the oxygen it needs. Heart disease most commonly results from arteriosclerosis or *hardening of the arteries*, which impairs circulation and increases the risk of a blood clot (thrombus). The most common form of arteriosclerosis is atherosclerosis—the buildup of fatty deposits called *plaque* in the lining of arteries (see Figure 15.3). Plaque results in the heart receiving insufficient blood and can cause a heart attack. A baseline electrocardiogram (abbreviated EKG or ECG), which is one measure of the health of the heart, is usually done around the age of 50 and repeated every two to three years.

The risk factors for heart disease are shown in Table 15.2. Several of these risk factors are beyond the

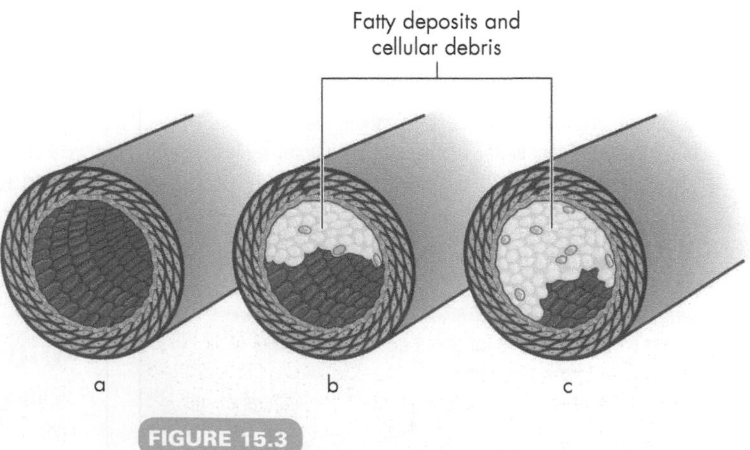

FIGURE 15.3

Atherosclerosis

Source: © Cengage Learning

control of the individual (age, race/ethnicity, and sex), but people can have some control over others (smoking, exercise, diet, and regular medical checkups).

LO3 The Immune System

The immune system is the body's defence against infections and other sources of disease. The immune system combats disease in several ways, one of which is the production of white blood cells, which engulf and kill worn-out and cancerous body cells and pathogens such as bacteria, fungi, and viruses. The technical term for white blood cells is leukocytes.

Leukocytes recognize foreign substances by their shapes. The foreign substances are termed *antigens* because the body reacts to them by generating specialized proteins, or *antibodies*. Antibodies attach themselves to the foreign substances, deactivating them and marking them for destruction. The immune system "remembers" how to battle antigens by maintaining their antibodies in the bloodstream, often for years. Inflammation is another function of the immune system. When injury occurs, blood vessels in the area first contract (to stem bleeding) and then dilate. Dilation increases the flow of blood, cells, and natural chemicals to the damaged area, causing redness, swelling, and warmth. The increased blood supply floods the region with white blood cells to combat invading microscopic life forms such as bacteria, which otherwise might use the local damage as a port of entry into the body.

Most people in middle adulthood lead rich sex lives (Duplassie & Daniluk, 2007; Vares et al., 2007).

Stress and the Immune System

Stress suppresses the immune system, as measured by the presence of substances in the blood that make up the immune system (Arranz, Guayerbas, & De la Fuente, 2007; Thornton et al., 2007), leaving us more vulnerable to infections such as the common cold (Barnard et al., 2005; Cohen, 2003).

leukocytes white blood cells

The stress hormones connected with anger—steroids, epinephrine, and norepinephrine—can constrict the blood vessels to the heart, leading to a heart attack in people who are vulnerable (Monat, Lazarus, & Reevy, 2007). The stress of chronic hostility and anger is related to higher cholesterol levels and a greater risk of heart disease (Richards, Hof, & Alvarenga, 2000).

© Blend Images/Jupiterimages

LO4 Sexuality

In the latter part of middle adulthood, the years of 57 to 64, nearly three quarters of adults remain sexually active (Lindau et al., 2007), but sexual problems often work their way into relationships. The most common problems among women are lack of sexual desire and difficulty becoming sexually aroused (Goldstein et al., 2006; Lindau et al., 2007). The most common problem among men is erectile dysfunction (Canadian Erectile Difficulties Research Centre, 2013).

But it is misleading to focus on the negative. Even women in middle adulthood whose partners use Viagra to obtain erections generally report heightened sexual satisfaction as a

Health Benefits to Having Sex

According to the Canadian Erectile Difficulties Research Centre (2013), the average middle-aged Canadian has sex seven times a month. Did you know that there are health benefits to having sex? Middle-aged adults can reap the following health benefits by engaging in regular sexual activity (WebMD, 2012):

- Less stress, better blood pressure
- A boost in immunity
- Burning of calories
- Improved heart health
- A boost in self-esteem
- Enjoyment of deeper intimacy
- Reduced pain when endorphins are released
- Lower risk of prostate cancer due to frequent ejaculations
- Stronger pelvic floor muscles for women, which reduces incontinence
- Better sleep

menopause the cessation of menstruation

perimenopause the beginning of menopause, usually characterized by 3 to 11 months of amenorrhea or irregular periods

climacteric the gradual decline in reproductive capacity of the ovaries, generally lasting about 15 years

result and often have an increase in sexual desire (Vares et al., 2007). Many middle-aged women who have chosen to remain single also report satisfying sex lives (Bridges, 2007).

Menopause, Perimenopause, and the Climacteric

Menopause, or the "change of life," is the cessation of menstruation. Menopause is a normal process that most commonly occurs between the ages of 46 and 50 and lasts for about two years. Perimenopause refers to the beginning of menopause and is usually characterized by 3 to 11 months of amenorrhea (lack of menstruation) or irregular periods.

EMERGING CANADA

Sexually transmitted infections (STIs) are on the rise among middle-aged (40- to 59-year-old) Canadians. In a study that compared 1997 and 2007 STI rates for this age group, chlamydia increased 166%, gonorrhea increased 210%, and syphilis increased 1,100%. Middle-aged men are overwhelmingly represented in this group. The Public Health Agency of Canada explains the rise of STIs on the shift toward more people being single and sexually active at that age. Other factors are impotence medication and middle-aged Canadians' belief that they are not at risk for STIs (Fang et al., 2010). Middle-aged adults may also associate the use of condoms with birth control, which is no longer an issue for middle-aged women. Condoms must continue to be used to protect against STIs.

Menopause is a specific event in a longer-term process known as the climacteric ("critical period"), the gradual decline in the reproductive capacity of the ovaries due to a decline in production of estrogen. The climacteric generally lasts about 15 years, from about age 45 to 60. After age 35 or so, the menstrual cycles of many women shorten, from an average of 28 days to 25 days at age 40 and to 23 days by the mid-40s. By the end of her 40s, a woman's cycles may become erratic, with some periods shortened and others missed.

DID YOU KNOW?

Sexuality continues to be an important part of a middle-aged woman's life.

In middle age, some women feel liberated because of the separation of sex from reproduction.

The estrogen deficit may lead to unpleasant perimenopausal sensations, such as night sweats, hot flashes (suddenly feeling hot), and hot flushes (suddenly looking reddened). Hot flashes and flushes may alternate with cold sweats (feeling suddenly cold and clammy). All of these sensations reflect *vasomotor instability*, disruptions in the body mechanisms that dilate or constrict the blood vessels to maintain an even body temperature. Additional signs of estrogen deficiency include dizziness, headaches, joint pain, tingling in the hands or feet, burning or itchy skin, and heart palpitations. The skin usually becomes drier. There is some loss of breast tissue and decreased vaginal lubrication during sexual arousal. However, menopause does not signal an end to women's sexual appetite.

Long-term estrogen deficiency has been linked to brittleness and porosity of the bones—osteoporosis. Osteoporosis can be handicapping, even life threatening. The brittleness of the bones increases the risk of serious fractures, especially of the hip, and many older women never recover from such injuries (Marwick, 2000). Estrogen deficiency also can impair cognitive functioning and feelings of psychological well-being (Ross et al., 2000; Yaffe et al., 2000).

Hormone Replacement Therapy

Some women with severe physical symptoms have been helped by hormone replacement therapy (HRT), which typically consists of synthetic estrogen or progesterone, or a combination of both. HRT may reduce the hot flushes, night sweats, and vaginal dryness brought about by hormonal deficiencies. Estrogen replacement also lowers the risks of osteoporosis while the woman is taking the medication (Canadian Women's Health Network, 2006). HRT may be beneficial for women who have a high risk of bone fracture and osteoporosis or who experience severe hot flashes and night sweats, as well as those with ovarian malfunction or who have had surgery to remove their ovaries.

HRT is controversial. The Canadian Women's Health Network warns of side effects associated with hormone therapy, including headaches, irritability, memory loss, and blood clots. Other serious risks associated with use over four years are heart disease, gallbladder disease, breast cancer, liver impairment, and endometrial cancer (Canadian Women's Health Network, 2006).

Do Men Undergo an "Andropause"?

For women, menopause is a time of relatively distinct age-related declines in sex hormones and fertility. In men, the decline in the production of male sex hormones and fertility is more gradual (Tan & Culberson, 2003). Thus, a man in his 70s or even older can father a child. However, many men in their 50s experience problems in achieving and maintaining erections (Conrad, 2007), which may reflect circulatory problems, hormone deficiencies, or other factors (Charlton, 2004).

To help with these symptoms, physicians write many prescriptions for testosterone and related drugs each year; however, the benefits are not fully proven, and the risks, including heightened risks of prostate cancer and heart disease, should inspire caution (Tan, 2002; Vastag, 2003).

Sexual Dysfunctions

Sexual dysfunctions are persistent or recurrent problems in becoming sexually aroused or reaching orgasm. Many people have sexual problems on occasion, but sexual dysfunctions are chronic and cause significant distress.

We do not have precise figures on the occurrence of sexual dysfunctions. The most accurate information may be based on the National Health and Social Life Survey (Laumann et al., 1994), in which the researchers found that sexual dysfunctions are quite common. Women more often reported painful sex, lack of pleasure, inability to reach orgasm, and lack of desire. Men were more likely to report reaching orgasm too soon ("premature ejaculation") and performance anxiety.

Dysfunctions that tend to begin or be prominent in men's middle adulthood include lack of interest in sex and erectile dysfunction. Premature ejaculation is more likely to affect them in early adulthood.

One challenge in both men and women in middle adulthood is a lessening of sexual desire. Lack of desire is more common among women than men (Goldstein et al., 2006), but contrary to popular belief, men can also experience a lack of desire. When one member of a couple is more interested in sex than the other, sex therapists often recommend that couples try to compromise and try to resolve problems in the relationship that may be dampening sexual ardour (Moore & Heiman, 2006). The reduction in testosterone levels that occurs in middle and later adulthood may in part explain men's gradual loss of sexual desire—along with some loss of muscle mass and strength (Janssen, 2006). Women's sexual desire may decline with age because of physical and psychological changes (Goldstein et al., 2006; Hayes & Dennerstein, 2005). Some medications, especially those used to control anxiety, depression, or hypertension, may also reduce desire. Viagra has helped a number of women whose sexual response has been hindered by antidepressants (Nurnberg et al., 2008).

Jade Lee/Asia Images/Getty Images

sexual dysfunctions persistent or recurrent problems in becoming sexually aroused or reaching orgasm

DID YOU KNOW?

Sexual dysfunctions are not rare.

According to some studies, sexual dysfunctions are actually common.

Repeated erectile problems, characterized by persistent difficulty in achieving or maintaining an erection during sexual activity, may make men anxious: when sexual opportunities arise, they expect failure rather than pleasure. As a result, they may avoid sex (Bancroft et al., 2005a, 2005b). Their partners may also avoid sexual contact because of their own frustration. The incidence of erectile disorder increases with age. A study of men aged 40–69 in Massachusetts found that nearly half reported problems in obtaining and maintaining erections. Men in the 50- to 59-year-old age group reported erectile problems two thirds as frequently as men in the 60- to 69-year-old age group (Johannes et al., 2000). Biological causes of erectile disorder affect the flow of blood to and through the penis, a problem that becomes more common as men age or experience damage to the nerves involved in erection (Goldstein, 1998, 2000). Erectile problems can arise when clogged or narrow arteries leading to the penis deprive the penis of oxygen (Thompson et al., 2005). Exercise seems to lessen the clogging of arteries, keeping them clear for the flow of blood into the penis. Oral medications—Viagra, Levitra, and Cialis—are commonly used to treat erectile disorder.

Fatigue may lead to erectile disorder in men; in women, fatigue may lead to inadequate lubrication, which can lead to them experiencing painful sex. But these will be isolated incidents unless the couple

EMERGING CANADA

Erectile dysfunction (ED) is difficulty getting or maintaining an erection. ED affects approximately half of all Canadian men over the age of 40. Experts believe that psychological factors, including stress, anxiety, guilt, depression, and fear of sexual failure are behind 10–20% of cases. Many physical factors may also be the cause and may be warning signs of other illnesses. Men who have concerns should talk with their doctor (Canadian Erectile Difficulties Resource Centre, 2013).

multidirectionality in the context of cognitive development, the notion that some aspects of intellectual functioning may improve while others remain stable or decline

attaches too much meaning to them and becomes concerned about future performances. Painful sex, however, can also reflect underlying infections or medical conditions.

Aging can affect the sexual response of women. Perimenopausal and postmenopausal women usually produce less vaginal lubrication than younger women, and the vaginal walls thin, which can render sex painful (Dennerstein & Goldstein, 2005) and possibly create performance anxiety (McCabe, 2005; Schultz et al., 2005).

© ColorBlind Images/Blend Images/Jupiterimages

Exercise is an important component of middle-aged health.

In such cases, artificial lubrication can help supplement the woman's own production, and estrogen replacement may halt or reverse some of the sexual changes of aging (Goldstein & Alexander, 2005). But partners also need to have realistic expectations and consider enjoyable sexual activities they can engage in without discomfort or high demands (McCarthy & Fucito, 2005).

LO5 Cognitive Development

Middle-aged adults continue to develop cognitively in various ways (Schaie, 2005; Willis & Schaie, 2006). For example, the overall Wechsler Adult Intelligence Scale score of a 53-year-old farmer in Saskatchewan decreases from the age of 27. His "verbal intelligence," as measured mainly by his knowledge of the meaning of words, remains pretty much the same, but his "performance subtest" scores, or his ability to perform on timed spatially related subtests, declines. A woman in her mid-40s, who had been "all-business" through her mid-20s in college, moved to Montreal at age 29 and is now extremely knowledgeable in art history and opera. She knew absolutely nothing about these areas as an undergraduate, when her math ability was at its height. A 47-year-old woman returns to college to complete her social work diploma. At first she is fearful of competing with the "kids," but she finds out quickly enough that her sense of purpose and her experiential skills, which are transferrable, more than compensate for what she thinks of as any "loss in brainpower."

Changes in Intellectual Abilities

Intellectual development in adulthood shows multidirectionality, interindividual variability, and plasticity. The concept of multidirectionality underscores the finding that some aspects of intellectual functioning may improve while others remain stable or decline. Rather than being measured strictly by academic degrees, intellectual functioning reflects the interaction of heredity and environmental factors—and, as discussed, the personal choice to engage in further study to increase one's facility in certain intellectual areas.

We discussed *interindividual variability* in terms of physical development, and we also find it in cognitive development. People mature differently in different cultural settings. Many women face sexism in educational environments. Some areas have better schools than others. Some youth find themselves in subcultures in which their peers disapprove if they earn high grades or seek approval from teachers. We also find interindividual variability in middle

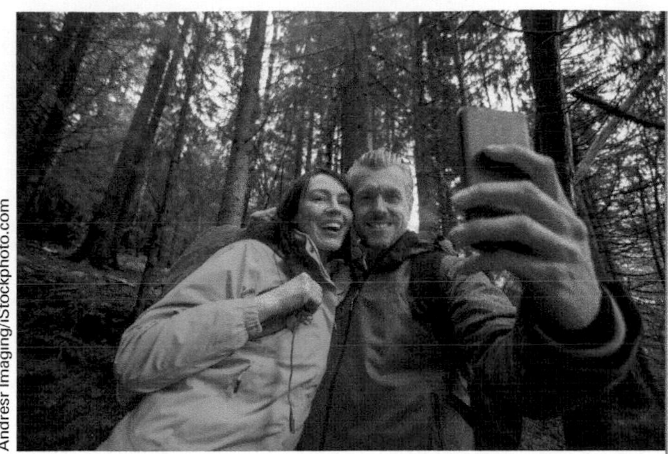
Andresr Imaging/iStockphoto.com

adulthood. Some people find themselves or allow themselves to be in "ruts" in which they gain little if any new knowledge. Others are hungry for the new and so read, travel, and visit museums in any spare moment they can find.

Plasticity refers to people's intellectual abilities not being absolutely fixed but being able to be modified under certain conditions at almost any time in life. The ideal period for language learning may be childhood, but you can pick up a new language in your 40s, 50s, or even later. You learn the meanings of new words for a lifetime (unless you lock yourself in a closet).

Cohort Effects

Consider the so-called "Flynn Effect." Philosopher and researcher John Flynn (2003) found that IQ scores increased some 18 points in the United States between the years 1947 and 2002. Psychologist Richard Nisbett (2007) argues that our genetic codes could not possibly have changed enough in half a century to account for this enormous difference and concludes that the reasons for the change must be social and cultural factors, such as the penetration of better educational systems and mass media.

The people who were middle-aged in 1947 and those who were middle-aged in 2002—those who illustrated the Flynn Effect—belong to different cohorts. Another important study, the Seattle Longitudinal Study, begun in 1956 by K. Warner Schaie, showed certain cohort effects. Participants were tested every seven years, and Schaie and his colleagues were able to assess both cohort effects and longitudinal effects on intellectual functioning. Groups of adults born more recently were superior to those born at earlier times in four of five mental abilities: assessing inductive reasoning, verbal meaning, spatial orientation, and word fluency (Schaie, 1994). The cohorts born earlier performed better in numeric ability. Schaie notes that the intellectual functioning of the members of a society reflects that society's technology and social functioning (Charness & Schaie, 2003). The Seattle study also indicates that the younger cohorts were actually exposed to a better educational system—one that encouraged them to think abstractly *(inductive reasoning)*, learn the meaning of words *(verbal meaning, word fluency)*, and interact with geometric figures *(spatial orientation)*.

> **DID YOU KNOW?**
>
> **The average IQ score of a nation may increase as a reflection of social changes.**
>
> IQ scores in Canada have actually risen over the past couple of generations.

plasticity
the capability of intellectual abilities to be modified, as opposed to being absolutely fixed

crystallized intelligence
a cluster of knowledge and skills that depend on accumulated information and experience, awareness of social conventions, and good judgment

fluid intelligence
a person's skills at processing information

Crystallized Intelligence versus Fluid Intelligence

Some might ask whether math ability and vocabulary size are accurate measures of "intelligence," when they are merely the types of items we find on intelligence tests, and a person's scores on intelligence tests can change as a result of experience. John Horn came up with a distinction that may be of some use. He spoke about the difference between crystallized and fluid intelligence.

> **DID YOU KNOW?**
>
> **Scores on the verbal subtests of standardized intelligence tests can increase for a lifetime.**
>
> An old dog *can* learn new tricks.

Crystallized intelligence is defined as the knowledge and skills that depend on accumulated information and experience, awareness of social conventions, and the capacity to make good decisions and judgments. Crystallized intelligence includes knowledge of a field's specialized vocabulary. Choosing to eat healthful foods could also be considered a sign of crystallized intelligence.

Fluid intelligence involves a person's skills at processing information. Let's do a quick comparison

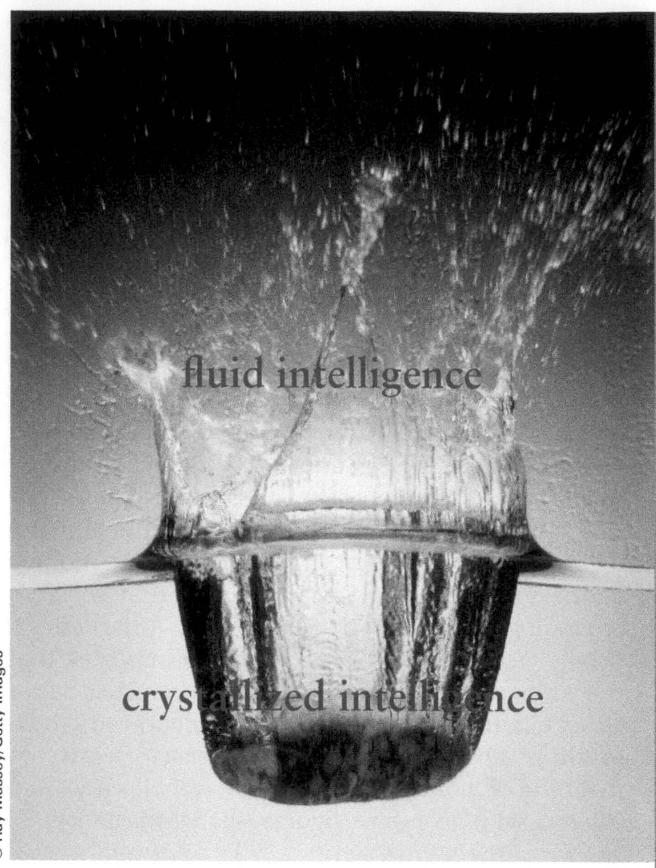

© Ray Massey/Getty Images

to a computer. Your crystallized intelligence is like the amount of information you have in storage. Your fluid intelligence is like a computer's processor and is part of your *working memory*—how much you can keep in mind at once, which works to access and manipulate information and arrive at answers quickly and accurately. Whereas researchers suggest a powerful role for environmental factors in the genesis of crystallized intelligence, they theorize a relatively stronger role for neurological factors in fluid intelligence (Horn & Noll, 1997; Salthouse & Davis, 2006).

Studies show that crystallized intelligence tends to increase with age through middle adulthood. In the absence of senile dementias, crystallized intelligence commonly increases throughout the lifespan, as does achievement on the verbal subtests of standardized intelligence tests. The studies that indicate that crystallized intelligence tends to increase throughout adulthood also show a decline for fluid intelligence (Escorial et al., 2003; Salthouse, 2001). K. Warner Schaie's (1994) longitudinal data shows that the intellectual factor of perceptual speed, which is most strongly related to fluid intelligence, is the factor that drops off most dramatically from early adulthood to late adulthood. Spatial orientation and numeric ability, both related to fluid intelligence, also decline dramatically in late adulthood. Verbal ability and inductive reasoning, which are more related to crystallized intelligence, show gains through middle adulthood and hold up in late adulthood.

Some group trends are revealed, despite interindividual variations. Schaie and his colleagues (2004) found that circumstances such as the following tend to stem cognitive decline into later adulthood:

- Good physical health
- Favourable environmental conditions, such as decent housing
- Remaining intellectually active through reading and keeping up with current events
- Being open to new ideas and new styles of life
- Being socially engaged
- Living with a partner who is intellectually active
- Being satisfied with one's achievements

The presence of these factors can help individuals maximize their potential at any age.

Information Processing

One of the interesting things about aging is that it can become more difficult to keep new information in working memory even when long-term memory remains relatively intact. Many older adults know too well the meaning of "in one ear and out the other."

Speed of Information Processing

The speed of information processing can be measured in several ways. One is simply physical: *reaction time*, which is the time it takes to respond to a stimulus. If you touch a hot stove, how long does it take to pull your hand away? In one assessment of reaction time, people push a button when a light is flashed. Compared with young adults, those in middle adulthood respond to the light more slowly—their reaction time is greater (Hartley, 2006). The difference in reaction time is only a fraction of a second, but it is enough to keep the typical middle-aged adult out of the firing line in the military and on the sidelines of professional sports (Salthouse & Berish, 2005). It can also make a difference when trying to avoid an accident on the highway.

Reaction time is only one aspect of processing speed. The broad cognitive aspect of perceptual speed is also intertwined with fluid intelligence. As with reaction time, the changes in middle adulthood are not that dramatic, but they are measurable. Because of continuous experience with reading and writing, educated individuals in middle adulthood may be better than ever at doing crossword puzzles (largely dependent on crystallized intelligence), but they might find it more difficult to navigate new cities than when they were younger (largely dependent on fluid intelligence) (Salthouse & Siedlecki, 2007).

Most researchers believe that the decline in processing speed reflects changes in the integrity of the nervous system through the death of neurons in the brain to changes in specific parts of the brain and changes in the secretion of neurotransmitters (Hartley, 2006).

Memory

K. Warner Schaie's (1994) longitudinal research found that memory is one intellectual factor that showed improvement through most of the years of middle adulthood and then stability from age 53 to 60. Not all researchers agree. Researchers use several kinds of memory tasks, they do not necessarily attain the same results (Salthouse, Siedlecki, & Krueger, 2006). Contrary to Schaie's results, most researchers conclude that people in middle adulthood and late adulthood perform less well than young adults at memorizing lists of words, numbers, and passages of prose (Salthouse & Davis, 2006).

The main strategies for memorization are *rote rehearsal* and *elaborative rehearsal*. Once we are in the latter part of middle adulthood, we are less likely than when we were younger to be able to learn new information by rote repetition (Salthouse & Babcock, 1991). We are also less capable of screening out distractions (Radvansky, Zacks, & Hasher, 2005). Elaborative rehearsal may also suffer because we are also apparently less capable of rapid classification or categorization (Hultsch et al., 1998).

We have been speaking of working, or short-term, memory. Let's look at storage, or long-term, memory. Not all types of memory functions decline in middle adulthood. We are typically more likely to retain or expand our general knowledge in middle adulthood (Prull, Gabrieli, & Bunge, 2000; Zacks, Hasher, & Li, 2000), such as by learning more about an area in which we have little knowledge or experience.

Procedural memory is a kind of motor memory of how to do things—how to ride a bicycle, how to use a keyboard, how to write with a pen, how to drive a car. Take, for example, a photo of the older Jean Piaget riding a bicycle. The "student of children" looks childlike, but the message for the student of psychology or education is that we can maintain procedural memories for a lifetime.

DID YOU KNOW?

Not all types of memory functioning decline in middle adulthood.

Long-term memory and general knowledge often improve with age.

Expertise and Practical Problem Solving

Any employer with some knowledge of human development would want to hire someone in middle adulthood. Middle-aged people have verbal abilities that match or exceed those of younger people, they have lost very little in the way of fluid intelligence, and they have a greater store of expertise and practical problem-solving skills (Leclerc & Hess, 2007).

Despite interindividual variations, as a group, middle-aged adults show their skills every day in every way. Over the years, they have acquired social skills that enable them to deal better with subordinates and with supervisors. They have a better feeling for other people's limitations and potential, and they have a better understanding of how to motivate them. They may also have experience that will help them remain calm in stressful situations. The parent who was so distraught when the first child cried may now be relaxed when the grandchildren cry. Part of the difference may be the "distance"—the generation of removal. But their patience is also the result of having learned that whether or not children cry, they will usually survive and develop into normal human beings—whatever that means.

The initial training or education of middle-aged people has now had the benefits of years of experience. People in middle adulthood have learned what works and what does not work for them. In terms of professions, for instance, "book learning" and perhaps internships have been supplemented by years of experience in the real world. Pianist Arthur Rubinstein became so accomplished as the years wore on that he often practised "mentally"—he needed the physical keyboard only intermittently. Although he lost some speed when playing rapid passages, he compensated by slowing before beginning those passages, and he created drama when he escalated his pacing.

LO6 Mental Health Issues

Mental health issues refer to a broad range of disorders that can affect "mood, thinking and behaviours" (Centre for Addiction and Mental Health, 2016). Mental health indicators are guided by psychological, social, and emotional well-being. Some of the most common mental health issues in middle adulthood are depression, anxiety disorders, biopolar disorder, schizophrenia, and substance abuse. Mental health issues have become the main cause of healthcare costs in Ontario at 1.5 times higher than all cancers, and 7 times more than infectious diseases (CAMH, 2016). Although highest amongst adolescents and young adults, mental health issues still greatly affect those in middle age.

Depression is the most common mental health issue for those in middle adulthood. The Centre for Disease Control predicts that by 2020, depression will be the second leading cause of disabilities throughout the world (Centers for Disease Control, 2016). Genetics, living in poverty, and environmental stresses are just some causes for mental health issues. Anxiety disorders are also on the rise, particularly in developed countries, where they are higher amongst women. Substance abuse and suicide are higher among men. Of all suicides in Canada, 75% involve men (CAMH, 2016). Men in their middle adulthood commit suicide at a rate of approximately 28 per 100,000, in comparison to women at 8.1 (Sheffield, 2013). Improved awareness and destigmatization of mental health issues is increasing in Canada, in spite of increasing prevalence rates.

LO7 Creativity and Mature Learning

Middle adulthood offers numerous opportunities for exercising creativity, expanding knowledge, and enjoying the intellectual experience.

Creativity

People in middle adulthood can be creative, and many middle-aged adults are at the height of their creativity. Inventor Thomas Edison built the kinetoscope, an early peephole method for watching films, at age 44. At age 56, Pablo Picasso painted *Guernica*, one of the best-known images in art and a protest against the Spanish Civil War. Author Toni Morrison wrote the Pulitzer Prize–winning novel *Beloved* at age 57. Canadian legend Leonard Cohen was in his 50s when he wrote his classic song *Hallelujah*. Yet researchers have found some differences in creativity between young adults and middle adults. Aspects of creativity that are relatively more likely to be found among young adults include creativity in music, mathematics, and physics (Norton et al., 2005; Simonton, 2006b). Strengths in middle age include practical problem-solving skills, critical thinking, and improved decision making. In many ways "we do get better with age!"

DID YOU KNOW?

Creativity continues well into middle adulthood.

Pablo Picasso, Leonard Cohen, and Thomas Edison all had great creative achievements during middle age.

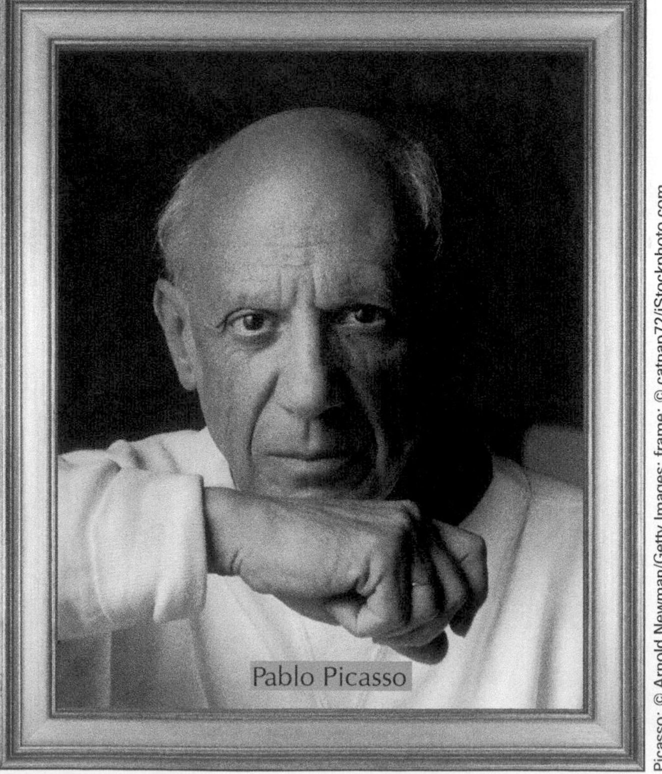
Pablo Picasso

Picasso: © Arnold Newman/Getty Images; frame: © catnap72/iStockphoto.com

Hero Images/Getty Images

In spite of greater socio-economic demands, mature learners are often more committed, motivated, and engaged than younger learners.

Writers and visual artists often continue to improve into middle adulthood, although their most emotional and fervent works may be produced at younger ages.

Mature Learners

For most adults, learning is a perpetual process. We learn when a new store opens in the neighbourhood or when we watch or listen to the media. We learn when we hear what is happening with a family member or when we observe a pet. But when psychologists and educators use the term "adult learning," they are usually speaking of learning as it occurs within a formal educational setting.

Even when we limit our discussion to educational settings, we find vast diversity and inter-individual variation. But research on mature learners suggests that they are likely to have some things in common: they are apt to be highly motivated, and they are more likely than younger learners to find the subject matter interesting for its own sake (Bye, Pushkar, & Conway, 2007).

> Research on mature learners suggests that they are apt to be highly motivated, and they are more likely than younger learners to find the subject matter interesting for its own sake.

Canada has the second highest rate of postsecondary attainment in the world, bettered only by Korea. You might assume that women who have families and have returned to school would be the women with the least exacting combinations of family and work demands. Actually, it's the other way around (Hostetler, Sweet, & Moen, 2007). Women with the greatest demands on them from family and work are those most likely to return to school. But once they're back, their major source of stress is time constraints; those who receive the emotional support of their families and employers experience the least stress and do best (Kirby et al., 2004).

Government assistance programs, such as Ontario's Second Careers, report an increasing number of laid-off adult workers are enrolling in postsecondary schools. Others in middle adulthood may choose to pursue educational goals they were not able to realize in their youth.

STUDY TOOLS

CHAPTER 15

Located at **nelson.com/student**

- ☐ Prepare for tests with a variety of exercises and activities
- ☐ Review Key Terms Flashcards (online or print)
- ☐ Create your own study tools with Build a Summary
- ☐ Watch Observing Development videos to expand your knowledge

Middle Adulthood: Social and Emotional Development

Rinelle/iStockphoto.com

LEARNING OUTCOMES

LO1 Discuss theories of development in middle adulthood

LO2 Analyze stability and change in social and emotional development in middle adulthood

LO3 Consider career developments typical of middle adulthood

LO4 Discuss trends in relationships in middle adulthood, focusing on grandparenting and being in the "sandwich generation"

> "Many of us 'launch' our children into the outside world during middle adulthood and help them establish themselves."

Social perceptions have changed greatly. Robert Havighurst's vision of normalcy was based on "typical" American families when he proposed his "developmental tasks" of middle adulthood in the 1970s. He didn't account for same-sex families, people who cannot or choose not to have children, people who choose the single life, or people who do not undertake "meaningful" social and civic responsibilities. He also did not account for various socio-economic and cultural influences. Havighurst did arrive at a list of issues that affect many of us at ages 40 to 64 years, and we will discuss many of these issues in this chapter.

Many people "launch" their children into the outside world during middle adulthood, and help them establish themselves. Sometimes parents are finding that their children need their help and support for much longer than they might have anticipated.

Those in middle adulthood may find that their preferences in leisure activities have changed over the years, or they may continue activities they have long enjoyed—athletic, cultural, and social pursuits. Some are establishing deeper relationships with life partners, and others are living alone, having never partnered or perhaps having divorced. Some are living in blended families facing the challenges of new family dynamics as a step-parent. Many middle-aged adults are involved in meaningful social or civic activities, but some are not.

Havighurst sounds pessimistic about work—when he mentions keeping performance at a satisfactory level. Many people reach peak performance or first come into their own in middle adulthood. As noted in Chapter 15, the ability to gain expertise and abilities remains generally intact.

Those in middle adulthood may have issues in adjusting to physical aging. Their bodies will be changing and they may encounter illnesses they weren't considering in young adulthood.

Middle-aged children may also need to come to the aid of aging parents, a responsibility that adds challenges to their lives. On the other hand, they may also find new rewards in relationships with aging parents, now they are "all grown up."

Erikson Today

Time & Life Pictures/Getty Images

Stage 7: Generativity versus Stagnation (40–64 years)

Family life and career are the defining features of this stage of development. Middle adulthood is defined by greater responsibility and a more established sense of control. Middle-aged individuals are working toward establishing stability in their life. Erikson spoke of generativity, which is the attempt to produce something that will be long-lasting and worthwhile. Inactivity and meaninglessness are feared. Major life shifts also occur during this stage of development, as children leave home, careers come to an end, and aging parents die. The challenge is to find purpose. Those who are successful boldly step into this step in the lifespan. Those who fail to capture a sense of accomplishment can be ill-equipped for the later stages of life.

Consider THIS

Should middle-aged parents be focused on their own futures, given that their children are now adults?

Please see page 274 for a discussion on this topic.

LO1 Theories of Development in Middle Adulthood

Theories of development in middle adulthood largely deal with the issue of whether we can even consider middle adulthood to be a distinct stage or phase of life.

generativity the ability to generate or produce, as in bearing children or contributing to society.

stagnation the state of no longer developing, growing, or advancing.

Erik Erikson's Theory of Psychosocial Development

Erikson believed that the major psychological challenge of the middle years is *generativity versus stagnation*. **Generativity** is the ability to generate or produce. We have an instinctive drive to leave something of meaning behind for future generations. Failure to achieve this goal leads to **stagnation**. For those that have raised their families and completed their careers, grandparenting offers an interesting opportunity for satisfying generativity in later adulthood.

Daniel Levinson's Seasons

When we walk down the street and encounter others, we may begin a sociological process of categorizing each person into three dimensions: race, gender, and age. For decades, researchers

Robert Havighurst's Developmental Tasks of Middle Adulthood

- ✓ Helping children establish themselves in the outside world
- ✓ Developing a range of enjoyable leisure activities
- ✓ Establishing a deeper relationship with a life partner
- ✓ Becoming involved in meaningful social and civic responsibilities
- ✓ Keeping performance at work at a satisfactory level
- ✓ Adjusting to the physical changes that accompany aging through the midlife period
- ✓ Adjusting to the demands and responsibilities of caring for aging parents

© Cengage Learning

Consider THIS

Should middle-aged parents be focused on their own futures, given that their children are now adults?

In earlier chapters, we looked at "the boomerang" generation, referring to the children of baby boomers, who just keep coming back home. The boomerang generation has created a unique set of problems for their parents. Canada's baby boomers face the financial worries of reduced pensions, low returns on their savings, and high debt. One more additional burden is their boomerang kids. According to a survey, one in five Canadian baby boomers is prepared to risk their own financial security to help out their adult children. Free room and board is the most common financial strain, followed by major purchases (such cars and furniture), rent expenses, groceries, and credit lines for their children. But by taking on these expenses, the baby boomers run the risk of placing their retirement plans in jeopardy (Beltrame, 2013).

As Canada's largest demographic group moves closer to retirement, 46% of Canadians aged 45–64 are still working to pay off their mortgage—including 33% of those between 55 and 64 years of age (Toneguzzi, 2011). According to Erikson, middle-aged adults are trying to establish stability in their life. They are torn between helping their adult children gain a financial footing, ensuring their own financial security, and leaving behind a legacy that proves to themselves and others that their time has made a difference. Naturally, parents are inclined to help their children find a place in the world but at what cost to themselves? How do aging parents protect their own futures? Should they be helping their adult children, or should they be focusing on their own financial stability and security? What impact will these choices have on late adulthood?

© Digital Vision/Getty Images

have studied the influence of race- and gender-based categorization, but what about ageism? Ageism includes all prejudices that are based on age. In our society, a billion-dollar industry is devoted toward making us look and feel younger. Aging is seen to be undesirable, particularly for women. The roots of ageism begin to become firmly established in middle age (Nelson, 2005). A **social clock** guides our judgment regarding the "appropriateness" of certain behaviours, life events, and trajectories (Paglia & Room, 1998).

David Svetlik/Shutterstock.com

According to Daniel Levinson and his colleagues, the years from 40 to 45 comprise a **midlife transition**—a psychological shift into middle adulthood that can be accompanied by a crisis during which people fear they have more to look back on than to look forward to. In the 1960s, Canadian psychoanalyst Elliott Jaques coined the term *midlife crisis* based on his studies of clinical patients who were dealing with depression and angst about getting older. The term became an instant popular culture sensation because, after all, everyone knew someone who fit the stereotype, so it must be true (Nixon, 2011). A **midlife crisis** is a time of dramatic self-doubt and anxiety, during which people sense the passing of their youth and become preoccupied with concerns about the imminence of their own mortality. Levinson believed that marker events such as menopause, the death of a parent or a friend, a divorce, or a child's leaving "the nest" could trigger the crisis.

Once beset by the crisis, some people attempt to deny the realities of aging, such as by having an extramarital affair to prove to themselves they are still sexually attractive, buying a sports car (red, of course), or suddenly shifting careers. Many people, however, view the years from age 45 onward as a type of second adulthood, filled with opportunities for new direction and fulfillment.

social clock
the social norms that guide our judgment regarding the age-related "appropriateness" of certain behaviours

midlife transition
a psychological shift into middle adulthood that is theorized to occur between the ages of 40 and 45, as people begin to believe they have more to look back on than to look forward to

midlife crisis
a time of dramatic self-doubt and anxiety, during which people sense the passing of their youth and become concerned with their own aging and mortality

DID YOU KNOW?

The midlife crisis is more the creation of Hollywood than a reflection of real life.

A midlife crisis may be more the exception than the rule.

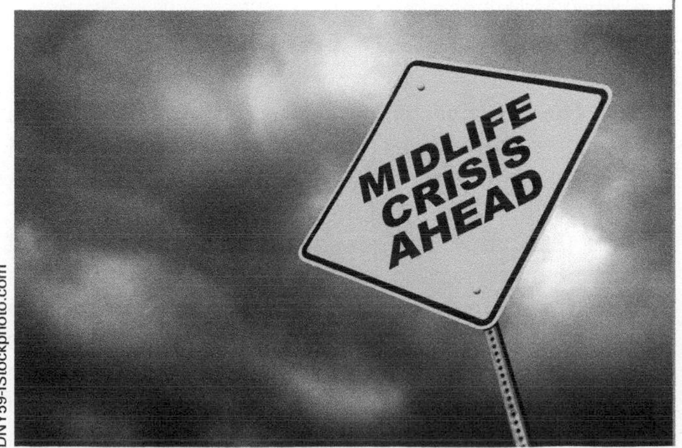

DNY59-iStockphoto.com

Entering Midlife: Crisis, Turning Point, or Prime of Life?

Daniel Levinson and his colleagues (1978) considered the transition to midlife at about the age of 40 to be a crisis, a midlife crisis, characterized by taking stock and often recognizing that one has fallen short of one's dream or dreams. The promising lead vocalist in a local band never made it. The Queen's University business major never sat at the Fortune 500 merger that brought in $25 million. The police college graduate at the top of her class never made RCMP commissioner. Thus, argues Becker (2006), the value of psychotherapy at this time of life should not be minimized.

Who's Having a Crisis?

According to psychiatrist Richard A. Friedman (2008), one excuse for messing up is "My dog ate my homework." Another is "I'm going through a midlife crisis." As mortality begins to loom on the horizon, some people experience the impulse to do things in denial of their age, such as buy a new, fast, expensive car; suddenly quit a job; or leave a loyal spouse for a younger version.

Friedman reports on the experiences of middle-aged men who cheated on their wives, claiming to have had midlife crises. They may say that they love their wives and don't know what got into them, but they're usually seeking novelty and risking too much for a few moments of fun. They behave this way because they feel they have missed opportunities, or because of a heightened sense of mortality.

empty nest syndrome
a feeling of loneliness or loss of purpose that parents, and especially mothers, are theorized to experience when the youngest child leaves home

These portraits are negative, to say the least. Other observers of adult development note that while some theorists present portraits of middle-aged people suddenly focusing on tragedy, loss, or doom, others find people to be in or entering the "prime of life" (Almeida & Horn, 2004; Lachman, 2004).

For First Nations, Métis, and Inuit peoples, the medicine wheel provides life teachings for maintaining inner, community, and ancestral balance. On the medicine wheel, middle adulthood is represented by the western doorway. The western direction, or *Epangishmok* in Ojibway, is often represented by the berry. It is with growth that things ripen and harvesting begins. The western doorway is also connected with the season of autumn. The west teaches about the heart and evaluates what's going on in life. It is a place of transformation and change. In adulthood, death and loss become more and more immediate (4D Interactive, 2006). Death doesn't have negative connotations; it is seen as freedom, including freedom to go on in another capacity (4D Interactive, 2006). Each stage of life is significant on the medicine wheel, and midlife doesn't connote crisis but rather is a time of reflection and transformation. It is also a time to find balance when guiding and caring for children and honouring and respecting elders.

People can develop certain illnesses at almost any time of life, but most people in middle adulthood encounter little decline in physical prowess. Intellectually, little fluid intelligence, if any, is lost, and crystallized intelligence is growing.

Middle-aged adults, especially professionals, are also often earning more money than young adults. They are more likely to be settled geographically and vocationally, although they may experience midlife career changes and movement from one organization or business to another, or being laid off due to national economic changes. By now, many have built systems of social support and may be involved in enduring romantic and social relationships and have children.

The flip side, as we will see, may be overwhelming responsibility, such as caring for adolescent children, a spouse, aging parents, and remaining in the workplace all at once. But many in middle adulthood are at the height of their productivity and resilience, despite these challenges.

The Life-Events Approach

The life-events approach to middle age focuses on the particular challenges and changes that people are likely to face at this time of life rather than on phases or stages of life. Numerous researchers have found that the most stressful life events of middle adulthood tend to include the death of a spouse or a child; the death of a parent or a sibling; marital divorce or separation, or separation from a cohabitant; hospitalization or change in the health status of oneself, one's child, parent, or sibling; the need to care for elderly parents; a change in the relationship with children; financial difficulties; concern about appearance, weight, or aging; moving; change or loss of employment; a change in a relationship with an important friend; or a change in responsibilities at work (Etaugh & Bridges, 2006; Lorenz et al., 2006).

One common change in middle adulthood occurs when the last child leaves the home. Although we once assumed that parents whose children have moved out would experience a painful "**empty nest syndrome**," this time can just as often be a positive stage (Etaugh & Bridges, 2006). Today, many middle-aged women and men in developed nations find they are "as young as they feel."

As sources of stress, negative life events, including physical illness and depression, have been shown to be harmful to people's health in middle adulthood (Lorenz et al., 2006; Ryff, Singer, & Seltzer, 2002). Some people who are under stress resort to a host of medicines, both prescribed and over the counter, or alcohol and drugs (Outram, Murphy, & Cockburn, 2006). An accumulation of stressful life events even seems capable of accelerating age-related declines in memory functioning (VonDras et al., 2005).

DID YOU KNOW?

Many parents no longer experience an "empty-nest syndrome" when the last child leaves home.

Having the last child leave home is often a positive event for middle-aged women.

The positive aspects of middle-aged people's situations—such as having understanding and helpful family members or friends—and a positive outlook can have moderating effects on stressors (Etaugh & Bridges, 2006). A sense of control has been shown to override the effects of stress and foster feelings of well-being among midlife adults (Windsor et al., 2008). Middle-aged adults are less likely to be depressed by negative life events when they perceive such events as capable of being changed and as specific rather than

Life Events

- ✓ Death of a spouse
- ✓ Marriage
- ✓ Illness
- ✓ Financial problems
- ✓ Marital separation or divorce
- ✓ Change in appearance
- ✓ Loss of a job

© Image Source

global problems (Adler, Kissel, & McAdams, 2006). Also, stress management strategies, such as exercise, socializing, journalling, meditation, and talk therapy, can prove useful.

© Stuart McClymont/Getty Images

EMERGING CANADA

Freedom 55 Financial is a financial institution that offers planning and advice on investments, retirement income, and life insurance, the implication being that if you plan with them, you will be financially confident and free at age 55 to do whatever you want (Freedom 55, 2016). When it comes to Freedom 55, however, Canadians aren't retiring; rather, they are leaving their spouses. The divorce rate in 2008 was highest in the Yukon province, followed by Alberta, then Ontario. Despite an overall decline in the national divorce rate, the over-50 crowd is the only age group experiencing more divorces. In 2007, the divorce rate for those over age 65 had doubled since 1980. As the lifespan unfolds, children leave the family, and couples have limited years left to be truly happy. This realization seems to be affecting people's decisions to remain married, leading to the new trend of the "27-year itch" (Kingston, 2007).

LO2 Stability and Change in Middle Adulthood

Many researchers use five basic factors of personality isolated by Robert McCrae and Paul Costa and their colleagues to study stability and change in the personality development of adults over several decades (McCrae & Costa, 2006; Terracciano, Costa, & McCrae, 2006). These factors are extraversion, agreeableness, conscientiousness, neuroticism (emotional instability), and openness to experience (see Table 16.1) (McCrae & Costa, 1997). A study of more than 5,000 German, British, Spanish, Czech, and Turkish people suggests that the factors are related to people's basic

TABLE 16.1

The "Big Five": The Five-Factor Model of Personality

Factor	Name	Traits
I	Extraversion	Contrasts talkativeness, assertiveness, and activity with silence, passivity, and reserve
II	Agreeableness	Contrasts kindness, trust, and warmth with hostility, selfishness, and distrust
III	Conscientiousness	Contrasts organization, thoroughness, and reliability with carelessness, negligence, and unreliability
IV	Neuroticism	Contrasts nervousness, moodiness, and sensitivity to negative stimuli with coping ability
V	Openness to experience	Contrasts imagination, curiosity, and creativity with shallowness and lack of perceptiveness

Source: © Cengage Learning

"big five" personality traits basic personality traits derived from contemporary statistical methods: extraversion, agreeableness, conscientiousness, neuroticism (emotional instability), and openness to experience

temperaments, which are considered to be largely inborn (McCrae et al., 2000). The researchers interpret the results to suggest that our personalities tend to mature rather than be shaped by environmental conditions, although the expression of personality traits is certainly affected by culture. (For example, a person who is "basically" open to new experiences is less likely to believe in a traditional, fundamentalist society than in an open society.)

Are There Sudden Shifts in Personality?

The notions of crises or turning points in emotional development also suggest that people undergo rather sudden changes or shifts in personality. As pointed out by Robert McCrae and Paul Costa, Jr. (2006), we have widely assumed that our personalities are deeply affected by adult life events such as getting married, working our way up in a vocation, and having and rearing children. However, according to two decades of longitudinal research, the "big five" personality traits tend to show a good deal of stability over time, at least after age 30 (Roberts & DelVecchio, 2000).

Longitudinal and cross-sectional research has shown some consistent trends in group personality change over the years. By and large, however, those who are, say, most extraverted in young adulthood will remain most extraverted in middle adulthood (Roberts & DelVecchio, 2000; Roberts, Walton, & Viechtbauer, 2006). On the other hand, for adults as a group, male and female, the traits of agreeableness and conscientiousness tend to increase from young adulthood to middle adulthood. Neuroticism declines throughout the same period, meaning that people become more emotionally stable. Extraversion and openness to new experience either remain the same or decline slightly in middle adulthood. The trait of being open to new experience decreases once more in late adulthood.

DID YOU KNOW?

Age differences play a role in personality trends.

Unlike childhood and adolescence, where there can be negative trends in personality development, during middle adulthood there tends to be greater maturity and adjustment (Soto, Oliver, Gosling, & Potter, 2011).

LO3 Work in Middle Adulthood

As suggested by Erikson and Levinson, many workers are at their peak in middle adulthood. They have had years to "learn the ropes," and many have advanced into the highest ranks of their trades or professions. One's work can continue to provide social benefits, a sense of identity, and self-esteem.

Job Satisfaction

Canadians are among the most satisfied workers in the world. In a global study of workers in 23 countries, only those in Denmark and Norway had a higher satisfaction level with their current employer (Fortier, 2010).

A study of more than 2,000 university employees found that job satisfaction increased steadily throughout middle adulthood (Hochwarter et al., 2001). The gains were greatest for men, ,especially for men who were white-collar workers, for example, professors. Some workers—particularly blue-collar workers—reported feelings of alienation and dissatisfaction. Some complained that supervisors treated them with disrespect and failed to ask them how to improve working conditions and productivity (Judge & Klinger, 2008). These feelings are particularly painful for middle-aged workers when their supervisors are young adults. Middle-aged women are often balancing the demands of the workplace and a family, and they may still experience a "glass ceiling" on the job (Casini & Sanchez-Mazas, 2005). Although women may be sought out in the hiring process, they will not necessarily have an easy time advancing. Still, most women and blue-collar workers reported more satisfaction on the job throughout middle age—just not as much as white-collar men.

The growing job satisfaction throughout middle age can be linked to factors such as increases in both expertise and income. Workers in middle adulthood may also have more realistic perceptions of their career goals. They may have come to terms with recognition that they (most of them) will never be the CEO of Apple, Inc. or the lead singer in a famous rock band.

DID YOU KNOW?

Women who have a college or university education experience less personal distress as they advance from middle adulthood to late adulthood.

Aside from increased concern with aging, this is generally true.

Art Babych/Shutterstock.com

Justin Trudeau, age 45, became the second-youngest Prime Minister of Canada when he won the federal election in 2015.

Career Change in Middle Adulthood

People change careers for many reasons—for more money, more job security, greater prestige, and more stimulation, among other reasons (Jepsen & Choudhuri, 2001; Sullivan et al., 2003). Most people who change their careers do so in young adulthood. By middle adulthood, people tend to have greater responsibilities and to have become more "entrenched" in their pursuits. They may also wonder whether they have the time and the ability to start over.

For reasons such as these, most career changes in midlife involve shifts into related fields (Shultz & Adams, 2007). For example, in the entertainment world, an actor might become a director or a producer. In the field of education, a teacher might move into educational administration. More radical shifts can occur, and they can also be successful (Hall, 2004). A laboratory chemist who has spent 20 years working for a pharmaceuticals company might decide she wants to work with people and have more time for herself, so she might choose to teach high-school chemistry and travel during the summers. These are all voluntary, planned changes.

EMERGING CANADA

Second Careers is a government program designed to fund and retrain Ontarians who are unemployed and have been forced into a career change at a time when most didn't expect it. With the emergence of a knowledge economy, it is projected that by 2026, 77% of the Canadian labour force will need a postsecondary education to be employable. Currently, only 60% of the Canadian workforce aged 35 or older meets this requirement, so the government is sending them back to school. This opportunity is exciting for some middle-aged students and terrifying for others. By 2032, a projected 1.73 million workers will need to be retrained for a second career in Ontario alone (Miner, 2010).

Not all career changes are planned, though. Some middle-aged people change careers following a personal crisis such as a divorce, conflict with co-workers, or being fired. In such cases, middle-aged people sometimes pick up whatever work they can to sustain themselves (Shultz & Adams, 2007).

Unemployment

This scenario is playing out all too frequently: a well-educated and accomplished woman lost her executive position in her late 40s, when her company was bought out and a new management team came in. She knew she was in a vulnerable position because the company taking over usually "chops off the head" of the acquired company; still, she thought she might have enough seniority to escape notice. Not so. New management cut in half the number of professionals at her level. At first she focused on her generous severance package. She thought she would take a month off to relax and then use the head-hunting firm hired by the company to relocate. However, she soon found that hers was a relatively small industry, and very few openings approximated her level. Former work friends clustered around her at first, but began to drift away. After four months, she had sunk into a deep clinical depression.

One group of researchers (McKee-Ryan et al., 2005) used meta-analysis to average out the findings of 104 studies of the effects of unemployment on the health of young and middle-aged adults. Unemployed subjects had lower physical and psychological well-being than employed subjects, and unemployed middle-aged subjects had lower well-being than unemployed young adults. Within the samples of unemployed middle-aged adults, those who fared worst were those for whom work was more important, those who had fewer financial resources and less social support, and those who tended to blame themselves for having lost their job. Those who fared best were those who had emotional and financial resources and social support, those who could structure their time, and those who had realistic strategies for job hunting or finding substitutes for jobs.

When we consider women who are unemployed, we find age differences in the intensity of their search for employment and their willingness to accept certain kinds of jobs. In a study of married women in four age groups, post-adolescents (up to age 21) spent more time trying to find employment than did women aged 22–35, 36–49, or 50–62 (Kulik, 2000). The women aged 50–62 were most likely to accept jobs low in pay, as long as they liked the work; those aged 22–49 were most likely to reject jobs because they conflicted with family life or because of work conditions. As in the study by McKee-Ryan and her colleagues (2005), the older women in the study were more likely to experience declines in their well-being following the loss of employment. On the other hand, the older women were least likely to suffer financial strain.

LO4 Relationships in Middle Adulthood

The term *middle adulthood* is a convenient term for describing people whose ages lie between young adulthood and late adulthood. In terms of their family relationships, their generation is in the middle in another way—often "sandwiched" in between their parents and their children (and sometimes their grandchildren).

Evolving Parent–Child Relationships

When children become emerging adults or young adults, most parents in Canada are content to "launch" their children to live on their own or with roommates. In many cases, the children remain at least partly financially dependent, sometimes for several years (Aquilino, 2005). Children who have been close to their parents may also remain in some ways emotionally dependent, even after they are out on their own—or at the very least, they may be hurt when their parents disapprove of their personal choices.

Parents are usually satisfied with their children living apart from them, providing they call or email regularly and drop by (or allow the parents to drop by) with reasonable frequency. Parents often try to find a balance between staying in touch and "interfering," especially once their children have partners or children of their own.

For some, leaving home is not a choice. Child marriage—under the age of 18, is common practice for some sects in international communities. It's assumed that once a girl is married she is a woman, and a boy, once married, becomes a man. In spite of the Early Marriage and the Convention on the Rights of the Child (CRC), which is meant to prevent marriage below the age of 18, there are many child brides today throughout the world. Child marriage occurs as a way to secure property and family wealth, in keeping with traditional custom, or to create stronger bonds between families. A recent study found that in six West African countries 44% of 20–24 year old women were married under the age of 15. Girls orphaned or living in poverty are more susceptible; they may become an additional wife to an older man. In areas of Albania, young girls are encouraged to "catch a husband" before migrating for work, as well as to avoid possible kidnapping when going to school (UNICEF, 2001).

When adult children take partners or marry, new challenges can emerge for their parents. First of all, parents may feel that nobody can be "good enough" for their child, and sometimes their child makes what the parents consider to be a poor choice. The parents must then deal with the issues as to whether, and how, they express their feelings about it. Regardless of the partner or spouse chosen by their child, parents must deal with in-laws and the extended family of the in-laws. Sometimes the families of both partners get along well, but more often the families would not have chosen each other as friends. Still, for the sake of their child, the parents usually try to act friendly on the occasions when the families are together. But such relationships can be another source of stress.

Grandparenting

As baby boomers age, they enter into the social role of grandparenting. The term *grandboomers* has been coined to describe them (Grandparenting in the twenty-first century, 2005). Let's begin this section by selecting one of the following two statements. Which statement will you live by— or forever destroy your relationship with your child by?

- As a grandparent, you have the right to tell your son or daughter how to raise your grandchild.
- As a grandparent, you have to keep your mouth tightly shut when you see your son-in-law or daughter-in-law doing what you consider to be the wrong thing with your grandchild.

One of the most challenging jobs of the newly minted grandparent is to navigate carefully between the treacherous rocks of reckless interference and painful neglect.

Young adulthood is the time of life when most of those who will bear children do so, and middle

Jupiterimages/Getty Images

Ashok Sinha/Getty Images

adulthood is the time of life when most of us who will become grandparents begin that role. Having and relating to grandchildren, like having and relating to one's children, has its pluses and its minuses. But research generally finds that the balance is more positive in the case of having grandchildren. For example, a study of grandparenting conducted in China, Greece, and Poland found that having grandchildren was viewed as an overwhelmingly positive event in each culture and was beneficial to grandparents, both socially and psychologically (Filus, 2006). The study also found that grandparents, like parents, participated in the care of grandchildren and in their recreational and educational activities. In situations in which the grandparents do not live in the same household with the grandchildren, parents spend a higher proportion of their time with their children in care-taking activities, whereas grandparents spend relatively more time in recreational and educational activities.

Cross-cultural studies also find gender differences in grandchildren's relationships with their grandparents that tend to parallel their relationships with their parents. Studies in the United States, Poland, Greece, Germany, and China all find that grandchildren through adolescence spend more time involved in activities with their grandmothers than with their grandfathers (Filus, 2006; Höpflinger & Hummel, 2006). Grandchildren are also relatively more involved with their mother's parents than their father's parents. It may come as a surprise, but the sex of the grandchild has little effect on these overall findings. Even male grandchildren, who would toss the football back and forth with the grandfather and not the grandmother, tend to gravitate more toward contacts with grandmothers than with grandfathers. Despite the greater involvement with grandmothers, grandchildren say they value their grandfathers just as highly—but researchers are not about to devise an experiment that would put children's lip service to the test!

LGBTQ Grandparents

One study that relied on extensive interviews with lesbian and bisexual grandmothers found that the experiences of these women were in some ways similar to those of heterosexual people, and in other ways quite different (Orel, 2006). Like most heterosexual grandparents, the lesbian and bisexual grandmothers believed that they were important sources of emotional support for their grandchildren. They also reported that their children either helped (facilitated) or hindered (discouraged) their relationships with their grandchildren, and that the pattern might shift from time to time. Recent research shows that younger children are likely to be more open and more accepting of the disclosure of sexual orientation than teenage children, who are likely struggling with their own sexual identity and may have the mistaken belief that older adults are largely asexual (Goldberg & Allen, 2013).

One of the "hyped" advantages of being a grandparent is being able to play with grandchildren but then being able to "send them home," leaving the "real work" to the children's parents. In many cases, however, this mindset assumes that the parents have lots of money and the grandparents have leisure time. It fails to address all the complications of family separations or divorce, or loss of identity as a family unit, situations that are so common today (Bridges et al., 2007; Soliz, 2007). It also doesn't address the fact that some grandparents hardly—or never—see their grandchildren because of geographical separation or harsh feelings following family conflict.

The notion of grandparents enjoying the best of the grandchild while escaping responsibility also ignores the thousands of grandparents who bear the primary responsibility for rearing grandchildren which is increasingly common, particularly for first generation immigrants in Canada (Goodman, 2007a; Hayslip & Kaminski, 2006).

Grandparents in Charge

In most cases, one or two biological parents determine the course of child rearing of their own children. But sometimes grandparents play a major role—or *the* major role (Goodman, 2007a). For example, an Israeli study of immigrants from Ethiopia and Eastern European countries found that grandparents who lived with their single-parent children and their grandchildren had a strong influence on their grandchildren and contributed to the overall adjustment of the family (Doron & Markovitzky, 2007).

Many studies (e.g., Doron & Markovitzky, 2007; Goodman, 2007b) show that grandparents have less

sandwich generation the term for middle-aged people who need to meet the demands of both their own children and their aging parents

influence when they live with their married children and their grandchildren; under these circumstances, they are less likely to contribute to the adjustment of the family. Rather than "filling a hole," they frequently become a source of discord between their son or daughter and their son- or daughter-in-law.

In some cases, grandparents are the sole caregivers of their grandchildren. These arrangements typically begin when the grandchild has a single parent (Hayslip & Kaminski, 2006; Park & Greenberg, 2007). Now and then, the parent dies, or the parent may be in the military and be sent on a tour of duty; the parent may place the child with grandparents while she or he "tries" living in another location, with or without a new job, and the time extends. The parent may even run off, perhaps mired in personal troubles.

Regardless of the reasons that grandparents—usually grandmothers—assume the responsibility for parenting grandchildren, becoming a parent, again, in middle adulthood, can be particularly stressful (Gerard, Landry-Meyer, & Roe, 2006; Leder et al., 2007) particularly if there are extenuating circumstances for grandparents parenting, like being a single grandparent, or having financial or health concerns. It would seem, however, that many grandparents do enjoy their roles in their grandchildren's lives. Their grandchildren value them deeply, even when they do not see them as often as they might wish (Bridges et al., 2007). Grandparents' find the child-rearing experience often allows them to relate to their grandchildren in a more relaxed way than parents can.

Middle-Aged Children and Aging Parents

Because of increasing life expectancy, more than half of the middle-aged people in developed nations have at least one living parent, and they frequently go on to experience late adulthood together (Callahan, 2007; U.S. Bureau of the Census, 2008). In Far Eastern nations such as China, Japan, and Korea, older parents tend to live with their children and their grandchildren; not so in Canada and the United States (Kwok, 2006).

The relationships between middle-aged children and their older parents can grow quite close,

AP Photo/Eric Risberg/Canadian Press

especially as tensions and expectations from earlier years tend to slip into history. If an older mother had been disappointed in her now middle-aged daughter's choice of a husband, the marriage may have since ended or worked itself out, or there might be grandchildren to focus on. The passing years and other events place relationships in perspective.

If the aging parents require assistance, in the United States and Canada, the task usually falls to a middle-aged daughter, who then becomes part of what has been dubbed the sandwich generation. She is "sandwiched" between several generations, caring for or contributing to the support of her own children at the same time she is caring for one or two parents (Grundy & Henretta, 2006). She may also be helping out with her own grandchildren. If she is fortunate, a sibling living in the vicinity can share the task. Given that she is also likely to be in the workforce, her role overload is multiplied (Gans & Silverstein, 2006).

Most grandparents do enjoy their roles in their grandchildren's lives. Their grandchildren value them deeply, even when they do not see them as often as they might wish.

In 2002, about 2.6 million people between the ages of 45 and 64 had children under the age of 25 living with them. Of these, about 27% also provided elder care, usually for their parents or parents-in-law. Most of these people in the sandwich generation were employed; some were forced to change work hours, refuse a job offer, or have a reduced income. In fact, 1 in 7 had reduced their hours over a one-year period and 10% suffered an income cut. Most (82%) who worked and had to juggle child and elder care were able to cope. The results for workers aged 45–64, however, showed that only 1 in 10 workers who were caring for an elderly family member, either with or without children at home, struggled with balancing home and work needs as well as meeting other responsibilities (Williams, 2004).

In other societies, particularly in northern Asia, grandparents are expected to help with child rearing. If their child/children move, they will travel sometimes for long periods of time, or move altogether, to where their children are so that they can assist their children with child rearing. This helps to reduce daycare costs, but can be a burden on aging or ill grandparents.

Siblings

For most North Americans, sibling relationships continue into late adulthood. The majority of people in middle adulthood have at least one living brother or sister. Most adult sibling relationships are close, but they tend to reflect the nature of sibling relationships in childhood. Sisters tend to have more intimate relationships than brothers (Bedford & Avioli, 2006). Sometimes, the sibling relationships that were antagonistic or competitive in childhood or adolescence grow closer in middle adulthood if the siblings cooperate in caring for a disabled parent (Leone, 2000). Conversely, a sibling relationship that had been close can grow distant if one sibling allows another to do all the work in caring for a parent.

Friends

Adolescents often belong to cliques and crowds, and young adults often have large numbers of friends. In middle adulthood, the number of friends tends to dwindle, and the adults tend to place more value on the friends they keep, both as couples and as individuals (Adams & Ueno, 2006). In midlife, people become less willing to spend their time with "just anybody"; therefore, their remaining friends are still more likely to be "close matches" in terms of interests, activities, and, often, years of mutual experience. For this reason, the loss of a friend is felt more deeply. But as in earlier years, friendships have sex differences. Male friends are more likely to be competitive and less likely to be intimate than female friends (Adams & Ueno, 2006; Muhlbauer & Chrisler, 2007).

Toni Antonucci and Kira Burditt (2004) report that men are more likely than women not to have friends or other close social relationships, and that social isolation is related to poorer physical and psychological health and with mortality. In a survey of 1,421 men ranging in age from 20 to 93, men without close social ties were found to be significantly more depressed than men with relationships.

© Blend Images/Jupiterimages

DID YOU KNOW?

Middle-aged people tend to have fewer friends than young adults do.

Middle-aged people tend to have fewer friends than young adults, but they have more in common with the friends who remain.

STUDY TOOLS

CHAPTER 16

Located at **nelson.com/student**

- ☐ Prepare for tests with a variety of exercises and activities
- ☐ Review Key Terms Flashcards (online or print)
- ☐ Create your own study tools with Build a Summary
- ☐ Watch Observing Development videos to expand your knowledge

CHAPTER 17

Late Adulthood: Physical and Cognitive Development

Tomas Rodriguez/Getty Images

LEARNING OUTCOMES

LO1 Describe trends in physical development in late adulthood, focusing on life expectancy

LO2 Compare programmed and cellular damage theories of aging

LO3 Identify common health concerns associated with late adulthood

LO4 Discuss cognitive development in late adulthood

"People aged 65 and older are the most rapidly growing segment of the Canadian population."

An Agequake Is Coming. People aged 65 and older are the most rapidly growing segment of the Canadian population. So many people are living longer that we are in the midst of a "greying of Canada," an aging of the population that is having significant effects on many aspects of society.

LO1 Physical Development

In 1900, only 1 person in 25 was over the age of 65. Today, that figure has more than tripled, to 1 in 8 of us. Since the 1960s seniors have increased from 8% to 14% of the population in 2009. There will continue to be a steady increase, and by 2036 it is projected that 23 to 25% of the Canadian population will be seniors, and 24 to 28% by 2061 (Statistics Canada, 2016b). To put these numbers in historical context, consider that through virtually all of human history, until the beginning of the 19th century, only a small fraction of humans lived to the age of 50.

Life expectancy varies from province to province and between the provinces and the territories.

The population over age 65 is usually divided into the young-old (65–74), the old-old (75–84), and the oldest-old (85 and over). The groups are assigned according to the likelihood that they will be dependent on family members or the medical community.

DID YOU KNOW?

Canadians have a higher life expectancy than our neighbours in the United States.

This difference is likely due to our healthcare system.

Longevity and Life Expectancy

Life span, or longevity, is the length of time a person can live under the best of circumstances. The life span of a species, including humans, depends on its genetic programming. With the right genes and environment, and with the good fortune to avoid serious accidents or illnesses, people have a life span of about 115 years (Dong, Milholland, & Vijg, 2016).

life span (longevity) the maximum amount of time a person can live under optimal conditions

life expectancy the amount of time a person can actually be expected to live in a given setting

One's life expectancy refers to the number of years a person in a given population group can actually expect to live. The average European American child born 100 years ago in the United States could expect to live 47 years. The average African American could expect a shorter life of 35.5 years (Andersen & Taylor, 2009). Great strides have been made in increasing life expectancy. A century ago, lower life expectancy rates were, in part, the result of high infant mortality rates due to diseases such as German measles, smallpox, polio, and diphtheria. These diseases have since been brought under control or eliminated. Other major killers, including bacterial infections such as tuberculosis, are now largely controlled by antibiotics. Other factors that contribute to longevity include public health measures such as safer water supplies, improved dietary habits, and more accessible healthcare. Life expectancy across the provinces has also changed significantly.

Thomas Fricke/First Light/Getty Images

Being a centenarian means you have celebrated your 100th birthday.

Sex Differences in Life Expectancy

Although the longevity gap between men and women is narrowing, life expectancy among men trails that among women by about 4.7 years (78 years for men versus 82.7 years for women) (CBC News, 2008).

Why the gap? For one thing, heart disease typically develops later in life in women than in men because estrogen provides women some protection against heart disease. Also, men are more likely to die from accidents, cirrhosis of the liver, strokes, suicide, homicide, HIV/AIDS, and some forms of cancer. Many of these causes of death reflect unhealthy habits.

Many men are reluctant to have regular physical examinations or to talk about health concerns with their doctors. Many men avoid medical attention until problems that could have been easily prevented or treated become serious or life-threatening. For example, women are more likely to examine themselves for signs of breast cancer than men are to examine their testicles for unusual lumps.

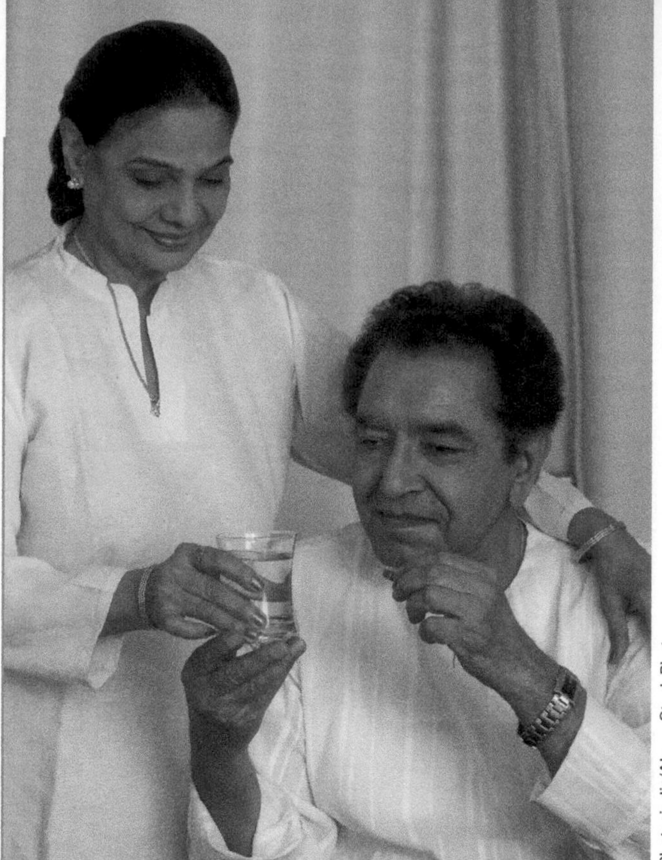
Photosindia/Alamy Stock Photo

After we reach our physical peak in our 20s, our biological functions begin a gradual decline.

Physical and Social Changes

After we reach our physical peak in our 20s, our biological functions begin a gradual decline. Aging also involves adapting to changing physical and social realities. People who were once "newbies" in the workplace become the "old guard." One-time newlyweds celebrate their silver and golden anniversaries. Yet aging can involve more than adjustment; it can also bring about personal growth and exciting changes. Even advanced age can bring greater harmony and integration to our personalities. However, we must learn to adapt to changes in our mental skills and abilities. Although older people's memories and fluid intelligence may not be as keen as they once were,

Is Poverty among the Elderly a Problem in Canada?

Canada ranks third in an international comparison of poverty rates among the elderly. Data reveals that there are currently 600,000, or 6.7% of, seniors living in poverty in Canada. Poverty rates are highest among women, particularly widows, who are over the age of 75. Despite beliefs that most older people are impoverished, however, Canadians aged 65 and older are actually less likely than the general population to live under the poverty level.

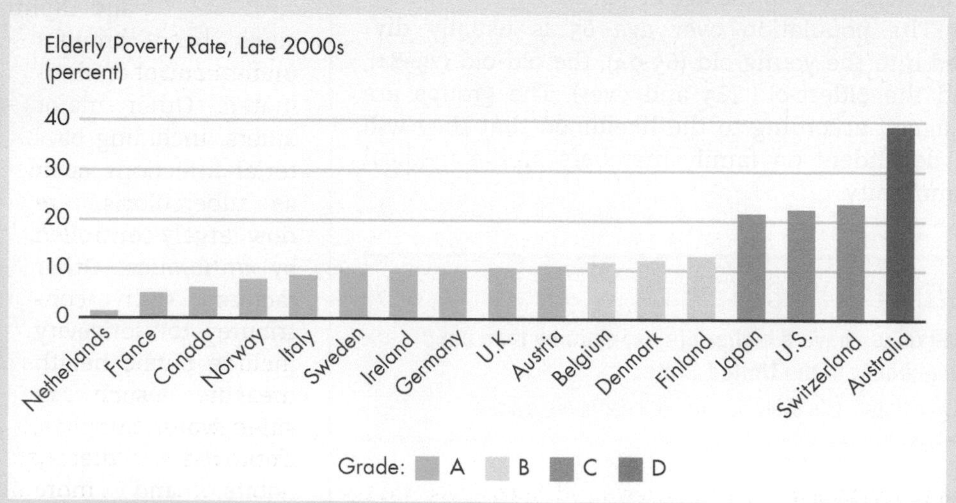

Sources: The Conference Board of Canada. (2016). How Canada performs. Retrieved October 28, 2016, from http://www.conferenceboard.ca/hcp/details/society/elderly-poverty.aspx; CARP. (2014). 600,000 seniors in Canada living in poverty. http://www.carp.ca/2014/12/11/600000-seniors-canada-live-poverty/

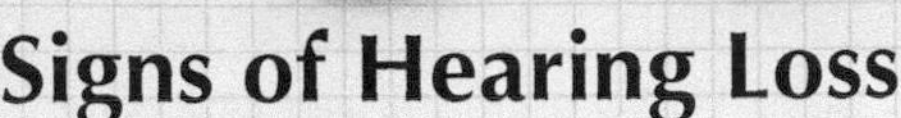

Signs of Hearing Loss

- Speaking more loudly than necessary in conversation
- Constantly asking for words to be repeated
- Straining to hear
- Misunderstanding conversations, especially in noisy situations
- Favouring one ear
- Thinking that people always mumble
- Turning the television or radio up louder than usual
- Having difficulty hearing on the telephone
- Withdrawing from social contact
- Ringing or buzzing in one or both ears
- Appearing dull and disinterested, slow to respond, or just not quite "with it"

If you are experiencing any of these signs of hearing loss, contact CHS to make an appointment for a hearing test.

Source: Canadian Hearing Society, http://www.chs.ca/signs-hearing-loss

© Radius Images/Jupiterimages

older people often have the maturity and experience that make them sources of wisdom.

Aging also has social aspects. Our self-concepts and behaviour as "young," "middle-aged," or "old" stem in large measure from cultural beliefs, personal or family beliefs, and our social clock. In historical times, "mature" people had great prestige, leading men to routinely claim to be older than they were. Women, whose reproductive capacity was valued, did not want to be viewed as being older than they were.

DID YOU KNOW?

In historical times, aging was viewed so positively that men often claimed to be older than they actually were.

Maturity was considered a mark of prestige but asking job applicants their age is illegal in Canada.

By contrast, the modern era has been marked by **ageism**—prejudice against people because of their age. Stereotypes that paint older people as grouchy, incapable, sluggish, forgetful, and fixed in their ways, shape the way people respond to older people and can actually impair the older people's performance (Horton, 2008).

ageism
prejudice against people because of their age.

cataract
a condition characterized by clouding of the lens of the eye

glaucoma
a condition involving abnormally high fluid pressure in the eye

presbycusis
loss of acuteness of hearing due to age-related degenerative changes in the ear

Changes in Sensory Functioning

Beginning in middle age, the lenses of the eyes become brittle, leading to presbyopia, as discussed in Chapter 15. In later adulthood, chemical changes of aging can lead to vision disorders such as cataracts and glaucoma. **Cataracts** cloud the lenses of the eyes, reducing vision. Today, outpatient surgery for correcting cataracts is routine. If performed before the condition progresses too far, the likelihood of regained sight is excellent. **Glaucoma** is a buildup of fluid pressure inside the eyeball. Glaucoma can lead to tunnel vision (lack of peripheral vision) or blindness. Glaucoma rarely occurs before age 40, but affects about 1 in 250 people over the age of 40, and 1 in 25 people over 80. Rates are higher among diabetics than non-diabetics. Glaucoma is treated with medication or surgery.

Blend Images/Jupiterimages

The sense of hearing, especially the ability to hear higher frequencies, also declines with age. **Presbycusis** is age-related hearing loss that affects about 1 person in 3 over the age of 65 (Sommers, 2008). Hearing ability tends to decline more quickly in men than in women. Hearing aids magnify sound and can compensate for hearing loss. The Ten Ways to Recognize Hearing Loss questionnaire from the National Institute on Deafness and other Communication Disorders shows how to recognize hearing loss.

Taste and smell become less acute as we age. The sense of smell decreases significantly from youth to advanced late adulthood. We also lose taste buds in the tongue with aging. As a result, foods may need to be more strongly spiced to yield the same flavour.

osteoporosis
a disorder in which bones become more porous, brittle, and subject to fracture, due to loss of calcium and other minerals

sleep apnea
temporary suspension of breathing while asleep

Bone Density

Bones begin to lose density in middle adulthood, becoming more brittle and vulnerable to fracture. Bones in the spine, hip, thigh, and forearm lose the most density as we age. **Osteoporosis** is a disorder in which bones lose so much calcium that they become dangerously prone to breakage. Osteoporosis can lead to bone fractures, the most serious of which are hip fractures, that is, breaks in the thigh bone, just below the hip joint. Hip fractures often result in hospitalization, loss of mobility, and, as is often the case in people in advanced late adulthood, death from complications.

Osteoporosis is, in most cases, a manageable disorder. Osteoporosis can shorten one's stature by centimetres and deform one's posture, causing the curvature in the spine known as "dowager's hump." Both men and women are at risk of osteoporosis, but women are at greater risk. Men typically have a larger bone mass, which provides greater protection against the disorder. Following the decline in bone density that women experience after menopause, women stand about twice the risk of hip fractures and about eight times the risk of spine fractures that men do. But older women who engage in walking as a form of regular exercise are less likely than their sedentary counterparts to suffer hip fractures (USDHHS, 2005).

Facts and Stats from Osteoporosis Canada:

- In adults over age 50, 1 in 4 women and at least 1 in 8 men have osteoporosis (the gender difference is due to drops in estrogen in women).
- Osteoporotic hip fractures consume more hospital bed days than strokes or heart attacks.
- Adults aged 19–50 need 1,000 mg of calcium a day. Adults older than age 50 need 1,200 mg of calcium a day (see the calculator on the Osteoporosis Canada website).
- Routine vitamin D supplementation is recommended for all Canadian adults.
- Regular physical activity, in particular weight-bearing activities, can help build and maintain bone mass throughout life.
- Smoking and excess alcohol consumption contribute to bone loss.
- It is never too late to take steps to reduce further bone loss.

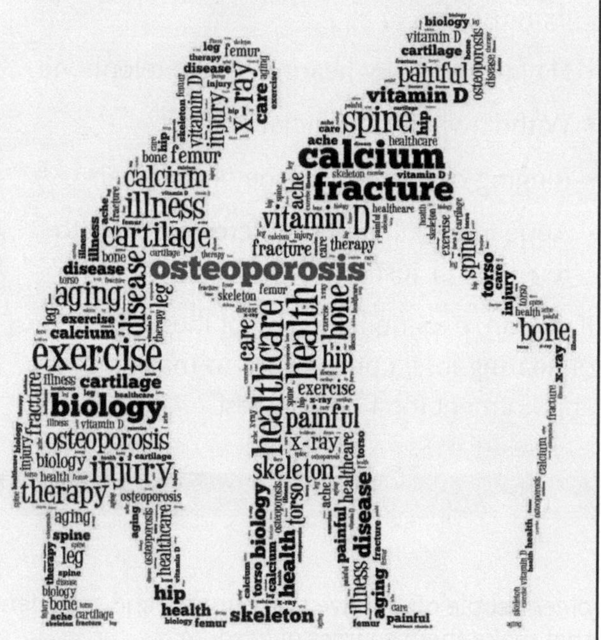

Mypokcik/Shutterstock.com

Source: Osteoporosis Canada. (2010). Facts and statistics: About osteoporosis. Retrieved from http://www.osteoporosis.ca/index.php/ci_id/8867/la_id/1.htm Used with permission.

Sleep

Older people need about 7 hours of sleep per night, yet sleep disorders such as insomnia and **sleep apnea** become more common in later adulthood (Wickwire et al., 2008). People who have sleep apnea stop breathing repeatedly during the night, causing awakenings. Apnea may be more than a sleep problem. For reasons that are not yet entirely clear, apnea is linked to increased risk of heart attacks and strokes.

Sleep problems in late adulthood may be related to other changes of late adulthood. Sometimes these changes are symptoms of psychological disorders such as depression, anxiety, or dementia. Men with enlarged prostate glands commonly need to urinate during the night, causing awakening. Loneliness can also contribute to sleeplessness, especially after the death of a close friend, spouse, or life partner.

Sleep medications are the most common treatment for insomnia (Wickwire et al., 2008). Alternatives may include keeping a regular sleep schedule, calming worries, and using relaxation techniques, natural remedies, and exercise.

Sexuality

According to unfounded cultural myths, older people are sexless and older men with sexual interests are "dirty old men." If older people believe these myths, they may renounce sex or feel guilty if they remain sexually active. Older women stop being sexualized in North American mainstream societies and are often no longer considered "desirable." This may be due to a societal preoccupation with being youthful. Another cultural myth is that older women aren't interested in sex. This is as opposed to older men who may be seen still to be virile and attractive as they age, as in the case of George Clooney.

People do not lose their sexuality as they age.

Sexuality doesn't decrease with aging. Sexual daydreaming, sex drive, and sexual activity all tend to decline with age, but sexual satisfaction may remain high (Barnett & Dunning, 2003). Older people with partners usually remain sexually active (Laumann et al., 2006). Most older people report that they like sex and may have their most sexually fulfilling years (Trudel et al., 2007). Sexual activity among older people, as among other groups, is influenced not only by physical structures and changes but also by psychological well-being, feelings of intimacy, and cultural expectations (Laumann et al., 2006).

EMERGING CANADA

The growing spread of sexually transmitted infections (STIs) among older Canadians might be partly a result of the Internet dating boom, as well as the belief that older seniors may not have STI's. Rapid intimacy often develops online before a couple even meets, which seems to accelerate the likelihood of sexual contact when the man and woman do meet. The phenomenon seems to be particularly common among middle-aged and older people, who are flooding online dating sites. The increased intimacy of social media seems to reduce the likelihood of safe-sex practices.

Changes in Women

Many of the physical changes in older women stem from a decline in estrogen production. The vaginal walls lose much of their elasticity and grow paler and thinner. Thus, sexual activity may become irritating. The thinning of the walls may also place greater pressure against the bladder and urethra during sex, sometimes leading to urinary urgency and a burning sensation during urination.

The vagina also shrinks. The labia majora lose some of their fatty deposits and become thinner. The vaginal opening constricts, and penile entry may become difficult. Following menopause, women also produce less vaginal lubrication, and lubrication may take minutes, not seconds, to appear. Lack of adequate lubrication is a key reason for painful sex. Additional lubrication can be used. Women's nipples still become erect as they are sexually aroused, but the spasms of orgasm become less powerful and fewer in number. Thus, orgasms may feel less intense, even though the experience of orgasm may remain just as satisfying. Despite these changes, women can retain their ability to reach orgasm well into their advanced years.

Changes in Men

Male adolescents may achieve erection in seconds, but after about age 50, men take progressively longer to achieve erection. Erections become less firm, perhaps because of lowered testosterone levels (Laumann et al., 2006).

Testosterone production usually declines gradually from about age 40 to age 60, and then begins to level off. However, the decline is not inevitable and may be related to a man's general health. Sperm production tends to decline, but viable sperm may be produced by men in their 70s, 80s, and 90s.

Nocturnal erections diminish in intensity, duration, and frequency as men age, but they do not normally disappear altogether (Perry et al., 2001). An adolescent may require but a few minutes to regain erection and ejaculate again after a first orgasm, whereas a man in his 30s may require half an hour. Past age 50, regaining erection may require several hours.

An older male may enjoy orgasm as thoroughly as he did at a younger age. Following orgasm, erection subsides more rapidly than in a younger man.

DID YOU KNOW?

Age-related sexual changes occur more gradually for men.

Unlike many women's changes, which are related to menopause, men's changes are not clearly related to one biological event.

Patterns of Sexual Activity

Despite decline in physical functions, older people can lead fulfilling sex lives. Years of sexual experience may more than compensate for any lessening of physical response (Laumann et al., 2006). Frequency of sexual activity tends to decline with age because of hormonal changes, physical problems, boredom, and cultural attitudes. Yet sexuality among older people is variable (Laumann et al., 2006). Many older people engage in sexual activity as often as or more often than when younger; some develop an aversion to sex; others lose interest.

cellular clock theory a theory of aging focusing on the limits of cell division

telomeres protective segments of DNA located at the tips of chromosomes

hormonal stress theory a theory of aging that suggests stress hormones, left at elevated levels, make the body more vulnerable to chronic conditions

Couples may adapt to the physical changes of aging by broadening their sexual repertoire to include more diverse forms of stimulation. The availability of a sexually interested and supportive partner may be the most important determinant of continued sexual activity (Laumann et al., 2006). The Internet has opened new doors of access and creativity for the older generation, just as it has for today's younger generations.

LO2 Theories of Aging

Although we can list all the things that happen as we age, we don't know exactly why they happen. Theories of aging fall into two broad categories:

- *Programmed theories* see aging as the result of genetic instructions.
- *Cellular damage theories* propose that aging results from damage to cells.

© Yoshida-Fujifotos/The Image Works

Twins Gin Kanie (left) and Kin Narita lived to the ages of 108 and 107.

Programmed Theories of Aging

Both environmental and genetic factors dictate our longevity. Programmed theories propose that aging and longevity are determined by a biological clock that ticks at a rate governed by genes. Many people who live to be 80 and over do so, in part, thanks to genetic factors. A person can have specific gene variations that make them less susceptible or resistant to certain diseases.

Centenarians are people who live beyond 100. In developed countries, 1 out of 6,000 live beyond the age of 100. Supercentenarians are older than 110. Only 1 in 7 million falls into this category. Ongoing data about the environmental and epidemiological components that contribute to health and well-being are important to understanding longevity (Zeliadt, 2010).

Programmed aging theorists believe that adaptive species survive long enough to reproduce and transmit their genes to future generations. From the evolutionary perspective, a species has no advantage (and probably a disadvantage given limited food supplies) if it were able to repair cell machinery and body tissues to maintain life indefinitely.

Cellular clock theory focuses on the built-in limits of cell division. After dividing about 50 times, human cells cease dividing and eventually die (Hayflick, 1996). Researchers find clues to the limits of cell division in **telomeres**, the protective segments of DNA at the tips of chromosomes. Telomeres shrink each time cells divide. When the loss of telomeres reaches a critical point after a number of cell divisions, the cell may no longer be able to function (Epel et al., 2006). The length of the telomeres for a species may determine the number of times a cell can divide and survive.

Hormonal stress theory focuses on the endocrine system, which releases hormones into the bloodstream. Hormonal changes foster age-related changes such as puberty and menopause. As we age, stress hormones, including corticosteroids and adrenaline, are left at elevated levels following illnesses, making the body more vulnerable to chronic conditions such as diabetes, osteoporosis, and heart disease. The changes in

Pogonici/iStockphoto.com

The cellular clock theory of aging implies that eventually our cells run out of time.

the production of stress hormones over time may be preprogrammed by genes.

Immunological theory holds that the immune system is preset to decline by an internal biological clock. For example, the production of antibodies declines with age, rendering the body less able to fight off infections. Age-related changes in the immune system also increase the risk of cancer and may contribute to general deterioration.

Cellular Damage Theories of Aging

Programmed theories assume that our genes preset our internal bodily processes to age. In contrast, cellular damage theories propose that internal bodily changes and external environmental assaults (such as carcinogens and toxins) cause cells and organ systems to malfunction, leading to death. For example, the wear-and-tear theory suggests that over the years, our bodies—as machines that wear out through use—become less capable of repairing themselves.

The free-radical theory attributes aging to damage caused by the accumulation of unstable molecules called *free radicals*. Free radicals are produced during metabolism by oxidation, possibly damaging cell proteins, membranes, and DNA (Sierra, 2006). Most free radicals are naturally disarmed by nutrients and enzymes called *antioxidants*. Most antioxidants are either made by the body or found in food. As we age, our bodies produce fewer antioxidants (Rattan, Kristensen, & Clark, 2006). People whose diets are rich in antioxidants are less likely to develop heart disease and some cancers.

As we age, cell proteins bind to one another in a process called *cross-linking*, thereby toughening tissues. Cross-linking stiffens collagen—the connective tissue supporting tendons, ligaments, cartilage, and bone. One result is coarse, dry skin. Cross-linking theory holds that the stiffening of body proteins accelerates and eventually breaks down bodily processes, leading to some of the effects of aging (Rattan et al., 2006). The immune system combats cross-linking, but becomes less able to do so as we age.

When considering the many theories of aging, remember that aging is an extremely complex biological process that may not be explained by any single theory or cause. Aging likely involves a combination of these and other factors.

immunological theory a theory of aging that holds that the immune system is preset to decline by an internal biological clock

wear-and-tear theory a theory of aging that suggests that over time our bodies become less capable of repairing themselves

free-radical theory a theory of aging that attributes aging to damage caused by the accumulation of unstable molecules called free radicals

cross-linking theory a theory of aging that holds that the stiffening of body proteins eventually breaks down bodily processes, leading to aging

LO3 Health Concerns and Aging

Although aging takes a toll on our bodies, many gerontologists believe that disease is not inevitable. They distinguish between *normal aging* and *pathological aging*. In normal aging, physiological processes decline slowly with age, enabling the person to enjoy many years of health and vitality into late adulthood. In pathological aging, chronic diseases or degenerative processes, such as heart disease, diabetes, and cancer, lead to disability or premature death. Figure 17.1 illustrates how older adults typically need more healthcare than

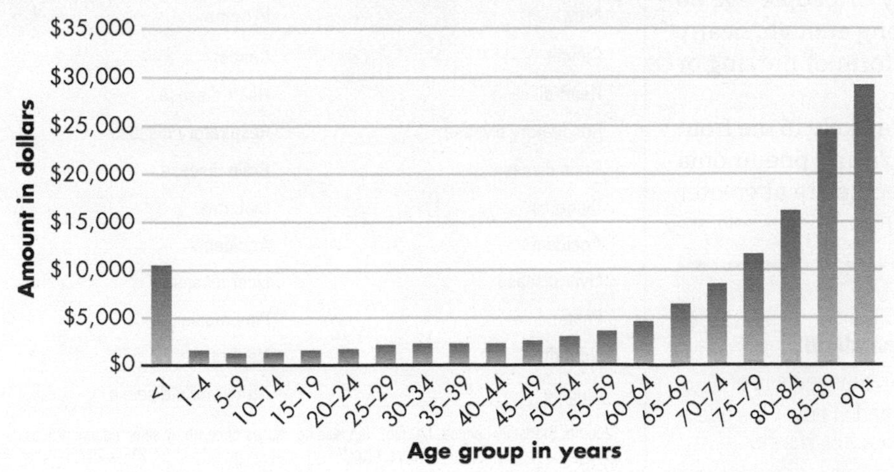

FIGURE 17.1

Provincial/Territorial Government Health Expenditure per Capita, by Age Group, Canada, 2012

Source: "Figure 9: Provincial/territorial government health expenditure per capita, by age group, Canada, 2012," p. 19, *National Health Expenditure Trends, 1975–2005 Report*, October 2015 from Canadian Institute for Health Information (CIHI).

EMERGING CANADA

The baby boomers are aging into the *silver tsunami*. For health-care researchers and policy analysts, the *silver tsunami* refers to the significant social changes that will result in 20 years, when seniors aged 65 and older will make up almost one-quarter of the population. Canada's healthcare dollars will be directed to the needs of older Canadians, and the financial strain will be significant. The Canadian Institute for Health Information (CIHI) focuses attention on the 44% of all government health spending in 2008 on seniors 65 and older, even though they made up only 13.7% of the population. We need to plan for the near future, when the silver tsunami increases their numbers significantly (Barua & Rovere, 2012).

Fernando Zabala/Alamy

Healthcare researchers refer to the silver tsunami—the financial strain that will wash over the Canadian healthcare system.

younger persons. Health expenditures in 2012 were highest among those 80 years of age and over. Although people over the age of 65 make up about 12% of the population, they occupy 25% of the hospital beds. As the numbers of older people increase in the 21st century, so will the cost of healthcare (2008).

Free radicals, which may contribute to the effects of aging, are produced during metabolism by oxidation, possibly damaging cell proteins, membranes, and DNA.

It is not true that most older adults require institutional care, such as nursing homes or residential-care facilities. The majority of older adults remain in their own communities after retirement; more than 66% of adults age 65 and older live in their own homes. Less than 10% of older adults live in nursing homes or other long-term care facilities. The population of nursing homes is made up largely of people age 80 and older. Yet if older adults live long enough, nearly half will eventually require some form of nursing or home healthcare.

In 1900, older people were more likely to die from infectious diseases such as influenza and pneumonia than they are today. Today, older people are at greater

DID YOU KNOW?

Most older adults remain living independently.

Most older Canadians do NOT spend their later years in a retirement community. More than 66% of adults over the age of 65 live in their own homes.

Mikadun/Shutterstock.com

risk of dying from chronic diseases such as heart disease and cancer. More than 4 out of 5 people over the age of 65 have at least one chronic health problem (Heron, 2007). Some health issues, such as varicose veins, are minor. Others, such as heart disease, pose serious health risks. While longevity is increasing, so too are the number of years older persons are living with one or more chronic health problems.

Cancer, Heart Disease, and Respiratory Disease

Cancer is the leading cause of death in men and women over the age of 65, followed by heart disease and respiratory disease (see Table 17.1).

As we age, the risk of most cancers rises because the immune system becomes less able to rid the body of precancerous and cancerous cells. Many older people are not adequately

TABLE 17.1

Ten Leading Causes of Death in Canada by Gender, 65–74

Men	Women
Cancer	Cancer
Heart disease	Heart disease
Respiratory disease	Respiratory disease
Brain disease	Brain disease
Diabetes	Diabetes
Accidents	Accidents
Liver disease	Liver disease
Pneumonia	Pneumonia
Nephritis	Nephritis
Suicide	Alzheimer's disease

Source: Statistics Canada. (2009b). Ten leading causes of death by selected age groups, by sex, Canada — 65 to 74 years. http://www.statcan.gc.ca/pub/84-215-x/2012001/tbl/t008-eng.htm

Is Calorie Restriction the Fountain of Youth?

Calorie restriction (CR) is a key intervention for weight loss and inhibiting cancers. Obesity-associated issues increase the risk and progression of cancer. CR affects growth factors, inflammation, pathways, and cancer growth and is also being used in cancer prevention strategies. In subjects (primarily animals) who received a 20–40% reduction in energy intake compared to an unrestricted group, there was a reversal of weight gain and an inhibiting of cancer growth. New research also suggests CR decreases the risk of diabetes and neurological degeneration in rhesus monkeys. CR, therefore, positively affects metabolism and reduces chronic diseases, as observed primarily in animals (Hursting, Dunlap, Ford, Hursting, Lashinger, 2013).

It remains to be seen whether, and to what degree, calorie restriction extends the life expectancy of people who have access to modern healthcare. Moreover, many people have difficulty keeping their weight within normal limits. How willing would we be to lower our calorie intake even further? Researchers are therefore also seeking alternative ways of triggering the anti-aging responses caused by calorie restriction.

Anna Hoychuk/Shutterstock.com

screened or treated for cancer or heart disease. One reason for the gap in diagnosis and treatment is *elder bias* (Ludwick & Silva, 2003), or discrimination against older people, by some health professionals.

Among the top chronic conditions, which are listed in Figure 17.2, several are also leading causes of death or pose significant risk factors for mortality. Hypertension, which affects about 50% of Canadians over the age of 65, is a major risk factor for heart attacks and strokes. Diabetes, the fifth most common chronic illness, is the fifth leading cause of death. Other chronic conditions, such as asthma, chronic bronchitis, cataracts, chronic sinusitis, visual impairment, and varicose veins, are rarely fatal but can lead to disability and reduced quality of life.

Arthritis

Arthritis is joint inflammation that results from conditions affecting the structures inside and surrounding the joints. Symptoms progress from redness to heat, swelling, pain, and loss of function. Children can also be affected by arthritis, but it is more common with advancing age. Arthritis is more common in women than men. Osteoarthritis and rheumatoid arthritis are the two most common forms of arthritis.

Osteoarthritis is a painful, degenerative disease characterized by wear and tear on joints. By the age of 60, more than half of Canadians show some signs of the disease. Among people over the age of 65, two thirds have the disease. The joints most commonly affected are in the knees, hips, fingers, neck, and lower back. Osteoarthritis is caused by erosion of cartilage, the pads of fibrous tissue that cushion the ends of bones. As cartilage wears down, bones grind together, causing pain (Axford et al., 2008). Osteoarthritis is more common among obese people because excess weight adds to the load on the hip and knee joints. Health professionals suggest using over-the-counter anti-inflammatory drugs (aspirin, acetaminophen, ibuprofen, naproxen) and prescription anti-inflammatory drugs to help relieve pain and discomfort (Axford et al., 2008). Specific exercises are also sometimes prescribed. In severe cases, joint replacement surgery may be needed.

arthritis
inflammation of the joints

osteoarthritis
a painful, degenerative disease characterized by wear and tear on joints

rheumatoid arthritis
a painful, degenerative disease characterized by chronic inflammation of the membranes that line the joints

Rheumatoid arthritis is characterized by chronic inflammation of the membranes that line the joints as a result of the body's immune system attacking its own tissues. The condition affects the entire body. It can produce unrelenting pain and eventually lead to severe disability. Bones and cartilage may also be affected. Onset of the disease usually occurs between the ages of 40 and 60. Anti-inflammatory drugs are used to treat it.

Substance Abuse

According to a 2007 to 2011 Canadian Health Measures Survey, prescription drug use rose with age from 12% among 6- to 14-year-olds to 83% among 65- to 79-year-olds.

Prescription drug use was also associated with physical and mental health conditions. Among people

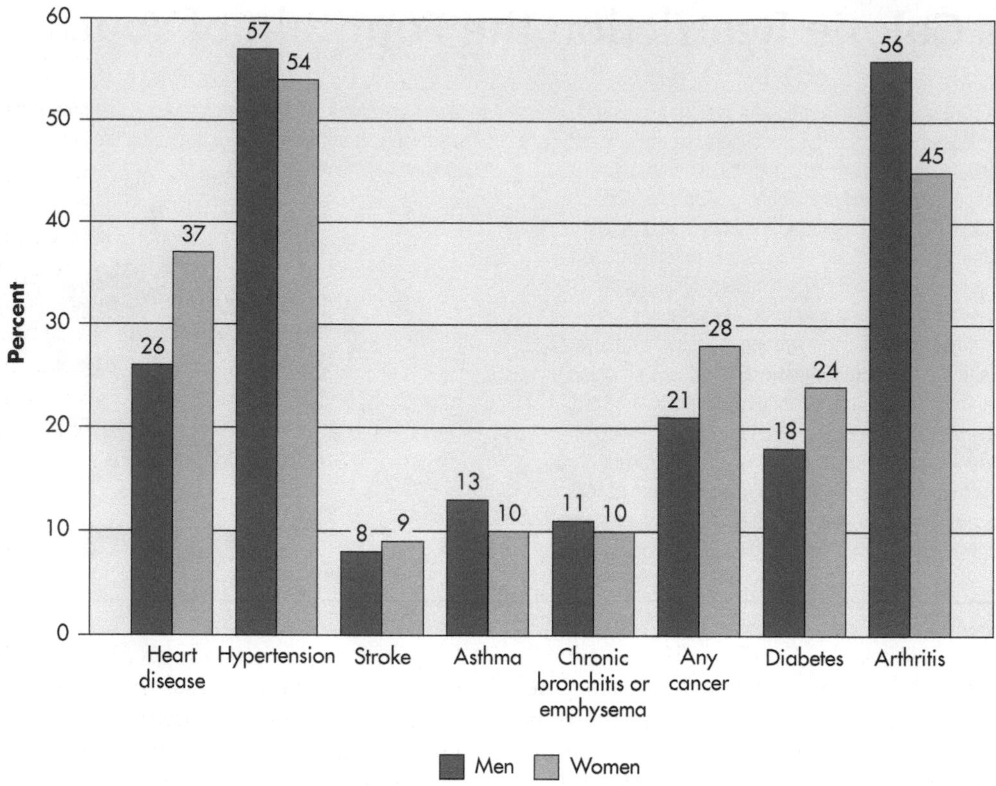

FIGURE 17.2

Chronic Health Conditions among People Age 65 and Over

The leading chronic health conditions affecting people in late adulthood are hypertension, arthritis, and heart disease.

Source: (2009) U.S. Government, Health Promotion and Aging. http://lghttp.48653.nexcesscdn.net/80223CF/springer-static/media/samplechapters/9780826131881/mobile/9780826131881_Chapter1.html

with at least three chronic conditions, the percentage of drug use was more than 90%. The percentage of people reporting prescription medication use rose with increasing levels of disability and pain, and with lower levels of self-perceived health and emotional well-being (Statistics Canada, 2015g). Among the most commonly used drugs are blood pressure and heart disease medication, tranquilizers, sleeping pills, and antidepressants. Taken correctly, prescription drugs can be of help; used incorrectly, they can be harmful.

Substance abuse is, unfortunately, not rare in late adulthood. Millions of older adults are addicted to, or risk becoming addicted to, prescription drugs, especially tranquilizers. According to the Centre for Addiction and Mental Health, medication issues in older adults are a significant problem. An estimated 50% of prescriptions are not taken properly. In addition, up to 20% of Canadian hospitalizations are the result of problems with medication. Further, the following signs of medication issues are sometimes mistaken for signs of aging: slurred speech, increased confusion, lethargy or sleepiness, and stumbling and falls (Centre for Addiction and Mental Health, 2009).

Although alcohol consumption is lower overall among older people, compared with among younger adults, many older adults suffer from long-term alcoholism. The health risks of alcohol abuse increase with age. The slowdown in the metabolic rate reduces the body's ability to metabolize alcohol, increasing the likelihood of intoxication. The combination of alcohol and other drugs,

DID YOU KNOW?

Medication issues are common in older adults.

Medication issues can be mistaken for signs of aging.

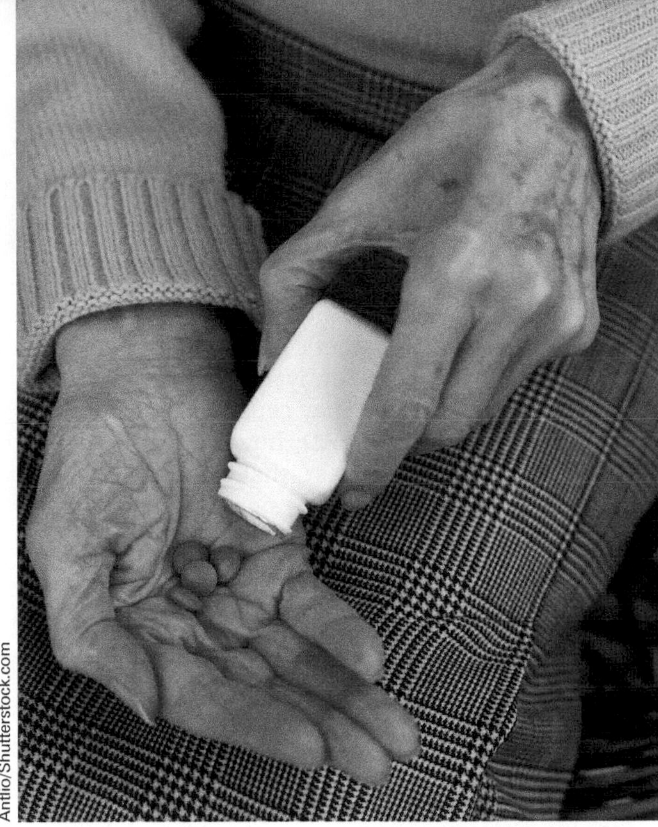

Antlio/Shutterstock.com

including prescription drugs, can be dangerous or even lethal. Alcohol can also either diminish or intensify the intended effects of prescription drugs.

Accidents

Although accidents can occur at any age, older people face greater risks of unintentional injuries from falls, motor vehicle accidents, residential fires, and non-fatal poisoning. Accidents are the sixth leading cause of death among older Canadians. Falls are especially dangerous for older adults who have osteoporosis because of their increased risks of fractures (Facts about Falling, 2008).

dementia
a condition characterized by deterioration of cognitive functioning

Many accidents involving older adults can be prevented by equipping the home with safety features, such as railings and non-skid floors. Wearing proper glasses and using hearing aids can reduce the risk of accidents resulting from vision or hearing problems, including many motor vehicle accidents. Adherence to safe driving speeds is especially important among older drivers because they have slower reaction times than younger drivers.

Substance Abuse in Older Adults

- 6–10% of older adults who drink will experience problems.
- 12% of men 65 to 74 years and 5% over 75 years were considered heavy drinkers (5 or more drinks on a single occasion at least once per month in the last year).
- Alcohol use by people 65 and older increased from 58.5% in 1997 to 73.5% in 2007.
- Alcohol and prescribed and over-the-counter medications are currently the drugs of most concern for seniors.
- The number of seniors with a history of illicit drug use is projected to increase.
- Cannabis is increasingly prevalent in older populations and has increased by 4% from 1998 to 2007.

Source: Permission granted by The Addictions Sub Group of the SHRTN (Seniors Health Research Transfer Network) Collaborative Geriatric Mental Health, Addictions and Behavioural Issues Community of Practice, Ontario.

Dementia and Alzheimer's Disease

Dementia is a condition characterized by dramatic deterioration of mental abilities involving thinking, memory, judgment, and reasoning. Dementia is not a consequence of normal aging but of disease processes that damage brain tissue. Some causes of dementia include strokes; Parkinson's disease; brain infections such as meningitis, HIV infection,

© Sean Murphy/Getty Images

Alzheimer's disease a severe form of dementia characterized by memory lapses, confusion, emotional instability, and progressive loss of cognitive functioning

and encephalitis; chronic alcoholism; infections; and tumors (Lippa, 2008; see Figure 17.3). The most common cause of dementia is **Alzheimer's disease** (Alzheimer Society, 2010). Approximately 500,000 Canadians have dementia. Within a generation, experts predict, dementia will affect 1.1 million Canadians who will require 756 million hours of care, at an estimated cost of $153 billion (Alzheimer Society, 2010).

Although some dementias may be reversible, especially those caused by tumours and treatable infections and those resulting from depression or substance abuse, the dementia resulting from AD is progressive and irreversible (Lippa, 2008).

Alzheimer's disease progresses in several stages. At first, subtle cognitive and personality changes occur, in which people with Alzheimer's have trouble managing finances and recalling recent events. As the disease progresses, they find it harder to manage daily tasks, select clothes, recall names and addresses, and drive. Later, they have trouble using the bathroom and maintaining hygiene. They no longer recognize family and friends or speak in full sentences. They may become restless, agitated, confused, and aggressive. They may get lost in stores, parking lots, and even their own homes. They may experience hallucinations or paranoid delusions, believing that others are attempting to harm them. People with Alzheimer's may eventually become unable to walk or communicate, rendering them completely dependent on others.

Although the cause or causes of Alzheimer's disease remain a mystery, scientists believe that both environmental and genetic factors are involved (Goldman et al., 2008; Tomiyama et al., 2008). The accumulation of plaque may cause the memory loss and other symptoms of AD; however, experiments with non-humans suggest that memory deficits may precede the formation of significant deposits of plaque (Jacobsen et al., 2006).

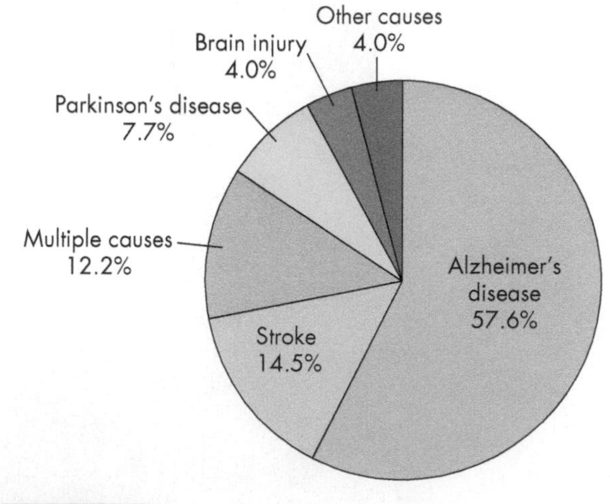

FIGURE 17.3

Causes of Dementia

Alzheimer's disease is the leading cause of dementia.

Source: Melanie P. Heron. (2007). *National Vital Statistics Reports, 56*(5). Centers for Disease Control and Prevention. www.cdc.gov/nchs/data/nvsr/nvsr56/nvsr56_05

LO4 Cognitive Development

When artist Jack Tworkov was in his 30s, his paintings were realistic. In his 50s, his works were abstract expressionistic, like those of Jackson Pollock. In his 60s, his paintings remained abstract and became hard-edged with geometric precision. Just before his death at age 82, he was experimenting with a loosely flowing calligraphic style that he never showed to the public.

Although Tworkov's body was in decline, he once commented, "Every morning I go to the easel in a fever." Tworkov was fortunate in that his cognitive processes were clear. Given the scores of new works in his later years, his processing speed had remained good—or at least good enough. His visual and motor memory and his capacity to rivet his attention to a task all remained superb. All these skills are part of what we labelled *fluid intelligence*. We have no personal way of comparing his skills in late adulthood with what they were 20 or 40 years earlier, but based simply on what can be observed, his abilities were stunning.

Crystallized intelligence can continue to improve throughout much of late adulthood (Mangina & Sokolov, 2006). However, all cognitive skills, on average, tend to decline in advanced age.

Memory

In a classic study of memory, Harry Bahrick and his colleagues (1975) sought to learn how well high-school graduates would recognize photographs of their classmates. Some of their subjects had graduated 15 years earlier, and others had been out of school for some 50 years. The experimenters interspersed photos of actual classmates with four times as many photos of strangers. People who had graduated 15 years earlier correctly recognized persons who were former schoolmates 90% of the time. But those who had graduated about 50 years earlier still recognized former classmates 75% of the time. Thus, the visual recognition memories had lasted half a century in people who were now in late adulthood.

Developmentalists speak of various kinds of memories. First we can distinguish between retrospective and prospective memories—memories of the past ("retro") and memories of the things we plan to do in the future. We can then divide retrospective memories into explicit and implicit memories.

Explicit versus Implicit Memories

Explicit memories are of specific information, such as things we did or things that happened to us (episodic or autobiographical memories) and general knowledge, such as the author of Hamlet (semantic memory). Implicit memories are more automatic and recall the performance of tasks such as reciting the alphabet or multiplication tables, riding a bicycle, or using a doorknob.

It is said that you never forget how to ride a bicycle or use a keyboard: these activities are also implicit memories—in these cases, sensorimotor habits.

Older adults often complain that they struggle to remember the names of people they know, even people they know very well. They are frustrated by the awareness that they knew the name yesterday, perhaps even a half hour ago, but "now" it is gone. When they do recall it, or another person reminds them of the name, they think, "Of course!" They are experiencing slippage in their explicit memory.

The temporal memory of older adults—that is, their recall of the order in which events have occurred—may become confused (Dumas & Hartman, 2003; Hartman & Warren, 2005). Older adults may have difficulty discriminating actual events from illusory events (Rybash & Hrubi-Bopp, 2000).

Older adults usually do not fare as well as younger adults in tasks that measure explicit memory, but they tend to do as well, or nearly as well, in tasks that assess **implicit memory** (Mitchell & Bruss, 2003). Implicit memory tasks tend to be automatic and do not require any conscious effort. They may reflect years of learning and repetition. Implicit memory includes remembering multiplication tables and the alphabet. When asked which letter comes after *p* or to recite the alphabet, the second task is easier. Reciting is how we learned, and overlearned, the 26 letters of the alphabet. It is said that we never forget how to ride a bicycle or use a keyboard; these activities are also implicit memories—in these cases, sensorimotor habits.

implicit memory automatic memories based on repetition and apparently not requiring any conscious effort to retrieve

Associative Memory

We use associative learning and associative memory to remember that the written letter A has the sound of an "A." We also use associative memory to develop a sight vocabulary; that is, we associate the written *the* with the sound of the word; we do not decode it as we read.

It turns out that aging has more of a detrimental effect on associative memory than on memory for single items (Naveh-Benjamin, Brav, & Levy, 2007). Older adults are impaired primarily in associating items with one another, but not in remembering individual items (Cohn, Emrich, & Moscovitch, 2008). Figure 17.4 identifies the different lobes in the brain. The aging brain atrophies in the frontal lobe and in the

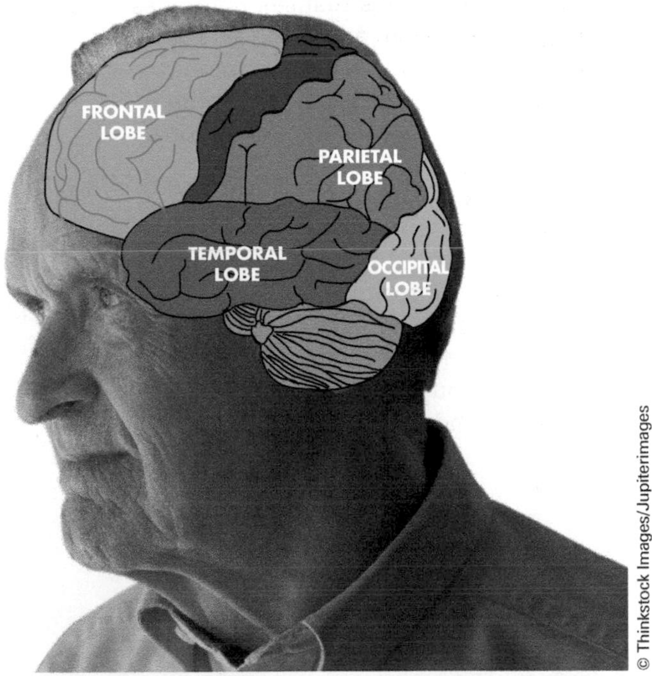

FIGURE 17.4

The Aging Brain

In the aging brain, atrophy in the frontal lobe and in the middle (medial) part of the temporal lobe may account for deficits in associative memory.

prospective memory memory of things one has planned for the future

middle part of the temporal lobe, which may account for this reduction in associative memory.

Long-Term Memory

Long-term memory has no known inherent limits, as noted in Chapter 9. Memories may reside for a lifetime, to be recalled by the proper cues. But long-term memories are also subject to distortion, bias, and even decay.

In typical studies of long-term memory, researchers present older adults with timelines that list ages from early childhood to the present day and ask them to fill in key events and to indicate how old they were at the time. Using this technique, people seem to recall events from the second and third decades of life in greatest detail and with the most emotional intensity (Glück & Bluck, 2007). These include early romances (or their absence), high-school days, musical groups, public figures, sports heroes, "life dreams," and early disappointments. Many psychologists look to psychological explanations for these findings. They may be right in pursuing this angle because "coming of age" and the development of "identity" usually occur during the second and third decades of life. However, another explanation is that sex hormones have their strongest effects in adolescence and early adulthood. The secretion of these hormones is related to the release of neurotransmitters involved in memory formation (Lupien et al., 2007).

Researchers have just discovered that the use of optogenetics, the use of light on brain and other tissues, has the potential to positively affect the neurons related to long-term memory and fear. There was recently a scientific breakthrough when research with mice and optogenetics was used the first time for specific memory neurons (PsyPost, 2016). These specific types of neurons allow for the treatment of various illnesses including obsessive-compulsive disorder, phobias, and post-traumatic stress disorders. They also help with the effects of traumatic events, minimizing suffering from trauma. The treatment has also shown to improve long-term memory problems in healthy adults (PsyPost, 2016).

Because of the decline in working memory and because of impairments in hearing, many older adults find it more difficult to understand spoken language.

Prospective Memory

Why do we need electronic organizers, desktop calendars, and shopping lists? To help us remember all the things we need to do. Retrospective memory helps us retrieve information from the past. **Prospective memory** aids us in remembering things we have planned to do in the future, despite the passage of time and despite the occurrence of interfering events. For prospective memory to succeed, we need to have foolproof strategies, such as alarm reminders on our cellphones, or we need to focus our attention and keep it focused. Distractibility will prevent us from reaching the goal.

A Swiss study examined the relationships between processing speed, working memory (the amount of information a person can keep in mind at once), prospective memory, and retrospective memory among 361 people between the ages of 65 and 80 (Zeintl, Kliegel, & Hofer, 2007). The researchers found that age-related declines in processing speed and working memory—aspects of fluid intelligence—had important effects on retrospective memory. However, some age-related declines in prospective memory appeared to be independent of processing speed and working memory. In other words, even if fluid intelligence remained intact, prospective memory might decline, suggesting the powerful effects of attention and distractibility.

Language Development

People aged 75 and older tend to show a decline in reading comprehension that is related to a decrease in the scope of working memory (De Beni, Borella, & Carretti, 2007). Because of the decline in working memory and because of impairments in hearing, many older adults find it more difficult to understand the spoken language (Burke & Shafto, 2008). However, when the speaker slows down and articulates more clearly, comprehension increases (Gordon-Salant, Fitzgibbons, & Friedman, 2007).

Rocketclips/Shutterstock.com

Older adults may also show deficiencies in language production. Although they may retain their receptive vocabularies, they often show a gradual decline in their expressive vocabularies—that is, the number of words they produce (Hough, 2007). Declines in associative memory and working memory appear to decrease the likelihood that words will "be there" when older people try to express ideas (Burke & Shafto, 2008). Similarly, older people are more likely to experience the frustrating "tip-of-the-tongue" phenomenon, in which they know a word but temporarily cannot produce it (Shafto et al., 2007).

Problem Solving

Figure 17.5 shows the so-called Duncker Candle Problem, which is sometimes used to challenge problem-solving skills. The goal is to use only the objects shown to attach the candle to the wall so that it will burn properly. Rather than trying to solve the problem, notice your thoughts as you looked at the objects in the figure. Even if you haven't yet thought of a solution, you have probably used mental trial and error to visualize what might work. (You will find the answer to the Duncker Candle Problem in Figure 17.6.)

Standard problem-solving methods require three elements whose fluid components tend to decline with age (Hassing & Johanssom, 2005): executive functioning to select strategies, working memory to hold the elements of the problem in mind, and processing speed to accomplish the task while the elements remain in mind. Experiments with young and older adults consistently show that the older adults use fewer strategies and display slower processing speed in solving complex math problems (Allain et al., 2007; Lemaire & Arnaud, 2008).

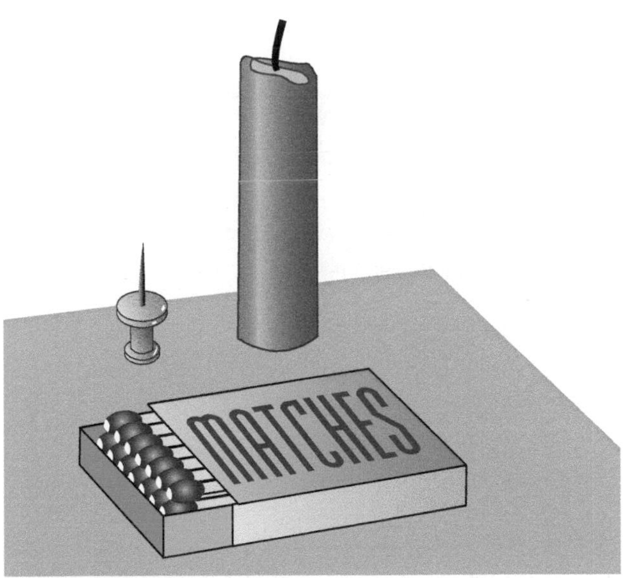

FIGURE 17.5

The Duncker Candle Problem

Can you use the objects shown on the table to attach the candle to the wall so that it will burn properly?

Source: © Cengage Learning

You might be asking yourself, how important is it for older people to solve complex math problems or "teasers" like the Duncker Candle Problem? The answer depends on what people are attempting to accomplish in life. However, research suggests that for the vast majority of older adults, abstract problem-solving ability, as in complex math problems, is not related to their quality of life. "Real-world" or everyday problem-solving skills are usually of greater concern (Gilhooly et al., 2007).

Moreover, when older adults encounter interpersonal conflicts, they tend to regulate their emotional responses differently from young and middle-aged adults. Whereas younger groups are relatively more likely to express feelings of anger or frustration, to seek support from other people, or to find solutions to interpersonal problems, older adults are more likely to focus on remaining calm and unperturbed (Coats & Blanchard-Fields, 2008). The difference appears to be partially due to older adults' decreased tendency to express anger and increased priority on regulating emotion. Perhaps the older adults do not wish to be "jarred," but it also sounds a bit like wisdom.

Wisdom

We may seek athletes who are in their 20s, but we prefer coaches who are decades older. It may be desirable to hire high-school teachers and college and university professors who have recently graduated, but we usually seek high-school principals and department chairs who are older. It is helpful to have 18-year-olds who are bursting with energy knocking on doors to get out the vote, but we want our presidential candidates to be older. Why? Because we associate age with wisdom.

Among the numerous cognitive hazards of aging, older people tend to be more distractible than young adults. Developmental psychologist Lynn Hasher (2008) suggests that distractibility can enable older adults to take a broader view of various situations: "A broad attention span may enable older adults to ultimately know more about a situation and... what's going on than their younger peers... [This] characteristic may play a significant role in why we think of older people as wiser."

FIGURE 17.6

Answer to the Duncker Candle Problem

Source: © Cengage Learning

Kunzmann and Baltes (2005) note that wise people approach life's problems in a way that addresses the meaning of life. They consider not only the present but also the past, the future, and the contexts in which the problems arise. They tend to be tolerant of other people's value systems and to acknowledge that life holds uncertainties and that they can only attempt to find workable solutions in an imperfect world. Ardelt (2008a, 2008b) adds emotional and philosophical dimensions to the definition of wisdom. She suggests that wise people tend to possess an unselfish love for others and tend to be less afraid of death.

"I'm a teenager trapped in an old body."
—Betty White

Helga Esteb/Shutterstock.com

STUDY TOOLS

CourseMate CHAPTER 17

Located at **nelson.com/student**

- ☐ Prepare for tests with a variety of exercises and activities
- ☐ Review Key Terms Flashcards (online or print)
- ☐ Create your own study tools with Build a Summary
- ☐ Watch Observing Development videos to expand your knowledge

bikeriderlondon/Shutterstock.com

CHAPTER 18

Late Adulthood: Social and Emotional Development

LEARNING OUTCOMES

LO1 Evaluate various theories of social and emotional development in late adulthood

LO2 Discuss psychological development in late adulthood, focusing on self-esteem and maintaining independence

LO3 Outline the social contexts in which people age, focusing on housing, religion, and family

LO4 Examine factors that contribute to adjustment to retirement

LO5 Discuss factors in "successful aging"

> "For many people, the later years are the best years—especially when they are filled with meaningful activity."

LO1 Theories of Social and Emotional Development in Late Adulthood

Life Review

Erikson labelled his eighth and final life stage as the crisis of ego integrity or despair. The crisis was defined by the battle between two competing states. Having ego integrity means that life is meaningful and worthwhile despite physical decline and impending death. The other state, despair, views life and death as overwhelming, resulting in feelings of depression and hopelessness.

ego integrity maintenance of the belief that life is meaningful and worthwhile despite physical decline and the inevitability of death

Erikson Today

Time & Life Pictures/Getty Images

Stage 8: Ego Integrity vs. Despair (65 years to death)

Much of our early life is spent preparing for midlife, but the last stage is characterized by reflection. As older adults look back to review their life's meaning, many do so with a feeling of integrity, which results from their sense of contentment and fulfillment. They realize that they have led a life that had meaning and value and that they have been contributing members of society. Many older adults may also be enthusiastic and hopeful about their lives and all they still plan to do. Those that feel they have not been successful in their life journey, on the other hand, will often feel a sense of despair with the realization that it's too late to make changes, or that they have run out of time. They may feel they have led a meaningless life.

Consider THIS

How do you want to be perceived, and treated, in your final years?

Please see page 315 for discussions on this topic.

Robert Peck's Developmental Tasks

Robert Peck (1968) amplified Erikson's stage of ego integrity versus despair by outlining three developmental tasks that people face in late adulthood:

- *Ego differentiation versus work-role preoccupation.* After retirement, people need to find new ways of defining their self-worth outside of their achievements in the workplace, perhaps in terms of roles in the community, activities with friends and family, or spiritual undertakings.
- *Body transcendence versus body preoccupation.* At some point in late adulthood, people face inevitable physical decline, and it is in their best interests to come to terms with it by shifting more value to cognitive activities and social relationships. Some people, of course, run into chronic illnesses or disabilities years earlier and must face the need to transcend body preoccupation prior to late adulthood.
- *Ego transcendence versus ego preoccupation.* Ego transcendence means preparing in some way to go beyond the physical limitations of one's own life expectancy. As death comes nearer, some prepare to transcend death by helping secure the futures of their children or grandchildren. Others work more broadly to benefit their church, synagogue, or mosque, or to leave planet Earth in "better shape" than they found it.

DID YOU KNOW?

Worldwide the number of people aged 80 years will almost quadruple by 2050, reaching 295 million (World Health Organization, 2012).

The majority of people aged 65 and older now consider themselves to be in good or excellent health, compared with other people of their age. Perhaps the same will be true of 80-year-olds in 2050.

Based on extensive interviews with a small sample of seniors, Monika Ardelt (2008b) writes that ego transcendence grows out of self-reflection and a willingness to learn from experience. She believes ego transcendence—which she also calls *the quieting of the ego*—is characterized by a concern for the well-being of humankind in general, not only for the self and close loved ones.

Kosobu/Shutterstock.com

The Importance of Reminiscence

Daniel Levinson theorized that one aspect of the "midlife crisis" was that people realized they had more to look back on than to look forward to. Older adults often engage in reminiscence—-that is, relating stories from the distant past. At times, some older people may seem to live in the past, possibly in denial of their current decline and the approach of death.

Reminiscence was once considered a symptom of dementia, but contemporary researchers now consider it to be a normal aspect of aging (Kunz, 2007). In working with healthy older volunteers as individuals and in groups, Robert Butler (2002) found that life reviews can be complex and nuanced; incoherent and self-contradictory; or even replete with irony, tragedy, and comedy. Butler believes that older people engage in life reviews in an attempt to make life meaningful, to move on with new relationships as contemporaries die, and to help them find ego integrity and accept the end of life.

Reminiscence treatment, involving the process of seniors reminiscing about their lives, is less reliant on drugs for relieving depression and other psychological problems in older adults than other treatments (Bohlmeijer et al., 2005). In a study in 2009 of Taiwanese seniors with dementia, for example, reminiscence treatment in the form of focused group work through cooking classes showed a reduction in depression, as well as improved sense of achievement with greater emotional stability. A family atmosphere was created, and physical needs of the participants were met (Huang et al., 2009).

Consider THIS

Why are elders so important in First Nations, Métis, and Inuit cultures in Canada?

Elders are not just people who have reached late adulthood. They are considered the "heart" of First Nations, Métis, and Inuit learning and are the gatekeepers of wisdom, knowledge, cultural practices, ceremonies, and history. Elders are seen as an important source of cultural power and voice within their communities (First Nations Pedagogy Online, 2009) as they pass down tradition, culture, values, and lessons using oral storytelling and ceremonies, and by role-modelling traditional practices. Community members look to elders for guidance on how to live a "good life," in keeping with traditional ways. Greatly honoured, elders often eat before others at feasts and community events, and are given tobacco as an offering of respect. As central figures to families, communities, and nations (Statistics Canada, 2010a), at the end of life, elders are deeply grieved when they pass.

disengagement theory the view that older adults and society withdraw from one another as older adults approach death

Activity Theory

It seems that well-being among older adults is generally predicted by pursuing goals, rather than the stereotype of the older adult who withdraws socially (Frazier, Newman, & Jaccard, 2007). This stereotype is supported by disengagement theory, which is

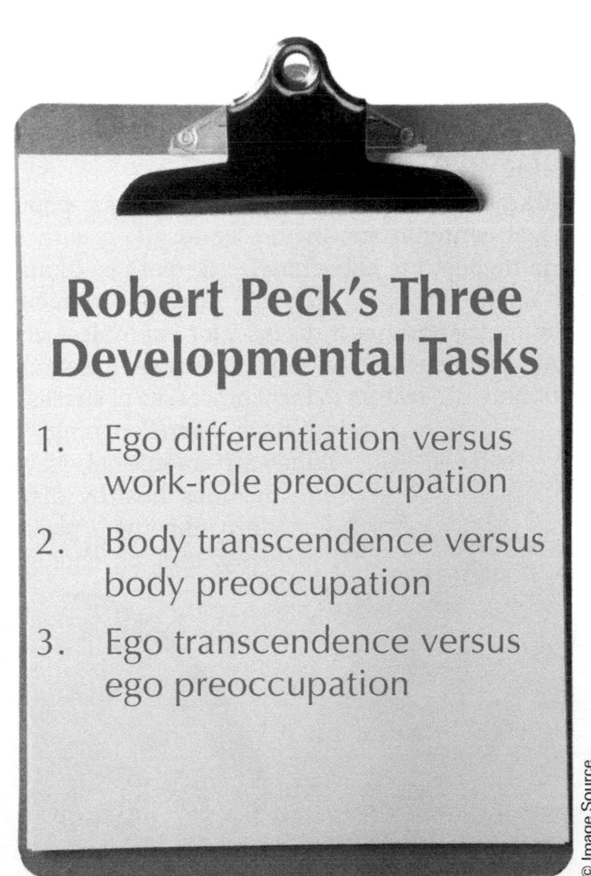
Robert Peck's Three Developmental Tasks
1. Ego differentiation versus work-role preoccupation
2. Body transcendence versus body preoccupation
3. Ego transcendence versus ego preoccupation
© Image Source

Spotmatik/iStockphoto.com

According to activity theory, older adults are more content when they are active and social.

activity theory the view that older adults fare better when they engage in physical and social activities

socio-emotional selectivity theory the view that people place increasing emphasis on emotional experience as they age but limit their social contacts to regulate their emotions

the view that older adults and society withdraw from one another as older adults approach death. A less stereotypical view is rooted in activity theory, which states that older adults are better adjusted when they are more active and involved in physical and social activities. Activity theory perceives many barriers in social attitudes, such as the beliefs that older people should "take it easy," or be forced into retirement, rather than considering the desires of the individual.

Okinawa, Japan, has one of the highest populations of centenarians in the world along with one of the highest life expectancies. Seniors in Okinawa have few of the chronic diseases—dementia, Alzheimer's, and heart disease, for example—which plague the elderly in western countries. Research to determine the factors in local processes of successful aging have been ongoing. The Okinawan traditional way of life includes healthy dietary habits, ongoing physical activity, and psychological and social aspects; these have been found to be key contributing factors for longevity (Okinawa Centenarian Study, n.d.).

© Andrea Pistolesi/Getty Images

Research shows that physical activity is associated with a lower mortality rate in late adulthood (Talbot et al., 2007). Leisure and informal social activities also contribute to life satisfaction among retired people (Joung & Miller, 2007). An Israeli study found particular benefits for life satisfaction in activities involving the next generation, the visual and performing arts, and spiritual and religious matters (Nimrod, 2007). However, older adults also found value in independent activities in the home.

Socio-Emotional Selectivity Theory

Socio-emotional selectivity theory addresses the development of older adults' social networks. Charles and Carstensen (2007) hypothesize that as we age, increasing emphasis is placed on emotional experience, leading to a greater focus on emotionally fulfilling experiences.

To regulate their emotional lives as they grow older, people limit their social contacts to a few individuals who are of major importance. By the time older adults reach their 80s, they are likely to have a small social network of family members and friends. This small social grouping does not mean that older adults are antisocial. It means that they may be more risk-averse, or wanting to be with those with whom they have a shared history and common values and interests.

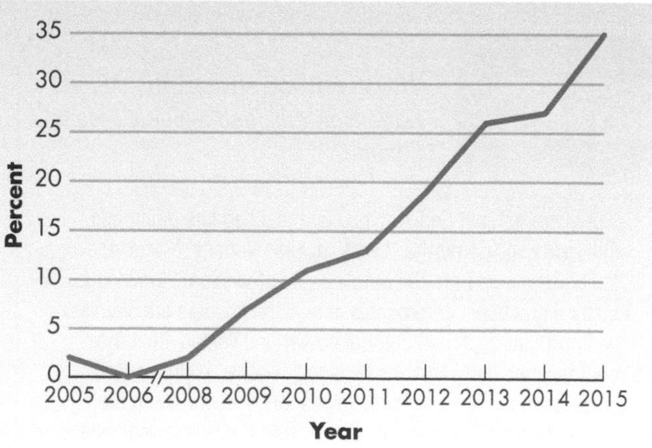

FIGURE 18.1

Social Media Usage among Seniors

The use of social media by seniors is on the rise. Using social media is a convenient way for seniors to socialize, keep in touch with family, and date. It is particularly useful for seniors with mobility issues.

Source: Pew Research Center. (2015, October 8). "Social Media Usage: 2005–2015." http://www.pewinternet.org/2015/10/08/social-networking-usage-2005-2015/

LO2 Psychological Development

Self-esteem, as we will see, is tied to both independence and dependence. Also, the psychological problems of depression and anxiety can affect us at any age, but they warrant special focus in late adulthood.

Self-Esteem

To study the lifetime development of self-esteem, Richard Robins and his colleagues (2002) recruited more than 300,000 individuals to complete an extensive online questionnaire that provided demographic information (age, sex, ethnic background, and so forth) and measures of self-esteem (see Figure 18.2). About 66% of the respondents were from the United States, and 57% were female. In general, the self-esteem of males was higher than that of females. Self-esteem was highest in childhood (likely an inflated estimate) and dipped precipitously in adolescence but it then rose gradually throughout middle adulthood and declined in late adulthood, with most of the decline occurring between the ages of 70 and 85. However, these results are all relative. Even for people in their 80s, self-esteem levels were above the midpoint of the questionnaire.

Robins and Trzesniewski (2005) suggest that the drop in self-esteem among people in their 80s is due to life changes such as retirement, loss of a spouse or partner, reduced social support, declining health, and downward movement in socio-economic status. The other hypothesis is more optimistic, namely that older people are wiser and more content and have reached Erikson's stage of ego transcendence, leading people to accept themselves as they are, "warts and all" (1968).

As the years wear on in late adulthood, people express progressively less "body esteem"—that is, less pride in the appearance and functioning of their bodies. There is also a gender difference, with older

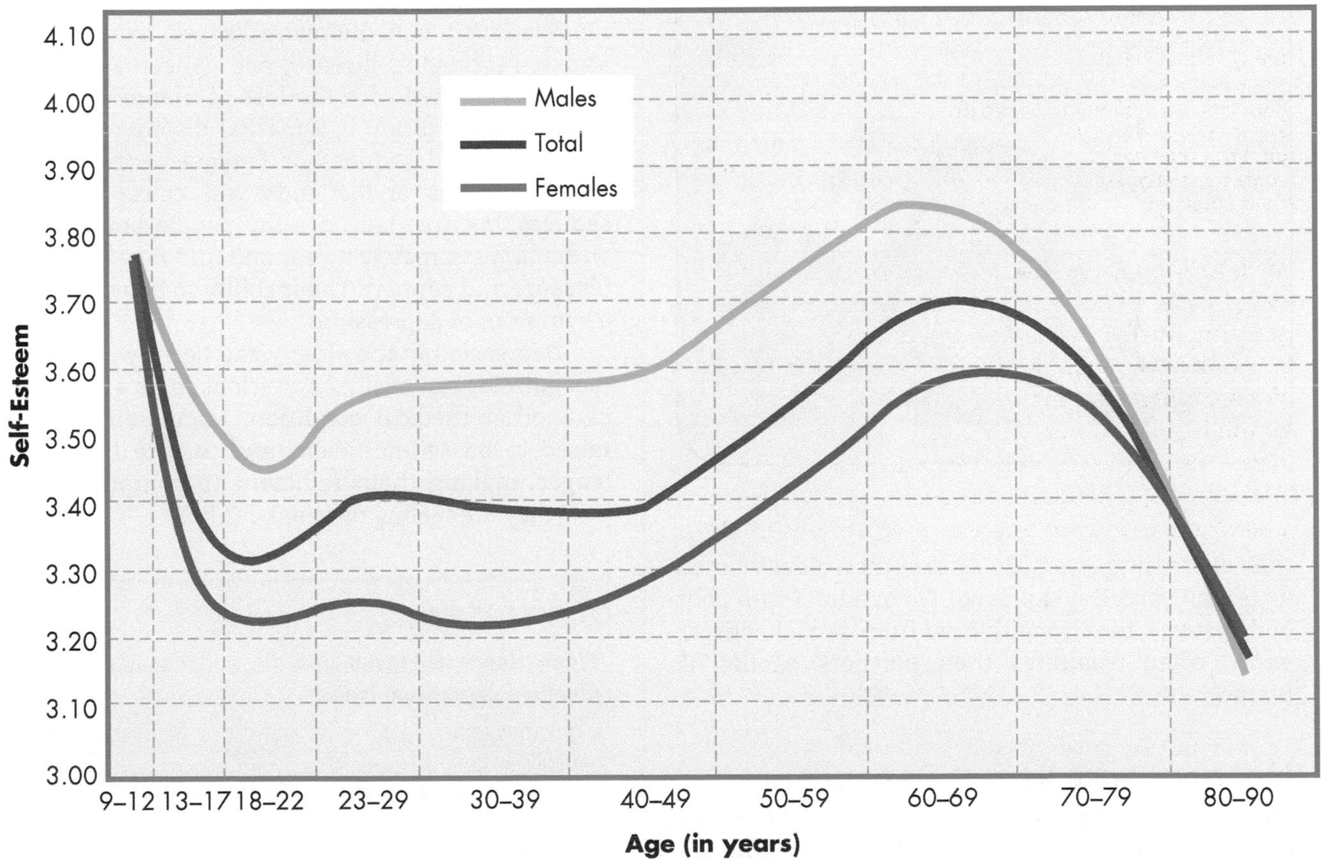

FIGURE 18.2

Mean Level of Self-Esteem as a Function of Age, for Total Sample, Males, and Females

Self-esteem is highest in childhood, dips in adolescence, rises gradually throughout middle adulthood, and declines in late adulthood.

Source: Richard W. Robins, Kali H. Trzesniewski, Jessica L. Tracy, Samuel D. Gosling, & Jeff Porter. Global self-esteem across the lifespan. *Psychology and Aging*, 17(3), 423–434, 2002, copyright American Psychological Association, Inc., adapted with permission.

Volunteering and the Older Adult in Canada

Being able to care for oneself is important but caring for others is also important in personal well-being and in achieving ego integrity during this stage. Volunteers help charitable and non-profit organizations deliver needed programs and services. Volunteering provides a social outlet and structure that allow older generations to be valuable and involved in the community where they live, and to "pass it forward." Canadians volunteer an estimated two billion hours yearly, the equivalent of 1.1 million fulltime jobs. In 2010 almost half of all Canadians were volunteering an average 156 hours each year (Fish, 2014). But the landscape for volunteering is changing.

It was assumed that there would be a large volunteer pool with baby boomers retiring, but this hasn't been the case. Many baby boomers are not retiring, but are instead continuing to work; they are not available for volunteering. Many other people are interested in volunteering but don't want a "till death do we part" position. Also, finding volunteer positions can be challenging. In previous generations anyone could volunteer, but volunteer positions are increasingly competitive and often agencies want specific skills and capabilities.

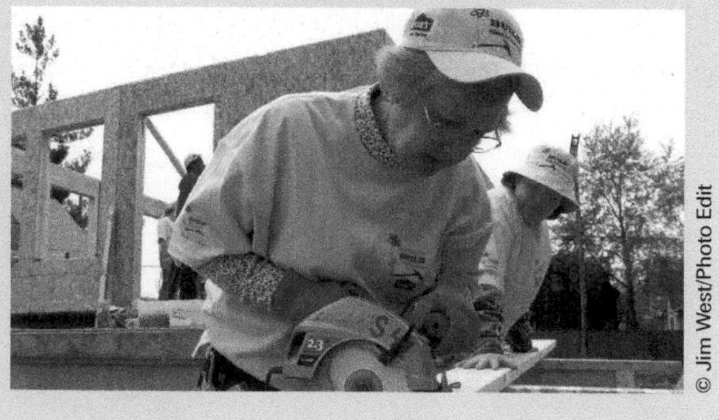

© Jim West/Photo Edit

men expressing less body esteem than older women do (Kaminski & Hayslip, 2006). Older adults with poor body esteem tend to withdraw from sexual activity, which often frustrates their partners (Mohan & Bhugra, 2005).

Independence versus Dependence

Being able to care for oneself appears to be a core condition of successful aging. Older people who are independent tend to think of themselves as leading a "normal life," whereas those who are dependent on others, even if they are only slightly dependent, tend to worry more about aging and encountering physical disabilities and stress (Sousa & Figueiredo, 2002). A study of 441 healthy people aged 65 to 95 found that dependence on others to carry out the activities of daily living increased with age (Perrig-Chiello et al., 2006). A particularly sensitive independence issue is toileting. Independence in toileting is especially important in enabling older people to avoid a loss in their self-esteem (Clark & Rugg, 2005).

Mental Health and Illness

Psychological problems, including depression and anxiety, are among the problems of aging.

Depression

Depression affects some 10% of people aged 65 and older (Kvaal et al., 2008). Depression in older people can be either a continuation of depression from earlier periods of life, or a new development (Fiske, 2006). Depression can be related to the personality factors (Duberstein et al., 2008), neurological changes in the brain (Ballmaier et al., 2008), or a possible genetic predisposition to imbalances of the neurotransmitter norepinephrine (Togsverd et al., 2008). Researchers are investigating links between depression and physical illnesses such as Alzheimer's disease, heart disease, stroke, Parkinson's disease, and cancer. Depression is also associated with the loss of friends and loved ones, but depression is a mental disorder that goes beyond normal sadness or bereavement. The loss of companions and friends will cause profound sadness, but mentally healthy people bounce back within approximately a year and find new sources of pleasure and support. The inability to bounce back is a symptom of depression.

Depression in the elderly can be very difficult to recognize. It can easily be overlooked as a symptom of another medical condition. Many seniors were raised to be self-sufficient and to face life's challenges, making them reluctant to complain about how they are feeling or to ask for help.

DID YOU KNOW?

When friends and loved ones die, sadness is a normal reaction; depression is not.

It is normal to be sad when we suffer loss. Depression is a mental illness.

Anxiety Disorders

Anxiety disorders affect at least 3% of people aged 65 and older, and co-exist with depression in about 8–9% of older adults (Kvaal et al., 2008). Older women are approximately twice as likely to be affected as older men (Stanley & Beck, 2000). The most common

Depression in Seniors—What to Look For

Depression often goes undetected as health care providers also tend to focus more on older people's physical health than their mental health. Many older people are reluctant to admit to depression because mental health issues often carry a stigma. Depression is also associated with memory lapses and other cognitive impairment, such as difficulty concentrating (Ballmaier et al., 2008). Some cases of depression are wrongly attributed to the effects of aging or are misdiagnosed as dementia or Alzheimer's disease. Depression in older people can usually be treated successfully through antidepressant drugs, cognitive-behavioural psychotherapy, and other methods (Schuurmans et al., 2006).

The main symptom of depression is a sad, despairing mood that

- is present most days and lasts most of the day
- lasts for more than two weeks
- impairs the person's performance at work, at school or in social relationships.

Other symptoms of depression include the following:

- changes in appetite and weight
- sleep problems
- loss of interest in work, hobbies, people, or sex
- withdrawal from family members and friends
- feeling useless, hopeless, excessively guilty, and/or pessimistic, or having low self-esteem
- agitation or feeling slowed down
- irritability
- fatigue
- trouble concentrating, remembering, and making decisions
- crying easily, or feeling like crying but being unable to
- thoughts of suicide (which should always be taken seriously)
- a loss of touch with reality, hearing voices (hallucinations), or having strange ideas (delusions).

Source: Centre for Addiction and Mental Health. (2013). Depression. https://www.camh.ca/en/hospital/health_information/a_z_mental_health_and_addiction_information/depression/Pages/default.aspx

anxiety disorders among older adults are generalized anxiety disorder and phobic disorders. Most cases of agoraphobia affecting older adults tend to be of recent origin and may involve the loss of social support systems due to the death of a spouse or close friends. Anxiety disorders can be harmful to older people's physical health. When older adults with anxiety disorders are subjected to stress, their levels of cortisol (a stress hormone) rise, then take some time to subside (Chaudieu et al., 2008). Cortisol

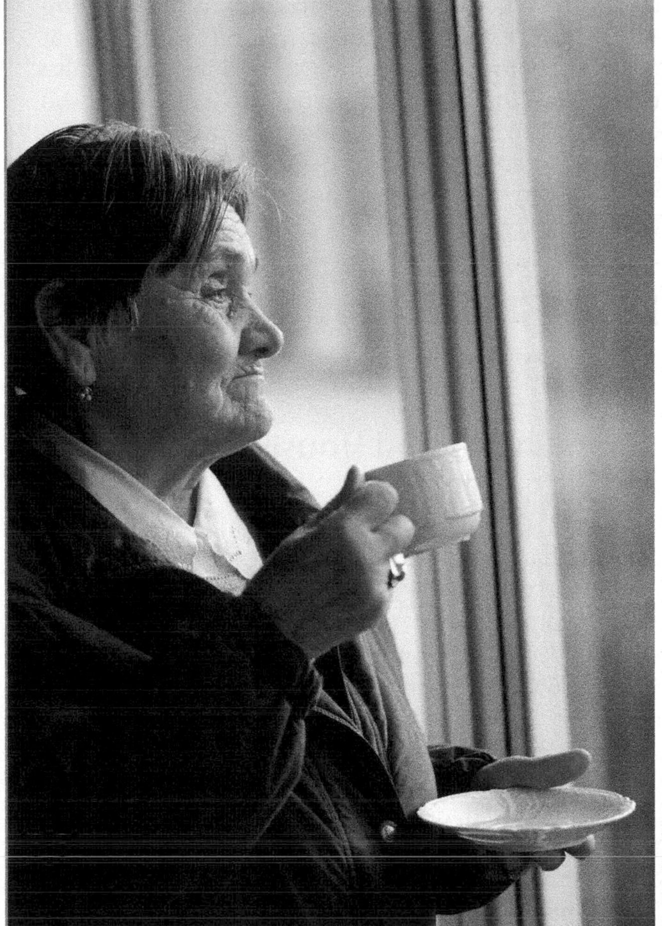
Zurijeta/Shutterstock.com

suppresses the functioning of the immune system, making anxious people more vulnerable to illness.

Changes in living conditions—selling a home, immigrating, moving into a retirement residence, or moving in with family, or simply the perception that one is losing control of their lives—can contribute to anxiety disorders.

generalized anxiety disorder extreme and/or persistent feelings of dread, worry, foreboding, and concern that are frequent and unrealistic

phobic disorder irrational, exaggerated fear of an object or situation

agoraphobia fear of open, crowded places

Suicide

Untreated depression can lead to suicide, which is not uncommon among older people. The highest rates of suicide are found among older men who have lost their wives or partners, no longer have their social networks, or fear the consequences of physical illnesses and loss of freedom (Johnson, Zhang, & Prigerson, 2008; Schmidtke, Sell, & Lohr, 2008). The Canadian Medical Association suggests that suicide is likely under-reported and not accurately captured by statistics because of the difficulty in determining a self-inflicted death from a natural or accidental death. Ageism is also at play. Our society has a faulty notion that mental health issues are just par for the course when it comes to elderly people. We expect they experience a level of depression because they are losing loved ones and dealing with more chronic illnesses (Monette, 2012).

LO3 Social Contexts of Aging

Communities and Housing for Older People

The 2011 Census reported that 39% of Canadians changed their place of residence within the last five years. Almost one quarter (23%) of those who moved were between ages 55 to 64, and 16% aged 75 and older. Seniors move for different reasons: they want to downsize, they move to live with family, they are newly separated or widowed, or they are facing a change in their health or finances. Many seniors remain homeowners. It's estimated that more than one third of the Canadian population will be 55 or older by 2038, and almost one quarter will be 65 or older. With the ongoing growth of the 55-plus age group, from 4.6 million in 2013 to an estimated 5 million in 2038, there will be a housing demand "for decades to come" (Canadian Mortgage and Housing Corporation).

When older people can no longer manage living on their own, they may consider utilizing the services of in-home care and visiting nurses to help them remain in the home. Others may move in with adult children. Still others may move into assisted-living residences, where they have their own apartment, a community dining room, 24-hour nursing support, and on-call physician care.

> Older adults may be reluctant to relocate to a nursing home; this move signifies their loss of independence.

DID YOU KNOW?

Elder abuse occurs when an elderly person is intentionally physically, emotionally, or mentally harmed, mistreated or neglected by family members or caregivers.

Approximately 7% of seniors report emotional or financial abuse by an adult child, spouse, or caregiver, and 1% report physical or sexual abuse (CBC, 2011). In 32% of reported cases, the offender is a family member.

Some older adults may be reluctant to relocate to a nursing home (often referred to as a long-term care facility), because the move signifies their loss of independence. Also, when older adults relocate, their existing social networks and routines tend to be disrupted.

Surveys indicate that older adults are relatively more willing to enter into long-term care when they perceive themselves to be in poor health and when one or more close family members live nearby (Jang et al., 2008).

Many countries around the world don't have nursing homes; many cultures frown upon institutional care for the elderly. People in these countries prefer to have seniors reside with family. This may be due to cultural norms, for financial reasons, or when independence isn't possible. Many families in Canada choose this option as well, for financial reasons, or to respect their family's cultural norms.

Some frightening stories have emerged about what happens in nursing homes. Occasionally, cases of elder abuse occur. Elder abuse is completely unacceptable and illegal. A well-selected and well-trained staff can deal well with impaired residents, many of whom are disoriented and frightened (Kazui et al., 2008) without resorting to abusive tactics.

Legislation protects adults living in residential care. Elder abuse is defined by the Government of Canada in this way:

- Intentionally causing bodily harm,
- Intentionally causing harm, including, but not limited to, threatening, intimidating, humiliating, harassing, coercing or restricting from appropriate social contact,
- Intentionally administering or prescribing medication for an inappropriate purpose,
- Subjecting to non-consensual sexual contact, activity or behaviour,
- Intentionally misappropriating or improperly or illegally converting money or other valuable possessions, or
- Intentionally failing to provide adequate nutrition, adequate medical attention or other necessity of life without a valid consent (Department of Justice Canada).

Religious and Cultural Practices

Religion involves beliefs and practices centred on claims about the nature of reality and moral behaviour, usually codified as rituals, religious laws, and prayers. Cultural traditions, customs, and practices are often part of faith, spiritual experience, and private and communal engagement. Often religious and cultural practices become a central part of life for older adults.

Rene Johnson/*Toronto Star* via Getty Images

Religious and cultural practices are part of a social context for many people. They offer the opportunity to worship, and to participate in social, educational, community, and charitable activities. Therefore, religious and cultural undertakings provide older adults with a vast arena for social networking.

It is not surprising, therefore, that studies find that religious involvement in late adulthood is usually associated with less depression (Braam et al., 2008) and more life satisfaction (Korff, 2006). Frequent religious attendance has also been shown to be associated with fewer problems in older people's activities of daily living (Park et al., 2008). Here, of course, we can assume that older people reap benefits both from social networking and from faith-based or cultural participation.

Consider some of the benefits of frequent churchgoing found in studies of older African Americans. Older African Americans who attend services more than once a week were found to live 13.7 years longer, on average, than their counterparts who *never* attend church (Marks et al., 2005). In-depth interviews with the churchgoers found several reasons for their relative longevity, including having a sense of hopefulness, having social support, avoiding being victimized by violence, and not falling into negative coping methods such as aggressive behaviour and alcohol consumption.

DID YOU KNOW?

African Americans who attend church more than once a week live more than 13.7 years longer than African Americans who never attend.

Faith-based beliefs and practices may be a factor in longevity.

Family and Social Relationships

Family and social relationships provide some of the most obvious—and most important—elements in the social lives of older adults.

Marriage

Approximately 38% of Canadian marriages end in divorce; but for many people, marriage lasts, "until death do us part." Married people face very different life tasks as young adults, middle-aged adults, and older adults. Also likely to vary from stage to stage are the qualities in relationships that help people fulfill these tasks. For example, the core issues in early adulthood are the selection of a partner, the development of a shared life, and emotional intimacy. Given these needs, two people's similarities in personality may foster their feelings of attachment and intimacy, providing them with a sense of equity in contributing to the relationship (Shiota & Levenson, 2007).

By middle adulthood, the partners' concerns appear to shift toward meeting their shared and individual responsibilities (Moen, Kim, & Hofmeister, 2001). The partnership needs to handle tasks such as finances, household chores, and parenting. Conflicts may easily arise over a division of labour unless the couple can divide the tasks readily (Hatch & Bulcroft, 2004; Shiota & Levenson, 2007). At this stage, similarity in personality may work against the couple. For example, Shiota and Levenson (2007) found in their study of marital satisfaction and the Big Five personality factors (see Chapter 16) in middle-aged adults, difference rather than similarity in conscientiousness and extraversion predicts marital satisfaction when the couple are in their 40s. Conscientious people want to get things done, but by middle adulthood they have their own way of doing things. When two people in close quarters each want a task completed in their own way, conflicts are likely. The relationship is likely smoother if one partner is detail-oriented while the other is more easygoing.

When couples reach their 60s, many midlife responsibilities such as child rearing and work have declined, allowing the partners to spend more time together. As a result, intimacy becomes a central issue once more. In this stage, couples report less disagreement over finances, household chores, and parenting (or grandparenting), but may have concerns about emotional expression and companionship (Hatch & Bulcroft, 2004). A similarity in personality is less of a contributor to conflict than it is in midlife.

DID YOU KNOW?

Older married couples are focused on each other, and intimacy becomes a primary focus of their relationship.

Because work and child rearing are removed from the relationship, many couples can now focus primarily on each other and intimacy. Some couples complain that they have too much time together!

Kelly Nelson/Shutterstock.com

In a study of 120 older Israeli couples, Kulik (2004) found that sharing power in the relationship and dividing household tasks contributed to satisfaction in the relationships. Past assistance from one's spouse in a time of need also positively affected the quality of the marriage and life satisfaction for both partners.

Divorce, Cohabitation, and Remarriage

Having worked out most of the problems in their relationships and having learned to live with those issues that remain, older adults are less likely than younger adults to seek divorce. The ideal of lifelong marriage retains its strength (Amato et al., 2007). Because of fear of loss of assets, family disruption, or stigmatization, and because of faith-based beliefs, older adults do not enter into divorce lightly. When they do consider divorce, although there are many causes, it is often because they are in an unacceptable marriage that is particularly negative, or because one of the partners has taken up a relationship with an outsider (Bengtson et al., 2005).

Older people are increasingly likely to cohabit today, making up about 4% of the unmarried population (Brown, Lee, & Bulanda, 2006). Nearly 90% of cohabiting older adults have previously been married, and they are less likely than younger people to want to remarry (Mahay & Lewin, 2007). Although they are less likely than younger cohabiters to marry their partners, older cohabiters report being in more intimate, stable relationships (King & Scott, 2005). They cite reasons for avoiding remarriage, such as concern about ramifications for pensions and disapproval by adult children, who may be concerned about their inheritance (King & Scott, 2005).

LGBTQ Relationships

Most of the research on LGBTQ people has focused on adolescents and young adults (Grossman, D'Augelli, & O'Connell, 2003). However, a growing body of information about LGBTQ has shown that, similar to heterosexual couples, LGBTQ in long-term partnerships tend to enjoy higher self-esteem, less depression, fewer suicidal urges, and less alcohol and drug abuse (D'Augelli et al., 2001). Research conducted by SAGE (Services and Advocacy for Gay, Lesbian, Bisexual, and Transgendered Elders), however, found that, compared with heterosexual seniors, LGBTQ seniors are twice as likely to age alone, four-and-a-half times more likely to have no children to rely on, and five times less likely to access seniors' services. In Canada, inclusive retirement homes, with specific diversity training for staff are increasingly popular, as many LGBTQ seniors have reported not being well served within the mainstream healthcare systems (Thomson, Ahluwalia, & Huang, 2013).

LGBTQ couples often experience discrimination and do not receive the same treatment or benefits as heterosexual couples. In most regions of the world, LGBTQ people are not entitled to the same rights at heterosexual couples. In 2005, Canada became one of the few countries in the world to implement a Civil Marriage Act, allowing same-sex couples to be recognized by the Government of Canada. LGBTQ people, however, continue to face a great deal of discrimination despite anti-discrimination laws.

The Canadian Mental Health Association estimates that hates crimes related to "sexual orientation, doubled in Canada from 2007 to 2008, and were the most violent of all hate crimes. Trans people continue to report high levels of violence, harassment, and discrimination when seeking stable housing, employment, health or social services" (Canadian Mental Health Association, n.d.). Additionally, suicide rates remain very high amongst transgender people.

Widowhood

By the age of 65, about 50% of all women and 10% of all men have experienced the loss of a spouse. By the age of 85, these figures rise to 80% and 40%. The

William Perugini/Shutterstock.com

EMERGING CANADA

"Coming out" isn't uncommon in late adulthood. The Olympic athlete and reality star Bruce Jenner surprised the world when he transitioned as a transgender woman in late adulthood. Like many older LGBTQ who decide to come out, Jenner—now Caitlyn—was not able to "live a lie anymore."

loss of a life partner is one of the most traumatic experiences of life. Most older adults emerge from such a loss as resilient individuals; however, the loss of a loved one has a profoundly negative impact on life for 10–20% of individuals. A severe grief reaction places the individual at a higher risk for high blood pressure, heart problems, cancer, and thoughts of suicide (Holland et al., 2013).

Men in their 70s seem to have the most difficulty coping, especially when they have retired and were expecting to spend more time with their wives during the coming years (Lund & Caserta, 2001).

Widowhood leads to a decline in physical and mental health, including increased mortality and deterioration in memory functioning (Aartsen et al., 2005). Loss of a spouse also heightens the risks of depression and suicide among older adults, more so among men than women (Ajdacic-Gross et al., 2008).

A popular bumper sticker declares, "If I had known grandchildren would be this much fun, I would have had them first."

Among people who are widowed, men are more likely than women to remarry, or at least to form new relationships. One reason is simply that women tend to outlive men, so there are more older women available. Also, women, more so than men, make use of the web of kinship relations and close friendships available to them. Men are also socialized to be less adept than women at various aspects of self and household care, and therefore seek that help from a new partner.

Singles and Older People without Children

Single, never-married, and non-cohabiting adults without children make up a small minority of the adult Canadian population. According to data from the United States, Japan, Europe, Australia, and Israel, single older adults without children are just as likely as people who have had children—married or not—to be socially active and involved in volunteer work (Wenger et al., 2007). They also tend to maintain close relationships with siblings and long-time friends. Very old (mean age = 93) mothers and women who have not had children report equally positive levels of well-being (Hoppmann & Smith, 2007).

On the other hand, married older men without children appear to be especially dependent on their spouses (Wenger et al., 2007). Parents also seem to be more likely than people without children to have a family network that permits them to avoid nursing homes or other residential care when their physical health declines (Wenger et al., 2007).

Siblings

In general, older sibling pairs tend to shore each other up with emotional support (Taylor, Clark, & Newton, 2008). This support is especially seen among sisters who are close in age and geographically near one another. After a spouse dies, the widowed person's siblings (and children) tend to ramp up their social contacts and emotional support (Guiaux, van Tilburg, & van Groenou, 2007).

A longitudinal developmental study of twin relationships found that, compared with other sibling relationships, twin relationships were more intense in terms of frequency of contacts, intimacy, conflict, and emotional support (Neyer, 2002). Frequency of contact and emotional closeness declined from early to middle adulthood, but increased again in late adulthood (mean age at time of study = 71.5 years).

Friendships

Older people have often narrowed their friendships to friends who are most like them and enjoy the same kinds of activities. As a way of regulating their

© Purestock/Jupiterimages

emotions, they tend to avoid people with whom they have had conflict over the years. Friends serve many functions in the lives of older adults, including providing social networks, acting as confidants, and offering emotional closeness and support.

Grandchildren

Although grandparent–grandchild relationships have great variation, research suggests that both cohorts view each other in a positive light and see their ties as deep and meaningful (Kemp, 2005). They often conceptualize their relationship as a distinct family connection that involves unconditional love, emotional support, obligation, and respect. Grandparents and their adult grandchildren often act as friends and confidants. The grandparent–grandchild relationship often differs from the relationship the grandparents had with their own children. A popular bumper sticker declares, "If I had known grandchildren would be this much fun, I would have had them first."

LO4 Retirement

Once upon a time, people retired as soon as they could afford to do so, usually at age 65. According to the Statistics Canada data surveyed earlier in this text, at age 65, the average person has two decades of life to look forward to. That number has been increasing and is likely to continue to increase. Moreover, because of medical advances, 65-year-olds are more and more likely to be robust. Therefore, many people, especially professionals, are working beyond the age of 65.

Retirement Planning

One of the keys of a successful retirement is retirement planning (Reitzes & Mutran, 2004). Retirement planning may include regularly putting money aside in plans such as a Registered Retirement Savings Plan (RRSP) and various pension plans in the workplace; or it could involve investing in stocks, bonds, or a second property.

People who live alone may do their retirement planning as individuals. However, couples in relationships—including married and cohabiting heterosexual and LGBGQ couples—usually make their retirement plans collaboratively (Mock, Taylor & Savin-Williams, 2006; Moen et al., 2006). By and large, the greater the satisfaction in the relationship, the more likely the partners are to make their retirement plans together (Mock & Cornelius, 2007).

Adjustment to Retirement

It is estimated that by 2050, 20% of the population will be retired (Barnett, van Sluijs, Ogilvie 2012). According to a recent study, the landscape of retirement is changing worldwide. Retirement has become more multifaceted. There is also no singular consensus on what satisfactory retirement means. For many, retirement is no longer about permanently leaving working life; it has become more individualized and may involve a longer transition. Bridge employment or restricted retirement are not uncommon in current retirement processes (Barnett, van Sluijs, Ogilvie 2012).

Research has consistently shown that older adults who are best adjusted to retirement are highly involved in a variety of activities, such as community activities and organizations (Kloep & Hendry, 2007). In the case of community activities, the experience and devotion of retirees renders their participation an important asset for the community, and activities promote the adjustment of older adults to retirement.

DID YOU KNOW?

The key to successful retirement is knowing how to relax.

However, "relaxing" does not necessarily mean doing as little as possible.

Pinquart and Schindler (2007) found in a retirement study that retirees could be divided into three groups, according to their satisfaction with retirement and various other factors. The group that was most satisfied with retirement maintained leisure and other non-work-related activities as sources of life satisfaction, or replaced work with more satisfying activities. They retired at a typical retirement age, were married, in good health, and had a high socioeconomic status. The majority of a second group retired at a later age and tended to be female; the

RETIREMENT FUND

Gods_Kings/Shutterstock.com

majority of the third group retired at a younger age and tended to be male. The second and third groups were not as satisfied with retirement. They were in poorer health, less likely to be married, and lower in socio-economic status than the first group. The third group had a spotty employment record, suggesting that retirement didn't change these people's lives in major ways.

A 2-year longitudinal study found that the adjustment of older retirees was affected by their pre-retirement work identities (Reitzes & Mutran, 2006). For example, upscale professional workers continued to be well-adjusted and had high self-esteem. They weren't simply "retirees"; they were retired professors or retired doctors or retired lawyers and the like. On the other hand, hourly wage earners and other blue-collar workers tended to have lower self-esteem and were more likely to think of themselves as simply "retirees." Socio-economic statuses may, therefore, influence the identity of retirees, as well as physical activity levels and general attitudes towards retirement.

Just before retirement, retirees tend to experience a wide range of feelings about giving up work. Some people are relieved; others are worried—about finances, about surrendering their work roles, or both. Even so, most retirees report that their well-being has increased a year after they have retired, and that much of the stress they felt before retiring has diminished (Nuttman-Shwartz, 2007).

Leisure Activities and Retirement

Once people retire, they have the opportunity to fill most of their days with activities they enjoy. Research has shown that engaging in recreational and leisure activities is essential for retirees' physical and psychological health (Hansen, Dik, & Zhou, 2008). A recent study looking at leisure activities among Korean seniors revealed that participation in leisure activities enhances the quality of life and life satisfaction in late adulthood. Leisure activities can improve physical functioning, enhance positive feelings, and increase social interactions. Further, those who participate in community-based exercise programs benefited psychologically, physically, and socially (Kim, Yamada, Heo, & Han, 2014).

Joint leisure activities also contribute to the satisfaction of marital and other intimate relationships and to family well-being (Ton & Hansen, 2001). Such activities reduce stress (Melamed, Meir, & Samson, 1995) and help retirees avert boredom (Sonnentag, 2003). Contributing to civic activities or volunteering at hospitals and the like also enhances retirees' self-esteem and fosters feelings of self-efficacy (Self-efficacy is Bandura's notion that our belief in our abilities can help us to complete tasks.) (Siegrist, Von Dem Knesebeck, & Pollack, 2004).

TABLE 18.1

Factor Analysis of Leisure Activities of Retirees

Factor #	Name	Items
I	Athletic-Competitive-Outdoors	Adventure sports, team sports, hunting & fishing, individual sports, camping & outdoors, building & repair, cards & games, computer activities, collecting
II	Artistic-Cultural-Self Expressive	Shopping, arts & crafts, entertaining & culinary arts, cultural arts, dancing, literature & writing, socializing, gardening & nature, community involvement, travel
III	Social	Partying

Source: Jo-Ida C. Hansen, Bryan J. Dik, & Shuangmei Zhou. (2008). An examination of the structure of leisure interests of college students, working-age adults, and retirees. *Journal of Counseling Psychology*, *55*(2), 133–145.

A British study of adults with an average age of 72 reported that 23% engaged in "active leisure" (sailing, walking); 18%, "passive leisure" (listening to music, watching television); 24%, social activities; 20%, hobbies; and 15%, other activities (Ball et al., 2007). The key motives for leisure activity were pleasure and relaxation.

In a questionnaire about leisure activities distributed to 194 retirees at an average age of 72, Jo-Ida Hansen and her colleagues (Hansen et al., 2008) mathematically correlated the respondents' self-reported leisure activities and found that they fell into three clusters or factors, as shown in Table 18.1. Factor I included athletic, competitive, and outdoor activities. Factor II involved artistic, cultural, and self-expressive activities. Partying was the sole activity that defined Factor III. Partying isn't just for youngsters.

LO5 Successful Aging

A recent study found that 44% of seniors perceive their health to be excellent or very good. In the same year, 37% of seniors reported that they had taken some action to improve their health: 71% said they had increased their physical activity, 21% said they had lost weight, and 13% had changed their eating habits (Public Health Agency of Canada, 2010b).

There are many definitions of successful aging. Physical activity, social contacts, self-rated good

EMERGING CANADA

The Public Health Agency of Canada (2010b) released a report indicating a positive relationship between the number of social activities seniors participate in and their self-perceived health, level of loneliness, and life satisfaction. Social activities decrease the odds of loneliness and life dissatisfaction. It is not the number of social interactions that seems to make the difference, but the quality of the activities. Seniors reported that barriers to participating in social activities included health issues, being too busy, and lack of income (CBC News, 2012b).

selective optimization with compensation reshaping of one's life to concentrate on what one finds to be important and meaningful in the face of physical decline and possible cognitive impairment

health, the absence of cognitive impairment and depression, nonsmoking, and the absence of disabilities and chronic diseases such as arthritis and diabetes are often defined as successful aging (Depp & Jeste, 2006).

Selective Optimization with Compensation

A different view of successful aging has been advanced by researchers who focus on the processes by which individuals attempt to provide better person–environment fits to the changing physical, cognitive, and social circumstances in late adulthood (e.g., Baltes & Baltes, 1990). Selective optimization with compensation can maximize older people's gains while minimizing their losses. Successful aging over the lifespan is about an ongoing process of selection (setting goals), optimization (increasing gains), and compensation (avoiding losses) (Baltes, 2008). An action-theoretical approach to these processes provides for a deeper understanding of successful aging (Baltes, 2008) and demonstrates how the environment and individual adapt.

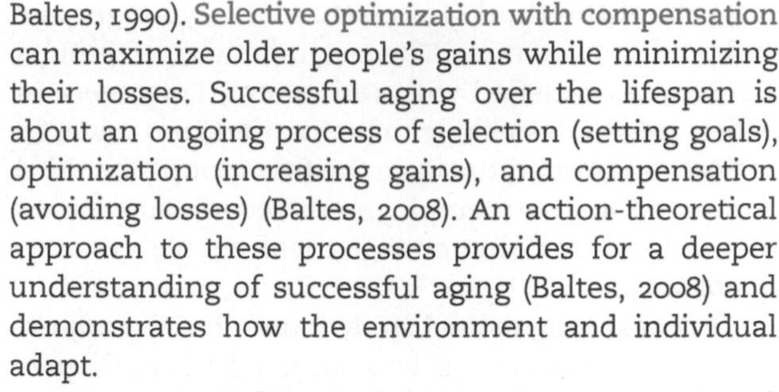

Though late adulthood is often viewed as a time to sit back and rest, it is an excellent opportunity to engage in new challenges and activities, such as going back to school.

Margaret Baltes and Laura Carstensen (2003) noted that a good deal of the research carried on by developmentalists focuses on decline and loss as major themes associated with late adulthood, and therefore the results tend to deflect attention from the many older people who experience late adulthood as a satisfying and productive stage of life. The concept of selective optimization with compensation is related to socio-emotional selectivity theory and is a key theme in adaptive aging (now also known as successful aging). In keeping with socio-emotional selectivity theory, successful agers tend to seek emotional fulfillment by reshaping their lives to concentrate on what they find to be important and meaningful.

Research on people aged 70 and older reveals that successful agers form emotional goals that bring them satisfaction (Löckenhoff & Carstensen, 2004). In applying the principle of selective optimization with compensation, successful agers may no longer compete in certain athletic or business activities (Bajor & Baltes, 2003; Freund & Baltes, 2002). Instead, they focus on matters that allow them to maintain a sense of control over their own lives.

Successful agers also tend to be optimistic. Such an outlook may be derived from transcendence of the ego, from spirituality, or sometimes from one's genetic heritage. (Yes, there is a genetic component to happiness [Lykken & Csikszentmihalyi, 2001].) However, retaining social contacts and building new ones also contributes to a positive outlook, as does, where possible, one's artistic and cultural activities.

The stereotype is that retirees look forward to late adulthood as a time when they can rest from life's challenges. But sitting back and allowing the world to pass by is a prescription for depression, not for living life to its fullest.

Canada is ranked as one of the best countries in the world in which to be a senior. Reasons for this

© Journal-Courier/Clayton Stalter/The Image Works

may include a comprehensive healthcare system, decent employment rates and pensions, lower rates of poverty as compared to many other countries, and an overall good standard of living. Many successful agers challenge themselves by taking up new pursuits such as painting, photography, or writing. Some travel to new destinations. Others return to school, taking special courses for older students, sitting in on regular college or university classes, or participating in seminars on special topics of interest. What will your retirement years look like?

Consider THIS

How do you want to be perceived, and treated, in your final years?

A 2012 survey of 1,500 seniors questioned whether ageism had become the most tolerated form of social discrimination, and of the Canadians surveyed, 89% associated aging with negative outcomes, such as being alone and losing independence. According to the survey, the three most common forms of discrimination faced by Canadian seniors are treated as if they are invisible (41%), as if they have nothing to contribute (38%), and as if they are incompetent (27%). These findings pose a significant obstacle for life review and the completion of Erikson's stage of ego integrity vs. despair (CTV News, 2012). Consider this: what is your perception of aging in Canada? How do you want to be perceived and treated in your final years? And are you cognizant of ageism in dealing with seniors?

STUDY TOOLS

CHAPTER 18

Located at **nelson.com/student**

- ☐ Prepare for tests with a variety of exercises and activities
- ☐ Review Key Terms Flashcards (online or print)
- ☐ Create your own study tools with Build a Summary
- ☐ Watch Observing Development videos to expand your knowledge

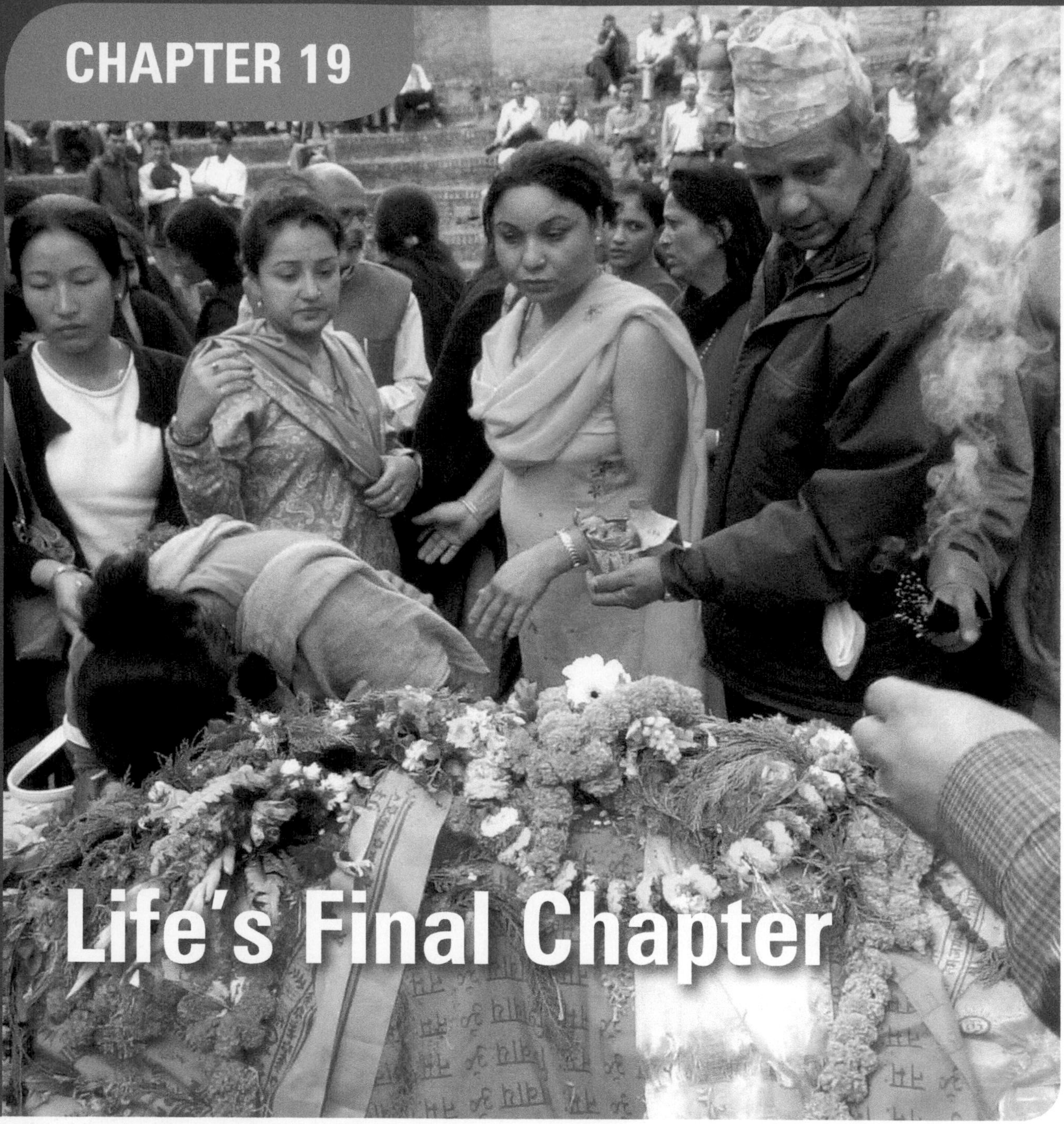

Devendra M. Singh/AFP/Getty Images

CHAPTER 19

Life's Final Chapter

LEARNING OUTCOMES

LO1 Define death and dying, and evaluate views on stages of dying

LO2 Identify settings in which people die, distinguishing between hospitals and hospices

LO3 Discuss the various types of euthanasia and their controversies

LO4 Discuss people's perspectives on death at various stages of development

LO5 Discuss coping with death, focusing on the funeral, and on working through the possible stages, or processes, of grieving

> “Today, only a small minority of Canadians die in their own homes—typically those who are in advanced old age or those who are gravely or terminally ill.”

When we are young we may not be concerned with getting older, let alone with our own mortality. It may seem that we will live forever. Eating well, exercising, and taking caring of ourselves may seem like all we need to do, in order to have a long life. We may have but a dim awareness of our own mortality. We parcel thoughts about death and dying into a mental file cabinet to be opened later in life, along with items like retirement, Old Age Security, and varicose veins. But death can occur at any age—by accident, violence, or illness. We can also be affected deeply at any stage of life through the deaths of others.

Our exposure to death and understanding of mortality is greatly influenced by our religious, cultural, and individual beliefs. The denial of death is deeply embedded in mainstream Canadian society. Many people prefer not to think about their own eventual death, struggle to find ways to grieve, and avoid planning ahead for their dissolution. Many First Nations, Métis, and Inuit peoples have a more collectivist approach to dying and death, conducting community-based ceremonies—preparing death feasts, and making traditional caskets, star blankets, and “give-aways” to commemorate the death of a loved one.

When we think about death and dying, many questions arise:

- How do we know when a person has died?
- Are there stages of dying?
- What is meant by the “right to die”? Do people have a right to die?
- What is a living will?
- How do we mourn? Are there stages of grieving? Are these stages accurate?

This chapter addresses these questions and many more.

LO1 Understanding Death and Dying

Death is commonly defined as the cessation of life. Many people think of death as a part of life, but death is the termination of life, not a part of it. Dying, though, is a part of life. It is the universal end-stage of life in which bodily processes decline, leading to death. Yet life holds significance and meaning even in the face of impending death.

death
the irreversible cessation of vital life functions

dying
the end-stage of life in which bodily processes decline, leading to death

brain death
cessation of activity of the cerebral cortex

whole-brain death
cessation of activity of the cerebral cortex and brain stem

Charting the Boundaries between Life and Death

How do we know when a person has died? Is it the stoppage of their hearts? Of their breathing? Of their brain activity?

Medical authorities generally use brain death as the basis for determining that a person has died (Appel, 2005). The most widely used criterion for establishing brain death is the absence of activity of the cerebral cortex, as shown by a flat EEG (electroencephalography) recording. When the cerebral cortex no longer shows signs of activity, consciousness—the sense of self and all psychological functioning—has ceased. The broader concept of whole-brain death includes death of the brain stem, which is responsible for certain automatic functions, such as the reflex of breathing. Thus, a person who is “brain dead” can continue to breathe. On the other hand, some people who are "whole-brain dead" can be been kept "alive" by life-support equipment that takes over their breathing and circulation.

Death is also a legal matter. In Canada, a person is considered legally dead when there is an irreversible cessation of breathing and circulation or when an irreversible cessation of brain activity occurs, including activity in the brain stem, which controls breathing (Appel, 2005).

> **DID YOU KNOW?**
>
> **A person may stop breathing and have no heartbeat but still be alive.**
>
> People whose hearts and lungs have ceased functioning can often be revived using cardiopulmonary resuscitation (CPR).

Are There Stages of Dying?

Responses to dying and death will vary across cultures, religions, and ethnicities.

The study of the processes of dying has been greatly influenced by the work of Elisabeth Kübler-Ross (1969). Her observations of terminally ill patients has provided analysis of some important and common responses to news of impending death. She hypothesized that dying patients pass through five stages of dying (see Table 19.1). She suggested that both younger patients and older people who suspect that death is near may undergo similar responses (Kübler-Ross, 1969). These five stages provide insight into common individual experiences of dying, but they shouldn't be used as a template, as other factors affect the adjustment of the dying individual.

TABLE 19.1

Stages of Dying

1. Denial	In this stage, people think, "It can't be me. The diagnosis must be wrong." Denial can be flat and absolute, or it can fluctuate so that one minute the patient accepts the medical verdict, and the next, the patient chats animatedly about future plans.
2. Anger	Denial usually gives way to anger and resentment toward the young and healthy, and, sometimes, toward the medical establishment: "It's unfair. Why me?" or "They didn't catch it in time."
3. Bargaining	People may bargain with a religious or culturally appropriate (omnipotent) force/s to try to postpone death, promising, for example, to do good deeds if they are given another six months, or another year.
4. Depression	With depression come feelings of grief, loss, and hopelessness—at the prospect of leaving loved ones and life itself.
5. Final Acceptance	Ultimately, inner peace or serenity may come as a quiet acceptance of the inevitable. This "peace" may not be contentment as such, as the patient may still fear death, but he or she comes to accept it with a sense of peace and dignity.

Much current "death education" suggests that hospital staff and family members can help support dying people by understanding the stages they are going through, by not imposing their own expectations, and by helping patients achieve final acceptance when they are ready to do so. But critics note that staff may be imposing Kübler-Ross's expectations.

Another critic, Joan Retsinas (1988), notes that Kübler-Ross's stages are limited to cases in which people receive a diagnosis of a terminal illness. As Retsinas points out, most people die because of their advanced years, not because of a specific terminal diagnosis. Thus, Kübler-Ross's approach may not be of much use in helping us understand reactions under circumstances other than terminal illness.

Edwin Shneidman (1977) acknowledges that dying people may have feelings such as those described by Kübler-Ross, but his research shows that individuals behave in dying more or less as they behaved during their earlier life when they experienced stress, failure, and threat. A gamut of emotional responses and psychological defences emerge, especially denial, and these responses can be observed in every death. However, according to Shneidman, the process of dying does not necessarily follow any progression of stages, as suggested by Kübler-Ross. The key factors that appear to affect the adjustment of the dying individual include the type and extent of organic cerebral impairment, pain and weakness, the time or phase of the person's life, the person's philosophy of life (and death), and prior experiences with crises.

> **DID YOU KNOW?**
>
> **In the Jewish tradition the bereavement process involves loved ones gathering for a mourning period of seven days.**
>
> This tradition is known as Shiva. Covering mirrors, not "bathing for pleasure," and sitting on low chairs are part of the process of mourning, or being present in grief.

Life and Death Issues: Bioethics and the "Erlangen Baby"

Marion Ploch was considered brain-dead after a car crash at thirteen weeks pregnant. The identity of the father of the unmarried woman's baby was know only to her. The decision about the normally developing fetus was then left up to the ethics committee of doctors and lawyers at the University Clinic at Erlangen in southern Germany (Fisher, 1992). The situation crept into public discourse. One side demanded that Ploch and her unborn child be left to die in a dignified manner. The other side referred to the unborn child's right to live and, therefore, wanted the body of the woman maintained until the fetus could be born. Under German law, the ethics panel decided they had an obligation to save the life of the fetus, while other doctors signed petitions against the decision, calling it a "shameless human experiment" (Caplan, 1993). The Ploch case became a media frenzy, and debates on bioethics ensued. A TV station tried to buy an ultrasound image of the fetus, and received a lawyer's letter stating that "the unborn obviously have a right to control their own image" (Fisher, 1992). One Catholic theologian argued an unusual position that "nature should take its course" (Fisher, 1992).

In a handful of cases in the United States, Britain, and Germany, babies have been brought to term in the dead bodies of their mothers. Some of the babies lived, some died. In another instance, a mother died at fifteen weeks pregnant. Her son was born with diabetes, pneumonia, and heart problems, but he is healthy and happy (Fisher, 1992).

In the Ploch case, the grandparents wanted the machines turned off, but after the ethics committee recommended keeping the fetus alive, they changed their minds. Although deemed medically dead, the nursing staff provided care for Ploch, as they might have for a living patient; they talked to her and even brushed her hair. The hospital bill was approximately $70,000 and was paid by the government. The fetus didn't survive.

Sources: Marc Fisher, "Brain-dead Woman Provides Life-support for Fetus Hospital Committee's Decision Provokes Ethics Controversy, *The Washington Post*, November 1, 1992, http://articles.mcall.com/1992-11-01/news/2889311_1_fetus-ethics-panel-unborn-child, and Arthur Caplan, "Should we maintain a corpse to rescue a fetus?" *The Baltimore Sun*, September 1, 1993, http://articles.baltimoresun.com/1993-09-01/news/1993244122_1_fetus-ploch-life-support

LO2 Where People Die

Many people throughout the world die at home surrounded by loved ones, but only a small minority of Canadians die in their own homes—typically those who are in advanced old age or who are gravely or terminally ill. When asked, 75% of Canadians said they would prefer to die in their home (Canadian Hospice Palliative Care Association, 2014), yet 70% of Canadians die in a hospital (Canadian Hospice Palliative Care Association, 2010). Of course, sudden death can happen at any time and anywhere, either because of accidents, heart attacks, or other unanticipated events.

hospice
an organization that treats dying patients by focusing on palliative care rather than curative treatment

In the Hospital

Dying in a hospital can seem impersonal. Hospitals function to treat diseases, not to help prepare patients and their families for death, although some hospitals do provide social workers and other psychosocial support services. Many patients and their families may assume that going to the hospital gives them the best chance of averting death, and although they may be without their familial surroundings, they are still comforted by family and friends. Some patients do, however, face death alone, cut off from their usual supports.

Hospice Care

Increasing numbers of dying people and their families are turning to **hospices** to help make their final days as meaningful and pain-free as possible. The word *hospice* derives from the Latin *hospitium*, meaning "hospitality"—the same root as the words *hospital* and *hospitable*. Hospices provide a homelike atmosphere to help terminally ill patients approach death with a maximum of dignity and a minimum of pain and discomfort. When necessary, hospice care is provided in inpatient settings, such as hospitals, nursing facilities, or hospice centres; but most hospice care is provided in the patient's home.

Depending on where they live, only 16–30% of Canadians who die will have access to or will receive hospice, palliative care, and end-of-life services (Canadian Hospice Palliative Care Association, 2014). Because of the "greying of Canada"—a rapidly aging population—the demand for these services will continue to rise.

Hospice workers typically work in teams that include physicians, nurses, social workers, mental health or pastoral counsellors, and home care aides; they provide physical, medical, spiritual, and emotional support to the entire family, not just the patient. Bereavement specialists assist the family to prepare for the loss and help them through grieving after the death. In contrast to hospitals, hospices provide the patient and family with as much control over

palliative care
treatment focused on the relief of pain and suffering, not on a cure

euthanasia
the purposeful taking of life to relieve suffering

decision making as possible. Hospice workers honour the patient's wishes when they choose not to be resuscitated or not to be kept alive on life-support equipment. Patients are given pain-killing medications to alleviate their discomfort.

Compared with hospital care, hospice care provides a more supportive environment for both the patient and the family; it is also less costly, especially when provided in the patient's home.

Hospice care has the following characteristics:

- Hospices offer 24-hour palliative care, not a curative treatment. They control pain and symptoms to enable the patient to live as fully and comfortably as possible.
- Hospices treat the person, not the disease. The hospice team addresses the medical, emotional, psychological, and spiritual needs of patients, family, and friends, including bereavement counselling after the death.
- Hospices emphasize the quality of life, not the length of life, neither hastening nor postponing death.

Hospices treat the person, not the disease. The hospice team addresses the medical, emotional, psychological, and spiritual needs of patients, family, and friends.

Supporting a Dying Person

According to the *Hospice* website, there are a number of ways to support someone with a life-threatening illness.

- **Give the gift of availability:** The greatest gift someone can offer a person who is dying is being available. Hospital or home visits and sharing in activities that are manageable for the dying person are very useful. Respecting the person's need for alone time and acknowledging their energy levels are also key (Wolfelt, 2016).
- **Listen actively:** Open discussion about their illness and death should not be avoided, but should be discussed at the person's discretion. Providing a safe space, and not criticizing, judging, or advice-giving are important when listening (Wolfelt, 2016).

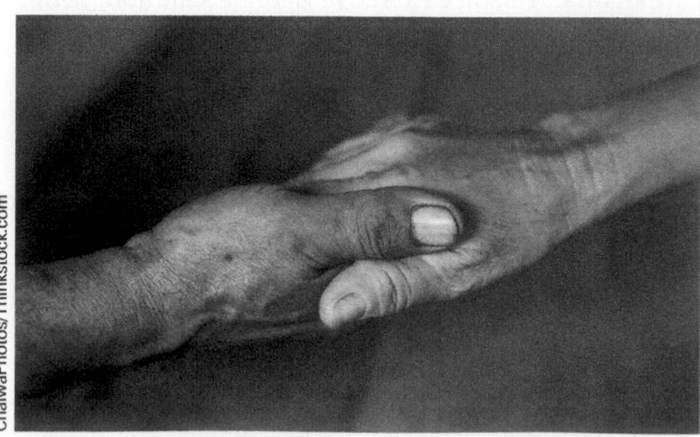
ChaiwaPhotos/Thinkstock.com

EMERGING CANADA

Blogging is a very popular option for many Canadian families and friends facing health events. Daily journal entries can keep loved ones updated. Blogs often include guest books that allow for messages of support and written words of encouragement without burdening the patient with having to respond to multiple well-meaning messages. CaringBridge is a nonprofit organization providing social-media support for anyone coping with illness (CaringBridge, 2013).

CaringBridge.org

Courtesy of The Caring Bridge

- **Know about the condition:** Where appropriate, it is good to educate yourself about what illness the person is dealing with. This provides for a greater understanding. Again, it's about listening and not advice-giving.
- **Show compassion:** The dying person will appreciate having the time and space to express his or her feelings. "Walking with and not behind or in front of" (Wolfelt, 2016) a dying person can provide much-needed care and support.
- **Give practical support and help:** Making food, washing clothes, cleaning the house, or acting as chauffeur to and from appointments or the hospital are practical ways to show support and care.
- **Keep in contact; communicate:** Not everyone can visit regularly because of personal and profession commitments, as well as geographic distance. Writing emails, texts, and letters, and making phone calls or even videos is a great way to show you care and have the person on your mind.
- **How are you coping?** Caring for someone who is dying can be very emotional and difficult. How are you feeling about the illness and your sick friend or family member? Do you need someone to talk through your thoughts and feelings with too? You're no help to your terminally ill friend or relative if you are sick or depressed yourself.

LO3 Dying and Human Rights

The word euthanasia, literally meaning "good death," is derived from the Greek roots *eu* ("good") and *thanatos* ("death"). Also called "mercy killing," it refers to the purposeful taking of a person's life through gentle or painless means to relieve the person's pain or suffering. There are several types of euthanasia.

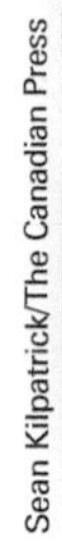

Sean Kilpatrick/The Canadian Press

Lee Carter, daughter of right-to-die pioneer Kay Carter, at the Supreme Court ruling.

DID YOU KNOW?

As of June 2016, the Supreme Court ruled that physician-assisted suicide will be legal in Canada.

Euthanasia and physician-assisted suicide are deaths caused by a lethal drug prescribed by a physician. Canadian law allows these procedures under very restricted circumstances.

End-of-Life Definitions

The Canadian Medical Association (CMA) has developed several definitions to be used when discussing end-of-life medical decisions. Euthanasia means knowingly and intentionally performing an act intended to end another person's life. In euthanasia, the subject (the patient) has an incurable illness, the agent (the person who assists) is aware of the life-threatening condition, the primary intent of the agent's act is to end life, and the act is undertaken with empathy and compassion and without personal gain.

"Dying with dignity" refers to a patient's dying following the guidelines that she or he has specified in advance. This includes how they are to be cared for near and at the end of their lives. Dying with dignity doesn't necessarily mean euthanasia or physician-assisted death (Canadian Medical Association Policy, 2014).

The CMA identifies three types of euthanasia. **Voluntary euthanasia** refers to an assisted death where the subject is competent, informed, and voluntarily asks to have his or her life ended. **Non-voluntary euthanasia** refers to an assisted death where the person has not expressed his or her preference in terms of an assisted death. **Involuntary euthanasia** refers to an assisted death where the person has made an informed choice and expressed his or her refusal to accept assistance in dying (Canadian Medical Association, 2007).

Assisted suicide differs from physician-assisted suicide in that it refers to a death that is self-inflicted as a result of someone else intentionally providing the knowledge or means to die by suicide. An example of assisted suicide is a physician who prescribes barbiturates to a patient with advanced amyotrophic lateral sclerosis (ALS), who then uses the drugs to kill herself (Canadian Medical Association, 2016). **Terminal sedation** is the medical practice of relieving distress in a terminally ill patient in the last hours or days of his or her life, usually by means of a continuous intravenous infusion of a sedative drug, such as a tranquilizer. Terminal sedation is not intended to hasten death, although whether it has that effect is often debated (Cellarius, 2008).

voluntary euthanasia the intentional ending of life as a result of a competent, informed person having made a personal decision to have an assisted death

non-voluntary euthanasia the intentional ending of the life of a person who has not expressed his or her preference in terms of an assisted death

involuntary euthanasia the intentional ending of the life of a person who made an informed choice and expressed his or her refusal to have an assisted death

assisted suicide a self-inflicted death as a result of someone intentionally providing the knowledge or means to die by suicide

terminal sedation the practice of relieving distress in the last hours or days of life with the use of sedatives

Euthanasia and Assisted Suicide in Canada under the New Legislation

Under legislation enacted in June 2014 in Quebec and in June 2016 throughout Canada, euthanasia continues to be illegal, but physician-assisted suicide in Canada will be legal under these circumstances: a "competent adult person . . . (1) clearly consents to the termination of life and (2) has a grievous and irremediable medical condition (including an illness, disease or disability) that causes enduring suffering that is intolerable to the individual in the circumstances of his or her condition" (Health Law Institute, 2016).

Canadian Physicians' Points of View

Euthanasia and assisted suicide are the most important issues facing Canadian society today. At the CMA's annual meeting in August 2015, a number of doctors expressed discomfort about

Studio Smart/Shutterstock.com

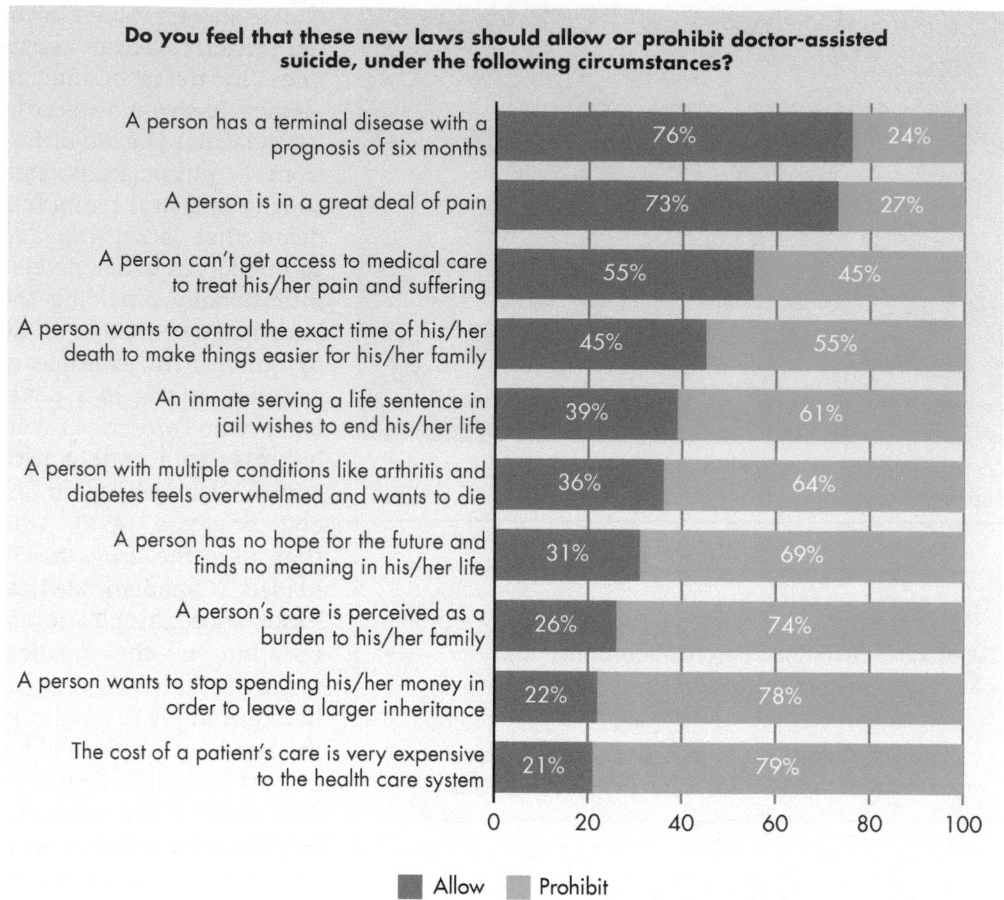
Do you feel that these new laws should allow or prohibit doctor-assisted suicide, under the following circumstances?
A person has a terminal disease with a prognosis of six months
76%
24%
A person is in a great deal of pain
73%
27%
A person can't get access to medical care to treat his/her pain and suffering
55%
45%
A person wants to control the exact time of his/her death to make things easier for his/her family
45%
55%
An inmate serving a life sentence in jail wishes to end his/her life
39%
61%
A person with multiple conditions like arthritis and diabetes feels overwhelmed and wants to die
36%
64%
A person has no hope for the future and finds no meaning in his/her life
31%
69%
A person's care is perceived as a burden to his/her family
26%
74%
A person wants to stop spending his/her money in order to leave a larger inheritance
22%
78%
The cost of a patient's care is very expensive to the health care system
21%
79%
0
20
40
60
80
100
Allow
Prohibit

FIGURE 19.1

Assisted Suicide Poll

Source: Angus Reid Institute

offering assisted death; also, they didn't want to refer patients to other physicians. Consequently, a Special Joint Committee on Physician-Assisted Dying has been established to examine legislative and regulatory frameworks in order to achieve an appropriate balance between physician rights of conscience and patient rights to access to assisted dying under the law. The CMA has also developed a framework for a pan-Canadian approach to assisted dying, which includes principles-based approaches to assisted dying. The proposed framework accounts for different points of views and differences of conscience; it strongly recommends that resources be in place to facilitate patient access (CMA, 2016). The Special Joint Committee on Physician-Assisted Suicide brought forward the proposal in February 2016 to the Parliament for review. Physicians are cooperating with legislators in order to establish new legislation and meet Supreme Court deadlines, as they want to have clarity for physicians and patients to avoid conflicting approaches, and the develop stellar pan-Canadian approaches.

The section above represents the official stand of the CMA, but how do individual doctors feel? The CMA polled more than 2,000 doctors. Only 20% said they would be willing to perform physician-assisted suicide. More than double that number, 42% said they would refuse to do so. Some 23% were not sure how they would respond, and 15% chose not to answer (see Figure 19.1).

Recent Court Decisions and Public Opinion

Gloria Taylor, a British Columbia woman with ALS, won her legal fight to obtain doctor-assisted suicide in Canada. The B.C. court ruled that it was unconstitutional to deny her this right if she could find a physician prepared to help her. Gloria died before pursuing this option (CBC News, 2012a). Canadians will also remember Sue Rodriquez's brave fight against ALS, and her ongoing fight to "the right to die."

Before the legislative change, many Canadians did not have the opportunity to die the way they wanted, or when they wanted. Due to laws against physician-assisted suicide in 2010, Kay Carter, a mother of seven who was dying from spinal stenosis, travelled to Switzerland, where assisted suicide is legal, to end her life. Carter's case became paramount to legal changes in Canada, when her daughter, Lee, became a plaintiff in the case of Carter vs. Canada, "to challenge our existing laws" (Dying with Dignity Canada, 2015). Lee Carter is a longstanding patron of Dying With Dignity Canada, and an advocate for voluntary death. She helped to shape Bill C-14, the act to amend medically assisted dying. Many advocates feel that the Bill was a victory, but many "failed" components were not passed. Advocates continue to push for amendments to the Bill (openparliament, 2016).

The Living Will

Pierre was in a tragic accident that left him in an irreversible coma and dependent on artificial life support—a respirator to maintain his breathing and feeding tubes to supply his body with nutrients. Would Pierre want his life to be maintained by whatever means were at the disposal of modern medicine, or would he prefer doctors to withdraw life support, allowing him to die naturally?

Keisha has been in pain day after day. She has a terminal disease, and her heart suddenly stops due to cardiac arrest. Would she want the doctors to resuscitate her by whatever means necessary in an effort to prolong her life for another few days or weeks?

Who decides when it is time for Keisha or Pierre to die—the patients themselves, their families, or the doctors managing their care?

A living will, also known as a healthcare directive, is a legal document that people draft when they are well. It can direct healthcare workers not to use aggressive medical procedures or life-support equipment to prolong vegetative functioning in the event they became permanently incapacitated and unable to communicate their wishes. Terminally ill patients can insist, for example, that "Do Not Resuscitate" orders be included in their charts, directing doctors not to use CPR in the event they have a cardiac arrest.

Living wills must be drafted in accordance with provincial or territorial laws. The terms of the document take effect only when patients are unable to speak for themselves. For this reason, living wills usually identify a proxy, such as the next of kin, who can make decisions in the event that the signer cannot communicate.

Still, many living wills are ignored. Some are disregarded by their proxies, often because the proxies don't judge the patient's wishes accurately or because they can't bear the emotional burden of asking healthcare workers to remove life support. Physicians are more likely to follow specific healthcare directives (e.g., "Do not resuscitate") than general guidelines.

living will
a document, prepared when a person is well, that outlines the person's desires concerning medical care should he or she become incapacitated or unable to speak for him/herself. It can provide directives for healthcare providers to terminate life-sustaining treatment.

DID YOU KNOW?

People who have living wills can hope their wishes will be carried out if they become unable to speak for themselves.

A living will may not be carried out for many reasons. Specific healthcare directives have a better chance of being carried out than general guidelines.

LO4 Lifespan Perspectives on Death

Psychologists have found interesting development in people's understanding of death and their reactions to death. Children, for example, seem to follow something of a Piagetian route in their cognitive development. Older people who truly understand the finality of death appear to take some reasonable steps to avert it, even "risk-taking" adolescents (Mills, Reyna, & Estrada, 2008).

Religious, cultural, and individual perspectives are part of people's understanding about what happens after we die: the Christian concept of heaven or hell, the Islamic belief of a journey into another existence, Hindu beliefs concerning reincarnation, Indigenous perspectives which include ancestral and spiritual realms, or agnostic or atheist beliefs that don't necessarily support the concept of an afterlife.

Children

Younger children lack the cognitive ability to understand the permanent nature of death (Slaughter & Griffiths, 2007). Preschoolers may think that death is reversible or temporary, a belief reinforced by cartoon characters who die and come back to life (Poltorak & Glazer, 2006). Nevertheless, their thinking becomes increasingly realistic as they progress through the ages of 4, 5, and 6 (Li-qi & Fu-xi, 2006). Children's understanding of death appears to increase as they learn about the biology of the human body and how

Organ, Tissue, and Blood Donation: The Gift of Life

Organ Donation

One winter day, I lost a dear student and friend to a sudden brain aneurism. Greg died as he had lived, with dignity and with charity. Upon his death, seven people received a gift of life because Greg had previously agreed to donate his organs. One donor can save up to eight lives, and the gift of tissue donation can enhance the lives of another 75.

Donating organs for transplant after death gives the gift of hope to someone else in need. Living donors—often family members—can sometimes donate a kidney or a portion of their liver for transplant. In deceased donation, all organs and tissues must be taken from the donor shortly after death. The organs and tissues that can be donated include heart, kidneys, liver, lungs, pancreas, skin, small bowel, stomach, bone, and heart valves. Only organs that are healthy at the time of death are suitable for transplantation.

Blood Donation

Blood and blood products are very important in everyday medical care. For heart surgery and some cancer treatments, it takes up to five blood donors for someone who requires a blood transfusion. For car accidents, it can take up to fifty donors (Canadian Blood Services, 2016). According to Canadian Blood Services you can donate if you meet these qualifications:

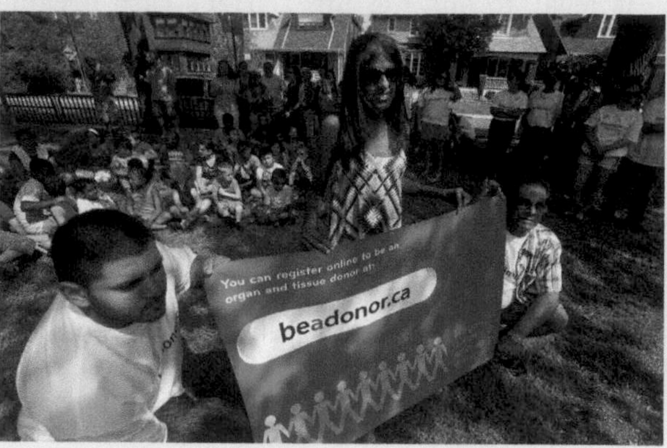

Chris So/Toronto Star via Getty Images

- In good health and feeling well enough to perform regular activities
- Are a minimum of 17 years old
- Meet specific height and weight requirements

Source: Canadian Blood Services, 2016. https://www.blood.ca/en/blood/who-does-my-donation-help

various organs contribute to the processes of life (Slaughter & Griffiths, 2007).

Loss is difficult for children to bear, especially when a parent dies (Greidanus, 2007). Death of a loved one strikes at the core of a child's sense of security and well-being. Older children may feel guilty because of the mistaken belief that they brought about the death by once wishing for the person to die. The loss of security may lead to anger, which may be directed toward surviving family or expressed in aggressive play. Children may show regressive or infantile behaviours, such as reverting to "baby talk" or becoming more demanding of food or attention. Some children may persist for several weeks in maintaining the belief that the deceased person is still alive. Although some child psychiatrists believe this response is normal, prolonged denial can be an indication of more severe problems (Crenshaw, 2007).

Children will be taught about death in keeping with their cultural, ethnic, and religious customs. Children may be taught that it is possible to survive death, either through reincarnation, as in some Eastern religions, or as in the transcendence of the soul, as in Christianity. Many children may fear death when they learn about it. To mitigate this fear, children in North America are sometimes told, "Your father is now in heaven and you will see him there again. Meanwhile, he is watching over you." Caregivers will

After children experience the death of someone close to them, encourage them to express all of their emotions honestly and openly. Watch for the following danger signs that may indicate a need for professional help:

- loss of sleep or appetite
- depressed mood for several weeks
- excessive fears (e.g., the fear of being alone)
- refusal to go to school
- withdrawal from friends

© Ryan McVay/Photodisc/Getty Images

sometimes try to comfort children by telling them that their loved one is "in a better place." The concept of surviving death renders death less permanent and less frightening to many children—and adults (Lattanzi-Licht, 2007).

Adolescents

Adolescents are "in between" in many ways. They know full well that when life functions come to an end, they cannot be restored, yet they are not beyond

How to Help Children and Young Teens When Someone Has Died

Victoria Hospice Bereavement Services and Helpguide.org makes these recommendations for helping a child or teen when someone has died.

Children ages 3–5 think magically, egocentrically, and in a physical manner. Seeing themselves at the centre of most things, they believe that their thoughts and even behaviours are the cause of events. Anxious behaviours can ensue when they are separated from primary caregivers; they may feel scared, worried, or concerned when an important adult in their lives is in distress.

When the caregiver needs to tell the child that someone has died, it is helpful to explain that the person can no longer feel,that their heart doesn't beat, and that they cannot see anymore. Telling the child about the upcoming funeral services as well as explaining who will be attending, what will happen, what is expected of the child him or herse;f, and other pertinent facts, help to prepare the child. The caregiver should also allow for opportunities to think, share, and talk about the person who has passed away. Adults model the processes of grieving, so if they aren't seen to be discussing feelings or sharing memories, this may make the child feel that they shouldn't either.

Objects that provide a connection to the person who has died may prove helpful.

Children ages 6–8 are similar to younger children, but at this age they may become concerned about their own health and that of their caregivers: "Can my mother or father die?" They may also need support from key adults in their lives, such as teachers, coaches, or religious figures. Children's grieving processes are different from adults and can be intense, brief, and sporadic; they can last over a long period of time.

Children ages 12–14 are entering the formal operational thought stage. Since young teens are learning to understand what will have changed when someone dies, they may experience powerful feelings of anger, sadness, guilt, fear, and hope. Teens are pushing for independence at this stage, but they can feel hurt or abandoned if their parents are withdrawn as a result of grieving.

Teens need detailed information. Talking with them about their feelings, allowing for less responsibility with household chores and employment, allowing for grieving processes, and watching for destructive behaviours—these are all supportive ways to help a teen when someone has died (Helpguide.org, 2016; Victoria Hospice Bereavement Services, 2014).

Dolgachov/Thinkstock.com

constructing magical, spiritual, or pseudoscientific theories as to how some form of life or thought might survive (Balk et al., 2007). Adolescents also speak of death in terms of concepts such as light, darkness, transition, and nothingness (Oltjenbruns & Balk, 2007).

Compared with young children, adolescents are more exposed to the deaths of older family members such as grandparents, and even of fellow adolescents, some of whom may have died of illness or from accidents, suicide, or foul play. Adolescents are more likely than young children to attend funerals, including funerals with open caskets. These experiences challenge the adolescent's sense of immortality that is associated with the personal fable (see Chapter 11; Noppe & Noppe, 2004). Even though adolescents come to recognize that the concept of death applies to them, they continue to engage in riskier behaviour than adults do. On the other hand, those adolescents who perceive certain behaviours to be highly risky are less likely to engage in them (Mills et al., 2008).

Even though adolescents come to recognize that the concept of death applies to them, they continue to engage in riskier behaviour than adults do.

© BananaStock/Jupiterimages

Adults

The leading causes of death in early adulthood are accidents and suicide. In middle adulthood, heart disease and cancer have become the leading causes of death in Canada. People are advised to become proactive in their screenings for cardiovascular problems and for several kinds of cancer. Some cancers have sex differences, but educated women and men are aware that age is a risk factor in both heart disease and cancer, and they are likely aware of middle-aged people who died "untimely" deaths from one or the other.

Heart disease and cancer remain the leading causes of death in late adulthood. As people move into advanced old age, many no longer drive due to loss of sensory acuity and slowed reaction time. Older adults are also more prone to falls, Alzheimer's disease, and other dementias. Some older people come to fear disability and discomfort nearly as much as they fear death.

Theorists of social and emotional development in late adulthood suggest that ego transcendence, or concern for the well-being of humankind in general, enables some people to begin to face death with an inner calm (see Chapter 18; Ardelt, 2008b). On the other hand, continuing with physical, leisure, and informal social activities are all associated with greater life satisfaction among older, retired people (Joung & Miller, 2007; Talbot et al., 2007). Psychosocial and cultural aspects will influence adaptability to aging, physical stamina and decline, and dying and death.

LO5 Coping with Death

For most, coping with someone else's death can be complicated, painful, and disorienting. Losing a loved one is considered to be one of the most stressful life changes we can endure.

What to Do When Someone Dies

If you are present at someone's death, call the family doctor, the police, or 911. A doctor is needed to complete the death certificate and to indicate the cause of death. If the cause of death cannot be readily determined, a coroner or medical examiner may become involved to determine the cause of death. Once the the doctor has examined the body and completed the death certificate, a funeral director may be contacted to remove the body from the home or the hospital, and to make arrangements for burial, cremation, or placement in a mausoleum. If death occurs unexpectedly or foul play is involved or suspected, an autopsy may be performed to determine the cause and circumstances of death. An autopsy might also be performed, with the family's consent, if the knowledge gained from the procedure could benefit medical science.

Funeral Arrangements

Funerals respond to death in an organized way that is tied to religious custom and cultural tradition. Funerals offer family and community a ritual for grieving publicly and saying farewell to the person who died. Funerals grant a closure that can help observers begin to move on with their lives.

Family members of the deceased decide how simple or elaborate they would like the funeral to be, whether they want the deceased's body to be buried or cremated. Sometimes these matters are spelled out by religious, cultural, or family custom, and sometimes these decisions can lead to family conflicts.

After their homes, automobiles, and children's educations, funerals may be a Canadian family's next largest expense. When arranging a funeral, people should consider these guidelines in order to meet their needs while remaining on budget:

- Make decisions based on reason and good sense, not on emotions or guilt.
- If a funeral home has not yet been selected, shop around; you can and should ask about their services and costs.
- Be aware that some cemeteries offer the plot for free but then make their profit from charging exorbitant maintenance fees, opening and closing fees, costs for monuments, and other fees.
- Caskets are often the major burial expense and can range from \$500 to \$50,000 or even more! Recognize that the type of casket you choose makes no difference to the deceased person, and tell the funeral director to show you models that fall within a comfortable price range.

Funerals can be expensive. Make decisions based on reason and good sense, not on emotions or guilt.

Legal and Financial Matters

Many legal and financial matters require attention following a death. Family members will need to deal with issues concerning estates, inheritance, outstanding debts, insurance, and amounts owed for funeral expenses. Focusing on these matters can be difficult during a time of grief. Family members should seek legal counsel to protect their own financial interests and for guidance on handling the deceased person's affairs. An

© Sylvain Grandadam/Getty Images

Different cultures often have very different approaches to funerary traditions. These musicians are part of a cremation ceremony in Bali, Indonesia.

DID YOU KNOW?

The average burial in Canada costs $10,000, while cremations cost 25% of the cost of a burial.

This may be why 60% of deceased people are now cremated (Demont, 2012).

attorney is usually needed to settle the estate, especially when it is sizeable or when complex matters arise in sorting through the deceased person's affairs.

Grief and Bereavement

The death of a close friend or family member can be a traumatic experience. It typically leads to a state of bereavement, an emotional state of longing and deprivation characterized by feelings of grief and a deep sense of loss. Mourning is synonymous with grief over the death of a person, but also describes culturally prescribed ways of displaying grief. Different cultures prescribe different periods of mourning and different rituals for expressing grief. The tradition of wearing unadorned black clothing for mourning goes back at least to the Roman Empire. In rural parts of Mexico, Italy, and Greece, widows are often still expected to wear black for the remainder of their lives. In England and North America, the wearing of black is on the decline, replaced by wearing joyous colours as the life of the deceased person is celebrated.

Photo by Peter Moon, *Wawatay News*, Sioux Lookout, Ontario

Canadian elder and Ranger Peter Fiddler uses an eagle feather to smudge the new military grave marker for Ranger Delilah Meekis of Sandy Lake First Nation.

bereavement
the state of deprivation brought about by the death of a family member or close friend

grief
emotional suffering resulting from a death

mourning
customary methods of expressing grief

disenfranchised grief
grief that is not acknowledge by society

Coping with loss requires time and the ability to come to terms with the loss and move ahead with one's life. Having a supportive social network is important in navigating this major transition, and grief counselling may also be useful.

LGBTQ Disenfranchised Grief

Experiences of grief among LGBTQ who have encountered the death of their partner remain largely invisible within larger society (McNutt &Yakushko, 2013). Disenfranchised grief, or grief that is not acknowledged by society, can occur for LGBTQ people. Loss and grieving of a loved one may be deemed as "less than," or stigmatized. Often family members and professionals don't see LGBTQ relationships as "real relationships," and their feelings may be minimized by family members and society. Access, privileges, and rights throughout terminal illness, dying, and death may also be lower for LGBTQ partners. This can create additional stress and feelings of loss for partners, close friends, family, and community members.

Grieving

There is no one right way to grieve and no fixed period of time for which grief should last. Sometimes, especially for parents who have lost a child, grief never ends, though people do learn over time to live with the loss. People grieve in different ways. Some grieve more publicly, while others reveal their feelings only in private. Other people may not always know when someone is grieving. Early experiences of the non-acceptance of loss are the best predictors of later grief experiences. Early non-acceptance indicates a much higher likelihood for a prolonged grief response (Holland et al., 2013).

Russell Underwood/Corbis/Getty Images

Grief usually involves a combination of emotions, especially depression, loneliness, feelings of emptiness, disbelief and numbness, apprehension about the future ("What will I do now?"), guilt ("I could have done something"), even anger ("They could have handled this better"). Grief may also be punctuated by relief that the deceased person is no longer suffering intense pain, or by a heightened awareness of one's own mortality. Grief can compromise well-being, leaving the person more vulnerable to illness and disease (Ajdacic-Gross et al., 2008).

Theories of Stages of Grieving

John Bowlby (1961), the attachment theorist, was the first to propose a stage theory of grief for coping with bereavement. It included four stages: shock–numbness, yearning–searching, disorganization–despair, and reorganization. Elisabeth Kübler-Ross (1969) adapted Bowlby's stage theory to describe the five-stage reaction, already discussed, of terminally ill patients to knowledge of their own impending death: 1. denial–isolation, 2. anger, 3. bargaining, 4. depression, and 5. acceptance. Kübler-Ross's stage theory has become generally accepted when applied to various kinds of losses, including children's responses to parental separation, adults' responses to marital separation (Gray, Koopman, & Hunt, 1991), and hospital staff's responses to the death of a patient. Medical education currently relies heavily on the Kübler-Ross model of grief (Kübler-Ross & Kessler, 2005; Maciejewski et al., 2007).

Jacobs (1993) modified Kübler-Ross's stage theory of grief to include numbness–disbelief, separation distress (yearning–anger–anxiety), depression–mourning, and recovery. Jacobs' stage theory, like the theories that preceded it, is largely based on anecdotes and case studies.

To test Jacobs' theory, Paul Maciejewski and his colleagues (2007) administered five items measuring disbelief, yearning, anger, depression, and acceptance of death to 233 bereaved individuals from 1 to 24 months following their losses. Several findings are clear. Disbelief was highest just after the loss and gradually waned over the course of two years. Acceptance of the loss shows the opposite course, being non-existent at the outset, growing gradually, and peaking two years later. Yearning, anger, and depression rise suddenly in the predicted order and then each wanes gradually.

Maciejewski and his colleagues (2007) believe they found support for the Jacobs theory, and to some degree they did. The predicted feelings were present and arose in the predicted order. However, others reviewing the same data noted that the investigators tested for only these five emotions; emotions they neglected could have been more powerful (Bonanno & Boerner, 2007; Silver & Wortman, 2007).

McClintock Greenberg (2011) argues against the stage model for grieving and loss. She says that people react to loss in different ways and that if we subscribe to the stage theory, we make certain erroneous assumptions: that grief follows a specific pattern, that the experience of grief is finite, that grief occurs in stages, and that prolonged grief is abnormal. This type of framing of "normal" grief reactions sets patients up for being pathologized (considered psychologically abnormal), and when they show too much emotion or, contrastingly, not enough, they are perceived to be grieving in the "wrong way," says McClintock Greenberg (2011). She argues that relationships are unique. If a relationship was close, grieving might be more intense. If not, then grieving might be less intense. On the other hand, even people in close relationships may not necessarily grieve intensely. People

The Widow Who Isn't a Widow?

What do you call a widow who isn't a widow? According to Shatz (2006), part of the problem is that we have no word for a woman who has cohabited with a partner who has died, even if she has been with him/her for decades. In "The widow who wasn't a bride," Shatz describes the experiences of nine women who experienced disenfranchised grief following the loss of their partners. The bereaved women felt marginalized by society and cut off from their partners' biological children.

have all kinds of different strategies for managing emotions.

Supporting a Grieving Person

What can you do if someone you know is faced with the death of a close family member or friend? Consider some combination of the following: First, encourage them to take care of themselves. When people are grieving, they can become so absorbed with their loss that they fail to attend to their own personal needs. Some people do not eat or bathe. They may feel guilty doing things for themselves and avoid any pleasurable experiences. Reassure them that they can grieve without withdrawing from life.

Encourage them to feel their loss. Some people prefer to bottle up their feelings, but covering up feelings or trying to erase them with drugs or alcohol may prolong the grieving process. When they feel the time is right, they will turn to a trusted friend. Make yourself available and invite the person to lean on you for support. Suggesting grief counselling where appropriate may also be helpful.

Encourage the individual to join a bereavement support group or seek counselling. They will find that they are not alone in their suffering. Sharing experiences can help people cope better with grief in a supportive environment. Of all family members enrolled in hospice, 70% do not access post-loss bereavement services; of those who have major depressive disorders, less than 50% draw on outside resources. These findings suggest that many of the people who could benefit from bereavement services do not seek them out (Holland et al., 2013). Encouragement and identification of the right support services may be helpful for the bereaved person, as well as being an advocate. A supportive friend will offer to go with the bereaved individual so he or she can get the help that is needed.

Reassure the individual that it takes time to come to terms with loss. There is no fixed timetable for grief to run its course. Remind them not to let other people push them into moving on "to the next stage" unless they are prepared to do so. Don't be afraid to talk about the deceased person. Take your cue from the bereaved person. Not talking about the departed person brings down a curtain of silence that can make it more difficult for the bereaved person to work through feelings of grief. By the same token, don't force bereaved persons to talk about their feelings.

You may fear that you'll say the wrong thing. Don't worry about what to say. Just spending time with the bereaved person can help. Don't expect to have all the answers; sometimes there are no answers. Sometimes what matters is simply being a good listener.

Alina Solovyova-Vincent/iStockphoto.com

Bereaved persons can find comfort knowing that they are not alone in their suffering; sharing experiences can help bereaved persons cope and process what they are feeling.

DID YOU KNOW?

Facing your feelings and expressing them creatively can help in the process of grieving.

Looking after your health, not letting anyone tell you how to feel, and planning ahead can be useful too (Helpguide.org, 2016).

"It's not the things we do in life that we regret on our deathbed; it is the things we do not."

—Randy Pausch

Find the Lesson

Death is a universal developmental event that we all encounter. Some of us fear the shadow that it casts, while others embrace the lessons that come from the loss of our loved ones. Fittingly, those who have taken us by the hand in life can also serve as our most insightful teachers through their death.

Randy Pausch is an excellent example of this. A famous lecture series asks the question, "If you knew you were going to die, and you had one last lecture, what would you say to your students?" Randy brought an interesting perspective to this question as he was dying of pancreatic cancer and he delivered his famous last lecture at Carnegie Mellon University on September 18, 2007. He chose not to speak about death, but about the lessons to be learned in life.

"Goodbyes are only for those who love with their eyes. Because for those who love with heart and soul there is no such thing as separation."

—Rumi

Pausch spoke about moments that change our lives forever. He explored the notion that lessons are learned through disappointment and that we need to realize that brick walls aren't designed to keep us out but to show us how much we want to achieve something. Experience is what we get when we don't get what we want. He talked about embracing the negative feedback that you receive in life because when people stop saying anything to you anymore, they have given up on you. Pausch asked, "Do we search for the fun in every situation, or do we choose to wallow in self-misery?" (Pausch & Zaslow, 2008)

Photo by Jonathan Wiggs/The Boston Globe via Getty Images

End-of-life celebrations are an alternative to traditional funerals or may be in keeping with cultural values or beliefs. They are a way to celebrate the life of a loved one that has died.

STUDY TOOLS

CH 19

Located at **nelson.com/student**

- ☐ Prepare for tests with a variety of exercises and activities
- ☐ Review Key Terms Flash Cards (online or print)
- ☐ Create your own study tools with Build a Summary
- ☐ Watch Observing Development videos to expand your knowledge

References

A

AAIDD. (2007). American Association on Intellectual and Developmental Disabilities. Retrieved from www.aamr.org. Accessed May 24, 2007.

Aalsma, M. C., Lapsley, D. K., & Flannery, D. J. (2006). Personal fables, narcissism, and adolescent adjustment. *Psychology in the Schools, 43*(4), 481–491.

Aartsen, M. J., et al. (2005). Does widowhood affect memory performance of older persons? *Psychological Medicine, 35*(2), 217–226.

Abdelaziz, Y. E., Harb, A. H., & Hisham, N. (2001). *Textbook of clinical pediatrics.* Philadelphia: Lippincott Williams & Wilkins.

Abel, K. (2016). Why basic toys may be best. *Family Education*. http://fun.familyeducation.com/games/29698.html.

Aber, J. L., Bishop-Josef, S. J., Jones, S. M., McLearn, K. T., & Phillips, D. A. (Eds.). (2007). *Child development and social policy: Knowledge for action. APA Decade of Behavior volumes*. Washington, DC: American Psychological Association.

Abraham, L. (2012). Holiday toys: Canadian Toy Association lists hottest toys for 2012. Retrieved from http://www.huffingtonpost.ca/2012/11/01/holiday-toys-_n_2060340.html.

Abravanel, E., & DeYong, N. G. (1991). Does object modeling elicit imitative-like gestures from young infants? *Journal of Experimental Child Psychology, 52,* 22–40.

Acevedo, A., & Loewenstein, D. A. (2007). Nonpharmacological cognitive interventions in aging and dementia. *Journal of Geriatric Psychiatry and Neurology, 20*(4), 239–249.

Active Healthy Kids Canada. (2010). Healthy habits start earlier than you think: The Active Healthy Kids Canada report card on physical activity for children and youth. Toronto: Author. Retrieved from http://www.activehealthykids.ca/ecms.ashx/2010 ActiveHealthyKids CanadaReportCard-longform.pdf

A.D.A.M. Medical Encyclopedia. (2012). Premenstrual dysphoric disorder. Retrieved from http://www.ncbi.nlm.nih.gov/pubmedhealth/PMH0004461/.

Adams, G. R., Berzonsky, M. D., & Keating, L. (2006). Psychosocial resources in first-year university students: The role of identity processes and social relationships. *Journal of Youth and Adolescence, 35*(1), 81–91.

Adams, R. G., & Ueno, K. (2006). Middle-aged and older adult men's friendships. In V. H. Bedford & B. Formaniak Turner (Eds.), *Men in relationships: A new look from a life course perspective* (pp. 103–124). New York: Springer Publishing Co.

Adler, J. M., Kissel, E. C., & McAdams, D. P. (2006). Emerging from the CAVE: Attributional style and the narrative study of identity in midlife adults. *Cognitive Therapy and Research, 30*(1), 39–51.

Adler, P. A., & Adler, P. (1998). Peer power: Preadolescents cuture and identity. New Brunswick, NJ: Rutgers University Press.

Adolph, K. E., & Berger, S. E. (2005). Physical and motor development. In M. H. Bornstein & M. E. Lamb (Eds.), *Developmental science: An advanced textbook* (5th ed.) (pp. 223–281). Hillsdale, NJ: Erlbaum.

Aguiar, A., & Baillargeon, R. (2002). Developments in young infants' reasoning about occluded objects. *Cognitive Psychology, 45*(2), 267–336.

Ainsworth, M. D. S. (1989). Attachments beyond infancy. *American Psychologist, 44,* 709–716.

Ainsworth, M. D. S., Blehar, M. C., Waters, E., & Wall, S. (1978). *Patterns of attachment: A psychological study of the strange situation.* Hillsdale, NJ: Erlbaum.

Ainsworth, M. D. S., & Bowlby, J. (1991). An ethological approach to personality development. *American Psychologist, 46*(4), 333–341.

Ajdacic-Gross, V., et al. (2008). Suicide after bereavement. *Psychological Medicine, 38*(5), 673–676.

Akman, Y. (2007). Identity status of Turkish university students in relation to their evaluation of family problems. *Social Behavior and Personality, 35*(1), 79–88.

Alberta Association of Midwives. (2015). What is a midwife? Retrieved October 11, 2016 from abmidwives.ca.

Alberta Health Services. (n.d.). *Healthy Parents, Healthy Children: Young Babies: Birth To 6 Months.* Retrieved from http://www.healthyparentshealthychildren.ca/young-babies-birth-to-6-months/.

Alberta SBS Prevention Campaign. (2010). Parents and caregivers of young children. Retrieved from http://www.shakenbaby.ca.

Alfirevic, Z., Sundberg, K., & Brigham, S. (2003). Amniocentesis and chorionic villus sampling for prenatal diagnosis. *Cochrane Database of Systematic Reviews*, DOI: 10.1002/14651858.CD003252.

Allain, P., Kauffmann, M., Dubas, F., Berrut, G., & Le Gall, D. (2007). Executive functioning and normal aging: A study of arithmetic word-problem-solving. *Psychologie & NeuroPsychiatrie Du Vieillissement, 5*(4), 315–325.

Alloway, T. P., Gathercole, S. E., Willis, C., & Adams, A. (2004). A structural analysis of working memory and related cognitive skills in young children. *Journal of Experimental Child Psychology, 87*(2), 85–106.

Almeida, D. M., & Horn, M. C. (2004). Is daily life more stressful during middle adulthood? In O. G. Brim, C. D. Ryff, & R. C. Kessler (Eds.), *How healthy are we? A national study of well-being at midlife* (pp. 425–451). *The John D. and Catherine T. MacArthur Foundation series on mental health and development. Studies on successful midlife development.* Chicago: University of Chicago Press.

Alphonso, C. (2012, November 26). Canada's first childhood obesity program targets unhealthy lifestyles. Retrieved from http://www.theglobeandmail.com/news/national/canadas-first-childhood-obesity-program-targets- unhealthy-lifestyles/article5711928/.

Alzheimer Society. (2010). *Rising tide: The impact of dementia on Canadian society.* Retrieved from http://www.alzheimer.ca/~/media/Files/national/Advocacy/ASC _Rising%20Tide _Full%20Report_Eng.ashx.

Amato, P. (2000). Consequences of divorce for adults and children. *Journal of Marriage and the Family, 62*(4), 1269–87.

Amato, P. (2010). Research on divorce: Continuing trends and newdevelopments. *Journal of Marriage and Family, 72*, 650–666.

Amato, P. R. (2006). Marital discord, divorce, and children's well-being: Results from a 20-year longitudinal study of two generations. In A. Clarke-Stewart & J. Dunn (Eds.), *Families count: Effects on child and adolescent development. The Jacobs Foundation series on adolescence* (pp. 179–202). New York: Cambridge University Press.

Amato, P. R., Booth, A., Johnson, D. R., & Rogers, S. J. (2007). *Alone together: How marriage in America is changing.* Cambridge, MA: Harvard University Press.

Amato, P. R., & Keith, B. (1991). Parental divorce and adult well-being: A meta-analysis. *Journal of Marriage and Family 53*(1), 43–58.

Amato, P. R., & Previti, D. (2003). People's reasons for divorcing. *Journal of Family Issues, 24,* 602–626.

Ambert, A.-M. (2005). *Cohabitation and marriage: How are they related.* Contemporary Family Trends series. Ottawa: The Vanier Institute of the Family. Retrieved from http://www.vifamily.ca/sites/default/files/cohabitation _and_marriage.pdf.

Ambert, A.-M. (2009). *Divorce: Facts, causes & consequences* (3rd. ed.). Ottawa: Vanier Institute of the Family. Retrieved from http://www.vifamily.ca/node/80.

American Cancer Society. (2007). www.cancer.org.

American Fertility Association. (2007). Retrieved from http://www.theafa.org/fertility/malefactor/index.html. Accessed February 6, 2007.

American Heart Association. (2007). Overweight in children. Retrieved from http://www.americanheart.org/presenter.jhtml?identifier=4670. Accessed May 18, 2007.

American Psychiatric Association. (1998). *Diagnostic and statistical manual of mental disorders: DSM-IV-TR*, (4th ed.). Washington, DC: Author.

American Society for Reproductive Medicine. (2012). Endometriosis. Retrieved June 14, 2016, from https://www.asrm.org/BOOKLET_Endometriosis/.

Ammaniti, M., Speranza, A. M., & Fedele, S. (2005). Attachment in infancy and in early and late childhood: A longitudinal study. In K. A Kerns & R. A. Richardson (Eds.), *Attachment in middle childhood* (pp. 115–136). New York: Guilford.

Amodio, D. M., & Showers, C. J. (2005). "Similarity breeds liking" revisited: The moderating role of commitment. *Journal of Social and Personal Relationships, 22*(6), 817–836.

Andersen, M. L., & Taylor, H. H. (2009). *Sociology: The essentials* (5th ed.). Belmont, CA: Wadsworth.

Anderson, C. A., Gentile, D. A., & Buckley, K. E. (2007). *Violent video game effects on children and adolescents: Theory, research, and public policy*. New York: Oxford University Press.

Andreou, G., Krommydas, G., Gourgoulianis, K. I., Karapetsas, A., & Molyvdas, P. A. (2002). Handedness, asthma, and allergic disorders: Is there an association? *Psychology, Health, and Medicine, 7*(1), 53–60.

Andrews, G., Clark, M., & Luszcz, M. (2002). Successful aging in the Australian longitudinal study of aging: Applying the MacArthur Model cross-nationally. *Journal of Social Issues, 58,* 749–765.

Angier, N. (2007, June 12). Sleek, fast, and focused: The cells that make dad dad. *New York Times,* pp. F1, F6.

Annett, M. (1999). Left-handedness as a function of sex, maternal versus paternal inheritance, and report bias. *Behavior Genetics, 29*(2), 103–114.

Annett, M., & Moran, P. (2006). Schizotypy is increased in mixed-handers, especially right-handed writers who use the left hand for primary actions. *Schizophrenia Research, 81*(2–3), 239–246.

Antonucci, T. C., & Birditt, K. S. (2004). Lack of close relationships and well-being across the life span. Paper presented to the American Psychological Association.

Anwar, M. (2014). Sweden's new gender neutral pronoun is a step towards equality, and it's catching on quickly. *Bustle.* Retrieved from http://www.bustle.com/articles/43304-swedens-new-gender-neutral-pronoun-is-a-step-towards-equality-and-its-catching-on-quickly.

Anxiety BC. (2010). Separation anxiety. Retrieved from http://www.anxietybc.com/parent/separation.php.

Appel, J. M. (2005). Defining death. *Journal of Medical Ethics, 31*(11), 641–642.

Appleyard, K., & Berlin, L. J. (2007). Supporting healthy relationships between young children and their parents. Policy brief. Center for Child and Family Policy, Duke University. Retrieved from https://childandfamilypolicy.duke.edu/pdfs/pubpres/SupportingHealthyRelationships.pdf.

Aquilino, W. S. (2005). Impact of family structure on parental attitudes toward the economic support of adult children over the transition to adulthood. *Journal of Family Issues, 26*(2), 143–167.

Arai, A., et al. (2007). Association between lifestyle activity and depressed mood among home-dwelling older people. *Aging & Mental Health, 11*(5), 547–555.

Archer, J. (2006). Testosterone and human aggression: An evaluation of the challenge hypothesis. *Neuroscience & Biobehavioral Reviews, 30*(3), 319–345.

Archibald, L. M. D., & Gathercole, S. E. (2006). Short-term memory and working memory in specific language impairment. In T. P. Alloway & S. E. Gathercole (Eds.), *Working memory and neurodevelopmental disorders* (pp. 139–160). New York: Psychology Press.

Ardelt, M. (2008a). Wisdom, religiosity, purpose in life, and death attitudes of aging adults. In A. Tomer, G. T. Eliason, T. Grafton, & P. T. P. Wong (Eds.), *Existential and spiritual issues in death attitudes* (pp. 139–158). Mahwah, NJ: Erlbaum.

Ardelt, M. (2008b). Self-development through selflessness: The paradoxical process of growing wiser. In H. A. Wayment, & J. J. Bauer (Eds.), *Transcending self-interest: Psychological explorations of the quiet ego. Decade of behavior* (pp. 221–233). Washington, DC: American Psychological Association.

Arija, V., et al. (2006). Nutritional status and performance in test of verbal and non-verbal intelligence in 6-year-old children. *Intelligence, 34*(2), 141–149.

Arnett, J. J. (2007). Socialization in emerging adulthood: From the family to the wider world, from socialization to self-socialization. In J. E. Grusec & P. D. Hastings (Eds.), *Handbook of socialization: Theory and research* (pp. 208–231). New York: Guilford.

Arnon, S., et al. (2006). Live music is beneficial to preterm infants in the neonatal intensive care unit environment. *Birth: Issues in Perinatal Care, 33*(2), 131–136.

Aronson, E., Wilson, T. D., & Akert, R. M. (2010). *Social psychology* (7th ed.). Upper Saddle River, NJ: Prentice Hall.

Arranz, L., Guayerbas, N., & De la Fuente, M. (2007). Impairment of several immune functions in anxious women. *Journal of Psychosomatic Research, 62*(1), 1–8.

Aschermann, E., Gülzow, I., & Wendt, D. (2004). Differences in the comprehension of passive voice in German- and English-speaking children. *Swiss Journal of Psychology, 63*(4), 235–245.

Ash, D. (2004). Reflective scientific sense-making dialogue in two languages: The science in the dialogue and the dialogue in the science. *Science Education, 88*(6), 855–884.

Aslin, R. N., & Schlaggar, B. L. (2006). Is myelination the precipitating neural event for language development in infants and toddlers? *Neurology, 66*(3), 304–305.

Aspy, C. B., et al. (2007). Parental communication and youth sexual behaviour. *Journal of Adolescence, 30*(3), 449–466.

Assembly of First Nations. (2008). *Health of First Nations Children and the Environment*. Retrieved from http://www.afn.ca/uploads/files/rp-discussion_paper_re_childrens_health_and_the_environment.pdf.

Association of American Colleges & Universities. (2007). Case study facilitation guidelines: February Fifth Forum: Cultivating community. Retrieved from http://www.diversityweb.org/diversity_innovations/institutional_leadership/institutional_statements_plans/knox.cfm. Accessed November 1, 2007.

Astington, J. W. & Edwards M., J. (2010). The development of theory of mind in early childhood. *Encyclopedia of infant and early childhood development*. Retrieved July 31, 2016 from http://www.child-encyclopedia.com/sites/default/files/textes-experts/en/588/the-development-of-theory-of-mind-in-early-childhood.pdf.

Atkinson, G., & Davenne, D. (2007). Relationships between sleep, physical activity and human health. *Physiology & Behavior, 90*(2–3), 229–235.

Auger, R. W., Blackhurst, A. E., & Wahl, K. H. (2005). The development of elementary-aged children's career aspirations and expectations. *Professional School Counseling, 8*(4), 322–329.

August, D., Carlo, M., Dressler, C., & Snow, C. (2005). The critical role of vocabulary development for English language learners. *Learning Disabilities Research & Practice, 20*(1), 50–57.

Autism Speaks Canada (2016). What is Autism? What is Autism Spectrum Disorder? Retrieved on October 15, 2016 from http://www.autismspeaks.ca/about-autism/what-is-autism/.

Autism Society of Canada. (2009). What are autism spectrum disorders? Retrieved from http://www.autismsocietycanada.ca/understanding_autism/what_are_asds/index_e.htm.

Axford, J., Heron, C., Ross, F., & Victor, C. R. (2008). Management of knee osteoarthritis in primary care: Pain and depression are the major obstacles. *Journal of Psychosomatic Research, 64*(5), 461–467.

B

Bäckström T., et al. (2003). The role of hormones and hormonal treatments in premenstrual syndrome. *CNS Drugs, 17*(5), 325–342.

Bahrick, H. P., Bahrick, P. O., & Wittlinger, R. P. (1975). Fifty years of memory for names and faces: A cross-sectional approach. *Journal of Experimental Psychology: General, 104*(1), 54–75.

Bahrick, H. P., Hall, L. K., & Da Costa, L.A. (2008). Fifty years of memory of college grades: Accuracy and distortions. *Emotion,* 8(1), 13–22.

Bailey, J. M., & Pillard, R. C. (1991). A genetic study of male sexual orientation. *Archives of General Psychiatry, 48*, 1089–1096.

Baillargeon, R., & DeVos, J. (1991). Object permanence in young infants: Further evidence. *Child Development, 62*, 1227–1246.

Bajor, J. K., & Baltes, P. B. (2003). The relationship between selection optimization with compensation, conscientiousness, motivation, and performance. *Journal of Vocational Behavior, 63*(3), 347–367.

Bakker, D. J. (2006). Treatment of developmental dyslexia: A review. *Pediatric Rehabilitation, 9*(1), 3–13.

Balk, D., Wogrin, C., Thornton, G., & Meagher, D. (2007). *Handbook of thanatology.* New York: Routledge/Taylor & Francis Group.

Ball, J. (2008). Aboriginal early language promotion and early intervention. In *Encyclopedia of language and literacy development* (pp. 1–8). London, ON: Canadian Language and Literacy Research Network. Retrieved from http://www.literacyencyclopedia.ca/pdfs/topic.php?topId=257.

Ball, V., Corr, S., Knight, J., & Lowis, M. J. (2007). An investigation into the leisure occupations of older adults. *British Journal of Occupational Therapy, 70*(9), 393–400.

Ballmaier, M., et al. (2008). Hippocampal morphology and distinguishing late-onset from early-onset elderly depression. *American Journal of Psychiatry, 165*(2), 229–237.

Baltes, P. B., & Baltes, M. M. (1990). Psychological perspectives on successful aging: The model of selective optimization with compensation. In P. B. Baltes & M. M. Baltes (Eds.), *Successful aging: Perspectives from the behavioral sciences* (pp. 1–34). New York: Cambridge University Press.

Baltes, M., & Carstensen, L. L. (2003). The process of successful aging: Selection, optimization and compensation. In U. M. Staudinger, & U. Lindenberger (Eds.), *Understanding human development: Dialogues with lifespan psychology* (pp. 81–104). Dordrecht, Netherlands: Kluwer Academic Publishers.

Bancroft, J., Carnes, L., & Janssen, E. (2005a). Unprotected anal intercourse in HIV-positive and HIV-negative gay men: The relevance of sexual arousability, mood, sensation seeking, and erectile problems. *Archives of Sexual Behavior, 34,* 299–305.

Bancroft, J, Carnes, L. & Janssen, E., Goodrich, D., & Long, J. S. (2005b). Erectile and ejaculatory problems in gay and heterosexual men. *Archives of Sexual Behavior, 34,* 285–297.

Bandura, A. (1986). *Social foundations of thought and action: A social-cognitive theory.* Englewood Cliffs, NJ: Prentice Hall.

Bandura, A. (2006a). Going global with social cognitive theory: From prospect to paydirt. In S. I. Donaldson, D. E. Berger, & K. Pezdek (Eds.), *Applied psychology: New frontiers and rewarding careers* (pp. 53–79). Hillsdale, NJ: Lawrence Erlbaum Associates Publishers.

Bandura, A. (2006b). Toward a psychology of human agency. *Perspectives on Psychological Science, 1(2*), 164–180.

Bandura, A., Barbaranelli, C., Vittorio Caprara, G., & Pastorelli, C. (2001). Self-efficacy beliefs as shapers of children's aspirations and career trajectories. *Child Development, 72*(1), 187–206.

Barnard, C. J., Collins, S. A., Daisley, J. N., & Behnke, J. M. (2005). Maze performance and immunity costs in mice. *Behaviour, 142*(2), 241–263.

Barnett, I., van Sluijs, E. M. F., & Ogilvie, D. (2012). Physical activity and transitioning to retirement: A systematic review. *American Journal of Preventive Medicine*, *43*(3), 329–336. Retrieved from http://www.ncbi.nlm.nih.gov/pmc/articles/PMC3830178/.

Barnett, J. E., & Dunning, C. (2003). Clinical perspectives on elderly sexuality. *Archives of Sexual Behavior, 32*(3), 295–296.

Barr, M. (n.d.). What is the period of PURPLE crying? Retrieved from http://www.purplecrying.info/what-is-the-period-of-purple-crying.php.

Barr, R. G., Paterson, J. A., MacMartin, L. M., Lehtonen, L., & Young, S. N. (2005). Prolonged and unsoothable crying bouts in infants with and without colic. *Journal of Developmental & Behavioral Pediatrics, 26*(1), 14–23.

Barr, R., Rovee-Collier, C., & Campanella, J. (2005). Retrieval protracts deferred imitation by 6-month-olds. *Infancy, 7*(3), 263–283.

Barry, C. M., & Wentzel, K. R. (2006). Friend influence on prosocial behavior: The role of motivational factors and friendship characteristics. *Developmental Psychology, 42*(1), 153–163.

Barua, B., & Rovere, M. (2012). Canada's aging Medicare burden. *Fraser Forum*, May/June. Retrieved from http://www.fraserinstitute.org/uploadedFiles/fraser-ca/Content/research-news/research/articles/canadas-aging-medicare-burden.pdf.

Basic Behavioral Science Task Force of the National Advisory Mental Health Council. (1996). Basic behavioral science research for mental health: Sociocultural and environmental practices. *American Psychologist, 51*, 722–731.

Batsche, G. M., & Porter, L. J. (2006). Bullying. In G. G. Bear & K. M. Minke (Eds.), *Children's needs III: Development, prevention, and intervention* (pp. 135–148). Washington, DC: National Association of School Psychologists.

Bauer, K. W., Yang, Y. W., & Austin, S. B. (2004). "How can we stay healthy when you're throwing all of this in front of us?" Findings from focus groups and interviews in middle schools on environmental influences on nutrition and physical activity. *Health Education and Behavior, 31*(1), 33–46.

Bauman, M. L., Anderson, G., Perry, E., & Ray, M. (2006). Neuroanatomical and neurochemical studies of the autistic brain: Current thought and future directions. In S. O. Moldin & J. L. R. Rubenstein (Eds.), *Understanding autism: From basic neuroscience to treatment* (pp. 303–322). Boca Raton, FL: CRC Press.

Baumrind, D. (1989). Rearing competent children. In W. Damon (Ed.), *Child development today and tomorrow.* San Francisco: Jossey-Bass.

Baumrind, D. (1991a). The influence of parenting style on adolescent competence and substance use. *Journal of Early Adolescence, 11,* 56–95.

Baumrind, D. (1991b). Parenting styles and adolescent development. In J. Brooks-Gunn, R. Lerner, & A. C. Petersen (Eds.), *Encyclopedia of adolescence.* New York: Garland.

Baumrind, D. (2005). Taking a stand in a morally pluralistic society: Constructive obedience and responsible dissent in moral/character education. In L. Nucci (Ed.), *Conflict, contradiction, and contrarian elements in moral development and education* (pp. 21–50). Mahwah, NJ: Erlbaum.

BC Partners for Mental Health and Addictions Information. (2004). *Wellness module 2: Stress and well-being.* Retrieved from http://www.heretohelp.bc.ca/skills/module2.

Beaulieu, M-D., et al. (2008). When is knowledge ripe for primary care? *Evaluation & the Health Professions, 31*(1), 22–42.

Beck, E., Burnet, K. L., & Vosper, J. (2006). Birth-order effects on facets of extraversion. *Personality and Individual Differences, 40*(5), 953–959.

Becker, D. (2006). Therapy for the middle-aged: The relevance of existential issues. *American Journal of Psychotherapy, 60*(1), 87–99.

Bedford, V. H., & Avioli, P. S. (2006). "Shooting the bull": Cohort comparisons of fraternal intimacy in midlife and old age. In V. H. Bedford & B. Formaniak Turner (Eds.), *Men in relationships: A new look from a life course perspective* (pp. 81–101). New York: Springer Publishing Co.

Beidel, D. C., & Turner, S. M. (2007). Clinical presentation of social anxiety disorder in children and adolescents. In D. C. Beidel & S. M. Turner (Eds.), *Shy children, phobic adults: Nature and treatment of social anxiety disorders* (2nd ed.) (pp. 47–80). Washington, DC: American Psychological Association.

Beilei, L., Lei, L., Qi, D., & von Hofsten, C. (2002). The development of fine motor skills and their relations to children's academic achievement. *Acta Psychologica Sinica, 34*(5), 494–499.

Bell, J. H., & Bromnick, R. D. (2003). The social reality of the imaginary audience: A grounded theory approach. *Adolescence, 38*: 205–219.

Belsky, J. (2006). Determinants and consequences of infant–parent attachment. In L. Balter & C. S. Tamis-LeMonda (Eds.), *Child psychology: A handbook of contemporary issues* (2nd ed.) (pp. 53–77). New York: Psychology Press.

Belsky, J., et al. (2007). Are there long-term effects of early child care? *Child Development, 78*(2), 681–701.

Beltrame, J. (2013, May 7). Unemployed kids a burden for boomer parents: Report. *Huffington Post*. Retrieved from http://www.huffingtonpost.ca/2013/05/07/baby-boomers-children-money_n_3230204.html.

Bem, S. L. (1974). The measurement of psychological androgyny. *Journal of Consulting and Clinical Psychology, 42*, 155–162.

Bem, S. L. (1993). The lenses of gender: Transforming the debate on sexual inequality. New Haven, CT: Yale University Press.

Bender, H. L., et al. (2007). Use of harsh physical discipline and developmental outcomes in adolescence. *Development and Psychopathology, 19*(1) 227–242.

Bengtson, V. L., et al. (Eds.). (2005). *Sourcebook of family theory and research*. Thousand Oaks, CA: Sage Publications, Inc.

Berenbaum, S. A., & Bailey, J. M. (2002). Effects on gender identity of prenatal androgens and genital appearance: Evidence from girls with congenital adrenal hyperplasia. *The Journal of Endocrinology and Metabolism, 88*(3), 1102–1106.

Berg, C. J., Chang, J., Callaghan, W. M., & Whitehead, S. J. (2003). Pregnancy-related mortality in the United States,

1991–1997. *Obstetrics and Gynecology, 101*, 289–296.

Bergland, C. (2013, October). Loving touch is key to healthy brain development. *Psychology Today*. Retrieved from https://www.psychologytoday.com/blog/the-athletes-way/201310/loving-touch-is-key-healthy-brain-development

Berndt, T. J. (2004). Friendship and three A's (aggression, adjustment, and attachment). *Journal of Experimental Child Psychology, 88*(1), 1–4.

Berndt, T. J., Miller, K. E., & Park, K. E. (1989). Adolescents' perceptions of friends and parents' influence on aspects of their school adjustment. *Journal of Early Adolescence, 9*, 419–435.

Bernstein, I. M., et al. (2005). Maternal smoking and its association with birth weight. *Obstetrics & Gynecology, 106*, 986–991.

Berscheid, E. (2003). On stepping on land mines. In Sternberg, R. J. (Ed.). *Psychologists defying the crowd: Stories of those who battled the establishment and won*. (pp. 33–44). Washington, DC: American Psychological Association.

Berscheid, E. (2006). Searching for the meaning of "love." In R. J. Sternberg & K. Weis (Eds.), *The new psychology of love* (pp. 171–183). New Haven, CT: Yale University Press.

Bertoni, A., et al. (2007). Stress communication, dyadic coping and couple satisfaction: A cross-sectional and cross-cultural study. *Età Evolutiva, 86*, 58–66.

Bertrand, L. D., MacRae-Krisa, L. D., Costello, M., & Winterdyk, J. (2013). Ethnic diversity and youth offending: An examination of risk and protective factors. *International Journal of Child, Youth and Family Studies, 1*, 166–188.

Berzonsky, M. D. (2005). Ego identity: A personal standpoint in a postmodern world. *Identity, 5*(2), 125–136.

Berzonsky, M. D., & Kuk, L. S. (2005). Identity style, psychosocial maturity, and academic performance. *Personality and Individual Differences, 39*(1), 235–247.

Beth Israel Deaconess Medical Center. (2001). NICU programs benefit premature babies and their parents. Retrieved from http://www.bidmc.org/YourHealth/HealthNotes/WomensHealth/Pregnancy/NICUProgramsBenefitPrematureBabiesandTheirParents.aspx.

Bhat, S., Acharya, U. R., Adeli, H., Bairy, G. M., & Adeli, A. Autism: Cause factors, early diagnosis and therapies. *Reviews in the Neurosciences, 25*(6), 841–850.

Bialystok, E., & Senman, L. (2004). Executive processes in appearance–reality tasks: The role of inhibition of attention and symbolic representation. *Child Development, 75*(2), 562–579.

Bialystok, E. (2015). Bilingualism and the development of executive function: The role of attention. *Child Development Perspectives 9*(2), 117–121.

Bialystok, E. K., & Craik, F. I. M. (2007). Bilingualism and naming: Implications for cognitive assessment. *Journal of the International Neuropsychological Society, 13*(2), 209–211.

Bibby, R. (2004). The Future Families Project: A survey of Canadian hopes and dreams. Ottawa: Vanier Institute of the Family. Retrieved from http://www.vifamily.ca/node/177.

Bielski, Z. (2012, June 8). Dating violence on the rise, Statistics Canada finds. *Globe and Mail.* Retrieved from http://www.theglobeandmail.com/life/relationships/dating-violence-on-the-rise-statistics-canada-finds/article4240601.

Bierman, K. L. (2003). *Peer rejection: Developmental processes and intervention strategies*. New York: The Guilford Press.

Bird, A., Reese, E., & Tripp, G. (2006). Parent–child talk about past emotional events: Associations with child temperament and goodness-of-fit. *Journal of Cognition and Development, 7*(2), 189–210.

Bissell, M., & McKay, A. (2005). Taking action on chlamydia literature review. Retrieved from http://www.toronto.ca/health/sexualhealth/checkuponchlamydia/pdf/chlamydia_research_3.pdf.

Black, D. W. (2007). Antisocial personality disorder, conduct disorder, and psychopathy. In J. E. Grant, & M. N. Potenza (Eds.), *Textbook of men's mental health* (pp. 143–170). Washington, DC: American Psychiatric Publishing, Inc.

Blackwell, D. L., & Lichter, D. T. (2004). Homogamy among dating, cohabiting, and married couples. *Sociological Quarterly, 45*(4), 719–737.

Blackwell, T. (2012, March 11). Downside of online dating: More STDs, some experts say. *National Post*. Retrieved from http://news.nationalpost.com/2012/03/11/downside-of-online-dating-more-stds-some-experts-say/.

Blass, E. M., & Camp, C. A. (2003). Changing determinants in 6- to 12-week-old human infants. *Developmental Psychobiology, 42*(3), 312–316.

Blazina, C., Eddins, R., Burridge, A., & Settle, A. G. (2007). The relationship between masculinity ideology, loneliness, and separation-individuation difficulties. *The Journal of Men's Studies, 15*(1), 101–109.

Boccia, M., & Campos, J. J. (1989). Maternal emotional signals, social referencing, and infants' reactions to strangers. In N. Eisenberg (Ed.), *New directions for child development, No. 44, Empathy and related emotional responses*. San Francisco: Jossey-Bass.

Bohlmeijer, E., Valenkamp, M., Westerhof, G., Smith, F., & Cuijpers, P. (2005). Creative reminiscence as an early intervention for depression. *Aging & Mental Health, 9*(4), 302–304.

Bohon, C., Garber, J., & Horowitz, J. L. (2007). Predicting school dropout and adolescent sexual behavior in offspring of depressed and nondepressed mothers. *Journal of the American Academy of Child & Adolescent Psychiatry, 46*(1), 15–24.

Boivin, M., Vitaro, F., & Poulin, F. (2005). Peer relationships and the development of aggressive behavior in early childhood. In R. E. Tremblay, W. W. Hartup, & J. Archer (Eds.), *Developmental origins of aggression* (pp. 376–397). New York: Guilford.

Boland, M. (2009). Exclusive breastfeeding should continue to six months. *Paediatrics & Child Health, 10*(3): 148. Retrieved from http://www.cps.ca/english/statements/n/breastfeedingmar05.htm.

Bonanno, G. A., & Boerner, K. (2007). The stage theory of grief. *Journal of the American Medical Association,* 297, 2693.

Boom, J., Wouters, H., & Keller, M. (2007). A cross-cultural validation of stage development: A Rasch re-analysis of longitudinal socio-moral reasoning data. *Cognitive Development, 22*(2), 213–229.

Booth-LaForce, C., et al. (2006). Attachment, self-worth, and peer-group functioning in middle childhood. *Attachment & Human Development, 8*(4), 309–325.

Bosi, M. L., & de Oliveira, F. P. (2006). Bulimic behavior in adolescent athletes. In P. I. Swain (Ed.), *New developments in eating disorders research* (pp. 123–133). Hauppauge, NY: Nova Science Publishers.

Boston Children's Hospital. (2011). Newborn senses. Retrieved from http://www.childrenshospital.org/az/Site1356/mainpageS1356P0.html.

Botelho-Urbanski, J. (2016, July 11). Baby Storm five years later: Preschooler on top of the world. *The Toronto Star*. Retrieved August 6, 2016 from https://www.thestar.com/news/gta/2016/07/11/baby-storm-five-years-later-preschooler-on-top-of-the-world.html.

Bouchard, T. J., Jr., Lykken, D. T., McGue, M., Segal, N. L., & Tellegen, A. (1990). Sources of human psychological differences: The Minnesota study of twins reared apart. *Science, 250*, 223–228.

Bowlby, J. (1961). Processes of mourning. *International Journal of Psychoanalysis, 42*, 317–339.

Bowlby, J. (1980). *A secure base: Clinical applications of attachment theory*. Routledge: New York.

Bowlby, J. (1988). *A secure base*. New York: Basic Books.

Boyle, T. (2013, May 21). Canadian children don't walk to school, study says. *Toronto Star*. Retrieved from http://www.thestar.com/life/health_wellness/2013/05/21/canadian_children_dont_walk_to_school_study_says.html.

Bozionelos, N., & Wang, L. (2006). The relationship of mentoring and network resources with career success in the Chinese organizational environment. *International Journal of Human Resource Management, 17*(9), 1531–1546.

Braam, A. W., et al. (2008). God image and mood in old age. *Mental Health, Religion, & Culture, 11*(2), 221–237.

Bracht, M. (2007). Toilet training 101. *ParentsCanada.com*. Retrieved from http://www.parentscanada.com/developing/pre-school/articles.aspx?listingid=181.

Bradley, R. H. (2006). The home environment. In N. F. Watt et al. (Eds.), *The crisis in youth mental health: Critical issues and effective programs*, Vol. 4, Early intervention programs and policies, Child psychology and mental health (pp. 89–120). Westport, CT: Praeger/Greenwood.

Bradshaw, J. (2012, May 16). Canada's only registered male midwife knew his calling all along. *The Globe and Mail*. Retrieved from http://www.theglobeandmail.com/news/national/canadas-only-registered-male-midwife-knew-his-calling-all-along/article4184592/.

Brady, E. M. (2007). Review of adulthood: New terrain. *Educational Gerontology, 33*(1), 85–86.

Branco, J. C., & Lourenço, O. (2004). Cognitive and linguistic aspects in 5- to 6-year-olds' class-inclusion reasoning. *Psicologia Educação Cultura, 8*(2), 427–445.

Brandstätter, H., & Farthofer, A. (2003). Influence of part-time work on university students' academic performance. *Zeitschrift für Arbeits- und Organisationspsychologie, 47*(3), 134–145.

Brase, G. L. (2006). Cues of parental investment as a factor in attractiveness. *Evolution and Human Behavior, 27*(2), 145–157.

Brazier, A., & Rowlands, C. (2006). PKU in the family: Working together. *Clinical Child Psychology and Psychiatry, 11*(3), 483–488.

Bremner, A., & Bryant, P. (2001). The effect of spatial cues on infants' responses in the AB task, with and without a hidden object. *Developmental Science, 4*(4), 408–415.

Brennan, S., & Taylor-Butts, A. (2008). Sexual assault in Canada: 2004 and 2007. (Statistics Canada Catalogue no. 85F0033M). Canadian Centre for Justice Statistics Profile Series, no. 19. Retrieved from http://www.statcan.gc.ca/pub/85f0033m/85f0033m2008019-eng.pdf.

Bretherton, I., Ridgeway, D., & Cassidy, J. (1990). Assessing internal working models of the attachment relationship: An attachment story completion task for 3-year-olds. *Attachment in the preschool years: Theory, research, and intervention* (pp. 273–308). Chicago: University of Chicago Press.

Bridges, A. J. (2007). Successful living as a (single) woman. *Psychology of Women Quarterly, 31*(3), 327–328.

Bridges, L. J., Roe, A. E. C., Dunn, J., & O'Connor, T. G. (2007). Children's perspectives on their relationships with grandparents following parental separation: A longitudinal study. *Social Development, 16*(3), 539–554.

Briones, T. L., Klintsova, A. Y., & Greenough, W. T. (2004). Stability of synaptic plasticity in the adult rat visual cortex induced by complex environment exposure. *Brain Research, 1018*(1), 130–135.

British Columbia Ministry of Education. (2010). Full Day Kindergarten Program Guide. Retrieved from http://www.bced.gov.bc.ca/early_learning/fdk/pdfs/fdk_program_guide.pdf.

Brockman, D. D. (2003). From late adolescence to young adulthood. Madison, CT: International Universities Press, Inc.

Bronfenbrenner, U., & Morris, P. A. (2006). The bioecological model of human development. In R. M. Lerner & W. Damon (Eds.), *Handbook of child psychology* (6th ed.), Vol. 1, *Theoretical models of human development* (pp. 793–828). Hoboken, NJ: Wiley.

Bronson, G. W. (1990). Changes in infants' visual scanning across the 2- to 14-week age period. *Journal of Experimental Child Psychology, 49*, 101–125.

Bronson, G. W. (1991). Infant differences in rate of visual encoding. *Child Development, 62*, 44–54.

Bronson, G. W. (1997). The growth of visual capacity: Evidence from infant scanning patterns. *Advances in Infancy Research, 11*, 109–141.

Broomhall, H. S., & Winefield, A. H. (1990). A comparison of the affective well-being of young and middle-aged unemployed men matched for length of unemployment. *British Journal of Medical Psychology, 63*(1), 43–52.

Brown, I., & Schormans, A. F. (2003). Maltreatment and life stressors in single mothers who have children with developmental delay. *Journal on Developmental Disabilities, 10*(1), 61–66.

Brown, R. (1973). *A first language: The early stages*. Cambridge, MA: Harvard University Press.

Brown, S. L., Lee, G. R., & Bulanda, J. R. (2006). Cohabitation among older adults. *Journals of Gerontology: Series B: Psychological Sciences and Social Sciences*, 61B(2), S71–S79.

Brownell, C. A., & Carriger, M. S. (1990). Changes in cooperation and self-other differentiation during the second year. *Child Development, 61*, 1164–1174.

Bruck, M., Ceci, S. J., & Principe, G. F. (2006). The child and the law. In K. Renninger, I. E. Sigel, W. Damon, & R. M. Lerner (Eds.), *Handbook of child psychology* (6th ed.), Vol. 4, *Child psychology in practice* (pp. 776–816). Hoboken, NJ: Wiley.

Brunner, L. C., Eshilian-Oates, L., & Kuo, T. Y. (2003). Hip fractures in adults.

American Family Physician, 67(3), 537–543.

Bryden, P. J., Bruyn, J., & Fletcher, P. (2005). Handedness and health: An examination of the association between different handedness classifications and health disorders. *Laterality: Asymmetries of Body, Brain and Cognition, 10*(5), 429–440.

Budney, A. J., Vandrey, R. G., Hughes, J. R., Moore, B. A., & Bahrenburg, B. (2007). Oral delta-9-tetrahydrocannabinol suppresses cannabis withdrawal symptoms. *Drug and Alcohol Dependence, 86*(1), 22–29.

Bugental, D. B., & Happaney, K. (2004). Predicting infant maltreatment in low-income families: The interactive effects of maternal attributions and child status at birth. *Developmental Psychology, 40*(2), 234–243.

Buhl, H. M., Wittmann, S., & Noack, P. (2003). Child–parent relationship of university students and young employed adults. *Zeitschrift für Entwicklungspsychologie und Pädagogische Psychologie, 35*(3), 144–152.

Buote, V. M., Wood, E., & Pratt, M. (2009). Exploring similarities and differences between online and offline friendships: The role of attachment style. *Human Behavior, 25*, 560–567.

Burke, D. M., & Shafto, M. A. (2008). Language and aging. In F. I. M. Craik, & T. A. Salthouse (Eds.), *The handbook of aging and cognition* (3rd ed.) (pp. 373–443). New York: Psychology Press.

Bushman, B. J. (1998). Priming effects of media violence on the accessibility of aggressive constructs in memory. *Personality and Social Psychology Bulletin, 24*(5), 537–545.

Bushnell, E. W. (1993, June). A dual-processing approach to cross-modal matching: Implications for development. Paper presented at the Society for Research in Child Development, New Orleans, LA.

Bushnell, I. W. R. (2001). Mother's face recognition in newborn infants: Learning and memory. *Infant and Child Development, 10*(1–2), 67–74.

Bushnik, T. (2006). Child care in Canada. (Statistics Canada, Catalogue no. 89-599-MIE — No. 003). Retrieved from http://www.statcan.gc.ca/pub/89-599-m/89-599-m2006003-eng.pdf.

Buss, D., & Schmitt, D. (2011). Evolutionary psychology and feminism. Springer Science+Business Media. Retrieved from http://www.bradley.edu/dotAsset/196924.pdf.

Buss, D. M. (1994). *The evolution of desire: Strategies of human mating*. New York: Basic Books.

Buss, D. M. (Ed.). (2005). *The handbook of evolutionary psychology*. Hoboken, NJ: John Wiley & Sons, Inc.

Buss, D. M., & Duntley, J. D. (2006). The evolution of aggression. In M. Schaller, J. A. Simpson, & D. T. Kenrick (Eds.), *Evolution and social psychology: Frontiers of social psychology* (pp. 263–285). Madison, CT: Psychosocial Press.

Buston, K., Williamson, L., & Hart, G. (2007). Young women under 16 years with experience of sexual intercourse: Who becomes pregnant? *Journal of Epidemiology & Community Health, 61*(3) 221–225.

Butler, M., Tiedemann, M., Nicol, J., & Valiquet, D. (2013). *Euthanasia and assisted suicide in Canada*. Ottawa: Parliamentary Information and Research Service. Retrieved from http://www.parl.gc.ca/Content/LOP/ResearchPublications/2010-68-e.pdf.

Butler, R. N. (2002). The life review. *Journal of Geriatric Psychology, 35*(1), 7–10.

Butterfield, S. A., & Loovis, E. M. (1993). Influence of age, sex, balance, and sport participation on development of throwing by children in grades K–8. *Perceptual and Motor Skills, 76*, 459–464.

Buunk, B. P., et al. (2002). Age and gender differences in mate selection criteria for various involvement levels. *Personal Relationships, 9*(3), 271–278.

Bye, D., Pushkar, D., & Conway, M. (2007). Motivation, interest, and positive affect in traditional and nontraditional undergraduate students. *Adult Education Quarterly, 57*(2), 141–158.

Bynum, M. S. (2007). African American mother–daughter communication about sex and daughters' sexual behavior: Does college racial composition make a difference? *Cultural Diversity & Ethnic Minority Psychology, 13*(2), 151–160.

C

Cai, X., Wardlaw, T. and Brown, D. (2012). Global trends in exclusive breast-feeding. *International Breastfeeding Journal* 7(12). Retrieved from http://www.ncbi.nlm.nih.gov/pmc/articles/PMC3512504/.

Callahan, J. J. (2007). Sandwich anyone? *Gerontologist, 47*(4), 569–571.

Calvert, S. L., & Kotler, J. A. (2003). Lessons from children's television: The impact of the Children's Television Act on children's learning. *Journal of Applied Developmental Psychology, 24*(3), 275–335.

Campanella, J., & Rovee-Collier, C. (2005). Latent learning and deferred imitation at 3 months. *Infancy, 7*(3), 243–262.

Campbell, A., Shirley, L., & Caygill, L. (2002). Sex-typed preferences in three domains: Do two-year-olds need cognitive variables? *British Journal of Psychology, 93*(2), 203–217.

Campbell, A., Shirley, L., Heywood, C., & Crook, C. (2000). Infants' visual preference for sex-congruent babies, children, toys and activities: A longitudinal study. *British Journal of Developmental Psychology, 18*(4), 479–498.

Campbell, D. W., Eaton, W. O., & McKeen, N. A. (2002). Motor activity level and behavioural control in young children. *International Journal of Behavioral Development, 26*(4), 289–296.

Campbell, S. B., et al. (2004). The course of maternal depressive symptoms and maternal sensitivity as predictors of attachment security at 36 months. *Development and Psychopathology, 16*(2), 231–252.

Campos, J. J., Hiatt, S., Ramsey, D., Henderson, C., & Svejda, M. (1978). The emergence of fear on the visual cliff. In M. Lewis & L. Rosenblum (Eds.), *The origins of affect.* New York: Plenum.

Campos, J. J., Langer, A., & Krowitz, A. (1970). Cardiac responses on the visual cliff in prelocomotor human infants. *Science, 170,* 196–197.

Campos, P. (2013). What is the semicolon project? Retrieved from http://kisselpaso.com/what-is-the-semicolon-project/.

Camras, L. A., et al. (2007). Do infants show distinct negative facial expressions for fear and anger? Emotional expression in 11-month-old European American, Chinese, and Japanese Infants. *Infancy, 11*(2), 131–155.

Canadian Assisted Reproductive Technologies Registry (CARTR) Plus. Preliminary treatment cycle data for 2014. *Better Outcomes Registry & Network Ontario*. Ottawa ON, October 2015.

Canadian Blood Services. (2016). Who does my donation help? Retrieved from https://www.blood.ca/en/blood/who-does-my-donation-help.

Canadian Cancer Society. (2007, January 18). Smoking rates dropping, but lung cancer deaths still leading cause of cancer death. Media release.

Canadian Cancer Society. (2016). Cancer statistics at a glance. Retrieved from http://www.cancer.ca/en/cancer-information/cancer-101/cancer-statistics-at-a-glance/?region=on.

Canadian Children's Rights Council. (n.d.). Youth suicides in Canada and elsewhere. Retrieved from http://canadiancrc.com/Youth_Suicide_in_Canada.aspx.

Canadian Cystic Fibrosis Foundation. (2014). Cystic fibrosis in Canada. Retrieved from http://www.cysticfibrosis.ca/about-cf/living-with-cystic-fibrosis/resources.

Canadian Down Syndrome Society. (2016). General information. Retrieved from http://www.cdss.ca/index.php?option=com_content&task=blogcategory&id=13&Itemid=52.

Canadian Erectile Difficulties Resource Centre. (2013). So how do I know if I have erectile difficulties? Retrieved from http://www.edhelp.ca/en/men/how/.

Canadian Federation for Sexual Health. (2007). *Sexual health in Canada: Baseline 2007.* Retrieved from http://www.cfsh.ca/files/publications/sexual_health_in_canada_baseline_2007_final.pdf.

Canadian Foundation for the Study of Infant Deaths. (2010). Babies' 'flat heads' can be prevented: Health coalition—Growing public awareness of SIDS prompts concern about positional plagiocephaly. Retrieved from http://www.sidscanada.org/resource-news 4html.

Canadian Geographic. (2010). Who we are: Canada by demographics—Top 10 languages. *The Canadian Atlas Online.* Retrieved from http://magazine.canadiangeographic.ca/Atlas/themes.aspx?id =whoweare&sub=whoweare_demographics _work&lang=En.

Canadian Hospice Palliative Care Association (2010). Fact Sheet: Hospice palliative care in Canada. Retrieved from http://www.chpca.net/resource_doc_library/Fact_Sheet _HPC_in_Canada.pdf.

Canadian Hospice Palliative Care Association. (2014). Fact sheet: Hospice palliative care in Canada. Retrieved from http://www.chpca.net/media/330558/Fact_Sheet_HPC_in_Canada%20Spring%2014%20Final.pdf.

Canadian Institute for Health Information. (2010a). *National Health Expenditure Trends, 1975 to 2010. Table E.1.6–E.1.11 Estimate of Total Provincial/Territorial Government Health Expenditures by Age and Sex, by Province/Territory and Canada (2003–2008)*. Ottawa: CIHI.

Canadian Institute for Health Information. (2010b). *National Health Expenditure Trends, 1975 to 2010. Appendix C.9–C.14. Population by Age and Sex, by Province/Territory and Canada (2003–2008)*. Ottawa: CIHI.

Canadian Institute for Health Information. (2013). *Canadian Organ Replacement Register Annual Report: Treatment of End-Stage Organ Failure in Canada, 2002 to 2011*. Ottawa: CIHI. Retrieved from https://secure.cihi.ca/free_products/2013_CORR_Annua_Report_EN.pdf.

Canadian Institute of Child Health. (2010). The health of Canada's children: A CICH profile—Low birth weight. Retrieved from http://www.cich.ca/PDFFiles/ProfileFactSheets/English/LBWEng.pdf.

Canadian Lung Association. (2012). Children and second-hand smoke. Retrieved from http://www.lung.ca/protect-protegez/tobacco-tabagisme/second-secondaire/children-enfants_e.php.

Canadian Medical Association. (2007). Euthanasia and assisted suicide (Update 2007). CMA policy. Retrieved from http://policybase.cma.ca/dbtw-wpd/Policypdf/PD07-01.pdf.

Canadian Medical Association. (2014). Euthanasia and assisted death. *CMA Policy*. Retrieved from https://www.cma.ca/Assets/assets-library/document/en/advocacy/EOL/CMA_Policy_Euthanasia_Assisted%20Death_PD15-02-e.pdf#search=euthanasia.

Canadian Medical Association. (2016, January 2). CMA takes recommendations for assisted dying legislation to Parliament Hill. Retrieved from https://www.cma.ca/En/Pages/cma-takes-recommendations-for-assisted-dying-legislation-to-parliament-hill.aspx.

Canadian Mental Health Association. (2013a). Children and depression. Retrieved from http://www.cmha.ca/mental_health/children-and-depression.

Canadian Mental Health Association. (2013b). Eating disorders. Retrieved from http://www.cmha.ca/mental-health/understanding-mental-illness/eating-disorders/.

Canadian Mental Health Association. (2013c). Fast facts about mental illness. Retrieved from http://www.cmha.ca/media/fast-facts-about-mental-illness/#.UguRfdKTiSo.

Canadian Mental Health Association. (2016e). *Lesbian, gay, bisexual, trans & queer identified people and mental health.* Retrieved from http://ontario.cmha.ca/mental-health/lesbian-gay-bisexual-trans-people-and-mental-health/.

Canadian Mental Health Association. (2013d). Youth and suicide. Retrieved from http://www.cmha.ca/mental_health/youth-and-suicide/#.Uicv-tKTiSo.

Canadian Mental Health Association. (n.d.). Lesbian, gay, bisexual, trans and queer identified people and mental health. Retrieved from http://ontario.cmha.ca/mental-health/lesbian-gay-bisexual-trans-people-and-mental-health/.

Canadian Mortgage and Housing Corporation. (2015). *Housing for older Canadians: The definitive guide to the over-55 market*. Retrieved from http://www.cmhc-schl.gc.ca/odpub/pdf/67514.pdf.

Canadian Obesity Network. (n.d.). What's really driving the childhood obesity epidemic. Retrieved August 11, 2016, from http://www.obesitynetwork.ca/Whats-really-driving-the-childhood-obesity-epidemic-110.

Canadian Paediatric Society. (2007). Bedwetting. Retrieved from http://www.cps.ca/caringforkids/growing&learning/bedwetting.htm.

Canadian Paediatric Society. (2010, June 24). When your child is sick. Retrieved from http://www.cps.ca/caringforkids!whensick/colds.htm.

Canadian Paediatric Society. (2013a). Growing up: Information for boys about puberty. Retrieved from http://www.caringforkids.cps.ca/handouts/information_for_boys_about_puberty.

Canadian Paediatric Society. (2013b). Growing up: Information for girls about puberty. Retrieved from http://www.caringforkids.cps.ca/handouts/information_for_girls_about_puberty.

Canadian PKU and Allied Disorders. (2008). About PKU. Retrieved from http://www.canpku.org/.

Canadian Premature Babies Foundation. (2016). Retrieved on October 11, 2016, on cpbf-fbpc.org.

Canadian Press. (2011, November 3). *Infant formula ads reduce breastfeeding.* Retrieved July 21, 2016, from *The Canadian Press*. http://www.cbc.ca/news/health/infant-formula-ads-reduce-breastfeeding-1.1011144.

Canadian Press. (2013, May 8). Early infant mortality in Canada called 2nd worst in developed world. Retrieved from http://www.cbc.ca/news/health/early-infant-mortality-in-canada-called-2nd-worst-in-developed-world-1.1314423.

Canadian Press. (2015, July 15). By the numbers: The rise of Canada's online dating scene. Retrieved from http://globalnews.ca/news/2111560/by-the-numbers-the-rise-of-canadas-online-dating-scene/.

Canadian Press. (2016, February 19). Rising food prices push Canadian inflation to 2%. *The Star.* https://www.thestar.com/business/2016/02/19/rising-food-prices-push-canadian-inflation-to-2.html.

Canadian Psychological Association. (2000). *Canadian code of ethics for psychologists* (3rd ed.). Retrieved (May 12, 2010) from http://www.cpa.ca/cpasite/userfiles/Documents/Canadian%20Code%20of%20Ethics%20for%20Psycho.pdf.

Canadian Psychological Association. (2011). Survey findings: Canadians face "significant barriers" to accessing psychological care: National poll. Retrieved from http://www.cpa.ca/polls./

Canadian Toy Association (2016). Hot indoor toys for 2016. Retrieved August 6, 2016 from http://www.canadiantoyassociation.ca/ToyStore/.

Canadian Women's Health Network. (2006). Hormone therapy. Retrieved June 10, 2016, from http://www.cwhn.ca/node/40788.

Cancer Care Ontario. (2013). Screen for life. Retrieved from https://www.cancercare.on.ca/pcs/screening/.

Cancer Prevention and Control. (2004). *Health Disparities, Minority Cancer Awareness.* National Center for Chronic Disease Prevention and Health Promotion, Centers for Disease Control.

Candy, T. R., Crowell, J. A., & Banks, M. S. (1998). Optical, receptoral, and retinal constraints on foveal and peripheral vision in the human neonate. *Vision Research, 38*(24), 3857–3870.

Canitano, R. (2007). Epilepsy in autism spectrum disorders. *European Child & Adolescent Psychiatry, 16*(1), 61–66.

Cappadocia, M. C., Pepler, D., Cummings, J. G., & Craig, W. (2012). Individual motivations and characteristics associated with bystander intervention during bullying episodes among children and youth. *Canadian Journal of School Psychology, 27*(3), 201–216.

Caplan, A. (1993, September 1). Should we maintain a corpse to rescue a fetus? *The Baltimore Sun.* Retrieved from http://articles.baltimoresun.com/1993-09-01/news/1993244122_1_fetus-ploch-life-support.

Caplan, M., Vespo, J., Pedersen, J., & Hale, D. F. (1991). Conflict and its resolution in small groups of one and two-year-olds. *Child Development, 62,* 1513–1524.

Capron, C., Thérond, C., & Duyme, M. (2007). Brief report: Effect of menarcheal status and family structure on depressive symptoms and emotional/behavioural problems in young adolescent girls. *Journal of Adolescence, 30*(1), 175–179.

Carey, B. (2006). The rules of attraction in the game of love. *LiveScience.com*. Retrieved from http://www.livescience.com/7023-rules-attraction-game-love.html.

Carey, B. (2007a, March 26). Poor behavior is linked to time in day care. *New York Times online.*

Carey, B. (2007b, June 22). Research finds firstborns gain the higher I.Q. *The New York Times online.*

CaringBridge. (2013). About us. Retrieved from http://www.caringbridge.org/about.

Carmichael, D. (2008). *Youth sport vs. youth crime.* Retrieved from http://www.isrm.co.uk/news/docs/132 Sport%20and%20Crime.pdf.

CARP. (2014). 600,000 seniors in Canada living in poverty. http://www.carp.ca/2014/12/11/600000-seniors-canada-live-poverty/.

Carrère, S., Buehlman, K. T., Gottman, J. M., Coan, J. A., & Ruckstuhl, L. (2000). Predicting marital stability and divorce in newlywed couples. *Journal of Family Psychology, 14*(1), 42–58.

Carroll, J. S., et al. (2007). So close, yet so far away: The impact of varying marital horizons on emerging adulthood. *Journal of Adolescent Research, 22*(3), 219–247.

Carver, L. J., & Vaccaro, B. G. (2007). 12-month-old infants allocate increased neural resources to stimuli associated with negative adult emotion. *Developmental Psychology, 43*(1), 54–69.

Casas, J. F., et al. (2006). Early parenting and children's relational and physical aggression in the preschool and home contexts. *Journal of Applied Developmental Psychology, 27*(3), 209–227.

Casini, A., & Sanchez-Mazas, M. (2005). "This job is not for me!": The impact of the gender norm and the organizational culture on professional upward mobility. *Cahiers Internationaux de Psychologie Sociale, Sep-Dec Vol* (67–68), 101–112.

Cassia, V. M., Simion, F., & Umilta, C. (2001). Face preference at birth: The role of an orienting mechanism. *Developmental Science, 4*(1), 101–108.

Caton, D., et al. (2002). Anesthesia for childbirth: Controversy and change. *American Journal of Obstetrics & Gynecology, 186*(5), S25–S30.

Cattell, R. B. (1949). *The culture-fair intelligence test.* Champaign, IL: Institute for Personality and Ability Testing.

Caudle, D. D., et al. (2007). Cognitive errors, symptom severity, and response to cognitive behavior therapy in older adults with generalized anxiety disorder. *American Journal of Geriatric Psychiatry, 15*(8), 680–689.

Caulfield, R. (2000). Beneficial effects of tactile stimulation on early development. *Early Childhood Education Journal, 27*(4), 255–257.

Cavallini, A., et al. (2002). Visual acuity in the first two years of life in healthy term newborns: An experience with the Teller Acuity Cards. *Functional Neurology: New Trends in Adaptive and Behavioral Disorders, 17*(2), 87–92.

Cavell, T. A. (2001). Updating our approach to parent training. I. The case against targeting noncompliance. *Clinical Psychology: Science and Practice, 8*(3), 299–318.

CBC Digital Archives. (2013). Umbilical cord blood: Stem cells for the future? Retrieved from http://www.cbc.ca/archives/categories/science-technology/biotechnology/stem-cells-scientific-promise-ethical-protest-1/umbilical-cord-blood-stem-cells-for-the-future.html.

CBC News. (2000, August 20). Mother who killed son dies of injuries. Retrieved from http://www.cbc.ca/news/canada/story/2000/08/20/subway_000820.html.

CBC News. (2003, March 17). Father calls sickle cell anemia 'neglected' disease. Retrieved from http://www.cbc.ca/health/story/2003/03/17/sickle_cell030317.html.

CBC News. (2007a, September 12). Married people outnumbered for first time: Census. Retrieved from http://www.cbc.ca/canada/story/2007/09/12/censusfamilies.html.

CBC News. (2007b, April 20). *Newborn screening.* Retrieved from http://www.cbc.ca/news/background/health/newborn_screen.html.

CBC News. (2008, January 14). Life expectancy hits 80.4 years: Statistics Canada. Retrieved from http://www.cbc.ca/canada/story/2008/01/14/death-stats.html.

CBC News. (2009a, February 5). Assisted human reproduction: Regulating and treating conception problems. Retrieved from http://www.cbc.ca/health/story/2009/02/05/f- reprotech. html.

CBC News. (2009b, February 11). Daycare: The debate over space. Retrieved from http://www.cbc.ca/news/story/2009/02/06/f-daycare.html.

CBC News. (2010, July 13). Quebec to pay for IVF treatment. Retrieved from http://www.cbc.ca/canada/montreal/story/2010/07/13/quebec-ivf-treatment.html.

CBC News. (2010a, August 28). Bullying and sexual orientation by the numbers. Retrieved August 20, 2016, from http://www.cbc.ca/news/canada/bullying-and-sexual-orientation-by-the-numbers-1.909444.

CBC News. (2011, March 1). Elder abuse: A growing dilemma in an aging population. Retrieved from http://www.cbc.ca/news/canada/elder-abuse-a-growing-dilemma-in-an-aging-population-1.1050233.

CBC News. (2012a, October 12). Inside Gloria Taylor's battle for the right to die. Retrieved from http://www.canada.com/news/Only+cent+doctors+would+perform+eut hanasia+legal+poll+finds/7939308/story.html.

CBC News. (2012b, October 17). Socializing key to "successful aging." Retrieved from http://www.cbc.ca/news/health/socializing-key-to-successful-aging-1.1260922.

CBC News. (2013, April 10). Dad shattered over death of Rehtaeh Parsons. Retrieved from http://www.cbc.ca/news/canada/nova-scotia/story/2013/04/10/ns-reteah-parsons-father.html.

Cellarius, V. (2008). Terminal sedation and the "imminence condition." *Journal of Medical Ethics, 34*(2), 69–72.

Centers for Disease Control and Prevention. (2005). National Center for Health Statistics. *America's children, 2005. America's children: Key national indicators of well-being 2005*. Childstats.gov. Retrieved from http://www.childstats.gov/amchildren05/hea8.asp.

Centers for Disease Control and Prevention. (2006). HIV/AIDS Surveillance Report, 2005, v. 17. Atlanta: U.S. Department of Health and Human Services, Centers for Disease Control and Prevention. Retrieved from http://www.cdc.gov/hiv/topics/surveillance/resources/reports/.

Centre for Addiction and Mental Health. (2009). Responding to older adults with substance use, mental health and gambling challenges. Retrieved from http://www.camh.net/Publications/Resources_for_Professionals/Older_Adults/index.html.

Centre for Addiction and Mental Health. (2013). Depression. https://www.camh.ca/en/hospital/health_information/a_z_mental_health_and_addiction_information/depression/Pages/default.aspx.

Centre for Addiction and Mental Health. (2016). Mental illness and addictions: Facts and statistics. Retrieved June 5, 2016, from http://www.camh.ca/en/hospital/about_camh/newsroom/for_reporters/pages/addictionmentalhealthstatistics.aspx.

Centre for ADHD Awareness, Canada. (n.d.). What is attention deficit hyperactivity disorder? Retrieved August 12, 2016, from http://www.caddac.ca/cms/page.php?67.

Centre for Research on Youth at Risk. (n.d.). *Restorative justice fact sheet.* Retrieved from http://www.stthomasu.ca/research/youth/restorative.htm.

Chalmers, B., Kaczorowski, J., O'Brien, B., & Royle, C. (2012). Rates of interventions in labor and birth across Canada: Findings of the Canadian Maternity Experiences Survey. *Birth: Issues in Perinatal Care*, *39*(3), 203–210. doi:10.1111/j.1523-536X.2012.00549.x

Chapman, M., & McBride, M. C. (1992). Beyond competence and performance: Children's class inclusion strategies, superordinate class cues, and verbal justifications. *Developmental Psychology, 28,* 319–327.

Charles, S. T., & Carstensen, L. L. (2007). Emotion regulation and aging. In J. J. Gross (Ed.), *Handbook of emotion regulation* (pp. 307–327). New York: Guilford Press.

Charles, S. T., Reynolds, C. A., & Gatz, M. (2001). Age-related differences and change in positive and negative affect over 23 years. *Journal of Personality and Social Psychology, 80,* 136–151.

Charlton, R. (2004). Ageing male syndrome, andropause, androgen decline or mid-life crisis? *Journal of Men's Health & Gender, 1*(1), 55–59.

Charness, N., & Schaie, K. W. (2003). *Impact of technology on successful aging*. New York: Springer.

Chaudieu, I., et al. (2008). Abnormal reactions to environmental stress in elderly persons with anxiety disorders. *Journal of Affective Disorders, 106*(3), 307–313.

Cheng, H., & Furnham, A. (2002). Personality, peer relations, and self-confidence as predictors of happiness and loneliness. *Journal of Adolescence, 25*(3), 327–339.

Cheng, S-T., & Chan, A. C. M. (2007). Multiple pathways from stress to suicidality and the protective effect of social support in Hong Kong adolescents. *Suicide and Life- Threatening Behavior, 37*(2), 187–196.

Chesley, N., & Moen, P. (2006). When workers care: Dual-earner couples' caregiving strategies, benefit use, and psychological well- being. *American Behavioral Scientist, 49*(9), 1248–1269.

Chess, S., & Thomas, A. (1991). Temperament. In M. Lewis (Ed.), *Child and adolescent psychiatry: A comprehensive textbook.* Baltimore: Williams & Wilkins.

Child Welfare Information Gateway. (2013). *Long-term consequences of child abuse and neglect.* Washington, DC: U.S. Department of Health and Human Services, Children's Bureau.

Choi, J. S., Koren, G., & Nulman, I. (2013). Pregnancy and isotretinoin therapy. *CMAJ: Canadian Medical Association Journal*, *185*(5), 411–413.

Chong, L., McDonald, H., & Strauss, E. (2004). Deconstructing aging. *Science, 305*(5689), 1419.

Chou, T-L., et al. (2006). Developmental and skill effects on the neural correlates of semantic processing to visually presented words. *Human Brain Mapping, 27*(11), 915–924.

Christian, P., et al. (2003). Effects of alternative maternal micronutrient supplements on low birth weight in rural Nepal: Double blind randomised community trial. *British Medical Journal, 326,* 571–576.

Christophersen, E. R., & Mortweet, S. L. (2003). Establishing bedtime. In E. R. Christophersen & S. L. Mortweet (Eds.), *Parenting that works: Building skills that last a lifetime* (pp. 209–228). Washington, DC: American Psychological Association.

Chronis, A. M., et al. (2007). Maternal depression and early positive parenting predict future conduct problems in young children with attention-deficit/hyperactivity disorder. *Developmental Psychology, 43*(1), 70–82.

Chua, A. (2011). *Battle hymn of the tiger mother*. New York: Penguin Press.

Cillessen, A. H. N. (2009). Sociometric methods. In K. H. Rubin, W. M. Bukowsk, & B. Laursen, (Eds.). *Handbook of peer interactions, relationships and groups*. New York: The Guilford Press.

Clancy, B., & Finlay, B. (2001). Neural correlates of early language learning. In M. Tomasello & E. Bates (Eds.), *Language development: The essential readings*. Malden, MA: Blackwell.

Clark, E. V. (1973). What's in a word? On the child's acquisition of semantics in his first language. In E. Moore (Ed.), *Cognitive development and the acquisition of language.* New York: Academic Press.

Clark, E. V. (1975). Knowledge, context, and strategy in the acquisition of meaning. In D. P. Date (Ed.), *Georgetown University roundtable on language and linguistics.* Washington, DC: Georgetown University Press.

Clark, J. (2005). Sibling relationships: Theory and issues for practice. *Child & Family Social Work, 10*(1), 90–91.

Clark, J., & Rugg, S. (2005). The importance of independence in toileting. *British Journal of Occupational Therapy, 68*(4), 165–171.

Clark, R. (1983). *Family life and school achievement: Why poor black children succeed or fail.* Chicago: University of Chicago Press.

Clark, S., & Symons, D. (2000). A longitudinal study of Q-sort attachment security and self-processes at age five. *Infant and Child Development, 9*, 91–104.

Clark, W. (2009). Kids' sports. Retrieved from http://www.statcan.gc.ca/pub/11-008-x/2008001/article/10573-eng.htm.

Clayton, R., & Crosby, R. A. (2006) Measurement in health promotion. In R. A. Crosby, R. J. DiClemente, & L. F. Salazar (Eds.), *Research methods in health promotion* (pp. 229–259). San Francisco: Jossey-Bass.

Cleary, D. J., Ray, G. E., LoBello, S. G., & Zachar, P. (2002). Children's perceptions of close peer relationships: Quality, congruence and meta-perceptions. *Child Study Journal, 32*(3), 179–192.

Cleveland Clinic. (2016). Diseases and conditions. Presbycusis. Retrieved from http://my.clevelandclinic.org/health/diseases_conditions/hic_What_is_Presbycusis.

Clode, D. (2006). Review of A left-hand turn around the world: Chasing the mystery and meaning of all things southpaw. *Laterality: Asymmetries of Body, Brain and Cognition, 11*(6) 580–581.

Cnattingius, S. (2004). The epidemiology of smoking during pregnancy: Smoking prevalence, maternal characteristics, and pregnancy outcomes. *Nicotine & Tobacco Research, 6*(Supp. I2), S125–S140.

Coats, A. H., & Blanchard-Fields, F. (2008). Emotion regulation in interpersonal problems: The role of cognitive-emotional complexity, emotion regulation goals, and expressivity. *Psychology and Aging, 23*(1), 39–51.

Cochran, S. V. (2005). Assessing and treating depression in men. In G. E. Good, & G. R. Brooks (Eds.), *The new handbook of psychotherapy and counseling with men* (pp. 121–133). San Francisco: Jossey-Bass.

Cohen, L. S., et al. (2006). Relapse of major depression during pregnancy in women who maintain or discontinue antidepressant treatment. *Journal of the American Medical Association, 295*(5), 499–507.

Cohen, S. (2003). Psychosocial models of the role of social support in the etiology of physical disease. In P. Salovey & A. J. Rothman (Eds.), *Social psychology of health* (pp. 227–244). New York: Psychology Press.

Cohen-Bendahan, C. C. C., Buitelaar, J. K., van Goozen, S. H. M., & Cohen-Kettenis, P. T. (2004). Prenatal exposure to testosterone and functional cerebral lateralization: A study in same-sex and opposite-sex twin girls. *Psychoneuroendocrinology, 29*(7), 911–916.

Cohn, D. (2013, July 10). In Canada most babies now born to women 30 and older. Pew Research Center. Retrieved from http://www.pewresearch.org/fact-tank/2013/07/10/in-canada-most-babies-now-born-to-women-30-and-older/.

Cohn, M., Emrich, S. M., & Moscovitch, M. (2008). Age-related deficits in associative memory. *Psychology and Aging, 23*(1), 93–103.

Cole, S., & Lanham, J. (2011). Failure to thrive: An update. *American Family Physician, 83*(7), 829–834.

Coleman, P. K. (2003). Perceptions of parent–child attachment, social self-efficacy, and peer relationships in middle childhood. *Infant and Child Development, 12*(4), 351–368.

Collaer, M. L., & Hill, E. M. (2006). Large sex difference in adolescents on a timed line judgment task: Attentional contributors and task relationship to mathematics. *Perception, 35*(4), 561–572.

Collins, W. A., & Laursen, B. (2006). Parent–adolescent relationships. In P. Noller & J. A. Feeney (Eds.), *Close relationships: Functions, forms and processes* (pp. 111–125). Hove, England: Psychology Press/Taylor & Francis.

Collins, W. A., Maccoby, E. E., Steinberg, L., Hetherington, E. M., & Bornstein, M. H. (2003). Contemporary research on parenting: The case for nature and nurture. In M. E. Hertzig & E. A. Farber (Eds.), *Annual progress in child psychiatry and child development: 2000–2001* (pp. 125–153). New York: Brunner-Routledge.

Colombo, J. (1993). *Infant cognition.* Newbury Park, CA: Sage.

Colombo, J., & Carlson, S. (2012). Is the measure the message: The BSID and nutritional interventions pediatrics. Retrieved from http://pediatrics.aappublications.org/content/early/2012/05/23/peds.2012-0934.

Colour Blindness Awareness. (n.d). Colour Blindness. Retrieved on October 10, 2016 from http://www.colourblindawareness.org/colour-blindness/.

Commons, M. L. (2004). The state of the art on Perry and epistemological development? *Journal of Adult Development, 11*(2), 59–60.

Commons, M. L., Galaz-Fontes, J. F., & Morse, S. J. (2006). Leadership, cross- cultural contact, socio-economic status, and formal operational reasoning about moral dilemmas among Mexican non-literate adults and high school students. *Journal of Moral Education, 35*(2), 247–267.

Conel, J. L. (1959). *The postnatal development of the human cerebral cortex, 5.* Cambridge, MA: Harvard University Press.

Conference Board of Canada. (2016). How Canada performs. Retrieved October 28, 2016, from http://www.conferenceboard.ca/hcp/details/society/elderly-poverty.aspx.

Conner, K. R., & Goldston, D. B. (2007). Rates of suicide among males increase steadily from age 11 to 21:

Developmental framework and outline for prevention. *Aggression and Violent Behavior, 12*(2), 193–207.

Connolly, J., Furman, W., & Konarski, R. (2000). The role of peers in the emergence of heterosexual romantic relationships in adolescence. *Child Development, 71*(5), 1395–1408.

Connolly, M. (2016). Late diagnosis, little treatment: What ADHD looks like in girls and women. Retrieved from http://www.additudemag.com/adhd/article/1626.html.

Connor, P. D., Sampson, P. D., Streissguth, A. P., Bookstein, F. L., & Barr, H. M. (2006). Effects of prenatal alcohol exposure on fine motor coordination and balance: A study of two adult samples. *Neuropsychologia, 44*(5), 744–751.

Conrad, P. (2007). *The medicalization of society: On the transformation of human conditions into treatable disorders.* Baltimore, MD: Johns Hopkins University Press.

Constantino, J. N., et al. (2006). Autistic social impairment in the siblings of children with pervasive developmental disorders. *American Journal of Psychiatry, 163*(2), 294–296.

Coo, H., Ouellette-Kuntz, H., Lloyd, J., Kasmara, L., Holden, J., & Lewis, P. (2008). Trends in autism prevalence: Diagnostic substitution revisited. *Journal of Autism Development Disorders, 38*(6), 1036–1046.

Cook, J. L., & Cook, G. (2010). Friendships during the preschool and childhood years. *Child Development: Principles and Perspectives*. Toronto: Pearson Allyn Bacon Prentice Hall.

Cooke, B. M., Breedlove, S. M., & Jordan, C. L. (2003). Both estrogen receptors and androgen receptors contribute to testosterone-induced changes in the morphology of the medial amygdala and sexual arousal in male rats. *Hormones & Behavior, 43*(2), 336–346.

Cooper, J., Appleby, L., & Amos, T. (2002). Life events preceding suicide by young people. *Social Psychiatry and Psychiatric Epidemiology, 37*(6), 271–275.

Coovadia, H. (2004). Antiretroviral agents: How best to protect infants from HIV and save their mothers from AIDS. *New England Journal of Medicine, 351*(3), 289–292.

Coren, S. (1992). *The left-hander syndrome.* New York: Free Press.

Corliss, R. (2003, January 20). Is there a formula for joy? *Time Magazine*, 44–46.

Cornwell, A. A., C., & Feigenbaum, P. (2006). Sleep biological rhythms in normal infants and those at high risk for SIDS. *Chronobiology International, 23*(5), 935–961.

Costello, E. J., Sung, M., Worthman, C., & Angold, A. (2007). Pubertal maturation and the development of alcohol use and abuse. *Drug and Alcohol Dependence, 88*, S50–S59.

Costigan, C. L., Cauce, A. M., & Etchison, K. (2007). Changes in African American mother– daughter relationships during adolescence: Conflict, autonomy, and warmth. In B. J. R. Leadbeater & N. Way (Eds.), *Urban girls revisited: Building strengths* (pp. 177–201). New York: New York University Press.

Courage, M. L., Howe, M. L., & Squires, S. E. (2004). Individual differences in 3.5-month olds' visual attention: What do they predict at 1 year? *Infant Behavior and Development, 27*(1), 19–30.

Covenant House. (2015). Facts & stats. Retrieved from http://www.covenanthousetoronto.ca/homeless-youth/facts-and-stats.

Cowan, P. A., & Cowan, C. P. (2005). Five-domain models: Putting it all together. In P. A. Cowan, C. P. Cowan, J. C. Ablow, V. K. Johnson, & J. R. Measelle (Eds.), *The family context of parenting in children's adaptation to elementary school, Monographs in parenting series* (pp. 315–333). Mahwah, NJ: Erlbaum.

Cramer, D. (2003). Facilitativeness, conflict, demand for approval, self-esteem, and satisfaction with romantic relationships. *Journal of Psychology, 137*(1), 85–98.

Crenshaw, D. A. (2007). Life span issues and assessment and intervention. In D. Balk, et al. (Eds.), *Handbook of thanatology* (pp. 227–234). New York: Routledge/Taylor & Francis Group.

Critical Media Project. (2016). Who are you? Retrieved from http://www.criticalmediaproject.org/cml/topicbackground/lgbt/.

Crombie, G., & Desjardins, M. J. (1993, March). *Predictors of gender: The relative importance of children's play, games, and personality characteristics.* Paper presented at the meeting of the Society for Research in Child Development, New Orleans, LA.

Crowther, C., et al. (2006). Neonatal respiratory distress syndrome after repeat exposure to antenatal corticosteroids: A randomised control trial. *Lancet, 367*(9526), 1913–1919.

Cruz, N. V., & Bahna, S. L. (2006). Do foods or additives cause behavior disorders? *Psychiatric Annals, 36*(10), 724–732.

CTV News. (2012, November 2). "Ageism" widespread, survey finds. Retrieved from http://www.ctvnews.ca/canada/ageism-widespread-in-canada-survey-finds-1.1021641.

Cuellar, J., & Curry, T. R. (2007). The prevalence and comorbidity between delinquency, drug abuse, suicide attempts, physical and sexual abuse, and self-mutilation among delinquent Hispanic females. *Hispanic Journal of Behavioral Sciences, 29*(1), 68–82.

Cukier, A. (2014). Tips for caring for near-term babies. *Parents Canada.* Retrieved from http://www.parentscanada.com/baby/tips-for-caring-for-near-term-babies.

Cumming, S. P., Eisenmann, J. C., Smoll, F. L., Smith, R. E., & Malina, R. M. (2005). Body size and perceptions of coaching behaviors by adolescent female athletes. *Psychology of Sport and Exercise, 6*(6), 693–705.

Cunningham, R. L., & McGinnis, M. Y. (2007). Factors influencing aggression toward females by male rats exposed to anabolic androgenic steroids during puberty. *Hormones and Behavior, 51*(1), 135–141.

Curtis, S. (2012). Early puberty is on the rise. Retrieved from http://www.parentscanada.com/school/early-puberty-is-on-the-rise.

D

D'Augelli, A. R., Grossman, A. H., Hershberger, S. L., & O' Connell, T. S. (2001). Aspects of mental health among older lesbian, gay, and bisexual adults. *Aging & Mental Health, 5*(2), 149–158.

Daman-Wasserman, M., Brennan, B., Radcliffe, F., Prigot, J., & Fagen, J. (2006). Auditory-visual context and memory retrieval in 3-month-old infants. *Infancy, 10*(3) 201–220.

Damon, W. (1991). Adolescent self-concept. In R. M. Lerner, A. C. Petersen, & J. Brooks-Gunn (Eds.), *Encyclopedia of adolescence.* New York: Garland.

Dandy, J., & Nettelbeck, T. (2002). The relationship between IQ, homework, aspirations and academic achievement for Chinese, Vietnamese and Anglo-Celtic Australian school children. *Educational Psychology, 22*(3), 267–276.

Dane, S., & Erzurumluoglu, A. (2003). Sex and handedness differences in eye–hand visual reaction times in handball players. *International Journal of Neuroscience, 113*(7), 923–929.

Dang-Vu, T. T., Desseilles, M., Peigneux, P., & Maquet, P. (2006). A role for sleep in brain plasticity. *Pediatric Rehabilitation, 19*(2) 98–118.

Daniels, S. R. (2006). The consequences of childhood overweight and obesity. *The Future of Children, 16*(1), 47–67.

Davis, L., Edwards, H., Mohay, H., & Wollin, J. (2003). The impact of very premature birth on the psychological health of mothers. *Early Human Development, 73*(1–2), 61–70.

De Beni, R., Borella, E., & Carretti, B. (2007). Reading comprehension in aging: The role of working memory and metacomprehension. *Aging, Neuropsychology, and Cognition, 14*(2), 189–212.

De Haan, M., & Groen, M. (2006). Neural bases of infants' processing of social information in faces. In P. J. Marshall & N. A. Fox (Eds.), *The development of social engagement: Neurobiological perspectives. Series in affective science* (pp. 46–80). New York: Oxford University Press.

de Villiers, J. G., & de Villiers, P. A. (1999). Language development. In M. H. Bornstein & M. E. Lamb (Eds.), *Developmental psychology: An advanced textbook* (4th ed.) (pp. 313–373). Mahwah, NJ: Erlbaum.

Deary, I. J., Whiteman, M. C., Starr, J. M., Whalley, L. J., & Fox, H. C. (2004). The impact of childhood intelligence on later life: Following up the Scottish mental surveys of 1932 and 1947. *Journal of Personality and Social Psychology, 86*(1), 130–147.

DeCasper, A. J., & Fifer, W. P. (1980). Of human bonding: Newborns prefer their mothers' voices. *Science, 208,* 1174–1176.

DeCasper, A. J., & Spence, M. J. (1991). Auditorially mediated behavior during the perinatal period: A cognitive view. In M. J. Weiss & P. R. Zelazo (Eds.), *Infant attention* (pp. 142–176). Norwood, NJ: Ablex.

de Guzman, M. R. T. (2007). Friendship, peer influence, and peer pressure during the teenage years. *NebGuide.* Retrieved from http://www.ianrpubs.unl.edu/live/g1751/build/g1751.pdf.

Delgado, A. R., & Prieto, G. (2004). Cognitive mediators and sex-related differences in mathematics. *Intelligence, 32*(1), 25–32.

Demont, J. (2012, September 5). It cost a lot to die in Nova Scotia, survey says. *Chronicle Herald.* Retrieved from http://thechronicleherald.ca/business/133001-it-costs-a-lot-to-die-in-nova-scotia-survey-says.

Dennerstein, L., & Goldstein, I. (2005). Postmenopausal female sexual dysfunction: At a crossroads. *Journal of Sexual Medicine, 2*(Suppl3), 116–117.

Department of Justice Canada. (2009). *If your child is in trouble with the law.* Retrieved from http://www.justice.gc.ca/eng/pi/yj-jj/information/information.html.

Department of Justice Canada. (2013). Age of consent to sexual activity: Frequently asked questions. Retrieved from http://www.justice.gc.ca/eng/rp-pr/other-autre/clp/faq.html.

Department of Justic Canada. (2015). Legal definitions of elder abuse and neglect. Retrieved from http://www.justice.gc.ca/eng/rp-pr/cj-jp/fv-vf/elder-aines/def/p211.html.

Depp, C. A., & Jeste, D. V. (2006). Definitions and predictors of successful aging: A comprehensive review of larger quantitative studies. *American Journal of Geriatric Psychiatry, 14,* 6–20.

Depression and Bipolar Support Alliance. (n.d.) Postpartum depression. Retrieved from http://www.dbsalliance.org/site/PageServer?pagename=education_depression_postpartum&gclid=CPWSrr3KgrkCFYtDMgodKjoAM.

Derby, C. A. (2000, October 2). Cited in study finds exercise reduces the risk of impotence. *The Associated Press.*

Dezoete, J. A., MacArthur, B. A., & Tuck, B. (2003). Prediction of Bayley and Stanford– Binet scores with a group of very low birth-weight children. *Child: Care, Health and Development, 29*(5), 367–372.

DiLalla, D. L., Gottesman, I. I., Carey, G., & Bouchard, T. J., Jr. (1999). Heritability of MMPI Harris–Lingoes and Subtle–Obvious subscales in twins reared apart. *Assessment, 6*(4), 353–366.

Disabled World. (2008). Height chart of men and women in difference countries. Retrieved from http://www.disabled-world.com/artman/publish/height-chart.shtml#ixzz12uF838KX.

Dishion, T. J., & Stormshak, E. A. (2007). Family and peer social interaction. In T. J. Dishion & E. A. Stormshak. (Eds.), *Intervening in children's lives: An ecological, family-centered approach to mental health care* (pp. 31–48). Washington, DC: American Psychological Association.

Doherty, W. J., Carroll, J. S., & Waite, L. J. (2007). In A. S. Loveless & T. B. Holman (Eds.), Supporting the institution of marriage: Ideological, research, and ecological perspectives. *The family in the new millennium: World voices supporting the "natural" clan Vol 2: Marriage and human dignity* (pp. 21–51). Praeger perspectives. Westport, CT: Praeger Publishers/Greenwood Publishing Group.

Dollfus, S., et al. (2005). Atypical hemispheric specialization for language in right-handed schizophrenia patients. *Biological Psychiatry, 57*(9), 1020–1028.

Dombrowski, M. A. S., et al. (2000). Kangaroo skin-to-skin care for premature twins and their adolescent parents. *American Journal of Maternal/Child Nursing, 25*(2), 92–94.

Donald, M., et al. (2006). Risk and protective factors for medically serious suicide attempts. *Australian and New Zealand Journal of Psychiatry, 40*(1), 87–96.

Dong, X., Milholland, B., & Vijg, J. (2016, October 13). Evidence for a limit to human lifespan. *Nature, 538*, 257–259. doi:10.1038/nature19793.

Donohue, K. F., Curtin, J. J., Patrick, C. J., & Lang, A. R. (2007). Intoxication level and emotional response. *Emotion, 7*(1), 103–112.

Donovan, D. M., & Wells, E. A. (2007). "Tweaking 12-Step": The potential role of 12-Step self-help group involvement in methamphetamine recovery. *Addiction, 102*(Suppl. 1), 121–129.

Dorling, J., et al. (2006). Data collection from very low birthweight infants in a geographical region: Methods, costs, and trends in mortality, admission rates, and resource utilisation over a five–year period. *Early Human Development, 82*(2), 117–124.

Doron, H., & Markovitzky, G. (2007). Family structure and patterns and psychological adjustment to immigration in Israel. *Journal of Ethnic & Cultural Diversity in Social Work, 15*(1–2), 215–235.

Drasgow, E., Halle, J. W., & Phillips, B. (2001). Effects of different social partners on the discriminated requesting of a young child with autism and severe language delays. *Research in Developmental Disabilities, 22*(2), 125–139.

Drewett, R., Blair, P., Emmett, P., Emond, A., & The ALSPAC Study Team. (2004). Failure to thrive in the term and preterm infants of mothers depressed in the postnatal period: A population-based birth cohort study. *Journal of Child Psychology and Psychiatry and Allied Disciplines, 45*(2), 359–366.

Drigotas, S. M., Rusbult, C. E., & Verette, J. (1999). Level of commitment, mutuality of commitment, and couple well-being. *Personal Relationships, 6*(3) 389–409.

Duberstein, P. R., Pálsson, S. P., Waern, M., & Skoog, I. (2008). Personality and risk for depression in a birth cohort of 70-year-olds followed for 15 years. *Psychological Medicine, 38*(5), 663–671.

Duffy, R. D., & Sedlacek, W. E. (2007). What is most important to students' long-term career choices. *Journal of Career Development, 34*(2), 149–163.

Duggan, A., et al. (2004). Evaluating a statewide home visiting program to prevent child abuse in at-risk families of newborns: Fathers' participation and outcomes. *Child Maltreatment: Journal of the American Professional Society on the Abuse of Children, 9*(1), 3–17.

Dumas, J. A., & Hartman, M. (2003). Adult age differences in temporal and item memory. *Psychology and Aging, 18*(3), 573–586.

Dunn, J., Davies, L. C., O'Connor, T. G., & Sturgess, W. (2001). Family lives and friendships: The perspectives of children in step-, single-parent, and nonstep families. *Journal of Family Psychology, 15*(2), 272–287.

Duplassie, D., & Daniluk, J. C. (2007). Sexuality: Young and middle adulthood. In M S. Tepper & A. F. Owens (Eds.), *Sexual health Vol. 1: Psychological foundations* (pp. 263–289). *Praeger perspectives: Sex, love, and psychology.* Westport, CT: Praeger Publishers/Greenwood Publishing Group.

Dupuis-Blanchard, S. M. (2008). Social engagement in relocated older adults. *Dissertation Abstracts International: Section B: The Sciences and Engineering. 68*(7-B), 4387.

Durkin, S. J., Paxton, S. J., & Sorbello, M. (2007). An integrative model of the impact of exposure to idealized female images on adolescent girls' body satisfaction. *Journal of Applied Social Psychology, 37*(5), 1092–1117.

Dyer, S. J. (2007). The value of children in African countries—Insights from studies on infertility. *Journal of Psychosomatic Obstetrics & Gynecology, 28*(2), 69–77.

Dying with Dignity Canada. (2015). Lee Carter. Available at http://www.dyingwithdignity.ca/lee_carter.

E

Eccles, J. S., et al. (2000). Gender-role socialization in the family: A longitudinal approach. In T. Eckes & H. M. Trautner (Eds.), *The developmental social psychology of gender* (pp. 333–360). Mahwah, NJ: Erlbaum.

Eckerman, C. O., Hsu, H.-C., Molitor, A., Leung, E. H. L., & Goldstein, R. F. (1999). Infant arousal in an en-face exchange with a new partner: Effects of prematurity and perinatal biological risk. *Developmental Psychology, 35*(1), 282–293.

Eddleston, M., Dissanayake, M., Sheriff, M. H. R., Warrell, D. A., & Gunnell, D. (2006). Physical vulnerability and fatal self-harm in the elderly. *British Journal of Psychiatry, 189*(3),

Edler, C., Lipson, S. F., & Keel, P. K. (2007). Ovarian hormones and binge eating in bulimia nervosa. *Psychological Medicine, 37*(1), 131–141.

Egerton, A., Allison, C., Brett, R. R., & Pratt, J. A. (2006). Cannabinoids and prefrontal cortical function: Insights from preclinical studies. *Neuroscience & Biobehavioral Reviews, 30*(5), 680–695.

Eimas, P. D., Sigueland, E. R., Juscyk, P., & Vigorito, J. (1971). Speech perception in infants. *Science, 171,* 303–306.

Eisenbeiss, S. (2015, August 24). #BabyTalk, #Motherese, Caretaker Talk, #ChildDirectedSpeech,... – Are they all names for the same thing? Boston University Conference on Language Development. Retrieved July 25, 2016, from https://childdirectedspeech.wordpress.com/2015/08/24/babytalk-motherese-caretaker-talk-childdirectedspeech-are-they-all-names-for-the-same-thing/.

Eisenberg, M. E., Neumark-Sztainer, D., & Paxton, S. J. (2006). Five-year change in body satisfaction among adolescents. *Journal of Psychosomatic Research, 61*(4), 521–527.

Eisner, E. W. (1990). The role of art and play in children's cognitive development. In E. Klugman & S. Smilansky (Eds.), Children's play and learning: Perspectives and policy implications. New York: Teachers College Press.

Eliot L. (2011). The trouble with sex differences. *Neuron 72*, 895–898.

El-Sheikh, M. (2007). Children's skin conductance level and reactivity: Are these measures stable over time and across tasks? *Developmental Psychobiology, 49*(2), 180–186.

Elkind, D. (1967). Egocentrism in adolescence. *Child Development, 38,* 1025–1034.

Elkind, D. (1985). Egocentrism redux. *Developmental Review, 5,* 218–226.

Elkind, D. (2007). *The power of play: How spontaneous imaginative activities lead to happier, healthier children*. Cambridge, MA: Da Capo Press.

Ellis, A., & Dryden, W. (1996). *The practice of rational emotive behavior therapy.* New York: Springer.

Else-Quest, N. M., Hyde, J. S., Goldsmith, H. H., & Van Hulle, C. A. (2006). Gender differences in temperament: A meta-analysis. *Psychological Bulletin, 132*(1), 33–72.

Eltzschig, H., Lieberman, E., & Camann, W. (2003). Regional anesthesia and analgesia for labor and delivery. *New England Journal of Medicine, 348*(4), 319–332.

Emery, R. E. (1989). Family violence. *American Psychologist,* 44, 321–328.

Emler, N., Tarry, H., & St. James, A. (2007). Post-conventional moral reasoning and reputation. *Journal of Research in Personality, 41*(1), 76–89.

Epel, E. S., et al. (2006). Cell aging in relation to stress arousal and cardiovascular disease risk factors. *Psychoneuroendocrinology, 31*(3), 277–287.

Erikson, E. H. (1963). *Childhood and society.* New York: Norton.

Erikson, E. H. (1968). *Identity: Youth and crisis.* New York: Norton.

Ersner-Hershfield, H., Mikels, J. A., Sullivan, S. J., & Carstensen, L. L. (2008). Poignancy: Mixed emotional experience in the face of meaningful endings. *Journal of Personality and Social Psychology, 94*(1) 158–167.

Escorial, S., et al. (2003). Abilities that explain the intelligence decline: Evidence from the WAIS-III. *Psicothema, 15*(1), 19–22.

Etaugh, C. A., & Bridges, J. S. (2006). Midlife transitions. In J. Worell & C. D. Goodheart (Eds.), *Handbook of girls' and women's psychological health: Gender and well-being across the lifespan* (pp. 359–367). *Oxford series in clinical psychology.* New York: Oxford University Press.

F

Facts About Falling (2008, January 28). *The Washington Post.*

Fagan, J., Holland, C., & Wheeler, K. (2007). The prediction, from infancy, of adult IQ and achievement. *Intelligence*, *35*(3), 225–231.

Fagot, B. I. (1990). A longitudinal study of gender segregation: Infancy to preschool. In F. F. Strayer (Ed.), *Social interaction and behavioral development during early childhood.* Montreal: La Maison D'Ethologie de Montreal.

Fagot, B. I., Rodgers, C. S., & Leinbach, M. D. (2000). Theories of gender socialization. In T. Eckes & H. M. Trautner (Eds.), *The developmental social psychology of gender* (pp. 65–89). Mahwah, NJ: Erlbaum.

Fair, R. C. (2007). Estimated age effects in athletic events and chess. *Experimental Aging Research, 33*(1), 37–57.

Fang L., Oliver, A., Jayaraman, G., Wong, T., et al. (2010). Trends in age disparities between younger and middle-age adults among reported rates of chlamydia, gonorrhea, and infectious syphilis infections in Canada: Findings from 1997 to 2007. *Sexually Transmitted Diseases*. *37*(1), 18–25.

Fantz, R. L. (1961). The origin of form perception. *Scientific American, 204,* 66–72.

Fantz, R. L., Fagan, J. F., III, & Miranda, S. B. (1975). Early visual selectivity. In L. B. Cohen & P. Salapatek (Eds.), *Infant perception: From sensation to cognition,* Vol. 1. New York: Academic Press.

Faris, M., & McCarroll, E. (2010). Crying babies: Answering the call of infant cries. *Texas Child Care*, *34*(2), 14–21.

Farmer, A., Elkin, A., & McGuffin, P. (2007). The genetics of bipolar affective disorder. *Current Opinion in Psychiatry, 20*(1), 8–12.

Feijó, L., et al. (2006). Mothers' depressed mood and anxiety levels are reduced after massaging their preterm infants. *Infant Behavior & Development, 29(*3), 476–480.

Feiring, C. (1993, March). *Developing concepts of romance from 15 to 18 years.* Paper presented at the meeting of the Society for Research in Child Development, New Orleans, LA.

Feldman, M. (2005). Management of primary nocturnal enuresis. *Pediatric Child Health 10*(10), 611-614. Retrieved from http://www.cps.ca/documents/position/primary-nocturnal-enuresis.

Feldman, R., & Masalha, S. (2007). The role of culture in moderating the links between early ecological risk and young children's adaptation. *Development and Psychopathology, 19*(1), 1–21.

Fergusson, A. (2007). What successful teachers do in inclusive classrooms: Research-based teaching strategies that help special learners succeed. *European Journal of Special Needs Education, 22*(1), 108–110.

Fernandes, L. (2011). Turn off the TV! Why you need to worry about family screen time. Retrieved from http://tvoparents.tvo.org/article/turn-tv-why-you-need-worry-about-family-screen-time.

Fernandez-Twinn, D. S., & Ozanne, S. E. (2006). Mechanisms by which poor early growth programs type-2 diabetes, obesity and the metabolic syndrome. *Physiology & Behavior, 88*(3), 234–243.

Féron, J., Gentaz, E., & Streri, A. (2006). Evidence of amodal representation of small numbers across visuo-tactile modalities in 5-month-old infants. *Cognitive Development, 21*(2), 81–92.

Field, A. P. (2006). The behavioral inhibition system and the verbal information pathway to children's fears. *Journal of Abnormal Psychology, 115*(4), 742–752.

Field, T. (1999). Sucking and massage therapy reduce stress during infancy. In M. Lewis & D. Ramsay (Eds.), *Soothing and stress* (pp. 157–169). Hillsdale, NJ: Erlbaum.

Field, T., Hernandez-Reif, M., Feijo, L., & Freedman, J. (2006). Prenatal, perinatal and neonatal stimulation: A survey of neonatal nurseries. *Infant Behavior & Development, 29*(1), 24–31.

Filus, A. (2006). Being a grandparent in China, Greece and Poland. *Studia Psychologiczne, 44*(1), 35–46.

Finkel, E. J., Eastwick, P. W., Karney, B. R., Reis, H. T., & Sprecher, S. (2012). Online dating: A critical analysis from the perspective of psychological science. *Psychological Science in the Public Interest, 13*(1), 3–66.

Finkelman, J. M. (2005). Sexual harassment. In A. Barnes (Ed.). *The handbook of women, psychology, and the law.* (pp. 64–78). Hoboken, NJ: Wiley.

First Nations Pedagogy Online. (2009). Elders. Retrieved from http://firstnationspedagogy.ca/elders.html.

Fisch, S. M. (2004). Children's learning from educational television: Sesame Street and beyond. Mahwah, NJ: Erlbaum.

Fish, S. (2014, July 2). The changing face of volunteering in Canada. Retrieved from https://charityvillage.com/Content.aspx?topic=The_changing_face_of_volunteering_in_Canada#.V0Rj4pErLIU.

Fisher, M. (1992, November 1). Brain-dead woman provides life-support for fetus. Hospital committee's decision provokes ethics controversy. *The Washington Post*. Retrieved from http://articles.mcall.com/1992-11-01/news/2889311_1_fetus-ethics-panel-unborn-child.

Fiske, A. (2006). The nature of depression in later life. In S. H. Qualls, & B. G. Knight (Eds.), *Psychotherapy for depression in older adults* (pp. 29–44). Hoboken, NJ: John Wiley & Sons Inc.

Fitzgerald, H. E., et al. (1991). The organization of lateralized behavior during infancy. In H. E. Fitzgerald, B. M. Lester, & M. W. Yogman (Eds.), *Theory and research in behavioral pediatrics.* New York: Plenum.

Fivush, R. (2002). Scripts, schemas, and memory of trauma. In N. L. Stein et al. (Eds.), *Representation, memory, and development: Essays in honor of Jean Mandler* (pp. 53–74). Mahwah, NJ: Erlbaum.

Fivush, R., & Hammond, N. R. (1990). Autobiographical memory across the preschool years: Toward reconceptualizing childhood amnesia. In R. Fivush & J. A. Hudson (Eds.), *Knowing and remembering in young children.* Cambridge: Cambridge University Press.

Fivush, R., Sales, J, M., Goldberg, A., Bahrick, L., & Parker, J. (2004). Weathering the storm: Children's long-term recall of Hurricane Andrew. *Memory, 12*(1), 104–118.

Flanders, D. (2013, September 16) Sorry kid. Spend the school day in your soiled soggy underwear; we don't do dirty bums. *Kindercare Pediatrics*. Retrieved August 1, 2016 from kindercarepediatrics.ca/education/sorry-kid-spend-the-school-day-in-your-soiled-soggy-underwear-we-dont-do-dirty-bums/.

Flavell, J. H. (1993). Young children's understanding of thinking and consciousness. *Current Directions in Psychological Science, 2,* 40–43.

Flavell, J. H., Miller, P. H., & Miller, S. A. (2002). *Cognitive development* (4th ed.). Upper Saddle River, NJ: Prentice Hall.

Florsheim, P. (Ed.). (2003). *Adolescent romantic relations and sexual behavior:*

Theory, research, and practical implications. Mahwah, NJ: Erlbaum.

Flouri, E., & Buchanan, A. (2003). The role of father involvement and mother involvement in adolescents' psychological well- being. *British Journal of Social Work, 33*(3), 399–406.

Flynn, J. R. (2003). Movies about intelligence: The limitations of g. *Current Directions in Psychological Science, 12*(3), 95–99.

Foley, G. M. (2006). Self and social–emotional development in infancy: A descriptive synthesis. In G. M. Foley & J. D. Hochman (Eds.), *Mental health in early intervention: Achieving unity in principles and practice* (pp. 139–173). Baltimore: Paul H. Brookes.

Fontaine, A-M. (2005). Écologie développementale des premières interactions entre enfants: Effet des matériels de jeu. *Enfance, 57*(2), 137–154.

Food and Drug Administration. (2004, July 20). *Decreasing the chance of birth defects.* Retrieved from http://www.fda.gov/fdac/features/996_bd.html.

Forman-Hoffman, V. L., Ruffin, T., & Schultz, S. K. (2006). Basal metabolic rate in anorexia nervosa patients: Using appropriate predictive equations during the refeeding process. *Annals of Clinical Psychiatry, 18*(2), 123–127.

Fortier, J. (2010, April 10). Canada a nation of "satisfied" workers: Survey. *Financial Post.* Retrieved from http://www.working.com/national/sectors/Canada+nation+satisfied+workers+Survey/2901739/story.html.

Fouad, N. A., & Arredondo, P. (2007). Implications for Psychologists as Researchers. In N. A. Fouad & P. Arredondo (Eds.), *Becoming culturally oriented: Practical advice for psychologists and educators* (pp. 81–93). Washington, DC: American Psychological Association.

4D Interactive. (2016). http://www.fourdirectionsteachings.com/transcripts/ojibwe.pdf.

Fozard, J. L., & Gordon- Salant, S. (2001). Changes in vision and hearing with aging. In J. E. Birren, & K. W. Schaie (Eds.), *Handbook of psychology of aging* (5th ed.) (pp. 241–266). San Diego: Academic Press.

Fraley, R. C. (2002). Attachment stability from infancy to adulthood: Meta-analysis and dynamic modeling of developmental mechanisms. *Personality and Social Psychology Review, 6*(2), 123–151.

Fraley, R. C., Vicary, A. M., Brumbaugh, C. C., & Roisman, G. I. (2011, June 27). Patterns of stability in adult attachment: An empirical test of two models of continuity and change. *Journal of Personality and Social Psychology, 101*(5), 974–992.

Franklin, A., Pilling, M., & Davies, I. (2005). The nature of infant color categorization: Evidence from eye movements on a target detection task. *Journal of Experimental Child Psychology, 91*(3), 227–248.

Frazier, L. D., Newman, F. L., & Jaccard, J. (2007). Psychosocial outcomes in later life. *Psychology and Aging, 22*(4), 676–689.

Freedom 55. (2016). Freedom today, freedom tomorrow. Retrieved from https://www.freedom55financial.com/#.

Freeman, J., & Luu, K. (2011). *The health of Canada's young people: A mental health focus.* Ottawa, ON: Public Health Agency of Canada. Retrieved from http://www.sexualityandu.ca/sexual-health/statistics1/statistics-on-sexual-intercourse-experience-among-canadian-teenagers.

Frerichs, L., Andsager, J. L., Campo, S., Aquilino, M., & Dyer, C. S. (2006). Framing breastfeeding and formula-feeding messages in popular U.S. magazines. *Women & Health, 44*(1), 95–118.

Freund, A. M. (2008, May 21). Successful aging as management of resources: The role of selection, optimization, and compensation. *Research in Human Development, 5*(2). Retrieved from http://www.tandfonline.com/doi/full/10.1080/15427600802034827.

Freund, A. M., & Baltes, P. B. (2002). The adaptiveness of selection, optimization, and compensation as strategies of life management. *Journals of Gerontology: Series B: Psychological Sciences & Social Sciences, 57B*(5), P426–P434.

Fried, P. A., & Smith, A. M. (2001). A literature review of the consequences of prenatal marijuana exposure: An emerging theme of a deficiency in aspects of executive function. *Neurotoxicology and Teratology, 23*(1), 1–11.

Friedman, R. A. (2008, January 15). Crisis? Maybe he's a narcissistic jerk. *The New York Times online.*

Frisch, R. (1997). Speech reported in N. Angier (1997), Chemical tied to fat control could help trigger puberty, *New York Times,* pp. C1, C3.

Frisch, R. E. (1994). The right weight: Body fat, menarche and fertility. *Proceedings of the Nutrition Society, 53,* 113–129.

Fromkin, V., et al. (2004).*The development of language in Genie: A case of language acquisition beyond the "critical period."* New York: Psychology Press.

Fry, D. P. (2005). Rough-and-tumble social play in humans. In A. D. Pellegrini & P. K. Smith (Eds.), *The nature of play: Great apes and humans* (pp. 54–85). New York: Guilford Press.

Furman, W., Rahe, D., & Hartup, W. W. (1979). Social rehabilitation of low-interactive preschool children by peer intervention. *Child Development, 50,* 915–922.

Furnham, A., Petrides, K. V., & Constantinides, A. (2005). The effects of body mass index and waist-to-hip ratio on ratings of female attractiveness, fecundity, and health. *Personality and Individual Differences, 38*(8), 1823–1834.

G

Gallagher, F., Bell, L., Waddell, G., Benoît, A., & Côté, N. (2012). Requesting cesareans without medical indications: An option being considered by young Canadian women. *Birth: Issues in Perinatal Care, 39*(1), 39–47. doi:10.1111/j.1523-536X.2011.00511.x.

Gans, D., & Silverstein, M. (2006). Norms of filial responsibility for aging parents across time and generations. *Journal of Marriage and Family, 68*(4), 961–976.

Gardner, H. (1983). *Frames of mind: The theory of multiple intelligences.* New York: Basic Books.

Gardner, H. (2006). *The development and education of the mind: The selected works of Howard Gardner*. Philadelphia: Routledge/Taylor & Francis.

Garmon, L. (Writer & Director). (1997). Secret of the wild child [Television series episode]. *Nova.* Arlington, VA: PBS.

Gartstein, M. A., Slobodskaya, H. R., & Kinsht, I. A. (2003). Cross-cultural differences in temperament in the first year of life: United States of America (U.S.) and Russia. *International Journal of Behavioral Development, 27*(4), 316–328.

Gathercole, S. E., Pickering, S. J., Ambridge, B., & Wearing, H. (2004a). The structure of working memory from 4 to 15 years of age. *Developmental Psychology, 40*(2), 177–190.

Gathercole, S. E., Pickering, S. J., Knight, C., & Stegmann, Z. (2004b). Working memory skills and educational attainment: Evidence from national curriculum assessments at 7 and 14 years of age. *Applied Cognitive Psychology, 18*(1), 1–16.

Gavin, N. I., et al. (2005). Perinatal depression: A systematic review of prevalence and incidence. *Obstetrics & Gynecology, 106,* 1071–1083.

Ge, X., et al. (2003). It's about timing and change: Pubertal transition effects on symptoms of major depression among African American youths. *Developmental Psychology, 39*(3), 430–439.

Geary, D. C. (2006). Sex differences in social behavior and cognition: Utility of sexual selection for hypothesis generation. *Hormones and Behavior, 49*(3), 273–275.

Gender Diversity. (2016). Education and support services. Retrieved from http://www.genderdiversity.org/support/.

Georgiades, S., et al. (2007). Structure of the autism symptom phenotype: A proposed multidimensional model. *Journal of the American Academy of Child & Adolescent Psychiatry, 46*(2), 188–196.

Gerard, J. M., Landry-Meyer, L., & Roe, J. G. (2006). Grandparents raising grandchildren: The role of social support in coping with caregiving challenges. *International Journal of Ageing & Human Development, 62*(4), 359–383.

Geschwind, D. H. (2000). Interview cited in D. E. Rosenbaum (2000, May 16), On left- handedness, its causes and costs, *New York Times,* pp. F1, F6.

Gesell, A. (1928). *Infancy and human growth.* New York: Macmillan.

Gesell, A. (1929). Maturation and infant behavior patterns. *Psychological Review, 36,* 307–319.

Ghetti, S., & Alexander, K. W. (2004). "If it happened, I would remember it": Strategic use of event memorability in the rejection of false autobiographical events. *Child Development, 75*(2), 542–561.

Gibson, E. J. (1969). *Principles of perceptual learning and development.* New York: Appleton-Century-Crofts.

Gibson, E. J. (1991). *An odyssey in learning and perception.* Cambridge, MA: MIT Press.

Gibson, E. J., & Walk, R. D. (1960). The visual cliff. *Scientific American, 202,* 64–71.

Gilhooly, M. L., et al. (2007). Real-world problem solving and quality of life in older people. *British Journal of Health Psychology, 12*(4), 587–600.

Gilligan, C. (1982). *In a different voice.* Cambridge, MA: Harvard University Press.

Gilligan, C. (1990). Remapping the moral domain: New images of the self in relationship. In C. Zanardi (Ed.), *Essential papers on the psychology of women. Essential papers in psychoanalysis* (pp. 480–495). New York: New York University Press.

Gilmore, J. (2010). Trends in dropout rates and the labour market outcomes of young dropouts. Ottawa: Statistics Canada. Retrieved from http://www.statcan.gc.ca/pub/81-004-x/2010004/article/11339-eng.htm#b.

Giussani, D. A. (2006). Prenatal hypoxia: Relevance to developmental origins of health and disease. In P. Gluckman & M. Hanson (Eds.), *Developmental origins of health and disease* (pp. 178–190). New York: Cambridge University Press.

Gleason, T. R. (2002). Social provisions of real and imaginary relationships in early childhood. *Developmental Psychology, 38*(6), 979–992.

Gleason, T. R. (2004). Imaginary companions and peer acceptance. *International Journal of Behavioral Development, 28*(3), 204–209.

Gleason, T. R., Gower, A. L., Hohmann, L. M., & Gleason, T. C. (2005). Temperament and friendship in preschool-aged children. *International Journal of Behavioral Development, 29*(4), 336–344.

Gleason, T. R., & Hohmann, L. M. (2006). Concepts of real and imaginary friendships in early childhood. *Social Development, 15*(1), 128–144.

Gleason, T. R., Sebanc, A. M., & Hartup, W. W. (2003). Imaginary companions of preschool children. In M. E. Hertzig & E. A. Farber (Eds.), *Annual progress in child psychiatry and child development: 2000–2001* (pp. 101–121). New York: Brunner-Routledge.

Glück, J., & Bluck, S. (2007). Looking back across the life span: A life story account of the reminiscence bump. *Memory & Cognition, 35*(8), 1928–1939.

Gobet, F., & Simon, H. A. (2000). Five seconds or sixty? Presentation time in expert memory. *Cognitive Science, 24*(4), 651–682.

Goel, P., Radotra, A., Singh, I., Aggarwal, A., & Dua, D. (2004). Effects of passive smoking on outcome in pregnancy. *Journal of Postgraduate Medicine, 50*(1), 12–16.

Golan, H., & Huleihel, M. (2006). The effect of prenatal hypoxia on brain development: Short- and long-term consequences demonstrated in rodent models. *Developmental Science, 9*(4), 338–349.

Goldberg A., & Allen, K. (2013). *LGBT-parent families: Innovations in research and implication for practice.* New York: Springer.

Goldman, J. S., Adamson, J., Karydas, A., Miller, B. L., & Hutton, M. (2008). New genes, new dilemmas: FTLD genetics and its implications for families. *American Journal of Alzheimer's Disease and Other Dementias, 22*(6), 507–515.

Goldschmidt, L., Day, N. L., & Richardson, G. A. (2000). Effects of prenatal marijuana exposure on child behavior problems at age 10. *Neurotoxicology and Teratology, 22*(3), 325–336.

Goldsmith, H. H., et al. (2003). Part III: Genetics and development. In R. J. Davidson et al. (Eds.), *Handbook of affective sciences.* London: Oxford University Press.

Goldstein, H. (2004). International comparisons of student attainment. *Assessment in Education: Principles, Policy & Practice, 11*(3), 319–330.

Goldstein, I. (1998). Cited in Kolata, G. (1998, April 4). Impotence pill: Would it also help women? *The New York Times,* pp. A1, A6.

Goldstein, I. (2000). Cited in Norton, A. (2000, September 1). Exercise helps men avoid impotence. *Reuters News Agency online*.

Goldstein, I., & Alexander, J. L. (2005). Practical aspects in the management of vaginal atrophy and sexual dysfunction in perimenopausal and postmenopausal women. *Journal of Sexual Medicine, 2*(Suppl3), 154–165.

Goldstein, I., Meston, C., Davis, S., & Traish, A. (Eds.). (2006). *Female sexual dysfunction.* New York: Parthenon.

Goldstein, S., & Brooks, R. B. (2005). *Handbook of resilience in children*. New York: Kluwer Academic/Plenum.

Gonzalez, V. (2005). Cultural, linguistic, and socioeconomic factors influencing monolingual and bilingual children's cognitive development. In V. Gonzalez & J. Tinajero (Eds.), *Review of research and practice,* Vol. 3 (pp. 67–104). Mahwah, NJ: Erlbaum.

González, Y. S., Moreno, D. S., & Schneider, B. H. (2004). Friendship expectations of early adolescents in Cuba and Canada. *Journal of Cross-Cultural Psychology, 35*(4), 436–445.

Goodman, C. G. (2007a). Intergenerational triads in skipped-generation grandfamilies. *International Journal of Ageing & Human Development, 65*(3), 231–258.

Goodman, C. G. (2007b). Family dynamics in three-generation grandfamilies. *Journal of Family Issues, 28*(3), 355–379.

GoodTherapy.org. (2013). Albert Bandura. Retrieved from http://www.goodtherapy.org/famous-psychologists/albert-bandura.html.

Gopnik A., & Astington, J. W. (1988). Children's understanding of representational change and its relation to the understanding of false belief and the appearance-reality distinction. *Child Development 59*(1), 26–37.

Gopnik, A., & Meltzoff, A. N. (1992). Categorization and naming: Basic-level sorting in eighteen-month-olds and its relation to language. *Child Development, 63,* 1091–1103.

Gopnik, A., & Slaughter, V. (1991). Young children's understanding of changes in their mental states. *Child Development, 62,* 98–110.

Gordon-Salant, S., Fitzgibbons, P. J., & Friedman, S. A. (2007). Recognition of time-compressed and natural speech with selective temporal enhancements by young and elderly listeners. *Journal of Speech, Language, and Hearing Research, 50*(5), 1181–1193.

Gormally, S., et al. (2001). Contact and nutrient caregiving effects on newborn infant pain responses. *Developmental Medicine and Child Neurology, 43*(1), 28–38.

Gottesman, N. (2012). Generation XL. *Parenting School Years, 26*(7), 72–76.

Gottlieb, B. H., Still, E., & Newby-Clark, I. R. (2007). Types and precipitants of growth and decline in emerging adulthood. *Journal of Adolescent Research, 22*(2), 132–155.

Gottman, J. M., Coan, J., Carrère, S. & Swanson, C. (1998). Predicting marital happiness and stability from newlywed interactions. *Journal of Marriage and the Family, 60,* 5–22.

Gottman Institute. The six things that predict divorce. Retrieved from https://www.gottman.com/blog/the-6-things-that-predict-divorce/.

Government of Canada. (2014). Get the facts about immunization. Retrieved October 15, 2016, from http://healthycanadians.gc.ca/healthy-living-vie-saine/immunization-immunisation/children-enfants/fact-fait-eng.php.

Government of Canada. (2016). *Assisted human reproductive act*. Retrieved on October 10, 2016 from http://laws-lois.justice.gc.ca/eng/acts/a-13.4/FullText.html.

Government of Canada. (n.d.) Family life—Divorce. Retrieved June 11, 2016, from http://well-being.esdc.gc.ca/misme-iowb/.3ndic.1t.4r@-eng.jsp?iid=76.

Graber, J. A., Seeley, J. R., Brooks-Gunn, J., & Lewinsohn, P. M. (2004). Is pubertal timing associated with psychopathology in young adulthood? *Journal of the American Academy of Child and Adolescent Psychiatry, 43*(6), 718–726.

Grandparenting in the twenty-first century: The times they are a changin'. (2005). *Ontario Health Promotion E-Bulletin, 2005*(434). Retrieved from http://www.ohpe.ca/node/6892.

Grandi, G., Ferrari, S., Xholli, A., Cannoletta, M., Palma, F., Romani, C., Vope, A., & Cagnacci, A. (2012). Prevalence of menstrual pain in young women: What is dysmenorrhea? *Journal of Pain Research, 5,* 169–174.

Gray, C., Koopman, E., & Hunt, J. (1991). The emotional phases of marital separation: an empirical investigation. *American Journal of Orthopsychiatry, 1991*(61), 138–143.

Gray, S. L., et al. (2008). Antioxidant vitamin supplement use and risk of dementia or Alzheimer's disease in older adults. *Journal of the American Geriatrics Society, 56*(2), 291–295.

Green, R. (1978). Sexual identity of 37 children raised by homosexual or transsexual parents. *American Journal of Psychiatry, 135,* 692–697.

Greene, S. M., Anderson, E. R., Doyle, E. A., Riedelbach, H., & Bear, G. G. (2006). Divorce. In K. M. Minke (Ed.), *Children's needs III: Development, prevention, and intervention* (pp. 745–757). Bethesda, MD: National Association of School Psychologists.

Greenough, W. T., Black, J. E., & Wallace, C. S. (2002). Experience and brain development. In M. H. Johnson, Y. Munakata, & R. O. Gilmore (Eds.), *Brain development and cognition: A reader* (2nd ed.) (pp. 186–216). Malden, MA: Blackwell.

Greidanus, J. A. (2007). A narrative inquiry into the experiences of bereaved children. *Dissertation Abstracts International Section A: Humanities and Social Sciences, 67*(9-A), 3447.

Grigorenko, E. L. (2007). Triangulating developmental dyslexia: Behavior, brain, and genes. In D. Coch, G. Dawson, & K. W. Fischer. (Eds.). *Human behavior, learning, and the developing brain: Atypical development.* (pp. 117–144). New York: Guilford.

Grindrod, C. M., & Baum, S. R. (2005). Hemispheric contributions to lexical ambiguity resolution in a discourse context: Evidence from individuals with unilateral left and right hemisphere lesions. *Brain and Cognition, 57*(1), 70–83.

Grolnick, W. S., McMenamy, J. M., & Kurowski, C. O. (2006). Emotional self-regulation in infancy and toddlerhood. In L. Balter & C. S. Tamis-LeMonda (Eds.), *Child psychology: A handbook of contemporary issues* (2nd ed.) (pp. 3–25). New York: Psychology Press.

Grossman, A. H., D'Augelli, A. R., & O'Connell, T. S. (2003). Being lesbian, gay, bisexual, and sixty or older in North America. In L. D. Garnets, & D. C. Kimmel (Eds.), *Psychological perspectives on lesbian, gay, and bisexual experiences* (2nd ed.) (pp. 629–645). New York: Columbia University Press.

Grossmann, K., et al. (2002). The uniqueness of the child–father attachment relationship: Fathers' sensitive and challenging play as a pivotal variable in a 16-year longitudinal study. *Social Development, 11*(3), 307–331.

Grundy, E., & Henretta, J. C. (2006). Between elderly parents and adult children: A new look at the intergenerational care provided by the "sandwich generation." *Ageing & Society, 26*(5), 707–722.

Grusec, J. E. (2002). Parenting socialization and children's acquisition of values. In M. H. Bornstein (Ed.), *Handbook of parenting* (2nd ed.), Vol. 5, *Practical issues in parenting* (pp. 143–167). Mahwah, NJ: Erlbaum.

Grusec, J. E. (2006). The development of moral behavior and conscience from a socialization perspective. In M. Killen & J. G. Smetana (Eds.), *Handbook of moral development* (pp. 243–265). Mahwah, NJ: Erlbaum.

Guerin, D. W., Gottfried, A. W., & Thomas, C. W. (1997). Difficult temperament and behaviour problems: A longitudinal study from 1.5 to 12 years. *International Journal of Behavioral Development, 21*(1), 71–90.

Guerrini, I., Thomson, A. D., & Gurling, H. D. (2007). The importance of alcohol misuse, malnutrition and genetic susceptibility on brain growth and plasticity. *Neuroscience & Biobehavioral Reviews, 31*(2), 212–220.

Guiaux, M., van Tilburg, T., & van Groenou, M. B. (2007). Changes in contact and support exchange in personal networks after widowhood. *Personal Relationships, 14*(3), 457–473.

Gulli, C. (2009, April 10). Youth survey: Teen girls in charge. *Macleans*. Retrieved from http://www2.macleans.ca/2009/04/10/teen-girls-in-charge/.

Gunby, J. (n.d.). Assisted reproductive technologies (ART) in Canada: 2011 results from the Canadian ART Register. *Canadian Fertility and Andrology Society.* Retrieved from http://www.fqpn.qc.ca/main/wp-content/uploads/2014/07/CARTR_2011_v3.pdf.

Güntürkün, O. (2006). Letters on nature and nurture. In P. B. Baltes et al. (Eds.), *Life span development and the brain: The perspective of biocultural co-constructivism* (pp. 379–397). New York: Cambridge University Press.

Gurba, E. (2005). On the specific character of adult thought: Controversies over post-formal operations. *Polish Psychological Bulletin, 36*(3), 175–185.

Gutknecht, L. (2001). Full-genome scans with autistic disorder: A review. *Behavior Genetics, 31*(1), 113–123.

H

Hack, M., Taylor, H. G., Drotar, D., Schluchter, M., Cartar, I., Wilson-Costello, D., . . . Morrow, M. (2005) Poor predictive validity of the Bayley Scales of Infant Development for cognitive function of extremely low birth weight children at school age. *Pediatrics, 116*(2).

Haith, M. M. (1979). Visual cognition in early infancy. In R. B. Kearsly & I. E. Sigel (Eds.), *Infants at risk: Assessment of cognitive functioning.* Hillsdale, NJ: Erlbaum.

Haith, M. M. (1990). Progress in the understanding of sensory and perceptual processes in early infancy. *Merrill–Palmer Quarterly, 36,* 1–26.

Halgin, R. P., & Whitbourne, S. K. (1993). *Abnormal psychology.* Fort Worth, TX: Harcourt Brace Jovanovich.

Hall, D. T. (2004). The protean career: A quarter-century journey. *Journal of Vocational Behavior, 65*(1), 1–13.

Hall, G. S. (1904). *Adolescence: Its psychology and its relations to physiology, anthropology, sociology sex, crime, religion and education, Vol. II.* New York: D Appleton & Company.

Halliday, L. F., & Bishop, D. V. M. (2006). Auditory frequency discrimination in children with dyslexia. *Journal of Research in Reading, 29*(2), 213–228.

Halpern, D. F. (2003). Sex differences in cognitive abilities. *Applied Cognitive Psychology, 17*(3), 375–376.

Halpern, D. F. (2004). A cognitive-process taxonomy for sex differences in cognitive abilities. *Current Directions in Psychological Science, 13*(4), 135–139.

Hamm, J. V. (2000). Do birds of a feather flock together? The variable bases for African American, Asian American, and European American adolescents' selection of similar friends. *Developmental Psychology, 36*(2), 209–219.

Hammer, K. (2012b). Full-day kindergarten in Ontario gets failing grade. Retrieved from http://www.theglobeandmail.com/news/toronto/kindergarten/full-day-kindergarten- in-ontario-gets-failing-grade/article1379499/.

Hammer, K. (2012a). The challenge of teaching empathy to stop bullying. Retrieved from http://www.theglobeandmail.com/news/national/education/the-challenge-of-teaching-empathy-to-stop-bullying/article5328473/.

Hangal, S., & Aminabhavi, V. A. (2007). Self-concept, emotional maturity, and achievement motivation of the adolescent children of employed mothers and homemakers. *Journal of the Indian Academy of Applied Psychology, 33*(1), 103–110.

Hanlon, T. E., Bateman, R. W., Simon, B. D., O'Grady, K. E., & Carswell, S. B. (2004). Antecedents and correlates of deviant activity in urban youth manifesting behavioral problems. *Journal of Primary Prevention, 24*(3), 285–309.

Hannon, P., Bowen, D. J., Moinpour, C. M., & McLerran, D. F. (2003). Correlations in perceived food use between the family food preparer and their spouses and children. *Appetite, 40*(1), 77–83.

Hansen, J. C., Dik, B. J., & Zhou, S. (2008). An examination of the structure of leisure interests of college students, working-age adults, and retirees. *Journal of Counseling Psychology, 55*(2), 133–145.

Harel, J., & Scher, A. (2003). Insufficient responsiveness in ambivalent mother–infant relationships: Contextual and affective aspects. *Infant Behavior and Development, 26*(3), 371–383.

Harlow, H. F., & Harlow, M. K. (1966). Learning to love. *American Scientist, 54,* 244–272.

Harlow, H. F., Harlow, M. K., & Suomi, S. J. (1971). From thought to therapy: Lessons from a primate laboratory. *American Scientist, 59,* 538–549.

Harris, G. (2004, September 14). *FDA links drugs to being suicidal.* Retrieved from http://www.nytimes.com.

Harris, S. R., Megens, A. M., Backman, C. L., & Hayes, V. E. (2005). Stability of the Bayley II Scales of Infant Development in a sample of low-risk and high-risk infants. *Developmental Medicine & Child Neurology, 47*(12), 820–823.

Harter, S. (2006). The self. In K. A. Renninger, I. E. Sigel, W. Damon, & R. M. Lerner (Eds.), *Handbook of child psychology* (6th ed.), Vol. 4, *Child psychology in practice* (pp. 505–570). Hoboken, NJ: Wiley.

Harter, S., & Pike, R. (1984). The pictorial scale of perceived competence and social acceptance for young children. *Child Development, 55,* 1969–1982.

Harter, S., & Whitesell, N. R. (2003). Beyond the debate: Why some adolescents report stable self-worth over time and situation, whereas others report changes in self-worth. *Journal of Personality, 71*(6), 1027–1058.

Hartley, A. (2006). Changing role of the speed of processing construct in the cognitive psychology of human aging. In J. E. Birren & K. W. Schaie (Eds.), *Handbook of the psychology of aging* (6th ed.) (pp. 183–207). Amsterdam, Netherlands: Elsevier.

Hartman, M., & Warren, L. H. (2005). Explaining age differences in temporal working memory. *Psychology and Aging, 20*(4), 645–656.

Hartup, W. W. (1983). The peer system. In P. H. Mussen (Ed.), *Handbook of child* psychology, Vol. 4, Socialization, personality, and social development. New York: Wiley.

Hartup, W. W. (1986). On relationships and development. In W. W. Hartup & Z. Rubin (Eds.), *Relationships and development* (pp. 1–26). Hillsdale, NJ: Erlbaum.

Hasher, L. (2008, May 20). Cited in Reistad-Long, S. Older brain, wiser brain. *The New York Times online*. Accessed October 5, 2008.

Hassett, J. M., Siebert, E. R., & Wallen, K. (2008). Sex differences in rhesus monkey toy preferences parallel those of children. *Hormone and Behavior, 54*(3), 359–364.

Hassing, L. B., & Johanssom, B. (2005). Aging and cognition. *Nordisk Psykologi, 57*(1), 4–20.

Hassman, R. (2014, April 4). Rights and restlessness: Rhoda Hassmann on human rights: 21st century malnutrition among Canada's Aboriginal peoples. [Web log post]. Retrieved from http://rhodahassmann.blogspot.ca/2014/04/malnutrition-among-canadas-aboriginal.html.

Hastings, P. D., Zahn-Waxler, C., Robinson, J., Usher, B., & Bridges, D. (2000). The development of concern for others in children with behavior problems. *Developmental Psychology, 36*(5), 531–546.

Hatch, L. R., & Bulcroft, K. (2004). Does long-term marriage bring less frequent disagreements? *Journal of Family Issues, 25,* 465–495.

Hatcher, R. A., et al. (Eds.). (2007). *Contraceptive technologies* (18th rev. ed.). New York: Ardent Media.

Hatfield, E., & Rapson, R. L. (2002). Passionate love and sexual desire: Cultural and historical perspectives. In A. L. Vangelisti, H. T. Reis, et al. (Eds.), *Stability and change in relationships. Advances in personal relationships* (pp. 306–324). New York: Cambridge University Press.

Havighurst, R. (1972). In Robert Havighurst: Developmental theorist. Retrieved from http://faculty.mdc.edu/jmcnair/EDF3214.Topic.Outline/Robert.Havighurst.htm. Accessed October 2, 2008.

Hawkley, L. C., Burleson, M. H., Berntson, G. G., & Cacioppo, J. T. (2003). Loneliness in everyday life: Cardiovascular activity, psychosocial context, and health behaviors. *Journal of Personality & Social Psychology, 85*(1), 105–120.

Hay, D. F., Payne, A., & Chadwick, A. (2004). Peer relations in childhood. *Journal of Child Psychology and Psychiatry. 45*(1), 84–108.

Hayes, R., & Dennerstein, L. (2005). The impact of aging on sexual function and sexual dysfunction in women: A review of population-based studies. *Journal of Sexual Medicine, 2*(3), 317–330.

Hayflick, L. (1996). *How and why we age.* New York: Ballantine Books, 1994.

Hayne, H., & Fagen, J. W. (Eds.). (2003). *Progress in infancy research,* Vol. 3. Mahwah, NJ: Erlbaum.

Hayslip, B., Jr., & Kaminski, P. L. (2006). Custodial grandchildren. In G. G. Bear & K. M. Minke (Eds.), *Children's needs III: Development, prevention, and intervention* (pp. 771–782). Washington, DC: National Association of School Psychologists.

Hayslip, B., Jr., Neumann, C. S., Louden, L., & Chapman, B. (2006). Developmental stage theories. In J. C. Thomas, D. L. Segal, & M. Hersen. (Eds.), *Comprehensive handbook of personality and psychopathology, Vol. 1: Personality and everyday functioning* (pp. 115–141). Hoboken, NJ: John Wiley & Sons, Inc.

Health Canada. (2000). *Because life goes on... Helping children and youth live with separation and divorce.* Retrieved from http://www.phac-aspc.gc.ca/publicat/mh-sm/pdf/booklet_e.pdf.

Health Canada. (2003). Canadian guidelines for body weight classification in adults. Reproduced with permission from Her Majesty the Queen in Right of Canada©, represented by the Minister of Health, 2013.

Health Canada. (2007a). Breastfeeding. Retrieved from http://www.hc-sc.gc.ca/fn-an/pubs/infant-nourrisson/nut_infant_nourrisson_term_3-eng.php.

Health Canada. (2007b). Eating well with Canada's food guide. Retrieved from http://www.hc-sc.gc.ca/fn-an/pubs/res-educat/res-educat_3-eng.php

Health Canada. (2007c). How much food you need every day. Retrieved from http://www.hc-sc.gc.ca/fn-an/food-guide-aliment/basics-base/quantit-eng.php

Health Canada. (2009). Aboriginal Head Start on Reserve. Retrieved from http://www.hc-sc.gc.ca/fniah-spnia/famil/develop/ahsor-papa_intro-eng.php.

Health Canada. (2012). Breastfeeding initiation in Canada: Key statistics and graphics. Retrieved from http://www.hc-sc.gc.ca/fn-an/surveill/nutrition/commun/prenatal/initiation-eng.php#a2.

Health Canada. (2013, September 5). *Healthy babies*. Retrieved July 21, 2016, from http://www.hc-sc.gc.ca/hl-vs/babies-bebes/index-eng.php.

Health Journal. (2010). Canadian women over 30 at risk as infertility rates predicted to double. Retrieved from http://www.thehealthjournal.ca/site/content/view/136/1/.

Health Law Institute. (2016). End of life law and policy in Canada. *Dalhousie University*. Retrieved from http://eol.law.dal.ca/?page_id=236.

Healy, M. D., & Ellis, B. J. (2007). Birth order, conscientiousness, and openness to experience. Tests of the family-niche model of personality using a with-in-family methodology. *Evolution and Human Behavior, 28*(1), 55–59.

Heart and Stroke Foundation. (2008). Healthy weight in children and youth. Retrieved from http://www.heartandstroke.com/site/c.ikIQLcMWJtE/b.3484293/k.D60A/Healthy_living__Healthy_weight_in_children_and_youth.htm

Heart and Stroke Foundation of Canada. (1993). *Position statement on physical activity.* Unpublished report. Ottawa: Author. Retrieved from http://www.pembinatrails.ca/program/physicaleducation/Documents/MPESA/Articles/Health%20Related/children%20stats.doc.

Heart and Stroke Foundation of Canada. (2013). Statistics: Cardiovascular disease deaths. Retrieved from http://www.heartandstroke.com/site/c.ikIQLcMWJtE/b.3483991/k.34A8/Statistics.htm.

Hebert, T. P. (2000). Gifted males pursuing careers in elementary education: Factors that influence a belief in self. *Journal for the Education of the Gifted, 24*(1), 7–45.

Heilman, K. M., Nadeau, S. E., & Beversdorf, D. O. (2003). Creative innovation: Possible brain mechanisms. *Neurocase, 9*(5), 369–379.

Heindel, J. J., & Lawler, C. (2006) Role of exposure to environmental chemicals in developmental origins of health and disease. In P. Gluckman & M. Hanson (Eds.), *Developmental origins of health and disease* (pp. 82–97). New York: Cambridge University Press.

Held, L. (2010). Profile of Mary Ainsworth. In A. Rutherford (Ed.), *Psychology's feminist voices multimedia Internet archive.* Retrieved from http://www.feministvoices.com/mary-ainsworth/.

Helpguide.org. (2016). Coping with grief and loss: Understanding the grieving process. Retrieved from http://www.helpguide.org/articles/grief-loss/coping-with-grief-and-loss.htm.

Henry, D., et al. (2000). Normative influences on aggression in urban elementary school classrooms. *American Journal of Community Psychology, 28*(1) 59–81.

Henzi, S. P., et al. (2007). Look who's talking: developmental trends in the size of conversational cliques. *Evolution and Human Behavior, 28*(1), 66–74.

Heron, M. P. (2007). National Vital Statistics Reports, 56(5). Centers for Disease Control and Prevention. Retrieved from http://www.cdc.gov/nchs/data/nvsr/nvsr56/nvsr56_05.pdf.

Hertenstein, M. J., & Campos, J. J. (2004). The retention effects of an adult's emotional displays on infant behavior. *Child Development, 75*(2), 595–613.

Hetherington, E. M. (1989). Coping with family transition: Winners, losers, and survivors. *Child Development, 60,* 1–14.

Hetherington, E. M. (2006). The influence of conflict, marital problem solving and parenting on children's adjustment in nondivorced, divorced and remarried families. In A. Clarke-Stewart & J. Dunn (Eds.), *Families count: Effects on child and adolescent development, The Jacobs Foundation series on adolescence* (pp. 203–237). Cambridge, UK: Cambridge University Press.

Hicks, B. M., et al. (2007). Genes mediate the association between P3 amplitude and externalizing disorders. *Psychophysiology, 44*(1), 98–105.

Higuera, V. (2016). Shaken baby syndrome. *Healthline.* Retrieved from http://www.healthline.com/health/shaken-baby-syndrome.

Hill, R. A., Donovan, S., & Koyama, N. F. (2005). Female sexual advertisement reflects resource availability in twentieth-century UK society. *Human Nature, 16*(3), 266–277.

Hill, S. E., & Flom, R. (2007). 18- and 24-month-olds' discrimination of gender- consistent and inconsistent activities. *Infant Behavior & Development, 30*(1) 168–173.

Hill, S. Y., et al., (2007). Cerebellar volume in offspring from multiplex alcohol dependence families. *Biological Psychiatry, 61*(1), 41–47.

Hincks-Dellcrest Centre. (2014). The child with poor social relations–rejected: Parent resource. Retrieved on August 20, 2016, from https://www.hincksdellcrest.org/ABC/Parent-Resource/The-Child-with-Poor-Social-Relations/Rejected.aspx.

Hinojosa, T., Sheu, C., & Michel, G. F. (2003). Infant hand-use preferences for grasping objects contributes to the development of a hand-use preference for manipulating objects. *Developmental Psychobiology, 43*(4), 328–334.

HIV Edmonton. (2010). *HIV/AIDS.* Retrieved from http://www.hivedmnton.com/hivinfo.htm.

Hochwarter, W. A., Ferris, G. R., Perrewé, P. L., Witt, L. A., & Kiewitz, C. (2001). A note on the nonlinearity of the age-job-satisfaction relationship. *Journal of Applied Social Psychology, 31*(6), 1223–1237.

Hoecker, J. L. (2011). Infant and toddler health: Is it okay to play Baby Einstein DVDs for my 6-month-old? I've heard that such programming can promote a child's development. Retrieved from http://www.mayoclinic.com/health/baby-einstein/AN01990.

Hoegh, D. G., & Bourgeois, M. J. (2002). Prelude and postlude to the self: Correlates of achieved identity. *Youth and Society, 33*(4), 573–594.

Hoff, E. (2006). Language experience and language milestones during early childhood. In K. McCartney & D. Phillips (Eds.), *Blackwell handbook of early childhood development, Blackwell handbooks of developmental psychology* (pp. 233–251). Malden, MA: Blackwell.

Hoff, E. V. (2005). A friend living inside me—The forms and functions of imaginary companions. *Imagination, Cognition and Personality, 24*(2), 151–189.

Hoffman, J. (2009).When grandparents parent. *Today's Parent*. Retrieved from http://www.todaysparent.com/family/parenting/when-grandparents-parent.

Hogan, A. M., de Haan, M., Datta, A., & Kirkham, F. J. (2006). Hypoxia: An acute, intermittent and chronic challenge to cognitive development. *Developmental Science, 9*(4), 335–337.

Hogan, A. M., Kirkham, F. J., Isaacs, E. B., Wade, A. M., & Vargha-Khadem, F. (2005). Intellectual decline in children with moyamoya and sickle cell anaemia. *Developmental Medicine & Child Neurology, 47*(12), 824–829.

Holland, J. J. (2000, July 25). *Groups link media to child violence.* Retrieved from http://www.ap.org/.

Holland, J. L. (1997). *Making vocational choices: A theory of vocational personalities and work environments* (3rd ed.). Odessa, FL: Psychological Assessment Resources.

Holland, J. M., Futterman, A., Thompson, L. W., Moran, C., Gallagher-Thompson, D. (2013). Difficulties accepting the loss of a spouse: A precursor for intensified grieving among widowed older adults. *Death Studies, 37*(2), 126–144.

Homer, B. D., & Nelson, K. (2005). Seeing objects as symbols and symbols as objects: Language and the development of dual representation. In B. D. Homer & C. S. Tamis- LeMonda (Eds.), *The development of social cognition and communication* (pp. 29–52). Mahwah, NJ: Erlbaum.

Homish, G. G., & Leonard, K. E. (2007). The drinking partnership and marital satisfaction: The longitudinal influence of discrepant drinking. *Journal of Consulting and Clinical Psychology, 75*(1) 43–51.

Honzik, M. P., Macfarlane, J. W., & Allen, L. (1948). The stability of mental test performance between two and eighteen years. *Journal of Experimental Education, 17,* 309–324.

Höpflinger, F., & Hummel, C. (2006). Heran wachsende Enkelkinder und ihre Großeltern: Im Geschlechtervergleich. *Zeitschrift für Gerontologie und Geriatrie, 39*(1), 33–40.

Hoppmann, C., & Smith, J. (2007). Life- history related differences in possible selves in very old age. *International Journal of Aging & Human Development, 64*(2), 109–127.

Horizons Women's Health Care. (2013). What are STIs? Retrieved from http://www.horizonswomens.com/what-are-stis.

Horn, I. B., Brenner, R., Rao, M., Cheng, T. L. (2006). Beliefs about the appropriate age for initiating toilet training: Are there racial and socioeconolmic differences? *The Journal of Pediatrics, 149*(2), 165–168.

Horn, J. L., & Noll, J. (1997). Human cognitive capabilities: Gf-Gc theory. In D. P. Flanagan, J. L. Genshaft, & P. L. Harrison (Eds.), *Contemporary intellectual assessment: Theories, tests, and issues* (pp. 53–91). New York: Guilford Press.

Horton, S. M. (2008). Aging stereotypes: Effects on the performance and health of seniors. *Dissertation Abstracts International Section A: Humanities and Social Sciences. 68*(8-A), 3540.

Hossain, M., Chetana, M., & Devi, P. U. (2005). Late effect of prenatal irradiation on the hippocampal histology and brain weight in adult mice. *International Journal of Developmental Neuroscience, 23*(4), 307–313.

Hostetler, A. J., Sweet, S., & Moen, P. (2007). Gendered career paths: A life course perspective on returning to school. *Sex Roles, 56*(1–2), 85–103.

Hough, M. S. (2007). Adult age differences in word fluency for common and goal-directed categories. *Advances in Speech Language Pathology, 9*(2), 154–161.

Huang, J. (2007). Hormones and female sexuality. In A. F. Owens & M. S. Tepper

(Eds.), Sexual health (Vol 2): Physical foundations (pp. 43–78). *Praeger perspectives: Sex, love, and psychology*. Westport, CT: Praeger Publishers/ Greenwood Publishing Group.

Huang, S-L., Li, C-M, Yang, C-Y., Chen, J-J. (2009, June). Application of reminiscence treatment on older people with dementia: A case study in Pingtung, Taiwan. *Journal of Nursing Research, 17*(2). Retrieved from http://journals.lww.com/jnr-twna/Abstract/2009/06000/Application_of_Reminiscence_Treatment_on_Older.6.aspx.

Huerta, M., Adema, W., Baxter, J., Corak, M., Deding, M., Gray, M.C., et al. (2011). Early maternal employment and child development in five OECD countries, OECD Social, Employment and Migration Working Papers, No. 118, OECD Publishing. Retrieved from http://dx.doi.org/10.1787/5kg5dlmtxhvh-en.

Huestis, M. A., et al. (2002). Drug abuse's smallest victims: in utero drug exposure. *Forensic Science International, 128*(2), 20.

Huizink, A. C., & Mulder, E. J. H. (2006). Maternal smoking, drinking or cannabis use during pregnancy and neurobehavioral and cognitive functioning in human offspring. *Neuroscience & Biobehavioral Reviews, 30*(1), 24–41.

Hultsch, D. F., Hertzog, C., Dixon, R.A., & Small, B. J. (1998). *Memory change in the aged.* New York: Cambridge University Press.

Human Resources and Skills Development Canada. (2010a). *Family life—Age of mother at childbirth.* Retrieved from http://www4.hrsdc.gc.ca/.3ndic.1t.4r@-eng.jsp?iid=75.

Human Resources and Skills Development Canada. (2010b). Indicators of Well Being in Canada: Social participation—Volunteering. Retrieved from http://www4.hrsdc.gc.ca/.3ndic.1t.4r@-eng.jsp?iid=74.

Human Resources and Skills Development Canada. (2013a). Family life: Age of mother at childbirth. Retrieved from http://www4.hrsdc.gc.ca/.3ndic.1t.4r@-eng.jsp?iid=75.

Human Resources and Skills Development Canada. (2013b). Family life: Marriage. Retrieved from http://www4.hrsdc.gc.ca/.3ndic.1t.4r@-eng.jsp?iid=78.

Human Resources and Skills Development Canada. (2013c). Health—Low birth rate. Retrieved from http://www4.hrsdc.gc.ca/.3ndic.1t.4r@-eng.jsp?iid=4.

Human Resources and Skills Development Canada. (2013d). Health—Self-rated health. Retrieved from http://www4.hrsdc.gc.ca/.3ndic.1t.4r@-eng.jsp?iid=10.

Human Rights Campaign Foundation. (2013). A resource guide to coming out. Retrieved from http://www.hrc.org/resources/entry/resource-guide-to-coming-out.

Hunt, C. E., & Hauck, F. R. (2006). Sudden infant death syndrome. *Canadian Medical Association Journal, 174*(13), 1861–1869.

Hunter, M. (2016). Children as young as three convinced they are born in the wrong body: Toddlers are among 1,500 under-16s sent to a 'transgender identity clinic.' *MailOnline*. Retrieved from http://www.dailymail.co.uk/news/article-3590175/Children-young-THREE-convinced-born-wrong-body-Toddlers-1-500-16s-sent-transgender-identity-clinic.html.

Huntington Society of Canada. (n.d.). What is Huntington disease? Retrieved from http://www.huntingtonsociety.ca/english/index.asp.

Hurd, Y. L., et al. (2005). Marijuana impairs growth in mid–gestation fetuses. *Neurotoxicology and Teratology, 27*(2), 221–229.

Hursting, D., Dunlap, S., Ford, N., Hursting, M., & Lashinger, L. (2013). Calorie restriction and cancer prevention: A mechanistic perspective. *BioMed Central.*

https://cancerandmetabolism.biomedcentral.com/articles/10.1186/2049-3002-1-10.

Hursting, S. D., Lavigne, J. A., Berrigan, D., Perkins, S. N., & Barrett, J. C. (2003). Calorie restriction, aging, and cancer prevention: Mechanisms of action and applicability to humans. *Annual Review of Medicine, 54*(131–152).

Hussain, A. (2002, June 26) It's official. Men really are afraid of commitment. Reuters.

Hyde, J. S., Fennema, E., & Lamon, S. J. (1990). Gender differences in mathematics performance: A meta-analysis. *Psychological Bulletin, 107,* 139–155.

Hyde, J. S., Lindberg, S. M., Linn, M. C., Ellis, A. B., & Williams, C. C. (2008). Gender similarities characterize math performance. *Science, 321,* 494–495.

Hynes, M., Sheik, M., Wilson, H. G., & Spiegel, P. (2002). Reproductive health indicators and outcomes among refugee and internally displaced persons in postemergency phase camps. *Journal of the American Medical Association, 288,* 595–603.

I

Immunization Action Coalition. (n.d.). Evidence shows vaccines unrelated to autism.

Retrieved July 21, 2016 from http://www.immunize.org/catg.d/p4028.pdf

National Institutes of Health. (2007, April 10). Infant and toddler nutrition. National Institutes of Health, Department of Health and Human Services. Retrieved from http://www.nlm.nih.gov/medlineplus/infantandtoddlernutrition.html.

International Human Genome Sequencing Consortium (2006). A global map of p53 transcription-factor binding sites in the human genome. *Cell, 124*(1), 207–219.

Intersex Society of North America. (2008). What is intersex? Retrieved on October 15, 2016, from http://www.isna.org/faq/frequency.

Ipsos Reid. (2006). 1/2 of Canadians say they have no control over stress levels. Retrieved from http://www.marketwire.com/press-release/-of Canadians-Say-They-Have-No-Control-Over-Stress-Levels-598798.htm.

J

Jacobs, D. M., Levy, G., & Marder, K. (2006). Dementia in Parkinson's disease, Huntington's disease, and related disorders. In M. J. Farah & T. E. Feinberg (Eds.), *Patient-based approaches to cognitive neuroscience* (2nd ed.) (pp. 381–395). Cambridge, MA: MIT Press.

Jacobs, J. E., Davis-Kean, P., Bleeker, M., Eccles, J. S., & Malanchuk, O. (2005). "I can, but I don't want to": The impact of parents, interests, and activities on gender differences in math. In A. M. Gallagher & J. C. Kaufman (Eds.), *Gender differences in mathematics: An integrative psychological approach* (pp. 246–263). New York: Cambridge University Press.

Jacobs, S. (1993). *Pathologic grief: Maladaptation to loss.* Washington, DC: American Psychiatric Press.

Jacobsen, J. S., et al. (2006). Early-onset behavioral and synaptic deficits in a mouse model of Alzheimer's disease. *Proceedings of the National Academy of Sciences, 103,* 5161–5166.

Jacobson, P. F., & Schwartz, R. G. (2005). English past tense use in bilingual children with language impairment. *American Journal of Speech-Language Pathology, 14*(4), 313–323.

Jang, Y., Kim, G., Chiriboga, D. A., & Cho, S. (2008). Willingness to use a nursing home. *Journal of Applied Gerontology, 27*(1), 110–117.

Janssen, E. (Ed). (2006). *The psychophysiology of sex.* Bloomington, IN: Indiana University Press.

Janssen, I. (2012). Healthy weights. In Public Health Agency of Canada, *The health of Canada's young people: A mental health focus.* Retrieved from http://www.phac-aspc.gc.ca/hp-ps/dca-dea/publications/hbsc-mental-mentale/weight-poids-eng.php.

Janz, T. (2012). Health at a glance: Current smoking trends. Ottawa: Statistics Canada. Retrieved from http://www.statcan.gc.ca/pub/82-624-x/2012001/article/11676-eng.htm.

Jayson, S. (2008, June 8). More view cohabitation as acceptable choice. *USA Today.* Retrieved from http://www.usatoday.com/news/nation/2008-06-08-cohabitation-study_N.htm. Accessed October 2, 2008.

Jepsen, D. A., & Choudhuri, E. (2001). Stability and change in 25-year occupational career patterns. *Career Development Quarterly, 50*(1), 3–19.

Johannes, C. B., et al. (2000). Incidence of erectile dysfunction in men 40 to 69 years old: Longitudinal results from the Massachusetts male aging study. *The Journal of Urology, 163,* 460.

Johnson, A. (2011, March 7). Latimer: No regrets about killing disabled daughter. Retrieved from http://www.ctvnews.ca/latimer-no-regrets-about-killing-disabled-daughter-1.615463.

Johnson, J. G., Zhang, B., & Prigerson, H. G. (2008). Investigation of a developmental model of risk for depression and suicidality following spousal bereavement. *Suicide and Life-Threatening Behavior, 38*(1), 1–12.

Johnson, K. (2008). Fostering attachment in the child care setting for infants and toddlers. Retrieved from http://www.earlychildhoodnews.com/earlychildhood/article_view.aspx?ArticleID=715.

Johnson, S. K. (2008, May). "I don't want to nap." *Parents Magazine*. Retrieved from http://www.parents.com/toddlers-preschoolers/sleep/naps/i-dont-wanna-nap/.

Johnson, W., & Bouchard, T. J., Jr., (2007). Sex differences in mental abilities: g masks the dimensions on which they lie. *Intelligence, 35*(1), 23–39.

Johnson, W., & Krueger, R. F. (2006). How money buys happiness: Genetic and environmental processes linking finances and life satisfaction. *Journal of Personality and Social Psychology, 90*(4), 680–691.

Jones, A., Gulbis, A., & Baker, E. H. (2010). Differences in tobacco use between Canada and the United States. *International Journal of Public Health, 55*(3), 167–175.

Jones B. C., et al. (2008). Effects of menstrual cycle phase on face preferences. *Archives of Sexual Behaviour, 37*(1), 78–84.

Jones, D. C., & Crawford, J. K. (2006). The peer appearance culture during adolescence: Gender and body mass variations. *Journal of Youth and Adolescence, 35*(2), 257–269.

Jones, E., & Herbert, J. (2006). Exploring memory in infancy: Deferred imitation and the development of declarative memory. *Infant and Child Development, 15*, 195–205.

Jones, S. S., & Hong, H-W. (2005). How some infant smiles get made. *Infant Behavior & Development, 28*(2), 194–205.

Jonkman, S. (2006). Sensitization facilitates habit formation: Implications for addiction. *Journal of Neuroscience, 26*(28), 7319–7320.

Jordan, J. V., Kaplan, A. G., Miller, J. B., Stiver, I. P., & Surrey, J. L. (1991). *Women's growth in connection.* New York: Guilford Press.

Jorgensen, G. (2006). Kohlberg and Gilligan: Duet or duel? *Journal of Moral Education, 35*(2), 179–196.

Joshi, R. M. (2003). Misconceptions about the assessment and diagnosis of reading disability. *Reading Psychology, 24*(3–4), 247–266.

Joung, H-M., & Miller, N. J. (2007). Examining the effects of fashion activities on life satisfaction of older females: Activity theory revisited. *Family & Consumer Sciences Research Journal, 35*(4), 338–356.

Judge, T. A., & Klinger, R. (2008). Job satisfaction: Subjective well-being at work. In M. Eid, & R. J. Larsen (Eds.), *The science of subjective well-being* (pp. 393–413). New York: Guilford Press.

K

Kail, R. V., & Cavanaugh, J. C. (2009). *Human Development* (2nd ed.). Nelson Education Ltd.

Kagan, L. J., MacLeod, A. K., & Pote, H. L. (2004). Accessibility of causal explanations for future positive and negative events in adolescents with anxiety and depression. *Clinical Psychology and Psychotherapy, 11*(3), 177–186.

Holt, T., Greene, L., & Davis, J. (2003). *National Survey of Adolescents and Young Adults: Sexual health knowledge, attitudes, and experiences.* Menlo Park, CA: Henry J. Kaiser Family Foundation.

Kaminski, P. L., & Hayslip, B., Jr. (2006). Gender differences in body esteem among older adults. *Journal of Women & Aging, 18*(3), 19–35.

Kaminski, R. A., & Stormshak, E. A. (2007). Project STAR: Early intervention with preschool children and families for the prevention of substance abuse. In P. Tolan, J. Szapocznik, & S. Sambrano (Eds.), *Preventing youth substance abuse: Science-based programs for children and adolescents* (pp. 89–109). Washington, DC: American Psychological Association.

Kanevsky, L., & Geake, J. (2004). Inside the zone of proximal development: Validating a multifactor model of learning potential with gifted students and their peers. *Journal for the Education of the Gifted, 28*(2), 182–217.

Kang, S. (2004). Substance use disorders in pregnancy and postpartum. Retrieved from http://heretohelp.bc.ca/visions/women-vol2/substance-use-disorders-in-pregnancy-and-postpartum.

Karatekin, C., Marcus, D. J., & White, T. (2007). Oculomotor and manual indexes of incidental and intentional spatial sequence learning during middle childhood and adolescence. *Journal of Experimental Child Psychology, 96*(2), 107–130.

Karavasilis, L., Doyle, A. B., & Markiewicz, D. (2003). Associations between parenting style and attachment to mother in middle childhood and adolescence. *International Journal of Behavioral Development, 27*(2), 153–164.

Katz, R., Lowenstein, A., Phillips, J., & Daatland, S. O. (2005). Theorizing inter-generational family relations: Solidarity, conflict, and ambivalence in cross-national contexts. In V. L. Bengtson et al. (Eds.), *Sourcebook of family theory & research* (pp. 393–420). Thousand Oaks, CA: Sage.

Katzman, D. K. (2005). Medical complications in adolescents with anorexia nervosa: A review of the literature. *International Journal of Eating Disorders, 37*(Suppl), S52–S59.

Kauff, N. D., & Offit, K. (2007). Modeling genetic risk of breast cancer. *Journal of the American Medical Association, 297,* 2637–2639.

Kavanagh, K., et al. (2007). Characterization and heritability of obesity and associated risk factors in vervet monkeys. *Obesity, 15*(7), 1666–1674.

Kavanaugh, R. D. (2006). Pretend play. In B. Spodek & O. N. Saracho (Eds.), *Handbook of research on the education of young children* (2nd ed.) (pp. 269–278). Mahwah, NJ: Erlbaum.

Kavcic, T., & Zupancic, M. (2005). Sibling relationship in early/middle childhood: Trait- and dyad-centered approach. *Studia Psychologica, 47*(3), 179–197.

Kavšek, M. (2012). The comparator model of infant visual habituation and dishabituation: Recent insights. *Developmental Psychobiology*, doi: 10.1002/dev.21081.

Kawas, C. H., & Brookmeyer, R. (2001). Aging and the public health effects of dementia. *The New England Journal of Medicine, 344,* 1160–1161.

Kaye, W. H., et al. (2004). Genetic analysis of bulimia nervosa: Methods and sample description. *International Journal of Eating Disorders, 35*(4), 556–570.

Kazdin, A. E. (2000). Treatments for aggressive and antisocial children. *Child and Adolescent Psychiatric Clinics of North America, 9*(4), 841–858.

Kazui, H., et al. (2008). Association between quality of life of demented patients and professional knowledge of care workers. *Journal of Geriatric Psychiatry and Neurology, 21*(1), 72–78.

Kearney, C. A., & Bensaheb, A. (2007). Assessing anxiety disorders in children and adolescents. In S. R. Smith & L. Handler (Eds.), *The clinical assessment of children and adolescents: A practitioner's handbook* (pp. 467–483). Mahwah, NJ: Erlbaum.

Keen, D., Rodger, S., Doussin, K., & Braithwaite, M. (2007). A pilot study of the effects of a social-pragmatic intervention on the communication and symbolic play of children with autism. *Autism, 11*(1), 63–71.

Keller, H., Kärtner, J., Borke, J., Yovsi, R., & Kleis, A. (2005). Parenting styles and the development of the categorical self: A longitudinal study on mirror self-recognition in Cameroonian Nso and German families. *International Journal of Behavioral Development, 29*(6), 496–504.

Kellman, P. J., & Arterberry, M. E. (2006). Infant visual perception. In D. Kuhn et al. (Eds.), *Handbook of child psychology: Vol. 2, Cognition, perception, and language* (6th ed.) (pp. 109–160). Hoboken, NJ: Wiley.

Kellogg, R. (1959). *What children scribble and why.* Oxford: National Press.

Kellogg, R. (1970). Understanding children's art. In P. Cramer (Ed.), *Readings in developmental psychology today.* Del Mar, CA: CRM.

Kemp, C. L. (2005). Dimensions of grandparent–adult grandchild relationships: From family ties to intergenerational friendships. *Canadian Journal on Aging, 24*(2), 161–178.

Kempes, M., Matthys, W., de Vries, H., & van Engeland, H. (2005). Reactive and proactive aggression in children: A review of theory, findings and the relevance for child and adolescent psychiatry. *European Child & Adolescent Psychiatry, 14*(1), 11–19.

Kendler, K. S., Gardner, C. O., Gatz, M., & Pedersen, N. L. (2007). The sources of co-morbidity between major depression and generalized anxiety disorder in a Swedish national twin sample. *Psychological Medicine, 37*(3), 453–462.

Kennard, J. (2012). Health sperm: Maximize your fertility. Retrieved from http://menshealth.about.com/cs/stds/a/healthy_sperm.htm.

Kennedy, B. (2013). Ontario youth soccer to stop keeping score, standings. Retrieved from http://www.thestar.com/sports/soccer/2013/02/16/ontario_youth_soccer_to_stop_keeping_score_standings.html.

Kennedy-Moore, E. (2013). Popular kids: Why are some children popular? *Psychology Today*. Retrieved August 20, 2016, from https://www.psychologytoday.com/blog/growing-friendships/201312/popular-kids.

Keogh, A. F., & Whyte, J. (2006). Exploring children's concepts of intelligence through ethnographic methods. *Irish Journal of Psychology, 27*(1–2), 69–78.

Kerns, K. A., Abraham, M. M., Schlegelmilch, A., & Morgan, T. A. (2007). Mother–child attachment in later middle childhood: Assessment approaches and associations with mood and emotion regulation. *Attachment & Human Development, 9*(1), 33–53.

Khamsi, R. (2007). Active parents make for active kids. Retrieved from http://www.newscientist.com/article/dn12950-active-parents-make-for-active-kids.html#.UheyxNKTiSp.

Kidd, E., & Bavin, E. L. (2007). Lexical and referential influences on on-line spoken language comprehension: A comparison of adults and primary-school-age children. *First Language, 27*(1), 29–52.

Kidsafe Foundation (2016). Be your kid's best parent, not their best friend! Retrieved from http://www.modernmom.com/bd0adc74-3b35-11e3-be8a-bc764e04a41e.html.

Kidshealth. (2010). Infections: Toxoplasmosis. Retrieved from http://kidshealth.org/parent/infections/parasitic/toxoplasmosis.html

Kids Help Phone. (2014). Cyberbullying. Retrieved from http://www.kidshelpphone.ca/Kids/InfoBooth/Bullying/Cyberbullying.aspx.

Killen, M., & Smetana, J. G. (Eds.). (2006). *Handbook of moral development*. Mahwah, NJ: Erlbaum.

Kim, J., Yamada, N., Heo, J., & Han, A. (2014). Health benefits of serious involvement in leisure activities among older Korean adults. *International Journal of Qualitative Studies on Health and Well-Being, 9*:1–9.

Kim, J-Y., McHale, S. M., Osgood, D. W., & Crouter, A. C. (2006). Longitudinal course and family correlates of sibling relationships from childhood through adolescence. *Child Development, 77*(6), 1746–1761.

King, J., MacKay, M., Sirnick, A., & The Canadian Shaken Baby Group. (2003). Shaken baby syndrome in Canada: Clinical characteristics and outcomes of hospital cases. *Canadian Medical Association Journal, 168*(2), 155–159. Retrieved from http://www.cmaj.ca/cgi/content/full/168/2/155.

King, P. M., & Kitchener, K. S. (2004). Reflective judgment. *Educational Psychologist, 39*(1), 5–18.

King, V., & Scott, M. E. (2005). A comparison of cohabiting relationships among older and younger adults. *Journal of Marriage and Family, 67*(2), 271–285.

Kingston, A., (2007, January 29). The 27-year itch. *Maclean's*. Retrieved from http://www.macleans.ca/article.jsp? content=20070129_140063_140063.

Kinsbourne, M. (2003). The corpus callosum equilibrates the cerebral hemispheres. In E. Zaidel & M. Iacoboni (Eds.), *The parallel brain: The cognitive neuroscience of the corpus callosum* (pp. 271–281). Cambridge, MA: MIT Press.

Kirby, P. G., Biever, J. L., Martinez, I. G., & Gómez, J. P. (2004). Adults returning to school: The impact on family and work. *Journal of Psychology: Interdisciplinary and Applied, 138*(1), 65–76.

Kirkcaldy, B. D., Shephard, R. J., & Siefen, R. G. (2002). The relationship between physical activity and self-image and problem behaviour among adolescents. *Social Psychiatry and Psychiatric Epidemiology, 37*(11), 544–550.

Kirkey, S. (2013). Only 20 per cent doctors would perform euthanasia if legal, poll of MDs finds. Retrieved from CBC News. (2012a, October 12). Inside Gloria Taylor's battle for the right to die. Retrieved from http://www.canada.com/news/Only+cent+doctors+would+perform+ euthanasia+legal+poll+finds/7939308/story.html.

Kistner, J. (2006). Children's peer acceptance, perceived acceptance, and risk for depression. In T. E. Joiner, J. S. Brown, & J. Kistner (Eds.), *The interpersonal, cognitive, and social nature of depression* (pp. 1–21). Mahwah, NJ: Erlbaum.

Kjelsås, E., Bjornstrom, C., & Götestam, K. G. (2004). Prevalence of eating disorders in female and male adolescents (14–15 years). *Eating Behaviors, 5*(1), 13–25.

Kleiber, D. A., & Kelly, J. R. (1980). Leisure, socialization, and the life cycle. In S. E. Iso-Ahola (Ed.), *Social psychological perspectives on leisure and recreation* (pp. 91–137). Springfield, IL: Charles C. Thomas.

Kliegel, M., Jäger, T., & Phillips, L. H. (2008). Adult age differences in event-based prospective memory: A meta-analysis on the role of focal versus nonfocal cues. *Psychology and Aging, 23*(1), 203–208.

Klein, P. J., & Meltzoff, A. N. (1999). Long-term memory, forgetting and deferred imitation in 12-month-old infants. *Developmental Science, 2*(1), 102–113.

Klier, C. M. (2006). Mother–infant bonding disorders in patients with postnatal depression: The Postpartum Bonding Questionnaire in clinical practice. *Archives of Women's Mental Health, 9*(5), 289–291.

Klintsova, A. Y., & Greenough, W. T. (1999). Synaptic plasticity in cortical systems. *Current Opinion in Neurobiology, 9*(2), 203–208.

Kloep, M., & Hendry, L. B. (2007). Retirement: A new beginning? *The Psychologist, 20*(12), 742–745.

Klohnen, E. C., & Luo, S. (2003). Interpersonal attraction and personality: What is attractive–self similarity, ideal similarity, complementarity or attachment security? *Journal of Personality and Social Psychology, 85*(4), 709–722.

Knaak, S. (2005). Breast-feeding, bottle-feeding and Dr. Spock: The shifting context of choice. *Canadian Review of Sociology and Anthropology, 42*(2), 197–216.

Knafo, A., & Plomin, R. (2006a). Parental discipline and affection and children's prosocial behavior: Genetic and environmental links. *Journal of Personality and Social Psychology, 90*(1), 147–164.

Knafo, A., & Plomin, R. (2006b). Prosocial behavior from early to middle childhood: Genetic and environmental influences on stability and change. *Developmental Psychology, 42*(5), 771–786.

Kniffin, K. M., & Wilson, D. S. (2004). The effect of nonphysical traits on the perception of physical attractiveness: Three naturalistic studies. *Evolution and Human Behavior, 25*(2), 88–101.

Kochanska, G., Coy, K. C., Murray, K. T. (2001). The development of self-regulation in the first four years of life. *Child Development, 72*(4), 1091–1111.

Kohl, C. (2004). Postpartum psychoses: Closer to schizophrenia or the affective spectrum? *Current Opinion in Psychiatry, 17*(2), 87–90.

Kohl, J. V. (2007). The mind's eyes: Human pheromones, neuroscience, and male sexual preferences. *Journal of Psychology & Human Sexuality, 18*(4), 313–369.

Kohlberg, L. (1963). Moral development and identification. In H. W. Stevenson (Ed.), *Child psychology: 62nd yearbook of the National Society for the Study of Education.* Chicago: University of Chicago Press.

Kohlberg, L. (1966). Cognitive stages and preschool education. *Human Development, 9,* 5–17.

Kohlberg, L. (1969). Stage and sequence: The cognitive-developmental approach to socialization. In D. A. Goslin (Ed.), *Handbook of socialization theory and research.* Chicago: Rand McNally.

Kohlberg, L. (1981). *The meaning and measurement of moral development.* Worcester, MA: Clark University Press.

Kohlberg, L. (1985). *The psychology of moral development.* San Francisco: Harper & Row.

Kohlberg, L., & Kramer, R. (1969). Continuities and discontinuities in childhood and adult moral development. *Human Development, 12,* 93–120.

Kolata, G. (2007, May 8). Genes take charge, and diets fall by the wayside. *New York Times online.*

Kolb, B., & Gibb, R. (2007). Brain plasticity and recovery from early cortical injury. *Developmental Psychobiology, 49*(2), 107–118.

Konijn, E. A., Bijvank, M. N., & Bushman, B. J. (2007). I wish I were a warrior: The role of wishful identification in the effects of violent video games on aggression in adolescent boys. *Developmental Psychology, 43*(4), 1038–1044.

Kopp, C. B. (1989). Regulation of distress and negative emotions: A developmental view. *Developmental Psychology, 25,* 343–354.

Korff, S. C. (2006). Religious orientation as a predictor of life satisfaction within the elderly population. *Dissertation Abstracts International: Section B: The Sciences and Engineering. 67*(1-B), 2006, 550.

Krackow, E., & Lynn, S. J. (2003). Is there touch in the game of Twister®? The effects of innocuous touch and suggestive questions on children's eyewitness memory. *Law and Human Behavior, 27,* 589–604.

Krebs, D. L., & Denton, K. (2005). Toward a more pragmatic approach to morality: A critical evaluation of Kohlberg's model. *Psychological Review, 112*(3), 629–649.

Kristensen, P., & Bjerkedal, T. (2007). Explaining the relation between birth order and intelligence. *Science, 313*(5832), 1717.

Kroeger, K. A., & Nelson, W. M., III. (2006). A language programme to increase the verbal production of a child dually diagnosed with Down syndrome and autism. *Journal of Intellectual Disability Research, 50*(2), 101–108.

Krojgaard, P. (2005). Continuity and discontinuity in developmental psychology. *Psyke & Logos, 26*(2), 377–394.

Krueger, C., Holditch-Davis, D., Quint, S., & DeCasper, A. (2004). Recurring auditory experience in the 28- to 34-week-old fetus. *Infant Behavior & Development, 27*(4), 537–543.

Kübler-Ross, E. (1969). *On death and dying.* New York: Macmillan.

Kübler-Ross, E., & Kessler, D. (2005). *On grief and grieving.* New York: Scribner.

Kuczaj, S. A., II (1982). On the nature of syntactic development. In S. A. Kuczaj II (Ed.), *Language development,* Vol. 1, *Syntax and semantics.* Hillsdale, NJ: Erlbaum.

Kuczmarski, R. J., Ogden, C. L., Guo, S. S., Grummer-Strawn, L. M., Flegal, K. M., Mei, Z., . . . Johnson, C.L. (2002). 2000 Center for Disease Control growth charts for the United States: Methods and development. Center for Disease Control and Prevention, Vital and Health Statistics, Series 11, (no. 246), 1–190.

Kuhl, P. K., et al. (1997). Cross-language analysis of phonetic units in language addressed to infants. *Science, 277*(5326), 684–686.

Kuhl, P. K., et al. (2006). Infants show a facilitation effect for native language phonetic perception between 6 and 12 months. *Developmental Science, 9*(2) F13–F21.

Kuhn, D. (2007). Editorial. *Cognitive Development, 22*(1), 1–2.

Kulick, D. (2006). Regulating sex: The politics of intimacy and identity. *Sexualities, 9*(1), 122–124.

Kulik, L. (2000). Women face unemployment: A comparative analysis of age groups. *Journal of Career Development, 27*(1), 15–33.

Kulik, L. (2004). Perceived equality in spousal relations, marital quality, and life satisfaction. *Families in Society, 85*(2), 243–250.

Kumar, K. (2010). A journey towards creating an inclusive classroom: How Universal Design for Learning has transformed my teaching. *Transformative Dialogues: Teaching & Learning Journal, 4*(2). Retrieved from http://kwantlen.ca/TD/TD.4.2/TD.4.2.5_Kumar_Inclusive_Classroom.pdf.

Kunz, J. A. (2007). The life story matrix. In J. A. Kunz, & F. G. Soltys (Eds.), *Transformational reminiscence: Life story work* (pp. 1–16). New York: Springer Publishing Co.

Kunzmann, U., & Baltes, P. B. (2005). The psychology of wisdom: Theoretical and empirical challenges. In R. J. Sternberg, & J. Jordan (Eds.), *A handbook of wisdom: Psychological perspectives* (pp. 110–135). New York: Cambridge University Press.

Kurdek, L. A. (2005). What do we know about gay and lesbian couples? *Current Directions in Psychological Science, 14*(5), 251.

Kurdek, L. A. (2006). Differences between partners from hetersosexual, gay, and lesbian cohabiting couples. *Journal of Marriage and the Family, 68*(2), 509–528.

Kvaal, K., et al. (2008). Co-occurrence of anxiety and depressive disorders in a community sample of older people. *International Journal of Geriatric Psychiatry, 23*(3), 229–237.

Kwok, H-K. (2006). A study of the sandwich generation in Hong Kong. *Current Sociology, 54*(2), 257–272.

Kwok, H. W. M. (2003). Psychopharmacology in autism spectrum disorders. *Current Opinion in Psychiatry, 16*(5), 529–534.

L

Labouvie-Vief, G. (2006). Emerging structures of adult thought. In J. J. Arnett & J. L. Tanner (Eds.). *Emerging adults in America.* (pp. 59–84). Washington, DC: American Psychological Association.

Labouvie-Vief, G., & González, M. M. (2004). Dynamic integration: Affect optimization and differentiation in development. In D. Y. Dai & R. J. Sternberg (Eds.), *Motivation, emotion, and cognition* (pp. 237–272). Mahwah, NJ: Erlbaum.

Labrell, F., & Ubersfeld, G. (2004). Parental verbal strategies and children's capacities at 3 and 5 years during a memory task. *European Journal of Psychology of Education, 19*(2), 189–202.

Lachman, M. E. (2004). Development in midlife. *Annual Review of Psychology, 55,* 305–331.

Laflamme, D., Pomerleau, A., & Malcuit, G. (2002). A comparison of fathers' and mothers' involvement in childcare and stimulation behaviors during free-play with their infants at 9 and 15 months. *Sex Roles, 47*(11–12), 507–518.

Lai, H-L., et al. (2006). Randomized controlled trial of music during kangaroo care on maternal state anxiety and preterm infants' responses. *International Journal of Nursing Studies, 43*(2), 139–146.

Lam, K. S. L., Aman, M. G., & Arnold, L. E. (2006). Neurochemical correlates of autistic disorder: A review of the literature. *Research in Developmental Disabilities, 27*(3), 254–289.

Lam, T. H., Shi, H. J., Ho, L. M., Stewart, S. M., & Fan, S. (2002). Timing of pubertal maturation and heterosexual behavior among Hong Kong Chinese adolescents. *Archives of Sexual Behavior, 31*(4), 359–366.

Lamb, M. E., & Ahnert, L. (2006). Nonparental child care: Context, concepts, correlates, and consequences. In K. A. Renninger, I. E. Sigel, W. Damon, & R. M. Lerner (Eds.), *Handbook of child psychology* (6th ed.), Vol. 4, *Child psychology in practice* (pp. 950–1016). Hoboken, NJ: Wiley.

Lamers, C. T. J., Bechara, A., Rizzo, M., & Ramaekers, J. G. (2006). Cognitive function and mood in MDMA/THC users, THC users and non-drug using controls. *Journal of Psychopharmacology, 20*(2), 302–311.

Landsford, J. E. (2009). Parental divorce and children's adjustment. *Perspectives on Psychological Science 4*(2), 140–152.

Langlois, C. (2013). Stages of puberty: Help your children feel positive about the changes in their body. *Canadian Living.* Retrieved from http://www.canadianliving.com/moms/teens/stages_of _puberty.php.

Langlois, J. H., et al. (2000). Maxims or myths of beauty? A meta-analytic and theoretical review. *Psychological Bulletin, 126*(3), 390–423.

Lansford, J. E., Malone, P. S., Castellino, D. R., Dodge, K. A., Pettit, G. S., & Bates, J. E. (2006). Trajectories of internalizing, externalizing, and grades for children who have and have not experienced their parents' divorce or separation. *Journal of Family Psychology. 20*(2), 292–301.

Lantolf, J. P., & Thorne, S. L. (2007). Sociocultural theory and second language learning. In B. VanPatten & J. Williams (Eds.), *Theories in second language acquisition: An introduction* (pp. 201–224). Mahwah, NJ: Erlbaum.

LaPointe, L. L. (Ed.). (2005). Feral children. *Journal of Medical Speech-Language Pathology, 13*(1), vii–ix.

Lapsley, D. K. (2006). Moral stage theory. In K. Killen & J. G. Smetana (Eds.), *Handbook of moral development* (pp. 37–66). Mahwah, NJ: Erlbaum.

Larroque, B., et al. (2005). Temperament at 9 months of very preterm infants born at less than 29 weeks' gestation: The Epipage study. *Journal of Developmental & Behavioral Pediatrics, 26*(1), 48–55.

Latham, G. P., & Budworth, M.-H. (2007). The study of work motivation in the 20th century. In L. L. Koppes, (Ed.), *Historical perspectives in industrial and organizational psychology* (pp. 353–381). Mahwah, NJ: Erlbaum.

Lattanzi-Licht, Marcia. (2007). Religion, spirituality, and dying. In D. Balk, et al. (Eds.), *Handbook of thanatology* (pp. 11–17). New York: Routledge/Taylor & Francis Group.

Lau, A. S., Litrownik, A. J., Newton, R. R., Black, M. M., & Everson, M. D. (2006). Factors affecting the link between physical discipline and child externalizing problems in Black and White families. *Journal of Community Psychology, 34*(1), 89–103.

Laumann, E. O., et al. (2006). Sexual activity, sexual disorders and associated help-seeking behavior among mature adults in five Anglophone countries from the Global Survey of Sexual Attitudes and Behaviors. *Archives of Sexual Behavior, 35*(2), 145–161.

Laumann, E. O., Gagnon, J. H., Michael, R. T., & Michaels, S. (1994). *The social organization of sexuality.* Chicago: University of Chicago Press.

Laumann, E. O., Mahay, J., & Youm, Y. (2007). Sex, intimacy, and family life in the United States. In M. Kimmel (Ed.), *The sexual self: The construction of sexual scripts* (pp. 165–190). Nashville, TN: Vanderbilt University Press.

Launslager, D. (2009). *Helping families to prepare for multiple-birth children*. Ottawa: Multiple Births Canada. Retrieved from http://www.beststart.org/events/detail/bsannualconf09/webcov/presentations/B4-Report-Donna%20Laugslager.pdf.

Laurendeau, M., & Pinard, A. (1970). *The development of the concept of space in the child.* New York: International Universities Press.

Lawrence, E., Nylen, K., & Cobb, R. J. (2007). Prenatal expectations and marital satisfaction over the transition to parenthood. *Journal of Family Psychology, 21*(2), 155–164.

Lawrence, E. B., & Bradbury, T. N. (2007). Trajectories of change in physical aggression and marital satisfaction. *Journal of Family Psychology, 21*(2), 236–247.

Leaper, C. (2002). Parenting girls and boys. In M. H. Bornstein (Ed.), *Handbook of parenting* (2nd ed.), Vol. 1, *Children and parenting* (pp. 189–225). Mahwah, NJ: Erlbaum.

Lecanuet, J. P., Graniere-Deferre, C., Jacquet, A.-Y., & DeCasper, A. J. (2000). Fetal discrimination of low-pitched musical notes. *Developmental Psychobiology, 36*(1), 29–39.

Leclerc, C. M., & Hess, T. M. (2007). Age differences in the bases for social judgments: Tests of a social expertise perspective. *Experimental Aging Research, 33*(1), 95–120.

Leder, S., Grinstead, L. N., & Torres, E. (2007). Grandparents raising grandchildren: Stressors, social support, and health outcomes. *Journal of Family Nursing, 13*(3), 333–352.

Leerkes, E. M., & Crockenberg, S. C. (2006). Antecedents of mothers' emotional and cognitive responses to infant distress: The role of family, mother, and infant characteristics. *Infant Mental Health Journal, 27*(4), 405–428.

Lefkowitz, E. S., & Zeldow, P. B. (2006). Masculinity and femininity predict optimal mental health: A belated test of the androgyny hypothesis. *Journal of Personality Assessment, 87*(1), 95–101.

Legro, R. S., et al. (2007). Clomiphene, metformin, or both for infertility in the polycystic ovary syndrome. *New England Journal of Medicine, 356*(6), 551–566.

Lehman, J. (2016). Your child is not your friend. *Empowering Parents*. Retrieved from https://www.empoweringparents.com/article/your-child-is-not-your-friend/.

Lejeune, C., et al. (2006). Prospective multicenter observational study of 260 infants born to 259 opiate-dependent mothers on methadone or high-dose buprenophine substitution. *Drug and Alcohol Dependence, 82*(3), 250–257.

Le Mare, L., & Audet, K. (2006). A longitudinal study of the physical growth and health of postinstitutionalized Romanian adoptee. *Pediatrics & Child Health, 11*(2): 85–91.

Lemaire, P., & Arnaud, L. (2008). Young and older adults' strategies in complex arithmetic. *American Journal of Psychology, 121*(1), 1–16.

Lengua, L., J., Honorado, E., & Bush, N. R. (2007). Contextual risk and parenting as predictors of effortful control and social competence in preschool children. *Journal of Applied Developmental Psychology, 28*(1), 40–55.

Lenneberg, E. H. (1967). *Biological foundations of language.* New York: Wiley.

Leon, K. (2003). Risk and protective factors in young children's adjustment in parental divorce: A review of the research. *Family Relations: An Interdisciplinary Journal of Applied Family Studies 52*(3), 258–270.

Leonardo, E. D., & Hen, R. (2006). Genetics of affective and anxiety disorders. *Annual Review of Psychology. 57,* 117–137.

Leone, J. L. (2000). Psychosocial factors leading to harmony or disharmony in sibling relationships in mid-life when faced with caregiving responsibilities for aging parents. *Dissertation Abstracts International: Section B: The Sciences and Engineering, 61*(4-B), 2245.

Leung, C., McBride-Chang, C., & Lai, B. (2004). Relations among maternal parenting style, academic competence, and life satisfaction in Chinese early adolescents. *Journal of Early Adolescence, 24*(2), 113–143.

Lever, N., et al. (2004). A drop-out prevention program for high-risk inner-city youth. *Behavior Modification, 28*(4), 513–527.

Levine, D. (2000). Virtual attraction: What rocks your boat. *CyberPsychology & Behavior, 3*(4), 565–573.

Levinson, D. J. (1996). *The seasons of a woman's life.* New York: Knopf.

Levinson, D. J., Darrow, C. N, & Klein, E. B. (1978). *Seasons of a man's life.* New York: Knopf.

Levinthal, B. R., & Lleras, A. (2007). The unique contributions of retinal size and perceived size on change detection. *Visual Cognition, 15*(1), 101–105.

Levpušcek, M. P. (2006). Adolescent individuation in relation to parents and friends: Age and gender differences. European *Journal of Developmental Psychology, 3*(3), 238–264.

Lewinsohn, P. M., Rohde, P., Seeley, J. R., Klein, D. N., & Gotlib, I. H. (2000). Natural course of adolescent major depressive disorder in a community sample: Predictors of recurrence in young adults. *American Journal of Psychiatry, 157,* 1584–1591.

Lewis, B. A., et al. (2004). Four-year language outcomes of children exposed to cocaine in utero. *Neurotoxicology and Teratology, 26*(5), 617–627.

Lewis, H. L. (2003). Differences in ego identity among college students across age, ethnicity, and gender. *Identity, 3*(2), 159–189.

Lewis, M., & Feiring, C. (1989). Early predictors of childhood friendship. In T. J. Berndt & G. W. Ladd (Eds.), *Peer relationships in child development.* New York: Wiley.

Li, Q. (2007). New bottle but old wine: A research of cyberbullying in schools. *Computers in Human Behavior, 23*(4), 1777–1791.

Lickliter, R. (2001). The dynamics of language development: From perception to comprehension. *Developmental Science, 4*(1), 21–23.

Ligaya, A. (2013, October 1). Canada ranks in top 5 of world's best places to grow old. *The Financial Post*. Retrieved from http://business.financialpost.com/personal-finance/retirement/sweden-canada-age-watch.

Light, L. L., Patterson, M. M., Chung, C., & Healy, M. R. (2004). Effects of repetition and response deadline on associative recognition in young and older adults. *Memory & Cognition, 32,* 1182–1193.

Lin, Y., Reilly, M., & Mercer, V. S. (2010). Responses to a modified visual cliff by pre-walking infants born preterm and at term. *Physical & Occupational Therapy in Pediatrics*, *30*(1), 66–78.

Lindau, S. T., Schumm, L. P., Laumann, E. O., Levinson, W., O'Muircheartaigh, C. A., & Waite, L. J. (2007). A study of sexuality and health among older adults in the United States. *New England Journal of Medicine, 357*(8), 762–775.

Lindberg, L. D., Jones, R., & Santelli, J. S. (2007). Non-coital sexual activities among adolescents. Retrieved from http://www.guttmacher.org/pubs/JAH_Lindberg.pdf.

Linder, R. (2016). The importance of developing emotional intelligence through education. *The Exceptional Parent 46*(5), 51.

Lipman, E. L., et al. (2006). Testing effectiveness of a community-based aggression management program for children 7 to 11 years old and their families. *Journal of the American Academy of Child & Adolescent Psychiatry, 45*(9), 1085–1093.

Lippa, R. L. (2008). Non-Alzheimer's dementia: Clinical features, management, and genetics. *American Journal of Alzheimer's Disease and Other Dementias, 22*(6), 454–455.

Lipsitt, L. P. (2002). Early experience and behavior in the baby of the twenty-first century. In J. Gomes-Pedro et al. (Eds.), *The infant and family in the twenty-first century* (pp. 55–78). London: Brunner-Routledge.

Lipsitt, L. P. (2003). Crib death: A biobehavioral phenomenon? *Current Directions in Psychological Science, 12*(5), 164–170.

Li-qi, Z., & Fu-xi, F. (2006). Preschool children's understanding of death. *Chinese Journal of Clinical Psychology, 14*(1), 91–93.

Löckenhoff, C. E., & Carstensen, L. L. (2004). Socioemotional selectivity theory, aging, and health: The increasingly delicate balance between regulating emotions and making tough choices. *Journal of Personality, 72*(6), 1395–1424.

Lorant, V., et al. (2005). A European comparative study of marital status and socio-economic inequalities in suicide. *Social Science & Medicine, 60*(11), 2431–2441.

Lorenz, F. O., Wickrama, K. A. S., Conger, R. D., & Elder Jr., G. H. (2006). The short-term and decade-long effects of divorce on women's midlife health. *Journal of Health and Social Behavior, 47*(2), 111–125.

Lorenz, K. (1962). *King Solomon's ring.* London: Methuen.

Lorenz, K. (1981). *The foundations of ethology.* New York: Springer-Verlag.

Lovaas, O. I., Smith, T., & McEachin, J. J. (1989). Clarifying comments on the young autism study: Reply to Schapler, Short, and Mesibov. *Journal of Consulting and Clinical Psychology, 57,* 165–167.

Lubinski, D. (2004). Introduction to the Special Section on Cognitive Abilities: 100 Years After Spearman's (1904) "'General Intelligence,' Objectively Determined and Measured." *Journal of Personality and Social Psychology, 86*(1), 96–111.

Lubinski, D., & Benbow, C. P. (2000). States of excellence. *American Psychologist, 55,* 137–150.

Lucariello, J. M., Hudson, J. A., Fivush, R., & Bauer, P. J. (Eds.). (2004). *The development of the mediated mind: Sociocultural context and cognitive development.* Mahwah, NJ: Erlbaum.

Lucas-Stannard, P. (2013, January 8). 5 myths about gender neutral parenting. *Everyday Feminism*. Retrieved August 6, 2016, from http://everydayfeminism.com/2013/01/gender-neutral-parenting-myths/.

Ludwick, R., & Silva, M. C. (2003, December 19). Ethical challenges in the care of elderly persons. *The Online Journal of Issues in Nursing.* Retrieved from http://nursingworld.org/ojin. Accessed October 5, 2008.

Ludwig, F. M., Hattjar, B., Russell, R. L., & Winston, K. (2007). How caregiving for grandchildren affects grandmothers' meaningful occupations. *Journal of Occupational Science, 14*(1), 40–51.

Lunau, K. (2009, June 29). Are we blushing yet? *macleans.ca.* Retrieved from http://www2.macleans.ca/2009/06/29/are-we-blushing-yet/.

Lund, D. A., & Caserta, M. S. (2001). When the unexpected happens: Husbands coping with the deaths of their wives. In D. A. Lund (Ed.), *Men coping with grief* (pp. 147–167). Amityville, NY: Baywood Publishing Co.

Lupien, S. J., Maheu, F., Tu, M., Fiocco, A., & Schramek, T. E. (2007). The effects of stress and stress hormones on human cognition: Implications for the field of brain and cognition. *Brain and Cognition, 65*(3), 209–237.

Lykken, D. T. (2006a). In C. J. Patrick (Ed.), *Psychopathic personality: The scope of the problem* (pp. 3–13). New York: Guilford.

Lykken, D. T. (2006b). The mechanism of emergenesis. *Genes, Brain & Behavior, 5*(4), 306–310.

Lykken, D. T., & Csikszentmihalyi, M. (2001). Happiness—stuck with what you've got? *Psychologist, 14*(9), 470–472.

Lynne, S. D., Graber, J. A., Nichols, T. R., Brooks-Gunn, J., & Botvin, G. J. (2007). Links between pubertal timing, peer influences, and externalizing behaviors among urban students followed through middle school. *Journal of Adolescent Health, 40*(2), 181.e7–181.e13.

Lyon, G. R., Shaywitz, S. E., & Shaywitz, B. A. (2003). A definition of dyslexia. *Annals of Dyslexia, 53,* 1–14.

Lyons-Ruth, K., Easterbrooks, M. A., & Davidson, C. (1997). Infant attachment strategies, infant mental lag, and maternal depressive symptoms: Predictors of internalizing and externalizing problems at age 7. *Developmental Psychology*, *33*(4), 681–692.

M

Maccoby, E. E. (2002). Parenting effects: Issues and controversies. In J. G. Borkowski et al. (Eds.), *Parenting and the child's world: Influences on academic, intellectual, and social-emotional development* (pp. 35–46). Mahwah, NJ: Erlbaum.

Maccoby, E. E., & Jacklin, C. N. (1974). *The psychology of sex differences.* Stanford, CA: Stanford University Press.

MacDonald, N., Yanchar, N., & Hebert, P. (2007). What's killing and maiming Canada's youth? *Canadian Medical*

Association Journal, 176(6). Retrieved from http://www.cmaj.ca/cgi/content/full/176/6/737.

Macfarlane, A. (1975). Olfaction in the development of social preferences in the human neonate. In M. A. Hofer (Ed.), *Parent– infant interaction.* Amsterdam: Elsevier.

Macfarlane, A. (1977). *The psychology of childbirth.* Cambridge, MA: Harvard University Press.

Maciejewski, P. K., Zhang, B., Block, S. D., & Prigerson, H. G. (2007). An empirical examination of the stage theory of grief. *Journal of the American Medical Association, 297,* 716–723.

Mackic-Magyar, J., & McCracken, J. (2004). Review of autism spectrum disorders: A research review for practitioners. *Journal of Child and Adolescent Psychopharmacology, 14*(1), 17–18.

Maclean, A. M., Walker, L. J., & Matsuba, M. K. (2004). Transcendence and the moral self: Identity integration, religion, and moral life. *Journal for the Scientific Study of Religion, 43*(3), 429–437.

MacQueen, K. (2009). Youth survey: Polite, honest ... bigoted? Immigrant teens find that tolerance goes both ways in Canada. Retrieved from http://www2.macleans.ca/2009/04/10/polite-honest-bigoted/.

Madon, S., et al. (2001). Am I as you see me or do you see me as I am? Self-fulfilling prophecies and self-verification. *Personality and Social Psychology Bulletin, 27*(9), 1214–1224.

Magolda, M. B. B. (2004). Evolution of a constructivist conceptualization of epistemological reflection. *Educational Psychologist, 39*(1), 31–42.

Mahay, J., & Lewin, A. C. (2007). Age and the desire to marry. *Journal of Family Issues, 28*(5), 706–723.

Mahler, M. S., Pine, F., & Bergman, A. (1975). *The psychological birth of the human infant: Symbiosis and individuation.* New York: Basic Books.

Maimburg, R. D., & Vaeth, M. (2006). Perinatal risk factors and infantile autism. *Acta Psychiatrica Scandinavica, 114*(4), 257–264.

Major, G. C., Doucet, E., Trayhurn, P., Astrup, A., & Tremblay, A. (2007). Clinical significance of adaptive thermogenesis. *International Journal of Obesity, 31*(2), 204–212.

Makinodan, M., Rosen, K. M., Ito, S., & Corfas, G. (2012). A critical period for social experience–dependent oligodendrocyte maturation and myelination. *Science, 337*(6100), 1357–1360.

Malik, A. (2007). Relationship between media screen usage and communicative competence. (Unpublished doctoral dissertation). University of Denver, Denver, Colorado.

Malone, P. S., et al. (2004). Divorce and child behavior problems: Applying latent change score models to life event data. *Structural Equation Modeling, 11*(3), 401–423.

Mangina, C. A., & Sokolov, E. N. (2006). Neuronal plasticity in memory and learning abilities: Theoretical position and selective review. *International Journal of Psychophysiology, 60*(3), 203–214.

Mann, D. (2011). Infant growth spurts tied to more sleep. Retrieved from http://www.webmd.com/parenting/baby/news/20110502/infant-growth-spurts-tied-to-more-sleep.

Manning, M. A. (2007). Self-concept and self-esteem in adolescents. *Principal Leadership, 7*(6), 11–15. Retrieved from http://www.nasponline.org/families/selfconcept.pdf.

Maratsos, M. P. (2007). Commentary. *Monographs of the Society for Research in Child Development, 72*(1), 121–126.

Marchione, M. (2012). Multivitamins may lower cancer risk in men. Retrieved from http://www.benefitspro.com/2012/10/17/multivitamins-may-lower-cancer-risk-in-men.

Marcia, J. E. (1991). Identity and self-development. In R. M. Lerner, A. C. Peter sen, & J. Brooks-Gunn (Eds.), *Encyclopedia of adolescence.* New York: Garland.

Marcovitch, S., & Zelazo, P. D. (2006). The influence of number of A trials on 2-year-olds' behavior in two A-not-B-type search tasks: A test of the hierarchical competing systems model. *Journal of Cognition and Development, 7*(4), 477–501.

Marder, L., Tulloh, R., & Pascall, E. (2014). Caridac problems in Down syndrome. *Paediatrics and Child Health 25(1)*, 23–29.

Marean, G. C., Werner, L. A., & Kuhl, P. K. (1992). Vowel categorization by very young infants. *Developmental Psychology, 28,* 396–405.

Markham, B. (2006). Older women and security. In J. Worell & C. D. Goodheart (Eds.), *Handbook of girls' and women's psychological health: Gender and well- being across the lifespan* (pp. 388–396). *Oxford series in clinical psychology.* New York: Oxford University Press.

Marks, L., Nesteruk, O., Swanson, M., Garrison, B., & Davis, T. (2005). Religion and health among African Americans. *Research on Aging, 27*(4), 447–474.

Marquis, C. (2003, March 16). Living in sin. *The New York Times,* p. WK2.

Marron, D. J., & Rayman, J. R. (2002). Addressing the career development needs of adult students in research university settings. In S. G. Niles (Ed.), *Adult career development: Concepts, issues and practices* (3rd ed.) (pp. 321–337). Columbus, OH: National Career Development Association.

Martin, C. L., & Ruble, D. (2004). Children's search for gender cues: Cognitive perspectives on gender development. *Current Directions in Psychological Science, 13*(2), 67–70.

Martin, C. L., Ruble, D. N., & Szkrybalo, J. (2002). Cognitive theories of early gender development. *Psychological Bulletin, 128*(6), 903–933.

Marwick, C. (2000). Consensus panel considers osteoporosis. *Journal of the American Medical Association online,* 283(16), 2093–2095.

Mastin, L. (2012). Right left, right wrong? An investigation into handedness—some facts, myths, truths, opinions and research. Retrieved from http://www.rightleftrightwrong.com/statistics.html.

Matlin, M. W. (2008). *The psychology of women* (8th ed.). Belmont, CA: Thomson/Wadsworth.

Matthews, A. K., Hughes, T. L., & Tartaro, J. (2006). Sexual behavior and sexual dysfunction in a community sample of lesbian and heterosexual women. In A. M. Omoto & H. S. Kurtzman (Eds.), *Sexual orientation and mental health* (pp. 185–205). Washington, DC: American Psychological Association.

Matthews, R. A., Del Priore, R. E., Acitelli, L. K., & Barnes-Farrell, J. L. (2006). Work-to-relationship conflict: Crossover effects in dual-earner couples. *Journal of Occupational Health Psychology, 11*(3), 228–240.

Mauro, E. (2001, October 17). Ottawa teen details final suicidal thoughts on blog. *CTV News*. Retrieved from http://www.ctvnews.ca/ottawa-teen-details-final-suicidal-thoughts-on-blog-1.712337.

Maxwell, C. D., Robinson, A. L., & Post, L. A. (2003). The nature and predictors of sexual victimization and offending among adolescents. *Journal of Youth & Adolescence, 32*(6) 465–477.

Mayo Clinic Staff. (2016). Diseases and conditions: Sleep terrors (night terrors). Retrieved from http://www.mayoclinic.org/diseases-conditions/night-terrors/basics/definition/con-20032552.

McAdams, T. A., Rijsdijk, F. V., Neiderhiser, J. M., Narusyte, J., Shaw, D. S., Natsuaki, M. N. et al. (2015). The relationship between parental depressive symptoms and offspring psychopathology: evidence from a children-of-twins study and an adoption study. *Psychological Medicine, 45(12)*, 2583-94.

McCabe, M. P. (2005). The role of performance anxiety in the development and maintenance of sexual dysfunction in men and women. *International Journal of Stress Management, 12*(4), 379–388.

McCall, R. B., Applebaum, M. I., & Hogarty, P. S. (1973). *Developmental changes in mental performance.* Monographs of the *Society for Research in Child Development, 38*(3, ser. 150).

McCarthy, B. W., & Fucito, L. M. (2005). Integrating medication, realistic expectations, and therapeutic interventions in the treatment of male sexual dysfunction. *Journal of Sex & Marital Therapy, 31*(4), 319–328.

McCarthy, G., & Maughan, B. (2010). Negative childhood experiences and adult love relationships: The role of internal working models of attachment. *Attachment and Human Development, 12*(5), 445–461.

McCartney, K., Owen, M. T., Booth, C. L., Clarke-Stewart, K. A., & Vandell, D. L. (2004). Testing a maternal attachment model of behavior problems in early childhood. *Journal of Child Psychology and Psychiatry, 45*(4), 765–778.

McClellan, J. M., & Werry, J. S. (2003). Evidence-based treatments in child and adolescent psychiatry: An inventory. *Journal of the American Academy of Child and Adolescent Psychiatry, 42*(12), 1388–1400.

McClintock Greenberg, T. (2011, September 6). How we misinterpret (and pathologize) grief: What people who are grieving should know. *Psychology Today*. https://www.psychologytoday.com/blog/21st-century-aging/201109/how-we-misinterpret-and-pathologize-grief.

McCormick, B. (2010). Keeping score & changing youth sports. Retrieved from http://learntocoachbasketball.com/keeping-score-changing-youth-sports.

McCracken, K (2015, January) A patchwork of care: Midwifery in Canada. *Active History.* Retrieved from http://activehistory.ca/2015/01/a-patchwork-of-care-midwifery-in-canada/.

McCracken, M., Jiles, R., & Blanck, H. M. (2007). Health behaviors of the young adult U.S. population: Behavioral risk factor surveillance system, 2003. *Preventing Chronic Disease, 4*(2), A25.

McCrae, R. R., & Costa, P. T., Jr. (1997). Personality trait structure as a human universal. *American Psychologist, 52,* 509–516.

McCrae, R. R., & Costa Jr., P. T. (2006). Cross-cultural perspectives on adult personality trait development. In D. K. Mroczek, & T. D. Little (Eds.), *Handbook of personality development* (pp. 129–145). Mahwah, NJ: Lawrence Erlbaum Associates Publishers.

McCrae, R. R., et al. (2000). Nature over nurture: Temperament, personality, and life span development. *Journal of Personality and Social Psychology, 78*(1), 173–186.

McDevitt, T. M., & Ormrod, J. E. (2002). *Child development and education.* Upper Saddle River, NJ: Prentice Hall.

McDonough, L. (2002). Basic-level nouns: First learned but misunderstood. *Journal of Child Language, 29*(2), 357–377.

McGrath, M., et al. (2005). Early precursors of low attention and hyperactivity in a preterm sample at age four. *Issues in Comprehensive Pediatric Nursing, 28*(1), 1–15.

McHale, J. P., & Rotman, T. (2007). Is seeing believing? Expectant parents' outlooks on coparenting and later coparenting solidarity. *Infant Behavior & Development, 30*(1), 63–81.

McHale, S. M., Kim, J.-Y., & Whiteman, S. D. (2006). Sibling relationships in childhood and adolescence. In P. Noller & J. A. Feeney (Eds.), *Close relationships: Functions, forms and processes* (pp. 127–149). New York: Psychology Press/Taylor & Francis.

McIlvane, W. J., & Dube, W. V. (2003). Stimulus control topography coherence theory: Foundations and extensions. *Behavior Analyst, 26*(2), 195–213.

McKee-Ryan, F., Song, Z., Wanberg, C. R., & Kinicki, A. J. (2005). Psychological and physical well-being during unemployment: A meta-analytic study. *Journal of Applied Psychology, 90*(1), 53–76.

Mcleod, S. (2014). Biological theories of gender. *Simply Psychology*. Retrieved from http://www.simplypsychology.org/gender-biology.html.

McManus, C. (2003). Right hand, left hand: The origins of asymmetry in brains, bodies, atoms and cultures. *Cortex, 39*(2), 348–350.

McManus, I. C., et al. (1988). The development of handedness in children. *British Journal of Developmental Psychology, 6*, 257–273.

McNutt, B., & Yakushko, O. (2013). Disenfranchised grief among lesbian and gay bereaved individuals. *Journal of LGBT Issues in Counselling, 7*(1). Retrieved from http://www.tandfonline.com/doi/abs/10.1080/15538605.2013.758345.

Meaney, K. S., Dornier, L. A., & Owens, M. S. (2002). Sex-role stereotyping for selected sport and physical activities across age groups. *Perceptual and Motor Skills, 94*(3), 743–749.

Meier, B. P., Robinson, M. D., & Wilkowski, B. M. (2006). Turning the other cheek: Agreeableness and the regulation of aggression-related primes. *Psychological Science, 17*(2), 136–142.

Meijer, A. M., & van den Wittenboer, G. L. H. (2007). Contribution of infants' sleep and crying to marital relationship of first-time parent couples in the first year after childbirth. *Journal of Family Psychology, 21*(1) 49–57.

Meinert, C. L., & Breitner, J. C. S. (2008). Chronic disease long-term drug prevention trials: Lessons from the Alzheimer's Disease Anti-Inflammatory Prevention Trial (ADAPT). *Alzheimer's & Dementia, 4*(1, Suppl 1), S7–S14.

Melamed, S., Meir, E. I., & Samson, A. (1995). The benefits of personality-leisure congruence. *Journal of Leisure Research, 27,* 25–40.

Mellon, M. W. (2006). Enuresis and encopresis. In G. G.Bea, & K. M. Minke (Eds.), *Children's needs III: Development, prevention, and intervention* (pp. 1041–1053). Washington, DC: National Association of School Psychologists.

Mellon, M. W., & Houts, A. C. (2006). Nocturnal enuresis. In J. E. Fisher & W. T. O'Donohue (Eds.), *Practitioner's guide to evidence-based psychotherapy* (pp. 432–441). New York: Springer Science + Business Media.

Meltzoff, A. N. (1988). Imitation, objects, tools, and the rudiments of language in human ontogeny. *Human Evolution, 3*(1–2), 45–64.

Meltzoff, A. N., & Moore, M, K. (1977). Imitation of facial and manual gestures by human neonates. *Science, 198,* 75–78.

Meltzoff, A. N., & Prinz, W. (Eds.). (2002). *The imitative mind: Development, evolution, and brain bases.* New York: Cambridge University Press.

Mendle, J., et al. (2006). Family structure and age at menarche: A children-of-twins approach. *Developmental Psychology, 42*(3), 533–542.

Mendleson, R. (2009, April). Youth survey: The surprising optimism of Aboriginal youth. *Macleans*. Retrieved from http://www2.macleans.ca/2009/04/02/the-surprising- optimism-of-aboriginal-youth/.

Mental Health Canada. (2013). Children and adolescents with conduct disorder. Retrieved from http://www.mentalhealthcanada.com/ConditionsandDisordersDetail.asp?lang=e&category=69#204.

Metcalfe, J. S., et al. (2005). Development of somatosensory-motor integration: An event-related analysis of infant posture in the first year of independent walking. *Developmental Psychobiology, 46*(1), 19–35.

Metzger, K. L., et al. (2007). Effects of nicotine vary across two auditory evoked potentials in the mouse. *Biological Psychiatry, 61*(1), 23–30.

Meyerhoff, M. (2005). *A Parent's Guide to Avoiding the Super Baby Syndrome*. Tallahassee, FL: William Gladden Foundation.

Michael, R., Gagnon, J., Laumann, E., & Kolata, G. (1994). *Sex in America: A definitive survey.* Boston: Little Brown.

Mikkola, M. (2016). Feminist perspectives on sex and gender. In E. N. Zalta (Ed.), *The Stanford Encyclopedia of Philosophy* (Spring 2016 Edition). Retrieved from http://plato.stanford.edu/archives/spr2016/entries/feminism-gender/.

Milan , A. (2013). Marital status: Overview, 2011. Statistics Canada. Retrieved from http://www.statcan.gc.ca/pub/91-209-x/2013001/article/11788-eng.pdf.

Milan, A., LaFlamme, N., & Wong, I. (2015). Diversity of grandparents living with their grandchildren. Insights on Canadian Society. *Statistics Canada*. Retrieved from http://www.statcan.gc.ca/pub/75-006-x/2015001/article/14154-eng.pdf.

Milgram, R. M., & Livne, N. L. (2006). Research on creativity in Israel: A chronicle of theoretical and empirical development. In J. C. Kaufman & R. J. Sternberg (Eds.), *The international handbook of creativity* (pp. 307–336). New York: Cambridge University Press.

Millar, W. J., & Maclean, H. (2005). Breastfeeding practices. *Health Reports* (Statistics Canada, Catalogue 82-003-XIE) *16*(12): 23–31. Retrieved from http://www.statcan.gc.ca/pub/82-003-x/82-003-x2004002-eng.pdf.

Miller, C. F., Trautner, H. M., & Ruble, D. N. (2006). The role of gender stereotypes in children's preferences and behavior. In L. Balter & C. S. Tamis-LeMonda (Eds.), *Child psychology: A handbook of contemporary issues* (2nd ed.) (pp. 293–323). New York: Psychology Press.

Miller, S. M., Boyer, B. A., & Rodoletz, M. (1990). Anxiety in children: Nature and development. In M. Lewis & S. M. Miller (Eds.), *Handbook of developmental psychopathology.* New York: Plenum.

Mills, B., Reyna, V. F., & Estrada, S. (2008). Explaining contradictory relations between risk perception and risk taking. *Psychological Science, 19*(5), 429–433.

Miner, R. (2010). *People without jobs, jobs without people: Ontario's labour market Future*. Retrieved from http://www.collegesontario.org/policy-positions/MinerReport.pdf.

Minino, A. M., Heron, M. P., Murphy, S. L., & Kochanek, K. D. (2007, October 10). Deaths: Final data for 2004. *National vital statistics reports, 55*(19). Retrieved from http://www.cdc.gov/nchs/data/nvsr/nvsr55/nvsr55_19.pdf.

Ministry of Health and Long-Term Care (2015). Ontario's fertility program. Retrieved October 10, 2016 from http://www.health.gov.on.ca/en/pro/programs/fertility/.

Minkler, M., & Fuller-Thomson, E. (2005). African American grandparents raising grandchildren: A national study using the Census 2000 *American Community Survey. Journals of Gerontology: Series B: Psychological Sciences and Social Sciences, 60B*(2), S82–S92.

Mischo, C. (2004). Fördert Gruppendiskussion die Perspektiven-Koordination? *Zeitschrift für Entwicklungspsychologie und Pädagogische Psychologie, 36*(1), 30–37.

Mitchell, A. L. (2006). Medical consequences of cocaine. *Journal of Addictions Nursing, 17*(4), 249.

Mitchell, D. D., & Bruss, P. J. (2003) Age differences in implicit memory: Conceptual, perceptual, or methodological? *Psychology and Aging, 18*(4), 807–822.

Mock, S. E., & Cornelius, S. W. (2007). Profiles of interdependence: The retirement planning of married, cohabiting, and lesbian couples. *Sex Roles, 56*(11–12), 793–800.

Mock, S. E., Taylor, C. J., & Savin-Williams, R. C. (2006). Aging together: The retirement plans of same-sex couples. In D. Kimmel, T. Rose, & S. David (Eds.), *Lesbian, gay, bisexual, and transgender aging: Research and clinical perspectives* (pp. 152–174). New York: Columbia University Press.

Moen, P., Huang, Q., Plassmann, V., & Dentinger, E. (2006). Deciding the future. *American Behavioral Scientist, 49*(10), 1422–1443.

Moen, P., Kim, J. E., & Hofmeister, H. (2001). Couples' work/retirement transitions, gender, and marital equality. *Social Psychology Quarterly, 64,* 55–71.

Moens, E., Braet, C., & Soetens, B. (2007). Observation of family functioning at mealtime: A comparison between families of children with and without overweight. *Journal of Pediatric Psychology, 32*(1), 52–63.

Mohan, R., & Bhugra, D. (2005). Literature update. *Sexual and Relationship Therapy, 20*(1), 115–122.

Molinari, L., & Corsaro, W. A. (2000). Le relazioni amicali nella scuola dell'infanzia e nella scuola elementare: Uno studio longitudinale. *Eta Evolutiva, 67,* 40–51.

Monat, A., Lazarus, R. S , & Reevy, G. (Eds.). (2007). *The Praeger handbook on stress and coping* (Vol. 2). Westport, CT: Praeger Publishers/Greenwood Publishing Group.

Monette, M. (2012, October 15). Senior suicide: An overlooked problem. *Canadian Medical Association Journal*. Retrieved from http://www.cmaj.ca/site/earlyreleases/15oct12_senior_suicide.xhtml.

Monte, L. (2013). Portion size, then and now. Retrieved from http://www.divinecaroline.com/self/wellness/portion-size-then-vs-now.

Mood Disorders Society of Canada. (n.d.). Depression in elderly. Retrieved from http://www.mooddisorderscanada.ca/documents/Consumer%20and%20Family%20Support/Depression%20in%20Elderly%20edited%20Dec16%202010.pdf.

Moore, D. R. & Heiman, J. R. (2006). Women's sexuality in context:

Relationship factors and female sexual functioning. In I. Goldstein, C. Meston, S. Davis, & A. Traish (Eds.), *Female sexual dysfunction*. New York: Parthenon.

Moretti. M. M., & Peled, M. (2004). Adolescent-parent attachment: Bonds that support healthy development. *Pediatrics and Child Health, 9*(8): 551–555.

Morrell, J., & Steele, H. (2003). The role of attachment security, temperament, maternal perception, and care-giving behavior in persistent infant sleeping problems. *Infant Mental Health Journal, 24*(5), 447–468.

Morrow, A. (2010, Sept. 7). Canadians are among the best educated in the world. *Globe and Mail*. Retrieved from http://www.theglobeandmail.com/news/national/canadians-among-best-educated-in-the-world-report/article4326151/.

Morry, M. M., & Gaines, S. O. (2005). Relationship satisfaction as a predictor of similarity ratings: A test of the attraction-similarity hypothesis. *Journal of Social and Personal Relationships, 22*(4), 561–584.

Morton, S. M. B. (2006). Maternal nutrition and fetal growth and development. In P. Gluckman & M. Hanson (Eds.), *Developmental origins of health and disease* (pp. 98–129). New York: Cambridge University Press.

Moses, L. J., & Flavell, J. H. (1990). Inferring false beliefs from actions and reactions. *Child Development, 61,* 929–945.

Moshman, D. (2005). *Adolescent psychological development* (2nd ed.). Mahwah, NJ: Erlbaum.

Mueller, R., Pierce, K., Ambrose, J. B., Allen, G., & Courchesne, E. (2001). Atypical patterns of cerebral motor activation in autism: A functional magnetic resonance study. *Biological Psychiatry, 49*(8) 665–676.

Muhlbauer, V., & Chrisler, J. C. (Eds.). (2007). *Women over 50: Psychological perspectives.* New York: Springer Science + Business Media.

Muraco, A. (2006). Intentional families: Fictive kin ties between cross-gender, different sexual orientation friends. *Journal of Marriage and Family, 68*(5), 1313–1325.

Muris, P., Bodden, D., Merckelbach, H., Ollendick, T. H., & King, N. (2003). Fear of the beast: A prospective study on the effects of negative information on childhood fear. *Behaviour Research and Therapy, 41*(2), 195–208.

Murphy, L (2015) Canada's C-section crisis: Why are rates so high? *Today's Parent.* Retrieved from http://www.todaysparent.com/pregnancy/giving-birth/canadas-c-section-crisis-why-are-rates-so-high/.

Murray, D. (2013). Breastfeeding and infant growth. Retrieved from http://breastfeeding.about.com/od/breastfeedingbystage/a/Breastfeeding-And-Infant-Growth.htm.

Myers, J. E., Madathil, J., & Tingle, L. R. (2005). Marriage satisfaction and wellness in India and the United States: A preliminary comparison of arranged marriages and marriages of choice. *Journal of Counseling & Development, 83*(2), 183–190.

Myers, S. M. (2006). Religious homogamy and marital quality: Historical and generational patterns, 1980–1997. *Journal of Marriage and Family, 68*(2): 292–304.

N

Nadeau, L., et al. (2003). Extremely premature and very low birthweight infants: A double hazard population? *Social Development, 12*(2), 235–248.

Nader, P. R., O'Brien, M., Houts, R., Bradley, R., Belsky, J., Crosnoe, R., et al. (2008). Identifying risk for obesity in early childhood. *Pediatrics, 118*(3), 594–601.

Nagin, D. S., & Tremblay, R. E. (2001). Parental and early childhood predictors of persistent physical aggression in boys from kinder-garten to high school. *Archives of General Psychiatry, 58*(4), 389–394.

National Center for Children in Poverty. (2004). Low-income children in the United States. Retrieved from http://cpmcnet.columbia.edu/dept/nccp/.

National Center for Education Statistics. (2007, June). Dropout rates in the United States: 2005. Retrieved from http://nces.ed.gov/pubs2007/dropout05/. Accessed July 20, 2007.

National Center for Injury Prevention and Control, Office of Statistics and Programming, Centers for Disease Control and Prevention. (2007a, March 29). National Center for Health Statistics (NCHS), National Vital Statistics System. Accessed May 7, 2007. Available at http://webappa.cdc.gov/cgi-bin/broker.exe.

National Center for Injury Prevention and Control. (2007b, July 11). Suicide: Fact sheet. Available at http://www.cdc.gov/ncipc/factsheets/suifacts.htm.

National Eating Disorder Information Centre. (2012). Statistics: Eating disorders and disordered eating. Retrieved from http://www.nedic.ca/knowthefacts/statisticsArchive.shtml.

National Eating Disorders Association (NEDA). (2016). Anorexia in males. Retrieved June 18, 2016. http://www.nationaleatingdisorders.org/anorexia-nervosa-males.

National Guideline Clearinghouse. (2007). Use of clomiphene citrate in women. Available at http://www.guideline.gov/summary/summary.aspx?ss=15&doc_id=4843&nbr=3484. Last updated January 29, 2007.

National Initiative for the Care of the Elderly. (n.d.). Introduction to older adults and substance use. Retrieved from http://www.nicenet.ca/tools-introduction-to-older-adults-and-substance-use.

National Institutes of Health. (2002). Available at http://cerhr.niehs.nih.gov/genpub/topics/vitamin_a-ccae.html.

National Library of Medicine. (2007, January 11). "Miscarriage." Retrieved from http://www.nlm.nih.gov/medlineplus/ency/article/001488.htm.

National Sleep Foundation. (2011). Children and sleep. Retrieved from http://www.sleepfoundation.org/article/sleep-topics/children-and-sleep.

National Sleep Foundation (2016). Sleepwalking. Retrieved from https://sleepfoundation.org/sleep-disorders-problems/abnormal-sleep-behaviors/sleepwalking.

National Tay-Sachs and Allied Diseases Association. (2016). Tay-Sachs disease. Retrieved from https://www.ntsad.org/index.php/the-diseases/tay-sachs.

Natsopoulos, D., Kiosseoglou, G., & Xeromeritou, A. (1992). Handedness and spatial ability in children: Further support for Geschwind's hypothesis of "pathology of superiority" and for Annett's theory of intelligence. *Genetic, Social, and General Psychology Monographs, 118*(1) 103–126.

Nauert, R. (2013). National survey finds big jump in teen abuse of prescription drugs. Retrieved from http://www.habitude.ca/national-survey-finds-big-jump-in-teen-abuse-of-prescription-drugs/.

Nauta, M. M. (2007). Career interests, self- efficacy, and personality as antecedents of career exploration. *Journal of Career Assessment, 15*(2), 162–180.

Naveh-Benjamin, M., Brav, T. K., & Levy, O. (2007). The associative memory deficit of older adults: The role of strategy utilization. *Psychology and Aging, 22,* 202–208.

Neisser, U., et al. (1996). Intelligence: Knowns and unknowns. *American Psychologist, 51,* 77–101.

Nelson, C. A., de Haan, M., & Thomas, K. M. (2006). *Neuroscience of cognitive development: The role of experience and the developing brain*. Hoboken, NJ: Wiley.

Nelson, C. A., & Luciana, M. (Eds.). (2001). *Handbook of developmental cognitive neuroscience.* Cambridge, MA: MIT Press.

Nelson, C. A., & Ludemann, P. M. (1989). Past, current, and future trends in infant face perception research. *Canadian Journal of Psychology, 43,* 183–198.

Nelson, K. (1973). *Structure and strategy in learning to talk.* Monographs for the Society for Research in Child Development, 38(1–2, ser. 149).

Nelson, K. (1981). Individual differences in language development: Implications for development of language. *Developmental Psychology, 17,* 170–187.

Nelson, K. (2005). Cognitive functions of language in early childhood. In B. D. Homer & C. S. Tamis-LeMonda (Eds.), *The development of social cognition and communication* (pp. 7–28). Mahwah, NJ: Erlbaum.

Nelson, K. (2006). Advances in pragmatic developmental theory: The case of language acquisition. *Human Development, 49*(3), 184–188.

Nelson, K., & Fivush, R. (2004). The emergence of autobiographical memory: A social cultural developmental theory. *Psychological Review, 111*(2), 486–511.

Nelson, M. (2013). Neonatal abstinence syndrome: The nurse's role. *International Journal of Childbirth Education, 28*(1), 38–42.

Nelson, T. D. (2005). Ageism: Prejudice against our feared future self. *Journal of Social Issues, 61*(2), 207–221.

Nesdale, D., & Lambert, A. (2007). Effects of experimentally manipulated peer rejection on children's negative affect, self-esteem, and maladaptive social behavior. *International Journal of Behavioral Development, 31*(2), 115–122.

Newburn-Cook, C. V., et al. (2002). Where and to what extent is prevention of low birth weight possible? *Western Journal of Nursing Research, 24*(8), 887–904.

Newman, R., Ratner, N. B., Jusczyk, A. M., Jusczyk, P. W., & Dow, K. A. (2006). Infants' early ability to segment the conversational speech signal predicts later language development: A retrospective analysis. *Developmental Psychology, 42*(4), 643–655.

News-Medical.Net. (2013). Culture plays role in deciding what makes a mate attractive, says researcher. Retrieved from http://www.news-medical.net/news/20130531/Culture-plays-role-in-deciding-what-makes-a-mate-attractive-says-researcher.aspx?page=2.

Neyer, F. J. (2002). Twin relationships in old age. *Journal of Social and Personal Relationships, 19*(2), 155–177.

NIAAA (National Institute on Alcohol Abuse and Alcoholism). (2005). Cage questionnaire. Available at http://pubs.niaaa.nih.gov/publications/Assesing%20Alcohol/InstrumentPDFs/16_CAGE.pdf.

Nielsen, S., & Palmer, B. (2003). Diagnosing eating disorders: AN, BN, and the others. *Acta Psychiatrica Scandinavica, 108*(3), 161–162.

Nielsen, S. J., & Popkin, B. M. (2003). Patterns and trends in food portion sizes, 1977–1998. *Journal of the American Medical Association, 289*(4), 450–453.

Niemeier, H. M., Raynor, H. A., Lloyd-Richardson, E. E., Rogers, M. L., & Wing, R. R. (2006). Fast food consumption and breakfast skipping: Predictors of weight gain from adolescence to adulthood in a nationally representative sample. *Journal of Adolescent Health, 39*(6), 842–849.

Nigg, J. T., Goldsmith, H. H., & Sachek, J. (2004). Temperament and attention deficit hyperactivity disorder: The development of a multiple pathway model. *Journal of Clinical Child and Adolescent Psychology, 33*(1), 42–53.

Nigg, J. T., Hinshaw, S. P., & Huang-Pollock, C. (2006). Disorders of attention and impulse regulation. In D. Cicchetti & D. J. Cohen (Eds.), *Developmental psychopathology,* Vol. 3, *Risk, disorder, and adaptation* (2nd ed.) (pp. 358–403). Hoboken, NJ: Wiley.

Nimrod, G. (2007). Retirees' leisure. *Leisure Studies, 26*(1), 65–80.

Nisbett, R. E. (2007, December 9). All brains are the same color. *The New York Times online.*

Nixon, R. (2010). Studies reveal why children get bullied and rejected. *LiveScience.com*. Retrieved from http://www.livescience.com/6032-studies-reveal-kids-bullied-rejected.html.

Nixon, R. (2011). Midlife crisis is a myth. *LiveScience.com*. Retrieved from http://www.livescience.com/12930-midlife-crisis-total-myth.html.

Nock, M. K., Kazdin, A. E., Hiripi, E., & Kessler, R. C. (2006). Prevalence, subtypes, and correlates of DSM-IV conduct disorder in the National Comorbidity Survey Replication. *Psychological Medicine, 36*, 699–710.

Noel-Weiss, J, (2007). Medicalizing motherhood: Maternity care in Canada in the 1920s and 1930s. Retrieved from http://www.asklenore.info/parenting/resources/maternity_care.pdf.

Nolen-Hoeksema, S., Stice, E., Wade, E., & Bohon, C. (2007). Reciprocal relations between rumination and bulimic, substance abuse, and depressive symptoms in female adolescents. *Journal of Abnormal Psychology, 116*(1), 198–207.

Nomaguchi, K. M. (2006). Maternal employment, nonparental care, mother–child interactions, and child outcomes during preschool years. *Journal of Marriage and Family, 68*(5), 1341–1369.

Nonaka, A. M. (2004). The forgotten endangered languages: Lessons on the importance of remembering from Thailand's Ban Khor Sign Language. *Language in Society, 33*(5), 737–767.

Nonnemaker, J. M., & Homsi, G. (2007). Measurement properties of the Fagerström Test for nicotine dependence adapted for use in an adolescent sample. *Addictive Behaviors, 32*(1), 181–186.

Noppe, I. C., & Noppe, L. D. (2004). Adolescent experiences with death: Letting go of immortality. *Journal of Mental Health Counseling, 26*(2), 146–167.

Norlander, T., Erixon, A., & Archer, T. (2000). Psychological androgyny and creativity: Dynamics of gender-role and personality trait. *Social Behavior and Personality, 28*(5), 423–435.

Norton, A., et al. (2005). Are there pre-existing neural, cognitive, or motoric markers for musical ability? *Brain and Cognition, 59*(2), 124–134.

Nurnberg, H. G., et al. (2008). Sildenafil treatment of women with antidepressant-associated sexual dysfunction. *Journal of the American Medical Association, 300*(4), 395–404.

Nuttman-Shwartz, O. (2007). Is there life without work? *International Journal of Aging & Human Development, 64*(2) 129–147.

O

O'Boyle, M. W., & Benbow, C. P. (1990). Handedness and its relationship to ability and talent. In S. Coren (Ed.), *Left- handedness: Behavior implications and anomalies.* Amsterdam: North-Holland.

O'Brien, B., Chalmers, B., Fell, D., Heaman, M., Darling, E. K., & Herbert, P. (2011). The experience of pregnancy and birth with midwives: Results from the Canadian Maternity Experiences Survey. *Birth: Issues in Perinatal Care, 38*(3), 207–215. doi:10.1111/j.1523-536X.2011.00482.x.

O'Dea, J. A. (2006). Self-concept, self-esteem and body weight in adolescent females: A three-year longitudinal study. *Journal of Health Psychology, 11*(4), 599–611.

O'Doherty, J., et al. (2003). Beauty in a smile: The role of medial orbitofrontal cortex in facial attractiveness. *Neuropsychologia, 41*(2), 147–155.

O'Donnell, L., et al. (2003). Long-term influence of sexual norms and attitudes on timing of sexual initiation among urban minority youth. *Journal of School Health, 23*(2), 68–75.

O'Keeffe, M. J., O'Callaghan, M., Williams, G. M., Najman, J. M., & Bor, W. (2003). Learning, cognitive, and attentional problems in adolescents born small for gestational age. *Pediatrics, 112*(2), 301–307.

O'Neill, D. K., & Chong, S. C. F. (2001). Preschool children's difficulty understanding the types of information obtained through the five senses. *Child Development, 72*(3), 803–815.

O'Neill, D. K., & Gopnik, A. (1991). Young children's ability to identify the sources of their beliefs. *Developmental Psychology, 27,* 390–397.

O'Shea, R. P., & Corballis, P. M. (2005). Binocular rivalry in the divided brain. In D. Alais & R. Blake (Eds.), *Binocular rivalry*. (pp. 301–315). Cambridge, MA: MIT Press.

Oates, J., & Messer, D. (2007). Growing up with TV. *The Psychologist, 20*(1), 30–32.

Office of National Statistics. (2006). Multiple Birth Statistics. Available at http://www.multiplebirths.org.uk/media.asp.

Office of the Commissioner of Official Languages. (2005). Bilingualism in Canada. Retrieved from http://www.ocol-clo.gc.ca/html/biling_e.php.

O'Grady, K. (2008.) Early puberty for girls. The new 'normal' and why we need to be concerned. *Canadian Women's Health Network.* http://www.cwhn.ca/en/node/39365.

Ogunfowora, O. B., Olanrewaju, D. M., & Akenzua, G. I. (2005). A comparative study of academic achievement of children with sickle cell anemia and their healthy siblings. *Journal of the National Medical Association, 97*(3), 405–408.

Okinawa Centenarian Study. (n.d.). *Investigating the world's longest-lived people*. Retrieved from http://www.okicent.org/.

Oliveira, M. (2010, March 25). Canada a hotbed of online dating. *Globe and Mail*. Retrieved from http://www.theglobeandmail.com/technology/canada-a-hotbed-of-online-dating/article4312016/.

Olivo, L., Cotter, R., & Bromwich, R. (2007). *Youth and the law: New approaches to criminal justice and child protection.* Toronto: Emond Montgomery Publications Ltd.

Olson, S. L., Bates, J. E., Sandy, J. M., & Lanthier, R. (2000). Early developmental precursors of externalizing behavior in middle childhood and adolescence. *Journal of Abnormal Child Psychology, 28*(2), 119–133.

Oltjenbruns, K. A., & Balk, D. E. (2007). Life span issues and loss, grief, and mourning: Part 1: The importance of a developmental context: childhood and adolescence as an example. In D. Balk, et al. (Eds.), *Handbook of thanatology* (pp. 143–163). New York: Routledge/Taylor & Francis Group.

Olweus Bullying Prevention Program. (2010). What is bullying? Retrieved from http://www.olweus.org/public/bullying.page.

Omori, M., & Ingersoll, G. M. (2005). Health-endangering behaviours among Japanese college students: A test of psychosocial model of risk-taking behaviours. *Journal of Adolescence, 28*(1), 17–33.

Ontario Association of Children's Aid Societies. (2010). Your duty to report. Retrieved from http://www.oacas.org/childwelfare/duty.htm.

Ontario Ministry of Education. (2004). *The individual education plan (IEP): A resource guide.* Retrieved from http://www.edu.gov.on.ca/eng/general/elemsec/speced/guide/resource/iepresguid.pdf.

OpenParliament. (2015). Bill C-279. Retrieved from https://openparliament.ca/bills/41-1/C-279/.

Orel, N. (2006). Lesbian and bisexual women as grandparents: The centrality of sexual orientation in the grandparent – grandchild relationship. In D. Kimmel, T. Rose, & S. David (Eds.), *Lesbian, gay, bisexual, and transgender ageing: Research and clinical perspectives* (pp. 175–194). New York: Columbia University Press.

Organisation for Economic Co-operation and Development. (2005). *OECD urges Canadian governments to increase funding for childcare.* Retrieved from http://www.oecd.org/canada/rgescanadiangovernments toincreasefundingforchildcare.htm.

Örnkloo, H., & von Hofsten, C. (2007). Fitting objects into holes: On the development of spatial cognition skills. *Developmental Psychology, 43*(2), 404–416.

opengovernment. (2016). Bill C-14. Retrieved from https://openparliament.ca/bills/42-1/C-14/.

Orphan Nutrition. (2016). Understanding malnutrition. Retrieved from http://www.orphannutrition.org/understanding-malnutrition/causes-of-malnutrition-among-orphans/.

Orstavik, R. E., Kendler, K. S., Czajkowski, N., Tambs, K., & Reichborn-Kjennerud, T. (2007). Genetic and environmental contributions to depressive personality disorder in a population-based sample of Norwegian twins. *Journal of Affective Disorders, 99*(1–3), 181–189.

Ortega, V., Ojeda, P., Sutil, F., & Sierra, J. C. (2005). Culpabilidad sexual en adolescentes: Estudio de algunos factores relacionados. *Anales de Psicología, 21*(2), 268–275.

Osteoporosis Canada. (2010). Facts and statistics: About osteoporosis. Retrieved from http://www.osteoporosis.ca/index.php/ci_id/8867/la_id/1.htm.

Oster, H. (2005). The repertoire of infant facial expressions: an ontogenetic perspective. In J. Nadel, & D. Muir (Eds.), *Emotional development: Recent research advances* (pp. 261–292). New York: Oxford University Press.

Ouellette, G. P. (2006). What's meaning got to do with it: The role of vocabulary in word reading and reading comprehension. *Journal of Educational Psychology, 98*(3), 554–566.

Ouellette-Kuntz , H., Coo, H., Lam, M., Breitenbach, M., Hennessey, P., Jackman, P., … Chung, A. M. (2014). The changing prevalence of autism in three regions of Canada. *Journal of Autism and Developmental Disorders, 44*(1), 12–136.

Outram, S., Murphy, B., & Cockburn, J. (2006). Prevalence of and factors associated with midlife women taking medicines for psychological distress. *AeJAMH (Australian e-Journal for the Advancement of Mental Health), 5*(3), 1–13.

Oztop, E., Kawato, M., & Arbib, M. (2006) Mirror neurons and imitation: A computationally guided review. *Neural Networks, 19*(3), 254–271.

P

Paavola, L., Kemppinen, K., Kumpulainen, K., Moilanen, I., & Ebeling, H. (2006). Maternal sensitivity, infant co-operation and early linguistic development: Some predictive relations. *European Journal of Developmental Psychology*, 3(1), 13–30.

Paglia, A., & Room, R. (1998). How unthinkable and at what age: Adult opinions about the 'social clock' for contested behaviour by teenagers. *Journal of Youth Studies, 1*(3), 295–314.

Pailone, N. (2013). The ABCs of PKU: What early childhood educators and school administrators need to know. *Canadian PKU and Allied Disorders*. Retrieved from http://canpku.org/wp-content/uploads/2016/03/CanPKU-Elementary-School-Guide.pdf.

Park, H-O. H., & Greenberg, J. S. (2007). Parenting grandchildren. In J. Blackburn, & C. N. Dulmus (Eds.), *Handbook of gerontology: Evidence-based approaches to theory, practice, and policy* (pp. 397–425). Hoboken, NJ: John Wiley & Sons, Inc.

Park, N. S., et al. (2008). Religiousness and longitudinal trajectories in elders' functional status. *Research on Aging, 30*(3), 279–298.

Parke, R. D., & Buriel, R. (2006). Socialization in the family: Ethnic and ecological perspectives. In N. Eisenberg, W. Damon, & R. M. Lerner (Eds.), *Handbook of child psychology* (6th ed.), Vol. 3, *Social, emotional, and personality development* (pp. 429–504). Hoboken, NJ: Wiley.

Patenaude, J., Niyonsenga, T., & Fafard, D. (2003). Changes in students' moral development during medical school: A cohort study. *Canadian Medical Association Journal, 168*(7), 840–844.

Paterson, D. S., et al. (2006). Multiple serotonergic brainstem abnormalities in sudden infant death syndrome. *Journal of the American Medical Association, 296*, 2124–2132.

Patrick, S., Sells, J. N., Giordano, F. G., & Tollerud, T. R. (2007). Intimacy, differentiation, and personality variables as predictors of marital satisfaction. *The Family Journal, 15*(4), 359–367.

Patterson, C. J. (2006). Children of lesbian and gay parents. *Current Directions in Psychological Science, 15*(5), 241–244.

Patterson, G. R. (2005). The next generation of PMTO models. *The Behavior Therapist, 28*(2), 27–33.

Patterson, M. M., & Bigler, R. S. (2006). Preschool children's attention to environmental messages about groups: Social categorization and the origins of intergroup bias. *Child Development, 77*(4), 847–860.

Pauktuutit Inuit Women of Canada. (2006). *The Inuit Way: A Guide to Inuit Culture*. Retrieved from http://www.uqar.ca/files/boreas/inuitway_e.pdf.

Pauli-Pott, U., Mertesacker, B., & Beckmann, D. (2003). Ein Fragebogen zur Erfassung des fruhkindlichen Temperaments im Elternurteil. *Zeitschrift für Kinder-und Jugend-psychiatrie und Psychotherapie, 31*(2), 99–110.

Paulussen-Hoogeboom, M. C., Stams, G. J. J. M., Hermanns, J. M. A., & Peetsma, T. T. D. (2007). Child negative emotionality and parenting from infancy to preschool: A meta-analytic review. *Developmental Psychology, 43*(2), 438–453.

Paulussen-Hoogeboom, M. C., Stams, G. J. J. M., Hermanns, J. M. A., Peetsma, T. T. D., van den Wittenboer, G. L. H. (2008). Parenting style as a mediator between children's negative emotionality and problematic behavior in early childhood. *Journal of Genetic Psychology169*(3), 209–226.

Paus, T., et al. (1999). Structural maturation of neural pathways in children and adolescents: In vivo study. *Science, 283*(5409), 1908–1911.

Pausch, R., & Zaslow, J. (2008). *The last lecture: Lessons in living*. London: Hodder & Stoughton Ltd.

Paxton, S. J., Neumark-Sztainer, D., Hannan, P. J., & Eisenberg, M. E. (2006). Body dissatisfaction prospectively predicts depressive mood and low self-esteem in adolescent girls and boys. *Journal of Clinical Child and Adolescent Psychology, 35*(4), 539–549.

Paxton, S. J., Norris, M., Wertheim, E. H., Durkin, S. J., & Anderson, J. (2005). Body dissatisfaction, dating, and importance of thinness to attractiveness in adolescent girls. *Sex Roles, 53*(9–10), 663–675.

Peck, R. C. (1968). Psychological developments in the second half of life. In B. L. Neugarten (Ed.), *Middle age and aging* (pp. 88–92). Chicago: University of Chicago Press.

Pei, M., Matsuda, K., Sakamoto, H., & Kawata, M. (2006). Intrauterine proximity to male fetuses affects the morphology of the sexually dimorphic nucleus of the preoptic area in the adult rat brain. *European Journal of Neuroscience, 23*(5), 1234–1240.

Pelphrey, K. A., et al. (2004). Development of visuospatial short-term memory in the second half of the first year. *Developmental Psychology, 40*(5), 836–851.

Penn, H. E. (2006). Neurobiological correlates of autism: A review of recent research. *Child Neuropsychology, 12*(1), 57–79.

Pepler, D., & Craig, W. (2000). Making a difference in bullying. *Peaceful Schools International*. Retrieved August 20, 2016, from http://peacefulschoolsinternational.org/wpcontent/uploads/making_a_difference_in_bullying.pdf.

Perls, T. T. (2005). The oldest old. *Scientific American, 272*, 70–75.

Perls, T. T., et al. (2002). Life-long sustained mortality advantage of siblings of centenarians. *Proceedings of the National Academy of Sciences 99*, 8442–8447.

Perrault, S. (2013). Police-reported crime statistics in Canada, 2012. Ottawa: Statistics Canada. Retrieved from http://www.statcan.gc.ca/pub/85-002-x/2013001/article/11854-eng.htm#a7.

Perrig-Chiello, P., Perrig, W. J., Uebelbacher, A., & Stähelin, H. B. (2006). Impact of physical and psychological resources on functional autonomy in old age. *Psychology, Health & Medicine, 11*(4), 470–482.

Perrone, K. M., Webb, L. K., & Jackson, Z. V. (2007). Relationships between parental attachment, work and family roles, and life satisfaction. *The Career Development Quarterly, 55*(3), 237–248.

Perry, P. J., et al. (2001). Bioavailable testosterone as a correlate of cognition, psychological status, quality of life, and sexual function in aging males: Implications for testosterone replacement therapy. *Annals of Clinical Psychiatry, 13*(2), 75–80.

Perry-Jenkins, M., Goldberg, A. E., Pierce, C. P., & Sayer, A. G. (2007). Shift work, role overload, and the transition to parent-hood. *Journal of Marriage and Family, 69*(1), 123–138.

Persson, G. E. B. (2005). Developmental perspectives on prosocial and aggressive motives in preschoolers' peer interactions. *International Journal of Behavioral Development, 29*(1), 80–91.

Peters, B. (2013). How do sleep problems affect children's behavior? Retrieved from http://sleepdisorders. about.com/od/causesofsleepdisorder1/f/How-Do-Sleep-Problems-Affect-Childrens-Behavior.htm.

Pflag Canada. (2009). Sexual identity. Retrieved August 7, 2016, from http://www.pflagcanada.ca/en/sexual-identity-e.html.

Philip, J., et al. (2004). Late first-trimester invasive prenatal diagnostic results of an international randomized trial. *Obstetrics & Gynecology, 103*(6), 1164–1173.

Phillips, D. A., & Styfco, S. J. (2007). Child development research and public policy: Triumphs and setbacks on the way to maturity. In J. L. Aber et al. (Eds.), *Child development and social policy: Knowledge for action. APA Decade of Behavior volumes* (pp. 11–27). Washington, DC: American Psychological Association.

Phinney, J. S. (2006). Ethnic identity exploration in emerging adulthood. In J. J. Arnett & J. L. Tanner (Eds.), *Emerging adults in America: Coming of age in the 21st century* (pp. 117–134). Washington, DC: American Psychological Association.

Phinney, J. S., & Alipuria, L. L. (2006). Multiple social categorization and identity among multiracial, multiethnic, and multicultural individuals: Processes and implications. In R. J. Crisp & M. Hewstone (Eds.), *Multiple social categorization: Processes, models and applications* (pp. 211–238). New York: Psychology Press.

Phinney, J. S., & Ong, A. D. (2007). Conceptualization and measurement of ethnic identity: Current status and future directions. *Journal of Counseling Psychology, 54*(3), 271–281.

Phipps, M. G., Blume, J. D., & DeMonner, S. M. (2002). Young maternal age associated with increased risk of postneonatal death. *Obstetrics and Gynecology, 100,* 481–486.

Physical Activity Fact Sheet. (2005). The President's Council on Physical Fitness and Sports, Department of Human Services.

Physical and Health Education Canada. (2009). Physical education in school. Retrieved from http://www.phecanada.ca/physical-education-school.

Piaget, J. (1962). *Play, dreams, and imitation in childhood.* New York: Norton. (Originally published in 1946.)

Piaget, J. (1963). *The origins of intelligence in children.* New York: Norton. (Originally published in 1936.)

Piaget, J. (1976). *The grasp of consciousness: Action and concept in the young child.* Cambridge, MA: Harvard University Press.

Piaget, J., & Inhelder, B. (1956). *The child's conception of space*. London: Routledge & Kegan Paul.

Picard, A. (2013). Midwives: Underused and misused assets in Canada. Retrieved from http://www.theglobeandmail.com/life/health-and-fitness/health/midwives-underused-and-misused-assets/article13133123/.

Pichichero, M. E. (2006). Prevention of cervical cancer through vaccination of adolescents. *Clinical Pediatrics, 45*(5), 393–398.

Pickert, K. (2012, May 21). The man who remade motherhood. *Time*, 179(20), 32–39.

Piek, J. P. (2006). *Infant motor development*. Champaign, IL: Human Kinetics.

Piek, J. P., Baynam, G. B., & Barrett, N. C. (2006). The relationship between fine and gross motor ability, self-perceptions and self-worth in children and adolescents. *Human Movement Science, 25*(1), 65–75.

Pierce, K. M., & Vandell, D. L. (2006). Child care. In G. G. Bear & K. M. Minke (Eds.), *Children's needs III: Development, prevention, and intervention* (pp. 721–732). Washington, DC: National Association of School Psychologists.

Pinker, S., & Jackendoff, R. (2005). The faculty of language: What's special about it? *Cognition, 95*(2), 201–236.

Pinquart, M., & Schindler, I. (2007). Changes of life satisfaction in the transition to retirement. *Psychology and Aging, 22*(3), 442–455.

Pitetti, K.H., Baynard, T. & Agiovlasitis, S. (2013). Children and adolescents with Down syndrome, physical fitness and physical activitiy. *Journal of Sport and Health Science 2(1)*, 47–57.

Pittman, G. (2010, September 1). First-time mothers drive up C-section rate: Study. *Reuters.* Retrieved from http://www.canada.com/health/First+time+mothers+drive+section+rate+Study/3470332/story.html.

Plomin, R., Owen, M. J., & McGuffin, P. (1994). The genetic basis of complex human behaviors. *Science, 264,* 1733–1739.

Plomin, R., & Walker, S. O. (2003). Genetics and educational psychology. *British Journal of Educational Psychology, 73*(1), 3–14.

Poisson, J. (2011). The "genderless baby" who caused a Storm of controversy in 2011. Retrieved from http://www.thestar.com/news/gta/2011/12/26/the_genderless_baby_who_caused_a_storm_of_controversy_in_2011.html.

Poltorak, D. Y., & Glazer, J. P. (2006). The development of children's understanding of death. *Child and Adolescent Psychiatric Clinics of North America, 15*(3), 567–573.

Popenoe, D., & Whitehead, B. D. (2006). *The state of our unions, 2006: The social health of marriage in America.* New Brunswick, NJ: Rutgers University.

Popma, A., et al. (2007). Cortisol moderates the relationship between testosterone and aggression in delinquent male adolescents. *Biological Psychiatry, 61*(3), 405–411.

Porfeli, E. J. (2007). Work values system development during adolescence. *Journal of Vocational Behavior, 70*(1), 42–60.

Posey, D. J., et al. (2007). Positive effects of methylphenidate on inattention and hyperactivity in pervasive developmental disorders: An analysis of secondary measures. *Biological Psychiatry, 61*(4), 538–544.

Posner, M. I., & Rothbart, M. K. (2007). *Relating brain and mind. Educating the human brain.* Washington, DC: American Psychological Association.

Powlishta, K. K. (2004). Gender as a social category: Intergroup processes and gender-role development. In M. Bennett & F. Sani (Eds.), *The development of the social self* (pp. 103–133). New York: Psychology Press.

Powlishta, K. K., Sen, M. G., Serbin, L. A., Poulin-Dubois, D., & Eichstedt, J. A. (2001). From infancy through middle childhood: The role of cognitive and social factors in becoming gendered. In R. K. Unger (Ed.), *Handbook of the psychology of women and gender* (pp. 116–132). New York: Wiley.

Prato-Previde, E., Fallani, G., & Valsecchi, P. (2006). Gender differences in owners interacting with pet dogs: An observational study. *Ethology, 112*(1), 64–73.

Pratt, C., & Bryant, P. (1990). Young children understand that looking leads to knowing (so long as they are looking into a single barrel). *Child Development, 61,* 973–982.

Pressley, M., & Hilden, K. (2006). Cognitive strategies. In D. Kuhn, R. S. Siegler, W. Damon, & R. M. Lerner (Eds.), *Handbook of child psychology* (6th ed.), Vol. 2, *Cognition, perception, and language* (pp. 511–556). Hoboken, NJ: Wiley.

Pressman, S. D., et al. (2005). Loneliness, social network size, and immune response to influenza vaccination in college freshmen. *Health Psychology. 24*(3), 297–306.

Priner, R., Freeman, S., Perez, R., & Sohmer, H. (2003). The neonate has a temporary conductive hearing loss due to fluid in the middle ear. *Audiology & Neurotology, 8*(2), 100–110.

Prostate Cancer Canada. (2013). Prostate Cancer Canada releases new recommendations. Retrieved from http://prostatecancer.ca/In-The-News/Foundation-News-Releases/Prostate-Cancer-Canada-Releases-New-Recommendation#.Ui4tD9KTiSo.

Province of British Columbia. (2010). *Baby's best chance: Parents' handbook of pregnancy and health care* (6th ed., 2nd rev.). Retrieved from http://www.hls.gov.bc.ca/publications/year/2010/bbc.pdf.

Prull, M. W., Gabrieli, J. D. E., & Bunge, S. A. (2000). In Craik, F. I. M., & Salthouse, T. A. (Eds.), *Age-related changes in memory: A cognitive neuroscience perspective. The handbook of aging and cognition* (2nd ed.) (pp. 91–153). Mahwah, NJ: Lawrence Erlbaum Associates Publishers.

Public Health Agency of Canada. (2005). Helping children at every age: Looking at divorce through the eyes of your child. Younger children. Retrieved from http://www.phac-aspc.gc.ca/publicat/mh-sm/divorce/2-eng.php.

Public Health Agency of Canada. (2010a). *Canadian incidence study of reported child abuse and neglect—2008: Major findings*. Retrieved from http://cwrp.ca/sites/default/files/publications/en/CIS-2008-rprt-eng.pdf.

Public Health Agency of Canada. (2010b). The health and well-being of Canadian seniors. In *The Chief Public Health Officer's report on the state of public health in Canada*. Retrieved from http://www.phac-aspc.gc.ca/cphorsphc-respcacsp/2010/fr-rc/cphorsphc-respcacsp-06-eng.php.

Public Health Agency of Canada (2011a). Benefits of physical activity. Retrieved August 11, 2016 from http://www.phac-aspc.gc.ca/hp-ps/hl-mvs/pa-ap/02paap-eng.php.

Public Health Agency of Canada. (2011b). The health and well-being of Canadian youth and young adults. In *The Chief Public Health Officer's report on the state of public health in Canada.* Retrieved from http://www.phac-aspc.gc.ca/cphorsphc-respcacsp/2011/cphorsphc-respcacsp-06-eng.php.

Public Health Agency of Canada (2012). Joint statement on safe sleep. Retrieved on October 11, 2016 at phac-aspc.gc.ca.

Public Health Agency of Canada (2014). Safe sleep. Retrieved on October 11, 2016, at phac-aspc.gc.ca.

Public Safety Canada. (2010). *Bullying prevention: Nature and extent of bullying in Canada.* Retrieved from http://www.publicsafety.gc.ca/res/cp/res/2008-bp-01-eng.aspx.

Puente, S., & Cohen, D. (2003). Jealousy and the meaning (or nonmeaning) of violence. *Personality & Social Psychology Bulletin, 29*(4), 449–460.

Pujol, J., et al. (2006). Myelination of language-related areas in the developing brain. *Neurology, 66*(3), 339–343.

Pulverman, R., Hirsh-Pasek, K., Golinkoff, R. M., Pruden, S., & Salkind, S. J. (2006). Conceptual foundations for verb learning: Celebrating the event. In K. Hirsh-Pasek & R. M. Golinkoff (Eds.), *Action meets word: How children learn verbs* (pp. 134–159). New York: Oxford University Press.

Q

Qin, W., et al. (2006). Calorie restriction attenuates Alzheimer's disease type brain amyloidosis in Squirrel monkeys (Saimiri sciureus). *Journal of Alzheimer's Disease, 10*(4), 417–422.

Quigley, N. R., & Tymon, Jr., W. G. (2006). Toward an integrated model of intrinsic motivation and career self management. *Career Development International, 11*(6), 522–543.

R

Radvansky, G. A., Zacks, R. T., & Hasher, L. (2005). Age and inhibition: The retrieval of situation models. *Journals of Gerontology: Series B: Psychological Sciences and Social Sciences, 60B*(5), P276–P278.

Raikes, H., et al. (2006). Mother–child bookreading in low-income families: Correlates and outcomes during the first three years of life. *Child Development, 77*(4), 924–953.

RAINN. (n.d.) What consent looks like. Retrieved October 22, 2016, from https://www.rainn.org/articles/what-is-consent.

Ramage-Morin, P. L. (2009). Medication use among senior Canadians. *Health Reports,* March 2009. (Statistics Canada, Catalogue no. 82-003-X). Retrieved from http://www.statcan.gc.ca/pub/82-003-x/2009001/article/10801/findings-resultats-eng.htm.

Ramchandani, P. G., Domoney, J., Sethna, V., Psychogiou, L., Vlachos, H., & Murray, L. (2013). *Journal of Child Psychology and Psychiatry, 54*(1), 56–64.

Ramey, C. T., Campbell, F. A., & Ramey, S. L. (1999). Early intervention: Successful pathways to improving intellectual development. *Developmental Neuropsychology, 16*(3), 385–392.

Randel, B., Stevenson, H. W., & Witruk, E. (2000). Attitudes, beliefs, and mathematics achievement of German and Japanese high school students. *International Journal of Behavioral Development, 24*(2), 190–198.

Rapin, I. (1997). Autism. *New England Journal of Medicine, 337,* 97–104.

Rat-Fischer, L., O'Regan, J. K., & Fagard, J. (2012). Handedness in infants' tool use. *Developmental Psychobiology,* doi: 10.1002/dev.21078.

Rathus, J. H., & Miller, A. L. (2002). Dialectical Behavior Therapy adapted for suicidal adolescents. *Suicide and Life-Threatening Behavior, 32*(2), 146–157.

Rathus, S. A., Nevid, J. S., & Fichner-Rathus, L. (2008). *Human sexuality in a world of diversity* (7th ed.). Boston: Allyn & Bacon.

Rattan, S. I. S., Kristensen, P., & Clark, B. F. C. (Eds.). (2006). *Understanding and modulating aging.* Malden, MA: Blackwell Publishing.

Reddy, L. A., & De Thomas, C. (2007). Assessment of attention-deficit/hyperactivity disorder with children. In S. R. Smith & L. Handler (Eds.), *The clinical assessment of children and adolescents: A practitioner's handbook* (pp. 365–387). Mahwah, NJ: Erlbaum.

Redshaw, M., & van den Akker, O. (2007). Editorial. *Journal of Reproductive and Infant Psychology, 25*(2), 103–105.

Reef, S., Zimmerman-Swain, L., & Coronado, V. (2004). Disease description: Rubella is a viral illness caused by a togavirus of the genus *Rubivirus*. Available at http://www.cdc.gov/nip/diseases/rubella/default.htm.

Rees, S., Harding, R., & Inder, T. (2006). The developmental environment and the origins of neurological disorders. In P. Gluckman & M. Hanson (Eds.), *Developmental origins of health and disease* (pp. 379–391). New York: Cambridge University Press.

Reijneveld, S. A., et al. (2004). Infant crying and abuse. *Lancet, 364*(9442), 1340–1342.

Reiner, W. G., & Gearhart, J. P. (2004). Discordant sexual identity in some genetic males with cloacal exstrophy assigned to female sex at birth. *The New England Journal of Medicine, 350*, 333–341.

Reis, O., & Youniss, J. (2004). Patterns in identity change and development in relationships with mothers and friends. *Journal of Adolescent Research, 19*(1), 31–44.

Reitzes, D. C., & Mutran, E. J. (2004). The transition to retirement. *International Journal of Aging & Human Development, 59*(1), 63–84.

Reitzes, D. C., & Mutran, E. J. (2006). Lingering identities in retirement. *Sociological Quarterly, 47*(2), 333–359.

Rennie, S. (2012, Sept. 20). Boomerang kids mean empty nest not quite so empty—Census. *Globe and Mail*. Retrieved from http://www.theglobeandmail.com/news/politics/boomerang-kids-mean-empty-nests-not-quite-so-empty-census/article4553426/.

Rest, J. R. (1983). Morality. In P. H. Mussen (Ed.), *Handbook of child psychology,* Vol. 3, *Cognitive development.* New York: Wiley.

Retsinas, J. (1988). A theoretical reassessment of the applicability of Kübler-Ross's stages of dying. *Death Studies, 12*(3), 207–216.

Reynolds, C. A., Barlow, T., & Pedersen, N. L. (2006). Alcohol, tobacco and caffeine use: Spouse similarity processes. *Behavior Genetics, 36*(2), 201–215.

Richards, J. C., Hof, A., & Alvarenga, M. (2000). Serum lipids and their relationships with hostility and angry affect and behaviors in men. *Health Psychology, 19*(4), 393–398.

Rivers, C. & Barnett, R. (2011). *The truth about girls and boys: Challenging toxic stereotypes about our children.* New York: Columbia University Press.

Rizzolatti, G., Fadiga, L., Fogassi, L., & Gallese, V. (2002). From mirror neurons to imitation: Facts and speculations. In A. N. Meltzoff & W. Prinz (Eds.), *The imitative mind: Development, evolution, and brain bases.* New York: Cambridge University Press.

Roberts, B. W., & DelVecchio, W. F. (2000). The rank-order consistency of personality traits from childhood to old age: A quantitative review of longitudinal studies. *Psychological Bulletin, 126*(1), 3–25.

Roberts, B. W., Walton, K. E., & Viechtbauer, W. (2006). Patterns of mean-level change in personality traits across the life course: A meta-analysis of longitudinal studies. *Psychological Bulletin, 132*(1). 1–25.

Roberts, K. C., Shields, M., de Groh, M., Aziz, A., & Gilbert, J. (2012). *Overweight and obesity in children and adolescents: Results from the 2009 to 2011 Canadian Health Measures Survey*. Ottawa: Statistics Canada. Retrieved from http://www.statcan.gc.ca/pub/82-003-x/2012003/article/11706-eng.htm.

Roberts, K., C., Shields, M., de Groh, M., Aziz, A., & Gilbert, J.-A. (2012). Overweight and obesity in children and adolescents: Results from the 2009 to 2011 Canadian Health Measures Survey. *Health Reports*, *23* (3), Statistics Canada, Catalogue no. 82-003-XPE.

Robins, R. W., & Trzesniewski, K. H. (2005). Self-esteem development across the life span. *Current Directions in Psychological Science, 14*(3), 158–162.

Robins, R. W., Trzesniewski, K. H., Tracy, J. L., Gosling, S. D., & Potter, J. (2002). Global self-esteem across the lifespan. *Psychology and Aging, 17*(3), 423–434.

Robins Wahlin, T., Lundin, A., & Dear, K. (2007). Early cognitive deficits in Swedish gene carriers of Huntington's disease. *Neuropsychology, 21*(1), 31–44.

Robinson, A. L., Dolhanty, J., & Greenberg, L. (2013). Emotion focused family therapy for eating disorders in children and adolescents. *Journal of Clinical Psychology and Psychotherapy 22*(1), 75–82.

Robinson, M. (2011). Monogamy and polyamory as strategic identities. American Psychological Association Convention, Washington, DC. Retrieved from http://www.academia.edu/3004497/Monogamy_and_Polyamory_as_Strategic_identities.

Roebers, C. M., & Schneider, W. (2002). Individual differences in young children's suggestibility: Relations to event memory, language abilities, working memory, and executive functioning. *Cognitive Development, 20*, 427–447.

Roeser, R. W., Peck, S. C., & Nasir, N. S. (2006). Self and identity processes in school motivation, learning, and achievement. In P. A. Alexander & P. H. Winne (Eds.), *Handbook of educational psychology* (pp. 391–424). Mahwah, NJ: Erlbaum.

Roffwarg, H. P., Muzio, J. N., & Dement, W. C. (1966). Ontogenetic development of the human sleep–dream cycle. *Science, 152,* 604–619.

Rogue Community College. (2012). Holland code quiz. Retrieved from http://www.roguecc.edu/counseling/hollandcodes/test.asp.

Rojahn, J., Komelasky, K., & Man, M. (2008). Implicit attitudes and explicit ratings of romantic attraction of college students toward opposite-sex peers with physical disabilities. *Journal of Developmental and Physical Disabilities, 20* (4). Retrieved from http://link.springer.com/article/10.1007/s10882-008-9108-6.

Rondal, J. A., & Ling, L. (2006). Neurobehavioral specificity in Down's Syndrome. *Revista de Logopedia, Foniatría y Audiología, 26*(1), 12–19.

Roopnarine, J. L., Krishnakumar, A., Metindogan, A., & Evans, M. (2006). Links between parenting styles, parent–child academic interaction, parent–school interaction, and early academic skills and social behaviors in young children of English-speaking Caribbean immigrants. *Early Childhood Research Quarterly, 21*(2), 238–252.

Roots of Empathy. (2013). What we do: Research and effectiveness of the program. Retrieved from http://www.rootsofempathy.org/en/what-we-do/research.html.

Rosander, K., & Hofsten, C. (2004). Infants' emerging ability to represent occluded object motion. *Cognition, 91*, 1–22.

Rose, A. J., Swenson, L. P., & Carlson, W. (2004). Friendships of aggressive youth: Considering the influences of being disliked and of being perceived as popular. *Journal of Experimental Child Psychology, 88*(1), 25–45.

Rose, S. A., Feldman, J. F., & Jankowski, J. J. (2001). Visual short-term memory in the first year of life: Capacity and recency effects. *Developmental Psychology, 37*(4), 539–549.

Rose, S. A., Feldman, J. F., & Jankowski, J. J. (2004). Infant visual recognition memory. *Developmental Review, 24,* 74–100.

Rose, S. A., Feldman, J. F., & Jankowski, J. J. (2005). The structure of infant cognition at 1 year. *Intelligence, 33*(3), 231–250.

Rose, S. A., Feldman, J. F., & Wallace, I. F. (1992). Infant information processing in relation to six-year cognitive outcomes. *Child Development, 63,* 1126–1141.

Rosen, M. (2012). Sad dads. *Parents.* Retrieved from http://www.parents .com/parenting/dads/sad-dads/.

Rosen, T., Pillemer, K., & Lachs, M. (2008). Resident-to-resident aggression in long-term care facilities. *Aggression and Violent Behavior, 13*(2), 77–87.

Rosenstein, D., & Oster, H. (1988). Differential facial responses to four basic tastes. *Child Development, 59,* 1555–1568.

Rosenthal, R., & Jacobson, L. (1968). *Pygmalion in the classroom.* New York: Holt, Rinehart & Winston.

Rospenda, K. M., et al. (2005). Is workplace harassment hazardous to your health? *Journal of Business and Psychology, 20*(1), 95–110.

Ross, H., Ross, M., Stein, N., & Trabasso, T. (2006). How siblings resolve their conflicts: The importance of first offers, planning, and limited opposition. *Child Development. 77*(6) 1730–1745.

Ross, J. L., Roeltgen, D., Feuillan, P., Kushner, H., & Cutler, W. B. (2000). Use of estrogen in young girls with Turner syndrome: Effects on memory. *Neurology, 54*(1), 164–170.

Rotenberg, K. J., et al. (2004). Cross-sectional and longitudinal relations among peer-reported trustworthiness, social relationships, and psychological adjustment in children and early adolescents from the United Kingdom and Canada. *Journal of Experimental Child Psychology, 88*(1), 46–67.

Roterman, M. (2012). Sexual behaviour and condom use of 15 - to 24-year-olds in 2003 and 2009/10. *Statistics Canada.* Retrieved from http://www.statcan .gc.ca/pub/82-003-x/2012001/ article/11632-eng.htm.

Rotermann, M., Sanmartin, C., Hennessy, D., and Arthur, M. (2015). Prescription medication use by Canadians aged 6 to 79.. Retrieved from Statistics Canada website, http://www.statcan .gc.ca/pub/82-003-x/2014006/ article/14032-eng.htm.

Roth, G. S., et al. (2004). Aging in rhesus monkeys: Relevance to human health interventions. *Science, 305*(5689), 1423–1426.

Rothbart, M. K., Ellis, L. K., & Posner, M. I. (2004). Temperament and self-regulation. In R. F. Baumeister & K. D. Vohs (Eds.), *Handbook of self-regulation: Research, theory, and applications.* New York: Guilford.

Rothbart, M. K., & Sheese, B. E. (2007). Temperament and emotion regulation. In J. J. Gross (Ed.), *Handbook of emotion regulation* (pp. 331–350). New York: Guilford.

Rottinghaus, P. J., Betz, N. E., & Borgen, F. H. (2003). Validity of parallel measures of vocational interests and confidence. *Journal of Career Assessment, 11*(4), 355–378.

Rottinghaus, P. J., Coon, K. L.,Gaffey, A. R., & Zytowski, D. G. (2007). Thirty-year stability and predictive validity of vocational interests. *Journal of Career Assessment, 15*(1), 5–22.

Roulet-Perez, E., & Deonna, T. (2006). Autism, epilepsy, and EEG epileptiform activity. In R. Tuchman & I. Rapin (Eds.), *Autism: A neurological disorder of early brain development* (pp. 174–188). *International review of child neurology*. London: Mac Keith Press.

Rowan, C. (2011). A research review regarding the impact of technology on child development, behavior, and academic performance. *Zone In*. Retrieved August 11, 2016, from http://www .sd23.bc.ca/ProgramsServices/ earlylearning/parentinformation/ Documents/Impact%20of%20 Technology%20on%20Young%20 Children's%20Development.pdf.

Rowland, D. T. (2009). Global population aging: History and prospects. In P. Uhlenberg (Ed.), *International handbook of population aging* (pp. 37–65). New York: Springer Science + Business Media.

Rubia, K., et al. (2006). Progressive increase of frontostriatal brain activation from childhood to adulthood during event- related tasks of cognitive control. *Human Brain Mapping, 27*(12), 973–993.

Rubin, K. H., Bukowski, W. M., & Parker, J. G. (2006). Peer interactions, relationships, and groups. In N. Eisenberg, W. Damon, & R. M. Lerner (Eds.), *Handbook of child psychology* (6th ed.), Vol. 3, *Social, emotional, and personality development* (pp. 571–645). Hoboken, NJ: Wiley.

Ruble, D. N., Martin, C. L., & Berenbaum, S. A. (2006). Gender development. In N. Eisenberg, W. Damon, & R. M. Lerner (Eds.), *Handbook of child psychology* (6th ed.), Vol. 3, *Social, emotional, and personality development.* (pp. 858–932). Hoboken, NJ: Wiley.

Rudolph, K. D., & Flynn, M. (2007). Childhood adversity and youth depression: Influence of gender and pubertal status. *Development and Psychopathology, 19*(2), 497–521.

Rudy, D., & Grusec, J. E. (2006). Authoritarian parenting in individualist and collectivist groups: Associations with maternal emotion and cognition and children's self-esteem. *Journal of Family Psychology, 20*(1), 68–78.

Rumbold, A. R., et al. (2006). Vitamins C and E and the risks of preeclampsia and perinatal complications. *New England Journal of Medicine, 354*, 1796–1806.

Runyon, M. K., & Kenny, M. C. (2002). Relationship of attributional style, depression, and posttrauma distress among children who suffered physical or sexual abuse. *Child Maltreatment: Journal of the American Professional Society on the Abuse of Children, 7*(3), 254–264.

Rusconi, A. (2004). Different pathways out of the parental Home: A comparison of West Germany and Italy. *Journal of Comparative Family Studies, 35*(4), 627–649.

Rushowy, Kristen (2014, April 28). Special needs kids often told to stay home from school, says People for Education report. *The Toronto Star*. Retrieved from https://www.thestar.com/yourtoronto/ education/2014/04/28/special_needs _kids_often_told_to_stay_home_from _school_says_people_for_education _report.html.

Rushton, J. P., & Bons, T. A. (2005). Mate choice and friendship in twins: Evidence for genetic similarity. *Psychological Science, 16*(7), 555–559.

Rushton, J. P., & Jensen, A. R. (2005). Thirty years of research on race differences in cognitive ability. *Psychology, Public Policy and Law, 11*(2), Retrieved from http://psychology.uwo.ca/faculty/ rushtonpdfs/PPPL1.pdf.

Rushton, J. P., Skuy, M., & Fridjhon, P. (2003). Performance on Raven's Advanced Progressive Matrices by African, East Indian, and White engineering students in South Africa. *Intelligence, 31*(2), 123–137.

Russ, S. W. (2006). Pretend play, affect, and creativity. In P. Locher, C. Martindale, & L. Dorfman (Eds.), *New directions* in aesthetics, creativity and the arts, Foundations and frontiers in aesthetics (pp. 239–250). Amityville, NY: Baywood.

Rybash, J. M., & Hrubi-Bopp, K. L. (2000). Source monitoring and false recollection: A life span developmental perspective. *Experimental Aging Research, 26*(1), 75–87.

Ryff, C. D., Singer, B. H., & Seltzer, M. M. (2002). Pathways through challenge: Implications for well-being and health. In L. Pulkkinen, & A. Caspi (Eds.), *Paths to successful development: Personality in the life course* (pp. 302–328). New York: Cambridge University Press.

S

Sabattini, L., & Leaper, C. (2004). The relation between mothers' and fathers' parenting styles and their division of labor in the home: Young adults' retrospective reports. *Sex Roles, 50*(3–4), 217–225.

Sabia, J. J. (2008). There's no place like home: A hazard model analysis of aging in place among older homeowners in the PSID. *Research on Aging, 30*(1), 3–35.

Sadker, D. M., & Silber, E. S. (Eds.) (2007). *Gender in the classroom: Foundations, skills, methods, and strategies across the curriculum.* Mahwah, NJ: Erlbaum.

Saffran, J. R., Werker, J. F., & Werner, L. A. (2006). The infant's auditory world: Hearing, speech, and the beginnings of language. In D. Kuhn, R. S. Siegler, W. Damon, & R. M. Lerner (Eds.), *Handbook of child psychology,* Vol. 2, *Cognition, perception, and language* (6th ed.) (pp. 58–108). Hoboken, NJ: Wiley.

Saggino, A., Perfetti, B., Spitoni, G., & Galati, G. (2006). Fluid intelligence and executive functions: New Perspectives. In L. V. Wesley (Ed.), *Intelligence: New research* (pp. 1–22). Hauppauge, NY: Nova Science Publishers.

Saigal, S., et al. (2006). Transition of extremely low-birth-weight infants from adolescence to young adulthood: Comparison with normal birth-weight controls. *Journal of the American Medical Association, 295*(6), 667–675.

Saiki, J., & Miyatsuji, H. (2007). Feature binding in visual working memory evaluated by type identification paradigm. *Cognition, 102*(1), 49–83.

Saito, S., & Miyake, A. (2004). On the nature of forgetting and the processing–storage relationship in reading span performance. *Journal of Memory and Language, 50*(4), 425–443.

Salapatek, P. (1975). Pattern perception in early infancy. In L. B. Cohen & P. Salapatek (Eds.), *Infant perception: From sensation to cognition.* New York: Academic Press.

Sales, J. M., Fivush, R., & Peterson, C. (2003). Parental reminiscing about positive and negative events. *Journal of Cognition and Development, 4*(2), 185–209.

Salmivalli, C., Ojanen, T., Haanpää, J., & Peets, K. (2005). "I'm OK but you're not" and other peer-relational schemas: Explaining individual differences in children's social goals. *Developmental Psychology, 41*(2), 363–375.

Salthouse, T. A. (2001). Structural models of the relations between age and measures of cognitive functioning. *Intelligence, 29*(2), 93–115.

Salthouse, T. A., & Babcock, R. L. (1991). Decomposing adult age differences in working memory. *Developmental Psychology, 27*(5), 763–776.

Salthouse, T. A., & Berish, D. E. (2005). Correlates of within-person (across-occasion) variability in reaction time. *Neuropsychology, 19*(1), 77–87.

Salthouse, T. A., & Davis, H. P. (2006). Organization of cognitive abilities and neuropsychological variables across the lifespan. *Developmental Review, 26*(1), 31–54.

Salthouse, T. A., & Siedlecki, K. L. (2007). Efficiency of route selection as a function of adult age. *Brain and Cognition, 63*(3), 279–286.

Salthouse, T. A., Siedlecki, K. L., & Krueger, L. E. (2006). An individual differences analysis of memory control. *Journal of Memory and Language, 55*(1), 102–125.

Salzarulo, P., & Ficca, G. (Eds.). (2002). *Awakening and sleep–wake cycle across development.* Amsterdam: John Benjamins.

Sandman, C., & Crinella, F. (1995). Cited in Margoshes, P. (1995). For many, old age is the prime of life. *APA Monitor, 26*(5), 36–37.

Santelli, J. S., Lindberg, J. D., Abma, J., McNeely, C. S., & Resnick, M. (2000). Adolescent sexual behavior: Estimates and trends from four nationally representative surveys. *Family Planning Perspectives, 32*(4), 156–165, 194.

Santos, D. C. C., Gabbard, C., & Goncalves, V. M. G. (2000). Motor development during the first 6 months: The case of Brazilian infants. *Infant and Child Development, 9*(3), 161–166.

Saroglou, V., & Galand, P. (2004). Identities, values, and religion: A study among Muslim, other immigrant, and native Belgian young adults after the 9/11 attacks. *Identity, 4*(2), 97–132.

Sarrazin, P., Trouilloud, D., & Bois, J. (2005a). Attentes du superviseur et performance sportive du pratiquant. Amplitude et fonctionnement de l'effet Pygmalion en contexte sportif. *Bulletin de Psychologie, 58*(1), 63–68.

Sarrazin, P., Trouilloud, D., Tessier, D., Chanal, J., & Bois, J. (2005b). Attentes de motivation et comportements différenciés de l'enseignant d'éducation physique et sportive à l'égard de ses élèves: une étude en contexte naturel d'enseignement. *Revue Européenne de Psychologie Appliquée, 55*(2), 111–120.

Sasaki, C. (2007). Grounded-theory study of therapists' perceptions of grieving process in bereaved children. *Dissertation Abstracts International: Section B: The Sciences and Engineering, 68*(1-B), 635.

Save the Children. (2004). *State of the world's mothers 2004.* Available at http://www.savethechildren.org/mothers/report_2004/index.asp. Accessed June 2004.

Savickas, M. L. (2005). The theory and practice of career construction. In S. D. Brown & R. W. Lent (Eds.). *Career development and counseling.* (pp. 42–70). Hoboken, NJ: Wiley.

Savin-Williams, R. C. (2007). Girl-on-girl sexuality. In B. J. R. Leadbeater & N. Way (Eds.), *Urban girls revisited: Building strengths* (pp. 301–318). New York: New York University Press.

Savin-Williams, R. C., & Diamond, L. M. (2004). Sex. In R. M. Lerner & L. Steinberg (Eds.), *Handbook of adolescent psychology* (2nd ed.) (pp. 189–231). Hoboken, NJ: Wiley.

Schafer, A. (2007, December). Should spanking still be legal in Canada? Canadian Children's Right Council. Retrieved from http://canadiancrc.com/Alyson_Schafer_on_Corporal_Punishment.aspx.

Schaie, K. W. (1994). The course of adult intellectual development. *American Psychologist, 49,* 304–313. Copyright © American Psychological Association.

Schaie, K. W. (2005). What can we learn from longitudinal studies of adult development? *Research in Human Development, 2*(3), 133–158.

Schaie, K. W., Willis, S. L., & Caskie, G. I. L. (2004). The Seattle longitudinal study: Relationship between personality and cognition. *Aging, Neuropsychology, and Cognition, 11*(2–3), 304–324.

Schafer, M., Mustillo S., & Ferraro, K. (2013). Age and the tenses of life satisfaction. *The Journals of Gerontology.* Retrieved October 27, 2016, from http://psychsocgerontology.oxfordjournals.org/content/early/2013/05/21/geronb.gbt038.full.

Scharf, M., Shulman, S., & Avigad-Spitz, L. (2005). Sibling relationships in emerging adulthood and in adolescence. *Journal of Adolescent Research, 20*(1), 64–90.

Schmidtke, A., Sell, R., & Lohr, C. (2008). Epidemiology of suicide in older persons. *Zeitschrift für Gerontologie und Geriatrie, 41*(1), 3–13.

Schneewind, K. A., & Kupsch, M. (2007). Patterns of neuroticism, work-family stress, and resources as determinants of personal distress: A cluster analysis of young, dual-earner families at the individual and couple level. *Journal of Individual Differences, 28*(3), 150–160.

Schonfeld, A. M., Mattson, S. N., & Riley, E. P. (2005). Moral maturity and delinquency after prenatal alcohol exposure. *Journal of Studies on Alcohol, 66*(4), 545–554.

Schoppe-Sullivan, S. J., Mangelsdorf, S. C., Brown, G. L., & Sokolowski, M. S. (2007). Goodness-of-fit in family context: Infant temperament, marital quality, and early coparenting behavior. *Infant Behavior & Development, 30*(1), 82–96.

Schraf, M., & Hertz-Lazarowitz, R. (2003). Social networks in the school context: Effects of culture and gender. *Journal of Social and Personal Relationships, 20*(6), 843–858.

Schuetze, P., Lawton, D., & Eiden, R. D. (2006). Prenatal cocaine exposure and infant sleep at 7 months of age: The influence of the caregiving environment. *Infant Mental Health Journal, 27*(4), 383–404.

Schultz, D. P., & Schultz, S. E. (2008). A history of modern psychology (9th Ed.). Belmont, CA: Thomson/Wadsworth.

Schultz, W. W., et al. (2005). Women's sexual pain and its management. *Journal of Sexual Medicine, 2*(3), 301–316.

Schumacher, D., & Queen, J. A. (2007). *Overcoming obesity in childhood and adolescence: A guide for school leaders.* Thousand Oaks, CA: Corwin Press.

Schuurmans, J., et al. (2006). A randomized, controlled trial of the effectiveness of cognitive-behavioral therapy and sertraline versus a waitlist control group for anxiety disorders in older adults. *American Journal of Geriatric Psychiatry, 14*(3), 255–263.

Schwartz, S. J. (2001). The evolution of Eriksonian and neo-Eriksonian identity theory and research: A review and integration. *Identity, 1*(1), 7–58.

Science Daily. (2011). A second language gives toddlers an edge. Retrieved from http://www.sciencedaily.com/releases/2011/01/110119120409.htm.

Science Daily. (2012, September 13). How early social deprivation impairs long-term cognitive function. Retrieved July 28, 2016, from https://www.sciencedaily.com/releases/2012/09/120913141413.htm.

Science Daily. (2013). Children with autism show increased positive social behaviors when animals are present. Retrieved from http://www.sciencedaily.com/releases/2013/02/130227183504.htm.

Scoffield, H. (2012). Canada family census 2011: New structure means new rules. Retrieved from http://www.huffingtonpost.ca/2012/09/19/canada-family-census-2011_n_1896307.html.

Scott, J. R. (2006). Preventing eclampsia. *Obstetrics & Gynecology, 108*, 824–825.

Scourfield, J., Van den Bree, M., Martin, N., & McGuffin, P. (2004). Conduct problems in children and adolescents: A twin study. *Archives of General Psychiatry, 61*, 489–496.

Seabrook, J. A., & Avison, W. R. (2015). Family structure and children's socioeconomic attainment: A Canadian sample. *Canadian Review of Sociology, 52*(1), 66–88.

Sears, W., & Sears, M. (2001). *The attachment parenting book: A commonsense guide to understanding and nurturing your baby.* Boston: Little, Brown & Co.

Secker-Walker, R. H., & Vacek, P. M. (2003). Relationships between cigarette smoking during pregnancy, gestational age, maternal weight gain, and infant birthweight. *Addictive Behaviors, 28*(1), 55–66.

Sefcek, J. A., Brumbach, B. H., Vasquez, G., & Miller, G. F. (2007). The evolutionary psychology of human mate choice: How ecology, genes, fertility, and fashion influence mating strategies. *Journal of Psychology & Human Sexuality, 18*(2–3) 125–182.

Segrin, C., Powell, H. L., Givertz, M., & Brackin, A. (2003). Symptoms of depression, relational quality, and loneliness in dating relationships. *Personal Relationships, 10*(1), 25–36.

Seidah, A., & Bouffard, T. (2007). Being proud of oneself as a person or being proud of one's physical appearance: What matters for feeling well in adolescence? *Social Behavior and Personality, 35*(2), 255–268.

Selman, R. L. (1976). Social-cognitive understanding. In T. Lickona (Ed.), *Moral development and behavior: Theory, research, and social issues.* New York: Holt, Rinehart & Winston.

Selman, R. L. (1980). *The growth of interpersonal understanding: Developmental and clinical analysis.* New York: Academic Press.

Selman, R. L., & Dray, A. J. (2006). Risk and prevention. In K. A. Renninger, I. E. Sigel, W. Damon, & R. M. Lerner (Eds.), *Handbook of child psychology* (6th ed.), Vol. 4, *Child psychology in practice* (pp. 378–419). Hoboken, NJ: Wiley.

Serbin, L. A., Poulin-Dubois, D., Colburne, K. A., Sen, M. G., & Eichstedt, J. A. (2001). Gender stereotyping in infancy: Visual preferences for and knowledge of gender-stereotyped toys in the second year. *International Journal of Behavioral Development, 25*(1), 7–15.

Service Canada. (2013). Employment insurance maternity and parental benefits. Retrieved October 14, 2016, from http://www.servicecanada.gc.ca/eng/ei/types/maternity_parental.shtml.

Sessoms, G. (2010). Activities for obese children to lose weight. Retrieved from http://www.livestrong.com/article/320821-activities-for-obese-children-to-lose-weight/.

Seto, C. (2012, December 17). When your toddler is a late walker. *Today's Parent*. Retrieved from http://www.todaysparent.com/toddler/toddler-development/toddler-is-a-late-walker/.

Seward, R. R. (2005). Family and community in Ireland. *Journal of Comparative Family Studies, 36*(2), 343–344.

Sexual Information and Education Council of Canada (SIECCAN). (2004). Sexual health education in the schools: Questions and answers. *Canadian Journal of Human Sexuality,* 13(3–4): 129–144. Retrieved from http://www.sieccan.org/pdf/sexual_health_qs.pdf.

Sexton, S. A. (2008). The influence of social support systems on the degree of PTSD symptoms in the elderly. *Dissertation Abstracts International: Section B: The Sciences and Engineering, 68*(7-B), 2008, 4846.

Sexuality and U. (2012). Statistics on Canadian teen pregnancies. Retrieved from http://www.sexualityandu.ca/sexual-health/statistics1/statistics-on-canadian-teen-pregnancies.

Shafto, M. A., Burke, D. M., Stamatakis, E. A., Tam, P. P., & Tyler, L. K. (2007). On the tip-of-the-tongue: Neural correlates of increased word-finding failures in normal aging. *Journal of Cognitive Neuroscience, 19*(12), 2060–2070.

Sharma, A. (2011). Childhood obesity ssue. The solution is not "eat less, move more."*Conduit 5*(1). Retrieved August 11, 2016, from http://www.obesitynetwork.ca/files/CONDUIT_Fall11_themesection.pdf.

Shatz, K. H. (2006). The widow who wasn't a bride. *Dissertation Abstracts International Section A: Humanities and Social Sciences, 67*(2-A), 739.

Shaw, G. (2013, March 13). Amanda Todd's mother speaks out about her daughter, bullying (with video). *Vancouver Sun*. Retrieved from http://www.vancouversun.com/news/Amanda+Todd+speaks+about+daughter+death/7384521/story.html.

Shaywitz, B. A., Lyon, G. R., & Shaywitz, S. E. (2006a). The role of functional magnetic resonance imaging in understanding reading and dyslexia. *Developmental Neuropsychology, 30*(1), 613–632.

Shaywitz, S. E., Mody, M., & Shaywitz, B. A. (2006b). Neural mechanisms in dyslexia. *Current Directions in Psychological Science, 15*(6), 278–281.

Sheeber, L. B., Davis, B., Leve, C., Hops, H., & Tildesley, E. (2007). Adolescents' relationships with their mothers and fathers: Associations with depressive disorder and subdiagnostic symptomatology. *Journal of Abnormal Psychology, 116*(1), 144–154.

Sheffield, C. (2013). Middle-aged men suffer mentally in the new economy. *Forbes*. http://www.forbes.com/sites/carriesheffield/2013/11/13/middle-aged-men-suffer-mentally-in-the-new-economy/#6fefdd27f2d0

Sherwin-White, S. (2006). The social toddler: Promoting positive behaviour. *Infant Observation, 9*(1), 95–97.

Shinohara, H., & Kodama, H. (2012). Relationship between duration of crying/fussy behavior and actigraphic sleep measures in early infancy. *Early Human Development*, *88*(11): 847–852.

Shiota, M. N., & Levenson, R. W. (2007). Birds of a feather don't always fly farthest. *Psychology and Aging, 22*(4), 666–675.

Shirk, S., Burwell, R., & Harter, S. (2003). Strategies to modify low self-esteem in adolescents. In M. A. Reinecke et al. (Eds.), *Cognitive therapy with children and adolescents: A casebook for clinical practice* (2nd ed.) (pp. 189–213). New York: Guilford.

Shneidman, E. S. (1977). Aspects of the dying process. *Psychiatric Annals, 17*(8), 391–397.

Shroff, H., et al. (2006). Features associated with excessive exercise in women with eating disorders. *International Journal of Eating Disorders, 39*(6), 454–461.

Shultz, K. S., & Adams, G. A. (Eds.). (2007). *Aging and work in the 21st century.* New York: Lawrence Erlbaum Associates, Inc.

Siegel, L. S. (1992). Infant motor, cognitive, and language behaviors as predictors of achievement at school age. In C. Rovee-Collier & L. P. Lipsitt (Eds.), *Advances in infancy research,* Vol. 7. Norwood, NJ: Ablex.

Siegler, R. S., & Alibali, M. W. (2005). *Children's thinking* (4th ed.). Upper Saddle River, NJ: Prentice Hall.

Siegrist, J., Von Dem Knesebeck, O., & Pollack, C. E. (2004). Social productivity and well- being of older people. *Social Theory & Health, 2*(1), 1–17.

Sierra, F. (2006). Is (your cellular response to) stress killing you? *Journals of Gerontology: Series A: Biological Sciences and Medical Sciences, 61A*(6), 557–561.

Signal Hill. (2009). *Healthy sexuality.* Retrieved from http://www.prolifebc.ca/hs-std.html.

Signorello, L. B., & McLaughlin, J. K. (2004). Maternal caffeine consumption and spontaneous abortion: A review of the epidemiologic evidence. *Epidemiology, 15*(2), 229–239.

Silbereisen, R. K. (2006). Development and ecological context: History of the psychological science in a personal view and experience—An interview with Urie Bronfenbrenner. *Psychologie in Erziehung und Unterricht, 53*(1), 241–249.

Silventoinen, K., et al. (2007). Genetic and environmental factors in relative weight from birth to age 18: The Swedish young male twins study. *International Journal of Obesity, 31*(4), 615–621.

Silver, R. C., & Wortman, C. B. (2007). The stage theory of grief. *Journal of the American Medical Association,* 297, 2692.

Simion, F., Cassia, V. M., Turati, C., & Valenza, E. (2001). The origins of face perception: Specific versus non-specific mechanisms. *Infant and Child Development, 10*(1–2), 59–65.

Simonelli, A., Monti, F., & Magalotti, D. (2005). The complex phenomenon of failure to thrive: Medical, psychological and relational-affective aspects. *Psicologia Clinica dello Sviluppo, 9*(2), 183–212.

Simonelli, A., Vizziello, G. F., Bighin, M., De Palo, F., & Petech, E. (2007). Transition to triadic relationships between parenthood and dyadic adjustment. *Età Evolutiva, 86,* 92–99.

Simon Fraser University. (2011). The Silver Surfer Project. Retrieved from http://www.sfu.ca/silversurfers/?page_id=26.

Simonton, D. K. (2006a). Creative genius, knowledge, and reason: The lives and works of eminent creators. In J. C. Kaufman & J. Baer (Eds.). *Creativity and reason in cognitive development.* (pp. 43–59). New York: Cambridge University Press.

Simonton, D. K. (2006b). Creativity around the world in 80 ways … but with one destination. In J. C. Kaufman & R. Sternberg (Eds.), *The international handbook of creativity* (pp. 490–496). New York: Cambridge University Press.

Simonton, D. K. (2007). Creative life cycles in literature: Poets versus novelists or conceptualists versus experimentalists? *Psychology of Aesthetics, Creativity, and the Arts, 1*(3), 133–139.

Sims, C. S., Drasgow, F., & Fitzgerald, L. F. (2005). The effects of sexual harassment on turnover in the military. *Journal of Applied Psychology, 90*(6), 1141–1152.

Singer, L. T., et al. (2005). Prenatal cocaine exposure and infant cognition. *Infant*

Behavior & Development, 28(4), 431–444.

Sinnema, J. (2009, March 12). Bad habits priming kids for chronic diseases: Study. *Edmonton Journal.* Retrieved from http://www.canada.com/health/healthy-living/habits+pri-ming+kids+chronic+diseases+Study/1385622/story.html.

Sirrs, S. M., et al. (2007). Normal-appearing white matter in patients with phenylketonuria: Water content, myelin water fraction, and metabolite concentrations. *Radiology, 242*, 236–243.

Skinner, B. F. (1957). *Verbal behavior.* New York: Appleton.

Skinner, R., & McFaull, S. (2012). Suicide among children and adolescents in Canada: Trends and sex differences, 1980–2008. *CMAJ, 184*(9), 1029–1034.

Skoczenski, A. M. (2002). Limitations on visual sensitivity during infancy: Contrast sensitivity, vernier acuity, and orientation processing. In J. W. Fagen & H. Hayne (Eds.), *Progress in infancy research,* Vol. 2. Mahwah, NJ: Erlbaum.

Slaughter, V., & Griffiths, M. (2007). Death understanding and fear of death in young children. *Clinical Child Psychology and Psychiatry, 12*(4), 525–535.

Slavin, R. E. (2006). *Educational psychology: Theory and practice* (8th ed.). Boston: Allyn & Bacon.

Sloan, S., Sneddon, H., Stewart, M., & Iwaniec, D. (2006). Breast is best? Reasons why mothers decide to breastfeed or bottlefeed their babies and factors influencing the duration of breastfeeding. *Child Care in Practice, 12*(3), 283–297.

Slobin, D. I. (2001). Form/function relations: How do children find out what they are? In M. Tomasello & E. Bates (Eds.), *Language development: The essential readings.* Malden, MA: Blackwell.

Smetana, J. G. (1990). Morality and conduct disorders. In M. Lewis & S. M. Miller (Eds.), *Handbook of developmental psychopathology.* New York: Plenum.

Smetana, J. G. (2005). Adolescent–parent conflict: Resistance and subversion as developmental process. In L. Nucci (Ed), *Conflict, contradiction, and contrarian elements in moral development and education* (pp. 69–91). Mahwah, NJ: Erlbaum.

Smetana, J. G., Campione-Barr, N., & Metzger, A. (2006). Adolescent development in interpersonal and societal contexts. *Annual Review of Psychology, 57,* 255–284.

Smiley, P. A., & Johnson, R. S. (2006). Self- referring terms, event transitivity and development of self. *Cognitive Development, 21*(3), 266–284.

Smith, C. L., Calkins, S. D., Keane, S. P., Anastopoulos, A. D., & Shelton, T. L. (2004). Predicting stability and change in toddler behavior problems: Contributions of maternal behavior and child gender. *Developmental Psychology, 40*(1), 29–42.

Smith, J. (2015, December 21). Liberal government commits to repealing so-called "spanking law." *Toronto Star.* Retrieved from http://www.thestar.com/news/canada/2015/12/21/liberal-government-commits-to-repealing-spanking-law.html.

Smith, P. K. (2005). Play: Types and functions in human development. In B. J. Ellis & D. F. Bjorklund (Eds.), *Origins of the social mind: Evolutionary psychology and child development* (pp. 271–291). New York: Guilford Press.

Smolka, E., & Eviatar, Z. (2006). Phonological and orthographic visual word recognition in the two cerebral hemispheres: Evidence from Hebrew. *Cognitive Neuropsychology, 23*(6), 972–989.

Snarey, J. R., & Bell, D. (2003). Distinguishing structural and functional models of human development. *Identity, 3*(3), 221–230.

Snedeker, J., Geren, J., & Shafto, C. L. (2007). Starting over: International adoption as a natural experiment in language development. *Psychological Science, 18*(1), 79–87.

Snegovskikh, V., Park, J. S., & Norwitz, E. R. (2006). Endocrinology of parturition. *Endocrinology and Metabolism Clinics of North America, 35*(1), 173–191.

Snow, C. (2006). Cross-cutting themes and future research directions. In D. August & T. Shanahan (Eds.), *Developing literacy in second-language learners: Report of the National Literacy Panel on Language-Minority Children and Youth* (pp. 631–651). Mahwah, NJ: Erlbaum.

Snyderman, M., & Rothman, S. (1990). *The IQ controversy.* New Brunswick, NJ: Transaction.

Society of Obstetricians and Gynaecologists of Canada. (2009a). Facts and statistics: Sexual health and Canadian youth–Teen pregnancy rates. Retrieved from http://www.sexualityandu.ca/teachers/data-6.aspx.

Society of Obstetricians and Gynaecologists of Canada. (2009b). Fact sheets: Sex facts in Canada 2006. Retrieved from http://www.sexualityandu.ca/media-room/fact-sheets-1.aspx.

Society of Obstetricians and Gynaecologists of Canada. (2012a). Sexual health: Masturbation. Retrieved from http://www.sexualityandu.ca/sexual-health/what_is_masturbation.

Society of Obstetricians and Gynaecologists of Canada. (2012b). Sexual health: Sexual orientation and coming out. Retrieved from http://www.sexualityandu.ca/sexual-health/sexual-orientation-and-coming-out.

Society of Obstetricians and Gynaecologists of Canada. (2012c). Statistics on Canadian teen pregnancies. Retrieved from Society of Obstetricians and Gynaecologists of Canada. (2012c). Statistics on sexual intercourse experience among Canadian teenagers. Retrieved from http://www.sexualityandu.ca/sexual-health/statistics1/statistics-on-canadian-teen-pregnancies.

Society of Obstetricians and Gynaecologists of Canada. (2012d). Statistics on sexual intercourse experience among Canadian teenagers. Retrieved from http://www.sexualityandu.ca/sexual-health/statistics1/statistics-on-sexual-intercourse-experience-among-canadian-teenagers.

Society of Obstetricians and Gynaecologists of Canada. (2012e). Types of STIs–STDs. Retrieved from http://www.sexualityandu.ca/stis-stds/types-of-stis-stds.

Solano, C. H., Batten, P. G., & Parish, E. A. (1982). Loneliness and patterns of self-disclosure. *Journal of Personality and Social Psychology, 43,* 524–531.

Soliz, J. (2007). Communicative predictors of a shared family identity: Comparison of grandchildren's perceptions of family-of-origin grandparents and stepgrandparents. *Journal of Family Communication, 7*(3), 177–194.

Sommerfeld, J. (2000, April 18). Lifting the curse: Should monthly periods be optional? MSNBC online.

Sommers, M. S. (2008). Age-related changes in spoken word recognition. In D. B. Pisoni, & R. E. Remez (Eds.), *The handbook of speech perception. Blackwell handbooks in linguistics* (pp. 469–493). Malden, MA: Blackwell Publishing.

Sonnentag, S. (2003). Recovery, work engagement, and proactive behavior. *Journal of Applied Psychology, 88,* 518–528.

Sontag, L. W., & Richards, T. W. (1938). *Studies in fetal behavior: Fetal heart rate as a behavioral indicator.* Child Development Monographs, *3*(4).

Sorce, J., Emde, R. N., Campos, J. J., Klinnert, M. D. (2000). Maternal emotional signaling: Its effect on the visual cliff behavior of 1-year-olds. In D. Muir & A. Slater, (Eds.), *Infant development: The essential readings. Essential readings in developmental psychology* (pp. 282–292). Malden, MA: Blackwell.

Soto, C., Oliver, J., Gosling, S., & Potter, J. (2011). *Journal of Personality and Social Psychology,* 100(2), 330–348. Retrieved from http://psycnet.apa.org/journals/psp/100/2/330/.

Sousa, L., & Figueiredo, D. (2002). Dependence and independence among old persons. *Reviews in Clinical Gerontology, 12*(3), 269–273.

Soussignan, R., & Schaal, B. (2005). Emotional processes in human newborns: a functionalist perspective. In J. Nadel, & D. Muir (Eds.), *Emotional development: Recent research advances* (pp. 127–159). New York: Oxford University Press.

South, S. J., Haynie, D. L., & Bose, S. (2007). Student mobility and school dropout. *Social Science Research, 36*(1), 68–94.

Spelke, E. S., & Owsley, C. (1979). Intermodal exploration and knowledge in infancy. *Infant Behavior and Development, 2,* 13–27.

Spieker, S. J., et al. (2003). Joint influence of child care and infant attachment security for cognitive and language outcomes of low-income toddlers. *Infant Behavior and Development, 26*(3), 326–344.

Sprecher, S. (1998). Insiders' perspectives on reasons for attraction to a close other. *Social Psychology Quarterly, 61*(4), 287–300.

Sroufe, L. A. (1998). Cited in S. Blakeslee (1998, August 4), Re-evaluating significance of baby's bond with mother, *New York Times,* pp. F1, F2.

Sroufe, L. A., Waters, E., & Matas, L. (1974). Contextual determinants of infant affectional response. In M. Lewis & L. Rosenblum (Eds.), *The origins of fear.* New York: Wiley.

Staff, J., Mortimer, J. T., & Uggen, C. (2004). Work and leisure in adolescence. In R. Lerner & L. Steinberg, (Eds.), *Handbook of adolescent psychology* (2nd ed.) (pp. 429–450). Hoboken, NJ: Wiley.

Stagnitti, K., Unsworth, C., & Rodger, S. (2000). Development of an assessment to identify play behaviours that discriminate between the play of typical preschoolers and preschoolers with pre-academic problems. *Canadian Journal of Occupational Therapy, 67*(5), 291–303.

Stahmer, A. C., Ingersoll, B., & Koegel, R. L. (2004). Inclusive programming for toddlers autism spectrum disorders: Outcomes from the Children's Toddler School. *Journal of Positive Behavior Interventions, 6*(2), 67–82.

Stams, G. J. M., Juffer, F., & IJzendoorn, M. H. van (2002). Maternal sensitivity, infant attachment, and temperament in early childhood predict adjustment in middle childhood: The case of adopted children and their biologically unrelated parents. *Developmental Psychology, 38*(5), 806–821.

Stanford, J. N., & McCabe, M. P. (2005). Sociocultural influences on adolescent boys' body image and body change strategies. *Body Image, 2*(2), 105–113.

Stankoff, B., et al. (2006). Imaging of CNS myelin by positron-emission tomography. *Proceedings of the National Academy of Sciences of the United States of America, 103*(24), 9304–9309.

Stanley, M. A., & Beck, J. G. (2000). Anxiety disorders. *Clinical Psychology Review, 20*(6), 731–754.

Statistics Canada. (2005). Divorces. *The Daily.* Retrieved from http://www.statcan.gc.ca/daily-quotidien/050309/dq050309b-eng.htm.

Statistics Canada. (2008a). Back-to-school factbook: Working while in school. Retrieved from http://www.statcan.gc.ca/pub/81-004-x/2006003/9341-eng.htm#e.

Statistics Canada. (2008b). *Leading causes of death in Canada.* (Statistics Canada, Catalogue no. 84-215-X.) Retrieved from www.statcan.gc.ca/pub/84-215-x/2008000/hl-fs-eng.htm#3.

Statistics Canada. (2008c). *National longitudinal study of children and youth (NLSCY).* Record no. 4450. Retrieved from http://www.statcan.gc.ca/cgi-bin/imdb/p2SV.pl?Function=getSurvey&SDDS=4450&lang=en&db=imdb&adm=8&dis=2.

Statistics Canada. (2009a). *Gay pride... by the numbers*. Retrieved from http://www42.statcan.ca/smr08/smr08_118-eng.htm.

Statistics Canada. (2009b). Ten leading causes of death by selected age groups, by sex, Canada—65 to 74 years. Retrieved from http://www.statcan.gc.ca/pub/84-215-x/2008000/tbl/t008-eng.htm.

Statistics Canada. (2009c). *2006 Census: The evolving linguistic portrait, 2006 Census: Sharp increase in population with a mother tongue other than English or French.* Retrieved from http://www12.statcan.ca/census-recensement/2006/as-sa/97-555/p2-eng.cfm.

Statistics Canada. (2010a). Aboriginal seniors in Canada. In *A portrait of seniors in Canada*. Retrieved from http://www.statcan.gc.ca/pub/89-519-x/2006001/4122091-eng.htm.

Statistics Canada. (2010b). Infant mortality rates, by province and territory (Table 102-0504). Retrieved from http://www40.statcan.gc.ca/101/cst01/health21a-eng.htm.

Statistics Canada. (2010c). Internet use by individuals, by selected frequency of use and age. Retrieved from http://www.statcan.gc.ca/tables-tableaux/sum-som/l01/cst01/comm32a-eng.htm.

Statistics Canada. (2010d.) Overweight and obese adults (self-reported), 2010. Retrieved from http://www.statcan.gc.ca/pub/82-625-x/2011001/article/11464-eng.htm.

Statistics Canada (2011). Pregnancy outcomes by age group (total pregnancies). Birth 2008. Cat. N. 84F0210x. Retrieved from http://www.statcan.gc.ca/tables-tableaux/sum-som/l01/cst01/hlth65a-eng.htm.

Statistics Canada (2011b). Fertility: Overview, 2009–2011. Retrieved on October 10, 2016 from http://www.statcan.gc.ca/pub/91-209-x/2013001/article/11784-eng.htm.

Statistics Canada (2011c). Portrait of families and living arrangements in Canada. Retrieved on August 20, 2016, from http://www12.statcan.ca/census-recensement/2011/as-sa/98-312-x/98-312-x2011001-eng.cfm.

Statistics Canada. (2012a). Body mass index of Canadian children and youth, 2009 to 2011. Retrieved from http://www.statcan.gc.ca/pub/82-625-x/2012001/article/11712-eng.htm.

Statistics Canada. (2012b). 2011 Census: Age and sex. *The Daily*, May 29. Retrieved from http://www.statcan.gc

.ca/daily-quotidien/120529/dq120529a-eng.pdf.

Statistics Canada. (2012c). 2011 Census of Population: Linguistic Characteristics of Canadians. Retrieved from http://www.statcan.gc.ca/daily-quotidien/121024/dq121024a-eng.htm.

Statistics Canada. (2013). Distribution (number and percentage) and percentage change of census families by family structure, Canada, provinces and territories, 2011. Retrieved from http://www12.statcan.ca/census-recensement/2011/as-sa/98-312-x/2011001/tbl/tbl2-eng.cfm.

Statistics Canada. (2013a). Canadian Households in 2011: Type and growth. Retrieved from http://www12.statcan.gc.ca/census-recensement/2011/as-sa/98-312-x/98-312-x2011003_2-eng.cfm.

Statistics Canada. (2013b). Fifty years of families in Canada: 1961 to 2011. Retrieved from http://www12.statcan.gc.ca/census-recensement/2011/as-sa/98-312-x/98-312-x2011003_1-eng.cfm.

Statistics Canada. (2013c). Generations in Canada.l Retrieved from http://www12.statcan.gc.ca/census-recensement/2011/as-sa/98-311-x/98-311-x2011003_2-eng.cfm.

Statistics Canada. (2013d). Linguistic characteristics of Canadians. Retrieved from http://www12.statcan.gc.ca/census-recensement/2011/as-sa/98-314-x/98-314-x2011001-eng.cfm.

Statistics Canada. (2013e). Police-reported crime statistics, 2012. *The Daily*, July 25. Retrieved from http://www.statcan.gc.ca/daily-quotidien/130725/dq130725b-eng.htm.

Statistics Canada. (2013f). The Canadian incidence study of reported child abuse and neglect. Retrieved from http://www5.statcan.gc.ca/bsolc/olc-cel/olc-cel?catno=85-224-X20010006459&lang=eng.

Statistics Canada. (2014a). *Health trends*. Statistics Canada Catalogue No. 82-213-XWE,Ottawa. Retrieved July 21, 2016 from http://www12.statcan.gc.ca/health-sante/82-213/index.cfm?Lang=ENG.

Statistics Canada. (2014b). Perceived life stress. Retrieved June 18, 2016, from http://www.statcan.gc.ca/pub/82-625-x/2015001/article/14188-eng.htm.

Statistics Canada. (2014c). Canadian post-secondary enrolments and graduates, 2012/2013. Retrieved June 17, 2016 from http://www.statcan.gc.ca/daily-quotidien/141125/dq141125d-eng.htm.

Statistics Canada. (2015a, November 27). Table 5.5 Leading causes of death of children and youth, by age group, 2006 to 2008. Retrieved from http://www5.statcan.gc.ca/cansim/a05?lang=eng&id=1020562.

Statistics Canada. (2015b). Health at a glance: Breastfeeding trends in Canada. Retrieved October 15, 2016. Retrieved from http://www.statcan.gc.ca/pub/82-624-x/2013001/article/11879-eng.htm.

Statistics Canada. (2015c). Percentage distribution of children and adolescents, by body mass index (BMI) category (based on World Health Organization cut-offs), age group and sex, household population aged 5 to 17, 2009 to 2011. Retrieved from http://www.statcan.gc.ca/pub/82-003-x/2012003/article/11706/tbl/tbl1-eng.htm.

Statistics Canada. (2015d). Childhood condition. Section C. Retrieved on August 16, 2016, from http://www.statcan.gc.ca/pub/82-619-m/2012004/sections/sectionc-eng.htm.

Statistics Canada. (2015e). Motor vehicle accidents causing death, by sex and by age group. http://www.statcan.gc.ca/tables-tableaux/sum-som/l01/cst01/health112a-eng.htm.

Statistics Canada. (2015f). 10 leading causes of death. Retrieved from http://www.statcan.gc.ca/pub/82-625-x/2014001/article/11896/c-g/c-g01-eng.htm.

Statistics Canada. (2015g). Percentage using prescription, 2007 to 2011. Retrieved from http://www.statcan.gc.ca/pub/82-003-x/2014006/article/14032/tbl/tbl1-eng.htm.

Statistics Canada. (2015h). Same-sex couples and sexual orientation…by the numbers. Retrieved from http://www.statcan.gc.ca/eng/dai/smr08/2015/smr08_203_2015.

Statistics Canada. (2016). Body mass index, overweight or obese, self-reported, youth, by sex, provinces and territories (percent). Retrieved from http://www.statcan.gc.ca/tables-tableaux/sum-som/l01/cst01/health84b-eng.htm.

Statistics Canada. (2016a, February 16). Youth crime in Canada, 2014. *The Daily.* http://www.statcan.gc.ca/daily-quotidien/160217/dq160217b-eng.htm.

Statistics Canada. (2016b). Population projections. Section 3: Analysis of the results of the long-term projections. Retrieved from http://www.statcan.gc.ca/pub/91-520-x/2010001/part-partie3-eng.htm.

Statistics Canada. (2016, June 11). Mixed unions in Canada. https://www12.statcan.gc.ca/nhs-enm/2011/as-sa/99-010-x/99-010-x2011003_3-eng.cfm.

Stauffacher, K., & DeHart, G. B. (2006). Crossing social contexts: Relational aggression between siblings and friends during early and middle childhood. *Journal of Applied Developmental Psychology, 27*(3), 228–240.

Steele, H. (2005b). Editorial. *Attachment & Human Development, 7*(4), 345.

Steele, H. (2005a). Editorial: Romance, marriage, adolescent motherhood, leaving for college, plus shyness and attachment in the preschool years. *Attachment & Human Development, 7*(2), 103–104.

Stein, D. J., Collins, M., Daniels, W., Noakes, T., & Zigmond, M. (2007). Mind and muscle: The cognitive–affective neuroscience of exercise. *CNS Spectrums, 12*(1), 19–22.

Steingraber, S. (2007). The Falling Age of Puberty in U.S. Girls: What We Know, What We Need to Know. The Breast Cancer Fund. Retrieved October 21, 2016, from http://www.breastcancerfund.org/assets/pdfs/publications/falling-age-of-puberty.pdf.

Stemberger, J. P. (2004). Phonological priming and irregular past. *Journal of Memory and Language, 50*(1), 82–95.

Sternberg, R. J. (2000). In search of the zipperump-a-zoo. *Psychologist, 13*(5), 250–255.

Sternberg, R. J. (2006a). A duplex theory of love. In R. J. Sternberg, & K. Weis (Eds.), *The new psychology of love* (pp. 184–199). New Haven, CT: Yale University Press.

Sternberg, R. J. (2006b). The nature of creativity. *Creativity Research Journal, 18*(1), 87–98.

Sternberg, R. J. (2007). A systems model of leadership: WICS. *American Psychologist, 62*(1), 34–42.

Sternberg, R. J., & Williams, W. M. (1997). Does the Graduate Record Examination predict meaningful success in the graduate training of psychologists? *American Psychologist, 52,* 630–641.

Stevenson, H. W., Chen, C., & Lee, S. (1993). Mathematics achievement of Chinese, Japanese, and American children: Ten years later. *Science, 259,* 53–58.

Stevenson, J. (1999). The treatment of the long-term sequelae of child abuse.

Journal of Child Psychology and Psychiatry, 40(1) 99–111.

Stifter, C. A., & Wiggins, C. N. (2004). Assessment of disturbances in emotion regulation and temperament. In R. DelCarmen-Wiggins & A. Carter (Eds.), *Handbook of infant, toddler, and preschool mental health assessment* (pp. 79–103). New York: Oxford University Press.

Stipek, D., & Hakuta, K. (2007). Strategies to ensure that no child starts from behind. In J. L. Aber et al. (Eds.), *Child development and social policy: Knowledge for action, APA Decade of Behavior volumes* (pp. 129–145). Washington, DC: American Psychological Association.

Stipek, D., Recchia, S., & McClintic, S. (1992). *Self-evaluation in young children.* Monographs of the Society for Research in Child Development, 57(1, ser. 226).

Stoel-Gammon, C. (2002). Intervocalic consonants in the speech of typically developing children: Emergence and early use. *Clinical Linguistics and Phonetics, 16*(3), 155–168.

Stokes, S. (n.d.). Increasing expressive skills for verbal children with autism. National Association for Special Education Teachers. Retrieved July 25, 2016 from http://marquisstudios.org/wp-content/uploads/2016/03/Autism-Spectrum-Disorder-Series-Increasing-Expressive-Skills-for-Verbal-Children-with-Autism.pdf.

Storch, E. A., et al. (2007). Peer victimization, psychosocial adjustment, and physical activity in overweight and at-risk-for-overweight youth. *Journal of Pediatric Psychology, 32*(1), 80–89.

Stores, G., & Wiggs, L. (Eds.). (2001). *Sleep disturbance in children and adolescents with disorders of development: Its significance and management.* New York: Cambridge University Press.

Strassberg, D. S., & Holty, S. (2003). An experimental study of women's Internet personal ads. *Archives of Sexual Behavior, 32*(3), 253–260.

Stratton, T. D., et al. (2005). Does students' exposure to gender discrimination and sexual harassment in medical school affect specialty choice and residency program selection? *Academic Medicine, 80*(4), 400–408.

Strayer, J., & Roberts, W. (2004). Children's anger, emotional expressiveness, and empathy: Relations with parents' empathy, emotional expressiveness, and parenting practices. *Social Development, 13*(2), 229–254.

Streri, A. (2002). Hand preference in 4-month-old infants: Global or local processing of objects in the haptic mode. *Current.*
Psychology Letters: Behaviour, Brain and Cognition, 7, 39–50.

Stright, A. D., Neitzel, C., Sears, K. G., & Hoke-Sinex, L. (2001). Instruction begins in the home: Relations between parental instruction and children's self-regulation in the classroom. *Journal of Educational Psychology, 93*(3), 456–466.

Strock, M. (2004). *Autism spectrum disorders (pervasive developmental disorders).* NIH Publication NIH-04-5511. Bethesda, MD: National Institute of Mental Health, National Institutes of Health, U.S. Department of Health and Human Services. Available at http://www.nimh.nih.gov/publicat/autism.cfm.

Sukhodolsky, D. G., Golub, A., Stone, E. C., & Orban, L. (2005). Dismantling anger control training for children: A randomized pilot study of social problem-solving versus social skills training components. *Behavior Therapy, 36*, 15–23.

Sullivan, S. E., Martin, D. F., Carden, W. A., & Mainiero, L. A. (2003). The road less traveled. *Journal of Leadership & Organizational Studies, 10*(2), 34–42.

Sulloway, F. J. (2007). Birth order and intelligence. *Science, 316*(5832), 1711–1712.

Summers, J. (2014). Kids and screen time: What does the research say? Retrieved from http://www.npr.org/sections/ed/2014/08/28/343735856/kids-and-screen-time-what-does-the-research-say.

Sun, S. S., et al. (2005). Is sexual maturity occurring earlier among U.S. children? *Journal of Adolescent Health, 37*(5), 345–355.

Suomi, S. J., Harlow, H. F., & McKinney, W. T. (1972). Monkey psychiatrists. *American Journal of Psychiatry, 128,* 927–932.

Supple, A. J., & Small, S. A. (2006). The influence of parental support, knowledge, and authoritative parenting on Hmong and European American adolescent development. *Journal of Family Issues, 27*(9), 1214–1232.

Sylva, K., et al. (2007). Curricular quality and day-to-day learning activities in preschool. *International Journal of Early Years Education, 15*(1), 49–65.

Szaflarski, J. P., et al. (2006). A longitudinal functional magnetic resonance imaging study of language development in children 5 to 11 years old. *Annals of Neurology, 59*(5), 796–807.

Szalavitz, A. (2010). Touching empathy. *Psychology Today*. Retrieved from https://www.psychologytoday.com/blog/born-love/201003/touching-empathy.

T

Takahashi, M., & Sugiyama, M. (2003). Improvement and prevention of misbehavior in a junior high school student: An analysis of behavioral contingency and change of stimulus function in a social setting. *Japanese Journal of Counseling Science, 36*(2), 165–174.

Talbot, L. A., Morrell, C. H., Fleg, J., L., & Metter, E. J. (2007). Changes in leisure time physical activity and risk of all-cause mortality in men and women. *Preventive Medicine: An International Journal Devoted to Practice and Theory, 45*(2–3), 169–176.

Tamis-LeMonda, C. S., Bornstein, M. H., & Baumwell, L. (2001). Maternal responsiveness and children's achievement of language milestones. *Child Development, 72*(3), 748–767.

Tamis-LeMonda, C. S., Cristofaro, T. N., Rodriguez, E. T., & Bornstein, M. H. (2006). Early language development: Social influences in the first years of life. In L. Balter & C. S. Tamis-LeMonda (Eds.), *Child psychology: A handbook of contemporary issues* (2nd ed.) (pp. 79–108). New York: Psychology Press.

Tan, R. S. (2002). Managing the andropause in aging men. *Clinical Geriatrics.* Available at http://www.mmhc.com/cg/articles/CG9907/Tan.html.

Tan, R. S., & Culberson, J. W. (2003). An integrative review on current evidence of testosterone replacement therapy for the andropause. *Maturitas, 45*(1), 15–27.

Tanner, J. L. (2006). Recentering during emerging adulthood: A critical turning point in life span human development. In J. J. Arnett & J. L. Tanner (Eds.), *Emerging adults in America: Coming of age in the 21st century* (pp. 21–55). Washington, DC: American Psychological Association.

Tanner, J. M. (1989). *Fetus into man: Physical growth from conception to maturity.* Cambridge, MA: Harvard University Press.

Tapper, K., & Boulton, M. J. (2004). Sex differences in levels of physical, verbal, and indirect aggression amongst primary school children and their associations with beliefs about aggression. *Aggressive Behavior, 30*(2), 123–145.

Tashiro, T., Frazier, P., & Berman, M. (2006). Stress-related growth following divorce and relationship dissolution. In M. A. Fine & J. H. Harvey (Eds.), *Handbook of divorce and relationship dissolution* (pp. 361–384). Mahwah, NJ: Erlbaum.

Tassi, F., Schneider, B. H., & Richard, J. F. (2001). Competitive behavior at school in relation to social competence and incompetence in middle childhood. *Revue Internationale de Psychologie Sociale, 14*(2), 165–184.

Taylor, C., & Peter, T. (2011). *Every class in every school: The first national climate survey on homophobia, biphobia, and transphobia in Canadian schools. Final report*. Toronto: Egale Canada Human Rights Trust.

Taylor, M. (1999). *Imaginary companions and the children who create them.* London: Oxford University Press.

Taylor, M., & Hort, B. (1990). Can children be trained in making the distinction between appearance and reality? *Cognitive Development, 5*(1), 89–99.

Taylor, M. F., Clark, N., & Newton, E. (2008). Counselling Australian baby boomers. *British Journal of Guidance & Counselling, 36*(2), 189–204.

Teen Challenge Canada. (2013). Alcohol abuse facts. Retrieved from http://www.teenchallenge.ca/get-help/educational-resources/alcohol-abuse-facts.

Terracciano, A., Costa Jr., P. T., & McCrae, R. R. (2006). Personality plasticity after age 30. *Personality and Social Psychology Bulletin, 32*(8), 999–1009.

Thapar, A., Langley, K., Asherson, P., & Gill, M. (2007). Gene-Environment interplay in attention-deficit hyperactivity disorder and the importance of a developmental perspective. *British Journal of Psychiatry, 190*(1), 1–3.

The Infinity Project. (2013). Retrieved from www.facebook.com/TogetherWeCanbeInfinite?filter=3.

Thomas, A., & Chess, S. (1989). Temperament and personality. In G. A. Kohnstamm, J. E. Bates, & M. K. Rothbart (Eds.), *Temperament in childhood.* Chichester, England: Wiley.

Thompson, A. M., Baxter-Jones, A. D. G., Mirwald, R. L., & Bailey, D. A. (2003). Comparison of physical activity in male and female children: Does maturation matter? *Medicine and Science in Sports and Exercise. 35*(10), 1684–1690.

Thompson, I. M., et al. (2005). Erectile dysfunction and subsequent cardiovascular disease. *Journal of the American Medical Association, 294*(23). 2996–3002.

Thompson, R. A. (2006). The development of the person: Social understanding, relationships, conscience, self. In N. Eisenberg, W. Damon, & R. M. Lerner (Eds.), *Handbook of child psychology* (6th ed.), Vol. 3, *Social, emotional, and personality development* (pp. 24–98). Hoboken, NJ: Wiley.

Thompson, R. A., Easterbrooks, M. A., & Padilla-Walker, L. M. (2003). Social and emotional development in infancy. In R. M. Lerner et al. (Eds.), *Handbook of psychology: Developmental psychology.* New York: Wiley.

Thompson, R. A., & Limber, S. P. (1990). "Social anxiety" in infancy: Stranger and separation reactions. In H. Leitenberg (Ed.), *Handbook of social and evaluation anxiety.* New York: Plenum.

Thompson, R. A., & Meyer, S. (2007). Socialization of emotion regulation in the family. In J. J. Gross (Ed.), *Handbook of emotion regulation* (pp. 249–268). New York: Guilford.

Thomson, J., Ahluwalia, M., & Huang, S. (2013, April 15). Gay seniors struggling to find "safe" retirement housing. Retrieved from http://www.cbc.ca/news/canada/gay-seniors-struggling-to-find-safe-retirement-housing-1.1405867.

Thornton, L. M., Andersen, B. L., Crespin, T. R., & Carson, W. E. (2007). Individual trajectories in stress covary with immunity during recovery from cancer diagnosis and treatments. *Brain, Behavior, and Immunity, 21*(2), 185–194.

Timmerman, L. M. (2006). Family care versus day care: Effects on children. In B. M. Gayle et al. (Eds.), *Classroom communication and instructional processes: Advances through meta-analysis* (pp. 245–260). Mahwah, NJ: Erlbaum.

Tjepkema, M. (2005). *Adult obesity in Canada: Measured height and weight* (Statistics Canada, Catalogue no. 82-620-MWE). Retrieved from http://www.statcan.gc.ca/pub/82-620-m/2005001/article/adults-adultes/8060-eng.htm.

Tobbell, J. (2003). Students' experiences of the transition from primary to secondary school. *Educational and Child Psychology, 20*(4), 4–14.

Togsverd, M., et al. (2008). Association of a dopamine beta-hydroxylase gene variant with depression in elderly women possibly reflecting noradrenergic dysfunction. *Journal of Affective Disorders, 106*(1-2), 169–172.

Tomaka, J., Thompson, S., & Palacios, R. (2006). The relation of social isolation, loneliness, and social support to disease outcomes among the elderly. *Journal of Aging and Health, 18*(3), 359–384.

Tomiyama, T., et al. (2008). A new amyloid ß variant favoring oligomerization in Alzheimer's-type dementia. *Annals of Neurology, 63*(3), 377–387.

Ton, M., & Hansen, J. C. (2001). Using a person-environment fit framework to predict satisfaction and motivation in work and marital roles. *Journal of Career Assessment, 9,* 315–331.

Toneguzzi, M. (2011, August 17). Nearly half of Canada's baby boomers still paying. *Calgary Herald*. Retrieved from http://blogs.calgaryherald.com/2011/08/17/nearly-half-of-canadas-baby-boomers-still-paying-down-mortgage/.

Toronto District School Board. (2013). International Day of Silence. Retrieved from http://www2.tdsb.on.ca/_site/ViewItem.asp?siteid=15&menuid=35317&pageid=29911.

Towse, J. (2003). Lifespan development of human memory. *Quarterly Journal of Experimental Psychology: Human Experimental Psychology, 56A*(7), 1244–1246.

Towse, J., & Cowan, N. (2005). Working memory and its relevance for cognitive development. In W. Schneider, R. Schumann- Hengsteler, & B. Sodian (Eds.), *Young children's cognitive development: Interrelationships among executive functioning, working memory, verbal ability, and theory of mind* (pp. 9–37). Mahwah, NJ: Erlbaum.

Trainor, L. J., & Desjardins, R. N. (2002). Pitch characteristics of infant-directed speech affect infants' ability to discriminate vowels. *Psychonomic Bulletin & Review, 9*(2), 335–340.

Trehub, S. E., & Hannon, E. E. (2006). Infant music perception: Domain-general or domain-specific mechanisms? *Cognition, 100*(1), 73–99.

Tremblay, M., S., LeBlanc, A. G., Janssen, I., Kho, M. E., Hicks, A., Murumets, K., et al. (2011). Canadian sedentary behaviour guidelines for children and youth. *Applied Physiology, Nutrition and Metabolism 36*(1), 59–64.

Trevarthen, C. (2003). Conversations with a two-month-old. In J. Raphael-Leff (Ed.), *Parent–infant psychodynamics: Wild things, mirrors, and ghosts.* London: Whurr.

Troxel, W. M., & Matthews, K. A. (2004). What are the costs of marital conflict and dissolution to children's physical health? *Clinical Child and Family Psychology Review, 7*(1), 29–57.

Trudel, G. A., Goldfarb, M. R., Preville, M., & Boyer, R. (2007). Relationship between psychological distress and marital functioning in the elderly. American Psychological Association, Conference abstract.

Tsuneishi, S., & Casaer, P. (2000). Effects of preterm extrauterine visual experience on the development of the human visual system: A flash VEP study. *Developmental Medicine and Child Neurology, 42*(10), 663–668.

Turkheimer, E., Haley, A., Waldron, M., D'Onofrio, B., Gottesman, I. I. (2003). Socioeconomic status modifies heritability of IQ in young mothers. *Psychological Science, 14*(6), 623–628.

Twist, M. (2005). Review of relationship therapy with same-sex couples. *Journal of Marital & Family Therapy, 31*(4), 413–417.

U

U.S. Bureau of the Census. (2008). *Statistical abstract of the United States* (128th ed.). Washington, DC: U.S. Government Printing Office.

U.S. Department of Education. (2006). *Teaching children with attention deficit hyperactivity disorder: Instructional strategies and practices*. Washington, DC.

Umek, L. M., Podlesek, A., & Fekonja, U. (2005). Assessing the home literacy environment: Relationships to child language comprehension and expression. *European Journal of Psychological Assessment, 21*(4), 271–281.

UNAIDS. (2006). *Report on the global AIDS epidemic: Executive summary.* Joint United Nations Programme on HIV/AIDS (UNAIDS). UNAIDS. 20 Avenue Appia. CH-1211. Geneva 27 Switzerland.

UNICEF. (2001). *Innocenti Digest.* Early marriage: Child spouses, 7.

UNICEF. (2006). *The state of the world's children: 2007*. New York: United Nations.

UNICEF. (2010). The Breastfeeding Initiative Exchange: Facts and figures. Retrieved from http://www.unicef.org/programme/breastfeeding/facts.htm.

UNICEF Canada. (2009). *The State of the World's Children 2009: Aboriginal children's health: Leaving no child behind,* Canadian supplement. Toronto: Author. Retrieved from http://www.unicef.ca/portal/Secure/Community/502/WCM/HELP/take_action/Advocacy/Leaving%20no%20child%20behind%2009.pdf.

Universitat Autonoma de Barcelona. (2016, June 1). Researchers use optogenetics to increase long-term memory in mice. *PsyPost.* Retrieved from http://www.psypost.org/2016/06/researchers-use-optogenetics-increase-long-term-memory-mice-43221.

University of Ottawa. (2013). Suicide in Canada: Facts and figures. Retrieved from http://www.med.uottawa.ca/sim/data/Suicide_e.htm.

University of Michigan. (n.d.). Understanding the perpetrator. Retrieved June 19, 2016, from https://sapac.umich.edu/article/196.

USDHHS. (2005, January 10). *Bone health and osteoporosis: A report of the Surgeon General*. http://www.surgeongeneral.gov/library/bonehealth. Accessed October 5, 2008.

Uylings, H. B. M. (2006). Development of the human cortex and the concept of "critical" or "sensitive" periods. *Language Learning, 56*(Suppl. 1), 59–90.

V

van IJzendoorn, M. H., & Juffer, F. (2006). The Emanuel Miller Memorial Lecture 2006: Adoption as intervention. Meta-analytic evidence for massive catch-up and plasticity in physical, socio-emotional, and cognitive development. *Journal of Child Psychology and Psychiatry, 47*(12), 1228–1245.

van Solinge, H., & Henkens, K. (2005). Couples' adjustment to retirement: A Multi-Actor Panel Study. *Journals of Gerontology: Series B: Psychological Sciences and Social Sciences, 60B*(1), S11–S20.

Vandello, J. A., & Cohen, D. (2003). Male honor and female fidelity: Implicit cultural scripts that perpetuate domestic violence. *Journal of Personality & Social Psychology, 84*(5), 997–1010.

Vander Ven, T., & Cullen, F. T. (2004). The impact of maternal employment on serious youth crime: Does the quality of working conditions matter? *Crime & Delinquency, 50*(2), 272–291.

Vares, T., Potts, A., Gavey, N., & Grace, V. M. (2007). Reconceptualizing cultural narratives of mature women's sexuality in the Viagra era. *Journal of Aging Studies, 21*(2), 153–164.

Vartanian, O., Martindale, C., & Kwiatkowski, J. (2003). Creativity and inductive reasoning: The relationship between divergent thinking and performance on Wason's 2-4-6 task. *Quarterly Journal of Experimental Psychology: Human Experimental Psychology. 56A*(4), 641–655.

Vastag, B. (2003). Many questions, few answers for testosterone replacement therapy. *Journal of the American Medical Association, 289,* 971–972.

Vellas, B., Gillette-Guyonnet, S., & Andrieu, S. (2008). Memory health clinics—A first step to prevention. *Alzheimer's & Dementia, 4*(1, Suppl 1), S144–S149.

Veldhuis, L., Vogel, I., Renders, C. M., van Rossem, L., Oenema, A., HiraSing, R. A., & Raat, H. (2012). Behavioral risk factors for overweight in early childhood; the 'Be active, eat right' study. *International Journal of Behavioral Nutrition and Physical Activity, 9*, 74. Retrieved from https://ijbnpa.biomedcentral.com/articles/10.1186/1479-5868-9-74.

Vellutino, F. R., Fletcher, J. M., Snowling, M. J., & Scanlon, D. M. (2004). Specific reading disability (dyslexia): What have we learned in the past four decades? *Journal of Child Psychology and Psychiatry, 45*(1), 2–40.

Verissimo, M., & Salvaterra, F. (2006). Maternal secure-base scripts and children's attachment security in an adopted sample. *Attachment & Human Development, 8*(3), 261–273.

Victoria Hospice Bereavement Services. (2014). I am grieving a death. Retrieved from http://www.victoriahospice.org/how-we-can-help-you/i-am-grieving-death.

Virji-Babul, N., Kerns, K., Zhou, E., Kapur, A., & Shiffrar, M. (2006). Perceptual-motor deficits in children with Down syndrome: Implications for intervention. *Down Syndrome: Research & Practice, 10*(2), 74–82.

Visscher, W. A., Feder, M., Burns, A. M., Brady, T. M., & Bray, R. M. (2003). The impact of smoking and other substance use by urban women on the birthweight of their infants. *Substance Use and Misuse, 38*(8), 1063–1093.

Vitiello, B. (Ed.). (2006). Guest editorial: Selective serotonin reuptake inhibitors (SSRIs) in children and adolescents. *Journal of Child and Adolescent Psychopharmacology, 16*(1–2), 7–9.

Volkova, A., Trehub, S. E., & Schellenberg, E. G. (2006). Infants' memory for musical performances. *Developmental Science, 9*(6), 583–589.

Volling, B. L. (2003). Sibling relationships. In M. H. Bornstein et al. (Eds.), *Well-being: Positive development across the life course* (pp. 205–220). Mahwah, NJ: Erlbaum.

Volterra, M. C., Caselli, O., Capirci, E., & Pizzuto, E. (2004). Gesture and the emergence and development of language. In M. Tomasello & D. I. Slobin (Eds.), *Beyond nature–nurture.* Mahwah, NJ. Erlbaum.

von Gontard, A. (2007). Encopresis. *Praxis der Kinderpsychologie und Kinderpsychiatrie, 56*(6),492–510.

VonDras, D. D., Powless, D. R., Olson, A. K., Wheeler, D., & Snudden, A. L. (2005). Differential effects of everyday stress on the episodic memory test performances of young, mid-life, and older adults. *Aging & Mental Health, 9*(1), 60–70.

Vorauer, J. D., Cameron, J. J., Holmes, J. G., & Pearce, D. G. (2003). Invisible overtures: Fears of rejection and the signal amplification bias. *Journal of Personality & Social Psychology, 84*(4), 793–812.

Vukman, K. B. (2005). Developmental differences in metacognition and their connections with cognitive development in adulthood. *Journal of Adult Development, 12*(4), 211–221.

Vygotsky, L. S. (1962). *Thought and language.* Cambridge, MA: MIT Press.

Vygotsky, L. S. (1978). *Mind in society: The development of higher psychological processes.* Cambridge, MA: Harvard University Press.

W

Wachs, T. D. (2006). The nature, etiology, and consequences of individual differences in temperament. In L. Balter & C. S. Tamis- LeMonda (Eds.), *Child psychology: A handbook of contemporary issues* (2nd ed.) (pp. 27–52). New York: Psychology Press.

Wahler, R. G., Herring, M., & Edwards, M. (2001). Coregulation of balance between children's prosocial approaches and acts of compliance: A pathway to mother–child cooperation? *Journal of Clinical Child Psychology, 30*(4), 473–478.

Wainright, J. L., Russell, S. T., & Patterson, C. J. (2004). Psychosocial adjustment, school outcomes, and romantic relationships of adolescents with same-sex parents. *Child Development, 75*(6), 1886–1898.

Wald, J., & Losen, D. J. (2007). Out of sight: The journey through the school-to-prison pipeline. In S. Books (Ed.), *Invisible children in the society and its schools* (3rd ed.) (pp. 23–37). Mahwah, NJ: Erlbaum.

Walitza, S., et al. (2006). Genetic and neuroimaging studies in attention deficit hyperactivity disorder. *Nervenheilkunde: Zeitschrift für interdisziplinaere Fortbildung, 25*(6), 421–429.

Wall, A. (2007). Review of integrating gender and culture in parenting. *The Family Journal, 15*(2), 196–197.

Wall, G., & Arnold, S. (2007). How involved is involved fathering? *Gender & Society, 21*(4), 508–527.

Wallerstein, J., Lewis, J., Blakeslee, S., Hetherington, E. M., & Kelly, J. (2005). Issue 17: Is divorce always detrimental to children? In R. P. Halgin (Ed.), *Taking sides: Clashing views on controversial issues in abnormal psychology,* (3rd ed.) (pp. 298–321). New York: McGraw-Hill.

Wallerstein, J. S. (1987). Children of divorce: Report of a ten year follow-up of early latency children. *American Journal of Orthopsychiatry, 57*, 199–211.

Walter, J. L., & LaFreniere, P. J. (2000). A naturalistic study of affective expression, social competence, and sociometric status in preschoolers. *Early Education and Development, 11*(1), 109–122.

Wang, L. (2005). Correlations between self-esteem and life satisfaction in elementary school students. *Chinese Mental Health Journal, 19*(11), 745–749.

Wang, S.-H., Baillargeon, R., & Paterson, S. (2005). Detecting continuity violations in infancy: A new account and new evidence from covering and tube events. *Cognition, 95*(2), 129–173.

Washburn, D. A. (Ed.). (2007). *Primate perspectives on behavior and cognition.* Washington, DC: American Psychological Association.

Watson, J. B. (1924). *Behaviorism.* New York: Norton.

Waxman, S. R., & Lidz, J. L. (2006). Early word learning. In D. Kuhn, R. S. Siegler, W. Damon, & R. M. Lerner (Eds.), *Handbook of child psychology* (6th ed.), Vol. 2, *Cognition, perception, and language* (pp. 299–335). Hoboken, NJ: Wiley.

WebMD. (2010). Tay-Sachs test. Retrieved from www.webmd.com/parenting/baby/tay-sachs-test.

WebMD. (2012). 10 surprising health benefits of sex. Retrieved from http://www.webmd.com/sex-relationships/guide/10-surprising-health-benefits-of-sex?page=1.

WebMD. (2013). What's it like in the womb? Retrieved from http://www.webmd.com/baby/features/in-the-womb.

Wechsler, D. (1975). Intelligence defined and undefined: A relativistic appraisal. *American Psychologist, 30,* 135–139.

Weckerly, J., Wulfeck, B., & Reilly, J. (2004). The development of morphosyntactic ability in atypical populations: The acquisition of tag questions in children with early focal lesions and children with specific- language impairment. *Brain and Language, 88*(2), 190–201.

Weeks, C. (2009, March 30). Interracial relationships rise 30 per cent in five years. *Globe and Mail.* Retrieved from http://www.theglobeandmail.com/life/article677491.ece.

Weinberg, R. A. (2004). The infant and the family in the twenty-first century. *Journal of the American Academy of Child and Adolescent Psychiatry, 43*(1), 115–116.

Weinshenker, M. N. (2006). Adolescents' expectations about mothers' employment: Life course patterns and parental influence. *Sex Roles, 54*(11–12), 845–857.

Weisler, R. H., & Sussman, N. (2007). Treatment of attention-deficit/hyperactivity disorder. *Primary Psychiatry, 14*(1), 39–42.

Wellbeing Institute. (1010, February). Failure to launch: The 'E' generation & depression in young adults. Retrieved from http://wellbeinginstitute.ca/failure-to-launch-the-e-generation-depression-in-young-adults/.

Wellman, H. M., Cross, D., & Bartsch, K. (1986). *Infant search and object permanence: A meta-analysis of the A-not-B error.* Monographs of the Society for Research in Child Development, 5(3, ser. 214).

Wellman, H. M., Fang, F., Liu, D., Zhu, L., & Liu, G. (2006). Scaling of theory-of-mind understandings in Chinese children. *Psychological Science, 17*(12), 1075–1081.

Weng, X., Odouli, R., & Li, D-K. (2008, January 25). Maternal caffeine consumption during pregnancy and the risk of miscarriage: a prospective cohort study. *American Journal of Obstetrics and Gynecology, available online.*

Wenger, G. C., Dykstra, P. A., Melkas, T., & Knipscheer, K. C. P. M. (2007). Social embeddedness and late-life parenthood: Community activity, close ties, and support. *Journal of Family Issues, 28*(11), 1419–1456.

Wenger, G. C., & Jerrome, D. (1999). Change and stability in confidant relationships. *Journal of Aging Studies, 13*(3), 269–294.

Wennergren, A.-C., & Rönnerman, K. (2006). The relation between tools used in action research and the zone of proximal development. *Educational Action Research, 14*(4), 547–568.

Wentworth, N., Benson, J. B., & Haith, M. M. (2000). The development of infants' reaches for stationary and moving targets. *Child Development, 71*(3), 576–601.

Wentzel, K. R., Barry, C. M., & Caldwell, K. A. (2004). Friendships in middle school: Influences on motivation and school adjustment. *Journal of Educational Psychology, 96*(2), 195–203.

Werker, J. F. (1989). Becoming a native listener. *American Scientist, 77,* 54–59.

Werker, J. F., et al. (2007). Infant-directed speech supports phonetic category learning in English and Japanese. *Cognition, 103*(1), 147–162.

Werker, J. F., & Tees, R. C. (2005). Speech perception as a window for understanding plasticity and commitment in language systems of the brain. *Developmental Psychobiology, 46*(3), 233–234.

Werner, E. E. (1988). A cross-cultural perspective on infancy. *Journal of Cross-Cultural Psychology, 19,* 96–113.

Werner, L. A., & Bernstein, I. L. (2001). Development of the auditory, gustatory, olfactory, and somatosensory systems. In E. B. Goldstein (Ed.), *Blackwell handbook of perception., Handbook of experimental psychology series* (pp. 669–708). Boston: Blackwell.

Wethington, E., Kessler, R. C., & Pixley, J. E. (2004). Turning points in adulthood. In O. G. Brim, C. D. Ryff, & R. C. Kessler (Eds.), *How healthy are we?: A national study of well-being at midlife* (pp. 586–613). *The John D. and Catherine T. MacArthur foundation series on mental health and development. Studies on successful midlife development.* Chicago: University of Chicago Press.

Whitehouse, E. M. (2006). Poverty. In G. G. Bear & K. M. Minke (Eds.), *Children's needs III: Development, prevention, and intervention* (pp. 835–845). Washington, DC: National Association of School Psychologists.

Wickwire Jr., E. M., Roland, M. M. S., Elkin, T. D., & Schumacher, J. A. (2008). Sleep disorders. In M. Hersen & D. Michel (Eds.), *Handbook of psychological assessment, case conceptualization, and treatment.* Vol 2, *Children and adolescents* (pp. 622–651). Hoboken, NJ: Wiley.

Wierzalis, E. A., Barret, B., Pope, M., & Rankins, M. (2006). Gay men and aging: Sex and intimacy. In D. Kimmel, T. Rose, & S. David (Eds.), *Lesbian, gay, bisexual, and transgender aging: Research and clinical perspectives* (pp. 91–109). New York: Columbia University Press.

Willett, W. C. (2005). Diet and cancer. *JAMA: Journal of the American Medical Association, 293,* 233–234.

Willetts, M. C. (2006). Union quality comparisons between long-term heterosexual cohabitation and legal marriage. *Journal of Family Issues, 27*(1), 110–127.

Williams, C. (2004, September). The sandwich generation. *Perspectives on Labour and Income, 5* (9). Retrieved from http://www.statcan.gc.ca/pub/75-001-x/10904/7033-eng.htm.

Williams, M. S. (2004). The psychology of eating. *Psychology and Health, 19*(4), 541–542.

Willis, S. L., & Schaie, K. W. (2006). Cognitive functioning in the baby boomers: Longitudinal and cohort effects. In S. K. Whitbourne, & S. L. Willis (Eds.), *The baby boomers grow up: Contemporary perspectives on midlife* (pp. 205–234). Mahwah, NJ: Lawrence Erlbaum Associates Publishers.

Wilson, D. R., Langlois, S., & Johnson, J. (2007). Mid-trimester amniocentesis fetal loss rate: Committee opinion. *Journal of Obstetrics and Gynaecology Canada, 29*(7):586–590). Retrieved from http://www.sogc.org/guidelines/documents/gui194CPG0707.pdf

Wilson, E. O. (2004). *On Human Nature.* Cambridge, MA: Harvard University Press.

Wilson, J. M. B., Tripp, D. A., & Boland, F. J. (2005). The relative contributions of waist-to-hip ratio and body mass to judgments of attractiveness. *Sexualities, Evolution & Gender, 7*(3), 245–267.

Wilson, P. (2004). A preliminary investigation of an early intervention program: Examining the intervention effectiveness of the Bracken Concept Development Program and the Bracken Basic Concept Scale–Revised with Head Start students. *Psychology in the Schools, 41*(3), 301–311.

Windsor, T. D., Anstey, K. J., Butterworth, P., & Rodgers, B. (2008). Behavioral approach and behavioral inhibition as moderators of the association between negative life events and perceived control in midlife. *Personality and Individual Differences, 44*(5), 1080–1092.

Winner, E. (2000). The origins and ends of giftedness. *American Psychologist, 55,* 159–169.

Witherington, D. C., Campos, J. J., Anderson, D. I., Lejeune, L., & Seah, E. (2005). Avoidance of heights on the visual cliff in newly walking infants. *Infancy, 7*(3), 285–298.

Witkowska, E., & Gådin, K. G. (2005). What female high school students regard as harassment. International Journal of *Adolescent Medicine and Health, 17*(4), 391–406.

Wocadlo, C., & Rieger, I. (2006). Educational and therapeutic resource dependency at early school-age in children who were born very preterm. *Early Human Development, 82*(1), 29–37.

Wodrich, D. L. (2006). Sex chromosome anomalies. In L. Phelps (Ed.), *Chronic health-related disorders in children: Collaborative medical and psychoeducational interventions* (pp. 253–270). Washington, DC: American Psychological Association.

Wojslawowicz Bowker, J. C., Rubin, K. H., Burgess, K. B., Booth-Laforce, C., & Rose- Krasnor, L. (2006). Behavioral characteristics associated with stable and fluid best friendship patterns in middle childhood. *Merrill-Palmer Quarterly, 52*(4), 671–693.

Wolchik, S. A., Wilcox, K. L., Tein, J. Y., & Sandler, I. N. (2000). Maternal acceptance and consistency of discipline as buffers of divorce stressors on children's psychological adjustment problems. *Journal of Abnormal Psychology, 28*(1), 87–102.

Wolf, M. (2014, May 13). 10 youth movements that changed history. *Huffington Post*. http://www.huffingtonpost.com/matt-wolf/10-youth-movements-that-c_b_4958409.html.

Wolfelt, A. (2016). How to support a friend who is dying. Hospice. Retrieved from http://www.hospicenet.org/html/help_a_friend.html.

Wolfenden, L. E., & Holt, N. L. (2005). Talent development in elite junior tennis: Perceptions of players, parents, and coaches. *Journal of Applied Sport Psychology, 17*(2), 108–126.

Woolfolk, A. (2008). *Educational psychology, active learning edition* (10th ed.). Boston: Allyn & Bacon.

World Health Organization. (2004). *HIV transmission through breastfeeding: A review of available evidence*. Retrieved from http://www.unfpa.org/webdav/site/global/shared/documents/publications/2004/hiv_transmission.pdf.

World Health Organization. (2012). Are you ready? What you need to know about aging. Retrieved from http://www.who.int/world-health-day/2012/toolkit/background/en/

World Health Organization. (2016a). Exclusive breastfeeding. Retrieved October 15, 2016, from http://www.who.int/nutrition/topics/exclusive_breastfeeding/en/.

World Health Organization. (2016b) Children: Reducing mortality. Retrieved from http://www.who.int/mediacentre/factsheets/fs178/en/.

Worell, J., & Goodheart, C. D. (Eds.), (2006). *Handbook of girls' and women's psychological health: Gender and well-being across the lifespan*. New York: Oxford University Press.

Wozniak, J. R., & Lim, K. O. (2006). Advances in white matter imaging: A review of in vivo magnetic resonance methodologies and their applicability to the study of development and aging. *Neuroscience & Biobehavioral Reviews, 30*(6), 762–774.

Wright, C., & Birks, E. (2000). Risk factors for failure to thrive: A population-based survey. *Child: Care, Health, and Development, 26*(1), 5–16.

Wright, D. W., & Young, R. (1998). The effects of family structure and maternal employment on the development of gender-related attitudes among men and women. *Journal of Family Issues, 19*(3), 300–314.

Wulff, K., & Siegmund, R. (2001). Circadian and ultradian time patterns in human behaviour. Part 1: Activity monitoring of families from prepartum to postpartum. *Biological Rhythm Research, 31*(5), 581–602.

X

Xie, H. L., Yan, B., Signe M., Hutchins, B. C., & Cairns, B. D. (2006). What makes a girl (or a boy) popular (or unpopular)? African American Children's perceptions and developmental differences. *Developmental Psychology, 42*(4), 599–612.

Y

Yaffe, K., Haan, M., Byers, A., Tangen, C., & Kuller, L. (2000). Estrogen use, APOE, and cognitive decline: Evidence of gene- environment interaction. *Neurology, 54*(10), 1949–1953.

Yamada, H., et al. (2000). A milestone for normal development of the infantile brain detected by functional MRI. *Neurology, 55*(2), 218–223.

Yang, H.-C., & Noel, A. M. (2006). The developmental characteristics of four- and five-year-old pre-schoolers' drawing: An analysis of scribbles, placement patterns, emergent writing, and name writing in archived spontaneous drawing samples. *Journal of Early Childhood Literacy,6*(2), 145–162.

Yeo, J. (2010). Childbirth experience of participants in Lamaze childbirth education [Korean]. *Korean Journal of Women Health Nursing, 16*(3), 215–223

Yip, T. (2014, spring). The effects of racial/ethnic discrimination and sleep quality on depressive symptoms and self-esteem trajectories among diverse adolescents. *Science and Business Media.* Retrieved from http://link.springer.com/article/10.1007/s10964-014-0123-x.

Yost, M. R., & Zurbriggen, E. L. (2006). Gender differences in the enactment of sociosexuality. *Journal of Sex Research, 43*(2), 163–173.

Z

Zacks, R. T., Hasher, L., & Li, K. Z. H. (2000). Human memory. In F. I. M. Craik & T. A. Salthouse (Eds.), *Age-related changes in memory: A cognitive neuroscience perspective. The handbook of aging and cognition* (2nd ed.) (pp. 293–357). Mahwah, NJ: Lawrence Erlbaum Associates Publishers.

Zaidi, A. U., & Shyraydi, M. (2002). Perceptions of arranged marriages by young Pakistani Muslim women living in a Western society. *Journal of Comparative Family Studies, 33*(4), 495–514.

Zajonc, R. B. (2001). The family dynamics of intellectual development. *American Psychologist, 56*(6/7), 490–496.

Zan, B., & Hildebrandt, C. (2003). First graders' interpersonal understanding during cooperative and competitive games. *Early Education and Development, 14*(4), 397–410.

Zarbatany, L., McDougall, P., & Hymel, S. (2000). Gender-differentiated experience in the peer culture: Links to intimacy in preadolescence. *Social Development, 9*(1), 62–79.

Zeifman, D. M. (2004). Acoustic features of infant crying related to intended caregiving intervention. *Infant and Child Development, 13*(2), 111–122.

Zeintl, M., Kliegel, M., & Hofer, S. M. (2007). The role of processing resources in age-related prospective and retrospective memory within old age. *Psychology and Aging, 22*(4), 826–834.

Zelazo, P. R. (1998). McGraw and the development of unaided walking. *Developmental Review, 18*(4), 449–471.

Zeliadt, N. (2010) Live long and proper: Genetic factors associated with increased longevity identified. *Scientific America*. Retrieved from http://www.scientificamerican.com/article/genetic-factors-associated-with-increased-longevity-identified/.

Zimmerman, B. J. (2000). Self-efficacy: An essential motive to learn. *Contemporary Educational Psychology, 25*(1), 82–91.

Zimmermann, P., Maier, M. A., Winter, M., & Grossmann, K. E. (2001). Attachment and adolescents' emotion regulation during a joint problem-solving task with a friend. *International Journal of Behavioral Development, 25*(4), 331–343.

Zweigenhaft, R. L., & Von Ammon, J. (2000). Birth order and civil disobedience: A test of Sulloway's "born to rebel" hypothesis. *Journal of Social Psychology, 140*(5), 624–627.

Name Index

L

M

S

T

U

V

W

X

Y

Z

Subject Index

Note: A page number followed by f indicates a figure; a page number followed by t indicates a table

D

E

F

G

H

I

Q

T

U

V

W

X

Y

Z

Chapter in Review

1

LO1 **developmental psychology**
the biological, psychological, and socio-cultural study of human change across the lifespan. (p. 3)

LO2 **behaviourism**
Watson's view that science must study observable behaviour only and investigate relationships between stimuli and responses. (p. 3)

maturation
the unfolding of genetically determined traits, structures, and functions. (p. 4)

psychosexual development
the process by which libidinal energy is expressed through different erogenous zones during different stages of development. (p. 4)

stage theory
a theory of development characterized by distinct periods of life. (p. 4)

defence mechanism
a method to reduce anxiety when the id and superego are too demanding. (p. 4)

Oedipal Complex
the rivalry between a boy and his father for his mother's love. (p. 5)

Electra Complex
the rivalry between a girl and her mother for her father's love. (p. 5)

psychosocial development
Erikson's theory, which emphasizes the importance of social relationships and conscious choice throughout eight stages of development. (p. 6)

life crisis
an internal conflict that attends each stage of psychosocial development. (p. 6)

identity crisis
according to Erikson, a period of inner conflict during which individuals examine their values and make decisions about their life roles. (p. 7)

classical conditioning
a simple form of learning in which one stimulus comes to bring forth the response usually brought forth by a second stimulus as a result of being paired repeatedly with the second stimulus. (p. 7)

operant conditioning
a simple form of learning in which an organism learns to engage in behaviour that is reinforced. (p. 7)

reinforcement
the process of providing stimuli following responses in an effort to increase the frequency of the responses. (p. 7)

positive reinforcer
a reinforcer that, when applied, increases the frequency of a response. (p. 8)

negative reinforcer
a reinforcer that, when removed, increases the frequency of a response. (p. 8)

LO1 **Explain the history of the study of human development.** The philosopher John Locke focused on the role of experience in development. Jean-Jacques Rousseau argued that children are good by nature, and if allowed to express their natural impulses, will develop into moral people. Hall founded child development as an academic discipline. All these theories are integrated to form a definition of developmental psychology, which is the biological, psychological, and socio-cultural study of development across the lifespan.

LO2 **Compare and contrast theories of human development.** Psychoanalytic theory focuses on the roles of internal conflict. Sigmund Freud believed that children undergo five stages of psychosexual development. Erik Erikson focused on social relationships and included adulthood by extending Freud's five developmental stages to eight.

Erikson's Stages

0–18 months	Trust vs. Mistrust
19 months–3 years	Autonomy vs. Shame and Doubt
4–5 years	Initiative vs. Guilt
6–11 years	Industry vs. Inferiority
Adolescence (12–18 years)	Identity vs. Role Confusion
Young Adulthood (19–39 years)	Intimacy vs. Isolation
Middle Adulthood (40–64 years)	Generativity vs. Stagnation
Later Life (65 years to death)	Ego Integrity vs. Despair

Learning theorists focus on how learning influences behaviour.

- John B. Watson and B.F. Skinner stress classical and operant conditioning. Social cognitive theorists, such as Albert Bandura, argue that much learning occurs by observation and that we choose whether we engage in learned behaviour.
- Jean Piaget's cognitive developmental theory hypothesizes that children's cognitive processes develop in an invariant series of stages, culminating with *formal operational* reasoning.
- Information-processing theory deals with how we encode information, manipulate it, place it in memory, and retrieve it.
- The biological perspective refers to genetics and developments such as conception, puberty, and peak performance and decline in adulthood.
- Ethology involves instinctive behaviour patterns.
- Urie Bronfenbrenner's ecological theory explains development in terms of the *reciprocal interaction* between children and the settings where development occurs.
- The socio-cultural perspective broadly addresses the richness of diversity by noting the influences of ethnicity and gender on development. This perspective is of particular importance to Canadians, given the more than 200 cultures within our borders.

LO3 **Enumerate key controversies in human development.** Theories of human growth and development have led to three major debates:

Nature and Nurture	What aspects of behaviour are determined by our genetic programming (nature)? What aspects of behaviour can be traced to nutrition, cultural and family backgrounds, and learning opportunities (nurture)?

punishments
aversive events that suppress or decrease the frequency of the behaviour they follow. (p. 8)

extinction
the cessation of a response that is performed in the absence of reinforcement. (p. 9)

social cognitive theory
a cognitively oriented learning theory that emphasizes observational learning. (p. 9)

cognitive-developmental theory
the stage theory that suggests children's abilities to mentally represent the world and solve problems are a result of the interaction of experience and the maturation of neurological structures. (p. 9)

schema
an action pattern or mental structure involved in the acquisition and organization of knowledge. (p. 10)

adaptation
the interaction between the organism and the environment, consisting of assimilation and accommodation. (p. 10)

assimilation
the incorporation of new events or knowledge into existing schemas. (p. 10)

accommodation
the modification of existing schemas to permit the incorporation of new events or knowledge. (p. 10)

equilibration
the creation of an equilibrium, or balance, between assimilation and accommodation. (p. 10)

ethology
the study of behaviours that are specific to a species from the evolutionary perspective. (p. 11)

fixed action pattern (FAP)
a stereotyped pattern of behaviour that is evoked by a "releasing stimulus"; an instinct. (p. 11)

ecology
the branch of biology that studies the relationships between living organisms and their environment. (p. 12)

ecological systems theory
the view that explains child development in terms of the reciprocal influences between children and their environmental settings. (p. 12)

microsystem
the immediate settings with which the child interacts, such as the home, the school, and peers. (p. 12)

mesosystem
the interlocking settings that influence the child, such as the interaction of the school and the larger community. (p. 12)

exosystem
community institutions and settings that indirectly influence the child, such as the school board and the parents' workplaces. (p. 13)

macrosystem
the basic institutions and ideologies that influence the child. (p. 13)

Continuity and Discontinuity	Maturational, psychoanalytic, and cognitive-developmental theorists see development as discontinuous (occurring in stages), whereas learning theorists see development as a continuous process.
Active and Passive Roles	Some educators, such as John Locke, view children as passive, requiring external motivation to learn. Other educators, many of them more modern, view children as active, having a natural love of learning.

LO4 Describe ways in which researchers study human development.

Development is studied by first gathering information and conducting research. Naturalistic observation is conducted in "the field"—the settings in which people develop. The case study is a carefully drawn account or biography of behaviour. Correlational studies reveal relationships between variables but not cause and effect. Experiments seek to determine cause and effect by exposing subjects to treatments and observing the results.

Longitudinal research, such as Canada's National Longitudinal Survey of Children and Youth (NLSCY), studies the same people repeatedly over time. Cross-sectional research observes and compares people of different ages. Ethical standards outlined by the Canadian Psychiatric Association require that researchers not use treatments that harm participants.

chronosystem
the environmental changes that occur over time and have an effect on the child. (p. 13)

zone of proximal development (ZPD)
Vygotsky's term for the range of tasks a child can carry out with the help of someone who is more skilled. (p. 13)

scaffolding
Vygotsky's term for temporary cognitive structures or methods of solving problems that help children as they learn to function independently. (p. 13)

gender
characterized by social constructs and identity, not fixed or definitive. It isn't as simple as physiology or anatomy. (p. 13)

LO3

nature
the processes within an organism that guide it to develop according to its genetic code. (p. 15)

nurture
environmental factors that influence development. (p. 15)

empirical
based on observation and experimentation. (p. 15)

LO4

case study
a carefully written account of the behaviour of an individual. (p. 16)

standardized test
a test that compares an individual's score with the scores of a group of similar individuals. (p. 16)

correlation coefficient
a number ranging from +1.00 to −1.00 that expresses the direction (positive or negative) and strength of the relationship between two variables. (p. 17)

positive correlation
a relationship between two variables in which one variable increases as the other increases. (p. 17)

negative correlation
a relationship between two variables in which one variable increases as the other decreases. (p. 17)

experiment
a method of scientific investigation that seeks to discover cause-and-effect relationships by introducing independent variables and observing their effects on dependent variables. (p. 17)

hypothesis
a proposition to be tested. (p. 17)

independent variable
a condition in a scientific study that is manipulated so that its effects can be observed. (p. 17)

dependent variable
a measure of an assumed effect of an independent variable. (p. 17)

experimental group
a group of subjects who receive a treatment in an experiment. (p. 18)

control group
a group of subjects in an experiment who do not receive the treatment but for whom all other conditions are comparable with those of the experimental group. (p. 18)

longitudinal research
the study of developmental processes by taking repeated measures of the same group of participants at various stages of development. (p. 18)

cross-sectional research
the study of developmental processes by taking measures of participants of different age groups at the same time. (p. 18)

cohort effect
similarities in behaviour among a group of peers as a result of being of approximately the same age. (p. 19)

2 Chapter in Review

LO1 heredity
the transmission of genetic material from one generation to another. (p. 21)

genetics
the branch of biology that studies heredity. (p. 21)

chromosomes
rod-shaped structures that are composed of genes and are found within the nuclei of cells. (p. 21)

genes
the basic units of heredity. Genes are composed of deoxyribonucleic acid (DNA). (p. 21)

polygenic
resulting from many (poly) genes. (p. 21)

deoxyribonucleic acid (DNA)
genetic material that takes the form of a double helix and is composed of phosphates, sugars, and bases. (p. 21)

mitosis
the form of cell division in which each chromosome splits lengthwise to double in number. Half of each chromosome combines with chemicals to retake its original form and then moves to the new cell. (p. 21)

mutation
a sudden, or accidental, variation in a heritable characteristic that affects the composition of genes. (p. 21)

meiosis
the form of cell division in which each pair of chromosomes splits so that one member of each pair moves to the new cell. As a result, each new cell has 23 chromosomes. (p. 22)

autosome
a pair of chromosomes (with the exception of sex chromosomes). (p. 22)

sex chromosome
a chromosome in the shape of a Y (male) or X (female) that determines the sex of the child. (p. 22)

monozygotic (MZ) twins
twins that derive from a single zygote that has split into two; identical twins. Each MZ twin carries the same genetic code. (p. 22)

dizygotic (DZ) twins
twins that derive from two separate zygotes; fraternal twins with separate genetic codes. (p. 22)

allele
a member of a pair of genes. (p. 22)

homozygous
having two identical alleles. (p. 22)

heterozygous
having two different alleles. (p. 22)

ovulation
the releasing of an ovum from an ovary. (p. 22)

dominant trait
a trait that is expressed. (p. 23)

LO1 Describe the influences of heredity on development.

Heredity is the biological transmission of traits from one generation to another. People normally have 46 strands of deoxyribonucleic acid (DNA) called chromosomes, which are organized into 23 pairs. Genes, which regulate the development of traits, are segments of chromosomes.

Sperm and ova are produced by meiosis and have 23 rather than 46 chromosomes. Monozygotic (MZ), or identical, twins develop from a single fertilized ovum that splits in two (see Figure 2.2). Dizygotic (DZ), or fraternal, twins develop from two fertilized ova. Traits are determined by pairs of genes, either from "averaging" the genetic instructions, or by dominant genes. Carriers of a trait bear one dominant gene and one recessive gene for it.

FIGURE 2.2

Difference between Identical and Fraternal Twins Cell Division

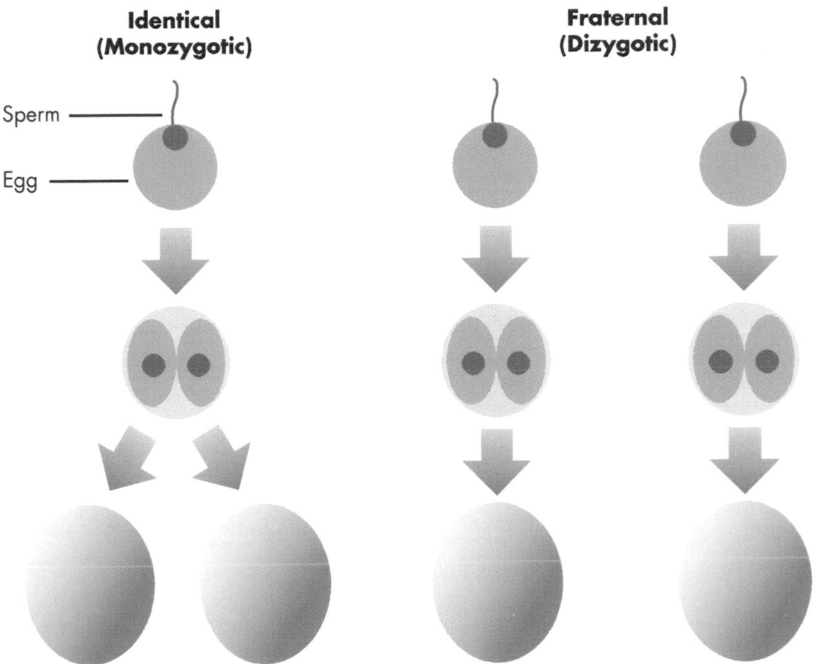

Source: https://commons.wikimedia.org/wiki/File:Identical-fraternal-sperm-egg.svg

Chromosomal abnormalities in offspring are more likely as parents age. Down syndrome is caused by an extra chromosome on the 21st pair. People with sex-linked disorders experience many differences, some of them associated with "maleness" or "femaleness," such as colour blindness. Genetic disorders include phenylketonuria (PKU), Huntington's disease, sickle-cell anemia, Tay-Sachs disease, cystic fibrosis, and hemophilia. Prenatal blood tests, ultrasound, and amniocentesis can determine the presence of various genetic and chromosomal abnormalities.

LO2 Describe the influences of the environment on development.

Our genotypes are the sets of traits that we inherit. But environmental conditions can vary their expression, resulting in our phenotypes. Researchers can study the heritability of a trait by observing its expression among relatives who differ in genetic closeness. Parents and children have a 50% overlap in genes, as do siblings, with the exception of monozygotic (MZ) twins, who have 100% overlap. MZ twins resemble each other more closely than dizygotic

recessive trait
a trait that is not expressed when the gene or genes involved have been paired with dominant genes. (p. 23)

carrier
a person who carries and transmits characteristics but does not exhibit them. (p. 23)

multifactorial problems
problems that stem from the interaction of heredity and environmental factors. (p. 23)

Down syndrome
a chromosomal abnormality characterized by intellectual challenges and caused by an extra chromosome in the 21st pair. (p. 24)

sex-linked chromosomal abnormalities
abnormalities that are transmitted from generation to generation and are carried on the sex chromosome. (p. 25)

phenylketonuria (PKU)
a genetic abnormality in which phenylalanine builds up and causes intellectual challenges. (p. 25)

Huntington disease (HD)
a fatal genetic neurologic disorder whose onset takes place is in middle age. It is a dominant trait, which is rare for a fatal genetic disorder. (p. 25)

sickle-cell anemia
a genetic disorder that decreases the blood's capacity to carry oxygen. (p. 25)

Tay-Sachs disease
a fatal genetic neurological disorder that causes degeneration and premature death. (p. 25)

cystic fibrosis
a fatal genetic disorder in which mucus obstructs the lungs and pancreas. (p. 26)

hemophilia
a genetic disorder in which blood does not clot properly. (p. 26)

sex-linked genetic abnormalities
abnormalities resulting from genes that are found on the X sex chromosome. They are more likely to be shown by male offspring (who do not have an opposing gene from a second X chromosome) than by female offspring. (p. 26)

muscular dystrophy
a chronic disease characterized by a progressive wasting away of the muscles. (p. 27)

colour blindness
a sex-linked condition that makes it difficult to differentiate various colours. (p. 27)

prenatal
before birth. (p. 27)

amniocentesis
a procedure for drawing and examining fetal cells sloughed off into amniotic fluid to determine the presence of various disorders. (p. 27)

chorionic villus sampling (CVS)
a method for the prenatal detection of genetic abnormalities that samples the membrane enveloping the amniotic sac and fetus. (p. 27)

(DZ) twins on physical and psychological traits, even when reared apart. Traits are likely to have a strong genetic basis if adopted children are closer to their natural parents than to their adoptive parents in their expression.

LO3 **Explain what happens in the process of conception.** Conception is the union of an ovum and a sperm cell and usually occurs in a fallopian tube (see Figure 2.7). More boys are conceived than girls, but they have a higher rate of miscarriage. Once a sperm cell has entered an ovum, the chromosomes from the sperm cell line up across from the corresponding chromosomes in the egg cell. They form 23 new pairs with a unique set of genetic instructions.

FIGURE 2.7

Female Reproductive Organs

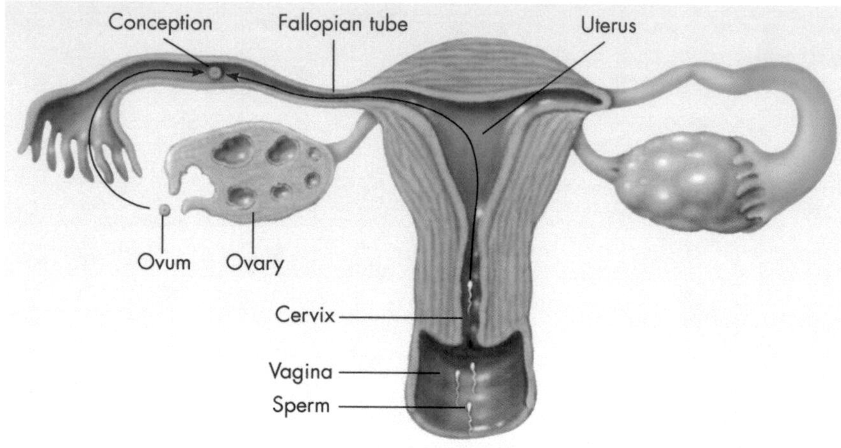

A low sperm count—or lack of sperm—is the most common infertility problem in men. The most common infertility problem in women is irregular ovulation or lack of ovulation; other reasons for infertility include infections such as pelvic inflammatory disease (PID), endometriosis, and obstructions. Fertility drugs regulate ovulation. Other ways of conceiving include artificial insemination and in vitro fertilization (IVF). Both of these procedures fall under a larger term called assisted reproductive technology.

Source: © Cengage Learning

placenta
the organ that provides oxygen and vital nutrients to the fetus and removes waste products from the blood. (p. 27)

ultrasound
sound waves too high in pitch to be sensed by the human ear. (p. 27)

alpha-fetoprotein (AFP) assay
a blood test that assesses the mother's blood level of alpha-fetoprotein, a substance that is linked to fetal neural tube defects. (p. 28)

LO2 **reaction range**
the interaction between nature (genetic potential) and nurture (the set of circumstances that we encounter in life). (p. 28)

genotype
the genetic form or constitution of a person as determined by heredity. (p. 28)

phenotype
the actual form or constitution of a person as determined by heredity and environmental factors. (p. 29)

LO3 **conception**
the union of a sperm cell and an ovum that occurs when the chromosomes of each of these cells combine to form 23 new pairs. (p. 29)

endometrium
the inner lining of the uterus. (p. 30)

spontaneous abortion
unplanned miscarriage of the developing organism. (p. 30)

pelvic inflammatory disease (PID)
an infection of the abdominal region that may have various causes and may impair fertility. (p. 31)

endometriosis
inflammation of endometrial tissue sloughed off into the abdominal cavity rather than out of the body during menstruation; the condition is characterized by abdominal pain and sometimes infertility. (p. 31)

motility
the movement of sperm. (p. 31)

assisted reproductive technology (ART)
the term for any medical assistance provided that enables conception to take place. (p. 32)

artificial insemination
injection of sperm into the uterus to fertilize an ovum. (p. 32)

in vitro fertilization (IVF)
fertilization of an ovum in a laboratory dish. (p. 32)

donor IVF
the transfer of a donor's ovum, fertilized in a laboratory dish, to the uterus of another woman. (p. 32)

LO4

germinal (zygotic) stage
the period of development between conception and the implantation of the embryo. (p. 34)

blastocyst
a cluster of cells that are formed around a cavity of fluid; some of the cells will become the fetus and some of the cells will become the placenta nourishing the fetus. (p. 34)

embryonic disk
the platelike inner part of the blastocyst that differentiates into the ectoderm, mesoderm, and endoderm of the embryo. (p. 34)

embryonic stage
the stage of prenatal development that lasts from implantation through the eighth week of pregnancy; it is characterized by the development of the major organ systems. (p. 34)

cephalocaudal
from head to tail. (p. 34)

proximodistal
from the inner part (or axis) of the body outward. (p. 34)

ectoderm
the outermost cell layer of the newly formed embryo from which the skin and nervous system develop. (p. 35)

neural tube
a hollowed-out area in the blastocyst from which the nervous system develops. (p. 35)

endoderm
the inner layer of the embryo from which the lungs and digestive system develop. (p. 35)

mesoderm
the central layer of the embryo from which the bones and muscles develop. (p. 35)

androgens
male sex hormones. (p. 35)

amniotic sac
the sac containing the fetus. (p. 36)

amniotic fluid
fluid within the amniotic sac that suspends and protects the fetus. (p. 36)

FIGURE 2.11

A Human Embryo at 7 Weeks

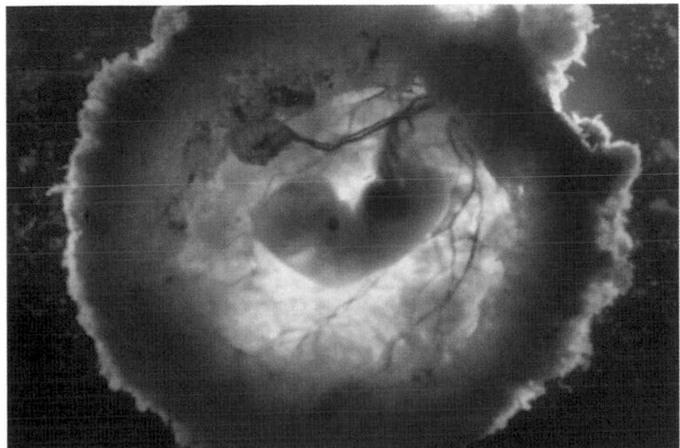

© Petit Format/Nestle/Science Source/Photo Researchers

LO4 Recount the major events of prenatal development.

Recount the major events of prenatal development. During the germinal stage, the zygote divides repeatedly and travels through a fallopian tube to the uterus, where it implants. Before implantation, it is nourished by the yolk of the original egg cell. Once implanted in the uterine wall, it is nourished by the mother. The embryonic stage lasts from implantation until the eighth week of development, during which time the major organ systems differentiate. Development follows cephalocaudal and proximodistal trends. The heart begins to beat during the fourth week. By the end of the second month, facial features are becoming distinct, teeth buds have formed, the kidneys are working, and the liver is producing red blood cells. Male sex hormones spur development of the male reproductive system. The embryo and fetus exchange nutrients and wastes with the mother through the placenta. Some disease organisms, such as those that cause syphilis and rubella, can pass through the placenta. Some drugs also pass through, including aspirin, narcotics, and alcohol.

The fetal stage is characterized by maturation of organs and gains in size. It lasts from the end of the embryonic stage until birth. The fetus begins to turn at the ninth or tenth week. It responds to sound waves by the 13th week of pregnancy. By the end of the second trimester, the fetus opens and shuts its eyes, sucks its thumb, and alternates between wakefulness and sleep. During the third trimester, it becomes increasingly capable of sustaining independent life.

fetal stage
the stage of development that lasts from the beginning of the ninth week of pregnancy through birth; it is characterized by gains in size and weight and by maturation of the organ systems. (p. 36)

stillbirth
the birth of a dead fetus. (p. 37)

teratogens
environmental influences or agents that can damage the embryo or fetus. (p. 38)

toxemia
a life-threatening disease that can afflict pregnant women; characterized by high blood pressure. (p. 38)

Rh incompatibility
a condition in which antibodies produced by the mother are transmitted to the child, possibly causing brain damage or death. (p. 38)

critical periods
periods during which an embryo is particularly vulnerable to a certain teratogen. (p. 38)

thalidomide
a treatment for insomnia used in the 1960s that cause birth defects. (p. 39)

fetal alcohol spectrum disorder (FASD)
a cluster of symptoms shown by children of women who drank heavily during pregnancy, including characteristic facial features and intellectual challenges. (p. 39)

accutane (isotretinoin)
a frequently prescribed acne medication that can cause significant physical and neurological birth defects. (p. 41)

progestin
a hormone used to maintain pregnancy that can cause masculinization of the fetus. (p. 41)

DES
diethylstilbestrol, an estrogen that has been linked to cancer in the reproductive organs of children of women who used the hormone when pregnant. (p. 41)

pathogenic
anything that causes disease. (p. 42)

syphilis
a sexually transmitted infection that, in advanced stages, can attack major organ systems. (p. 42)

congenital
present at birth; resulting from the prenatal environment. (p. 42)

HIV/AIDS
HIV stands for human immunodeficiency virus, which cripples the body's immune system. AIDS stands for acquired immunodeficiency syndrome, a condition in which the immune system is weakened such that it is vulnerable to diseases it would otherwise be able to fight off. (p. 42)

rubella
a viral infection that can cause retardation and heart disease in the embryo. Also called German measles. (p. 42)

premature
born before the full term of gestation. Also referred to as preterm. (p. 42)

Maternal malnutrition is linked to low birth weight, prematurity, and cognitive and behavioural problems. Environmental agents that can harm the embryo and fetus include accutane, thalidomide, tetracycline, DES (diethylstilbestrol), toxoplasmosis, high doses of vitamins A and D, narcotics, marijuana, cocaine, alcohol, cigarette smoke, heavy metals, PCBs (polychlorinated biphenyls), prescribed medication, food-borne substances, and radiation. Teratogens are most harmful during critical periods, when certain organs are developing. Women who contract rubella may bear children who suffer from deafness, intellectual challenges, heart disease, or cataracts. Syphilis can cause miscarriage or stillbirth. Toxemia is characterized by high blood pressure and is often seen in preterm or small babies. In Rh incompatibility, the mother's antibodies can cause brain damage or death.

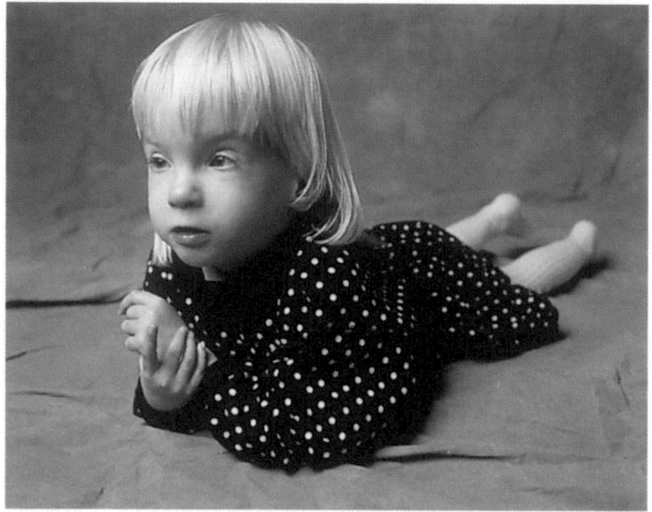

Teenage mothers have a higher incidence of infant mortality and children with low birth weight. Older parents run an increasing risk of chromosomal abnormalities and stillborn or preterm babies.

The rapid pace of scientific technology has caused Canadians to closely examine medical ethics and to enact legislation to ensure that research in reproductive technology remains ethically sound.

Chapter in Review

3

LO1 Braxton-Hicks contractions
the first, usually painless, contractions of childbirth. (p. 46)

prostaglandins
hormones that stimulate uterine contractions. (p. 46)

oxytocin
a hormone that stimulates labour contractions. (p. 46)

efface
to become thin. (p. 46)

dilate
to widen. (p. 46)

transition
movement of the head of the fetus into the birth canal. (p. 47)

LO2 midwife
an individual who cares for women during pregnancy, labour and delivery, and after the child is born. (p. 48)

natural childbirth
childbirth without medical intervention, including anaesthesia, being given to the mother during labour and delivery. (p. 49)

Lamaze method
a childbirth method in which women are educated about childbirth, breathe in patterns that reduce pain during birth, and have a coach present. (p. 49)

anaesthetics
agents that lessen pain. (p. 49)

general anaesthesia
an agent that eliminates pain by putting a person to sleep. (p. 49)

local anaesthetic
an agent that reduces pain in an area of the body. (p. 49)

Caesarean section (C-section)
delivery of a baby by abdominal surgery. (p. 50)

LO3 anoxia
absence of oxygen. (p. 50)

hypoxia
less oxygen than required. (p. 50)

breech (bottom-first) presentation
buttocks-first childbirth. (p. 51)

preterm
born prior to 37 weeks of gestation. (p. 51)

lanugo
fine, downy hair on premature babies. (p. 51)

vernix
oily white substance on the skin of premature babies. (p. 51)

respiratory distress syndrome
weak and irregular breathing, typical of preterm babies. (p. 51)

LO1 Identify the stages of childbirth. An expectant woman's first uterine contractions are Braxton-Hicks contractions, or false labour contractions. A day or so before labour begins, women may spot blood. About 1 woman in 10 has a rush of amniotic fluid. Maternal hormones stimulate contractions strong enough to expel the baby.

Childbirth begins with the onset of regular contractions of the uterus, which efface and dilate the cervix. The first stage may last from hours to more than a day. During transition, the head of the fetus moves into the birth canal. The second stage begins when the baby appears at the opening of the birth canal and ends with birth of the baby. Mucus is suctioned from the baby's mouth so that breathing is not obstructed. The umbilical cord is severed. During the third stage, the placenta is expelled.

LO2 Describe the different methods of childbirth. The most common method of childbirth is vaginal birth by medical doctor. For pain management, general anaesthesia and analgesics may be used; but they put the woman to sleep, decrease the strength of uterine contractions, and lower the responsiveness of the newborn. Local anaesthetics may be used instead to lessen pain in parts of the body. Birth may be natural, as in no pain or other medications, at home or in the hospital. Midwives are becoming increasingly popular. The midwife teaches women relaxation exercises to help deal with the discomfort of contractions. Midwives will also use various medical interventions when necessary. Prepared childbirth also uses relaxation methods such as the Lamaze method to help manage the pain of childbirth. Only a medical doctor can perform a Caesarean section (C-section), which means that the baby is delivered surgically through the abdomen. C-sections are most likely when the baby is large or in distress. Herpes and HIV infections can be bypassed by using C-section.

LO3 Discuss potential problems with childbirth. Prenatal oxygen deprivation can impair development of the nervous system and can be fatal. A baby is preterm when birth occurs at or before 37 weeks of gestation. A baby has a low birth weight when it weighs less than 2.5 kg (5.5 lb.). Risks of prematurity include infant mortality and delayed neurological and motor development. Preterm babies are relatively thin. Their sucking may be weak, and they may show respiratory distress. Preterm babies usually remain in the hospital in incubators, but they profit from early stimulation. Canadians want to ensure that all children have an equal opportunity to access health care services. The UNICEF Report, Leaving No Child Behind, looks at disparities between health statistics of Aboriginal and non-Aboriginal children in Canada.

LO4 Describe the key events of the postpartum period. Women may encounter the baby blues, or postpartum depression. These problems probably reflect hormonal changes following birth, although stress can play a role.

Postpartum depression symptoms include the following:

- feelings of hopelessness, helplessness, and worthlessness
- mood swings
- abnormal sleep patterns (frequently insomnia)

Treatment includes medication, social support, counselling, and psychoeducation to help work through her depressive symptoms and to adjust to parenting. Fathers may experience depression after the birth of a child possibly due to the major changes that take place adjusting to parenthood, stress in the relationship with his wife, and anxiety.

Early infant bonding is advantageous for both the baby and the mother.

incubators
heated, protective containers for premature infants. (p. 52)

small for dates
description of newborns who are small for their age. (p. 53)

LO4 **postpartum period**
the period immediately following childbirth. (p. 53)

postpartum depression (PPD)
serious maternal depression following delivery; characterized by sadness, apathy, and feelings of worthlessness. (p. 55)

bonding
formation of parent–infant attachment. (p. 55)

LO5 **Apgar scale**
a measure of a newborn's health that assesses appearance, pulse, grimace, activity level, and respiratory effort. (p. 56)

Brazelton Neonatal Behavioural Assessment Scale
a measure of a newborn's motor behaviour, response to stress, adaptive behaviour, and control over physiological state. (p. 56)

reflexes
unlearned responses to a stimulus. (p. 57)

rooting reflex
the response of turning the mouth and head toward the stroking of the cheek or the corner of the mouth. (p. 57)

Moro reflex
the response of arching the back, flinging out the arms and legs, and drawing them back to the chest in response to a sudden change in position. (p. 57)

grasping reflex
the response of grasping objects that touch the palms. (p. 57)

stepping reflex
the response of taking steps when held under the arms and leaned forward so the feet press the ground. (p. 57)

Babinski reflex
the response of fanning the toes when the soles of the feet are stroked. (p. 57)

tonic-neck reflex
the response of turning the head to one side, extending the arm and leg on that side, and flexing the limbs on the opposite side. (p. 57)

visual accommodation
automatic adjustments of the lenses to focus on objects. (p. 58)

convergence
inward movement of the eyes to focus on an object that is drawing nearer. (p. 58)

amplitude
loudness (of sound waves). (p. 58)

pitch
highness or lowness (of a sound), as determined by the frequency of sound waves. (p. 58)

TABLE 3.2

The APGAR Scale

Points	0	1	2
Appearance: Colour	Blue, pale	Body pink, extremities blue	Entirely pink
Pulse: Heart Rate	Absent (not detectable)	Slow—below 100 beats/minute	Rapid—100–140 beats/minute
Grimace: Reflex Irritability	No response	Grimace	Crying, coughing, sneezing
Activity level: Muscle tone	Completely flaccid, limp	Weak, inactive	Flexed arms and legs; resists extension
Respiratory effort: Breathing	Absent (infant is not breathing)	Shallow, irregular, slow	Regular breathing; lusty crying

LO5 **Describe the characteristics of the newborn.** The newborn's health is usually evaluated by the Apgar scale, see Table 3.2. The Brazelton Neonatal Behavioural Assessment Scale screens for behavioural and neurological problems. The newborn's rooting and sucking reflexes are basic to survival. Other key reflexes include the startle reflex, the grasping reflex, the stepping reflex, the Babinski reflex, and the tonic-neck reflex. Most reflexes disappear or are replaced by voluntary behaviour within months. If reflexes do not appear or disappear when developmentally appropriate, the infant may have neurological issues.

Newborns are nearsighted. Newborns are particularly responsive to the sounds and rhythms of speech. The taste preferences of neonates are similar to those of older children and adults. The sensations of skin against skin may contribute to attachment. Touch is the most advanced of all senses at birth; it is so important that a lack of touch could lead the infant to become depressed and eventually die. Neonates spend two-thirds of their time in sleep, distributing their sleep throughout the day and night in a series of naps. Neonates spend about half their time sleeping in rapid-eye-movement (REM) sleep, but as time goes on, REM sleep accounts for less of their sleep. REM sleep may be related to brain development.

Sudden infant death syndrome (SIDS) is the most common cause of death in infants between the ages of 1 month and 1 year. SIDS is more common among babies who are put to sleep on their stomachs, preterm and low-birth-weight infants, male infants, and infants whose mothers smoked during or after pregnancy The mortality rate of First Nation infants is higher than the national average by 1.5 times. SIDS occurs 3 to 10 times more often in this community. Babies cry mainly because of pain and discomfort. Crying communicates hunger, anger, pain, and the presence of health problems. "Purple crying" can be frightening for parents but is developmentally normal. Shaken baby syndrome (SBS) is the impulsive act of an exhausted or frustrated caregiver. Harm to a child is preventable when caregivers seek help and the proper support systems are in place.

rapid-eye-movement (REM) sleep
a sleep period when dreams are likely, as suggested by rapid eye movements. (p. 60)

non-rapid-eye-movement (non-REM) sleep
a sleep period when dreams are unlikely. (p. 60)

sudden infant death syndrome (SIDS)
the death, while sleeping, of apparently healthy babies who stop breathing. (p. 61)

pacifier
a device such as an artificial nipple or teething ring that soothes babies when sucked. (p. 63)

shaken baby syndrome (SBS)
the violent shaking of an infant often to stop it from crying. (p. 63)

4 Chapter in Review

LO1

differentiation the processes by which behaviours and physical structures become specialized. (p. 67)

failure to thrive (FTT) a disorder of infancy and early childhood characterized by variable eating and inadequate gains in weight. (p. 68)

canalization the tendency of growth rates to return to normal after undergoing environmentally induced change. (p. 68)

micronutrients nutrients required in small doses, such as vitamins and minerals, that are required for physical growth. (p. 70)

macronutrients nutrients required in large quantities, such as protein, carbohydrates, and fat, and are responsible for physical growth. (p. 70)

vaccines a small amount of dead or weakened germs that, when taken in by the infant's body, allows the immune system to protect itself against the disease by creating antibodies. (p. 70)

LO2

neurons cells in the nervous system that transmit messages. (p. 70)

dendrites rootlike parts of neurons that receive impulses from other neurons. (p. 71)

axon a long, thin part of a neuron that transmits impulses to other neurons through branching structures called axon terminals. (p. 71)

neurotransmitters chemicals that transmit neural impulses across a synapse from one neuron to another. (p. 71)

myelin sheath a fatty, whitish substance that encases and insulates axons. (p. 71)

myelination the coating of axons with myelin. (p. 72)

multiple sclerosis a disorder in which hard fibrous tissue replaces myelin, impeding neural transmission. (p. 72)

medulla an area of the hindbrain involved in heartbeat and respiration. (p. 72)

cerebellum the part of the hindbrain involved in coordination and balance. (p. 72)

cerebrum the part of the brain responsible for learning, thought, memory, and language, and muscle control. (p. 72)

LO1 Describe the physical development of the infant. Three key sequences of physical development are cephalocaudal development, proximodistal development, and differentiation. Infants usually double their birth weight in 5 months and triple it by their first birthday. Height increases by about half in the first year and usually occurs in spurts after extended periods of sleep. Infants grow another 10 to 15 cm (4 to 6 in.) and gain another 1.8 to 3.2 kg (4 to 7 lb.) in their second year. The head diminishes in proportion to the rest of the body. Failure to thrive (FTT) impairs growth in infancy and early childhood. FTT can have organic causes or nonorganic causes, possibly including deficiencies in caregiver–child interaction.

Breast milk is the optimal food for infants and it is recommended that women breastfeed their infants for 2 years and beyond although most women stop when they return to work. Alternatively, iron-fortified formula may be given for women who choose not to breastfeed or who are unable to for a variety of reasons. Introduction of solid foods is recommended at 4–6 months of age. Breastfeeding is related to the mother's availability, knowledge of the advantages of breastfeeding, support in caregiving, and availability of alternatives. Breast milk is tailored to human digestion, contains essential nutrients, contains the mothers' antibodies, helps protect against infant diarrhea, and is less likely than formula to lead to allergies. Malnutrition is connected with a small brain, fewer neurons, and less myelination. Micronutrients and macronutrients are required for growth development. This is particularly an issue in the Aboriginal community in Canada.

Children are vaccinated in Canada against numerous otherwise fatal diseases. To date, no evidence has been found linking vaccination to autism, a worry some parents fear.

LO2 Describe the development of the brain and the nervous system in infancy. Neurons receive and transmit messages in the form of neurotransmitters. As the child matures, axons grow in length, dendrites and axon terminals proliferate, and many neurons become wrapped in myelin, making them more efficient. The brain triples in weight by the first birthday, reaching nearly 70% of its adult weight. The brain has two major prenatal growth spurts: neurons proliferate during the first, and the second spurt is due mainly

FIGURE 4.2

Structures of the Brain

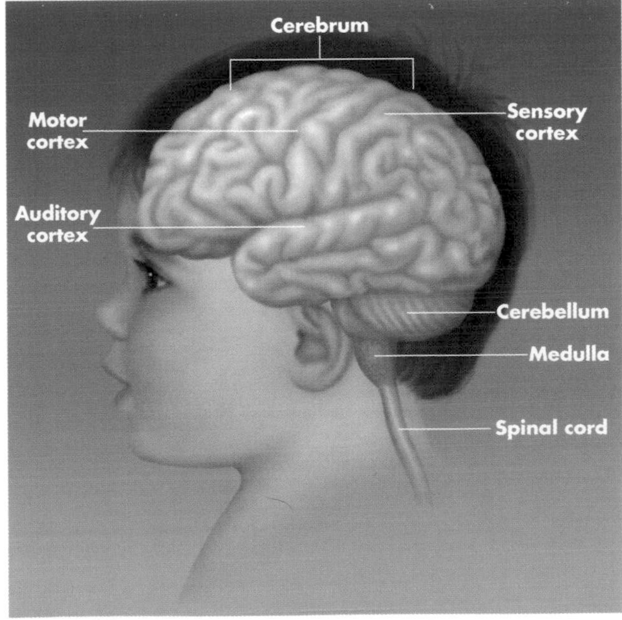

Source: © Cengage Learning

plasticity
the ability of the brain to compensate for injuries in particular areas by developing new neural pathways. (p. 74)

LO3 **palmar grasp**
grasping objects between the fingers and the palm. (p. 74)

pincer grasp
grasping objects between the fingers and the thumb. (p. 74)

locomotion
movement from one place to another. (p. 74)

toddler
a child who walks with short, uncertain steps. (p. 75)

LO4 **habituation**
becoming used to a stimulus and therefore paying less attention to it. (p. 79)

FIGURE 4.4

Preferences for Visual Stimuli in 2-Month-Olds

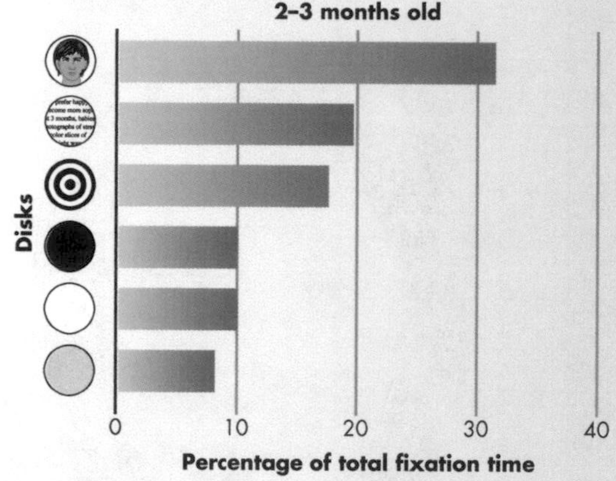

Source: © Cengage Learning

to the proliferation of dendrites and axon terminals. Sensory and motor areas of the brain begin to develop because of maturation, but sensory stimulation and motor activity spur development The brain shows plasticity especially between 1 to 2 years of age. This means the brain has the ability to compensate for injuries to certain areas that might occur for various reasons; new neural pathways can be found to send messages.

LO3 Describe the development of gross motor milestones during infancy.

Motor development is related to changes in posture, movement, and coordination. Children gain the ability to move their bodies through a sequence of activities that includes rolling over, sitting up, crawling, walking, and running. Although the sequence remains stable, some children skip a step. Both maturation (nature) and experience (nurture) play roles in motor development. Development of motor skills can be accelerated by training, but the effect is generally slight. Extreme deprivation can be overcome as seen in the example of Romanian orphans adopted by Canadians.

LO4 Outline patterns of sensory and perceptual development in infancy.

Newborns are nearsighted and have poor peripheral vision. Their acuity and peripheral vision approximate adult levels by the age of 6 months. Newborns look longer at stripes than at blobs, and by 8 to 12 weeks of age, they prefer curved lines to straight ones. Two-month-olds fixate longer on the human face than on other stimuli. Infants can discriminate their mother's face from a stranger's after about 8 hours of contact. Newborns direct their attention to the edges of objects, but 2-month-olds scan objects from the edges inward.

Researchers use the visual cliff apparatus to study depth perception. Most infants refuse to venture out over the cliff by the time they can crawl. Perhaps infants need some experience crawling before they develop a fear of heights. Newborns reflexively orient their heads toward a sound. Infants discriminate caregivers' voices by 3 1/2 months of age. Early infants can perceive most of the speech sounds throughout the languages of the world, but by 10 to 12 months of age, this ability diminishes.

Newborns seem to be at the mercy of external stimuli, but later intentional action replaces "capture." Systematic search replaces unsystematic search, attention becomes selective, and irrelevant information gets ignored. Sensory changes are linked to maturation of the nervous system (nature), but experience (nurture) also plays a crucial role. Children have critical periods in their perceptual development when their sensory experience is required to optimize—or maintain—sensory capacities.

FIGURE 4.6

Declining Ability to Discriminate the Sounds of Foreign Languages

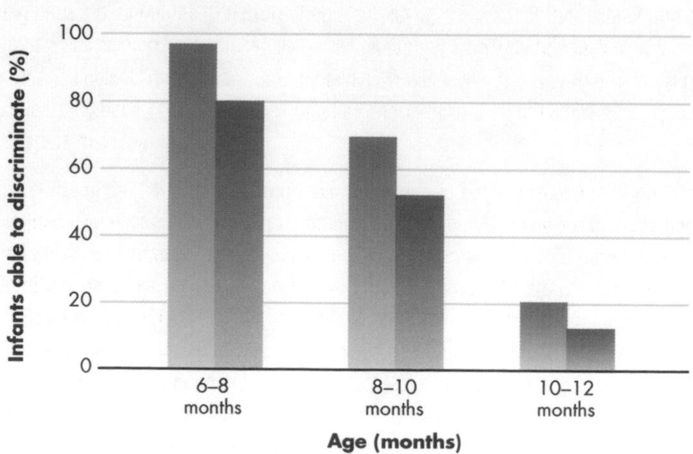

Source: Werker, 1989.

INFANCY: COGNITIVE DEVELOPMENT

5 Chapter in Review

LO1 **schema**
a mental structure that categorizes information based on similarity. (p. 83)

assimilation
new information is added to an existing schema. (p. 83)

accommodation
new information must be modified to fit an existing schema as new information is acquired. (p. 83)

primary circular reactions
the repetition of actions that first occurred by chance and that focus on the infant's own body. (p. 84)

secondary circular reactions
the repetition of actions that produce an effect on the environment. (p. 84)

tertiary circular reactions
the purposeful adaptation of established schemas to new situations. (p. 85)

object permanence
recognition that objects continue to exist when they are not in view. (p. 86)

deferred imitation
imitation of a behaviour that was seen earlier. (p. 87)

LO3 **visual recognition memory**
the kind of memory shown in an infant's ability to discriminate previously seen objects from novel objects. (p. 91)

LO4 **prelinguistic**
vocalizations made by the infant before the use of language. (p. 91)

cooing
prelinguistic vowel-like sounds that reflect feelings of positive excitement. (p. 91)

babbling
the child's first vocalizations that have the sounds of speech. (p. 91)

echolalia
the automatic repetition of sounds or words. (p. 92)

intonation
the use of pitches of varying levels to help communicate meaning. (p. 92)

receptive vocabulary
the number of words one understands. (p. 92)

expressive vocabulary
the number of words one can use in the production of language. (p. 92)

referential language style
use of language primarily as a means for labelling objects. (p. 93)

expressive language style
use of language primarily as a means for engaging in social interaction. (p. 93)

LO1 Examine Jean Piaget's studies of cognitive development. Piaget labelled children's concepts of the world as schemas. A schema is a mental filter that categorizes knowledge so that similar information can be grouped together. Information that fits an existing schema is processed by way of assimilation. Information that is new altogether and doesn't fit is acquired through accommodation.

Piaget hypothesized that cognitive processes develop in an orderly sequence of four stages: sensorimotor, preoperational, concrete operational, and formal operational. The sensorimotor stage refers to the first 2 years of cognitive development and involves the progression from responding to events with reflexes to displaying goal-oriented behaviour (see table below). A critical milestone in the sensorimotor stage is the appearance of early signs of object permanence, or the ability of an infant to appreciate that an object continues to exist physically even when out of view.

Researchers who question the validity of Piaget's claims argue the following:

- development is not tied to discrete stages
- adult and peer influences play a role in cognitive development
- infants are more competent than Piaget estimated

Piaget's Stages of Cognitive Development

Stage	Age	Hallmarks
1. Simple reflexes	0–1 month	Assimilation of new objects into reflexive responses. Infants "look and see." Inborn reflexes can be modified by experience.
2. Primary circular reactions	1–4 months	Repetition of actions that may have initially occurred by chance but that have satisfying or interesting results. Infants "look in order to see." The focus is on the infant's body. Infants do not yet distinguish between themselves and the external world.
3. Secondary circular reactions	4–8 months	Repetition of schemas that have interesting effects on the environment. The focus shifts to external objects and events. Infants gain initial cognitive awareness that schemas influence the external world.
4. Coordination of secondary schemas	8–12 months	Coordination of secondary schemas, such as looking and grasping to attain specific goals. Infants' activities show signs of the beginning of intentionality and means–end differentiation. Infants demonstrate an imitation of actions not already in their repertoires.
5. Tertiary circular reactions	12–18 months	Purposeful adaptation of established schemas to specific situations. Infants' behaviour takes on an experimental quality. Infants exhibit overt trial and error in problem solving.
6. Invention of new means through mental combinations	18–24 months	Mental trial and error in problem solving. Infants take "mental detours" based on cognitive maps. Infants engage in deferred imitation and symbolic play. Infants' cognitive advances are made possible by mental representations of objects and events and by the beginnings of symbolic thought.

overextension
use of words in situations in which their meanings become extended. (p. 93)

holophrase
a single word that is used to express complex meanings. (p. 94)

telegraphic speech
type of speech in which only the essential words are used. (p. 94)

syntax
the language rules for placing words in an order to form sentences. (p. 94)

models
in learning theory, those whose behaviours are imitated by others. (p. 95)

extinction
decrease in the frequency of a response due to the absence of reinforcement. (p. 96)

shaping
gradual building of complex behaviour by reinforcing successive approximations to the target behaviour. (p. 96)

sensitive period
the period from about 18 months to puberty when the brain is especially capable of learning language. (p. 98)

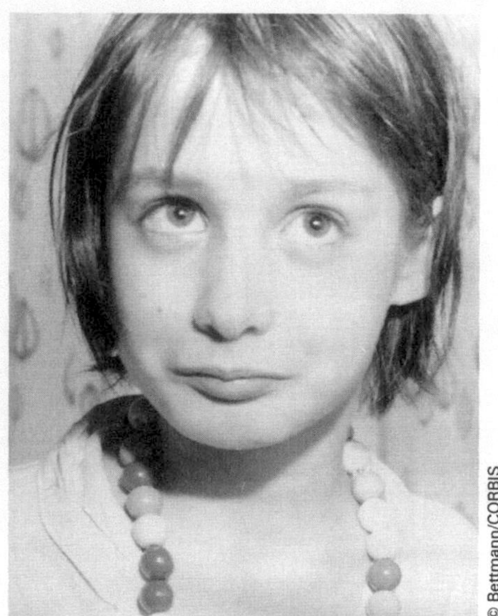

© Bettmann/CORBIS

Genie's tragically unique experience provides support for the *sensitive period hypothesis* of language development.

LO2 Discuss the information-processing approach.

The information-processing approach focuses on how children manipulate or process information from the environment or already stored in the mind. Two primary tools used in this processing are memory and imitation. Even newborns demonstrate memory to stimuli, and between 2 and 6 months of age, infants' memory develops dramatically. Deferred imitation occurs as early as 6 months of age.

LO3 Identify individual differences in intelligence among infants.

The Bayley Scales of Infant Development make up one of the most important tests of intellectual development among infants. A total of 289 scale items test for mental skills (verbal communication, perceptual skills, learning and memory, and problem-solving skills) and motor skills (gross and fine). Infant intelligence is tested to determine the presence of handicaps, and although the Bayley scales can identify gross lags in development and relative strengths and weaknesses, infant intelligence scores are generally poor predictors of intelligence scores taken more than a year later.

Assessing visual recognition memory is another way of studying infant intelligence. Longitudinal studies by Susan Rose and her colleagues showed that the capacity for visual recognition memory is stable and the trait shows predictive validity for broad cognitive abilities throughout childhood, including intelligence and language ability. Furthermore, it appears that speed at which a baby habituates to an object it has seen numerous times is related to intelligence. Studies have found a modest correlation between information processing in infancy (6 to 12 months) and academic achievement in adulthood (21 years).

LO4 Examine language development in children.

Children develop language according to an invariant sequence of steps or stages. The first stage involves prelinguistic vocalizations, such as cooing, babbling, and echolalia. Because of the repetition of sounds, echolalia is often called "parroting." Children who are diagnosed on the autism spectrum or who have Tourettes syndrome often display echolalia after the stage when it usually ends. Vocabulary development refers to the child's learning the meanings of words. Most children acquire receptive vocabulary faster than expressive vocabulary. In other words, children understand the words they use before they can speak them.

Children's first words usually appear between 11 and 13 months of age but these appearances range between 8 to 18 months. Once children can express themselves with words, they try to talk about more objects than they have words for. First, the words are simple syllabic combinations, and first sentences are often single words called holophrases, which express simple but complete ideas. In early language acquisition, children use telegraphic speech to communicate full ideas. When children's speech or language is delayed, further investigation is required to discover the root of the issue.

Theories on language development are divided into those emphasizing nurture and those emphasizing nature. Proponents of nurture theories build on the work of B.F. Skinner and cite the roles of imitation and reinforcement in language development. One way to speak to children that involves nurturing is called "motherese" or baby talk. Some individuals worry that this will prevent children from learning adult speech because of a lack of modelling; there is, however, little evidence if any to support this idea.

Proponents of the nativist view argue that the ability to acquire language is innate and therefore biological. The work of Steven Pinker, among others, shows, however, that language acquisition results from an interaction of biological and environmental factors (in other words, it results from a combination of nature and nurture). This notion is reinforced through the tragic story studied in *The Genie Project*, which allows us to see the impact of severe environmental conditions on language acquisition. Related to this, early deprivation has been found to have significant impact on the brain. The neglect need not be as severe as the case of Genie to have lasting effects. It has been found that children who have been severely neglected such as those raised in orphanages have cognitive impairments well into adulthood.

Chapter in Review

6

LO1 **attachment** an affectional bond characterized by seeking closeness with another and distress upon separation. (p. 101)

separation anxiety fear of separation from an attachment figure. (p. 101)

contact comfort the pleasure derived from physical contact with another. (p. 102)

ethologists scientists who study the behaviour patterns characteristic of various species. (p. 102)

social smile a smile that occurs in response to a human voice or face. (p. 102)

critical period a period during which imprinting can occur. (p. 102)

imprinting the process by which waterfowl become attached to the first moving object they follow. (p. 102)

pre-attachment phase lasts from birth to 6 weeks; characterized by random attachment. (p. 102)

attachment-in-the-making phase occurs from 6 weeks to 6 months; characterized by preference for familiar figures. (p. 103)

clear-cut attachment phase occurs from 6 to 7 months and lasts until 18 to 24 months; characterized by dependence on the primary caregiver, usually the mother. (p. 103)

formation of reciprocal relationships occurs from 18 months until 2 years and beyond; characterized by awareness of factors that predict the parent's return (p. 103)

internal working model a set of expectations and beliefs about the self, others, and the relationship between self and others. (p. 103)

secure attachment a type of attachment characterized by mild distress when a caregiver leaves and being readily soothed by reunion. (p. 103)

avoidant attachment a type of insecure attachment characterized by apparent indifference to leave-takings by and reunions with an attachment figure. (p. 104)

anxious-ambivalent attachment a type of insecure attachment characterized by severe distress at the caregiver's departure and ambivalent behaviour at reunions. (p. 104)

disorganized–disoriented attachment a type of insecure attachment characterized by dazed and contradictory behaviours toward an attachment figure. (p. 104)

Milestones in Language Development in Infancy

Psychosocial Stage	Personality Crisis (Challenge)	Important Life Event	Outcome
Infancy (birth to 18 months)	Trust vs. Mistrust	Feeding	Trust is developed when caregivers are reliable and affectionate. Mistrust is developed when care is unpredictable and/or lacking in affection.

LO1 **Describe the development of attachment in infancy and theoretical views of how it evolves.** There are different theories developed to explain attachment behaviour from a psychoanalytical view that explains attachment as the result of oral gratification, to cognitive theories that align attachment with object permanence, to ethological theories that explain that attachment is a biological need that guarantees survival of a species.

First, psychoanalysts suggest that the primary caregiver becomes a love object. The Harlows' experiments with monkeys suggest that contact comfort is a key to attachment. Rhesus monkeys were found to prefer cloth monkeys over wired monkeys especially when they were frightened. Ethologists view attachment as an instinct (i.e., a fixed-action pattern) that occurs during a critical period. Bowlby advanced the attachment literature by applying the concepts developed by ethologists to human infants. Bowlby said that infants form an internal working model of attachments which includes beliefs that an infant is worthy of love and that others will be available and will be able to protect or soothe the child when in need as well as a general belief about the self and others.

Most infants in Canada are securely attached. In the strange-situation method, pioneered by Canadian researcher Mary Ainsworth, secure infants mildly protest the mother's departure and, on her return, are readily comforted by her. The three major types of insecure attachment are avoidant attachment, anxious-ambivalent attachment, and disorganized-disoriented attachment. Compared with insecure infants, secure infants are happier, more sociable, and more competent. They use their mother as a secure base from which to explore their environment. Parents of securely attached infants are more likely to be affectionate and sensitive to their needs. Children who are adopted may develop secure attachments to adoptive parents; however, some adoptive children who lived in orphanages as infants have a difficult time bonding with caregivers and may develop a reactive attachment disorder. The prototype hypothesis says that the first attachment a child has with a caregiver serves as the foundation for all others, including relationships with romantic partners. Attachments may change, however, if an individual is cared for by someone who has a secure attachment with their own caregivers but this takes a lot of time and exposure to the securely attached individual.

LO2 **Discuss the effects of social deprivation, abuse and neglect, and autism spectrum disorders on attachment.** The Harlows found that rhesus infants reared in isolation later avoided contact with other monkeys. Isolated females who later had offspring tended to neglect or abuse them. Many institutionalized children who receive little social stimulation temporarily develop withdrawal and depression. Mistreated children are less intimate with peers and are more aggressive, angry, and non-compliant than other children. Child abuse tends to run in families, perhaps because abusive parents serve as role models. The 2008 Canadian Incidence Study of Reported Child Abuse and Neglect (Public Health Agency of Canada, 2010) concluded that incidents of child abuse are under-reported and remain a significant Canadian social issue. The causes of child abuse

reactive attachment disorder
characterized as disturbed or inappropriate social interactions across a number of social situations, developed before age 5 years. (p. 104)

prototype hypothesis
the belief that the initial relationship between child and caregiver serves as the foundation of all other relationships, including romantic ones. (p. 104)

LO2

physical abuse
any type of deliberate force that leads to non-accidental injury to any part of the body. (p. 106)

sexual abuse
the molestation or exploitation of a child. (p. 106)

emotional abuse
verbal abuse or inadequate attention. (p. 107)

neglect
failing to supervise a child which may result in the child receiving injury. (p. 107)

autism spectrum disorders (ASDs)
developmental disorders characterized by impairment in social communication and social interaction across various contexts, and by repetitive, stereotyped behaviour. (p. 109)

mutism
refusal to speak. (p. 110)

echolalia
automatic repetition of sounds or words. (p. 110)

LO4

social referencing
using another person's reaction to a situation to form one's own response. (p. 114)

emotional regulation
techniques for controlling one's emotional states. (p. 114)

LO5

separation–individuation
the process of becoming separate from and independent of the mother. (p. 115)

temperament
individual difference in style of reaction, which is present early in life. (p. 115)

goodness of fit
agreement between the parents' expectations of a child and the child's temperament. (p. 116)

sex
a way of classifying individuals usually as male or female, due to a combination of biological and physiological features. (p. 116)

intersex
individuals who are born with variations to their chromosomes or genitals such that their sex doesn't match binary notions of male or female. (p. 116)

gender
a cultural view of what it means to be masculine or feminine according to one's sex. (p. 116)

include having been abused as children, low tolerance for what is considered normal infant or child behaviour, misinterpreting children's behaviour as negative, and relying on coercion and physical punishment to change behaviour.

Researchers believe that 1 in 68 children will be diagnosed with autism spectrum disorder. Autism spectrum disorders (ASDs) are characterized by impairment in social communication and social interaction across contexts as well as restricted, repetitive patterns of behaviour, activities, or interests. ASD is four to five times more common among boys than girls. Features of the disorder include communication problems, intolerance of change, and self-harm. Studies of twins suggest that autism may involve heredity, and neurological impairment is also suspected. Behaviour modification has been used to increase social play and the child's attention to others. The Autism Society of Canada reminds us that individuals with autism should be valued for their differences and not viewed as persons who should be changed. Avoid referring to "an autistic child," but instead refer to "a child with autism" to avoid having the disorder define the individual.

LO3 Discuss the effects of childcare on development. Daycare was once seen as a second alternative to home care, but research now shows that daycare has many advantages. Infants with daycare experience are more independent, self-confident, outgoing, affectionate, and cooperative with peers and adults than infants who are not in daycare. In terms of cognitive development, children in high-quality day care outperform children who remain in the home. On the other hand, children in daycare are more aggressive than other children. A population increase will require a closer examination of Canadian daycares.

LO4 Describe the emotional development of the infant. Researchers debate whether the emotional expression of newborns begins in an undifferentiated state of diffuse excitement or whether several emotions are present. Infants' initial emotional expressions appear to comprise either a positive attraction to pleasant stimulation or withdrawal from aversive stimulation. By the age of 2 to 3 months, social smiling has replaced reflexive smiling. Most infants develop a fear of strangers at about 6 to 9 months.Infants display social referencing as early as 6 months of age, when they use caregivers' facial expressions or tones of voice for information on how to respond in novel situations. Emotional regulation is emotional self-control. Securely attached children are more likely to regulate their emotions well.

LO5 Describe the personality development of the infant, focusing on the self-concept, temperament, and sex differences. Research using the mirror technique finds that the self-concept develops by about 18 months of age. Self-awareness enables the child to develop concepts of sharing and cooperation and emotions such as embarrassment, envy, empathy, pride, guilt, and shame.

Infants' temperament (see Table 6.2) involves their activity level, regularity, approach or withdrawal, adaptability, response threshold, response intensity, quality of mood, distractibility, attention span, and persistence. Thomas and Chess found that most infants can be classified as having one of three temperaments: easy, difficult, or slow-to-warm-up. Temperament remains moderately consistent from infancy through young adulthood.

Female infants sit, crawl, and walk earlier than boys do. By 12 to 18 months of age, girls prefer to play with dolls and similar toys, whereas boys prefer sports equipment and transportation toys.

Sex is a way of classifying individuals, usually as male or female. Some individuals are born intersex, possessing biological and/or physiological features of both sexes. Gender refers to a cultural view of what it means to act masculine or feminine according to one's sex. It is socially constructed and thus means different things to different people living across parts of the world and throughout history. Children are socialized to believe certain things about what toys they should play with and what subjects they are good at. Gender stereotypes limit opportunities for children who must conform to standards determined by a culture, standards that don's necessarily fit with the individual child's sense of self.

Chapter in Review

LO1 corpus callosum
the thick bundle of nerve fibres that connects the left and right hemispheres of the brain. (p. 121)

plasticity
the tendency of new parts of the brain to take up the functions of injured parts. (p. 121)

LO2 gross motor skills
skills employing the large muscles used in locomotion. (p. 121)

fine motor skills
skills employing the small muscles used in manipulation, such as those in the fingers. (p. 122)

LO5 nightmares
dreams of disturbing and vivid content. (p. 127)

sleep terrors
frightening dreamlike experiences that occur during the deepest stage of non-REM sleep, shortly after the child has gone to sleep. (p. 127)

somnambulism
sleepwalking. (p. 127)

LO6 enuresis
failure to control the bladder (urination) once the normal age for control has been reached. (p. 128)

bed-wetting
failure to control the bladder during the night. (p. 128)

encopresis
failure to control the bowels once the normal age for bowel control has been reached; also called soiling. (p. 128)

LO7 preoperational stage
the second stage in Piaget's scheme, characterized by inflexible and irreversible mental manipulation of symbols. (p. 129)

symbolic play
play in which children make believe that objects and toys are other than what they are. Also called pretend play. (p. 129)

egocentrism
putting oneself at the centre of things such that one is unable to perceive the world from another person's point of view. (p. 129)

precausal
a type of thought in which natural cause-and-effect relationships are attributed to will and other preoperational concepts. (p. 130)

transductive reasoning
faulty reasoning that links one specific isolated event to another specific isolated event. (p. 130)

LO1 Describe trends in physical development in early childhood. Children gain about 5 to 8 cm (2 to 3 in.) in height and 2 to 3 kg (4 to 6 lb.) in weight per year in early childhood. Boys are slightly larger than girls. The brain develops more quickly than any other organ in early childhood, in part because of myelination. The left hemisphere is relatively more involved in logical analysis, language, and computation. The right hemisphere is usually superior in visual–spatial functions, emotional responses, and creative mathematical reasoning. But the hemispheres work together. The brain shows plasticity in early childhood. Two factors involved in the brain's plasticity are the growth of new dendrites and the redundancy of neural connections.

LO2 Describe motor development in early childhood. Preschoolers make great strides in the development of gross motor skills. Girls tend to be better in balance and precision; boys have some advantage in throwing and kicking. Physically active parents are likely to have physically active children. Fine motor skills develop gradually. Kellogg identified 20 scribbles that she considered the building blocks of art. Free drawing should be encouraged. Handedness emerges by 6 months. Left-handedness may be related to some language and health problems, yet a disproportionately large number of artists, musicians, and mathematicians are left-handed.

LO3 Describe nutritional needs in early childhood. Health Canada recommends that young children's diet should focus on food servings rather than caloric intake. During the second and third years, children's appetites typically wane and grow erratic. Many children eat too much sugar and salt. Experts are concerned about the rising trend in childhood obesity. Obesity is an issue that begins in early childhood. This is an important time for parents to intervene as preschool-aged children who are overweight are five times as likely to be overweight at 12 years. Factors that contribute to being overweight for this age group include not eating breakfast, drinking more than two glasses of a sugary drink, playing outside less than an hour daily, and watching more than two hours a of television a day.

LO4 Describe trends in health and illness in early childhood. In developing countries, diarrheal diseases are a leading cause of death and are almost always related to unsafe drinking water and lack of adequate sanitation. Immunization and antibiotics reduce the incidence of disease. Children are at greater risk of dying if they live in rural areas, are from poor households, and are born to mothers who are uneducated.

LO5 Explain sleep patterns in early childhood. Most 2- and 3-year-olds sleep about 10 hours at night and nap during the day. Getting children to sleep during the day can be very difficult for caregivers as children may protest; however, children during early childhood still require between 12 to 14 hours of sleep a day. Sleep terrors are more severe than nightmares. Sleep terrors and sleepwalking usually occur during deep sleep. Sleepwalkers' eyes are usually open; if awakened, they may show confusion but are unlikely to be violent. Adequate sleep is necessary, as a lack of sleep is associated with behavioural difficulties.

LO6 Discuss elimination disorders. Most Canadian children are toilet trained by age 2 or 3 years but may continue to have "accidents." Enuresis is apparently related to slowed physical development and stress. Encopresis can stem from constipation and stress. Most of these concerns are outgrown.

animism
the attribution of life and intentionality to inanimate objects. (p. 131)

artificialism
the belief that environmental features were made by people. (p. 131)

conservation
in cognitive psychology, the principle that properties of substances such as weight and mass remain the same (are conserved) when superficial characteristics such as their shapes or arrangement are changed. (p. 131)

LO8

scaffolding
Vygotsky's term for the situation in which a child carries out tasks with the help of someone who is more skilled, to advance their skills. (p. 132)

zone of proximal development (ZPD)
the gap between what children are capable of doing now and what they could do with help from others. (p. 132)

LO9

theory of mind
the understanding that people are mental beings that have their own mental states including thoughts, wishes, and feelings that differ from our own. (p. 133)

appearance–reality distinction
the difference between real events on the one hand and mental events, fantasies, and misleading appearances on the other hand. (p. 134)

LO10

scripts
abstract, generalized accounts of familiar repeated events. (p. 135)

autobiographical memory
the memory of specific episodes or events. (p. 135)

rehearsal
a strategy that uses repetition to remember information. (p. 135)

LO11

fast mapping
a process of quickly determining a word's meaning, which facilitates children's vocabulary development. (p. 136)

overregularization
the application of regular grammatical rules for forming inflections to irregular verbs and nouns. (p. 136)

pragmatics
the practical aspects of communication, such as adaptation of language to fit the social situation. (p. 137)

inner speech
Vygotsky's concept of the ultimate binding of language and thought. Inner speech originates in vocalizations that may regulate the child's behaviour and become internalized by age 6 or 7. (p. 138)

LO7 **Describe Piaget's preoperational stage.** Piaget's preoperational stage lasts from about age 2 to 7 and is characterized by the use of symbols. Preoperational thinking is characterized by pretend play, egocentrism, precausal thinking, confusion between mental and physical events, and the ability to focus on only one dimension at a time. Conservation is lacking because it requires focusing on two aspects of a situation at once.

LO8 **Discuss influences on cognitive development in early childhood.** Vygotsky envisions scaffolding and the zone of proximal development as two factors in cognitive development. When caregivers provide appropriate play materials and stimulating experiences, children show gains in social and language development. For example, every time parents sit down and review the sounds letters make with their preschool children, scaffolding is occurring. Canadians are increasingly concerned about the quality control of childcare centres. Head Start programmes have been found to enhance cognitive skills for children and foster a sense of pride in learning. Television and screen time continue to be primary challenges to children's learning. Fortunately, some viewing (e.g., *Sesame Street*) shows mild to productive influences on cognitive development.

LO9 **Explain how "theory of mind" affects cognitive development.** Children come to understand the distinctions between external and mental events and between appearances and realities. By age 3 years, most children begin to realize that people gain knowledge through the senses, and by age 4 years, they understand which senses provide certain kinds of information. Also, children begin to use a theory of mind meaning that they can start to infer the thoughts, wishes, and feelings of others that differ from our own. Children who have a well-developed theory of mind have been found to be better communicators, to resolve conflicts with their friends, and to be more popular with their peers.

LO10 **Outline memory development in early childhood.** Memory is significantly related to intelligence. Preschoolers recognize more items than they can recall. Autobiographical memory is linked to language skills. Factors affecting memory include what the child is asked to remember, interest level and motivation, the availability of retrieval cues, and the memory measure being used. When preschoolers are trying to remember, they engage in behaviour such as looking, pointing, and touching.

LO11 **Outline language development in early childhood.** Preschoolers acquire about nine new words per day, some of which occur due to fast mapping. During the third year, children usually add articles, conjunctions, possessive adjectives, pronouns, and prepositions. Between the ages of 3 and 4 years, children combine phrases and clauses into complex sentences. Preschoolers overregularize irregular verbs and nouns as they learn grammar. To Vygotsky, inner speech is the ultimate binding of language and thought.

8 EARLY CHILDHOOD: SOCIAL AND EMOTIONAL DEVELOPMENT
Chapter in Review

LO1 **authoritative** a child-rearing style in which parents are restrictive and demanding yet communicative and warm. (p. 141)

authoritarian
a child-rearing style in which parents demand submission and obedience. (p. 141)

permissive–indulgent
a child-rearing style in which parents are warm and not restrictive. (p. 141)

rejecting–neglecting
a child-rearing style in which parents are neither restrictive and controlling nor supportive and responsive. (p. 141)

inductive
based on an attempt to foster understanding of the principles behind parental demands; characteristic of disciplinary methods, such as reasoning. (p. 142)

LO2 **regression** a return to behaviour characteristic of earlier stages of development. (p. 144)

dramatic play
play in which children enact social roles. (p. 145)

disinhibit
stimulate a response that has been suppressed by showing a model engaging in that response. (p. 148)

LO3 **Categorical self** the definitions of the self that refer to external traits. (p. 149)

LO4 **gender roles socialization** learning to acquire clusters of traits and behaviours that are considered stereotypical of females and males. (p. 151)

gender identity
a person's innate, deeply felt sense of being female or male (or sometimes both, or neither). (p. 152)

gender stability
the concept that one's sex is unchanging. (p. 152)

gender constancy
the concept that one's sex remains the same despite changes in appearance or behaviour. (p. 152)

gender-schema theory
the view that society's gender-based concepts shape our assumptions of gender-typed preferences and behaviour patterns. (p. 152)

gender-neutral parenting (GNP)
the decision not to assign a specific gender to children based on their biological sex. (p. 153)

Psychosocial Stage	Personality Crisis (Challenge)	Important Life Event	Outcome
Early Childhood (18 months to 3 years)	Autonomy vs. Shame and Doubt	Toilet Training	Children develop a sense of personal control, skill, and independence. Success leads to feelings of self-rule and independence, whereas failure results in feelings of shame and self-doubt.
Preschool (4 to 5 years)	Initiative vs. Guilt	Exploration	Children need to take control over their own environment, which leads to a sense of purpose. If children exert too much power, they will encounter disapproval and resulting guilt. Failure to control their environment will lead to a sense of inadequacy.

LO1 **Describe the dimensions of child rearing and styles of parenting.** Approaches to child rearing can be classified according to the dimensions of warmth–coldness and restrictiveness–permissiveness. Consistent control and firm enforcement of rules can lead to positive consequences for the child. Authoritative parents are restrictive but warm and tend to have the most competent and achievement-oriented children. Authoritarian parents are restrictive and cold. The sons of authoritarian parents tend to be hostile and defiant; the daughters tend to be low in independence. Children of rejecting–neglecting parents show the least competence and maturity. To enforce rules, parents tend to use inductive methods, power assertion, and withdrawal of love. Inductive methods use "reasoning," or explaining why one sort of behaviour is good and another is not. Hartup discusses the bidirectional relationship between parents and children. Individuals are changed by relationships just as changes in relationship are precipitated by changes in the individual. Young children experience divorce as a disruption to their sense of security and safety. They worry about abandonment and being separated from their parent. Change to their family structure significantly impacts their well-being. They are helped through this family transition when parents talk to them about the separation.

LO2 **Explain how siblings, birth order, peers, and other factors that affect social development during early childhood.** Siblings provide caregiving, emotional support, advice, role models, social interaction, restrictions, and cognitive stimulation. However, they are also sources of conflict, control, and competition. First-born and only children are generally more highly motivated to achieve, more cooperative, more helpful, more adult-oriented, and less aggressive, but later-born children tend to have greater social skills with peers. From their peers, children learn social skills, such as sharing, taking turns, and coping with conflict. Peers also provide emotional support. Preschoolers' friendships are characterized by shared activities and feelings of attachment.

Play develops motor, social, and cognitive skills; but unfortunately, even preschoolers spend 2 hours a day using their screens such as tablets, television, and computers to entertain themselves. Technology has become addictive, and this means children aren't playing outside getting much needed exercise or socializing with their peers.

Prosocial behaviour begins to develop in the first year, when children begin to share. The development of prosocial behaviour is linked to the development of empathy and perspective

gender bending
when an individual dresses or acts in a manner opposite to their identified gender or in a gender-neutral way. (p. 153)

cisgender
when an individual's gender is consistent with that individual's biological sex. (p. 153)

taking. Girls show more empathy than boys do. This may be due to the socialization of girls to be attuned to the emotions of others rather than actual sex differences. Preschool aggression is often instrumental. By age 6 or 7 years, aggressive behaviour can be seen as a way to obtain something valuable, like a toy. It also becomes person oriented such that children taunt and criticize each other at this age. Aggressive behaviour appears to be stable and can predict problems in adulthood. Genetic factors may be involved in aggressive behaviour. Social cognitive theory suggests that children become aggressive as a result of frustration and observational learning. Aggressive children are often rejected by their less aggressive peers. Children who are physically punished are more likely to behave aggressively. Observing aggressive behaviour teaches aggressive skills, disinhibits children, and habituates them to violence. Those who view aggression as socially acceptable behaviour are more likely to be aggressive themselves. All-day kindergarten in Canada has been found to lead to higher achievement and greater independence, but critics wonder whether children are being rushed through their early childhood.

LO3 **Discuss personality and emotional development during early childhood, focusing on the self, Erikson's views, and fears.** Children as young as age 3 years can describe themselves in terms of their behaviour and their internal states. Secure attachment and competence contribute to self-esteem. Preschoolers are most likely to fear animals, imaginary creatures, and the dark.

LO4 **Discuss the development of gender roles and sex differences.** Although gender and sex are often used interchangeably, they have different meanings. Gender refers to socio-cultural factors that give rise to the terms *girl* and *boy*. Gender is considered on a continuum, rather than as a binary term. Sex refers to biological features of males and females due to chromosomes, hormones, and genitalia. Theories of gender development include the role of nature or the influence of the environment, including nurture. From an evolutionary perspective, women were designed to bear children and to feed them, leaving the men to be the hunter–gatherers. The man's body evolved to better suit the role of hunter–gatherer. Also, hormones have been found to play some role in gender development. Girls and boys are born with both sex hormones; however, the amount each impact on their bodies differs. Children who were born with a rare genetic condition resulting in sex reassignment at birth have found mixed results. Some males who are reassigned as females develop male identities, and some maintain their female identities. Thus, biology is only partially responsible for gender development. Gender role socialization is the process of learning gender stereotypes according to one's cultural expectations. Cultural expectations of being female and male are called gender roles. Social cognitive theorists explain the development of gender-typed behaviour in terms of observational learning and socialization. According to Kohlberg's cognitive-developmental theory, gender-typing involves the emergence of gender identity, gender stability, and gender constancy. According to gender-schema theory, preschoolers attempt to conform to the cultural gender schema. This theory asserts that gender identity alone leads to gender-appropriate behaviour as children understand the labels *girl* and *boy* and try to live up to expectations of what is considered gender-appropriate behaviour. Some parents are deciding to raise their children gender-neutral, not assigning a specific gender to their children based on their biological sex. Children regardless of their biological sex are able to determine what activities and style of dress they prefer without limitations as opposed to what is ascribed to them.

TABLE 8.1

Baumrind's Patterns of Parenting

Parental Style	Restrictiveness and Control	Warmth and Responsiveness
Authoritative	↑	↓
Authoritarian	↑	↓
Permissive–Indulgent	↓	↓
Rejecting–Neglecting	↓	↓

Chapter in Review

9

LO1 **growth spurt** a period during which growth advances at a dramatically rapid rate compared with other periods. (p. 153)

LO2 **reaction time** the amount of time required to respond to a stimulus. (p. 157)

LO3 **attention-deficit hyperactivity disorder (ADHD)** a disorder characterized by excessive inattention, impulsiveness, and hyperactivity. (p. 158)

hyperactivity excessive restlessness and overactivity; a characteristic of ADHD. (p. 158)

stimulants drugs that increase the activity of the nervous system. (p. 158)

learning disabilities disorders characterized by inadequate development of specific academic, language, and speech skills. (p. 159)

dyslexia a reading disorder characterized by letter reversals, mirror reading, slow reading, and reduced comprehension. (p. 159)

classroom inclusion placing children with disabilities in classrooms with children without disabilities. (p. 159)

LO4 **concrete operations** the third stage in Piaget's scheme, characterized by flexible, reversible thought concerning tangible objects and events. (p. 160)

decentration simultaneous focusing on more than one aspect or dimension of a problem or situation. (p. 160)

transitivity the principle that if A > B and B > C, then A > C. (p. 161)

seriation placing objects in an order or series according to a property or trait. (p. 161)

LO5 **preconventional level** according to Kohlberg, a period during which moral judgments are based largely on expectations of rewards or punishments. (p. 163)

conventional level according to Kohlberg, a period during which moral judgments largely reflect social rules and conventions. (p. 163)

postconventional level according to Kohlberg, a period during which moral judgments are derived from moral principles, and people look to themselves to set moral standards. (p. 163)

LO1 **Describe trends in physical development in middle childhood.** Children tend to gain a little over 5 cm (2 in.) in height and 2 to 3 kg (5 to 7 lb.) in weight per year during middle childhood. Boys are slightly heavier and taller than girls through ages 9 or 10, until girls begin the adolescent growth spurt. Overweight children usually do not outgrow their baby fat. Parents can promote children's healthy living by eliminating unhealthy snack foods from the home, controlling portion sizes, and acting as a positive role model. Heredity plays a role in weight. Sedentary habits also foster weight gain. It is recommended that children reduce their screen time to no more than 2 hours a day, walk to school, decrease time spent sitting, and increase time spent outdoors. Healthy food choices from the Canada's Food Guide should be coupled with regular physical activity. Some reasons for childhood obesity include the fast food industry that caters to children; inexpensive, high-calorie foods; reduced physical education in schools; and a hectic family schedules that limit family mealtime.

Wara Jenny/iStockphoto.com

LO2 **Describe changes in motor development in middle childhood.** Middle childhood is marked by increases in speed, strength, agility, and balance. Children improve in gross and fine motor skills as the pathways that connect the cerebellum to the cortex become more myelinated. Reaction time decreases. Boys have slightly greater overall strength, whereas girls have better coordination and flexibility. Many Canadian children are not physically fit, in part because of the amount of time spent watching TV.

LO3 **Discuss ADHD and learning disabilities.** Attention-deficit hyperactivity disorder (ADHD) is a neurological condition that runs in families and may involve differences in the brain. ADHD is marked by excessive inattention, impulsivity, and/or hyperactivity. Not all children with this disorder are hyperactive. Many children with the disorder have difficulties socially as a result of their unique constellation of symptoms. Children with ADHD are sometimes treated with stimulants, which trigger the cerebral cortex to inhibit more primitive areas of the brain. Non-medical treatment of ADHD is also recommended including behaviour modification. Dyslexia also runs in families. Some children with learning disabilities benefit from being in mainstream classrooms. Universal classroom design and individual education plans are two strategies implemented to meet the needs of Canada's diverse classrooms.

LO4 **Describe Piaget's concrete operational stage.** By the age of 11, children's thought processes become more logical and complex. Piaget characterized children during this period as entering the concrete operational stage, in which children begin to think in logical terms but focus on tangible objects rather than abstract ideas. Concrete operational children are less egocentric, engage in decentration, and understand concepts such as conservation, transitivity, seriation, and class inclusion.

LO6 **sensory memory**
the structure of memory first encountered by sensory input. Information is maintained in sensory memory for only a fraction of a second. (p. 164)

short-term memory
the structure of memory that can hold a sensory stimulus for up to 30 seconds after the trace decays. (p. 164)

encode
to transform sensory input into a form that is more readily processed. (p. 165)

rehearsing
repeating that aids in recall. (p. 165)

long-term memory
the memory structure capable of relatively permanent storage of information. (p. 165)

elaborative strategy
a method for increasing retention of new information by relating it to well-known information. (p. 166)

metacognition
awareness of and control of one's cognitive abilities. (p. 166)

metamemory
knowledge of the functions and processes involved in one's storage and retrieval of information. (p. 167)

LO7 **intelligence**
defined by Wechsler as the "capacity ... to understand the world [and the] resourcefulness to cope with its challenges." (p. 167)

achievement
acquired competencies that are attained by an individual's efforts and are presumed to be made possible by that individual's abilities. (p. 167)

intelligence quotient (IQ)
a score on an intelligence test. (p. 168)

mental age (MA)
the intellectual level at which a child is functioning. (p. 169)

chronological age (CA)
a person's actual age. (p. 169)

cultural bias
a factor in intelligence tests that provides an advantage for test takers from certain cultural backgrounds. (p. 170)

culture-free
descriptive of a test in which cultural biases have been removed. (p. 170)

cultural–familial developmental challenges
substandard intellectual performance stemming from lack of opportunity to acquire knowledge and skills. (p. 172)

heritability
the degree to which the variations in a trait from one person to another can be attributed to genetic factors. (p. 172)

LO5 **Discuss Kohlberg's theories of moral development.** Kohlberg concluded that moral reasoning in children was related to overall cognitive development. Kohlberg's theory emphasized the importance of being able to view a situation from multiple perspectives. The reasoning on which people base their judgments reflects their level of moral development. At a preconventional level, moral judgments are based on the positive or negative consequences of one's actions. At the conventional level, moral judgments are based on conformity to conventional standards. At a postconventional level, moral judgments are based on personal moral standards. Roots of Empathy is a character-based curriculum being taught in Canadian classrooms. It aims to reduce the incidence of aggression and bullying and to promote behaviour based on empathy.

LO6 **Describe developments in information processing in middle childhood.** Key elements in children's information-processing capabilities include development in selective attention; development in the storage and retrieval of sensory, short-term, and long-term memory; development of recall memory; and development of metacognition and metamemory.

LO7 **Describe intellectual development in middle childhood, focusing on theories of intelligence.** Intelligence is usually perceived as a child's underlying competence or *learning ability,* whereas achievement involves a child's acquired competencies or *performance*. Sternberg proposed a three-part theory of intelligence (see Figure 9.5). Gardner theorized that intelligence reflected more than academic achievement, with nine different categories of intelligence (see Figure 9.6).

The Wechsler Intelligence Scale for Children-V (WISC-V) and Stanford–Binet Intelligence Scale (SB5), fifth edition, have been developed to measure intelligence. Many psychologists and educational specialists have developed culture-free tests to avoid cultural biases they feel are present in the WISC-V and the SB5. About half of children score between 90 and 110 on IQ (intelligence quotient) tests. Most tests indicate only a moderate relationship between IQ scores and creativity.

LO8 **Describe language development in middle childhood, including reading and bilingualism.** Children's language ability grows more sophisticated in middle childhood. During this stage, most children learn to read. Exposure to a variety of languages affects children's cognitive development. Bilingualism is of special interest in Canada, where more than 100 languages are spoken. Bilingualism has been found to have a positive impact on the brain as it trains executive functioning through language selection. When you learn more than one language, you are always selecting among many words for the correct one and this strengthens the ability to selectively attend to information.

LO8 **word-recognition method**
a method for learning to read in which children come to recognize words through repeated exposure to them. (p. 174)

phonetic method
a method for learning to read in which children decode the sounds of words based on their knowledge of the sounds of letters and letter combinations. (p. 174)

sight vocabulary
words that are not decoded but are immediately recognized because of familiarity with their overall shapes. (p. 174)

bilingual
using or capable of using two languages with equal or nearly equal facility. (p. 174)

10 Chapter in Review

LO1 reciprocal determinism
the interplay between one's personality, environment, and behaviour. (p. 177)

social cognition
one's understanding of the relationship between oneself and others. (p. 177)

LO2 co-regulation
a gradual transferring of control from parent to child, beginning in middle childhood. (p. 179)

transsexuals
individuals who prefer to be of the other sex and who may undergo hormone treatments, cosmetic surgery, or both to achieve the appearance of being of the other sex. (p. 179)

blended families
families that include the biological children of at least one of the partners in a relationship. (p. 181)

skip-generation families
families whose grandparents parent the grandchildren with little or no help from their adult child. (p. 182)

LO3 peer rejection
when children are rejected by their peers. Divided into two groups: one is withdrawn–rejected, as they are disliked by their peers due to some perceived difference; the other is aggressive–rejected, and they are rejected due to aggressive behaviour that is disruptive. (p. 185)

bullying
an act of intentional harm, repeated over time, in a relationship characterized by an imbalance of power. (p. 185)

bystanders
peers who watch a bullying episode take place but do not take part in the bullying, at least, initially. (p. 186)

cyberbullying
using some form of technology to bully and harass another person. (p. 186)

LO4 Pygmalion effect
a self-fulfilling prophecy; an expectation that is confirmed because of the behaviour of those who hold the expectation. (p. 188)

self-fulfilling prophecy
an event that occurs because of the behaviour of those who expect it to occur. (p. 188)

sexism
discrimination or bias on the basis of a person's sex. (p. 188)

LO5 serotonin
a neurotransmitter that is involved in mood disorders such as depression. (p. 189)

Psychosocial Stage	Personality Crisis (Challenge)	Important Life Event	Outcome
School Age (6 to 11 years)	Industry vs. Inferiority	School	Children learn to cope with new social and academic demands. Success leads to a sense of ability and accomplishment. Failure leads to a sense of inferiority.

LO1 Explain theories of social and emotional development in middle childhood. Erikson saw middle childhood as the stage of industry versus inferiority. Social cognitive theorists note that children in middle childhood depend less on external rewards and punishments and increasingly regulate their own behaviour. Bandura coined the term reciprocal determinism as the interplay between individuals' personality, their environment, and their behaviour. Thus, when children are aggressive, they receive feedback that they are powerful and the environment changes allowing the children to maintain their power out of fear. Cognitive-developmental theory notes that concrete operations enhance social development. In middle childhood, children become more capable of taking the role or perspective of another person. Selman theorizes that children move from egocentricity to seeing the world through the eyes of others in five stages.

In early childhood, children's self-concepts focus on external traits. In middle childhood, children begin to include abstract internal traits. Social relationships and group membership assume importance. In middle childhood, competence and social acceptance contribute to self-esteem, but self-esteem tends to decline as the self-concept becomes more realistic. Authoritative parenting fosters self-esteem.

LO2 Discuss the impact of the family on social development in middle childhood. In middle childhood, the family continues to play a key role in socialization. Parent–child interactions focus on school-related issues, chores, and peers. Parents do less monitoring of children, as children's "co-regulation" develops. The Canadian family has evolved to the point that there is no longer a "typical" family. Research does not indicate a difference in development when a child is raised by same-sex parents. The sexual orientation of these children is generally heterosexual.

Divorce disrupts children's lives and usually lowers the family's financial status. Children are likely to greet divorce with sadness, shock, and disbelief. Children of divorce fare better when parents cooperate in child rearing. Stepparents and blended families have become increasingly common. One difficulty of stepparents is disciplining their non-biological child. Single parents are mostly women, and this has also become a common family arrangement. The impact of divorce on children in this age group suggests that they are more likely to experience conduct disorders, drug abuse, poor grades, lowered self-esteem, and disruptions in interpersonal functioning although many children are able to rebound 1 year after their parents divorce. Children appear to suffer as much from marital conflict as they do from divorce.

Grandparents who raise their grandchildren without the help of their adult children have also become more common in recent years. This arrangement is sometimes called the skip-generation family. Having both parents in the workforce may lead to lack of supervision, but there is little evidence that maternal employment harms children. Research shows that having a mother who works fosters children's greater independence and flexibility in their gender-role stereotypes.

attributional style
one's disposition toward interpreting outcomes (successes or failures), as in tending to place blame or responsibility on oneself or on external factors. (p. 190)

generalized anxiety disorder (GAD)
an anxiety disorder in which anxiety appears to be present continuously and is unrelated to the situation. (p. 191)

phobias
irrational, excessive fears that interfere with one's functioning. (p. 191)

separation anxiety disorder (SAD)
an extreme form of separation anxiety characterized by anxiety about separating from parents; SAD often takes the form of refusal to go to school. (p. 191)

school phobia
fear of attending school, marked by extreme anxiety at leaving parents. (p. 192)

conduct disorders
disorders marked by persistent breaking of the rules and violations of the rights of others. (p. 193)

LO3 Discuss the influences of peers on social development in middle childhood. Peers take on increasing importance in middle childhood and exert pressure to conform. Peers provide practice in social skills, sharing, relating to leaders, and coping with aggressive impulses. Early in middle childhood, friendships are based on proximity. Between the ages of 8 and 11 years, children become more aware that friends meet each other's needs and have traits such as loyalty. Children who are accepted by their peers are often socially savvy and know how to join play groups. They tend to be attractive, mature for their age, and successful at sports or academics. Some children who are socially aggressive by gossiping or manipulating others may be perceived as popular if they are socially competent and considered "cool" by their peers. These are often children who are feared by their peers. Children who are rejected fall into two groups. The first group is withdrawn–rejected; these are children who tend to be disliked by their peers because they are perceived to be different in some way. The second group of children are aggressive–rejected; these children disrupt and act uncooperatively. They tend to be more impulsive and inattentive and do not learn to conform.

Bullying occurs when there is intent to harm, repeated behaviour over time, imbalance of power, and when it causes the victim distress. Cyberbullying occurs when some form of technology is used to harass or bully another person. One of the greatest issues of cyberbullying is that hurtful comments or pictures may reappear well after the incident has seemed to have gone away and thus individuals feel that they cannot escape from their bully.

LO4 Explain the importance of the school on development in middle childhood. Schools make demands for mature behaviour and nurture positive physical, social, and cognitive development. Readiness for school is related to children's early life experiences, individual differences in development and learning, and the school's expectations. An effective school has an orderly atmosphere, empowers teachers and students, holds high expectations of children, and has solid academics. Teachers' expectations can become self-fulfilling prophecies.

LO5 Discuss social and emotional problems that tend to develop in middle childhood. Depressed children tend to complain of poor appetite, insomnia, lack of energy, and feelings of worthlessness. They blame themselves excessively for any shortcomings. Psychotherapy focuses on cognitive errors; antidepressants are sometimes helpful but controversial. Separation anxiety disorder (SAD) is diagnosed when separation anxiety is persistent and excessive and interferes with daily life. Children may refuse school due to school phobia or because they find it to be unpleasant or hostile. The central aspect of treatment of school refusal is to insist that the child attend school. Finally, conduct disorders may have a genetic component, but other contributing factors are antisocial family members, physical punishment, and family stress.

Vlue/Shutterstock.com

The Infinity Project is a youth initiative encouraging others to speak out if they are struggling with depression, self-harm, anxiety, or any issue that overwhelms them.

Chapter in Review

LO1 puberty the biological stage of development characterized by physiological and cognitive changes that are associated with reproduction. (p. 195)

feedback loop a system in which glands regulate each other's functioning through a series of hormonal messages. (p. 195)

primary sex characteristics the structures that make reproduction possible. (p. 195)

secondary sex characteristics physical indicators of sexual maturation—such as changes to the voice and growth of bodily hair—that do not directly involve reproductive structures. (p. 195)

asynchronous growth imbalanced growth, such as the growth that occurs during the early part of adolescence and causes many adolescents to appear gawky. (p. 196)

secular trend a historical trend toward increasing adult height and earlier puberty. (p. 197)

semen the fluid that contains sperm and substances that nourish and help transport sperm. (p. 197)

nocturnal emission emission of seminal fluid while asleep. (p. 197)

gynecomastia enlargement of breast tissue in males. (p. 197)

epiphyseal closure the process by which the cartilage that separates the long end of a bone from the main part of the bone turns to bone. (p. 198)

menarche the onset of menstruation. (p. 198)

LO2 anorexia nervosa an eating disorder characterized by irrational fear of weight gain, distorted body image, and severe weight loss. (p. 202)

osteoporosis a condition involving progressive loss of bone tissue. (p. 202)

bulimia nervosa an eating disorder characterized by cycles of binge eating and vomiting as a means of controlling weight gain. (p. 203)

LO3 formal operations the fourth stage in Piaget's cognitive-developmental theory, characterized by the capacity for flexible, reversible operations concerning abstract ideas and concepts, such as symbols, statements, and theories. (p. 203)

LO1 Describe the key events of puberty and their relationship to social development. G. Stanley Hall believed that adolescence is marked by "storm and stress." Current views challenge the idea that storm and stress are normal or beneficial. Puberty is a stage of physical development that is characterized by reaching sexual maturity. Sex hormones trigger the development of primary and secondary sex characteristics. Adolescents grow about 20 cm (8 inches), but puberty is a process that takes a long time. Precocious puberty (or early onset puberty) is becoming a common trend in Canada. Adolescents may look gawky because of asynchronous growth. Having a resource that is knowledgeable and non-judgmental is important for teens who are experiencing so many physical changes. The effects of early maturation are generally positive for boys and often negative for girls.

LO2 Discuss health in adolescence, focusing on causes of death and eating disorders. Unintentional injuries are the number one cause of death for Canadian adolescents. Car accidents are the most common cause of death. To fuel the adolescent growth spurt, adolescents need to increase their food intake by making more healthy choices from Canada's Food Guide. The use of recreational drugs (both illegal and prescription) is a social reality for the Canadian teenager. Other issues that workers with teens should be aware of include eating disorders such as anorexia nervosa and bulimia nervosa, which may develop because of fear of gaining weight resulting from cultural idealization, particularly for females.

LO3 Outline adolescent cognitive development and the key events of Piaget's stage of formal operations. In Western societies, formal operational thought begins at about the time of puberty. The major achievements of the stage involve classification, logical thought (deductive reasoning), and the ability to hypothesize. Adolescent egocentrism is shown in the concepts of the imaginary audience and the personal fable.

Sanjagrujic/iStockphoto.com

LO4 Discuss sex differences in cognitive abilities. The stage of formal operations is Piaget's final stage of development. Many children, but not all, reach this stage during adolescence. The formal operational stage is characterized by the individual's increased ability to classify objects and ideas, engage in logical thought, hypothesize, and demonstrate a sophisticated use of symbols. Females tend to excel in verbal ability. Males tend to excel in visual–spatial ability. Females and males show equal ability in math. Boys are more likely than girls to have reading problems. Sex differences in cognitive abilities have been linked to biological factors and to gender stereotypes and social influences.

imaginary audience
the belief that others around us are as concerned with our thoughts and behaviours as we are; one aspect of adolescent egocentrism. (p. 204)

personal fable
the belief that our feelings and ideas are special and unique and that we are invulnerable; one aspect of adolescent egocentrism. (p. 204)

LO5 postconventional level
according to Kohlberg, a period during which moral judgments are derived from moral principles and people look to themselves to set moral standards. (p. 206)

LO5 Discuss Kohlberg's theory of moral development in adolescence. In the postconventional level, according to Kohlberg, moral reasoning is based on the person's own moral standards. Moral judgments are derived from personal values, not from conventional standards or authority figures. Postconventional thought, when found, first occurs during adolescence, apparently because formal operational thinking is a prerequisite for it.

LO6 Explain the roles of the school in adolescence, focusing on dropping out. The school has a significant role in the adolescent's life. The transition to middle school, junior high, or high school generally involves a shift to a larger, more impersonal setting. This transition is often accompanied by a decline in grades and a drop in self-esteem. More Canadian teenagers are graduating than in previous generations, but we must continue to address the issue of dropping out. High-school dropouts are more likely to be unemployed and to earn lower salaries in their adult lives.

Wunderimages/iStockphoto.com

LO7 Discuss career development and work experience during adolescence. Student employment can be a positive influence if working is kept to a reasonable amount (10 hours per week). If employment hours are greater than 10, or if the employment takes place late at night, working can be a barrier to completing high school. John Holland's Vocational Preference Inventory is a tool that students can use to match their personal interests and strengths with possible future careers.

ADOLESCENCE: SOCIAL AND EMOTIONAL DEVELOPMENT

12 Chapter in Review

LO1 **ego identity**
according to Erikson, individuals' sense of who they are and what they stand for. (p. 211)

psychological moratorium
a time-out period when adolescents experiment with different roles, values, beliefs, and relationships. (p. 211)

identity crisis
a turning point in development during which people examine their values and make decisions about life roles. (p. 211)

identity diffusion
an identity status that characterizes those who who are non-committal to specific beliefs and who are not in the process of exploring alternatives. (p. 211)

foreclosure
an identity status that characterizes those who have made commitments without considering alternatives. (p. 212)

moratorium
an identity status that characterizes those who are actively exploring alternatives in an attempt to form an identity. (p. 212)

identity achievement
an identity status that characterizes those who have explored alternatives and have developed commitments. (p. 212)

ethnic identity
a sense of belonging to an ethnic group. (p. 213)

unexamined ethnic identity
the first stage of ethnic identity development; similar to the diffusion or foreclosure identity statuses. (p. 213)

ethnic identity search
the second stage of ethnic identity development; similar to the moratorium identity status. (p. 213)

achieved ethnic identity
the final stage of ethnic identity development; similar to the identity achievement status. (p. 213)

LO2 **clique**
a group of five to ten individuals who may be exclusive of others, and who share activities and confidences. (p. 216)

crowd
a large, loosely organized group of people who may or may not spend much time together and who are identified by the activities of the group. (p. 216)

LO3 **masturbation**
sexual self-stimulation. (p. 218)

LO4 **youth in conflict with the law**
a child or adolescent whose behaviour is characterized by illegal activities. (p. 221)

Psychosocial Stage	Personality Crisis (Challenge)	Important Life Event	Outcome
Adolescence (12 to 18 years)	Identity vs. Role Confusion	Social Relationships	Teens develop a sense of their personal identity. Success leads to their ability to define themselves clearly and to stay true to who they believe they are. Failure leads to unclear standards and a weak sense of self.

LO1 **Discuss the formation of identity in adolescence.** Erikson's adolescent stage of psychosocial development is identity versus identity diffusion. The primary task of this stage is for adolescents to develop a sense of who they are and what they stand for. Marcia's identity statuses represent the four combinations of the dimensions of exploration and commitment: identity diffusion, foreclosure, moratorium, and identity achievement. Development of identity is more complicated for adolescents who belong to ethnic minority groups; they are faced with two sets of cultural values that may conflict.

Self-esteem tends to decline as the child progresses from middle childhood into early adolescence, perhaps because of increasing recognition of the disparity between the ideal self and the real self. Self-esteem then gradually improves.

LO2 **Examine relationships with parents and peers during adolescence.** During adolescence, children spend much less time with parents than during childhood. Although adolescents become more independent of their parents, they generally continue to love and respect them. The role of peers increases markedly during the teen years. Adolescents are more likely than younger children to stress intimate self-disclosure and mutual understanding in friendships. The two major types of peer groups are cliques and crowds. Romantic relationships begin to appear during early and middle adolescence. Dating is a source of fun, prestige, and experience in relationships. Dating is also a preparation for adult intimacy. Online friendships are important to teens, although insecure attachment has been linked to unsafe disclosures in online relationship. Cyberbullying is a concern, although social media can also support positive social messages.

RawPixel.com/Shutterstock.com

LO3 Discuss sexuality during adolescence, focusing on sexual identity and teenage pregnancy. Issues regarding lesbian, gay, bisexual, transgendered, and queer (LGBTQ) youth are becoming part of our mainstream Canadian culture. The process of "coming out" may be a painful struggle but as society becomes more inclusive, these adjustments will likely become a more positive experience. Early onset of puberty can lead to earlier sexual activity. Adolescents who have close relationships with their parents are less likely to initiate sexual activity early. Peer pressure is a powerful contributor to adolescent sexual activity. Many girls who become pregnant have received little advice about how to resist sexual advances. Many do not have access to contraception. Others misunderstand reproduction or miscalculate the odds of conception. Graduating from high school becomes more difficult for these young mothers, which lowers their potential for future income earning. Young Canadian women are becoming more comfortable with their sexuality.

TABLE 12.2

Percentages of Canadian Adolescents Grade 9 and 10 Who Report Ever Having Had Intercourse, 2002, 2006, 2010

	2002	2006	2010
Male Grade 9	20%	20%	24%
Female Grade 9	18%	19%	19%
Male Grade 10	27%	25%	31%
Female Grade 10	25%	27%	31%

Source: *The health of Canada's young people: a mental health focus.* John G. Freeman, Matthew King, William Pickett, with Wendy Craig, et al., 2011. Adapted and reproduced with permission from the Minister of Health, 2016.

LO4 Review the statistics specific to youth in conflict with the law and measures that can reduce youth crime in Canada. Although Canada is experiencing a decrease in national crime rates, youth crimes (assaults, drug-related crimes, and school-related offences) are on the rise. The important link between youth and crime seems to be socio-economic deprivation, not race or ethnicity. Empowerment and community involvement are primary philosophies of the Youth Criminal Justice Act (2003), which favours community programs (such as those involving sports) over incarceration as a way to reduce these crime trends. Restorative justice focuses on community ownership and involvement, giving a voice to the victims, the offenders, the family and friends of both, and society as a whole. First Nations, Métis, and Inuit youth report feeling optimistic about their futures, despite their over-representation in the youth justice system as a result of residential schooling and intergenerational psychosocial issues including poverty.

LO5 Outline risk factors in adolescent suicide. Suicide is the second leading cause of death among Canadian adolescents. Most suicides among adolescents and adults are linked to stress, feelings of depression, identity problems, impulsivity, and social problems. Warning signs of suicide include sudden changes in behaviour, isolation, withdrawal, and feelings of hopelessness.

EARLY ADULTHOOD: PHYSICAL AND COGNITIVE DEVELOPMENT

13 Chapter in Review

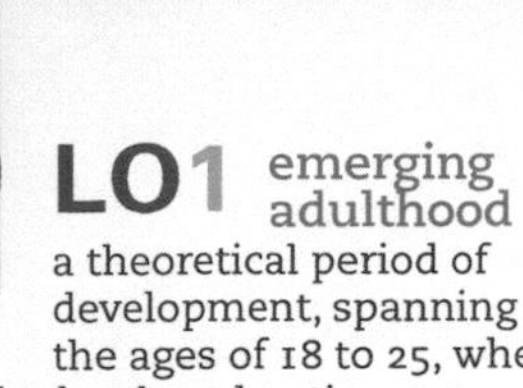

LO1 emerging adulthood
a theoretical period of development, spanning the ages of 18 to 25, when young people in developed nations engage in extended role exploration. (p. 226)

LO3 adaptive thermogenesis
the process by which the body converts food energy (calories) to heat at a lower rate when a person eats less, because of, for example, famine or dieting. (p. 229)

substance abuse
a persistent pattern of use of a substance characterized by frequent intoxication and impairment of physical, social, or emotional well-being. (p. 230)

substance dependence
a persistent pattern of use of a substance that is accompanied by physiological addiction. (p. 230)

tolerance
habituation to a drug such that increasingly higher doses are needed to achieve similar effects. (p. 230)

abstinence syndrome
a characteristic cluster of symptoms that results from a sudden decrease in the level of usage of a substance. (p. 230)

hallucinogenics
drugs that give rise to hallucinations. (p. 231)

LO4 dysmenorrhea
painful menstruation. (p. 234)

prostaglandins
hormones that cause muscles in the uterine wall to contract, as during labour. (p. 234)

amenorrhea
the absence of menstruation. (p. 234)

premenstrual syndrome (PMS)
the discomforting symptoms that affect many women during the 4- to 6-day interval preceding their periods. (p. 234)

premenstrual dysphoric disorder (PMDD)
a condition similar to but more severe than PMS. (p. 234)

dating violence
assaults such as verbal threats, pushing, and slapping committed by an individual in an intimate relationship and often leading to injuries that require first aid. (p. 235)

sexual harassment
deliberate or repeated unwanted comments, gestures, or physical contact. (p. 236)

LO5 crystallized intelligence
one's intellectual attainments, as shown, for example, by vocabulary and accumulated knowledge. (p. 237)

LO1 Discuss the (theoretical) stage of emerging adulthood. Emerging adulthood is a period of development, spanning the ages of 18 to 25, in which young people engage in extended role exploration. Many developmental theorists consider emerging adulthood to be a new stage of development that bridges adolescence and early adulthood.

Michael Jung/Shutterstock.com

LO2 Describe trends in physical development in early adulthood. Physical development peaks in early adulthood. During this stage, most people are at their height of sensory sharpness, strength, reaction time, and cardiovascular fitness. Peak fitness is followed by gradual declines in the cardiovascular, respiratory, and immune systems but regular exercise can reduce these effects. Fertility in both sexes declines as early adulthood progresses.

LO3 Examine health in early adulthood, focusing on causes of death, diet, exercise, and substance abuse. Accidents are the leading cause of death in early adulthood. Most young adults do not eat the recommended five fruits and vegetables each day. About four in ten report insufficient exercise and being overweight, which has become a Canadian health concern. Substance abuse is use of a substance despite its social, occupational, psychological, or physical effects. Depressants such as alcohol, narcotics, and barbiturates are addictive substances that slow the activity of the nervous system. Alcohol also lowers inhibitions, relaxes, and intoxicates. Stimulants such as nicotine, cocaine, and amphetamines accelerate the heartbeat and other bodily functions but depress the appetite. Hallucinogenics such as marijuana and LSD give rise to perceptual distortions called hallucinations. Stress is a concern in a busy Canadian lifestyle.

LO4 Discuss sexuality in early adulthood, focusing on LGBTQ, menstrual problems, sexual coercion, and sexual violence. Sexual activity with a partner tends to peak in the 20s. An international report found that Canadians are quite comfortable with their sexuality, reporting more partners and more time spent on sex than people in most other countries. Sexually transmitted infections (STIs) include bacterial infections such as chlamydia, gonorrhea, and syphilis; viral infections such as HIV/AIDS (human immunodeficiency virus/acquired immune deficiency syndrome), HPV (human papillomavirus), and genital herpes; and some others. Most women experience at least some discomfort prior to or during menstruation. Sexual assault is significantly under-reported in Canada, perhaps partly because victims usually know their attackers. Dating violence is also increasing at an alarming rate. Addressing aggressive sexual behaviour is needed to address the root of this social issue.

LO5 Discuss cognitive development in early adulthood, focusing on "post-formal" developments and effects of life after high school. Young adults are more cognitively complex than adolescents with fluid and crystalized intelligence increasing. They are able to weigh several factors at one time, and they encounter diverse ideas and people when attending postsecondary education, as a majority of Canadian youth do. Their previous dualistic thinking may be replaced by relativistic thinking. Labouvie-Vief's theory of pragmatic thought notes that "cognitively healthy" adults are more willing than

fluid intelligence
mental flexibility; the ability to process information rapidly. (p. 237)

dualistic thinking
dividing the cognitive world into opposites, such as good and bad, or us versus them. (p. 237)

relativistic thinking
recognition that judgments are often not absolute but are made from a certain belief system or cultural background. (p. 237)

pragmatic thought
decision making characterized by willingness to accept reality and compromise. (p. 237)

cognitive–affective complexity
a mature form of thinking that permits people to harbour positive and negative feelings about their career choices and other matters. (p. 237)

egocentric adolescents to compromise and deal within the world as it is, not as they would like it to be; they develop cognitive–affective complexity that enables them to harbour both positive and negative feelings about their choices.

LO6 **Describe career choice and development during early adulthood.** Careers are central to the lives of Canadian adults. People work for extrinsic rewards, such as money and benefits, and for intrinsic rewards, such as self-identity and self-fulfillment. Developmental tasks when beginning a job include accepting subordinate status, learning to get along with co-workers and supervisors, finding a mentor, and showing progress.

Intrinsic reasons for working include the following (Duffy & Sedlacek, 2007):

- **The work ethic.** This view believes that we are morally obligated to avoid idleness.
- **Self-identity.** Our occupational identity can become intertwined with our self-identity.
- **Self-fulfillment.** We often express our personal needs and interests through our work.
- **Self-worth.** Recognition and respect for a job well done contribute to self-esteem.
- **Socialization.** The workplace extends our social contacts.
- **Public roles.** Work roles help define our functions in the community.

Career development has numerous stages. The first or *fantasy stage* involves unrealistic conception of self-potential and of the world of work, which dominates from early childhood until about age 11 (Auger et al., 2005). During the second or *tentative choice stage*, from about age 11 through high school, children base their choices on their interests, abilities, and limitations, as well as glamour. In the *realistic choice stage,* choices become narrow as students weight job requirements with their own interests, abilities, and values. During the *maintenance stage*, young adults begin to settle into a career role.

Michael Svoboda/iStockphoto.com

14 Chapter in Review

LO1 **individuation** the young adult's process of becoming an individual by means of integrating his or her own values and beliefs with those of his or her parents and society at large. (p. 242)

LO2 **intimacy versus isolation** according to Erik Erikson, the central conflict or life crisis of early adulthood, in which a person develops an intimate relationship with a significant other or risks heading down a path toward social isolation. (p. 243)

LO3 **the dream** according to Daniel Levinson and his colleagues, the drive to become someone, to leave one's mark on history, which serves as a tentative blueprint for the young adult. (p. 243)

LO4 **attraction–similarity hypothesis** the view that we tend to develop romantic relationships with people who are similar to ourselves in physical attractiveness and other traits. (p. 246)

reciprocity the tendency to respond in kind when we feel admired and complimented. (p. 246)

romantic love a form of love fuelled by passion and feelings of intimacy. (p. 246)

intimacy the experience of warmth toward another person that arises from feelings of closeness and connectedness. (p. 247)

passion intense sexual desire for another person. (p. 247)

commitment the decision to devote oneself to a cause or another person. (p. 247)

LO6 **serial monogamy** a series of exclusive sexual relationships. (p. 250)

celibacy abstention from sexual activity, whether from choice or lack of opportunity. (p. 250)

LO7 **cohabitation** living together with a romantic partner without being married. (p. 250)

LO8 **monogamy** the practice of having a sexual relationship with only one person at a time. (p. 252)

Psychosocial Stage	Personality Crisis (Challenge)	Important Life Event	Outcome
Young Adulthood (19 to 39 years)	Intimacy vs. Isolation	Relationships	Young adults need to form intimate and loving relationships. Success leads to patterns of strong relationship building. Failure to enter into loving relationships results in loneliness and isolation.

LO1 **Examine the issues involved in early adulthood separation.** Havighurst's "tasks" for early adulthood include getting started in an occupation and finding a life partner, though his view might now be seen as a dated notion of early adulthood. Traditional or insecure parents may find a child's leaving for college or university to be stressful. Young adults are returning home (the boomerang generation) in very high numbers, making the "empty nest" not so empty anymore. Adult children most often return because of financial troubles or relationship issues. Young adults need to become individuals by integrating their own values with those of their parents and society.

LO2 **Describe the conflict between intimacy and isolation.** Erikson's core conflict for early adulthood is intimacy versus isolation. Young adults who develop ego identity during adolescence are more ready to marry and develop friendships. A variety of different types of relationships are available to young Canadians starting out in life.

LO3 **Discuss the stage of life for entry into adulthood.** Levinson labels the ages of 17 to 33 the entry phase of adulthood for young men—when they leave home and strive for independence. Young women may take longer to leave home because of the social constraints of sexism, both from their families and from society. Many young adults adopt "the dream," which serves as a tentative blueprint for life. Young adults undergo an age-30 transition, when they commonly reassess their lives. Young adults often settle down during their later 30s.

LO4 **Examine the emotional forces of attraction and love.** Physical appearance is a key in selection of romantic partners. People in mainstream Canadian culture tend to prefer slenderness in both sexes. People prefer partners who are similar to them in attractiveness and attitudes. People tend to reciprocate feelings of attraction. Berscheid and Hatfield define romantic love in terms of arousal and cognitive appraisal of that arousal as love. Sternberg's "triangular theory" of love includes the building blocks of intimacy, passion, and commitment. Jealousy can lead to insecurity and loss of feelings of affection. Nonphysical traits, such as familiarity, respect, and sharing of values and goals, also influence attractiveness of a partner.

LO5 **Explain why people get lonely and what they do in response.** Loneliness can be related to low self-confidence, depression, and physical health problems. Lonely people can lack social skills, interest in other people, and empathy. Many people remain lonely because of fear of rejection. There is an important difference between being lonely and being alone.

polyamory
the practice of consenting partners who maintain an "open" sexual relationship. (p. 252)

same-sex marriage
marriage between two gay males or between two lesbians. (p. 252)

homogamy
marriage between two similar individuals. (p. 253)

Nandy Photos/iStockphoto.com

LO6 **Discuss the lifestyle of being single.** Being single is the most common Canadian lifestyle of people in their early 20s. Many people postpone marriage to pursue educational and career goals. Many choose to live together without being married. Some have not found the right partner. Some single people are lonely, but most are well adjusted. Online dating is becoming a common way to meet potential partners in Canada. Many singles engage in serial monogamy, while many others choose celibacy.

LO7 **Describe the practice of living together.** The number of people living together in Canada has surged in the last two decades. In 2006, Statistics Canada recorded same-sex unions for the first time, as a result of Canada's legalization of same-sex marriages. Relationships are much more likely to dissolve when cohabitation precedes marriage. Cohabitants tend to have less traditional views of marriage and gender roles.

LO8 **Describe the practice of marriage.** Families, for all of their different descriptions and labels, remain our most common form of Canadian lifestyle. Marriage legitimizes sexual relations, provides an institution for rearing children, and permits the orderly transmission of wealth from one generation to another. Types of marriage include monogamy, arranged marriage, and same-sex marriages. Similarity in physical attractiveness, attitudes, background, and interests play a role in marital choices. Most marriages where partners are very similar in physical attractiveness, values, and family backgrounds enjoy a higher rate of stability than other unions. Intimacy and support of one's spouse are related to marital satisfaction. Couple satisfaction does not seem to be measurably different between same-sex couples and opposite-sex couples, but household chores are more evenly distributed in same-sex unions, leading to less bickering.

Dragon Images/Shutterstock.com

LO9 **Discuss the state of parenthood.** Young Canadians are delaying parenthood into their later 20s. Most Canadians choose to have children for personal happiness, but having a child is unlikely to save a troubled marriage. The quality of a couple's adjustment declines the first year of a child's life. Role overload can be a serious challenge, especially for single parents. Postpartum depression is another stressor for new parents. Workplace tension affects home life, and vice versa.

LO10 **Discuss divorce and its repercussions.** In a survey of Canadian teenagers, 90% stated that when they marry it will be forever; yet the Canadian divorce rate is currently 40%. Changes in divorce laws and increased economic independence of women contribute to the divorce rate. Divorce hits women in the pocketbook harder than men, especially when women do not have careers. Divorced and separated people have the highest rates of physical and mental illness.

15 Chapter in Review

LO1 **baby boomers** postwar babies whose births between 1946 and 1965 spiked the Canadian population by 11%. (p. 258)

inter-individual variability the notion that people do not age in the same way or at the same rate. (p. 258)

presbyopia loss of elasticity in the lens that makes it harder to focus on nearby objects. (p. 258)

presbycusis loss of hearing over time. (p. 258)

LO2 **metastases** the transference of malignant or cancerous cells to other parts of the body. (p. 260)

arteriosclerosis hardening of the arteries. (p. 262)

atherosclerosis the buildup of fatty deposits (plaque) on the lining of arteries. (p. 262)

LO3 **leukocytes** white blood cells. (p. 263)

LO4 **menopause** the cessation of menstruation. (p. 264)

perimenopause the beginning of menopause, usually characterized by 3 to 11 months of amenorrhea or irregular periods. (p. 264)

climacteric the gradual decline in reproductive capacity of the ovaries, generally lasting about 15 years. (p. 264)

sexual dysfunctions persistent or recurrent problems in becoming sexually aroused or reaching orgasm. (p. 265)

LO5 **multidirectionality** in the context of cognitive development, the notion that some aspects of intellectual functioning may improve while others remain stable or decline. (p. 266)

plasticity the capability of intellectual abilities to be modified, as opposed to being absolutely fixed. (p. 267)

crystallized intelligence a cluster of knowledge and skills that depend on accumulated information and experience, awareness of social conventions, and good judgment. (p. 267)

fluid intelligence a person's skills at processing information. (p. 267)

LO1 **Describe trends in physical development in middle adulthood.** The baby boomers have grown up and are now Canada's middle-aged generation. In middle adulthood, hair begins to grey, and hair loss accelerates. The skin loses elasticity. It becomes harder for eyes to focus on nearby objects or fine print. Reaction time is slower. Breathing capacity declines. Fat replaces lean tissue and the basal metabolic rate declines. Strength decreases. Bone begins to lose density and strength. The cardiovascular system becomes less efficient. There is an increased risk of adult onset diabetes.

FIGURE 15.1

Leading Causes of Death in Middle Adulthood*

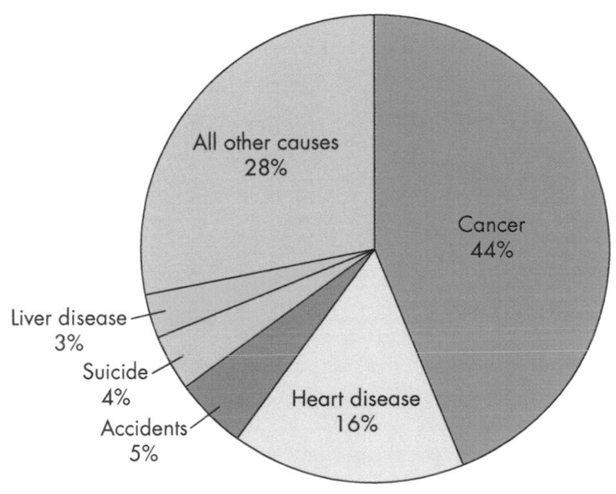

*Not indicated in Figure 15.1 is women's sharply increased incidence of death due to heart disease after menopause.

Source: Statistics Canada. (2011). *The 10 leading causes of death*. http://www.statcan.gc.ca/pub/82-625-x/2014001/article/11896/c-g/c-g01-eng.htm

LO2 **Discuss the major health concerns of middle adulthood, including cancer and heart disease.** In middle adulthood, cancer and heart disease are the two leading causes of death in Canada. Risk factors for cancer include heredity, problems in the immune system, hormonal factors, and carcinogens. Positive lifestyle habits can reduce the risks associated with cancer. The risk factors for heart disease include family history, high blood pressure, high serum cholesterol, smoking, sedentary lifestyle, and arteriosclerosis.

LO3 **Discuss the functioning of the immune system.** The immune system combats disease by producing white blood cells (leukocytes), which engulf and kill pathogens. Leukocytes recognize foreign substances (antigens), deactivate them, and mark them for destruction. Stress suppresses the immune system. Stress hormones connected with anger can constrict the blood vessels to the heart, leading to a heart attack.

LO4 **Discuss sexuality in middle adulthood, focusing on menopause and sexual difficulties.** Most people in middle adulthood lead rich sex lives, but the frequency of sex tends to decline. The climacteric generally lasts about 15 years and is caused by decline in estrogen production. Menopause is part of the climacteric and is a normal process lasting about 2 years; it results in the female no longer ovulating. Estrogen deficiency can cause night sweats, hot flashes, hot flushes—even dizziness, headaches, joint pain, tingling in the hands or feet, burning or itchy skin, heart palpitations, and brittleness and porosity of the bones (osteoporosis). Hormone replacement therapy (HRT) can help women deal with these symptoms but using HRT comes with considerable health risks.

Men show a more gradual decline in sex hormones and fertility, but sexual difficulties often begin in middle adulthood. Sexual activity can, however, yield surprising health benefits.

There is an increase in sexually transmitted infections (STIs) in middle age, possibly because condom use tends to be associated with preventing pregnancy, which is no longer an issue for middle-aged women; a shift toward more single, sexually active people; greater use of male impotence medication; and middle-aged adults' mistaken belief that they are not at risk for STIs. Condoms must continue to be used to protect against STIs.

LO5 **Describe cognitive development in middle adulthood, distinguishing between crystallized and fluid intelligence.** Intellectual development in adulthood shows multidirectionality, inter-individual variability, and plasticity. Schaie's Seattle Longitudinal Study found that adults born more recently were superior to those born at earlier times in inductive reasoning, verbal meaning, spatial orientation, and word fluency. The earlier cohorts performed better in numeric ability. Neurological factors apparently play a powerful role in fluid intelligence. Crystallized intelligence tends to increase with age through middle adulthood, but a decline occurs in fluid intelligence, which relates to perceptual speed, spatial orientation, and numeric ability. Verbal ability and reasoning mainly reflect crystallized intelligence; they increase through middle adulthood and hold up in late adulthood. Good health and staying intellectually active help stem cognitive decline in late adulthood.

LO6 **Describe mental health concerns and issues of stress.** Mental illness is a broad range of disorders which include but are not limited to depression, anxiety disorders, bipolar, schizophrenia, and substance abuse. Mental health issues are the main cause of disability in Canada and greatly affect those in middle age. Genetics, living in poverty, and environmental stresses are just some causes. Improved awareness and destigmatization of mental health issues is increasing in Canada.

LO7 **Discuss opportunities for exercising creativity and continuing education in middle adulthood.** Writers and visual artists often continue to improve into middle adulthood, although their most emotional and fervent works may be produced at younger ages. Mature learners in higher education are likely to be highly motivated and to find the subject matter interesting for its own sake. Ironically, women with the greatest family and work demands are most likely to return to school. Canada has the second highest rate of postsecondary attainment in the world.

SportPoint/Shutterstock.com

16 Chapter in Review

LO1 **generativity** the ability to generate or produce, as in bearing children or contributing to society. (p. 274)

stagnation the state of no longer developing, growing, or advancing. (p. 274)

social clock the social norms that guide our judgment regarding the age-related "appropriateness" of certain behaviours. (p. 275)

midlife transition a psychological shift into middle adulthood that is theorized to occur between the ages of 40 and 45, as people sometimes begin to believe they have more to look back on than to look forward to. (p. 275)

midlife crisis a time of dramatic self-doubt and anxiety, during which people sense the passing of their youth and become concerned with their own aging and mortality. (p. 275)

empty nest syndrome a feeling of loneliness or loss of purpose that parents are theorized to experience when the youngest child leaves home. (p. 276)

LO2 **"big five" personality traits** basic personality traits derived from contemporary statistical methods: extraversion, agreeableness, conscientiousness, neuroticism (emotional instability), and openness to experience. (p. 278)

LO4 **sandwich generation** the term for middle-aged people who need to meet the demands of both their own children and their aging parents. (p. 282)

Psychosocial Stage	Personality Crisis (Challenge)	Important Life Event	Outcome
Middle Adulthood (40 to 64 years)	Generativity vs. Stagnation	Work and Parenthood	Adults thrive when they create and nurture things that will outlast them. Raising children, or creating a positive change, leads to feelings of usefulness and accomplishment. Failure results in shallow involvement, and a realization that they will leave nothing lasting behind.

LO1 **Discuss theories of development in middle adulthood.** Havighurst's tasks for middle adulthood include helping our children establish themselves, adjusting to physical changes, and adjusting to caring for aging parents. Erikson believed that the major psychological challenge of the middle years is generativity versus stagnation. Canadian Elliott Jaques developed the concept of a midlife crisis. Levinson characterizes the years of 40 to 45 as a midlife transition that is often accompanied by a midlife crisis, but many people at this age are at the height of their productivity and resilience. Although it was once assumed that parents without children in the home would undergo an "empty nest syndrome," this time can be a positive event. The social clock has begun and ageism colours much of middle life.

DNY59-iStockphoto.com

LO2 **Analyze stability and change in social and emotional development in middle adulthood.** Longitudinal research finds that the "big five" personality traits show a good deal of stability after age 30, but the traits of agreeableness and conscientiousness tend to increase and neuroticism declines.

LO3 **Consider career developments typical of middle adulthood.** A study of university employees found that job satisfaction increased through middle adulthood. Most career changes in midlife involve shifts into related fields. Unemployed middle-aged people show lower well-being than unemployed young adults. Second Careers is a provincial government initiative designed to send middle-aged workers back to school, creating a more vital economy.

Art Babych/Shutterstock.com

Justin Trudeau, age 45, became the second-youngest Prime Minister of Canada when he won the federal election in 2015.

LO4 Discuss trends in relationships in middle adulthood, focusing on grandparenting and being in the "sandwich generation." When their children take partners or get married, middle-aged people need to adjust to having in-laws. Research generally finds that grandchildren are beneficial to grandparents socially and psychologically. Parents spend a higher proportion of their time with their children in childcare activities, whereas grandparents spend relatively more time in recreational and educational activities. Grandchildren spend more time in activities with their grandmothers than with their grandfathers, and are relatively more involved with their mother's parents.

In some cases, grandparents bear the primary responsibility for rearing grandchildren, and sometimes they are the sole caregivers. Such arrangements typically begin when the grandchild has a single parent. Acting as the parent again can be highly stressful for grandparents.

Grandparents "coming out" to their grandchildren in early childhood seems to meet with greater acceptance than when the grandchildren are in the teen years.

When aging parents need help, the task usually falls to a middle-aged daughter, who then becomes "sandwiched" between caring for her parents while also caring for or helping her children (and sometimes her grandchildren). Sibling relationships that were antagonistic in childhood can grow closer in middle adulthood if the siblings cooperate in caring for parents. In middle adulthood, the number of friends tends to decline, and people tend to place more value on the friends they retain.

AP Photo/Eric Risberg/Canadian Press

17 Chapter in Review

LO1 **life span (longevity)**
the maximum amount of time a person can live under optimal conditions. (p. 285)

life expectancy
the amount of time a person can actually be expected to live in a given setting. (p. 285)

ageism
prejudice against people because of their age. (p. 287)

cataract
a condition characterized by clouding of the lens of the eye. (p. 287)

glaucoma
a condition involving abnormally high fluid pressure in the eye. (p. 287)

presbycusis
loss of acuteness of hearing due to age-related degenerative changes in the ear. (p. 287)

osteoporosis
a disorder in which bones become more porous, brittle, and subject to fracture, due to loss of calcium and other minerals. (p. 288)

sleep apnea
temporary suspension of breathing while asleep. (p. 288)

LO2 **cellular clock theory**
a theory of aging focusing on the limits of cell division. (p. 290)

telomeres
protective segments of DNA located at the tips of chromosomes. (p. 290)

hormonal stress theory
a theory of aging that suggests stress hormones, left at elevated levels, make the body more vulnerable to chronic conditions. (p. 290)

immunological theory
a theory of aging that holds that the immune system is preset to decline by an internal biological clock. (p. 291)

wear-and-tear theory
a theory of aging that suggests that over time our bodies become less capable of repairing themselves. (p. 291)

free-radical theory
a theory of aging that attributes aging to damage caused by the accumulation of unstable molecules called free radicals. (p. 291)

cross-linking theory
a theory of aging that holds that the stiffening of body proteins eventually breaks down bodily processes, leading to aging. (p. 291)

LO1 **Describe trends in physical development in late adulthood, focusing on life expectancy.** Old age is divided into the young-old, the old-old, and the oldest-old. One in eight North Americans is over the age of 65, and seniors have increased from 8% to 14% since 2009. The life span of a species depends on its genetic programming. Our life expectancy is the number of years we can actually expect to live. Disease prevention and treatment contribute to longevity. The average Canadian baby can expect to live about 80 years, but there are differences due to sex, race, geographic location, and behaviour. Men's life expectancy trails women's by about 4 years. Leading causes of death include cancer, heart disease, respiratory disease, brain disease, diabetes, and accidents.

After we reach our physical peak in our 20s, our biological functions gradually decline. Chemical changes of aging can lead to vision disorders such as cataracts and glaucoma. Presbycusis affects one senior citizen in three. Taste and smell become less acute. Osteoporotic hip fractures consume many hospital bed days in Canada. Insomnia and sleep apnea become more common in later adulthood. Sexual daydreaming, sex drive, and sexual activity decline with age, but sexual satisfaction may remain high. Many of the physical changes in older women stem from a decline in estrogen production. Sexual frequency declines with age.

LO2 **Compare programmed and cellular theories of aging.** Theories of aging have two main categories: (1) programmed theories such as cellular clock theory, hormonal stress theory, and immunological theory, and (2) cellular damage theories such as wear-and-tear theory, free-radical theory, and cross-linking theory.

LO3 **Identify common health concerns associated with late adulthood.** The three major causes of death of Canadians age 65 and older are cancer, heart disease, and respiratory disease (see Table 17.1). Hypertension is a major risk factor for heart attacks and strokes. Arthritis becomes more common with advancing age and is more common in women. Many older adults are addicted to prescription drugs; many have adverse drug reactions. Older adults have a greater risk of accidents, especially falls. Dementia is not a normal result of aging; however, Alzheimer's disease is the leading cause of dementia.

TABLE 17.1

Ten Leading Causes of Death in Canada by Gender, 65–74

Men	Women
Cancer	Cancer
Heart disease	Heart disease
Respiratory disease	Respiratory disease
Brain disease	Brain disease
Diabetes	Diabetes
Accidents	Accidents
Liver disease	Liver disease
Pneumonia	Pneumoniaa
Nephritis	Nephritis
Suicide	Alzheimer's disease

Source: Statistics Canada. (2009b). Ten leading causes of death by selected age groups, by sex, Canada — 65 to 74 years. http://www.statcan.gc.ca/pub/84-215-x/2012001/tbl/t008-eng.htm

LO3 **arthritis**
inflammation of the joints. (p. 293)

osteoarthritis
a painful, degenerative disease characterized by wear and tear on joints. (p. 293)

rheumatoid arthritis
a painful, degenerative disease characterized by chronic inflammation of the membranes that line the joints. (p. 293)

dementia
a condition characterized by deterioration of cognitive functioning. (p. 295)

Alzheimer's disease (AD)
a severe form of dementia characterized by memory lapses, confusion, emotional instability, and progressive loss of cognitive functioning. (p. 296)

LO4 **implicit memory**
automatic memories based on repetition and apparently not requiring any conscious effort to retrieve. (p. 297)

prospective memory
memory of things one has planned for the future. (p. 298)

LO4 **Discuss cognitive development in late adulthood.** Fluid intelligence is most vulnerable to decline in late adulthood. Crystallized intelligence can improve throughout much of late adulthood. Older adults have relatively more difficulty naming public figures than uncommon objects. The working memories of older adults hold less information than the working memories of young adults. Older adults usually do as well as younger adults in tasks that measure implicit memory, such as memory of multiplication tables or the alphabet. Aging has a more detrimental effect on associative memory than on memory for single items, perhaps because of impairment in binding and in use of strategies for retrieval. Long-term memories are subject to distortion, bias, and even decay. Older people recall events from their teens and 20s in greatest detail and emotional intensity, perhaps because of the effects of sex hormones.

Knowledge of meanings of words can improve well into late adulthood, but a decline in reading comprehension is related to a decrease in working memory. Because of this and also because of impairments in hearing, many older adults find it more difficult both to understand the spoken language and to produce language. Older people are more likely to experience the "tip-of-the-tongue" phenomenon. Problem solving requires executive functioning to select strategies, working memory to hold the elements of the problem in mind, and processing speed to accomplish the task while the elements remain in mind. All of these have fluid components that decline with age.

Older adults tend to regulate their emotional responses when they experience conflict. Older adults tend to take a broader view of situations, contributing to wisdom. People with wisdom tolerate other people's views and admit that life has its uncertainties and that we seek workable solutions in an imperfect world.

FIGURE 17.4

The Aging Brain

In the aging brain, atrophy in the frontal lobe and in the middle (medial) part of the temporal lobe may account for deficits in associative memory.

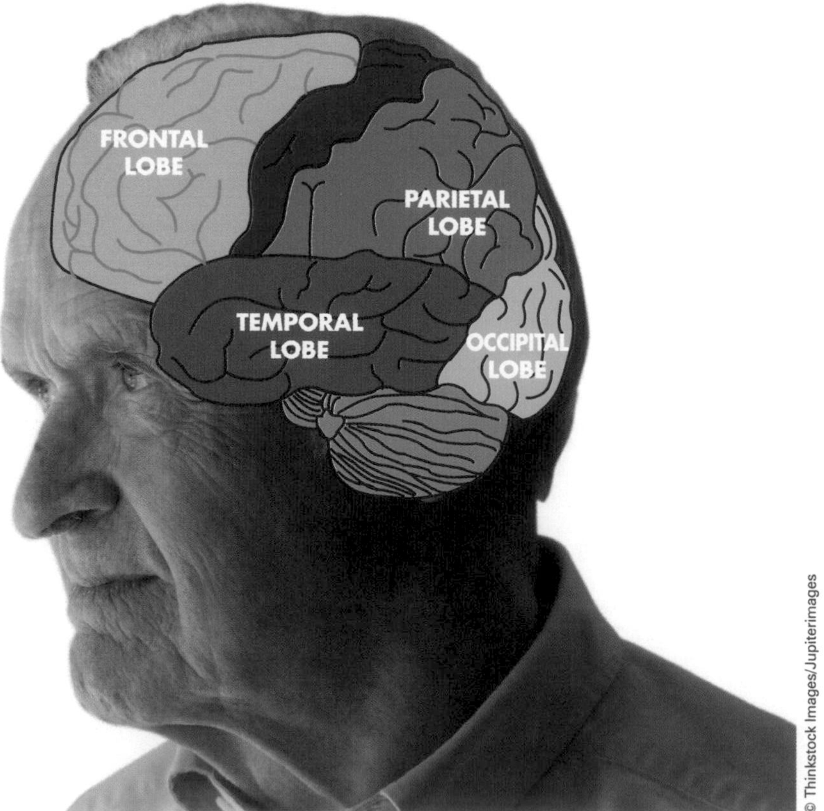

18 Chapter in Review

LO1 **ego integrity** maintenance of the belief that life is meaningful and worthwhile despite physical decline and the inevitability of death. (p. 302)

disengagement theory the view that older adults and society withdraw from one another as older adults approach death. (p. 303)

activity theory the view that older adults fare better when they engage in physical and social activities. (p. 304)

socio-emotional selectivity theory the view that we place increasing emphasis on emotional experience as we age but limit our social contacts to regulate our emotions. (p. 304)

LO2 **generalized anxiety disorder** extreme and/or persistent feelings of dread, worry, foreboding, and concern that are frequent and unrealistic. (p. 307)

phobic disorder irrational, exaggerated fear of an object or situation. (p. 307)

agoraphobia fear of open, crowded places. (p. 307)

Spotmatik/iStockphoto.com

LO5 **selective optimization with compensation** a person reshaping his or her life to concentrate on what the person finds to be important and meaningful in the face of physical decline and possible cognitive impairment. (p. 314)

Psychosocial Stage	Personality Crisis (Challenge)	Important Life Event	Outcome
Later Life (65 years to death)	Ego Integrity vs. Despair	Reflection on Life (Life Review)	Older adults need to actively look back on life and feel a sense that their life mattered. Success at this stage leads to feelings of wisdom and contribution. Death is the logical next step and is received with grace. Failure to navigate this stage results in regret, bitterness, despair, and fear of death.

Gods_Kings/Shutterstock.com

LO1 **Evaluate various theories of social and emotional development in late adulthood.** Erikson's final stage is ego integrity versus despair; the challenge is to continue to see life as meaningful and worthwhile in the face of physical decline and the approach of death. Peck's three developmental tasks of late adulthood are ego differentiation versus work-role preoccupation, body transcendence versus body preoccupation, and ego transcendence versus ego preoccupation. Butler proposes that reminiscence, or life reviews, attempt to make life meaningful and accept the end of life. Well-being among older adults is generally predicted by pursuing goals rather than withdrawal. Activity theory argues that older adults are better adjusted when they are more active and involved. According to socio-emotional selectivity theory, older people limit their social contacts to regulate their emotional lives.

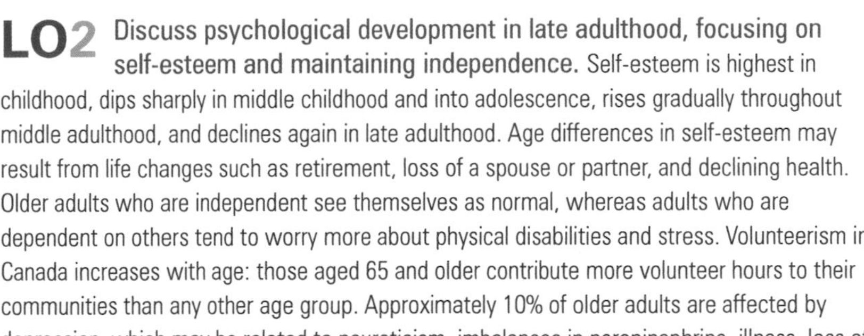

LO2 **Discuss psychological development in late adulthood, focusing on self-esteem and maintaining independence.** Self-esteem is highest in childhood, dips sharply in middle childhood and into adolescence, rises gradually throughout middle adulthood, and declines again in late adulthood. Age differences in self-esteem may result from life changes such as retirement, loss of a spouse or partner, and declining health. Older adults who are independent see themselves as normal, whereas adults who are dependent on others tend to worry more about physical disabilities and stress. Volunteerism in Canada increases with age: those aged 65 and older contribute more volunteer hours to their communities than any other age group. Approximately 10% of older adults are affected by depression, which may be related to neuroticism, imbalances in norepinephrine, illness, loss of loved ones, and cognitive impairment. Depression can lead to suicide. Suicide in late adulthood is sometimes underestimated, likely due to ageism. The most common anxiety disorders among older adults are generalized anxiety disorder and phobic disorders.

LO3 **Discuss the social contexts in which people age, focusing on housing, religion, and family.** Older Canadians prefer to remain in their homes as long as their physical and mental conditions permit. Older Canadians worry about crime, although they are less likely than younger people to be victimized. Older people who cannot live alone may hire in-house care, move in with adult children, or enter assisted-living residences or nursing homes (also called long-term facilities). Relocation disrupts social networks. Religious and cultural involvement often provides social, educational, and charitable activities as well as the promise of an afterlife. Religious and cultural involvement in late adulthood is usually associated with less depression and more life satisfaction.

A majority of Canadians will fulfill their marital commitment "until death do us part." A study of the Big Five personality factors and marital satisfaction found that similarity in conscientiousness and extraversion predicts marital satisfaction for couples in their 60s. By that age, many midlife responsibilities such as child rearing and work have declined, and intimacy re-emerges as a central issue. As compared with couples in midlife, older couples are more affectionate when they discuss conflicts, and they disagree less. Sharing power in the relationship and dividing household tasks contributes to satisfaction. Older adults are less likely than younger adults to seek divorce. As with heterosexuals, LGBTQ in long-term partnerships tend to enjoy higher self-esteem and less depression. Losing a spouse in late adulthood is a traumatic experience and can lead to a decline in health. Widowed men are more likely to remarry than widowed women. Older sibling pairs support each other emotionally. Older people often narrow their friendships to people who are most like them. Grandparents and their adult grandchildren often have very close relationships.

LO4 **Examine factors that contribute to adjustment to retirement.** Retirement planning is a key to successful retirement—e.g., putting money aside and investigating areas where one might relocate. The best adjusted and most satisfied retirees are involved in a variety of activities.

LO5 **Discuss factors in "successful aging."** Definitions of successful aging often focus on physical activity, social contacts, the absence of cognitive impairment and depression, and health. Baltes and Carstensen focus on person–environment fit and see successful aging in terms of selective optimization with compensation, which is related to socio-emotional selectivity theory. Successful agers also tend to be optimistic and to challenge themselves. Social media usage is on the rise among seniors. It is playing an increasingly important role in socializing. 56% of Facebook users are 65 and older.

FIGURE 18.1

Social Media Usage among Seniors

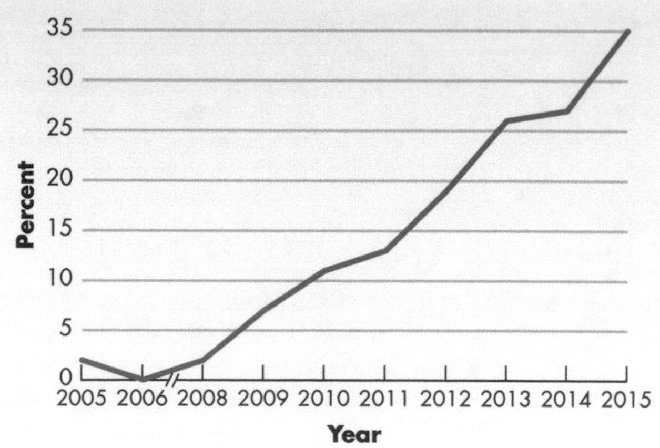

Source: Pew Research Center. (2015, October 8). "Social Media Usage: 2005–2015." http://www.pewinternet.org/2015/10/08/social-networking-usage-2005-2015/

LIFE'S FINAL CHAPTER

Chapter in Review

19

LO1 **death**
the irreversible cessation of vital life functions. (p. 317)

dying
the end-stage of life in which bodily processes decline, leading to death. (p. 317)

brain death
cessation of activity of the cerebral cortex. (p. 317)

whole brain death
cessation of activity of the cerebral cortex and brain stem. (p. 317)

LO2 **hospice**
an organization that treats dying patients by focusing on palliative care rather than curative treatment. (p. 319)

palliative care
treatment focused on the relief of pain and suffering, not on a cure. (p. 320)

LO3 **euthanasia**
the purposeful taking of life to relieve suffering. (p. 320)

voluntary euthanasia
the intentional ending of life as a result of a competent, informed person having made a personal decision to have an assisted death. (p. 321)

non-voluntary euthanasia
the intentional ending of the life of a person who has not expressed his or her preference in terms of an assisted death. (p. 321)

involuntary euthanasia
the intentional ending of the life of a person who made an informed choice and expressed his or her refusal to have an assisted death. (p. 321)

assisted suicide
a self-inflicted death as a result of someone intentionally providing the knowledge or means to die by suicide. (p. 321)

terminal sedation
the practice of relieving distress in the last hours or days of life with the use of sedatives. (p. 321)

living will
a document, prepared when a person is well, that outlines the person's desires concerning medical care should he or she become incapacitated or unable to speak for him/herself. It can provide directives for health-care providers to terminate life-sustaining treatment. (p. 323)

LO5 **bereavement**
the state of deprivation brought about by the death of a family member or close friend. (p. 327)

grief
emotional suffering resulting from a death. (p. 327)

LO1 **Define death and dying, and evaluate views on stages of dying.** Death is the end of life, but *dying* is a part of life. Medical authorities usually use brain death—absence of activity in the cerebral cortex—as the standard for determining whether a person has died. Whole brain death includes death of the brain stem. Kübler-Ross hypothesized five stages of dying: denial, anger, bargaining, depression, and final acceptance. But Kübler-Ross's view applies only to people who have been diagnosed with terminal illness, and other investigators find that dying does not necessarily follow a progression of stages.

FIGURE 19.1

Assisted Suicide Poll

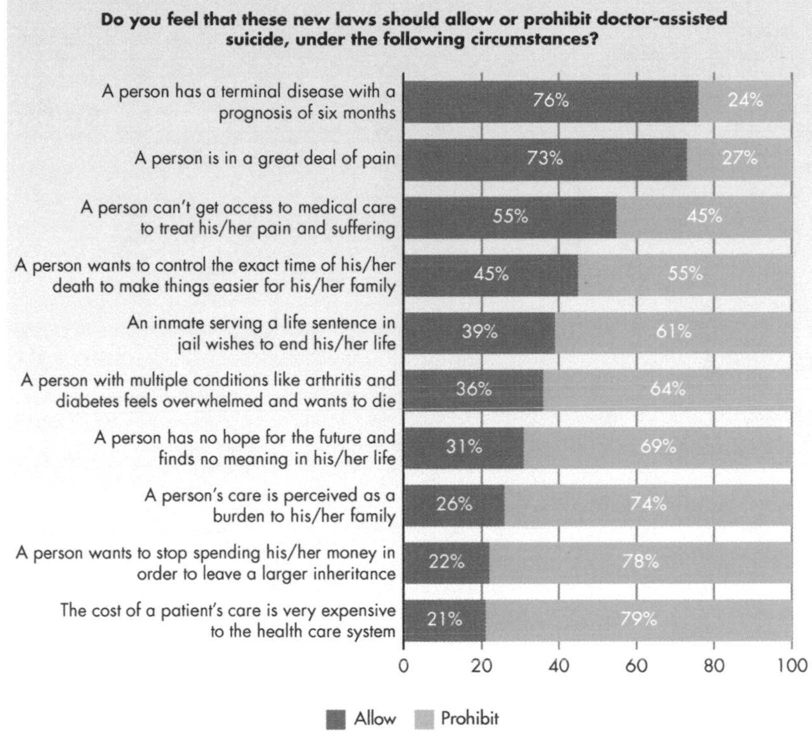

Do you feel that these new laws should allow or prohibit doctor-assisted suicide, under the following circumstances?
A person has a terminal disease with a prognosis of six months
76%
24%
A person is in a great deal of pain
73%
27%
A person can't get access to medical care to treat his/her pain and suffering
55%
45%
A person wants to control the exact time of his/her death to make things easier for his/her family
45%
55%
An inmate serving a life sentence in jail wishes to end his/her life
39%
61%
A person with multiple conditions like arthritis and diabetes feels overwhelmed and wants to die
36%
64%
A person has no hope for the future and finds no meaning in his/her life
31%
69%
A person's care is perceived as a burden to his/her family
26%
74%
A person wants to stop spending his/her money in order to leave a larger inheritance
22%
78%
The cost of a patient's care is very expensive to the health care system
21%
79%
0
20
40
60
80
100
Allow
Prohibit

Source: Angus Reid Institute

LO2 **Identify settings in which people die, distinguishing between hospitals and hospices.** About 70% of all Canadians die in hospitals. Only a few die at home —usually those who are very old or terminally ill. Between 16% and 30% of Canadians who die have access to hospice services. Hospices provide palliative care, not curative care; they help the whole family, not just the patient. People who are dying often want to focus on topics other than their situation and may enjoy hearing about humorous events or a companion's life experiences. Social-media websites such as CaringBridge can assist in creating a support group for those who are ill, while minimizing the energy needed to stay in touch with loved ones.

LO3 **Discuss the various types of euthanasia and their controversies.** The Canadian Medical Association has taken a leadership role in end-of-life medical issues. This organization has defined voluntary euthanasia (requested by a competent patient), non-voluntary euthanasia (the patient's consent has not been received and his or her preference is unknown), and involuntary euthanasia (the patient does not want euthanasia).

mourning
customary methods of expressing grief. (p. 327)

disenfranchised grief
grief that is not acknowledge by society (p. 327)

Terminal sedation, or continuous sedation, can be administered to the dying person to prevent discomfort, but some argue that it might hasten death.

Physicians are not unified on end-of-life issues. Assisted suicide in Canada has recently been legalized for competent persons who clearly consent to the termination of life and have a grievous medical condition causing enduring suffering that is intolerable (Health Law Institute, 2016). But many doctors at the Canadian Medical Association's (CMA) general meeting expressed discomfort about offering assisted death; also, they did not want to refer patients to other physicians. A special committee is tasked with looking at legislative and regulatory frameworks to achieve a balance between physician rights of conscience and patient rights to access to assisted dying.

LO4 Discuss people's perspectives on death at various stages of development. Preschoolers may think that death is reversible or temporary, but their view of death becomes progressively more realistic at the ages of 4, 5, and 6. Death of a parent is usually most difficult for a child to bear. It is normal for children to fear death. Adolescents know that when someone dies, life cannot be restored, but they may construct magical, spiritual, or pseudoscientific theories to try to explain how some form of life or thought might survive. Most young adults in developed nations need not think too much about death. In middle adulthood, death comes more to the fore, often when screening for various deadly diseases is prescribed. Older people may come to fear disability almost as much as death. Some theorists suggest that ego transcendence enables some people to begin to face death with calmness.

Photo by Jonathan Wiggs/The Boston Globe via Getty Images

End-of-life celebrations are increasingly popular ways to celebrate the passing of a friend or family member.

LO5 Discuss coping with death, focusing on the funeral, and on working through the possible stages, or processes, of grieving. If you are present at someone's death, call the family doctor or 911.

Funerals provide an organized response to death that is tied to religious and cultural traditions. Ritual allows people to grieve publicly and bid farewell to the deceased person. In multicultural Canada, this ritual can be expressed in many forms. For example, many First Nations, Métis, and Inuit peoples have death feasts, making traditional caskets, star blankets and "give-aways" to commemorate the death of a loved one. The family of a deceased person may find it difficult to focus on financial and legal matters, such as organ donation or the costs of funerals.

A death can lead to bereavement and mourning. Grief can involve a variety of feelings—depression, loneliness, emptiness, numbness, fear, guilt, even anger. A person's early responses to grief can be predictors of their later experiences of grief. Death is universal—a developmental event that we all encounter.